second edition

Abnormal Psychology

AN INTEGRATIVE APPROACH

David H. Barlow
Boston University

V. Mark Durand
University at Albany
State University of New York

NEW MEDIA ADDITION WITH DSM-IV TABLES

WADSWORTH

THOMSON LEARNING

Australia • Canada • Mexico • Singapore • Spain • United Kingdom • United States

WADSWORTH
THOMSON LEARNING ™

Psychology Editor: *Marianne Taflinger*
Development Editor: *Penelope Sky*
Editorial Assistant: *Rachael Bruckman*
Marketing Managers: *Margaret Parks, Marc Linsenman*
Project Editors: *Keith Faivre, Teri Hyde*
Senior Print Buyer: *Karen Hunt*
Permissions Editor: *Lillian Campobasso*
Text and Cover Designer: *Vernon T. Boes*

Art Editor: *Lisa Torri*
Photo Editors: *Bob Western, Terry Powell*
Photo Researcher: *Joan Meyers–Murie/Myers Photo Art*
Interior Illustration: *Precision Graphics*
Cover Image: *Bill Tucker/Photo Network*
Compositor: *Graphic World, Inc.*
Cover and Text Printer: *Von Hoffmann Press*

Printed in the United States of America
1 2 3 4 5 6 7 04 03 02 01 00

Library of Congress Cataloging-in-Publication Data

Barlow, David H.
    Abnormal psychology : an integrative approach / David H. Barlow,
V. Mark Durand. — 2nd ed.
        p.   cm.
    Includes bibliographical references and index.
    ISBN 0-534-50731-x
    1. Psychology, Pathological.   2. Mental Illness.   I. Durand,
Vincent Mark.   II. Title.
    [DNLM: 1. Mental Disorders.   2. Psychopathology.   WM 100
B258a 1998]
RC454.B345   1998
616.89—dc21
DNLM/DLC
for Library of Congress   98-20270
                                                     CIP

Wadsworth/Thomson Learning
10 Davis Drive
Belmont, CA 94002-3098
USA

For more information about our products, contact us:
Thomson Learning Academic Resource Center
1-800-423-0563
http://www.wadsworth.com

International Headquarters
Thomson Learning
International Division
290 Harbor Drive, 2nd Floor
Stamford, CT 06902-7477
USA

UK/Europe/Middle East/South Africa
Thomson Learning
Berkshire House
168-173 High Holborn
London WC1V 7AA
United Kingdom

Asia
Thomson Learning
60 Albert Street, #15-01
Albert Complex
Singapore 189969

Canada
Nelson Thomson Learning
1120 Birchmount Road
Toronto, Ontario M1K 5G4
Canada

I dedicate this book to my mother, Doris Elinor Barlow-Lanigan, for her multi-dimensional influence across my life span.
D.H.B.

To Wendy and Jonathan, whose patience, understanding, and love provided me the opportunity to complete such an ambitious project.
V.M.D.

about the authors

David H. Barlow is an internationally recognized pioneer and leader in clinical psychology. A professor at Boston University, Dr. Barlow also directs the clinical psychology programs and the Center for Anxiety and Related Disorders, one of the largest research clinics of its kind in the world. Previously, he was distinguished professor at the University at Albany–State University of New York. From 1975 to 1979 he was professor of psychiatry and psychology at Brown University, where he also founded the clinical psychology internship program. From 1969 to 1975 he was professor of psychiatry at the University of Mississippi, where he founded the Medical School psychology residency program. Dr. Barlow received his B.A. from the University of Notre Dame, his M.A. from Boston College, and his Ph.D. from the University of Vermont.

A fellow of every major psychological association, Dr. Barlow has received many awards in honor of his excellence in scholarship, including the National Institute of Mental Health Award; the Distinguished Scientist Award of the Society for a Science of Clinical Psychology of the American Psychological Association; the Distinguished Contribution to Applied Research Award from the American Association of Applied and Preventive Psychology; a certificate of appreciation from the APA section on the clinical psychology of women, for "outstanding commitment to the advancement of women in psychology"; in addition, the annual Grand Rounds in Clinical Psychology at Brown University was named in his honor, and he was awarded the first graduate alumni scholar award at the University of Vermont. During the 1997–1998 academic year he was Fritz Redlich Fellow at the Center for Advanced Study in the Behavioral Sciences in Menlo Park, California.

Dr. Barlow has served on the editorial boards of 19 different journals, published more than 400 scholarly articles, and written 20 books, including *Anxiety and Its Disorders,* Guilford Press; *Clinical Handbook of Psychological Disorders: A Step-by-Step Treatment Manual,* 2nd edition, Guilford Press; *Single-Case Experimental Designs: Strategies for Studying Behavior Change,* 2nd edition, Allyn & Bacon (with Michael Herson); *The Scientist-Practitioner: Research and Accountability in the Age of Managed Care,* 2nd edition, Allyn & Bacon (with Steve Hayes and Rosemery Nelson); and *Mastery of Your Anxiety and Panic,* Graywind Publications (with Michelle Craske).

From 1990 to 1994, Dr. Barlow was one of three psychologists on the task force that was responsible for reviewing the work of more than 1000 mental health professionals who participated in the creation of the new DSM-IV. He also chaired the APA Task Force on Psychological Intervention Guidelines, which created a template for clinical practice guidelines. His current research program focuses on the nature and treatment of anxiety and related emotional disorders.

At leisure he plays golf, skis, and retreats to his home in Nantucket, where he loves to write, walk on the beach, and visit with his island friends.

V. Mark Durand is a world authority in the area of developmental disabilities and is currently professor of psychology at the University at Albany–State University of New York, where he has administered more than $2 million in federal research and training grants in the areas of functional communication, assistive technology, home-school training, and improving the problem behaviors of children and adults with severe disabilities. He served as associate director for clinical training for the doctoral psychology program from 1987 to 1990 and as chair of the psychology department from 1995 to 1998; he currently directs the Albany Center for the Study of Developmental and Behavioral Disabilities and the New York Autism Network. He received his B.A., M.A., and Ph.D.—all in psychology—at the State University of New York–Stony Brook.

Dr. Durand was awarded the University Award for Excellence in Teaching at SUNY–Albany in 1991 and in 1989 was named Distinguished Reviewer of the Year for the *Journal of the Association for Persons with Severe Handicaps.* He has served on various editorial boards, reviewed for numerous journals, and written many scholarly articles and dozens of chapters on functional communication, educational programming, and behavior therapy. His five books include *Severe Behavior Problems: A Functional Communication Training Approach* and, most recently, *Sleep Better! A Guide to Improving Sleep for Children with Special Needs.*

Dr. Durand developed a unique treatment for severe behavior problems that is currently mandated by states across the country and is used worldwide. He also developed an assessment tool that is used internationally and has been translated into more than 15 languages. In 1993 he was the keynote speaker for the Australian National Conference on Behaviour Modification; he has also lectured throughout Norway. He has been consulted by the departments of education in numerous states and by the U.S. Departments of Justice and Education. His current research program includes the study of prevention models and treatments for such serious problems as self-injurious behavior.

In his leisure time he enjoys jogging, soccer, playing with his son, Jonathan, and long drives with his wife, Wendy.

brief contents

contents

2 An Integrative Approach to Psychopathology 27

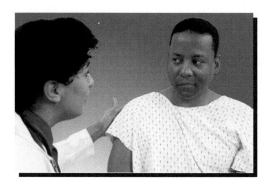

3 Clinical Assessment and Diagnosis 63

4 **Research Methods** *89*

5 **Anxiety Disorders** *III*

6 Somatoform and Dissociative Disorders *152*

7 Mood Disorders *182*

8 **Eating and Sleep Disorders** *228*

9 Physical Disorders and Health Psychology 264

10 Sexual and Gender Identity Disorders 298

11 **Substance-Related Disorders** *336*

Danny: Multiple Dependencies 337

Perspectives on Substance-Related Disorders *338*
Levels of Involvement *338*
Diagnostic Issues *341*

Depressants *342*
Alcohol Use Disorders *343*
Sedative, Hypnotic, or Anxiolytic
   Substance Use Disorders *348*

12 **Personality Disorders** *374*

An Overview *375*
Categorical and Dimensional Models *375*
Personality Disorder Clusters *376*
Statistics and Development *376*
Gender Differences *378*
Comorbidity *379*

Specific Personality Disorders *380*

13 Schizophrenia and Other Psychotic Disorders *404*

14 Developmental Disorders *438*

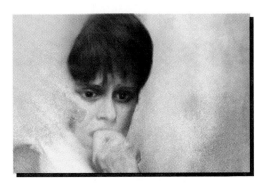

preface

Every once in a while something dramatic happens in science. For example, evolutionary biologists, who long assumed that the process of evolution was gradual, suddenly had to adjust to evidence that it happens in fits and starts in response to such cataclysmic environmental events as meteor impacts. Similarly, geology has been revolutionized by the discovery of plate tectonics.

Until now, the science of psychopathology has been compartmentalized, with psychopathologists examining the separate effects of psychological, biological, and social influences. This approach is still reflected in popular media accounts that describe, for example, a newly discovered gene, a biological dysfunction, or early childhood experiences as a "cause" of a psychological disorder. This way of thinking still dominates discussions of causality and treatment in most psychology textbooks: "The psychoanalytic views of this disorder are . . . the biological views are . . . ," and, often in a separate chapter, "psychoanalytic treatment approaches for this disorder are . . . cognitive behavioral treatment approaches are . . . biological treatment approaches are. . . ."

The success of the first edition of this book confirms our belief that this approach is no longer useful. Recent explosive advances in knowledge demonstrate that genetic and neuroscientific research depends on our understanding that psychological and social factors directly affect neurotransmitter function and even genetic expression. Similarly, we cannot study behavioral, cognitive, or emotional processes without appreciating the contribution of biological and social factors to psychological and psychopathological expression. Thus, we have abandoned the traditional compartmentalized approach to psychopathology, which, in any case, usually confused our students. Instead, we use a more accessible approach that accurately reflects the current state of our clinical science.

As colleagues, you are aware that we understand some disorders better than others. But we hope you will share our excitement in conveying to the student both what we currently know about the causes and treatment of psychopathology and how far we have yet to go in understanding these complex interactions.

Our Approach

This is clearly the first of a new generation of abnormal psychology textbooks that offers an integrative and multidimensional perspective. (We acknowledge such one-dimensional approaches as biological, psychosocial, and supernatural as historic trends). We include substantial current evidence of the reciprocal influences of biology and behavior and of psychological and social influences on biology. Our examples hold students' attention; for example, we discuss genetic contributions to divorce, the effects of early social and behavioral experience on later brain function and structure, new information on the relation of social networks to the common cold, and new data on psychosocial treatments for cancer. We emphasize the fact that in the phenomenon of implicit memory and blind sight, which may have parallels in dissociative experiences, psychological science verifies the existence of the unconscious (although it does not much resemble the seething caldron of conflicts envisioned by Freud). We acknowledge the often neglected area of emotion theory for its rich contributions to psychopathology. We weave scientific findings from the study of emotions together with behavioral, biological, cognitive, and social discoveries to create an integrated tapestry of psychopathology.

Life-Span Developmental Influences

No modern view of abnormal psychology can ignore the importance of life-span developmental factors to the manifestation and treatment of psychopathology. Accordingly, we do not relegate "disorders of childhood" to a separate chapter; we discuss childhood anxiety, for example, in the context of the other anxiety disorders. This organization, which is for the most part consistent with DSM-IV, helps students appreciate the need to study each disorder from childhood through adulthood. We note findings on developmental considerations in separate sections of each disorder chapter and, as appropriate, discuss how specific developmental factors affect causation and treatment.

Scientist-Practitioner Approach

We go to some length to explain why the scientist-practitioner approach to psychopathology is both practical and ideal. Like most of our colleagues, we view this as something more than simple awareness of how scientific findings apply to psychopathology. We show how every clinician contributes to general scientific knowledge through astute and systematic clinical observations, functional analyses of individual case studies, and systematic observations of series of cases in clinical settings. For example, we explain how information on dissociative phenomena provided by early psychoanalytic theorists remains relevant today. We also describe the formal methods used by scientist-practitioners, showing how abstract research designs are applied to research programs.

Clinical Cases

We have enriched the book with authentic clinical histories to illustrate scientific findings on the causes and treatment of psychopathology. We have both run active clinics for years, so 95% of the cases are from our own files, and they provide a fascinating frame of reference for the findings we describe. Most chapters begin with a case description, and most discussion of the latest theory and research is related to these very human cases.

Disorders in Detail

We cover the major psychological disorders in 11 chapters, focusing on three broad categories: clinical description, causal factors, and treatment and outcomes. We pay considerable attention to case studies and DSM-IV criteria, and we include statistical data, such as prevalence and incidence rates, sex ratio, age of onset, and the general course or pattern for the disorder as a whole. Throughout, we explore how biological, psychological, and social dimensions may interact to cause a particular disorder. Finally, by covering treatment and outcomes within the context of specific disorders, we provide a realistic sense of clinical practice.

Treatment

One of the best received innovations in the first edition was that we discussed treatment in the context of the disorders that are its target instead of in a separate chapter, an approach that is supported by the development of specific psychosocial and pharmacological treatment procedures for specific disorders. We have retained this integrative format and improved upon it, and we include treatment procedures in the key terms and glossary.

Legal and Ethical Issues

In our closing chapter we integrate many of the approaches and themes that have been discussed throughout the text. We include case studies of people who have been involved directly with many legal and ethical issues and with the delivery of mental health services. We also provide a historical context for current perspectives so students will understand the effects of social and cultural influences on legal and ethical issues.

Special Photo Feature

We have included photos of actual clients who were diagnosed with psychological disorders (for an example of this feature, see page 113). In every case, we have the individual's permission to use the photo; in cases where we felt a person might not truly understand our purpose, we have not used the image. By showing these faces, which represent both genders and most races, cultures, and stages of development, we hope to convey the hardship imposed by psychological disorders and help reduce the stigma, anxiety, and isolation that add to the burden of people who struggle with them.

DSM-IV

Much has been said about the mix of political and scientific considerations that resulted in DSM-IV, and naturally we have our own opinions (David Barlow had the interesting experience of sitting on the task force). Psychologists are often concerned about turf issues in what has become, for better or worse, the nosological standard in our field, and with good reason: In previous DSM editions, scientific findings sometimes gave way to personal opinions. However, this time most professional biases were left at the door while the task force almost endlessly debated the data. This process produced enough new information to fill every psychopathology journal for a year with integrative reviews, reanalysis of existing databases, and new data from field trials (a sampling of papers and data are still in the process of being published in four volumes to accompany the DSM-IV). From a scholarly point of view, the process was both stimulating and exhausting.

In this book are highlights of various debates that created the nomenclature and recent updates. For example, we summarize the data and discussion of premenstrual dysphoric disorder and mixed anxiety depression, two disorders that did not make it into the final criteria. Students can thus see the process of making diagnoses as well as the mix of data and inference that are part of it.

We also describe the intense continuing debate on categorical and dimensional classifications and discuss some of the compromises the task force made to accommodate data. For example, we discuss why it does not yet seem possible to dimensionalize personality disorders, although almost everyone agrees that when we can we will prefer to do so.

Diversity

Issues of culture and gender are integral to the study of psychopathology. Throughout the text we describe current thinking about which aspects of the disorders are culturally specific and which are universal, and about the strong and sometimes puzzling effects of gender roles. Clearly, our field will grow in depth and detail as these subjects become standard research topics. For example, why do some disorders overwhelmingly affect females and others appear predominately in males? And why does this apportionment sometimes change from one culture to another? In answering questions like these, we adhere closely to science, emphasizing that each gender and culture are each one dimension among several that constitute psychopathology.

New to This Edition

Organization and Condensation

We have slightly reorganized the contents in order to present all the necessary material in a convenient 16 chapters. The chapters on sleeping disorders and eating disorders are now combined so we can demonstrate the impact of psychological and social factors on "activities of survival," a theme we also apply in the chapter on physical disorders and health psychology. We devote an entire chapter to developmental disorders, which now logically precedes the chapter on cognitive disorders.

Hundreds of new references appear for the first time in this edition and some of the information they contain stuns the imagination. We have also added extensive coverage of Alzheimer's disease to the chapter on cognitive disorders. Yet we have condensed the text without sacrificing a writing style that has been commended as lively, conversational, and engaging. Nonessential material has been eliminated, and we have incorporated DSM-IV criteria into the text instead of presenting them in tables.

Pedagogy

Each chapter now contains several Concept Checks that let students verify their comprehension at regular intervals. Answers are at the end of each chapter, along with a more detailed Summary; the Key Terms are now listed in text order rather than alphabetically and thus form a sort of outline that students can study.

"From the Inside"

The popularity of the case studies (which now have descriptive titles) indicates that students appreciate the humanization of data that might otherwise appear dry and lifeless. To emphasize that psychological disorders affect real people who respond in a variety of ways, almost all of the 11 disorder chapters now conclude with a compassionate review of a first-person memoir by someone who survived or is living with a challenging psychological condition. These stories were chosen for the value of their deeply personal points of view; they complement the research-based text without pretending to be scientific. In addition, quotations from the featured memoir appear as chapter-opening epigraphs and as displayed quotations in the body of the chapter, so a "real" voice can be heard as a counterpoint to our objective discussion.

Visual Summaries

At the end of each disorder chapter is a colorful two-page chart that succinctly summarizes the causes, development, symptoms, and treatment of each disorder covered in the chapter. Our integrative approach is instantly evident in these diagrams, which show the interaction of biological, psychological, and social factors in the etiology and treatment of disorders. The visual summaries will help the instructor wrap up discussions and students will appreciate them as study aids.

Major Content Changes

Chapter 1, Abnormal Behavior in Historical Context

- Substantially condensed without any loss of content
- Updated definitions and citations
- More precise headings

Chapter 2, An Integrative Approach to Psychopathology

- New discussion of methodological developments in genetics
- Updated information on neurotransmitter systems
- New material on the plasticity of the CNS in response to psychological and environmental input
- Support for the potential influence of the cognitive and emotional systems on the development of psychological disorders
- New summary reflecting current views of what is culturally specific and what is universal in psychopathy

Chapter 3, Clinical Assessment and Diagnosis

- Revised explanation of neuroimaging
- Updated section on creating a diagnosis
- Recent thinking on future alternatives to DSM-IV

Chapter 4, Research Methods

- New references on genetics and new discussion of recent association study paradigms
- Deleted section on necessary and sufficient conditions

Chapter 5, Anxiety Disorders

- Full description of the latest information on genetic contributions to anxiety and the role of specific chromosomal locations of "anxious" genes
- New data on separate neurobiological contributions to anxiety and panic, including an integration of fact and theory from Gray's behavioral inhibition and fight-flight systems and LeDoux's emphasis on the amygdala
- New information on generalized anxiety disorder, including different presentations by children and the elderly, chronicity, and theories of development

- New data on the epidemiology, causes, and treatment of panic disorder with and without agoraphobia, as well as the latest detailed information from a large national multicenter study comparing psychosocial and drug treatments
- New studies on panic disorder and associated suicidal tendencies
- New data on the treatment of social phobia, from multisite collaborative studies comparing the effects of drugs and psychosocial treatments
- Revised data on the prevalence of posttraumatic stress disorder (PTSD) as a result of various kinds of trauma
- New evidence of changes in brain structure as a result of PTSD, with implications for long-term course

Chapter 6, Somatoform and Dissociative Disorders

- New data from the World Health Organization on the prevalence of somatic complaints and somatization disorder worldwide
- New data on the prevalence and structure of pathological dissociation in the general population and on environmental and genetic contributions, including evidence that pathological dissociation is a categorically separate experience from normal dissociation
- New observations on the high frequency of suicide attempts by people with body dysmorphic disorder and on successful psychological treatment of the condition
- Cross-cultural influences on the prevalence of dissociative identity disorder
- Updated information on the causes of dissociative identity disorder and its relation to early trauma
- Substantial review of the controversy over real versus false memories of trauma and their relation to dissociative amnesia

Chapter 7, Mood Disorders

- 1998 data on manic episodes that emphasizes "dysphoric" mania
- New data demonstrating that previous estimates of recurrent depressive disorders were greatly underestimated and that almost all mood disorders are recurrent
- New information on the prevalence and presentation of mood disorders in different cultural groups
- Updates on the prevalence and course of mood disorders in children and adolescents and the distinctive presentation of depressive disorders in adolescents
- New data on frontal EEG asymmetry as a potential biological marker for vulnerability to depression
- New discussion of possible causes of gender imbalance in depressive disorders, including the role of marriage in the etiology of depression
- Updated information on psychosocial treatment of mood disorders and efforts to prevent depression in vulnerable individuals

Chapter 8, Eating and Sleep Disorders

- Discussion of increasing global prevalence of eating disorders
- New data on eating disorders in different cultural groups (including African-American, Hispanic, Asian-American, Native American, and Caucasian)
- New information on how cultural factors influence the gender imbalance in eating disorders
- New evidence on numbers of people in weight loss programs who meet criteria for binge eating disorder
- Recent data on the economic costs of insomnia
- New research on the effects of sleep deprivation on the immune system
- Discussion of sleep abnormalities as preceding and therefore indicating imminent clinical depression
- Implications of the discovery that light on the skin, as well as through the eyes, affects the biological clock
- New data on excessive sleepiness among the elderly and among black men
- New discussion of nocturnal eating syndrome

Chapter 9, Physical Disorders and Health Psychology

- Fewer topics covered in greater depth illustrate the influence of psychological factors on biological and physical processes
- New data on the relationship of unemployment to higher mortality among males
- New illustrations of how psychosocial mechanisms may influence the immune system
- New data on the inability of world health organizations to diminish the spread of AIDS and on the discouraging results of new drug combinations to suppress HIV
- Encouraging updates on the effects of psychosocial treatments on symptoms, immune system functioning, and survival time among cancer patients
- New data on how blood pressure is influenced by culture
- New model of the etiology of chronic fatigue syndrome

Chapter 10, Sexual and Gender Identity Disorders

- Updates on surveys of normal sexual behavior
- Worldwide societal views of gender identity disorder as reflected in new laws
- Updated information on how biology and environment interact in contributing to gender identity
- Advances in the medical treatment of sexual dysfunctions, including reports of the effectiveness of Sildenafil (Viagra)
- Current descriptions of paraphilias and new data on potential biological contributions

Chapter 11, Substance-Related Disorders

- The drug use of Americans as reported in the 1996 National Household Survey on Drug Abuse
- New information on the benzodiazepine Rohypnol, the "date rape drug"
- New evidence that smoking during pregnancy may increase likelihood of smoking by offspring
- Updated Kendler studies of female twins and alcoholism
- Recent research on the consequences of cigarette advertising and teen smoking
- Outcomes of Project MATCH, which matched treatments with different groups of people with alcoholism
- Recent negative evaluations of preventive programs like DARE

Chapter 12, Personality Disorders

- Report on the cross-cultural five-factor model of personality (in German, Portuguese, Hebrew, Chinese, Korean, and Japanese)
- New data on clinicians' subjective impressions for axis II disorders integrated with potential gender bias in diagnosing these disorders
- Discussion of recent prospective research on children who later develop schizotypal personality disorder, which found them to be passive, unengaged, and acutely sensitive to criticism
- Recent study by Cadoret, Yates, Troughton, Woodworth, and Stewart of gene-environment interaction in antisocial personality disorder
- Results from new study connecting combat trauma with antisocial behavior
- Discussion of new data indicating a lower density of dopamine receptors in people who score high on a measure of detachment, which may help explain schizoid personality disorder
- New section on the combination of abuse and/or neglect and personality style in the etiology of borderline personality disorder

Chapter 13, Schizophrenia and Other Psychotic Disorders

- Section on symptoms reorganized to incorporate latest thinking on positive, negative, and disorganized categories
- New data that people with flat affect respond physiologically as well as verbally to emotionally laden stimuli
- New material on cultural and gender differences in schizophrenia
- Updated research from Kendler's Roscommon Family Study on the familial risks of psychotic disorders
- Revised section on psychosocial interventions, including recent advances in supportive employment interventions

Chapter 14, Developmental Disorders

- New chapter includes disorders that were previously covered in Chapter 15 (mental retardation; learning disorders) and Chapter 16 (autistic, Asperger's, Rett's disorders; childhood disintegrative disorder; ADHD; tic disorder; communication disorders; stuttering, selective mutism, and expressive language disorders)
- New opening section emphasizes that this is not a "childhood disorders" chapter, but instead covers life-long impairments that first manifest during childhood
- ADHD section expanded to include more discussion of treatment options
- Learning disorders updated to include recent genetic research, neuropsychological findings, and treatment approaches
- Updated and condensed section of autistic disorder
- Implications of recent research on genetic screening and treatment for mental retardation

Chapter 15, Cognitive Disorders

- New chapter covers cognitive disorders exclusively
- Recent information on prescription drug use delirium among older adults
- New data on the economic costs of Alzheimer's disease
- Addition of the Mini Mental State Exam for assessing dementia of the Alzheimer's type
- Discussion of new study that found a correlation between early journal entries by nuns and later development of Alzheimer's disease
- New genetic data and table on Alzheimer's disease
- Expanded section on caregivers of people with amnestic disorders

Chapter 16, Mental Health Services: Legal, Ethical, and Professional Issues

- New section on the misperception of dangerousness among women and ethnic minorities and its effect on involuntary civil commitment
- Recent data on homelessness among first-time psychiatric hospital admissions
- New section on civil commitment and sex offenders

Teaching Aids for the Instructor and Student

- *From the Inside,* by Inner Images, produced by Sonia Blackman, Ph.D. Dramatic re-creations of the inner experiences of people with posttraumatic stress syndrome, bulimia, and schizophrenia in one 60-minute videotape (each segment averages 20 minutes).
- *Abnormal Psychology: Inside Out,* Volume I, produced by Only Child Productions, producer Ira Wohl, M.S.W. A two-volume set of diagnostic interviews of 147 minutes on videotape with ten clients whose disorders include major depressive disorder, bipolar disorder, sexual disorder, panic disorder, obsessive-compulsive disorder, schizophrenia, cognitive disorder, antisocial personality disorder, alcohol abuse, and anorexia. The client with bipolar disorder is depicted in both her manic and depressive phases, showing the student the marked differences in each phase. Interviews were conducted with client volunteers by a team of experienced therapists at Washington University School of Medicine. Each interview segment lasts from 5 to 15 minutes.
- *Abnormal Psychology: Inside/Out,* Volume II, produced by Kwaamba, producer Art Kohn, Ph.D. Six additional clients with different disorders are shown in the context of their everyday lives on this 40-minute tape. Each segment ranges from 5 to 10 minutes in length.
- *Transparency Acetates* by John P. Forsyth is a careful selection of over 100 full-color figures that reflect art from the text and other sources. The labels have been upsized to allow easy reading in large lecture halls.
- *PowerPoint Presentation* by John P. Forsyth. This CD–ROM includes a series of fully customizable slides and integrated text, each of which is full of visually engaging, colorful images and graphics. The slides for each lecture are arranged by topic and cover most major chapters of the text. Also included are some acetates of new text art and overheads that may be integrated into the existing slides or modified depending on the instructor's preference. One of the strongest features of this ancillary is that it allows instructors the flexibility and choice in editing the graphical and textual content of the slides to suit their particular needs. The PowerPoint lectures are designed to be run on Windows 95 IBM/PC based systems; however, they may be converted readily to a variety of formats (e.g., MAC Platform or Internet). PowerPoint for Windows 95 or MAC is required to take full advantage of the CD–ROM package.
- *Web Resources:* Our online resource center offers a 20-item multiple-choice quiz and links to relevant sites for each chapter. Go to: **http://psychstudy.brookscole.com**
- *Test Bank* by David Santogrossi and Shari Stembel contains 100–125 items per chapter in multiple-choice, true/false, and essay formats, and are sorted into factual, conceptual, and applied questions. The items are all page-referenced to the main text and each chapter contains at least 10 items that are located on the psychstudy center on the World Wide Web. And each appropriate chapter contains questions that refer to the clients on the videotape *Abnormal Psychology: Inside Out,* Volume I.
- *Thomson World Class Learning and Testing Tools* (in Windows and Macintosh formats). All test items from the printed test bank are available in electronic format.

This fully integrated suite of test creation, delivery, and classroom management tools includes World Class Test, Test Online, and World Class Management software. World Class Testing Tools allows professors to deliver tests via print, floppy, hard drive, LAN, or Internet. With these tools, professors can create cross-platform exam files from publisher files or existing WESTest 3.2 test banks, edit questions, create questions, and provide their own feedback to objective test questions—enabling the system to work as a tutorial or an examination. In addition, professors can generate questions algorithmically, create tests that include multiple-choice, true/false, or matching questions. Professors can also track the progress of an entire class or an individual student. Testing and tutorial results can be integrated into the class management tool, which offers scoring, gradebook, and reporting capabilities.

• *Instructor's Manual* by Ronald Ruiz contains learning objectives, chapter outlines, chapter summaries, key terms, classroom activities, demonstrations, and lecture topics, supplementing reading material, book reviews, video resources, and Internet resources.

• *InfoTrac:* A fully searchable online university library for students that offers complete articles from more than 600 scholarly and popular publications, including such periodicals as the *American Journal of Psychology*. InfoTrac access is available on a password-protected Web Site that is updated daily.

Titles of Interest

• *Study Guide* by David Santogrossi encourages collaborative learning and active reading, listening, and study skills. It contains chapter summaries, key words, sample questions, and activities and questions related to the videotape *Abnormal Psychology: Inside Out*, Volume I.

• *Looking into Abnormal Psychology: Contemporary Readings* by Scott O. Lilienfeld is a fascinating 234-page reader compromised of 40 articles from popular magazines and journals. Each article explores ongoing controversies regarding mental illness and its treatment.

• *Casebook in Abnormal Psychology* by Timothy A. Brown and David H. Barlow is a comprehensive casebook that reflects the integrative approach, which considers the multiple influences of genetics, biology, familial, and environment factors into a unified model of causality as well as maintenance and treatment of the disorder. The casebook reflects treatment methods that are the most effective interventions developed for a particular disorder. It also presents two undiagnosed cases in order to give students an appreciation for the complexity of disorders. The cases are strictly teaching/learning exercises similar to what many instructors use on their examinations.

Acknowledgments

Finally, this book in both its editions would not have begun and certainly would not be finished without the inspiration and coordination of Marianne Taflinger, our senior editor at Brooks/Cole, who convinced us that we could truly accomplish something new and different and who put her own heart and soul into the process. One additional person has left her mark on every page. We owe a great deal to senior developmental editor Penelope Sky, who nudged, cajoled, and, on occasion, challenged us on topics from the placement of a comma to the broadest philosophical and cultural issues. Her perseverance and sense of humor in the face of unremitting deadlines deserve mention in the annals of remarkable psychological resilience.

In the production process, many individuals worked as hard as we did to complete this project in what seems like a shockingly brief period of time. Bette Selwyn assisted enormously in typing and integrating a vast amount of new information into each chapter and expertly formatting this material. It is an understatement to say that we couldn't have done it without you. Keith Faivre coordinated the innumerable details involved in the production of this book at Brooks/Cole, including the thankless job of making sure that every reference was correct and that the photos were in the right places.

Special thanks to the staff at the Center for Advanced Study in the Behavioral Sciences, where David H. Barlow had the good fortune to spend a sabbatical preparing the second edition. The staff report that their goal is to make the fellowship year the best of one's life for those fortunate enough to spend a year in residence, and they certainly succeeded. Thanks also to my colleague Sue Mineka, another fellow in residence, who shared materials and some ideas as we struggled with ironically similar tasks. Numerous colleagues and students provided superb feedback on the first edition, and to them we express our deepest gratitude. Although not all comments were favorable, all were important. Readers who take the time to communicate their thoughts offer the greatest reward to writers or scholars.

Finally, you share with us the task of communicating knowledge and discoveries in the exciting field of psychopathology, a challenge that none of us takes lightly. In the spirit of collegiality, we would greatly appreciate your comments on the content and style of this book and recommendations for improving it further.

David H. Barlow
Center for Advanced Study
in the Behavioral Sciences,
Stanford, California

V. Mark Durand
Somewhere in front of a computer screen

reviewers

Creating this book has been both stimulating and exhausting, and we could not have done it without the valuable assistance of colleagues who read one or more chapters and provided extraordinarily perceptive critical comments, corrected errors, pointed to relevant information and, on occasion, offered new insights that helped us achieve a successful integrative model of each disorder.

Frank Andrasik, *University of West Florida*
Robin Apple, *Stanford University Medical Center*
Dorothy Bianco, *Rhode Island College*
Susan Blumenson, *City University of New York, John Jay College of Criminal Justice*
Robert Bornstein, *Gettysburg College*
James Calhoun, *University of Georgia*
Montie Campbell, *Oklahoma Baptist University*
Antonio Cepeda-Benito, *Texas A & M University*
Juris Draguns, *Pennsylvania State University*
Mitchell Earlywine, *University of Southern California*
Elizabeth Epstein, *Rutgers University*
Donald Evans, *Drake University*
Ronald Evans, *Washburn University*
Anthony Fazio, *University of Wisconsin, Milwaukee*
Diane Finley, *Towson State University*
Allen Frances, *Duke University*
David Gleaves, *Texas A & M University*
Frank Goodkin, *Castleton State College*
Irving Gottesman, *University of Virginia*
Marjorie Hardy, *Muhlenberg College*
Brian Hayden, *Brown University*
Stephen Hinshaw, *University of California, Berkeley*
William Iacono, *University of Minnesota*
Heidi Inderbitzen-Nolan
Thomas Jackson, *University of Arkansas*
Boaz Kahana, *Cleveland State University*
Arthur Kaye, *Virginia Commonwealth University*
Ernest Keen, *Bucknell University*
Elizabeth Klonoff
Ann Kring, *Vanderbilt University*

Marvin Kumler, *Bowling Green State University*
Thomas Kwapil, *University of North Carolina, Greensboro*
Michael Lambert, *Brigham Young University*
Travis Langley, *Henderson State University*
Cynthia Ann Lease, *Virginia Polytechnic Institute and State University*
Richard Leavy, *Ohio Weslyan University*
Scott Lilienfeld, *Emory University*
Michael Lyons, *Boston University*
Jerald Marshall, *Valencia Community College*
Janet Matthews, *Loyola University*
Dean McKay, *Fordham University*
Thomas Miller, *Murray State University*
Scott Monroe, *University of Oregon*
Mary McNaughton-Cassill, *University of Texas at San Antonio*
Sumie Okazaki, *University of Wisconsin, Madison*
John Otey, *South Arkansas University*
P. B. Poorman, *University of Wisconsin*
Carol Rothman, *City University of New York, Herbert H. Lehman College*
Jerome Small, *Youngstown State University*
Irene Staik, *University of Montevallo*
Brian Stagner, *Texas A & M University*
Chris Tate, *Middle Tennessee State University*
Lisa Terre, *University of Missouri, Kansas City*
Michael Vasey, *Ohio State University*
Larry Ventis, *College of William and Mary*
Richard Viken, *Indiana University*
Philip Watkins, *Eastern Washington University*
Kim Weikel, *Shippensburg University of Pennsylvania*
Michael Wierzbicki, *Marquette University*
John Wincze, *Brown University*
Bradley Woldt, *South Dakota State University*
Ellen Zaleski, *Fordham University*
Raymond Zurawski, *St. Norbert College*

Abnormal Behavior in Historical Context

A clear and complete insight into the nature of madness, a correct and distinct conception of what constitutes the difference between the sane

and the insane has, as far as I know, not been found.

Shopenhauer
The World as Will and Idea

Today you may have gotten out of bed, had breakfast, gone to class, studied, and, at the end of the day, enjoyed the company of your friends before dropping off to sleep. It probably did not occur to you that there are many physically healthy people who are not able to do some or any of these things. What they have in common is a **psychological disorder,** which is a psychological dysfunction within an individual that is associated with distress or impairment in functioning and a response that is not typical or culturally expected. Before examining exactly what this means, let's look at one individual's situation.

Judy
The Girl Who Fainted at the Sight of Blood

Judy, a 16-year-old, was referred to our Anxiety Disorders Clinic after increasing episodes of fainting. About 2 years earlier, in her first biology class, the teacher showed a movie of a frog dissection to illustrate various points about anatomy. This was a particularly graphic film, with vivid images of blood, tissue, and muscle. About halfway through, Judy felt a bit lightheaded and left the room. But the images did not leave her. She continued to be bothered by them and occasionally felt slightly queasy. She began to avoid situations where she might see blood or injury. She stopped looking at magazines that might have gory pictures. She found it difficult to look at raw meat, or even Band-Aids, because they brought the feared images to mind. Eventually, anything her friends or parents said that evoked an image of blood or injury caused Judy to feel lightheaded. It got so bad that if one of her friends exclaimed, "Cut it out!" she felt faint. Beginning about 6 months before her visit to the clinic, Judy actually fainted when she unavoidably encountered something bloody. Her family physician could find nothing wrong with her, nor could several other physicians. By the time she was referred to our clinic she was fainting five to ten times a week, often in class. Clearly, this was problematic for her and disruptive in school; each time she fainted, the other students flocked around her, trying to help, and class was interrupted. Because no one could find anything wrong with her, the principal finally concluded that she was being manipulative and suspended her from school, even though she was an honor student.

Judy was suffering from what we now call *blood-injury–injection phobia.* Her reaction was quite severe, thereby meeting the criteria for **phobia,** a psychological disorder characterized by marked and persistent fear of an

object or situation. But many people have similar reactions that are *not* as severe when they receive an injection or see someone who is injured, whether blood is visible or not. For people who react as severely as Judy, this phobia can be very disabling. They may avoid certain careers, such as medicine or nursing, and, if they are so afraid of needles and injections that they avoid them even when necessary, they put their health at risk.

Definitions

Keeping in mind the real-life problems faced by Judy, let's look more closely at the definition of *psychological disorder,* or abnormal behavior: It is a *psychological dysfunction* within an individual that is associated with *distress or impairment* in functioning and *a response that is not typical or culturally expected* (see Figure 1.1). On the surface, these three criteria may seem obvious, but they were not easily arrived at, and it is worth a moment to explore what they mean. You will see, importantly, that no one criterion has yet been developed that fully defines abnormality.

Psychological dysfunction refers to a breakdown in cognitive, emotional, or behavioral functioning. If you are out on a date that should be fun, but you experience severe fear all evening and just want to go home, your emotions are not functioning properly. However, if all your friends agree that the person who asked you out is dangerous, then it would not be "dysfunctional" for you to be fearful and avoid the date.

A cognitive dysfunction is present if an individual displays psychotic behavior—that is, hallucinating and totally

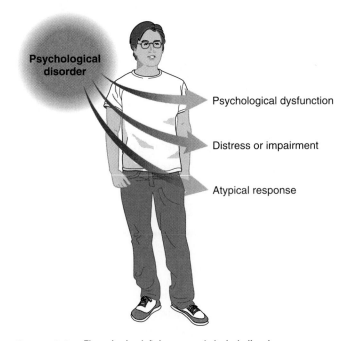

figure 1.1   The criteria defining a psychological disorder.

out of touch with reality as in schizophrenia and some other severe disorders. A dysfunction was present for Judy: She fainted at the sight of blood. But many people experience a mild version of this reaction (feeling queasy at the sight of blood) without meeting the criteria for the disorder, so knowing where to draw the line between normal and abnormal dysfunction is often difficult. For this reason, these problems are often considered to be on a *continuum* or as a *dimension,* rather than as categories that are either present or absent. This, too, is a reason why just having a dysfunction is not enough to meet the criteria for a psychological disorder.

That the disorder or behavior must be associated with *distress* adds an important component and seems clear: The criterion is satisfied if the individual is extremely upset. We can certainly say that Judy was very distressed and even suffered with her

Distress and suffering are a natural part of life and do not in themselves constitute a psychological disorder.

phobia. But remember, by itself this criterion does not define abnormal behavior. It is often quite normal to be distressed; for example, if someone close to you dies. The human condition is such that suffering and distress are very much part of life. This is not likely to change. Furthermore, for some disorders, by definition, suffering and distress are absent. Consider the person who feels extremely elated and may act impulsively as part of a manic episode. As we'll see in Chapter 7, one of the major difficulties with this problem is that people enjoy the manic state so much that they are reluctant to begin treatment or stay in treatment very long. Thus, defining psychological disorder by distress alone doesn't work, although the concept of distress contributes to a good definition.

The concept of *impairment* is useful, though not entirely satisfactory. For example, many people consider themselves shy or lazy. This doesn't mean that they're abnormal. But if you are so shy that you find it impossible to date or even interact with people, and you make every attempt to avoid interactions even though you would like to have friends, then your social functioning is impaired. Judy was clearly impaired by her phobia, but many people with similar, less severe reactions are not impaired. This difference again illustrates the important point that most psychological disorders are simply extreme expressions of otherwise normal emotions, behaviors, and cognitive processes.

Finally, the criterion that the response be *atypical or not culturally expected* is important but also insufficient to determine abnormality. At times, something is considered abnormal because it occurs infrequently; it deviates from the average. The greater the deviation, the more abnormal it is. You might say that someone is abnormally short or abnormally tall, meaning that the persons' height deviates sub-

stantially from average, but this obviously isn't a definition of disorder. Many people are far from the average in their behavior, but few would be considered disordered. We might call them talented or eccentric. Many artists, movie stars,

Some religious behaviors may seem unusual to us but are culturally or individually appropriate.

We accept extreme behaviors by entertainers, such as Marilyn Manson, that would not be tolerated in other members of our society.

and athletes fall in this category. For example, it's not normal to masturbate in public, but Madonna used to do it on stage. The novelist J. D. Salinger, who wrote *Catcher in the Rye,* retreated to a small town in New Hampshire and refused to see any outsiders for years, but he continued to write. The male singer Marilyn Manson wears heavy makeup on stage. These people are well paid and also seem to enjoy their careers. In most cases, the more productive you are in the eyes of society, the more eccentricities society will tolerate. Therefore, "deviating from the average" doesn't work very well as a definition.

Another view is that your behavior is abnormal if you are violating social norms, even if a number of people are sympathetic to your point of view. This definition is very useful in considering important cultural differences in psychological disorders. For example, to enter a trance state and believe you are possessed reflects a psychological disorder in most Western cultures but not in many other societies where the behavior is accepted and expected (see Chapter 6). (A cultural perspective is an important point of reference throughout this book.) However, a social standard of normal has been misused. Consider, for example, the practice of committing political dissidents to mental institutions because they protest the policies of their government, which was common in the former Soviet Union before the fall of communism. Although such dissident behavior clearly violates social norms, it should not alone be cause for commitment.

In conclusion, though it is difficult to define "normal" and "abnormal"—and the debate continues (Lilienfeld & Marino, 1995; Follette & Houts, 1996)—we can safely say that **behavioral, emotional, or cognitive dysfunctions that** **are unexpected in their cultural context and associated with personal distress or substantial impairment in functioning are abnormal.** This definition can be useful across cultures and subcultures if we pay very careful attention to what is "functional" or "dysfunctional" in a given society. This emphasizes a point made repeatedly throughout the book: To understand and treat psychopathology it is crucial that we attend to influential ethnic and cultural factors. (Jerome Wakefield [1992, 1997], in a very thoughtful analysis of the matter, uses the shorthand definition "harmful dysfunction.") A variant of this approach is most often used in current diagnostic practice, as outlined in the fourth edition of the *Diagnostic and Statistical Manual* (DSM–IV) (American Psychiatric Association, 1994), which contains the current listing of criteria for psychological disorders. And this approach guides our thinking in this book.

To leave you with a final challenge, take the problem of defining abnormal behavior a step further and consider this: What if Judy passed out so often that after a while neither her classmates nor her teachers even noticed because she regained consciousness quickly? Furthermore, what if Judy continued to get good grades? Would fainting all the time at the mere thought of blood be a disorder? Would it be impairing? dysfunctional? distressing? What do you think?

■ concept check 1.1

Check your understanding of the definitions of abnormal behavior. Write the letter for any, all, or none of the following definitions in the blanks: (a) societal norm violation, (b) impairment in functioning, (c) dysfunction, and (d) distress.

1. Jan's neighbor collects aluminum cans and attaches them to the inside walls of her house for decoration. She has two rooms completely "wallpapered" with cans and has started on a third. Jan knows of no one else who engages in similar behavior and, therefore, believes her neighbor to be abnormal. Jan could be using one of two definitions of abnormality. Which, if any, are they? _____

2. Miguel recently began feeling sad and lonely. While still able to function at work and fulfill his other responsibilities, he finds himself feeling down much of the time and he worries about what is happening to him. Which of the definitions of abnormality apply to Miguel's situation? _____

3. Three weeks ago, Tony, a thirty-five-year-old business executive, stopped showering, refused to leave his apartment, and started watching television talk shows. Threats of being fired have failed to bring Tony back to reality, and he continues to spend his days staring blankly at the television screen. Which of the definitions seem to describe Tony's situation? _____

4. Jane is afraid to leave her home. She used to force herself to go out in order to maintain contact with friends and relatives; however, more recently she refuses to go anywhere. Which definitions apply to this situation? _____

The Science of Psychopathology

Psychopathology is the scientific study of psychological disorders. Within this field are specially trained professionals, including clinical and counseling psychologists, psychiatrists, psychiatric social workers, and psychiatric nurses. *Clinical* and *counseling psychologists* receive the Ph.D. degree (or sometimes a Psy.D., doctor of psychology, or Ed.D., doctor of education) and follow a course of graduate-level study, lasting approximately 5 years, that prepares them to conduct research into the causes and treatment of psychological disorders and to diagnose, assess, and treat these disorders. Psychologists with other specialty training, such as experimental and social psychologists, concentrate on investigating the basic determinants of behavior but do not assess or treat psychological disorders. In addition, although there is a great deal of overlap, counseling psychologists tend to study and treat adjustment and vocational issues encountered by relatively healthy individuals, and clinical psychologists usually concentrate on more severe psychological disorders.

Psychiatrists first earn an M.D. degree in medical school, and then specialize in psychiatry during a 3- to 4-year residency training. Psychiatrists also investigate the nature and causes of psychological disorders, often from a biological point of view, make diagnoses, and offer treatments. Many psychiatrists emphasize drugs or other biological treatments, although most use psychosocial treatments as well.

Psychiatric social workers typically earn a master's degree in social work as they develop expertise in collecting information relevant to the social and family situation of the individual with a psychological disorder. Social workers also treat disorders, often concentrating on family problems associated with them. *Psychiatric nurses* have advanced degrees such as a master's or even a Ph.D., and specialize in the care and treatment of patients with psychological disorders, usually in hospitals as part of a treatment team.

The most important development in the recent history of psychopathology is the adoption of scientific methods to learn more about the nature of psychological disorders, their causes, and their treatment. Most mental health professionals take a scientific approach to their clinical work and therefore earn the title **scientist–practitioner** (Barlow, Hayes, & Nelson, 1984). Mental health practitioners may function as scientist–practitioners in one or more of three ways (see Figure 1.2). First, they may keep up with the latest scientific developments in their field and therefore use the most current diagnostic and treatment procedures. In this sense, they are consumers of the science of psychopathology to the advantage of their patients. Second, scientist–practitioners evaluate their own assessments or treatment procedures to see if they work. They are accountable not only to their patients but also to the government agencies and insurance companies that pay for the treatments, so they must demonstrate clearly that their treatments work. Third, scientist–practitioners might conduct research, often in clinics or hospitals, that produces

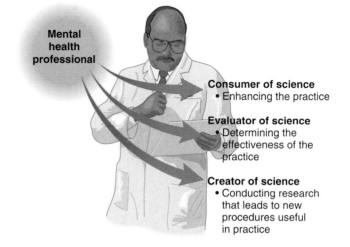

figure 1.2 Functioning as a scientist-practitioner.

new information about disorders or their treatment, thus becoming immune to the fads that plague our field, often at the expense of patients and their families. For example, new "miracle cures" for psychological disorders that are reported several times a year in popular media would not be used by a scientist–practitioner who did not have sound scientific data showing that they work. Such data flow from research that attempts three basic things: to describe psychological disorders, to determine their causes, and to treat them (see Figure 1.3). These three categories compose an organizational structure that recurs throughout this book, and that is formally evident in the discussions of specific disorders beginning in Chapter 5. A general overview of them now will give you a clearer perspective on our efforts to understand abnormality.

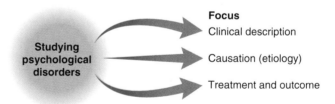

figure 1.3 Three major categories make up the study and discussion of psychological disorders.

Clinical Description

In hospitals and clinics we often say that a patient "presents" with a specific problem or set of problems, or we discuss the **presenting problem.** *Presents* is a traditional shorthand way of indicating why the person came to the clinic. Describing Judy's presenting problem is the first step in determining her **clinical description,** which represents the unique combination of behaviors, thoughts, and feelings that make up a specific disorder. The word *clinical* refers both to the types of problems or disorders that you would find in a clinic or hospital, and to the activities connected with assessment and treatment. Throughout this text are excerpts from many more individual cases, most of them from our personal files.

Children experience panic and anxiety differently from adults, so their reactions may be mistaken for symptoms of physical illness.

Clearly, one important function of the clinical description is to specify what makes the disorder different from normal behavior or from other disorders. Statistical data may also be relevant. For example, how many people in the population as a whole have the disorder? This figure is called the **prevalence** of the disorder. Statistics on how many new cases occur during a given period of time, such as a year, represent the **incidence** of the disorder. Other statistics include the *sex ratio*—that is, what percentage of males and females have the disorder—and the typical *age of onset,* which often differs from one disorder to another.

In addition to having different symptoms, age of onset, and possibly a different sex ratio and prevalence, most disorders follow a somewhat individual pattern, or **course.** For example, some disorders, such as schizophrenia (see Chapter 13), follow a *chronic course,* meaning that they tend to last a long time, sometimes a whole lifetime. Other disorders, like mood disorders (see Chapter 7), follow an *episodic course,* in that the individual is likely to recover within a few months, only to suffer a recurrence of the disorder at a later time. This pattern may repeat throughout a person's life. Still other disorders may have a *time-limited course,* meaning the disorder will improve without treatment in a relatively short period of time.

Closely related to differences in the course of disorders are differences in onset. Some disorders have an *acute onset,* meaning that they begin suddenly; others develop gradually over an extended period of time, which is sometimes called an *insidious onset.* It is important to know the typical course of a disorder so that we can know what to expect in the future and how best to deal with the problem. This is an important part of the clinical description. For example, if someone is suffering from a mild disorder with acute onset that we know is time limited, we might advise the individual not to bother with expensive treatment, because the problem will be over soon enough, like a common cold. However, if the disorder is likely to last a long time (become chronic), the individual might want to seek treatment and take other appropriate steps. The anticipated course of a disorder is called the **prognosis.** So we might say, "the prognosis is good," meaning the individual will probably recover, or "the prognosis is guarded," meaning the probable outcome doesn't look good.

The patient's age may be a very important part of the clinical description. A specific psychological disorder occurring in childhood may present very differently from the same disorder in adulthood or old age. Children experiencing severe anxiety and panic often assume that they are physically ill because they have difficulty understanding that there is nothing physically wrong. Because their thoughts and feelings are different from those experienced by adults with anxiety and panic, children are often misdiagnosed and treated for a medical disorder.

We call the study of changes in behavior over time *developmental psychology,* and we refer to the study of changes in abnormal behavior as *developmental psychopathology.* When you think of developmental psychology, you probably picture researchers studying the behavior of children. However, because we change throughout our lives, researchers also study development in adolescents, adults, and older adults. Study across the entire age span is referred to as *lifespan developmental psychopathology.* The field is relatively new but expanding rapidly.

Causation, Treatment, and Outcomes

Etiology, or the study of origins, has to do with why a disorder begins (what causes it) and includes biological, psychological, and social dimensions. Because the etiology of psychological disorders is so important to this field, we devote an entire chapter (Chapter 2) to it.

Treatment is often important to the study of psychological disorders. If a new drug or psychosocial treatment is successful in treating a disorder, it may give us some hints about the nature of the disorder and its causes. For example, if a drug with a specific known effect within the nervous system alleviates a certain psychological disorder, we know that something in that part of the nervous system might either be causing the disorder or helping maintain it. Similarly, if a psychosocial treatment designed to help clients regain a sense of control over their lives is effective with a certain disorder, a diminished sense of control may be an important psychological component of the disorder itself.

As we shall see in the next chapter, psychology is never that simple. This is because the *effect* does not necessarily imply the *cause.* To use a common example, you might take an aspirin to relieve a tension headache you developed during a grueling day of taking exams. If you then feel better, that does not mean that the headache was caused by a lack

■ **concept check 1.2**

A clinical description includes the unique combination of behaviors, thoughts, and feelings that make up a given psychological disorder. Match the following words that are used in clinical descriptions with their corresponding examples: (a) presenting problem, (b) prevalence, (c) incidence, (d) prognosis, (e) course, or (f) etiology.

1. Maria should recover quickly with no intervention necessary. Without treatment, John will deteriorate rapidly.

_____

2. Three new cases of bulimia have been reported in this county during the past month and only one in the next county. _____

3. Elizabeth visited the campus mental health center because of her increasing feelings of guilt and anxiety.

_____

4. Biological, psychological, and social influences all contribute to a variety of disorders. _____

5. The pattern a disorder follows can be chronic, time-limited, or episodic. _____

6. How many people in the population as a whole suffer from obsessive–compulsive disorder? _____

of aspirin in the first place. Nevertheless, many people seek treatment for psychological disorders, and treatment can provide interesting hints about the nature of the disorder.

In the past, textbooks emphasized treatment approaches in a very general sense, with little attention to the disorder being treated. For example, a mental health professional might be thoroughly trained in a single theoretical approach, such as psychoanalysis or behavior therapy (both described later in the chapter), and then use that approach on every disorder. More recently, as our science has advanced, we have developed specific effective treatments that do not always adhere neatly to one theoretical approach or another but that have grown out of a deeper understanding of the disorder in question. For this reason, there are no separate chapters in this book on such types of treatment approaches as psychodynamic, cognitive behavioral, or humanistic. Rather, the latest and most effective drug and psychosocial treatments are described in the context of specific disorders in keeping with our integrative multidimensional perspective.

We now survey many early attempts to *describe* and *treat* abnormal behavior, and more still to comprehend its *causes,* which will give you a better perspective on current approaches. In Chapter 2, we examine exciting contemporary views of causation and treatment. In Chapter 3, we discuss efforts to describe, or classify, abnormal behavior. In Chapter 4, we review research methods—our systematic efforts to discover the truths underlying description, cause, and treatment that allow us to function as scientist–practitioners. In Chapters 5 through 15, we examine specific disorders; our discussion is organized in each case in the now familiar triad of description, cause, and treatment. Finally, in Chapter 16 we examine legal, professional, and ethical issues that are relevant to psychological disorders and their treatment today. With that overview in mind, let us turn to the past.

The Past: Historical Conceptions of Abnormal Behavior

For thousands of years, humans have tried to explain and control problematic behavior. But our efforts always derive from the theories or models of behavior that are popular at the time. The purpose of these models is to explain why someone is "acting like that." Three major models that have guided us date back to the beginnings of civilization.

Humans have always supposed that agents outside our bodies and environment influence our behavior, thinking, and emotions. These agents, which might be divinities, demons, spirits, or other phenomena such as magnetic fields or the moon or the stars, are the driving forces behind the *supernatural model.* In addition, since ancient Greece, the mind has often been called the *soul* or the *psyche* and considered separate from the body. Although many have thought that the mind can influence the body and, in turn, the body can influence the mind, most philosophers looked for causes of abnormal behavior in one or the other. This split gave rise to two traditions of thought about abnormal behavior, summarized as the *biological model* and the *psychological model.*

These three models—the supernatural, the biological, and the psychological—are very old but continue to be used today.

The Supernatural Tradition

For much of our recorded history, deviant behavior has been considered a reflection of the battle between good and evil. When confronted with unexplainable, irrational behavior and by suffering and upheaval, people perceived evil. Barbara Tuchman, a noted historian, chronicled the second half of the 14th century, a particularly difficult time for humanity, in *A Distant Mirror* (1978). She very ably captures the conflicting tides of opinion on the origins and treatment of insanity during that bleak and tumultuous period.

One strong current of opinion put the causes and treatment of psychological disorders squarely in the realm of the supernatural. During the last quarter of the 14th century, religious and lay authorities supported these popular superstitions, and society as a whole began to believe in the reality and power of demons and witches. The Catholic church had split, and a second center, complete with a pope, emerged in the south of France to compete with Rome. In reaction to

During the Middle Ages, individuals with psychological disorders were sometimes thought to be possessed by evil spirits that had to be exorcised through rituals.

this schism, the Roman church fought back against the evil in the world that must have been behind this heresy.

People now turned increasingly to magic and sorcery to solve their problems. During these turbulent times, the bizarre behavior of people afflicted with psychological disorders was seen as the work of the devil and witches. It followed that individuals possessed by evil spirits were probably responsible for any misfortune experienced by the townspeople, which inspired drastic action against the possessed. Treatments included *exorcism,* in which various religious rituals were performed to rid the victim of evil spirits. Other approaches included shaving the pattern of a cross in the hair of the victim's head, and securing sufferers to a wall near the front of a church so that they might benefit from hearing Mass.

The conviction that sorcery and witches are causes of madness and other evils continued into the 15th century, and evil continued to be blamed for unexplainable behavior, even after the founding of our own country, as evidenced by the Salem witch trials.

An equally strong opinion, even during this period, reflected the enlightened view that insanity was a natural phenomenon, caused by mental or emotional stress, and that it was curable (Alexander & Selesnick, 1966; Maher & Maher, 1985a). Mental depression and anxiety were recognized as illnesses (Kemp, 1990; Schoeneman, 1977), although symptoms such as despair and lethargy were often identified by the church with the sin of *acedia,* or sloth (Tuchman, 1978). Common treatments were rest, sleep, and a healthy and happy environment. Other treatments included baths, ointments, and various potions. Indeed, during the 14th and 15th centuries, the insane, along with the physically deformed or disabled, were often moved from house to house in medieval

villages, as neighbors took turns caring for them. We now know that this medieval practice of keeping people who have psychological disturbances in their own community is beneficial (see Chapter 14). (We will return to this subject when we discuss biological and psychological models later in this chapter.)

One of the chief advisers to the king of France, a bishop and philosopher named Nicholas Oresme, also suggested that the disease of melancholy (depression) was the source of some bizarre behavior, rather than demons. Oresme pointed out that much of the evidence for the existence of sorcery and witchcraft, particularly among the insane, was obtained from people who were tortured and who, quite understandably, confessed to anything.

These conflicting crosscurrents of natural and supernatural explanations for mental disorders are represented more or less strongly in various historical works, depending on the sources consulted by historians. Some assumed that demonic influences were the predominant explanations of abnormal behavior during the Middle Ages (for example, Zilboorg & Henry, 1941); others believed that the supernatural had little or no influence. As we see in the handling of the severe psychological disorder experienced by the late-14th-century King Charles VI of France, both influences were strong, sometimes alternating in the treatment of the same case.

Charles VI
The Mad King

In the summer of 1392, King Charles VI of France was under a great deal of stress, due in part to the division of the Catholic church. As he rode with his army to the province of Brittany, a nearby aide dropped his lance with a loud clatter and the king, thinking he was under attack, turned on his own army, killing several prominent knights before being subdued from behind. The army immediately marched back to Paris. The king's lieutenants and advisers concluded that he was mad.

During the following years, at his worst the king hid in a corner of his castle believing he was made of glass, or roamed the

corridors howling like a wolf. At other times he couldn't remember who or what he was. He became fearful and enraged whenever he saw his own royal coat of arms, and would try to destroy it if it were brought near him.

The people of Paris were devastated by their leader's apparent madness. Some thought it reflected God's anger, because the king failed to take up arms to end the schism in the Catholic church; others thought it was God's warning *against* taking up arms; still others thought it was divine punishment for heavy taxes (a conclusion some people might make today). But most thought the king's madness was caused by sorcery, a belief strengthened by a great drought that dried up the ponds and rivers, causing cattle to die of thirst. Merchants claimed their worst losses in 20 years.

Naturally, the king was given the best care available. The most famous healer in the land was a 92-year-old physician whose treatment program included moving the king to one of his residences in the country where the air was thought to be the cleanest in the land. The physician prescribed rest, relaxation, and recreation. After some time, the king seemed to recover. The physician recommended that the king not be burdened with the responsibilities of running the kingdom, claiming that if he had few worries or irritations, his mind would gradually strengthen and further improve.

Unfortunately, the physician died, the king's insanity returned more seriously than before, and his new therapist insisted that the malady was caused by sorcery. Remedies and rituals of all kinds were tried, but none worked. High-ranking officials and doctors of the university called for the sorcerers to be discovered and punished. Even Charles himself came to believe during his lucid moments that the source of his madness was evil and sorcery.

If Judy had lived during the late 14th century, it is quite possible that she would have been seen as possessed and subjected to exorcism. You may remember the movie *The Exorcist*, in which a young girl, behaving very strangely, was screened for every possible mental and physical disorder before authorities reluctantly resorted to an exorcism.

Treatments for Possession

With a perceived connection between evil deeds and sin on the one hand, and psychological disorders on the other, it is logical to conclude that the sufferer is largely responsible for the disorder, which might well be a punishment for evil deeds. Does this sound familiar? The acquired immune deficiency syndrome (AIDS) epidemic reflects a very similar belief among some people in the 1990s. Since the human immunodeficiency virus (HIV) is in Western societies most prevalent among prac-

ticing homosexuals, many people believe it is a divine punishment for what they consider abhorrent behavior. This view is slowly dissipating as the AIDS virus spreads to other "less sinful" segments of the population, but it still persists.

Possession, however, is not always connected with sin, but may be seen as involuntary and the possessed individual as blameless. Furthermore, exorcisms at least have the virtue of being relatively painless. Interestingly, they sometimes work, as do other forms of faith healing, for reasons we will explore in subsequent chapters. But what if they did not? In the Middle Ages, if exorcism failed, some authorities thought that steps were necessary to make the body uninhabitable by evil spirits, and many people were subjected to confinement, beatings, and other forms of torture (Kemp, 1990).

Somewhere along the way, a creative "therapist" decided that hanging people over a pit full of poisonous snakes might scare the evil spirits right out of their bodies (to say nothing of terrifying the people themselves). Strangely, this approach sometimes worked; that is, the most disturbed, oddly behaving individuals would suddenly come to their senses and experience relief from their symptoms, if only temporarily. Naturally, this was reinforcing to the therapist and so snake pits were built in many institutions. Many other treatments based on the hypothesized therapeutic element of shock were developed, including dunkings in ice-cold water. We will discuss modern shock treatments such as electroconvulsive therapy later in the chapter.

Mass Hysteria

Another fascinating phenomenon is characterized by large-scale outbreaks of bizarre behavior. To this day these episodes puzzle historians and mental health practitioners. During the Middle Ages they lent support to the notion of

In hydrotherapy, patients were shocked back to their senses by being submerged in ice-cold water.

Emotions are contagious and can escalate into mass hysteria.

possession. In Europe, whole groups of people were simultaneously compelled to run out in the streets, dance, shout, rave, and jump around in patterns as if they were at a particularly wild party late at night, but without the music. This behavior was known by several names, including Saint Vitus's Dance and tarantism. It is most interesting that many people behaved in this strange way all at once. In an attempt to explain the inexplicable, several reasons were offered in addition to possession. One reasonable guess was reaction to insect bites. Another possibility was

what we now call "mass hysteria." Consider the following example.

Mass hysteria may simply demonstrate the phenomenon of *emotion contagion,* in which the experience of an emotion seems to spread to those around us (Hatfield, Cacioppo, & Rapson, 1994). If someone nearby becomes very frightened or very sad, chances are that for the moment you also will feel fear or sadness. When this kind of experience escalates into full-blown panic, whole communities are affected (Barlow, in press). People are also very suggestible when they are in states of high emotion. Therefore, if one person identifies a "cause" of the problem, others will probably assume that their own reactions have the same source. In popular language, this shared response is sometimes referred to as *mob psychology.*

Modern Mass Hysteria

One Friday afternoon an alarm sounded over the public address system of a community hospital calling all physicians to the emergency room immediately. Arriving from a local school in a fleet of ambulances were 17 students and 4 teachers who reported dizziness, headache, nausea, and stomach pains. Some were vomiting; most were hyperventilating.

All the students and teachers had been in four classrooms, two on each side of the hallway. The incident began when a 14-year-old girl reported a funny smell that seemed to be coming from a vent. She fell to the floor, crying and complaining that her stomach hurt and her eyes stung. Soon, many of the students and most of the teachers in the four adjoining classrooms, who could see and hear what was happening, experienced similar symptoms. Of 86 susceptible people (82 students and 4 teachers in the four classrooms), 21 patients (17 students and 4 teachers) experienced symptoms severe enough to be evaluated at the hospital. Inspection of the school building by public health authorities revealed no apparent cause for the reactions, and physical examinations by teams of physicians revealed no physical abnormalities. All the patients were sent home and quickly recovered (Rockney & Lemke, 1992).

The Moon and the Stars

Paracelsus, a Swiss physician who lived from 1493 to 1541, rejected notions of possession by the devil, suggesting instead that the movements of the moon and stars had profound effects on people's psychological functioning. This influential theory inspired the word *lunatic,* which is derived from the Latin word for moon, *luna.* You might hear some of your friends explain something crazy they did last night by saying, "It must have been the full moon."

The belief that heavenly bodies affect human behavior still exists, although there is no scientific evidence to support it. Despite much ridicule, millions of people around the world are convinced that their behavior is influenced by the stages of the moon or the position of the stars. This belief is most noticeable today in followers of astrology, who hold that their behavior and the major events in their lives can be predicted by their day-to-day relationship to the position of the planets. However, no serious evidence has ever confirmed such a connection.

Comments

The supernatural tradition in psychopathology is alive and well, although it is relegated, for the most part, to small religious sects in this country and to nontechnological cultures elsewhere. Members of organized religions in most parts of the world look to psychology and medical science for help with major psychological disorders; in fact, the Roman Catholic church requires that all health care resources be exhausted before spiritual solutions such as exorcism can be considered. Nonetheless, miraculous cures are sometimes achieved by exorcism, magic potions and rituals, and other methods that seem to have little connection with modern science. It is fascinating to explore them when they do occur, and we will return to this topic in subsequent chapters. But such cases are relatively rare, and almost no one would advocate supernatural treatment for severe psychological disorders except, perhaps, as a last resort.

The Biological Tradition

Physical causes of mental disorders have been sought since early in history. Important to the biological tradition are a man, Hippocrates; a disease, syphilis; and the early consequences of believing that psychological disorders are biologically caused.

Hippocrates and Galen

The Greek physician Hippocrates (460–377 B.C.) is considered to be the father of modern medicine. He and his associates left a body of work called the *Hippocratic Corpus* written between 450 and 350 B.C. (Maher & Maher, 1985a), in which they suggested that psychological disorders could be treated like any other disease. They did not limit their search for the causes of psychopathology to the general area of "disease," because they believed that psychological disorders might also be caused by brain pathology or head trauma and could be influenced by heredity (genetics). These are remarkably astute deductions for the time, and they have been supported in recent years. Hippocrates considered the brain to be the seat of wisdom, consciousness, intelligence, and emotion. Therefore, disorders involving these functions would logically be located in the brain. Hippocrates also recognized the importance of psychological and interpersonal contributions to psychopathology, such as the sometimes negative effects of family stress; on some occasions, he removed patients from their families.

The Roman physician Galen (ca. 129–198 A.D.) later adopted the ideas of Hippocrates and his associates and developed them further, creating a powerful and influential school of thought within the biological tradition that extended well into the 19th century. One of the more interesting and influential legacies of the Hippocratic–Galenic approach is the *humoral theory* of disorders. Hippocrates assumed that normal brain functioning was related to four bodily fluids or *humors:* blood, black bile, yellow bile, and phlegm. Blood came from the heart, black bile from the spleen, phlegm from the brain, and choler or yellow bile from the liver. Physicians believed that disease resulted from too much or too little of one of the humors; for example, too much black bile was thought to cause melancholia (depression). In fact, the term *melancholer,* which means black bile, is still used today in its derivative form *melancholy* to refer to aspects of depression. The humoral theory was, perhaps, the first example of associating psychological disorders with chemical imbalance, an approach that is widespread today.

The four humors were related to the Greeks' conception of the four basic qualities: heat, dryness, moisture, and cold. Each humor was associated with one of these qualities. Terms derived from the four humors are still sometimes applied to personality traits. For example, *sanguine* describes someone who is cheerful and optimistic, though insomnia and delirium were thought to be caused by excessive blood in the brain. *Melancholic,* of course, means depressive (depression was thought to be caused by black bile flooding the brain). *Phlegmatic* indicates apathy and sluggishness but can also mean being calm under stress. A *choleric* person is hot tempered (Maher & Maher, 1985a).

Excesses of one or more humors were treated by regulating the environment to increase or decrease heat, dryness, moisture, or cold, depending on which humor was out of balance. One reason King Charles VI's physician moved him to the less stressful countryside was to restore the balance in his humors (Kemp, 1990). In addition to rest, good nutrition, and exercise, two treatments were developed. In one, *bleeding* or *bloodletting,* a carefully mea-

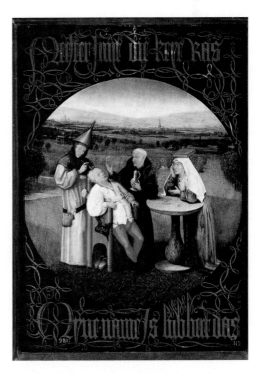

Bloodletting, the extraction of blood from patients, was intended to restore the balance of humors in the body.

sured amount of blood was removed from the body, often with leeches. The other was to induce vomiting; indeed, in a well-known treatise on depression published in 1621, *Anatomy of Melancholy,* Burton recommended eating tobacco and a half-boiled cabbage to induce vomiting (Burton, 1621/1977).

Three hundred years ago, Judy might have been diagnosed with an illness, a brain disorder, or some other physical problem, and given the proper medical treatments of the day, including bed rest, a healthful diet, exercise, and other ministrations as indicated.

Hippocrates also coined the word *hysteria* to describe a concept he learned about from the Egyptians, who had identified what we now call the *somatoform disorders.* In these disorders, the physical symptoms appear to be the result of an organic pathology for which no organic cause can be found, such as paralysis and some kinds of blindness. Because these disorders occurred primarily in women, the Egyptians (and Hippocrates) mistakenly assumed that they were restricted to women. They also presumed a cause: The empty uterus wandered to various parts of the body in search of conception (the Greek for "uterus" is *hysteron*). Numerous physical symptoms reflected the location of the wandering uterus. The prescribed cure might be marriage or, occasionally, fumigation of the vagina to lure the uterus back to its natural location (Alexander & Selesnick, 1966). Knowledge of physiology eventually disproved the wandering uterus theory; however, the tendency to stigmatize dramatic women as "hysterical" continued unabated well into the 1970s, when mental health professionals became sensitive to the prejudicial stereotype the term implied. As you will learn in Chapter 6, somatoform disorders (and the traits associated with them) are not limited to one sex or the other.

The Nineteenth Century

SYPHILIS

The biological tradition waxed and waned during the centuries after Hippocrates and Galen, but was reinvigorated in the 19th century by the discovery of the nature and cause of syphilis, a sexually transmitted disease caused by a bacterial microorganism entering the brain. Behavioral and cognitive symptoms of what we now know as advanced syphilis include believing that everyone is plotting against you (delusion of persecution) or that you are God (delusion of grandeur), as well as other bizarre behaviors. Although these symptoms are very similar to those of psychosis, researchers recognized that a subgroup of apparently psychotic patients deteriorated steadily, becoming paralyzed and dying within 5 years of onset. This course of events contrasted with that of most psychotic patients, who remained fairly stable. In 1825, the condition was designated a disease, *general paresis,* because it had consistent symptoms (presentation) and a consistent course that resulted in death. The relationship between general paresis and syphilis was only gradually established. Louis Pasteur's germ theory of disease, around 1870, facilitated the identification of the specific bacterial microorganism that caused syphilis. Pasteur stated that all the symptoms of a disease were caused by a germ bacterium that had invaded the body.

Of equal importance was the discovery of a cure for general paresis. Physicians observed a surprising recovery in patients who had contracted malaria, and deliberately injected others with blood from a soldier who was ill with malaria. Many recovered, because the high fever "burned out" the syphilis bacteria. Obviously, this type of experiment would not be ethically possible today. Ultimately, clinical investigators discovered that penicillin cures syphilis, but with the malaria cure, "madness" and associated behavioral and cognitive symptoms for the first time were traced directly to a curable infection. Many mental health professionals then assumed that comparable causes and cures might be discovered for all psychological disorders.

JOHN P. GREY

The biological tradition flourished in the Western world in the 19th century. Its champion in the United States was the most influential American psychiatrist of the time, John P. Grey (Bockoven, 1963). In 1854, Grey was appointed superintendent of the Utica State Hospital in New York, the largest in the country. He also became editor of the *American Journal of Insanity,* the precursor of the current *American Journal of Psychiatry,* the flagship publication of the American Psychiatric Association. Grey's position was that

In the 19th century, psychological disorders were attributed to mental or emotional stress, so patients were often treated sympathetically in a restful and hygienic environment.

insanity was *always* due to physical causes. Therefore, the mentally ill patient should be treated as physically ill. The emphasis was once again on rest, diet, and proper room temperature and ventilation, approaches used for centuries by previous therapists in the biological tradition. Grey even invented the rotary fan in order to ventilate his large hospital.

Under Grey's leadership, the conditions in hospitals greatly improved, and they became more humane, livable institutions. But in subsequent years they also became so large and impersonal that individual attention was not possible. In fact, leaders in psychiatry at the end of the 19th century were alarmed at the increasing size and impersonality of mental hospitals and recommended that they be downsized. It was almost 100 years before the community mental health movement was successful in reducing the population of mental hospitals with the very controversial policy of "de-institutionalization," in which patients were released into their communities. Unfortunately, this practice has as many negative consequences as positive ones, including a large increase in the number of chronically disabled patients homeless on the streets of our cities.

Consequences of the Biological Tradition

In the late 19th century, John P. Grey and his colleagues ironically reduced or eliminated interest in treating mental patients because they thought that mental disorders were due to some as yet undiscovered brain pathology and were therefore incurable. The only available course of action was to hospitalize these patients. In fact, around the turn of the century some nurses documented clinical success in treating mental patients but were prevented from treating others for fear of raising hopes of a cure among family members. In place of treatment, interest centered on diagnosis, legal questions concerning the responsibility of patients for their actions during periods of insanity, and the study of brain pathology itself.

Emil Kraepelin (1856–1926) was the dominant figure during this period, and one of the founding fathers of modern psychiatry. He was extremely influential in advocating the major ideas of the biological tradition but he was little involved in treatment. His lasting contribution was in the area of diagnosis and classification, which we'll discuss in detail in Chapter 3. Kraepelin (1913) was one of the first to distinguish among various psychological disorders, seeing that each may have a different age of onset and time course, with somewhat different clusters of presenting symptoms, and probably a different cause. Many of his descriptions of schizophrenic disorders are still useful today.

By the end of the 1800s, a scientific approach to psychological disorders and their classification had begun with the search for biological causes. Furthermore, treatment was based on humane principles. However, there were many drawbacks, the most unfortunate being that active intervention and treatment were all but eliminated in some settings, despite the fact that some very effective approaches were available. It is to these that we now turn.

■ **concept check** 1.3

For thousands of years, humans have tried to understand and control abnormal behavior. Check your understanding of these historical theories and match them to the treatments used to "cure" abnormal behavior: (a) marriage; fumigation of the vagina; (b) hypnosis; (c) bloodletting; induced vomiting; (d) patient placed in socially facilitative environments; and (e) exorcism; burning at the stake.

1. Supernatural causes; evil demons took over the victims' bodies and controlled their behaviors. _____

2. The humoral theory reflected the belief that normal functioning of the brain required a balance of four bodily fluids or humors. _____

3. Maladaptive behavior was caused by poor social and cultural influences within the environment. _____

The Twentieth Century

NEW TREATMENTS

Renewed interest in the biological origin of psychological disorders led, ultimately, to greatly increased understanding of biological contributions to psychopathology and to the development of new treatments. In the 1930s, the physical interventions of electric shock and brain surgery were often used. Their effects, and the effects of new drugs, were discovered quite by accident. For example, insulin was occasionally given to stimulate appetite in psychotic patients who were not eating, but it also seemed to calm them down. In 1927, a Viennese physician, Manfred Sakel, began using higher and higher dosages until, finally, patients convulsed and became comatose (Sakel, 1958). Some actually recovered their mental health, much to the surprise of everybody, and their recovery was attributed to the convulsions. The procedure became known as *insulin shock therapy*, but it was abandoned because it was too dangerous, often resulting in coma or even death. Other methods of producing convulsions had to be found.

In the 1920s, Joseph von Meduna observed that schizophrenia was very rarely found in epileptics (which ultimately did not prove to be true). Some of his followers concluded that induced brain seizures might cure schizophrenia. Following suggestions on the possible benefits of applying electric shock directly to the brain—notably, by two Italian physicians, Cerletti and Bini, in 1938—a surgeon in London treated a depressed patient by sending six small shocks directly through his brain, producing convulsions (Hunt, 1980). The patient recovered. Though greatly modified, shock treatment is still with us today, much to the distress of many. The controversial modern uses of *electroconvulsive therapy* (ECT) are described in Chapter 7. It is interesting that even now we have very little knowledge of how it works.

During the 1950s, the first effective drugs for severe psychotic disorders were developed in a systematic way.

Prior to that time, a number of medicinal substances, including opium (derived from poppies), had been used as sedatives, along with countless herbs and folk remedies (Alexander & Selesnick, 1966). With the discovery of *Rauwolfia serpentina* (later renamed *reserpine*) and another class of drugs called *neuroleptics* (major tranquilizers), for the first time hallucinatory and delusional thought processes could be diminished; these drugs also controlled agitation and aggressiveness. Other discoveries included *benzodiazepines* (minor tranquilizers), which seemed to reduce anxiety. By the 1970s, the benzodiazepines (known by such brand names as Valium and Librium) were among the most widely prescribed drugs in the world. As drawbacks and side effects of tranquilizers became apparent, along with their limited effectiveness, prescriptions decreased somewhat (we'll discuss the benzodiazepines in more detail in Chapters 5 and 11).

Throughout the centuries, as Alexander and Selesnick (1966) point out, "The general pattern of drug therapy for mental illness has been one of initial enthusiasm followed by disappointment" (p. 287). For example, bromides, a class of sedating drugs, were used at the end of the 19th and the beginning of the 20th century to treat anxiety and other psychological disorders. By the 1920s, they were reported as being effective for many serious psychological and emotional symptoms. By 1928, one of every five prescriptions in the United States was for bromides. When their side effects, including various undesirable physical symptoms, became widely known, and experience began to show that their overall effectiveness was relatively modest, bromides largely disappeared from the scene.

Neuroleptics have also been used less as attention has focused on their many side effects, such as tremors and shaking. However, the positive effects of these drugs on some patients' psychotic symptoms of hallucinations, delusions, and agitation revitalized both the search for biological contributions to psychological disorders and the search for new and more powerful drugs.

The Psychological Tradition

It is a long leap from evil spirits to brain pathology as causes of psychological disorders. In the intervening centuries, where was the body of thought that put psychological development, both normal and abnormal, in an interpersonal and social context? In fact, this approach has a long and distinguished tradition. Plato, for example, thought that the two causes of maladaptive behavior were the social and cultural influences in one's life and the learning that took place in that environment. If something was wrong in the environment, such as abusive parents, one's impulses and emotions would overcome reason. The best treatment was to reeducate the individual through rational discussion so that the power of reason would predominate (Maher & Maher, 1985a). This was very much a precursor to modern **psychosocial** approaches, which focus not only on psychological factors but on social and cultural ones as well. Other well-known early philosophers, including Aristotle, also emphasized the influence of social environment and early learning on later psychopathology. These philosophers wrote about the importance of fantasies, dreams, and cognitions and thus anticipated, to some extent, later developments in psychoanalytic thought and cognitive science. They also advocated humane and responsible care for the psychologically disturbed.

Moral Therapy

During the first half of the 18th century, a strong psychosocial approach to mental disorders called **moral therapy** became influential. The term *moral* really meant "emotional" or "psychological" rather than a code of conduct. Its basic tenets included treating institutionalized patients as normally as possible in a setting that encouraged and reinforced normal social interaction (Bockoven, 1963), thus providing them with many opportunities for appropriate social and interpersonal contact. Relationships were carefully nurtured. Individual attention clearly

Patients with psychological disorders were freed from chains and shackles as a result of the influence of Philippe Pinel (1745–1826), a pioneer in making mental institutions more humane.

emphasized positive consequences for appropriate interactions and behavior; the staff made a point of modeling this behavior. Lectures on various interesting subjects were provided, and restraint and seclusion were eliminated.

Once again, little is new under the sun. The principles of moral therapy date back to Plato and beyond. But moral therapy as a system originated with the well-known French psychiatrist, Philippe Pinel (1745–1826) (Zilboorg & Henry, 1941). A former patient, Pussin, long since recovered, was working in the Parisian hospital, La Bicêtre, when Pinel took over. Pussin had already instituted remarkable reforms, remembering, perhaps, being shackled as a patient himself. Pussin persuaded Pinel to go along with the changes. Much to Pinel's credit, he did, first at La Bicêtre and then at the women's hospital Salpêtrière (Maher & Maher, 1985b; Weiner, 1979), where a humane, socially facilitative atmosphere produced "miraculous" results.

After William Tuke (1732–1822) followed Pinel's lead in England, Benjamin Rush (1745–1813), often considered the founder of American psychiatry, introduced moral therapy in his early work at Pennsylvania Hospital. It then became the treatment of choice in the leading hospitals. *Asylums* had appeared in the 16th century, but they were more like prisons than hospitals. It was the rise of moral therapy in Europe and the United States that made institutions habitable and even therapeutic.

In 1833, Horace Mann, chairman of the board of trustees of the Worcester State Hospital, reported on 32 patients who had been given up as incurable. These patients were treated with moral therapy, cured, and released to their families. Of 100 patients who were viciously assaultive before treatment, no more than 12 continued to be violent a year after beginning treatment. Forty patients had routinely torn off any new clothes provided by attendants; only eight continued this behavior after a period of treatment. These were remarkable statistics then and would be remarkable even today (Bockoven, 1963).

Asylum Reform and the Decline of Moral Therapy

Unfortunately, after the mid-19th century, humane treatment declined because of a convergence of factors. First, it was widely recognized that moral therapy worked best when the number of patients in an institution was 200 or fewer, allowing for a great deal of individual attention. After the Civil War, enormous waves of immigrants arrived in the United States, yielding their own populations of mentally ill. Patient loads in existing hospitals increased to 1,000, 2,000, and more. Since immigrant groups were thought not to deserve the same privileges as "native" Americans (whose ancestors had immigrated perhaps only 50 or 100 years earlier!), they were not given moral treatments even when there were sufficient hospital personnel.

A second reason for the decline of moral therapy has an unlikely source. The great crusader Dorothea Dix (1802–1887) campaigned endlessly for reform in the treatment of the insane. A schoolteacher who had worked in various institutions, she had firsthand knowledge of the deplorable conditions imposed on the insane, and she made it her life's work to inform the American public and their leaders of these abuses. Her work became known as the **mental hygiene movement.**

In addition to improving the standards of care, Dix worked hard to make sure that everyone who needed care received it, including the homeless. Through her efforts, humane treatment became more widely available in American institutions. As her career drew to a close, she was rightly acknowledged as a hero of the 19th century.

Dorothea Dix (1802–1887) began the mental hygiene movement and spent much of her life campaigning for reform in the treatment of the mentally ill.

Unfortunately, an unforeseen consequence of Dix's heroic efforts was a substantial increase in the number of mental patients. This influx led to a rapid transition from moral therapy to custodial care because hospitals were inadequately staffed. Dix reformed our asylums and single-handedly inspired the construction of numerous new institutions here and abroad. But even her tireless efforts and advocacy could not ensure sufficient staffing to allow the individual attention necessary to moral therapy.

A final blow to the practice of moral therapy was the decision, in the middle of the 19th century, that mental illness was caused by brain pathology and, therefore, was incurable.

The psychological tradition lay dormant for a time, only to reemerge in several very different schools of thought in the 20th century. The first major approach was **psychoanalysis,** based on Sigmund Freud's (1856–1939) elaborate theory of the structure of the mind and the role of unconscious processes in determining behavior. The second was **behaviorism,** associated with John B. Watson, Ivan Pavlov, and B. F. Skinner, which focuses on how learning and adaptation affect the development of psychopathology.

Psychoanalytic Theory

Have you ever felt as if someone cast a spell on you? Have you ever been caught by a look across the room from a classmate, or a stare from a musician as you sat down in front at a large concert? If so, you have something in common with the patients of Anton Mesmer (1734–1815) and with millions of people since his time who have been hypnotized. Mesmer had his patients sit in a dark room around a large vat of chemicals with rods extending from it and touching

Anton Mesmer (1734–1815) and other early therapists used strong suggestions to cure their patients, who were often hypnotized.

them. Dressed in flowing robes, he suggested strongly that they were being cured. Because of his rather unusual techniques Mesmer was considered an oddity and maybe a charlatan, but he is also widely regarded as the father of hypnosis, a state in which extremely suggestible subjects sometimes appear to be in a trance.

Many distinguished scientists and physicians were very interested in Mesmer's powerful methods of suggestion. One of the best known, Jean Charcot (1825–1893), was head of the Salpêtrière Hospital in Paris, where Philippe Pinel had introduced psychological treatments several generations earlier. A distinguished neurologist, Charcot demonstrated that some of the techniques of mesmerism were effective with a number of psychological disorders, and

he did much to legitimize the fledgling practice of hypnosis. Significantly, in 1885 a young man named Sigmund Freud came from Vienna to study with Charcot.

After returning from France, Freud teamed up with Josef Breuer (1842–1925), who had experimented with a somewhat different hypnotic procedure. While his patients were in the highly suggestible state of hypnosis, Breuer asked them to describe their problems, conflicts, and fears in as much detail as they could. Breuer observed two extremely important phenomena during this process. First, patients often became extremely emotional as they talked, and felt quite relieved and improved after emerging from the hypnotic state. Second, seldom would they have gained an understanding of the relationship between their emotional problems and their psychological disorder. In fact, it was difficult or impossible for them to recall some of the details they had described under hypnosis. In other words, the material seemed to be beyond the awareness of

Josef Breuer (1842–1925) worked on the celebrated case of "Anna O." and, with Freud, developed the theory of psychoanalysis.

the patient. With this observation, Breuer and Freud had "discovered" the **unconscious** mind and its apparent influence on the production of psychological disorders. This is one of the most important developments in the history of psychopathology and, indeed, of psychology as a whole.

A close second was their discovery that it is therapeutic to recall and relive emotional trauma that has been made unconscious and to release the accompanying tension. This release of emotional material became known as **catharsis.** A fuller understanding of the relationship between current emotions and earlier events is referred to as *insight.* As we shall see throughout this book, particularly in Chapters 5 and 6 on anxiety and somatoform disorders, the existence of "unconscious" memories and feelings and the importance of "processing" emotion-laden information have been verified and reaffirmed.

Freud and Breuer's theories were based on case observations, some of which were made in a surprisingly systematic way for those times. An excellent example is Breuer's classic

Jean Charcot (1825–1893) studied hypnosis and influenced Sigmund Freud to consider psychosocial approaches to psychological disorders.

description of his treatment of "hysterical" symptoms in Anna O. in 1895 (Breuer & Freud, 1957). Anna O. was a bright, attractive young woman who was perfectly healthy until she reached 21 years of age. Shortly before her problems began, her father developed a serious chronic illness that led to his death. Throughout his illness, Anna O. had cared for him; she felt it necessary to spend endless hours at his bedside. Five months after her father became ill, Anna noticed that during the day her vision blurred, and that from time to time she had difficulty moving her right arm and both legs. Soon, additional symptoms appeared. She began to experience some difficulty speaking, and her behavior became very erratic. Shortly thereafter, she consulted Breuer.

Bertha Pappenheim (1859–1936), famous as "Anna O.," was described as "hysterical" by Breuer.

In a series of treatment sessions, Breuer dealt with one symptom at a time through hypnosis and subsequent "talking through," tracing each symptom to its hypothetical causation in circumstances surrounding the death of Anna's father. One at a time her "hysterical" ailments disappeared, but only after treatment was administered to each respective behavior. This process of treating one behavior at a time fulfills a basic requirement for drawing scientific conclusions about the effects of treatment in an individual case study, as we will see in Chapter 4. We will return to the fascinating case of Anna O. in Chapter 6.

Freud took these basic observations and expanded them into the **psychoanalytic model,** the most comprehensive theory yet constructed on the development and structure of our personalities. He also speculated on where this development could go wrong and produce psychological disorders. Though many of Freud's views changed over time, the basic principles of mental functioning that he originally proposed remained constant through his writings and are still applied by psychoanalysts today.

Psychoanalytic theory has had unprecedented influence; what follows is a brief outline of it. Our focus is on its three major facets: (a) the *structure of the mind* and the distinct functions of personality that sometimes clash with one another; (b) the *defense mechanisms* with which the mind defends itself from these clashes, or conflicts; and (c) *the stages of early psychosexual development* that provide grist for the mill of our inner conflicts.

Sigmund Freud (1856–1939), is considered the founder of psychoanalysis.

THE STRUCTURE OF THE MIND

The mind, according to Freud, has three major parts or functions: the *id, ego,* and *superego* (see Figure 1.4). These terms, like many from psychoanalysis, have found their way into our common vocabulary, but although you may have heard them, you may not be aware of their meaning.

The **id** is the source of our strong sexual and aggressive feelings or energies. It is, basically, the animal within us; if totally unchecked, it would make us all rapists or killers. The energy or drive within the id is the *libido.* Even today some people explain low sex drive as an absence of libido. A less important source of energy, not as well conceptualized by Freud, is the death instinct, or *thanatos.* Much like matter and antimatter, these two basic drives, toward life and fulfillment on the one hand and death and destruction on the other, are continually in opposition.

The id operates according to the *pleasure principle,* with an overriding goal of maximizing pleasure and eliminating any associated tension or conflicts. The goal of pleasure, which is particularly prominent in childhood, often conflicts with social rules and regulations, as we shall see later. The id has its own characteristic way of processing information; referred to as *primary process,* this type of thinking is very emotional, irrational, illogical, filled with fantasies, and preoccupied with sex, aggression, selfishness, and envy.

Fortunately for all of us, in Freud's view, the id's selfish and sometimes dangerous drives do not go unchecked. In fact, only a few months into life, we know we must adapt our basic demands to the real world. In other words, we must find ways to meet our basic needs without offending everyone around us. Put yet another way, we must act realistically. The part of our mind that ensures that we act realistically is called the **ego,** and it operates according to the *reality principle* instead of the pleasure principle. The cognitive operations or thinking styles of the ego are characterized by logic and reason and are referred to as the *secondary process,* as opposed to the illogical and irrational primary process of the id.

The third important structure within the mind, the **superego,** or what we might call *conscience,* represents the *moral principles* instilled in us by our parents and our culture. It is the voice within us that nags at us when we know we're doing something wrong. Since the purpose of the superego is to counteract the potentially dangerous aggressive and sexual drives of the id, the basis for conflict is readily apparent.

The role of the ego is to mediate conflict between the id and the superego, juggling their demands with the realities of the world. The ego is often referred to as the executive or

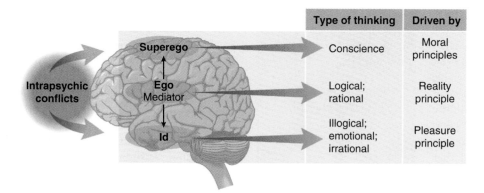

	Type of thinking	Driven by
Superego	Conscience	Moral principles
Ego Mediator	Logical; rational	Reality principle
Id	Illogical; emotional; irrational	Pleasure principle

figure 1.4 Freud's structure of the mind.

manager of our minds. If it mediates successfully, we can go on to the higher intellectual and creative pursuits of life. If it is unsuccessful, and the id or superego becomes too strong, conflict will overtake us and psychological disorders will develop. Because these conflicts are all within the mind, they are referred to as **intrapsychic conflicts.**

Now think back to the case of Anna O., in which Breuer observed that patients cannot always remember important but unpleasant emotional events. From these and other observations, Freud conceptualized the mental structures described in this section to explain unconscious processes. He believed that the id and the superego are almost entirely unconscious. We are fully aware only of the secondary processes of the ego, which is a relatively small part of the mind.

DEFENSE MECHANISMS

The ego fights a continual battle to stay on top of the warring id and superego. Occasionally, their conflicts produce anxiety that threatens to overwhelm the ego. The anxiety is a *signal* that alerts the ego to marshal **defense mechanisms,** unconscious protective processes that keep primitive emotions associated with conflicts in check so that the ego can continue its coordinating function.

Although Freud first conceptualized defense mechanisms, it was his daughter, Anna Freud, who developed the ideas more fully.

We all use defense mechanisms at times—sometimes they are adaptive and at other times maladaptive. For example, have you ever done poorly on a test because the professor was unfair in her grading? And then when you got home you yelled at your brother or perhaps even your dog? This is an example of the defense mechanism of *displacement*. The ego adaptively "decides" that expressing primitive anger at your professor might not be in your best interest. Because your brother and your dog don't have the authority to affect you in an adverse way, your anger is "displaced" to one of them. Some people may redirect energy from conflict or underlying anxiety into a more constructive outlet such as work, where they may be more efficient because of the redirection. This process is called *sublimation*.

More severe internal conflicts that produce a lot of anxiety or other emotions can trigger self-defeating defensive processes or symptoms. Phobic and obsessive symptoms are especially common self-defeating defensive reactions that, according to Freud, reflect an inadequate attempt to deal with an internally dangerous situation. Phobic symptoms typically incorporate elements of the danger. For example, a dog phobia may be connected to an infantile fear of castration; that is, a man's internal conflict involves a fear of being attacked and castrated, a fear that is consciously expressed as a fear of being attacked and bitten by a dog, even if he "knows" the dog is harmless.

Defense mechanisms have actually been subjected to scientific study, and there is some evidence that they may be of potential import in the study of psychopathology (Vaillant, Bond, & Vaillant, 1986). For example, different psychological disorders seem to be associated with different defense mechanisms (Pollack & Andrews, 1989), which might be important in planning treatment. Indeed, the current DSM–IV includes an axis of defense mechanisms in the appendix. Vaillant (1976) noted that healthy defense mechanisms, such as humor and sublimation, correlated with psychological health. Thus, the concept of defense mechanisms—"coping styles," in contemporary terminology—continues to be important to the study of psychopathology.

Examples of defense mechanisms are listed below (based on DSM–IV, APA, 1994).

Denial: Refuses to acknowledge some aspect of objective reality or subjective experience that is apparent to others

Displacement: Transfers a feeling about, or a response to, an object that causes discomfort onto another, usually less threatening, object or person

Projection: Falsely attributes own unacceptable feelings, impulses, or thoughts to another individual or object

Rationalization: Conceals the true motivations for actions, thoughts, or feelings through elaborate reassuring or self-serving but incorrect explanations

Reaction formation: Substitutes behavior, thoughts, or feelings that are the direct opposite of unacceptable ones

Repression: Blocks disturbing wishes, thoughts, or experiences from conscious awareness

Sublimation: Directs potentially maladaptive feelings or impulses into socially acceptable behavior

PSYCHOSEXUAL STAGES OF DEVELOPMENT

Freud also theorized that during infancy and early childhood we pass through a number of **psychosexual stages of development** that have a profound and lasting impact. This makes Freud one of the first to take a developmental perspective of the study of abnormal behavior, which we will look at in more detail throughout this book. The stages—oral, anal, phallic, latency, and genital—represent distinctive patterns of gratifying our basic needs and satisfying our drive for physical pleasure. For example, the oral stage, typically extending for approximately 2 years from birth, is characterized by a central focus on the need for food. In the act of sucking, necessary for feeding, the lips, tongue, and mouth become the focus of libidinal drives and, therefore, the principal source of pleasure. Freud hypothesized that, if we did not receive appropriate gratification during a specific stage or if a specific stage left a particularly strong impression (which he termed *fixation*), an individual's personality would reflect the stage throughout adult life. For example, fixation at the oral stage might result in excessive thumb sucking and emphasis on oral stimulation through eating, chewing pencils, or biting fingernails. Adult personality characteristics theoretically associated with oral fixation include dependency and passivity or, in reaction to these tendencies, rebelliousness and cynicism.

One of the more controversial and frequently mentioned psychosexual conflicts occurs during the phallic stage (from age 3 to age 5 or 6), which is characterized by early genital self-stimulation. This conflict is the subject of the Greek tragedy *Oedipus Rex*, in which Oedipus is fated to kill his father and, unknowingly, to marry his mother. Freud asserted that all young boys relive this fantasy when genital self-stimulation is accompanied by images of sexual interactions with their mothers. These fantasies, in turn, are accompanied by strong feelings of envy and perhaps anger toward their fathers, with whom they identify but whose place they wish to take. Furthermore, strong fears develop that the father may punish that lust by removing the son's penis—thus, the phenomenon of *castration anxiety*. This fear helps the boy keep his lustful impulses toward his mother in check. The battle of the lustful impulses on the one hand and castration anxiety on the other creates a conflict that is internal, or intrapsychic, called the *Oedipus complex*. The phallic stage passes uneventfully only if several things happen. First, the child must resolve his ambivalent relationship with his parents and reconcile the simultaneous anger and love he has for his father. If this happens, he may go on to channel his libidinal impulses into heterosexual relationships while retaining harmless affection for his mother.

The counterpart conflict in girls, called the *Electra complex*, is even more controversial. Freud viewed the young girl as wanting to replace her mother and possess her father. Central to this possession is the girl's desire for a penis, so as to be more like her father and brothers—hence the term *penis envy*. According to Freud, the conflict is successfully resolved when females develop healthy heterosexual relationships and look forward to having a baby, which he viewed as a healthy substitute for having a penis. Needless to say, this particular theory has provoked marked consterna-

tion over the years as being sexist and demeaning. It is important to remember that it is theory, not fact; no systematic research exists to support it.

In Freud's view, all nonpsychotic psychological disorders resulted from underlying unconscious conflicts, the anxiety that resulted from those conflicts, and the implementation of ego defense mechanisms. Freud called such disorders **neuroses,** or *neurotic disorders*, from an old term referring to disorders of the nervous system.

LATER DEVELOPMENTS IN PSYCHOANALYTIC THOUGHT

Freud's original psychoanalytic theories have been greatly modified and developed in a number of different directions, mostly by his students or followers. Some theorists simply took one component of psychoanalytic theory and developed it more fully. Others broke with Freud and went in entirely new directions.

Anna Freud (1895–1982), Freud's daughter, concentrated on the way in which the defensive reactions of the ego determine our behavior. In so doing, she was the first proponent of the modern field of **ego psychology** or self-psychology. Her book, *Ego and the Mechanisms of Defense* (1946), is still influential. According to Anna Freud, the individual slowly accumulates adaptational capacities, skill in reality testing, and defenses. Abnormal behavior develops when the ego is deficient in regulating such functions as delaying and controlling impulses, or in marshaling appropriate normal defenses to strong internal conflicts.

A related area that is quite popular today is referred to as **object relations.** In this school of thought are theorists

Anna Freud (1895–1982), here with her father, contributed the concept of defense mechanisms to the field of psychoanalysis.

Melanie Klein and Otto Kernberg. Kernberg's work on borderline personality disorder, in which some behavior "borders" on being out of touch with reality and thus psychotic, has been widely applied (see Chapter 12). Object relations is the study of how children incorporate the images, memories, and sometimes the values of a person who was very important to them and to whom they were (or are) emotionally attached. *Object* in this sense refers to these important people, and the process of incorporation is called *introjection*. Introjected objects can become an integrated part of the ego or may assume conflicting roles in determining the identity, or self. For example, your parents may have conflicting views on relationships or careers, which, in turn, may be different from your own partly developed point of view. To the extent that these varying positions have been incorporated, the potential for conflict arises. One day you may feel one way about your career direction, and the next day you may feel quite differently. According to object relations theory, you tend to see the world through the eyes of the person incorporated into your self. Object relations theorists focus on how these disparate images come together to make up a person's identity and on the conflicts that may emerge.

Carl Jung (1875–1961) and Alfred Adler (1870–1937) were students of Freud who came to reject his ideas and form their own schools of thought. Jung, rejecting many of the sexual aspects of Freud's theory, introduced the concept of the **collective unconscious,** a wisdom accumulated by society and culture over the millennia that is stored deep in individual memories and passed down from generation to generation. Jung also suggested that spiritual and religious drives are as much a part of human nature as sexual drives; this emphasis and the idea of the collective unconscious continues to draw the attention of mystics. Jung emphasized the importance of enduring personality traits such as introversion (the tendency to be shy and withdrawn) and extroversion (the tendency to be friendly and outgoing).

Adler focused on feelings of inferiority and the striving for superiority; he created the term *inferiority complex*. Unlike Freud, both Jung and Adler also believed that the basic quality of human nature is positive and that there is a strong drive toward self-actualization. Jung and Adler believed that by removing barriers to both internal and external growth the individual would improve and flourish.

Others took psychoanalytical theorizing in different directions, emphasizing development over the life span and the influence of culture and society on personality. Karen Horney (1885–1952) and Erich Fromm (1900–1980) are associated with these ideas, but the best-known theorist is Erik Erikson (1902–1994). Erikson's greatest contribution was his theory of development across the life span, in which he described in some detail the crises and conflicts that accompany eight specific stages. For example, in the last of these stages, the *mature age,* beginning at about 65, individuals review their lives and attempt to make sense of them, experiencing both the satisfaction of having completed some lifelong goals and despair at having failed at others. Scientific developments have borne out the wisdom of considering psychopathology from a developmental point of view.

PSYCHOANALYTIC PSYCHOTHERAPY

Many techniques of psychoanalytic psychotherapy, or *psychoanalysis,* are designed to reveal the nature of unconscious mental processes and conflicts through catharsis and insight. Freud developed techniques of **free association,** in which patients are instructed to say whatever comes to mind without the usual socially required censoring. Free association is intended to reveal emotionally charged material that may be repressed because it is too painful or threatening to bring into consciousness. Freud's patients lay on a couch, and he sat behind them so they would not be distracted. This is how the couch became the symbol of psychotherapy. Other techniques include **dream analysis** (still quite popular today), in which the content of dreams, supposedly reflecting the primary process thinking of the id, is systematically related to symbolic aspects of unconscious conflicts. The therapist interprets the patient's thoughts and feelings from free association and the content of dreams and relates them to various unconscious conflicts. This procedure is often difficult because the patient may resist the efforts of the therapist to uncover repressed and sensitive conflicts and may *deny* the interpretations. The goal of this stage of therapy is to help the patient gain insight into the nature of the conflicts.

The relationship between the therapist, called the **psychoanalyst,** and the patient is very important. In the context of this relationship as it evolves, the therapist may discover the nature of the patient's intrapsychic conflict. This is because, in a phenomenon called **transference,** patients come to relate to the therapist very much as they did toward important figures in their childhood, particularly their parents. Patients who resent the therapist but can verbalize no good reason for it may be reenacting childhood resentment toward a parent. More often, the patient will fall deeply in love with the therapist, which reflects strong positive feelings that existed earlier for a parent. In the phenomenon of *countertransference,* therapists project some of their own personal issues and feelings, usually positive, onto the patient. Therapists are trained to deal with their own feelings as well as their patients', whatever the mode of therapy, and it is strictly against all ethical canons of the mental health professions to accept overtures from patients that might lead to relationships outside therapy.

Classical psychoanalysis requires therapy four to five times a week for 2 to 5 years to analyze unconscious conflicts, resolve them, and restructure the personality to put the ego back in charge. Reduction of "symptoms" (psychological disorders) is relatively inconsequential, because they are only expressions of underlying intrapsychic conflicts that arise from psychosexual developmental stages. Thus, eliminating a phobia or depressive episode would be of little use unless the underlying conflict was dealt with adequately, because another set of "symptoms" would almost certainly emerge *(symptom substitution).* Because of the extraordinary expense of psychoanalysis, and the lack of evidence that it is effective in alleviating psychological disorders, this approach is seldom used today.

Classical psychoanalysis is still practiced, particularly in some large cities, but many psychotherapists employ a loosely related set of approaches referred to as **psychodynamic psychotherapy.** Although conflicts and unconscious processes are still emphasized, and efforts are made to identify trauma and active defense mechanisms, therapists use an eclectic mixture of tactics, with a social and interpersonal focus. Two additional features characterize psychodynamic psychotherapy. First, it is significantly briefer than classical psychoanalysis. Second, psychodynamic therapists deemphasize the goal of personality reconstruction, focusing instead on relieving the suffering associated with psychological disorders.

COMMENTS

Pure psychoanalysis is of historical more than current interest, and classical psychoanalysis as a treatment has been diminishing in popularity for years. In 1980, the term *neurosis,* which specifically implied a psychoanalytic view of the causes of psychological disorders, was dropped from the DSM, the official diagnostic system of the American Psychiatric Association.

A major criticism of psychoanalysis is that it is basically unscientific, relying on reports by the patient of events that happened years ago. These events have been filtered through the experience of the observer and then interpreted by the psychoanalyst in ways that certainly could be questioned and might differ from one analyst to the next. Finally, there has been no careful measurement of any of these psychological phenomena, and there is no obvious way to prove or disprove the basic hypotheses of psychoanalysis. This is important, because measurement and the ability to prove or disprove a theory are the foundations of the scientific approach.

Nevertheless, psychoanalytic concepts and observations have been very valuable, not only to the study of psychopathology and psychodynamic psychotherapy but also to the history of ideas in Western civilization. Careful scientific studies of psychopathology have supported the observation of unconscious mental processes, the notion that basic emotional responses are often triggered by hidden or symbolic cues, and the understanding that memories of events in our lives can be repressed and otherwise avoided in a variety of ingenious ways. These concepts, along with the importance of various coping styles or defense mechanisms, will appear repeatedly throughout this book.

Freud's revolutionary ideas that pathological anxiety emerges in connection with some of our deepest and darkest instincts brought us a long way from witch trials and incurable brain pathology. Before Freud, the source of good and evil and of urges and prohibitions was conceived as external and spiritual, usually in the guise of demons confronting the forces of good. Since Freud, we ourselves have become the battleground for these forces, and we are inexorably caught up in the battle, sometimes for better and sometimes for worse.

Humanistic Theory

We have already seen that Jung and Adler broke sharply with Freud. Their fundamental disagreement concerned the very nature of humanity. Freud portrayed life as a battleground where we are continually in danger of being overwhelmed by our darkest forces. Jung and Adler, by contrast, emphasized the positive, optimistic side of human nature. Jung talked about setting goals, looking toward the future, and realizing one's fullest potential. Adler believed that human nature reaches its fullest potential when we contribute to other individuals and to society as a whole. He believed that we all strive to reach superior levels of intellectual and moral development. Nevertheless, both Jung and Adler retained many of the principles of psychodynamic thought. Their general philosophies were adopted in the middle of the century by personality theorists and became known as *humanistic psychology.*

Self-actualizing was the watchword for this movement. The underlying assumption is that all of us could reach our highest potential, in all areas of functioning, if only we had the freedom to grow. Inevitably, a variety of conditions may block our actualization. Since every person is basically good and whole, most blocks originate outside the individual. Difficult living conditions or stressful life or interpersonal experiences may move you away from your true self.

Abraham Maslow (1908–1970) was most systematic in describing the structure of personality. He postulated a *hierarchy of needs,* beginning with our most basic physical needs for food and sex and ranging upward to our needs for self-actualization, love, and self-esteem. Social needs such as friendship fall somewhere in between. Maslow hypothesized that we cannot progress up the hierarchy until we have satisfied the needs at lower levels.

Carl Rogers (1902–1987) is from the point of view of therapy the most influential humanist. Rogers originated client-centered therapy, later known as **person-centered therapy** (Rogers, 1961). In this approach, the therapist takes a passive role, making as few interpretations as possible. The point is to give the individual a chance to develop during the course of therapy, unfettered by threats to the self. Humanist theorists have great faith in the ability of human relations to foster this growth. **Unconditional positive regard,** the complete and almost unqualified acceptance of most of the client's feelings and actions, is critical to the humanistic approach. *Empathy* is the sympathetic understanding of the individual's particular view of the world. The hoped-for result of person-centered therapy is that clients will be more straightforward and honest with themselves and will access their innate tendencies toward growth.

Like psychoanalysis, the humanistic approach has had a substantial effect on theories of interpersonal relationships. For example, the human potential movements so popular in the 1960s and 1970s were a direct result of humanistic theorizing. This approach also emphasized the importance of the therapeutic relationship in a way quite different from Freud's. Rather than seeing the relationship as a means to an end (transference), humanistic therapists believed that relationships, including the therapeutic relationship, were the single most positive influence in facilitating human growth. In fact, Rogers made substantial contributions to the scientific study of therapist–client relationships.

Nevertheless, the humanistic model contributed relatively little new information to the field of psychopathology. One reason for this is that its proponents, with some exceptions, have not been much interested in doing research that would discover or create new knowledge. Rather, they stress the unique, nonquantifiable experiences of the individual, emphasizing that people are more different than alike. As Maslow noted, the humanistic model found its greatest application among individuals without psychological disorders. The application of person-centered therapy to more severe psychological disorders has decreased substantially over the decades, although certain variations have periodically arisen in some areas of psychopathology.

The Behavioral Model

As psychoanalysis swept the world at the beginning of the 20th century, events in Russia and the United States would eventually provide an alternative psychological model that was every bit as powerful. The **behavioral model,** which is also known as the *cognitive-behavioral* or *social learning model,* brought the systematic development of a more scientific approach to psychological aspects of psychopathology.

PAVLOV AND CLASSICAL CONDITIONING

In his classic study examining why dogs salivate prior to the presentation of food, physiologist Ivan Petrovich Pavlov (1849–1936) of St. Petersburg, Russia, initiated the study of **classical conditioning,** a type of learning in which a neutral stimulus is paired with a response until it elicits that response. The word *conditioning* (or *conditioned response*) resulted from an accident in translation from the original Russian. Pavlov was really talking about a response that occurred only on the "condition" of the presence of a particular event or situation (stimulus)—in this case, the footsteps of the laboratory assistant at feeding time. Thus, "conditional response" would have been more accurate. Conditioning is one way we acquire new information, particularly information that is somewhat emotional in nature. This process is not as simple as it first seems, and we continue to

uncover many more facts about its complexity (Rescorla, 1988). But it can be quite automatic. Let's look at a powerful contemporary example.

Psychologists working in oncology units have studied a phenomenon well known to many cancer patients, their nurses and physicians, and their families. Chemotherapy, a common treatment for some forms of cancer, has some side effects including severe nausea and vomiting. But these patients often experience severe nausea and, occasionally, vomiting, when they merely see the medical personnel who administered the chemotherapy, or any equipment associated with the treatment itself, even on days when their treatment is not delivered (Morrow & Dobkin, 1988). For some patients, this reaction becomes associated with a wide variety of stimuli that evoke people or things present during chemotherapy—anybody in a nurse's uniform, or even the sight of the hospital itself. The strength of the response to similar objects or people is usually a function of *how* similar these objects or people are. This phenomenon is called *stimulus generalization* because the response "generalizes" to similar stimuli. In any case, this particular reaction, obviously, is very distressing and uncomfortable, particularly if it is associated with a wide variety of objects or situations. Psychologists have had to develop specific treatments to overcome this response (Redd & Andrykowski, 1982); they are described more fully in Chapter 9.

Whether the stimulus is food, as in Pavlov's laboratory, or chemotherapy, the classical conditioning process begins with a stimulus that would elicit a response in almost anyone and requires no learning; no conditions must be present for the response to occur. For these reasons, the food or chemotherapy is called the *unconditioned stimulus (UCS).* The natural or unlearned response to this stimulus—in these cases, salivation or nausea—is called the *unconditioned response (UCR).* Now the learning comes in. As we have already seen, any person or object that is *associated* with the unconditioned stimulus (food or chemotherapy) acquires the power to elicit the same response, but now the response, because it was elicited by the conditional or *conditioned stimuli (CS),* is termed a *conditioned response (CR).* Thus, the nurse who is associated with the chemotherapy becomes a conditioned stimulus. The nauseous sensation, which is almost the same as that experienced during chemotherapy, becomes the conditioned response.

With unconditioned stimuli as powerful as chemotherapy, a conditioned response can be learned in one trial. However, most learning of this type requires repeated pairing of the unconditioned stimulus (for example, chemotherapy) and the conditioned stimulus (for instance, nurses' uniforms or hospital equipment). When Pavlov began to investigate this phenomenon, he substituted a metronome for the footsteps of his laboratory assistants so that he could quantify the stimulus more accurately and, therefore, study the approach more precisely. What he also learned is that presentation of the CS (for example, the metronome) *without* the food for a long enough period of time would eventually eliminate the conditioned response to the food. In other words, the dog learned that the metronome no longer meant that a meal might be on the way. This process was called **extinction.**

Ivan Pavlov (1849–1936) identified the process of classical conditioning, which is important to many emotional disorders.

Because Pavlov was a physiologist, it was quite natural for him to study these processes in a laboratory and to be quite scientific about it. This required precision in measuring and observing relationships and in ruling out alternative explanations. Although this approach is common in biology, it was not at all common in psychology at that time. For example, it was impossible for psychoanalysts to measure unconscious conflicts precisely, or even observe them. Even early experimental psychologists such as Edward Titchener (1867–1927) emphasized the study of **introspection.** Subjects simply reported on their inner thoughts and feelings after experiencing certain stimuli, but the results of this "armchair" psychology were inconsistent and discouraging to many experimental psychologists.

WATSON AND THE RISE OF BEHAVIORISM

A young American psychologist, John B. Watson (1878–1958), is considered the founder of behaviorism. Strongly influenced by the work of Pavlov, Watson decided that to base psychology on introspection was to head in the wrong direction; that psychology could be made as scientific as physiology; and that psychology no more needs introspection or other nonquantifiable methods than do chemistry and physics (J. Watson, 1913, p. 158). This point of view is reflected in a famous quote from a seminal article published by Watson in 1913: "Psychology, as the behaviorist views it, is a purely objective experimental branch of natural science. Its theoretical goal is the prediction and control of behavior. Introspection forms no essential part of its methods" (p. 158). This, then, was the beginning of behaviorism and, like most revolutionaries, Watson took his cause to extremes. For example, he wrote that "thinking," for purposes of science, could be equated with subvocal talking and that one need only measure movements around the larynx to study this process objectively.

Most of Watson's time was spent developing behavioral psychology as a radical empirical science, but he did dabble briefly in the study of psychopathology. In 1920, he and a student, Rosalie Rayner, presented an 11-month-old boy named Albert with a harmless fluffy white rat to play with. Albert was not afraid of the small animal and enjoyed playing with it. However, every time Albert reached for the rat, the experimenters made a loud noise behind him. After only five trials, Albert showed the first signs of fear if the white rat came near. The experimenters then determined that Albert displayed mild fear of any white furry object, even a Santa Claus mask with a white fuzzy beard. You may not think that this is surprising, but keep in mind that this was one of the first examples ever recorded in a laboratory of actually producing fear of an object not previously feared.

Another student of Watson's, Mary Cover Jones, thought that if fear could be learned or classically conditioned in this way, perhaps it could also be unlearned or "extinguished." She worked with a boy named Peter, who at 2 years, 10 months old was already quite afraid of furry objects. Jones decided to bring a white rabbit into the room where Peter was playing for a short time each day. She also arranged for other children, whom she knew did not fear rabbits, to be in the same room. She noted that Peter's fear

Mary Cover Jones (1896–1987) was one of the first psychologists to use behavioral techniques to free a patient from phobia.

gradually diminished. Each time it diminished, she brought the rabbit closer. Eventually Peter was touching and even playing with the rabbit (Jones, 1924a, 1924b), and years later the fear had not returned.

THE BEGINNINGS OF BEHAVIOR THERAPY

The implications of Jones's research were largely ignored for two decades, given the fervor associated with more psychoanalytic conceptions of the development of fear. But in the late 1940s and early 1950s, Joseph Wolpe (1915–   ), a pioneering psychiatrist from South Africa, became dissatisfied with prevailing psychoanalytic interpretations of psychopathology and began looking for something else. He turned to the work of Pavlov and became familiar with the wider field of behavioral psychology. He developed a variety of behavioral procedures for treating his patients, many of whom suffered from phobias. His best-known technique was termed **systematic desensitization.** In principle, it was really very similar to the treatment of little Peter. Individuals were gradually introduced to the objects or situations they feared so that their fear could extinguish; that is, they could test reality and see that nothing bad really happened in the presence of the phobic object or scene. Wolpe added another element by having his patients do something that was *incompatible with fear* while they were in the presence of the dreaded object or situation. Because he could not always reproduce the phobic object in his office, Wolpe had his patients carefully and systematically *imagine* the phobic scene and the response he chose was relaxation, because it was convenient. For example, Wolpe treated a young man with a phobia of dogs by training him first to relax deeply and then imagine he was looking at a dog across the park. Gradually, he could imagine the dog across the park and remain relaxed, experiencing little or no fear, and Wolpe then had him imagine that he was closer to the dog. Eventually the young man imagined that he was actually touching the dog, while maintaining a very relaxed, almost trancelike state.

Wolpe reported great success with systematic desensitization, one of the first wide-scale applications of the new science of behaviorism to psychopathology. Wolpe, working with fellow pioneers Hans Eysenck and Stanley Rachman in London, called this approach **behavior therapy.**

B. F. Skinner and Operant Conditioning

Sigmund Freud's influence extended far beyond psychopathology, into many aspects of our cultural and intellectual history. Only one other behavioral scientist has made a similar impact, Burrhus Frederic (B. F.) Skinner (1904–1990). In 1938 he published *The Behavior of Organisms,* in which he laid out, in a comprehensive manner, the principles of *operant conditioning,* a type of learning in which behavior changes as a function of what follows the behavior. Skinner observed early on that a large part of our behavior is not automatically elicited by an unconditioned stimulus (UCS) and that we must account for this. In the ensuing years, Skinner did not confine his ideas to the laboratories of experimental psychology. He ranged far and wide in his writings, describing, for example, the potential applications of a science of behavior to our culture. Some of the best-known examples of his ideas are in the novel *Walden Two* (Skinner, 1948), in which he depicts a fictional society run on the principles of operant conditioning. In another well-known work, *Beyond Freedom and Dignity* (1971), Skinner lays out a broader statement of problems facing our culture and suggests solutions based on his own view of a science of behavior.

Skinner was strongly influenced by Watson's conviction that a science of human behavior must be based on observable events and relationships among those events. The work of psychologist Edward L. Thorndike (1874–1949) also influenced Skinner. Thorndike is best known for the *law of effect,* which states that behavior is either strengthened (likely to be repeated more frequently) or weakened (likely to occur less frequently) depending on the consequences of that be-

B.F. Skinner (1904–1990) studied operant conditioning, a form of learning that is central to psychopathology.

havior. Skinner took the very simple notions that Thorndike had tested in the animal laboratories, using food as a reinforcer, and developed them in a variety of complex ways to apply to much of our behavior. For example, if a 5-year-old boy starts shouting at the top of his lungs in McDonald's, much to the annoyance of the people around him, it is unlikely that his behavior was automatically elicited by an unconditioned stimulus (UCS). Also, he will be less likely to do it in the future if his parents scold him, take him out to the car to sit for a bit, or consistently reinforce more appropriate behavior. Then again, if the parents think his behavior is cute and laugh, chances are he will do it again.

Skinner coined the term *operant conditioning* because behavior "operates" on the environment and changes it in some way. For example, the boy's behavior affects his parents' behavior and probably the behavior of other customers as well. Therefore, he changes his environment. Most things that we do socially provide the context for other people to respond to us in one way or another, thereby providing consequences for our behavior. The same is true of our physical environment, although the consequences may be long-term (polluting the air eventually will poison us). Skinner preferred the term *reinforcement* to "reward" because it connotes the effect on the behavior. Skinner once said that he found himself a bit embarrassed to be talking continually about reinforcement, much as Marxists used to see class struggle everywhere. But he pointed out that all of our behavior is governed to some degree by reinforcement, which can be arranged in an endless variety of ways, in *schedules of reinforcement.* Skinner wrote a whole book on different schedules of reinforcement (Ferster & Skinner, 1957). He also believed that using punishment as a consequence is relatively ineffective in the long run and that the primary way to develop new behavior is to positively reinforce desired behavior. Much like Watson, Skinner did not see the need to go beyond the observable and quantifiable to establish a satisfactory science of behavior. He did not deny the influence of biology or the existence of subjective states of emotion or cognition; he simply explained these phenomena as relatively inconsequential side effects of a particular history of reinforcement.

The subjects of Skinner's research were usually animals, mostly pigeons and rats. Using his new principles, Skinner and his disciples actually taught the animals a variety of tricks, including dancing, playing Ping-Pong, and playing a toy piano. To do this he used a procedure called **shaping,** a process of reinforcing successive approximations to a final behavior or set of behaviors. If you want a pigeon to play Ping-Pong, first you provide it with a pellet of food every time it moves its head slightly toward a Ping-Pong ball tossed in its direction. Gradually you require the pigeon to move its head ever closer to the Ping-Pong ball until it touches it. Finally, receiving the food pellet is contingent on the pigeon's actually hitting the ball back with its head.

Pavlov, Watson, and Skinner contributed significantly to behavior therapy (e.g., Wolpe, 1958), in which scientific principles of psychology are applied to clinical problems. Their ideas have substantially contributed to current psychosocial treatments, and so will be referred to repeatedly in this book.

Comments

The behavioral model has contributed greatly to the understanding and treatment of psychopathology, as will be apparent in the chapters that follow. Nevertheless, this model is incomplete in itself and inadequate to account for what we now know about psychopathology. In the past there was little or no room for biology in behaviorism, because disorders were considered to be, for the most part, environmentally determined reactions. The model also fails to account for development of psychopathology across the life span. Recent advances in our knowledge of how information is processed, both consciously and subconsciously, have added a layer of complexity. Integrating all these dimensions requires a new model of psychopathology.

The Present: The Scientific Method and an Integrative Approach

As Shakespeare wrote, "What's past is prologue." We have just reviewed three different traditions or ways of thinking about causes of psychopathology: the supernatural, the biological, and the psychological (further subdivided into two major historical components: psychoanalytic and behavioral).

Supernatural explanations of psychopathology are still with us. Superstitions prevail, including beliefs in the effects of the moon and the stars on our behavior. However, this tradition has little influence on scientists and other professionals. Biological, psychoanalytic, and behavioral models, by contrast, continue to further our knowledge of psychopathology, as we will see in the next chapter.

Each tradition has failed in at least one important way. First, scientific methods were not often applied to the theories and treatments within a tradition, mostly because methods that would have produced the evidence necessary to confirm or disconfirm the theories and treatments had not been developed. Lacking such evidence, various fads and superstitions were widely accepted that ultimately proved to be untrue or useless. New fads often superseded truly useful theories and treatment procedures. This trend was at work in the "discovery" of the drug reserpine, which, in fact, had been around for thousands of years. King Charles VI was subjected to a variety of procedures, some of which have since been proved useful and others that were mere fads or even harmful. How we use scientific methods to confirm or disconfirm findings in psychopathology will be described in Chapter 3. Second, health professionals tend to look at psychological disorders very narrowly, from their own point of view alone. John Grey assumed that psychological disorders were the result of brain disease and that other factors had no influence whatsoever. John Watson assumed that all behaviors, including disordered behavior, were the result of psy-

chological and social influences and that the contribution of biological factors was inconsequential.

In the 1990s, two developments have come together as never before to shed light on the nature of psychopathology: (a) the increasing sophistication of scientific tools and methodology and (b) the realization that no one influence—biological, behavioral, cognitive, emotional, or social—ever occurs in isolation. Literally, every time we think, feel, or do something, the brain and the rest of the body are hard at work. Perhaps not as obvious, however, is the fact that our thoughts, feelings, and actions inevitably influence the function and even the structure of the brain, sometimes permanently. In other words, our behavior, both normal and abnormal, is the product of a continual interaction of psychological, biological, and social influences.

The view that psychopathology is multiply determined had its early adherents. Perhaps the most notable was Adolf Meyer (1866–1950), often considered the dean of American psychiatry. Whereas most professionals during the first half of the century held narrow views of the cause of psychopathology, Meyer steadfastly emphasized the equal contributions of biological, psychological, and sociocultural determinism. Although Meyer had some proponents, it was 100 years before the wisdom of his advice was fully recognized in the field.

In the late 1990s, a veritable explosion of knowledge about psychopathology occurred, and it was clear that a new model was needed that would consider biological and psychological as well as social influences on behavior. This approach to psychopathology would combine findings from all areas with our rapidly growing understanding of how we experience life during different developmental periods, from infancy to old age. In the remainder of this book we will explore some of these reciprocal influences and demonstrate that the only currently valid model of psychopathology is multidimensional and integrative.

Summary

Definitions

- A psychological disorder is (a) a *psychological dysfunction* within an individual that is (b) *associated with distress or impairment* in functioning and (c) *a response that is not typical or culturally expected*. All three basic criteria must be met; no one criterion alone has yet been identified that defines the essence of abnormality.

The Science of Psychopathology

- The field of psychopathology is concerned with the scientific study of psychological disorders. Trained mental health professionals range from clinical and counseling psychologists to psychiatrists and psychiatric social workers and nurses. Each profession requires a specific type of training.
- Using scientific methods, mental health professionals can function as scientist–practitioners. They not only keep up with the latest findings but also use scientific data to eval-

uate their own work, and they often conduct research within their clinics or hospitals.

• Research about psychological disorders falls into three basic categories: description, causation, and treatment and outcomes.

The Past: Historical Conceptions of Abnormal Behavior

• Historically, there have been three prominent approaches to abnormal behavior. In the supernatural tradition, abnormal behavior is attributed to agents outside our bodies or social environment, such as demons, spirits, or the influence of the moon and stars; though still alive, this tradition has been largely replaced by biological and psychological perspectives. In the biological tradition, disorders are attributed to disease or biochemical imbalances; in the psychological tradition, abnormal behavior is attributed to faulty psychological development and to social context.

• Each tradition has its own way of treating individuals who suffer from psychological disorders. Supernatural treatments include exorcism to rid the body of the supernatural spirits. Biological treatments typically emphasize physical care and the search for medical cures, especially drugs. Psychological approaches use psychosocial treatments, beginning with moral therapy and including modern psychotherapy.

• Sigmund Freud, the founder of psychoanalytic therapy, offered an elaborate conception of the unconscious mind. In therapy, Freud focused on tapping into the mysteries of the unconscious through such techniques as catharsis, free association, and dream analysis. Though Freud's followers steered from his path in many ways, Freud's influence can still be felt today.

• One outgrowth of Freudian therapy is humanistic psychology, which focuses more on human potential and self-actualizing than on psychological disorders. Therapy that has evolved from this approach is known as person-centered therapy; the therapist shows almost unconditional positive regard for the client's feelings and thoughts.

• The behavioral model moved psychology into the realm of science. Both research and therapy focus on things that are measurable, including such techniques as systematic desensitization, reinforcement, and shaping.

The Present: The Scientific Method and the Integrative Approach

• With the increasing sophistication of our scientific tools, we now realize that no contribution to psychological disorders ever occurs in isolation. Our behavior, both normal and abnormal, is a product of a continual interaction of psychological, biological, and social influences.

Key Terms

psychological disorder
phobia
psychopathology
scientist–practitioner
presenting problem
clinical description
prevalence
incidence
course
prognosis
etiology
psychosocial
moral therapy
mental hygiene movement
psychoanalysis
behaviorism
unconscious
catharsis
psychoanalytic model
id
ego
superego
intrapsychic conflicts
defense mechanisms
psychosexual stages of development
neurosis
ego psychology
object relations
collective unconscious
free association
dream analysis
psychoanalyst
transference
psychodynamic psychotherapy
self-actualizing
person-centered therapy
unconditional positive regard
behavioral model
classical conditioning
extinction
introspection
systematic desensitization
reinforcement
behavior therapy
shaping

Answers to Concept Checks

1.1
1. a, c   2. d   3. b, c   4. b

1.2
1. d   2. c   3. a
4. f   5. e   6. b

1.3
1. e   2. c   3. d

An Integrative Approach to Psychopathology

2

One-Dimensional or Multidimensional Models
Genetic Contributions to Psychopathology
Neuroscience and Its Contributions to
Psychopathology
Behavioral and Cognitive Science
Emotions
Cultural, Social, and Interpersonal Factors
Life-Span Development

The spirit within nourishes,
and the mind, diffused
through all the members,
sways the mass and mingles
with the whole frame.
Virgil
The Aeneid

Remember Judy from Chapter 1? We knew she suffered from blood–injury–injection phobia, but we did not know why. Here we will address the issue of causation. In this chapter we examine the specific components of a **multidimensional integrative approach** to psychopathology (see Figure 2.1). *Biological* dimensions include causal factors from the fields of genetics and neuroscience. *Psychological* dimensions include causal factors from behavioral and cognitive processes, including learned helplessness, social learning, prepared learning, and even unconscious processes (in a different guise than in the days of Freud). *Emotional* influences contribute in a variety of ways to psychopathology, as do *social* and *interpersonal* influences. Finally, *developmental* influences figure in any discussion of causes of psychological disorders. You will become familiar with these areas as

they relate to psychopathology and learn about some of the latest developments that are relevant to psychological disorders. But keep in mind what we confirmed in the last chapter: No influence operates in isolation. Each dimension, biological or psychological, is strongly influenced by the others and by development, and they weave together in various complex and intricate ways to create a psychological disorder.

We will explain briefly why we have adopted a multidimensional integrative model of psychopathology. Then we preview various causal influences and interactions, using Judy's case as background. After that we look more deeply at specific causal influences in psychopathology, examining both the latest research and integrative ways of viewing what we know.

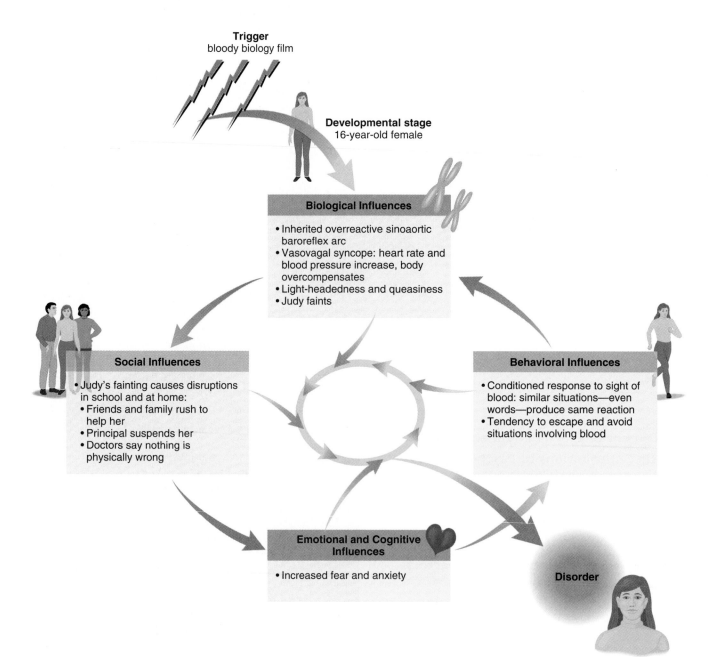

figure 2.1   Judy's case

One-Dimensional or Multidimensional Models

To say that psychopathology is caused by a physical abnormality or by conditioning is to accept a linear or one-dimensional model, which attempts to trace the origins of behavior to a single cause. A linear causal model might hold that schizophrenia or a phobia is caused by a chemical imbalance or by growing up surrounded by overwhelming conflicts among family members. In psychology and psychopathology, we still encounter this type of thinking occasionally, but most scientists and clinicians believe that abnormal behavior results from various influences. A system, or feedback loop, may have independent inputs at many different points, but as each input becomes part of the whole it can no longer be considered independent. This perspective on causality is *systemic*, which derives from the word *system;* it implies that any particular influence contributing to psychopathology cannot be considered out of context. Context, in this case, is the biology and behavior of the individual, as well as the cognitive, emotional, social, and cultural environment, because any one component of the system inevitably affects the other components.

What Caused Judy's Phobia?

From a multidimensional perspective, let's look at what might have caused Judy's phobia (see Figure 2.1).

BEHAVIORAL INFLUENCES

The cause of Judy's phobia might at first seem obvious. She saw a movie with graphic scenes of blood and injury and had a bad reaction to it. Her reaction, an unconditioned response, became associated with situations similar to the scenes in the movie, depending on how similar they were. But Judy's reaction reached such an extreme that even hearing someone say, "Cut it out!" evoked queasiness. Is Judy's phobia a straightforward case of classical conditioning? It might seem so, but one puzzling question arises: Why didn't the other kids in Judy's class develop the same phobia? As far as Judy knew, nobody else even felt queasy!

BIOLOGICAL INFLUENCES

We now know that much more is involved in blood–injury–injection phobia than a simple conditioning experience, although, clearly, conditioning and stimulus generalization contribute. In fact, we have learned a lot recently about this phobia (Marks, 1988; Page 1994, 1996).

Physiologically, Judy experienced a *vasovagal syncope,* which is a common cause of fainting. When she saw the film she became mildly distressed, as many people would, and her heart rate and blood pressure increased accordingly, which she probably did not notice. Then her body took over, immediately compensating by decreasing her vascular resistance, lowering her heart rate and, eventually, lowering her blood pressure. The amount of blood reaching her brain diminished until she lost consciousness. *Syncope* means "sinking feeling" or "swoon" due to low blood pressure in the head. If Judy had quickly bent down and put her head between her knees, she might have avoided fainting, but it happened so quickly she had no time to use this strategy.

People who experience the same traumatic event will have different long-term reactions.

A possible cause of the vasovagal syncope is an overreaction of a mechanism called the *sinoaortic baroreflex arc,* which compensates for sudden increases in blood pressure by lowering it. Interestingly, the tendency to overcompensate seems to be inherited, a trait that may account for the high rate of blood–injury–injection phobia in families. Do you ever feel queasy at the sight of blood? If so, chances are your mother or father or someone else in your immediate family has the same reaction. In a recent study, 61% of the family members of individuals with this phobia had a similar condition, although somewhat milder in most cases (Öst, 1992).

You might think, then, that we have discovered the cause of blood–injury–injection phobia, and that all we need to do is develop a pill to regulate the baroreflex. But many people with rather severe syncope reaction tendencies do *not* develop phobias. They cope with their reaction in various ways, including tensing their muscles whenever they are confronted with blood. Tensing your muscles very quickly raises blood pressure and prevents the fainting response.

Furthermore, some people with little or no syncope reaction develop the phobia anyway (Öst, 1992). Therefore, the cause of blood–injury–injection phobia is more complicated than it seems. If we said that the phobia is caused by a biological dysfunction (an overactive vasovagal reaction probably due to a particularly sensitive baroreflex mechanism) or a traumatic experience (seeing a gruesome film) and subsequent conditioning, we would be partly right on both counts, but in adopting a one-dimensional causal model we would miss the most important point: To cause blood–injury–injection phobia, a complex *interaction* must occur between behavioral and biological factors. Inheriting a strong syncope reaction definitely puts a person at risk for developing this phobia, but other influences are at work as well.

EMOTIONAL INFLUENCES

Judy's case is a good example of biology influencing behavior. But behavior, thoughts, and feelings can also influence biology, sometimes dramatically. What role did Judy's fear and anxiety play in the development of her phobia, and where did they come from? Emotions can affect physiological responses such as blood pressure, heart rate, and respiration, particularly if we know rationally that there is nothing to fear, as Judy did. In her case, rapid increases in heart rate, caused by her emotions, may have triggered a stronger and more intense baroreflex. Emotions also changed the way she thought about situations involving blood and injury and motivated her to behave in ways she didn't want to, avoiding all situations connected with blood and injury, even if it was important not to avoid them. As we shall see throughout this book, emotions play a substantial role in the development of many disorders.

SOCIAL INFLUENCES

We are all social animals; by our very nature we tend to live in groups such as families. Social and cultural factors make direct contributions to biology and behavior. Judy's friends and family rushed to her aid when she fainted. Did their support help or hurt? Her principal rejected her and dismissed her problem. What effect did this behavior have on her phobia? Rejection, particularly by authority figures, can make psychological disorders worse than they otherwise would be. Then again, being supportive only when somebody is experiencing symptoms is not always helpful because the strong effects of social attention may actually increase the frequency and intensity of the reaction.

DEVELOPMENTAL INFLUENCES

One more influence affects us all—*time*. With the passage of time, many things about ourselves and our environments change in important ways, causing us to react differently at different ages. Thus, at certain times we may enter a *developmental critical period* when we are more or less reactive to a given situation or influence than at other times. To go back to Judy, it is possible that she was previously exposed to other situations involving blood. Important questions to ask are these: Why did this problem develop when she was 16 years old and not before? Is it possible that her suscepti-

bility to having a vasovagal reaction was highest in her teenage years? It may be that the timing of her physiological reaction, along with viewing the disturbing biology film, provided just the right (but unfortunate) combination to initiate her severe phobic response.

■ concept check 2.1

Theorists have abandoned the notion that any one factor can explain abnormal behavior in favor of a multidimensional model. The following influences are discussed in your textbook: (a) behavioral, (b) biological, (c) emotional, (d) social, and (e) developmental. Match each term to its description below. As we acknowledge that behaviors have multiple causes, you may be able to justify citing more than one influence for each situation.

1. The fact that some phobias are more common than others (for example, fear of heights and snakes) and may have contributed to survival of the species at an earlier time suggests that they may be genetically "prewired." This would be evidence for which of the influences? _____

2. Jan's husband, Jinx, was an unemployed jerk who spent all his time chasing other women. Jan, happily divorced for several years, cannot understand why she still becomes nauseous when she smells the aftershave that Jinx wore. Which influence best explains her response? _____

3. The fact that 16-year-old Nathan is finding it more difficult than his 7-year-old sister to adjust to and accept his parents' recent separation may be explained in part by _____ influences.

4. Five-year-old Taylor hates naptime at preschool. After she threw a noisy tantrum that threatened to wake the other children, Taylor's teachers allowed her to play a game with them during naptime. The teachers should not be surprised that this behavior occurs again the next day, as _____ influences can have powerful effects upon behavior.

5. Although a traumatic ride on a ferris wheel when she was young is likely to have been the initial cause of Jennifer's fear of heights, her strong emotional reaction to heights is likely to maintain or even increase her fear. The initial development of the phobia is likely a result of _____ influences; however, _____ influences are likely maintaining the fear.

Outcome and Comments

Fortunately for Judy, she responded very well to brief but intensive treatment at one of our clinics, and she was back in school within 7 days. Judy was gradually exposed, with her full cooperation, to words, images, and situations describing or depicting blood and injury while a sudden drop in blood pressure was prevented. We began with something mild, such as the phrase "cut it out!" By the end of the week Judy was witnessing surgical procedures at the local hospital. Judy required close therapeutic supervision during this program.

At one point, while driving home with her parents from an evening session, she had the bad luck to pass a car crash, and she saw a bleeding accident victim. That night, she dreamed about bloody accident victims coming through the walls of her bedroom. This experience made her call the clinic and request emergency intervention to reduce her distress, but it did not slow her progress. (Programs for treating phobias and related anxiety disorders will be described more fully in Chapter 5. It is the issue of etiology or causation that concerns us here.)

As you can see, finding the causes of abnormal behavior is a complex and fascinating process. Focusing on biological or behavioral factors would not have given us a full picture of the causes of Judy's disorder; we had to consider a variety of other influences and how they might interact. A discussion in more depth follows, examining the research underlying the many biological, psychological, and social influences that must be considered as causes of any psychological disorder.

 Genetic Contributions to Psychopathology

What causes you to look like one or both of your parents or, perhaps, your grandparents? Obviously, the genes that you inherit from your parents and from your ancestors before them. **Genes** are very long molecules of DNA (deoxyribonucleic acid) at various locations on chromosomes, within the cell nucleus. Ever since Gregor Mendel's pioneering work in the 19th century, we have known that physical characteristics such as hair color and eye color and, to a certain extent, height and weight are determined—or at least strongly influenced—by our genetic endowment. However, other factors in the environment influence our physical appearance as well. To some extent, our weight and even our height are affected by nutritional, social, and cultural factors. Consequently, our genes seldom determine our physical development in any absolute way. They do provide some boundaries to our development. Exactly where we go within these boundaries depends on environmental influences.

Although this is true for most of our characteristics, it is not true for all of them. Some of our characteristics are very strongly determined by one or more genes, including natural hair and eye color. Some rare disorders are determined in this same kind of way, including Huntington's disease, a degenerative brain disease that appears in early to middle age, usually the early 40s. This disease has been traced to a genetic defect that causes deterioration in a specific area of the brain, the basal ganglia. It causes broad-based changes in personality, cognitive functioning and, particularly, motor behavior, including involuntary shaking or jerkiness throughout the body. We have not yet discovered a way to environmentally influence the course of Huntington's disease.

Another example of genetic influence is a disorder known as phenylketonuria (PKU), which can result in mental retardation. This disorder, present at birth, is caused by the inability of the body to metabolize (break down) phenylalanine, a chemical compound that is found in many foods. Like Huntington's disease, PKU is caused by a defect in a single gene, with little contribution from other genes or the environmental background. PKU is inherited when both parents are carriers of the gene and pass it on to the child.

Given the genetic determination of PKU, how do you think we could best intervene to prevent or correct this disorder? One possibility, of course, is genetic counseling. If the risk for a PKU baby is high, people might be advised not to have children. Fortunately, researchers have discovered a much simpler way. We can change the way the environment interacts with and affects the genetic expression of this disorder. Specifically, by detecting PKU early enough (which is now routinely done), we can simply restrict the amount of phenylalanine in the baby's diet until the child develops to the point where a normal diet does not harm the brain, usually at about 6 or 7 years of age. Disorders such as Huntington's disease and PKU, in which cognitive impairment of various kinds is the prominent characteristic, are covered in more detail in Chapter 15.

Except for identical twins, every person has a unique set of genes unlike those of anyone else in the world. Since there is some room for the environment to influence our development within the constraints set by our genes, there are many reasons for the development of individual differences.

What about our behavior and traits, our likes and dislikes? Do genes influence personality and, by extension, abnormal behavior? This question of nature (genes) versus nurture (upbringing and other environmental influences) is age-old in psychology, and the answers that are beginning to emerge are fascinating. Before discussing them, let's review briefly what we know.

The Nature of Genes

We have known for a long time that each normal human cell has 46 chromosomes arranged in 23 pairs. One chromosome

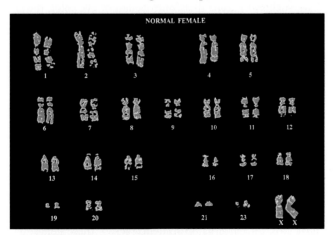

A normal female has 23 pairs of chromosomes.

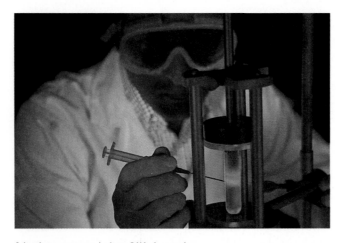

Scientists can now isolate DNA for study.

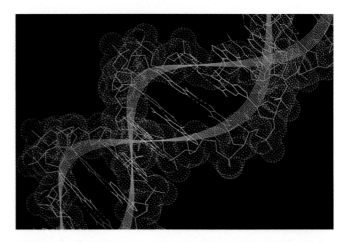

A DNA molecule, which contains genes, resembles a double spiral, or helix.

in each pair comes from your father and one from your mother. We can actually see these chromosomes through a microscope, and we can sometimes tell when one is faulty and predict what problems it will cause.

The first 22 pairs of chromosomes provide programs for the development of the body and brain, and the last pair, called the *sex chromosomes,* determines an individual's sex. In females, both chromosomes in the 23rd pair are called *X chromosomes.* In males, the mother contributes an X chromosome but the father contributes a *Y chromosome.* This one difference is responsible for the variance in biological sex. Abnormalities in the sex chromosomal pair can cause ambiguous sexual characteristics.

The DNA molecules that contain genes have a certain structure, a "double helix," that was discovered only a few decades ago. The shape of a helix is like a spiral staircase. A double helix is two spirals intertwined, turning in opposite directions. Located on this double spiral are simple pairs of molecules bound together and arranged in different orders. On the X chromosome are approximately 160 million pairs. The ordering of these "base pairs" determines how the body develops and works.

If something is wrong in the ordering of these molecules on the double helix, we have a *defective gene,* which may or may not lead to problems. If it is a single dominant gene, such as the type that controls hair or eye color, the effect can be quite noticeable. A *dominant gene* is one of a pair of genes that determines a particular trait. A *recessive gene,* by contrast, must be paired with another recessive gene to determine a trait. When we have a dominant gene, using Mendelian laws' of genetics we can predict fairly accurately how many offspring will develop a certain trait, characteristic, or disorder, depending on whether one or both of the parents carry that dominant gene.

Most of the time, predictions are not so simple. Much of our development and, interestingly, most of our behavior, personality, and even IQ is probably *polygenic*—that is, influenced by many genes, each contributing only a tiny effect. For this reason, most scientists have decided that we must look for patterns of influence across these genes, us-

ing procedures called *quantitative genetics* (Plomin, 1990; Plomin, De Fries, McClearn, & Rutter, 1997). Quantitative genetics basically sums up all the tiny effects across many genes without necessarily telling us which genes are responsible for which effects, although researchers are now using molecular genetic techniques (the study of the actual structure of genes) in an attempt to identify some of the specific genes that contribute to individual differences (e.g., Gottesman, 1997; Plomin et al., 1995). In Chapter 3, we'll look at the actual methods scientists use to study the influence of genes. Here, our interest is on what they are finding.

New Developments in the Study of Genes and Behavior

Scientists have now identified, in a preliminary way, the genetic contribution to psychological disorders and related behavioral patterns. The best estimates attribute about half our enduring personality traits and cognitive abilities to genes. For example, it now seems quite clear that the heritability of general cognitive ability (IQ) is approximately 62%, and that this figure is relatively stable throughout adult life (Gottesman, 1997). This estimate is based on a landmark study by McClearn et al. (1997), who compared 110 Swedish identical twin pairs of at least 80 years old with 130 same-sex fraternal twin pairs of a similar age. This work built on earlier important twin studies with different age groups showing similar results (e.g., Bouchard, Lykken, McGue, Segal, & Tellegen, 1990). In the McClearn et al. (1997) study, heritability estimates for specific cognitive abilities, such as memory or ability to perceive spatial relations, ranged from 32% to 62%. In other studies, the same calculation for personality traits such as shyness or activity levels ranges between 30% and 50% (Bouchard et al., 1990; Loehlin, 1992; Saudino & Plomin, 1996; Saudino, Plomin, & De Fries, 1996). For psychological disorders, the evidence indicates that genetic factors contribute to the full range but account for less than half of the explanation. If one of a pair of identical twins has schizophrenia, there is a less than 50% likelihood that the other twin will also (Gottesman, 1991). Similar or lower rates exist for other psychological disorders (Plomin et al., 1997), with the possible exception of alcoholism (Kendler et al., 1995).

Behavioral geneticists have reached general conclusions on the role of genes and psychological disorders that are relevant to our purposes. First, *no individual genes* have been identified that contribute substantially to the major psychological disorders, despite occasional reports to the contrary in the press. For example, in 1987 a report claimed that a gene linked to bipolar disorder had been found in a group of closely related Amish families (see Chapter 7). However, this result could not be replicated. Similar reports on schizophrenia appear periodically; most recently, interest has focused on Chromosome 6 (e.g., Peltonen, 1995). It is likely that specific genes may be found to be associated with certain psychological disorders, and in Chapter 3 we will discuss one major effort to identify them. But all the evidence suggests that contributions to psychological disorders come from many genes, each having a relatively small effect. It is extremely important that we recognize this probability and make every attempt to track the genes. Advances in gene mapping and molecular genetics help with this very difficult research (e.g., Plomin et al., 1997).

Genetic contributions to behavior are evident in twins who were raised apart. When these brothers were finally reunited, they were both firemen, and they discovered many other shared characteristics and interests.

Genetic research leads to discoveries that border on science fiction. One fascinating new development is the ability to "knock out" certain genes through breeding or other methods, which might, in the future, prevent certain genetically determined diseases. However, because psychological disorders are partly the product of numerous genes that contribute a small amount each, it is unlikely that this technology will reduce a person's vulnerability to psychological disorders. In any case, such a step is decades in the future. The more important questions now are how genetic and environmental factors interact to influence both the development of psychological disorders and their treatment.

The Interaction of Genetic and Environmental Effects

In 1983, the distinguished neuroscientist Eric Kandel speculated that the process of learning affects more than behavior. He suggested that the very genetic structure of cells may actually change as a result of learning, if genes that were in-active or dormant interact with the environment in such a way that they become active. In other words, the environment may occasionally "turn on" certain genes. This type of mechanism may lead to changes in the number of receptors at the end of a neuron, which, in turn, would affect biochemical functioning in the brain.

Although Kandel was not the first to propose this idea, it had enormous impact. Most of us assume that the brain, like other parts of the body, may well be influenced by environmental changes during development. But we also assume that once maturity is reached, the structure and function of our internal organs and most of our physiology are pretty much set or, in the case of the brain, "hardwired." The competing idea is that the brain and its functions are plastic, subject to continual change in response to the environment, even at the level of genetic structure. Now there is evidence supporting that view (Owens, Mulchahey, Stout, & Plotsky, 1997). In order to explore gene–environment interactions as they relate to psychopathology, we can look at two models: diathesis–stress and reciprocal gene–environment.

Eric Kandel is a pioneer in establishing the effects of learning on biological functioning.

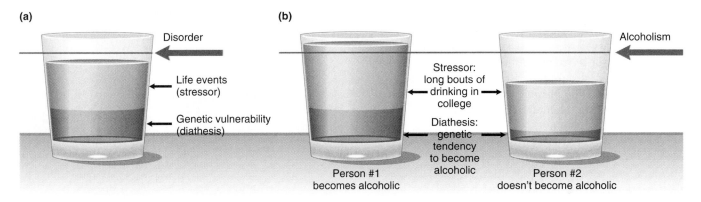

figure 2.2   In the diathesis–stress model, the greater the underlying vulnerability, the less stress is needed to trigger a disorder.

THE DIATHESIS–STRESS MODEL

For years, scientists have assumed a specific method of interaction between genes and the environment. According to this **diathesis–stress model,** individuals inherit, from multiple genes, tendencies to express certain traits or behaviors, which may then be activated under conditions of stress (see Figure 2.2). Each inherited tendency is a *diathesis,* which means, literally, a condition that makes one susceptible to developing a disorder. When the right kind of life event, such as a certain type of stressor, comes along, the disorder develops. For example, according to the diathesis–stress model, Judy inherited a *tendency* to faint at the sight of blood. This tendency is the diathesis, or **vulnerability.** It would not become prominent until certain environmental events occurred. For Judy, this event was the sight of an animal being dissected when she was in a situation in which escape, or at least closing her eyes, was not acceptable. The stress of seeing the dissection under these conditions activated her genetic tendency to faint. Together, these factors led to her developing a disorder. If she had not taken biology, she might have gone through life without ever knowing she had the tendency, at least to such an extreme, although she might have felt queasy about minor cuts and bruises. You can see that the "diathesis" is genetically based, and that the "stress" is environmental, but they must interact to produce a disorder.

We might also take the case of someone who inherits a vulnerability to alcoholism, which would make him substantially different from a close friend who does not have the same tendency. During college, both engage in extended drinking bouts, but only the individual with the "addictive" genes begins the long downward spiral into alcoholism. His friend doesn't.

Having a particular vulnerability doesn't mean that you will develop the associated disorder. The smaller the vulnerability, the greater the life stress required to produce the disorder; conversely, with greater vulnerability, less life stress is required. This model of gene–environment interactions has been very popular although, in view of the relationship of the environment to the structure and function of the brain, it is greatly oversimplified.

THE RECIPROCAL GENE–ENVIRONMENT MODEL

There is now some evidence that genetic endowment may actually *increase the probability* that an individual will experience stressful life events (e.g., Saudino, Pedersen, Lichtenstein, McClearn, & Plomin, 1997). For example, people with a genetic vulnerability to develop a certain disorder, such as blood–injury–injection phobia, may also have a personality trait—let's say impulsiveness—that makes them more likely to be involved in minor accidents that would result in their seeing blood. In other words,

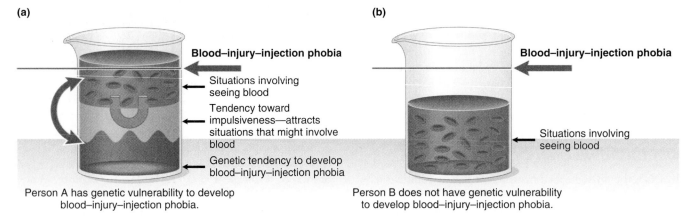

figure 2.3   Reciprocal gene–environment model

they may be accident prone because they are continually rushing to complete things or to get to places without regard for their physical safety. These people, then, might have a genetically determined tendency to create the very environmental risk factors that trigger a genetic vulnerability to blood–injury–injection phobia. This **reciprocal gene–environment model** (see Figure 2.3) has been proposed only recently (Rende & Plomin, 1992), but there is some evidence that it applies to the development of depression, because some people may tend to seek out difficult relationships or other circumstances that lead to depression (Bebbington et al., 1988; Kendler et al., 1995; McGuffin, Katz, & Bebbington, 1988).

McGue and Lykken (1992) have even applied the reciprocal gene–environment model to some fascinating data on the influence of genes on the divorce rate. Many of us think that divorces occur because people simply marry the wrong partner. Some people, of course, may stick it out, because their religion forbids divorce or for other reasons. But a successful marriage depends on finding the ideal partner, right? Not necessarily! For example, if you and your spouse each have an identical twin, and both identical twins have been divorced, the chance that you will also divorce increases greatly. Furthermore, if your identical twins and your parents and your spouse's parents have been divorced, the chance that you will divorce is 77.5%. Conversely, if none of your family members on either side has been divorced, the probability that you will divorce is only 5.3%.

Of course, this is the extreme example, but McGue and Lykken (1992) demonstrated that the probability of your divorcing doubles over the probability in the population at large if your fraternal twin is also divorced, but increases *six-fold* if your identical twin is divorced. Obviously, no one gene causes divorce. To the extent that it is genetically determined, the tendency to divorce is almost certainly related to various inherited traits, such as being high-strung, impulsive, or short-tempered (Jockin, McGue, & Lykken, 1996). Another possibility is that an inherited trait makes it *more likely* that we will choose an incompatible spouse. To take a simple example, if you are passive and unassertive, you may well choose a strong, dominant mate who turns out to be impossible to live with. You get divorced, but then find yourself attracted to another individual with the same personality traits, who is also impossible to live with. Some people write this kind of pattern off to poor judgment. Social, interpersonal, psychological, and environmental factors play major roles in whether we stay married but, just possibly, our genes contribute to how we create our own environment.

In summary, there is a very complex interaction between genes and the environment that plays an important role in every psychological disorder (Kendler, 1995). Our genetic endowment *does* influence our behavior, our emotions, and our cognitive processes. Environmental events, in turn, seem to affect our very genetic structure. Neither nature (genes) nor nurture (environmental events) alone influences the development of our behavior and personalities, but a complex interaction of the two.

Neuroscience and Its Contributions to Psychopathology

Knowing how the nervous system and, especially, the brain work is central to any understanding of our behavior, emotions, and cognitive processes. This is the focus of **neuroscience.** To comprehend the newest research in this field, we first need an overview of how the brain and the nervous system function. The human nervous system includes the *central nervous system,* consisting of the brain and the spinal cord, and the *peripheral nervous system,* consisting of the somatic nervous system and the autonomic nervous system (see Figure 2.4).

The Central Nervous System

The central nervous system (CNS) processes all information received from our sense organs and reacts as necessary. It sorts out what is relevant, such as a certain taste or a new sound, from what isn't, such as a familiar view or ticking clock; checks the "memory banks" to determine why the information is relevant; and implements the right reaction, whether it is to answer a question or to play a Chopin étude. This is a lot of exceedingly complex work. The spinal cord is part of the central nervous system, but its primary function is to facilitate the sending of messages to and from the brain, which is the other major component of the CNS and the most complex organ in the body. The brain uses an average of 140 billion nerve cells, called **neurons,** to control our every thought and action. Neurons transmit information throughout the nervous system. Understanding how they work is important for our purposes because current research has confirmed that neurons contribute to psychopathology.

The typical neuron contains a central cell body with two kinds of branches. One kind of branch is called a *dendrite.* Dendrites have numerous *receptors* that receive messages in the form of chemical impulses from other nerve cells, which are converted into electrical impulses. The other kind of branch, called an *axon,* transmits these impulses to other neurons. Any one nerve cell may have multiple connections to other neurons. The brain has billions of nerve cells, so you can see how complicated the system becomes, far more complicated than the most powerful computer that has ever been built (or will be for some time). In the 1997 victory of a powerful computer over the reigning world chess champion, the computer was programmed to estimate probabilities only of one move versus another among possible moves on a chessboard. The CNS, on the other hand, must organize every facet of our existence.

Nerve cells are not actually connected. There is a small space through which the impulse must pass to get to the next neuron. The space between the axon of one neuron and

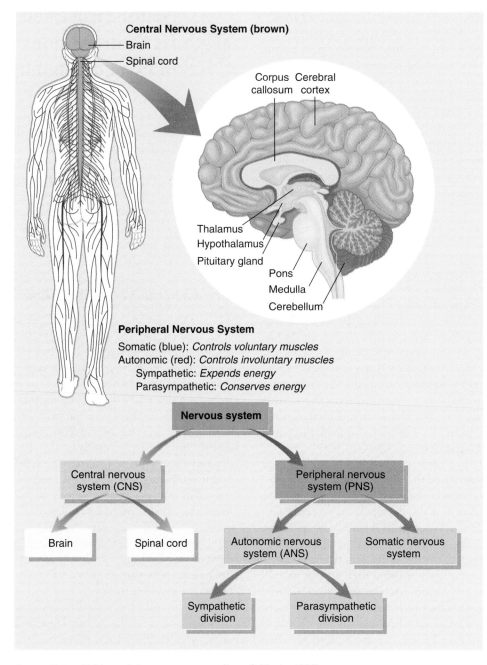

figure 2.4   Divisions of the nervous system (from Goldstein, 1994)

the dendrite of another is called the **synaptic cleft** (see Figure 2.5). What happens in this space is of great interest to psychopathologists. The chemicals that are released from the axon of one nerve cell and transmit the impulse to the receptors of another nerve cell are called **neurotransmitters.** Only in the past several decades have we begun to understand their complexity. Now, using increasingly sensitive equipment and techniques, scientists have identified many different types of neurotransmitters.

Major neurotransmitters that are relevant to psychopathology include *norepinephrine* (also known as noradrenaline), *serotonin, dopamine,* and *gamma aminobutyric acid (GABA).* You will see these terms many times in this book. Excesses or insufficiencies in some neurotransmitters are

associated with different groups of psychological disorders. For example, reduced levels of *GABA* are associated with excessive anxiety (Costa, 1985). Early research (S. Snyder, 1976, 1981) linked increases in dopamine activity to schizophrenia. Other early research found correlations between depression and high levels of norepinephrine (Schildkraut, 1965) and, possibly, low levels of serotonin (Siever, Davis, & Gorman, 1991). However, more recent research, described later in this chapter, indicates that these early interpretations are probably much too simplistic. Many types and subtypes of neurotransmitters are just being discovered, and they interact in very complex ways. In view of their importance, we will return to the subject of neurotransmitters shortly.

The central nervous system screens out information that is irrelevant to the current situation. From moment to moment we notice what moves or changes more than what remains the same.

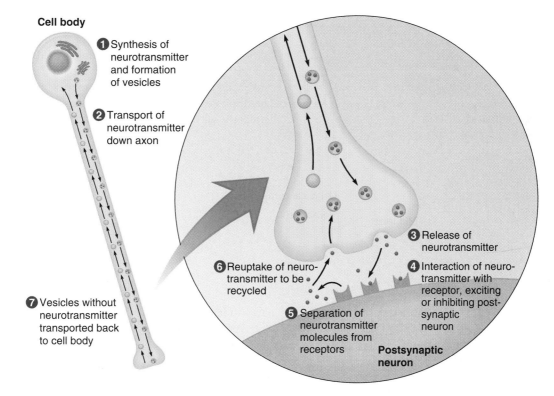

figure 2.5 The transmission of information from one neuron to another

The Structure of the Brain

Having an overview of the brain is useful because many of the structures described here are later mentioned in the context of specific disorders. One way to view the brain (see Figure 2.6) is to see it in two parts—the *brain stem* and the *forebrain*. The brain stem is the lower and more ancient part of the brain. Found in most animals, this structure handles most of the essential automatic functions such as breathing, sleeping, and moving around in a coordinated way. The forebrain is more advanced, and has evolved more recently.

The lowest part of the brain stem, the *hindbrain*, contains the *medulla*, the *pons*, and the *cerebellum*. The hindbrain regulates many automatic activities, such as breathing, the pumping action of the heart (heartbeat), and digestion. The cerebellum controls motor coordination, and recent research suggests that abnormalities in the cerebellum may be associated with the psychological disorder autism (Courchesne, 1997) (see Chapter 14).

The *midbrain* coordinates movement with sensory input, and contains parts of the *reticular activating system (RAS)*, which contributes to processes of arousal and tension such as whether we are awake or asleep.

At the very top of the brain stem are the *thalamus* and *hypothalamus*, which are involved very broadly with the regulation of behavior and emotion. These structures function primarily as a relay between the forebrain and the remaining lower areas of the brain stem. Some anatomists even consider the thalamus and hypothalamus to be parts of the forebrain.

At the base of the forebrain, just above the thalamus and hypothalamus is the *limbic system. Limbic* means "border." The limbic system, which figures prominently in much of psychopathology, includes such structures as the *hippocampus* (sea horse), *cingulate gyrus* (girdle), *septum* (partition), and *amygdala* (almond), all of which are named for their approximate shapes. This system helps regulate our emotional experiences and expressions and, to some extent, our ability to learn and to control our impulses. It is also involved with the basic drives of sex, aggression, hunger, and thirst.

The *basal ganglia*, also at the base of the forebrain, includes the *caudate* (tailed) *nucleus*. Because damage to these structures may make us change our posture or twitch or shake, they are believed to control motor activity. Later in this chapter we will review some very interesting findings on the relationship of this area to obsessive–compulsive disorder.

The largest part of the forebrain is the *cerebral cortex*, which contains more than 80% of all the neurons in the central nervous system. This part of the brain provides us with our distinctly human qualities, allowing us to look to the future and plan, to reason, and to create. The cerebral cortex is divided into two hemispheres. Although the hemispheres look very much alike structurally and operate relatively independently (both are capable of perceiving, thinking, and remembering), recent research indicates that each has different specialties. The left hemisphere seems to be chiefly responsible for verbal and other cognitive processes. The right hemisphere seems to be better at perceiving the world around us and creating images. The hemispheres may play differential roles in specific psychological disorders. For example, current theories about dyslexia (a learning disability involving reading) suggest that it may be a result of the two hemispheres not specializing adequately or communicating properly with each other (Gladstone, Best, & Davidson,

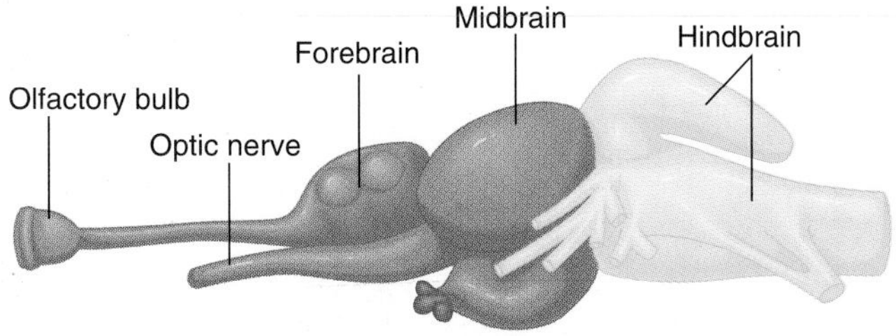

figure 2.6a   Three divisions of the brain

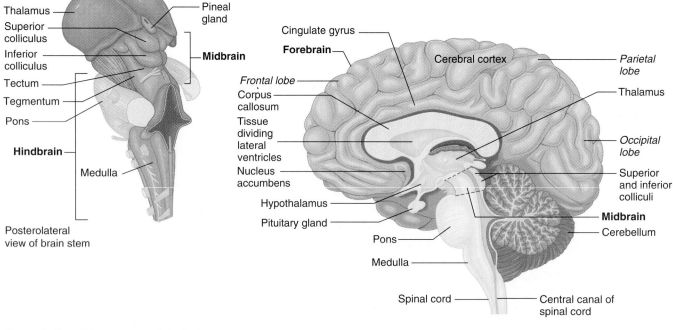

figure 2.6b   Major structures of the brain

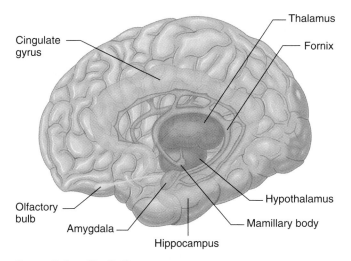

figure 2.6c   The limbic systems

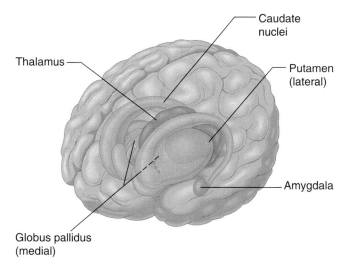

figure 2.6d   The basal ganglia

1989). Each hemisphere consists of four separate areas or lobes: *temporal, parietal, occipital,* and *frontal* (see Figure 2.7). Each is associated with different processes: the temporal lobe with recognizing various sights and sounds and with long-term memory storage; the parietal lobe with recognizing various sensations of touch; the occipital lobe with integrating and making sense of various visual inputs. The three lobes, located toward the back (posterior) of the brain, work together to process sight, touch, hearing, and other signals from our senses.

The frontal lobe is the most interesting from the point of view of psychopathology. It carries most of the weight of our thinking and reasoning abilities as well as memory. It also enables us to relate to the world around us and the people in it, to behave as social animals. When studying areas of the brain for clues to psychopathology, most researchers focus on the frontal lobe of the cerebral cortex, as well as on the limbic system and the basal ganglia.

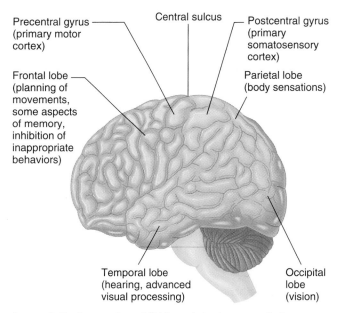

figure 2.7   Some major subdivisions of the human cerebral cortex and a few of their primary functions (adapted from Kalat, 1995).

The Peripheral Nervous System

The peripheral nervous system coordinates with the brain stem to make sure that the body is working properly. Its two major components are the *somatic nervous system* and the *autonomic nervous system (ANS)*. The somatic nervous system controls the muscles, so damage in this area might make it difficult for us to engage in any voluntary movement, including talking. The autonomic nervous system includes the *sympathetic nervous system (SNS)* and *parasympathetic nervous system (PNS)*. The primary duties of the ANS are to regulate the cardiovascular system (for example, the heart and blood vessels) and the endocrine system (for instance, the pituitary, adrenal, thyroid, and gonadal glands) and to perform various other functions, including aiding digestion and regulating body temperature (see Figure 2.8).

■ **concept check 2.2**

Check your understanding of the structures of the brain by listing which is being described in the sentences below: (a) frontal lobe, (b) brain stem, (c) midbrain, or (d) cerebral cortex.

1. Movement, breathing, and sleeping depend on this ancient part of the brain, which is present in most animals.

2. This area contains parts of the reticular activating system and coordinates movement with sensory output.

3. More than 80% of the neurons in the human central nervous system are contained in this part of the brain, which gives us distinct qualities.

4. This area is responsible for most of our memory, thinking, and reasoning capabilities, and makes us "social animals."

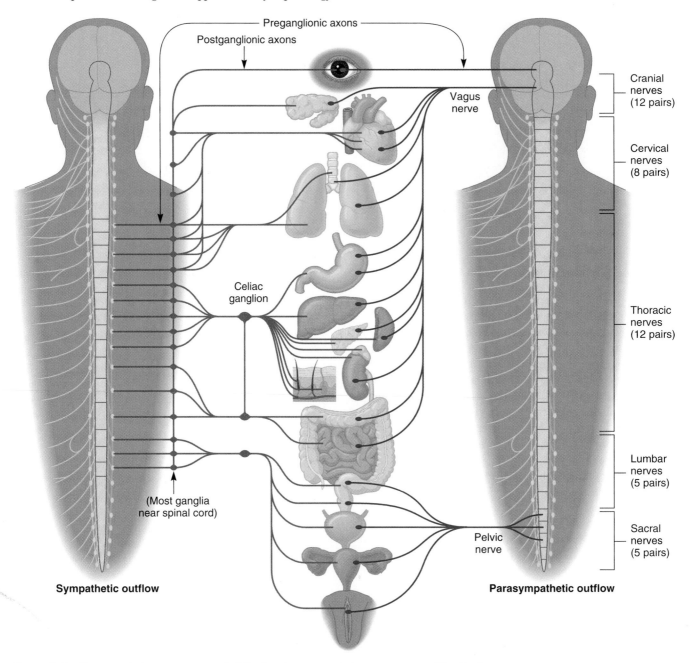

figure 2.8   The sympathetic nervous system (red lines) and parasympathetic nervous system (blue lines)

The *endocrine system* works a bit differently from other systems in the body. Each endocrine gland produces its own chemical messenger, called a **hormone,** and releases it directly into the bloodstream. The adrenal glands produce epinephrine (also called *adrenaline*) in response to stress, as well as salt-regulating hormones; the thyroid gland produces thyroxine, which facilitates energy metabolism and growth; the pituitary is a master gland that produces a variety of regulatory hormones; and the gonadal glands produce sex hormones such as estrogen and testosterone. The endocrine system is closely related to the immune system; it is also implicated in a variety of disorders, particularly the stress-related physical disorders discussed in Chapter 9.

The sympathetic and parasympathetic divisions of the ANS often operate in a complementary fashion. The SNS is primarily responsible for mobilizing the body during times of stress or danger, by rapidly activating the organs and glands under its control. When the sympathetic division goes on alert, the heart beats faster, thereby increasing the flow of blood to the muscles; respiration increases, allowing more oxygen to get into the blood and brain; and the adrenal glands are stimulated. All these changes help mobilize us for action. If we are threatened by some immediate danger, such as a mugger coming at us on the street, we are able to run faster or defend ourselves with greater strength than if the sympathetic nervous system had not innervated our internal organs. When you read in the newspaper that a woman lifted a heavy object to free a trapped child, you can be sure that her sympathetic nervous system was working overtime. This system mediates a substantial part of our "emergency"

This brief overview should give you a general sense of the structure and function of the brain and nervous system. New procedures for studying brain structure and function that involve photographing the working brain will be discussed in Chapter 3. Here, our focus is on what these studies reveal about the nature of psychopathology.

Neurotransmitters

The biochemical neurotransmitters in the brain and nervous system that carry messages from one neuron to another are receiving intense attention by psychopathologists (Bloom & Kupfer, 1995). These chemicals were discovered only in the past several decades, and only in the past few years have we developed the extraordinarily sophisticated procedures necessary to study them. One way to think of neurotransmitters is as narrow currents flowing through the ocean of the brain. Sometimes they run parallel with other currents, only to separate once again. Often they seem to meander aimlessly, looping back on themselves before moving on. Neurons that are sensitive to one type of neurotransmitter cluster together and form paths from one part of the brain to the other. Often these paths overlap with the paths of other neurotransmitters but, as often as not, they end up going their separate ways (Dean, Kelsey, Heller, & Ciaranello, 1993). There are thousands, perhaps tens of thousands, of these **brain circuits,** and we are just beginning to discover and map them. Recently, neuroscientists have identified several that seem to play roles in various psychological disorders.

Almost all drug therapies work by either increasing or decreasing the flow of specific neurotransmitters. Some drugs directly inhibit, or block, the production of a neurotransmitter. Other drugs increase the production of competing biochemical substances that may deactivate the neurotransmitter. Yet other drugs do not affect neurotransmitters directly but prevent the chemical from reaching the next neuron by closing down, or occupying, the receptors in that neuron. After a neurotransmitter is released, it is quickly drawn back from the synaptic cleft into the same neuron. This process is called **reuptake.** Some drugs work by blocking the reuptake process, thereby causing continued stimulation along the brain circuit.

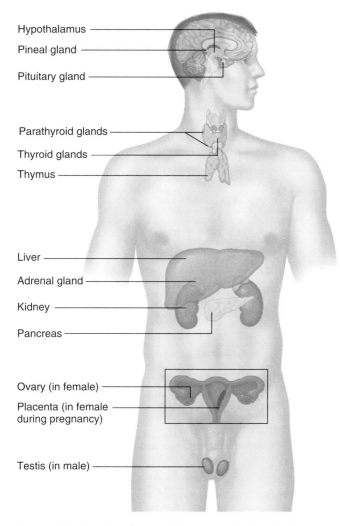

figure 2.9 Location of some of the major endocrine glands

or "alarm" reaction, discussed later in this chapter and in Chapter 5.

One of the functions of the parasympathetic system, is to balance the sympathetic system. In other words, because we could not operate in a state of hyperarousal and preparedness forever, the PNS takes over after a while, normalizing our arousal and facilitating the storage of energy by helping the digestive process.

One brain connection that is implicated in some psychological disorders involves the hypothalamus and the endocrine system. The hypothalamus connects to the adjacent pituitary gland, which is the master or coordinator of the endocrine system. The pituitary gland, in turn, may stimulate the cortical part of the adrenal glands on top of the kidneys. As noted previously, surges of epinephrine tend to energize us, arouse us, and get our bodies ready for threat or challenge. When athletes say their adrenaline was really flowing, they mean they were highly aroused and up for the game. The cortical part of the adrenal glands also produces the stress hormone *cortisol*. This system is called the *hypothalamic–pituitary–adrenalcortical axis* or *HYPAC axis* (see Figure 2.9); it has been implicated in several psychological disorders and will be mentioned in Chapters 5, 7, and 9.

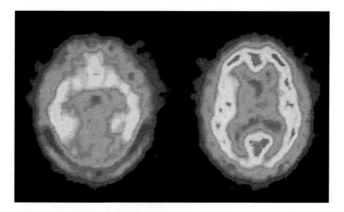

A PET scan shows the distribution of serotonergic neurons.

New neurotransmitters are discovered every year, and existing neurotransmitter systems must be subdivided into separate classifications. Because this very dynamic field of research is in a state of considerable flux, the neuroscience of psychopathology is a very exciting area of study; however, research findings that seem to apply to psychopathology today may no longer be relevant tomorrow. Many years of study will be required before it is all sorted out.

You may still read reports that certain psychological disorders are caused by biochemical imbalances, excesses, or deficiencies in certain neurotransmitter systems. For example, abnormal activity of the neurotransmitter serotonin is often described as causing depression, and abnormalities in the neurotransmitter dopamine have been implicated in schizophrenia. However, increasing evidence indicates that this is an enormous oversimplification. We are now learning that the effects of neurotransmitter activity are more general and less specific. They often seem to be related to the way we process information (Depue, in press; Depue, Luciana, Arbisi, Collins, & Leon, 1994). Changes in neurotransmitter activity may make people more or less likely to exhibit certain kinds of behavior in certain situations without causing the behavior directly. In addition, broad-based disturbances in our functioning are almost always associated with *interactions* of the various neurotransmitters rather than with *alterations* in the activity of any one system (Depue & Spoont, 1986; Depue & Zald, 1993; Owens et al., 1997). In other words, the currents intersect so often that changes in one result in changes in the other, often in an unpredictable way.

Research on neurotransmitter function focuses primarily on what happens when activity levels change. We can study this in several ways. We can introduce substances called **agonists** that effectively *increase* the activity of a neurotransmitter by mimicking its effects, substances called **antagonists** that *decrease,* or block, a neurotransmitter, or substances called **inverse agonists** that produce effects *opposite* to those produced by the neurotransmitter. By systematically manipulating the production of a neurotransmitter in different parts of the brain, scientists are able to learn more about its effects. In fact, most drugs could be classified as either agonistic or antagonistic, although they may achieve these results in a variety of ways. We now describe the four neurotransmitter systems most often mentioned in connection with psychological disorders.

Serotonin

The technical name for **serotonin** is 5-Hydroxytryptamine (5HT). Approximately six major circuits of serotonin spread from the midbrain, looping around its various parts (Azmitia, 1978) (see Figure 2.10). Because of the widespread nature of these circuits, many of them ending up in the cortex, serotonin is believed to influence a great deal of our behavior,

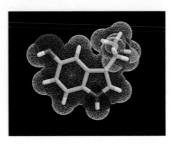

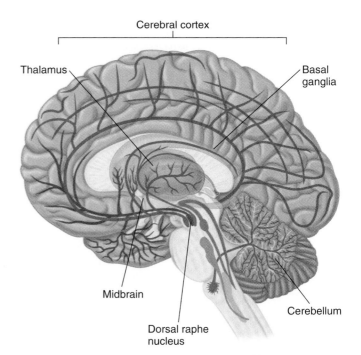

figure 2.10   Major serotonin pathways in the brain

particularly the way we process information (Depue & Spoont, 1986; Spoont, 1992).

The serotonin system regulates our behavior, moods, and thought processes. Extremely low activity levels of serotonin are associated with less inhibition and with instability, impulsivity, and the tendency to overreact to situations. Low serotonin activity has been associated with aggression, suicide, and impulsive overeating and excessive sexual behavior. However, these behaviors do not *necessarily* happen if serotonin activity is low. Other currents in the brain, or other psychological or social influences, may well compensate for low serotonin activity. Therefore, low serotonin activity may make us more vulnerable to certain problematic behavior without directly causing it. (The same fact is emerging about other neurotransmitter systems.) To add to the complexity, serotonin has slightly different effects depending on the type or subtype of receptors that are involved, and we now know that there are at least 15 different receptors in the serotonin system (Owens et al., 1997). Several different classes of drugs primarily affect the serotonin system, including the tricyclic antidepressants such as imipramine (known by its brand name Tofranil), but a new class of serotonin specific reuptake inhibitors (SSRIs), including fluoxetine (Prozac) (see Figure 2.11), affect serotonin more directly than other drugs such as tricyclic antidepressants. These drugs are used to treat a number of psychological disorders, particularly anxiety, mood, and eating disorders. You may also have heard of "fen/phen" and similar antiobesity drugs that boost levels of serotonin and, it is hoped, reduce impulsive food intake. The fact that this class of drugs was removed from the market in 1997 due to a newly discovered risk of heart valve damage reminds us that there is a lot to learn about the complex action of these

How Neurotransmitters Work
Neurotransmitters are stored in tiny sacs at the end of the neuron Ⓐ. An electric jolt makes the sacs merge with the outer membrane, and the neurotransmitter is released into the synapse Ⓑ. The molecules diffuse across the gap and bind receptors, specialized proteins, on the adjacent neuron Ⓒ. When sufficient neurotransmitter has been absorbed, the receptors release the molecules, which are then broken down or reabsorbed by the first neuron and stored for later use Ⓓ.

How Serotonin Drugs Work
Prozac enhances serotonin's effects by preventing it from being absorbed Ⓔ. Redux and fenfluramine (antiobesity drugs) cause the release of extra serotonin into the synapse Ⓕ.

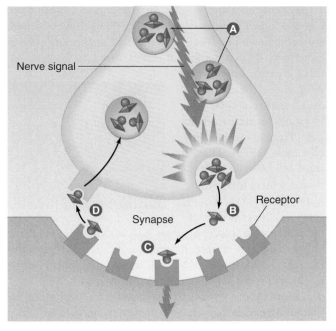

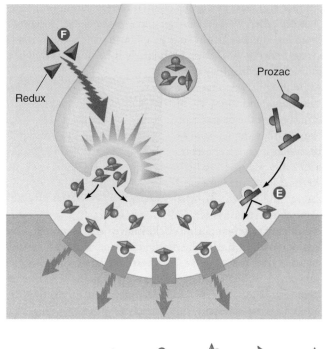

Receptor Variation
There are at least 15 different serotonin receptors, each associated with a different function.

figure 2.11 Manipulating serotonin in the brain

drugs. The herbal medication St. John's-wort, available in health stores, also affects serotonin levels.

GAMMA AMINOBUTYRIC ACID (GABA)
The neurotransmitter **gamma aminobutyric acid, GABA** for short, reduces postsynaptic activity, which, in turn, inhibits a wide variety of behaviors and emotions; its best known effect, however, is to reduce anxiety. Scientists have discovered that a particular class of drugs, the *benzodiazepines,* or mild tranquilizers, make it easier for GABA molecules to attach themselves to the receptors of specialized neurons. Thus, the higher the level of benzodiazepine, the more GABA becomes attached to neuron receptors and the calmer we become 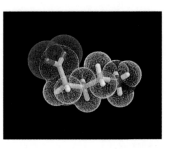 (to a point). Neuroscientists thus assume that we must have within us substances very much like the benzodiazepine class of drugs—in other words, natural benzodiazepines. However, we have yet to discover them (Bloom & Kupfer, 1995).

As with other neurotransmitter systems, we now know that GABA's effect is not specific to anxiety but has a much broader influence. Like serotonin, the GABA system rides on many circuits distributed widely throughout the brain. GABA seems to reduce overall arousal somewhat and to temper our emotional responses. For example, in addition to reducing anxiety, minor tranquilizers also have an anticonvulsant effect, relaxing muscle groups that may be subject to spasms. Further, this system seems to reduce levels of anger, hostility, aggression and, perhaps, even positive emotional states such as eager anticipation and pleasure (Bond & Lader, 1979; Lader, 1975). Thus, this system may specifically act to process information relevant to arousal associated with emotional and physical states. We are also learning that the GABA system may not be unitary, but composed of a number of subsystems. Different types of GABA receptors seem to act in different ways, with perhaps only one of the subtypes having an affinity for the benzodiazepine component (Gray, 1985; Pritchett, Lüddens, & Seeburg, 1989). Therefore, the conclusion that this system is responsible for anxiety seems just as out of date as concluding that the serotonin system is responsible for depression.

NOREPINEPHRINE

A third neurotransmitter system that is important to psychopathology is **norepinephrine** (also known as *noradrenaline*) (see Figure 2.12). We have already seen that norepinephrine, like epinephrine, (referred to as a *catecholamine*), is also part of the endocrine system. Catecholamines are secreted by the adrenal glands. Norepinephrine seems to stimulate at least two groups (and probably a lot more) of receptors called *alpha-adrenergic* and *beta-adrenergic* receptors. Someone in your family may be taking a widely used class of drugs called *beta blockers,* particularly if he or she has hypertension or difficulties with regulating heart rate. As the name indicates, these drugs block the beta receptors so that their response to a surge of norepinephrine is reduced, which keeps blood pressure and heart rate down. In the central nervous system, a

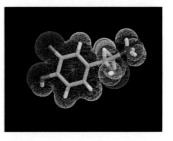

number of norepinephrine circuits have been identified. One major circuit begins in the hindbrain, in an area that controls basic bodily functions such as respiration. Another circuit appears to influence the emergency reactions or alarm responses (Gray, 1987; Gray & McNaughton, 1996) that occur when we suddenly find ourselves in a very dangerous situation, suggesting that norepinephrine may bear some relationship to states of panic (Charney et al., 1990; Gray & McNaughton, 1996). More likely, however, is that this system, with all its varying circuits coursing through the brain, acts in a more general way to regulate or modulate certain behavioral tendencies and is not directly involved in specific patterns of behavior or in psychological disorders.

DOPAMINE

Finally, **dopamine** is a major neurotransmitter that is also classified as a catecholamine. Dopamine has been implicated in psychological disorders such as schizophrenia (see Figure 2.13). Remember the wonder drug reserpine mentioned in Chapter 1 that reduced psychotic behaviors associated with schizophrenia? This drug and more modern antipsychotic treatments affect a number of neurotransmitter systems, but their greatest impact may be that they block specific dopamine receptors, thus lowering dopamine activity (for example, Snyder, Burt, & Creese, 1976). Thus, it was long thought possible that in schizophrenia dopamine circuits may be too active. The recent develop-

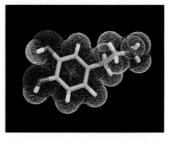

ment of new antipsychotic drugs such as clozapine, which has only weak effects on certain dopamine receptors, suggests this idea may need revising. We will explore the dopamine hypothesis in some detail in Chapter 13.

In its various circuits throughout specific regions of the brain, dopamine also seems to have a more general effect, best described as a *switch* that turns on various brain circuits that may be associated with certain types of behavior. Once the switch is turned on, other neurotransmitters may then inhibit or facilitate emotions or behavior (Oades, 1985; Spoont, 1992). Dopamine circuits merge and cross with

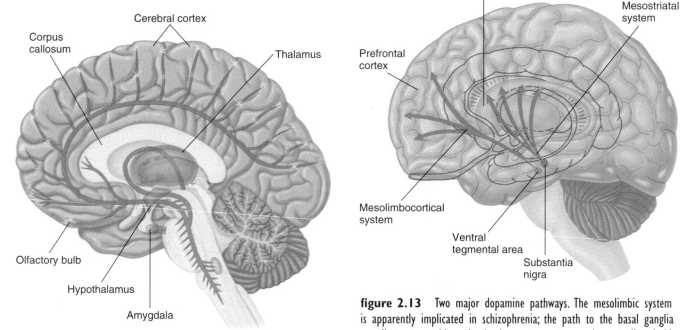

figure 2.12   Major norepinephrine pathways in the human brain (adapted from Kalat, 1995).

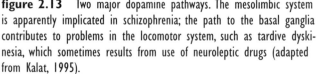

figure 2.13   Two major dopamine pathways. The mesolimbic system is apparently implicated in schizophrenia; the path to the basal ganglia contributes to problems in the locomotor system, such as tardive dyskinesia, which sometimes results from use of neuroleptic drugs (adapted from Kalat, 1995).

serotonin circuits at many points and therefore influence many of the same behaviors. For example, dopamine activity is associated with exploratory, outgoing, pleasure-seeking behaviors, and serotonin is associated with inhibition and constraint; thus, in a sense they balance each other (Depue et al., 1994). Once again, we see that the effects of a neurotransmitter—in this case, dopamine—are more complex than we originally thought. Researchers have thus far discovered at least five different receptor sites that are selectively sensitive to dopamine (Owens et al., 1997). One of a class of drugs that affects the dopamine circuits specifically is L-dopa, which is a dopamine agonist (increases levels of dopamine). One of the systems that dopamine switches on is the locomotor system, which regulates our ability to move in a coordinated way and, once turned on, is influenced by serotonin activity. Because of these connections, deficiencies in dopamine have been associated with disorders such as Parkinson's disease, in which a marked deterioration in motor behavior includes tremors, rigidity of muscles, and difficulty with judgment. L-dopa has been successful in reducing some of these motor disabilities.

■ concept check 2.3

Check your understanding of the major functions of four important neurotransmitters by matching them to the descriptions below: (a) GABA, (b) serotonin, (c) dopamine, and (d) norepinephrine.

1. Which neurotransmitter binds to neuron receptor sites, inhibiting postsynaptic activity and reducing overall arousal? _____

2. Which neurotransmitter is a switch that turns on various brain circuits? _____

3. Which neurotransmitter seems to be involved in your emergency reactions or alarm responses? _____

4. Which neurotransmitter is believed to influence the way we process information, as well as to moderate or inhibit our behavior? _____

Implications for Psychopathology

Psychological disorders typically mix emotional, behavioral, and cognitive symptoms, so identifiable lesions (or damage) localized in *specific* structures of the brain do not, for the most part, cause them. Even widespread damage most often results in motor or sensory deficits, which are usually the province of the medical specialty of neurology; neurologists often work with neuropsychologists to identify specific lesions. But psychopathologists are also beginning to theorize about the more *general* role of brain function in the development of personality, considering how different types of biologically driven personalities might be more

vulnerable to developing certain types of psychological disorders (e.g., Depue, in press). For example, genetic contributions might lead to patterns of neurotransmitter activity that influence personality. Thus, some impulsive risk takers may have low serotonergic activity and high dopaminergic activity.

Procedures for studying images of the functioning brain have recently been applied to *obsessive–compulsive disorder (OCD)*. Individuals with this severe anxiety disorder suffer from intrusive, frightening thoughts—for example, that they might have become contaminated with poison and will poison their loved ones if they touch them. To prevent this drastic consequence, they engage in compulsive rituals such as very frequent washing to try to scrub off the imagined poison. A number of investigators have found intriguing differences between the brains of patients with OCD and other people. Though the size and structure of the brain are the same, patients with OCD have increased activity in the part of the frontal lobe of the cerebral cortex called the *orbital surface*. Increased activity is also present in the cingulate gyrus and, to a lesser extent, in the caudate nucleus, a circuit that extends from the orbital section of the frontal area of the cortex to parts of the thalamus. Activity in these areas seems to be correlated; that is, if one area is active, the other areas are also. These areas contain several pathways of neurotransmitters, and one of the most concentrated is serotonin.

Remember that one of the roles of serotonin seems to be to moderate our reactions. Eating behavior, sexual behavior, and aggression are under better control with adequate levels of serotonin. Research, mostly on animals, demonstrates that lesions (damage) that interrupt serotonin circuits seem to impair the ability to ignore irrelevant external cues, making the organism overreactive. Thus, if we were to experience damage or interruption in this brain circuit, we might find ourselves acting on every thought or impulse that enters our heads.

To understand the brain of someone with obsessive–compulsive disorder, Thomas Insel, a biologically oriented psychopathologist, reviewed the most current literature.

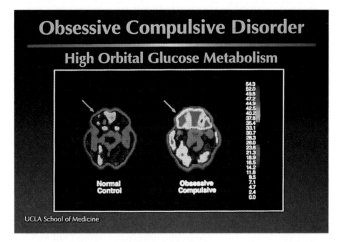

Brain function is altered in people with obsessive–compulsive disorder, but it normalizes after effective psychosocial treatment.

Insel (1992) described a case originally reported by Eslinger and Damasio (1985) of a man who had been successful as an accountant, husband, and father of two before undergoing surgery for a brain tumor. He made a good recovery from surgery and seemed to be fine, but in the following year his business failed and he separated from his family. Although his scores on IQ tests were as high as ever and all his mental functions were intact, he was unable to keep a job or even be on time for an appointment. What was causing all these problems? He was engaging in lengthy and uncontrollable compulsive rituals. Most of his days were consumed with washing, dressing, and rearranging things in the single room where he lived. In other words, he had classic obsessive–compulsive symptoms. The area of his brain that was damaged by removal of the tumor was a small area of his orbital frontal cortex.

This information seems to support very strongly a biological cause for psychopathology—in this case, OCD. You might think there is no need to consider social or psychological influences here. Maybe there is some wisdom to the strategy of adopting a one-dimensional or linear causal model that traces all psychopathology to certain brain circuits. But Insel and other neuroscientists interpret these findings very cautiously. First, this case involves only one individual. Other individuals with the *same* lesion might react differently. Also, brain imaging studies are often inconsistent with each other on many important details. Sometimes pinpointing the increased or decreased activity is difficult because brains differ in their structure, just as bodies and faces do. Finally, studies using brain imaging techniques have often cited interesting results, such as different brain functions in patients with panic disorder, but attempts to replicate the results have not been successful. Therefore, much more work has to be done, and perhaps technology has to improve further, before we can really be confident about the relation of the orbital frontal cortex to OCD. It is possible that activity in this area may simply be a result of the repetitive thinking and ritualistic behavior that characterizes OCD, rather than a cause. To take a simple analogy, if you were late for class and began running, massive changes would occur throughout your body and brain. If someone who did not know that you had just sprinted to class then examined you with brain scans, your brain functions would look different from those of the brain of a person who had walked to class. If you were doing very well in the class, the scientist might conclude, wrongly, that your unusual brain function "caused" your intelligence.

Psychosocial Influences on Brain Structure and Function

At the same time that psychopathologists are exploring the causes of psychopathology, whether in the brain or in the environment, people are suffering and require the best treatments we have. Sometimes the effects of treatment tell us something about the nature of psychopathology. For example, if a clinician thinks that obsessive–compulsive disorder is caused by a specific brain (dys)function or by learned anxiety to scary or repulsive thoughts, this view would determine choice of treatment, as noted in Chapter 1. Directing a treatment at one or the other of these theoretical causes of the disorder and then observing whether the patient gets better will prove or disprove the accuracy of the theory. This common strategy has one overriding weakness. Successfully treating a patient's particular feverish state or toothache with aspirin does not mean that the fever or toothache was caused by an aspirin deficiency, because an effect does not imply a cause. Nevertheless, this line of evidence gives us some hints about causes of psychopathology, particularly when it is combined with other, more direct experimental evidence.

If you knew that someone with OCD might have a somewhat faulty brain circuit, what treatment would you choose? Maybe you would recommend brain surgery. In fact, psychosurgery to correct severe psychopathology is an option still chosen today on occasion, particularly in the case of OCD when the suffering is severe (Jenike et al., 1991). For the accountant described previously, the removal of his brain tumor seems to have inadvertently eliminated an inhibitory part of the brain circuit implicated in OCD. Very precise surgical lesions might dampen the runaway activity that seems to occur in or near this particular area of the brain. This result would probably be welcome if all other treatments have failed, although psychosurgery is used very seldom and has not been studied systematically.

Nobody wants to do surgery if less intrusive treatments are available. To use the analogy of a television set that has developed the "disorder" of going fuzzy, if you had to rearrange and reconnect wires on the circuit board every time the disorder occurred, the correction would be a major undertaking. Alternatively, if you could simply turn a knob and eliminate the fuzziness, the correction would be simpler and less risky. The development of drugs affecting neurotransmitter activity has given us one of those knobs. We now have drugs that, although not a cure or even an effective treatment in all cases, do seem to be beneficial in treating OCD. As you might suspect, most of them act by increasing serotonin activity in one way or another.

But is it possible to get at this brain circuit without either surgery or drugs? Could psychological treatment be powerful enough to affect the circuit directly? The answer now seems to be yes. Lewis R. Baxter and his colleagues used brain imaging on patients who had not been treated and then took an additional, very important scientific step (Baxter et al., 1992). They treated the patients with a cognitive–behavioral therapy known to be effective in OCD called *exposure* and *response prevention* (described more fully in Chapter 5), and then repeated the brain imaging. In a bellwether finding, widely noted in the world of psychopathology, Baxter and his colleagues discovered that the brain circuit had been changed (normalized) by a psychological intervention. The same team of investigators then replicated the experiment with a different group of patients and found the same changes in brain function (Schwartz, Stoessel, Baxter, Martin, & Phelps, 1996). Is psychotherapy another knob on the TV set with which we can directly change brain circuits? Much more research needs to be done in this area, but there is a stream of evidence supporting the powerful effects of psychosocial factors on brain structure and function.

At this point we will consider just two examples of this phenomenon. Other examples will appear in subsequent chapters.

Psychosocial Dwarfism

At a clinic in a well-known city, a young boy presented for a medical evaluation. Detailed physical and psychological examination revealed a mental and social age of 8 years, with physical development in the same range.

This boy's mother was killed in an automobile accident shortly after his birth, along with his genetic father, with whom the mother had had an affair. The legal father, to whom the mother was married when the boy was born, remarried another woman when the boy was approximately 3 years old. Three half-brothers and half-sisters, the children of the mother and the legal father, were also in the home.

The boy's stepmother began a course of physical and psychological abuse that will make you cringe. For years the boy was locked in a closet day and night, sitting in his own excrement. He was deprived of food and water. Sometimes his brothers and sisters would sneak food to him. On occasions when he was let out, he would sneak food and water any way he could. Sometimes he drank out of the toilet bowl; sometimes he ate out of the garbage can. Once a week he was tied up and severely beaten with a broomstick. The mother made the other children do the beating. If they refused, she beat them. The boy's arm and skull had been fractured in several places. The arm had never been set.

The extreme abuse stunted the child's intellectual, emotional, and social growth. Another surprising finding that emerged from this study has since been documented, tragically, in a number of similar cases. The abuse stunted physical growth and maturation. In fact, this 8-year-old boy was really 16 years old. Rescue from an environment that was perhaps more hostile than the worst prisoner-of-war camp resulted in an enormous growth spurt of 13 inches in 3 years. It was almost as if growth hormones had been dammed up in his pituitary gland all those years. In fact, pituitary function had been markedly inhibited during the years of abuse. Although the boy never reached normal height, even at age 16 he was able to recover a large percentage of his growth. Intellectual and social functioning improved far less dramatically (Money, 1992; Money, Annecillo, & Hutchison, 1985).

Although a number of similar cases have been reported, more common is a condition often seen in young children called *failure to thrive,* which accounts for up to 5% of all pediatric hospital admissions and is estimated at 10% to 20% of hospital admissions in rural settings (Drotar & Sturm, 1991). Although many nonthriving children have identifiable medical conditions, a substantial number fall into the category of nonorganic or psychosocial failure to thrive, known officially as feeding disorder of infancy or early childhood. Reduced caloric intake, for whatever reason, always plays a role, but the causes of reduced caloric intake lie in the dysfunctional psychosocial setting. This is a factor we will discuss further in Chapter 8.

Cancer and Psychological Treatment

Consider an example of psychosocial influences on physical conditions in a very different context. There is good evidence that psychological treatments can increase survival time in patients with cancer that has metastasized (spread) and can prevent recurrence of cancer that has not spread. David Spiegel, a psychiatrist at Stanford University, and his colleagues (1989) studied 86 women with advanced breast cancer that had metastasized to other areas of their bodies and was expected to kill them within 2 years. Clearly, the prognosis was very poor indeed. Although Spiegel and his colleagues had little hope of affecting the disease itself, they thought that by treating these people in group psychotherapy at least they could relieve some of their anxiety, depression, and pain.

All patients had routine medical care for their cancer. In addition, 50 patients (of the 86) met with their therapist for psychotherapy once a week in small groups. Much to every-

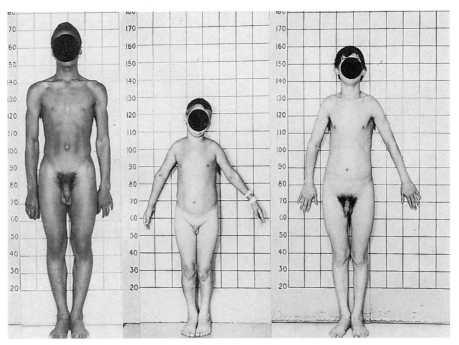

Left: Normal 16-year-old. *Center:* A 16-year-old boy with psychosocial dwarfism. *Right:* the same boy, after rescue, at 19.

one's surprise, including Dr. Spiegel's, the therapy group's survival time was significantly longer than that of the control group who did not receive psychotherapy but otherwise benefited from the best care available. In fact, the group receiving therapy lived twice as long on average (approximately 3 years) as the controls (approximately 18 months). Four years after the study began, one-third of the therapy patients were still alive, and all the patients receiving the best medical care available *without* therapy had died. Subsequently, a careful reanalysis of medical treatment received by each group revealed no differences that could account for the effects of psychosocial treatment (Kogon, Biswas, Pearl, Carlson, & Spiegel, 1997). Of course, these findings do not mean that psychosocial interventions cured advanced cancer. At 10 years, only three patients in the therapy group still survived.

Supporting these findings, Fawzy and his colleagues studied 56 cancer patients with malignant melanoma (skin cancer) who, unlike the patients in the Spiegel study, had a reasonably good prognosis at the start of the study. Thirty-eight of these patients received six weekly 1-hour treatment sessions delivered in small groups, where they were taught relaxation techniques, stress-management procedures, and generally how to cope with illness-related problems. Six months after treatment, immune functioning was higher in the group receiving psychotherapy than in a control group receiving only customary medical care (Fawzy, Cousins et al., 1990; Fawzy, Kemeny et al., 1990). More important, at a 5- to 6-year follow-up, control patients tended to have more recurrences of the cancer and were significantly more likely to die. Ten control patients and only three in the treatment group had died, replicating the findings of Spiegel and colleagues (1989) (Fawzy et al. 1993). What psychological factors directly affect the physical processes involved in life-threatening diseases? There is reasonably good evidence that reducing stress and giving patients better coping procedures and a sense of control seem to boost immune system functioning, but other factors are probably at work too. We will return to this fascinating topic in Chapter 9.

Interactions with Brain Function and Structure

Several recent experiments illustrate the interaction of psychosocial factors and brain function as reflected in neurotransmitter activity. Some even indicate that psychosocial factors directly affect levels of neurotransmitters. For example, Insel, Champoux, Scanlan, and Soumi (1986) raised two groups of rhesus monkeys identically except for their ability to control things in their cages. One group had free access to toys and food treats, but the second group got these toys and treats only when the first group did. In other words, the second group had the same number of toys and treats but they could not choose when they got them. Therefore, they had less control over their environment. In psychological experiments we say that the second group was "yoked" with the first group because their treatment depended entirely on what happened to the first group. In any case, the monkeys in the first group grew up, with a sense of control over things in their lives and those in the second group didn't.

Later in their lives, all these monkeys were administered a benzodiazepine inverse agonist, a neurochemical that has the *opposite* effect of the neurotransmitter GABA; the effect is an extreme burst of anxiety. (The few times this neurochemical has been administered to people, usually scientists administering it to each other, the recipients have reported the experience—which lasts only a short time—to be one of the most horrible sensations they had ever endured.) When this substance was injected into the monkeys, the results were interesting. The monkeys that had been raised with little control over their environment ran to a corner of their cage where they crouched and displayed signs of severe anxiety and panic. But the monkeys that had a sense of control behaved quite differently. They did not seem anxious at all. Rather, they seemed angry and aggressive, even attacking other monkeys near them. Thus, the very same level of a neurochemical substance, acting as a neurotransmitter, had very different effects, depending on the psychological histories of the monkeys.

Thomas Insel, the leading investigator in the monkey study, conducts research on the interaction of neurotransmitters and psychosocial factors at the National Institute of Mental Health.

Rhesus monkeys injected with a specific neurotransmitter react with anger or fear, depending on their early psychological experiences.

The Insel and colleagues (1986) experiment is an example of a significant interaction between neurotransmitters and psychosocial factors. Other experiments suggest that psychosocial influences directly affect the functioning and perhaps even the structure of the central nervous system. Scientists have observed that psychosocial factors routinely change the activity levels of many of our neurotransmitter systems, including norepinephrine and serotonin (Anisman, 1984; Maser & Gallup, 1974). It also seems that the structure of neurons themselves, including the number of receptors on a cell, can be changed by learning and experience (Kandel, 1983; Kandel, Jessell, & Schacter, 1991; Owens et al., 1997) and that these effects on the CNS continue throughout our lives.

We are now beginning to learn how this happens. For example, William Greenough and his associates (1990) studied the cerebellum, which coordinates and controls motor behavior. They discovered that the nervous systems of rats raised in a rich environment requiring a lot of learning and motor behavior develop differently from those in rats that were "couch potatoes." The active rats had many more connections between nerve cells in the cerebellum and grew many more dendrites. The researchers also observed that certain kinds of learning decreased the connections between neurons in other areas. In a follow-up study, Wallace, Kilman, Withers, and Greenough (1992) reported that these structural changes in the brain began in as little as 4 days in rats, suggesting enormous plasticity in brain structure as a result of experience. Similarly, stress during early development can lead to substantial changes in the functioning of the HYPAC axis described above that, in turn, makes primates more or less susceptible to stress later in life (Andrews & Rosenbloom, 1991; McEwen & Steller, 1993). So, we can conclude that early psychological experience affects the development of the nervous system and thus determines vulnerability to "psychological disorders" later in life. It seems that the very structure of our nervous system is constantly changing as a result of learning and experience, even into old age, and that some of these changes are permanent. Of course, this plasticity of the CNS helps us adapt more readily to our environment. These findings will be very important when we discuss the causes of anxiety disorders and mood disorders in Chapters 5 and 7.

Scientists have begun to pin down the complex interaction between psychosocial factors, brain structure, and brain function as reflected in neurotransmitter activity. Yeh, Fricke, and Edwards (1996) studied two male crayfish who were battling to establish dominance in their social group. When one of the crayfish won the battle and established dominance, the scientists found that serotonin made a specific set of neurons more likely to fire; but in the animal who lost the battle, serotonin made the same neurons less likely to fire. Thus, unlike the Insel et al. experiment above, where monkeys were injected with a neurotransmitter, Edwards et al. discovered that naturally occurring neurotransmitters have different effects depending on the previous psychosocial experience of the organism. Furthermore, this experience directly affects the structure of neurons at the synapse

William Greenough and his associates raised rats in a complex environment that required significant learning and motor behavior, which affected the structure of the rats' brains. This supports the role of psychological factors on biological development.

by altering the sensitivity of serotonin receptors. They also discovered that the effects of serotonin are reversible if the losers once again become dominant.

Comments

The specific brain circuits involved in psychological disorders are very complex systems identified by pathways of neurotransmitters traversing the brain. The existence of these circuits suggests that the structure and function of the nervous system play major roles in psychopathology. But other research suggests that the circuits are strongly influenced, perhaps even created, by psychological and social factors. Furthermore, both biological interventions, such as drugs, and psychological interventions or experience seem capable of altering the circuits. Therefore, we cannot consider the nature and cause of psychological disorders without examining both biological and psychological factors.

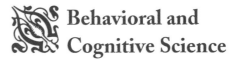

Behavioral and Cognitive Science

Enormous progress has been made in understanding behavioral and cognitive influences in psychopathology. Some new information has come from the recently established field of **cognitive science,** which is concerned with how we acquire and process information and how we store and ultimately retrieve it (one of the processes involved in memory). Scientists have also discovered that a great deal goes on inside our heads of which we are not necessarily aware. Because, technically, these cognitive processes are unconscious, some findings recall the unconscious mental processes that are so much a part of Freud's theory of psychoanalysis (although they do not look much like the ones he envisioned). A brief account of current thinking on what is happening during the process of classical conditioning will start us on our way.

Conditioning and Cognitive Processes

During the 1960s and 1970s, behavioral scientists in animal laboratories began to uncover the complexity of the basic processes of classical conditioning (Rapee, 1991). Robert Rescorla (1988) concluded that simply pairing two events closely in time (such as the meat powder and the metronome in Pavlov's laboratories) is not really what's important in this type of learning; at the very least, it is a very simple summary. Rather, a variety of different judgments and cognitive processes combine to determine the final outcome of this learning, even in lower animals such as rats.

To take just one simple example, Pavlov would have predicted that if the meat powder and the metronome were paired, say, 50 times, then a certain amount of learning would take place. But Rescorla and others discovered that if one animal never saw the meat powder at any time except for the 50 trials following the metronome sound, whereas the meat powder was brought to the other animal many times *in between* the 50 times it was paired with the metronome, the two animals would learn very different things; that is, even though the metronome and the meat powder were paired 50 times for each animal, the

metronome was *much less meaningful* to the second animal (see Figure 2.14). Put another way, the first animal learned that the sound of the metronome meant that meat powder came next; the second animal learned that the meat sometimes came after the sound and sometimes without the sound. That two different conditions produce two different learning outcomes is really a commonsense notion, but it demonstrates, along with many far more complex scientific findings, that basic classical (and operant) conditioning paradigms really facilitate the learning of the *relationship* among events in the environment. This type of learning makes us able to develop working ideas about the world that allow us to make appropriate judgments. We can then respond in a way that will benefit or at least not hurt us. In other words, complex cognitive as well as emotional processing of information is involved when conditioning occurs, even in animals.

Learned Helplessness

Along similar lines, Martin Seligman, also working with animals, described the phenomenon of **learned helplessness.** Learned helplessness occurs when rats or other animals encounter conditions over which they have no control whatsoever. If rats are confronted with a situation in which they receive occasional foot shocks, they can function very well if

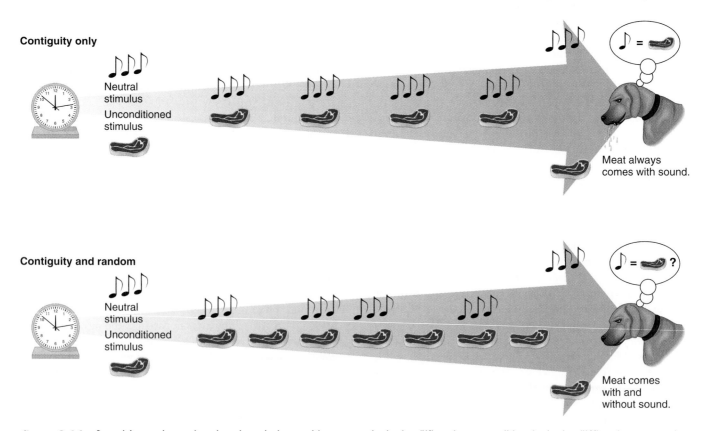

figure 2.14 Rescorla's experiment that showed contiguity—pairing a neutral stimulus (NS) and an unconditioned stimulus (UCS)—does not result in the same kind of conditioning. The dog in the contiguity-only group (top panel) experiences the usual conditioning procedure: pairing a tone and meat causes the tone to take on properties of the meat. For the dog in the contiguity-and-random group, the fact that the meat appeared away from the tones as well as with it makes the tone much less meaningful.

they learn they can cope with these shocks by doing something to avoid them (say, pressing a lever). But if the animals learn that their behavior has no effect whatsoever on their environment—sometimes they get shocked and sometimes they don't, no matter what they do—they become very "helpless"; in other words, they give up attempting to cope and seem to develop the animal equivalent of depression.

Martin Seligman first described the concept of learned helplessness.

Seligman drew some important conclusions from these observations. He theorized that the same phenomenon may happen with people who are faced with uncontrollable stress in their lives. Subsequent work revealed this to be true under one important condition: People become depressed if they "decide" or "think" they can do little about the stress in their lives, even if it seems to others that there *is* something they could do. People make an *attribution* that they have no control, and become depressed (Abramson, Seligman, & Teasdale, 1978; I. Miller & Norman, 1979). We will revisit this important psychological theory of depression in Chapter 7. It illustrates, once again, the necessity of recognizing that different people process information about events in the environment in different ways. These cognitive differences are an important component of psychopathology.

Social Learning

Another influential psychologist, Albert Bandura (1973, 1986), observed that organisms, including lower animals, do not have to actually experience certain events in their environment to learn effectively. Rather, they can learn just as much by observing what happens to someone else in a given situation. This fairly obvious discovery came to be known as **modeling** or **observational learning.** What is important is that, even in animals, this type of learning requires a symbolic integration of the experiences of others with judgments of what might happen to oneself; in other words, even an animal that is not very intelligent by human standards, such as a rat, must infer the conditions under which its own experiences would be very similar to those of the animal it is observing. Bandura expanded his observations into a network of ideas in which behavior, cognitive factors, and environmental influences converged to produce the complexity of behavior that confronts us. He also specified in some detail the importance of the social context of our learning; that is, much of what we learn depends on our interactions with other people around us.

The basic idea in all Bandura's work is that a careful analysis of cognitive processes may well produce the most accurate scientific predictions of behavior. Concepts of probability learning, information processing, and attention have become increasingly important in psychopathology (Craighead, Ilardi, Greenberg, & Craighead, 1997; Mathews & MacLeod, 1994).

Prepared Learning

It is clear that biology and, probably, our genetic endowment influence *what* we learn. This conclusion is based on the fact that we learn to fear some objects much more easily than others. In other words, we learn fears and phobias selectively (Mineka, 1985b; Seligman, 1971). Why might this be? According to the concept of **prepared learning,** we have become *highly prepared* for learning about certain types of objects or situations over the course of evolution because this knowledge contributes to the survival of the species. Even without any contact, we are more likely to learn to fear snakes or spiders than rocks or flowers, even if we know rationally that the snake or spider is harmless (e.g., Fredrikson, Annas, & Wik, 1997; Pury & Mineka, 1997). In the absence of experience, however, we are less likely to fear guns or electrical outlets, even though they are potentially much more deadly. Why do we so readily learn to fear snakes or spiders? One possibility is that when our ancestors lived in caves, those who avoided snakes and spiders eluded deadly varieties and therefore survived in greater numbers to pass down their genes to us, thus contributing to the survival of the species. This is just a theory, of course, but at present it seems a likely explanation. Something within us recognizes the connection between a certain signal and a threatening event. In other words, certain UCSs (unconditioned stimuli) and CSs (conditioned stimuli) "belong" to one another. If you've ever gotten sick on cheap wine or bad food, chances are you won't make the same mistake again. This very quick or "one-trial" learning also occurs in animals who eat something that tastes bad or may contain poison. It is easy to see that survival is associated with quickly learning to avoid poisonous food. When animals are shocked instead of poisoned when eating certain foods, however, they do not learn this association nearly as quickly, probably because in nature shock is not a consequence of eating, whereas being poisoned may be. Perhaps these selective associations are also facilitated by our genes (Cook, Hodes, & Lang, 1986; Garcia, McGowan, & Green, 1972).

Cognitive Science and the Unconscious

Advances in cognitive science have revolutionized our conceptions of the unconscious. We are not aware of much of what goes on inside our heads, but our unconscious is not necessarily the seething caldron of primitive emotional conflicts envisioned by Freud. Rather, we simply seem able to process and store information, and act on it, without having the slightest awareness of what the information is or why we are acting on it. Is this surprising? Consider briefly these two examples.

Lawrence Weiskrantz (1992) describes a phenomenon called *blind sight* or *unconscious vision*. He relates the case of a young man who, for medical reasons, had a small section of his visual cortex (the center for the control of vision in the brain) surgically removed. Though the operation was considered a success, the young man became blind in both eyes. Later, during routine tests, a physician raised his hand to the left of the patient who, much to the shock of his doctors, reached out and touched it. Subsequently, scientists determined that he could not only reach accurately for objects but could also distinguish among objects and perform most of the functions usually associated with sight. Yet, when asked about his abilities, he would say, "I couldn't see anything, not a darn thing," and that all he was doing was guessing.

The phenomenon in this case, of course, is associated with real brain damage. Much more interesting, from the point of view of psychopathology, is that the same thing seems to occur in healthy individuals who have been hypnotized (Hilgard, 1992; Kihlstrom, 1992); that is, normal individuals, provided with hypnotic suggestions that they are blind, are able to function visually but have no awareness or memory of their visual abilities. This condition, which illustrates a process of *dissociation* between behavior and consciousness, is the basis of the dissociative disorders discussed in Chapter 6.

A second example, which is more relevant to psychopathology, is called **implicit memory** (Craighead et al., 1997; Graf, Squire, & Mandler, 1984; Kihlstrom, Barnhardt, & Tataryn, 1992; Schacter, Chiu, & Ochsner, 1993). Implicit memory is apparent when someone clearly acts on the basis of things that have happened in the past, but can't remember the events. (A good memory for events is called *explicit memory*.) But implicit memory can be very selective for only certain events or circumstances. Clinically, we have already seen in Chapter 1 an example of implicit memory at work in the story of Anna O., the classic case first described by Breuer and Freud (1957) to demonstrate the existence of the unconscious. It was only after therapy that Anna O. remembered events surrounding her father's death and the connection of these events to her paralysis. Thus, Anna O.'s behavior (occasional paralysis) was evidently connected to implicit memories of her father's death. Many scientists have concluded that Freud's speculations on the nature and structure of the unconscious went beyond reality, but the existence of unconscious processes has since been demonstrated, and we must take them into account as we study psychopathology.

What methods do we have for studying the unconscious? The *black box* refers to unobservable feelings and cognitions inferred by an individual's self-report. In recent decades, psychologists, confident in an established science of behavior have returned to the black box with new methods, attempting to reveal the unobservable. Several methods for studying the unobservable unconscious have been made possible by advances in technology. One of them is the Stroop color-naming paradigm.

In the Stroop paradigm, subjects are shown a variety of

1. RED	6. GREEN	11. BLUE
2. PURPLE	7. PURPLE	12. PURPLE
3. GREEN	8. BROWN	13. BROWN
4. BLUE	9. BLUE	14. RED
5. BROWN	10. RED	15. GREEN

The Stroop paradigm. Have someone keep time as you name the colors of the words and not the words themselves, and again while you name the words and colors together.

words, each printed in a different color. They are shown these words very quickly and asked to name the colors in which they are printed while ignoring their meaning. Color naming is delayed when the meaning of the word attracts the subject's attention, despite his or her efforts to concentrate on the color; that is, the meaning of the word interferes with the subject's ability to process color information. For example, experimenters have determined that people with certain psychological disorders, like Judy, are much slower at naming the colors of words associated with their problem (for example, *blood, injury, dissect*) than the colors of words that have no relation to the disorder. Thus, psychologists can now uncover particular patterns of emotional significance, even if the subject cannot verbalize them or is not even aware of them. These developments in our understanding of the nature of psychopathology will come up repeatedly as we discuss specific disorders. Once again, note that these findings support Freud's theories about the unconscious, up to a point. But no assumptions are made about an elaborate structure existing within the mind that is continually in conflict (Freud's id, ego, superego). As cognitive science advances, it is less important to assume the existence of an unconscious with such a complex structure and array of functions.

■ **concept check 2.4**

Check your understanding of behavioral and cognitive influences by identifying the following descriptions. Choose your answers from (a) learned helplessness, (b) modeling, (c) prepared learning, and (d) implicit memory.

1. Karen noticed that every time Don behaved well at lunch, the teacher praised him. Karen decided to behave better to receive praise herself. _____

2. Josh stopped trying to please his father because he never knows whether his father will be proud or outraged.

_____

3. Greg fell into a lake as a baby and almost drowned. Even though Greg has no recollection of the event, he hates to be around large bodies of water. _____

4. Christal was scared to death of the tarantula, even though she knew it wasn't likely to hurt her.

_____

Cognitive–Behavioral Therapy

As scientists began to discover the important contributions of cognitive processes to behavioral development, psychologists began to integrate cognitive procedures and techniques directly into therapy. Among the originators of **cognitive-behavioral therapy** was Aaron T. Beck (1976), who developed methods for dealing with faulty attributions and attitudes associated with learned helplessness and depression (see Chapter 7). Albert Ellis (1962), in an approach he called *rational–emotive therapy,* also focused directly on the irrational beliefs that he thought were at the root of maladaptive feelings and behavior.

Cognitive–behavioral approaches to treatment will be described in some detail in later chapters, particularly in Chapter 5 on anxiety disorders, Chapter 7 on mood disorders, and Chapter 9, where we describe stress-reduction procedures. In general, cognitive–behavioral therapists examine in some detail the ongoing thinking processes of individuals who are anxious, depressed, or stressed. This is often accomplished by having patients monitor their thoughts during periods of distress. For example, a straight-A student who suffers from depression might assume before taking a particular course in college that she almost certainly will do very poorly; she is then likely to become more depressed. Such negative thoughts are clearly unrealistic and irrational. Similarly, individuals with severe anxiety might continually focus on dangers that could arise in normal situations. Individuals with these types of depression or anxiety are often not aware that their thinking is inappropriate or negative, because it is automatic or unconscious.

The point of cognitive-behavioral therapy is to reveal these thoughts and develop a different set of attitudes and attributions. Patients are also assigned specific behavioral tasks, such as entering fearful situations, in which they can work on their emotional and cognitive reactions. Procedures such as relaxation or exercise that change arousal or activity levels may also be a component of therapy. Thus, the cognitive–behavioral approach continually targets both aspects of the problem: clarifying and modifying attributions and attitudes (cognitive), and avoiding situations that provoke unrealistic anxiety or depression, increasing activity, or improving social skills (behavioral). Such therapy is usually short-term, requiring between 10 and 20 sessions. How specific cognitive–behavioral methods are used will be described in more detail in the chapters on specific disorders.

 **Emotions**

Emotions play an enormous role in our day-to-day lives, and can contribute in major ways to the development of psychopathology. Consider the emotion of fear. Have you ever found yourself in a really dangerous situation? Have you ever almost crashed your car, and known for several seconds beforehand what was going to happen? Have you ever been swimming in the ocean and realized that you were out too

Charles Darwin (1809–1882) drew this cat frightened by a dog to show the fight or flight reaction.

far or caught in a current? Have you ever almost fallen from a height, such as a cliff or a roof? In any of these instances you would have felt an incredible surge of arousal. As the first great emotion theorist, Charles Darwin (1872), pointed out over 100 years ago, this kind of reaction seems to be programmed in all animals, including humans, which suggests that it serves a useful function. The alarm reaction that activates during potentially life-threatening emergencies is called the **flight or fight response.** If you are caught in ocean currents, your almost instinctual tendency is to struggle toward shore. You might realize rationally that you're best off just floating until the current runs its course and then, more calmly, swimming in later. Yet somewhere, deep within, ancient instincts for survival won't let you relax, even though struggling against the ocean will only wear you out and increase your chance of drowning. Still, this same kind of reaction might momentarily give you the strength to lift a car off your trapped brother or fight off an attacker. The whole purpose of the physical rush of adrenaline that we feel in extreme danger is to mobilize us to escape the danger (flight) or to withstand it (fight).

The Physiology and Purpose of Fear

How do physical reactions prepare us to respond this way? The great physiologist Walter Cannon (1929) speculated on the reasons, and his ideas have been elaborated on by Beck and Emery (1985). Fear activates your cardiovascular system. Your blood vessels constrict, thereby raising arterial pressure and decreasing the blood flow to your extremities (fingers and toes). Excess blood is redirected to the skeletal muscles, where it is available to the vital organs that may be needed in an emergency. Often people seem "white with fear"; that is, they turn pale as a result of decreased blood flow to the skin. "Trembling with fear," with your hair standing on end, may be the result of shivering and piloerection (in which body hairs stand erect), reactions that conserve heat when your blood vessels are constricted. These defensive adjustments can also produce the hot and cold spells that often occur during extreme fear. Breathing becomes faster and, usually, deeper to provide necessary oxygen to rapidly circulating blood. Increased blood circulation carries oxygen to the brain, stimulating cognitive processes and sensory functions, which makes you more alert and able to think more quickly during emergencies. An increased amount of glucose (sugar) is released from the liver into the bloodstream, further energizing various crucial muscles and organs, including the brain. Pupils dilate, presumably to allow a better view of the situation. Hearing becomes more acute, and digestive activity is suspended, resulting in a reduced flow of saliva (the "dry mouth" of fear). In the short term, voiding the body of all waste material and eliminating digestive processes further prepare the organism for concentrated action and activity, so there is often pressure to urinate and defecate and, occasionally, to vomit. (This will also protect you if you have ingested poisonous substances during the emergency.)

It is easy to see why the flight or fight reaction is fundamentally important. Millennia ago, when our ancestors lived in very tenuous circumstances, those with strong emergency reactions were more likely to live through attacks and other dangers than those with weak emergency responses, and the survivors passed their genes down to us.

Emotional Phenomena

The **emotion** of fear is a subjective feeling of terror, a strong motivation for behavior (escaping or fighting), and a complex physiological response. To define "emotion" is difficult, but most theorists agree that it is an *action tendency* (Lang, 1979, 1985); that is, a tendency to behave in a certain way (for example, escape), elicited by an external event (a threat) and a feeling state (terror), accompanied by a (possibly) characteristic physiological response (Gross & Muñoz, 1995; Izard, 1992; R. S. Lazarus, 1991; Oatley & Jenkins, 1992; Ortony & Turner, 1990). One purpose of a feeling state is to *motivate* us to carry out a behavior: If we escape, our terror, which is unpleasant, will be decreased, so decreasing unpleasant feelings motivates us to escape. How do you think this works with anger or with love? What is the feeling state? What is the behavior?

Emotions are usually short-lived, temporary states lasting from several minutes to several hours, occurring in response to an external event. **Mood** is a more persistent period of emotionality. Thus, in Chapter 7 we will describe enduring or recurring states of depression or excitement (mania) as mood disorders. But anxiety disorders, described in Chapter 5, are characterized by enduring or chronic anxiety and, therefore, could also be called *mood disorders.* Alternatively, both anxiety disorders and mood disorders could be called *emotional disorders,* a term not formally used in psychopathology. This is only one exam-

ple of the occasional inconsistencies in the terminology of abnormal psychology. A related term you will see occasionally, particularly in Chapters 3 and 13 is **affect,** which refers to the momentary emotional tone that accompanies what we say or do. For example, if you just got an A+ on your test but you look sad, your friends might think your reaction strange because your *affect* is not appropriate to the event.

The Components of Emotion

Theorists tend to concentrate on one of three components of emotion: *behavior, physiology,* or *cognitive processes* (see Figure 2.15). Emotion theorists who concentrate on behavior think that basic patterns of emotion differ from one another in fundamental ways; for example, anger may differ from sadness not only in how it feels but also behaviorally and physiologically. These theorists also emphasize that emotion is a way of communicating between one member of the species and another. One function of fear is to motivate immediate and decisive action such as running away. But if you look scared, your facial expression will quickly communicate the possibility of danger to your friends, who may not have been aware that a threat is imminent. Your facial communication increases their chance for survival because they can now respond more quickly to the threat when it occurs. This may be one reason emotions are contagious, as we observed in Chapter 1 when discussing mass hysteria (Hatfield, Cacioppo, & Rapson, 1993).

Other scientists have concentrated on the physiology of emotions, most notably Cannon (1929), who viewed emotion as primarily a brain function. Research in this tradition

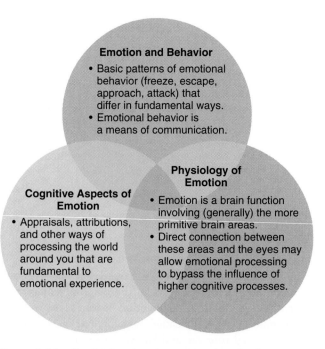

figure 2.15 Emotion has three important and overlapping components: behavior, cognition, and physiology.

Our emotional reaction depends on context. Fire, for example, can be threatening or comforting.

suggests that areas of the brain associated with emotional expression are generally more ancient and primitive than areas associated with higher cognitive processes such as reasoning. Other research indicates direct neurobiological connections between the emotional centers of the brain and parts of the eye (the retina) or ear that allow emotional activation without the influence of higher cognitive processes (LeDoux, 1993; Moore, 1973; Zajonc, 1984); in other words, you may experience various emotions quickly and directly without necessarily thinking about them or being aware of why you feel the way you do.

Finally, a number of prominent theorists concentrate on studying the cognitive aspects of emotion. Notable among these theorists is Richard S. Lazarus (for example, 1968, 1991), who proposes that changes in a person's environment are appraised in terms of their potential impact on that person. The type of appraisal you make determines the emotion that you experience. For example, if you see somebody holding a gun in a dark alley, you will probably appraise the situation as dangerous, and experience fear. You would make a very different appraisal if you saw a tour guide displaying an antique gun in a museum. Lazarus would suggest that thinking and feeling cannot be separated, but other cognitive scientists are concluding otherwise: Although cognitive and emotional systems interact and overlap, they are fundamentally separate (Teasdale, 1993). All these components of emotion—behavior, physiology, and cognition—are important, and theorists continue to study their interaction.

Anger and Your Heart

When we discussed Judy's blood phobia, we observed that behavior and emotion may strongly influence biology. Scientists have recently made important discoveries about the familiar emotion of anger. We have known for years that negative emotions such as hostility and anger increase a person's risk of developing heart disease (Chesney, 1986; MacDougall, Dembroski, Dimsdale, & Hackett, 1985). In fact, sustained hostility with angry outbursts contributes more strongly to death from heart disease than other well-known risk factors, including smoking, high blood pressure, and high cholesterol levels (Williams, Haney, Lee, Kong, & Blumenthal, 1980).

Why is this, exactly? Ironson and her colleagues (1992) asked a number of people with heart disease to recall something that made them very angry in the past. Sometimes these events had occurred many years earlier. In one case, an individual who had spent time in a Japanese prisoner-of-war camp during World War II became angry every time he thought about it, especially when he thought about reparations paid by the U.S. government to Japanese-Americans who had been held in internment camps during the war. Ironson and her associates compared the experience of anger to stressful events that increased heart rate but were *not* associated with anger. For example, some participants imagined making a speech to defend themselves against a charge of shoplifting. Others tried to figure out difficult problems in arithmetic within a time limit. Heart rates during these angry situations and stressful ones were then compared to heart rates that increased as a result of exercise (riding a stationary bicycle). The investigators found that the ability of the heart to pump blood efficiently through the body dropped significantly during anger but not during stress or exercise. In fact, remembering being angry was sufficient to cause the anger effect. If subjects were *really* angry, their heart-pumping efficiency dropped even more, putting them at risk for dangerous disturbances in heart rhythm (arrhythmias).

This study was the first to prove that anger affects the heart through decreased pumping efficiency at least in people who already have heart disease. Other studies, such as one by Williams and colleagues (1980), demonstrated that anger also affects people without heart disease. Medical students who were often angry were seven times more likely to die by the age of 50 than students in the same class who had lower levels of hostility. Shall we conclude that too much anger causes heart attacks? This would be another example of one-dimensional causal modeling. Increasing evidence, including the studies just mentioned, suggests that anger and hostility contribute to heart disease, but so do many other factors, including a genetically determined biological vulnerability. We will discuss cardiovascular disease in Chapter 9.

Emotions and Psychopathology

We now know that suppressing almost any kind of emotional response, such as anger or fear, increases sympathetic nervous system activity, which may contribute to psychopathology (Gross & Levenson, 1997). Other emotions seem to have a more direct effect. In Chapter 5 we will study the phenomenon of *panic* and its relationship to anxiety disorders. One interesting possibility is that a panic attack is simply the normal emotion of fear occurring at the wrong time, when there is nothing to be afraid of. In mood disorders some patients become overly excited and joyful. They think they have the world on a string and that they can do anything they want and spend as much money as they want because everything will turn out all right. Every little event is the most wonderful and exciting experience they have ever had. These individuals are suffering from *mania*, which is part of the very serious mood disorder discussed in Chapter 7. People who suffer from mania usually alternate periods of excitement with periods of extreme sadness and distress, when they feel that all is lost and that the world is a gloomy and hopeless place. During extreme sadness or distress, people are unable to experience any pleasure in life and often find it difficult even to get out of bed and move around. If hopelessness becomes acute, they are at risk for suicide. This emotional state is *depression*, a defining feature of many mood disorders.

Thus, basic emotions of fear, anger, sadness or distress, and excitement may contribute to many psychological disorders and may even define them. Emotions and mood also affect our cognitive processes: If one's mood is positive, then one's associations, interpretations, and impressions also tend to be positive (Bower, 1981). Your impression of people you first meet and even your memories of past events are colored to a great extent by your current mood. If you are consistently negative or depressed, then your memories of past events are likely to be unpleasant. The pessimist or depressed person sees the bottle as half-empty. On the other hand, the cheerful optimist is said to see the world through rose-colored glasses and to see the bottle as half-full. This is a rich area of investigation for cognitive scientists (M. Eysenck, 1992; Teasdale, 1993), particularly those interested in the close interconnection of cognitive and emotional processes. Leading psychopathologists are beginning to outline the nature of emotion disruption (or dysregulation) and to understand how these disruptions interfere with thinking and behavior in various psychological disorders (Gross & Muñoz, 1995; Kring & Bachorowski, in press).

Cultural, Social, and Interpersonal Factors

Given the welter of neurobiological and psychological variables impinging on our lives, is there any room for the influence of social, interpersonal, and cultural factors? Studies are beginning to demonstrate the substantial power and depth of such influences. In fact, researchers have now established that cultural and social influences can kill you. Consider the following example.

Voodoo, the Evil Eye, and Other Fears

In many cultures around the world, individuals may suffer from *fright disorders*, exaggerated startle responses, and other observable fear reactions. One example is the Latin American *susto*. Susto is characterized by various anxiety-based symptoms, including insomnia, irritability, phobias, and the marked somatic symptoms of sweating and increased heart rate (tachycardia). But susto has only one cause: The individual becomes the object of black magic, or witchcraft, and is suddenly badly frightened. In some cultures, the sinister influence is called the *evil eye* (Good & Kleinman, 1985; Tan, 1980), and the resulting fright disorder can be fatal. Cannon (1942), examining the Haitian phenomenon of voodoo death, suggested that the sentence of death by a medicine man may create an intolerable autonomic arousal in the subject, who has little ability to cope because there is absolutely no social support. Ultimately, the condition leads to damage to internal organs and death. Thus, from all accounts, an individual who is from a physical and psychological point of view functioning in a perfectly healthy and adaptive way suddenly dies because of marked changes in the social environment.

Fear and phobias are universal, occurring across all cultures. But *what* we fear is strongly influenced by our social environment. Israeli and

A "possessed" person receives treatment in a voodoo ritual.

Jewish children, whose culture emphasizes individuality and autonomy, have been found to be less fearful of outsiders than Bedouin children in the same community, whose culture emphasizes the group and the family.

Bedouin researchers recently studied the fears of hundreds of Jewish and Bedouin children living in the same region of Israel (Elbedour, Shulman, & Kedem, 1997). Although they all feared potentially life-threatening events, Jewish children, whose society emphasizes individuality and autonomy, have fewer fears than Bedouin children, who grow up in a strongly paternalistic society in which the group and family are central and who are taught to be cautious about the rest of the world. Thus, Bedouin and Jewish children have different fears, and the Bedouin children have more of them, many centering on the possible disintegration of the family. Thus, cultural factors influence the form and content of psychopathology and may differ even among cultures side by side in the same country.

Gender

Gender roles have a strong and sometimes puzzling effect on psychopathology. Everyone experiences anxiety and fear, and phobias are found all over the world. But phobias have a peculiar characteristic: The likelihood of your having a particular phobia is powerfully influenced by your gender! For example, someone who complains of an insect or small animal phobia severe enough to prohibit field trips or visits to friends in the country is almost certain to be female, as are 90% of the people with this phobia. But a social phobia strong enough to keep someone from parties or meetings affects men and women equally.

We think these substantial differences have to do with cultural expectations of men and women, or our *gender roles*. For example, an equal number of men and women may have an experience that could lead to an insect or small animal phobia, such as being bitten by one, but in our society it isn't always acceptable for a man to show or even admit fear. So a man is more likely to hide or endure the fear until he gets over it. It is more acceptable for women to acknowledge fearfulness, and so a phobia develops. It is also more acceptable for a man to be shy than to show fear, so he is more likely to admit social discomfort.

To avoid or survive a panic attack, an extreme experience of fear, some males drink alcohol instead of admitting they're afraid (see Chapter 5). In many cases this attempt to cope may lead to alcoholism, a disorder that affects many more males than females (see Chapter 11). One reason for this gender imbalance is that males are more likely than females to self-medicate their fear and panic with alcohol, and in so doing start down the slippery slope to addiction.

Bulimia nervosa, the severe eating disorder, occurs almost entirely in young females. Why? As we'll see in Chapter 8, a cultural emphasis on female thinness plagues our society and, increasingly, societies around the world. The pressures for males to be thin are less apparent, and of the few males who develop bulimia a substantial percentage belong to the gay subculture where cultural imperatives to be thin are present.

One's gender doesn't cause psychopathology, but as gender role is a social and cultural factor that influences the form and content of a disorder, we will attend closely to it in the chapters that follow.

Social Effects on Health and Behavior

A large number of studies have demonstrated that the greater the number and frequency of social relationships and contacts, the longer you are likely to live. Conversely, the lower you score on a "social index" that measures the richness of your social life, the shorter your life expectancy. Studies documenting this finding have been reported in the United States (Berkman & Syme, 1979; House, Robbins, & Metzner, 1982; Schoenbach, Kaplan, Fredman, & Kleinbaum, 1986) as well as in Sweden and Finland. They take into account existing physical health and other risk factors for dying young, such as high blood pressure, high cholesterol levels, and smoking habits, and still produce the same result. Studies also show that social relationships seem to protect individuals against many physical and psychological disorders, such as high blood pressure, depression, alcoholism, arthritis, and low birth weight in newborns (Cobb, 1976; House, Landis, & Umberson, 1988).

Now, a startling new study reports that whether or not we come down with a cold is strongly influenced by the quality and extent of our social network. Cohen, Doyle, Skoner, Rabin, and Gwaltney (1997) used nasal drops to expose 276 healthy volunteers to one of two different rhinoviruses (cold viruses), and then quarantined the subjects for a week. The authors measured the extent of participation in 12 different types of social relationships (e.g., spouse, parent, friend, colleague, etc.), as well as other factors, such as smoking and poor sleep quality, that are likely to increase susceptibility to colds. The surprising results were that the greater the extent of social ties, the smaller the chance of catching a cold, even after all other factors were taken into consideration (controlled for). In fact, those with the fewest social ties were more than four times more likely to catch a cold than those with the greatest number of ties. What could account for this? Once again, social and interpersonal factors seem to influence psychological and neurobiological variables—for example, the immune system—sometimes to a substantial degree. Thus, one cannot really study psychological and biological aspects of psychological disorders (or physical disorders, for that matter), without taking into account the social and cultural context of the disorder.

That a multidimensional point of view is necessary is shown time and again. Consider an experiment with primates that illustrates the dangers of ignoring social context. A large group of monkeys were injected with amphetamine, a central nervous system stimulant (Haber & Barchas, 1983). Surprisingly, the drug had no reliable effect on the average behavior of the monkeys as a group. When the investigators divided the monkeys according to social dominance and submissiveness, however, dramatic effects appeared. Amphetamine increased dominant behaviors in primates who were high in the social hierarchy and submissive behaviors in those who were low in the hierarchy. Thus, the effects of a biological factor (the drug) on psychological characteristics (behavior) were uninterpretable unless the social context of the experiment was considered.

Returning to human studies, how do social relationships have such a profound impact on our physical and psychological characteristics? We don't know for sure, but there are some intriguing hints. Some people think interpersonal relationships give meaning to life and that people who have something to live for can overcome physical deficiencies and even delay death. You may have known an elderly person who far outlived his or her expected time in order to witness a significant family event such as a grandchild's graduation from college. Once the event has passed, the person dies. Another common observation is that if one spouse in a longstanding marital relationship dies, particularly an elderly wife, the other often dies soon after, regardless of health status. It is also possible that social relationships facilitate health-promoting behaviors, such as restraint in the use of alcohol and drugs, getting proper sleep, and seeking appropriate health care (House, Landis, & Umberson, 1988).

Sometimes social upheaval is an opportunity for studying the impact of social networks on individual functioning. When the Sinai Peninsula was dismantled and evacuated as part of peace negotiations with Egypt, Steinglass, Weisstub, and Kaplan De-Nour (1988) studied residents of an Israeli community that was threatened with dissolution. They found that believing oneself embedded firmly in a social context was just as important as actually having a social network. Poor long-term adjustment was best predicted in those who *perceived* that their social network was disintegrating, whether it actually did or not. In another example, whether you live in a city or the country may be associated with your chances of developing schizophrenia, a very severe disorder. Lewis, David, Andreasson, and Allsbeck (1992) found that the incidence of schizophrenia was 38% greater in men who had been raised in cities than in those raised in rural areas. We have known for a long time that there is more schizophrenia in the city than in the country, but researchers thought that people with schizophrenia drifted to cities *after* developing schizophrenia, or that other endemic urban factors such as drug use or unstable family relationships, might be the real culprit. But Lewis and associates carefully controlled for such factors, and it now seems there may be something about cities over and above those influences that contributes to the development of schizophrenia. We do not yet know what it is. This finding, if it is replicated and shown to be true, may be very important in view of the mass migration of individuals, to overcrowded urban areas, particularly in less developed countries.

In summary, we cannot study psychopathology independently of social and interpersonal influences; and we still have much to learn. Juris Draguns (1990, 1995) has nicely summarized our knowledge in concluding that many major psychological disorders, such as schizophrenia and major depressive disorder, seem to occur in all cultures, but that they may look different from one culture to another because individual symptoms are strongly influenced by social and interpersonal context. For example, as we will see in Chapter 7, depression in Western culture is reflected in feelings of guilt and inadequacy, and in developing countries with physical distress such as fatigue or illness.

Social and Interpersonal Influences on the Elderly

Finally, the effect of social and interpersonal factors on the expression of physical and psychological disorders may differ with age. Grant, Patterson, and Yager (1988) studied 118 men and women 65 years old or older who lived independently. Those with fewer meaningful contacts and less social support from relatives had consistently higher levels of depression and more reports of unsatisfactory quality of life. However, if these individuals became physically ill, they had more substantial support from their families than those who were not physically ill. This finding raises the unfortunate possibility that it may be advantageous for elderly people to become physically ill, because illness allows them to reestablish the social support that makes life worth living. If further research indicates that this is true, involving their families before they get ill might help maintain their physical health (and significantly reduce health care costs).

A long and productive life usually includes strong social relationships and interpersonal relations.

The study of older adults is growing at a rapid pace. The Census Bureau has estimated that by the year 2080 the number of people age 85 and older will grow from the current 3.3 million to 18.7 million. With this growth will come a corresponding increase in the number of older adults with mental health problems, many of whom will not receive appropriate care (Gatz & Smyer, 1992). As you can see, to understand and treat the disorders experienced by older adults is necessary and important.

Social Stigma

Other factors make the consideration of social and cultural issues imperative to the study of psychopathology. Psychological disorders continue to carry a substantial stigma in our society. To be anxious or depressed is to be weak and cowardly. To be schizophrenic is to be unpredictable and crazy. For physical injuries in times of war, we award medals. For psychological injuries, the unfortunate soldiers earn scorn and derision, as anyone knows who has seen the movies *Patton* or *Born on the Fourth of July*. Often, a patient with psychological disorders does not seek health insurance reimbursement for fear that a co-worker might learn about the problem. With far less social support than for physical illness, there is less chance of full recovery. Some of the consequences of social attitudes toward psychological disorders will be discussed in Chapter 16.

Interpersonal Psychotherapy (IPT)

A form of psychotherapy with proven effectiveness for some disorders has been developed that emphasizes the resolution of interpersonal problems and stressors. As developed by Myrna Weissman and her late husband, Gerald Klerman

(Klerman, Weissman, Rounsaville, & Chevron, 1984; Weissman, 1995), **interpersonal psychotherapy** (IPT) grew from the work of the American psychiatrist Harry Stack Sullivan. Trained as a Freudian, Sullivan greatly emphasized current interpersonal relationships, in addition to interpersonal experiences during particular psychosexual stages of growth in childhood.

In IPT, the patient and therapist work together on identifying life stresses that precipitated the psychological disorder and current interpersonal problems that are either the source of the life stress or intimately connected with it. Typically, these include one or more of four kinds of interpersonal issues. One of the most common is an interpersonal role dispute, such as marital conflict. Experiencing the death of a loved one and making the necessary adjustments is a second common area of focus. Acquiring a new relationship through marriage or job change may be a third source of interpersonal stress. Finally, the fourth area is identifying and correcting deficits in social skills that make it difficult to form the relationships, particularly intimate relationships, that are so important to all of us. IPT, like cognitive–behavioral therapy, is brief, typically 10 to 15 sessions, and has proven highly effective for problems such as depression.

Global Incidence of Psychological Disorders

Behavioral and mental health problems in developing countries are exacerbated by political strife, technological change, and massive movements from rural to urban areas. An important study from the Center for the Study of Culture and Medicine, headed by Arthur Kleinman, reveals that 10% to 20% of all primary medical services in poor countries are sought by patients with psychological disorders, principally anxiety and mood disorders (including suicide attempts), as well as alcoholism, drug abuse,

In developing countries, personal upheaval due to political strife affects mental health.

of development may influence our vulnerability to other types of stress or to differing psychological disorders.

Important developmental changes occur at all points in life. For example, adulthood, far from being a relatively stable period, is highly dynamic, with important changes occurring into old age. Erik Erikson suggested that we go through eight major crises during our lives (Erikson, 1982), each determined by our biological maturation and the social demands made at particular times. Unlike Freud, who envisioned no developmental stages beyond adolescence, Erikson believed that we grow and change beyond the age of 65. During older adulthood, for example, we look back and view our lives either as rewarding or as disappointing. Although aspects of Erikson's theory of psychosocial development have been criticized as being too vague (Shaffer, 1993), it demonstrates the comprehensive approach to human development advocated by life-span developmentalists.

and childhood developmental disorders. Record numbers of young men are committing suicide in Micronesia. Alcoholism levels among adults in Latin America have risen to 20%. Treatments for disorders such as depression and addictive behaviors that are successful in the United States can't be administered in countries where mental health care is limited. In China, more than 1 billion people are served by approximately 3,000 mental health professionals. In the United States 200,000 mental health professionals serve 250 million people, and yet only one in three people with a psychological disorder in our country has ever received treatment of any kind. These shocking statistics suggest that in addition to their role in causation, social and cultural factors substantially maintain disorders, because most societies have not yet developed the social context for alleviating and ultimately preventing them. Changing society's attitude is just one of the challenges facing us in the next century.

Life-Span Development

Life-span developmental psychopathologists point out that we tend to look at psychological disorders from a snapshot perspective: We focus on a particular point in a person's life and assume it represents the whole person. The inadequacy of this way of looking at people should be clear. Think back on your own life over the past few years. The person you were, say, 3 years ago, is very different from the person you are now, and the person you will be 3 years from now will have changed in important ways. To understand psychopathology, we must appreciate how experiences during different periods

The Principle of Equifinality

Like a fever, a particular behavior or disorder may have a number of causes. The principle of **equifinality** is used in developmental psychopathology to indicate that we must consider a number of paths to a given outcome (Cicchetti, 1991). There are many examples of this principle; for example, a delusional syndrome may be an aspect of schizophrenia, but it can also arise from amphetamine abuse. Delirium, which involves difficulty focusing attention, often occurs in older adults after surgery, but it can also result from thiamine deficiency or renal (kidney) disease. Autism can sometimes occur in children whose mothers are exposed to rubella during pregnancy, but it can also occur in children whose mothers experience difficulties during labor.

Different paths can also result from the interaction of psychological and biological factors during various stages of development. How someone copes with impairment due to organic causes may have a profound effect on that person's overall functioning. For example, people with documented brain damage may have different levels of disorder. Those with healthy systems of social support, consisting of family and friends, as well as highly adaptive personality characteristics, such as marked confidence in their abilities to overcome challenges, may experience only mild behavioral and cognitive disturbance despite an organic pathology. Those without comparable support and personality may be incapacitated. This may be clearer if you think of people you know with physical disabilities. Some, paralyzed from the waist down by accident or disease (paraplegics), have nevertheless become superb athletes or accomplished in business or the arts. Others with the same condition are depressed and hopeless; they have withdrawn from life or, even worse, ended their lives. Even the content of delusions and hallucinations that may accompany a disorder, and the degree to which they are frightening or difficult to cope with, is determined in part by psychological and social factors.

Researchers are exploring not only what makes people experience particular disorders but also what protects others from having the same difficulties. If you were interested in why someone would be depressed, for example, you would first look at people who display depression. But you could also study people in similar situations and from similar backgrounds who are not depressed. An excellent example of this approach is research on "resilient" children, which suggests that social factors may protect some children from being hurt by stressful experiences, such as one or both parents suffering a psychiatric disturbance (Garmezy & Rutter, 1983; Hetherington & Blechman, 1996). The presence of a caring adult friend or relative can offset the negative stresses of this environment, as can the child's own ability to understand and cope with unpleasant situations. Those of us who were brought up in violent or otherwise dysfunctional families who have successfully gone on to college might want to look back for the factors that protected us. Perhaps if we better understand why some people do not encounter the same problems as others in similar circumstances, we can better understand particular disorders, assist those who suffer from them, and even prevent some cases from occurring at all.

Summary

- We have examined modern approaches to psychopathology and we have found the field to be complex indeed. In this brief overview (even though it may not seem brief), we have seen that contributions from (a) psychoanalytic theory, (b) behavioral and cognitive science, (c) emotional influences, (d) social and cultural influences, (e) genetics, (f) neuroscience, and (g) life-span developmental factors all must be considered when we think about psychopathology. Even though our knowledge is incomplete, you can see why we could never resume the one-dimensional thinking of the various historical traditions described in Chapter 1. In chapters covering specific psychological disorders, we will return to cases very much like Judy's and consider them from this multidimensional integrative perspective. But first we must explore the processes of assessment and diagnosis used to measure and classify psychopathology.

One-Dimensional or Multidimensional Models
- The causes of abnormal behavior are complex and fascinating. You can say that psychological disorders are caused by nature (biology) and by nurture (psychosocial factors),

and you would be right on both counts—but also wrong on both counts.
- To identify the causes of various psychological disorders, we must consider the interaction of all relevant dimensions: genetic contributions, the role of the nervous system, behavioral and cognitive processes, emotional influences, social and interpersonal influences, and developmental factors. Thus, we have arrived at a multidimensional integrative approach to the causes of psychological disorders.

Genetic Contributions to Psychopathology
- The genetic influence on much of our development and most of our behavior, personality, and even IQ is *polygenic*— that is, influenced by many genes, each contributing only a tiny effect. This is assumed to be the case in abnormal behavior as well, although individual genes have yet to be identified that relate to the major psychological disorders.
- In studying causal relationships in psychopathology, researchers look at the interactions of genetic and environmental effects. In the diathesis–stress model, individuals are assumed to inherit certain vulnerabilities that make them susceptible to a disorder when the right kind of stressor comes along. In the reciprocal gene–environment model, the individual's genetic vulnerability toward a certain disorder may make it more likely that he or she will experience the stressor that in turn triggers the genetic vulnerability and thus the disorder.

Neuroscience and its Contributions to Psychopathology
- The field of neuroscience promises much as we try to unravel the mysteries of psychopathology. Within the nervous system, levels of neurotransmitter and neuroendocrine activity interact in very complex ways to modulate and regulate emotions and behavior and contribute to psychological disorders.
- Critical to our understanding of psychopathology are the neurotransmitter currents called brain circuits. Of the neurotransmitters that may play a key role, we investigated four: serotonin, gamma aminobutyric acid (GABA), norepinephrine, and dopamine.

Behavioral and Cognitive Science
- The relatively new field of cognitive science provides a valuable perspective on how behavioral and cognitive influences affect the learning and adaptation each of us experience throughout life. Clearly, such influences not only contribute to psychological disorders but also may directly modify brain functioning, brain structure, and even genetic expression. We examined some of the research in this field by looking at learned helplessness, modeling, prepared learning, implicit memory, and cognitive–behavioral therapy.

Emotions
- Emotions have a direct and dramatic impact on our functioning and play a central role in many disorders. Mood, a persistent period of emotionality, is often evident in psychological disorders.

Social Factors

• Social and interpersonal influences profoundly affect both psychological disorders and biology. Interpersonal psychotherapy (IPT), a form of treatment that focuses on the resolution of social and interpersonal problems, has proven effectiveness for some disorders.

Life-Span Development

• In considering a multidimensional integrative approach to psychopathology, it is important to remember the principle of equifinality, which reminds us that we must consider the various paths to a particular outcome, not just the result.

Key Terms

multidimensional integrative approach
genes
diathesis–stress model
vulnerability
reciprocal gene–environment model
neuroscience
neurons
synaptic cleft
neurotransmitters
hormone
brain circuits
reuptake
agonist
antagonist
inverse agonist
serotonin
gamma aminobutyric acid (GABA)
norepinephrine (also nonadrenaline)
dopamine
cognitive science
learned helplessness
modeling (also observational learning)

prepared learning
implicit memory
cognitive–behavioral therapy
flight or fight response
emotion
mood
affect
interpersonal psychotherapy (IPT)
equifinality

Answers to Concept Checks

2.1
1. b
2. a (best answer) or c
3. e
4. a (reinforcement of tantrum) or d
5. a (initial development of phobia), c (maintenance of phobia)

2.2
1. b
2. c
3. d
4. a

2.3
1. a
2. c
3. d
4. b

2.4
1. b
2. a
3. d
4. c

Clinical Assessment and Diagnosis

3

Frank: Young, Serious, and Anxious
Assessing Psychological Disorders
Diagnosing Psychological Disorders

It is not the illness but the human being that needs help. As a doctor I am not concerned with the illness but with the human being.
Georg Goddeck,
The Meaning of Illness

The processes of clinical assessment and diagnosis are central to the study of psychopathology and, ultimately, to the treatment of psychological disorders. **Clinical assessment** is the systematic evaluation and measurement of psychological, biological, and social factors in an individual presenting with a possible psychological disorder. **Diagnosis** is the process of determining whether the particular problem afflicting the individual meets all the criteria for a psychological disorder, as set forth in the *Diagnostic and Statistical Manual of Mental Disorders, Fourth Edition* or *DSM-IV* (American Psychiatric Association, 1994). In this chapter, after demonstrating assessment and diagnosis within the context of an actual case, we examine the development of the DSM into a widely used classification system for abnormal behavior. Then we review the many assessment techniques available to the clinician. Next, we turn to diagnostic issues and the related challenges of classification.

Frank
Young, Serious, and Anxious

Frank was referred to one of our clinics for evaluation and possible treatment of severe distress and anxiety centering on his marriage. He arrived neatly dressed in his work clothes (he was a mechanic). He reported that he was 24 years old and that this was the first time he had ever seen a mental health professional. He wasn't sure that he really needed (or wanted) to be there, but he felt he was beginning to "come apart" a little bit due to his marital difficulties. He figured that it certainly wouldn't hurt to come once to see whether we could help. What follows is a transcript of parts of this first interview.

Therapist: What sorts of problems have been troubling you during the past month?
Frank: I'm beginning to have a lot of marital problems. I was married about 9 months ago, but I've been really tense around the house and we've been having a lot of arguments.
Therapist: Is this something recent?
Frank: Well, it wasn't too bad at first, but it's been worse lately. I've also been really uptight in my job, and I haven't been getting my work done.

Note that we always begin by asking the patient to describe the major difficulties that brought him or her to the office. With adults or with children old enough (or verbal enough) to tell us their story, this strategy tends to break the ice. It also allows us to relate details revealed later in the interview to the central problem as seen through the patient's eyes.

After Frank described his major problem in some detail, the therapist then asked more about his marriage, his job, and other current life circumstances. Frank reported that he had worked steadily in an auto body repair shop for the past 4 years and that he had married a 17-year-old woman. After getting a better picture of his current situation, we returned to his feelings of distress and anxiety.

Therapist: When you feel uptight at work, is it the same kind of feeling you have at home?
Frank: Pretty much. I just can't seem to concentrate, and lots of times I lose track of what my wife's saying to me, which makes her mad and then we'll have a big fight.
Therapist: Are you thinking about something else when you lose your concentration, such as your work, or maybe other things?
Frank: Oh, I don't know. I guess I just worry a lot.
Therapist: What do you find yourself worrying about most of the time?
Frank: Well, I worry about getting fired and then not being able to support my family. A lot of the time I feel like I'm going to catch something—you know, get sick and not be able to work. Basically I guess I'm afraid of getting sick and then failing at my job and in my marriage, and having my parents and her parents both telling me what an ass I was for getting married in the first place.

During the first 10 minutes or so of the interview, Frank seemed quite tense and anxious and often looked down at the floor while he talked, glancing up only occasionally to make eye contact. Sometimes his right leg twitched a bit. Although it was not easy to see at first because he was looking down, Frank also closed his eyes very tightly for 2 to 3 seconds. It was when his eyes were closed that his right leg would twitch.

The interview continued for half an hour, exploring marital and job issues. It became increasingly clear that Frank felt inadequate and anxious about handling situations in his life. Eventually he talked freely and looked up a little more at the therapist, but he continued to close his eyes and twitch his right leg slightly. When asked if he were aware of what he was doing, Frank said that he was, most of the time. He explained that he had a recurring fear that he was going to "take a fit," by which he meant have an epileptic seizure.

Frank: I've noticed if I really jerk my leg and pray real hard for a little while the thought will go away (Nelson & Barlow, 1981, p. 19).

What's wrong with Frank? The first interview reveals an insecure young man experiencing substantial stress as he questions whether he is capable of handling marriage and a job. He reports that he loves his wife very much and wants the marriage to work and that he is attempting to be as conscientious as possible on his job, a job from which he derives a lot of satisfaction and enjoyment. Also, for some reason, he is having troubling thoughts about seizures. So, where do we go from here? How do we determine whether Frank has a psychological disorder or if he is simply one of many young men suffering the normal stresses and strains of a new marriage who, perhaps, could benefit from counseling?

Assessing Psychological Disorders

The process of clinical assessment in psychopathology has been likened to a funnel (Hawkins, 1979; D. R. Peterson, 1968). The clinician begins by collecting a lot of information across a broad range of the individual's functioning to determine where the source of the problem may lie. After getting a preliminary sense of the overall functioning of the person, the clinician narrows the focus by ruling out problems in some areas and concentrating on areas that seem most relevant.

To understand the different ways clinicians assess psychological problems, we need to understand three basic concepts that help determine the value of our assessments: *reliability, validity,* and *standardization* (see Figure 3.1). Assessment techniques are subject to a number of strict requirements, not the least of which is some evidence (research) that they actually do what they are designed to do. One of the more important requirements of these assessments is that they are reliable. **Reliability** is the degree to which a measurement is consistent. Imagine how irritated you would be if you had stomach pain, and you went to four competent physicians and got four different diagnoses and four different treatments. The diagnoses would be said to be unreliable because two or more "raters" did not agree on the conclusion. We expect, in general, that presenting the same symptoms to different physicians will result in similar diagnoses. One way psychologists improve their reliability is by carefully designing their assessment devices and then conducting research on them to ensure that two or more raters

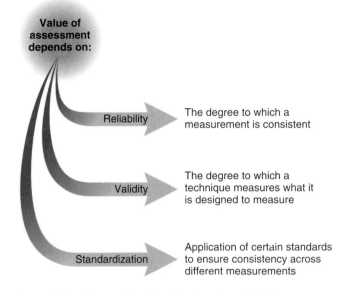

figure 3.1   Concepts that determine the value of clinical assessments

will get the same answers (called *interrater reliability*). They also determine whether these techniques are stable across time. In other words, if you go to a clinician on Tuesday and are told you have an IQ of 110, you should expect a similar result if you take the same test again on Thursday. This is known as *test-retest reliability*. We return to the concept of reliability when we talk of diagnoses and classification.

Validity is whether something measures what it is designed to measure; in this case, whether a technique assesses what it is supposed to. Comparing the results of one assessment measure with the results of others allows you to begin to determine its validity. This comparison is called *concurrent* or *descriptive validity*. *Predictive validity* is how well your assessment tells you what will happen in the future. For example, does it predict who will succeed in school and who will not, which is one of the goals of an IQ test?

Standardization is the process by which a certain set of standards or norms is determined for a technique in order to make its use consistent across different measurements. The standards might apply to the procedures of testing, scoring, and evaluating data. For example, the assessment might be given to large numbers of people who differ on important factors such as age, race, gender, socioeconomic status, and diagnosis; their scores would then be used as a standard, or norm, for comparison purposes. For example, if you are an African-American male, 19 years old, and from a middle-class background, your score on a psychological test should be compared to the scores of others like you and not to the scores of very different people, such as a group of women of Asian descent in their 60s from working-class backgrounds. Reliability, validity, and standardization are important to all forms of psychological assessment.

Clinical assessment consists of a number of strategies and procedures that help clinicians acquire the information they need to understand their patients and assist them. These procedures include a *clinical interview* and, within the

During their first meeting, the mental health professional focuses on the problem that brought the person to treatment.

context of the interview, a *mental status exam* that can be administered either formally or informally, often a thorough *physical examination, behavioral observation and assessment,* and *psychological tests* (if needed).

The Clinical Interview

The clinical interview is the core of most clinical work and is used by psychologists, psychiatrists, and other mental health professionals. The interview gathers information on current and past behavior, attitudes, and emotions, as well as a detailed history of the individual's life in general and of the presenting problem. Clinicians determine when the specific problem first started and identify other events (for example, life stress, trauma, physical illness) that might have occurred about the same time. In addition, most clinicians gather at least some information on the patient's current and past interpersonal and social history, including family makeup (for instance, marital status, number of children, college student currently living with parents) and on the individual's upbringing. Information on sexual development, religious attitudes (current and past), relevant cultural concerns (such as stress induced by discrimination), and educational history are also routinely collected. To organize information obtained during an interview, many clinicians use a **mental status exam.**

THE MENTAL STATUS EXAM

In essence, the mental status exam involves the systematic observation of somebody's behavior. This type of observation occurs when any one person interacts with another. All of us, clinicians and nonclinicians alike, perform daily pseudo-mental status exams. The trick for clinicians, of course, is to organize their observations of other people in a way that gives them sufficient information to determine whether a psychological disorder might be present (Nelson & Barlow, 1981). Mental status exams can be very structured and detailed (J. K. Wing, Cooper, & Sartorius, 1974) but, for the most part, they are performed relatively quickly by experienced clinicians in the course of interviewing or observing a patient. The exam covers five categories: appearance and behavior, thought processes, mood and affect, intellectual functioning, and sensorium.

1. *Appearance and behavior.* The clinician notes any overt physical behaviors such as Frank's leg twitch, as well as the individual's dress, general appearance, posture, and facial expression. For example, very slow and effortful motor behavior, sometimes referred to as psychomotor retardation, may indicate severe depression.

2. *Thought processes.* When clinicians listen to a patient talk, they're getting a good idea of that person's thought processes. They might look for several things here. For example, what is the rate or flow of speech? Does the person talk really fast or really slowly? What about continuity of speech? In other words, does the patient make sense when he

or she talks or are ideas presented with no apparent connection? In some patients with schizophrenia, a disjointed speech pattern is quite noticeable and is referred to as "looseness of association." Clinicians sometimes ask very specific questions. If the patient shows difficulty with continuity or rate of speech, they might ask, "Can you think clearly or is there some problem putting your thoughts together? Do your thoughts tend to be mixed up or come slowly?"

In addition to rate or flow and continuity of speech, what about the content? Is there any evidence of *delusions* (distorted views of reality)? The individual might also have *ideas of reference,* where everything everyone else does somehow relates back to her or him. *Hallucinations* are things a person perceives (most commonly, sees or hears) that aren't really there. For example, the clinician might say, "Let me ask you a couple of routine questions that we ask everybody. Do you ever see things or maybe hear things when you know there is nothing there?"

3. *Mood and affect.* Determining mood and affect is an important part of the mental status exam. "Mood" is the predominant feeling state of the individual. Does the person appear to be down in the dumps or continually elated? Does she or he talk in a depressed or hopeless fashion? How pervasive is this mood? Are there times when the depression seems to go away? "Affect," by contrast, refers to the feeling state that accompanies what we say at a given point in time. Usually our affect is "appropriate"; that is, we laugh when we say something funny or look sad when we talk about something sad. If a friend just told you his or her mother died and is laughing about it, or if your friend has just won the lottery and is crying, you would think it strange, to say the least. A mental health clinician would note that your friend's affect is "inappropriate." Then again, you might observe your friend talking about a range of happy and sad things with no affect whatsoever. In this case, a mental health clinician would say the affect is "blunted" or "flat."

4. *Intellectual functioning.* Clinicians make a rough estimate of others' intellectual functioning just by talking to them. Do they seem to have a reasonable vocabulary? Can they talk in abstractions and metaphors (as most of us do much of the time)? How is the person's memory? We usually make some gross or rough estimate of intelligence that is noticeable only if it deviates from normal, such as concluding the person is above or below average intelligence.

5. *Sensorium.* Sensorium is our general awareness of our surroundings. Do subjects know what the date is, what time it is, where they are, who they are, and who you are? Most of us, of course, are fully aware of these facts. People with permanent brain damage or dysfunction—or temporary brain damage or dysfunction, often due to drugs or other toxic states—may not know the answer to these questions. If the patient knows who he or she is and who the clinician is and has a good idea of the time and place, the clinician would say that the patient's sensorium is "clear" and is "oriented times three" (to person, place, and time).

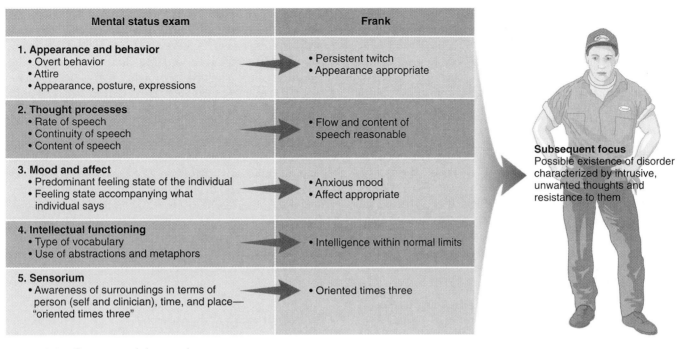

Mental status exam	Frank
1. Appearance and behavior • Overt behavior • Attire • Appearance, posture, expressions	• Persistent twitch • Appearance appropriate
2. Thought processes • Rate of speech • Continuity of speech • Content of speech	• Flow and content of speech reasonable
3. Mood and affect • Predominant feeling state of the individual • Feeling state accompanying what individual says	• Anxious mood • Affect appropriate
4. Intellectual functioning • Type of vocabulary • Use of abstractions and metaphors	• Intelligence within normal limits
5. Sensorium • Awareness of surroundings in terms of person (self and clinician), time, and place— "oriented times three"	• Oriented times three

Subsequent focus
Possible existence of disorder characterized by intrusive, unwanted thoughts and resistance to them

figure 3.2 Components of the mental status exam

What can we conclude from these informal behavioral observations? Basically, they allow the clinician to make a preliminary determination of which areas of the patient's behavior and condition should be assessed in more detail and perhaps more formally. If psychological disorders remain a possibility, the clinician may begin to hypothesize which disorders might be present. This process, in turn, provides more focus for the assessment and diagnostic activities to come.

Returning to our case, what have we learned from this mental status exam (see Figure 3.2)? Observing Frank's persistent motor behavior in the form of a twitch led to the discovery of a functional relationship with some troublesome thoughts regarding seizures. Beyond this, his appearance was appropriate, and the flow and content of his speech was reasonable; his intelligence was well within normal limits, and he was oriented times three. He did display an anxious mood; however, his affect was appropriate to what he was saying. These observations suggested that we direct the remainder of the clinical interview and additional assessment and diagnostic activities to identify the possible existence of a disorder characterized by intrusive, unwanted thoughts and the attempt to resist them—in other words, *obsessive–compulsive disorder*. Below we will describe some of the specific assessment strategies, from among many choices, that we would use with Frank.

Patients usually have a pretty good idea of their major concerns in a general sense ("I'm depressed"; "I'm phobic"); occasionally, the problem reported by the patient may not, after assessment, be the major issue in the eyes of the mental health clinician. The case of Frank illustrates this point well: He complained of distress relating to marital problems, but the clinician decided, on the basis of the initial interview, that the principal difficulties lay elsewhere. Frank

wasn't attempting to hide anything from the clinician. Frank just didn't think his intrusive thoughts were the major problem; additionally, talking about them was very difficult for him because they were quite frightening.

This example illustrates the importance of conducting the clinical interview in a way that elicits the patient's trust and empathy. Psychologists and other mental health professionals are trained extensively in methods that put patients at ease and facilitate communication, including nonthreatening ways of seeking information as well as appropriate listening skills. Information provided by patients to psychologists and psychiatrists is protected by laws of "privileged communication" or confidentiality in most states; that is, even if authorities want the information the therapist has received from the patient, they cannot have access to it without the expressed consent of the patient. The only exception to this rule occurs when the clinician judges that, because of the patient's condition, some harm or danger to either the patient or someone else is imminent. At the outset of the initial interview, the therapist should inform the patient of the confidential nature of their conversation and the (quite rare) conditions under which that confidence would not hold.

Despite these assurances of confidentiality and the clinician's interview skills, patients sometimes find it difficult to volunteer sensitive information. In our own files is the case of a man in his early 20s who came to therapy once a week for 5 months. He wanted help with what he viewed as deficient interpersonal skills and anxieties that were impeding his ability to relate to other people. Only after 5 months, and quite by chance during a particularly emotional session, did he reveal his secret. He was strongly sexually attracted to small boys and confessed that he found their feet and associated objects such as socks and shoes to be nearly irresistible. In fact, he had hidden in his home a large collection of small socks and shoes. Confidentiality had been assured, and the therapist was there to help. Nevertheless, the patient found it almost impossible to volunteer this information. There may well have been signs that something else was going on during the 5 months of treatment, but if there were, the therapist missed them.

■ concept check 3.1

Identify which part of the mental status exam is being performed in each of the following situations.

1. Dr. Swan listened carefully to Joyce's speech pattern, noting its speed, content, and continuity. She noticed no looseness of association but did hear indications of delusional thoughts and visual hallucinations. _____

2. Andrew arrived at the clinic accompanied by police, who had found him dressed only in shorts although the temperature was 23 degrees. He was reported to the police by someone who saw him walking very slowly down the street making strange faces and talking to himself. _____

3. When Lisa was brought to Dr. Miller's office, he asked if she knew the date and time, her identity, and where she was. _____

4. Dr. Jones viewed Tim's laughter after discussing his near-fatal incident as inappropriate and also noted that Tim appeared to be elated. _____

5. Mark's vocabulary and memory seemed adequate, leading Dr. Adams to estimate that Mark was of average intelligence. _____

SEMISTRUCTURED CLINICAL INTERVIEWS

Until relatively recently most clinicians, after training, developed their own methods of collecting necessary information from patients. Different patients seeing different psychologists or other mental health professionals might encounter markedly different types and styles of interviews. *Unstructured interviews* follow no systematic format. *Semistructured interviews* are made up of questions that have been carefully phrased and tested to elicit useful information in a consistent manner, so clinicians can be sure they have inquired about the most important aspects of particular disorders. Clinicians may also depart from set questions to follow up on specific issues—thus the label "semistructured." Because the wording and sequencing of questions has been carefully worked out over a number of years, the clinician can feel confident that a semistructured interview will accomplish its purpose. The disadvantage, of course, is that it robs the interview of some of the spontaneous quality of two people talking about a problem. Also, if applied too rigidly, this type of interview may inhibit the patient from volunteering useful information that is not directly relevant to the questions being asked. For these reasons, fully structured interviews administered wholly by a computer have not caught

on, although they are used in some settings. An increasing number of mental health professionals routinely use semistructured interviews. Some are quite specialized. For example, Frank's clinician, in probing further into a possible obsessive–compulsive disorder, might use the *Anxiety Disorders Interview Schedule for DSM-IV (ADIS-IV)* (DiNardo, Brown, & Barlow, 1994). According to this interview schedule, the clinician first asks if the patient is bothered by thoughts, images, or impulses (obsessions) or currently feels driven to repeat some behavior or thought over and over again (compulsions). Based on an 8-point rating scale that ranges from "never" to "occasionally" to "constantly," the patient then rates each obsession on two measures: *persistence–distress* (how often it occurs and how much distress it causes) and *resistance* (types of attempts the patient makes to get rid of the obsession). For compulsions, the patient rates their *frequency*.

Physical Examination

Many patients with problems first go to a family physician and are given a physical. If the patient presenting with psychological problems has not had a physical exam in the past year, a clinician might recommend one, with particular attention to the medical conditions sometimes associated with the specific psychological problem. Many problems presenting as disorders of behavior, cognition, or mood may, on careful physical examination, have a clear relationship to a temporary toxic state. This toxic state could be caused by bad food, the wrong amount or type of medicine, or the onset of a medical condition. For example, thyroid difficulties, particularly hyperthyroidism (overactive thyroid gland), may produce symptoms that mimic certain anxiety disorders, such as generalized anxiety disorder. Hypothyroidism (underactive thyroid gland) might produce symptoms consistent with depression. Certain psychotic symptoms, including delusions or hallucinations, might be associated with the development of a brain tumor. Withdrawal from cocaine often produces panic attacks, but many patients presenting with panic attacks are reluctant to volunteer information about their addiction, which may lead to an inappropriate diagnosis and improper treatment.

Usually, psychologists and other mental health professionals are well aware of the medical conditions and drug use and abuse that may contribute to the kinds of problems described by the patient. If a current medical condition or substance abuse situation exists, the clinician must ascertain whether it is merely coexisting or causal, usually by looking at the onset of the problem. If a patient has suffered from severe bouts of depression for the past 5 years, but within the past year also developed hypothyroid problems or began taking a sedative drug, then we would not conclude that the depression was caused by the medical or drug condition. If the depression developed simultaneously with the initiation of sedative drugs and diminished considerably when the drugs were discontinued, we would be likely to conclude that the depression was part of a substance-induced mood disorder.

Behavioral Assessment

The mental status exam is one way to begin to sample how people think, feel, and behave and how these actions might contribute to or explain their problems. **Behavioral assessment** takes this process one step further by using direct observation to formally assess an individual's thoughts, feelings, and behavior in specific situations or *contexts;* this information should explain why he or she is having difficulties at this time. Indeed, behavioral assessment may be much more appropriate than any interview in terms of assessing individuals who are not old enough or skilled enough to report their problems and experiences. Clinical interviews provide limited assessment information. Young children or individuals who are not verbal because of the nature of their disorder or because of cognitive deficits or impairments are not good candidates for clinical interviews. As mentioned above, sometimes people deliberately withhold information because it is embarrassing or because they aren't aware that it is important. In addition to talking with a client in an office about a problem, some clinicians go to the person's home or workplace or even into the local community to observe the person and the reported problems directly. Others set up role-play simulations in a clinical setting to see how people might behave in similar situations in their daily lives. These techniques are all types of behavioral assessment.

In behavioral assessment, *target behaviors* are identified and observed with the goal of determining the factors that seem to influence them. It may seem easy to identify what is bothering a particular person (that is, the target behavior), but even this aspect of assessment can be challenging. For example, when the mother of a 7-year-old child with a severe conduct disorder came to one of our clinics for assistance, she told the clinician, after much prodding, that her son "didn't listen to her" and that he sometimes had an "attitude." The boy's schoolteacher, however, painted a very different picture. She spoke candidly of his verbal violence—of his threats toward other children and to herself, threats she took very seriously. To get a clearer picture of the situation at home, the clinician visited one afternoon. Approximately 15 minutes after the visit began, the boy got up from the kitchen table without removing the drinking glass he was using. When his mother quite meekly asked him to put the glass in the sink, he picked it up and threw it across the room, sending broken glass throughout the kitchen. He giggled and went into his room to watch TV. "See," she said. "He doesn't listen to me!"

Obviously, this mother's description of her son's behavior at home didn't give a good picture of what he was really like. It also didn't accurately portray her response to his violent outbursts. Without the home visit, the clinician's assessment of the problem and recommendations for treatment would have been very different. Clearly this was more than simple disobedience. We developed strategies to teach the mother how to make requests of her son and how to follow up if he was violent.

To go back to Frank and his anxiety about his marriage, how do we know he is telling the "truth" about his relationship with his wife? Is what he is *not* telling us important? What would we find if we observed Frank and his wife interacting in their home, or if they had a typical conversation in front of us in a clinical setting? Most clinicians assume that a complete picture of a person's problems requires direct observation in naturalistic environments. But going into a person's home, workplace, or school isn't always possible or practical, so clinicians sometimes set up analog settings. For example, one of us studies children with autism (a disorder that is characterized by social withdrawal and communication problems; see Chapter 14). The reasons for self-hitting (called *self-injurious*) behavior are discovered by placing the children in simulated classroom situations, such as sitting alone at a desk, working in a group, or being asked to complete a difficult task (Durand & Crimmins, 1988). Observing how they behave in these different situations helps us determine why they hit themselves, so we can design a successful treatment to eliminate the behavior. David Wolfe (1991) uses contrived situations to assess the emotional reactions of parents with a history of abuse toward their children. By asking parents to have their children put away favorite toys, which usually results in problem behavior by the child, the therapist can see how the parents respond. These observations are later used to develop treatments.

THE ABCs OF OBSERVATION

Observational assessment is usually focused on the here and now. Therefore, the clinician's attention is usually directed to the immediate behavior, its antecedents, and its consequences (Baer, Wolf, & Risley, 1968). To use the example of the young boy, an observer would note that the sequence of events was (a) his mother asking him to put his glass in the sink (antecedent), (b) the boy throwing the glass (behavior), and (c) his mother's lack of response (consequence). This Antecedent-Behavior-Consequence sequence (the ABCs) might suggest that the boy was being reinforced for his violent outburst by not having to clean up his mess. And because there was no negative consequence for his behavior (his mother didn't scold or reprimand him), he will probably act violently the next time he doesn't want to do something (see Figure 3.3).

This is an example of a relatively *informal observation.* During the home visit, the clinician took rough notes about

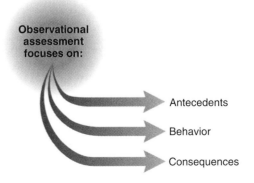

figure 3.3 The ABCs of observation

what occurred. Later, in his office, he elaborated on the notes. A problem with this type of observation is that it relies on the observer's recollection as well as on his or her interpretation of the events. *Formal observation* involves identifying specific behaviors that are observable and *measurable* (called an *operational definition*). It would be hard for two people to agree on what "having an attitude" looks like. An operational definition might further specify this as "any time the boy does not comply with his mother's reasonable requests." Once the target behavior is selected and defined, an observer writes down each time it occurs, along with what happened just before (antecedent) and just after (consequence). The goal of collecting this information is to see whether there are any obvious patterns of behavior and then to design a treatment based on these patterns.

People can also observe their own behavior to find patterns, a technique known as *self-monitoring* or self-observation. People trying to quit smoking may write down the number of cigarettes they smoke and the times and places where they smoke. This observation can tell them exactly how big their problem is (for example, they smoke two packs a day) and what situations lead them to smoke more (for example, talking on the phone). When behaviors occur only in private (such as purging by people with bulimia), self-monitoring is essential. Because the people with the problem are in the best position to observe their own behavior throughout the day, clinicians often ask clients to self-monitor their behavior to get more detailed information on the problem.

A more formal and structured way to observe behavior is through checklists and *behavior rating scales,* which are used as assessment tools prior to treatment and then periodically during treatment to assess changes in the patient's behavior. Of the many such instruments for assessing a variety of behaviors, the Brief Psychiatric Rating Scale (Overall & Hollister, 1982), which can be completed by staff, assesses 18 general areas of concern. Each symptom is rated on a 7-point scale from 0 (not present) to 6 (extremely severe). The rating scale includes such items as *somatic concern* (preoccupation with physical health, fear of physical illness, hypochondriasis), *guilt feelings* (self-blame, shame, remorse for past behavior), and *grandiosity* (exaggerated self-opinion, arrogance, conviction of unusual power or abilities).

A phenomenon known as *reactivity* can distort any observational data. Any time you observe how people behave, the mere fact of your presence may cause them to change their behavior (Kazdin, 1979). To test reactivity, you can tell a friend you are going to record every time she or he says the word *like.* Just before you reveal your intent, however, count the times your friend uses this word in a 5-minute period. You will probably find that he or she uses the word much less often when you are recording it. Your friend will "react" to the observation by changing the behavior. The same phenomenon occurs if you observe your own behavior, or self-monitor. Behaviors people want to increase, such as talking more in class, tend to increase, and behaviors people want to decrease, such as smoking, tend to decrease when they are self-monitored (Cavior & Marabotto, 1976; Sieck & McFall, 1976). Clinicians sometimes depend on the reactivity

of self-monitoring to increase the effectiveness of their treatments.

Psychological Testing

We are confronted with "psychological" tests in the popular press almost every week: "12 Questions to Test Your Relationship," "New Test to Help You Assess Your Lover's Passion," "Are You a Type 'Z' Personality?" Although we may not want to admit it, many of us have probably purchased a magazine at some point to take one of these tests. Many are no more than entertainment, designed to make you think about the topic (and to make you buy the magazine). They are typically made up for the purposes of the article and include questions that, on the surface, seem to make sense. We are interested in these tests because we want to understand better why we and our friends behave the way we do. In reality, they usually tell us little.

In contrast, the tests used to assess psychological disorders must meet the strict standards we have noted. They must be *reliable*—so that two or more people administering the same test to the same person will come to the same conclusion about the problem—and they must be *valid*—so that they measure what they say they are measuring.

Psychological tests include specific tests to determine cognitive, emotional, or behavioral responses that might be associated with a specific disorder and more general tests that assess long-standing personality features. Specialized areas include *intelligence testing* to determine the structure and patterns of cognition. *Neuropsychological testing* determines the possible contribution of brain damage or dysfunction to the patient's condition. Neurobiological procedures use imaging to assess brain structure and function.

PROJECTIVE TESTING

We saw in Chapter 1 how Freud brought to our attention the presence and influence of unconscious processes in psychological disorders. At this point we should ask, "If people aren't aware of these thoughts and feelings, how do we assess them?" To address this intriguing problem, psychoanalytic workers developed several assessment measures known as **projective tests.** They include a variety of methods in which ambiguous stimuli, such as pictures of people or things, are presented to a person who is asked to describe what he or she sees. The theory here is that people "project" their own personality and unconscious fears onto other people and things—in this case, the ambiguous stimuli—and, without realizing it, reveal their unconscious thoughts to the therapist.

Because these tests are based in psychoanalytic theory, they have been, and remain, controversial. Even so, the use of projective tests is quite common, with a majority of clinicians administering them at least occasionally and most doctoral programs providing training in their use (Durand, Blanchard, & Mindell, 1988). Three of the more widely used are the *Rorschach inkblot test*, the *Thematic Apperception Test*, and the *sentence-completion method*.

figure 3.4 This inkblot resembles the ambiguous figures presented in the Rorschach test.

More than 80 years ago, a Swiss psychiatrist named Hermann Rorschach developed a series of inkblots, initially to study perceptual processes, then to diagnose psychological disorders. The *Rorschach inkblot test* is one of the early projective tests. In its current form, the test includes 10 inkblot pictures that serve as the ambiguous stimuli (see Figure 3.4). The examiner presents the inkblots one by one to the person being assessed, who responds by telling what he or she sees.

Though Rorschach advocated a scientific approach to studying the answers to the test (Rorschach, 1951), he died at the age of 38, before he had fully developed his method of systematic interpretation. Unfortunately, much of the early use of the Rorschach is extremely controversial, because of the lack of data on reliability or validity, among other things. Until relatively recently, therapists administered the test any way they saw fit, although one of the most important tenets of assessment is that the same test be given in the same way each time—that is, according to standardized procedures. If you encourage someone to give more detailed answers during one testing session but not during a second session, you may get different responses as the result of your administering the test differently on the two occasions—not because of problems with the test or administration by another person (interrater reliability).

To respond to the concerns about reliability and validity, John Exner developed a standardized version of the Rorschach inkblot test, called the *Comprehensive System* (Exner, 1974, 1978, 1986; Exner & Weiner, 1982). Exner's system of administering and scoring the Rorschach specifies how the cards should be presented, what the examiner

should say, and how the responses should be recorded (Erdberg, 1996). Varying these steps can lead to varying responses by the client. Recent work on this new system indicates that when used in a standard way, the test may indeed be a useful assessment device for identifying some forms of psychopathology (Acklin, McDowell, & Orndoff, 1992).

The *Thematic Apperception Test* (TAT) is perhaps the best known projective test, after the Rorschach. It was developed in 1935 by Morgan and Murray at the Harvard Psychological Clinic (Bellak, 1975). The TAT consists of a series of 31 cards (see Figure 3.5); 30 with pictures on them and one blank card, although only 20 cards are typically used during each administration. Unlike the Rorschach, which involves asking for a fairly straightforward description of what the test taker sees, the instructions for the TAT ask the person to tell a dramatic story about the picture. The tester presents the pictures and tells the client, "This is a test of imagination, one form of intelligence." The person being assessed can "let your imagination have its way, as in a myth, fairy story, or allegory" (M. I. Stein, 1978, p. 186). Again like the Rorschach, the TAT is based on the notion that people will reveal their unconscious mental processes in their stories about the pictures (Dana, 1996).

Several variations of the TAT have been developed for different groups, including a Children's Apperception Test (CAT) and a Senior Apperception Technique (SAT). In addition, modifications of the test have evolved for use with a variety of racial and ethnic groups, including African-

figure 3.5 Example of a picture resembling those in the Thematic Apperception Test.

Americans, Native Americans, and people from India, South Africa, and the South Pacific Micronesian culture (Bellak, 1975; Dana, 1996). These modifications have included changes not only in the appearance of people in the pictures but also in the situations that are depicted.

Unfortunately, unlike recent trends in the use of the Rorschach, the TAT and its variants continue to be used inconsistently. How the stories people tell about these pictures are interpreted depends on the examiner's frame of reference as well as what the patient may say. It is not surprising, therefore, that there is little reliability across raters using this system (Lundy, 1985). Despite these problems, the TAT is still widely used, and some clinicians continue to report that they find it valuable in guiding their diagnostic and treatment decisions.

Despite their popularity and increasing standardization, most clinicians who use projective tests have their own methods of administration and interpretation. When used as icebreakers, for getting people to open up and talk about how they feel about things going on in their lives, the ambiguous stimuli in these tests can be valuable tools. However, their relative lack of reliability and validity make them less useful as diagnostic tests (Anastasi, 1988). Concern over the inappropriate use of projective tests should remind readers of the importance of the scientist–practitioner approach. Clinicians are not only responsible for knowing how to administer tests but also need to be aware of research that suggests they have limited usefulness as a means of diagnosing psychopathology.

PERSONALITY INVENTORIES

The questions in "psychological" tests published in mainstream magazines typically make sense when you read them. This is called having *face validity:* The wording of the questions seems to fit the type of information desired. But is this necessary? A prominent psychologist, Paul Meehl, presented his position on this issue more than 50 years ago and subsequently influenced a whole field of study on **personality inventories** (Meehl, 1945). Put simply, Meehl pointed out that what is necessary from these types of tests is not whether the questions necessarily make sense on the surface but, rather, what the answers to these questions predict. If we find that people who have schizophrenia tend to respond "true" to "I have never been in love with anyone," then it doesn't matter whether we have a theory of love and schizophrenia. If people with certain disorders tend, as a group, to answer a variety of questions in a certain way, this pattern may predict who else has this disorder. The content of the questions becomes irrelevant. The importance lies in what the answers predict.

Although many personality inventories are available, we will look at the most widely used personality inventory in the United States, the *Minnesota Multiphasic Personality Inventory (MMPI)*, which was developed in the late 1930s and early 1940s and first published in 1943 (Hathaway & McKinley, 1943). In stark contrast to projective tests, which rely heavily on theory for an interpretation, the MMPI and similar inventories are based on an *empirical* approach; that is, the collection and evaluation of data. The administration of the MMPI is straightforward. The individual being assessed reads statements and answers either "true" or "false." Following are some statements from the MMPI:

> I cry easily.
> I am happy most of the time.
> I believe I am being followed.
> Someone has been trying to poison me.

Obviously, there is little room for interpretation of MMPI responses, unlike responses to projective tests such as the Rorschach and the TAT. A problem with administering the MMPI, however, is the time and tedium of responding to the 550 items on the original version and now the 567 items on the MMPI-2. Individual responses are *not* examined; instead, the pattern of responses is reviewed to see if it resembles patterns from groups of people who have specific disorders (for example, a pattern similar to a group with schizophrenia). Each group is represented on 1 of 10 separate standard scales:

1. *Hypochondriasis (HS),* such as degree of bodily complaints
2. *Depression (D),* such as negativity, low morale, hopelessness
3. *Hysteria (Hy),* such as physical symptoms that allow escape from responsibilities or stress
4. *Psychopathic deviation (Pd),* such as lack of ability to form warm, stable bonds or appreciate customs and social rules
5. *Masculinity/femininity (MF),* such as personality features that distinguish homosexual men with "feminine" interests
6. *Paranoia (Pa),* such as feelings of persecution, hypersensitivity, rigid thinking
7. *Psychasthenia (Pt),* such as excessive self-doubt, obsessive preoccupations, compulsive urges and acts, low self-confidence
8. *Schizophrenia (Sc),* such as having unusual thoughts, very suspicious
9. *Hypomania (Ma),* such as heightened activity levels, easy distractibility, over-optimism
10. *Social introversion (Si),* such as an introversion–extroversion measure

Fortunately, clinicians can have these responses scored by computer; the program also includes an interpretation of the results, thereby reducing problems of reliability. One concern that arose early in the development of the MMPI was the potential of some people to answer in ways that would downplay their problems; skilled individuals would ascertain the intent of statements such as "Someone has control over my mind," and fake the answers. To assess this possibility, the MMPI includes four additional scales that determine the validity of each administration. For example, on the Lie Scale (L), one statement is "I have never had a bad night's sleep." Answering "true" to this is an indication

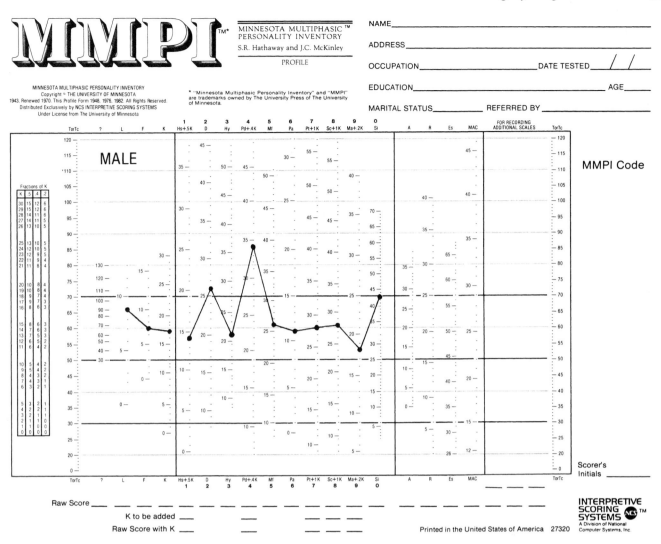

figure 3.6 An MMPI profile (from MMPI, 1982)

that the person may be falsifying answers in order to look good. The other scales are the "F" or Infrequency scale, which measures false claims about psychological problems or determines whether the person is answering randomly; the "K" or Defensiveness scale, which assesses whether the person sees himself or herself in unrealistically positive ways; and the "?" or Cannot-Say scale, which simply measures the number of items the test taker did not answer.

Figure 3.6 is an MMPI *profile* or summary of scores from an individual being clinically assessed. Before we tell you why this 27-year-old man (we'll call him James S.) was being evaluated, let's see what his MMPI profile tells us about him. The first three data points represent scores on the L, F, and K scales; the high scores on these scales were interpreted to mean that James S. made a naive attempt to look good for the evaluator and may have been trying to fake an appearance of having no problems. Another important part of his profile is the very high score on the Pd (Psychopathic deviation) scale, which measures the tendency to behave in antisocial ways. The interpretation of this score is that James S. is "aggressive, unreliable, irresponsible; unable

to learn from experience; may initially make a good impression but then psychopathic features will surface in longer interactions or under stress."

Why was James S. being evaluated? He is a young man with a criminal record that begins in his childhood. He was evaluated as part of his trial for kidnapping, raping, and murdering a middle-aged woman. Throughout his trial, he made up a number of contradictory stories to make himself look innocent (remember his high scores on the L, F, and K scales), including blaming his brother. However, there was overwhelming evidence of his guilt, and he was sentenced to life in prison. His answers on the MMPI resembled those of others who act in violent and antisocial ways.

The MMPI is one of the most extensively researched assessment instruments in psychology, with more than 8,000 research references published about it (Anastasi, 1988). The original standardization sample—the people who first responded to the statements and set the standard for answers—included many people from Minnesota who had no psychological disorders and several groups of people who had particular disorders. A more recent version of this test,

This child is concentrating on a standard psychological assessment test.

the MMPI-2, as well as a version for adolescents—the MMPA-A—(Archer & Krishna Murthy, 1996), eliminates problems with the original version, problems in part due to the original selective sample of people and in part to the wording of questions (Helmes & Reddon, 1993; Newmark & McCord, 1996). For example, some questions were sexist. One item on the original version asks the respondent to say whether she has ever been sorry that she is a girl (Worell & Remer, 1992). Another item states, "Any man who is willing to work hard has a good chance of succeeding." Other items were criticized as insensitive to cultural diversity. Items dealing with religion, for example, referred almost exclusively to Christianity (Butcher, Graham, Williams, & Ben-Porath, 1990). The MMPI-2 has also been standardized with a sample that reflects the 1980 U.S. Census figures, including African-Americans and Native Americans for the first time. In addition, new items have been added that deal with contemporary issues such as type A personality, low self-esteem, and family problems.

Reliability of the MMPI is excellent when it is interpreted according to standardized procedures, and thousands of studies on the original MMPI attest to its validity with a range of psychological problems (Anastasi, 1988). But a word of caution is necessary here. As they might with any other form of assessment, some clinicians look at an MMPI profile and interpret the scales on the basis of their own clinical experience and judgment only. By not relying on the standard means of interpretation, this practice compromises the instrument's reliability and validity.

INTELLIGENCE TESTING

"She must be very smart. I hear her IQ is 180!" What is "IQ"? What is "intelligence"? And how are they important in psychopathology? As many of you know from your introductory psychology course, intelligence tests were developed for one specific purpose: to predict who would do well in school. In 1904, a French psychologist, Alfred Binet, and his colleague, Théodore Simon, were commissioned by the French government to develop a test that would identify "slow learners" who would benefit from remedial help. The two psychologists identified a series of tasks that presumably measured the skills children need to succeed in school, including tasks of attention, perception, memory, reasoning, and verbal comprehension. Binet and Simon gave their original series of tasks to a large number of children; they then eliminated those that did not separate the slow learners from the children who did well in school. After several revisions and sample administrations, they had a test that was relatively easy to administer and that did what it was designed to do—predict academic success. In 1916, Lewis Terman of Stanford University translated a revised version of this test for use in the United States; it became known as the *Stanford-Binet*.

The test provided a score known as an **intelligence quotient,** or *IQ*. Initially, IQ scores were calculated by using the child's *mental age (MA)*. For example, a child who passed all the questions on the 7-year-old level and none of the questions on the 8-year-old-level received a mental age of 7. This mental age was then divided by the child's *chronological age (CA)* and multiplied by 100 to get the IQ score. However, there were problems with using this type of formula for calculating an IQ score. For example, a 4-year-old needed to score only 1 year above his or her chronological age to be given an IQ score of 125, although an 8-year-old had to score 2 years above his or her chronological age to be given the same score (Bjorklund, 1989). Current tests use what is called a *deviation IQ*. A person's score is compared only to scores of others of the same age. The IQ score, then, is really an estimate of how much a child's performance in school will deviate from the average performance of others of the same age.

In addition to the revised version of the Stanford-Binet (Thorndike, Hagen, & Sattler, 1986), there is another widely used set of intelligence tests, developed by psychologist David Wechsler. The Wechsler tests include versions for adults (*Wechsler Adult Intelligence Scale-III* [*WAIS-III*]), children (*Wechsler Intelligence Scale for Children-Third Edition* [*WISC-III*]), and for young children (*Wechsler Preschool and Primary Scale of Intelligence-Revised* [*WPPSI-R*]). All these tests contain *verbal scales* (which measure vocabulary, knowledge of facts, short-term memory, and verbal reasoning skills) and *performance scales* (which assess psychomotor abilities, nonverbal reasoning, and ability to learn new relationships).

One of the biggest mistakes nonpsychologists (and a distressing number of psychologists) make is to confuse IQ with intelligence. An IQ is a score on one of the intelligence tests we just described. An IQ score significantly higher than average means that the person has a significantly greater than average chance of doing well in our educational system. By contrast, a score that is significantly lower than average suggests that the person will probably not do well in school. Does a lower-than-average IQ score mean that a person is not intelligent? Not necessarily. First of all, there are numerous reasons for a low score. If the IQ test is administered in English and that is not the person's native language, the results will be affected.

Perhaps more important, however, is the lack of general agreement about what constitutes intelligence (Weinberg, 1989). Remember that the IQ tests measure abilities such as attention, perception, memory, reasoning, and verbal comprehension. But do these skills represent the totality of what we consider intelligence? Some recent theorists believe that what we think of as intelligence involves much more, including the ability to adapt to the environment, the ability to generate new ideas, and the ability to process information efficiently (Sternberg, 1988). We will discuss disorders that involve cognitive impairment, such as delirium and mental retardation, and IQ tests are typically used in assessing these disorders. Keep in mind, however, that we will be discussing IQ and not necessarily intelligence. In general, however, IQ tests tend to be reliable, and to the extent that they predict academic success, they are valid assessment tools.

Neuropsychological Testing

Sophisticated tests have been developed that can pinpoint the location of brain dysfunction. Fortunately, these techniques are generally available and relatively inexpensive. **Neuropsychological testing** measures abilities in areas such as receptive and expressive language, attention and concentration, memory, motor skills, perceptual abilities, and learning and abstraction in such a way that the clinician can make educated guesses about the person's performance and the possible existence of brain impairment. In other words, this method of testing assesses brain dysfunction by observing its effects on the person's ability to perform certain tasks. Although you do not see damage, you can see its effects.

A fairly simple neuropsychological test often used with children is the *Bender Visual–Motor Gestalt Test* (Canter, 1996). A child is given a series of cards on which are drawn various lines and shapes. The task is for the child to copy what is drawn on the card. The errors on the test are compared to test results of other children of the same age; if the number of errors exceeds a certain amount, then brain dysfunction is suspected. This test is less sophisticated than other neuropsychological tests because the nature or location of the problem cannot be determined with this test. The Bender Visual–Motor Gestalt Test can be useful for psychologists, however, because it

provides a simple screening instrument that is easy to administer and that can detect possible problems. Two of the most popular advanced tests of organic damage that allow more precise determinations of the location of the problem are the *Luria–Nebraska Neuropsychological Battery* (Golden, Hammeke, & Purisch, 1980) and the *Halstead–Reitan Neuropsychological Battery* (Reitan & Davison, 1974). These offer an elaborate battery of tests to assess a variety of skills. For example, the Halstead–Reitan Neuropsychological Battery includes the *Rhythm Test* (which asks the person to compare rhythmic beats, to test sound recognition, attention, and concentration), the *Strength of Grip Test* (which compares the grip of the right and left hands), and the *Tactile Performance Test* (which requires the test taker to place wooden blocks in a form board while blindfolded, to test learning and memory skills) (Macciocchi & Barth, 1996).

Many of the skills assessed in neuropsychological testing are also assessed in intelligence tests. There is a great deal of overlap in these two approaches; however, research on the validity of neuropsychological tests suggests that they may be useful for detecting organic damage. One study found that the Halstead–Reitan and the Luria–Nebraska test batteries were equivalent in their abilities to detect damage and were about 80% correct (G. Goldstein & Shelly, 1984). However, these types of studies raise the issue of **false positives** and **false negatives** (Boll, 1985). For any assessment strategy, there will be times when the test shows a problem when none exists (false positives) and times when no problem is found when indeed some difficulty is present (false negatives). The possibility of false results is particularly troublesome for tests of brain dysfunction; a clinician who fails to find damage that exists might miss an important medical problem that needs to be treated. Fortunately, neuropsychological tests are used primarily as screening devices and are routinely paired with other assessments to improve the likelihood that real problems will be found. They do well with regard to measures of reliability and validity. On the downside, they can require hours to administer and are therefore not used routinely unless brain damage is suspected.

Neuroimaging: Pictures of the Brain

For more than a century we have known that many of the things that we do, think, and remember are partially controlled by specific areas of the brain. In recent years we have developed the ability to look inside the brain and take increasingly accurate "pictures" of its structure and function, using a technique called **neuroimaging** (Andreasen & Swayze, 1993; Baxter, Guze, & Reynolds, 1993). Neuroimaging can be divided into two categories. One category includes procedures that examine the *structure* of the brain, such as the size of various parts and whether there is any damage. In the second category are procedures that examine the actual *functioning* of the brain by mapping blood flow and other metabolic activity.

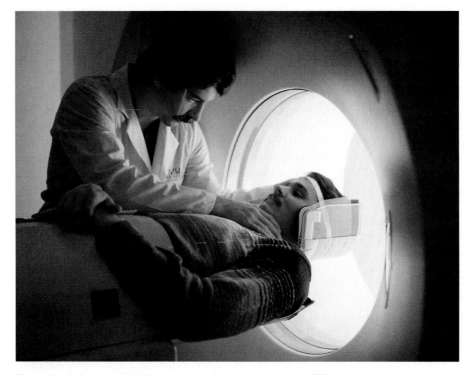

The patient is being positioned for a magnetic resonance imaging (MRI) scan.

IMAGES OF BRAIN STRUCTURE

The first technique, developed in the early 1970s, utilizes multiple X-ray exposures of the brain from different angles; that is, X-ray are passed directly through the head. As with any X-rays, these are partially blocked or attenuated more by bone and less by brain tissue. The degree of attenuation is picked up by detectors in the opposite side of the head. A computer then reconstructs pictures of various "slices" of the brain. This procedure, which takes about 15 minutes, is called *computerized axial tomography (CAT), CAT scan,* or sometimes *CT scan.* It is relatively noninvasive and has proven very useful in identifying and locating abnormalities in the structure or shape of the brain. It is particularly useful in locating brain tumors, injuries, and other structural and anatomical abnormalities. One difficulty, however, is that these scans, like all X-rays, involve repeated X-radiation, which poses some risk of cell damage (Baxter et al., 1993).

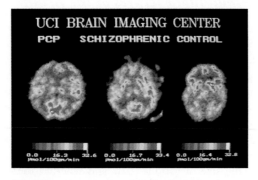

The PET scans compare activity in the brain of a drug abuser (left), a person with schizophrenia (center), and in a normal brain (right).

More recently a procedure has been developed that gives greater resolution (specificity and accuracy) than a CAT scan without the inherent risks of X-rays. This scanning technique is called nuclear *magnetic resonance imaging (MRI).* The patient's head is placed in a high-strength magnetic field through which radio frequency signals are transmitted. These signals "excite" the brain tissue, altering the protons in the hydrogen atoms. The alteration is measured, along with the time it takes the protons to "relax" or return to normal. Where there is slight damage, the signal is lighter or darker (Andreasen & Swayze, 1993). Technology now exists that allows the computer to view the brain in layers, which enables very precise examination of the structure. Although MRI is more expensive than a CAT scan and originally took as long as 45 minutes, this is changing as technology improves. Newer versions of MRI procedures take as little as 10 minutes; the time and cost are decreasing yearly. Another disadvantage of MRI at present is that someone undergoing the procedure is totally enclosed inside a narrow tube with a magnetic coil surrounding the head. People who are somewhat claustrophobic often cannot tolerate an MRI.

Although neuroimaging procedures are very useful for identifying damage to the brain, only recently have they been used to determine structural or anatomical abnormalities that might be associated with various psychological disorders. Some tantalizing preliminary studies are reviewed in subsequent chapters on specific disorders.

IMAGES OF BRAIN FUNCTIONING

Two procedures, recently developed and widely used, are capable of measuring the actual functioning of the brain, as opposed to its structure. The first is called *positron emission tomography (PET).* Subjects undergoing a *PET scan* are injected with a tracer substance attached to radioactive isotopes, groups of atoms that react distinctively. This substance interacts with blood, oxygen, or glucose. When parts of the brain become active, blood, oxygen, or glucose rushes to these areas of the brain, creating "hot spots" picked up by detectors that identify the location of the isotopes. Thus, we can learn what parts of the brain are working and what parts are not. To obtain clear images, the individual undergoing the procedure must remain motionless for 40 seconds or more. These images can be superimposed on MRI images to show the precise location of the active areas. The PET scans are also useful in supplementing MRI and CAT scans in localizing the sites of trauma due to head injury or stroke as well as in localizing brain tumors. More important, PET scans are used increasingly to look at varying

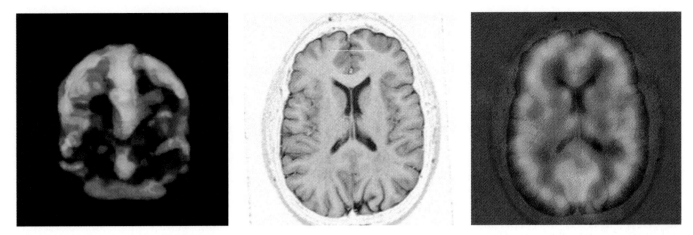

A horizontal brain section (a) in a SPECT image clearly reveals parietal lobe damage in a person with schizophrenia. Images (b) and (c) are MRI photographs. SPECT images show metabolic activity and thus indicate the relationship between the brain and behavior. The higher-resolution MRI images show tissue variations.

patterns of metabolism that might be associated with different disorders. Recent PET scans have demonstrated that many patients with early Alzheimer's-type dementia show reduced glucose metabolism in the parietal lobes. Other intriguing findings have been reported for obsessive–compulsive disorder and bipolar disorder (see Chapters 5 and 7). PET scanning is very expensive: The cost is about $6 million to set up a PET facility and $500,000 a year to run it. Therefore, these facilities are available only in large medical centers.

A second procedure used to assess brain functioning is called *single photon emission computed tomography (SPECT)*. It works very much like PET, although a different tracer substance is used, and it is somewhat less accurate. It is also less expensive, however, and requires far less sophisticated equipment to pick up the signals. For this reason it is used more frequently.

Recently, MRI procedures have been developed that work much more quickly than the regular MRI (Barinaga, 1997; M. Cohen, Rosen, & Brady, 1992). Using sophisticated computer technology, these procedures take only milliseconds and, therefore, can actually take pictures of the brain at work, recording its changes from one second to the next. Because these procedures measure the functioning of the brain, they are called functional MRI or f MRI. In just the last year or 2, f MRI has largely replaced PET scans in the leading brain imaging centers, because it allows researchers to see the immediate response of the brain to a brief event, such as seeing a new face. This response is called an event-related f MRI. Even more powerful technology based on light sources is on the way (Baringa, 1997). Shining infrared light through the head and picking up changes as the light is scattered by brain tissue at work may be a less expensive and more accurate way of learning how the brain works.

Although we have learned little to date, brain imagery procedures hold enormous potential for illuminating the contribution of neurobiological factors to psychological disorders.

Psychophysiological Assessment

Yet another method for assessing brain structure and function specifically and nervous system activity more generally is called **psychophysiological assessment.** As the term implies, *psychophysiology* refers to measurable changes in the nervous system that reflect emotional or psychological events. The measurements may be taken either directly from the brain or peripherally, from other parts of the body.

Frank feared that he might have seizures. If we had any reason to suspect that he might really have periods of memory loss or exhibit bizarre, trancelike behavior, if only for a short period of time, it would be important for him to have an **electroencephalogram (EEG).** Measuring electrical activity in the head related to the firing of a specific group of neurons reveals brain wave activity, the low-voltage electrical current ongoing in the brain, usually from the cortex. A person's brain waves can be assessed in both waking and sleeping states. In an EEG, electrodes are placed directly on various places on the scalp to record the different low-voltage currents.

We have learned much about EEG patterns in the past decades (Fein & Callaway, 1993). Usually we measure *ongoing* electrical activity in the brain. When brief periods of EEG patterns are recorded in response to specific events, such as hearing a psychologically meaningful stimulus, the response is called an *event-related potential (ERP)* or *evoked potential.* We have learned that EEG patterns are often affected by psychological or emotional factors and can be an index of these reactions, or a psychophysiological measure. In a normal, healthy, relaxed adult, waking activities are characterized by a very regular pattern of changes in voltage that we term *alpha waves.* Many types of stress-reduction treatments attempt to *increase* the frequency of the alpha waves, often by relaxing the patients in some way. The alpha wave pattern is associated with relaxation and calmness. During sleep, we pass through several different stages of brain activity, at least partially identified by EEG patterns. During the deepest, most relaxed stage, typically occurring 1 to 2 hours after a person falls asleep, EEG recordings show a pattern of *delta waves*. These brain waves are slower and more irregular than the alpha waves, which is perfectly normal for this stage of sleep. We will see in Chapter 5 that panic attacks occurring while a person is sound asleep come almost exclusively during the delta wave stage. If frequent delta wave activity occurred during the waking state, it might indicate dysfunction of localized areas of the brain.

Extremely rapid and irregular "spikes" on the EEG recordings of someone who is awake may reflect significant seizure disorders, depending on the pattern. The EEG recording is one of the primary diagnostic tools for identifying seizure disorders. Psychophysiological assessment of other bodily responses may also play a role in assessment. These responses include heart rate, respiration, and *electrodermal responding* (skin conductance), formerly referred to as *galvanic skin response* (GSR), which is a measure of sweat gland activity controlled by the peripheral nervous system. Remember from Chapter 2 that the peripheral nervous system and, in particular, the sympathetic division of the autonomic nervous system (ANS) are very responsive to stress and emotional arousal.

Assessing psychophysiological *responding* to emotional stimuli is very important in many disorders, one being posttraumatic stress disorder. Stimuli such as sights and sounds associated with the trauma evoke strong psychophysiological responding, even if the patient is not fully aware of the nature of the trauma because memories of it are inaccessible.

Psychophysiological assessment is also used with many sexual dysfunctions and disorders. For example, sexual arousal can be assessed through direct measurement of penile circumference in males or vaginal blood flow in females in response to erotic stimuli, usually movies or slides (see Chapter 10). Sometimes the individual might be unaware of specific patterns of sexual arousal.

Physiological measures are also important in the assessment and treatment of conditions such as headaches and hypertension (E. Blanchard, 1992; E. Blanchard, Martin, & Dubbert, 1988); they form the basis for the treatment we call *biofeedback*. In biofeedback, as we shall see in Chapter 9, levels of physiological responding, such as blood pressure readings, are "fed back" to the patient (provided on a continuous basis) by meters or gauges so that the patient can try to regulate these responses.

Nevertheless, physiological assessment is not without its limitations, for it requires a great deal of skill and some technical expertise. Even when administered properly, the measures often produce inconsistent results because of procedural or technical difficulties or the nature of the response itself. For this reason, and because the technology is relatively expensive, only clinicians specializing in certain disorders where these measures are particularly important are likely to use psychophysiological recording equipment. It is most often used in theoretical investigations of the nature of certain psychological disorders, particularly emotional disorders (Barlow, 1988).

■ **concept check 3.2**

In assessing psychological disorders, the reliability and validity of the techniques used to measure behavior cannot be overlooked. Without these two factors, accurate assessment is impossible. Check your understanding of reliability and validity by marking each test R (reliable) or NR (not reliable) and V (valid) or NV (not valid).

1. EEG to show electrical activity in the brains of people who have seizures _____

2. Rorschach inkblots _____

3. Structured interviews with definite answers

_____

4. Sentence completion _____

Diagnosing Psychological Disorders

Thus far, we have looked at Frank's functioning on a very individual basis; that is, we have closely observed his behavior, cognitive processes, and mood, and conducted semistructured interviewing, behavioral assessment, and psychological tests. These operations tell us what is *unique* about Frank, not what he may have in common with other individuals.

Learning how Frank may resemble other people in terms of the problems he presents is also very important, for several reasons. If in the past people came in with similar problems or psychological profiles, we can go back and find a lot of information from their cases that might be applicable to Frank's. We can see how the problems began for those other individuals, what factors seemed influential, and how long the problem or disorder lasted. Did the problem in the other cases just go away on its own? If not, what kept it going? Did it need treatment? Most important, what treatments seemed to relieve the problem for those other individuals? These general questions are very useful because they evoke a wealth of clinical and research information that enables the investigator to make certain inferences about what will happen next and what treatments may work. In other words, the clinician can establish a *prognosis*, a term we discussed in Chapter 1 that refers to the likely future course of a disorder under certain conditions. If you can make these general conclusions, you don't have to start at square one every time someone new comes into your office.

If we want to determine what is unique about an individual's personality, cultural background, or circumstances, we use what is known as an **idiographic strategy.** This information lets us tailor our treatment to the person. On the other hand, to take advantage of the information already accumulated on a particular problem or disorder, we must be able to determine a general class of problems to which the presenting problem belongs. This requires a **nomothetic**

strategy. In other words, we attempt to name or classify the problem. When we identify a specific psychological disorder, such as a mood disorder, in the clinical setting, we are making a *diagnosis*. We can also identify a general class or grouping of problems by determining a particular personality profile on a psychological test such as the MMPI. Before proceeding, we will define some additional terms more precisely.

Since classification is such an integral part of science and, indeed, of our human experience, we describe its various aspects individually (Millon, 1991). The term **classification** itself is very broad, referring simply to any effort to construct groups or categories and to assign objects or people to these categories on the basis of their shared attributes or relations—a nomothetic strategy. If the classification is in a scientific context, it is most often called **taxonomy,** which is the classification of entities for scientific purposes, such as insects or rocks or, if the subject is psychology, behaviors. If you apply a taxonomic system to psychological or medical phenomena or other clinical areas, you use the word **nosology.** The term **nomenclature** describes the names or labels of the disorders that make up the nosology (e.g., anxiety or mood disorders). Most mental health professionals use the classification system contained in the *Diagnostic and Statistical Manual of Mental Disorders, Fourth Edition, (DSM-IV).* This is the official system in the United States and is used widely throughout the world. A clinician refers to the DSM-IV to identify a specific psychological disorder in the process of making a diagnosis.

During the past several years we have seen enormous changes in how we think about classifying psychopathology. Because these developments affect so much of what we do, we will examine carefully the processes of classification and diagnosis as they are used in psychopathology. We look first at different approaches, examine the concepts of reliability and validity as they pertain to diagnosis, and then discuss our current system of classification, the DSM-IV.

Classification Issues

Classification is at the heart of any science, and much of what we have said about it is common sense. If we could not order and label objects or experiences, scientists could not communicate with each other and our knowledge would not advance. Everyone would have to develop a personal system, which, of course, would mean nothing to anyone else. In your biology or geology courses, when you study insects or rocks, classification is fundamental. Knowing how one species of insects differs from another allows us to study its functioning and origins.

When we are dealing with human behavior or human behavioral disorders, however, the subject of classification becomes controversial. Some people have questioned whether it is proper or ethical to classify human behavior. Even among those who recognize the necessity of classification, major controversies have arisen in several areas. Within

Despite their wide physical variation, all dogs belong to the same class of animals.

psychopathology, for example, definitions of "normal" and "abnormal" are questioned, and so is the assumption that a behavior or cognition is part of one category or disorder and not another. Some would prefer to talk about behavior and feelings on a continuum from happy to sad or fearful to nonfearful, rather than to create such categories as mania, depression, and phobia. Of course, for better or worse, classifying behavior and people is something that we all do. Few of us talk about our own emotions or those of our friends by using a number on a scale (where 0 is totally unhappy and 100 is totally happy), although this approach might be more accurate. ("How do you feel about that?" "About 65.") Rather, we talk about being happy, sad, angry, depressed, fearful, and so on.

CATEGORICAL AND DIMENSIONAL APPROACHES

To avoid reinventing the wheel every time we see a new set of problem behaviors and to seek general principles of psychopathology, in what different ways can we classify human behavior? We have already alluded to two possibilities. We can have distinct *categories* of disorders that have little or nothing in common with one another; for example, you either hear voices talking to you from the refrigerator (auditory hallucination) and have other symptoms of schizophrenia, or you don't. Alternatively, we can quantify the various attributes of a psychological disorder along several *dimensions,* coming up with a composite score. An MMPI profile is a good example; another is "dimensionalizing" depression on a continuum of severity, from feeling mildly depressed in the morning (something most of us experience once in a while) to feeling so deeply depressed and hopeless that suicide is the only solution. Which system is better? In fact, each has its strengths and its faults. We'll look at both.

The **classical** (or pure) **categorical approach** to classification originates in the work of Emil Kraepelin (1856–1926) and the biological tradition in the study of psychopathology. Here we assume that every diagnosis has a clear underlying pathophysiological cause, such as a bacterial infection or a malfunctioning endocrine system, and that each disorder is unique. When diagnoses are thought of in this way, the causes could be psychological or cultural, instead of pathophysiological, but there is still only one set of causative factors per disorder, which does not overlap at all with other disorders. Because each disorder is fundamentally different from every other, we need only one set of defining criteria, which everybody in the category has to meet. If the criteria for a major depressive episode are (a) the presence of depressed mood, (b) significant weight loss or gain when not dieting, (c) diminished ability to think or concentrate, and 7 additional specific symptoms, then, in order to be diagnosed with depression, an individual would have to meet all 10 criteria. In that case, according to the classical categorical approach, the clinician would know the cause of the disorder.

Emil Kraepelin (1856–1926) was one of the first psychiatrists to classify psychological disorders from a biological point of view.

Classical categorical approaches are quite useful in medicine. It is extremely important for a physician to make accurate diagnoses. If a patient has a fever accompanied by stomach pain, the doctor must determine quickly if the cause is stomach flu or an infected appendix. This is not always easy, but physicians are trained to examine the signs and symptoms closely, and they usually reach the correct conclusion. To understand the cause of symptoms (infected appendix) is to know what treatment will be effective (surgery). But if someone is depressed or anxious, is there a similar type of underlying cause? As we saw in Chapter 2, probably not. Most psychopathologists believe that psychological and social factors interact with biological factors to produce a disorder. Therefore, despite the beliefs of Kraepelin and other early biological investigators, the mental health field has not adopted a classical categorical model of psychopathology. As A. Frances and Widiger (1986) point out, the classical categorical approach is clearly inappropriate to the complexity of psychological disorders.

A second strategy is a **dimensional approach,** in which we note the variety of cognitions, moods, and behaviors with which the patient presents and quantify them on a scale. For example, on a scale of 1 to 10, a patient might be rated as severely anxious (10), moderately depressed (5), and mildly manic (2) to create a profile of emotional functioning (10, 5, 2). Although dimensional approaches have been applied to psychopathology, they are relatively unsatisfactory. Most theorists can't agree on how many dimensions are

required; some say one dimension is enough; others have identified as many as 33 (Millon, 1991).

A third strategy for organizing and classifying behavioral disorders has found increasing support in recent years as an alternative to classical categorical or dimensional approaches. It is a categorical approach but with the twist that it basically combines some of the features of each of the former approaches. Called a **prototypical approach,** this alternative identifies certain essential characteristics of an entity so you (and others) can classify it, but it also allows for certain nonessential variations that do not necessarily change the classification. For example, if someone were to ask you to describe a dog, you could very easily give a general description (the essential, categorical characteristics), but you might not exactly describe a specific dog. Dogs come in different colors, sizes, and even species (the nonessential, dimensional variations), but they all share certain doggish characteristics that allow you to classify them separately from cats. Thus, requiring a certain number of prototypical criteria and only some of an additional number of criteria is adequate. Of course, this system is not perfect because there is a greater blurring at the boundaries of categories, because some symptoms apply to more than one disorder. However, it has the advantage of fitting best with the current state of our knowledge of psychopathology, and it is relatively user-friendly.

When this approach is used in classifying a psychological disorder, many of the different possible features or properties of the disorder are listed, and any candidate must meet enough (but not all) of them to fall into that category. Consider the DSM-IV criteria defining a major depressive episode.

Criteria for Major Depressive Episode

A. Five (or more) of the following symptoms have been present during the same 2-week period and represent a change from previous functioning; at least one of the symptoms is either (a) depressed mood or (b) loss of interest or pleasure.

   Note: Symptoms that are clearly due to a general medical condition or mood-incongruent delusions or hallucinations should not be included.

   1. Depressed mood most of the day
   2. Markedly diminished interest or pleasure in all, or almost all, activities
   3. Significant weight loss (when not dieting) or weight gain
   4. Insomnia or hypersomnia nearly every day
   5. Psychomotor agitation or retardation
   6. Fatigue or loss of energy nearly every day
   7. Feelings of worthlessness or excessive or inappropriate guilt
   8. Diminished ability to think or concentrate or indecisiveness
   9. Recurrent thoughts of death

As you can see, the criteria include many nonessential symptoms, but if you have either depressed mood or marked loss of interest or pleasure in most activities *and* at least four of the remaining eight symptoms, you come close enough to the prototype to meet the criteria for a major depressive episode. One person might have depressed mood, significant weight loss, insomnia, psychomotor agitation, and loss of energy, whereas another person who also meets the criteria for major depressive episode might have markedly diminished interest or pleasure in activities, fatigue, feelings of worthlessness, difficulty thinking or concentrating, and suicidal ideation. Although both have the requisite five symptoms that bring them close to the prototype; they look very different because they share only one symptom. This is a good example of a prototypical category. The DSM-IV is based on this approach.

RELIABILITY

Any system of classification should describe specific subgroups of symptoms that are clearly evident and can be readily identified by experienced clinicians. If two clinicians interview the patient at separate times on the same day (and assuming that the patient's condition does not change during the day), the two clinicians should see, and perhaps measure, the same set of behaviors and emotions. The psychological disorder can thus be identified *reliably*. Obviously, if the disorder is not readily apparent to both clinicians, the resulting diagnoses might represent bias. For example, someone's clothes might provoke some comment. One of your friends might later say, "She looked kind of sloppy tonight." Another might comment, "No, that's just a real funky look; she's right in style." Perhaps a third friend would say, "Actually, I thought she was dressed kind of neatly." You might wonder if they had all seen the same person. In any case, there would be no *reliability* to their observations. Getting your friends to agree about someone's appearance would require a careful set of definitions, which you all accept.

As noted before, unreliable classification systems are subject to bias by clinicians making diagnoses. One of the most unreliable categories in current classification is the whole area of personality disorders—chronic, traitlike sets of inappropriate behaviors and emotional reactions that characterize a person's way of interacting with the world. Although great progress has been made, determining the presence or absence of this type of disorder during one interview is still very difficult. Morey and Ochoa (1989) asked 291 mental health professionals to describe an individual with a personality disorder whom they had recently seen, along with their diagnoses. Morey and Ochoa also collected detailed information on the actual signs and symptoms present in these patients. They were able to determine whether the actual diagnosis matched the objective criteria as determined by the symptoms.

Morey and Ochoa found substantial bias in making diagnoses. For example, for some reason clinicians who were either less experienced or female diagnosed borderline personality disorder more frequently than the criteria indicated. More experienced clinicians and male clinicians diagnosed the condition less frequently than the criteria indicated. Patients who were white, female, or poor were diagnosed

with borderline personality disorder more often than the criteria indicated. Although bias among clinicians is always a potential problem, the more reliable the nosology, or system of classification, the less likely it is to creep in during diagnosis.

VALIDITY

In addition to being reliable, a system of nosology must be valid. Earlier we described *validity* as whether something measures what it is designed to measure. There are several different types of diagnostic validity. For one, the system should have *construct validity*. This means that the signs and symptoms chosen as criteria for the presence of the diagnostic category are consistently associated, and that what they identify differs from other categories. Someone meeting the criteria for depression should be discriminable from someone meeting criteria for social phobia. This discriminability might be evident not only in presenting symptoms but also in the course of the disorder and possibly in the choice of treatment. It may also predict familial aggregation, the extent to which the disorder would be found among the patient's relatives (Blashfield & Livesley, 1991; Cloninger, 1989).

In addition, a valid diagnosis tells the clinician what is likely to happen with the prototypical patient; it may predict the course of the disorder and the likely effect of one treatment or another. This type of validity is often referred to as *predictive validity*, and sometimes *criterion validity*, when the outcome is the criterion by which we judge the usefulness of the category.

Finally, there is *content validity*, which simply means that if you create criteria for a diagnosis of, say, social phobia, it should reflect the way most experts in the field think of social phobia, as opposed to, say, depression. In other words, you need to get the label right.

DSM-III

The year 1980 brought a landmark in the history of nosology: the third edition of the *Diagnostic and Statistical Manual (DSM-III)* (American Psychiatric Association, 1980). Under the leadership of Robert Spitzer, DSM-III departed radically from its predecessors. Three changes stood out. First, DSM-III attempted to take an atheoretical approach to diagnosis, relying on precise descriptions of the disorders as they presented to clinicians rather than on psychoanalytic or biological theories of etiology. With this focus, DSM-III became a tool for clinicians with a variety of different points of view. For example, rather than classifying *phobia* under the broad category "neurosis," defined by intrapsychic conflicts and defense mechanisms, it was assigned its own category within a new broader group, the *anxiety disorders*.

The second major change in DSM-III was that the specificity and detail with which the criteria for identifying a disorder were listed made it possible to study their reliability and validity. Although not all the categories in DSM-III (and its 1987 revision, DSM-III-R) achieved perfect reliability and validity, this system was a vast improvement over what we had before.

Third, DSM-III (and III-R) allowed individuals with possible psychological disorders to be rated on five different dimensions, or *axes*. The disorder itself, such as a schizophrenia or mood disorder, was represented only on the first axis. More enduring (chronic) disorders of personality were listed on Axis II. Axis III comprised physical disorders and conditions. On Axis IV the clinician rated, in a dimensional fashion, the amount of psychosocial stress the person reported, and the current level of adaptive functioning on Axis V. This framework allowed the clinician to gather information about the individual's functioning in a number of different areas rather than limiting it to the disorder itself.

Allen Francis chaired the task force that produced the fourth edition of the *Diagnostic and Statistical Manual (DSM-IV)*. The project took seven years (1988–1994) and involved hundreds of mental health professionals.

PROBLEMS WITH DSM-III AND III-R

Despite the conceptual advances of DSM-III and its revision, DSM-III-R (American Psychiatric Association, 1987), a number of problems remained. First, the reliability of some of the diagnostic categories was often unacceptably low. Researchers discovered that, even under optimal conditions, experienced interviewers watching videotapes could not always agree on whether a disorder was present. This lack of consensus occurred more for some disorders, such as somatoform and personality disorders, than for others (for example, Hyler, Williams, & Spitzer, 1982; Spitzer, Forman, & Nee, 1979). Even when reliability was better, as with the anxiety disorders, it was difficult for clinicians to agree on the presence or absence of some specific disorders, such as generalized anxiety disorder or even simple phobia (DiNardo, Moras, Barlow, Rapee, & Brown, 1993; DiNardo, O'Brien, Barlow, Waddell, & Blanchard, 1983). Identifying a phobia seems to be a fairly straightforward task, but clinicians often could not agree if the condition was severe enough to be a disorder. This lack of consensus is just one example of how complex a challenge it is to categorize psychopathology.

In addition, many of the criteria for DSM-III and III-R, although empirically based and potentially measurable, were established by committee consensus (Spitzer, 1991); that is, a group of experts attempted to decide what should be part of the diagnosis and what should not. Decisions by consensus sometimes produce strange results. For example, one of the criteria for panic disorder in DSM-III-R was four panics in a 4-week period. Why four? Did this reflect some study indicating that three panics in a

4-week period are qualitatively different from four or five? Of course not—the criterion was simply the result of a committee offering a ball-park figure that sounded reasonable. Of course, committee members knew the figure was nothing more than a convenient approximation, but tens of thousands of other clinicians subsequently operated under the assumption that the criteria were hard-and-fast and that a person with three attacks didn't have a panic disorder, despite cautions published in the DSM itself. Such a mind-set reflects a tendency by some clinicians, often inexperienced ones, to "reify" a diagnostic category, which means to take it too literally. This is a mistake. Systems of nosology are simply our best working estimate of the optimal ways of classifying psychopathology and should not be taken as a permanent gold standard.

In spite of these shortcomings, DSM-III and III-R had a substantial impact. Maser, Kaelber, and Weise (1991) surveyed the international usage of various diagnostic systems and found that DSM-III had become very popular for a number of reasons. Primary among them were its precise descriptive format and its neutrality with regard to presuming a cause for diagnosis. The multiaxial format, which emphasizes a broad consideration of the whole individual rather than a narrow focus on the disorder alone, was also very useful. For these reasons, more clinicians around the world used DSM-III-R at the beginning of the 1990s than the International Classification of Disease (ICD) system, a World Health Organization (WHO) System for classifying all physical and mental disorders that was designed to be applicable internationally.

DSM-IV

By the late 1980s, clinicians and researchers realized the need for a consistent, worldwide system of nosology. The 10th edition of the *International Classification of Diseases* (ICD-10) would be published in 1993, and the United States is required by treaty obligations to use the ICD-10 codes in all matters related to health. To make the ICD-10 and DSM as compatible as possible, work proceeded on both the ICD-10 and the fourth edition of the DSM (DSM-IV) more or less simultaneously. Concerted efforts were made to share research data and other information in order to create an empirically based worldwide system of nosology for psychological disorders.

The DSM-IV task force decided to rely as little as possible on a consensus of experts. Any changes in the diagnostic system were to be based on sound scientific data. The revisers attempted to review the voluminous literature in all areas pertaining to the diagnostic system (cf. Widiger et al., 1996), and to identify large sets of data that might have been collected for other reasons but that, with reanalysis, would be useful to DSM-IV. Finally, 12 different independent studies or field trials examined the reliability and validity of alternative sets of definitions or criteria and, in some cases, the possibility of creating a new diagnosis. (A description of one of these field trials follows on p. 86.)

Perhaps the most substantial change in DSM-IV is that the distinction between organically based disorders and psychologically based disorders that was present in previous editions has been eliminated. As we saw in Chapter 2, we now know that even disorders associated with known brain pathology are substantially affected by psychological and social influences. Similarly, disorders previously described as psychological in origin certainly have biological components and, most likely, identifiable brain circuits.

The multiaxial system remains in DSM-IV, with some changes in the five axes. Specifically, only personality disorders and mental retardation are now coded on Axis II. Pervasive developmental disorders, learning disorders, motor skills disorders, and communication disorders, previously coded on Axis II, are now all coded on Axis I. Axis IV, which rated the patient's amount of psychosocial stress, was not useful and has been replaced. The new Axis IV is used for reporting psychosocial and environmental problems that might have an impact on the disorder. Axis V is essentially unchanged. In addition, optional axes have been included for rating dimensions of behavior or functioning that may be important in some cases. There are axes for defense mechanisms or coping styles, social and occupational functioning, and relational functioning; one might use them to describe the quality of relationships that provide the interpersonal context for the disorder. Finally, a number of new disorders were introduced in DSM-IV, and some disorders in DSM-III-R have been either deleted or subsumed into other DSM-IV categories.

The DSM-IV diagnostic guidelines take cultural considerations into account.

DSM-IV AND FRANK

In Frank's case, initial observations indicate an anxiety disorder on Axis I, specifically obsessive–compulsive disorder. However, he might also have long-standing personality traits that lead him systematically to avoid social contact. If so, there might be a diagnosis of schizoid personality disorder on Axis II. Unless Frank has an identifiable medical condition, there is nothing on Axis III. Job and marital difficulties would be coded on Axis IV, where we note psychosocial or environmental problems that are not part of the disorder but might make it worse. Frank's difficulties with work would be noted by checking "occupational problems" and specifying "threat of job loss"; for problems with the primary support group, marital difficulties would be noted. On Axis V, the clinician would rate the highest overall level of Frank's current functioning on a 0 to 100 scale (100 indicates superior functioning in a wide variety of situations). At present, Frank's score is 55, which indicates moderate interference with functioning at home and at work.

This multiaxial system organizes a range of important information that might be relevant to the likely course of the disorder and, perhaps, treatment. For example, two people might present with obsessive–compulsive disorder but look very different on Axes II through V; such differences would greatly affect the clinician's recommendations for the two cases.

SOCIAL AND CULTURAL CONSIDERATIONS IN DSM-IV

By emphasizing levels of stress in the environment, DSM-III and DSM-IV facilitate a more complete picture of the individual. Furthermore, DSM-IV corrects a previous omission by including a plan for integrating important social and cultural influences on diagnosis. The plan allows the disorder to be described from the perspective of the patient's personal experience and in terms of the primary social and cultural group, such as Hispanic or Chinese. The following are suggestions for accomplishing these goals (Mezzich et al., 1993).

What is the primary cultural reference group of the patient? For recent immigrants to the country as well as other ethnic minorities, how involved are they with their "new" culture versus their old culture? Have they mastered the language of their "new" country (for example, English in the United States) or is language a continuing problem?

Does the patient use terms and descriptions from his or her "old" country to describe the disorder? For example, *ataques de nervios* in the Hispanic subculture is a type of anxiety disorder close to panic disorder. Does the patient accept Western models of disease or disorder in which treatment is available in health care systems, or does the patient also have an alternative health care system in another culture (for instance, traditional herbal doctors in Chinese subcultures)?

What does it mean to be "disabled"? What kinds of "disabilities" are acceptable in a given culture, and which are not? For example, is it acceptable to be physically ill but not anxious or depressed? What are the typical family, social, and religious supports in the culture? Are they

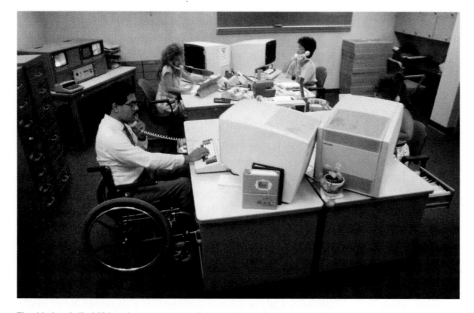

The kinds of disabilities that are accepted in a given culture are socially determined.

available to the patient? Does the clinician understand the first language of the patient as well as the cultural significance of the disorder?

These cultural considerations must not be overlooked in making diagnoses and planning treatment, and they are assumed throughout this book.

CRITICISMS OF DSM-IV

Because the collaboration among groups creating the ICD-10 and DSM-IV was largely successful, it is clear that DSM-IV (and the closely related ICD-10 mental disorder section) is the most advanced, scientifically based system of nosology ever developed. Nevertheless, we still cannot assume that the system is final, or even completely correct. In fact, any nosological system should be considered a work in progress.

We still have "fuzzy" categories that blur at the edges, making diagnostic decisions difficult at times. As a consequence, individuals are often assigned more than one psychological disorder at the same time, sometimes as many as three or four. (Several disorders exist in a state of **comorbidity.**) How can we conclude anything definite about the course of a disorder, the response to treatment, or the likelihood of associated problems if we are dealing with combinations of disorders (Follette & Houts, 1996)? The answers to these difficult questions are hard to establish when only one disorder is present. In the future, people who require an assignment of three or four disorders may have an entirely new class in our nosological system. Resolution of these tough problems simply awaits the long, slow process of science.

Criticisms center on two other aspects of DSM-IV and ICD-10. First, they very strongly emphasize reliability, sometimes at the expense of validity. This is understandable, because reliability is so difficult to achieve *unless* you are willing to sacrifice validity. If the sole criterion for establish-

ing depression were to hear the patient say at some point during an interview, "I feel depressed," one could theoretically achieve perfect reliability (unless the clinician didn't hear the client, which sometimes happens). But this achievement would be at the expense of validity because many people with differing psychological disorders, or none, occasionally say they are depressed. Thus, clinicians could agree that the statement occurred, but it would be of little use (Carson, 1991; Meehl, 1989). Second, as Carson (1996) points out, methods of constructing our nosology have a way of perpetuating definitions handed down to us from past decades, even if they might be fundamentally flawed. Carson (1991) makes a strong argument that it might be better to start fresh every once in a while and create a whole new system of disorders based on emerging scientific knowledge rather than simply fine-tune old definitions, but this is very unlikely to happen.

A thoughtful alternative was offered recently by Follette and Houts (1996), who argue that our system of nosology should become more theoretical. For example, depression can have a number of different causes. One individual might be depressed because a loved one died; another because it results in attention from a girlfriend. Mild depression might lead to drug abuse, which deepens the depression. If we can't include *why* someone is depressed, we will never truly advance our system of classification; and, without testing one theory (e.g., biochemical changes resulting from stress) against another theory (e.g., changes in social support), we won't really understand causation. This theoretical approach emphasizes the function of behavior (why it occurs) rather than just the fact that it exists. It has been applied to alcoholism and pedophilia (Wulfert, Greenway, & Dougher, 1996) (see Chapters 10 and 11), and to anxiety disorder (Hayes, Wilson, Gifford, Follette, & Strosahl, 1996) (see Chapter 5). But the perspective still requires considerable development and testing to determine whether it will be a useful addition to systems of classification.

In addition to the frightful complexity of categorizing psychopathology in particular and human behavior in general, systems are also subject to misuse, some of which can be dangerous and harmful. Diagnostic categories are really just a convenient format for organizing observations, that help professionals communicate, study, and plan. But if we reify a category, we literally make it a "thing," assuming it has a meaning that, in reality, does not exist. Categories may change from time to time with the advent of new knowledge, so none can be written in stone. If a case falls on the fuzzy borders between diagnostic categories, we should not expend all our energy attempting to force it into one cate-

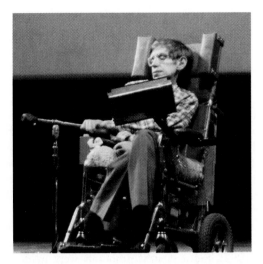

Would we label this man? Stephen Hawking, one of the world's leading physicists, is severely disabled by amyotrophic lateral sclerosis (ALS), a rare progressive degenerative disease of the spinal cord. Because he cannot activate his voice box or move his lips, Hawking types his words into an electronic voice synthesizer that "speaks" for him. He uses his thumbprint to autograph his books. "I have been lucky," he says. "I don't have anything to be angry about."

gory or another. It is a mistaken assumption that everything has to fit neatly somewhere.

A related problem that occurs any time we categorize people is **labeling.** You may remember Kermit the Frog from *Sesame Street* sharing with us that "It's not easy being green." Something in human nature causes us to use a label, even one as superficial as skin color, to characterize the totality of an individual ("He's green . . . he's different from me"). We see the same phenomenon among psychological disorders ("He's a schizo"). Furthermore, if the disorder is associated with an impairment in cognitive or behavioral functioning, the label itself has negative connotations, and becomes pejorative.

Once labeled, individuals with a disorder may identify with the negative connotations associated with the label. This affects their self-esteem. Attempts to document the detrimental effects of labeling have produced mixed results (S. Segal, 1978), but if you think of your own reactions to the mentally ill, you will probably recognize the tendency to generalize inappropriately from the label. We have to remember that terms in psychopathology do not describe people, but identify patterns of behavior that may or may not occur in certain circumstances. Thus, whether the disorder is medical or psychological, we must resist the temptation to identify the person with the disorder: Note the different implications of "John is a diabetic" and "John is a person who has diabetes."

Creating a Diagnosis

During the extensive deliberations by thousands of people that led to the publication of DSM-IV, a number of potentially new diagnostic categories were considered. Since one of us was a member of the task force, we can offer brief examples to illustrate how diagnostic categories are created.

MIXED ANXIETY–DEPRESSION

Family physicians' offices, clinics, hospitals, and so on are called *primary care settings* because they are where a person goes first with a problem. For years, people coming to these primary care clinics have complained of minor aches and pains that prove to have no physical basis. They also complain of feeling up-tight, down in the dumps, and anxious. Health care professionals examining these individuals report that their symptoms of both anxiety and depression are classic, but not frequent or severe enough to meet criteria for an existing anxiety or mood disorder.

The DSM-IV task force was concerned about issues like this for several reasons. First, since many individuals present with some minor symptoms of a given disorder, it is important to set thresholds high enough that only people who clearly are suffering some impairment will qualify for the category. ("Thresholds" are the minimum number of criteria required to meet the definition of a disorder.) The primary reason for this concern is that substantial legal and policy implications are contingent on a diagnosis. That is, someone who presents with a psychological disorder that clearly qualifies for a diagnosis becomes part of the loosely organized medico-legal system and is eligible to ask (or sue) the government or private insurance companies for financial reimbursement or disability payments. This money actually comes from taxpayers who are already burdened by skyrocketing health care costs. Clearly, if the diagnostic system includes people who have only minor symptoms, who are not particularly impaired and just "feel down" from time to time, or who don't like their job and want disability (an all too common request in mental health clinics), the health care system would be even more strained and have fewer resources to treat the seriously impaired. On the other hand, if people are experiencing considerable suffering and impairment in functioning, it is important that they be covered in any health care system. For these reasons, minor complaints of dysphoric mood, characterized by vague complaints of anxiety and depression, were not considered sufficiently severe to constitute a formal diagnosis.

In 1989, Klerman, reporting on a large study by Wells et al. (1989), found that patients who claimed to be anxious and mildly depressed *were* impaired in a number of areas, when compared with normal controls and with patients with chronic medical conditions. Substantial impairment was present in the areas of physical and social functioning, not only causing patients to miss work but also interfering with their functioning in the home; it was *worse* than the impairment of many patients with chronic medical conditions. The evidence also suggested that these individuals were already imposing an *enormous* burden on the health care system by appearing in large numbers at community clinics and the offices of family doctors. Barrett, Barrett, Oxman, and Gerber (1988), assessing patients from a rural primary care practice, found that as many as 14.4% of patients presented with principal complaints of anxiety and depression. Other studies also supported this finding (Katon & Roy-Byrne, 1991). Finally, evidence suggested that such people were at greatly increased risk of developing more severe mood or anxiety disorders (Moras et al., 1996).

Therefore, we concluded that it might be very valuable to identify these people and find out more about the etiology, course, and maintenance of the problem. The authors of the ICD–10, recognizing that this phenomenon is prevalent throughout the world, had created a category of mixed anxiety–depression, but they had not defined it or created any criteria that would allow further examination of the potential disorder. Therefore, to explore the possibility of creating a new diagnostic category (Zinbarg & Barlow, 1996; Zinbarg et al., 1994), a study was undertaken that had three specific goals. First, if mental health professionals carefully administered semistructured interviews (the Anxiety Disorders Interview Schedule), would they find patients who fit the new category? Or would careful examination find the criteria for already existing disorders that had been overlooked by health professionals not well trained in identifying psychological disorders? Second, if mixed anxiety–depression did exist, was it really more prevalent in medical primary care settings than in outpatient mental health settings? Third, what set of criteria (for example, types and number of symptoms) would best identify the disorder?

The study to answer these questions was conducted simultaneously in seven different sites around the world (Zinbarg et al., 1994). Results indicated that people presenting with a number of anxious and depressed symptoms, who *did not meet* criteria for an existing anxiety or mood disorder (because they did not have the right mix and/or severity of anxious or depressed symptoms), were common in primary care settings. Furthermore, they were substantially impaired in their occupational and social functioning and experienced a great deal of distress. Additional analysis revealed that such people could be distinguished from people with existing anxiety or mood disorders on the basis of their symptoms. Specifically, they presented with a set of emotional and behavioral symptoms that fall into the general category of *negative affect,* including behaviors such as difficulty sleeping and difficulty concentrating. These behaviors are often part of anxiety and mood disorders but are not specific to either. (Negative affect and its symptoms are described more fully in Chapter 7.) In any case, because these people appeared both anxious and depressed, the potential new category possessed content validity.

This study also established some of the criteria important in determining *construct validity* for the new category of mixed anxiety–depression. However, since the category is so new, we do not have information on additional criteria important in establishing construct validity, such as course, response to treatment, and the extent to which the disorder aggregates in families, and we cannot yet verify the reliability of the diagnosis or anything about predictive validity.

Therefore, the decision of the DSM-IV task force was to place this mixed anxiety–depression diagnosis in the Appendix, which is reserved for new diagnoses under study. It is likely to become a full diagnostic category in future editions, but more research needs to be done first.

PREMENSTRUAL DYSPHORIC DISORDER

This disorder evokes a very different issue that must be considered in the creation of any diagnostic category: bias and stigmatization. Evaluation of this extremely controversial category actually began well before the publication of DSM-III-R in 1987. Clinicians had identified a small group of women who presented with severe and sometimes incapacitating emotional reactions associated with the late luteal phase of their menstrual period (Rivera-Tovar, Pilkonis, & Frank, 1992). Subsequently, proposals were made to consider inclusion of this disorder in the DSM-III-R. In view of the suffering and impairment associated with the condition, the proponents argued, women deserved the attention, care, and financial support that inclusion in a diagnostic category would provide. In addition, as with mixed anxiety–depression, the creation of this category would promote a substantial increase in research into the nature and treatment of the problem.

Nevertheless, arguments against the category were marshaled along several fronts. First, opponents noted that there was relatively little scientific information in either the clinical or research literature on this topic. The existing information was insufficient to warrant the creation of a new diagnostic category. More important were substantial objections that what could be a "normal" endocrinological stage experienced by all or most women would be stigmatized as a psychiatric disorder. The seeming similarities with the once widely accepted category of "hysteria" described in Chapter 1 were also noted. (Remember that this "disorder," characterized by a variety of incapacitating physical complaints without a medical basis, was thought to be caused by the wandering of the uterus.) Questions were raised about whether the disorder would best be described as endocrinological or gynecological rather than mental. Since premenstrual dysphoric disorder occurs only in women, should we include a comparable disorder associated with, for example, aggressiveness related to excessive male hormones?

The DSM-III-R task force decided to place this disorder in the Appendix in the hope of promoting further study. We also wanted to clearly differentiate this syndrome from premenstrual syndrome (PMS), which has less severe and specific premenstrual symptomatology. One way of accomplishing this was by naming the condition *late luteal phase dysphoric disorder* (LLPDD).

After the publication of DSM-III-R, LLPDD attracted a great deal of research attention. By 1991 some observers estimated that one research article per month on LLPDD was published (Gold et al., 1996). A variety of scientific findings began to accrue that supported the inclusion of this disorder in DSM-IV. For example, although the rather vague and less severe symptoms of premenstrual syndrome (PMS) occur in 20% to 40% of women (Severino & Moline, 1989), only a very small proportion of them—about 4.6%—suffer from the more severe and incapacitating symptoms associated with LLPDD (Rivera-Tovar & Frank, 1990). In addition, a substantial number of women with no other psychological disorder meet the criteria for LLPDD. Among other findings supporting the inclusion of this disorder in DSM-IV are abnormalities in several biological systems that are associated with clinically significant premenstrual dysphoria (Gold et al., 1996) and the revelation that several different types of treatment show some promise of being effective against LLPDD (for example, Stone, Pearlstein, & Brown, 1991). Hurt and colleagues, in a reanalysis of data from 670 women, recommended a set of criteria for this disorder that were not very different from those proposed in DSM-III-R (Hurt et al., 1992).

Nevertheless, arguments continue against including this disorder in the diagnostic system. Most of them cite the issue of stigmatization, warning that recognition might confirm the cultural belief that menstruation and resulting disability make women unfit for positions of responsibility. (There have been several cases where accusations of the less severe condition of PMS have been used against a mother in an attempt to win child custody for the father; see Gold et al., 1996). Also, elevating the condition to the category of a disorder might sustain and strengthen religious and cultural taboos associated with the menstrual cycle that range from prohibition of sexual intercourse to actual banishment from regular living quarters. In Orthodox Judaism, women are required to take a ritual communal bath called the *mikvah* after each period to cleanse themselves of menstrual impurities. Only then can they resume physical and sexual contact with their husbands (Reik, 1964). Those arguing against the disorder also point out that some of the symptoms are associated with anger, which would not be viewed as inappropriate in a male. Only in a female does society presume that anger signifies something is wrong.

What would you do? Would you call this condition a disorder in order to ensure that women suffering from it receive the attention and treatment they need? Or would you be more concerned with the potential for misuse of the diagnosis, particularly the social stigmatization? It is interesting that many women with this disorder are quite comfortable with the label. Some women presenting with other psychological disorders, such as depression, refuse to accept the suggestion that they have a "psychiatric problem," insisting that it is really premenstrual syndrome (Rapkin, Chang, & Reading, 1989). Early in 1994 the DSM-IV task force decided to retain the disorder in the Appendix as needing further study. Among other problems, the committee wanted to see more epidemiological data using the new criteria and to examine more carefully the data on the relation of this problem to existing mood disorders.

Several additional research findings indicated that the name *late luteal phase dysphoric disorder* was not entirely ac-

curate, because the symptoms may not be exclusively related to the endocrine state of the late luteal phase. Therefore, the name has been changed to *premenstrual dysphoric disorder*.

Conclusions

The process of changing the criteria for existing diagnoses and creating new ones will continue as our science advances. New findings on brain circuits, cognitive processes, and cultural factors that affect our behavior could date diagnostic criteria relatively quickly. Nevertheless, the enormous international effort that went into the construction of DSM-IV and ICD-10 is not likely to be repeated soon. At present, the best estimates are that attempts will not be made to update the system for another 10 years or so. With this in mind, we can turn our attention to the current state of our knowledge about a variety of major psychological disorders. Beginning with Chapter 5, we attempt to predict the next major scientific breakthroughs affecting diagnostic criteria and definitions of disorders. But first we review the all-important area of research methods and strategies used to establish new knowledge of psychopathology.

 **Summary**

Assessing Psychological Disorders

- Clinical assessment is the systematic evaluation and measurement of psychological, biological, and social factors in an individual with a possible psychological disorder; diagnosis is the process of determining that those factors meet all the criteria for a specific psychological disorder.
- Reliability, validity, and standardization are important components in determining the value of a psychological assessment.
- To assess various aspects of psychological disorders, clinicians may first interview and take an informal mental status exam of the patient. More systematic observations of behavior are called behavioral assessment.
- A variety of psychological tests can be used during assessment, including projective tests, in which the patient responds to ambiguous stimuli by "projecting" unconscious thoughts; personality inventories, in which the patient takes a self-report questionnaire designed to assess personal traits; and intelligence testing that provides a score known as an intelligence quotient.
- Biological aspects of psychological disorders may be assessed through neuropsychological testing that is designed to identify possible areas of brain dysfunction. Neuroimaging can be used more directly to identify brain structure and function. Finally, psychophysiological assessment refers to measurable changes in the nervous system reflecting emotional or psychological events that might be relevant to a psychological disorder.

Diagnosing Psychological Disorders

• The term *classification* refers to any effort to construct groups or categories and to assign objects or people to the categories on the basis of their shared attributes or relations. Methods of classification include classical categorical, dimensional, and prototypical approaches. Our current system of classification, the *Diagnostic and Statistical Manual, Fourth Edition (DSM-IV)*, is based on a prototypical approach, in which certain essential characteristics are identified but certain "nonessential" variations do not necessarily change the classification. The DSM-IV categories are based on empirical findings to identify the criteria for each diagnosis. Although this system is the best to date in terms of scientific underpinnings, it is far from perfect, and research continues on the most useful way to classify psychological disorders.

Key Terms

clinical assessment
diagnosis
reliability
validity
standardization
mental status exam
behavioral assessment
projective tests
personality inventories
intelligence quotient
neuropsychological testing
false positives
false negatives
neuroimaging
psychophysiological assessment
electroencephalogram (EEG)
idiographic strategy
nomothetic strategy
classification
taxonomy
nosology
nomenclature
classical categorical approach
dimensional approach
prototypical approach
comorbidity
labeling

Answers to Concept Checks

3.1
1. thought processes
2. appearance and behavior
3. sensorium
4. mood and affect
5. intellectual functioning

3.2
1. R, V
2. NR, NV
3. R, V
4. NR, NV

Research Methods

To a person uninstructed in natural history, his country or seaside stroll is a walk through a gallery filled with wonderful works of art, nine-tenths

of which have their faces turned to the wall.

Thomas Henry Huxley
On the Educational Value of the Natural History Sciences

Behavioral scientists explore human behavior the same way other scientists study the path of a comet or the AIDS virus: They use the scientific method. As we've already seen, abnormal behavior is a challenging subject because of the interaction of biological and psychological dimensions. Rarely are there any simple answers to such questions as "Why do some people have hallucinations?" or "How do you treat someone who is suicidal?"

In addition to the obvious complexity of human nature, another factor that makes an objective study of abnormal behavior difficult is the inaccessibility of many important aspects of this phenomenon. We can't "get inside the minds" of people except indirectly. Fortunately, some very creative individuals have accepted this challenge and have developed many ingenious methods for scientifically studying *what* behaviors constitute problems, *why* people suffer from behavioral disorders, and *how* to treat these problems. Some of you will ultimately contribute to this important field by applying the methods described in this chapter. Many critical questions regarding abnormal behavior have yet to be answered, and we hope that some of you will be inspired to take them on. However, understanding research methods is extremely important for all of you. You or someone close to you may need the services of a psychologist, psychiatrist, or other mental health provider. You may have questions such as these:

- Should childhood aggression be cause for concern, or is it a phase that my child will grow out of?
- The *Today* show just reported that increased exposure to sunlight alleviates depression. Instead of seeing a therapist, should I buy a ticket to Hawaii?
- I read a story about the horrors of shock therapy. Should I advise my neighbor not to let her daughter have this treatment?
- My brother has been in therapy for 3 years but doesn't seem to be any better. Should I tell him to look elsewhere for help?
- My mother is still in her fifties but seems to be forgetting things. Friends tell me this is natural as you grow older. Should I be concerned?

To answer such questions you need to be a good consumer of research. When you understand the correct ways of obtaining information—that is, research methodology—you will know when you are dealing with fact and not fiction.

Knowing the difference between a fad and an established approach to a problem can be the difference between months of suffering and a quick resolution to a disturbing problem.

Important Concepts

As we have said from the start, we will examine several aspects of abnormal behavior. First, "What problems cause distress and impair functioning?" Second, "Why do people behave in unusual ways?" And third, "How do we help them behave in more adaptive ways?" The first question is about the nature of the problems people report; we explore research strategies that help us answer this question. The second question considers the causes, or *etiology,* of abnormal behavior; we explore strategies for discovering why a disorder occurred. Finally, because we want to help people who have disorders, we describe how researchers evaluate treatments. Before we discuss specific strategies, however, we must consider several general ways of evaluating research.

Basic Components of a Research Study

The basic research process is really very simple. You start with an educated guess, called a **hypothesis,** about what you expect to find. When you decide how you want to test this hypothesis, you have a **research design** that includes the aspects you want to measure in the people you are studying (the **dependent variable**), and the influences on their behaviors (the **independent variable**). Finally, two forms of validity are specific to research studies: **internal** and **external validity.** Internal validity is the extent to which we can be confident that the independent variable is causing the dependent variable to change. External validity refers to how well the results relate to things outside your study; that is, how well your findings describe similar individuals who were not among the study subjects. Although we will discuss a variety of research strategies, they all have these basic elements. Table 4.1 shows the essential components of a research study.

HYPOTHESIS
A close friend lost his younger brother in a motorcycle accident. The senseless loss of this fine young man created a tremendous amount of grief and bitterness. The family wanted to know *why*—what was the purpose, the reason for this tragedy?

Human beings look for order and purpose in our lives. We want to know why the world works as it does, why people behave the way they do. Kegan (cited in Lefrancois, 1990) describes us as "meaning-making" organisms, constantly striving to make sense of what is going on around us. It is interesting to note that this orientation is reflected in such physiological processes as vision. We often see only

table 4.1 The Basic Components of a Research Study

Component	Description
Hypothesis	An educated guess or statement to be supported by data.
Research design	The plan for testing the hypothesis. Affected by the question addressed, by the hypothesis, and by practical considerations.
Dependent variable	Some aspect of the phenomenon that is measured and is expected to be changed or influenced by the independent variable.
Independent variable	The aspect that is manipulated or that is thought to influence the change in the dependent variable.
Internal validity	The extent to which the results of the study can be attributed to the independent variable.
External validity	The extent to which the results of the study can be generalized or applied outside the immediate study.

parts of things—the side of a person's head, the way she walks down a hall. Yet the brain can take these parts and put them together to make a meaningful whole—your best friend.

The familiar search for meaning and order also characterizes the field of abnormal behavior. Almost by definition, abnormal behavior defies the regularity and predictability we want. It is this departure from the norm that makes the study of abnormal behavior so intriguing. In an attempt to make sense of these phenomena, behavioral scientists construct hypotheses and then test them. Hypotheses are nothing more than educated guesses about the world. You may believe that watching violent television programs will cause children to be more aggressive. You may think that bulimia is influenced by media depictions of "ideal" female body types. You may suspect that someone who is abused as a child is likely to become a spouse and child abuser later on. These concerns are all testable hypotheses about different phenomena.

Once a scientist decides what to study, the next step is to put it in words that are unambiguous and in a form that is testable. A study of depression among women can serve as an example. Kenneth Kendler and his associates (Kendler, Kessler, Neale, Heath, & Eaves, 1993) studied 680 female–female twins (both identical and fraternal) for several years to examine the incidence of depression. These researchers posed the following hypothesis: "The probability that a woman will experience an episode of major depression is influenced by a number of 'risk factors,' such as premature loss of a parent, stressful life events, previous episodes of depression, and genetic influences." The way the hypothesis is stated suggests the researchers already know the answer to their question. Obviously, they won't know what they will find until the study is completed, but phrasing the hypothesis in this way makes it testable. If, for example, major depression isn't predicted by any of these risk factors, they may not be involved in depression; if only one of the risk factors is involved, then the other factors may not be involved. This concept of **testability** (the ability to support the hypothesis) is important for science because it allows us to say that in this case, either (a) depression is predicted by these multiple influences, so let's study them more, or (b) depression is not predicted by these multiple influences, so let's look elsewhere.

When they develop an experimental hypothesis, researchers also specify dependent and independent variables. A dependent variable is what is expected to change or be influenced by the study. Psychologists studying abnormal behavior typically measure an aspect of the disorder such as overt behaviors, thoughts, and feelings, or biological symptoms. In Kendler's study the main dependent variable was episodes of major depression among twins, as measured across several years by structured interviews of the kind we described in Chapter 3, with the goal of predicting what would cause similar episodes. Independent variables are those factors thought to affect the dependent variables. In Kendler's study, they included stressful life events, previous episodes of depression, and genetics. In treatment studies, the treatment itself is expected to influence behavior and is therefore another independent variable.

INTERNAL AND EXTERNAL VALIDITY

Suppose Kendler found that, unknown to him, many of the twins took antidepressant drugs during the entire time he was studying them. The drugs would have affected the number of episodes of depression they experienced, in a way not related to factors such as stressful life events or genetics, which would completely change the meaning of his results. This situation, which relates to internal validity, is called a **confound,** and is any factor occurring in a study that makes the results uninterpretable. In the Kendler study, we wouldn't know how antidepressant drugs affected the results or what the results would mean for women not taking such drugs. The degree to which confounds are present in a study is a measure of internal validity, the extent to which the results can be explained by the independent variable. Such a hypothetical confound in Kendler's study would have made his research internally *in*valid because it would have reduced his ability to explain the results in terms of the independent variables of stressful life events, previous depressive episodes, and genetics.

Scientists use many strategies to ensure internal validity in their studies, three of which we discuss here: control groups, randomization, and analog models. In a **control group,** people are similar to the experimental group in every way *except* that members of the experimental group are exposed to the independent variable and those in the control group are not. Because researchers can't prevent people from being exposed to many things around them that could affect the outcomes of the study, they try to compare people who receive the treatment with people who go through similar experiences except for the treatment (control group). Control groups help rule out alternative explanations for results, thereby strengthening internal validity.

Randomization is the process of assigning people to different research groups in such a way that each person has an equal chance of being placed in any group. Placing people in groups by flipping a coin or using a random number table helps improve internal validity by eliminating any systematic bias in assignment, but it does not necessarily eliminate bias in your group. We will see later that people sometimes "put themselves in groups" and that this self-selection can affect the study results. Perhaps a researcher treating people with depression offers them the choice of being either in the treatment group, which requires coming into the clinic twice a week for two months, or in a wait-list control group, which means waiting until some later time to be treated. The most severely depressed individuals will probably not be motivated to come to frequent treatment sessions and so will choose the wait-list group. If members of the treated group are less depressed after several months, it could be because of the treatment or because group members were less depressed to begin with. Groups assembled randomly avoid these problems.

Analog models create in the controlled conditions of the laboratory aspects that are comparable (analogous) to the phenomenon under study. A bulimia researcher could ask volunteers to binge eat in the laboratory, questioning them before they ate, while they were eating, and after they finished to learn whether eating in this way made them feel more or less anxious, guilty, and so on. If she used volunteers of any age, gender, race, or background, she could rule out influences on the subjects' attitudes about eating that she might not be able to dismiss if the group contained only people with bulimia. In this way, such "artificial" studies help improve internal validity.

In a research study, internal and external validity often seem to be in opposition. On the one hand, we want to be able to control as many different things as possible in order to conclude that the independent variable (the aspect of the study we manipulated) was responsible for the changes in the dependent variables (the aspects of the study we expected to change). On the other hand, we want the results to apply to people other than the subjects of the study and in other settings; this is **generalizability,** the extent to which results apply to *everyone* with a particular disorder. If we control the total environment of the people who participate in the study so that only the independent variable changes, the result is not relevant to the "real world." Kendler and his associates limited the participants in their study to women partly to control for gender-related causes of depression. Although this limitation eliminates gender differences, thereby increasing internal validity, it also prohibits conclusions about males, thereby decreasing external validity. Internal and external validity are in this way often inversely related. Researchers constantly try to balance these two concerns

and, as we see later in this chapter, the best solution for achieving both internal and external validity may be to conduct several related studies.

Statistical versus Clinical Significance

Moving from purely subjective to more objective ways of studying behavior has led to extraordinary advances in our understanding of abnormality. Yet one aspect of this evolution has received considerable criticism: the use of statistical significance to determine the presence of effects in research.

Statistics is part of psychology's evolution from a pre-scientific to a scientific discipline. Statisticians gather, analyze, and interpret data from research. In psychological research, statistical significance typically means that the probability of obtaining the observed effect by chance is small. As an example, consider a group of older adults with mental retardation who also have self-injurious behavior—hitting, slapping, or scratching themselves until they cause physical damage. Suppose they participate in a treatment program and are observed to hurt themselves less often than a similar group of adults who do not receive treatment. If a statistical test of these results indicates that the difference in behavior is expected to occur by chance less than five times in every 100 experiments, then we can say that the difference is statistically significant. But is it an *important* difference? The difficulty is in the difference between **statistical** and **clinical significance.**

Suppose we were researching a new drug treatment for the self-injurious behaviors of older adults with retardation. We examined one group that received medication and a second group that received a placebo. To learn whether the new drug diminished self-injury, we used a rating scale to note how frequently each person hit himself or herself. At the beginning of the study, all the subjects hit themselves an average of 10 times per day. At the end of the study, we added all the scores on the rating scales and found that the group on medication received lower scores than the untreated group and that the results were statistically significant. Is this new treatment something we should recommend for all people who hit themselves?

Closer examination of the results leads to concern about *the size of the effect.* Suppose when you look at the people who were rated as improved you find that they still hit themselves about six times per day. Even though the frequency is lower, they are still hurting themselves. Some hit themselves just a few times but produce serious cuts, bruises, and contusions. This suggests that your statistically significant results may not be clinically significant; that is, important to the people who hurt themselves. The distinction would be particularly important if there were another medical treatment that did not reduce the incidence of self-hitting so much but reduced the severity of the blows, causing less harm.

Fortunately, concern for the clinical significance of results has led researchers to develop statistical methods that address not just the fact that groups are different, but how large these differences are, or *effect size* (for example, Sedlmeier & Gigerenzer, 1989). Calculating the actual statistical measures involves fairly sophisticated procedures that take into account how much each treated and untreated person in a research study improves or worsens (Jacobson & Truax, 1991; Speer, 1992). In other words, instead of just looking at the results of the group as a whole, individual differences are considered as well. Some researchers have used more subjective ways of determining whether truly important change has resulted from treatment. The behavioral scientist Montrose Wolf (1978) advocated the assessment of what he calls *social validity*. This technique involves obtaining input from the person being treated as well as significant others about the importance of the changes that have occurred. In the example

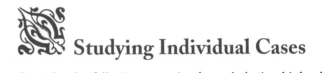
Studying people as part of a group sometimes masks individual differences.

above, we might ask employers and family members if they thought the medication led to truly important reductions in self-injurious behavior. If the effect of the treatment is large enough to impress those who are directly involved, the treatment effect is clinically significant. Statistical techniques of measuring effect size and assessing subjective judgments of change will let us better evaluate the results of our treatments.

The "Average" Client

Too often we look at results from studies and make generalizations about the group, ignoring individual differences. Kiesler (1966) labeled the tendency to see all participants as one homogeneous group the *patient uniformity myth*. Comparing groups according to their mean scores ("Group A improved by 50% over Group B") hides important differences in individual reactions to our interventions.

The patient uniformity myth leads researchers to make inaccurate generalizations about disorders and their treatments. It would not be surprising if a researcher studying the treatment of self-injurious behavior concluded that a drug was a good treatment. Yet suppose we found that, although some participants did improve with treatment, others actually got worse. Such differences would be averaged out in the analysis of the group as a whole, but for the person whose head banging increased with the new drug, it would make little difference that "on the average" people improved. Because people who display self-injurious behavior differ in such ways as age, cognitive abilities, gender, and history of treatment, a simple group comparison may be misleading. Practitioners who deal with all types of disorders understand the heterogeneity of their clients and therefore do not know whether treatments that are statistically significant will be

effective for a given individual. In our discussions of various disorders, we will return to this issue.

Studying Individual Cases

Consider the following scenario: A psychologist thinks she has discovered a new disorder. She has observed several men who seem to have very similar characteristics. All complain of a specific sleep disorder: falling asleep at work. Each man has obvious cognitive impairments that were evident during the initial interviews, and are very similar physically, each with significant hair loss and a pear-shaped physique. Finally, their personality styles are extremely egocentric, or self-centered. On the basis of these preliminary observations, the psychologist has come up with a tentative name, the *Homer Simpson Disorder*, and she has decided to investigate this condition and possible treatments. But what is the best way to begin exploring a relatively unknown disorder? One way is to use the **case study method,** investigating intensively one or more individuals who display the behavioral and physical patterns (Kazdin, 1981).

One way to describe the case study method is by noting what it is not. It does not use the scientific method. Few efforts are made to ensure internal validity and, typically, many confounding variables are present that can interfere with conclusions. Instead, the case study method relies on a clinician's observations of differences between one person or group with a disorder, people with other disorders, and people with no psychological disorders. The clinician usually collects as much information as possible, to obtain a detailed description of the person. Historically, interviewing the person under study yields a great deal of information on personal and family background, education, health, and work history, as well as the person's opinions about the nature and causes of the problems being studied.

Case studies are important in the history of psychology. Sigmund Freud developed psychoanalytic theory and the methods of psychoanalysis on the basis of his observations of dozens of cases. Freud and Breuer's description of Anna O. (see Chapter 1) led to development of the clinical technique known as free association. Sex researchers Virginia Johnson and William Masters based their work on many case studies and helped shed light on numerous myths regarding sexual behavior (Masters & Johnson, 1966). Joseph Wolpe, author of the landmark book *Psychotherapy by Reciprocal Inhibition* (1958), based his work with systematic desensitization on over 200 cases. As our knowledge of psychological disorders has grown, we have relied less and less on the case study method.

One difficulty with depending heavily on individual cases is that sometimes coincidences occur that are irrelevant to the condition under study. As a student, I learned firsthand the power of coincidence. I was in a large lab room working on the university computer system. There were almost 100 terminals. I was just learning how to use the keyboard, which included a rather ominous looking red button with nothing written on it. As I worked, the button seemed to call out to be pressed. During a lull in my work, I pressed the button and every terminal in the room went blank. Feeling panicky, I looked around to see if anyone knew I was to blame for this catastrophe. There was a great deal of exasperation and cursing, but it was not directed at me. For weeks, I was convinced that I had knocked out the mainframe computer, even though the shutoff was the result of a technical problem in the mainframe itself. Only after describing the incident to a good friend did I learn that I could not have caused the shutdown. I had been part of a rather convincing coincidence.

Unfortunately, more meaningful coincidences in people's lives often lead to mistaken conclusions about what causes certain conditions and what treatment appears to be effective. Because a case study does not have the controls of an experimental study, the results may be unique to a particular person without our realizing it or may derive from a special combination of factors that are not obvious. We are constantly exposed to abnormal behavior through the media. Just before mass murderer Ted Bundy was executed in Florida, he proclaimed that pornography was to blame for his abhorrent behavior. The case of Jeffrey Dahmer, who killed, mutilated, and cannibalized his victims, is known throughout the world. Attempts have been made to discover childhood experiences that could possibly explain his adult behavior. What conclusions should we draw? Did Ted Bundy have valuable insight into his own behavior, or was he attempting to evade responsibility? Can acquaintances and friends of the Dahmer family shed accurate light on his development? We must be careful about concluding anything from such sensational portrayals.

Researchers in cognitive psychology point out that the general public and researchers themselves are often, unfor-

tunately, more highly influenced by dramatic accounts than by scientific evidence (Nisbett & Ross, 1980). Remembering our tendency to ignore this fact, we highlight research findings in this book. To advance our understanding of the nature, causes, and treatment of abnormal behavior, we must guard against premature and inaccurate conclusions.

Research by Correlation

One of the fundamental questions posed by scientists is whether two variables relate to each other. A statistical relationship between two variables is called a **correlation.** For example, is autism related to damage in the cerebellum? Are people with depression more likely to have negative attributions? Is the frequency of hallucinations higher among older people? The answers depend on determining how one variable (number of hallucinations) is related to another (age). Unlike experimental designs, which involve manipulating or changing conditions, correlational designs are used to study phenomena just as they occur. The result of a correlational study—whether variables occur together—is important to the ongoing search for knowledge about abnormal behavior.

One of the clichés of science is that a correlation does not imply causation. Two things occurring together do not imply that one caused the other. For example, the occurrence of marital problems in families is correlated with behavior problems in children (Emery, 1982; Reid & Crisafulli, 1990). If you conduct a correlational study in this area you will find that in families with marital problems you tend to see children with behavior problems; in families with fewer marital problems, you are likely to find children with fewer behavior problems. The most obvious conclusion is that having marital problems will cause children to misbehave. If only it were as simple as that! The nature of the relationship between marital discord and childhood behavior problems can be explained in a number of ways. It may be that problems in a marriage cause disruptive behavior in the children. However, some evidence suggests that the opposite may be true as well: The disruptive behavior of children may cause marital problems (Rutter & Giller, 1984). In addition, evidence suggests genetic influences may play a role in conduct disorders (Rutter et al., 1990) and in marital discord (McGue & Lykken, 1992).

This example points out the problems in interpreting the results of a correlational study. We know that variable "A" (marital problems) is correlated with variable "B" (child behavior problems). We do not know from these studies whether A causes B (marital problems cause child problems), whether B causes A (child problems cause marital problems), or whether some third variable "C" causes both (genes influence both marital problems and child problems).

In another example, allergies and depression may be related. Research reveals a surprisingly high correlation between allergic reactions and depressive symptoms (I. R. Bell, Jasnoski, Kagan, & King, 1991). But what causes what?

Does depression make people more likely to have allergies (A causes B)? Does the presence of allergies cause people to be depressed (B causes A)? Or does some common underlying biological factor make people susceptible to both allergies and depression (C causes A and B)? At least one theory of this relationship points to the last explanation, with a complex neurochemical susceptibility resulting in a predisposition to both allergies and depression (C causes A and B) (Marshall, 1993).

The associations between marital discord and child problems and between allergies and depression represent a **positive correlation.** This means that great strength or quantity in one variable (a great deal of marital distress) is associated with great strength or quantity in the other variable (more child disruptive behavior). At the same time, lower strength or quantity in one variable (marital distress) is associated with lower strength or quantity in the other (disruptive behavior). If you have trouble conceptualizing statistical concepts, you can think about this mathematical relationship in the same way you would a social relationship. Two people who are getting along well tend to go places together: "Where I go, you will go!" The correlation (or **correlation coefficient**) is represented as +1.00. The plus sign means there is a positive relationship, and the 1.00 that it is a "perfect" relationship, in which the people are inseparable. Obviously, two people who like each other do not go everywhere together. The strength of their relationship ranges between 0.00 and 1.00 (0.00 means no relationship exists). The higher the number, the stronger the relationship, whether the number is positive or negative (for example, a correlation of −.80 is "stronger" than a correlation of +.75). You would expect two strangers, for example, to have a relationship of 0.00 because their behavior is not related; they sometimes end up in the same place together, but this occurs rarely and randomly. Two people who know each other but do not like each other would be represented by a negative sign, with the range of −1.00 to 0.00, and a strong negative relationship would be −1.00, which means "Anywhere you go, I won't be there!"

Using this analogy, allergies and depression have a relatively strong positive correlation represented by a number such as +.50. They tend to go together. On the other hand, other variables are strangers to each other. Schizophrenia

and height are not related at all, so they don't go together, and probably would be represented by a number close to 0.00. If A and B have no correlation, their correlation coefficient would approximate 0.00. Other factors have negative relationships: As one increases, the other decreases. (See Figure 4.1 for an illustration of positive and negative correlations.) We used an example of **negative correlation** in Chapter 2, when we discussed social supports and illness. The more social supports that are present, the less likely it is that a person will become ill. The negative relationship between social supports and illness could be represented by a number such as −.40. The next time someone wants to break up with you, ask if the goal is to weaken the strength of your positive relationship to something like +.25 (friends), to become complete strangers at 0.00, or to have an intense negative relationship approximating −1.00 (enemies).

A correlation allows us to see whether a relationship exists between two variables, but not to draw conclusions about whether either variable *causes* the effects. This is a problem of **directionality.** In this case, it means that we do not know whether A causes B, B causes A, or a third variable C causes A and B. Therefore, even an extremely strong relationship between two variables (+.90) means nothing about the direction of causality.

Epidemiological Research

Scientists often think of themselves as detectives, finding the truth by studying clues. One type of correlational research that is very much like the efforts of detectives is called **epidemiology.** Epidemiology is the study of the incidence, distribution, and consequences of a particular problem or set of problems in one or more populations. Epidemiologists expect that by tracking a disorder among many people, they will find important clues to why the disorder exists. One strategy is to determine the **incidence** of a disorder, the estimated number of new cases during a specific period of time. For example, as we will see in Chapter 11, the incidence of new cases of eighth graders using marijuana and cocaine is increasing. A related strategy involves determining **prevalence,** the number of people with a disorder at any one time.

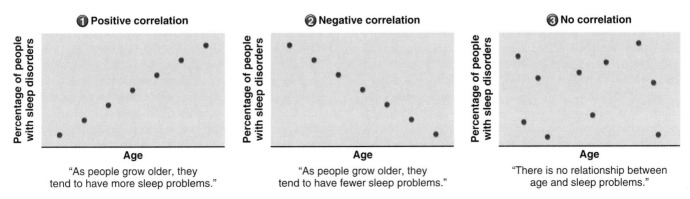

figure 4.1 These three graphs represent hypothetical correlations between age and sleep problems.

The more social supports people have, the less likely it is that they will become ill.

For example, the prevalence of alcohol dependence among Americans in 1990 was estimated at 10.5 million adults (U.S. Department of Health and Human Services, 1990). Epidemiologists study the incidence and prevalence of disorders among different groups of people. For instance, data from epidemiological research indicate that the prevalence of alcohol dependence among African-Americans is lower than among whites (McCreery & Walker, 1993).

Although the primary goal of epidemiology is to determine the extent of medical problems, it is also useful in the study of psychological disorders. In the early 1900s a number of Americans displayed symptoms of a strange mental disorder. Its symptoms were similar to those of organic psychosis, which is often caused by mind-altering drugs or great quantities of alcohol. Many patients appeared to be catatonic (immobile for long periods of time), or exhibited symptoms similar to those of paranoid schizophrenia. Victims were likely to be poor and African-American, which led to speculation about racial and class inferiority. However, using the methods of epidemiological research, Joseph Goldberger found correlations between the disorder and diet, and he identified the cause of the disorder as a deficiency of the B vitamin niacin among people with poor diets. The symptoms were successfully eliminated by niacin therapy and improved diets among the poor. A long-term, widespread benefit of Goldberger's findings was the introduction of vitamin-enriched bread in the 1940s (Gottesman, 1991).

Researchers have used epidemiological techniques to study the effects of stress on psychological disorders. In the spring of 1980, the Mount St. Helens volcano erupted, creating extensive property damage and loss of life. Shore, Tatum, and Vollmer (1986) interviewed families who had lived near the erupting volcano and were directly affected. When these subjects were compared to members of a comparable (control) community that was similar in demographics but had not experienced a similar traumatic event, the researchers found a significantly higher number of psychological disorders in the people who lived near Mount St. Helens. This is a correlational study because the investigators did not manipulate the independent variable. (They didn't set off the volcano!) Despite its correlational nature, the study did show a relationship between stress and psychological problems.

If you have followed the work on the AIDS virus, you have seen how epidemiologists study a problem. By tracking the incidence of this disease among several populations (gay men, intravenous drug users, spouses and children of infected individuals), researchers have obtained important information about how the virus is passed from person to person. They inferred from the types of behaviors engaged in by members of these groups that the virus was probably spread by the transfer of bodily fluids through unprotected sex or by nonsterile hypodermic needles. Like other types of correlational research, epidemiological research can't tell us conclusively what causes a particular phenomenon. However, knowledge about the prevalence and course of psychological disorders is extremely valuable to our understanding because it points researchers in the right direction.

Research by Experiment

An **experiment** involves the manipulation of an independent variable and the observation of its effects. We manipulate the independent variable to answer the question of causality. If we observe a correlation between social supports and psychological disorders, we can't conclude which of these factors influenced the other. We can, however, change the extent of social supports and see whether there is an accompanying change in the prevalence of psychological disorders—in other words, do an experiment.

What will this experiment tell us about the relationship between these two variables? If we increase social supports and find no change in the frequency of psychological disorders, it *may* mean that lack of such supports does not cause psychological problems. On the other hand, if we find that psychological disorders diminish with increased social support, we can be more confident that nonsupport does contribute to them. However, because we are never 100% confident that our experiments are internally valid—that there are no other possible explanations—we are cautious about interpreting our results. In the following section, we describe different ways researchers conduct experiments and consider how each one brings us closer to understanding abnormal behavior.

Group Experimental Designs

Correlational researchers observe groups to see how different variables are associated. In group experimental designs, researchers are more active. They actually change an independent variable to see how the behavior of the people in the group is affected.

Suppose researchers design an intervention to help reduce insomnia in older adults, who are particularly affected by the condition (Mellinger, Balter, & Uhlenhuth, 1985). They treat 20 individuals and follow them for 10 years to learn whether their sleep patterns improve. The treatment is the independent variable; that is, it would not have occurred naturally. They then assess the members to learn whether their behavior changed as a function of what the researchers did. Introducing or withdrawing a variable in a way that would not have occurred naturally is also called *manipulating a variable.*

Unfortunately, a decade later the researchers find that the adults that were treated for sleep problems still, as a group, sleep less than eight hours per night. Is the treatment a failure? Maybe not. The question that can't be answered in this study is what would have happened to group members if they hadn't been treated. Perhaps their sleep patterns would have been worse. But we can't go back in time like Kathleen Turner in *Peggy Sue Got Married* or Michael J. Fox in *Back to the Future* to see what would have happened with no help, so how is it possible to find out?

CONTROL GROUPS

One answer to the "what if" dilemma is to use a control group—people who are similar to the experimental group in every way except that they are not exposed to the independent variable. The researchers also follow this group of people, assess them 10 years later, and look at their sleep patterns over this time. They probably observe that, without intervention, people tend to sleep fewer hours as they get older (Bootzin, Engle-Friedman, & Hazelwood, 1983). Members of the control group, then, might sleep significantly less than people in the treated group, who might themselves sleep somewhat less than they did 10 years earlier. The control group allows the researchers to see that their treatment did help the treated subjects keep their sleep time from decreasing further.

Ideally, a control group is nearly identical to the subject group in such things as age, gender, socioeconomic backgrounds, and the problems they are reporting. Furthermore, a researcher would do the same assessments before and after the independent variable manipulation (for example, a treatment) to people in both groups. Any later differences between the groups after the change would, therefore, be attributable only to what was changed.

People in a treatment group often expect to get better. When behavior changes as a result of a person's expectation of change rather than as a result of any manipulation by an experimenter, the phenomenon is known as a **placebo effect.** Conversely, people in the control group may be disappointed that they are not receiving treatment. Depending on the type of disorder they experience (for instance, depression), disappointment may make them worse. This phenomenon would also make the treatment group look better by comparison.

One way researchers have addressed the expectation concern is through **placebo control groups.** The word *placebo* (which means "I shall please") typically refers to inactive medications such as sugar pills. The placebo is given to members of the control group to make them believe they are getting treatment (Parloff, 1986). A placebo control in a medication study can be carried out with relative ease because people in the untreated group receive something that *looks like* the medication that is administered to the treatment group. In psychological treatments, however, it is not always easy to devise something that people believe may help them but does not include the component the researcher believes is effective. Clients in these types of control groups are often given part of the actual therapy—for example, the same homework as the treated group—but not the portions the researchers believe are responsible for improvements.

It is important to note that you can look at the placebo effect as one portion of any treatment (Lambert, Shapiro, & Bergin, 1986). If someone you provide with a treatment improves, you would have to attribute the improvement to a combination of your treatment and the client's expectation of improving (placebo effect). In fact, therapists want their clients to expect improvement; this helps strengthen the treatment. However, when researchers conduct an experi-

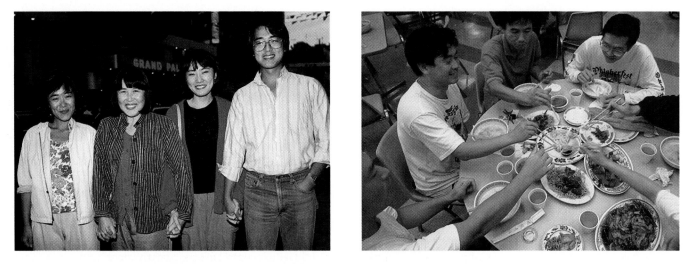

In comparative treatment research, different treatments are administered to comparable groups of people.

ment to determine the portion of a particular treatment that is responsible for the observed changes, the placebo effect is a confound that can dilute the validity of the research. Thus, researchers use a placebo control group to help distinguish the results of positive expectations from the results of actual treatment.

The **double-blind control** is a variant of the placebo control group procedure. As the name suggests, not only are the participants in the study "blind," or unaware of what group they are in or what treatment they are given (single blind), but so are the researchers or therapists providing treatment (double blind). This type of control eliminates the possibility that an investigator might bias the outcome. For example, a researcher comparing two treatments who expected one to be more effective than the other might "try harder" if the "preferred" treatment wasn't working as well as expected. On the other hand, if the treatment that wasn't expected to work seemed to be failing, the researcher might not push as hard to see it succeed. This behavior might not be deliberate, but it could happen. If, however, both the participants and the researchers or therapists are "blind," there is less chance that bias will affect the results.

A double-blind placebo control does not work perfectly in all cases. If medication is part of the treatment, participants and researchers may be able to tell whether or not they have received it by the presence or absence of physical reactions (side effects). Even with purely psychological interventions, participants often know whether or not they are receiving a powerful treatment, and they may alter their expectations for improvement accordingly.

Comparative Treatment Research

As an alternative to using no-treatment control groups to help evaluate results, some researchers compare different treatments. In this design, the researcher gives different treatments to two or more comparable groups of people with a particular disorder, and can then assess how or whether each

treatment helped the people who received it. This is called **comparative treatment research.** In the sleep study we discussed, two groups of older adults could be selected, with one group given medication for insomnia, the other given a cognitive-behavioral intervention, and the results compared.

The *process* and *outcome* of treatment are two important issues to be considered when different approaches are studied. Process research focuses on the mechanisms responsible for behavior change. In an old joke, someone goes to a physician for a new miracle cold cure. The physician prescribes the new drug, and tells the patient that the cold will be gone in 7 to 10 days. As most of us know, colds typically improve in 7 to 10 days without "miracle drugs." The new drug probably does nothing to further the improvement of the patient's cold. The "process" aspect of testing medical interventions involves evaluating the biological mechanisms responsible for change. Does the medication cause lower serotonin levels, for example, and does this account for the changes we observe? Similarly, in looking at psychological interventions, we determine what is "causing" the observed changes. This is important for several reasons. First, if we understand what the "active ingredients" of our treatment are, we can often eliminate aspects that are not important, thereby saving clients time and money. Additionally, knowing what is important about our interventions can help us create more powerful newer versions that may be more effective.

Outcome research focuses on the positive and/or negative results of the treatment. In other words, does it work? Remember, treatment process involves finding out why or how your treatment works. In contrast, treatment outcome involves finding out what changes occur *after* treatment. You probably have guessed by now that even this seemingly simple task becomes more complicated the closer we look at it. Depending on what dependent variables you select to measure, and when and where you assess them, your view of "success" may vary considerably. For example, Greta Francis and Kathleen Hart (1992), who described their work with depressed adolescents in an inpatient (hospital) setting, used a treatment that includes "activity increase" strategies. The goal is to help adolescents become more involved in activities that give them access to positive experiences. Francis and Hart note that, although they observe improvements in depression when the adolescents are in the structured hospital environment, this improvement often disappears outside the hospital.

Do activity increase strategies result in positive treatment outcomes for depressed adolescents? That depends on where you assess their depression. If you look at their outcomes in the hospital, you may see improvement. If you follow them home after discharge, you might conclude that the treatment wasn't effective at all. Again, in evaluating whether a treatment is effective, researchers must carefully define success.

To avoid assembling groups that differ in some important way, researchers use randomization (L. M. Hsu, 1989). They can assign participants to groups in an unbiased way with a variety of techniques, such as using a random numbers table or flipping a coin. The goal of this process is to reduce the chances that the participants are different in a way that will influence the results. Suppose the women in the depression treatment group were also more motivated to improve, and that's why they were willing to come in during the day for treatment. If this were so, the positive results might be related to how motivated the women are. By randomly assigning people to groups, researchers eliminate factors that might influence the outcomes.

Single-Case Experimental Designs

B. F. Skinner's innovations in scientific methodology were among his most important contributions to psychopathology. Skinner formalized the concept of **single-case experimental designs.** This method involves the systematic study of one individual under a variety of experimental conditions; the researcher manipulates an independent variable in ways that reduce the likelihood of confounding explanations. Skinner thought it was much better to know a lot about the behavior of one individual than to make only a few observations of a large group for the sake of presenting the "average" response. Psychopathology is concerned with the suffering of specific people, and this methodology has greatly helped us understand the factors involved in individual psychopathology (Barlow & Hersen, 1984). Many applications throughout this book reflect Skinnerian methods.

Single-case experimental designs differ from case studies in their use of various strategies to improve internal validity, thereby reducing the number of confounding variables. As we will see, these strategies have strengths and weaknesses in comparison with traditional group designs. Although we use examples from treatment research to illustrate the single-case experimental designs, they, like other

research strategies, can help explain why people engage in abnormal behavior as well as how to treat them.

Repeated Measurements

One of the more important strategies used in single-case experimental design is *repeated measurement,* in which a behavior is measured several times instead of only once before you change the independent variable and once afterward. The researcher takes the same measurements over and over to learn how variable the behavior is (how much it changes day to day) and whether it shows any obvious trends (is it getting better or worse?). Suppose a young woman, Wendy, comes into the office complaining about feelings of anxiety. When we ask her to rate the level of her anxiety, she gives it a 9 (10 is the worst). After several weeks of treatment Wendy rates her anxiety at 6. Can we say that the treatment reduced her anxiety? Not necessarily.

Suppose we had measured Wendy's anxiety each day during the weeks before her visit to the office (repeated measurement) and observed that they differed greatly. On particularly good days, she rated her anxiety from 5 to 7. On bad days, it was up between 8 and 10. Suppose further that, even after treatment, her daily ratings continued to range from 5 to 10. The rating of 9 before treatment and 6 after treatment may only have been part of the daily variations she experienced normally. In fact, Wendy could just as easily have had a good day and reported a 6 before treatment, and then had a bad day and reported a 9 after treatment, which would imply that the treatment made her worse!

Repeated measurement is part of each single-subject experimental design. It helps identify how a person is doing before and after intervention and whether the treatment accounted for any changes. Figure 4.2 summarizes Wendy's anxiety and the added information obtained by repeated measurement. The top graph shows Wendy's original before-and-after ratings of her anxiety. The middle graph shows that with daily ratings her reports are variable and that just by chance the previous measurement was probably very misleading. She had good and bad days both before and after treatment and doesn't seem to have changed much.

The bottom graph shows that Wendy's anxiety was on its way down before the treatment, which would also have been obscured with just before-and-after measurements. Maybe she was getting better on her own, and the treatment didn't have much effect. Although the middle graph shows how the **variability** from day to day could be important in an interpretation of the effect of treatment, the bottom graph shows how the **trend** itself can also be important in determining the cause of any change. The three graphs illustrate important parts of the repeated measurements: (a) the **level** or degree of behavior change with different interventions (top); (b) the *variability* or degree of change over time (middle); and (c) the trend or direction of change (bottom). Again, before-and-after scores alone do not necessarily show what is responsible for behavioral changes.

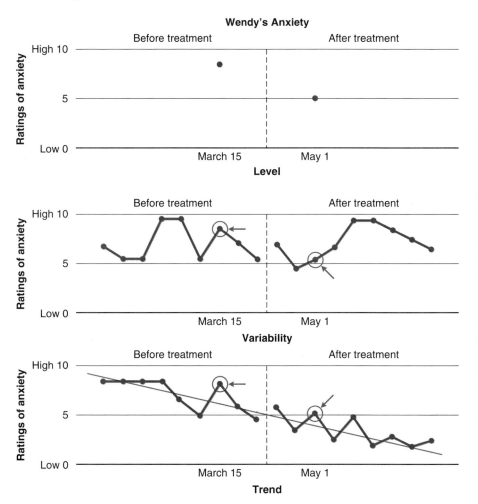

figure 4.2   While graph I gives the impression that Wendy's anxiety level changed significantly, graphs 2 and 3 demonstrate how examining variability and trend can provide much more information about the true nature of the change.

Withdrawal Designs

One of the more common strategies used in single-subject research is a **withdrawal design,** in which a researcher tries to determine whether the independent variable is responsible for changes in behavior. The effect of Wendy's treatment could be tested by stopping it for a period of time to see whether her anxiety increased. A simple withdrawal design has three parts. First, a person's condition is evaluated before treatment, to establish a **baseline.** Then comes the change in the independent variable—in Wendy's case, the beginning of treatment. Last, treatment is withdrawn ("return to baseline") and the researcher assesses whether Wendy's anxiety level changes again as a function of this last step. If with the treatment her anxiety lessens in comparison to baseline, and then worsens again after treatment is withdrawn, the researcher can conclude that the treatment has reduced Wendy's anxiety.

How is this design different from a case study? An important difference is that the change in treatment is designed specifically to show whether treatment caused the changes in behavior. Although case studies often involve treatment, they don't include any effort to learn whether the

person would have improved without the treatment. A withdrawal design gives researchers a better sense of whether or not the treatment itself caused behavior change.

In spite of their advantages, withdrawal designs are not always appropriate. The researcher is required to remove what might be an effective treatment, a decision that is sometimes difficult to justify for ethical reasons. In Wendy's case, a researcher would have to decide there was a sufficient reason to deliberately make her anxious again. A withdrawal design is also unsuitable when the treatment can't be removed. Suppose Wendy's treatment involved visualizing herself on a beach on a tropical island. It would be very difficult—if not impossible—to stop her from imagining something. Similarly, some treatments involve teaching people skills, which might be impossible to unlearn. If Wendy learned how to be less anxious in social situations, how could she revert to being socially apprehensive? Another single-case experimental design, the multiple baseline, addresses this limitation, as we will see shortly.

Several counterarguments support the use of withdrawal designs (Barlow & Hersen, 1984). Treatment is routinely withdrawn when medications are involved. *Drug holidays* are periods of time when the medication is withdrawn so clinicians can determine whether it is responsible for the treatment effects. Any medication can have negative side effects, and unnecessary medication should be avoided. Sometimes treatment withdrawal happens naturally. Withdrawal does not have to be prolonged; a very brief withdrawal may still clarify the role of the treatment.

Multiple Baselines

Another single-case experimental design strategy that is used frequently and that doesn't have some of the drawbacks of a withdrawal design is the **multiple baseline.** Rather than stopping the intervention to see whether it is effective, the researcher starts treatment at different times across settings, (home versus school), behaviors (yelling at spouse or boss), or people. After waiting a period of time and taking repeated measures of Wendy's anxiety both at home and at her office (the baseline), the clinician could treat her first at home. When the treatment begins to be effective, intervention could begin at work. If she improves only at home after beginning treatment, but improves at work after treatment is used there also, we could conclude that the treatment was effective. This is an example of using a multiple baseline across settings.

Does internal validity improve with a multiple baseline? Yes. Any time other explanations for results can be ruled out, internal validity is improved. Wendy's anxiety improved only in the settings where it was treated, which rules out competing explanations. If she had won the lottery at the same time treatment started and her anxiety decreased in all situations, we couldn't conclude that her condition was affected by treatment.

Suppose a researcher wanted to assess the effectiveness of a treatment for a child's problem behaviors. Treatment could first focus on the child's crying, then on a second problem, such as fighting with siblings. If the treatment was first effective only in reducing crying, and effective for fighting only after the second intervention, the researcher could conclude that the treatment, not something else, accounted for the improvements. This is a multiple baseline conducted across behaviors.

Single-case experimental designs are sometimes criticized because they tend to involve only a small number of cases, leaving their external validity in doubt. In other words, we can't say that the results we saw with a few people would be the same for everyone. However, although they are called *single-case*, researchers can and often do use these designs with several people at once, in part to address the issue of external validity. We recently studied the effectiveness of a treatment for the severe behavior problems of children with autism and other developmental disabilities (Durand & Carr, 1992). We taught the children to communicate instead of misbehave, using a procedure known as *functional communication training* (we will discuss this in more detail in Chapter 14). Using a multiple

baseline, we introduced this treatment to a group of six children. Our dependent variables were the incidence of the children's behavior problems and their newly acquired communication skills. As Figure 4.3 shows, only when we began

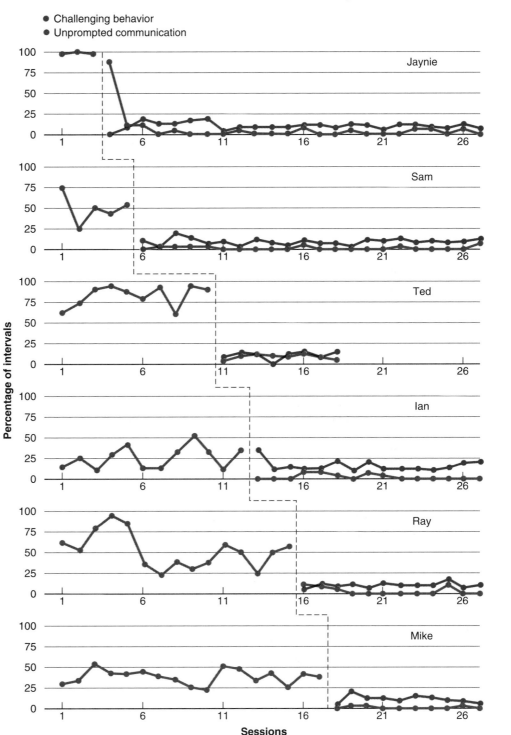

figure 4.3 This figure shows how a multiple baseline design was used to illustrate that the treatment—functional communication training—was responsible for improvements in the children's behaviors. The green circles represent how often each child exhibited behavior problems (called *challenging behavior*), and the blue circles show how often they communicated without help from the teacher (referred to as *unprompted communication*) (adapted from Durand & Carr, 1992).

treatment did each child's behavior problems improve and verbal communication begin. This design let us rule out coincidence or some other change in the children's lives as explanations for the improvements.

Among the advantages of the multiple baseline design in evaluating treatments is that it does not require withdrawal of treatment and, as we've seen, withdrawing treatment is sometimes difficult or impossible. Furthermore, the multiple baseline typically resembles the way treatment would naturally be implemented. A clinician can't help a client with numerous problems simultaneously, but can take repeated measures of the relevant behaviors and observe when they change. A clinician who sees predictable and orderly changes related to where and when the treatment is used can conclude that the treatment is causing the change. It is unlikely that we could provide treatment for all the children with autism at the same time. The delay in delivering treatment therefore helped us determine whether functional communication training was what caused improvements.

■ concept check 4.1

Different areas of study call for different forms of research. Check your understanding of research methods by indicating which would be most appropriate in each of the following situations. Choose from (a) case study; (b) correlation; (c) epidemiology; (d) experiment; and (e) single-case experimental design.

1. A researcher is interested in how noise levels affect a person's concentration. _____

2. A researcher wants to investigate the hypothesis that as children go through adolescence, they listen to louder music. _____

3. A researcher is interested in studying a woman who had no contact with civilization and created her own language.

_____

4. A researcher wants to know how different kinds of music will affect a 5-year-old who has never spoken.

_____

Studying Genetics

We tend to think of genetics in terms of what we inherit from our parents: "He's got his mother's eyes!" "She's thin just like her dad." "She's stubborn like her mother." This very simple view of how we become the people we are suggests that how we look, think, feel, and behave is predetermined. Yet, as we saw in Chapter 2, we now know that the interaction between our genetic makeup and our experiences is what determines how we will develop. The goal of behavioral geneticists (people who study the genetics of behavior) is to tease out the role of genetics in these interactions.

Genetic researchers examine both **phenotypes,** the observable characteristics or behavior of the individual, and **genotypes,** the unique genetic makeup of individual people. For example, a person with Down syndrome typically has some level of mental retardation and a variety of other physical characteristics such as slanted eyes and a thick tongue. These characteristics are the phenotype. The genotype is the extra 21st chromosome that causes Down syndrome.

Our knowledge of the phenotypes of different psychological disorders exceeds our knowledge of the genotypes, but that may soon change. Ever since the discovery of the double helix, scientists have known that we have to map the structure and location of every gene on all 46 chromosomes if we are to fully understand our genetic endowment. Beginning in 1990, scientists around the world, in a coordinated effort, began the **human genome project** (*genome* means all the genes of an organism). Using the latest advances in molecular biology, scientists working on this project are attempting to complete a comprehensive mapping of human genes. This work has identified over 75 genes that contribute to inherited diseases. These exciting findings represent truly astounding progress in deciphering the nature of genetic endowment and its role in psychological disorders.

What follows is a brief review of four traditional research strategies scientists use as they study the interaction between environment and genetics in psychological disorders: family studies, adoption studies, twin studies, and genetic linkage analysis.

Family Studies

In **family studies,** scientists simply examine a behavioral pattern or emotional trait in the context of the family. The member with the trait singled out for study is called the **proband.** If there is a genetic influence, presumably the trait should occur more often in first-degree relatives (parents, siblings, or offspring) than in second-degree or more distant relatives. The presence of the trait in distant relatives, in turn, should be somewhat greater than in the population as a whole. In Chapter 1, we met Judy, the adolescent with blood–injury–injection phobia who fainted at the sight of blood. The tendency of a trait to run in families, or *familial aggregation,* is as high as 60% for this disorder; that is, 60% of the first-degree relatives of someone with blood–injury–injection phobia have the same reaction at least to some degree. This is one of the highest rates of familial aggregation for any psychological disorder we have studied.

The problem with family studies is that family members tend to live together, and there might be something in their shared environment that causes the high familial aggregation. For example, Mom might have developed a very bad reaction to blood as a young girl after witnessing a serious accident. Every time she sees blood she has a very strong emotional response. Because emotions are contagious, the

Although family members often resemble each other, genetics has to do with far more than what we inherit from our parents.

young children watching Mom probably react similarly. In adulthood, they pass it on, in turn, to their own children.

Adoption Studies

How do we separate environmental from genetic influences in families? One way is through **adoption studies.** Scientists identify adoptees who have a particular behavioral pattern or psychological disorder, and attempt to locate first-degree relatives who were raised in different family settings. Suppose a young man has a disorder and scientists discover that his brother was adopted as a baby and brought up in a different home. The researchers would then attempt to find many similar case examples. If they can identify enough sibling pairs (and they usually do after a lot of hard work), they can assess whether siblings brought up in different families display the disorder to the same extent as the original subject. If the brothers raised with different families have the disorder more frequently than would be expected by chance, the researchers can infer that genetic endowment is a contributor.

Twin Studies

Nature presents an elegant experiment that gives behavioral geneticists their closest possible look at the role of genes in development: identical (monozygotic) twins. These twins not only look alike but they have identical genes. Fraternal

(dizygotic) twins, on the other hand, come from different eggs and have only about 50% of their genes in common, as do all first-degree relatives. In **twin studies,** the obvious scientific question is whether identical twins share the same trait—say, fainting at the sight of blood—more often than fraternal twins. Determining whether a trait is shared is easy with some physical traits, such as height. As Plomin (1990) points out, correlations in height for both first-degree relatives and fraternal twins are 0.45, and 0.90 for identical twins. These findings show that heritability of height is about 90%, so approximately 10% of the variance is due to environmental factors. But the case of the child with psychosocial dwarfism (see Chapter 2) reminds us that the 90% estimate is the *average* contribution. An identical twin who was severely physically abused or selectively deprived of proper foods might be substantially different in height from the other twin.

Michael Lyons and his colleagues (1995) conducted a study of antisocial behavior among members of the Vietnam Era Twin Registry. The individuals in the study were about 8,000 twin men who served in the military from 1965 to 1975. The investigators found that among monozygotic (identical) twins there was a greater degree of resemblance for antisocial traits than among dizygotic (fraternal) twins. The difference was greater for adult antisocial behavior than for juvenile antisocial behavior. The researchers concluded that the family environment was a stronger influence than genetic factors on juvenile antisocial traits, and that antisocial behavior in adulthood is more strongly influenced by genetic factors. In other words, after the individual grew up and left his family of origin, early environmental influences mattered less and less.

This way of studying genetics isn't perfect. You can assume that monozygotic twins have the same genetic makeup and that dizygotic twins do not. However, a complicating concern is whether monozygotic twins have the same experiences or environment as dizygotic twins. Some identical twins are dressed alike and are even given similar names. Yet the twins themselves influence each other's behavior, and in some cases, monozygotic twins may affect each other more than dizygotic twins (Carey, 1992).

One way to address this problem is by combining the adoption study and twin study methods. If you can find identical twins, one of whom was adopted as an infant, you can estimate the relative roles of genes and the environment (nature versus nurture) in the development of behavioral patterns.

Genetic Linkage and Association Studies

The results of a series of family, twin, and adoption studies may suggest that a particular disorder has a genetic component, but they can't provide the *location* of the implicated gene or genes. To locate a defective gene, there are two general strategies: **genetic linkage analysis** and **association studies** (Plomin, Owen, & McGuffin, 1994).

The basic principle of genetic linkage analysis is very simple. When a family disorder is studied, other inherited characteristics are assessed at the same time. These other characteristics—called **genetic markers**—are selected because we know their exact location. If a match or "link" is discovered between the inheritance of the disorder and the inheritance of a genetic marker, the genes for the disorder and the genetic marker are probably close together on the same chromosome. For example, bipolar affective disorder (manic depression) was studied in a large Amish family (Egeland et al., 1987). Researchers found that two markers on chromosome 11, genes for insulin and a known cancer gene, were linked to the presence of mood disorder in this family, suggesting that a gene for bipolar affective disorder might be on chromosome 11. Unfortunately, although this is a genetic linkage study, it also illustrates the danger of drawing premature conclusions from research. This linkage study and a second study that purported to find a linkage between bipolar disorder and the X chromosome (Biron et al., 1987) have yet to be replicated; that is, different researchers have not been able to show similar linkages in other families (Gottesman, 1991). This failure casts doubt on the conclusion that one gene is responsible for such a complex disorder. Be mindful of such limitations the next time you read in a newspaper or hear on TV that a gene has been identified as causing some disorder.

Researchers are having a bit more luck with linkage studies of schizophrenia (see Chapter 2, where we note the interest in chromosome 6). The schizophrenia collaborative linkage group (1996) analyzed 11 different studies. They confirmed evidence for linkage on chromosome 22, but the supposed schizophrenia gene accounted for only about 2% of the probability of developing the disorder, a very small contribution indeed. The genetic contributions to schizophrenia continue to be explored.

The second strategy for locating specific genes, association studies, also uses genetic markers. Whereas linkage studies compare markers in a large group of people with a particular disorder, association studies compare such people and people without the disorder. If certain markers occur significantly more often in the people with the disorder, it is assumed that the markers are close to the genes involved with the disorder. Association studies are thus better able to identify genes that may only weakly be associated with a disorder. Both strategies for locating specific genes shed new light on the origins of specific disorders and may inspire new approaches to treatment (Sherman et al., 1997).

Studying Behavior Over Time

Sometimes we want to ask, "How will a disorder or behavior pattern change (or remain the same) over time?" This question is important for several reasons. First, the answer helps us decide whether to treat a particular person. For example, should we begin an expensive and time-consuming program for a young adult who is depressed over the loss of a grandparent? You might not, if you knew that with normal social supports the depression is likely to diminish over the next few months without treatment. On the other hand, if you have reason to believe that a problem isn't likely to go away on its own, you might decide to begin treatment. For example, as we will see below, aggression among very young children does not usually go away naturally and should be dealt with as early as possible.

It is also important to understand the developmental changes in abnormal behavior because sometimes these can provide insight into how problems are created and become more serious. For example, we will see that some researchers identify people who are at risk for schizophrenia by virtue of their family histories, and follow them through the entire risk period (18–45 years of age) (Sameroff & Seifer, 1990). The goal is to discover the factors (e.g., social status, family psychopathology) that predict who will ultimately manifest the disorder. (This complex and fascinating research is described in Chapter 13.)

Several research strategies for examining psychopathology across time combine individual and group research methods, including both correlational and experimental designs. We'll look next at two of the most frequently used: cross-sectional and longitudinal designs.

Cross-Sectional Designs

A variation of correlation research is to compare different people at different ages. For a **cross-sectional design,** researchers take a "cross-section" of a population across the different age groups and compare them on some characteristic. For example, if they were trying to understand the development of alcohol abuse and dependence, they could take groups of adolescents at 12, 15, and 17 years of age and assess their beliefs about alcohol use. In such a comparison, J. Brown and Finn (1982) made some interesting discoveries. They found that 36% of the 12-year-olds thought the primary purpose of drinking was to get drunk. This percentage increased to 64% with 15-year-olds, but dropped again to 42% for the 17-year-old students. The researchers also found that 28% of the 12-year-olds reported drinking with their friends at least sometimes, a rate that increased to 80% for the 15-year-olds and to 88% for the 17-year-olds. Brown and Finn used this information to develop the hypothesis that the reason for excessive drinking among teens is a deliberate attempt to get drunk rather than a mistake in judgment once they are under the influence of alcohol. In other words, teenagers do not, as a group, appear to drink too much because once they've had a drink or two they show poor judgment and drink excessively. Instead, their attitudes before drinking seem to influence how much they drink later.

In cross-sectional designs, the participants in each age group are called **cohorts;** Brown and Finn studied three cohorts: 12-year-olds, 15-year-olds, and 17-year-olds. The members of each cohort are the same age at the same time, and thus have all been exposed to similar experiences. At the same time, members of one cohort differ from members of other cohorts in age and in their exposure to cultural and historical experiences. You would expect a group of 12-year-olds in the early 1990s to have received a great deal of education about drug and alcohol use ("Just Say No"), whereas the 17-year-olds may not have. Differences among cohorts in their opinions about alcohol use may be related to their respective cognitive and emotional development at these different ages and to their dissimilar experiences. This **cohort effect,** the confounding of age and experience, is a limitation of the cross-sectional design.

Researchers prefer cross-sectional designs to study changes over time partly because they are easier to use than longitudinal designs (discussed next). Additionally, some phenomena are less likely to be influenced by different cultural and historical experiences and are therefore less susceptible to cohort effects. For example, the prevalence of Alzheimer's disease among people at ages 60 and 70—assumed to be strongly influenced by biology—is not likely to be greatly affected by different experiences among the study subjects.

One question that is not answered by cross-sectional designs is how problems develop in individuals. For example, do children who refuse to go to school grow up to have anxiety disorders? A researcher cannot answer this question simply by comparing adults with anxiety problems and children who refuse to go to school. He could ask the adults whether they were anxious about school when they were children, but this **retrospective information** (looking back) is usually less than accurate. To get a better picture of how individuals develop over the years, researchers use longitudinal designs.

Longitudinal Designs

Rather than looking at different groups of people of differing ages, researchers may follow one group over time and assess change in its members directly. The advantage of **longitudinal designs** is that they do not suffer from cohort effect problems and they allow the researchers to assess individual change. (Figure 4.4 illustrates both longitudinal and cross-sectional designs.) Susan Nolen-Hoeksema, Joan Girgus, and Martin Seligman (1992) conducted a longitudinal study on depression among children. They assessed symptoms among 508 third-grade children through structured interviews conducted every 6 months over a 5-year period. In addition to measuring depressive symptoms such as sadness and troubles with eating and sleeping, the researchers also determined the number of negative events the children experienced, their "explanatory style," or degree of expectation that bad things would happen. The researchers found that negative events most affected young children; as they grew up, their pessimism, along with actual negative events, predicted depression. In other words, young children are almost exclusively influenced by the bad things that really happen to them, but as they grow older, their attitudes more strongly determine whether they become depressed (see Chapter 7).

Longitudinal design

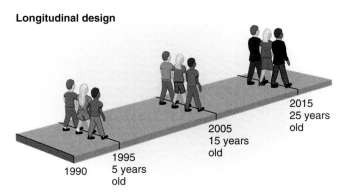

Same people followed across time

Cross-sectional design

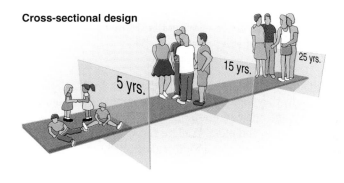

People of different ages viewed at the same time

figure 4.4 Two research designs

Imagine conducting a major longitudinal study. Not only must the researcher persevere over months and years but so must the people who participate in the study. They must remain willing to continue in the project, and the researcher must hope they will not move away, or worse, die! Longitudinal research is costly and time-consuming; it is also subject to the distinct possibility that the research question will have become irrelevant by the time the study is complete. Finally, longitudinal designs can suffer from a phenomenon similar to the cohort effect on cross-sectional designs. The **cross-generational effect** involves trying to generalize the findings to groups whose experiences are very different from those of the study participants. For example, the drug use histories of people who were young adults in the 1960s and early 1970s will be vastly different from those of people who were born in the 1990s.

Sometimes psychopathologists combine longitudinal and cross-sectional designs in a strategy called the **sequential design,** which involves repeated study of different cohorts over time. Julia Wallace and Michael O'Hara (1992) studied depression among rural elderly adults. They used both a cross-sectional and a longitudinal design to learn whether and how depression among these older adults (65 years of age and older) changed over time. Their ambitious project involved conducting a structured interview with over 3,500 older residents of two counties in rural Iowa. Following the first interview, they compared the results among the

Longitudinal studies can be complicated by the cross-generational effect; for example, young people in the '60s shared experiences that were very different from those of young people in the '90s.

adults in different age groups. In the cross-sectional part of the study, they looked at depression among older adults in different age ranges (cohorts): 65–69, 70–74, 75–79, 80–84, 85–89, and 90 and older. Wallace and O'Hara reinterviewed the subjects for the longitudinal part of the study 3 and 6 years later. Both parts of the sequential design produced similar findings: Depression seemed to increase as adults grew older, but social supports mitigated the increases. In other words, having more social supports seemed to help prevent some depression later in life.

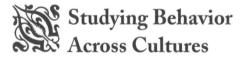 ## Studying Behavior Across Cultures

Just as we can become narrowly focused when we study people only at a certain age, we can also miss important aspects by studying people from only one culture. Studying the differences in behavior of people from different cultures can tell us a great deal about the origins and possible treatments of abnormal behaviors. Unfortunately, most research literature originates in Western cultures (Lambert et al., 1992), producing an ethnocentric view of psychopathology that can limit our understanding of disorders in general and can also restrict the way we approach treatment. Researchers in Malaysia have described a disorder they call *gila,* which has some of the features of schizophrenia, but also differs in important ways (Resner & Hartog, 1970). Could we learn more about schizophrenia (and gila) by comparing the disorders themselves *and* the cultures in which they are found? Increasing awareness of the limited cultural scope of our research is creating a corresponding increase in cross-cultural research on psychopathology.

The designs we have described are adapted for studying abnormal behavior across cultures. Some researchers view the effects of different cultures as though they were different

treatments (Malpass & Poortinga, 1986). In other words, the independent variable is the effect of different cultures on behavior, rather than, say, the effect of cognitive therapy versus simple exposure for the treatment of fears. The difference between looking at culture as a "treatment" and our typical design, however, is important. In cross-cultural research, we can't randomly assign infants to different cultures and observe how they develop. People from varying cultures can differ in any number of important ways—their genetic backgrounds, for one—that could explain variations in their behavior for reasons other than culture.

The characteristics of different cultures can also complicate research efforts. Symptoms or descriptions of them can be very dissimilar in different societies. Nigerians who are depressed complain of heaviness or heat in the head, crawling sensations in the head or legs, burning sensations in the body, and a feeling that the belly is bloated with water (Ebigno, 1982). In contrast, people in the United States report feeling worthless, being unable to start or finish anything, losing interest in usual activities, and thinking of suicide. Natives of China, on the other hand, do not report loss of pleasure, the helplessness or hopelessness, guilt, or suicidal thoughts seen in depressed North Americans (Kleinman, 1982). These few examples illustrate that applying a standard definition of depression across different cultures will result in vastly different outcomes.

An additional complicating factor is varying tolerances or "thresholds" for abnormal behavior. If people in different cultures see the same behaviors very differently, researchers will have trouble comparing incidence and prevalence rates. Lambert and colleagues (1992) found that Jamaican parents and teachers report fewer incidents of abnormal child behavior than do their American counterparts. Does this represent a biological or environmental difference in the children themselves, the effects of different thresholds of tolerance in the societies, or a combination of both? Understanding cultural attitudes and customs is essential to such research.

The same behaviors—for example, that of women in public—may be viewed very differently in different cultures.

Finally, treatment research is also complicated by cross-cultural differences. Cultures develop treatment models that reflect their own values. In Japan, psychiatric hospitalization is organized in terms of a family model, with caregivers assuming parental roles. A family model was also common in psychiatric institutions in 19th-century North America until it was replaced with the medical model that is common today (Blue & Gaines, 1992; Dwyer, 1992). In Saudi Arabia, women are veiled when outside the home, which prevents them from uncovering their faces in the presence of therapists; custom thus complicates efforts to establish a trusting and intimate therapeutic client–therapist relationship (Dubovsky, 1983). Because in the Islamic view medicine and religion are inseparable, medical and religious treatments are combined (Horikoshi, 1980). As you can see, something as basic as comparing treatment outcomes is highly complex in a cross-cultural context.

The Power of a Program of Research

When we examine different research strategies independently, as we have done here, we often have the impression that some approaches are better than others. It is important to understand that this is not true. Depending on the type of question you are asking and the practical limitations inherent in the inquiry, any of the research techniques would be appropriate. In fact, significant issues often get resolved not by one perfectly designed study, but rather by a *series* of studies that examine different aspects of the problem—in a *program* of research. In an outstanding example of this approach, Gerald Patterson and his colleagues at the University of Oregon studied the aggressive behavior of children.

Their earliest research focused on basic concerns, such as why children are aggressive. The researchers first did a series of correlational studies to determine what variables were associated with aggression in children. One study was conducted in a state institution for girls with various problem behaviors (Buehler, Patterson, & Furniss, 1966). Researchers found that the "delinquent" behaviors—including rule breaking, criticizing adults, and aggressiveness—were likely to be reinforced by the girls' peers, who encouraged them.

Using strategies from epidemiology, Patterson also looked at the prevalence of aggression in children. He found that the likelihood of inappropriate behavior among children who are identified as *not* having a disorder ranged from 41% to 11%, with a mean of approximately 25% (Patterson, Cobb, & Ray, 1972). In other words, some level of aggression appears to be normal. Children are seen as "deviant" not for displaying a behavior, but when that behavior exceeds an acceptable level of frequency or intensity.

As you remember, interpreting the results from correlation studies can be difficult, especially if the intent is to determine causation. To forestall this criticism, Patterson also conducted experimental studies. One strategy he used was a single-case experimental design (withdrawal design), in which he observed how a 5-year-old boy reacted to his mother's attempts to change his problem behavior (Patterson, 1982). Patterson asked the boy's mother to restrain the child if he was aggressive but not to talk to him during this time. Patterson observed that the boy whined and complained when he was restrained. In the experimental condition, Patterson asked the mother to talk with her son in a positive way when he complained. Later, Patterson had her again ignore her son's complaints (a withdrawal design). What was found was that the boy was more likely to complain about being restrained when his mother talked with him. One conclusion was that reinforcement (verbal communication) from the mother encouraged the boy to try to escape her restraint by complaining. By observing both the boy's behavior (the dependent variable) and the mother's behavior (the independent variable), Patterson could make stronger conclusions about the role of the mother in influencing her son's behavior.

One of the questions about aggression in children concerns development. How does aggressiveness change over time? Patterson used cross-sectional research to observe children at different ages. In one study he found that the rate of aggression decreases as children get older (Patterson, 1982). It seems that children are less often aggressive as they get older, but their aggression may become more intense or destructive.

Using **treatment outcome research,** this group of researchers has also examined the effects of a treatment package on the aggressive behavior of children. Patterson and Fleischman (1979) introduced a behavioral treatment involving parent training (see Chapter 12) and described the results of the treatment on the behavior of both parents and their children. The researchers found that they could reduce inappropriate child behavior and improve the parenting skills of the parents, and that these changes persisted a year after treatment.

As this example indicates, research is conducted in stages, and a complete picture of any behavior can be seen only after looking at it from many different perspectives. An integrated program of research can help researchers explore various aspects of abnormal behavior.

Replication

The motto of the state of Missouri is "Show Me." The motto of science could be "Show Me Again." Scientists in general, and behavioral scientists, in particular, are never really convinced that something is "true." People are very skeptical when it comes to claims about causes or treatment outcomes. Replicating findings is what makes researchers confident that what they are observing isn't a coincidence. We noted when we described the case study method that if we look at a disorder in only one person, no matter how carefully we describe and document what we observe, we cannot draw strong conclusions.

The strength of a research program is in its ability to replicate findings in different ways to build confidence in the results. If you look back at the research strategies we have described, you will find that replication is one of the most important aspects of each. The more times a researcher repeats a process (and the behavior he is studying changes as expected) the more sure he is about what caused the changes.

Research Ethics

A final issue, though not the least important, involves the ethics of doing research in abnormal psychology. For example, the appropriateness of a clinician's delaying treatment to people who need it, just to satisfy the requirements of an ex-

perimental design, is frequently questioned. One single-case experimental design, the withdrawal design, can involve removing treatment for a period of time. Treatment is also withheld when placebo control groups are used in group experimental designs. When does a scientist's interest in preserving the internal validity of a study outweigh a client's right to treatment?

One answer to this question involves **informed consent**—a research participant's formal agreement to cooperate in a study following full disclosure of the nature of the research and the participant's role in it. The concept of informed consent is actually derived from the war trials after World War II. Revelations that the Nazis had forced prisoners into "medical experiments" helped establish the informed consent guidelines that are still used today. In studies using some form of treatment delay or withdrawal, the participant is told about why it will occur and the risks and benefits, and permission to proceed is then attained. In placebo control studies, participants are told that they may not receive an active treatment (all participants are blind to or unaware of which group they are placed in), but they are usually given the option of receiving treatment after the study ends.

True informed consent is at times elusive. The basic components are competence, voluntarism, full information, and comprehension on the part of the subject (Imber et al., 1986). In other words, research participants must be capable of consenting to participation in the research, they must volunteer or not be coerced into participating, they must have all the information they need to make the decision, and they must understand what their participation will involve. In some circumstances, all these conditions are difficult to attain. Children, for example, often do not fully appreciate what will occur during research. Similarly, individuals with cognitive impairments such as mental retardation or schizophrenia may not understand their role or their rights as participants. In institutional settings there is concern that participants not feel coerced into taking part in research.

Certain general protections help assure that these concerns are properly addressed. First, research in university and medical settings must be approved by an institutional review board (IRB) (Ceci, Peters, & Plotkin, 1985). These are committees made up of university faculty and nonacademic people from the community, and their purpose is to see that the rights of research participants are protected. The committee structure allows people other than the researcher to look at the research procedures to determine whether sufficient care is being taken to protect the welfare and dignity of the participants.

To safeguard those who participate in psychological research and to clarify the responsibilities of researchers, the American Psychological Association has published *Ethical Principles of Psychologists,* which includes general guidelines for conducting research (American Psychological Association, 1992). People in research experiments must be protected from both physical and psychological harm. In addition to the issue of informed consent, these principles also stress the investigators' responsibility for the research participants' welfare, because the researcher ultimately must ensure that the welfare of the research participants is given priority over any other consideration, including experimental design.

Psychological harm is difficult to define, but its definition remains the responsibility of the investigator. Researchers must hold in confidence all information obtained from participants, who have the right to concealment of their identity on all data, either written or informal. Whenever deception is considered essential to research, the investigator must satisfy a committee of peers that this judgment is correct. If deception or concealment is used, participants must be debriefed—that is, told in language they can understand the true purpose of the study and why it was necessary to deceive them.

The Society for Research in Child Development (1990) has endorsed ethical guidelines for research that address some of the issues unique to research with children. For example, not only do these guidelines call for confidentiality, protection from harm, and debriefing, but they also require informed consent from children's caregivers and from the children themselves if they are age 7 and older. These guidelines specify that the research must be explained to children in language they can understand so that they can decide whether they wish to participate.

Many other ethical issues extend beyond protection of the participants, including how researchers deal with errors in their research, fraud in science, and the proper way to give credit to others. "Doing a study" involves much more than selecting the appropriate design. Researchers must be aware of numerous concerns that involve the rights of the people in the experiment itself as well as their own conduct.

■ concept check 14.2

Ethics are important to the research process. Ethical guidelines are spelled out by various professional organizations to ensure the well-being of research subjects. In each of the situations below, write N if it is necessary or X if it is untrue or not required for the experiment to be ethical.

1. After the nature of the experiment and their role in it are disclosed to the participants, they must be allowed to refuse or agree to sign an informed consent form.

_____

2. If the participant is in the control group or taking a placebo, an informed consent form is not needed.

_____

3. Research in universities or medical settings must be approved by the institution's review board whether or not the participants lack the cognitive skills to protect themselves from harm. _____

4. Participants have a right to concealment of their identity on all data collected and reported. _____

5. When deception is essential to the research, participants do not have to be debriefed regarding the true purpose of the study. _____

Summary

- Research involves establishing a hypothesis that is then tested. In abnormal psychology, research focuses on hypotheses meant to explain the nature, the causes, or the treatment of a disorder.
- The individual case study is used to study one or more individuals in depth. Though case studies have an important role in the theoretical development of psychology, they are not subject to experimental control and must necessarily be suspect in terms of both internal and external validity.
- Research by correlation can tell us whether a relationship exists between two variables, but it does not tell us if that relationship is a causal one. Epidemiological research is a type of correlational research that reveals the incidence, distribution, and consequences of a particular problem in one or more populations.
- Research by experiment can follow one of two designs: group or single case. In both designs, a variable (or variables) is manipulated and the effects are observed in order to determine the nature of a causal relationship.
- Genetic research focuses on the role of genetics in behavior. These research strategies include family studies, adoption studies, twin studies, genetic linkage analyses, and association studies.
- Research strategies that examine psychopathology across time include cross-sectional and longitudinal designs. Both focus on differences in behavior or attitudes at different ages, but the former does so by looking at different individuals at different ages while the latter looks at the same individuals at different ages.
- The clinical picture, causal factors, and treatment process and outcome can all be influenced by cultural factors.
- The more the findings of a research program are replicated, the more they gain in credibility.
- Ethics are important to the research process, and ethical guidelines are spelled out by many professional organizations in an effort to ensure the well-being of research subjects.

Key Terms

hypothesis
research design
dependent variable
independent variable
internal validity
external validity
testability
confound
control group
randomization
analog model
generalizability
statistical significance
clinical significance

case study method
correlation
positive correlation
correlation coefficient
negative correlation
directionality
epidemiology
incidence
prevalence
experiment
placebo effect
placebo control group
double-blind control
comparative treatment research
single-case experimental design
variability
trend
level
withdrawal design
multiple baseline
baseline
phenotype
genotype
human genome project
family studies
proband
adoption studies
twin studies

genetic linkage analysis
association studies
genetic markers
cross-sectional design
cohort
cohort effect
retrospective information
longitudinal design
cross-generational effect
sequential design
treatment outcome research
informed consent

Answers to Concept Checks

4.1
1. d
2. b
3. a
4. e

4.2
1. N
2. X
3. N
4. N
5. X

Anxiety Disorders

One thing is certain, that the problem of anxiety is a nodal point, linking up all kinds of the most important questions; a riddle, of which the

solution must cast a flood of light upon our whole mental life.

Sigmund Freud
Introductory Lectures on Psychoanalysis

Anxiety is complex and mysterious, as Freud realized many years ago. In some ways, the more we learn about it, the more baffling it seems. "Anxiety" is a specific type of disorder, but it is much more than that. It is an emotion implicated so heavily across the full range of psychopathology that we begin by exploring its general nature, both biological and psychological. Next, we consider fear, a somewhat different but clearly related emotion. We suggest that panic is fear that occurs, perhaps, at an inappropriate time. With these important ideas clearly in mind, we focus on specific anxiety disorders.

Anxiety, Fear, and Panic

Have you ever experienced anxiety? A silly question, you might say, since most of us feel some anxiety almost every day of our lives. Did you have a test in school today for which you weren't "perfectly" prepared? Did you have a date last weekend with somebody new? And how about that job interview coming up? Even *thinking* about that might make you nervous. But have you ever stopped to think about the nature of anxiety? What is it? What causes it?

Anxiety is a mood-state characterized by marked negative affect, bodily symptoms of tension, and apprehension about the future (American Psychiatric Association, 1994; Barlow, 1988, in press). It is important to note that anxiety is *very* hard to study. In humans it can be a subjective sense of unease, a set of behaviors (looking worried and anxious, fidgeting), or a physiological response originating in the brain and reflected in elevated heart rate and muscle tension. Because anxiety is difficult to study in humans, much of the research has been done with animals. For example, we might teach laboratory rats that a light signals an impending shock. The animals certainly look and act anxious when the light comes on. They may fidget, tremble, and perhaps cower in a corner. We might give them an anxiety-reducing drug and notice a reduction of anxiety in their

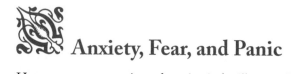

[I] found it difficult to focus my attention on anything except my own internal agony.*

reaction to the light. But is the rats' experience of anxiety the same as humans'? It seems to be similar, but we don't know for sure; research with animals provides only general information about the nature of anxiety in humans. Thus, anxiety remains a mystery, and we are only beginning our journey of discovery. Anxiety is also closely related to depression (Barlow, Chorpita, & Turovsky, 1996; Mineka, Watson, & Clark, 1998), so much of what we say here is relevant to Chapter 7.

Anxiety is not very pleasant, so why do we seem programmed to experience it almost every time we do something important? Surprisingly, anxiety is good for us, at least in moderate amounts. Psychologists have known for nearly a century that we perform better when we are a little anxious (Yerkes & Dodson, 1908). You would not have done so well on that test the other day if you had had no anxiety. You were a little more charming and lively on that date last weekend because you were anxious. And you will be better prepared for that job interview coming up if you are anxious. In short, physical and intellectual performances are driven and enhanced by anxiety. Without it, very few of us would get much done. Howard Liddell (1949) first proposed this idea when he called anxiety the "shadow of intelligence." He thought that the human ability to plan in some detail for the future was connected to that gnawing feeling that things could go wrong and we had better be prepared for them. This is why anxiety is a future-oriented mood-state. If you were to put it into words you might say, "Something might go wrong, and I'm not sure I can deal with it, but I've got to be ready to try." "Maybe I'd better study a little harder (or check the mirror one more time before my date, or do a little more research on that company before the interview.)"

But what happens when you have too much anxiety? You might actually fail the exam because you can't concentrate on the questions. All you can think about when you're too anxious is how terrible it will be if you fail. You might blow the interview for the same reason. On that date with a new person, you might spend the evening with perspiration running off your face, a sick feeling in your stomach, unable to think of even one reasonably interesting thing to say. Too much of a good thing can be harmful, and there are very few sensations more harmful than severe anxiety that is out of control.

What makes the situation worse is that severe anxiety usually doesn't go away—that is, even if we "know" that there is really nothing to be afraid of, we remain anxious. We constantly see examples of this kind of irrationality. John Madden, the well-known sports announcer and former professional football coach, suffers from claustrophobia. He has written about his anxiety and used it as a source of humor in several television commercials. Despite his imposing size (6 feet 4 inches, 260 pounds), Madden has had to overcome the stigma, embarrassment, and effect of anxiety on his everyday life, but he hasn't overcome the claustrophobia itself. Madden, who may have to announce a game in New York one Sunday and in San Francisco the next, cannot travel by air. For a long time he

---

*Featured quotations in this chapter are from Daryl M. Woods, *Afraid of Everything: A Personal History of Agoraphobia* (R & E Publishers, 1984).

took trains around the country; now he uses a well-equipped private bus. Madden and countless other individuals who suffer from anxiety-based disorders are well aware that there is little to fear in the situations they find so stressful. Madden must have long since realized that, since flying is the safest way to travel, it is in his best interest to fly in order to save time and help maintain his lucrative career. And yet he cannot abandon his self-defeating behavior. All the disorders discussed in this chapter are characterized by excessive anxiety, which takes many different forms.

In Chapter 2 we saw that **fear** is an immediate alarm reaction to danger. Like anxiety, fear can be good for us. It protects us by activating a massive response from the autonomic nervous system (increased heart rate and blood pressure, for example), which, along with our subjective sense of terror, motivates us to escape (flee) or, possibly, to attack (fight). As such, this emergency reaction is often called the "flight or fight" response.

Although not all emotion theorists agree, there is much evidence that fear and anxiety reactions differ psychologically and physiologically (Barlow, Chorpita, & Turovsky, 1996). As noted above, anxiety is a future-oriented mood-state, characterized by apprehension because one cannot predict or control upcoming events. Fear, on the other hand, is an immediate emotional reaction to current danger characterized by strong escapist action tendencies and, often, a surge in the sympathetic branch of the autonomic nervous system (Barlow, Brown, & Craske, 1994). Someone experiencing fear might say, "I've got to get out of here right now or I may not make it."

What happens if you experience the alarm response of fear when there is nothing to be afraid of, if you have a false alarm? Consider the case of Gretchen, who appeared at one of our clinics.

Gretchen
Attacked by Panic

I was 25 when I had my first attack. It was a few weeks after I'd come home from the hospital. I had had my appendix out. The surgery had gone well, and I wasn't in any danger, which is why I don't understand what happened. But one night I went to sleep and I woke up a few hours later—I'm not sure how long—but I woke up with this vague feeling of apprehension. Mostly I remember how my heart started pounding. And my chest hurt; it felt like I was dying—that I was having a heart attack. And I felt kind of queer, as if I were detached from the experience. It seemed like my bedroom was covered with a haze. I ran to my sister's room, but I felt like I was a puppet or a robot who was under the control of somebody else while I was running. I think I scared her almost as much as I was frightened myself. She called an ambulance (Barlow, in press).

"First time it happened to me, I was driving down the highway, and I had a kind of a knot in my chest. I felt like I had swallowed something and it got stuck, and it lasted pretty much overnight. . . . I felt like I was having a heart attack. . . . I assumed that's what was happening. I felt very panicky. A flushed feeling came over my whole body. I felt as though I was going to pass out. . . ."

The roots of the panic experience are deeply embedded in our cultural myths. Pan, the Greek god of nature, lived in the country, presiding over rivers, woods, streams, and grazing animals. But Pan did not look like the typical god. He was very ugly and short, with legs resembling a goat's. Unfortunately for travelers, Pan habitually napped in a small cave or thicket near the road. When traveling Greeks disturbed him, he let out a bloodcurdling scream that was so intense that many terrified travelers died of fright. This sudden overwhelming reaction came to be known as **panic,** after the irate god. In psychopathology, a **panic attack** is defined as an abrupt experience of intense fear or acute discomfort, accompanied by physical symptoms that usually include heart palpitations, chest pain, shortness of breath and, possibly, dizziness.

There are three basic types of panic attacks described in DSM-IV: situationally bound, unexpected, and situationally predisposed. If you know you are afraid of high places or of driving over long bridges, you might have a panic attack in these situations but not anywhere else; this is a *situationally bound* (cued) panic attack. By contrast, you might experience *unexpected* (uncued) panic attacks. The third type of panic attack, the *situationally predisposed,* is in between. You are more likely, but not inevitably, to have an attack where you have had one before; for example, in a large mall. If you don't know whether it will happen today, and it does, the attack is situationally predisposed. We mention these types of attacks because they play a role in several anxiety disorders. Unexpected and situationally predisposed attacks are important in *panic disorder.* Situationally bound attacks are more common in *specific phobias* or *social phobia* (see Figure 5.1).

Remember that fear is an intense emotional alarm accompanied by a surge of energy in the autonomic nervous system that motivates us to flee from danger. Does Gretchen's panic attack sound like it could be the emotion of fear? A variety of evidence suggests that it is (Barlow, 1991, Barlow et al., 1996) including similarities in reports of the experience of fear and panic, similar behavioral tendencies to escape, and similar underlying neurobiological processes.

Over the years we have recorded panic attacks during physiological assessments of patients (e.g., Hofmann & Barlow, 1996). The physiological surge recorded in one pa-

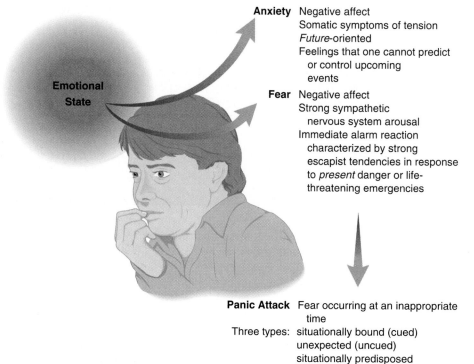

figure 5.1 The relationships among anxiety, fear, and panic attack

tient is shown in Figure 5.2. Notice the sudden doubling of heart rate from minute 11 through minute 13, accompanied by increases in muscle tension (frontalis EMG) and finger temperature. This massive autonomic surge peaked and subsided within three minutes. The panic attack in the laboratory occurred quite unexpectedly from the patient's point of view and from ours. As the figure shows, fear and panic are experienced very suddenly, which is necessary to mobilize us for instantaneous reaction to impending danger.

Causes

You learned in Chapters 1 and 2 that excessive emotional reactions have no simple one-dimensional cause, but come from multiple sources.

BIOLOGICAL CONTRIBUTIONS

There is increasing evidence that we inherit a tendency to be tense or uptight (Eysenck, 1967; Gray & McNaughton, 1996; Lader & Wing, 1964; McGuffin & Reich, 1984). As with almost all psychological disorders, and unlike hair or eye color, no single gene seems to cause anxiety. Instead, weak contributions from many genes in several different areas on chromosomes, collectively make us vulnerable to anxiety (Kendler et al., 1995; Lesch et al., 1996; Plomin et al., 1997) when the right psychological and social factors are in place.

The tendency to panic also seems to run in families and may have a genetic component (Barlow, in press). There is

some evidence that genetic contributions to panic and anxiety differ (Kendler et al., 1995); but in both situations genetic vulnerability, particularly in a person who is under stress, may create the condition for panic but does not cause it directly. Recently, sophisticated methods of studying genetics, called quantitative trait loci (see Chapters 2 and 4), have allowed investigators to identify relevant areas on a number of chromosomes in animals, including 1, 12, and 15. Numerous genes in these areas seem to create a tendency to be uptight, overemotional, or anxious (Flint et al., 1995).

Anxiety is also associated with specific brain circuits, the GABA-benzodiazepine system in particular. Depleted levels of this neurotransmitter are associated with increased anxiety, although the relationship is not quite so direct. The noradrenergic system has also been implicated in anxiety, and recent evidence from basic animal studies, as well as studies of normal anxiety in humans, suggest that the serotonergic neurotransmitter system is particularly involved (Deakin & Graeff, 1991; Lesch et al., 1996; Maier, 1997).

The area of the brain most often associated with anxiety is the limbic system (Davis, 1992; Gray & McNaughton, 1996; LeDoux, 1995, 1996), which acts as a mediator between the brain stem and the cortex. The more primitive brain stem monitors and senses changes in bodily functions and relays these potential danger signals to higher cortical processes through the limbic system. Jeffrey Gray, a prominent British neuropsychologist, identified a brain circuit in the limbic system of animals that seems heavily involved in anxiety (Gray, 1982, 1985, in press) and that may be relevant to humans. This circuit leads from the septal and hippocampal area in the limbic system to the frontal cortex. (The septal-hippocampal system is activated by serotonergic and noradrenergic mediated pathways originating in the brain stem.) The system that Gray calls the **behavioral inhibition system (BIS)** is activated by signals from the brain stem of unexpected events, such as major changes in body functioning that might signal danger. Danger signals in response to something we see that might be threatening descend from the cortex to the septal–hippocampal system. The BIS also receives a big boost from the amygdala (Davis, 1992; LeDoux, 1996). When the BIS is activated by signals that arise from the brain stem or descend from the cortex, our tendency is to freeze, experience anxiety, and apprehensively evaluate the situation to confirm that danger is present.

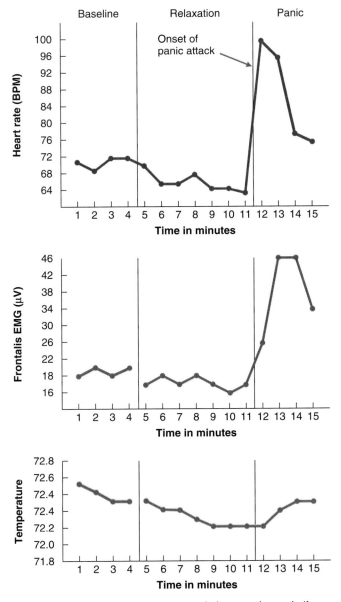

figure 5.2 Physiological measurements during a panic attack (from Cohen, Barlow, & Blanchard, 1985).

The behavioral inhibition system circuit is distinct from the circuit involved in panic. Gray (1982; Gray & McNaughton, 1996) and Graeff (1987, 1993; Deakin & Graeff, 1991) identified what Gray calls the **fight/flight system (FFS).** This circuit originates in the brain stem, perhaps in the raphe nucleus, and travels through several midbrain structures, including the amygdala, the ventromedial nucleus of the hypothalamus, and the central gray matter. When stimulated in animals, this circuit produces an immediate alarm-and-escape response that looks very much like panic in humans (Gray & McNaughton, 1996). Gray and McNaughton (1996) and Graeff (1993) think the FFS is activated in part by deficiencies in serotonin.

Research into the neurobiology of anxiety and panic is still very new, but we have made exciting progress by implicating two seemingly different brain systems and confirming the crucial role of the amygdala. Brain-imaging procedures will undoubtedly yield much more information in the years to come.

Psychological Contributions

In Chapter 2 we reviewed some theories on the nature of psychological causes of anxiety. Remember that Freud thought anxiety was a psychic reaction to danger surrounding the reactivation of an infantile fearful situation. Behavioral theorists view anxiety as a product of early classical conditioning, modeling, or other forms of learning (Bandura, 1986).

Evidence is accumulating (for example, Barlow, in press; Mineka, 1985a; Mineka & Zinbarg, 1996) that supports an integrated model of anxiety that involves a variety of factors. In childhood we may acquire an awareness that events are not always in our control (Chorpita & Barlow, in press). The continuum of this perception may range from total confidence in our control of all aspects of our lives to deep uncertainty about ourselves and our ability to deal with upcoming events. The perception is most evident as a set of danger-laden beliefs. If you are anxious about schoolwork, you may think you will do poorly on the next exam and that there is no way you can pass the course, even though all your grades have been As and Bs. A general "sense of uncontrollability" may develop early as a function of upbringing and other environmental factors. It seems to be the psychological factor that makes us most vulnerable to anxiety in later life.

Most psychological accounts of panic invoke *conditioning* and *cognitive* explanations that are difficult to separate. Thus, a strong fear response initially occurs during extreme stress or perhaps as a result of a dangerous situation in the environment (a true alarm). This emotional response then becomes associated with a variety of external and internal cues. In other words, the cues provoke the fear response and an assumption of danger, whether or not danger is actually present (Martin, 1983; Mineka, 1985a; Razran, 1961). External cues are places or situations similar to the one where the initial panic attack occurred. Internal cues are increases in heart rate or respiration that were associated with the initial panic attack, even if they are now due to perfectly normal circumstances, such as exercise. Thus, when your heart is beating fast you are more likely to think of and, perhaps, experience a panic attack than when it is beating normally.

Social Contributions

Stressful life events trigger our biological and psychological vulnerabilities to anxiety. Most are interpersonal in nature—marriage, divorce, difficulties at work, death of a loved one, and so on. Some might be physical such as an injury or illness. Social pressures, perhaps to excel in school, might also provide sufficient stress to trigger anxiety.

The same stressors can trigger physical reactions such as headaches or hypertension and emotional reactions such as panic attacks (Barlow, in press). The particular way we react to stress seems to run in families. If you get headaches, chances are other people in your family also get headaches.

If you have panic attacks, other members of your family probably do also. This finding suggests a possible genetic contribution, at least to initial panic attacks.

An Integrated Model

Putting the factors together, we can see that a tendency to be uptight or high strung might be inherited. But a biological vulnerability to anxiety is not anxiety itself. You might also grow up believing that the world is not controllable and that you might not be able to cope when things go wrong. If this perception is strong, you have a *psychological vulnerability* to anxiety. Finally, you might be under a lot of pressure, particularly from interpersonal stressors. A given stressor could activate your biological tendencies to anxiety and your psychological tendencies to feel that you might not be able to deal with the situation and control the stress. Once this cycle starts, it tends to feed on itself so that it might not stop even when the particular life stressor has long since passed.

Anxiety can be very general, evoked by many aspects of your life. But it is usually focused on one area, such as grades. When this focus becomes intense, it determines the nature of a particular anxiety disorder.

Panic is also a characteristic response to stress that runs in families and may have a genetic component. Because an individual associates the panic attack with internal or external cues (conditioning is one form of learning), the attacks are called *learned alarms*. Even if you have a legitimate fear response to a dangerous situation (true alarm), your reaction can become associated with a variety of cues that may then trigger an attack *in the absence* of any danger, making it a learned alarm. Furthermore, anxiety and panic are closely related (Barlow, in press), in that anxiety increases the likelihood of panic. This relationship makes sense from an ethological point of view, since sensing possible future threat or danger (anxiety) should prepare us to react instantaneously with an alarm response if the danger becomes imminent. Anxiety and panic need not occur together, but it makes sense that they often do.

Generalized Anxiety Disorder

Clinical Description

Is somebody in your family a worrywart? Is somebody in your family perfectionistic? Perhaps it is you! Most of us worry to some extent. As we have said, worry can be very useful. It helps us plan for the future, make sure that we're prepared for that test, or double-check that we've thought of everything before we head home for the holidays. The worry process itself is not pleasant, but without it nothing would go very smoothly. But what if you worry indiscriminately about everything? Furthermore, what if worrying is unproductive: No matter how much you worry, you can't seem to decide what to do about an upcoming problem or situation. And what if you *can't stop* worrying, even if you know it is

doing you no good and probably making everyone else around you miserable? These features characterize **generalized anxiety disorder (GAD).** Consider the following case.

Irene
Ruled by Worry

Irene was a 20-year-old college student, with an engaging personality but not many friends. She came to the clinic complaining of excessive anxiety and general difficulties in controlling her life. *Everything* was a catastrophe for Irene. Although she carried a 3.7 grade point average she was convinced that she would flunk every test she took. As a result, she repeatedly threatened to drop courses after only several weeks of classes because she feared that she would not understand the material.

Irene worried until she dropped out of the first college she attended after 1 month. She felt depressed for a while, then decided to take a couple of courses at a local junior college, believing she could handle the work there better. After achieving straight As at the junior college for 2 years, she enrolled once again in a 4-year college as a junior. After a short time she began calling the clinic in a state of extreme agitation, saying that she had to drop this or that course because she couldn't handle it. With great difficulty, her therapist and parents persuaded her to stay in the courses and to seek further help. In any course Irene completed, her grade was between an A and a B-minus, but she still worried about every test and every paper, afraid that she would fall apart and be unable to understand and complete the work.

Irene did not worry only about school. She was also concerned about relationships with her friends, and whenever she was with her new boyfriend she feared making a fool of herself and losing his interest. In fact, she reported that each date went extremely well, but she knew the next one would probably be a disaster. As the relationship progressed and some sexual contact seemed natural, Irene was worried sick that her inexperience would make her boyfriend consider her naive and stupid. Nevertheless, she reported enjoying the early sexual contact and admitted that he seemed to enjoy it also, but she was convinced that the next time a catastrophe would happen.

Irene was also concerned about her health. She had minor hypertension, probably because she was somewhat overweight. She then approached every meal as if death itself might result if she ate the wrong types or amounts of food. She became reluctant to have her blood pressure checked for fear that it would be very high, or to weigh herself for fear that she was not losing weight. She severely restricted her eating, and as a result had an occasional episode of binge eating, although not often enough to warrant concern.

In addition, Irene worried about her religious faith and about her relationships with her family, particularly her mother and sister. Although Irene had an occasional panic attack, this was not a major issue to her. As soon as the panic subsided she focused on the next possible catastrophe. In addition to high blood pressure, Irene had tension headaches and a "nervous stomach," with a lot of gas, occasional diarrhea, and some abdominal pain.

> Irene's life was a series of impending catastrophes. Her mother reported that she dreaded a phone call from Irene, let alone a visit, because she knew that she would have to see her daughter through a crisis. For the same reason, Irene had very few friends. Even so, when she temporarily gave up her anxiety she was really fun to be with.

Irene suffered from generalized anxiety disorder, which is, in many ways, the basic syndrome that characterizes every anxiety disorder considered in this chapter (T. A. Brown, Barlow, & Liebowitz, 1994). Specific anxiety disorders are complicated by panic attacks or other features that are the *focus* of the anxiety. In GAD, the focus is generalized to the events of everyday life. For that reason we consider GAD first.

The DSM-IV criteria specify that for at least 6 months excessive anxiety and worry (apprehensive expectation) must be ongoing more days than not. Furthermore, it must be very difficult to turn off or control the worry process. This is what distinguishes pathological worrying from the normal kind we all experience from time to time as we get ready for an upcoming event or challenge. Most of us worry for a time but can set the problem aside and go on to another task. Even if the upcoming challenge is a big one, as soon as it is over the worrying stops. For Irene, it never stopped. She turned to the next crisis as soon as the current one was over.

The physical symptoms associated with generalized anxiety and GAD differ somewhat from those associated with panic attacks and panic disorder (covered next). Whereas panic is associated with autonomic arousal, presumably as a result of a sympathetic nervous system surge (for instance, heart rate increases and palpitations, perspiration, trembling, and so on), GAD is characterized by muscle tension, mental agitation (T. A. Brown, Marten, & Barlow, 1995), susceptibility to fatigue (probably the result of chronic excessive muscle tension), some irritability, and difficulty sleeping. Focusing attention is difficult, as the mind quickly switches from crisis to crisis. For children, only one physical symptom is required, and a recent study validates this strategy (Tracey, Chorpita, Douban, & Barlow, 1997).

People with GAD worry about minor, everyday life events for the most part, a characteristic that distinguishes GAD from other anxiety disorders. When asked, "Do you worry excessively about minor things?" 100% of individuals with GAD respond "yes" compared to approximately 50% of individuals with other anxiety disorder categories, as displayed in Figure 5.3. Such a difference is statistically significant. Of course, major events quickly become the focus of anxiety and worry, too. Adults typically focus on possible misfortune to their children, family health, job responsibilities, and more minor things such as household chores or being on time for appointments. Children with GAD most often worry about academic, athletic, or social performance and physical injury (Silverman, La Greca, & Wasserstein, 1995). The elderly tend to focus, understand-

ably, on health (Person & Borkovec, 1995); they also have difficulty sleeping, which seems to make the anxiety worse (Beck & Stanley, 1997).

Statistics

Although worry and physical tension are very common, the severe generalized anxiety experienced by Irene is quite rare. Approximately 4% of the population meet criteria for GAD during a given 6-month period (Blazer, Hughes, George, Swartz, & Boyer, 1991; Kessler et al., 1994). This is still quite a large number, making GAD one of the most common anxiety disorders, second only to specific and social phobia and, perhaps, to panic disorder with agoraphobia. However, relatively few people with GAD come for treatment compared to patients with panic disorder. Anxiety clinics like ours report that only approximately 10% of their patients meet criteria for GAD compared to 30% to 50% for panic disorder.

Between 55% and 65% of individuals with GAD are female (Borkovec & Mathews, 1988; T. A. Brown et al., 1994; DiNardo, 1991; Sanderson, DiNardo, Rapee, & Barlow, 1990). In epidemiological studies, which include people who do not necessarily seek out treatment, the sex ratio is approximately 67% female to 33% male (Blazer, George, & Hughes, 1991; Wittchen, Zhao, Kessler, & Eaton, 1994).

Some people with GAD report onset in early adulthood, usually in response to a life stressor. Nevertheless, most studies find that GAD is associated with an earlier and more gradual onset than most other anxiety disorders (D. J. Anderson, Noyes, & Crowe, 1984; Barlow, in press; T. A. Brown et al., 1994; Sanderson & Barlow, 1990). Like Irene, many people have felt anxious and tense all their lives. Once it develops, GAD is chronic. One recent study found only

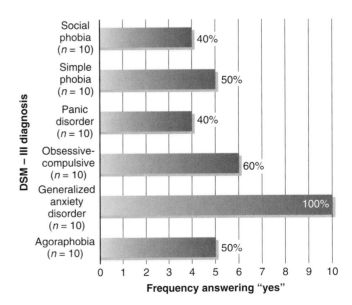

figure 5.3 Clients' answers to interviewer's question, "Do you worry excessively about minor things?" (from Sanderson & Barlow, 1986, November)

an 8% probability of becoming symptom free after 2 years of follow-up (Yonkers, Warshaw, Massion, & Keller, 1996).

Anxiety in its various forms is very prevalent among the elderly. Himmelfarb and Murrell (1984) found that 17% of elderly men and 21.5% of elderly women surveyed in a community sample had sufficiently severe anxiety symptoms to warrant treatment, although it is not clear that everyone met criteria for GAD. We also know that the use of minor tranquilizers in the elderly is very high, ranging from 17% to 50% in one study (Salzman, 1991). It is not entirely clear why drugs are prescribed with such frequency for the elderly. One possibility is that the drugs may not be entirely intended for anxiety. Prescribed drugs may be primarily for sleeping problems or other secondary effects of medical illnesses. In any case, benzodiazepines put the elderly at greater risks for falling down and breaking bones, particularly their hips. Major difficulties that hamper the investigation of anxiety in the elderly include the lack of good assessment instruments and treatment studies (Hersen, Van Hasselt, & Goreczny, 1993), largely due to a lack of sufficient research interest (Beck & Stanley, 1997; Sheikh, 1992).

According to studies reported by Judith Rodin and her colleagues (described in Chapter 2), the elderly may be particularly susceptible to anxiety about failing health or other life situations that begin to diminish whatever control they retain over events in their lives. This increasing lack of control, failing health, and the gradual loss of meaningful functions may be a particularly unfortunate by-product of the way the elderly are treated in Western culture. If it were possible to change our attitudes and behavior, we might well reduce the frequency of anxiety, depression, and early death among our elderly citizens.

Causes

What causes GAD? We have learned a great deal in the past several years. As with most anxiety disorders, there may be a genetic contribution. This conclusion is based on studies showing that GAD tends to run in families (Noyes, Clarkson, Crowe, Yates, & McChesney, 1987; Noyes et al., 1992). Twin studies strengthen this suggestion. Kendler, Neale, Kessler, Heath, and Eaves (1992a) found that the risk of GAD was somewhat greater for both members of monozygotic (identical) female twin pairs when one twin already had GAD than in dizygotic female twins. But in a later study, Kendler et al. (1995) confirmed that what seems to be inherited is the tendency to become anxious rather than GAD itself. Other twin studies (for example, Torgersen, 1983) have not found a strong heritable factor in GAD. As noted at the beginning of this chapter, investigations of anxiety as a human trait show a clear heritable factor, and there is every reason to think that, when all the appropriate studies are done, GAD will be proved at least as strongly heritable as is the trait of anxiety (Barlow, in press).

For a long time, generalized anxiety disorder has posed a real puzzle to investigators. Although the definition of

the disorder is relatively new, originating in 1980 with DSM-III, clinicians and psychopathologists were working with people with generalized anxiety long before diagnostic systems were developed. For years, clinicians thought that people who were generally anxious had simply not focused their anxiety on anything specific. Thus, such anxiety was described as "free floating." But now scientists have looked more closely and have discovered some very interesting distinctions.

The first hints of difference were found in the physiological responsivity of individuals with GAD. It is interesting that individuals with GAD do not respond as strongly as individuals with anxiety disorders in which panic is more prominent. In fact, several studies have found that individuals with GAD show *less responsiveness* on most physiological measures, such as heart rate, blood pressure, skin conductance, and respiration rate (Borkovec & Hu, 1990; Hoehn-Saric, McLeod, & Zimmerli, 1989), than do individuals with other anxiety disorders. For this reason people with GAD have been called *autonomic restrictors* (Barlow, Chorpita, & Turovsky, 1996; Thayer, Friedman, & Borkovec, 1996).

When individuals with GAD are compared to nonanxious normal subjects, the one physiological measure that consistently distinguishes the anxious group is muscle tension (Marten et al., 1993). People with GAD are chronically tense. To understand this phenomenon we may have to know what's going on in the minds of people with GAD. With new methods from cognitive science, we are beginning to uncover the sometimes unconscious mental processes ongoing in GAD (McNally, 1996).

The evidence indicates that individuals with GAD are highly sensitive to threat in general, particularly to a threat that has personal relevance. That is, they allocate their attention much more readily to sources of threat than people who are not anxious (Butler & Mathews, 1983; MacLeod, Mathews, & Tata, 1986; Mathews, 1997; Mogg, Mathews, & Weinman, 1989). Furthermore, this acute awareness of potential threat, particularly if it is personal, seems to be entirely automatic or *unconscious*. Using the Stroop color-naming task described in Chapter 2, MacLeod and Mathews (1991) presented threatening words on a screen for only *20 milliseconds* and still found that individuals with GAD were slower to name the colors of the words than were nonanxious individuals. Remember that in this task words in colored letters are presented very briefly and subjects are asked to name the *color* rather than the word. The fact that the colors of threatening words were named more slowly suggests that the *words* were more relevant to people with GAD, which interfered with their naming the color—even though the words *were not present long enough* for the individuals to be conscious of them! Investigators using other paradigms have come to similar conclusions (M. W. Eysenck, 1992; Mathews, 1997; McNally, 1996).

How do mental processes link up with the tendency of individuals with GAD to be autonomic restrictors? Tom Borkovec and his colleagues have suggested some possibilities. These researchers noticed that although the peripheral autonomic arousal of individuals with GAD is restricted, they showed marked increases in EEG beta activity, reflecting intense cognitive processing in the frontal lobes, particularly in the left hemisphere. This finding suggests to Borkovec and Inz (1990) that people with GAD engage in frantic, intense thought processes or worry *without* accompanying images (which would be reflected by activity in the right hemisphere of the brain). Borkovec suggests that this kind of worry may be ex-

Tom Borkovec and his colleagues theorized that people with generalized anxiety disorder worry excessively in order to avoid images of deep-seated emotional threat. Borkovec has also developed effective psychosocial treatments for GAD.

actly what causes these individuals to be autonomic restrictors (Borkovec, Shadick, & Hopkins, 1991; Roemer & Borkovec, 1993). That is, they are thinking so hard about upcoming problems that they don't have the attentional capacity left for the all-important process of *creating images* of the potential threat, images that would elicit more substantial negative affect and autonomic activity. In other words, they *avoid* all the negative affect associated with the threat. But from the point of view of therapy, it is very important to "process" the images and negative affect associated with anxiety (Craske & Barlow, 1988). Since people with GAD do not seem to engage in this process, they may avoid much of the unpleasantness and pain associated with the negative affect and imagery, but they are never able to work through their problems and arrive at solutions. Therefore they become *chronic worriers*, with accompanying autonomic inflexibility and quite severe muscle tension. Thus, intense worrying for an individual with GAD may serve the same maladaptive purpose as avoidance does for people with phobias. It prevents the person from facing the feared situation, and so adaptation never occurs.

In summary, some people inherit a tendency to be tense. Significant stress makes them apprehensive and vigilant. This sets off intense worry with resulting physiological changes, leading to generalized anxiety disorder (Turovsky & Barlow, 1996). This model is very current, as it combines findings from cognitive science with biological data from both the central and peripheral nervous systems. Time will tell if the model is correct, although supporting data continue to come in (DiBartolo, Brown, & Barlow, 1997). In any case, it is consistent with our view of anxiety as a future-oriented mood-state focused on potential danger or threat, as opposed to an emergency or alarm reaction to actual present danger. A model of generalized anxiety disorder is presented in Figure 5.4.

Treatment

Generalized anxiety disorder is quite common, but available treatments, both drug and psychological, are relatively weak and not well developed—although we are making progress. Benzodiazepines (minor tranquilizers) are most frequently prescribed for generalized anxiety and the evidence indicates that they give some relief, at least in the short term. Very few studies have looked at the effects of these drugs for a period longer than 8 weeks. Those that have suggest that benefits seem to continue for approximately 6 months (Schweizer & Rickles, 1996). But the therapeutic effect is relatively modest. Furthermore, benzodiazepines carry some risks. First, they seem to impair both cognitive and motor functioning (for instance, Hindmarch, 1986, 1990; O'Hanlon, Haak, Blaauw, & Riemersma, 1982). Specifically, people don't seem to be as alert on the job or at school when they are taking benzodiazepines. The drugs may impair driving, and in the elderly they seem to be associated with falls resulting in hip fractures (Ray, Gurwitz, Decker, & Kennedy, 1992).

More important, benzodiazepines seem to produce both psychological and physical dependence, making it very diffi-

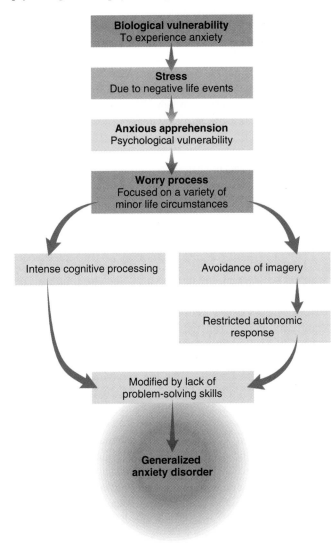

figure 5.4 An integrative model of generalized anxiety disorder

cult for people to stop taking them (Noyes, Garvey, Cook, & Suelzer, 1991; Rickels, Schweizer, Case, & Greenblatt, 1990; Schweizer, Rickels, Case, & Greenblatt, 1990). There is reasonably wide agreement that the optimal use of benzodiazepines is for the short-term relief of anxiety associated with a temporary crisis or stressful event, such as a family problem. Under these circumstances, a physician may prescribe a benzodiazepine until the crisis is resolved, but for no more than several days or a week or two at most. There is increasing evidence for the usefulness of antidepressants in the treatment of GAD (e.g., Rickels, Downing, Schweizer, & Hassman, 1993), and these drugs may, ultimately, prove to be a better choice.

The panic was in my legs, in my throat, and I felt compelled to run. . . .

In the short term, psychological treatments seem to confer about the same benefit as drugs in the treatment of generalized anxiety disorder but are probably better in the long term (Barlow & Lehman, 1996; Borkovec & Whisman, 1996; Gould, Otto, Pollack, & Yap, 1997). Recent reports of new innovations in brief psychological treatments are encouraging. As we learn more about generalized anxiety, we may find that helping people with this disorder to focus on what is actually threatening is useful. Because we now know that individuals with GAD seem to avoid "feelings" of anxiety and the negative affect associated with images, clinicians have designed treatments to help them process the information on an emotional level, using images, so that they will feel anxious. Of course, these treatments have other components, such as teaching patients how to relax deeply to combat tension. Borkovec and his colleagues found such a treatment to be significantly better than a placebo psychological treatment, not only at posttreatment but at a 1-year follow-up (Borkovec & Costello, 1993). This may be the beginning of a new generation of effective psychological treatments for anxiety. In our clinic we have developed a cognitive behavioral treatment (CBT) for GAD in which patients evoke the worry process during therapy sessions and confront anxiety-provoking images and thoughts head-on. The patient learns to use cognitive therapy and other coping techniques to counteract and control the worry process. Preliminary evidence shows that this treatment is also effective (Craske, Barlow, & O'Leary, 1992). Recent studies indicate that brief psychological treatments alter the sometimes unconscious cognitive biases associated with GAD (Mathews, Mogg, Kentish, & Eysenck, 1995; Mogg, Bradley, Millar, & White, 1995).

There is particularly encouraging evidence that psychological treatments are effective with children who suffer from generalized anxiety. Barrett, Dadds, and Rapee (1996) found significant benefit in children with severe GAD when cognitive behavioral procedures were combined with family therapy. After treatment, 95% of the children receiving this combination of therapies no longer met criteria for the diagnosis. Kendall et al. (1997) randomly assigned 94 children from 9 to 13 years of age to cognitive–behavioral therapy (CBT) or a wait list control group. The majority of the children were diagnosed with GAD but some had social phobia or separation anxiety. Based on teacher ratings, fully 70% of the treated children were functioning normally after treatment, gains that were maintained for at least 1 year. Similarly, we are also making progress in adapting our treatments for the elderly, as important new studies show (Beck & Stanley, 1997; Stanley, Beck, & Glassco, 1997).

After trying a number of different drugs, Irene was treated with the CBT approach developed at our clinic and found herself much more able to cope with life. She completed college and graduate school, married, and is successful in her career as a counselor in a nursing home. But even now, Irene finds it difficult to relax and stop worrying. She continues to experience mild to moderate anxiety, particularly when under stress; she takes minor tranquilizers on occasion to support her psychological coping skills.

Panic Disorder with and without Agoraphobia

Did you have a relative, an eccentric aunt, for example, who never seemed to leave the house? Family reunions or visits always had to be at her house. She never went anywhere else. Most people attributed their old aunt's behavior to her being a little odd or perhaps just not fond of travel. She was very warm and friendly when people came to visit, so she retained contact with the family.

In fact, your aunt may not be just odd or eccentric. She may suffer from a very debilitating anxiety disorder called **panic disorder with agoraphobia (PDA),** in which individuals experience severe unexpected panic attacks; they may think they're dying or otherwise losing control. Since they never know when an attack might occur, they develop **agoraphobia,** fear and avoidance of situations in which they would feel unsafe in the event of a panic attack or symptoms. These situations include those from which it would be hard or embarrassing to escape to get home or to a hospital. In severe cases, people with PDA are totally unable to leave the house, sometimes for years on end, as in the following example.

Mrs. M.
Self-Imprisoned

Mrs. M. was 67 years old and lived in a second-floor walk-up apartment in a lower-middle-class section of the city. Her adult daughter, one of her few remaining contacts with the world, had requested an evaluation, with Mrs. M.'s consent. I rang the bell and entered a narrow hallway; Mrs. M. was nowhere in sight. Knowing that she lived on the second floor, I walked up the stairs and knocked on the door at the top. When I heard Mrs. M. ask me to come in, I opened the door. She was sitting in her living room, and I could quickly see the layout of the rest of the apartment. The living room was in the front; the kitchen was in the back, adjoining a porch. To the right of the stairs was the one bedroom, with a bathroom opening from it.

Mrs. M. was glad to see me and very friendly offering me coffee and home-made cookies. I was the first person she had seen in 3 weeks. In fact, Mrs. M. had not left that apartment in 20 years, and she had suffered from panic disorder with agoraphobia for over 30 years.

As she told her story, Mrs. M. conveyed vivid images of a wasted life. And yet she continued to struggle in the face of adversity and to make the best she could of her limited existence. Even areas in her apartment signaled the potential for terrifying panic attacks. She had not answered the door herself for the past 15 years because she was afraid to look into the hallway. She could enter her kitchen and go into the areas containing the stove and refrigerator, but for the past 10 years she had not been to the part of the room that overlooked the backyard or out onto the back porch. Thus, her life for the past decade had been confined to her bedroom, her living room, and the front half of her kitchen. She relied on her adult daughter to bring groceries and visit once a week. Her only other visitor was the parish priest, who came to deliver communion every 2 to 3 weeks when he could. Her only other contact with the outside world was through the television and the radio. Her husband, who had abused both alcohol and Mrs. M., had died 10 years earlier of alcohol-related causes. Early in her very stressful marriage she had her first terrifying panic attack and had gradually withdrawn from the world. As long as she stayed in her apartment, she was relatively free of panic. For this reason, and because in her mind there were few reasons left near the end of her life to venture out, she declined treatment.

Clinical Description

At the beginning of the chapter we talked about the related phenomena of anxiety and panic. In PDA, anxiety and panic are combined with *phobic avoidance* in an intricate relationship that can become as devastating as it was for Mrs. M. Many people who have panic attacks do not necessarily develop panic disorder. Similarly, many people experience anxiety and panic without developing agoraphobia. In those cases, the disorder is called **panic disorder without agoraphobia (PD).**

To meet criteria for panic disorder (with or without agoraphobia) a person must experience an unexpected panic attack *and* develop substantial anxiety over the possibility of having another attack *or* about the implications of the attack or its consequences. In other words, he or she must think that each attack is a sign of impending death or incapacitation. A few individuals do not report concern about another attack but still change their behavior in a way that indicates the distress the attacks cause them. They may avoid going to certain places or neglect their duties around the house for fear that an attack might occur if they are too active.

THE DEVELOPMENT OF AGORAPHOBIA

Many people with panic disorder develop agoraphobia. The term *agoraphobia* was coined in 1871 by Westphal and, in the original Greek, refers to fear of the marketplace. This is a very appropriate term since the *agora*, the Greek marketplace, was a very busy, bustling area. One of the most stressful places for modern agoraphobics is the shopping mall, the modern-day agora.

All the evidence now points to the conclusion that agoraphobic avoidance behavior is simply one complication of severe unexpected panic attacks (Craske & Barlow, 1988). Simply put, if you have had unexpected panic attacks and are afraid you may have another one, you want to be in a safe place or at least with a safe person who knows what you are experiencing if another attack occurs, so you can quickly get to a hospital or at least go into your bedroom and lie down (the home is usually a safe place). We know that anxiety is diminished for individuals with agoraphobia if they think a location or person is "safe," even if there is nothing effective the person could do if something bad did happen. If you are in a shopping mall or a crowded movie theater or church, not only is it difficult to leave but you are probably going to embarrass yourself if you try. You may think you will have to climb over everyone in church to get out, or get up in the middle of the movie and run out, or worse, faint in the movie theater (in fact, individuals with agoraphobia seldom if ever do any of these things). For these reasons, when they do go to church or to the movies, agoraphobics always sit very near the door. A list of typical situations commonly avoided by someone with agoraphobia is found in Table 5.1.

Though agoraphobic behavior initially is closely tied to the occasions of panic, it can become relatively independent

table 5.1 Typical Situations Avoided by a Person with Agoraphobia

Shopping malls
Cars (as driver or passenger)
Buses
Trains
Subways
Wide streets
Tunnels
Restaurants
Theaters
Being far from home
Staying at home alone
Waiting in line
Supermarkets
Stores
Crowds
Planes
Elevators
Escalators

Source: Adapted from Barlow & Craske, 1994

Willard Scott, the former *Today Show* weatherman, endures frequent panic attacks yet remains able to function.

Michelle Craske demonstrated that agoraphobic avoidance is simply one way of coping with panic. She and Ron Rapee also developed an effective psychosocial treatment for panic disorder.

internal physical sensations (Barlow, in press; Barlow & Craske, 1989; Craske & Barlow, 1993; Shear et al., 1997). These behaviors involve removing yourself from situations or activities that might produce the physiological arousal that somehow resembles the beginnings of a panic attack. Some patients might avoid exercise because it produces increased cardiovascular activity or faster respiration that reminds them of panic attacks. Other patients might avoid sauna baths or any rooms in which they might perspire. Psychopathologists are beginning to recognize that this cluster of avoidance behaviors is every bit as important as more classical agoraphobic avoidance. A list of situations or activities typically avoided within the interoceptive cluster is found in Table 5.2.

of panic attacks (Craske & Barlow, 1988; Craske, Rapee, & Barlow, 1988). In other words, an individual who has not had a panic attack for years may still have strong agoraphobic avoidance, like Mrs. M. Agoraphobic avoidance seems to be determined by the extent to which you think or expect you might have another attack rather than by how many attacks you actually have or how severe they are. Thus, agoraphobic avoidance is simply one way of coping with unexpected panic attacks.

Other methods of coping with panic attacks include using (and eventually abusing) drugs and/or alcohol. Some individuals do not actually avoid agoraphobic situations but endure them with "intense dread." For example, people who simply must go to work each day or, perhaps, travel as part of the job will suffer untold agonies of anxiety and panic simply to achieve their goals. Thus DSM-IV notes that agoraphobia may be characterized either by avoiding the situations or by enduring them with marked distress.

One of the best examples of someone who toughs it out is the former weatherman on the *Today* show, Willard Scott. One day, after doing the show successfully for years, he went on camera and suddenly felt his heart pounding and his chest getting tight; he also experienced the sheer terror of being totally unsure of what he was going to do or say next. He thought he was having a heart attack and was about to die on camera. He reports that many times when he goes on camera he experiences these panic attacks, although most viewers would never know it. Somehow he makes it through. Although most people think all the world sees their panic, only their families—and sometimes not even they—know what the person is going through.

Most patients with severe agoraphobic avoidance (and some with little) also display another cluster of avoidant behaviors that we call *interoceptive avoidance* or avoidance of

Statistics

Panic disorder with or without agoraphobia is fairly common. Approximately 3.5% of the population meet the criteria for panic disorder at some point during their lives, two-thirds of them women (Eaton, Kessler, Wittchen, & Magee, 1994) and another 5.3% meet the criteria for agoraphobia (Kessler et al., 1994). The rates of agoraphobia may be somewhat overestimated as a result of methodological difficulties, but most people with panic disorder do have agoraphobic avoidance.

Onset of panic disorder usually occurs in early adult life—from mid-teens through about 40 years of age. The mean age of onset is between 25 and 29 (Öst, 1987). Prepubescent children have been known to experience unexpected panic attacks and occasionally panic disorder, although this is quite rare (Albano, Chorpita, & Barlow, 1996; Kearney, Albano, Eisen, Allan, & Barlow, 1997; Moreau & Weissman, 1992). Most initial unexpected panic attacks begin at or after puberty. In fact, puberty seems a better predictor of unexpected panic attacks than age, since higher rates of panic attacks are found in physically mature girls (Hayward et al., 1992). Furthermore, many prepubertal children who are seen by general medical practitioners have symptoms of hyperventilation that may well be panic attacks. However, these children do not report fear of dying or losing control—perhaps because they are not at a stage of their cognitive development where they can make these attributions (Nelles & Barlow, 1988).

Important work on anxiety in the elderly has been carried out by Pat Wisocki and her colleagues (Wisocki, 1988;

table 5.2 Interoceptive Daily Activities Typically Avoided by People with Agoraphobia

Running up flights of stairs
Walking outside in intense heat
Hot, stuffy rooms
Hot, stuffy cars
Hot, stuffy stores or shopping malls
Walking outside in very cold weather
Aerobics
Lifting heavy objects
Dancing
Sexual relations
Watching horror movies
Eating heavy meals
Watching exciting movies or sports events
Getting involved in "heated" debates
Having showers with the doors and windows closed
Having a sauna
Hiking
Sports
Drinking coffee or any caffeinated beverages
Eating chocolate
Standing quickly from a sitting position
Getting angry

Source: Adapted from Barlow & Craske, 1994

Wisocki, Handen, & Morse, 1986), who discovered that health and vitality are the primary focus of anxiety in the elderly population. Lindesay (1991) studied 60 confirmed cases of phobic disorder in the elderly and found that they differed from younger adults in several ways. The primary phobia in this group was agoraphobia which had a late onset (after age 50) and was often related to a very stressful life event, usually an illness or injury. In general, panic disorder seems less pervasive among the elderly, but our estimates are not yet firm (e.g., Beck & Stanley, 1997).

As we have said, 75% or more of those who suffer from agoraphobia are women (Barlow, 1988; Myers et al., 1984; Thorpe & Burns, 1983). For a long time we didn't know why, but now it seems that the most logical explanation is cultural: It is more accepted for women to report fear and to avoid numerous situations. Men, on the other hand, are expected to be stronger and braver, to "tough it out." In fact, the higher the severity of agoraphobic avoidance, the greater the proportion of women. For example, in our clinic, out of a group of patients suffering from panic disorder with mild agoraphobia, 72% were women; but if the agoraphobia was moderate, the percentage was 81%. Similarly, if agoraphobia was severe, the percentage was 89%.

What happens to men who have severe unexpected panic attacks? Is cultural disapproval of fear in men so strong that most of them simply endure panic? The answer seems to be "no." A large proportion of males with

Sometimes just writing a check for my purchases required all the control I could muster.

unexpected panic attacks cope in a culturally acceptable way: They consume large amounts of alcohol. The problem is that they become dependent on alcohol, and many begin the long downward spiral into serious addiction. Thus, males may end up with an even more severe problem than panic disorder with agoraphobia. Because these men are so impaired by alcohol abuse, clinicians may not realize that they also have PDA. Furthermore, even if they are successfully treated for their addiction, the anxiety disorder still requires treatment (Chambless, Cherney, Caputo, & Rheinstein, 1987; Cox, Swinson, Shulman, Kuch, & Reichman, 1993; Himle & Hill, 1991; Kushner, Sher, & Beitman, 1990).

CULTURAL INFLUENCES

Panic disorder exists worldwide, although its expression may vary from place to place. In Lesotho, Africa, the prevalence of panic disorder (and generalized anxiety disorder) was found to be equal to or greater than in North America (Hollifield, Katon, Spain, & Pule, 1990). In a more comprehensive study, prevalence rates for panic disorder were remarkably similar in the U.S., Canada, Puerto Rico, New Zealand, Italy, Korea, and Taiwan, with only Taiwan showing somewhat lower rates (Horwath & Weissman, 1997). Rates are also similar among different ethnic groups in the United States, including African-Americans. Furthermore, black and white patients with panic disorder show no significant differences in symptoms (Friedman, Paradis, & Hatch, 1994). However, it is very important to note that panic disorder co-occurs very frequently with hypertension in African-American patients (Neal, Nagle-Rich, & Smucker, 1994; Neal-Barnett & Smith, 1997).

Somatic symptoms of anxiety may be emphasized in third world cultures. Feelings of dread or angst may not be part of the cultural idiom. In Chapter 2 we described a fright disorder called *susto* in Latin America. An anxiety-related, culturally defined syndrome prominent among Hispanic-Americans, particularly those from the Caribbean, is called *ataques de nervios* (Liebowitz et al., 1994). The symptoms of an ataque seem quite similar to those of panic attacks, although such manifestations as shouting uncontrollably or bursting into tears may be associated more frequently with ataque than with panic.

NOCTURNAL PANIC

Think back to the case of Gretchen, whose panic attack is described on page 113. Is there anything unusual about her report? She was sound asleep when it happened! Approximately 60% of the people with panic disorder have experienced such nocturnal attacks (Craske & Rowe, 1997; Uhde, 1994). In fact, panic attacks occur more frequently between 1:30 a.m. and 3:30 a.m. than at any other time (C. B. Taylor et al., 1986). In some cases, people are afraid to go to sleep at night! What's happening to them? Are they having nightmares?

Nocturnal attacks are studied in a sleep laboratory. Patients spend a few nights sleeping while attached to an electroencephalograph (EEG) machine that monitors their brain waves (see Chapter 3). We all go through various stages of sleep that are reflected by different patterns on the electroencephalogram. (Stages of sleep are discussed fully in Chapter 8.) We have learned that nocturnal panics occur during delta wave or slow wave sleep, which typically occurs several hours after we fall asleep and is the deepest stage of sleep. People with panic disorder often begin to panic when they start sinking into delta sleep, and then they awaken in the midst of an attack. Since there is no obvious reason for them to be anxious or panicky when they are sound asleep, most of these individuals think they are dying (Craske & Barlow, 1988; Craske & Rowe, 1997).

What causes nocturnal panic? We thought it might be nightmares, but nightmares and other dreamlike activity occur only during a stage of sleep characterized by rapid eye movement (REM sleep), which typically occurs much later in the sleep cycle. Therefore, people are not dreaming when they have nocturnal panics, a conclusion that is consistent with patient reports. Some therapists are not aware of the stage of sleep associated with nocturnal panic attacks, and so assume that patients are "repressing" their dream material, perhaps because it might relate to an early trauma too painful to be admitted to consciousness. As we've seen, this is virtually impossible because nocturnal panic attacks do not occur during REM sleep, so there is no well-developed dream or nightmare activity going on when they happen. Thus, it is not possible for these patients to be dreaming anything.

Some therapists assume that patients with nocturnal panic might have a breathing disorder called *sleep apnea*, an interruption of breathing during sleep that may feel like suffocation. This condition is often found in people who are substantially overweight. But sleep apnea has a cycle of awakening and falling back to sleep that is not characteristic of nocturnal panics.

A related phenomenon occurring in children is called sleep terrors, which is described in more detail in Chapter 8. Often children awake imagining that something is chasing them around the room. It is common for them to scream and actually get out of bed as if something were after them. However, they *do not wake up*, and have no memory of the event in the morning. In contrast individuals experiencing nocturnal panic attacks do wake up and later remember the event very clearly. Sleep terrors also tend to occur at a later stage of sleep (stage 4 sleep), a stage that is associated with sleepwalking.

Finally, there is a fascinating condition called *isolated sleep paralysis* that seems culturally determined. Have you ever heard the expression "the witch is riding you"? If you're white, you probably haven't, but if you're African-American, chances are you at least know somebody who has had this frightening experience (Bell, Dixie-Bell, & Thompson, 1986).

Isolated sleep paralysis occurs during the transitional state between sleep and waking, when a person is either falling asleep or waking up. During this period the individual

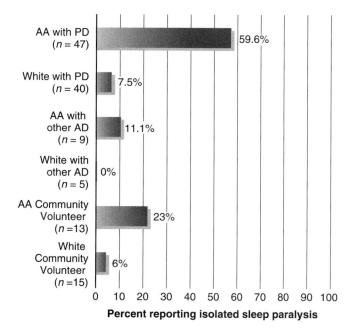

figure 5.5 Isolated sleep paralysis in African-Americans (AA) and whites with panic disorder (PD), other anxiety disorder (AD) but not panic disorder and community volunteers with no disorder. Adapted from Paradis, Friedman, & Hatch (1997).

is unable to move and experiences a surge of terror that resembles a panic attack; occasionally, there are also vivid hallucinations. This event is interesting in that it occurs much less frequently in Caucasians. In this country it is a common experience of African-Americans with panic disorder (Neal-Barnett & Smith, 1997; Paradis, Friedman, & Hatch, 1997). Since a high proportion of these individuals also suffer traditional panic attacks, Bell et al. (1986) hypothesized that panic disorder in African-Americans may well be accompanied by the additional feature of isolated sleep paralysis. Now evidence confirms this hypothesis. Paradis et al. (1997) found that the occurrence of isolated sleep paralysis was significantly higher in African-Americans with panic disorder (59.6%) as compared with other groups (see Figure 5.5). Thus, isolated sleep paralysis seems to be common in African-Americans with panic disorder. Even more interesting is that the disorder does not seem to occur in Nigerian blacks. In fact, the prevalence in Nigerian blacks is about the same as it is in American whites. The reasons for this distribution are not clear, although all factors point to a cultural explanation.

SUICIDE

Based on epidemiological data, Weissman and her colleagues found that 20% of patients with panic disorder had attempted suicide, and they concluded that such attempts were associated with panic disorder. They also concluded that the risk of someone with panic disorder attempting suicide is comparable to that for individuals with major depression (Johnson, Weissman, & Klerman, 1990; Weissman, Klerman, Markowitz, & Ouellette, 1989). This finding is frightening, because panic disorder is quite prevalent and clinicians have generally not been on the lookout for possible suicide attempts in such patients. The investigators also found that even patients with panic disorder who did not have accompanying depression were still at risk for suicide.

Other researchers, however (Beck, Steer, Sanderson, & Skeie, 1991; S. Friedman, Jones, Chernen, & Barlow, 1992), examined hundreds of patients with panic disorder in outpatient clinics and did not find a suicide risk in those who had no additional disorders. They did find that the risk of suicidal thoughts and attempts was greater in patients with panic disorder who also had borderline personality disorder, in which suicidal attempts are a prominent characteristic. Hornig and McNally (1995), in a reanalysis of Weissman et al. (original data), came to a similar conclusion.

Discrepant findings of this type are common in research in psychopathology and almost always force scientists to look closely at their methods and examine what might account for very different findings in two or more studies. When several possibilities are recognized, scientists have some guidance in determining which possibility (or hypothesis) seems to account for the discrepancy. Thus does science advance.

What caused the discrepancy here? Among the several possibilities, the method of assessment and the type of interview used in the studies differed considerably. The epidemiological studies reported by Weissman et al. (1989) were conducted by lay interviewers who were not necessarily trained in determining suicidal risk. Also, the lay interviewers were interviewing a random sample of the population rather than a sample drawn from clinic outpatients. In addition, the lay interviewers did not necessarily

identify other disorders individuals with panic disorder might have had in the past that could have accounted for suicidal ideation.

But there are other possibilities. The epidemiological study may have included individuals who were unaware that treatment existed. As a result, they might have become particularly hopeless and begun to think about suicide. All the patients at the outpatient clinics, on the other hand, were about to receive treatment and therefore had some hope of recovering. Although Hornig and McNally's 1995 analysis does not support this interpretation, we must continue to conduct research that clarifies the true relationship between panic disorder and suicide.

Causes

It is not possible to understand panic disorder (with or without agoraphobia) without referring to the triad of contributing factors mentioned throughout this book: biological, psychological, and social. Strong evidence indicates that agoraphobia develops after a person has unexpected panic attacks (or panic-like sensations); but whether agoraphobia develops and how severe it becomes seem to be socially and culturally determined, as noted above. Panic attacks and panic disorder, on the other hand, seem to be related most strongly to biological and psychological factors and their interaction.

At the beginning of the chapter we discussed how biological, psychological, and social factors may contribute to

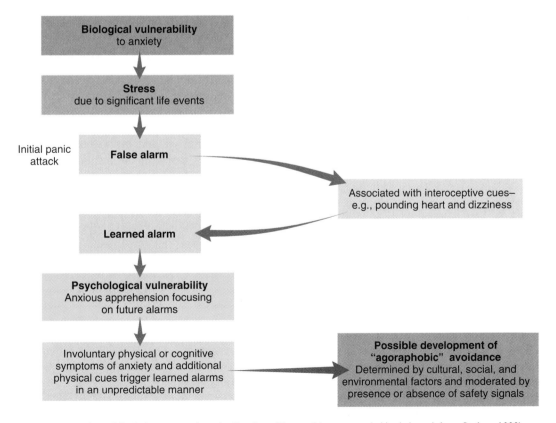

figure 5.6 A model of the causes of panic disorder with or without agoraphobia (adapted from Barlow, 1988)

the development and maintenance of anxiety and to an initial unexpected panic attack. Elsewhere we have suggested a model of the etiology of panic disorder that takes into consideration what we know about the development of anxiety and panic (see Figure 5.6).

As noted earlier, we all inherit some vulnerability to stress, a tendency to be neurobiologically overreactive to the events of daily life. Thus, some people are more likely than others to have an emergency alarm reaction (unexpected panic attack) when confronted with stress-producing events. These may include stress on the job or at school, death of a loved one, divorce, and positive events that are nevertheless stressful, such as graduating from school and starting a new career, getting married, or changing jobs. (Remember that other people might have headaches or high blood pressure in response to the same kinds of stress.) Particular situations quickly become associated in an individual's mind with external and internal cues that were present during the attack. The next time the person's heart rate increases during exercise, she might assume she is having a panic attack (conditioning). Harmless exercise is an example of an internal cue or a conditioned stimulus (CS) for a panic attack. Being in a movie theater when panic first occurred would be an external cue that might become a CS for future panics. Since these cues become associated with a number of different internal and external stimuli through a learning process, we call them "learned alarms."

But none of this would make much difference without the next step. The individuals must develop *anxiety* over the possibility of having another panic attack. That is, they think that the physical sensations associated with the panic attack mean that something terrible is about to happen, perhaps death. This is what creates panic disorder. In other words, when people have a tendency to expect the worst when they experience strong physical sensations, some of them focus their anxiety on the possibility of *future* panic attacks whereas other people experiencing these attacks do not.

We know that approximately 8% to 12% of the population will have an occasional unexpected panic attack, often during a period of intense stress (Norton, Harrison, Hauch, & Rhodes, 1985; Salge, Beck, & Logan, 1988; M. J. Telch, Lucas, & Nelson, 1989). Most of these people do not develop anxiety (M. J. Telch et al., 1989). Only approximately 3% go on to develop anxiety over future panic attacks and thereby meet the criteria for panic disorder. What happens to those individuals who don't develop anxiety? They seem to attribute the attack to events of the moment, such as an argument with a friend, something they ate, or a bad day, and go on with their lives, perhaps experiencing an occasional panic attack when they are under stress again.

The influential cognitive theories of David Clark (1986, 1996) explicate in more detail some of the cognitive processes that may be ongoing in panic disorder. Clark emphasizes the psychological vulnerability of people with this

I stepped into therapy like an innocent into the water, trusting in some guiding hand to help me stay afloat.

disorder to interpret normal physical sensations in a catastrophic way. In other words, although we all typically experience rapid heartbeat after exercise, if you have a psychological or cognitive vulnerability, you might interpret the response as dangerous, and feel a surge of anxiety. This anxiety, in turn, produces more physical sensations because of the action of the sympathetic nervous system, you perceive these additional sensations as even more dangerous, and a vicious cycle begins that results in a panic attack. Thus, Clark emphasizes as most important the cognitive process in panic disorder.

Supporting this model, Ehlers and Breuer (1992) had panic disorder patients and several control groups try to estimate how fast their hearts were beating. The exercise demonstrated that patients with panic disorder paid much closer attention to their internal somatic sensations because they were much more *accurate* at estimating how fast their hearts were beating than individuals without panic disorder. In other words, because they are anxious about bodily sensations to begin with, because these sensations might indicate an unexpected panic is about to occur, the patients are more *vigilant* for internal sensations, or more *interoceptively aware.* But this awareness helps maintain the vicious cycle because they quickly notice *any* somatic response and interpret it as dangerous. Some studies however, could not replicate this finding (Antony et al., 1993), so we need to study the phenomenon more closely.

One hypothesis that panic disorder and agoraphobia evolve from psychodynamic causes suggested that early object loss and/or separation anxiety might predispose someone to develop the condition as an adult. Object loss, or separation anxiety, is what a child might feel at the threat of separation or upon actual separation from an important caregiver, such as the mother or father. Dependent personality tendencies often characterize a person with agoraphobia. These characteristics were hypothesized as a possible reaction to early separation. Nevertheless, despite some intriguing suggestions, there is very little evidence that patients who have panic disorder with agoraphobia experienced separation anxiety during childhood more frequently than individuals with other psychological disorders or, for that matter, normals (Barlow, 1988; Thyer, 1993; van der Molen, van den Hout, van Dieren, & Griez, 1989). It is still possible, however, that the trauma of early separation might predispose someone to psychological disorders in general. (Separation anxiety disorder is discussed in the section on specific phobias.)

Treatment

MEDICATION

As noted in Chapter 1, research on the effectiveness of new treatments is important to psychopathology. Responses to certain specific treatments, whether drug or psychological, may indicate the causes of the disorder. For example, in some of his pioneering work, Donald Klein (1964) analyzed the effects of various drugs on panic and anxiety. He noticed that drugs affecting primarily the serotonergic and noradrenergic neurotransmitter systems, specifically a tricyclic antidepressant drug called imipramine, blocked panic attacks but did not seem to affect generalized anxiety. Benzodiazepines, on the other hand, reduced anxiety but did not seem to block panic attacks. Thus, he developed his theory that panic was different from anxiety, which led to biological theories suggesting different locations in the brain for panic and anxiety responses.

Although subsequent studies strongly suggest that anxiety and panic may well be separate processes, the differential effects of the two classes of drugs have not been as strongly supported. It seems that some high-potency benzodiazepines are just as effective for panic disorder as are tricyclic antidepressants such as imipramine, as well as the newer serotonin specific reuptake inhibitors (SSRIs) such as Prozac and Paxil. In fact, a large number of drugs affecting either the noradrenergic, serotonergic, or benzodiazepine-GABA neurotransmitter systems seem effective in treating panic disorder.

There are advantages and disadvantages to each class of drugs. Imipramine, one of the tricyclic antidepressants, produces strong side effects that include dizziness, dry mouth and, on occasion, sexual dysfunction, so many patients refuse to stay on it for very long. But a person who can become accustomed to the side effects or wait until they wear off may find that the drug can reduce panic attacks and associated anxiety. SSRIs are just as effective, but produce fewer immediate side effects, so that individuals usually continue taking their pills (e.g., Lecrubier, Bakker, et al., 1997; Lecrubier, Judge, et al., 1997). SSRIs are currently the preferred drug for panic disorder, although we are now learning that the side effect of sexual dysfunction seems to occur in most people taking these medications. On the other hand, high-potency benzodiazepines such as *alprazolam* (Xanax), commonly used for panic disorder, work very fast but are hard to stop taking due to psychological and physical dependence and addiction. Also, all benzodiazepines adversely affect cognitive and motor functions to some degree. Therefore, people taking them in high doses often find their ability to drive a car or study somewhat reduced.

Approximately 60% of patients with panic disorder are free of panic as long as they stay on an effective drug (Ballenger et al., 1988; Klosko, Barlow, Tassinari, & Cerny, 1990; Lecrubier, Bakker, et al., 1997), but relapse rates are high once the medication is stopped. Approximately 20% to 50% of patients relapse after stopping tricyclic antidepressants (M. J. Telch, 1988; M. J. Telch, Tearnan, & Taylor, 1983). The relapse rate is closer to 90% for those who stop taking benzodiazepines (for example, Fyer et al., 1987).

PSYCHOLOGICAL INTERVENTION

Psychological treatments have proven quite effective for panic disorder. Originally, such treatments concentrated on reducing agoraphobic avoidance, using strategies based on exposure to feared situations. The strategy of exposure-based

---

table 5.3	**Situation-Exposure Tasks (from least to most difficult)**

Shopping in a crowded supermarket for 30 minutes alone
Walking five blocks away from home alone
Driving on a busy highway for five miles with spouse, and alone
Eating in a restaurant, seated in the middle
Watching a movie while seated in the middle of the row

Source: Barlow & Craske, 1994

---

treatments is to arrange conditions in which the patient can gradually face the feared situations and learn that there is really nothing to fear. Of course, most patients with phobias are well aware of this rationally, but they must be convinced on an emotional level as well by "reality testing" the situation. Sometimes the therapist accompanies the patients on their exposure exercises. At other times, the therapist simply helps patients structure their own exercises and provides them with a variety of psychological coping mechanisms to help them complete the exercises, which are typically arranged from least to most difficult. A sample of these are listed in Table 5.3. The therapist identifies situations that are relevant to the patient and then arranges them in order of difficulty.

Gradual exposure exercises combined with anxiety-reducing coping mechanisms, such as relaxation or breathing retraining, have proven effective in helping patients overcome agoraphobic behavior. As many as 70% of patients undergoing these treatments substantially improve as their anxiety and panic are reduced and their agoraphobic avoidance greatly diminished. Very few, however, are cured, because many still experience some anxiety and panic attacks, though at a less severe level.

Effective psychological treatments have recently been developed that treat panic attacks directly (Barlow & Craske, 1989, 1994; D. M. Clark et al., 1994; Klosko et al., 1990). **Panic control treatment (PCT)** concentrates on exposing patients with panic disorder to the cluster of interoceptive sensations that remind them of their panic attacks. The therapist attempts to create "mini" panic attacks in the office by having the patients exercise to elevate their heart rates or perhaps by spinning them in a chair to make them dizzy. A variety of exercises have been developed for this purpose (see Table 5.4). Patients also receive cognitive therapy. Basic attitudes and perceptions concerning the dangerousness of the feared but objectively harmless situations are identified and modified. As we learned above, many of these attitudes and perceptions are beyond the patient's awareness. Uncovering these unconscious cognitive processes requires a great deal of therapeutic skill. In addition to exposure to interoceptive sensations and cognitive therapy, patients are taught relaxation or breathing retraining to help them cope with increases in anxiety and to reduce excess arousal.

These psychological procedures are highly effective for panic disorder. Between 80% and 100% of patients are free of panic after approximately 12 weekly sessions. Follow-up studies of patients who receive PCT indicate that they re-

table 5.4 Exercises to Create the Sensation of Panic

1. Shake your head loosely from side to side for 30 seconds (to produce dizziness or disorientation).
2. Place your head between your legs for 30 seconds and then lift it quickly (to produce lightheadedness or blood rushing).
3. Take one step up, using stairs or a box or a footstool, and immediately step down. Do this repeatedly at a fast enough rate to notice your heart pumping quickly for 1 minute (to produce racing heart and shortness of breath).
4. Hold your breath for as long as you can or about 30–45 seconds (to produce chest tightness and smothering feelings).
5. Tense every part of your body for 1 minute without causing pain. Tense your arms, legs, stomach, back, shoulders, face—everything. Alternatively, try holding a push-up position for 1 minute or for as long as you can (to produce muscle tension, weakness, and trembling).
6. Spin in a chair for 1 minute. If you have a chair that spins,

such as a desk chair, this is ideal. It's even better if someone is there to spin you around. Otherwise, stand up and turn around quickly to make yourself dizzy. Be near a soft chair or couch that you can sit in after 1 minute is up. This will produce dizziness and perhaps nausea as well.
7. Hyperventilate for 1 minute. Breathe deep and fast, using a lot of force. Sit down as you do this. This exercise might produce unreality, shortness of breath, tingling, cold or hot feelings, dizziness, or headache.
8. Breathe through a thin straw for 1 minute. Don't allow any air through your nose; hold your nostrils together (to produce feelings of restricted air flow or smothering).
9. Stare at a small spot on the wall or stare at yourself in the mirror for 2 minutes. Stare as hard as you can to produce feelings of unreality.

Source: Barlow & Craske, 1994

main better after at least 2 years (Craske, Brown, & Barlow, 1991). Remaining agoraphobic behavior can then be treated with more standard exposure exercises. Although these treatments are quite effective, they are relatively new and not yet available to many individuals who suffer from panic disorder because administering them requires therapists to have advanced training.

NEW EVIDENCE ON COMBINED TREATMENT

Preliminary results are in from a major study sponsored by the National Institute of Mental Health that looked at the separate and combined effects of psychological and drug treatments (Barlow, Gorman, Shear, & Woods, 1997; Shear, Woods, Gorman, & Barlow, 1997; Woods, Barlow, Gorman, & Shear, 1997). In this double-blind study, 304 carefully screened patients with panic disorder were treated at four different sites, two known for their expertise with medication treatments and two known for their expertise with psychological treatments. The purpose of this arrangement was to control for any bias that might affect the results because of the allegiance of investigators committed to one type of treatment or the other. Patients were randomized into five different treatment conditions: psychological treatment alone (PCT), drug treatment alone (imipramine—IMI—a tricyclic antidepressant, was used), a combined treatment condition (IMI + PCT), and two "control" conditions, one using placebo alone (PLA), and one using placebo + PCT (to determine the extent to which any advantage for combined treatment was due to placebo contribution).

Table 5.5 shows the results in terms of the percentage of patients who responded to treatment at the end of 3 months, based on the judgement of an independent evaluator, and includes patients who dropped out along the way, counting them as failures. The data reveal an advantage of the combined treatment over individual treatments; but, surprisingly, this advantage was almost entirely due to placebo contributions to PCT. Both PCT + IMI and PCT + PLA were

significantly more effective than IMI alone. PCT alone occupied an intermediate position in effectiveness between the combined treatments and IMI alone. Table 5.5 also presents the results after 6 additional months of maintenance treatment when patients were seen once per month. At this point the results looked very much as they did after initial treatment, except that all treatments were substantially better than the placebo alone condition since the number of placebo responses had diminished. Table 5.5 also shows the last set of results, 6 months after treatment was discontinued (15 months after it was initiated). At this point patients on medication, whether combined with PCT or not, had deteriorated somewhat, and those receiving PCT without the drug had retained most of their gains. Thus, treatments containing CBT without the drug tended to be superior.

Conclusions from this large and important study suggest that there is no advantage to combining drug and PCT treatments, since any incremental effect of combined treatment seems to be a placebo effect, not a true drug effect. Furthermore, the psychological treatments seemed to perform better in the long run (6 months after treatment had stopped). The public health recommendation emanating from this study, based on the principle of utilizing the least intrusive treatment first, suggests that the psychological treatment should be offered initially, followed by drug treatment for those patients who do not respond adequately or for whom psychological treatment is not available. Since this was such a large study involving so many different research centers, it is likely to have a substantial impact on national health care policy.

Specific Phobia

Remember Judy in Chapter 1? When she saw a film of the frog being dissected, Judy began feeling queasy. Eventually

table 5.5 Results from the Multicenter Collaborative Study

	CBT + IMI	CBT + PLA	CBT Alone	IMI Alone	PLA Alone
Percent of patients responding after 3 months of initial treatment	67%	65%	56%	49%	38%
Percent of patients responding after 6 months of maintenance treatment (9 months after treatment began)	59%	53%	44%	38%	13%
Percent responding 6 additional months after treatment was discontinued (15 months after treatment began)	28%	43%	33%	20%	13%

she reached the point of fainting if someone simply said "Cut it out." Earlier in this chapter you read about John Madden's difficulties with flying. Judy and John Madden have in common what we call a specific phobia.

Clinical Description

A **specific phobia** is an irrational fear of a specific object or situation that markedly interferes with an individual's ability to function. Prior to DSM-IV this category was called "simple" phobia to distinguish it from the more complex agoraphobia condition, but we now recognize that there is nothing simple about it. Many of you might be afraid of something that is not dangerous, such as going to the dentist, or have a greatly exaggerated fear of something that is only mildly dangerous, such as driving a car or flying. For this reason, most people can identify to some extent with a phobia. Recent surveys indicate that specific fears of a variety of objects or situations occur in a majority of the population (Myers et al., 1984). But the very commonness of fears, even severe fears, often causes people to trivialize the psychological disorder known as a specific phobia. These phobias, in their severe form, can be extremely disabling, as we saw with Judy.

For people such as John Madden, on the other hand, phobias are a nuisance, sometimes an extremely inconvenient nuisance; but one can adapt to life with a phobia by simply working around it somehow. In upstate New York and New England where we live and work, some people are afraid to drive in the snow. We have had people come to our clinics who have been so severely phobic that during the winter they were ready to uproot, change their jobs and their lives, and move south. That is one way of dealing with a phobia. We will discuss some other ways at the end of this chapter.

The major characteristic held in common by Judy and John Madden, of course, is the DSM-IV criterion of marked and persistent fear that is set off by a specific object or situation. Both also have recognized that their fear and anxiety are excessive or unreasonable. Finally, both went to considerable lengths to avoid situations where their phobic response might occur.

There the similarities end. In fact, there are as many phobias as there are objects and situations. The variety of Greek and Latin names contrived to describe phobias stuns the imagination. Table 5.6 gives only the phobias beginning with the letter "a" from a long list compiled by Jack D. Maser from medical dictionaries and other diverse sources (Maser, 1985). Of course, this sort of list has little or no value for people studying psychopathology, but it does show the extent of the named phobias.

Before the publication of DSM-IV in 1994, no meaningful classification of specific phobias existed. However, we have now learned that the cases of Judy and of John Madden represent types of specific phobia that differ in major ways. Four major subtypes of specific phobia have been identified: (a) animal type, (b) natural environment type (for instance, heights, storms, and water), (c) blood-injection-injury type, and (d) situational type (such as planes, elevators, or enclosed places). A fifth category, "other," includes phobias that do not fit any of the four major subtypes (for instance, situations that may lead to choking, vomiting, or contracting an illness; or, in children, avoidance of loud sounds or costumed characters). Although this subtyping strategy is useful, we also know that most people who suffer from phobia tend to have multiple phobias of several types (Hofmann, Lehman, & Barlow, 1997). This fact weakens the utility of subtyping a bit.

BLOOD-INJECTION-INJURY PHOBIA

How do phobia subtypes differ from each other? We have already seen one major difference in the case of Judy. Rather than the usual surge of activity in the sympathetic nervous system and increased heart rate and blood pressure, Judy experienced a marked drop in heart rate and blood pressure and fainted as a consequence. Many people who suffer from phobias and experience panic attacks in their feared situations report that they feel like they are going to faint but they never do, because their heart rate and blood pressure are actually increasing. Therefore, those with **blood-injection-injury phobias** almost always differ in their physiological reaction from people with other types of phobia (Barlow & Liebowitz, 1995; Öst, 1992). We also noted in Chapter 2 that blood-injection-injury phobia runs in families more strongly than any phobic disorder we know. This is probably because people with this phobia inherit a strong vasovagal response to blood, injury, or the possibility

table 5.6   Phobias Beginning with "A"

Term	Fear of:
Acarophobia	Insects, mites
Achluophobia	Darkness, night
Acousticophobia	Sounds
Acrophobia	Heights
Aerophobia	Air currents, drafts, wind
Agoraphobia	Open spaces
Agyiophobia	Crossing the street
Aichmophobia	Sharp, pointed objects; knives; being touched by a finger
Ailurophobia	Cats
Algophobia	Pain
Amathophobia	Dust
Amychophobia	Laceration; being clawed, scratched
Androphobia	Men (and sex with men)
Anemophobia	Air currents, wind, drafts
Anginophobia	Angina pectoris
Anthropophobia	Human society
Antlophobia	Floods
Apeirophobia	Infinity
Aphephobia	Physical contact, being touched
Apiphobia	Bees, bee stings
Astraphobia	Thunderstorms, lightning
Ataxiophobia	Disorder
Atephobia	Ruin
Auroraphobia	Northern lights
Autophobia	Being alone; solitude; oneself; being egotistical

Source: Maser, 1985

of an injection, all of which cause a drop in blood pressure and a tendency to faint. The phobia develops over the possibility of having this response. The average age of onset for this phobia is approximately 9 years (Antony, Brown, & Barlow, 1997a; Öst, 1989).

SITUATIONAL PHOBIA

Phobias characterized by fear of public transportation or enclosed places are called **situational phobias.** Claustrophobia, a fear of small enclosed places, is situational, as is a phobia of planes. Psychopathologists first thought that situational phobia was similar to panic disorder with agoraphobia (PDA). One similarity in these two disorders is age of onset. Both situational phobia and PDA tend to emerge in an individual's early to mid-twenties (Antony et al., 1997a). The extent to which PDA and situational phobias run in families is also very similar (Curtis, Hill, & Lewis, 1990; Curtis, Himle, Lewis, & Lee, 1989; Fyer et al., 1990), with approximately 30% of first-degree relations having the same or a similar phobia. But more recent analyses, both descriptive (Antony et al., 1997a) and laboratory based (Antony, Brown, & Barlow, 1997) do not support the similarity as anything more than superficial. The main difference between situational phobia and PDA is that people with situational phobia never experience panic attacks outside the context of their phobic object or situation. Therefore, they can relax when they don't have to confront their phobic situation. People with panic disorder, on the other hand, might experience unexpected, uncued panic attacks at any time.

NATURAL ENVIRONMENT PHOBIA

Sometimes very young people develop fears of situations or events occurring in nature. These fears are called **natural environment phobias.** The major examples are heights, storms, and water. These fears also seem to cluster together (Barlow, in press; Hofmann et al., 1997): If you fear one situation or event, such as deep water, you are likely to fear another, such as storms. Many of these situations have some danger associated with them and, therefore, mild to moderate fear can be very adaptive. For example, one should be careful in a high place or in deep water. It is entirely possible that we are somewhat prepared to be afraid of these situations; as we discussed in Chapter 2, something in our genes makes us very sensitive to these situations if any sign of danger is present. In any case, these phobias have a peak age of onset of about 7 years. They are not phobias at all if they are only passing fears. They have to be persistent and to interfere substantially with the person's functioning, leading to avoidance of boat trips or summer vacations in the mountains where there might be a storm.

ANIMAL PHOBIA

Fears of animals and insects are called **animal phobias.** Once again, these fears are common but become phobic only if severe interference with functioning occurs. For example, we have seen cases in our clinic where people with snake or mice phobias are unable to read magazines for fear of unexpectedly coming across a picture of one of these animals. There are many places that these people are unable to go, even if they want to very badly, such as to the country to visit someone. The fear experienced by people with animal phobias is very different from an ordinary mild revulsion. The age of onset for these phobias, like that of natural environment phobias, peaks at around 7 years (Antony et al., 1997a; Öst, 1987).

OTHER PHOBIAS

Several additional types of phobias from the "other" category are described briefly here since they appear in considerable numbers and can cause substantial problems. If you are afraid of contracting a disease and go to excessive and irrational lengths to avoid exposure to that disease, it is possible that you have an *illness phobia.* In these cases, the individuals do not believe they have the disease but are afraid they might acquire it in any number of ways (Barlow & Liebowitz, 1995; Salkovskis, Warwick, & Clark, 1990). When this fear occurs in severe form it can be very incapacitating, since individuals with illness phobia may avoid all contact with people or places where they might catch something. Illness phobia has become more prevalent during the AIDS epidemic. People may have no reason to believe they have AIDS, and they will test negatively for HIV, but they

People who develop a natural environment phobia intensely fear such places as heights and events such as lightning.

may avoid public restrooms, some restaurants, and any contact whatsoever with strangers for fear of contracting the disease. Illness phobia can also resemble other disorders, such as obsessive-compulsive disorder (see p. 144) or hypochondriasis (see Chapter 6), but is sufficiently different to be classified as a type of specific phobia. We will return to this issue when we discuss these two disorders.

Choking phobia is characterized by fear and avoidance of swallowing pills, foods, or fluids and can produce significant weight loss. Other names for choking phobia include "hypersensitive gag reflex" or "globus hystericus" (McNally, 1994). Phobias of choking and vomiting are relatively common and almost always originate in the traumatic experience of choking on a piece of food. In some people the consequences are that they are unable to eat solid food and, in addition to weight loss, suffer severe nutritional and dental problems. If the phobia is prolonged, the person is likely to experience deterioration in gum tissue and tooth structure from lack of use and, ultimately, tooth loss. These people often maintain themselves on liquid diets. Fortunately, the condition does respond to direct, structured treatment (Ball & Otto, 1994; Chorpita, Vitali, & Barlow, 1997).

SEPARATION ANXIETY DISORDER

All the anxiety disorders described in this chapter may occur during childhood, and there is one additional anxiety disorder unique to children. **Separation anxiety disorder** is characterized by a child's unrealistic and persistent worry that something will happen to his parents or other important people in his life, or that something will happen to the child himself that will separate him from his parents (for example, he will be lost, kidnapped, killed, or hurt in an accident). The child often refuses to go to school or even to leave home, not because he is afraid of school but because he is afraid of separating from his loved ones. These fears can result in the child refusing to sleep alone and may be characterized by nightmares involving possible separation and by physical symptoms, distress, and anxiety (Albano et al., 1996).

Of course, all young children experience separation anxiety to some extent; this fear usually decreases as the child grows older. Therefore, a clinician must judge whether the separation anxiety is greater than would be expected at that particular age (Ollendick & Huntzinger, 1990). It is also important to differentiate separation anxiety from school phobia. In school phobia, the fear is clearly focused on something specific to the school situation; the child can leave the parents or other attachment figures to go somewhere other than school. In separation anxiety, the act of separating from the parent or attachment figure provokes anxiety and fear.

Tom Ollendick in a leading investigator into the nature and treatment of anxiety disorders in children.

Francis, Last, and Strauss (1987) found that the prevalence of certain symptoms varies as a function of age. For example, the prominent symptom among the youngest children was worry that something would happen to their loved ones. Excessive distress upon being separated was prominent in the middle age group of children, and physical complaints on school days characterized separation anxiety in adolescents.

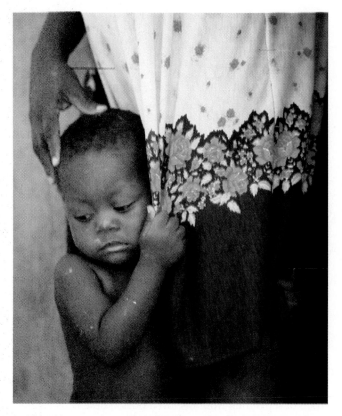

A child with separation anxiety disorder persistently worries that parting with an important person drastically endangers either the loved one or the child.

■ **concept check 5.1**

Identify the following examples of specific phobias. Select your answer from the following: (a) blood-injection-injury; (b) acrophobia; (c) animal; (d) situational; (e) natural environment; (f) other.

1. Dennis fears and strenuously avoids storms. Not surprisingly, on his first oceangoing cruise, he found that deep water terrified him, too. _____

2. Rita was comfortable at the zoo until the old terror gripped her at the insect display. _____

3. Armando would love to eat fish with his fishing buddies, but he experiences an inordinate fear of choking on a bone. _____

4. John had to give up his dream of becoming a surgeon because he faints at the sight of blood. _____

5. Farrah can't visit her rural friends because of her fear of snakes. _____

Statistics

Specific fears occur in a majority of people. The ones most commonly found in the population at large, categorized by Agras, Sylvester, and Oliveau (1969), are presented in Table 5.7. Not surprisingly, fears of snakes and heights rank near the top. Notice also that the sex ratio among common fears is overwhelmingly female with a couple of exceptions. Among these exceptions is fear of heights, for which the sex ratio is approximately equal.

Very few people who report specific fears qualify as having a phobia, but for approximately 11% of the population, their fears are at some point severe enough to be classified as disorders and earn the label "phobia," and these numbers seem to be increasing in younger generations (Magee, Eaton, Wittchen, McGonagle, & Kessler, 1996). This is a very high percentage, making specific phobia one of the most common psychological disorders in the United States. As with common fears, the sex ratio for specific phobias is, at 4:1, overwhelmingly female. Even though phobias may interfere with an individual's functioning, only the most severe cases actually come for treatment, because affected people tend to work around their phobias; for example, someone with a fear of heights arranges her life so that she never has to be in a tall building or other high place. Table 5.8 presents the distribution of the 48 patients who recently came to our anxiety disorders clinic with a specific phobia as their primary problem; these are broken down by type. As you can see, people with situational phobias of such things as driving, flying, or small enclosed places most frequently come for treatment. However, there is reason to believe that people with blood-injury-injection phobias are quite prevalent in the population (Agras et al., 1969; Myers et al., 1984); they might seek help if they knew good treatments are available.

Once a phobia develops, it tends to last a lifetime (run a chronic course) (for instance, Antony, Brown, & Barlow, 1997a; Barlow, in press); thus, the issue of treatment, described shortly, becomes important.

Although most anxiety disorders look pretty much the same in adults and children, clinicians must be very aware of the types of normal fears and anxieties experienced throughout childhood so they can distinguish them from specific phobias (Albano et al., 1996; King, 1993; Silverman & Rabian, 1993). Infants, for example, show marked fear of loud noises and strangers. At 1 to 2 years of age, children quite normally are very anxious about separating from parents, and fears of animals and the dark also develops and may persist into the fourth or fifth year of life. Fear of various monsters and other imaginary creatures may begin at about age 3 and last for several years. At age 10, children may fear evaluation by others and feel anxiety over their physical appearance. Generally, reports of fear decline with age, although performance-related fears of such activities as taking a test or talking in front of a large group may increase with age. Specific phobias seem to decline with old age (Blazer, George, et al., 1991; Sheikh, 1992).

The prevalence of specific phobias varies from one culture to another. Hispanics are two times more likely to report specific phobias than white Americans (Magee et al., 1996), for reasons that are not entirely clear. A variant of phobia in Chinese cultures is called *Pa-leng*, sometimes *frigo phobia* or "fear of the cold." Pa-leng can be understood only in the context of traditional ideas—in this case the Chinese

table 5.7 Prevalence of Intense Fears and Phobia

Intense Fear	Prevalence per 1,000 Population	Sex Distribution	SE by Sex	Phobia	Prevalence per 1,000 Population*	Sex Distribution	SE by Sex
Snakes	253	M: 118 / F: 376	M: 34 / F: 48	Illness/injury	31 (42%)	M: 22 / F: 39	M: 15 / F: 20
Heights	120	M: 109 / F: 128	M: 33 / F: 36	Storms	13 (18%)	M: 0 / F: 24	M: 0 / F: 15
Flying	109	M: 70 / F: 144	M: 26 / F: 38	Animals	11 (14%)	M: 6 / F: 18	M: 8 / F: 13
Enclosures	50	M: 32 / F: 63	M: 18 / F: 25	Agoraphobia	6 (8%)	M: 7 / F: 6	M: 8 / F: 8
Illness	33	M: 31 / F: 35	M: 18 / F: 19	Death	5 (7%)	M: 4 / F: 6	M: 6 / F: 8
Death	33	M: 46 / F: 21	M: 21 / F: 15	Crowds	4 (5%)	M: 2 / F: 6	M: 5 / F: 7
Injury	23	M: 24 / F: 22	M: 15 / F: 15	Heights	4 (5%)	M: 7 / F: 0	M: 9 / F: 0
Storms	31	M: 9 / F: 48	M: 9 / F: 22				
Dentists	24	M: 22 / F: 26	M: 15 / F: 16				
Journeys alone	16	M: 0 / F: 31	M: 0 / F: 18				
Being alone	10	M: 5 / F: 13	M: 7 / F: 11				

*Percentages of the total of those with phobias are in parentheses.
Source: Adapted from Agras, Sylvester, & Oliveau, 1969

concept of yin and yang (Tan, 1980). Chinese medicine holds that there must be a balance of yin and yang forces in the body for health to be maintained. Yin represents the cold, dark, windy, energy-sapping aspects of life; yang refers to the warm, bright, energy-producing aspects of life. Individuals with Pa-leng have a morbid fear of the cold. They ruminate over loss of body heat, and may wear several layers of clothing even on a hot day. They may complain of belching and flatulence, which indicate the presence of wind and therefore of too much yin in the body.

Causes

For a long time we thought that most specific phobias began with an unusual traumatic event. For example, if you were bitten by a dog you would develop a phobia of dogs. We now know this is not always the case (Barlow, in press; Öst, 1985). As we explained briefly in Chapter 2, "conditioning" experiences do not play a major role in the etiology of most phobias. This is not to say that traumatic conditioning experiences do not result in subsequent phobic behavior. Almost every person with a choking phobia has had some kind of a choking experience. An individual with claustrophobia who recently came to our clinic reported being trapped in an elevator for an extraordinarily long period of time. These are examples of phobias acquired by *direct experience,* where real danger or pain results in an alarm response (a true alarm).

This is one way of developing a phobia, and there are at least three others: *experiencing* a false alarm (panic attack) in a specific situation, *observing* someone else experience severe fear (vicarious experience) or, under the right conditions, *being told* about danger.

Remember our earlier discussion of unexpected panic attacks? Studies show that many phobics do not necessarily experience a true alarm resulting from real danger at the onset of their phobia. Many initially have an unexpected panic attack in a specific situation, related, perhaps, to current life stress. A phobia of that situation may then develop. Munjack (1984) studied people with specific phobias of driving. He noted that about 50% of the people who could remember when their phobia started experienced a true alarm

table 5.8 Forty-Eight Patients with Specific Phobia as the Primary Problem

Type of Phobia	Number
Animal	3
Natural environment	3
Blood and injury	3
Situational	29
Other	10

Note: Patients were seen at the authors' anxiety disorders clinic between November 4, 1994, and April 29, 1998.

Chinese medicine is based on the concept that *yin* (dark, cold, enervating forces) and *yang* (bright, warm, energizing forces) must harmonize in the body. In this traditional representation of the yin/yang balance, note that each aspect contains something of the other.

due to a traumatic experience such as a car accident. The others had had nothing terrible happen to them while they were driving, but they had experienced an unexpected panic attack during which they felt they were going to lose control of the car and wipe out half the people on the highway. In fact, their driving was not impaired and their catastrophic thoughts were simply part of the panic attack.

We also learn fears vicariously. Seeing someone else have a traumatic experience or endure intense fear may be enough to instill a phobia in the watcher. Remember, we noted above that emotions are very contagious. If someone you are with is either happy or fearful, you will probably feel a tinge of happiness or fear also. Öst (1985) describes how a severe dental fear developed in this way. An adolescent boy sat in the waiting room at the school dentist's office partly observing, but fully hearing, his friend who was being treated. Evidently, the boy's reaction to pain caused him to move suddenly, and the drill punctured his cheek. The boy in the waiting room who overheard the accident bolted from the room and developed a severe and long-lasting fear of dental situations. Nothing actually happened to the second person but you can certainly understand why he developed his phobia. Susan Mineka and her colleagues in an elegant series of experiments have shown that a monkey can develop a phobia simply by watching another monkey experience fear (Mineka, Davidson, Cook, & Keir, 1984).

Sometimes just being warned repeatedly about a potential danger is sufficient for someone to develop a phobia. Öst (1985) describes the case of a woman with an extremely severe snake phobia who had never encountered a snake in her life. Rather, she had been told repeatedly while growing up about the dangers of snakes in the high grass. She was encouraged to wear high rubber boots to guard against this imminent threat—and she did so even when walking down the street. We call this mode of developing a phobia *information transmission.*

Terrifying experiences alone do not create phobias. As we have said, a true phobia also requires anxiety over the possibility of another extremely traumatic event or false alarm. Remember, when we are anxious, we persistently anticipate something terrible, and we are likely to avoid situations where that terrible thing might occur. If we don't develop anxiety, our reaction would presumably be in the category of normal fears experienced by over half the population. Normal fear can cause mild distress, but it is usually ignored and forgotten.

This point is best illustrated by Peter DiNardo and his colleagues (1988), who studied a group of dog phobics as well as a matched group who did not have the phobia. Like Munjack's (1984) driving phobics, about 50% of the dog phobics had had a frightening encounter with a dog, usually involving a bite. However, in another group of individuals who did *not* have dog phobia, about 50% had also had a frightening encounter with a dog. Why hadn't they become phobics as well? They had not developed anxiety about another encounter with a dog, unlike the people who did become phobic. A diagram of the etiology of specific phobia is presented in Figure 5.7.

In summary, several things have to occur for a person to develop a phobia. First, a traumatic conditioning experience often plays a role, (even hearing about a frightening event is sufficient for some individuals). Second, fear is more likely to develop if we are "prepared"; that is, we seem to carry an inherited tendency to fear situations that have always been dangerous to the human race, such as being threatened by wild animals or trapped in small places (see Chapter 2).

We also have to be susceptible to developing anxiety that the event will happen again. We have discussed the biological and psychological reasons for anxiety and have seen that at least one phobia, blood-injection-injury phobia, is highly heritable (Öst, 1989). Öst found that 64% of 25 patients had at least one first-degree relative with blood phobia. Patients with blood phobia probably also inherit a strong vasovagal response that makes them susceptible to fainting. This alone would not be sufficient to ensure their becoming phobic, but combines with anxiety to produce strong vulnerability.

Several years ago, Fyer et al. (1990) demonstrated that approximately 31% of

Peter DiNardo and his colleagues, who studied people with dog phobias, made important discoveries about the causes of phobias in general.

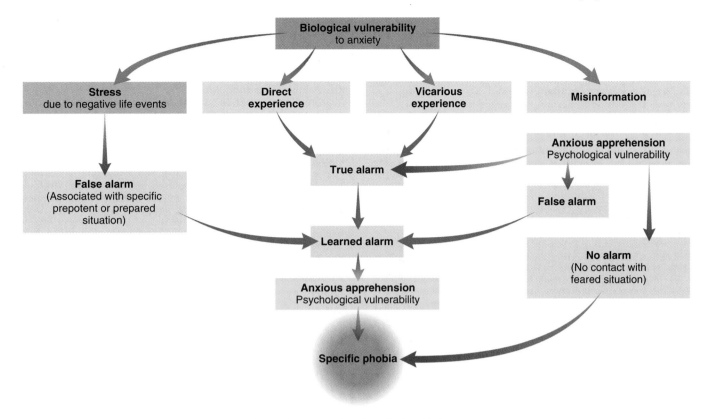

figure 5.7 A model of the various ways a specific phobia may develop (from Barlow, 1988)

the first-degree relatives of people with specific phobias also had a phobia, compared with 11% of the first-degree relatives of normal controls. More recently, in a collaborative study between Dr. Fyer's clinic and our center, we replicated these results, finding a 28% prevalence in the first-degree relatives of patients with phobia compared to 10% in relatives of controls. More interestingly, it seemed that each sub-type of phobia "bred true," in that relatives were likely to have identical types of phobia. We do not know whether the tendency for phobias to run in families is due to genes or to modeling, but the finding is at least suggestive of a genetic contribution.

Finally, social and cultural factors are very strong determinants of who ultimately develops and reports a specific phobia. In most societies around the world it is almost unacceptable for males to express fears and phobias. Thus, the overwhelming majority of reported specific phobias occur in women. What happens to the males? Very possibly they work hard to overcome their fears by repeatedly exposing themselves to their feared situations. Another possibility is that they simply endure their fears without telling anyone about them and without seeking any treatment.

Treatment

Although the development of phobias is relatively complex, the treatment is fairly straightforward. Almost everyone agrees that specific phobias require structured and consistent exposure-based exercises. Nevertheless, most patients who expose themselves gradually to what they fear must be under therapeutic supervision. Individuals who attempt to carry out the exercises alone often attempt to do too much too soon and end up escaping the situation, which may strengthen the phobia. In addition, if they fear having another unexpected panic attack in this situation, it is helpful to direct therapy at panic attacks in the manner described for panic disorder (Antony, Craske, & Barlow, 1995; Craske, Antony, & Barlow, 1997). Finally, in cases of blood-injury-injection phobia, where fainting is a real possibility, graduated exposure-based exercises must be done in very specific ways. Individuals must *tense* various muscle groups during exposure exercises to keep their blood pressure sufficiently high to complete the practice (Öst & Sterner, 1987). New developments make it possible to treat many specific phobias, including blood phobia, in a single day-long session (e.g., Öst, Ferebee, & Furmark, 1997; Antony et al., 1995; Craske et al., 1997). Basically, the therapist spends most of the day with the individual, working through exposure exercises with the phobia object or situation. The patient then practices approaching the phobic situation at home, checking in occasionally with the therapist. It is interesting that in these cases not only does the phobia disappear, but the tendency to experience the vasovagal response at the sight of blood also lessens considerably.

Social Phobia

Clinical Description

Are you shy? If so, you have something in common with 20% to 50% of college students, depending on which survey you read. A much smaller number of people, who suffer severely around others, have **social phobia.** Consider the following case of a 13-year-old boy.

Billy
Too Shy

Billy was the model boy at home. He did his homework, stayed out of trouble, obeyed his parents, and was generally so quiet and reserved he didn't attract much attention. However, when he got to junior high school, something his parents had noticed earlier became painfully evident. Billy had no friends. He was unwilling to attend social or sporting activities connected with school, even though most of the other kids in his class went to these events. When his parents decided to check with the guidance counselor, they found that she had been about to call them. She reported that Billy did not socialize or speak up in class, and was sick to his stomach all day if he knew he was going to be called on. His teachers had difficulty getting anything more than a yes or no answer from him. More troublesome was that he had been found hiding in a stall in the boy's restroom during lunch, which he said he had been doing for several months instead of eating. After Billy was referred to our clinic, we diagnosed a severe case of social phobia, an irrational and extreme fear of social situations. Billy's phobia took the form of extreme shyness. He was afraid of being embarrassed or humiliated in the presence of almost everyone except his parents.

Social phobia is more than exaggerated shyness (Schneier et al., 1996). The following cases are typical of many that appear from time to time in the press.

Star Player?

In the second inning of an All-Star game, Los Angeles Dodger second baseman Steve Sax fielded an easy grounder, straightened up for the lob to first, and bounced the ball past first baseman Al Oliver, who was less than 40 feet away. It was a startling error even in an All-Star game studded with bush-league mishaps. But hard-core baseball fans knew it was one more manifestation of a leading mystery of the 1983 season: Sax, 23, the National League Rookie of the Year, could not seem to make routine throws to first base. (Of his first 27 errors that season, 22 were bad throws.)

Steve Sax overcame his problem and went on to play for a number of major league teams. Many other athletes are not so fortunate. This problem is not limited to athletes but is also developed by well-known lecturers and performers. Singer Carly Simon actually gave up live shows for several years because of intolerable performance anxiety. The inability of a skilled athlete to throw a baseball to first base or a seasoned performer to appear on stage certainly does not match the concept of "shyness" with which we are all familiar. In fact, many of these performers may well be among our more gregarious citizens. What holds these two seemingly different conditions together?

Billy, Steve Sax, and Carly Simon all experienced marked and persistent fear of one or more social or performance situations. In Billy's case, these situations were any in which he might have to interact with people. For Steve Sax and Carly Simon, they were specific to performing in public. Individuals with performance anxiety usually have no difficulty with social interaction, but when they must do something in front of people, anxiety takes over and they focus on the possibility that they will embarrass themselves.

The most common type of performance phobia, to which most people can relate, is public speaking. Other common situations are eating in a restaurant; signing a paper in front of a clerk; or urinating in a public restroom ("bashful bladder"). Males with this problem must wait until a stall is available, a difficult task at times. What these examples have in common is that the individual is required to *do* something while others are watching and, to some extent, evaluating the behavior. This is truly a social phobia because the people have no difficulty eating, writing, or urinating in private. Only when others are watching does the behavior deteriorate.

Individuals who are extremely and painfully shy in almost all social situations meet DSM-IV criteria for the subtype *social phobia generalized type,* occasionally called *social anxiety disorder.* It is particularly prominent in children. In the child program in one of our clinics, 100% of children and adolescents with social phobia met criteria for generalized type (Albano, DiBartolo, Heimberg, & Barlow, 1995). Billy also fits this subtype (Schneier et al., 1996).

Statistics

As many as 13.3% of the general population suffer from social phobia at some point in their lives (Kessler et al., 1994). This makes social phobia the most prevalent psychological disorder, afflicting over 35 million people in the United States alone, based on current population estimates. Of course, many more people are shy, but not severely enough to meet criteria for social phobia. The sex ratio favors females only somewhat (1.4 to 1.0), unlike other anxiety disorders where females predominate (Magee et al., 1996). This distribution differs a bit from the sex ratio of social phobics appearing at clinics, which is nearly 50-50 (Barlow, in press; Marks, 1985), suggesting that males may seek help more frequently, perhaps because of career-related issues. Social phobia usually begins during adolescence, with a peak age of onset at about 15 years, later than specific phobias but earlier than panic disorder. Social phobia also tends to be more prevalent in people who are young (18–29 years), undereducated, single, and of low socioeconomic class. Alarmingly, the number of young people with social phobia seems to be increasing somewhat (Magee et al., 1996). Prevalence declines slightly among the elderly (Magee et al., 1996; Sheikh, 1992). Considering their difficulty meeting people, it is not surprising that a greater percentage of individuals with social phobia are single than in the population at large.

Social phobias distribute relatively equally among different ethnic groups (Magee et al., 1996). In Japan, the clinical presentation of anxiety disorders is best summarized under the label *shinkeishitsu.* One of the most common subcategories is referred to as *taijin kyōfushō* (Kirmayer, 1991; Kleinknecht, Dinnel, Kleinknecht, Hiruma, & Hirada, 1997). Japanese people with this form of social phobia strongly fear looking people in the eye and are afraid that some aspect of their personal presentation (blushing, stuttering, body odor, and so on) will appear reprehensible.

Causes

We have noted that we seem to be prepared by evolution to fear certain wild animals and dangerous situations in the natural environment. Similarly, it seems we are also prepared to fear angry, critical, or rejecting people (Mineka & Zinbarg, 1995, 1996; Öhman, 1986). In a series of studies, Öhman and colleagues (for example, Dimberg & Öhman, 1983; Öhman & Dimberg, 1978) noted that we learn more quickly to fear angry expressions than other facial expressions, and that this fear diminishes much more slowly than other types of learning. More recently, Lundh and Öst (1996) demonstrated that social phobics who saw a number of pictures of faces were likely to remember critical expressions, whereas normals remembered the accepting expressions. Why should we inherit a tendency to fear angry faces? Our ancestors probably avoided hostile, angry, domineering people who might attack or kill them. In fact, in all species, dominant aggressive individuals, high in the social hierarchy, tend to be avoided. Possibly, individuals who avoided people with angry faces were more likely to survive and pass their genes down to us. Of course, this is just a theory.

Jerome Kagan and his colleagues (for example, Kagan, Reznick, & Snidman, 1988a; Kagan & Snidman, 1991) have demonstrated that some infants are born with a temperamental pro-

Jerome Kagan discovered that shyness is evident as early as 4 months of age and is probably inherited.

file or trait of inhibition or shyness that is evident as early as 4 months of age. Four-month-old infants with this trait become more agitated and cry more frequently when presented with toys or other normal stimuli than infants without the trait. There is now evidence that individuals with excessive behavioral inhibition are at increased risk for developing phobic behavior (Biederman et al., 1990; Hirschfeld et al., 1992). In any case, inhibition relates more to generalized social phobia than to discrete performance anxiety such as public speaking. A model of the etiology of social phobia would look somewhat like models of panic disorder and specific phobia.

Three pathways to social phobia are possible. First, one could inherit a biological vulnerability to develop anxiety and/or a biological tendency to be very socially inhibited. Second, when under stress, one might have an unexpected panic attack (false alarm) in a social situation and then become anxious about having additional false alarms (panic attacks) in the same or similar social situations. Third, someone might experience a real social trauma resulting in a true alarm. Anxiety would then develop (be conditioned) in the same or similar social situations. Traumatic social experiences may also extend back to difficult periods in childhood. Early adolescence—usually ages 12 through 15—is when children may be brutally taunted by peers who are attempting to assert their own dominance. This treatment may produce anxiety and panic that are reproduced in future social situations. A diagram of the etiology of social phobia is presented in Figure 5.8.

There is also evidence that some social phobics are predisposed to focus their anxiety on events involving social evaluation. Some investigators (Bruch & Heimberg, 1994; Rapee & Melville, 1997) suggest that the parents of people with social phobia are significantly more socially fearful and concerned with the opinions of others than are the parents of patients with panic disorder, and that they pass this concern on to their children. Fyer, Mannuzza, Chapman, Liebowitz, and Klein (1993) reported that the relatives of people with social phobia had a significantly greater risk of developing it than the relatives of individuals without social phobia (16% vs. 5%). Thus, a combination of biological and psychological events may lead to the development of social phobia.

Treatment

Effective treatments have been developed for social phobia only in the past several years (Barlow & Lehman, 1996; Hope & Heimberg, 1993; S. Taylor, 1996). Rick Heimberg and colleagues developed a program in which groups of patients rehearse or role play their socially phobic situations in front of each other (Heimberg et al., 1990; Hope & Heimberg, 1993). The group members participate in the role-playing, for example, acting as audience for someone who has extreme difficulty giving a speech. At the same time the therapist conducts rather intensive cognitive therapy

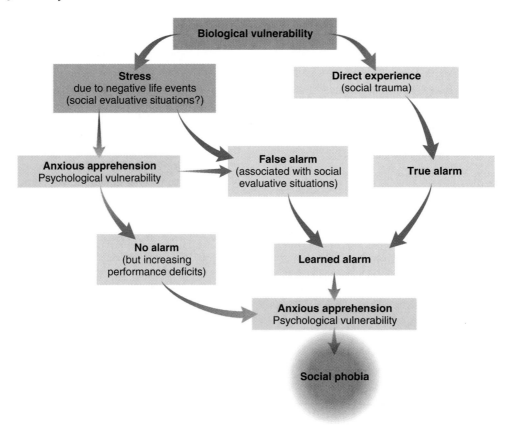

figure 5.8   A model of the various ways a social phobia may develop (from Barlow, 1988)

aimed at uncovering and changing the automatic or unconscious perceptions of danger that the socially phobic client assumes to exist. These treatments have been much more effective than education about anxiety and social phobia and social support for stressful life events. More important, a follow-up after 5 years indicates that the therapeutic gains are maintained (Heimberg, Salzman, Holt, & Blendell, 1993). Recent studies suggest that the behavioral rehearsal is a more important part of treatment than the cognitive therapy component (Feske & Chambless, 1995). We have adapted these protocols for use with adolescents, directly involving parents in the group treatment process. Preliminary results suggest that severely socially phobic adolescents can attain relatively normal functioning in school and other social settings (Albano & Barlow, 1996).

Effective drug treatments have been discovered as well. For a time clinicians assumed that beta blockers worked well, particularly for performance anxiety, but the evidence does not seem to support that contention (Liebowitz et al., 1992). Most recently, tricyclic antidepressants and, particularly, monoamine oxidase (MAO) inhibitors, have been found to be more effective than placebo in the treatment of severe social anxiety (Liebowitz et al., 1992), although relapse is common when drugs are stopped. Studies comparing MAO inhibitors to the psychological treatments described earlier are now complete, and show that both treatments are highly and equally effective, but that relapse is more common among those taking medication after treatment stops (Heimberg et al., 1997; Liebowitz et al., 1997).

The combined effect of these treatments is currently being evaluated.

Posttraumatic Stress Disorder

Clinical Description

In recent years we have heard a great deal about the severe and long-lasting emotional disorders that can occur after a variety of traumatic events. Perhaps the most impressive traumatic event is war, but emotional disorders also occur after physical assault (particularly rape), car accidents, natural catastrophes, or the sudden death of a loved one. The emotional disorder that follows a trauma is known as **posttraumatic stress disorder (PTSD)**.

DSM-IV describes the setting event for PTSD as exposure to a traumatic event during which one feels fear, helplessness, or horror. Afterward, victims reexperience the event through memories and nightmares. When memories occur very suddenly and the victims find themselves reliving the event, they are having a *flashback*. Victims avoid anything that reminds them of the trauma. They display a characteristic restriction or numbing of emotional responsiveness, which may be very disruptive to interpersonal relationships. They are sometimes unable to remember certain aspects of the event. It is possible that victims unconsciously

Exposure to a traumatic event may create profound fear and helplessness. People who suffer from posttraumatic stress disorder may reexperience such feelings in flashbacks, involuntarily reliving the horrifying event.

attempt to avoid the experience of emotion itself, like people with panic disorder, since intense emotions could bring back memories of the trauma. Finally, victims typically are chronically overaroused, easily startled, and quick to anger.

Posttraumatic stress disorder was first named in 1980 in DSM-III (American Psychiatric Association, 1980), but it has a long history. In 1666, the British diarist Samuel Pepys witnessed the Great Fire of London that caused substantial loss of life and property and threw the city into total chaos for a time. He captured the events in an account that is still read today. But Pepys did not escape the effects of the horrific event. Six months later he wrote, "It is strange to think how to this very day I cannot sleep a night without great terrors of fire; and this very night could not sleep to almost 2 in the morning through thoughts of fire" (Daly, 1983, p. 66). The DSM-IV criteria show that difficulty sleeping and recurring intrusive dreams of the event are prominent features of PTSD. Pepys described his guilt at saving himself and his property while others died. He also experienced a sense of detachment and a numbing of his emotions concerning the fire, common experiences in posttraumatic stress disorder.

Consider the following case from one of our clinics.

The Joneses
One Victim, Many Traumas

Mrs. Betty Jones and her four children arrived at a farm to visit a friend. (Mr. Jones was at work.) Jeff, the oldest child, was 8 years old. Marcie, Cathy, and Susan were 6, 4, and 2

years of age. Mrs. Jones parked the car in the driveway, and they all started across the yard to the front door. Suddenly Jeff heard growling somewhere near the house. Before he could warn the others, a large German Shepherd charged and leapt at Marcie, the 6-year-old, knocking her to the ground and tearing viciously at her face. The family, too stunned to move, watched the attack helplessly. After what seemed like an eternity, Jeff lunged at the dog and it moved away. The owner, in a state of panic, ran to a nearby house to get help. Mrs. Jones immediately put pressure on Marcie's facial wounds in an attempt to stop the bleeding. The owner had neglected to retrieve the dog, and it stood a short distance away, growling and barking at the frightened family. Eventually the dog was restrained and Marcie was rushed to the hospital. Marcie, who was hysterical, had to be restrained on a padded board so emergency room physicians could stitch her wounds.

This case is unusual because not only did Marcie develop PTSD, but so did her 8-year-old brother. In addition, Cathy, four, and Susan, two, although quite young, also showed symptoms of the disorder, as did their mother (see Table 5.9) (Albano, Miller, Zarate, Côté, & Barlow, 1997). Jeff evidenced classic survivor guilt symptoms, reporting that he should have saved Marcie or at least put himself between Marcie and the dog. Both Jeff and Marcie regressed developmentally, wetting the bed (nocturnal enuresis) and experiencing nightmares and separation fears. In addition Marcie, having been strapped down and given local anesthetic and stitches, became very frightened of any medical procedures and even of such routine daily events as having her nails trimmed or taking a bath. Furthermore, she refused to be tucked into bed, something she had enjoyed all her life, probably because it reminded her of the hospital board. Jeff started sucking his fingers, which he had not done for years. These behaviors, along with intense separation anxiety, are common, particularly in younger children (Eth, 1990). Cathy, the 4-year-old, evidenced considerable fear and avoidance when tested, but denied having any problems when she was interviewed by a child psychologist. Susan, the 2-year-old, also had some symptoms, as shown in Table 5.9, but was too young to talk about them. However, for several months following the trauma she repeatedly said, without provocation, "Doggy bit sister."

Children's memories of traumatic events can become embellished over the years. For example, some children incorporate a superhero coming to the rescue. These intense memories are very malleable and subject to distortion.

As indicated in the criteria, PTSD is subdivided into *acute* and *chronic*. *Acute PTSD* can be diagnosed between 1 and 3 months after the event occurs. When PTSD continues longer than 3 months, it is considered chronic. *Chronic PTSD* is usually associated with more prominent avoidance behaviors (J.R.T. Davidson, Hughes, Blazer, & George, 1991), as well as with the more frequent co-occurrence of additional diagnoses such as social phobia. In delayed onset PTSD, individuals show few if any symptoms immediately after a trauma, but later, perhaps years afterward, they develop full-blown PTSD. Why onset is delayed in some individuals is not yet clear.

As noted above, PTSD cannot be diagnosed until a month after the trauma. New to DSM-IV is a disorder called acute stress disorder. This is really PTSD occurring within the first month after the trauma, but the different name emphasizes the very severe reaction that some people have immediately. PTSD-like symptoms are accompanied

by severe dissociative symptoms, such as amnesia for all or part of the trauma, emotional numbing, and *derealization*, or feelings of unreality. According to new studies, approximately 40% of individuals with acute stress disorder go on to develop PTSD (APA, 1994). Acute stress disorder was included in DSM-IV because many people with very severe early reactions to trauma could not otherwise be diagnosed and, therefore, could not receive insurance coverage for immediate treatment.

Statistics

Determining the prevalence rates for PTSD seems relatively straightforward: Simply observe victims of a trauma and see

---

■ concept check 5.2

Match the correct preliminary diagnosis with the following cases: (a) generalized anxiety disorder; (b) "nervous breakdown"; (c) social phobia; (d) panic disorder; (e) acute posttraumatic stress disorder.

1. Bobby sang in the school play in first grade. Even then and still today, he's been afraid to perform in public. _____

2. Audrey worries about everything to an extreme degree. She worries most about her friends and family, but she also worries about things that she has no control over. _____

3. Tom hates to shop. Every time he goes to the mall, he sweats, becomes nauseous, and has trouble breathing. _____

4. Judy witnessed a car accident 5 weeks ago. Since then, she's had many flashbacks of the accident, and she's also had trouble sleeping. _____

---

table 5.9   Symptoms of Posttraumatic Stress Disorder (PTSD) Evidenced by Marcie and Her Siblings

Symptoms	Jeff	Marcie	Cathy	Susan
Repetitive play—trauma themes		x	x	x
Nightmares	x	x	x	x
Reexperiencing		x		
Distress at exposure to similar stimuli	x	x	x	x
Avoidance of talk of trauma		x	x	
Avoidance of trauma recollections		x		
Regressive behavior	x	x		
Detachment	x	x		
Restricted affect	x	x		
Sleep disturbance	x	x	x	x
Anger outbursts	x	x		
Hypervigilance	x	x		
Startle response	x	x		
DSM-III-R PTSD diagnosis met	x	x		

Source: Albano et al., 1997

how many are suffering from PTSD. But a number of studies have demonstrated the remarkably *low* prevalence of PTSD in populations of trauma victims. Rachman (1978) studied the British citizenry who endured numerous life-threatening air raids during World War II. He concluded that "a great majority of people endured the air raids extraordinarily well, contrary to the universal expectation of mass panic. Exposure to repeated bombings did not produce a significant increase in psychiatric disorders. Although short lived fear reactions were common, surprisingly few persistent phobic reactions emerged" (Rachman, 1991, p. 162). Similar results have been observed after disastrous fires, earthquakes, and floods (Green, Grace, Lindy, Titchener, & Lindy, 1983).

Phillip Saigh (1984) made some interesting observations when he was teaching at the American University in Beirut, Lebanon, just before and during the Israeli invasion in the early 1980s. Saigh had been collecting questionnaires measuring anxiety among university students just before the invasion. When the invasion began, half these students escaped to the surrounding mountains and were safe. The other half endured intense shelling and bombing for a period of time. Saigh continued administering the questionnaires and found a surprising result. There were no essential long-term differences between the group in the mountains and the group in the city, although a few students in the city who were closely exposed to danger and death did develop emotional reactions that progressed into PTSD.

On the other hand, some studies have found a very high incidence of PTSD after trauma. Kilpatrick et al. (1985) sampled more than 2,000 adult women who had personally experienced such trauma as rape, sexual molestation, robbery, and aggravated assault. Subjects were asked whether they had thought about suicide after the trauma, attempted suicide, or had a *nervous breakdown* (a lay term that has no meaning in psychopathology but is commonly used to refer to a severe psychological upset). The authors also analyzed the results based on whether the attack was completed or attempted, as shown in Table 5.10. Rape had the most significant emotional impact. Compared to 2.2% of nonvictims, 19.2% of

rape victims had attempted suicide, and 44% reported suicidal ideation at some time following the rape. Similarly, Resnick, Kilpatrick, Dansky, Saunders, and Best (1993) found that 32% of rape victims met criteria for PTSD at some point in their lives. Looking at all types of trauma (e.g., physical assault, accidents) in a large sample of adult women in the U.S., Resnick et al. (1993) found that 17.9% experienced PTSD. S. Taylor and Koch (1995) found that 15 to 20% of people experiencing severe auto accidents developed PTSD. Recent surveys indicate that among the population as a whole, 7.8% have experienced PTSD (Kessler, Sonnega, Bromet, Hughes, & Nelson, 1995), and that combat and sexual assault are the most common traumas.

What accounts for the discrepancies between the low rate of PTSD in citizens who endured bombing and shelling in London and Beirut and the relatively high rate in victims of crime? Investigators have now concluded that during air raids many people *may not have directly experienced the horrors of dying, death, and direct attack*. Close exposure to the trauma seems to be necessary to developing this disorder (Barlow, in press; D. W. King, King, Foy, & Gudanowski, 1996).

But is this the whole story? It seems not. Some people experience the most horrifying traumas imaginable and emerge psychologically healthy. For others, even relatively mild stressful events are sufficient to produce a full-blown disorder. To understand how this can happen we must consider the etiology of PTSD.

Causes

PTSD is the one disorder for which we are sure of the etiology: Someone personally experiences a trauma and develops a disorder. However, whether one develops PTSD or not is a surprisingly complex issue involving biological, psychological, and social factors.

David Foy and his colleagues (Foy, Sipprelle, Rueger, & Carroll, 1984) concluded that the intensity of combat exposure contributed to the etiology of PTSD in a group of Viet-

table 5.10 Proportion of Victimization Groups Experiencing Major Mental Health Problems

	Problem					
	Nervous Breakdown		*Suicidal Ideation*		*Suicide Attempt*	
Group	*n*	*%*	*n*	*%*	*n*	*%*
Attempted rape	7	9.0	23	29.5	7	8.9
Completed rape	16	16.3	44	44.0	19	19.2
Attempted molestation	2	5.4	12	32.4	3	8.1
Completed molestation	1	1.9	12	21.8	2	3.6
Attempted robbery	0	0.0	3	9.1	4	12.1
Completed robbery	5	7.8	7	10.8	2	3.1
Aggravated assault	1	2.1	7	14.9	2	4.3
Nonvictims	51	3.3	106	6.8	34	2.2

Source: Kilpatrick et al., 1985

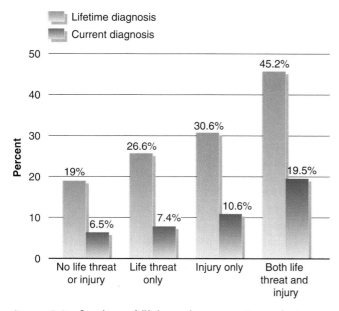

figure 5.9 Prevalence of lifetime and current posttraumatic stress disorder associated with assault characteristics (from Resnick et al., 1993)

nam war veterans but did not account for all of it. For example, approximately 67% of prisoners of war developed PTSD (Foy, Resnick, Sipprelle, & Carroll, 1987). This means that 33% of the prisoners who endured long-term deprivation and torture *did not* develop the disorder. Similarly, Resnick, Kilpatrick, Dansky, Saunders, and Best (1993) demonstrated that the percentage of female crime victims who developed PTSD increased as a function of the severity of the trauma (see Figure 5.9). At lower levels of trauma, some people develop PTSD but most do not. What accounts for these differences?

As with other disorders, we bring our own biological and psychological vulnerability with us. The greater the vulnerability, the more likely we are to develop PTSD. If certain characteristics run in your family, you have a much greater chance of developing the disorder (J. Davidson, Swartz, Storck, Krishnan, & Hammett, 1985; Foy et al., 1987). A family history of anxiety suggests a biological vulnerability for PTSD. True et al. (1993) reported that, given the same amount of combat exposure and one twin with PTSD, a monozygotic (identical) twin was more likely to develop PTSD than a dizygotic twin. The correlation of symptoms in identical twins was between .28 and .41, whereas for fraternal twins it was between .11 and .24, which suggests some genetic influence.

Breslau, David, and Andreski (1995) demonstrated among a random sample of 1,200 individuals that characteristics such as a tendency to be anxious as well as factors such as minimal education and ethnic group membership predict exposure to traumatic events in the first place and therefore an increased risk for PTSD. This is reminiscent of the studies on reciprocal gene environment interactions that we described in Chapter 2, in which existing vulnerabilities, some of them heritable, may help determine the kind of environment in which one lives and, therefore, the type of psychological disorder one may develop.

Also, there seems to be a psychological contribution based on early experiences with unpredictable or uncontrollable events. Foy et al. (1987) discovered that at very high levels of trauma, these vulnerabilities did not matter as much, because most prisoners (67%) developed PTSD. However, at low levels of stress or trauma, vulnerability matters a great deal in determining whether the disorder will develop. Family instability is one factor that may instill a sense that the world is an uncontrollable place (Chorpita & Barlow, in press), so it is not surprising that individuals from unstable families are at risk for developing PTSD if they experience trauma. This factor was relevant in a study of over 1,600 male and female Vietnam veterans (D. W. King et al., 1996).

Basoglu et al. (in press) studied two different groups of torture victims in Turkey. Thirty-four survivors had no history of political activity, commitment to a political cause or group, or expectations of arrest and torture. Compared with 55 tortured political activists, the nonactivists were subjected to less horrendous abuse but showed higher levels of psychopathology. It seemed that the political activists were more prepared psychologically for torture, which they generally experienced as predictable, thereby reducing later psychological symptoms. This study further demonstrates psychological factors that either protect against or increase the risk of developing PTSD.

Finally, social and cultural factors play a major role in the development of PTSD (for example, E. M. Carroll, Rueger, Foy, & Donahoe, 1985). The results from a number of studies are very consistent in showing that, if you have a strong and supportive group of people around you, it is much less likely that you will develop PTSD after a trauma. In a particularly interesting study, Vernberg, LaGreca, Silverman, and Prinstein (1996) studied 568 elementary school children 3 months after Hurricane Andrew hit the coast of South Florida. More than 55% of these children reported moderate to very severe levels of PTSD symptoms. When the authors examined factors contributing to who developed PTSD symptoms and who didn't, social support from parents, close friends, classmates, and teachers was a very important protective factor. Similarly, positive coping strategies involving active problem solving seemed to be protective, whereas becoming angry and placing blame on others were associated with higher levels of PTSD. The broader and deeper the network of social support, the less chance of developing PTSD.

Why is this? As we saw in Chapter 2, we are all social animals and something about having a loving, caring group of people around us directly affects our biological and psychological responses to stress. It is likely that one reason for the very high prevalence of PTSD in Vietnam veterans is the tragic absence of social support when they returned from the war.

Dennis Charney and colleagues suggested that PTSD involves a number of neurobiological systems (Charney, Deutch, Krystal, Southwick, & Davis, 1993; Southwick, Krystal, Johnson, & Charney, 1992). These investigators worked with animals, mostly rats, who were exposed to strong uncontrollable stress, such as repeated shock. The effects are presented in Table 5.11. Southwick et al. (1992) suggest that the simultaneous alterations of numerous neu-

table 5.11 Effects of Uncontrollable Stress on Neurobiological Systems of Rats

Neurochemical System	Functional Alteration Produced by Uncontrollable Stress	Acute Adaptive Behavioral Responses
Noradrenergic	Increased regional norepinephrine turnover in limbic and cortical areas Increased responsiveness of locus ceruleus neurons	Anxiety, fear, autonomic hyperarousal, "fight" or "flight" readiness, encoding of traumatic memories, facilitation of sensory-motor responses
Dopaminergic	Increased dopamine release in frontal cortex and nucleus accumbens Activation of mesocortical dopamine neurons	Hypervigilance
Opiate	Increased endogenous opiate release in periaqueductal gray Decreased density of mu opiate receptors in cerebral cortex	Analgesia, emotional blunting, encoding of traumatic memories
Benzodiazepine	Decreased density of benzodiazepine receptors in hippocampus and cerebral cortex Reduced GABA*-dependent chloride flux	Fear, hyperarousal
Hypothalamic-pituitary-adrenal axis	Elevated glucocorticoid levels at the level of the hippocampus	Metabolic activation, learned behavioral responses

*GABA = gamma-aminobutyric acid.
Source: Southwick, Krystal, & Charney, 1992

rochemical systems and structures probably represent adaptive responses to stress. Of course, work with animals is only suggestive of what happens with humans. Some of these investigator have extended their work to patients with PTSD and confirmed the existence of elevated corticotropin-releasing factor (CRF), which indicates heightened activity in the HYPAC axis described in Chapter 2. You may remember that primates studied in the wild who are under extreme stress also have elevated levels of CRF and cortisol, the stress hormones. You may also remember that chronic activation of stress hormones in these primates seems to result in permanent damage to the hippocampus, which regulates the stress hormones. Thus, chronic arousal and some other symptoms of PTSD may be directly related to changes in brain function and structure (Bremner, Licinio, et al., 1997). New evidence of damage to the hippocampus has appeared in groups of patients with war-related PTSD (Gurvits et al., 1996) and adult survivors of childhood sexual abuse (Bremner, Randall, et al., 1997). Although these results are only correlational at present, further studies will confirm if the changes are a result of PTSD, and where they can be reversed by treatment.

Earlier we described a panic attack as an adaptive fear response occurring at an inappropriate time. It is not surprising that Southwick et al. (1992) trace a brain circuit for PTSD that is very similar to the brain circuit for panic attacks, originating in the locus coeruleus in the brain stem. We have speculated that the alarm reaction is much the same in both panic disorder and PTSD, but in panic disorder the alarm is false. In PTSD, the initial alarm is true in that real danger is present (J. C. Jones & Barlow, 1990). If the alarm is severe enough, we may develop a conditioned or learned alarm reaction to stimuli that reminds us of the trauma (for instance, being tucked into bed reminded Marcie of the emergency room board). We may also develop anxiety about the possibility of additional uncontrollable

emotional experiences (such as flashbacks, which are common in PTSD). Whether or not we develop anxiety depends in part on our vulnerabilities. This model of the etiology of PTSD is presented in Figure 5.10.

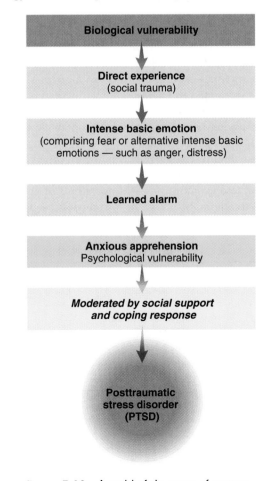

figure 5.10 A model of the causes of posttraumatic stress disorder (from Barlow, 1988)

Treatment

From the psychological point of view, most clinicians agree that victims of PTSD should face the original trauma in order to develop effective coping procedures and thus overcome the debilitating effects of the disorder. (Barlow & Lehman, 1996; Foa & Meadows, 1997). In psychoanalytic therapy, reliving emotional trauma to relieve emotional suffering is called *catharsis*. The trick, of course, is in arranging the reexposure so that it will be therapeutic rather than traumatic once again. Unlike the object of a specific phobia, a traumatic event is difficult to re-create, and very few therapists want to try. Therefore, *imaginal exposure*, in which the content of the trauma and the emotions associated with it are worked through systematically, has been used for decades under a variety of names.

Another complication is that trauma victims often repress their memories of the event. This happens automatically and unconsciously. On occasion, with treatment, the memories flood back and the patient very dramatically relives the episode. Although this may be very frightening to both patient and therapist, it is therapeutic if handled appropriately. Generally, reexposure to the trauma is best carried out very gradually. Mardi Horowitz (1986, p. 125), a psychodynamic psychotherapist, recommends that if the patient is "frozen in [an] overcontrolled state of denial and numbness," it is all the more important that the therapeutic reliving be gradual.

Both Marcie, the young girl bitten by the dog, and her brother were treated simultaneously. The primary difficulty was Marcie's reluctance to be seen by a doctor or to undergo any physical examinations, so a series of experiences was arranged from least to most intense (see Table 5.12). Mildly anxiety-provoking procedures for Marcie included having her pulse taken, lying on an examination table, and taking a bath after accidentally cutting herself. The most intense challenge was being strapped on a restraining board. First Marcie watched her brother go through these exercises. He was not afraid of these particular procedures, although he was anxious about being strapped to a board because of Marcie's terror at the thought. After she watched her brother experience these situations with little or no fear, Marcie tried each one in turn. The therapist took instant photographs of her that she kept after completing the procedures. Marcie was also asked to draw pictures of the situations. The therapist and her family warmly congratulated her as she completed each exercise.

Because of Marcie's age, she was not adept at imaginatively re-creating memories of the traumatic medical procedures. Therefore, her treatment offered experiences designed to alter her current perceptions of the situations. Marcie's PTSD was successfully treated, and her brother's guilt was greatly reduced as a function of helping in her treatment.

Some drug treatments have also been tried with PTSD but the investigation of effective ones is just beginning (Lydiard, Brawman-Mintzer, & Ballenger, 1996). Preliminary experience suggests that some of the same drugs, such as SSRIs (Prozac, Paxil), effective for anxiety disorders in general might be helpful with PTSD, perhaps because they relieve the severe anxiety and panic attacks that are so prominent in this disorder.

Obsessive-Compulsive Disorder

Clinical Description

A client with an anxiety disorder who needs hospitalization is likely to have **obsessive-compulsive disorder (OCD)**. A client who is referred for psychosurgery because every psychological and pharmacological treatment has failed and the suffering is unbearable probably has OCD. OCD is the devastating culmination of the anxiety disorders. It is not uncommon for someone with OCD to experience severe generalized anxiety, recurrent panic attacks, debilitating avoidance, and major depression, all occurring simultane-

---

table 5.12 Fear and Avoidance Hierarchy for Marcie

	Pretreatment Fear Rating	*Posttreatment Fear Rating*
Being strapped on a board	4	0
Having an electrocardiogram	4	0
Having a chest X-ray	4	0
Having M.D. listen to heart with stethoscope	3	0
Lying on examination table	3	0
Taking a bath after sustaining an accidentally inflicted cut	3	0
Allowing therapist to put Band-Aid on a cut	2	0
Letting therapist listen to heart with stethoscope	1	0
Having pulse taken	1	0
Allowing therapist to examine throat with tongue depressor	1	0

Source: Albano et al., 1997

ously in conjunction with obsessive-compulsive symptoms. With OCD, establishing even a foothold of control and predictability over the dangerous events in life seems so utterly hopeless that victims resort to magic and rituals.

In other anxiety disorders the danger is usually in an external object or situation, or at least in the memory of one. In OCD the dangerous event is a thought, image, or impulse that the client attempts to avoid as completely as someone with a snake phobia avoids snakes. For example, has anyone ever told you not to think of pink elephants? If you really concentrate on not thinking of pink elephants, using every mental means possible, you will realize how difficult it is to suppress a suggested thought or image. Individuals with OCD fight this battle all day, every day, sometimes for most of their lives, and usually fail miserably.

In Chapter 3 we discussed the case of Frank, who experienced involuntary thoughts of epilepsy or seizures and prayed or shook his leg to try to distract himself. **Obsessions** are intrusive and mostly nonsensical thoughts, images, or urges that the individual tries to resist or eliminate. **Compulsions** are the thoughts or actions used to suppress the obsessions and provide relief. Frank had both obsessions and compulsions but his disorder was mild compared to the following case.

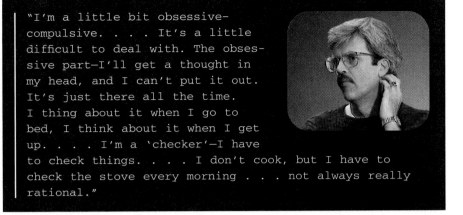

"I'm a little bit obsessive-compulsive. . . . It's a little difficult to deal with. The obsessive part—I'll get a thought in my head, and I can't put it out. It's just there all the time. I thing about it when I go to bed, I think about it when I get up. . . . I'm a 'checker'—I have to check things. . . . I don't cook, but I have to check the stove every morning . . . not always really rational."

Richard
Enslaved by Ritual

Richard, a 19-year-old college freshman majoring in philosophy, withdrew from school because of incapacitating ritualistic behavior. He abandoned personal hygiene because the compulsive rituals that he had to carry out during washing or cleaning were so time-consuming that he could do nothing else. Almost continual showering gave way to no showering. He stopped cutting and washing his hair and beard, brushing his teeth, and changing his clothes. He left his room infrequently and, to avoid rituals associated with the toilet, defecated on paper towels, urinated in paper cups, and stored the waste in the closet. He ate only late at night when his family was asleep. To be able to eat he had to exhale completely, making a lot of hissing noises, coughs, and hacks, and then fill his mouth with as much food as he could while no air was in his lungs. He would eat only a mixture of peanut butter, sugar, cocoa, milk, and mayonnaise. All other foods he considered contaminants. When he walked he took very small steps on his toes while continually looking back, checking and rechecking. On occasion he ran quickly in place. He withdrew his left arm completely from his shirt sleeve as if he were crippled and his shirt was a sling.

Like everyone with OCD, Richard experienced intrusive and persistent thoughts and impulses; in his case they were about sex, aggression, and religion. His various behaviors were efforts to suppress sexual and aggressive thoughts or to ward off the disastrous consequences that he thought would ensue if he did not perform his rituals. Richard performed most of the repetitive behaviors and mental acts mentioned in the DSM-IV criteria. Compulsions can be either behavioral (handwashing, checking) or mental (thinking about certain words in a specific order, counting, praying, and so on) (Foa et al., 1996). The important thing is that they are believed to reduce stress or prevent a dreaded event. Compulsions are often "magical" in that they frequently bear no logical relation to the obsession.

OBSESSIONS

Jenike, Baer, and Minichiello (1986) noted that the most common obsessions in a sample of 100 patients were contamination (55%), aggressive impulses (50%), sexual content (32%), somatic concerns (35%), and the need for symmetry (37%). Sixty percent of those sampled displayed multiple obsessions. "Need for symmetry" refers to keeping things in perfect order or doing something in a very specific way. As a child were you careful not to step on cracks in the sidewalk? You and your friends might have kept this up for a few minutes before tiring of it. But what if you had to spend your whole life avoiding cracks, on foot or in a car? You wouldn't have much fun. People with obsessive impulses may feel they are about to yell out a swear word in church. One client, a young, attractive, and very moral woman, was afraid to ride the bus for fear that if a man sat down beside her she would grab his crotch! In reality this would be the last thing she would do, but the impulse was so horrifying that she made every attempt possible to suppress it and to avoid situations where the impulse might occur.

COMPULSIONS

Leckman et al. (1997) analyzed types of compulsions in several large groups of patients and found that checking and ordering and arranging, along with washing and cleaning, were the major categories of rituals. Most clients with OCD present with cleaning and washing or checking rituals. For people who fear contact with objects or situations that may be contaminating, washing or cleaning restores a sense of safety and control. Checking rituals serve to prevent an imagined disaster or catastrophe. Most are logical, such as repeatedly checking the stove to see whether you turned it off, but severe cases can be illogical. For example, Richard thought that if he did not eat in a certain way he might become possessed. If he didn't take small steps and look back, some disaster might happen to his family. A mental act, such as counting, can also be a compulsion. Like Richard, many patients have both kinds of rituals.

Certain kinds of obsessions are strongly associated with certain kinds of rituals (Leckman et al., 1997). For example, aggression and sexual obsessions seem to lead to checking rituals. Obsessions with symmetry lead to ordering and arranging or repeating rituals; obsessions with contamination lead, of course, to washing rituals. In addition, a small group of patients compulsively hoard things, fearing that if they throw something away, even a 10-year-old newspaper, they then might urgently need it. One patient's house and yard were condemned by the city because junk was piled so high it was both unsightly and a fire hazard. Among her hoard was a 20-year collection of used sanitary napkins!

On rare occasions patients, particularly children, will present with few if any identifiable obsessions. We saw an 8-year-old child who felt compelled to undress, put on his pajamas, and turn down the covers in a very time-consuming fashion each night; he always repeated the ritual three times! He could give no particular reason for his behavior; he simply had to do it.

Statistics

A large epidemiological study put the lifetime prevalence of OCD at approximately 2.6% (Karno & Golding, 1991), although recent studies examining the same individuals more closely suggest that this may be an overestimate (M. B. Stein, Forde, Anderson, & Walker, 1997). Of course, not all cases meeting criteria for OCD are as severe as Richard's. Obsessions and compulsions can be arranged along a continuum, like most clinical features of anxiety disorders. Randy Frost and his colleagues found that between 10% and 15% of "normal" college students engaged in checking behavior substantial enough to score within the range of patients with OCD (Frost, Sher, & Geen, 1986).

It would be unusual *not* to have an occasional intrusive or strange thought. Many people have bizarre, sexual, or aggressive thoughts, particularly if they are bored—for example, when sitting in class. But most people let these thoughts go in one ear and out the other, so to speak. Certain individuals, however, are horrified by such thoughts, considering them signs of an alien, intrusive, evil force. The majority of individuals with OCD are female, but the ratio is not as large as for some other anxiety disorders. Rasmussen and Tsuang (1984, 1986) reported that 55% of 1,630 patients were female. The ECA epidemiology study noted 60% females in their sample of OCD (Karno & Golding, 1991). Interestingly, in children the sex ratio is reversed, with more males than females (Hanna, 1995). This seems to be because

boys tend to develop OCD earlier. By mid-adolescence the sex ratio is approximately equal before becoming predominantly female in adulthood (Albano et al., 1996). Average age of onset ranges from early adolescence to mid-twenties but typically peaks earlier in males (at 13 to 15) than in females (at 20 to 24) (Rasmussen & Eisen, 1990). Once OCD develops, it tends to become chronic.

In Arabic countries, obsessive-compulsive disorder is easily recognizable, although as always cultural beliefs and concerns influence the content of the obsessions and the nature of the compulsions. In Saudi Arabia and Egypt, obsessions are primarily related to religious practices, specifically the Moslem emphasis on cleanliness. Contamination themes are also highly prevalent in India. Nevertheless, OCD looks remarkably similar across cultures. Insel (1984) reviewed studies from England, Hong Kong, India, Egypt, Japan, and Norway and found essentially similar types and proportions of obsessions and compulsions.

Causes

Many of us sometimes have intrusive, even horrific thoughts and occasionally engage in ritualistic behavior, especially when we are under stress (Parkinson & Rachman, 1981a, 1981b). But very few of us develop obsessive-compulsive disorder. Once again, as with panic disorder and posttraumatic stress disorder, one must develop anxiety focused on the possibility of having additional intrusive thoughts.

The repetitive, intrusive, unacceptable thoughts of OCD may well be regulated by the hypothetical brain circuit described in Chapter 2. However, the tendency to develop anxiety over having additional compulsive thoughts may have the same biological and psychological precursors as anxiety in general.

Why would people with OCD focus their anxiety on the occasional intrusive thought rather than on the possibility of a panic attack or some other external situation? One hypothesis is that early experiences taught them that some thoughts are dangerous and unacceptable. They learn this through the same process of misinformation that convinced the person with snake phobia that snakes were dangerous and could be everywhere. Clients with OCD equate thoughts with the specific actions or activity represented by the thoughts, a characteristic of some individuals with fundamentalist religious beliefs. One patient believed that thinking about abortion was the moral equivalent of having an abortion. Richard finally admitted to having strong homosexual impulses that were unacceptable to him and to his minister father, and he believed that the impulses were as sinful as actual acts. Many people with OCD who believe in the tenets of fundamental religions, whether Christian, Jewish, or Islamic, present with similar attitudes. Of course, the vast majority of fundamentalists do not develop OCD. Once again, biological and psychological vulnerabilities must be present for this disorder to develop. Believing that some thoughts are unacceptable and therefore must be suppressed may put people at greater risk of OCD (Amir, Cashman, & Foa, 1997; Parkinson &

Rachman, 1981b; Salkovskis & Campbell, 1994). A model of the etiology of obsessive-compulsive disorder that is somewhat similar to other models of anxiety disorders is presented in Figure 5.11.

Treatment

Studies evaluating the effects of drugs on obsessive-compulsive disorder are showing some promise for medication (Riggs & Foa, 1993; Zohar et al., 1996). The most effective seem to be those that specifically inhibit the reuptake of serotonin, which benefit up to 60% of patients with OCD. However, the average treatment gain is moderate at best (Greist, 1990) and relapse frequently occurs when the drug is discontinued (Lydiard et al., 1996).

Highly structured psychological treatments work somewhat better than drugs but they are not readily available. The most effective approach is exposure and response prevention, a process whereby the rituals are actively prevented and the patient is systematically and gradually exposed to the feared thoughts or situations (Barlow & Lehman, 1996). Richard would be systematically exposed to harmless objects or situations that he thought were contaminated, including certain foods and household chemicals, and his washing and checking rituals would be prevented. Usually this can be done by simply working closely with patients to see that they do not wash or check. In severe cases, patients may be hospitalized and the faucets removed from the bathroom sink for a period of time to discourage repeated washing. However the rituals are prevented, the procedures seem to facilitate "reality testing," because the client soon learns, at an emotional level, that no harm will result whether he carries out the rituals or not. Studies now under way examine the combined effects of medication and psychological treatments.

Psychosurgery is one of the more radical treatments for obsessive-compulsive disorder. "Psychosurgery" is a misnomer that refers to neurosurgery for a psychological disorder. Jenike et al. (1991) recently reviewed the records of 33 patients with obsessive-compulsive disorder, most of them extremely severe cases who had failed to respond at all to either drug or psychological treatment. After a very specific surgical lesion to the cingulate bundle (cingulotomy), approximately 30% benefitted substantially. Considering that these patients seemed to have no hope whatsoever from other treatments, surgery deserves consideration as a last resort. Each year we understand more about the causes of OCD, and our treatments are improving. Before long, such radical treatments as psychosurgery will no longer be employed.

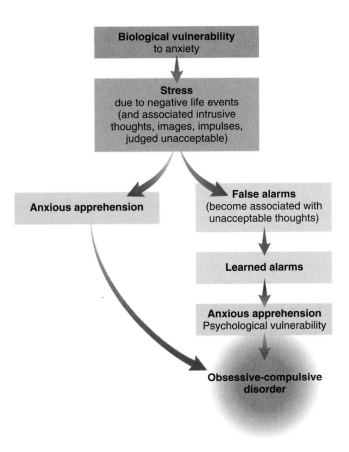

figure 5.11 A model of the causes of obsessive-compulsive disorder (from Barlow, 1988)

■ **concept check 5.3**

Match the anxiety disorder with the following cases: (a) agoraphobia; (b) obsessive-compulsive disorder; (c) posttraumatic stress disorder; (d) situational phobia; (e) generalized anxiety disorder.

1. Frank spends several hours each day making sure that his stove and iron are turned off, doors locked, and water faucets shut. Each must be checked in a particular order six times. He knows that his behavior is excessive, and he may be in danger of losing his job, but he fears disaster if he is not vigilant. _____

2. Darlene has always refused to use escalators. She knows that they are quite safe, but she walks far out of her way to find an elevator or stairs to avoid the anxiety she feels when she considers riding an escalator. Darlene wishes she could overcome this fear because she is a personal shopper and does most of her work at department stores in the mall.

_____

3. Stacy is a sophomore in high school. Since beginning her freshman year, she has had difficulty sleeping and concentrating. Her parents have also noticed that she is quite irritable. Stacy worries often about her performance in school, but has seen her grades drop because the uncontrollable worry takes up much of her time now. _____

4. Jack was involved in a car accident six weeks ago in which the driver of the other car was killed. Since then, Jack has been unable to get in a car because it brings back the horrible scene he witnessed. Nightmares of the accident haunt him and interfere with his sleep. He is irritable and has lost interest in his work and hobbies. _____

from the inside

Afraid of Everything: A Personal History of Agoraphobia
By Daryl M. Woods*

Just as she was about to complete her graduate work and begin a career, Daryl M. Woods found herself facing the confusing and debilitating symptoms of agoraphobia. "In the beginning I had no idea that my emotional slump and complete lack of motivation were the early signals my mind was giving me that something was wrong" (p. 1). In *Afraid of Everything: A Personal History of Agoraphobia*, Woods describes her gradual emotional decline:

> It was on my job [as realtor] that the first ominous sign showed itself. . . . I had taken a client to see some country property. When we got to the acreage and I stopped my car, I suddenly realized that I was afraid to open the car door for myself. . . . One day, after I had unlocked the front door and ushered the clients into the living room, I found that I was unable to follow them through the house. . . . I felt weak, particularly in my legs, my heart rate increased, my palms became wet, and what I could control of my thoughts told me to get away from the situation as fast as possible. (pp. 4–6)

What follows is Woods's highly insightful recollection of her ten-year struggle with what she calls "a condition whose outstanding characteristic is fear, neurotic fear. Fear of space, fear of confinement, fear of travel, fear of groups, and fear of being alone. Then, finally, the fear of fear itself" (p. 1).

Woods takes the reader on an intimate journey through the generalized anxiety, depression, and panic that she experienced in her bout with agoraphobia. "I seemed to fear being anywhere except in the safe confines of my own home. Simple routine things such as getting the paper from the front yard were major traumatic events for me" (p. 13).

In addition to telling her own story, the author also includes accurate and readable descriptions of the varying components of agoraphobia and their possible causes and treatments. With the help of antidepressants, lots of soul searching, and behavior modification therapy, Woods finally gains the upper hand over her illness:

> Where before I had been immobilized by anxiety, now I could see it coming and prepare myself to deal with it appropriately. . . . It may seem foolish and difficult to believe that a successful drive downtown, parking the car, and entering a store could be the reason for personal exhilaration and great celebration. But it was! Each event of this kind was progress back to normalcy and away from fear. (p. 75)

Probably the most compelling feature of the book is Woods's willingness to accept full responsibility for both her stumbles and her successes, from her denial of the seriousness of her symptoms to the obstacles she overcomes in the course of therapy.

Afraid of Everything: A Personal History of Agoraphobia is a candid exploration of one of the most misunderstood and often misdiagnosed anxiety disorders.

*This book is currently out of print, but may be found in many libraries.

Summary

Anxiety, Fear, and Panic

- Anxiety is a future-oriented state characterized by negative affect in which a person focuses on the possibility of uncontrollable danger or misfortune; in contrast, fear is a present-oriented state characterized by strong escapist tendencies and a surge in the sympathetic branch of the autonomic nervous system in response to current danger.

- A panic attack represents the alarm response of real fear, but there is no actual danger.

- Panic attacks may be (a) unexpected (completely without warning), (b) situationally bound (always occurring in a specific situation), or (c) situationally predisposed (likely but unpredictable in a specific situation).

- Panic and anxiety combine to create different anxiety disorders.

Generalized Anxiety Disorder

- In generalized anxiety disorder (GAD), anxiety focuses on minor everyday events, not one major worry or concern.

- Both genetic and psychological vulnerabilities seem to contribute to the development of GAD.

- Though drug and psychological treatments may be effective in the short term, drug treatments are no more effective in the long term than placebo treatments. Successful treatment may help individuals with GAD focus on what is really threatening to them in their lives.

Panic Disorder with and without Agoraphobia

- In panic disorder with or without agoraphobia (a fear and avoidance of situations considered to be "unsafe") anxiety is focused on the next panic attack.

- We all have some genetic vulnerability to stress, and many of us have had a neurobiological overreaction to some stressful event—that is, a panic attack. Individuals who develop panic disorder then develop *anxiety* over the possibility of having another panic attack.

- Both drug and psychological treatments have proven successful in the treatment of panic disorder. One method, *panic control treatment*, concentrates on exposing patients to clusters of sensations that remind them of their panic attacks.

Specific Phobia

- In phobic disorders, the individual avoids situations that produce severe anxiety and/or panic. In specific phobia, the fear is focused on a particular object or situation.

- Phobias can be acquired by experiencing some traumatic event; they can also be learned vicariously or even be taught.

- Treatment of phobias is rather straightforward, with a focus on structured and consistent exposure-based exercises.

Social Phobia
- Social phobia is a fear of being around others, particularly in situations that call for some kind of "performance" in front of other people.
- Though the causes of social phobia are similar to those of specific phobias, treatment has a different focus that includes rehearsing or role playing socially phobic situations. In addition, drug treatments have been effective.

Posttraumatic Stress Disorder
- Posttraumatic stress disorder (PTSD) focuses on avoiding thoughts or images of past traumatic experiences.
- The underlying cause of PTSD is obvious—a traumatic experience. But mere exposure is not enough. The intensity of the experience seems to be a factor in whether an individual develops PTSD; biological vulnerabilities, as well as social and cultural factors, appear to play a role as well.
- Treatment involves reexposing the victim to the trauma in order to overcome the debilitating effects of PTSD.

Obsessive-Compulsive Disorder
- Obsessive-compulsive disorder (OCD) focuses on avoiding frightening or repulsive intrusive thoughts (obsessions) or neutralizing these thoughts through the use of ritualistic behavior (compulsions).
- As with all of the anxiety disorders, biological and psychological vulnerabilities seem to be involved in the development of OCD.
- Drug treatment seems to be only modestly successful in treating OCD. The most effective treatment approach is exposure and response prevention.

Key Terms

anxiety
fear
panic
panic attack
behavioral inhibition system (BIS)
fight/flight system (FFS)
generalized anxiety disorder (GAD)
panic disorder with agoraphobia (PDA)
agoraphobia
panic disorder without agoraphobia (PD)
panic control treatments (PCT)
specific phobia
blood-injection-injury phobia
situational phobia
natural environment phobia
animal phobia
separation anxiety disorder
social phobia
posttraumatic stress disorder (PTSD)
acute stress disorder
obsessive-compulsive disorder (OCD)
obsessions
compulsions

Answers to Concept Checks

5.1
1. e   2. c   3. f   4. a   5. c

5.2
1. c   2. a   3. d   4. e

5.3
1. b   2. d   3. e   4. c

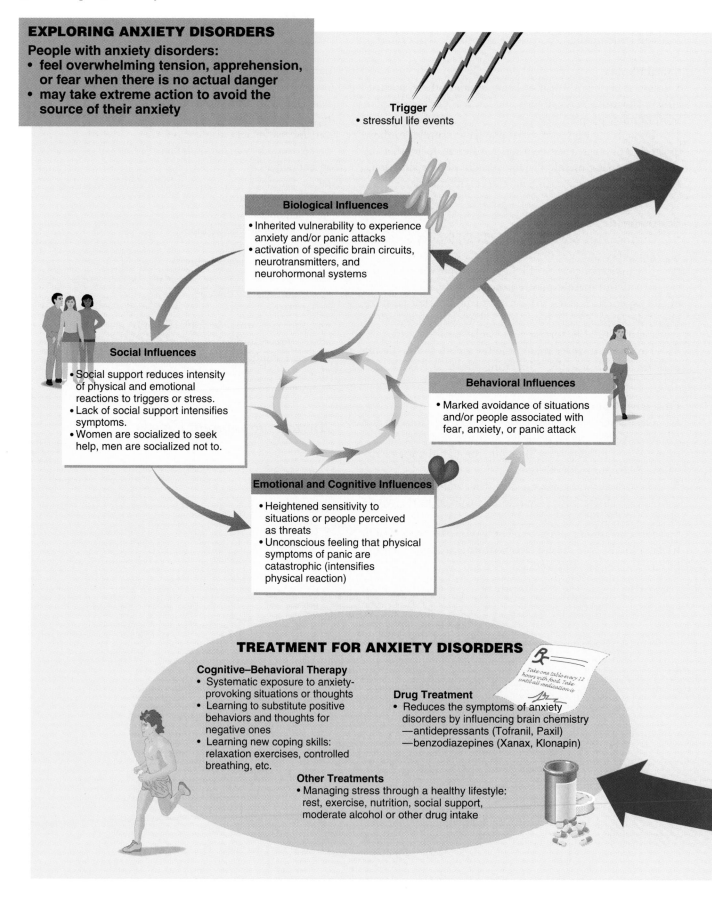

EXPLORING ANXIETY DISORDERS

People with anxiety disorders:
- feel overwhelming tension, apprehension, or fear when there is no actual danger
- may take extreme action to avoid the source of their anxiety

Trigger
- stressful life events

Biological Influences
- Inherited vulnerability to experience anxiety and/or panic attacks
- activation of specific brain circuits, neurotransmitters, and neurohormonal systems

Social Influences
- Social support reduces intensity of physical and emotional reactions to triggers or stress.
- Lack of social support intensifies symptoms.
- Women are socialized to seek help, men are socialized not to.

Behavioral Influences
- Marked avoidance of situations and/or people associated with fear, anxiety, or panic attack

Emotional and Cognitive Influences
- Heightened sensitivity to situations or people perceived as threats
- Unconscious feeling that physical symptoms of panic are catastrophic (intensifies physical reaction)

TREATMENT FOR ANXIETY DISORDERS

Cognitive–Behavioral Therapy
- Systematic exposure to anxiety-provoking situations or thoughts
- Learning to substitute positive behaviors and thoughts for negative ones
- Learning new coping skills: relaxation exercises, controlled breathing, etc.

Drug Treatment
- Reduces the symptoms of anxiety disorders by influencing brain chemistry
  —antidepressants (Tofranil, Paxil)
  —benzodiazepines (Xanax, Klonapin)

Other Treatments
- Managing stress through a healthy lifestyle: rest, exercise, nutrition, social support, moderate alcohol or other drug intake

TYPES OF ANXIETY DISORDERS

PANIC DISORDERS

People with PANIC DISORDERS have had one or more panic attacks and are very anxious and fearful about having future attacks.

What is a panic attack?
A person having a panic attack feels:
- Apprehension leading to intense fear
- Sensation of "going crazy," or of losing control
- Physical signs of distress: racing heartbeat, rapid breathing, dizziness, nausea, sensation of heart attack or imminent death

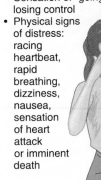

When/why do panic attacks occur?
Panic attacks can be:
- *Situationally bound:* always occurring in the same situation, which may lead to extreme avoidance of triggering persons, places, or events (see specific and social phobias)
- *Unexpected:* can lead to extreme avoidance of any situation or place felt to be unsafe (agoraphobia)
- *Situationally predisposed:* attacks may or may not occur in specific situations (between situationally bound and unexpected)

PHOBIAS

People with PHOBIAS avoid situations that produce severe anxiety and/or panic. There are three main types:

Agoraphobia
- Fear and avoidance of situations, people, or places where it would be unsafe to have a panic attack: malls, grocery stores, buses, planes, tunnels, etc.
- In the extreme, inability to leave the house or even a specific room
- Begins after a panic attack, but can continue for years even if no other attacks occur

Specific Phobia
- Fear of specific object or situation that triggers attack: heights, closed spaces, insects, snakes, flying
- Develops from personal or vicarious experience of traumatic event with the triggering object or situation, or from misinformation

Social Phobia
- Fear of being called for some kind of "performance" that may be judged: using a public restroom, speaking in public, meeting new people, etc.

OTHER TYPES OF ANXIETY DISORDERS

Generalized Anxiety Disorder
- Uncontrollable unproductive worrying about everyday events
- Feeling impending catastrophe even after successes
- Inability to stop the worry/ anxiety cycle: e.g., Irene's fear of failure about school, relationships, and health even though everything seemed fine
- Physical symptoms of muscle tension

Obsessive–Compulsive Disorder
- Fear of unwanted and intrusive thoughts (obsessions)
- Repeated ritualistic actions (compulsions) designed to neutralize the unwanted thoughts: e.g., Richard's attempts to suppress "dangerous" thoughts about sex, aggression, and religion with compulsive washing and cleaning rituals

Posttraumatic Stress Disorder
- Fear of reexperiencing a traumatic event: rape, war, life-threatening situation, etc.
- Nightmares of the traumatic event in flashbacks
- Avoidance of the intense feelings of the event through emotional numbing

6

Somatoform and Dissociative Disorders

Why I became more afraid of living and of dying than others will forever remain an enigma.
Carla Cantor
Phantom Illness: Shattering the Myth of Hypochondria

Do you know somebody who's a hypochondriac? Most of us do. Maybe it's you! The popular image of hypochondria is of someone who exaggerates the slightest physical symptom. Many people continually run to the doctor even though there is nothing really wrong with them. This is usually a harmless tendency that may even be worth some good-natured jokes. But for a few individuals, the preoccupation with their health or appearance becomes so great that it dominates their lives. Their problems fall under the general heading of **somatoform disorders.** *Soma* means body, and the problems preoccupying these people seem, initially, to be physical disorders. What the disorders have in common, however, is that there is usually no identifiable medical condition causing the physical complaints.

Have you ever felt "detached" from yourself or your surroundings? ("This isn't really me," or "That doesn't really look like my hand," or "There's something unreal about this place.") During these experiences some people feel as if they are dreaming. These very mild sensations that most people experience from time to time are slight alterations, or detachments, in consciousness, or identity, and are known as *dissociative experiences* or dissociation. For a few people, these experiences are so intense and extreme that they lose their identity entirely and assume a new one, or they lose their memory or sense of reality and are unable to function. We will discuss several types of **dissociative disorders** in the second half of this chapter.

Somatoform and dissociative disorders are very strongly linked historically and there is increasing evidence that they share common features (Kihlstrom, 1994; Prelior, Yutzy, Dean, & Wetzel, 1993). They used to be categorized under one general heading, "hysterical neurosis." You may remember (from Chapter 1) that the term *hysteria,* which dates back to the Greek Hippocrates, and the Egyptians before him, suggests that the cause of these disorders, which were thought to occur primarily in women, can be traced to a "wandering uterus." But the term *hysterical* came to refer more generally to physical symptoms without known organic cause, or to dramatic or "histrionic" behavior thought to be characteristic of women. Freud (1894/1962) suggested that in a condition called *conversion hysteria* unexplained physical symptoms indicated the conversion of unconscious emotional conflicts into a more acceptable form. The historical term *conversion* remains with us (without the theoretical implications); however, the prejudicial and stigmatizing term *hysterical* is no longer used.

The term *neurosis,* as defined in psychoanalytic theory, suggested a specific cause for certain disorders. Specifically, neurotic disorders resulted from underlying unconscious conflicts, anxiety that resulted from those conflicts, and the implementation of ego defense mechanisms. *Neurosis* was eliminated from the diagnostic system in 1980 because it was too vague, applying to almost all nonpsychotic disorders, and because it implied a specific but unproven cause for these disorders.

Somatoform and dissociative disorders are not well understood, but they have intrigued psychopathologists and the public for centuries. A fuller understanding provides a rich perspective on the extent to which normal, everyday traits found in all of us can evolve into distorted, strange, and incapacitating disorders.

Somatoform Disorders

DSM-IV lists five basic somatoform disorders: hypochondriasis, somatization disorder, conversion disorder, pain disorder, and body dysmorphic disorder. In each, individuals are pathologically concerned with the appearance or functioning of their bodies.

Hypochondriasis

CLINICAL DESCRIPTION

Like many terms in psychopathology, **hypochondriasis** has ancient roots. To the Greeks, the "hypochondria" was the region below the ribs, and the organs in this region affected mental state. For example, ulcers and abdominal disorders were once considered part of the hypochondriacal syndrome. As the actual causes of such disorders were discovered, physical complaints without a clear cause continued to be labeled "hypochondriasis" (Barsky, Wyshak, & Klerman, 1986). In hypochondriasis, severe anxiety is focused on the possibility of having a serious disease. The threat seems so real that no amount of reassurance, even from physicians, will help for long. Consider the following case.

> ### Gail
> #### Invisibly Ill
>
> Gail was married at 21 and looked forward to a new life. As one of many children in a lower-middle-class household, she felt weak and somewhat neglected and suffered from low self-esteem. An older stepbrother berated and belittled her when he was drunk. Her mother and stepfather refused to listen to her or believe her complaints. But she believed that marriage would solve everything; she was finally someone special. Unfortunately, it didn't work out that way. She soon discovered her husband was continuing an affair with an old girlfriend.
>
> Three years after her wedding Gail came to our clinic complaining of anxiety and stress. She was working part-time as a waitress and found her job extremely stressful. Although to the best of her knowledge her husband had stopped seeing his former girlfriend, she had trouble getting the affair out of her mind.
>
> Although Gail complained initially of anxiety and stress, it soon became clear that her major concerns were about her health. Any time she experienced minor physical symptoms such as breathlessness or a headache, she was afraid that she had a serious illness. A headache indicated a brain tumor. Breathlessness was an impending heart attack. Other sensations were quickly elaborated

into the possibility of AIDS or cancer. Gail was afraid to go to sleep at night for fear that she would stop breathing. She avoided exercise, drinking, and even laughing because the resulting sensations upset her. Public restrooms and, on occasion, public telephones were feared as sources of infection.

The major trigger of uncontrollable anxiety and fear was the news in the newspaper and on television. Each time an article or show appeared on the "disease of the month," Gail found herself irresistibly drawn into it, intently noting symptoms that were part of the disease. For days afterward she was vigilant, looking for the symptoms in herself and others. She even watched her dog closely to see whether he was coming down with the dreaded disease. Only with great effort could she dismiss these thoughts after several days. Real illness in a friend or relative would incapacitate her for days at a time.

Gail's fears developed during the first year of her marriage, around the time she learned of her husband's affair. At first, she spent a great deal of time and more money than they could afford going to doctors. Over the years she heard the same thing during each visit: "There's nothing wrong with you; you're perfectly healthy." Finally, she stopped going, as she became convinced that her concerns were excessive, but her fears did not go away and she was chronically miserable.

Gail's problems are fairly typical of hypochondriasis. Research indicates that hypochondriasis shares many features with the anxiety disorders, particularly panic disorder (Salkovskis, Warwick, & Clark, 1996), including similar age of onset, personality characteristics, and patterns of familial aggregation (running in families). Indeed, the two disorders are frequently comorbid; that is, if individuals with a hypochondriacal disorder have additional diagnoses, these are most likely to be anxiety disorders (Côté et al., 1996).

Hypochondriasis is characterized by anxiety or fear that one has a serious disease. Therefore, the essential problem is anxiety, but its expression is different from that of the other anxiety disorders. In hypochondriasis, the individual is preoccupied with bodily symptoms, misinterpreting them as indicative of illness or disease. Almost any physical sensation may become the basis for concern for individuals with hypochondriasis. Some may focus on normal bodily functions such as heart rate or perspiration, others on very minor physical abnormalities such as a cough. Some individuals complain of very vague symptoms, such as aches or fatigue.

Because a key feature of this disorder is preoccupation with physical symptoms, individuals with hypochondriasis almost always go initially to family physicians. They come to the attention of mental health professionals only after family physicians have ruled out realistic medical conditions as a cause.

Another important feature of hypochondriasis is that reassurances from numerous doctors that all is well and the individual is healthy have, at best, only a short-term effect. It isn't long before patients like Gail are back in the office of another doctor on the assumption that the previous doctors

have missed something. In studying this feature for purposes of modifying the diagnostic criteria in DSM-IV, researchers confirmed a subtle but interesting distinction (Côté et al., 1996; Kellner, Hernandez, & Pathak, 1992; Salkovskis et al., 1996). Individuals who fear *developing* a disease, and therefore avoid situations they associate with contagion, are different from those who are anxious that they actually *have* the disease. Individuals who have marked fear of *developing* a disease are classified as having an *illness phobia* (see Chapter 5). Individuals who mistakenly believe they currently *have* a disease are diagnosed with hypochondriasis. These two groups differ further. Individuals with high disease conviction are more likely to misinterpret physical symptoms and display higher rates of checking behaviors and trait anxiety than individuals with illness phobia (Côté et al., 1996). Individuals with illness phobia have an earlier age of onset than those with disease conviction. *Disease conviction* has become the core feature of hypochondriasis. Of course, some people may have both a disease conviction and a fear of developing additional diseases (Kellner, 1986). In one recent study, 60% of a group of patients with illness phobia went on to develop hypochondriasis as well as panic disorder (Benedette et al., 1997).

If you have just read Chapter 5, you may think that patients with panic disorder resemble patients with hypochondriasis. Patients with panic disorder also misinterpret physical symptoms as the beginning of the next panic attack, which they believe may kill them. Salkovskis et al., (1996) suggested that, although both disorders include characteristic concern with physical symptoms, patients with panic disorder typically fear *immediate* symptom-related catastrophes that may occur during the few minutes they are having a panic attack. Individuals with hypochondriacal concerns, on the other hand, focus on a long-term process of illness and disease (for example, cancer or AIDS). Hypochondriacal patients also continue to seek out the opinions of additional doctors in an attempt to rule out (or perhaps confirm) a disease process. Despite numerous assurances that they are healthy, they remain unconvinced and unreassured. In contrast, panic patients continue to believe that their panic attacks might kill them, but most learn rather quickly to stop going to doctors and emergency rooms, where they are told again and again that nothing is wrong with them. Finally, the anxieties of individuals with panic disorder tend to focus on the specific set of 10 or 15 sympathetic nervous system symptoms associated with a panic attack. Hypochondriacal concerns range much wider. Nevertheless, there are probably more similarities than differences between these groups.

Minor, seemingly hypochondriacal, concerns are common in young children, who frequently complain of abdominal aches and pains that do not seem to have a physical basis. In most cases these complaints are passing responses to stress and do not develop into a full-blown chronic hypochondriacal syndrome.

STATISTICS

We know very little about the prevalence of hypochondriasis in the general population. Early estimates indicate that anywhere between 1% and 14% of medical patients are diagnosed with hypochondriasis. Later estimates cite a range of 4% to 9% of patients in general medical practice (Barsky, Wyshak, Klerman, & Latham, 1990). Although historically considered one of the "hysterical" disorders unique to women, the sex ratio is actually 50–50 (Kellner, 1986; Kirmayer & Robbins, 1991). It was thought for a long time that hypochondriasis was more prevalent in elderly populations, but this does not seem to be true (Barsky, Frank, Cleary, Wyshak, & Klerman, 1991). In fact, hypochondriasis is spread fairly evenly

In hypochondriasis, normal experiences and sensations are often transformed into life-threatening illnesses.

across various phases of adulthood. Naturally, more elderly people go to see physicians, making the *absolute number* of patients in this age group somewhat higher than in the younger population. Hypochondriasis may emerge at any time of life, with the peak age periods found in adolescence, middle age (40s and 50s), and after age 60 (Kellner, 1986).

As with anxiety disorders, culture-specific syndromes seem to fit comfortably with hypochondriasis. Among these is the disorder of *koro*, in which there is the belief, accompanied by severe anxiety and sometimes panic, that the genitals are retracting into the abdomen. Most victims of this disorder are Chinese males, although it is also reported in females; there are very few reports of the problem in Western cultures. Why does *koro* occur in Chinese cultures? Rubin (1982) points to the central importance of sexual functioning among Chinese males. He notes that typical sufferers are guilty about excessive masturbation, unsatisfactory intercourse, or promiscuity. These kinds of events may predispose men to focus their attention on their sexual organs, which could exacerbate anxiety and arousal, much as it does in the anxiety disorders, thereby setting off an "epidemic."

Another culture-specific disorder, prevalent in India, is an anxious concern about losing semen, something that obviously occurs during sexual activity. The disorder is called *dhat,* and is associated with a vague mix of physical symptoms including dizziness, weakness, and fatigue that are not so specific as in *koro*. These low-grade depressive or anxious symptoms are simply attributed to a physical factor, semen loss. Other specific culture-bound somatic symptoms associated with emotional factors would include hot sensations in the head or a sensation of something crawling in the head, specific to African patients (Ebigno, 1986), and a sensation of burning in the hands and feet in Pakistani or Indian patients (Kirmayer & Weiss, 1993).

Whatever the symptom, I always interpreted it as a precursor of some crippling Illness.*

Somatic symptoms may be among the more challenging manifestations of psychopathology. First, a physician must rule out a physical cause for the somatic complaints before referring the patient to a mental health professional. Second, the mental health professional must determine the nature of the somatic complaints in order to know whether they are associated with a specific somatoform disorder or are part of some other psychopathological syndrome, such as a panic attack. Third, the clinician must be acutely aware of the specific culture or subculture of the patient, which often requires consultation with experts in cross-cultural presentations of psychopathology.

CAUSES

Investigators with generally differing points of view agree on psychopathological processes ongoing in hypochondriasis. Faulty interpretation of physical signs and sensations as evidence of physical illness is central, so almost everyone agrees that hypochondriasis is basically a *disorder of cognition or perception* with strong emotional contributions (Adler et al., 1994; Barsky & Wyshak, 1990; Clark & Salkovskis, 1992; Kellner, 1985).

Individuals with hypochondriasis experience physical sensations that are common to all of us, but they quickly focus their attention to these sensations. Remember that the very act of focusing on yourself increases arousal and makes the physical sensations seem more intense than they actually are (see Chapter 5). If you also tend to misinterpret these as symptoms of illness, your anxiety will increase further. Increased anxiety produces additional physical symptoms, in a vicious cycle (see Figure 6.1) (Warwick & Salkovskis, 1990).

Using procedures from cognitive science such as the Stroop test (see Chapter 2), Hitchcock and Mathews (1992) confirmed that subjects with hypochondriasis show enhanced perceptual sensitivity to illness cues. They also tend to interpret ambiguous stimuli as threatening. Thus, they quickly become aware (and frightened) of any sign of possible illness or disease. A minor headache, for example, might

*Featured quotations in this chapter are from Carla Cantor, *Phantom Illness: Shattering the Myth of Hypochondria* (Houghton Mifflin, 1996).

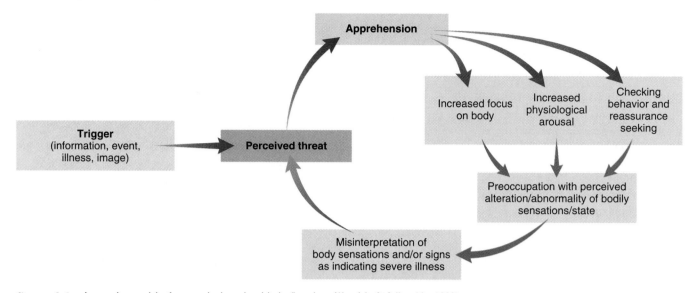

figure 6.1   Integrative model of causes in hypochondriasis (based on Warwick & Salkovskis, 1990).

be interpreted as a sure sign of a brain tumor. Once again, this cycle is similar to what happens in panic disorder (see Chapter 5).

What causes individuals to develop this pattern of somatic sensitivity and distorted beliefs? Although we are not sure, we can safely say the solution is unlikely to be found in isolated biological or psychological factors. There is every reason to believe that the fundamental causes of hypochondriasis are similar to those implicated in the anxiety disorders. For example, there is evidence that hypochondriasis runs in families (Kellner, 1985), suggesting (but not proving) a possible genetic contribution. But this contribution may be nonspecific, such as a tendency to over respond to stress, and thus may be indistinguishable from the nonspecific genetic contribution to anxiety disorders. Hyperresponsivity might combine with a tendency to view negative life events as unpredictable and uncontrollable and, therefore, to be guarded against at all times. As we noted in Chapter 5, these factors would constitute biological and psychological vulnerabilities to anxiety.

Why does this anxiety focus on physical sensations and illness? We know that children with hypochondriacal concerns often report the same kinds of symptoms that other family members may have reported at one time (Kellner, 1985; Pilowsky, 1970). It is therefore quite possible, as in panic disorder, that individuals who develop hypochondriasis have *learned* from family members to focus their anxiety on specific physical conditions and illness.

Three other factors may contribute to this etiological process (Côté et al., 1996; Kellner, 1985). First, hypochondriasis seems to develop in the context of a stressful life event, as do many disorders, including anxiety disorders. Such events often involve death or illness. (Gail's traumatic first year of marriage seemed to coincide with the beginning of her disorder.) Second, people who develop hypochondriasis tend to have had a disproportionate incidence of disease in their family when they were children. Thus, even if they did not develop hypochondriasis until adulthood, they carry

strong memories of illness that could easily become the focus of anxiety. Third, an important social and interpersonal influence may be operating. Some people who come from families where illness is a major issue seem to have learned that an ill person is often paid increased attention. The "benefits" of being sick might contribute to the development of the disorder. A "sick person" who thus receives more attention and less responsibility is described as adopting a "sick role." These issues may be even more significant in somatization disorder, described next.

TREATMENT

Unfortunately, we know very little about treating hypochondriasis. Scientifically controlled studies have appeared only recently. Warwick, Clark, Cobb, and Salkovskis (1996) randomly assigned 32 patients to either cognitive behavioral therapy or a no-treatment wait-list control group. Treatment focused on identifying and challenging illness-related misinterpretation of physical sensations and on showing patients how to create "symptoms" by focusing attention on certain body areas. Bringing on their own symptoms persuaded many patients that such events were under their control. Patients were also coached to seek less reassurance regarding their concerns. Patients in the treatment group improved an average of 76%, and those in the wait-list group only 5%; benefits were maintained for 3 months. Of course, results from one small study are far from conclusive.

Although it is common clinical practice to uncover unconscious conflicts through psychodynamic psychotherapy, results on the effectiveness of this kind of treatment have seldom been reported. In one study, Ladee (1966) noted that only 4 out of 23 patients seemed to derive any benefit.

Surprisingly, clinical reports indicate that reassurance seems to be effective in some cases (Kellner, 1992)—"surprisingly" because, by definition, patients with hypochondriasis are not supposed to benefit from reassurance about their health. However, reassurance is usually given only very briefly by family doctors who have little time to provide the ongoing support and reassurance that might be necessary. Mental health professionals may well be able to offer reassurance in a more effective and sensitive manner, devote sufficient time to all the concerns the patient may have, and attend to the "meaning" of the symptoms (for example, their relation to the patient's life stress). Participation in support groups may also give these people the reassurance they need. It is very likely we will see more research on the treatment of hypochondriasis in the future.

Somatization Disorder

CLINICAL DESCRIPTION

In 1859, Pierre Briquet, a French physician, described patients who came to see him with seemingly endless lists of somatic complaints for which he could find no medical basis (American Psychiatric Association, 1980). Despite his negative findings, patients returned shortly with either the same complaints or new lists containing slight variations. For over 100 years this disorder was called *Briquet's syndrome*, before being changed in 1980 to **somatization disorder.** Consider the following case.

Linda
Full-Time Patient

Linda, an intelligent woman in her 30s, came to our clinic looking distressed and pained. As she sat down she noted that coming into the office was very difficult for her, as she had trouble breathing and considerable swelling in the joints of her legs and arms. She was also in some pain from chronic urinary tract infections and might have to leave at any moment to go to the restroom, but she was extremely happy that she had kept the appointment. At least she was seeing someone who could help alleviate her considerable suffering. She said she knew we would have to go through a detailed initial interview, but she had something that might save time. At this point she pulled out several sheets of paper and handed them over. One section, some five pages long, described her contacts with the health care system for *major difficulties only*. Times, dates, potential diagnoses, and days hospitalized were noted. The second section, one and one-half single-spaced pages, consisted of a list of all the medications she had taken for various complaints.

Linda felt that she had any one of a number of chronic infections that nobody could properly diagnose. She had begun to have these problems in her teenage years. She often discussed her symptoms and fears with doctors and clergy. She was drawn to hospitals and medical clinics, and had entered nursing school after high school. However, during hospital training, she noticed her physical condition deteriorating rapidly: She seemed to pick up the diseases she was learning about. A series of stressful emotional events resulted in her leaving nursing school.

After developing unexplained paralysis in her legs, Linda was admitted to a psychiatric hospital, and after a year she regained her ability to walk. On discharge she obtained disability status, which freed her from having to work full time, and she volunteered at the local hospital. With her chronic but fluctuating incapacitation, on some days she could go in and on some days she could not. She was currently seeing a family practitioner and six specialists, who monitored various aspects of her physical condition. She was also seeing two ministers for pastoral counseling.

Linda easily met and exceeded all the DSM-IV diagnostic criteria for somatization disorder. Do you notice any differences between Linda, who presented with somatization disorder, and Gail, who presented with hypochondriacal disorder? Of course, Linda was more severely impaired and also had suffered in the past from symptoms of paralysis (which we now call conversion symptoms; see p. 163). But the more telling difference is that Linda was *not so afraid* as Gail that she had a disease. Linda was concerned with the symptoms themselves, not with what they might mean. Furthermore, Linda's entire life revolved around her symptoms; in fact, she once said that her symptoms were her identity: Without them she would not know who she was. She did not know how to relate to people except in terms of her symptoms. Her few friends who were not health care professionals had the patience to relate to her sympathetically, through the veil of her symptoms.

STATISTICS

Somatization disorder is very rare. DSM-III-R criteria required 13 or more symptoms from a list of 35, making diagnosis very difficult. The criteria were greatly simplified for DSM-IV with only eight symptoms required (Cloninger, 1996). These criteria have been validated as easier to use and more accurate than alternative or past criteria (Yutzy et al., 1995). Katon et al., (1991) demonstrated that somatization disorder occurs on a continuum: People with only a few somatic symptoms of unexplained origin may experience sufficient distress and impairment of functioning to be considered to have a "disorder." Although it has its own name, undifferentiated somatoform disorder, it is really just somatization disorder with fewer than eight symptoms. Using between four and six symptoms as criteria, Escobar and Canino (1989) found a prevalence of somatization disorder of 4.4% in one large city.

Linda's disorder developed during adolescence, apparently the typical age of onset. A number of studies have demonstrated that individuals with somatization disorder tend to be women, unmarried, and from lower socioeconomic groups (for example, Swartz et al., 1986). For instance, 68% of the patients in a large sample studied by Kirmayer and Robbins (1991) were female. In addition to a variety of somatic complaints, individuals may also have psychological complaints, usually anxiety or mood disorders (Adler et al., 1994; Kirmayer & Robbins, 1991). Suicidal attempts that appear to be manipulative gestures rather than true death efforts are frequent. Although symptoms may come and go, somatization disorder and the accompa-

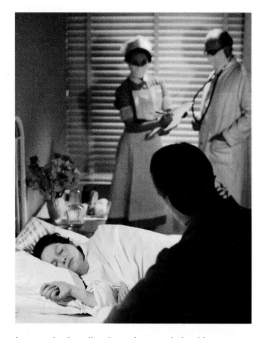

In somatization disorder, primary relationships are often with medical caregivers; one's symptoms are one's identity.

nying sick role behavior are chronic, often continuing into old age.

In some other cultures, males present with somatic complaints at least as often and sometimes more often than females (Swartz, Landerman, George, Blazer, & Escobar, 1991). Of course, one must be particularly careful to rule out medical causes of somatic complaints in third world countries, where parasitic and other infectious diseases and physical conditions associated with poor nutrition are common and not always easy to diagnose. Table 6.1 presents data from a large World Health Organization study on individuals presenting to primary care settings with either somatic complaints that would not be sufficient to meet criteria for disorder, or for somatization disorder. Notice that the rates are relatively uniform around the world for somatic complaints as is the sex ratio (Gureje, Simon, Ustin, & Goldberg, 1997). When the problem is severe enough to meet criteria for disorder, the sex ratio is approximately 2:1 female.

CAUSES

Somatization disorder shares some features with hypochondriasis, including family illness or injury during childhood. But this is a minor factor at best, since countless families experience chronic illness or injuries without passing on the sick role to children. Something else contributes strongly to somatization disorder.

Given the past difficulty in making a diagnosis, few etiological studies of somatization disorder have been done. Early studies of possible genetic contributions had mixed results. For example, in a sophisticated twin study, Torgersen (1986) found no increased prevalence of somatization disorder in monozygotic pairs, but most studies find substantial

evidence that the disorder runs in families and may have a heritable basis (Bell, 1994; Guze, Cloninger, Martin, & Clayton, 1986; Katon, 1993). A more startling finding emerged from these studies, however. Somatization disorder is strongly linked in family and genetic studies to antisocial personality disorder (ASPD) (see Chapter 13), which is characterized by vandalism, persistent lying, theft, irresponsibility with finances and at work, and outright physical aggression. Individuals with antisocial personality disorder seem insensitive to signals of punishment and to the negative consequences of their often impulsive behavior, and they apparently experience little anxiety or guilt.

Antisocial personality disorder occurs primarily in males and somatization disorder in females, but they share a number of features. Both begin early in life, typically run a chronic course, predominate among lower socioeconomic classes, are difficult to treat, and are associated with marital discord, drug and alcohol abuse, and suicide attempts, among other complications (Cloninger, 1978; Goodwin & Guze, 1984; Lilienfeld, 1992). Both family and adoption studies suggest that ASPD and somatization disorder tend to run in families and may well have a heritable component (for instance, Bohman, Cloninger, von Knorring, & Sigvardsson, 1984; Cadoret, 1978), although it is also possible that the behavioral patterns could be learned in a maladaptive family setting.

The aggressiveness, impulsiveness, and lack of emotion characteristic of antisocial personality disorder seem to be at the other end of the spectrum from somatization disorder. What could these two disorders possibly have in common? Although we don't yet have the answers, Lilienfeld (1992) reviews a number of hypotheses; we will look at some of them here because they are a fascinating example of integrative biopsychosocial thinking about psychopathology.

One model with some support suggests that somatization disorder and ASPD share a neurobiologically based disinhibition syndrome. How might this work? The well-known neuropsychologist Jeffrey Gray (1982, 1985) proposed three major functional systems: a behavioral inhibition system (BIS), a behavioral activation system (BAS), and a fight–flight system (FFS). As noted in Chapter 5, the BIS and the FFS may well play a prominent role in the expression of anxiety and panic. On the other hand, the BAS underlies, at least partly, impulsivity, thrill seeking, and excitability. A number of investigators (for example, Cloninger, 1987b; Gorenstein & Newman, 1980) have suggested that antisocial personality disorder and somatization disorder (as well as substance abuse and attention deficit-hyperactivity disorder; see Chapters 12 and 16) may have in common a *weak* BIS that is incapable of exerting sufficient control over the BAS.

To review, the BIS basically ensures that we are very sensitive to threat or danger and avoid situations or signals suggesting that threat or danger is imminent. When confronted with such signals, we normally feel anxiety. Individuals with antisocial personality disorder don't seem to experience anxiety, although they may experience panic on occasion (Fowles, 1993). Instead, they are overly responsive to short-term rewards (impulsive), even if the pursuit of these rewards gets them in trouble. There is accumulating evidence that impulsiveness is common in ASPD (for instance, Newman, Widom, & Nathan, 1985). How does this apply to people with somatization disorder? Many of the behaviors and traits associated with somatization disorder also seem to reflect short-term gain at the expense of long-term problems. The continual development of new somatic symptoms gains immediate sympathy and attention (for a while) but eventually social isolation (Goodwin & Guze, 1984). Other behaviors that seem to indicate short-term gratification are the novelty-seeking and provocative sexual behavior often present in people with somatization disorder (Kendall, Williams, & Agras, 1975).

The brain circuit mediating the BIS is relatively well established, as we saw in Chapter 5. It runs from the septal area through the hippocampus to the orbital frontal cortex. A variety of neurophysiological evidence suggests a dysfunction in this brain circuit not only in ASPD but also in somatization disorder, substance abuse, and perhaps, attention deficit hyperactivity disorder (Cloninger, 1987b; Lilienfeld, 1992). If individuals with ASPD and somatization disorder share the same underlying neurophysiological vulnerability, why do they behave so differently? The explanation is that social and cultural factors exert a strong effect. Both Cathy Spatz Widom (1984) and Robert Cloninger (1987b) have pointed out that the major difference between the disorders is their degree of *dependence*. Aggression is strongly associated with males in most mammalian species, including rodents (Gray & Buffery, 1971). Dependence and lack of aggression are strongly associated with females. Thus, both aggression and ASPD are strongly associated with males and dependence and somatization disorder are strongly associated with females. Gender roles are among the strongest components of identity. It is very possible that gender socialization accounts almost entirely for the profound differences in the expression of the same biological vulnerability among men and women.

These theoretical models are still preliminary and require a great deal more data before we can have confidence in their validity. But such ideas are at the forefront of our knowledge of psychopathology and reflect the kinds of integrative approach to psychopathology (described in Chapter 2) that will inevitably emerge as our knowledge increases.

Might these assumptions apply to Linda or her family? Linda's sister had been married briefly and had two children. She had been in therapy for most of her adult life. Occasionally, Linda's sister visited doctors with various somatic complaints, but her primary difficulty was unexplained periods of recurring amnesia that might last several days; these spells alternated with blackout periods during which she was rushed to the hospital.

Were there signs of sexual impulsivity or ASPD in this family? The sister's older daughter, after a very stormy adolescence characterized by truancy and delinquency, was sentenced to jail for violations involving drugs and assault. In the midst of one session with us, Linda noted that she had kept a list of people with whom she had had sexual intercourse. The list numbered well over 20, and most of the sexual episodes occurred in the offices of mental health professionals or clergy!

This development in Linda's relationship with caregivers was very important since she saw it as the ultimate sign that the caregivers were concerned about her as a person and that she was important to them. But the relation-

table 6.1 **Frequency of Two Forms of Somatization in a Cross-Cultural Study (N = 5,438)***

	ICD-10 Somatization Disorder (%)			Somatic Symptom Index (%)		
Center	*Men*	*Women*	*Overall Prevalence*	*Men*	*Women*	*Overall Prevalence*
Ankara, Turkey	1.3	2.2	1.9	22.3	26.7	25.2
Athens, Greece	0.4	1.8	1.3	7.7	13.5	11.5
Bangalore, India	1.3	2.4	1.8	19.1	20.0	19.6
Berlin, Germany	0.3	2.0	1.3	24.9	25.9	25.5
Groningen, the Netherlands	0.8	4.1	2.8	14.7	19.9	17.8
Ibadan, Nigeria	0.5	0.3	0.4	14.4	5.0	7.6
Mainz, Germany	1.0	4.4	3.0	24.9	17.3	20.6
Manchester, U.K.	0	0.5	0.4	21.4	20.0	20.5
Nagasaki, Japan	0	0.2	0.1	13.3	7.9	10.5
Paris, France	0.5	3.1	1.7	18.6	28.2	23.1
Rio de Janeiro, Brazil	1.5	11.2	8.5	35.6	30.6	32.0
Santiago, Chile	33.8	11.2	17.7	45.7	33.3	36.8
Seattle, USA	0.7	2.2	1.7	10.0	9.8	9.8
Shanghai, China	0.3	2.2	1.5	17.5	18.7	18.3
Verona, Italy	0	0.2	0.1	9.7	8.5	8.9
Total	1.9	3.3	2.8	19.8	19.7	19.7

*Weighted to the first-stage (intake) sample.
Adapted from Gureje et al., 1997. *The International Classification of Diseases* (10th ed.) (ICD 10), criteria were used in this study.

ships almost always ended tragically. Several of the caregivers' marriages disintegrated and at least one mental health professional committed suicide. Linda herself was never satisfied or fulfilled by the relationships but was greatly hurt when they inevitably ended. The American Psychological Association has decreed that it is *always* unethical to have *any* sexual contact with a patient at any time during treatment. Violations of this ethical canon have nearly always resulted in tragic consequences.

TREATMENT

Somatization disorder is exceedingly difficult to treat and there are no treatments with proven effectiveness that seem to "cure" the syndrome. In our clinic we concentrate on providing reassurance, reducing stress and, in particular, reducing the frequency of help-seeking behaviors. One of the most common patterns is the person's tendency to visit numerous medical specialists according to the symptom of the week. There is an extensive medical and physical workup with every visit to a new physician (or to one who has not been seen for a while). In treatment, to limit these visits a gatekeeper physician is assigned each patient to screen all physical complaints. Subsequent visits to specialists must be specifically authorized by this gatekeeper. In the context of a positive therapeutic relationship, most patients are amenable to this arrangement.

Additional therapeutic attention is directed at reducing the supportive consequences of relating to significant others on the basis of physical symptoms alone. More appropriate methods of interacting with others are encouraged. Because Linda, like many patients with this disorder, had managed to become eligible for disability payments from the state, additional goals involved encouraging at least part-time employment with the ultimate goal of discontinuing disability.

Other specialists in somatization disorder have enumerated similar therapeutic goals. For example, G. R. Smith, Monson, and Ray (1986) and R. J. Smith (1991) evaluated a similar procedure and found that, although it did not improve the patient's mental or physical health, it did substantially reduce the help-seeking behavior. This is an extremely important goal, because the cost in dollars—to the patient, to the medical system and, ultimately, to society—is enormous.

Conversion Disorder

CLINICAL DESCRIPTION

Conversion disorders generally have to do with physical malfunctioning, such as paralysis, blindness, or difficulty speaking (aphonia), without any physical or organic pathology to account for the malfunction. Most conversion symptoms suggest that some kind of neurological disease is affecting sensory-motor systems, although conversion symptoms can mimic the full range of physical malfunctioning.

Conversion disorders provide us with some of the most intriguing, sometimes astounding, examples of psychopathology. What could possibly account for somebody going blind when all visual processes are perfectly normal, or

experiencing paralysis of the arms or legs when there is no neurological damage? Consider the following case.

Eloise
Unlearning Walking

Eloise sat on a chair with her legs under her, refusing to put her feet on the floor. Her mother sat close by, ready to assist her if she needed to move or get up. Her mother had made the appointment and, with the help of a friend, had all but carried Eloise into the office. Eloise was a 20-year-old of borderline intelligence who was friendly and personable during the initial interview and who readily answered all questions with a big smile. She obviously enjoyed the social interaction.

Eloise's difficulty walking developed over a 5-year period. Her right leg had given way and she began falling. Gradually, the condition worsened to the point that 6 months before her admission to the hospital Eloise could move around only by crawling on the floor.

Physical examinations revealed no physical problems. Eloise presented with a classic case of conversion disorder. Although she was not paralyzed, her specific symptoms included weakness in her legs and difficulty keeping her balance, with the result that she fell frequently. This particular type of conversion symptom is called *astasia–abasia*.

Eloise lived with her mother, who ran a gift shop in the front of her house in a very small rural town. Eloise had been schooled through exceptional education programs until she was about 15; after this, no further programs were available. When Eloise began staying home, her walking began to deteriorate.

In addition to blindness, paralysis, and aphonia, conversion symptoms may include total mutism and the loss of the sense of touch. Some people have seizures, which may be psychological in origin since no significant EEG changes can be documented. Another relatively common symptom is globus hystericus, the sensation of a lump in the throat that makes it difficult to swallow, eat, or sometimes talk.

The term *conversion* has been used off and on since the Middle Ages (Mace, 1992), but was popularized by Freud, who believed that the anxiety resulting from unconscious conflicts somehow was "converted" into physical symptoms to find expression. This allowed the individual to discharge some anxiety without actually experiencing it. As in phobic disorders, the anxiety resulting from unconscious conflicts might be "displaced" onto another object.

CLOSELY RELATED DISORDERS

Distinguishing among conversion reactions, real physical disorders, and outright **malingering** (faking) is sometimes difficult. Several factors can help.

First, conversion reactions often have the same quality of indifference to the symptoms that is present in somatization disorder. This attitude has been referred to as *la belle indifférence*, and is considered a hallmark of conversion reactions but, unfortunately, it is not a foolproof sign. A blasé attitude toward illness is sometimes displayed by people with actual physical disorders and some people with conversion symptoms do become quite distressed.

Second, conversion symptoms are often precipitated by marked stress. C. V. Ford (1985) noted that the incidence of marked stress preceding a conversion symptom occurred in 52% to 93% of the cases. Thus, if one cannot identify a stressful event preceding the onset of the conversion symptom, one might more carefully consider the presence of a true physical condition.

Finally, although people with conversion symptoms can usually function normally, they seem truly unaware either of this ability or of sensory input. For example, individuals with the conversion symptom of blindness can usually avoid objects in their visual field, but they will tell you they can't see the objects. Similarly, individuals with conversion symptoms of paralysis of the legs might suddenly get up and run in an emergency, and then be astounded that they were able to do this. It is possible that some people who experience miraculous cures during religious ceremonies may have been suffering from conversion reactions. Although these factors may help in distinguishing between conversion and organically based physical disorders, clinicians often make mistakes. Fishbain and Goldberg (1991) describe three people, one of whom died, who were first diagnosed with conversion reaction and later found to have physical disorders. In one study, 25% of patients diagnosed with conversion reaction were later found to have physical disorders (G. C. Watson & Buranen, 1979).

It can also be very difficult to distinguish between individuals who are truly experiencing conversion symptoms in a seemingly involuntary way and malingerers who are very good at faking symptoms. Once malingerers are exposed, their motivation is clear: They are either trying to get out of something, such as work or legal difficulties, or they are attempting to gain something, such as a financial settlement. Malingerers are fully aware of what they are doing and are clearly attempting to manipulate others to gain a desired end.

More puzzling is a set of conditions called **factitious disorders** which fall somewhere between malingering and conversion disorders. The symptoms are feigned and under voluntary control, as with malingering, but there is *no good reason* for voluntarily producing the symptoms except, possibly, to assume the sick role and receive increased attention. Tragically, this disorder may extend to other members of the family. An adult with the disorder may purposely make the children sick, evidently for the attention and pity then given to the parent who is causing the symptoms. When an individual deliberately makes someone else sick, the condition is called *factitious disorder by proxy* or, sometimes, "Munchausen's syndrome by proxy."

UNCONSCIOUS MENTAL PROCESSES IN CONVERSION AND RELATED DISORDERS

Unconscious cognitive processes seem to play a role in much of psychopathology (although not necessarily as Freud envisioned it), but nowhere is this phenomenon more readily and dramatically apparent than when we attempt to distinguish between conversion disorders and related conditions.

To take a closer look at the "unconscious" mental process in these conditions, we'll review briefly the case of Anna O. (see Chapter 2).

As you may remember, when Anna O. was 21 years old she was nursing her dying father. This was a very difficult time for her. She reported that after many days by the sick bed, her mind wandered. Suddenly she found herself imagining (dreaming?) that a black snake was moving across the bed, about to bite her father. She tried to grab the snake, but her right arm had gone to sleep and she could not move it. Looking at her arm and hand, she imagined that her fingers had turned into little poisonous snakes. Horrified, all she could do was pray, and the only prayer that came to mind was in English (Anna O.'s native language was German). After this, she experienced paralysis in her right arm whenever she remembered this hallucination. The paralysis gradually extended to the right side of her body and, on occasion, to other parts of her body. She also experienced a number of other conversion symptoms such as deafness and, intriguingly, an inability to speak German, although she remained fluent in English.

In Breuer's treatment of Anna O., she relived her traumatic experiences in her imagination. Under hypnosis, she was able to re-create the memory of her horrific hallucination. As she recalled and processed the images, her paralysis left her and she regained her ability to speak German. Breuer called the therapeutic reexperiencing of emotionally traumatic events *catharsis* (purging, or releasing). Catharsis has proven to be an effective intervention with many emotional disorders, as noted in Chapter 5.

Were Anna O.'s symptoms really "unconscious," or did she realize at some level that she could move her arm and the rest of her body if she wanted to, and it simply served her purpose not to? This question has long bedeviled psychopathologists. Now, new information (reviewed in Chapter 2) on unconscious cognitive processes becomes important. We are all capable of receiving and processing information in a number of sensory channels (such as vision and hearing) without being aware of it. Remember the phenomenon of blind sight or unconscious vision? Weiskrantz (1980) and others discovered that people with small, localized damage to certain parts of their brains could identify objects in their field of vision, but they had no awareness whatsoever that they could see. Could this happen to people without brain damage? Consider the following case.

Celia
Seeing through Blindness

A 15-year-old girl named Celia suddenly was unable to see. Shortly thereafter she regained some of her sight but her vision was so severely blurred that she could not read. When she was brought to a clinic for testing, psychologists arranged a series of sophisticated vision tests that did not require her to report when she could or could not see. One of the tasks required her to examine three triangles displayed on three separate screens and to press a button under the screen containing an upright triangle. Celia performed perfectly on this test without being aware that she could see anything (Grosz & Zimmerman, 1970). Was Celia faking? Evidently not, or she would have purposely made a mistake.

Sackeim, Nordlie, and Gur (1979) evaluated the potential difference between real unconscious process and faking by hypnotizing two subjects and giving each a suggestion of total blindness. One subject was also told that it was extremely important that she appear to everyone to be blind. The second subject was not given further instructions. The first subject evidently following instructions to appear blind at all costs, performed far below chance on a visual discrimination task similar to the upright triangle task. On almost every trial she chose the wrong answer. The second subject with the hypnotic suggestion of blindness but no instructions to "appear" blind at all costs performed perfectly on the visual discrimination task—although, she reported that she could not see anything. How is this relevant to identifying malingering? In an earlier case, Grosz and Zimmerman (1965) evaluated a male who seemed to have conversion symptoms of blindness. They discovered that he performed much more poorly than chance on a visual discrimination task. Subsequent information from other sources confirmed that he was almost certainly malingering. To review these distinctions, someone who is truly blind would perform at a chance level on visual discrimination tasks. People with conversion symptoms, on the other hand, can see objects in their visual field and therefore would perform well on these tasks, but this experience is dissociated from their awareness of sight. Malingerers and, perhaps, individuals with factitious disorders simply do everything possible to pretend they can't see.

STATISTICS

We have already seen that conversion disorder may occur in conjunction with other disorders, particularly somatization disorder, as in the case of Linda. Linda's paralysis passed after several months and did not return, although on occasion she would report "feeling as if" it were returning. Conversion disorders are relatively rare in mental health settings, but remember that people who seek help for this condition are more likely to consult neurologists or other specialists. The prevalence estimates in neurological settings vary dramatically from 1% to 30% (Marsden, 1986; Trimbell, 1981).

Like somatization disorder, conversion disorders are found primarily in women (Folks, Ford, & Regan, 1984) and typically develop during adolescence or slightly thereafter. However, they occur relatively frequently in males at times of extreme stress (Chodoff, 1974). Conversion reactions are not uncommon in soldiers exposed to combat (Mucha & Reinhardt, 1970). The symptoms often disappear after a time, only to return later in the same or similar form when a new stressor occurs.

In other cultures, some conversion symptoms are very common aspects of religious or healing rituals. Seizures, paralysis, and trances are common in some rural fundamentalist religious groups in the United States (Griffith, English, & Mayfield, 1980), and are often seen as evidence of contact with God. Individuals who exhibit such symptoms are thus held in high esteem by their peers. These symptoms do not meet criteria for a "disorder" unless they persist and interfere with an individual's functioning.

CAUSES

Freud described four basic processes in the development of conversion disorder. First, the individual experiences a traumatic event—in Freud's view, an unacceptable, unconscious conflict. Second, since the conflict and the resulting anxiety are unacceptable, the person represses the conflict, making it unconscious. Third, since the anxiety continues to increase and threatens to emerge into consciousness, the person "converts" it into physical symptoms, thereby relieving the pressure of having to deal directly with the conflict. This reduction of anxiety is considered to be the *primary gain* or reinforcing event that maintains the conversion symptom. Fourth, the individual receives greatly increased attention and sympathy from loved ones and may also be allowed to avoid a difficult situation or task. Freud considered such attention or avoidance to be the *secondary gain* or the secondarily reinforcing set of events.

We believe Freud was basically correct on at least three counts and possibly a fourth, although firm evidence supporting any of these ideas is sparse and Freud's views were far more complex than represented here. What seems to happen is that individuals with conversion disorder have experienced a traumatic event that must be escaped at all costs. This might be combat, where death is imminent, or an impossible interpersonal situation. Since simply running away is unacceptable in most cases, the socially acceptable alternative of getting sick is substituted; but getting sick on purpose is also unacceptable, so this motivation is detached from the person's consciousness. Finally, since the escape behavior (the conversion symptoms) is successful to an extent in obliterating the traumatic situation, the behavior continues until the underlying problem is resolved.

The one step in Freud's progression of events about which some questions remain is the issue of primary gain. The notion of primary gain accounts for the feature of *la belle indifférence* (cited previously), where individuals seem not the least bit distressed about their symptoms. In other words, Freud thought that since the symptoms reflected an unconscious attempt to resolve a conflict, the patient would not be upset by them. But formal tests of this feature provide little support for Freud's claim. For example, Lader and Sartorius (1968) compared patients with conversion disorder with control groups of anxious patients without conversion symptoms. The patients with conversion disorder showed equal or greater anxiety and physiological arousal than the control group. The impression of indifference may be more in the mind of the therapist than true of the patient.

Social and cultural influences also contribute to conversion disorder which, like somatization disorder, tends to occur in less educated, lower socioeconomic groups where knowledge about disease and medical illness is not well developed (Swartz, Blazer, Woodbury, George, & Landerman, 1986). Prior experience with real physical problems, usually among other family members, tends to influence the later choice of specific conversion symptoms; that is, patients tend to adopt symptoms with which they are familiar (for example, Brady & Lind, 1961). Furthermore, the incidence of these disorders has decreased over the decades. The most likely explanation is that current knowledge eliminates much of the secondary gain that is so important in these disorders.

Finally, many conversion symptoms seem to be part of a larger constellation of psychopathology. Linda had broad-ranging somatization disorder as well as the severe conversion symptoms that resulted in her hospitalization. In similar cases, individuals may have a marked biological vulnerability to develop the disorder when under stress, with biological processes like those discussed in the context of somatization disorder. For countless other cases, however, biological contributory factors seem to be less important than the overriding influence of interpersonal factors, in this case the actions of Eloise's mother, as we will see. We will talk about Eloise's treatment in the next section. There you will see that the extent of her suffering and its successful resolution point primarily to a psychological and social etiology.

TREATMENT

Although there are few systematic controlled studies evaluating the effectiveness of treatment for conversion disorders, we often treat these conditions in our clinics and elsewhere, and our methods closely follow our thinking on etiology. Since conversion disorder has much in common with somatization disorder, many of the treatment principles are similar.

A principal strategy is to identify and attend to the traumatic or stressful life event, if it is still present (either in real life or in memory), and remove, if possible, sources of "secondary gain." As in the case of Anna O., therapeutic assistance in reexperiencing or "reliving" the event (catharsis) is a reasonable first step.

The therapist must also work very hard to reduce any reinforcing or supportive consequences of the conversion symptoms (secondary gain). For example, it was quite clear that Eloise's mother found it convenient if Eloise stayed pretty much in one place most of the day while her mother attended to the store in the front of the house. Eloise's immobility was thus strongly reinforced by motherly attention and concern. Any unnecessary mobility was punished. The therapist must collaborate with both the patient and the family to eliminate such self-defeating behaviors.

The seizures and trances that may be symptomatic of conversion disorder are also common in some rural fundamentalist religious groups in the United States.

Many times, removing the secondary gain is easier said than done. Eloise was successfully treated in the clinic. Through intensive daily work with the staff she was able to walk again. To accomplish this she had to practice walking every day with considerable support, attention, and praise from the staff. When her mother visited, the staff noticed that she verbalized her pleasure with Eloise's progress, but her facial expressions or "affect" conveyed a different message. The mother lived a good distance from the clinic, so she could not attend sessions, but she promised to carry out the program at home after Eloise was discharged. She didn't, however. A follow-up contact 6 months after Eloise was discharged revealed that she had totally relapsed and was once again spending almost all her time in a room in the back of the house while her mother attended to business out front.

Pain Disorder

A related somatoform disorder about which little is known is **pain disorder.** In pain disorder there may have been clear physical reasons for pain, at least initially, but psychological factors play a major role in maintaining it. In the placement of this disorder in DSM-IV, serious consideration was given to removing it entirely from the somatoform disorders and putting it in a separate section, because a person rarely presents with localized pain without some physical basis, such as an accident or illness. Therefore, it was very difficult to separate the cases where the causes were judged to be primarily psychological from the ones where the causes are primarily physical. Because pain disorder fits most closely within the somatoform cluster (an individual presents with physical symptoms judged to have strong psychological contributions), the decision was made to leave pain disorder in the somatoform section. However, the three subtypes of pain disorder run the gamut from pain judged to be due *primarily to psychological factors* to pain judged to be due *primarily to a general medical condition.*

An important feature of pain disorder is that the pain is real and it hurts, regardless of the causes (King & Strain, 1991). Consider the following two cases.

The Medical Student
Temporary Pain

During her first clinical rotation, a 25-year-old, third-year medical student in excellent health was seen at her student health service for intermittent abdominal pain of several weeks' duration. The student claimed no past history of similar pain. Physical examination revealed no physical problems, but she told the physician that she had recently separated from her husband. The student was referred to the health service psychiatrist. No other psychiatric problems were found. She was taught relaxation techniques and given supportive therapy to help her cope with her current stressful situation. The student's pain subsequently disappeared, and she successfully completed medical school.

The Woman with Cancer
Managing Pain

A 56-year-old woman with metastatic breast cancer who appeared to be coping appropriately with her disease had severe pain in her right thigh for a month. She initially obtained relief from a combination of drugs, and subsequently received hypnotherapy and group therapy. These treatment modalities provided additional pain relief and enabled the patient to decrease her narcotic intake with no increase in pain.

The medical student's pain was seen as purely psychological. In the case of the second woman, the pain was probably related to cancer. But we now know that whatever its cause, pain has a strong psychological component. If medical treatments for existing physical conditions are in place and pain remains, or if the pain seems clearly related to psychological factors, psychological interventions are appropriate. Because of the complexity of pain itself and the variety of narcotics and other medications prescribed for it, multidisciplinary pain clinics are part of most large hospitals. (In Chapter 9, we discuss health psychology and the contribution of psychological factors to physical disorders, and delve more deeply into types of pain disorders, their causes, and treatment.)

Body Dysmorphic Disorder

Did you ever wish you could change part of your appearance? Maybe your weight or the size of your nose or the way your ears stick out? Most people fantasize about improving something, but some relatively normal-looking people imagine they are so ugly they are unable to interact with others or otherwise function normally for fear that people will laugh at their ugliness. This curious affliction is called **body dysmorphic disorder (BDD),** and at its center is a preoccupation with some imagined defect in appearance by someone who actually looks reasonably normal. The disorder has been referred to as "imagined ugliness" (Phillips, 1991). Consider the following case.

Jim
Ashamed to Be Seen

In his mid-twenties, Jim was diagnosed with suspected social phobia; he was referred to our clinic by another professional. Jim had just finished rabbinical school and had been offered a position at a synagogue in a nearby city. However, he found himself unable to accept because of marked social difficulties. Lately he had given up leaving his small apartment for fear of running into people he knew and being forced to stop and interact with them.

Jim was a good-looking young man of about average height, with dark hair and eyes. Although he was somewhat depressed, a mental status exam and a brief interview focusing on current functioning and past history did not reveal any remarkable problems. There was no sign of a psychotic process (he was not out of touch with reality). We then focused on Jim's social difficulties. We expected the usual kinds of anxiety about interacting with people or "doing something" (performing) in front of them. But this was not Jim's concern. Rather, he was convinced that everyone, even his good friends, were staring at a part of his body that he himself found absolutely grotesque. He reported that strangers would never mention his deformity and that his friends felt too badly for him to mention it. Jim thought his head was square! Like the Beast in *Beauty and the Beast* who could not imagine people reacting to him with anything less than abhorrence, Jim could not imagine people getting past the fact that his head was square. To hide his condition as well as he could, Jim wore soft floppy hats and was most comfortable in winter, when he could all but completely cover his head with a large stocking cap. To us, Jim looked perfectly normal.

Clinical Description

To give you a better idea of the types of concerns people with body dysmorphic disorder present to health professionals, the locations of imagined defects in 30 patients are shown in Table 6.2.

Many people with this disorder become fixated on mirrors. They frequently check their presumed ugly feature to see if any change has taken place. Others avoid mirrors to an almost phobic extent. Quite understandably, suicidal ideation, suicide attempts, and suicide itself are frequent consequences of this disorder (Phillips, 1991). People with dysmorphic disorder have "ideas of reference," which means they think that everything that goes on in their world somehow is related to them—in this case, to their imagined defect. This disorder can cause considerable disruption in the patient's life. Many patients with severe cases become housebound for fear of showing themselves to other people.

If this disorder seems strange to you, you are not alone. For decades, this condition, previously known as *dysmorphophobia* (literally, fear of ugliness), was thought to represent a psychotic delusional state because the affected individuals were unable to realize, even for a fleeting moment, that their ideas were irrational. Whether this is true is still debated.

In the context of obsessive–compulsive disorder (see Chapter 5), a similar issue arose as to whether patients really *believe* in their obsessions or realize that they are irrational. A minority (10% or less) of people with OCD believe that their fears about contaminating others or need to prevent catastrophes with their rituals are perfectly realistic and reasonable. This brings up the very major issue of what is "delusional" and what isn't, which is even more important to body dysmorphic disorder.

For example, in the 30 cases examined by Phillips et al. (1993) and in 50 cases reported by Veale, Boocock, et al. (1996) about half the subjects were absolutely convinced that their imagined bodily defect was real and a reasonable source of concern. Is this delusional? Psychopathologists, including those on the DSM-IV Task Force, have wrestled long and hard with this issue, only to conclude that there are no clear answers and that more research is needed. For now, individuals with BDD whose beliefs are so firmly held that they could be called delusional receive a second diagnosis of delusional disorder: somatic type (see Chapter 14).

STATISTICS

The prevalence of body dysmorphic disorder is hard to estimate since by its very nature it tends to be kept secret. However, the best estimates are that it is far more common than we had previously thought and that without some sort of treatment it tends to run a lifelong course (Phillips, 1991; Veale, Boocock, et al., 1996). One of the patients with body dysmorphic disorder reported in Phillips et al. (1993) had suffered from her condition for 71 years, since the age of 9.

If you think a college friend seems to have at least a mild version of BDD, you're probably correct. A recent study suggested that as many as 70% of college students report at least some dissatisfaction with their bodies; 28% of these appear to meet all the criteria for the disorder (Fitts, Gibson, Redding, & Deiter, 1989). However, this study was done by questionnaire and may well have reflected the large percentage of students who are concerned simply with weight. In mental health clinics the disorder is also seen infrequently because most people with BDD seek out another type of health professional, the plastic surgeon (covered shortly).

BDD is not strongly associated with one sex or the other. According to published reports, slightly more females than males are affected in this country, but 62% of a large number of individuals with BDD in Japan were males. As you might suspect, very few people with this disorder get

table 6.2 Location of Imagined Defects in 30 Patients with Body Dysmorphic Disorder*

Location	N	%
Hair†	19	63
Nose	15	50
Skin‡	15	50
Eyes	8	27
Head/face§	6	20
Overall body build/bone structure	6	20
Lips	5	17
Chin	5	17
Stomach/waist	5	17
Teeth	4	13
Legs/knees	4	13
Breasts/pectoral muscles	3	10
Ugly face (general)	3	10
Ears	2	7
Cheeks	2	7
Buttocks	2	7
Penis	2	7
Arms/wrists	2	7
Neck	1	3
Forehead	1	3
Facial muscles	1	3
Shoulders	1	3
Hips	1	3

*Total is greater than 100% because most patients had "defects" in more than one location.
†Involved head hair in 15 cases, beard growth in two cases, and other body hair in three cases.
‡Involved acne in seven cases, facial lines in three cases, and other skin concerns in seven cases.
§Involved concerns with shape in five cases and size in one case.
Source: Phillips et al., 1993.

married. Age of onset ranges from early adolescence through the 20s, peaking at the age of 18 or 19 (Phillips et al., 1993; Veale, Boocock, et al., 1996). Individuals are somewhat reluctant to seek treatment. In many cases a relative will force the issue, demanding that the individual get help; this insistence may reflect the disruptiveness of the disorder for family members. Severity is also reflected in the high percentage (24%) of past suicide attempts among the 50 cases described by Veale, Boocock, et al. (1996).

Individuals with BDD react to what they think is a horrible or grotesque feature. Thus, the psychopathology lies in their reacting to a deformity that others cannot perceive. Of course, social and cultural determinants of beauty and body image define, in large part, what is "deformed." (Nowhere is this more evident than in the greatly varying cultural standards for body weight and shape, factors that play a major role in eating disorders, as we will see in Chapter 8.)

For example, in most cultures it is desirable for a woman's skin to be lighter and more perfectly smooth than a man's skin (Fallon, 1990; Liggett, 1974). Over the centuries freckles have not been popular, and in many cultures chemical solutions were used to remove them. Unfortu-

In various cultures a child's head or face is manipulated to produce desirable features, as in the addition of rings to lengthen the neck of this Burmese girl.

nately, whole layers of skin disappeared and the underlying flesh was severely damaged (Liggett, 1974).

Concerns with the width of the face, so common in BDD, can also be culturally determined. Until very recently, in some areas of France, Africa, Greenland, and Peru the head of a newborn infant was reshaped, either by hand or by very tight caps secured by strings. Sometimes the face was elongated; other times it was widened. Similarly, attempts were made to flatten the noses of newborn infants, usually by hand (Fallon, 1990; Liggett, 1974).

Other mutilations to enhance beauty are familiar to readers of the *National Geographic.* For example, in Uganda, it is common practice to insert a large disk or plate into the lower lip, stretching the skin to fit. In Australia and New Guinea, the two top front teeth are knocked out to celebrate adolescents' reaching adulthood. In some tribes, holes are drilled through the six front teeth and star-shaped plugs of brass inserted; these teeth are also filed to sharp points. In Burma, women wear brass neck rings from an early age to lengthen the neck. One woman's neck was nearly 16 inches long (D. Morris, 1985).

Finally, many are aware of the old practice in China of binding girls' feet, often preventing the foot from growing to more than one-third of its normal size. Women's bound feet forced them to walk in a way that was thought very seductive. As Brownmiller (1984) points out, the myth that an unnaturally small foot signifies extraordinary beauty and grace is still with us. Can you think of the fairy tale where a small foot becomes the identifying feature of the beautiful heroine?

What can we learn about body dysmorphic disorder from such practices of mutilation around the world? The behavior of individuals with BDD seems remarkably strange, because they go *against* current cultural practices that put less emphasis on altering facial features. In other words, people who simply conform to the expectations of their culture do not have a disorder (as noted in Chapter 1). Nevertheless, aesthetic plastic surgery, particularly for the nose and lips, is still widely accepted and, since it is most often undertaken by the wealthy carries an aura of elevated status. In this light, BDD may not be so strange. As with most psychopathology, its characteristic attitudes and behavior may simply be an exaggeration of normal culturally sanctioned behavior.

Causes and Treatment

We know very little about either the etiology or the treatment of body dysmorphic disorder. We have almost no information on whether it runs in families, and so we can't investigate a specific genetic contribution. Similarly, we do not have any meaningful information on biological or psychological predisposing factors or vulnerabilities. Of course, psychoanalytic speculations are numerous, but most center on the defensive mechanism of displacement—that is, an underlying unconscious conflict would be too anxiety-provoking to admit into consciousness, so the person displaces it onto a body part.

What little evidence we do have on etiology comes from a very weak source: the pattern of comorbidity of BDD with other disorders. BDD is a somatoform disorder because its central feature is a psychological preoccupation with somatic issues. For example, in hypochondriasis the focus is on physical sensations, and in BDD the focus is on physical appearance. We have already seen that many of the somatoform disorders tend to co-occur. Linda presented with somatization disorder but also had a history of conversion disorder. However, BDD does not tend to co-occur with the other somatoform disorders, nor does it occur in family members of patients with other somatoform disorders.

A disorder that does frequently co-occur with BDD and is also found among other family members is obsessive-compulsive disorder (Tynes, White, & Steketee, 1990). Is BDD a variant of OCD? There are certainly a lot of similarities. People with BDD complain of persistent, intrusive, and horrible thoughts about their appearance, and they engage in such compulsive behaviors as repeatedly looking in mirrors to check their physical features. BDD and OCD also have, approximately, the same age of onset and run the same course. Perhaps most significantly, there are two, and only two, treatments for BDD with any evidence of effectiveness. Drugs that block the reuptake of serotonin, such as clomipramine (Anafranil) and fluoxetine (Prozac), provide relief to at least some people (Hollender et al., 1994). Intriguingly, these are the same drugs that have the strongest effect in OCD. Similarly, exposure and response prevention, the type of cognitive behavior therapy that is effective with OCD, has also been successful with BDD (McKay et al.,

1997; Veale, Gourney, et al., 1996). If BDD does turn out to be a variant of obsessive-compulsive disorder, we will know a lot more about some of the biological and psychological factors that may lead to its development (Veale, Boocock, et al., 1996).

Another interesting lead on causes of BDD comes from cross-cultural explorations of similar disorders. You may remember the Japanese variant of social phobia, *taijin kyōfushō* (see in Chapter 5), in which individuals may believe they have horrendous bad breath or body odor and thus avoid social interactions. But people with *taijin kyōfushō* also have all the other characteristics of social phobia. In fact, patients who would be diagnosed with BDD in our culture might simply be considered to have severe social phobia in Japan and Korea. Possibly, then, anxiety is fundamentally related to BDD, a connection that would give us hints on the nature of the disorder.

Michael Jackson as a child and as an adult. Many people alter their features through surgery. However, people with body dysmorphic disorder are seldom satisfied with the results.

PLASTIC SURGERY

Since the concerns of people with BDD involve mostly the face or head, it is not surprising that the disorder is big business for the plastic surgery profession—but it's bad business. These patients do not benefit from surgery and may return for additional surgery or, on occasion, file malpractice lawsuits. Even worse, a recent study found that the preoccupation with imagined ugliness actually increased in people who had plastic surgery, dental work, or special skin treatments for their perceived problems (Phillips et al., 1993). It is very important that plastic surgeons screen out these patients; many do so by collaborating with medically trained psychologists (Pruzinsky, 1988). Some investigators estimate that as many as 2% of all patients who request plastic surgery may have BDD (Andreasen & Bardach, 1977), and recent direct surveys suggest a much higher percentage. The most common procedures are rhinoplasties (nose jobs), face-lifts, eyebrow elevations, and surgery to alter the jaw line. The problem is, surgery on people with BDD seldom produces the desired results. These individuals return for additional surgery on the same defect, or concentrate on some new defect. Hollander, Liebowitz, Winchel, Klumker, and Klein (1989) describe one patient who had four separate rhinoplasties, and then became concerned about his thinning hair and sloped shoulders. Andreasen and Bardach noted that some patients become "synthetic creations of artificial noses, breasts, ears, and hips." Phillips et al. (1993) report that, of 25 surgical or dental procedures, only 2 gave relief. In more than 20 cases, the severity of the disorder and accompanying distress actually *increased* after surgery.

> *I can point to a very early preoccupation with my body, not liking my nose, my wispy curls, my bushy eyebrows. . . .*

Dissociative Disorders

At the beginning of the chapter we said that when individuals feel detached from themselves or their surroundings, almost as if they are dreaming or living in slow motion, they are having dissociative experiences. Morton Prince, the founder of the *Journal of Abnormal Psychology*, noted over 90 years ago that many people experience something like dissociation occasionally (Prince, 1906–1907). It is most likely to happen after an extremely stressful event, such as an accident. It might also happen when you're very tired or under physical or mental pressure from, say, staying up all night cramming for an exam. Perhaps because you knew the cause, the dissociation may not have bothered you much (Dixon, 1963; Noyes, Hoenk, Kuperman, & Slymen, 1977). On the other hand, it may have been very, very frightening.

Recently, investigators at Stanford surveyed the reactions of journalists who witnessed one of the first executions in California in many decades (Freinkel, Koopman, & Spiegel, 1994). The prisoner, Robert Alton Harriss, had been found guilty of the particularly brutal murder of two 16-year-old boys. As is customary, a number of journalists were invited to witness the execution. Because there were a number of stays of execution, they ended up spending all night at the prison as Harriss was repeatedly led into and back out of the gas chamber before he was finally executed near daybreak. Several weeks later, the journalists filled out acute stress reaction questionnaires. Between 40% and 60% of the journalists experienced several dissociative symptoms. For example, during the execution things around them seemed unreal or dreamlike and they felt that time had stopped. They also felt estranged from other people and very distant from their own emotions; a number of them felt they were strangers to themselves.

These kinds of experiences can be divided into two types. During an episode of depersonalization, your perception alters so that you temporarily lose the sense of your own reality. During an episode of **derealization,** your sense of the reality of the external world is lost. Things may seem to change shape or size; people may seem dead or mechanical.

Symptoms of unreality are characteristic of the dissociative disorders because depersonalization is, in a sense, a psychological mechanism whereby one "dissociates" from reality. Depersonalization is often part of a serious set of conditions where reality, experience, and even one's identity seem to disintegrate. As we go about our day-to-day lives, we ordinarily have an excellent sense of who we are and a general knowledge of the identity of other people. We are also aware of events around us, of where we are, and of why we are there. Finally, except for occasional small lapses, our memories remain intact so that events leading up to the current moment are clear in our minds.

But what happens if we can't remember why we are in a certain place or even who we are? What happens if we lose our sense that our surroundings are real? Finally, what happens if we not only forget who we are but begin thinking that we are somebody else—somebody who has a different personality, different memories, and even different physical reactions, such as allergies that we never had? These are examples of disintegrated experience (Putnam, 1991; Spiegel & Cardena, 1991). In each case there are alterations in our relationship to the self, to the world, or to memory processes.

Although we have much to learn about these disorders, we will briefly describe four of them—depersonalization disorder, dissociative amnesia, dissociative fugue, and dissociative trance disorder—before examining the fascinating condition of dissociative identity disorder. As you will see, the influence of social and cultural factors is evident in dissociative disorders more than in some other classes of psychopathology. Dissociation is a basic emotional or behavioral pattern that is present to some degree across the human race and is perhaps "normal" in some contexts. But when it results in distress and impairment, it has become pathological. However, the expression of the pathology does not stray far from socially and culturally sanctioned forms.

Depersonalization Disorder

When feelings of unreality are so severe and frightening that they dominate an individual's life and prevent normal functioning, clinicians may diagnose the very rare **depersonalization disorder.** Consider the following case.

Bonnie
Dancing Away from Herself

Bonnie, a dance teacher in her late 20s, was accompanied by her husband when she first visited the clinic and complained of "flipping out." When asked what she meant, she said, "It's the most scary thing in the world. It often happens when I'm teaching my modern dance class. I'll be up in front and I will feel focused on. Then, as I'm demonstrating the steps, I just feel like it's not really me and that I don't really have control of my legs. Sometimes I feel like I'm standing in back of myself just watching. Also I get tunnel vision. It seems like I can only see in a narrow space right in front of me and I just get totally separated from what's going on around me. Then I begin to panic and perspire and shake." It turns out that Bonnie's problems began after she smoked marijuana for the first time about 10 years before. She had the same feeling then and found it very scary, but with the help of friends she got through it. Lately the feeling recurred more frequently and more severely, particularly when she was teaching dance class.

You may remember from Chapter 5 that during an intense panic attack many people (approximately 50%) experience feelings of unreality. People undergoing intense stress or experiencing a traumatic event may also experience these symptoms, which, in fact, characterize the newly defined *acute stress disorder.* Feelings of depersonalization and derealization are part of several different disorders (Boon & Draijer, 1991). But when severe depersonalization and derealization are the primary problem, the individual meets criteria for depersonalization disorder (Steinberg, 1991). Simeon et al. (1997) described 30 consecutive cases, 19 women and 11 men. Mean age of onset was 16.1 years and the course tended to be chronic, lasting on average of 15.7 years so far in those cases. All the patients were substantially impaired. Although none had any additional dissociative disorders, over 50% suffered from additional mood and anxiety disorders.

Dissociative Amnesia

Perhaps the easiest to understand of the severe dissociative disorders is one called **dissociative amnesia,** which includes several different patterns. People who are unable to remember anything, including who they are, are said to suffer from **generalized amnesia.** Generalized amnesia may be lifelong or may extend from a period in the more recent past, such as 6 months or a year previously.

The Woman Who Lost Her Memory

Several years ago a woman in her early 50s brought her daughter to one of our clinics because of the girl's refusal to attend school and other severely disruptive behavior. The father, who refused to come to the session, was very quarrelsome, a heavy drinker and, on occasion, abusive. The girl's brother, now in his mid-20s, lived at home and was a burden on the family. Several times a week a major battle erupted, complete with shouting, pushing, and shoving, as each member of the family blamed the others for all their problems. The mother, a very strong woman, was clearly the peacemaker responsible for holding the family together. Approximately every 6 months, usually after a family battle, the mother totally lost her memory and the family had her admitted to the hospital. After a few days away from the turmoil, the mother regained her memory and went home, only to repeat the cycle in the coming months. Although we did not treat this family (they lived too far away), the situation resolved itself when the children moved away and the stress decreased.

Far more common than general amnesia is **localized or selective amnesia,** a failure to recall specific events, usually traumatic, that occur during a specific period of time. In fact, dissociative amnesia is very common during war (Loewenstein, 1991; Spiegel & Cardena, 1991).

Sackeim and Devanand (1991) describe the interesting case of a woman whose father had deserted her when she was very young. She had also been forced to have an abortion at the age of 14. Years later, she came for treatment for frequent headaches. In therapy she reported early events (for example, the abortion) rather matter of factly; but under hypnosis she would relive, with intense emotion, the early abortion and remember the fact that subsequently she was raped by the abortionist. She also had images of her father attending a funeral for her aunt, one of the few times she ever saw him. Upon awakening from the hypnotic state she had no memory whatsoever of emotionally reexperiencing these events, and she wondered why she had been crying. In this case the woman did not have amnesia for the *events themselves* but rather for her intense *emotional reactions to the events.* In most cases of dissociative amnesia, the forgetting is very selective for traumatic events or memories rather than generalized.

Dissociative Fugue

A related disorder is referred to as **dissociative fugue,** with *fugue* literally meaning "flight" (*fugitive* is from the same root). In these curious cases, memory loss revolves around a specific incident—an unexpected trip (or trips). Mostly, individuals just take off, and later find themselves in a new place, unable to remember why or how they got there. Usually they have left behind an intolerable situation. During these trips a person sometimes assumes a new identity or at least becomes confused about the old identity. Consider the following case.

The Misbehaving Sheriff

Aktar and Brenner (1979) describe a 46-year-old sheriff who reported at least three episodes of dissociative fugue. On each occasion he found himself as far as 200 miles from his home. When he came to he immediately called his wife,

but he was never able to completely recall what he did while he was away, sometimes for several days. During treatment the sheriff remembered who he was during these trips. Despite his occupation, he became the outlaw type he had always secretly admired. He adopted an alias, drank heavily, mingled with a rough crowd, and went to brothels and wild parties.

Dissociative amnesia and fugue states usually do not appear before adolescence and usually occur in adulthood. It is rare for these states to appear for the first time after an individual reaches the age of 50 (Sackeim & Devanand, 1991). However, once they do appear, they may continue well into old age.

Fugue states usually end rather abruptly, like those of the misbehaving sheriff, and the individual returns home recalling most, if not all, of what happened. In this disorder, the disintegrated experience is more than memory loss, involving at least some disintegration of identity, if not the complete adoption of a new one.

An apparently distinct dissociative disorder not found in Western cultures is called *amok* (as in "running amok"). Most people with this disorder are males. Amok has attracted attention because individuals in this trancelike state often brutally assault and sometimes kill persons or animals. If the person is not killed himself, he probably will not remember the episode. Running amok is only one of a number of syndromes in which an individual enters a trancelike

Robert Clark awoke in a hospital in Yuma, Arizona, with no memory of how he got there. He had apparently arrived by bus from St. Petersburg, Florida. He carried only a little money and pictures that could be of his grandchildren. Despite his memory loss, Clark's cognitive functions were intact, and he had no organic impairment.

state and suddenly, imbued with a mysterious source of energy, runs or flees for a long time. Except for amok, the prevalence of running disorders is somewhat greater in women, as with most dissociative disorders. Among native peoples of the Arctic, running disorder is termed *pivloktoq*. Among the Navajo tribe it is called *frenzy witchcraft*. Despite their different culturally determined expression, running disorders seem to meet criteria for dissociative fugue, with the possible exception of amok.

■ concept check 6.1

Diagnose the disorders described below: (a) depersonalization disorder; (b) conversion disorder; (c) body dysmorphic disorder; (d) dissociative fugue.

1. Loretta is 32 and has been preoccupied with the size and shape of her nose for 2 years. She has been saving money for plastic surgery, after which, she is sure, her career will improve. Trouble is, three (honest) plastic surgeons have told her that her nose is fine as it is. _____

2. Henry is 64 and recently arrived in town. He does not know where he is from or how he got here. His driver's license proves his name, but he is unconvinced that it is his. He is in good health and is not taking any medication.
_____

3. Dan has been tested by several doctors, none of whom can find an organic reason for his blindness. Specially designed tests show that he is not faking his problem. Dan's blindness occurred suddenly, after his wife of 10 years died.
_____

Dissociative Trance Disorder

Dissociative disorders differ in very important ways across cultures. In many areas of the world, dissociative phenomena may occur as a trance or possession. The usual sorts of dissociative symptoms, such as sudden changes in personality, are attributed to possession by a spirit important in the particular culture. Often this spirit demands and receives presents or favors from the family and friends of the victim. Like other dissociative states, trance disorder seems to be most common in women and is often associated with stress or trauma, which, as in dissociative amnesia and fugue states, is current rather than in the past.

Of course, trance and possession are a common part of some traditional religious and cultural practices and is not considered abnormal in that context. Dissociative trances commonly occur in India, Nigeria (where they are called *vinvuza*), Thailand (*phii pob*), and other Asian and African countries (Mezzich et al., 1992; Saxena & Prasad, 1989). In the United States, culturally accepted dissociation commonly occurs during African-American prayer meetings (Griffith et al., 1980), Native American rituals (Jilek, 1982),

and Puerto Rican spiritist sessions (Comas-Diaz, 1981). Among Bahamians and Southern blacks, trance syndromes are often referred to colloquially as "falling out."

Only when the state is *undesirable* and considered pathological by members of the culture is it defined as a **dissociative trance disorder (DTD).** Although trance and possession are almost never seen in Western cultures, they are among the most common forms of dissociative disorders elsewhere. A category to include these states has been proposed for a future edition of DSM.

Dissociative Identity Disorder

CLINICAL DESCRIPTION

People with **dissociative identity disorder (DID)** may adopt as many as 100 new identities, all simultaneously coexisting inside one body and mind. In some cases, the identities are complete, each with its own behavior, tone of voice, and physical gestures. In other cases, only a few characteristics are distinct, because the identities are only partially independent. Consider the following case, originally reported by Ludwig, Brandsma, Wilbur, Bendfeldt, and Jameson (1972).

Jonah
Bewildering Blackouts

Jonah, 27 years old and black, suffered from severe headaches that were unbearably painful and lasted for longer and longer periods of time. Furthermore, he couldn't remember things that happened while he had a headache, except that sometimes a great deal of time passed. Finally, after a particularly bad night, when he could stand it no longer, he arranged for admission to the local hospital. What really prompted Jonah to come to the hospital, however, was that other people told him what he did during his severe headaches. For example, he was told that the night before he had a violent fight with another man and attempted to stab him. He fled the scene and was shot at during a high-speed chase by the police. His wife told him that during a previous headache he chased her and his 3-year-old daughter out of the house, threatening them with a butcher knife. During his headaches, and while he was violent, he called himself "Usoffa Abdulla, son of Omega." Once he attempted to drown a man in a river. The man survived and Jonah escaped by swimming a quarter of a mile upstream. He woke up the next morning in his own bed, soaking wet, with no memory of the incident.

During Jonah's hospitalization, the staff was able to observe his behavior directly, both when he had headaches and during other periods that he did not remember. He claimed other names at these times, acted differently, and generally seemed to be another person entirely. The staff distinguished three separate identities, or **alters,** in addition to Jonah. (*Alters* is the shorthand term for the different identities or personalities in DID.) The first alter was named Sammy. Sammy seemed rational, calm, and in control. The second alter, King Young, seemed to be in charge of all sexual activity and was particularly interested in having as many heterosexual interactions as possible. The third alter was the violent and dangerous Usoffa Abdulla.

Characteristically, Jonah knew nothing of the three alters. Sammy was most aware of the other personalities. King Young and Usoffa Abdulla knew a little bit about the others but only indirectly.

In the hospital, psychologists determined that Sammy first appeared when Jonah was about 6, immediately after Jonah saw his mother stab his father. Jonah's mother sometimes dressed him as a girl in private. On one of these occasions, shortly after Sammy emerged, King Young appeared. When Jonah was 9 or 10 he was brutally attacked by a group of white youths. At this point Usoffa Abdulla emerged, announcing that his sole reason for existence was to protect Jonah.

DSM-IV criteria for dissociative identity disorder include amnesia, as in dissociative amnesia and dissociative fugue. Here, however, identity has also fragmented. How many personalities live inside one body is relatively unimportant, whether there are 3, 4, or even 100 of them. Rather, the defining feature of this disorder is that certain aspects of the person's identity are dissociated. For this reason, the name was changed in DSM-IV from multiple personality disorder to dissociative identity disorder. This change also corrects the notion that multiple people somehow live inside one body.

CHARACTERISTICS

The person who becomes the patient and asks for treatment is usually a "host" identity. Host personalities usually attempt to hold various fragments of identity together but end up being overwhelmed. The first personality to seek treatment is seldom the original personality of the person. Usually the host personality develops later (Putnam, 1992). Many patients have at least one impulsive alter who handles sexuality and generates income, sometimes by acting as a prostitute. In other cases all alters may abstain from sex. Cross-gendered alters are not uncommon. For example, a small fragile woman might have a strong powerful male alter who serves as a protector.

The transition from one personality to another is called a *switch.* Usually the switch is instantaneous (although in movies and television it is often drawn out for dramatic effect). Physical transformations may occur during switches. Posture, facial expressions, patterns of facial wrinkling, and even physical disabilities may emerge. In one study, changes in handedness occurred in 37% of the cases (Putnam, Guroff, Silberman, Barban, & Post, 1986).

■ concept check **6.2**

Check your understanding of the criteria for dissociative disorders and the different ways in which they may be presented. In each situation below, write N if it does not fit the criteria for dissociative disorder. If it is a dissociative disorder, specify which type: (a) depersonalization disorder; (b) dissociative trance disorder; (c) generalized amnesia; (d) dissociative identity disorder.

1. Ann was found wandering the streets, unable to recall any important personal information. After searching her purse and finding an address, doctors were able to contact her mother. They then found out that Ann had just been in a terrible accident and was the only survivor. Ann could not remember her mother or any details of the accident. She was very distressed. _____

2. Judith, who has metastatic breast cancer, complained of a pain in her head. She seemed to be coping appropriately with her disease. No cause for the pain in her head could be determined. _____

3. Karl was brought to a clinic by his mother. She was concerned because at times his behavior was very strange. His speech and his way of relating to people and situations would change dramatically, almost as if he were a different person. What bothered her and Karl the most was that he could not recall anything he did during these periods of time. _____

4. Terry complained about feeling out of control. She said that she felt sometimes as if she were floating under the ceiling and just watching things happen to her. She also experienced tunnel vision and felt uninvolved in the things that went on in the room around her. This always caused her to panic and perspire. _____

CAN DID BE FAKED?

Are the fragmented identities "real" or is the person faking them to avoid responsibility or stress? As with conversion disorders, it is very difficult to answer this question, for several reasons. First, evidence indicates that individuals with DID are very suggestible (Bliss, 1984). It is possible that alters are created in response to leading questions from therapists, either during psychotherapy or while the person is in a hypnotic state.

The Hillside Strangler

During the late 1970s, Kenneth Bianchi brutally raped and murdered ten young women in the Los Angeles area and left their bodies naked and in full view on the sides of various hills. Despite overwhelming evidence that Bianchi was the "Hillside Strangler," he continued to assert his innocence, prompting some professionals to think he might have DID. His lawyer brought in a clinical psychologist, who hypnotized him and asked whether there were another part of Ken with whom he could speak. Guess what? Somebody called "Steve" answered, and said he had done all the killing. Steve also said that Ken knew nothing about the murders. With this evidence, the lawyer entered a plea of not guilty by reason of insanity.

The defense called on Martin Orne, a distinguished clinical psychologist and psychiatrist who is one of the world's leading experts on hypnosis and dissociative disorders (Orne, Dinges, & Orne, 1984). Orne used procedures similar to those we described in the context of conversion blindness to determine whether Bianchi was simulating DID or had a true psychological disorder. For example, Orne suggested during an in-depth interview with Bianchi that a true multiple personality disorder included at least three personalities. Bianchi soon produced a third personality. By interviewing Bianchi's friends and relatives, Orne established that there was no independent corroboration of different personalities before Bianchi's arrest. Psychological tests also failed to show significant differences among the personalities; true fragmented identities often score very differently on personality tests. Sev-

Martin Orne is a leading expert worldwide on hypnosis and dissociative disorders.

eral textbooks on psychopathology were found in Bianchi's room; therefore, he presumably had studied the subject. Orne concluded that Bianchi responded like someone simulating hypnosis, not someone deeply hypnotized. On the basis of Orne's testimony, Bianchi was found guilty and sentenced to life in prison.

Some investigators have studied the ability of individuals to fake dissociative experiences. Spanos, Weeks, and Bertrand (1985) demonstrated in an experiment that a college student could simulate an alter if it was suggested that faking was plausible, as in the interview with Bianchi. All the students in the group were told to play the role of an accused murderer claiming his innocence. The subjects received exactly the same interview as Bianchi, word for word. Over 80% simulated an alternate personality in order to avoid conviction. Groups that were given vaguer instructions, and no direct suggestion that an alternate personality might exist, were much less likely to use one in their defense.

In an important experiment along the same lines, Spanos, James, and de Groot (1990) compared subjects with hypnotically induced amnesia (similar to the type in dissociative disorders) with subjects who were instructed to *simulate* amnesia. All the subjects were asked to memorize a list of words. They were then given a list that included the memo-

rized words and many new ones. Subjects under hypnosis exhibited above-chance levels of recognition of the original words. Simulators, on the other hand, had below-chance recognition for the same words. Below-chance levels of recognition, of course, are more consistent with faked amnesia.

These findings on faking and the effect of hypnosis led Spanos (1994) to suggest that the symptoms of DID could be solely accounted for by therapists who inadvertently suggested the existence of alters, a model known as the "sociocognitive model" because the possibility of identity fragments and early trauma is socially reinforced by a therapist. (We will return to this point of view when we discuss false memories.)

Objective tests suggest that many people with fragmented identities are not consciously and voluntarily simulating (Kluft, 1991). Condon, Ogston, and Pacoe (1969) examined a film about Chris Sizemore, the real-life subject of the book and movie *The Three Faces of Eve.* They determined that one of the personalities (Eve Black) showed a *transient micro-strabismus* (divergence in conjugant lateral eye movements) that was not observed in the other personalities. These optical differences have been confirmed by S. D. Miller (1989), who demonstrated that DID subjects had 4.5 times the average number of changes in optical functioning in their alter identities than control subjects who simulated alter personalities. Miller concludes that optical changes, including measures of visual acuity, manifest refraction, and eye muscle balance, would be difficult to fake. Ludwig et al. (1972) found that Jonah's various identities had different physiological responses to emotionally laden words, including galvanic skin response (GSR), a measure of

Chris Sizemore's history of multiple personality disorder was dramatized in *The Three Faces of Eve.*

otherwise imperceptible sweat gland activity, and electroencephalogram (EEG) brain waves. A number of subsequent studies confirm that various alters have unique psychophysiological profiles (Putnam, 1995).

Anna O.
Revealed

We return one more time to the very famous case that prompted early insights into the unconscious and contributed to the development of psychoanalysis. Earlier we described Anna O.'s conversion symptoms of paralysis in her right arm, anesthesia of her right side, and the loss of the ability to speak her native German (although she retained perfect command of English). As Anna confronted her traumatic memories of watching her father die while she nursed him, she increasingly recovered her physical abilities.

Anna O.'s real name was Bertha Pappenheim and she was an extraordinary woman. What many people don't realize is that she was never completely cured by Breuer, who finally gave up on her in 1882. During the next decade she was institutionalized several times with severe recurrences of her conversion symptoms before beginning a slow recovery. She went on to become a pioneering social worker and staunch crusader against the sexual abuse of women (Putnam, 1992). She devoted her life to freeing women who were trapped in prostitution and white slavery throughout Europe, Russia, and the Near East. Risking her own life, she entered brothels to liberate women from their captors. She wrote a play, *Women's Rights*, about sadistic men and the ongoing abuse of women. She founded a league of Jewish women in 1904 and a home for unwed mothers in 1907. In recognition of her extraordinary contributions as one of the first militant feminists, a commemorative stamp was later issued in her honor by the West German government (Sulloway, 1979).

Pappenheim's friends remarked that she seemed to lead a "double life." On the one hand, she was a radical feminist and reformer. On the other hand, she belonged to the cultural elite in *fin de siècle* Vienna. It is clear from Breuer's notes that there were "two Anna O.'s" and that she suffered from dissociative identity disorder (DID). One personality was somewhat depressed and anxious but otherwise relatively normal. But in an instant she would turn dark and foreboding. Breuer was convinced that during these times "Anna" was someone else, someone who hallucinated and was verbally abusive. And it was the second Anna O. who experienced conversion symptoms. The second Anna O. spoke only English or garbled mixtures of four or five languages. The first Anna O. spoke fluent French and Italian as well as her native German. Characteristically, one personality had no memory of what happened when the other was "out." Almost anything might cause an instant switch in personalities—for example, the sight of an orange, which was Anna O.'s primary source of nourishment when she nursed her dying father. Putnam (1992) reports that when Bertha Pappenheim died of cancer in 1936, "It is said that she left two wills, each written in a different hand" (p. 36).

STATISTICS

Jonah had 4 identities, and Anna O. only 2, but the average number of alter personalities is reported by clinicians as closer to 15 (Ross, 1997; Sackeim & Devanand, 1991). Of people with DID, the ratio of females to males is as high as 9 to 1, although these data are based on accumulated case studies rather than survey research. The onset is almost always in childhood, often as young as 4 years of age, although it is usually approximately 7 years before the disorder is identified (Putnam et al., 1986). Once established, the disorder tends to last a lifetime in the absence of treatment. The form it takes does not seem to vary substantially over the person's life span, although there is some evidence that the frequency of switching decreases with age (Sakheim & Devanand, 1991). Different personalities may emerge in response to new life situations, as was the case with Jonah.

We don't have good epidemiological studies on the prevalence of the disorder in the population at large, although investigators now think it is more common than previously estimated (Kluft, 1991; Ross, 1997). For example, semi-structured interviews of large numbers of severely disturbed inpatients found prevalence rates of DID of between 3% and 6% (Ross, 1997; Ross et al., 1991; Saxe et al., 1993). Additional studies in nonclinical samples, using either the population of a large city (Ross, 1991, 1997) or a university (von Braunsberg, 1994), suggest that between 0.5% and 1% of these large samples (over 400 in each) suffer from DID.

A very large percentage of DID patients have simultaneous psychological disorders that may include substance abuse, depression, somatization disorder, borderline personality disorder, panic attacks, and eating disorders (Ross et al., 1990). In one sample of over 100 patients, more than seven additional diagnoses were noted on the average (Ellason & Ross, 1997). It seems likely that different personalities will present with differing patterns of comorbidity, but the research has not yet been done. In some cases this high rate of comorbidity may reflect the fact that certain disorders, such as borderline personality disorder, share many features with DID—for example, self-destructive, sometimes suicidal behavior and emotional instability. For the most part, however, the high frequency of additional disorders accompanying DID simply reflects an intensely severe reaction to what seems to be in almost all cases horrible child abuse. Because auditory hallucinations are very common, DID is often misdiagnosed as a psychotic disorder. But the voices in DID are reported by patients as coming from inside their heads, not outside as in psychotic disorders. Since patients with DID are usually aware that the voices are hallucinations, they don't report them and try to suppress them. Since these voices often encourage doing something against one's will, some individuals, particularly in other cultures, appear to be possessed by demons (Putnam, 1995). Although systematic studies are lacking, DID seems to occur in a variety of cultures throughout the world (Boon & Draijer, 1993; Coons, Bowman, Kluft, & Milstein, 1991; Ross, 1997). For example, Coons et al. (1994) found reports of DID in 21 different countries.

CAUSES

It is informative to examine current evidence on causes for all dissociative disorders, as we do below, but our emphasis is on the etiology of DID. Life circumstances that encourage the development of DID seem quite clear in at least one respect. Almost every patient presenting with this disorder reports that he or she was horribly, often unspeakably, abused as a child.

Sybil

You may have seen the movie that was based on Sybil's biography (Schreiber, 1973). Sybil's mother had schizophrenia and her father refused or was unable to intervene in the mother's brutality. Day after day throughout her childhood, Sybil was sexually tortured and occasionally nearly murdered. Before she was a year old her mother began tying her up in various ways and, on occasion, suspending her from the ceiling. Many mornings her mother placed Sybil on the kitchen table and forcefully inserted various objects into her vagina. Sybil's mother reasoned, psychotically, that she was preparing her daughter for adult sex. In fact, she so brutally tore the child's vaginal canal that scars were evident during adult gynecological exams. Sybil was also given very strong laxatives but prohibited from using the bathroom. Because of her father's detachment and the normal appearance of the family, the abuse continued without interruption throughout Sybil's childhood.

Imagine you are a child in a situation like this. What can you do? You're too young to run away. You're too young to call the authorities. Although the pain may be unbearable, you have no way of knowing that it is unusual or wrong. But you can do one thing! You can escape into a fantasy world; you can be somebody else. If the escape blunts the physical and emotional pain just for a minute or makes the next hour bearable, chances are you'll escape again. Your mind learns that there is no limit to the identities that can be created as needed. Fifteen? Twenty-five? A hundred? Such numbers have been recorded in some cases. You do whatever it takes to get through life.

Most surveys report a very high rate of childhood trauma in cases of DID (Gleaves, 1996; Ross, 1997). Putnam et al. (1986) examined 100 cases and found that 97% of the patients had experienced significant trauma, usually sexual or physical abuse. Sixty-eight percent reported incest. Ross et al. (1990) reported that, of 97 cases, 95% reported physical or sexual abuse. Unfortunately, the abuse seems often as bizarre and sadistic as what Sybil suffered. Some children were buried alive. Some were tortured with matches, steam irons, razor blades, or glass. Now investigators have corroborated the existence of early sexual abuse in 12 patients with DID, by examining early records, interviewing relatives and acquaintances, and so on (Lewis, Yeager, Swica, Pincus, & Lewis, 1997).

Not all of the trauma is caused by abuse. Putnam (1992) describes a young girl in a war zone who saw both her parents blown to bits in a mine field. In a heart-wrenching response, she tried to piece the bodies back together, bit by bit.

Such observations have led to wide-ranging agreement that DID is rooted in a natural tendency to escape or "dissociate" from the unremitting negative affect associated with severe abuse (Kluft, 1984, 1991). A lack of social support during or after the abuse also seems implicated. A recent study of 428 adolescent twins demonstrated that a surprisingly high 33% to 50% of the variance in dissociative experience could be attributed to a chaotic, nonsupportive family environment. The remainder of the variance was associated with individual experience and personality factors (Waller & Ross, 1997).

The behavior and emotions that make up disorders seem related to otherwise normal tendencies present in all of us to some extent. It is quite common for otherwise normal individuals to escape in some way from emotional or physical pain (Butler, Duran, Jasiukaitis, Koopman, & Spiegel, 1996; Spiegel & Cardena, 1991). Noyes and Kletti (1977) surveyed over 100 survivors of various life-threatening situations and found that most had experienced some type of dissociation, such as feelings of unreality, a blunting of emotional and physical pain, and even separation from their bodies. Dissociative amnesia and fugue states are clearly reactions to severe life stress. But the life stress or trauma is in the present rather than the past, as in the case of the overwrought mother who suffered from dissociative amnesia. Many patients are escaping from legal difficulties or severe stress at home or on the job (Sackeim & Devanand, 1991). But sophisticated statistical analyses indicate that "normal" dissociative reactions differ substantially from the pathological experiences we've described (Waller, Putnam, & Carlson, 1996; Waller & Ross, 1997), and that at least some people do not develop severe pathological dissociative experiences no matter how extreme the stress. These findings are consistent with our diathesis-stress model, in that only with the appropriate vulnerabilities (the diathesis) will one react to stress with pathological dissociation.

You may have noticed that DID seems very similar in its etiology to posttraumatic stress disorder (PTSD). Both conditions feature strong emotional reactions to experiencing a severe trauma (Butler et al., 1996). But remember that not everyone goes on to experience posttraumatic stress disorder after severe trauma. Only people who are biologically and psychologically vulnerable to anxiety are at risk for developing PTSD in response to moderate levels of trauma. However, as the severity of the trauma increases, a greater percentage of people develop PTSD as a consequence. But some people do not become victims of the disorder even after the most severe traumas, suggesting that individual psychological and biological factors interact with the trauma to produce PTSD.

There is a growing body of opinion that DID is a very extreme subtype of PTSD, with a much greater emphasis on the process of dissociation than on symptoms of anxiety, although both are present in each disorder (Butler et al., 1996). There is also some evidence that the "developmental window" of vulnerability to the abuse that leads to DID closes at approximately 9 years of age (Putnam, 1995). After that, DID is unlikely to develop, although severe PTSD might. This is a particularly good example of the role of development in the etiology of psychopathology.

We also must remember that we know relatively little about DID. Our conclusions are based on retrospective case studies or correlations rather than on the prospective examination of people who may have undergone the severe trauma that seems to lead to DID (Kihlstrom, Glisky, & Anguilo, 1994). Therefore, it is hard to say what psychological or biological factors might contribute, but there are hints concerning individual differences that might play a role.

Suggestibility

Suggestibility is a personality trait that is distributed normally across the population, much like weight and height. Some people are much more suggestible than others; some are relatively immune to suggestibility; and the majority fall in the midrange.

Did you ever have an imaginary childhood playmate? Many people did, and it is one sign of the ability to lead a rich fantasy life, which can be very helpful and adaptive. But it also seems to correlate with being suggestible or easily hypnotized (some people equate the terms *suggestibility* and *hypnotizability*). A hypnotic trance is also very similar to dissociation (Bliss, 1986; Butler et al., 1996; Carlson & Putnam, 1989). People in a trance tend to be totally focused on one aspect of their world, and they become very vulnerable to suggestions by the hypnotist. There is also the phenomenon of self-hypnosis, in which individuals can dissociate from most of the world around them and "suggest" to themselves that, for example, they won't feel pain in one of their hands.

According to the *autohypnotic model,* people who are suggestible may be able to use dissociation as a defense against extreme trauma (Putnam, 1991). As many as 50% of DID patients clearly remember imaginary playmates in childhood (Ross et al., 1990); whether they were created before or after the trauma is not entirely clear. When the trauma becomes unbearable, the person's very identity splits into multiple dissociated identities. Children's ability to distinguish clearly between reality and fantasy as they grow older may be what closes the developmental window for developing DID at approximately age 9. People who are less suggestible may develop a severe posttraumatic stress reaction but not a dissociative reaction. Once again, these explanations are all very speculative because there are no controlled studies of this phenomenon (Kihlstrom et al., 1994).

BIOLOGICAL CONTRIBUTIONS

As in posttraumatic stress disorder, where the evidence is more solid, there is almost certainly a biological vulnerability to DID, but it is difficult to pinpoint. For example, in the large twin study mentioned above (Waller & Ross, 1997) none of the variance, or identifiable causal factors was at-

A person in a hypnotic trance is very suggestible and may become very absorbed in a particular experience.

tributable to heredity: All of it was environmental. Of course, as with anxiety disorders, more basic heritable traits, such as tension, may increase vulnerability.

Interesting observations may provide some hints about brain activity during dissociation. Individuals with certain neurological disorders, particularly seizure disorders, experience many dissociative symptoms (Cardena, Lewis-Fernandez, Bear, Pakianathan, & Spiegel, 1996). Devinsky, Feldman, Burrowes, and Bromfield (1989) reported that approximately 6% of patients with temporal lobe epilepsy reported "out of body" experiences. About 50% of another series of patients with temporal lobe epilepsy displayed some kinds of dissociative symptoms (Schenk & Bear, 1981), including alternate identities or identity fragments.

Patients with dissociative experiences who have seizure disorders are clearly different from those who do not (Ross et al., 1997). The seizure patients develop dissociative symptoms in adulthood that are not associated with trauma, in clear contrast to DID patients without seizure disorders. This is certainly an area for future study (Putnam, 1991).

Head injury and resulting brain damage may induce amnesia or other types of dissociative experience. But these conditions are usually easily diagnosed since they are generalized and irreversible, and are associated with an identifiable head trauma (Butler et al., 1996).

REAL MEMORIES AND FALSE

One of the most controversial issues in the field of abnormal psychology today concerns the extent to which memories of early trauma, particularly sexual abuse, are really accurate or not. Some suggest that many such memories are simply the result of strong suggestions by careless therapists. The stakes in this controversy are enormous, with considerable opportunity for harm to innocent people on each side of the controversy.

On the one hand, if early sexual abuse did occur, but is not remembered because of dissociative amnesia, it is crucially important to reexperience aspects of the trauma under the direction of a skilled therapist in order to relieve current suffering. Without therapy the patient is likely to suffer from posttraumatic stress disorder or a dissociative disorder indefinitely. It is also important that perpetrators are held accountable for their actions, perhaps through the legal system, since abuse of this type is a crime, and prevention is an important goal.

On the other hand, if memories of early trauma are inadvertently created in response to a careless therapist, but seem real to the patient, false accusations against loved ones could lead to irreversible family breakup and, perhaps, unjust prison sentences for the falsely accused perpetrators. In recent years, allegedly inaccurate accusations as a result of false memories have led to substantial lawsuits against therapists resulting in awards of millions of dollars in damages. As with most issues that reach this level of contention and disagreement, it is clear that the final answer will not involve an all-or-none resolution. For there is incontrovertible evidence that false memories *can* be created by reasonably well understood psychological processes (Schacter, 1995; 1997). But, there is also incontrovertible evidence that early traumatic experiences can cause selective dissociative amnesia, with substantial implications for psychological functioning (Gleaves, 1996; Spiegel, 1995).

Victims of accusations deriving from allegedly false memories have formed a society called the False Memory Syndrome Foundation. One goal is to educate the legal profession and the public at large about false memories after psychotherapy, so that, in the absence of other objective evidence, such "memories" can not be used to convict innocent people.

Evidence supporting the existence of distorted or illusory memories comes from experiments like one by the distinguished cognitive psychologist Elizabeth Loftus and her colleagues. Loftus, Coan, and Pickrell (1996) successfully convinced a number of individuals that they had been lost for an extended period of time when they were approximately 5 years old, which was not true. A trusted companion was recruited to "plant" the memory. In one case, a 14-year-old boy was told by his older brother that he had been lost in a nearby shopping mall when he was 5 years old, rescued by an older man, and ultimately reunited with his mother and brother. Several days after receiving this suggestion, the boy reported remembering the event and even that he felt very frightened when he was lost. As time went by, the boy remembered more and more details of the event, beyond those described in the "plant," including an exact description of the older man. When he was finally told that the incident never happened, the boy was very surprised, and he continued to describe details of the event as if they were true.

Another study illustrates the same point in a somewhat different way (Bruck, Ceci, Francouer, & Renick, 1995). Thirty-five 3-year-old girls were given a genital exam as part of their routine medical checkup; another 35 girls were not. Shortly after the exam, with her mother present, each girl was asked to describe where the doctor had touched her. She was then presented with an anatomically correct doll and asked once again to point out where the doctor had touched her. The findings indicated that the children were very inaccurate in reporting what happened. Approximately 60% of those who were touched in the genital region refused to indicate

this, whether the dolls were used or not. On the other hand, of the children in the control group, approximately 60% indicated genital insertions or other intrusive acts by the doctor, even though nothing of the sort had occurred.

In another set of studies, preschool children were asked to think about actual events that they had experienced, such as an accident, and about fictitious events such as having to go to the hospital to get their fingers removed from a mousetrap. Each week for 10 consecutive weeks, an interviewer asked each child to choose one of the scenes and to "think very hard and tell me if this ever happened to you." The child thus experienced thinking hard and visualizing both real and fictitious scenes over an extended period of time. After 10 weeks the children were examined by a new interviewer who had not participated in the experiment.

Ceci and his colleagues conducted several experiments using this paradigm (Ceci, 1995). In one study, 58% of the preschool children described the fictitious event as if it had really happened. Twenty-five percent of the children described the fictitious events as real a majority of the time. Furthermore, the children's narratives were very detailed and coherent and embellished in ways that were not suggested originally. More telling was the fact that in one study 27% of the children, when told that their memory was false, claimed that they actually did remember the event.

But there is also plenty of evidence that therapists need to be very sensitive to signs of trauma that may not be fully remembered in patients presenting with symptoms of dissociative or posttraumatic stress disorders. Even if patients are unable to report or remember early trauma, it can sometimes be confirmed through corroborating evidence (Coons, 1994). In a compelling study, Williams (1994) interviewed 129 women with previously documented histories, such as hospital records, of having been sexually abused as children. Thirty-eight percent did not recall the incidents that had been reported to authorities at least 17 years earlier, even with extensive probing of their abuse histories. Dissociative amnesia was more extensive if the victim had been very young and knew the abuser. As noted above, Lewis et al. (1997) provided similar documentation of severe early abuse.

In a recent study, Elliot (1997) surveyed 364 individuals out of a larger group who had experienced substantial trauma such as a natural disaster, car accident, or physical abuse. Fully 32% reported delayed recall of the event, which suggested at least temporary dissociative amnesia. This phenomenon was most prevalent among combat veterans, people who had witnessed the murder or suicide of a family member, and those who had suffered sexual abuse. The severity of the trauma predicted the extent of the amnesia, and the most common trigger for recalling the trauma was a media presentation, such as a movie. As Brewin, Andrews, and Gotlib (1993) also point out, the available data from cognitive science do not necessarily support an extreme reconstructive model of (false) memory induced by careless therapists, since most individuals can recall important details of their childhood, particularly if they are unique and unexpected.

How will this controversy be resolved? Because false memories can be created through strong repeated suggestions by an authority figure, therapists must be fully aware of the conditions under which this is likely to occur, particularly when dealing with young children. This requires an extensive knowledge of the workings of memory and other aspects of psychological functioning and illustrates, once again, the dangers of dealing with inexperienced or inadequately trained psychotherapists. Elaborate tales of satanic abuse of children under the care of elderly women in day care centers are most likely cases of memories implanted by aggressive and careless therapists or law enforcement officials. In some cases, elderly caregivers have been sentenced to life in prison.

On the other hand, many people with dissociative and posttraumatic stress disorders have suffered documented extreme abuse and trauma, which then becomes dissociated from awareness. It may be that future research will find that the severity of dissociative amnesia is directly related to the severity of the trauma in vulnerable individuals, and is also likely to be proven as qualitatively different from "normal" dissociative experiences (e.g., Waller et al., 1996). In other words, are there two kinds of memories: traumatic memories that can be dissociated, and "normal" memories that cannot? At present, this is the scientific crux of the issue.

from the inside

Phantom Illness: Shattering the Myth of Hypochondria by Carla Cantor with Brian A. Fallon, M.D.*

"One warm June evening I found myself imprisoned, a patient on a psychiatric ward of a hospital a few miles from my New Jersey home. It was not at all what I had intended. I had come to the emergency room earlier that day in desperation: I had to talk to someone about the undiagnosed pain in my wrist, my thinning hair, and the unrelenting fear that I was morbidly ill" (p. 1).

Carla Cantor opens *Phantom Illness* with the story of a hospital stay that turned out to be the beginning of her road to recovery from lifelong hypochondria. Though not entirely a memoir, the book begins and ends with episodes and personal insights from Cantor's life as a hypochondriac. In between are straightforward chapters outlining current medical and psychiatric thinking on different types of somatic disorders, possible causes, and steps toward treatment. Throughout the book, Cantor weaves in strands of her personal experiences as well as revealing stories and insightful quotes from many people with different somatic disorders.

The hospital misadventure begins when an emergency-room physician misdiagnoses her condition as clinical depression. Cantor's reaction demonstrates the depths of her preoccupation with physical illness. "After the initial shock of hearing his words, I felt relief. . . . Finally, my illness would be diagnosed! Doctors would examine my inflamed wrist, psychiatrists would listen to me talk about the psychic pain of the past year, and they would all figure out whether I was really sick or just plain crazy" (p. 4). The hospital stay also seemed to promise relief from her stressful life. "Being in a hospital also seemed like a reasonable excuse for leaving behind the responsibilities and stresses that go with being a freelance writer and mother of two young children" (p. 4).

To her dismay, Cantor's overnight stay in the psychiatric ward was not the restful respite she had expected. "Suddenly, my undiagnosed illness didn't seem so terrible. I could live with it. In fact, maybe, just maybe, I thought, there really wasn't much wrong with me after all" (p.5). She left the next morning, determined to overcome the problem on her own. "Perhaps the best thing to do was leave the pain alone. Accept the symptoms, ignore them" (p.6)

However, Cantor's lifelong problem resisted solution. "My existence was peppered with episodes of illness. When the going got tough, I'd get sick. Or just the opposite: when things seemed to be going well, I'd come down with a symptom, or at least what I interpreted as one" (p.10). In addition, Cantor suffered the shame that is common to hypochondriacs. As one of the people she interviewed put it, "Unless you have it yourself, it's looked upon as a character flaw. . . . Hypochondria is not something you can admit to anyone. It's so embarrassing" (p. 51). She continued to suffer.

Help came to her by chance. Although Cantor had never before read anything about hypochondria, the moment she saw a newspaper article about the disorder, "suddenly something clicked for me. The myriad tests, the files of medical bills, the dozens of maladies for which doctors could never find a cause. There *was* something wrong with me, but not a deadly disease, which in my more rational moments, I believe I had always known" (p.6). For Cantor, the realization that she was not alone in her suffering was the catalyst to seek help.

After consulting with Brian Fallon, Cantor received treatment, including fluoxetine (Prozac), which helped her tremendously. She contacted Fallon with the idea of writing a book about hypochondria. Her rationale was that the book would spread information and hope to other hypochondriacs, whom she views as suffering intense psychological pain. "If you're lucky, as I was, you finally wake up, not just intellectually but deep in your soul, to a simple paradox: if you ar going to live out the rest of your life preparing for the day the tumor arrives, when you get the report of that terrible blood test, when you collapse in crushing pain, what's the point? Why would anyone want to live to 120 as a hypochondriac?" (p. 290)

In the end, Cantor can rightfully claim that she and Fallon have achieved their goals of providing solid information and relieving the suffering of many people who suffer from hypochondriacal worries about their health. "As I come to the close of my odyssey, I hope I have succeeded in accomplishing what I set out to do: erase a stigma, debunk some myths, lend some illumination to a puzzling, perpetually elusive malady" (p. 219).

*Carla Cantor with Brian A. Fallon, M.D., *Phantom Illness: Shattering the Myth of Hypochondria* (Houghton Mifflin, 1996).

Advocates on both sides of this issue agree that clinical science must proceed as quickly as possible to specify the processes under which the implantation of false memories is likely, and to define the presenting features that indicate a real but dissociated traumatic experience (Kihlstrom, 1997; Pope, 1996, 1997). Until then, mental health professionals must be extremely careful not to prolong unnecessary suffering, among both victims of actual abuse and victims falsely accused as abusers.

TREATMENT

Individuals who experience dissociative amnesia or a fugue state usually get better on their own and remember what they have forgotten. The episodes are so clearly related to current life stress that prevention of future episodes usually involves therapeutic resolution of the distressing situations and increasing the strength of personal coping mechanisms. When necessary, therapy focuses on recalling what happened during the amnesic or fugue states, often with the help of friends or family who know what happened, so patients can confront the information and integrate it into their conscious experience.

For DID, however, the process is not so easy. With the person's very identity shattered into many different elements, reintegrating the personality might seem hopeless. Fortunately, this is not always the case. Although no controlled research has been reported on the effects of treatment, there are many documented successes of attempts to reintegrate identities through long-term psychotherapy (Ellason & Ross, 1997; Putnam, 1989; Ross, 1997). Nevertheless, the prognosis for most people remains guarded. Coon (1986) found that only 5 out of 20 patients achieved a full integration of their identities. More recently, Ellason and Ross (1997) reported that 12 out of 54 (22.2%) patients had achieved integration 2 years after presenting for treatment, which in most cases, had been continuous.

The strategies that therapists use today in treating DID are based on accumulated clinical wisdom as well as on procedures that have been successful with posttraumatic stress disorder (see Chapter 5). The fundamental goal is to identify cues or triggers that provoke memories of trauma and/or dissociation and to neutralize them. More importantly, the patient must confront and relive the early trauma and gain control over the horrible events, at least as they recur in the patient's mind (Kluft, 1996; Ross, 1997). In order to instill this sense of control, the therapist must skillfully, and very slowly, help the patient visualize and relive aspects of the trauma until it is simply a terrible memory instead of a current event. Since the memory is unconscious, aspects of the experience are often not known to either the patient or the therapist until they emerge during treatment. Hypnosis is often used to access unconscious memories and bring various alters into awareness. As the process of dissociation may be very similar to the process of hypnosis, the latter may be a particularly efficient way to access traumatic memories. (Of course, there is as yet no evidence that hypnosis is a *necessary* part of treatment.) We know that DID seems to run a

chronic course and very seldom improves spontaneously, which confirms that current treatments, primitive as they are, have some effectiveness.

It is possible that reemerging memories of trauma may trigger further dissociation. The therapist must be on guard against this happening. Trust is important to any therapeutic relationships, but it is absolutely essential in the treatment of DID. Occasionally medication is combined with therapy, but there is little indication that it helps much. What little clinical evidence there is indicates that antidepressant drugs might be appropriate in some cases (Coon, 1986; Kluft, 1996; Putnam & Loewenstein, 1993).

■ **concept check 6.3**

Check your understanding of somatoform and dissociative disorders by identifying the type of disorder for each of these descriptions: (a) malingering, (b) factitious, (c) body dysmorphic, (d) pain disorder, and (e) localized amnesia.

1. Susan pretends to be sick so that she can get supportive attention from her mother. _____

2. Betty had considerable pain when she broke her arm. A year after it healed and all medical tests indicate that her arm is fine, she still complains of the pain. It seems to intensify when she fights with her husband. _____

3. William hated the way his ears stick out, so he has surgery to have them tacked down flat against his head. After the surgery, he still hates his ears. _____

4. Robert's car was rear-ended during a multiple-car accident. Even though extensive testing indicates that nothing is wrong with Robert's neck, he claims that he is in pain. On weekends, the pain apparently disappears during softball games. The driver of the vehicle that hit him has $1 million insurance coverage for all accidents. _____

5. Carol cannot remember what happened last weekend. On Monday she was admitted to a hospital, suffering from cuts, bruises, and contusions. It also appeared that she had been sexually assaulted. _____

Summary

Somatoform Disorders

• Individuals with somatoform disorders are pathologically concerned with the appearance or functioning of their bodies and bring these concerns to the attention of health professionals, who usually find no identifiable medical basis for the physical complaints.

• There are several types of somatoform disorders. Hypochondriasis is a condition in which individuals believe they are seriously ill and become very anxious over this possibility. Somatization disorder is characterized by a seemingly unceasing and wide-ranging pattern of physical complaints that dominate the individual's life and interpersonal relationships. In conversion disorder, there is physical malfunctioning, such as paralysis, without any apparent physical problems. In pain disorder, psychological factors are judged to play a major role in maintaining physical suffering. In body dysmorphic disorder, a person who looks normal is obsessively preoccupied with some imagined defect in appearance (imagined ugliness).

• Distinguishing among conversion reactions, real physical disorders, and outright malingering, or faking, is sometimes difficult. Even more puzzling can be factitious disorder, in which the person's symptoms are feigned and under voluntary control, as with malingering, but for no apparent reason.

• The causes of somatoform disorders are not well understood, but some, including hypochondriasis and body dysmorphic disorder, seem very closely related to anxiety disorders.

• Treatment of somatoform disorders ranges from very basic techniques of reassurance and social support to those meant to reduce stress and remove any secondary gain for the behavior. *Recently, specifically tailored cognitive behavioral therapy has proven successful with hypochondriasis.* Patients suffering from body dysmorphic disorder often turn to plastic surgery, which more often than not increases their preoccupation and distress.

Dissociative Disorders

• Dissociative disorders are characterized by alterations in perceptions: a sense of detachment from one's own self, from the world, or from memories.

• Dissociative disorders include depersonalization disorder, in which the individual's sense of personal reality is temporarily lost (depersonalization) and so is the reality of the external world (derealization). In dissociative amnesia, the individual may be unable to remember important personal information; in generalized amnesia the individual is unable to remember anything at all; more commonly, the individual is unable to recall specific events that occur during a specific period of time (localized *or selective* amnesia). In dissociative fugue, memory loss is combined with an unexpected trip (or trips). In the extreme, new identities, or alters, may be formed, as in dissociative identity disorder. Finally, the newly defined dissociative trance disorder, is considered to cover dissociations that may be culturally determined.

• The causes of dissociative disorders are not well understood but often seem related to the tendency to escape psychologically from memories of traumatic events.

• Treatment of dissociative disorders involves helping the patient reexperience the traumatic events in a controlled therapeutic manner in order to develop better coping skills. In the case of dissociative identity disorder, therapy is often long-term, and may include antidepressant drugs. Particularly essential with this disorder is a sense of trust between therapist and patient.

Key Terms

somatoform disorders
dissociative disorders
hypochondriasis
somatization disorder
conversion disorder
malingering
factitious disorders
pain disorder
body dysmorphic disorder (BDD)
depersonalization
derealization
depersonalization disorder
dissociative amnesia
generalized amnesia
localized or selective amnesia
dissociative fugue
dissociative trance disorder (DTD)
dissociative identity disorder (DID)
alters

Answers to Concept Checks

6.1
1. c   2. d.   3. b

6.2
1. c   2. N   3. d   4. a

6.3
1. b   2. d   3. c   4. a   5. e

EXPLORING SOMATOFORM AND DISSOCIATIVE DISORDERS

These two sets of disorders share some common features and are strongly linked historically as "hysterical neuroses." Both are relatively rare and not yet well understood.

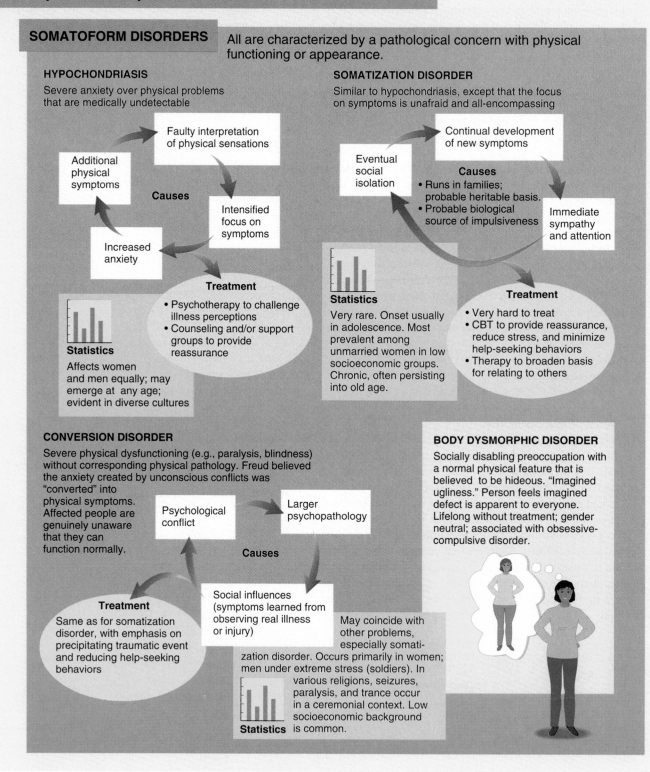

SOMATOFORM DISORDERS

All are characterized by a pathological concern with physical functioning or appearance.

HYPOCHONDRIASIS

Severe anxiety over physical problems that are medically undetectable

Faulty interpretation of physical sensations

Additional physical symptoms

Causes

Intensified focus on symptoms

Increased anxiety

Treatment
- Psychotherapy to challenge illness perceptions
- Counseling and/or support groups to provide reassurance

Statistics
Affects women and men equally; may emerge at any age; evident in diverse cultures

SOMATIZATION DISORDER

Similar to hypochondriasis, except that the focus on symptoms is unafraid and all-encompassing

Continual development of new symptoms

Eventual social isolation

Causes
- Runs in families; probable heritable basis.
- Probable biological source of impulsiveness

Immediate sympathy and attention

Statistics
Very rare. Onset usually in adolescence. Most prevalent among unmarried women in low socioeconomic groups. Chronic, often persisting into old age.

Treatment
- Very hard to treat
- CBT to provide reassurance, reduce stress, and minimize help-seeking behaviors
- Therapy to broaden basis for relating to others

CONVERSION DISORDER

Severe physical dysfunctioning (e.g., paralysis, blindness) without corresponding physical pathology. Freud believed the anxiety created by unconscious conflicts was "converted" into physical symptoms. Affected people are genuinely unaware that they can function normally.

Psychological conflict

Larger psychopathology

Causes

Social influences (symptoms learned from observing real illness or injury)

Treatment
Same as for somatization disorder, with emphasis on precipitating traumatic event and reducing help-seeking behaviors

Statistics
May coincide with other problems, especially somatization disorder. Occurs primarily in women; men under extreme stress (soldiers). In various religions, seizures, paralysis, and trance occur in a ceremonial context. Low socioeconomic background is common.

BODY DYSMORPHIC DISORDER

Socially disabling preoccupation with a normal physical feature that is believed to be hideous. "Imagined ugliness." Person feels imagined defect is apparent to everyone. Lifelong without treatment; gender neutral; associated with obsessive-compulsive disorder.

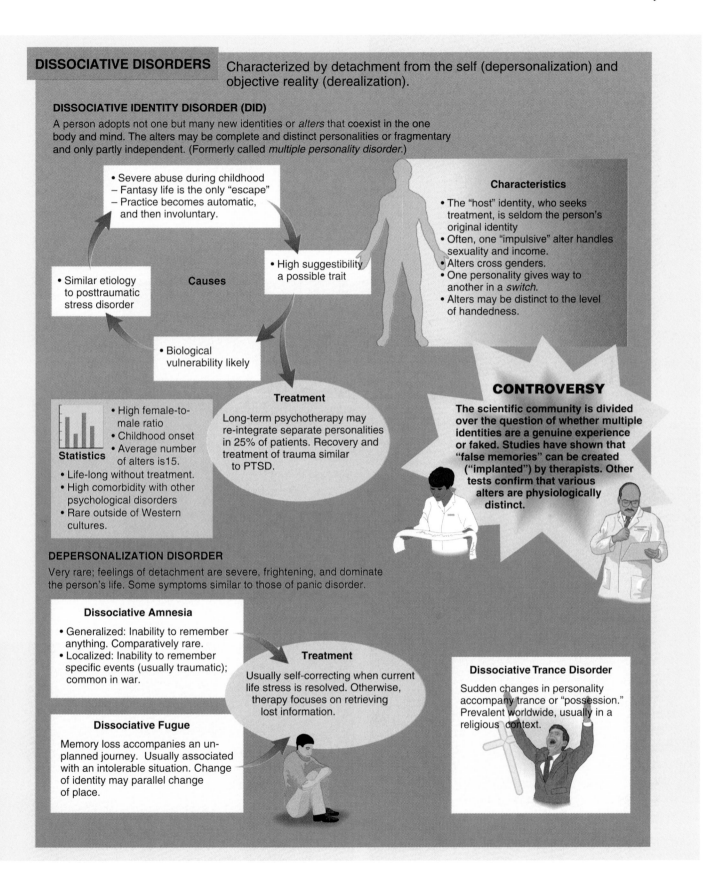

DISSOCIATIVE DISORDERS

Characterized by detachment from the self (depersonalization) and objective reality (derealization).

DISSOCIATIVE IDENTITY DISORDER (DID)

A person adopts not one but many new identities or *alters* that coexist in the one body and mind. The alters may be complete and distinct personalities or fragmentary and only partly independent. (Formerly called *multiple personality disorder*.)

Causes

- Severe abuse during childhood
  - Fantasy life is the only "escape"
  - Practice becomes automatic, and then involuntary.
- High suggestibility a possible trait
- Similar etiology to posttraumatic stress disorder
- Biological vulnerability likely

Characteristics

- The "host" identity, who seeks treatment, is seldom the person's original identity
- Often, one "impulsive" alter handles sexuality and income.
- Alters cross genders.
- One personality gives way to another in a *switch*.
- Alters may be distinct to the level of handedness.

Statistics

- High female-to-male ratio
- Childhood onset
- Average number of alters is 15.
- Life-long without treatment.
- High comorbidity with other psychological disorders
- Rare outside of Western cultures.

Treatment

Long-term psychotherapy may re-integrate separate personalities in 25% of patients. Recovery and treatment of trauma similar to PTSD.

CONTROVERSY

The scientific community is divided over the question of whether multiple identities are a genuine experience or faked. Studies have shown that "false memories" can be created ("implanted") by therapists. Other tests confirm that various alters are physiologically distinct.

DEPERSONALIZATION DISORDER

Very rare; feelings of detachment are severe, frightening, and dominate the person's life. Some symptoms similar to those of panic disorder.

Dissociative Amnesia

- Generalized: Inability to remember anything. Comparatively rare.
- Localized: Inability to remember specific events (usually traumatic); common in war.

Treatment

Usually self-correcting when current life stress is resolved. Otherwise, therapy focuses on retrieving lost information.

Dissociative Fugue

Memory loss accompanies an unplanned journey. Usually associated with an intolerable situation. Change of identity may parallel change of place.

Dissociative Trance Disorder

Sudden changes in personality accompany trance or "possession." Prevalent worldwide, usually in a religious context.

7

Mood Disorders

. . . my life is in ruins and . . . my body is uninhabitable. It is raging and weeping and full of destruction and wild energy gone amok. In the mirror I see

a creature I don't know but must live and share my mind with.

Kay Redfield Jamison
An Unquiet Mind

Think back over the last month of your life. It may seem normal in most respects; you studied during the week, socialized on the weekend, and thought about the future once in a while. Perhaps you were anticipating with some pleasure the next school break, or seeing an old friend or a lover. But maybe sometime during the past month you also felt kind of down, because you broke up with your boyfriend or girlfriend or, worse yet, somebody close to you died.

Think about your feelings during this period. Were you sad? Perhaps you remember crying. Maybe you felt listless, and you couldn't seem to get up the energy to go out with your friends. It may be that you feel this way once in a while for no good reason that you can think of, and your friends think you're moody.

If you are like most people, you know that your mood will pass. You will be back to your old self in a day or two. In fact, if you *never* felt down and always saw only what was good in a situation, it might be more remarkable than if you were depressed once in a while.

Feelings of depression (and joy) are universal, which makes it all the more difficult to understand disorders of mood, disorders that can be so incapacitating that violent suicide may seem by far the better option than living. Consider the following case.

Katie
Weathering Depression

Katie was an attractive but very shy 16-year-old who came to our clinic with her parents. For several years, Katie had seldom interacted with anybody outside her family because of her considerable social anxiety. Going to school was very difficult, and as her social contacts decreased her days became empty and dull. By the time she was 16, a deep, all-encompassing depression blocked the sun from her life. Here is how she described it later.

The experience of depression is like falling into a deep, dark hole that you cannot climb out of. You scream as you fall, but it seems like no one hears you. Some days you float upward without even trying; on other days, you wish that you would hit bottom so that you would never fall again. Depression affects the way you interpret events. It influences the way you see yourself and the way you see other people. I remember looking in the mirror and thinking that I was the ugliest creature in the world. Later in life, when some of these ideas would come back, I learned to remind

myself that I did not have those thoughts yesterday and chances were that I would not have them tomorrow or the next day. It is a little like waiting for a change in the weather.

But at 16, in the depths of her despair, Katie had no such perspective. She often cried for hours at the end of the day. She had begun drinking alcohol the year before, with the blessing of her parents, strangely enough, since the pills prescribed by her family doctor did no good. A glass of wine at dinner had a temporary soothing effect on Katie, and both she and her parents, in their desperation, were willing to try anything that might make her a more functional person. But one glass was not enough. She drank more and more often. She began drinking herself to sleep. It was a means of escaping what she felt: "I had very little hope of positive change. I do not think that anyone close to me was hopeful, either. I was angry, cynical, and in a great deal of emotional pain." Katie's life continued to spiral downward.

For several years, Katie had thought about suicide as a solution to her unhappiness. At 13, in the presence of her parents, she reported these thoughts to a psychologist. Her parents wept, and the sight of their tears deeply affected Katie. From that point on she never expressed her suicidal thoughts again, but they remained with her.

By the time she was 16, her preoccupation with her own death had increased.

I think this was just exhaustion. I was tired of dealing with the anxiety and depression day in and day out. Soon I found myself trying to sever the few interpersonal connections that I did have, with my closest friends, with my mother, and my oldest brother. I was almost impossible to talk to. I was angry and frustrated all the time. One day I went over the edge. My mother and I had a disagreement about some unimportant little thing. I went to my bedroom where I kept a bottle of whiskey or vodka or whatever I was drinking at the time. I drank as much as I could until I could pinch myself as hard as I could and feel nothing. Then I got out a very sharp knife that I had been saving and slashed my wrist deeply. I did not feel anything but the warmth of the blood running from my wrist.

The blood poured out onto the floor next to the bed that I was lying on. The sudden thought hit me that I had failed, that this was not enough to cause my death. I got up from the bed and began to laugh. I tried to stop the bleeding with some tissues. I stayed calm and frighteningly pleasant. I walked to the kitchen and called my mother. I cannot imagine how she felt when she saw my shirt and pants covered in blood. She was amazingly calm. She asked to see the cut and said that it was not going to stop bleeding on its own and that I needed to go to the doctor immediately. I remember as the doctor shot Novocaine into the cut he remarked that I must have used an anesthetic before cutting myself. I never felt the shot or the stitches.

After that, thoughts of suicide became more frequent and much more real. My father asked me to promise that I would never do it again and I said I would not, but that promise meant nothing to me. I knew it was to ease his pains and fears and not mine, and my preoccupation with death continued.

Think for a moment about your own experience of depression. What are the major differentiating factors between your feelings and Katie's? Clearly, Katie's depression was outside the boundaries of normal experience by virtue of its intensity and duration. In addition, her severe or "clinical" depression interfered substantially with her ability to function. Finally, a number of associated psychological and physical symptoms accompany clinical depression.

I was a senior in high school when I had my first attack of manic-depressive illness; once the siege began, I lost my mind rather rapidly.

Because of their sometimes tragic consequences, we need to develop as full an understanding as possible of mood disorders. In the following sections, we describe how various emotional experiences and symptoms interrelate to produce specific mood disorders. We offer detailed descriptions of different mood disorders, and examine the many criteria that define them. We discuss the relationship of anxiety and depression, and the causes and treatment of mood disorders. We conclude with a discussion of suicide.

An Overview of Depression and Mania

The disorders described in this chapter used to be categorized under several different general labels, such as "depressive disorders," "affective disorders," or even "depressive neuroses." Beginning with DSM-III-R, these problems have been grouped under the heading **mood disorders** because they are characterized by gross deviations in mood.

The fundamental experiences of depression and mania contribute, either singly or together, to all the mood disorders. We describe each state and discuss its contributions to the various mood disorders. Then we briefly describe the additional defining criteria, features, or symptoms that define the specific disorders.

The most commonly diagnosed and most severe depression is called a **major depressive episode.** The DSM-IV criteria indicate an extremely depressed mood state that lasts at least 2 weeks and includes cognitive symptoms (such as feelings of worthlessness and indecisiveness), and disturbed physical functions (such as altered sleeping patterns, significant changes in appetite and weight, or a very notable loss of energy) to the point that even the slightest activity or movement requires an overwhelming effort. The episode is typically accompanied by a marked general loss of interest and of the ability to experience any pleasure from life, including interactions with family or friends and accomplishments at work or at school. (The inability to experience pleasure is termed *anhedonia.*) Although all symptoms are important, recent evidence suggests that the physical changes (sometimes

called somatic or *vegetative* symptoms) are central to this disorder (Buchwald & Rudick-Davis, 1993; Keller et al., 1995), as they strongly indicate a full major depressive episode. The average duration of such an episode if untreated is approximately 9 months (Eaton et al., 1997; Tollefson, 1993).

The second fundamental state in mood disorders is abnormally exaggerated elation, joy, or euphoria. In **mania,** individuals find extreme pleasure in every activity; in fact, some patients compare their daily experience of mania to a continuous sexual orgasm. They become extraordinarily active (hyperactive), requiring very little sleep, and may develop grandiose plans, believing they can accomplish anything they desire. Speech is typically very rapid and may become incoherent, because the individual is attempting to express so many exciting ideas at once; this feature is typically referred to as *flight of ideas.*

DSM-IV criteria for a manic episode require a duration of only 1 week, less if the episode is severe enough to require hospitalization. Hospitalization could occur, for example, if the individual was engaging in self-destructive buying sprees, charging thousands of dollars in the expectation of making a million dollars the next day. Irritability is often part of a manic episode, usually near the end. Paradoxically, being anxious or depressed is also commonly part of mania, as described below. The average duration of an untreated manic episode is 6 months.

DSM-IV also defines a **hypomanic episode,** a less severe version of a manic episode that does not cause marked impairment in social or occupational functioning. (*Hypo* means "below"; thus the episode is below the level of a manic episode.) A hypomanic episode is not in itself necessarily problematic, but it does contribute to the definition of several mood disorders.

The Structure of Mood Disorders

Individuals who experience either depression *or* mania are said to suffer from a *unipolar mood disorder,* because their mood remains at one "pole" of the usual depression–mania continuum. Because mania by itself is extremely rare, almost everyone with a unipolar mood disorder suffers from unipolar depression. Someone who alternates between depression and mania is said to have a *bipolar mood disorder* traveling from one "pole" of the depression–elation continuum to the other and back again. However, this label is somewhat misleading, because depression and elation may not exactly be at opposite ends of the same mood state; in fact, though related, they are often relatively independent.

An individual can experience manic symptoms but feel somewhat depressed or anxious at the same time. This combination is called **dysphoric manic** or **mixed episode** (Cassidy, Forest, Murry, & Carroll 1998; McElroy et al., 1992). The patient usually experiences such symptoms of mania as being out of control or dangerous, and becomes anxious or depressed about them. Recent research suggests that manic episodes are characterized by dysphoric (anxious or depressive) features more commonly than was thought, and that dysphoria can be severe (Cassidy et al., 1998). The rare individual who suffers from manic episodes alone also meets criteria for bipolar mood disorder since experience shows that this individual can be expected to become depressed at a later time (Goodwin & Jamison, 1990).

Depression and mania may differ from one person to another in terms of their severity, their course (or the frequency with which they tend to recur) and, occasionally, the accompanying symptoms. An important feature of major depressive episodes is that they are *time-limited*, lasting from 2 weeks to 9 months if untreated (Tollefson, 1993). Almost all major depressive episodes eventually remit on their own without treatment, although approximately 10% last 2 years or longer. Manic episodes remit on their own without treatment after approximately 6 months (Goodwin & Jamison, 1990). Therefore, it is very important to determine the course or *temporal patterning* of the episodes. For example, do they tend to recur? If they do, does the patient recover fully between episodes? Do the depressive episodes alternate with manic or hypomanic episodes? All these different patterns come under the DSM-IV general heading of *course modifiers* for mood disorders.

Course modifiers characterize the mood state in the past, which helps us better predict the future of the disorder. We determine the pattern of recurrence, and whether there is a temporal association of the episode with other mood-related features or a certain time of the year (usually winter).

The importance of course makes the goals of treating mood disorders somewhat different than for other psychological disorders. Clinicians want to do everything possible to relieve people like Katie from their *current* depressive episode, but, an equally important goal is to prevent *future* episodes—in other words, to help people like Katie stay well for a longer period of time. Studies have appeared that evaluate the effectiveness of treatment in terms of this second goal (Fava, Grandi, Zielezny, Rafanelli, & Canestrari, 1996; Frank et al., 1990).

Either losing or gaining weight and either losing sleep (insomnia) or sleeping too much (hypersomnia) might contribute to the diagnosis of a major depressive episode. Similarly, in a manic episode one individual may present with clear and extreme euphoria and elation accompanied by inflated self-esteem or grandiosity, and another may appear irritable and exhibit flight of ideas. In reality, it is more common to see patients with a mix of such symptoms.

Depressive Disorders

Clinical Descriptions

The most easily recognized mood disorder is **major depressive disorder, single episode,** which is defined by the absence of manic or hypomanic episodes before or during the episode. We now know that an occurrence of just one isolated depressive episode in a lifetime is rare (Angst & Preizig, 1996; Judd, 1997).

If two or more major depressive episodes occurred and were separated by a period of at least 2 months during which the individual was not depressed, **major depressive disorder, recurrent,** is diagnosed. Otherwise, the criteria are the same as for major depressive disorder, single episode. Recurrence is very important in predicting the future course of the disorder as well as in choosing appropriate treatments. Individuals with recurrent major depression usually have a family history of depression, unlike people who experience single episodes. Approximately 80% of single-episode cases later experience a second episode and thus meet criteria for major depressive disorder, recurrent (Judd, 1997; Keller, Lavori, et al., 1992). Because of this finding, and others reviewed below, clinical scientists in just the last several years have concluded that unipolar depression is almost always a chronic condition that waxes and wanes over time but seldom disappears. The median lifetime number of major depressive episodes is four; in one large sample, 25% experienced six or more episodes (Angst, 1988; Angst & Preizig, 1996). The median duration of recurrent major depressive episodes is 5 months (Solomon et al., 1997), some-

While his bride awaited him, Abraham Lincoln was suffering from a depressive episode that was so severe he was unable to proceed with the wedding until several days later.

what shorter than the average length of the first episode (Eaton et al., 1997).

On the basis of these criteria, how would you diagnose Katie? Katie suffered from severely depressed mood, feelings of worthlessness, difficulty concentrating, recurrent thoughts of death, sleep difficulties, and loss of energy. She clearly met the criteria for major depressive disorder, recurrent. Katie's depressive episodes were quite severe when they occurred, but she tended to cycle in and out of them.

Dysthymic disorder shares many of the symptoms of major depressive disorder but differs in its course. The symptoms are somewhat milder but remain relatively unchanged over long periods of time, sometimes 20 or 30 years or more (Akiskal & Cassano, 1997; Keller, Baker, & Russell, 1993; J. A. Rush, 1993).

Dysthymic disorder is defined as a persistently depressed mood that continues for at least 2 years, during which the patient cannot be symptom-free for more than 2 months at a time. Dysthymic disorder differs from a major depressive episode only in the severity, chronicity, and number of its symptoms, which are milder and fewer but last longer.

DOUBLE DEPRESSION

Recently, individuals have been studied who suffer from both major depression episodes *and* dysthymic disorder, and who are therefore said to have **double depression.** Typically, dysthymic disorder develops first, perhaps at an early age, and then one or more major depressive episodes occur later (Eaton et al., 1997). Identifying this particular pattern is important because it is associated with severe psychopathology and a problematic future course (Akiskal & Cassano, 1997; Keller, Hirschfeld, & Hanks, 1997; D. N. Klein, Taylor, Dickstein, & Harding, 1988). For example, Keller, Lavori, Endicott, Coryell, and Klerman (1983) found that 61% of patients suffering from double depression had not recovered from the underlying dysthymic disorder 2 years after follow-up. The investigators also found that patients who had recovered from the superimposed major depressive episode experienced very high rates of relapse and recurrence. Consider the following case.

Jack
A Life Kept Down

Jack was a 49-year-old divorced white man who lived at his mother's with his 10-year-old son. He complained of chronic depression, saying he finally realized he needed help. Jack reported that he had been a pessimist and a worrier for much of his adult life. He consistently felt kind of down and depressed and did not have much fun. He had difficulty making decisions, was generally pessimistic about the future, and thought very little of himself. During the past 20 years, the longest period he could remember in which his mood was "normal" or less depressed lasted only 4 or 5 days.

Despite his difficulties, Jack had managed to finish college and obtain a master's degree in public administration.

People told him his future was bright and that he would be highly valued in state government. Jack did not think so. He took a job as a low-level clerk in a state agency, thinking that he could always work his way up. He never did, remaining at the same desk for 20 years.

Jack's wife, fed up with his continued pessimism, lack of self-confidence, and relative inability to enjoy day-to-day events, became discouraged and divorced him. Jack moved in with his mother so that she could help care for his son and share expenses.

About 5 years before coming to the clinic, Jack had experienced a bout of depression worse than anything he had previously known. His self-esteem went from low to nonexistent. From indecisiveness, he became totally unable to decide anything. He was exhausted all the time, and felt as if lead had filled his arms and legs, making it difficult even to move. He became unable to complete projects or to meet deadlines. Seeing no hope, he began to consider suicide. After tolerating a listless performance for years from someone they had expected to rise through the ranks, Jack's employers finally fired him.

After about 6 months, the major depressive episode resolved and Jack returned to his chronic but milder state of depression. He could get out of bed and accomplish some things, although he still doubted his own abilities. However, he was unable to obtain another job. After several years of waiting for something to turn up, he realized that he was totally unable to solve his own problems and that without help his depression would certainly continue. After a thorough assessment, we determined that Jack suffered from a classic case of double depression.

Onset and Duration

The mean age of onset for major depressive disorder is 25 years in community samples of subjects who are not in treatment (Burke, Burke, Regier, & Roe, 1990), and 29 years for patients who are in treatment (Judd et al., in press), but the average age of onset seems to be decreasing (Weissman, Bruce, Leaf, Florio, & Holzer, 1991). A frightening finding is that the incidence of depression and consequent suicide seem to be steadily increasing (Cross-National Collaborative Group, 1992; Lewinsohn, Rohde, Seeley, & Fischer, 1993). In 1989, Myrna Weissman and her colleagues published a survey of people in five different U.S. cities (Klerman & Weissman, 1989; Wickramaratne, Weissman, Leaf, & Holford, 1989) that revealed a greatly increased risk of developing depression in younger Americans. Among Americans born before 1905, only 1% had developed depression by age 75; of those born since 1955, 6% had become depressed by age 24. A later study based on very similar surveys conducted in Puerto Rico, Canada, Italy, Germany, France, Taiwan, Lebanon, and New Zealand (see Figure 7.1) suggests that this trend toward developing depression at increasingly earlier ages is occurring worldwide (Cross-National Collaborative Group, 1992).

As noted previously, the length of depressive episodes is variable, with some lasting as little as 2 weeks; in more severe cases, an episode might last for several years, with the average duration of the first episode being 6 to 9 months if untreated (Eaton et al., 1997; Tollefson, 1993). Although 9 months is a long time to suffer with a severe depressive episode, evidence indicates that even in the most severe cases, the probability of remission of the episode approaches 90% (Thase, 1990) within a 5-year period (Keller, Lavori, et al., 1992). Even in those severe cases where the episode lasts 5 years or longer, 38% can be expected to recover (Mueller et al., 1996). On occasion, however, episodes may not entirely clear up, leaving some residual symptoms. In this case, the likelihood of a subsequent episode is much higher. It is also likely that subsequent episodes will be associated with incomplete interepisode recovery. Knowing this is important to treatment planning, as treatment should be continued much longer in these cases.

Recent evidence also identifies important subtypes of dysthymic disorder. Although the typical age of onset has been estimated to be in the early 20s, Klein and colleagues (1988) found that onset before 21 years of age, and often much earlier, is associated with three characteristics: (a) greater chronicity (it lasts longer), (b) relatively poor prognosis (response to treatment), and (c) a stronger likelihood of the disorder running in the family of the affected

individual. These findings have been replicated (Akiskal & Cassano, 1997). A greater prevalence of current personality disorders has been found in patients with early onset dysthymia than in patients with major depressive disorder (Pepper et al., 1995). Adolescents who have recovered from dysthymic disorder have a lower level of social support and higher levels of stress than adolescents with major depressive disorders, or other nonmood disorders (Klein, Lewisohn, & Seely, 1997). These findings may further reflect the insidiousness of the psychopathology in early onset dysthymia. Investigators have found a rather high prevalence of dysthymic disorder in children (Kovacs, Gatsonis, Paulauskas, & Richards, 1989), and Kovacs, Akiskal, Gatsonis, and Parrone (1994) found that 76% of a sample of dysthymic children later developed major depressive disorder.

Dysthymic disorder may last 20 to 30 years or more, although a preliminary study reported a median duration of approximately 5 years in adults (Rounsaville, Sholomskas, & Prusoff, 1988) and 4 years in children (Kovacs et al., 1994). Barrett (1984) conducted a 2-year naturalistic follow-up of adults with dysthymic disorder and found that 63% reported no improvement in their disorder. In fact, the conditions of some had deteriorated. Kovacs et al. (1994), on the other hand, found that almost all children with dysthymia in their

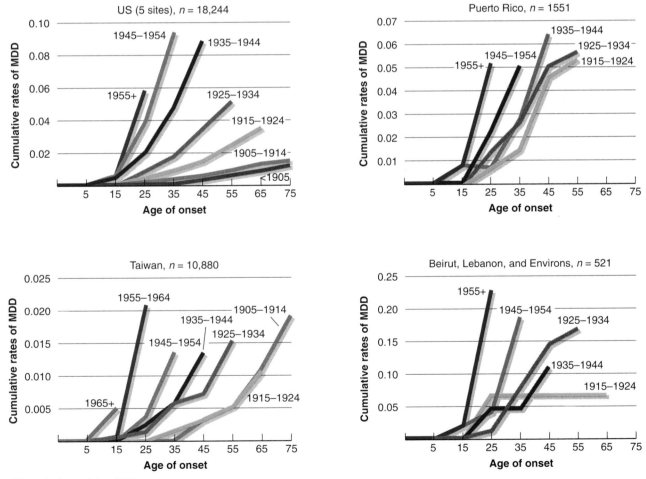

*Years indicate date of birth.

figure 7.1 Cross-cultural data on the onset of major depressive disorder (adapted from Cross-National Collaborative Group, 1992)

Queen Victoria remained in such deep mourning for her husband, Prince Albert, that she was unable to perform as monarch for several years after his death.

sample eventually recovered from it. It is relatively common for major depressive episodes and dysthymic disorder to co-occur (double depression). Among those who have had dysthymia, as many as 79% have also had a major depressive episode at some point in their lives.

From Grief to Depression

At the beginning of the chapter, we asked if you had ever felt down or depressed. Almost everyone has. But if someone you love has died—particularly if the death was unexpected and the person was a member of your immediate family—you may, after your initial reaction to the trauma, have experienced most of the symptoms of a major depressive episode: anxiety, emotional numbness, and denial. In fact, the frequency of severe depression following the death of a loved one is so high (approximately 62%) that mental health professionals do not consider it a disorder unless very severe symptoms appear, such as psychotic features or suicidal ideation, or the less-alarming symptoms last longer than 2 months (Jacobs, 1993). Some grieving individuals require immediate treatment because they are incapacitated by their symptoms (for example, severe weight loss, no energy whatsoever) that they cannot function.

It is important that we confront death and process it emotionally. All religions and cultures have rituals, such as funerals and burial ceremonies, to help us work through our losses with the support and love of our relatives and friends. Usually the natural grieving process resolves within the first several months, although some people grieve for a year or longer (Clayton & Darvish, 1979; Jacobs, Hansen, Berkman, Kasl, & Ostfeld, 1989). Grief often recurs at significant anniversaries, such as the birthday of the loved one,

holidays, and other meaningful occasions, including the anniversary of the death. Mental health professionals are concerned when someone does *not* grieve after a death, because grieving is our natural way of confronting and handling loss.

When grief lasts beyond the normal time, mental health professionals become concerned (C. G. Blanchard, Blanchard, & Becker, 1976). After a year or so, the chance of recovering from severe grief without treatment is considerably reduced and, for approximately 10%–20% of bereaved individuals (Jacobs, 1993; Midleton, Burnett, Raphael, & Martinek, 1996), a normal process becomes a disorder. Many of the psychological and social factors that are related to mood disorders in general, including a history of past depressive episodes (Horowitz et al., 1997; Jacobs et al., 1989), also predict the development of a normal grief response into a **pathological grief reaction** or **impacted grief reaction**. Particularly prominent symptoms include intrusive memories and distressingly strong yearnings for the loved one, and avoiding people or places that are reminders of the loved one (Horowitz et al., 1997). In cases of long-lasting grief, the rituals intended to help us face and accept death were ineffective. As with victims suffering from posttraumatic stress, one therapeutic approach is to help grieving individuals reexperience the trauma under close supervision. Usually the grieving person is encouraged to talk about the loved one, the death, and the meaning of the loss while experiencing all the associated emotions, until he or she can come to terms with reality. This procedure allows the individual to process negative emotions effectively and thus develop a sense of acceptance.

Bipolar Disorders

The key identifying feature of **bipolar disorders** is the tendency of manic episodes to alternate with major depressive episodes in an unending roller coaster ride from the peaks of elation to the depths of despair. Beyond that, bipolar disorders are parallel in many ways to depressive disorders. For example, a manic episode might occur only once or repeatedly. A milder but more chronic version of bipolar disorder called **cyclothymic disorder** is similar in many ways to dysthymic disorder. Consider the following case.

Jane
Funny, Smart, and Desperate

Jane was the wife of a well-known surgeon and the loving mother of three children. They lived in an old country house on the edge of town with plenty of room for the family and pets. Jane was nearly 50; the older children had moved out; the youngest son, 16-year-old Mike, was having substantial academic difficulties in school and seemed very anxious. Jane brought Mike to the clinic to find out why he was having problems.

As they entered the office, I observed that Jane was well-dressed, neat, vivacious, and personable; she had a bounce to her step. She began talking about her wonderful and successful family before she and Mike even reached their seats. Mike, by contrast, was very quiet and reserved. He seemed resigned and perhaps relieved that he would have to say very little during the session. By the time Jane sat down, she had mentioned the personal virtues and material achievement of her husband, and the brilliance and beauty of one of her older children, and she was proceeding to describe the second child. But before she finished she noticed a book on anxiety disorders and, having read voraciously on the subject, began a litany of various anxiety-related problems that might be troubling Mike.

In the meantime, Mike sat in the corner with a small smile on his lips that seemed to be masking considerable distress and uncertainty over what his mother might do next. It became clear as the interview progressed that Mike suffered from obsessive-compulsive disorder, which disturbed his concentration both in and out of school: He was failing all his courses.

It also became clear that Jane herself was in the midst of a *hypomanic episode,* evident in her unbridled enthusiasm, grandiose perceptions, "uninterruptable" speech, and report that she needed very little sleep these days. She was also easily distracted, as when she quickly switched from describing her children to the book on the table. When asked about her own psychological state, Jane readily admitted that she was a "manic depressive" (the old name for *bipolar disorder*) and that she alternated rather rapidly between feeling on top of the world and feeling very depressed; she was taking medication for her condition. I immediately wondered if Mike's obsessions had anything to do with his mother's condition.

Mike was treated intensively for his obsessions and compulsions, but made little progress. He said that life at home was very difficult when his mother was depressed. She sometimes went to bed and stayed there for 3 weeks. During this time, she seemed be in a depressive stupor, essentially unable to move for days. It was up to the children to care for themselves and their mother, whom they fed by hand. Because the older children had now left home, much of the burden had fallen on Mike. Jane's profound depressive episodes would remit after about 3 weeks, and she would immediately enter a hypomanic episode that might last several months or more. During hypomania, Jane was, for the most part, funny and entertaining and a delight to be with—if you could get a word in edgewise. Consultation with her therapist, an expert in the area, revealed that he had prescribed a number of medications but was so far unable to bring her mood swings under control.

Jane suffered from **bipolar II disorder,** in which major depressive episodes alternate with hypomanic episodes rather than full manic episodes. As noted above, hypomanic episodes are less severe. Although she was noticeably "up," Jane functioned pretty well while in this mood state. The criteria for **bipolar I disorder** are the same, except that the individual experiences a full manic episode. As in the criteria set for depressive disorder, for the manic episodes to be

considered separate, there must be a symptom-free period of at least 2 months between them. Otherwise, one episode is seen as a continuation of the last.

Another case illustrates a full manic episode. This individual was first encountered when he was admitted to a hospital.

Billy
The World's Best at Everything

Before Billy reached the ward you could hear him laughing and carrying on in a deep voice; it sounded like he was having a wonderful time. As the nurse brought Billy down the hall to introduce him to the staff, he spied the Ping-Pong table. Loudly, he exclaimed, "Ping-Pong! I love Ping-Pong! I have only played twice but that is what I am going to do while I am here; I am going to become the world's greatest Ping-Pong player! And that table is gorgeous! I am going to start work on that table immediately and make it the finest Ping-Pong table in the world. I am going to sand it down, take it apart, and rebuild it until it gleams and every angle is perfect!" Billy soon went on to something else that totally absorbed his attention.

The previous week, Billy had emptied his bank account, taken his credit cards and those of his elderly parents with whom he was living, and bought every piece of fancy stereo equipment he could find. He thought that he would set up the best sound studio in the city and make millions of dollars by renting it to people who would come from far and wide. This episode had precipitated his admission to the hospital.

During manic or hypomanic phases, patients often deny that they have a problem, which was characteristic of Billy. Even after spending inordinate amounts of money or making foolish business decisions, these individuals, particularly if they are in the midst of a full manic episode, are so wrapped up in their enthusiasm and expansiveness that their behavior seems perfectly reasonable to them. The high during a manic state is so pleasurable that people may stop taking their medication during periods of distress or discouragement in an attempt to bring on a manic state once again; this is a serious challenge to professionals.

Returning to the case of Jane, we continued to treat Jane's son Mike for several months. We made very little progress before the school year ended. Because Mike was doing so poorly, the school administrators informed his parents that he would not be accepted back the next year. Mike and his parents wisely decided it might be a good idea if he got away from the house and did something different for a while, and he began working and living at a ski and tennis resort. Several months later, his father called to tell us that Mike's obsessions and compulsions had completely lifted since he'd been away from home. The father thought Mike should continue living at the resort, where he had entered school and was doing better academically. He now agreed with our previous assessment that Mike's condition might be related to

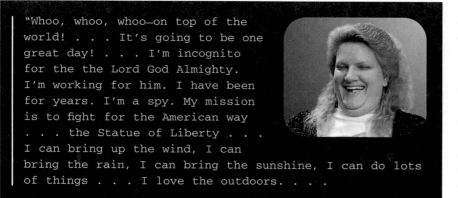

"Whoo, whoo, whoo—on top of the world! . . . It's going to be one great day! . . . I'm incognito for the the Lord God Almighty. I'm working for him. I have been for years. I'm a spy. My mission is to fight for the American way . . . the Statue of Liberty . . . I can bring up the wind, I can bring the rain, I can bring the sunshine, I can do lots of things . . . I love the outdoors. . . ."

his relationship with his mother. Several years later, we heard that Jane, in a depressive stupor, had killed herself, an all-too-tragic outcome in bipolar disorder.

Like dysthymic disorder, *cyclothymic disorder* is a chronic alternation of mood elevation and depression that does not reach the severity of manic or major depressive episodes. Individuals with cyclothymic disorder tend to be in one mood state or the other for many years with relatively few periods of neutral (or euthymic) mood. This pattern must last for at least 2 years (1 year for children and adolescents) to meet criteria for the disorder. Individuals with cyclothymic disorder alternate between the kinds of mild depressive symptoms Jack experienced during his dysthymic states and the sorts of hypomanic episodes Jane experienced. In neither case was the behavior severe enough to require hospitalization or immediate intervention. Much of the time, such individuals are just considered moody. However, the chronically fluctuating mood states are, by definition, substantial enough to interfere with functioning. Furthermore, people with cyclothymia should be treated because of their increased risk to develop the more severe bipolar I or bipolar II disorder (Akiskal, Khani, & Scott-Strauss, 1979; Depue et al., 1981; F. K. Goodwin & Jamison, 1990).

Onset and Duration

The average age of onset for bipolar I disorder is 18, and for bipolar II disorder it is 22, although cases of both can begin in childhood (Weissman et al., 1991). This is somewhat younger than the average age of onset for major depressive disorder, and bipolar disorders begin more acutely (Weissman et al., 1991; Winokur, Coryell, Endicott, & Akiskal, 1993). About one-third of the cases of bipolar disorder begin in adolescence (M. A. Taylor & Abrams, 1981), and the onset is often preceded by minor oscillations in mood or mild cyclothymic mood swings (Goodwin & Ghaemi, 1998; F. K. Goodwin & Jamison, 1990). Only 10% to 13% of bipolar II disorder cases progress to full bipolar I syndrome (Coryell, Endicott, et al., 1995; Depression Guideline Panel, 1993). The distinction between unipolar and bipolar mood disorder also seems well defined, since only 5.2% of a large group of 381 patients with unipolar depression experienced a manic episode during a 10-year follow-up period (Coryell, Endi-

cott, et al., 1995). If these disorders were more closely related, then we would expect to see more individuals moving from one to the other.

It is relatively rare for someone to develop bipolar disorder after the age of 40. Once it does appear, the course is chronic; that is, mania and depression alternate indefinitely. Therapy usually involves managing the disorder with ongoing drug regimens that prevent recurrence of episodes. Suicide is an all-too-common consequence of bipolar disorder, almost always occurring during depressive episodes, as it did in the case of Jane. Estimates of suicide in bipolar disorder range from 9% to as high as 60%, with an average rate of 19% (Jamison, 1986). Even with treatment, patients with bipolar disorder tend to do poorly, with one study showing 60% of a large group experiencing poor adjustment during the first 5 years after treatment (Goldberg, Harrow, & Grossman, 1995).

In typical cases, cyclothymia is chronic and lifelong. In about one-third of patients, cyclothymic mood swings develop into full-blown bipolar disorder (Waters, 1979). In one sample of cyclothymic patients, 60% were female, and the age of onset was quite young, often during the teenage years or before, with some data suggesting the most common age of onset to be 12 to 14 years (Depue et al., 1981). The disorder is often not recognized, and sufferers are thought to be high-strung, explosive, moody, or hyperactive (F. K. Goodwin & Jamison, 1990). One subtype of cyclothymia is based on the predominance of mild depressive symptoms, one on the predominance of hypomanic symptoms, and another on an equal distribution of both.

■ concept check 7.1

Match the word to its definition: (a) mania, (b) hypomanic episode, (c) anhedonia, (d) dysthymic episode, (e) major depressive episode, (f) bipolar disorder.

1. A tendency for manic episodes to alternate with major depressive episodes. _____

2. A period of abnormally extreme elation, joy, or euphoria. _____

3. The inability to experience pleasure. _____

4. Similar to major depressive disorder but differs in course. Symptoms are somewhat milder but remain unchanged over long periods of time. _____

5. Similar to a manic episode except that it is less severe. _____

Additional Defining Criteria

Other symptoms, or *specifiers,* may or may not accompany a mood disorder; when they do, they are often helpful in determining the most effective treatment. The specifiers are of two broad types: those that describe the most recent episode of the disorder, and those that describe its course or temporary pattern. We will briefly review these here. As a guide through this maze of specifiers, refer to Figure 7.2. What should be evident from the complexity of the figure is that diagnosing a mood disorder is not a straightforward task; great diversity of symptoms is possible within any of the diagnostic categories.

" . . . I've been sad, depressed most of my life. . . . I had a headache in high school for a year and a half. . . . There have been different periods in my life when I wanted to end it all. . . . I hate me, I really hate me. I hate the way I look, I hate the way I feel. I hate the way I talk to people . . . I do everything wrong . . . I feel really hopeless."

Six basic specifiers describe the most recent episode of a mood disorder: atypical, melancholic, chronic, catatonic, psychotic, and with postpartum onset.

1. *Atypical features specifier.* This specifier modifies depressive episodes and dysthymia but not manic episodes. Individuals with this specifier consistently oversleep and overeat during their episodes and therefore gain weight (e.g., J. Davidson, Miller, Turnbull, & Sullivan, 1982; Klein, 1989; Quitkin et al., 1988). Although they also have considerable anxiety, they can react with interest or pleasure to *some* things, unlike most depressed individuals. It is possible that people with these atypical symptoms differ from other depressed individuals in some important ways, such as response to treatment or age of onset (Lam & Stewart, 1996; Quitkin et al., 1991; Stewart, Rabkin, Quitkin, McGrath, & Klein, 1993). However, it may be that the symptoms simply represent an early stage of a depressive disorder that is characterized by slightly less severe symptoms and more anxiety (Casper et al., 1985; Himmelhoch & Thase, 1989; J. A. Rush, 1993).

2. *Melancholic features specifier.* This specifier applies only if the full criteria for a major depressive episode have been met; it does not apply in the case of dysthymia. Melancholic specifiers include some of the more severe somatic symptoms, such as early morning awakenings, weight loss, loss of libido (sex drive), excessive or inappropriate guilt, and anhedonia (partially diminished interest or pleasure in activities). Some studies suggest that this type of depression responds better to somatic treatments such as electroconvulsive therapy (ECT) or tricyclic antidepressant medication than do nonmelancholic depressive episodes, which may, in turn, respond better to psychological treatments (Crow et al., 1984; C. J. Robins, Block, & Peselow, 1990; Rush & Weissenburger, 1994; Simpson, Pi, Gross, Baron, & November, 1988). Other studies, however, have not replicated these findings (for instance, Copolov et al., 1986; Coryell & Turner, 1985; Norman, Miller, & Dow, 1988; Paykel, Hollyman, Freeling, & Sedgwich, 1988). There are also some hints that depressive episodes with melancholic features may occur more often in the absence of a stressful precipitating event, suggesting, perhaps, a stronger biological contribution to on-

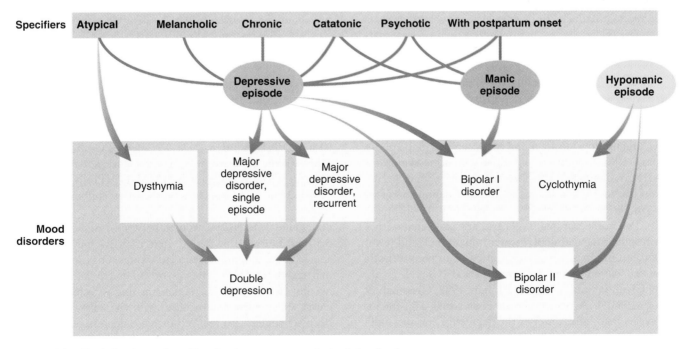

figure 7.2 Mood disorders and specifiers for the most recent episode of the disorder

set (Frank, Anderson, Reynolds, Ritenour, & Kupfer, 1994). Melancholia episodes also occur more frequently in older people (Depression Guideline Panel, 1993). The concept of "melancholic" does seem to signify, at the very least, a severe type of depressive episode. Whether this type is anything more than a different point on a continuum of severity remains to be seen (Rush & Weissenburger, 1994).

3. *Chronic features specifier.* This specifier applies only if the full criteria for a major depressive episode have been met *continuously* for at least the past 2 years. Dysthymic disorder is *not* considered here because, for that disorder, a duration of at least 2 years is a primary diagnostic criterion.

4. *Catatonic features specifier.* This specifier can be applied to major depressive episodes and even to manic episodes, though it is very rare, and rarer still in mania. This very serious condition involves a total absence of movement (a stuporous state, as in the case of Jane) or **catalepsy,** in which the muscles are waxy and semirigid, so that a patient's arms or legs remain in any position in which they are placed. Catatonic symptoms may also involve excessive but random or purposeless movement. Catalepsy is more commonly associated with schizophrenia.

5. *Psychotic features specifiers.* Some individuals in the midst of a major depressive or manic episode may experience psychotic symptoms, specifically **hallucinations** (seeing or hearing things that aren't there) and **delusions** (strongly held but inaccurate beliefs). Patients may also have somatic delusions; believing, for example, that their bodies are rotting internally and deteriorating into nothingness. Some may hear voices telling them how evil and sinful they are (*auditory hallucinations*). Such hallucinations and delusions are called *mood congruent* because they seem directly related to the depression. On rare occasions, depressed individuals might have other types of hallucinations or delusions such as *delusions of grandeur* (believing, for example, that they are supernatural or supremely gifted) that do not seem consistent with the depressed mood. This is a *mood incongruent* hallucination or delusion. Although quite rare, this condition signifies a very serious type of depressive episode that may progress to schizophrenia (or may be a symptom of schizophrenia to begin with). Delusions of grandeur accompanying a manic episode are mood congruent (as in the photo on page 190). Conditions in which psychotic symptoms accompany depressive episodes are relatively rare, occurring in 5% to 15% of identified cases of depression (Depression Guideline Panel, 1993; Spiker et al., 1985; Thase, 1990). Psychotic features in general are associated with a poor response to treatment, greater impairment, and fewer weeks with minimal symptoms, compared to nonpsychotic depressed patients over a 10-year period (Coryell et al., 1996; Chan, Janicak, Davis, & Altman, 1987; Glassman & Roose, 1981; J. A. Rush, 1993). Poor social adjustment, even years before the onset of the depressive episode, indicates the strong possibility of developing psychotic features

Profound melancholia is a day-in, day-out, night-in, night-out, almost arterial level of agony.

(Sands & Harrow, 1995). This type of depression may respond better to a combination of drugs that treat *both* psychotic symptoms and depression than to a single treatment (Kocsis et al., 1990).

6. *Postpartum onset specifier.* This specifier can apply to both major depressive and manic episodes. It is characterized by severe manic or depressive episodes of a psychotic nature that first occur during the postpartum period (the 4-week period immediately following childbirth), typically 2 to 3 days after delivery. These symptoms could be the initial warning that a full-blown bipolar disorder is developing (Dean & Kendell, 1981). The postpartum incidence, however, is quite low, approximately 1 per 1,000 deliveries (for example, Meltzer & Kumar, 1985). If a new mother experiences one of these severe postpartum episodes, the chances are approximately 50% that she will experience another episode with subsequent births (Davidson & Robertson, 1985; Depression Guideline Panel, 1993). Therefore, a severe postpartum episode helps to predict the future course of a mood disorder. Early recognition is important because in a few tragic cases, a mother in the midst of an episode has killed her newborn child (Purdy & Frank, 1993).

The postpartum onset specifier should not be applied to mild depressive episodes during the postpartum period. Most people, including the new mother herself, have difficulty understanding why she is depressed, because they assume this is a joyous time. Many new mothers forget that extreme stress can be brought on by physical exhaustion, new schedules, adjusting to nursing, and other changes that follow the birth.

However, some researchers have concluded that the risks for developing mood disorders during the postpartum period might be overestimated (Whiffen, 1992). O'Hara, Zekoski, Philipps, and Wright (1990) found no differences in the rates of minor and major depression in a group of childbearing women, either during pregnancy or after delivery, and in a well-matched control group. A close examination of women with postpartum depression revealed no essential differences between the characteristics of this mood disorder and others (Gotlib, Whiffen, Wallace, & Mount, 1991; Whiffen, 1992; Whiffen & Gotlib, 1993). In other words, postpartum depression does not seem to require a separate category in DSM-IV (Purdy & Frank, 1993). Minor reactions in adjustment to childbirth, sometimes called *postpartum blues,* typically last a few days and occur in 50% to 80% of women between 1 and 5 days after delivery. During this period, new mothers may be tearful and have some temporary mood swings, but these are normal responses to the stresses of childbirth and disappear quickly (Kendell, 1985). Not surprisingly, factors that increase stress, such as difficulties with the baby's feeding or sleep schedules, also seem to increase depressive symptoms in mothers.

Specifiers Describing Course of Mood Disorders

Three specifiers may accompany recurrent mania or depression: longitudinal course, rapid cycling, and seasonal pattern. Differences in course or temporal pattern may require different treatment strategies.

1. *Longitudinal course specifiers.* Whether the individual has had major episodes of depression or mania in the past is important, as is whether the individual fully recovered between past episodes. Other important determinations are whether the patient with a major depressive episode suffered from dysthymia before the episode (double depression), and whether the patient with bipolar disorder experienced a previous cyclothymic disorder. Antecedent dysthymia or cyclothymia predicts a *decreasing* chance of full interepisode recovery. Most likely, the patient will require a long and intense course of treatment to maintain a normal mood state for as long as possible after recovering from the current episode (J. A. Rush, 1993). Noting these longitudinal course specifiers—that is, whether there was full recovery between episodes and whether the patient had dysthymia or cyclothymia before the disorder—is important for recurrent major depressive disorder, bipolar I disorder, and bipolar II disorder.

2. *Rapid-cycling specifier.* This temporal specifier applies only to bipolar I and bipolar II disorders. Some people move very quickly in and out of depressive or manic episodes. An individual with bipolar disorder who experiences at least four manic or depressive episodes within a year is considered to have a *rapid-cycling pattern,* which is apparently a severe variety of bipolar disorder that does not respond well to standard treatments (Bauer et al., 1994; Dunner & Fieve, 1974). In addition, traditional antidepressant medication such as tricyclics may actually *provoke* rapid cycling, making clinicians very wary of prescribing these drugs to this group of patients (Bauer et al., 1994; Goodman & Ghaemi, 1998; Wehr & Goodwin, 1979). There is some evidence that alternative drug treatment such as anticonvulsants may be more effective with this group of patients (Post et al., 1989).

Approximately 20% of bipolar patients experience rapid cycling. As many as 90% are female, a higher rate than in other variations of bipolar disorder (for example, Wehr, Sack, Rosenthal, & Cowdry, 1988). Unlike bipolar patients in general, most people with rapid cycling begin with a depressive episode rather than a manic episode (McElroy & Keck, 1993). In most cases, rapid cycling tends to increase in frequency over time and can reach very severe states in which patients cycle between mania and depression without any break whatsoever. Fortunately, rapid cycling does not seem to be permanent, since fewer than 3% of patients continue with rapid cycling across a 5-year period (Coryell, Endicott, & Keller, 1992).

3. *Seasonal pattern specifier.* This temporal specifier applies both to bipolar disorders and to recurrent major depressive disorder. It accompanies episodes that occur during certain seasons (for instance, winter depression). Some

Most seasonal affective disorders involve depression in winter, when the light is low and the days are short.

mood disorders do seem tied to seasons of the year. The most usual pattern is a depressive episode that begins in the late fall and ends with the beginning of spring; in both major depressive disorder, recurrent, and in bipolar disorder, individuals may become depressed during the winter and manic during the summer. This condition is called **seasonal affective disorder (SAD).**

Although some studies have reported seasonal cycling of manic episodes, the overwhelming majority of seasonal mood disorders involve winter depression, which has been estimated to affect as many as 5% of North Americans (Lewy, 1993). Unlike more severe melancholic types of depression, people with winter depressions tend toward excessive sleep (rather than decreased sleep) and increased appetite and weight gain (rather than decreased appetite and weight loss), symptoms shared with atypical depressive episodes. Although SAD seems a bit different from other major depressive episodes, family studies have not yet revealed any differential aggregation that would suggest winter depressions are really a separate type (Allen, Lam, Remick, & Sadovnick, 1993).

Emerging evidence suggests that SAD may be related to daily and seasonal changes in the production of melatonin, a hormone secreted by the pineal gland. Because exposure to light suppresses melatonin production, it is produced only at night. Melatonin production also tends to increase in winter, when there is less sunlight. One theory is that increased production of melatonin might trigger depression in vulnerable people (F. K. Goodwin & Jamison, 1990). (We will return to this topic when we discuss biological contributions to depression.)

As you might expect, the prevalence of SAD is higher in extreme northern and southern latitudes because there is less winter sunlight. Studies have indicated less than 2% prevalence of SAD in Florida in contrast to nearly 10% prevalence in New Hampshire (Terman, 1988). (These numbers include only those individuals meeting criteria for major depressive disorder.) Many more people are troubled by "winter blues," a few depressive symptoms that do not meet criteria for a disorder. A popular name for this type of reaction is *cabin fever.* Seasonal affective disorder is quite prevalent in Fairbanks, Alaska, where 9% of the population appears to meet criteria for the disorder and another 19% have some seasonal symptoms of depression. The disorder also seems quite stable. In one group of 59 patients, 86% experienced winter depression during a 9-year period of observation, with only 14% recovering during that time. For 26 (44%) of these patients, whose symptoms were more severe to begin with, depressive episodes began to occur during other seasons as well (Schwartz, Brown, Wehr, & Rosenthal, 1996). Rates in children and adolescents are between 1.7% and 5.5%, according to one study, with higher rates in post-pubertal girls (Swedo et al., 1995), but the study needs replication.

Some clinicians reasoned that exposure to bright light might slow melatonin production in individuals with SAD (Blehar & Rosenthal, 1989; Lewy, Kern, Rosenthal, & Wehr, 1982). In phototherapy, a current treatment, most patients are exposed to 2 hours of very bright light (2,500 lux) immediately on awakening. If the light exposure is effective, the patient begins to notice a lifting of mood within 3 to 4 days and a remission of winter depression in 1 to 2 weeks. Patients are also asked to avoid bright lights in the evening (from shopping malls and the like), so as not to interfere with the effects of the morning treatments. But this treatment is not without side effects. Approximately 19% of patients will experience headaches, 17% eyestrain, and 14% will just feel "wired" (Levitt et al., 1993). Because phototherapy is relatively new, its effectiveness is not yet clear. No controlled studies have been conducted, and the mechanism of action or cause has not been established (Yoon, 1996). It may be that factors other than changes in melatonin production are responsible for winter depression, or that increased melatonin is only one of many causal factors.

Prevalence of Mood Disorders

One major epidemiological study found about 7.8% of people in North America have had a mood disorder at some point in their lives, and 3.7% have experienced a disorder over the past year (Weissman et al., 1991). A more recent study suggests higher rates, with 19% of the population experiencing a mood disorder at some point in their lives (Kessler et al., 1994). As Bland (1997) and others point out, different research methods may account for the differing rates of prevalence. Wittchen, Knauper, and

table 7.1	**Prevalences of Affective Disorders Reported in Epidemiological Surveys Conducted Since 1980 Using RDC, DSM-III or III-R, or ICD–10 Criteria**

	Median % (range)	
Disorder	6 months to 1 year	Lifetime
Major depression	6.5 (2.6 to 9.8)	16.1 (4.4 to 18.0)
Dysthymia	3.3 (2.3 to 4.6)	3.6 (3.1 to 3.9)
Bipolar	1.1 (1.0 to 1.7)	1.3 (0.6 to 3.3)

Source: Adapted from Wittchen et al., 1994

Kessler (1994) compiled a summary of major studies, as shown in Table 7.1. Median prevalence rates at both 6 months to 1 year and at some point during their lives are shown for the principal disorders. At present this table represents the best estimate of the worldwide prevalence of mood disorders. The studies agree that women are twice as likely to have mood disorders as men. Table 7.2 breaks down lifetime prevalence by four principal mood disorders. Notice here that the imbalance in prevalence between males and females is accounted for solely by major depressive disorder and dysthymia, because the bipolar disorders are distributed approximately equally across gender. It is interesting that the prevalence of major depressive disorder and dysthymia is significantly lower among blacks than among whites and Hispanics (Kessler et al., 1994; Weissman et al., 1991), although, once again, no differences appear in bipolar disorders. One recent study of major depressive disorder in a community sample of African-

table 7.2	**Lifetime Prevalence of Mood Disorder Subtypes by Age, Sex, and Ethnicity**

	Lifetime Prevalence in %			
	Bipolar I	Bipolar II	*Major Depression*	Dysthymia
Total	0.8	0.5	4.9	3.2
Age				
18–29	1.1	0.7	5.0	3.0
30–44	1.4	0.6	7.5	3.8
45–64	0.3	0.2	4.0	3.6
65+	0.1	0.1	1.4	1.7
Sex				
Men	0.7	0.4	2.6	2.2
Women	0.9	0.5	7.0	4.1
Ethnicity				
White	0.8	0.4	5.1	3.3
Black	1.0	0.6	3.1	2.5
Hispanic	0.7	0.5	4.4	4.0

Note: Significant variation within groups, adjusted for age, sex, or ethnicity
Source: Adapted from Weissman et al., 1991

Americans found a prevalence of 3.1% during the previous year, with fair or poor health status being the major predictor of depression in this population. Few of these individuals received appropriate treatment, with only 11% coming in contact with a mental health professional (Brown, Ahmed, Gary, & Milburn, 1995). Considering the chronicity and seriousness of mood disorders (Klerman & Weissman, 1992), the prevalence is very high indeed, demonstrating a substantial impact not only on the affected individuals and their families but also on society.

■ concept check 7.2

Check your understanding of mood disorders and their components by matching the following scenarios with the correct disorder or term: (a) major depressive episode, (b) mania, (c) bipolar I disorder, (d) dysthymic disorder, and (e) double depression.

1. Feeling certain he would win the lottery, Charles went on an all-night shopping spree, maxing out all his credit cards without a worry. We know he's done this before several times. _____

2. Last week, Ryan went out with his friends, buying rounds of drinks, socializing until early morning, and feeling on top of the world. Today Ryan will not get out of bed to go to work, see his friends, or even turn on the lights. This seems to be a recurring pattern. _____

3. For the past few weeks, Jennifer has been sleeping a lot. She can't get up the energy to leave the house. She's also lost a lot of weight. _____

4. Heather has had some mood disorder problems in the past, although some days she's better than others. All of a sudden, though, she seems to have fallen into a rut. She can't make any decisions because she doesn't trust herself.

_____

5. Sanchez is always down and a bit blue, but recently he seems so depressed that nothing pleases him.

_____

In Children and Adolescents

You might assume that depression requires some experience with life, that an accumulation of negative events or disappointments might create pessimism, which then leads to depression. Like many reasonable assumptions in psychopathology, this one is not uniformly correct. We now have evidence that 3-month-old babies can become depressed! Infants of depressed mothers display marked depressive behaviors (sad faces, slow movement, lack of responsiveness), even when interacting with a nondepressed adult (Field et al., 1988). Whether this behavior or temperament is due to a genetic tendency inherited from the mother, the result of early interaction patterns with a depressed mother, or a combination is not yet clear.

Most investigators agree that mood disorders are fundamentally similar in children and in adults (Lewinsohn, Hops,

Roberts, Seeley, & Andrews, 1993; Pataki & Carlson, 1990). Therefore, there are no "childhood" mood disorders in DSM-IV that are specific to a developmental stage, unlike anxiety disorders. However, it also seems clear that the "look" of depression changes with age (see Table 7.3). For example, children under 3 years of age might manifest depression by their facial expressions as well as by their eating, sleeping, and play behavior, quite differently from children between the ages of 9 and 12. Data collected by Carlson and Kashani confirmed that depressed adolescents, when compared to adolescents with nondepressive disorders, are particularly vulnerable to low self-esteem and self-consciousness. Adolescents who are forced to limit their activities because of illness or injury are at high risk for depression (Lewinsohn, Gotlib, & Seeley, 1997).

Estimates on the prevalence of mood disorders in children and adolescents vary widely, although more sophisticated studies are beginning to appear. The general conclusion is that depressive disorders occur *less frequently* in children than in adults but rise dramatically in adolescence, when, if anything, depression is *more frequent* than in adults (Kashani, Hoeper, Beck, & Corcoran, 1987; Lewinsohn et al., 1993; Petersen, Compas, Brooks-Gunn, Stemmler, & Grant, 1993). Furthermore, there is some evidence that, in young children, dysthymia is more prevalent than major depressive disorder, but this ratio reverses in adolescence. Like adults, adolescents experience major depressive disorder more frequently than dysthymia (Kashani et al., 1983; Kashani et al., 1987). Major depressive disorder in adolescents is also a largely female disorder, as it is in adults, although interestingly, this is not true for more mild depression. Only among the adolescents referred to treatment does the gender imbalance exist (Compas et al., 1997), though why more girls reach a more severe state requiring referral to treatment is not clear.

Children below the age of 9 seem to present with more irritability and emotional swings rather than classic manic states, and also are often mistaken as being hyperactive. After age 9, children appear more typically manic (Carlson, 1990; Fristad, Weller, & Weller, 1992). Bipolar disorder seems to be particularly rare in childhood, although case studies of children as young as 4 years of age displaying bipolar symptoms have been reported (Poznanski, Israel, & Grossman, 1984). However, the prevalence of bipolar disorder rises substantially in adolescence, which is not surprising in that many adults with bipolar disorder report a first onset during the teen years (Keller & Wunder, 1990).

One developmental difference between children and adolescents on the one hand and adults on the other is that children, especially boys, tend to become aggressive and even destructive during depressive episodes. For this reason, childhood depression is sometimes misdiagnosed as hyperactivity or, more often, conduct disorder in which aggression and even destructive behavior are common. Often conduct disorder and depression co-occur (Lewinsohn et al., 1993; Petersen et al., 1993; Sanders, Dadds, Johnston, & Cash, 1992). Puig-Antich (1982) found that one-third of prepubertal depressed boys met full criteria for a conduct disorder, which developed at approximately the same time as the de-

table 7.3   Speculative Manifestations of Depressive Symptoms Through Childhood

Adult Symptom	Childhood Symptom				
	0–36 Months	3–5 Years	6–8 Years	9–12 Years	13–18 Years
Dysphoric mood	Sad or expressionless face, gaze aversion, staring, irritability	Sad expression, somberness or labile mood, irritability	Prolonged unhappiness, somberness, irritability	Sad expression, apathy, irritability	Sad expression, apathy, irritability, increasing complaints of depression
Loss of interest or pleasure	No social play	Decreased socialization	Decreased socialization	Adult presentation	Adult presentation
Appetite or weight change	Feeding problems	Feeding problems	Adult presentation	Adult presentation	Adult presentation
Insomnia or hypersomnia	Sleep problems	Sleep problems	Sleep problems	Adult presentation	Adult presentation
Psychomotor agitation	Tantrums, irritability	Irritability, tantrums	Irritability, tantrums	Aggressive behavior	Aggressive behavior
Psychomotor retardation	Lethargy	Lethargy	Lethargy	Lethargy	Adult presentation
Loss of energy	Lethargy	Lethargy	Lethargy	Lethargy	Adult presentation
Feelings of worthlessness		Low self-esteem	Low self-esteem	Guilt, low self-esteem	Guilt
Diminished concentration			Poor school performance	Poor school performance	Poor school performance
Recurrent thoughts of death or suicide		Accident proneness	Accident proneness, morbid outlook	Adult presentation	Adult presentation
Anxiety	Separation/ attachment problems	School phobia	Phobias, separation anxiety	Phobias, separation anxiety	Adult presentation
Somatic complaints		Present	Present	Present	Present

Source: Carlson & Kashani, 1988

pressive disorder and remitted with the resolution of the depression. Biederman and colleagues (1987) found that 32% of children with attention deficit disorder also met criteria for major depression. In any case, successful treatment of the underlying depression (or spontaneous recovery) also resolves the associated problems in these specific cases. Adolescents with bipolar disorder may also become aggressive, impulsive, sexually provocative, and accident prone (Carlson, 1990; Keller & Wunder, 1990; Reiss, 1985).

Whatever the presentation, mood disorders in children and adolescents are very serious because of their likely consequences. Rates of attempted suicide skyrocket during adolescence (Keller & Wunder, 1990; Pataki & Carlson, 1990; Petersen et al., 1993). Fleming, Boyle, and Offord (1993), in an important prospective study, followed 652 adolescents with either a major depressive disorder or a conduct disorder for 4 years. These adolescents, by and large, continued to suffer from serious psychopathology and markedly impaired functioning. Similar findings were reported by Garber, Weiss, and Shanley (1993).

In the Elderly

Only recently have we seriously considered the problem of depression in the elderly. Some studies estimate that 18% to 20% of nursing home residents may experience major depressive episodes (Katz, Leshen, Kleban, & Jethanandani, 1989; Rockwood, Stolee, & Brahim, 1991), which are likely to be chronic if they appear first after the age of 60 (Rapp, Parisi, & Wallace, 1991). Late-onset depressions are associated with marked sleep difficulties, hypochondriasis, and agitation. It can be difficult to diagnose depression in the elderly because the presentation of mood disorders is often complicated by the presence of medical illnesses or symptoms of dementia (for example, Blazer, 1989; Small, 1991). That is, elderly people who become physically ill or begin to show signs of dementia might become depressed about it, but the signs of depression would be attributed to the illness or dementia and thus missed. Nevertheless, the overall prevalence of major depressive disorder is the same or slightly lower in the elderly as in the general population (Kessler et al., 1994; Weissman et al., 1991), perhaps because stressful life events that trigger major depressive episodes decrease with age. But milder symptoms that do not meet criteria for major depressive disorder may be more common among the elderly (Ernst & Angst, 1995; Gotlib & Nolan, in press), perhaps due to illness and infirmity (Roberts, Kaplan, Shema, & Strawbridge, 1997).

Depression can also contribute to physical disease in the elderly. Researchers have found that increasing feelings of

Among adolescents, severe major depressive disorder occurs mostly in girls.

helplessness, particularly in nursing home residents, can lead to depression and early death (Grant, Patterson, & Yager, 1988; House, Landis, & Umberson, 1988). Similar findings suggest that elderly people who become ill and are also depressed stay in the hospital longer than those who are ill but not depressed (Agbayewa & Cossette, 1990; Schubert, Burns, Paras, & Sioson, 1992).

An even more tragic finding is that symptoms of depression are increasing substantially in our growing population of elderly people. Wallace and O'Hara (1992) in a longitudinal study found that elderly citizens became increasingly depressed over a 3-year period. They suggest, with some evidence, that this trend is related to increasing illness and reduced social support; in other words, as we become frailer and more alone, the psychological result is depression, which, of course, increases the probability that we will become even frailer and have even less social support. This vicious cycle is deadly.

The earlier gender imbalance in depression disappears after the age of 65. In early childhood, boys are more likely to be depressed than girls, but an overwhelming surge of depression in adolescent girls produces an imbalance in the sex ratio that is maintained until old age, when just as many women are depressed, but increasing numbers of men are also affected (Wallace & O'Hara, 1992). From the perspective of the life span, this is the first time since early childhood that the sex ratio for depression is balanced.

Across Cultures

We noted the strong tendency of anxiety to take very physical or somatic forms in some cultures; instead of talking about fear, panic, or general anxiety, many people describe stomachaches, chest pains or heart distress, and headaches. Much the same tendency exists across cultures for mood dis-

orders, which is not surprising given the close relationship of anxiety and depression. Feelings of weakness or tiredness particularly characterize depression that is accompanied by mental or physical slowing or retardation. Some cultures have their own idioms for depression; for instance, the Hopi say they are "heartbroken" (Manson & Good, 1993).

Although somatic symptoms that characterize mood disorders seem roughly equivalent across cultures, it is difficult to compare subjective feelings. The way people think of depression may be influenced by the cultural view of the individual and the role of the individual in society (J. H. Jenkins, Kleinman, & Good, 1990). For example, in societies that focus on the *individual* instead of the *group*, it is common to hear statements such as "I feel blue" or "I am depressed." However, in cultures where the individual is tightly integrated into the larger group, someone might say, "Our life has lost its meaning," referring to the group in which the individual resides (Manson & Good, 1993). Despite these influences, it is generally agreed that the best way to study the nature and prevalence of mood disorders (or any other psychological disorder) in other cultures is first to determine their prevalence using standardized criteria (Neighbors, Jackson, Campbell, & Williams, 1989). The DSM criteria are increasingly used, along with semistructured interviews in which the same questions are asked, with some allowances for different words that might be specific to one subculture or another.

Weissman and colleagues (1991) looked at the lifetime prevalence of mood disorders in African-American and Hispanic-American ethnic groups (see Table 7.2). For each disorder, the figures are similar (although, as noted above,

Depression among the elderly is a serious problem that can be difficult to diagnose because the symptoms are often similar to those of physical illness or dementia.

somewhat lower for blacks in major depressive disorder and dysthymia), indicating no particular difference across subcultures. However, these figures were collected on a carefully constructed sample meant to represent the whole country. In specific locations, results can differ dramatically. Kinzie, Leung, Boehnlein, and Matsunaga (1992) used a structured interview to determine the percentage of adult members of a Native American village who met criteria for mood disorders. The lifetime prevalence for any mood disorder was 19.4% in men, 36.7% in women, and 28% overall, approximately four times higher than in the general population. Examined by disorder, almost all the increase is accounted for by greatly elevated rates of major depression. Findings in the same village for substance abuse are very similar to the results for major depressive disorder (see Chapter 11). The appalling social and economic conditions on many reservations fulfill all the requirements for chronic major life stress, which is so strongly related to the onset of mood disorders, particularly major depressive disorder.

Among the Creative

Early in the history of the United States, Benjamin Rush, one of the signers of the U.S. Constitution and a founder of American psychiatry, observed something very curious: "From a part of the brain preternaturally elevated, but not diseased, the mind sometimes discovers not only unusual strengths and acuteness, but certain talents it never exhibited before. Talents for eloquence, poetry, music and painting, and uncommon ingenuity in several of the mechanical arts, are often evolved in this state of madness" (Rush, 1812, p. 153). This clinical observation has been made many times for thousands of years and applies not only to creativity but also to leadership.

Is there truth in the enduring belief that genius is allied to madness? Several researchers, including Kay Redfield Jamison and Nancy Andreasen, have attempted to find out. The results are surprising. Table 7.4 lists a group of famous American poets, many of whom won the coveted Pulitzer Prize. As

As her diaries and letters demonstrate vividly, novelist Virginia Woolf suffered from both mania and depression. She committed suicide by drowning.

you can see, all almost certainly had bipolar disorder. Many committed suicide. These 8 poets are among the 36 born in this century who are represented in *The New Oxford Book of American Verse*, a collection reserved for the most distinguished poets in the country. It is certainly striking that about 20% of these 36 poets exhibited bipolar disorders, given the population prevalence of slightly less than 1%; but F. K. Goodwin and Jamison (1990) think that 20% is probably a conservative estimate, because the 28 remaining poets have not been studied in sufficient detail to determine whether they also suffered from bipolar disorder. Andreasen (1987) reported results similar to those shown in Table 7.5 in a study of 30 other creative writers.

Many artists and writers, whether suspected of mood disorders or not, speak of periods of inspiration when thought processes quicken, moods lift, and new associations are generated (K. R. Jamison, 1989). Perhaps something inherent in manic states fosters creativity. On the other hand, it is possible that the genetic vulnerability to mood disorders is independently accompanied by a predisposition to creativity (Richards, Kenney, Lunde, Benet, & Merzel, 1988). In other words, the genetic patterns associated with bipolar disorder may also carry the spark of creativity. These ideas are little more than speculations at present but the study of creativity and leadership, which are so highly valued in all cultures, may well be enhanced by a deeper understanding of "madness" (F. K. Goodwin & Jamison, 1990; Prien et al., 1984).

table 7.4   Partial Listing of Major 20th-Century American Poets, Born Between 1895 and 1935, with Documented Histories of Manic-Depressive Illness

Poet	*Pulitzer Prize in Poetry*	*Treated for Major Depressive Illness*	*Treated for Mania*	*Committed Suicide*
Hart Crane (1899–1932)		X	X	X
Theodore Roethke (1908–1963)	X	X	X	
Delmore Schwartz (1913–1966)		X	X	
John Berryman (1914–1972)	X	X	X	X
Randall Jarrell (1914–1965)		X	X	X
Robert Lowell (1917–1977)	X	X	X	
Anne Sexton (1928–1974)	X	X	X	X
Sylvia Plath* (1932–1963)	X	X		X

*Plath, although not treated for mania, was probably bipolar II.
Source: F. K. Goodwin & Jamison, 1990

Anxiety and Depression

One of the mysteries faced by psychopathologists is the apparent overlap of anxiety and depression. Some of the latest theories on the causes of depression are based, in part, on this research. Several theorists have concluded that the two moods are more alike than different. This may seem strange, because you probably do not feel the same when you are anxious as when you are depressed. However, we now know that almost everyone who is depressed, particularly to the extent of having a disorder, is also anxious (Barlow, in press; Di Nardo & Barlow, 1990; Sanderson, Di Nardo, Rapee, & Barlow, 1990), but not everyone who is anxious is depressed.

Let's examine this fact for a moment: *Almost all depressed patients are anxious, but not all anxious patients are depressed.* This means that certain core symptoms of depression are *not* found in anxiety and, therefore, reflect what is "pure" about depression. These core symptoms are the inability to experience pleasure (*anhedonia*) and a depressive "slowing" of both motor and cognitive functions until they are extremely labored and effortful (Brown, Chorpita, & Barlow, 1998; L. A. Clark & Watson, 1991; Moras et al., 1996; Tellegen, 1985; Watson & Kendall, 1989). Cognitive content (what is thought about) is usually more negative in depressed individuals than in anxious ones (Greenberg & Beck, 1989).

Recently, ongoing research in our own setting has identified symptoms that seem central to panic and anxiety. In panic, the symptoms reflect primarily autonomic activation (excessive physiological symptoms such as heart palpitations and dizziness); muscle tension and apprehension (excessive worrying about the future) seem to reflect the essence of anxiety (Brown et al., 1997; Zinbarg & Barlow, 1996; Zinbarg et al., 1994). Many people with depression also have symptoms of anxiety or panic. More important, a large number of symptoms help define *both* anxiety and depressive disorders. Because these symptoms are *not specific* to either kind of disorder, they are called symptoms of *negative affect* (Brown et al., 1998; Tellegen, 1985). In Chapter 3, we talked about the process of creating a new diagnosis of mixed anxiety and depression. We noted that people who met criteria presented with symptoms of negative affect *without* any specific symptoms of anxiety or depression. Identifying pure anxious or depressive symptoms as well as symptoms of negative affect that are common to both mood states was an important step in creating this diagnosis (Brown et al., 1998; Moras et al., 1996; Zinbarg et al., 1994). Other researchers have reported finding similar shared and discrete symptoms (for instance, L. Clark & Watson, 1991). Symptoms specific to anxiety, specific to depression, and common to both states are presented in Table 7.5. Ultimately, research in this area may cause us to rethink our diagnostic criteria and combine anxiety and mood disorders into one larger category.

Now think back for a minute to the case of Katie. You remember that she was severely depressed and clearly had experienced a major depressive episode along with serious suicidal ideation. A review of the list of depressive symptoms shows that Katie had all of them, thus meeting the criteria for major depressive disorder outlined in DSM-IV. However, remember that Katie's difficulty began with her dread of interacting with her classmates or teachers for fear of making a fool of herself. Finally, she became so anxious that she stopped going to school. After seeing a doctor who recommended that she be "persuaded" to attend school, her parents became firmer. As Katie explained, however,

> I felt nauseated and sick each time that I went into the school building and so each day I was sent home. Uncomfortable physical experiences like sweaty palms, trembling, dizziness, and nausea accompanied my anxiety and fear. For me, being in a classroom, being in the school building, even the anticipation of being in school, triggered anxiety and illness. All of the sensations of anxiety draw your attention away from your surroundings and toward your own physical feelings. All of this would be bearable if it wasn't so extremely intense. I found myself battling the desire to escape and seek comfort. And, each escape brings with it a

table 7.5   Symptoms Specific to Anxiety and to Depression as Well as Symptoms That Are Shared by Both States

Pure Anxiety Symptoms
Apprehension
Tension
Edginess
Trembling
Excessive worry
Nightmares

Pure Depression Symptoms
Helplessness
Depressed mood
Loss of interest
Lack of pleasure
Suicidal ideation
Diminished libido

Mixed Anxiety and Depression Symptoms (Negative Affect)
Anticipating the worst
Worry
Poor concentration
Irritability
Hypervigilance
Unsatisfying sleep
Crying
Guilt
Fatigue
Poor memory
Middle/late insomnia
Sense of worthlessness
Hopelessness
Early insomnia

Source: Adapted from Zinbarg et al., 1994

sense of failure and guilt. I understood that my physical sensations were inappropriate for the situation but I couldn't control them. I blamed myself for my lack of control.

Katie's case is rather typical in that severe anxiety eventually turned into depression. She never really lost the anxiety; she just became depressed, too. More recent epidemiological studies have confirmed that major depression almost always follows anxiety and may be a consequence of it (Breslaw, Schultz, & Peterson, 1995; Kessler et al., 1996). The finding that depression often follows anxiety leads us to the causes of depression and other mood disorders.

 # Causes

In Chapter 2 we described equifinality as the same end product resulting from possibly different causes. Just as there may be many reasons for a fever, there may also be a number of reasons for depression. For example, a depressive disorder that arises in winter has a different precipitant than a severe depression following a death, even though the episodes might look quite similar. Nevertheless, psychopathologists are identifying biological, psychological, and social factors that seem strongly implicated in the etiology of mood disorders, whatever the precipitating factor. An integrative theory of the etiology of mood disorders considers the interaction of biological, psychological, and social dimensions and also notes the very strong relationship of anxiety and depression. Before describing this, we will review evidence pertaining to each contributing factor.

Biological Dimensions

FAMILIAL AND GENETIC INFLUENCES

Studies that would allow us to determine the genetic contribution to a particular disorder or class of disorders would be very difficult to do. Three types of strategies can help us estimate this contribution, however. In *family studies,* we look at the prevalence of a given disorder in the first-degree relatives of an individual known to have the disorder (the *proband*). We have found that, despite wide variability, the rate in relatives of probands with mood disorders is consistently about two to three times greater than in relatives of controls who don't have mood disorders (Gershon, 1990). Interestingly, the most frequent mood disorder in the relatives of bipolar patients is not bipolar disorder but unipolar depression (e.g., Coryell et al., 1984; Rice et al., 1987; Tsuang et al., 1985). In other words, having bipolar disorder is associated with a *general* risk of having another mood disorder but not with a *specific* risk for bipolar disorder. For patients with unipolar depression, by contrast, there is little or no chance that their relatives have bipolar disorder to a greater degree than the normal population (e.g., Weissman

et al., 1984). One possibility is that there may not be a *specific or separate* genetic contribution to bipolar disorder; bipolar disorder may simply be a *more severe* manifestation of the underlying genetic vulnerability. This manifestation would be determined by other psychosocial or pathophysiological factors that would occur in addition to the genetic vulnerability, but this connection is not yet certain and investigators do not agree on whether unipolar and bipolar disorders are two disorders or one disorder on a continuum of severity (Blehar, Weissman, Gershon, & Hirschfeld, 1988).

The difficulty with family studies, of course, is that we cannot separate from true genetic contributions the effects of a common psychosocial environment. This problem is solved with a second strategy, *adoption studies,* in which we look at the biological relatives of an individual with a given disorder who was adopted at an early age. If a genetic contribution exists, the adopted probands with the disorder should have more biological relatives *with* the same disorder than the adopted probands *without* the disorder. Unfortunately, the data here are mixed. For example, some studies report a greater risk of mood disorder among the biological relatives of adoptees with a mood disorder (Mendlewicz & Rainer, 1977; Wender et al., 1986). In another study, no greater risk of having a mood disorder was found in the biological relatives of the adopted probands (Von Knorring, Cloninger, Bohman, & Sigvardsson, 1983).

The best evidence that genes have something to do with mood disorders comes from *twin studies,* in which we examine the frequency with which identical twins (with identical genes) have the disorder, compared to fraternal twins who share only 50% of their genes (as do all first-degree relatives). If a genetic contribution exists, the disorder should be present in identical twins to a much greater extent than in fraternal twins. One fascinating study with enough twins to draw reasonable conclusions has been conducted. Figure 7.3 presents the results (Bertelsen, Harvald, & Hauge, 1977). As you can see, if one twin presents with a mood disorder, an identical twin is approximately three times more likely than a fraternal twin to have a mood disorder. The probability is particularly high for bipolar disorder. When one twin had a bipolar I disorder, 80% of the identical twins also had some mood disorder (although not necessarily bipolar disorder). These results are similar to those found in earlier twin studies (Nurnberger & Gershon, 1992), but later twin studies show a somewhat weaker rate of concordance (for instance, McGuffin & Katz, 1989; Kendler, Neale, Kessler, Heath, & Eaves, 1993). Severity is also related to amount of concordance (the degree to which something is shared). For example, if one twin had severe depression (defined as three or more major depressive episodes), then 59% of the identical twins and 30% of the fraternal twins also presented with a mood disorder. If the individual presented with fewer than three episodes, the concordance rate dropped to 33% in identical twins and 14% in fraternal twins. This means that severe mood disorders may have a stronger genetic contribution than less severe disorders, a finding that holds true for most psychological disorders.

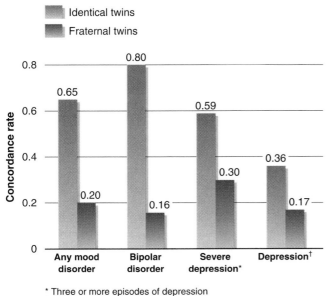

* Three or more episodes of depression
† Fewer than three episodes of depression

figure 7.3 Mood disorders among twins (adapted from Bertelsen, Harvald, & Hauge, 1977). Graphically depicted data were derived from evaluation of 110 pairs of twins. Identical twins shared mood disorders, especially bipolar disorder, more frequently than fraternal twins.

More recently, Kendler et al. (1993) estimates heritability of major depressive disorders in a large number of female twins to be from 41% to 46%, well within the range reported in Figure 7.3. Even in older adults, estimates of heritability remain in the moderate range of approximately 35% (McGue & Christensen, 1997). Note that bipolar disorder confers an increased risk of developing *some* mood disorder but not necessarily bipolar disorder. This conclusion supports findings noted previously that bipolar disorder may simply be a more severe variant of mood disorders rather than a fundamentally different disorder. Then again, of identical twins concordant for a mood disorder, 80% are also concordant for polarity. In other words, if one identical twin is unipolar, there is an 80% chance that the other twin is unipolar. This finding suggests that these disorders may be inherited separately and therefore be separate disorders after all (Nurnberger & Gershon, 1992). In any case, results from a number of other studies (Gershon, 1990) suggest that the Bertelsen and colleagues (1977) study overestimates the genetic contribution for bipolar disorder somewhat, probably because the diagnostic procedures used to define the patients or identify the mood disorder may have varied. Nevertheless, it strongly reinforces the idea of a genetic vulnerability to mood disorders.

Although these findings do raise continuing questions about the relative contributions of psychosocial and genetic factors to mood disorders, overwhelming evidence suggests that such disorders are familial and almost certainly reflect an underlying genetic vulnerability. However, as with other psychological disorders, it seems unlikely that we will find any single dominant gene that is responsible (Nurnberger &

Gershon, 1992), although occasional reports appear to the contrary. Think back to the section on genetic linkage analysis in Chapter 3. We noted the attention given several years ago to a study of Amish families in Pennsylvania who are very homogeneous genetically (Egeland et al., 1987). The findings from this study pointed to a specific location on chromosome 11 that might be the site of a single gene associated with bipolar disorder. However, a reanalysis of the data several years later (Kelsoe et al., 1989) revealed that the results did not support the original findings. Later studies have failed to find a specific gene associated with bipolar disorder (Kelsoe 1997; U.S. Congress, 1992), although occasional promising reports appear (Belliver et al., 1998). Thus, as with most psychological disorders, any genetic contribution appears to be the result of many genes, each adding to the cumulative effect.

JOINT HERITABILITY OF ANXIETY AND DEPRESSION

Although most studies have looked at specific disorders in isolation, a growing trend is to examine the heritability of related groups of disorders. Evidence supports the supposition of a close relationship among depression, anxiety, and panic. For example, data from family studies indicate that the more signs and symptoms of anxiety and depression there are in a given patient, the greater the rate of anxiety or depression or both in first-degree relatives and children (Hammen, Burge, Burney, & Adrian, 1990; Kovacs et al., 1989; Leckman, Weissman, Merikangas, Pauls, & Prusoff, 1983; Puig-Antich & Rabinovich, 1986; Weissman, 1985). In several important reports from a major set of data on over 2,000 female twins, Ken Kendler and his colleagues (Kendler, Heath, Martin, & Eaves, 1987; Kendler, Neale, Kessler, Heath, & Eaves, 1992b; Kendler et al., 1995) also found that the same genetic factors contribute to both anxiety and depression. Social and psychological explanations seemed to account for the factors that differentiate anxiety from depression. These findings suggest, once again, that the biological vulnerability for mood disorders may not be specific to that disorder but may reflect a more general predisposition to anxiety or mood disorders. The specific form of the disorder would be determined by psychological, social, or additional biological factors (Akiskal, 1997; Weissman, 1985).

NEUROTRANSMITTER SYSTEMS

Mood disorders have been the subject of more intense neurobiological study than almost any other area of psychopathology, with the possible exception of schizophrenia. New and exciting findings describing the relationship of specific neurotransmitters to mood disorders appear almost monthly and are punctuated by occasional reported "breakthroughs." In this difficult area, most breakthroughs prove to be illusory, but false starts provide us with an ever-deeper understanding of the enormous complexity of the neurobiological underpinnings of mood disorders (Green, Mooney, Posener, & Schildkraut, 1995).

In Chapter 2, we observed that we now know that neurotransmitter systems have many subtypes and interact in many complex ways, with each other and with neuro-modulators (products of the endocrine system). Research implicates low levels of serotonin in the etiology of mood disorders but only in relation to other neurotransmitters, including norepinephrine and dopamine (e.g., F. K. Goodwin & Jamison, 1990; Spoont, 1992). Remember that the apparent primary function of serotonin is to regulate our emotional reactions. For example, we are more impulsive, and our moods swing more widely, when our levels of serotonin are low. This may be because one of the functions of serotonin is to regulate systems involving norepinephrine and dopamine (Mandell & Knapp, 1979). According to the "permissive" hypothesis, when serotonin levels are low, other neurotransmitters are permitted to range more widely, become dysregulated, and contribute to mood irregularities, including depression. More recently, Mann et al. (1996) used sophisticated brain imaging procedures (PET scans) to confirm impaired serotonergic transmission in patients with depression. This theory is undoubtedly overly simplistic, but it does represent current strategies in the study of neurotransmitters and psychopathology. Current thinking is that the balance of the various neurotransmitters and their subtypes is more important than the absolute level of any one neurotransmitter.

In the context of this delicate balance, there is continued interest in the role of dopamine, particularly in relationship to manic episodes (Depue & Iacono, 1989). For example, the dopamine agonist L-dopa seems to produce hypomania in bipolar patients (for instance, Van Praag & Korf, 1975), along with other dopamine agonists (Silverstone, 1985). But, as with other research in this area, it is quite difficult to pin down any relationships with certainty.

THE ENDOCRINE SYSTEM

Investigators became interested in the endocrine system when they noticed that patients with diseases affecting this system sometimes became depressed. For example, hypothyroidism, or Cushing's disease, which affects the adrenal cortex, leads to excessive secretion of cortisol and, often, to depression.

In Chapter 2, we discussed the brain circuit called the HYPAC, beginning in the hypothalamus and running through the pituitary gland, which coordinates the endocrine system. One of the glands influenced by the pituitary is the cortical section of the adrenal gland, which produces the stress hormone cortisol that completes the HYPAC axis. Cortisol is called a *stress hormone* because it is elevated during stressful life events. (We will discuss this system in more detail in Chapter 9.) For now, it is enough to know that cortisol levels are elevated in depressed patients, a finding that makes sense considering the relationship between depression and severe life stress (Gibbons, 1964; Gold, Goodwin, & Chrousos, 1988; Ladd, Owens, & Nemeroff, 1996; Weller & Weller, 1988). This connection led to the development of what was thought to be a biological test for depression, the *dexamethasone suppression test* (DST). Dexamethasone is a glucocorticoid that suppresses cortisol secretion in normal subjects. However, when this substance was given to patients

who were depressed, much *less* suppression was noticed, and what did occur didn't last very long (Carroll, Martin, & Davies, 1968; Carroll et al., 1980). Approximately 50% of patients show this reduced suppression, particularly if their depression is severe (Rush et al., 1997). The thinking was that in depressed patients, the adrenal cortex secreted enough cortisol to overwhelm the suppressive effects of dexamethasone. This theory was heralded as very important, because it promised the first biological laboratory test for a psychological disorder. However, later research demonstrated that individuals with other disorders, particularly anxiety disorders, also demonstrate nonsuppression (Feinberg & Carroll, 1984; F. K. Goodwin & Jamison, 1990), which cast doubt on the usefulness of a test to diagnose depression. Thus, as with early theories about single neurotransmitters, our understanding of the role of cortisol in producing depression has proven overly simplistic.

Researchers nevertheless remain very interested in the relationship of cortisol to depression, and recent research has taken some exciting new turns. Investigators have discovered that neurotransmitter activity in the hypothalamus regulates the release of hormones that affect the HYPAC axis. **Neurohormones** are an increasingly important focus of study in psychopathology (e.g., Ladd, Owens, & Nemeroff, 1996). There are literally thousands of neurohormones. Sorting out their relationship to antecedent neurotransmitter systems (as well as determining their independent effects on the central nervous system) is likely to be a very complex task indeed.

SLEEP AND CIRCADIAN RHYTHMS

On page 193, we discussed the interesting new findings on seasonal affective disorder (SAD), noting that a characteristic symptom is an *increase* in sleeping. We have known for several years that sleep disturbances are a hallmark of most mood disorders. Most important, in people who are depressed there is a significantly shorter period of time after falling asleep before rapid eye movement (REM) sleep begins. As you may remember from your introductory psychology or biology course, there are two major stages of sleep: REM sleep and non-REM sleep (see also Chapter 8). When we first fall asleep we go through several substages of progressively deeper sleep during which we achieve most of our rest. After about 90 minutes, we begin to experience REM sleep, when the brain arouses, and we begin to dream. Our eyes move rapidly back and forth under our eyelids, hence the name "rapid eye movement" sleep. As the night goes on, we have increasing amounts of REM sleep. Depressed individuals have diminished slow wave sleep, which is the deepest, most restful part of sleep (Kupfer, 1995). (We will discuss the process of sleep in more detail in Chapter 8.) In addition to entering REM sleep *much more quickly*, depressed patients experience REM activity that is much more intense, and the stages of deepest sleep don't occur until later and sometimes not at all. It seems that some sleep characteristics occur only *while* we are depressed and not at other times (A. J. Rush et al., 1986), although more recent evidence suggests that disturbances in sleep continuity as well as reduction of deep sleep may be more trait-like in that they are present even when the individual is not depressed (Kupfer, 1995). It is not yet clear whether sleep disturbances also characterize bipolar patients (F. K. Goodwin & Jamison, 1990), although preliminary evidence suggests patterns of *increased* rather than *decreased* sleep (Kupfer, 1995).

David Kupfer and his colleagues discovered sleep abnormalities in depressed individuals that may help us understand the biological causes of mood disorders.

Another interesting finding is that *depriving* depressed patients of sleep, particularly during the second half of the night, causes temporary improvement in their condition (Wehr & Sack, 1988), although the depression returns when the patients start sleeping normally again. In any case, because sleep patterns reflect a biological rhythm, there may be a relationship between seasonal affective disorder, sleep disturbances in depressed patients, and a more *general* disturbance in biological rhythms.

An additional interesting finding is that patients with bipolar disorder and their children (who are at risk for the disorder) show increased sensitivity to *light* (for instance, Nurnberger et al., 1988); that is, they show greater suppression of melatonin when they are exposed to light at night. There is also evidence that extended bouts of insomnia trigger manic episodes (Wehr, Goodwin, Wirz-Justice, Breitmeier, & Craig, 1982). These findings and others suggest that mood disorders may be related to disruptions in our circadian (daily) rhythms. For example, sleep deprivation may temporarily readjust the biological rhythms of depressed patients. Light therapy for seasonal affective disorder may have a similar effect. F. K. Goodwin and Jamison (1990) suggest that the specific genetic vulnerability to mood disorders may well be related to low levels of serotonin, which somehow affect the regulation of our daily biological rhythms (Kupfer, 1995). Of course, many of the results cited here are very preliminary and this theory, although fascinating, is still only speculative.

Important research will look at the interaction of psychosocial factors and potentially important biological markers such as sleep characteristics. Monroe, Thase, and Simons (1992) reported that people with major depressive disorder who had experienced a major life stress just before their episode did *not* evidence reduced latency to REM sleep, but those *without* a precipitating life stress *did* have reduced REM latency values. Thase, Simons, and Reynolds (1996) report that abnormal sleep profiles predict a somewhat poorer response to psychosocial treatment. This type of research prefaces more integrated strategies to come.

A new and promising area of investigation focuses on characteristics of brain waves in depressed individuals.

Measuring electrical activity in the brain with electroencephalogram (EEG) was described in Chapter 3, where we also described a type of brain wave activity, alpha waves, that indicate calm, positive feelings. Davidson (1993) noted differential alpha activity in the two hemispheres of the brain in depressed individuals. Davidson and his colleagues demonstrated that depressed individuals exhibit greater right-side anterior activation of their cerebral hemispheres (and less left-side activation) than nondepressed individuals. Furthermore, right-sided anterior activation is also found in patients who are no longer depressed (Gotlieb, Ranginath, & Rosenfeld, in press), suggesting that this brain function might represent a vulnerability to depression. If these findings are confirmed (Gotlib & Abramson, in press), this type of brain functioning could become an indicator of a biological vulnerability to depression.

Psychological Dimensions

STRESSFUL LIFE EVENTS

Stress and trauma are among the most striking contributions to the etiology of psychological disorders. This is reflected throughout psychopathology and is evident in the wide adoption of the diathesis–stress model of psychopathology described in Chapter 2 (and referred to throughout this book), which describes possible genetic and psychological vulnerabilities. But in seeking what activates this vulnerability (diathesis), we usually look for a stressful or traumatic life event. It should be sufficient to ask people whether anything major had happened in their lives before they developed depression or some other psychological disorder. Most people do report losing a job, getting divorced, having a child, or graduating from school and starting a career. But, as with most issues in the study of psychopathology, the significance of a major event is not easily discovered (Kessler, 1997), so most investigators have stopped simply asking patients whether something bad (or good) happened and have begun to look at the *context* of the event as well as the *meaning* it has for the individual.

For example, losing a job is stressful for most people, but it is far more difficult for some than others. A few people might even see it as a blessing. If you were laid off as a manager in a large corporation due to a restructuring, but your wife is the president of another corporation and makes more than enough money to support the family, it might not be so bad. Furthermore, if you are an aspiring writer or artist who has not had time to pursue your art, becoming jobless might be the opportunity you have been waiting for, particularly if your wife has been telling you for years to devote yourself to your creative pursuits.

Now consider losing your job if you are a single mother of two young children living from day to day and, on account of a recent doctor's bill, you have to choose between paying the electric bill or buying food. The stressful life event is the same, but the context is very different and

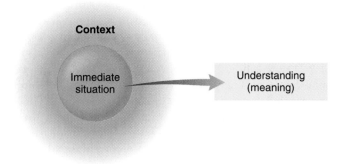

figure 7.4   Context and meaning in life stress situations (from Brown, 1989)

transforms the significance of the event substantially. To complicate the scenario further, think for a minute about how such a woman might react to losing her job. One woman might well decide that she is a total failure and thus becomes unable to carry on and provide for her children. Another woman might realize that the job loss was not her fault at all and take advantage of a job training program while scraping by somehow. Thus, both the *context* of the life event and its *meaning* are important. This approach to studying life events, developed by George W. Brown (1989) and associates in England, is represented in Figure 7.4.

Brown's considerable advance in studying life events is difficult to carry out and the methodology is still evolving. American psychologists such as Scott Monroe (Monroe & Roberts, 1990) and others (Dohrenwend & Dohrenwend, 1981; Shrout et al., 1989) are actively developing new methods. One crucial issue is the bias inherent in remembering events. If you ask people who are currently depressed what happened when they first became depressed more than 5 years ago, you will probably get different answers from those they would give if they were *not* currently depressed. Because current moods distort memories, many investigators have concluded that the only useful way to study stressful life events is to follow people *prospectively*, to determine more accurately the precise nature of events and their relation to subsequent psychopathology.

In any case, in summarizing a large amount of research it is clear that stressful life events are strongly related to the onset of mood disorders (Kessler, 1997). Measuring the *context* of events and their impact in a random sample of the population, a number of studies have found a marked relationship between severe and, in some cases, traumatic life events and the onset of depression (Brown, 1989; Brown, Harris, & Hepworth, 1994). Severe events precede *all* types of depression except, perhaps, for a small group of patients with melancholic or psychotic features who are experiencing subsequent episodes (Brown et al., 1994). In addition, for people with recurrent depression, the clear occurrence of a severe life stress before or early in the latest episode predicts a much poorer response to treatment and a longer time before remission (Monroe, Kupfer, & Frank, 1992), as well as a greater likelihood of recurrence

(Monroe, Roberts, Kupfer, & Frank, 1996). Again, the context and meaning are probably more important than the exact nature of the event itself.

Similar findings confirm the relationship of stressful events to the onset of episodes in bipolar disorder (Ellicott, 1988; F. K. Goodwin & Jamison, 1990; Johnson & Robert, 1995). However, several issues may be particularly relevant to the etiology of bipolar disorders (Goodwin & Ghaemi, 1958). First, stressful life events seem to trigger early mania and depression, but as the disorder progresses these episodes seem to develop a life of their own. In other words, once the cycle begins a psychological or pathophysiological process takes over and ensures that the disorder will continue (for example, Post, 1992; Post et al., 1989). Second, some of the precipitants of manic episodes seem related to loss of sleep, as in the postpartum period (F. K. Goodwin & Jamison, 1990) or as a result of jet lag, that is, disturbed circadian rhythms. In most cases of bipolar disorder, nevertheless, stressful life events are substantially indicated not only in provoking relapse, but also in preventing recovery (Johnson & Miller, 1997).

Finally, although almost everyone who becomes depressed has experienced a significant stressful event, most people who experience such events do not become depressed. Although the data are not yet as precise as we would like, somewhere between 20% and 50% of individuals who experience severe events become depressed. Thus, between 50% and 80% of individuals do *not* develop depression or, presumably, any other psychological disorder. Once again, data strongly support the *interaction* of stressful life events with some kind of vulnerability, either genetic, psychological, or, more likely, a combination of the two influences.

Given a genetic vulnerability (diathesis) and a severe life event (stress), what happens then? Research has isolated a number of psychological and biological processes. To illustrate one, let's return to Katie. Her life event was attending a new school.

Katie
No Easy Transitions

I was a serious and sensitive 11-year-old at the edge of puberty and at the edge of an adventure that many teens and preteens embark on—the transition from elementary to junior high school. A new school, new people, new responsibilities, new pressures. Academically, I was a good student up to this point but I didn't feel good about myself and generally lacked self-confidence.

Katie began to experience severe anxiety reactions. Then she became quite ill with the flu. After recovering and attempting to return to school, Katie discovered that her anxieties were worse than ever. More important, she began to feel she was losing control.

As I look back I can identify events that precipitated my anxieties and fears, but then everything seemed to happen suddenly and without cause. I was reacting emotionally and physically in a way that I didn't understand.

> I felt out of control of my emotions and body. Day after day I wished, as a child does, that whatever was happening to me would magically end. I wished that I would awake one day to find that I was the person I was several months before.

Katie's feeling of loss of control leads to another important psychological factor in depression: learned helplessness.

LEARNED HELPLESSNESS

To review our discussion in Chapter 2, Martin E. P. Seligman discovered that dogs and rats have a very interesting emotional reaction to events over which they have no control. If rats receive occasional shocks, they can function reasonably well, if they can cope with the shocks by doing something to avoid them, such as pressing a lever. But if they learn that nothing they do helps them to avoid the shocks, they eventually become very helpless, give up, and manifest an animal equivalent of depression (Seligman, 1975).

Do humans react the same way? Seligman suggests that we seem to, but only under one important condition: People become anxious and depressed when they make an *attribution* that they have no control over the stress in their lives (Abramson, Seligman, & Teasdale, 1978; I. Miller & Norman, 1979). These findings evolved into an important model called the **learned helplessness theory of depression.** Often overlooked is Seligman's point that anxiety is the first response to a stressful situation. Depression may follow marked hopelessness about coping with the difficult life events (Barlow, 1988; Mineka & Kelly, 1989). The depressive attributional style is (a) *internal,* in that the individual attributes negative events to personal failings ("it is all my fault"); (b) *stable,* in that, even after a particular negative event passes, the attribution that "additional bad things will always be my fault" remains; and (c) *global* in that the attributions extend across a wide variety of issues. Research continues on this interesting concept, but you can see how it applies to Katie. Early in her difficulties with attending school, she began to believe that events were totally out of her control and that she was unable even to begin to cope. More important, in her eyes the bad situation was all her fault: "I blamed myself for my lack of control." A downward spiral into a major depressive episode followed.

But a major question remains: Is learned helplessness a *cause* of depression or a correlated side effect of becoming depressed? If it were a *cause,* learned helplessness would have to exist *before* the depressive episode. Results from a 5-year longitudinal study in children may shed some light on this issue. Nolen-Hoeksema, Girgus, and Seligman (1992) reported that negative attributional style did not predict later symptoms of depression in *young* children; rather, stressful life events seemed to be the major precipitant of symptoms. However, as they *grew older,* they tended to develop more negative cognitive styles which *did* tend to predict symptoms of depression in reaction to additional negative events. Nolen-Hoeksema and colleagues speculate that meaningful negative events early in childhood may give rise to negative attributional styles in a developmental fashion, making these children more vulnerable to future depressive episodes when stressful events occur.

This thinking recalls the types of psychological vulnerabilities theorized to contribute to the development of anxiety disorders (Barlow, 1988). That is, in a person who has a nonspecific genetic vulnerability to either anxiety or depression, stressful life events activate a psychological sense that life events are uncontrollable (Barlow, in press; Barlow, Chorpita, & Turovsky, 1996). There is evidence that negative attributional styles are not specific to depression but characterize anxiety patients as well (Heimberg, Klosko, Dodge, & Shadick, 1989). This may indicate that cognitive vulnerability is no more specific for mood disorders than genetic vulnerability. Abramson, Metalsky, and Alloy (1989) revised the learned helplessness theory to deemphasize specific attributions and highlight the development of a *sense of hopelessness* as a crucial cause of many forms of depression. Attributions are important only to the extent that they contribute to a sense of hopelessness. This fits well with recent thinking on crucial differences between anxiety and depression. Both anxious and depressed individuals feel helpless and believe they lack control, but only in depression do they give up and become hopeless about ever regaining control (Alloy, Kelly, Mineka, & Clements, 1990; Barlow, 1991; Barlow et al., 1996).

There is some evidence that a pessimistic style of attributing negative events to one's own character flaws results in hopelessness (Abramson, Alloy, & Metalsky, 1995; Gotlib & Abramson, in press). This style may predate and there-

According to the learned helplessness theory of depression, people become depressed when they believe they have no control over the stress in their lives.

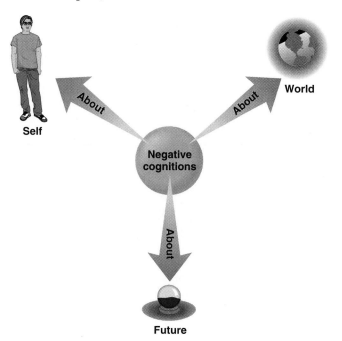

figure 7.5   Beck's cognitive triad for depression

fore, in a sense, contribute to anxious or depressive episodes that follow negative or stressful events (Gotlib & Abramson, in press).

In 1967 Aaron T. Beck (1967, 1976) suggested that depression may result from a tendency to interpret everyday events in a negative way, wearing gray instead of rose-colored glasses. According to Beck, people with depression make the worst of everything; for them, the smallest setbacks are major catastrophes. In his extensive clinical work, Beck observed that all of his depressed patients thought this way, and he began classifying the types of "cognitive errors" that characterized this style. From the long list he compiled, two representative examples are *arbitrary inference* and *overgeneralization.* Arbitrary inference is evident when a depressed individual emphasizes the negative rather than the positive aspects of a situation. A high school teacher may assume he is a terrible instructor because two students in his class fell asleep. He fails to consider other reasons they might be sleeping (up all night partying) and "infers" that his teaching style is at fault. As an example of overgeneralization, when your professor makes one critical remark on your paper you then assume that you will fail the class despite a long string of very positive comments and good grades on other papers. You are overgeneralizing from one small remark. According to Beck, people who are depressed think like this all the time. They make cognitive errors in thinking negatively about *themselves,* their *immediate world,* and their *future,* three areas that together are called the **(depressive) cognitive triad** (see Figure 7.5).

In addition, Beck theorized, after a series of negative events in childhood, individuals may develop a deep-seated *negative schema,* an enduring negative cognitive belief system about some aspect of life (A. T. Beck, Epstein, & Harrison, 1983; Gotlib, 1997; Gotlib & Krasnoperova, in press;

Gotlib & MacLeod, 1997). In a "self-blame" schema, individuals feel personally responsible for every bad thing that happens. With a negative self-evaluation schema, they believe they can never do anything correctly. In Beck's view, these cognitive errors and schemas are automatic; that is, not necessarily conscious. Indeed, an individual might not even be aware of thinking negatively and illogically. Thus, very minor negative events can lead to a major depressive episode.

A variety of evidence supports a cognitive theory of emotional disorders in general and depression in particular. The thinking of depressed individuals is consistently more negative than that of nondepressed individuals (Gotlib, 1997; Hollon, Kendall, & Lumry, 1986), in each dimension of the cognitive triad—the self, the world, and the future (for example, Bradley & Mathews, 1988; Segal, Hood, Shaw, & Higgins, 1988). Depressive cognitions seem to emerge from distorted and probably automatic methods of processing information. People are more likely to recall negative events when they are depressed than when they are not depressed or than nondepressed individuals (Gotlib, Roberts, & Gilboa, 1996; Lewinsohn & Rosenbaum, 1987).

The implications of this theory are very important. By recognizing cognitive errors and the underlying schemas, we can correct them and alleviate depression and related emotional disorders. In developing ways to do this, Beck became the father of cognitive therapy, one of the most important approaches in some time (see pp. 213–215).

Seligman and Abramson on the one hand, and Beck on the other, developed their theories independently, and there is good evidence that their models are independent, in that some people may have a negative outlook (dysfunctional attitudes) while others may explain things negatively (hopeless attributes) (Joiner & Rudd, 1996; Spangler, Simons, Monroe, & Thase, 1997). Nevertheless, the basic premises overlap a great deal and there is considerable evidence that depression is always associated with pessimistic explanatory style and negative cognitions. Evidence also exists that cognitive vulnerabilities predispose some people to view events in a very negative way, putting them at risk for depression. The most exciting evidence supporting this new conclusion comes from the ongoing Temple-Wisconsin study of cognitive vulnerability to depression (CVD) conducted by Lauren Alloy and Lyn Abramson. University freshmen who were not depressed at the time of the initial assessment were assessed every several months for up to 5 years to determine if they experienced any stressful life events or diagnosable episodes of depression or other psychopathology. Importantly, at the first assessment the investigators determined if the students were cognitively vulnerable to developing depression or not on the basis of their scores on questionnaires that measure dysfunctional attitudes and hopelessness attributions. Preliminary results from the first 2.5 years of follow-up suggest that negative cognitive styles do, in fact, indicate a vulnerability to later depression. Even if participants had never suffered from depression before in their lives, high-risk participants (who scored high on the measures of cognitive vulnerability) were far more likely than low-risk participants to experience a major depressive episode or at least depressive symptoms. Seventeen percent of the high-risk subjects versus only 1% of the low-risk subjects experienced major depressive episodes and 39% vs. 6% experienced minor depressive symptoms (Gotlib & Abramson, in press). Although we must await the final results of this study, preliminary data are very suggestive that cognitive vulnerabilities to developing depression do exist and, when combined with biological vulnerabilities, create a slippery path to depression.

Social and Cultural Dimensions

MARITAL RELATIONS

Marital dissatisfaction and depression are strongly related. Findings from a number of studies indicate that marital disruption often precedes depression. Bruce and Kim (1992) collected data on 695 women and 530 men and then reinterviewed them up to 1 year later. During this period a number of participants separated from or divorced their spouses, though the majority reported stable marriages. Approximately 21% of the women who reported a marital split during the study experienced severe depression, a rate three times higher than that for women who remained married. Nearly 17% of the men who reported a marital split developed severe depression, a rate *nine* times higher than that for men who remained married. However, when the researchers considered only those participants with no history of severe depression, 14% of the men who separated or divorced during the period experienced severe depression, as did approximately 5% of the women. In other words, *only the men* faced a heightened risk of developing a mood disorder for the first time immediately following a marital split. Is remaining married more important to men than to women? It would seem so.

Monroe, Bromet, Connell, and Steiner (1986), as well as O'Hara (1986), also implicated factors in the marital relationship as predicting the later onset of depression. Important findings from the Monroe group's (1986) study emphasize the necessity of separating *marital conflict* from *marital support*. In other words, it is possible that high marital conflict and strong marital social support may both be present the same time or may both be absent. High conflict, low support, or both, are particularly important in generating depression (Barnett & Gotlib, 1988; Gotlib & Beach, 1995).

Another finding with considerable support is that depression, particularly if it continues, may lead to substantial deterioration in marital relationships (Beach, Sandeen, & O'Leary, 1990; Coyne, 1976; Gotlib & Beach, 1995; Hokanson, Rubert, Welker, Hollander, & Hedeen, 1989; Paykel & Weissman, 1973; Whiffen & Gotlib, 1989). It is not hard to figure out why. Being around someone who is continually negative, ill-tempered, and pessimistic becomes pretty tiring after a while. Because emotions are contagious, the spouse probably begins to feel pretty bad also. These kinds of interactions precipitate arguments or, worse, make the nondepressed spouse want to leave (Biglan et al., 1985). But conflict within a marriage seems to have different effects on men and women. Depression seems to cause men to withdraw or otherwise disrupt the relationship. For women, on the other hand, it's problems in the relationship that most often causes depression. Thus, for both men and women, depression and problems in marital relations are associated, but the causal direction is different (Fincham, Beach, Harold, & Osborne, 1997), a result also found by Spangler, Simons, Monroe, and Thase (1996). Given these factors Beach et al., (1990) suggest that therapists treat disturbed marital relationships at the same time as the mood disorder to ensure the highest level of success for the patient and the best chance of preventing future relapses.

MOOD DISORDERS IN WOMEN

Data on the prevalence of mood disorders indicate dramatic gender imbalances. Although bipolar disorder is evenly divided between men and women, almost 70% of the individuals with major depressive disorder and dysthymia are women (Bland, 1997; Nolen-Hoeksema, 1987; Weissman et al., 1991). What is particularly striking is that this gender imbalance is constant around the world, even though overall rates of disorder may vary from country to country (Weissman & Olfson, 1995) (see Fig. 7.6). Often overlooked is the similar ratio for most anxiety disorders, particularly panic disorder and generalized anxiety disorder. Women represent an even greater proportion of specific phobias, as noted in Chapter 2. What could account for this?

It may be that gender differences in the development of emotional disorders are strongly influenced by perceptions of uncontrollability (Barlow, 1988, in press). If you feel a sense of mastery over your life and the difficult events that we all encounter, you might experience occasional stress but you will not feel the helplessness that is central to anxiety and mood disorders. The source of these differences is cultural, in the sex roles assigned to men and women in our society. Males are strongly encouraged to be independent, masterful, and assertive; females, by contrast, are expected to be more passive, sensitive to other people and, perhaps, to rely on others more than males do. Although these stereotypes are slowly changing, they still describe current sex roles, to a large extent. But this culturally induced dependence and passivity may well put women at severe risk for emotional disorders by increasing their feelings of uncontrollability and helplessness. Evidence has accumulated that parenting styles that encourage stereotypic gender roles are implicated in the development of early psychological vulnerability to later depression or anxiety (Chorpita & Barlow, in press); specifically, a smothering overprotective style which prevents the child from developing initiative.

Constance Hammen and her colleagues (Hammen, Marks, Mayol, & de Mayo, 1985) think that the value women place on intimate relationships may also put them at risk. Disruptions in such relationships, combined with an

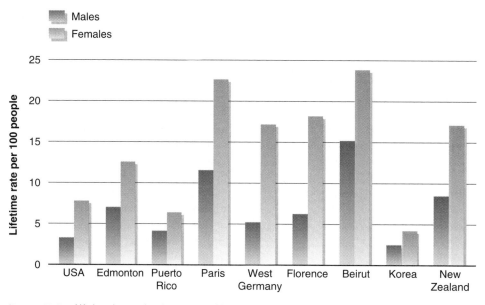

figure 7.6   Lifetime international rate per 100 people for major depression (adapted from Weissman et al., 1994)

inability to cope with the disruptions, may be far more damaging to women than to men. Data from Fincham et al. (1997) and Spangler et al. (1996), described above, seem to support this view. However, data from Bruce & Kim (1992), reviewed above, suggest that if the disruption actually reaches the stage of divorce, men who had previously been functioning well are at greater risk for depression.

Another potentially important gender difference has been suggested by Susan Nolen-Hoeksema (1987, 1990): Women tend to ruminate more than men about their situation and blame themselves for being depressed. Men tend to ignore their feelings, perhaps engaging in activity to take their minds off them. This male behavior may be therapeutic because "activating" people (getting them busy doing something) is a common element of successful therapy for depression (Lewinsohn & Gotlib, 1995).

As Strickland (1992) points out, women *are* at a disadvantage in our society: They experience more discrimination, poverty, sexual harassment, and abuse than do men. They also earn less respect and accumulate less power. Three-quarters of the people living in poverty in this country are women and children. Women, particularly single mothers, have a difficult time entering the workplace. Therefore, the meaning of conflict in a relationship is greater for women than for men, who are likely to respond more to problems at work. Married women who are employed full time outside the home report levels of depression no greater than those of employed married men. Single, divorced, and widowed women experience significantly more depression than men in the same categories (Weissman & Klerman, 1977). This does not necessarily mean that anyone should get a job to avoid becoming depressed. Indeed, for a man or woman, feeling mastery, control, and value in the strongly socially supported role of homemaker and parent should be associated with low rates of depression.

Finally, other disorders may reflect gender role stereotypes, but in the opposite direction. Disorders that are associated with aggressiveness, overactivity, and substance abuse occur far more frequently in men than in women (Barlow, 1988, in press). Identifying the reasons for gender imbalances across the full range of psychopathological disorders may prove important in discovering causes of disorders.

SOCIAL SUPPORT

In Chapter 2, we examined the powerful effect of social influences on our psychological and biological functioning. We cited several examples of how social influences seem to contribute to early death, such as the evil eye or lack of social support in old age. In general, the greater the number and frequency of your social relationships and contacts, the longer you are likely to live (for instance, House, Landis, & Umberson, 1988). It is not surprising, then, that social factors influence whether we become depressed.

In an early landmark study, G. W. Brown and Harris (1978) first suggested the important role of social support in the onset of depression. In a study of a large number of women who had experienced a serious life stress, they discovered that only 10% of the women who had a friend in whom they could confide became depressed, compared to 37% of the women who did not have a close supportive relationship. Later prospective studies have also confirmed the importance of social support (or lack of it) in predicting the onset of depressive symptoms at a later time (for instance, Cutrona, 1984; Joiner, 1997; Lin & Ensel, 1984; Monroe, Imhoff, Wise, & Harris, 1983; Phifer & Murrell, 1986). Other studies have established the importance of social support in speeding recovery from depressive episodes (Keitner et al., 1995; McLeod, Kessler, & Landis, 1992; Sherbourne, Hays, & Wells, 1995). These findings and others have led to an exciting new psychosocial therapeutic approach for emotional disorders called *interpersonal psychotherapy,* which we will discuss later in this chapter.

Let's return once again to Katie. In reflecting on her turbulent times and the days when death seemed more rewarding than life, one thing sticks out clearly in her mind.

> My parents are the true heroes of these early years. I will always admire their strength, their love, and their commitment. My father is a high school graduate and my mother has an eighth-grade education. They dealt with very complicated legal, medical, and psychological issues. They had little support from friends or professionals, yet they continued to do what they believed best. In my eyes there is no greater demonstration of courage and love.

Katie's parents did not have the social support that might have helped them through these difficult years, but they gave it to Katie. We will return to her case later.

An Integrative Theory

How do we put all this together? Basically, depression and anxiety may often share a common, genetically determined biological vulnerability (Barlow, in press; Barlow et al., 1996) that can be described as an overactive neurobiological response to stressful life events. Once again, this vulnerability is simply a general tendency to develop depression or anxiety rather than a specific vulnerability for depression or anxiety itself.

There is good evidence that stressful life events precede the onset of depression in most cases. How do the two factors interact? The best current thinking is that stressful life events activate stress hormones which, in turn, have wide-ranging effects on the neurotransmitter systems, particularly those involving serotonin and norepinephrine. There is also evidence that activation of stress hormones over the long term may actually "turn on" certain genes, producing long-term structural and chemical changes in the brain. For example, processes triggered by long-term stress may lead to atrophy of neurons in the hippocampus that help regulate emotions. Such structural change might permanently affect the regulation of neurotransmitter activity. The extended effects of stress may also disrupt the circadian rhythms in certain individuals, who then become susceptible to the recurrent cycling that seems so uniquely characteristic of the mood disorders (Post, 1992). What we have so far is a possible mechanism for the diathesis–stress model.

People who develop mood disorders also possess a psychological vulnerability experienced as feelings of inadequacy for coping with the difficulties confronting them. As with anxiety, we may develop this sense of control in childhood (Chorpita & Barlow, in press). It may range on a continuum from total confidence to a complete inability to cope. When vulnerabilities are triggered, the "giving up" process is crucial to the development of depression (Alloy et al., 1990). A variety of evidence indicates that these attitudes and attributions correlate rather strongly with such biochemical markers of stress and depression as by-products of norepinephrine (for example, Samson, Mirin, Hauser, Fenton, & Schildkraut, 1992), and with hemispheric lateral asymmetry (Davidson et al., in press). There is also evidence that early experience of stress, perhaps years before the onset of mood disorders, may leave an enduring cognitive vulnerability that intensifies the biochemical and cognitive response to stress later in life (Gotlib & Abramson, in press; Nolen-Hoeksema et al., 1992).

Finally, it seems clear that factors such as interpersonal relationships or our gender may protect us from the effects of stress and therefore from developing mood disorders. Alternatively, these factors may at least determine whether we quickly recover from these disorders or not.

In summary, biological, psychological, and social factors all influence the development of mood disorders, as depicted in Figure 7.7. This model does not account for the varied presentation of mood disorders—unipolar, bipolar, and so on. In other words, why would someone with an underlying genetic vulnerability who experiences a stressful life event develop a bipolar disorder rather than a unipolar disorder or, for that matter, an anxiety disorder? As with the anxiety disorders and other stress disorders, specific psychosocial circumstances, such as early learning experiences may interact

Of the impoverished people in the United States, three-quarters are women and children.

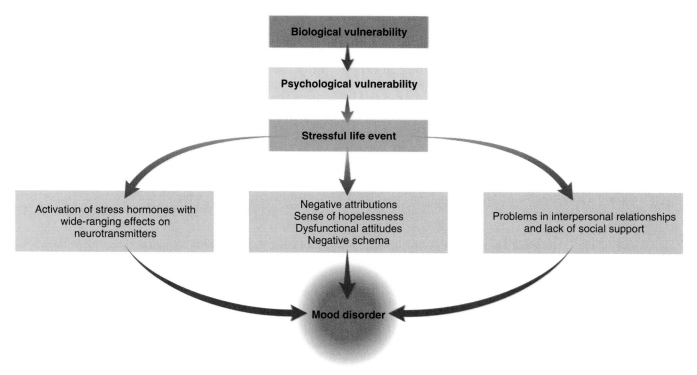

figure 7.7   An integrative model of mood disorders.

with specific genetic vulnerabilities and personality characteristics to produce the rich variety of emotional disorders. Only time will tell.

Treatment

We have learned a great deal about the neurobiology of mood disorders during the past several years. Findings on the complex interplay of neurochemicals are beginning to shed light on the nature of mood disorders. As we have noted, the principal effect of medications is to alter levels of these neurotransmitters and other related neurochemicals. Other biological treatments, such as electroconvulsive therapy (ECT), dramatically affect brain chemistry. A more interesting development, however, alluded to throughout this book, is that powerful psychological treatments also alter brain chemistry.

Medications

ANTIDEPRESSANTS

Three basic types of antidepressant medications are used to treat depressive disorders: *tricyclic antidepressants, monoamine oxidase* (MAO) *inhibitors,* and the newer *selective serotonergic reuptake inhibitors* (SSRIs).

Tricyclic antidepressants are widely used treatments for depression. The best-known variants are probably *imipramine* (Tofranil) and *amitriptyline* (Elavil). These drugs work partly by blocking the reuptake of certain neurotransmitters,

allowing them to pool in the synapse and, as the theory goes, eventually desensitize or *down-regulate* the transmission of that particular neurotransmitter (so that less of the neurochemical is transmitted). Tricyclic antidepressants seem to have their greatest effect by down-regulating norepinephrine, although other neurotransmitter systems, particularly serotonin, are also affected. They take a while to work because the down-regulating process often takes between 2 and 8 weeks. During this time, many patients feel a bit worse and develop a number of side effects such as blurred vision, dry mouth, constipation, difficulty urinating, drowsiness, weight gain (at least 13 pounds on average) and, perhaps, sexual dysfunction. For this reason, as many as 40% of these patients may stop taking the drug, thinking that the cure is worse than the disease. Nevertheless, with careful management, many side effects disappear. Tricyclics alleviate depression in approximately 50% of patients compared to approximately 25% to 30% of patients taking placebo pills, based on a summary analysis of over 100 studies (Depression Guideline Panel, 1993) (see Table 7.6). If dropouts are excluded and only those who complete treatment are counted, success rates increase to between 65% and 70%. Another issue clinicians must consider is that tricyclics are *lethal* if taken in excessive doses; therefore, they must be prescribed with great caution to patients with suicidal tendencies.

MAO inhibitors work very differently; as their name suggests, they block the enzyme MonoAmine Oxidase that breaks down such neurotransmitters as norepinephrine and serotonin. The result is roughly equivalent to the effect of the tricyclics. Because they are not broken down, the neurotransmitters pool in the synapse, ultimately leading to a down-regulation or desensitization. The MAO inhibitors seem to be as effective or slightly more effective than the tricyclics

(Depression Guideline Panel, 1993), with somewhat fewer side effects. Some evidence suggests that they are relatively more effective for depression with atypical features (Thase & Kupfer, 1996). But MAO inhibitors are used far less often because of two potentially serious consequences: Eating and drinking foods and beverages containing tyramine, such as cheese, red wine, or beer, can lead to severe hypertensive episodes and, occasionally, death. In addition, many other drugs that people take on a daily basis, such as cold medications, are dangerous and even fatal in interaction with an MAO inhibitor. For this reason, MAO inhibitors are usually prescribed only when tricyclics are not effective. Pharmaceutical companies have developed a new generation of more selective MAO inhibitors that are short-acting and do not interact negatively with tyramine (Baldessarini, 1989). Testing is still continuing on these new drugs, and they are not available in the United States, although they are in other countries.

Another class of drugs seems to have a specific effect on the serotonin neurotransmitter system (although they affect other systems to some extent). These *selective serotonergic reuptake inhibitors* (SSRIs) specifically block the reuptake of serotonin. This temporarily increases levels of serotonin at the receptor site, but the precise mechanism of action is unknown. Perhaps the best-known drug in this class is *fluoxetine* (Prozac). Like many other medications, Prozac was initially hailed as a breakthrough drug; it even made the cover of *Newsweek* (March 26, 1990). Then reports began to appear that it might lead to suicidal preoccupation, paranoid reactions and, occasionally, violence (for example, Mandalos & Szarek, 1990; Teicher, Glod, & Cole, 1990). Prozac went from being a wonder drug in the eyes of the press to a potential menace to modern society. Of course, neither conclusion was true. More recent findings indicate that the risks of suicide with this drug are no greater than with any other antidepressant, and the effectiveness is about the same (Fava & Rosenbaum, 1991). However, Prozac has its own set of side effects, the most prominent of which are physical agitation, sexual dysfunction or low desire (which is very prevalent), insomnia, and gastrointestinal upset. But these side effects, on the whole, seem to bother most patients less than the side effects associated with tricyclic antidepressants, with the possible exception of the sexual dysfunction. Recent studies suggest similar effectiveness of SSRIs and tricyclics with dysthmia (Lapierre, 1994).

Two new antidepressants seem to have somewhat different mechanisms of neurobiological action. Venlafaxine is related to tricyclic antidepressants but acts in a slightly different manner, reducing some of the associated side effects as well as the risk of damage to the cardiovascular system. Other typical side effects remain, including nausea and sexual dysfunction. Nefazodone is closely related to the SSRIs but seems to improve sleep efficiency instead of disrupting sleep. Both drugs are roughly comparable in effectiveness to older antidepressants (Preskorn, 1995; Thase & Kupfer, 1996). Finally, there has been a great deal of interest lately in the antidepressant properties of the natural herb St. John's Wort (*hypericum*). St. John's Wort is very popular in Europe, and the National Institutes of Health in the United States is beginning a large study to examine its effectiveness (Holden, 1997). The advantages of St. John's Wort are that it produces very few side effects and that it is relatively easy to produce. Some preliminary evidence suggests that the herb also somehow alters serotonin function. Only time will tell if it is truly effective.

Current studies indicate that drug treatments that are effective with adults are *not* necessarily effective with children (Boulos et al., 1991; Geller et al., 1992; Ryan, 1992). Sudden deaths of children under 14 who were taking tricyclic antidepressants have been reported, particularly during exercise, as in routine school athletic competition (Tingelstad, 1991). The causes imply cardiac side effects. Traditional antidepressant drug treatments are usually effective with the elderly, but administering them takes consider-

table 7.6   Efficacy of Various Antidepressant Drugs for Major Depressive Disorder

Drug	Drug Efficacy		Drug-Placebo	
	Inpatient	*Outpatient*	*Inpatient*	*Outpatient*
Tricyclics	50.0%	51.5%	25.1%	21.3%
SD	(6.5)	(5.2)	(11.5)	(3.9)
N	[33]	[102]	[8]	[46]
Monoamine oxidase inhibitors (MAOIs)	52.7%	57.4%	18.4%	30.9%
SD	(9.7)	(5.5)	(22.6)	(17.1)
N	[14]	[21]	[9]	[13]
Selective serotonin reuptake inhibitors (SSRIs)	54.0%	47.4%	25.5%	20.1%
SD	(10.1)	(12.5)	(21.7)	(7.8)
N	[8]	[39]	[2]	[23]

Note: The percentage shown in the *Drug Efficacy* column is the anticipated percentage of patients provided the treatment shown who will respond. The *Drug-Placebo* column shows the expected percentage difference in patients given a drug versus a placebo based on direct drug-placebo comparisons in trials that included at least these two cells. The numbers in parentheses are the standard deviations of the estimated percentage of responders. The bracketed numbers give the number of studies for which these estimates are calculated.
Source: Adapted from Depression Guideline Panel, 1993, April

Of the synthetic drugs for depression, *fluoxetine* (Prozac, *left*), is the most widely used; the common groundcover *hypericum* (St. John's Wort, *right*), is being tested as an effective natural treatment.

able skill because older people may suffer from a variety of side effects not experienced by younger adults, including memory impairment and physical agitation (for instance, Deptula & Pomara, 1990; Marcopulos & Graves, 1990).

Clinicians and researchers have concluded that recovery from depression, although important, may not be the most important therapeutic outcome (Frank et al., 1990; Prien & Kupfer, 1986). The large majority of people eventually recover from a major depressive episode, some rather quickly. A more important goal is often to delay the next depressive episode or even prevent it entirely (Prien & Potter, 1993; Thase, 1990; Thase & Kupfer, 1996). This is particularly important for patients who retain some symptoms of depression or have a past history of chronic depression or multiple depressive episodes. Because all these factors put people at risk for relapse, it is recommended that drug treatment go well beyond the termination of a depressive episode, continuing perhaps 6 to 12 months after the episode is over, or even longer. The drug is then gradually withdrawn over a period of weeks or months. (We will return to strategies for *maintaining* therapeutic benefits.)

Antidepressant medications have relieved severe depression and undoubtedly prevented suicide in tens of thousands of patients around the world. Although these medications are readily available, many people refuse or are not eligible to take them. Some are wary of long-term side effects. Women of childbearing age must protect themselves against the possibility of conceiving while taking antidepressants, because they can damage the fetus. In addition, 40% to 50% of patients do not respond to these drugs, and a substantial number of the remainder are left with residual symptoms.

Lithium

A fourth type of equally effective antidepressant drug, *lithium*, is a common salt widely available in the natural environment. It is found in our drinking water in amounts too small to have any effect. However, the side effects of therapeutic doses of lithium are potentially more serious than those of other antidepressants. Dosage has to be very carefully regulated to prevent toxicity (poisoning) and lowered thyroid

functioning, which might intensify the lack of energy associated with depression. Substantial weight gain is also common. Lithium, however, has one major advantage that distinguishes it from other antidepressants: It is often effective in preventing and treating manic episodes. For this reason it is most often referred to as a mood stabilizing drug. Because tricyclic antidepressants can induce manic episodes, even in individuals without preexisting bipolar disorder (F. K. Goodwin & Ghaemi 1998; F. K. Goodwin & Jamison, 1990; Prien et al., 1984), lithium is the treatment of choice.

We are not sure how lithium works. It may limit the availability of dopamine and norepinephrine, but may have more important effects on some of the neurohormones in the endocrine system, particularly those that influence the production and availability of sodium and potassium, electrolytes found in body fluids (F. K. Goodwin & Jamison, 1990). Results indicate that 30% to 60% of bipolar patients respond very well to lithium initially, 30% to 50% evidence a partial response, and 10% to 20% have a poor response (Prien & Potter, 1993; Show, 1985). Thus, while effective, lithium provides many people with inadequate therapeutic benefit.

Kay Redfield Jamison, an internationally respected authority on bipolar disorder, has suffered from the disease since adolescence.

Patients who don't respond can take other drugs with antimanic properties, including anticonvulsants such as carbamazepine and calcium channel blockers such as verapamil (Thase & Kupfer, 1996). But newer studies show that these drugs have one distinct disadvantage: They are less effective than lithium in preventing suicide (Theis-Flechtner et al., 1996; Tonde, Jamison, & Baldessarini, in press). Thus, lithium remains the preferred drug for bipolar disorder (F. K. Goodwin & Ghaemi, 1998).

For those patients who *do* respond to lithium, some studies suggest that maintaining adequate doses can prevent recurrence of manic episodes in approximately 66% of individuals (with 34% relapsing), based on 10 major double-blind studies comparing lithium to placebo. Relapse rates in the placebo group averaged a very high 81% over periods ranging from several months to several years (F. K. Goodwin & Jamison, 1990; Suppes, Baldessarini, Faedda, & Tohen, 1991). But newer studies following patients for up to 5 years report that approximately 70% ultimately relapse, even if they continue to take the lithium (Gitlin, Swendsen, Heller, & Hammen, 1995; Peselow, Fieve, Difiglia, & Sanfilipo, 1994). Nevertheless, for almost anyone with recurrent manic episodes, maintenance on lithium or a related drug is recommended to prevent relapse. Another problem with drug treatment of bipolar disorder is that people usually *like* the euphoric or high feeling that mania produces, and they often stop taking lithium in order to maintain or regain the state; that is, they do not comply with the medication regimen. Because the evidence now clearly indicates that individuals who stop their medication are at considerable risk for relapse, other methods, usually psychological in nature, are used to increase compliance.

Electroconvulsive Therapy (ECT)

When someone does not respond to medication (or in an extremely severe case), clinicians may consider a more dramatic treatment, **electroconvulsive therapy (ECT),** the most controversial treatment for psychological disorders, after psychosurgery. In Chapter 1, we described how ECT was used in the early 20th century. Despite many unfortunate abuses along the way, ECT is considerably changed today. It is now a safe and reasonably effective treatment for *very severe* depression that has not improved with other treatments (Black, Winokur, & Nasrallah, 1987; R. R. Crowe, 1984; Klerman, 1988). In current administrations, patients are anesthetized to reduce discomfort and given muscle-relaxing drugs to prevent bone breakage from convulsions during seizures. Electric shock is administered directly through the brain for less than a second, producing a seizure and a series of brief convulsions that usually lasts for several minutes. In current practice, treatments are administered once every other day for a total of 6 to 10 treatments (fewer if the patient's mood returns to normal). Side effects are surprisingly few and generally limited to short-term memory loss and confusion that disappear after a week or two, although some patients may have long-term memory problems. For severely depressed inpatients with psychotic features, controlled studies (including some in which the control group undergoes a "sham" ECT procedure and doesn't actually receive shocks) indicate that 50% to 70% of those *not responding* to medication will benefit. Continued treatment with medication or psychotherapy is then necessary because the relapse rate approaches 60% (Brandon et al., 1984; Depression Guideline Panel, 1993; Fernandez, Levy, Lachar, & Small, 1995; Prudic, Sackeim, & Devanand, 1990). It may not be in the best interest of psychotically depressed and acutely suicidal inpatients to wait 3 to 6 weeks to determine whether a drug or psychological treatment is working; in these cases, immediate ECT may be appropriate.

We do not really know why ECT works. Obviously, repeated seizures induce massive functional and perhaps structural changes in the brain, which seems to be therapeutic. Because of the controversial nature of this treatment, its use declined considerably during the 1970s and 1980s. In view of our broad ignorance of how it works, ECT is unlikely to become widely available again any time soon (American Psychiatric Association, 1990).

Psychosocial Treatments

Of the effective psychosocial treatments now available for depressive disorders, two major approaches are most effective. The first is cognitive-behavioral; Aaron T. Beck, the founder of *cognitive therapy*, is most closely associated with this approach. The second approach, *interpersonal psychotherapy*, was developed by Myrna Weissman and Gerald Klerman.

Cognitive Therapy

Beck's **cognitive therapy** grew directly out of his observations of the role of deep-seated negative thinking in generating depression (A. T. Beck, 1967, 1976; A. T. Beck & Young, 1985; J. E. Young, Beck, & Weinberger, 1993). Clients are taught to carefully examine their thought processes while they are depressed and to recognize "depressive" errors in thinking. This task is not always easy, because many thoughts are automatic and beyond clients' awareness. Negative thinking seems natural to them. Clients are taught that errors in thinking can directly cause depression. Treatment involves correcting cognitive errors and substituting less depressing and (perhaps) more realistic thoughts and appraisals. Later in therapy, underlying *negative cognitive schemas* (characteristic ways of viewing the world) that trigger specific cognitive errors are targeted, not only in the office but also as part of the client's day-to-day life. The therapist purposefully takes a Socratic approach, making it clear that therapist and client are working as a team to uncover faulty thinking patterns and the underlying schemas from which they are generated. Therapists must be skillful and highly trained. The following is an example of an actual interaction between Beck and a client.

Beck and Irene
A Dialogue

Because an intake interview had already been completed by another therapist, Beck did not spend time reviewing Irene's symptoms in detail or taking a history. Irene began by describing her "sad states." Beck almost immediately started to elicit her automatic thoughts during these periods.

Therapist: What kind of thoughts were you having during these 4 days when you said your thoughts kept coming over and over again?

Patient: Well, they were just—mostly, "Why is this happening again"—because, you know, this isn't the first time he's been out of work. You know, "What am I going to do"—like I have all different thoughts. They are all in different things like being mad at him, being mad at myself for being in this position all the time. Like I want to leave him or if I could do anything to make him straighten out and not depend so much on him. There's a lot of thoughts in there.

T: Now can we go back a little bit to the sad states that you have? Do you still have that sad state?

P: Yeah.

T: You have it right now?

P: Yeah, sort of. They were sad thoughts about—I don't know—I get bad thoughts, like a lot of what I'm thinking is bad things. Like not—there is like, ah, it isn't going to get any better, it will stay that way. I don't know. Lots of things go wrong, you know, that's how I think.

T: So one of the thoughts is that it's not going to get any better?

P: Yeah.

T: And sometimes you believe that completely?

P: Yeah, I believe it, sometimes.

T: Right now do you believe it?

P: I believe—yeah, yeah.

T: Right now you believe that things are not going to get better?

P: Well, there is a glimmer of hope but it's mostly. . . .

T: What do you kind of look forward to in terms of your own life from here on?

P: Well, what I look forward to—I can tell you but I don't want to tell you. *(Giggles).* Um, I don't see too much.

T: You don't want to tell me?

P: No, I'll tell you but it's not sweet and great what I think. I just see me continuing on the way I am, the way I don't want to be, like not doing anything, just being there, like sort of with no use, that like my husband will still be there and he will, you know, he'll go in and out of drugs or whatever he is going to do, and I'll just still be there, just in the same place.

By inquiring about Irene's automatic thoughts, the therapist began to understand her perspective—that she would go on forever, trapped, with her husband in and out of drug centers. This hopelessness about the future is characteristic of most depressed patients. A second advantage to this line of inquiry is that the therapist introduced Irene to the idea of looking at her own thoughts, which is central to cognitive therapy.

(J. E. Young et al., 1993, pp. 258–259)

Between sessions, clients are instructed to carefully *monitor and log* their thought processes, particularly in situations where they might feel depressed. They also attempt to change their behavior by carrying out specific activities assigned as homework, such as tasks in which clients can test their faulty thinking. For example, a client who has to participate in an upcoming meeting might think, "If I go to that meeting, I'll just make a fool of myself and all my colleagues will think I'm stupid." The therapist might instruct the client to go to the meeting, predict ahead of time the reaction of her colleagues, and then see what really happens. This part of treatment is called *hypothesis testing* because the client makes a hypothesis about what's going to happen (usually a depressing outcome) and then, most often, dis-

covers that it is incorrect ("My colleagues congratulated me on my presentation").

The therapist typically schedules other activities to *reactivate* depressed patients who have given up most activities, helping them put some fun back into their lives. Along similar lines, other investigators have shown that exercise and/or increased activities alone can improve self-concept and lift depression (Doyne et al., 1987; Jacobson et al., 1996; Ossip-Klein et al., 1989). Cognitive therapy typically takes from 10 to 20 sessions, scheduled weekly.

Related cognitive-behavioral approaches to depression were developed by Peter Lewinsohn and his colleagues (for example, Lewinsohn & Clarke, 1984; Lewinsohn & Gotlib, 1995) and Lynn Rehm and his colleagues (for example, Rehm, Kaslow, & Rabin, 1987). Initially, Lewinsohn focused on reactivating depressed patients and countering their mood by bringing them in contact with various kinds of reinforcing events. For example, they might be assigned the task of going to the kind of social event they used to enjoy with their friends. Lewinsohn's treatment originally concentrated on behavioral change. During the past several years, however, this successful program has included cognitive procedures as well and is now similar to the program developed by Beck. Similarly, Rehm emphasized behavioral change in developing self-control over moods and daily activities, an approach that also includes cognitive components.

INTERPERSONAL PSYCHOTHERAPY (IPT)

We have seen that major disruptions in our interpersonal relationships are an important category of stresses that can trigger mood disorders (Barnett & Gotlib, 1988; Coyne, 1976). In addition, people with few, if any, important social relationships seem at risk for developing and sustaining mood disorders (Sherbourne, Hays, & Wells, 1995). **Interpersonal psychotherapy (IPT)** (Klerman, Weissman, Rounsaville, & Chevron, 1984; Weissman, 1995; Weissman & Markowitz, 1994) focuses on resolving problems in existing relationships and learning to form important new interpersonal relationships.

Like cognitive-behavioral approaches, IPT is highly structured and seldom takes longer than 15 to 20 sessions, usually scheduled once a week. After identifying life stressors that seem to precipitate the depression, the therapist and patient work collaboratively on the patient's current interpersonal problems. Typically, these include one or more of four interpersonal issues: *dealing with interpersonal role disputes,* such as marital conflict; *adjusting to the loss of a relationship,* such as grief over the death of a loved one; *acquiring new relationships,* such as getting married or establishing professional relationships; and *identifying and correcting deficits in social skills* that prevent the person from initiating or maintaining important relationships.

To take a common example, the therapist's first job is to identify and define an interpersonal dispute (Weissman, 1995), perhaps with a wife who expects her spouse to support her but has had to take an outside job to help pay bills. The husband, might expect the wife to share equally in generating income. If this dispute seems to be associated with the onset of depressive symptoms and to result in a continuing series of arguments and disagreements without resolution, it would become the focus for IPT.

After helping to identify the dispute, the next step is to bring it to a resolution. First, the therapist helps the patient determine the stage of the dispute.

1. *Negotiation Stage:* Both partners are aware that it *is* a dispute, and they are trying to renegotiate it.
2. *Impasse Stage:* The dispute smolders beneath the surface and results in low-level resentment, but no attempts are made to resolve it.
3. *Resolution Stage:* The partners are taking some action, such as divorce or separation.

The therapist works with the patient to define the dispute clearly for both parties and develop specific strategies for resolving it. Along similar lines, Daniel O'Leary, Steve Beach, and their colleagues, as well as Neil Jacobson and his colleagues, have made marital therapy applicable to the large numbers of clients they see, particularly women, who are in the midst of very dysfunctional marriages (as is the case for as many as 50% of all depressed patients) (Beach et al., 1990; Jacobson, Dobson, Fruzzetti, Schmaling, & Salusky, 1991; Jacobson, Fruzzetti, Dobson, Whisman, & Hops, 1993; K. D. O'Leary & Beach, 1990).

Recent studies that have compared the results of cognitive therapy and IPT to those of tricyclic antidepressants and other control conditions have found that psychosocial approaches and medication are equally effective, and that all treatments are more effective than placebo conditions, brief psychodynamic treatments, or other appropriate control conditions for both major depressive disorder and dysthymia (A. T. Beck, Hollon, Young, Bedrosian, & Budenz, 1985; Blackburn & Moore, 1997; Hollon et al., 1992; I. W. Miller, Norman, & Keitner, 1989; Schulberg et al., 1996; Shapiro et al., 1995). Depending on how "success" is defined, approximately 50% to 70% or more of people benefit from treatment to a significant extent, compared to approximately 30% in placebo or control conditions. A study sponsored by the National Institutes of Mental Health (NIMH) and carried out in three different clinics in North America is the largest study reported to date (Elkin et al., 1989). The results indicate no essential differences in effectiveness among interpersonal psychotherapy, cognitive therapy, and tricyclic antidepressants, considering all patients who were treated. At one clinic medication was more effective than cognitive therapy if the patients were *severely* depressed (Elkin et al., 1995), a finding that may indicate less skillful cognitive therapists administering the treatment at that site (Hollon, 1993; Hollon, & Beck, in press; Jacobson & Hollon, 1996a, 1996b). Similar studies have not found a difference in treatment effectiveness based on severity of depression (Hollon et al., 1992; McLean &

> *No pill can help me deal with the problem of not wanting to take pills; likewise, no amount of psychotherapy alone can prevent my manias and depressions. I need both.*

Myrna Weissman and her husband, the late Gerald Klerman, developed interpersonal psychotherapy, which is effective with mood disorders and related conditions.

Taylor, 1992). In any case, when patients who *had* recovered were followed up for 18 months, the results were very disappointing (Shea et al., 1992). Of all patients entering treatment, only 30% of those who received cognitive therapy remained well compared to 26% of those who received IPT, 19% in the tricyclic drug group, and 20% in the placebo group. Shea et al. (1992) concluded that treatments were just not delivered long enough (or well enough) to effect meaningful change.

In view of the seriousness of mood disorders in children and adolescents, work has begun on preventing these disorders in these age groups (Munoz, 1993). Most researchers focus on instilling social and problem-solving skills in children that are adequate to prevent the kinds of social stress that are so often associated with depression. In fact, Sanders and colleagues (1992) and Dadds, Sanders, Morrison, and Rebgetz (1992) determined that disordered communication and problem-solving skills, particularly within the family, are characteristic of depressed children and a natural target for treatment. Now, Beardslee et al. (1997) have observed sustained effects from a preventive program directed at families with children between the ages of 8 and 15 in which one parent had experienced a recent episode of depression. Eighteen months after participating in 6 to 10 family sessions, these families were doing substantially better on most measures than the control families. In an even more intriguing preventive effort, Gilham, Reivich, Jaycox, and Seligman (1995) taught cognitive and social problem-solving techniques to 69 fifth- and sixth-grade children who were at risk for depression. Compared to children in a matched no-treatment control group, the prevention group reported fewer depressive symptoms during the 2 years they were followed. More importantly, moderate to severe symptoms were reduced by half and the positive effects of this program increased during the period of follow-up. This suggests that it might be possible to "psychologically immunize" children against depression by teaching appropriate cognitive and social skills before they enter puberty.

Combined Treatments

A few studies have tested the very important question of whether combining psychosocial treatments with medication is effective in treating depression (for instance, A. T. Beck et al., 1985; Blackburn & Moore, 1997; Hollon et al., 1992; I. W. Miller, Norman, Keitner, Bishop, & Down, 1989). The results thus far do not strongly suggest any *immediate* advantage of combined treatments over separate drug or psychosocial treatment. The treatments clearly operate in different ways. Medication, when it works, does so more quickly than psychosocial treatments, which in turn have the advantage of increasing the patient's long-range social functioning (particularly in the case of IPT) and also protecting against relapse or recurrence (particularly cognitive therapy). Combining treatments, therefore, might take advantage of the rapid drugs' action and the psychosocial protection against recurrence or relapse, thereby allowing eventual discontinuation of the medications. For example, Fava, Grandi, Zielezny, Rafanelli, and Canestrari (1996) assigned patients who had been successfully treated with antidepressant drugs to either cognitive–behavioral treatment of residual symptoms or standard clinical management. Four years later, patients treated with cognitive–behavioral procedures had a substantially lower relapse rate (35%) than patients in the clinical management position (70%).

Preventing Relapse

Given the high rate of recurrence in depression, it is not surprising that well over 50% of patients on antidepressant medication relapse if their medication is stopped within 4 months after their last depressive episode (Hollon, Shelton, & Loosen, 1991; Thase, 1990). Therefore, one important question has to do with **maintenance treatment** to *prevent* relapse or recurrence over the long term.

In a number of studies, cognitive therapy reduced rates of subsequent relapse in depressed patients by more than 50% over groups treated with antidepressant medication (for example, M. D. Evans et al., 1992; Kovacs, Rush, Beck, & Hollon, 1981; Simons, Murphy, Levine, & Wetzel, 1986). M. D. Evans et al. (1992) found that cognitive therapy prevented subsequent relapse to the same extent as did continuing medication over a 2-year period. Data on relapse presented in Figure 7.8 show that 50% of a group whose medication was stopped relapsed during the same period, compared to 32% of a group whose medication was continued at least 1 year. Relapse rates were only 21% for the group receiving cognitive therapy alone and 15% for those receiving cognitive therapy combined with medication. It is inter-

esting that the cognitive therapy was *not* continued beyond the initial 12-week period.

Ellen Frank and her colleagues (1990) found that IPT also significantly reduced the risk for recurrence among recovered depressed outpatients who, based on past history, were at substantial risk for relapse. These patients had been treated initially with a combination of tricyclic antidepressant medication and IPT. However, if patients were *maintained* on full therapeutic dosages of tricyclic medication across the 3-year period of study, their rate of relapse or recurrence was even lower than that of patients continuing to receive IPT. These findings provide strong support for continuing drug treatment in severely depressed patients who are at high risk for relapse and who have had an initial successful response to antidepressant medication. Specifically, 46% of a group of patients who were better after initial treatment (with medication and IPT) and were maintained on therapeutic doses of the drug for the 3-year period remained better (among those

who didn't, some dropped out while others had recurrences). This figure compares to 31% receiving monthly sessions of IPT alone across the 3 years (down from weekly during active treatment), and 9% of patients receiving placebo for 3 years. Combining drug and IPT did not significantly improve the result. More recently, Kupfer et al. (1992) substituted placebo tablets after 3 years with 50% of the people who had *done well* on drugs, and continued medication for the

Ellen Frank and her colleagues were the first to use psychosocial treatments to prevent recurring episodes of mood disorders.

other half of the group. After 2 more years, 82% of those who stayed on drugs were still better, compared to only 33% who were switched to placebo. These findings provide strong additional support for continuing drug treatment in *severe* patients who are at high risk for relapse and who have had an initial successful response to antidepressant medication.

Frank, Kupfer, Wagner, McEachran, and Cornes (1991) analyzed tape recordings of the IPT sessions to determine whether *how* the treatment was delivered was important. When the treatment was rated by experts as qualitatively better, the average number of months that patients did not relapse was twice as long as the overall average (2 years instead of 1) and four times as long as for patients who received lower-quality therapy (2 years instead of 6 months).

In summary, both brief psychosocial treatments and continuing medication *may* be effective in preventing relapse and recurrence. If further study confirms this, psychosocial treatments may be a desirable initial strategy so that people can avoid the various medical risks associated

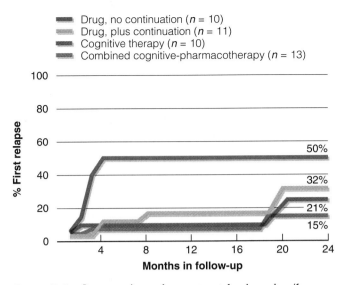

figure 7.8 Data on relapse after treatment for depression (from Evans et al., 1992).

of establishing specific treatments for certain types of depression.

Psychosocial Treatments for Bipolar Disorder

Although medication, particularly lithium, is the preferred treatment for bipolar disorder, most clinicians emphasize the need for psychosocial intervention to manage interpersonal and practical problems (for example, marital and job difficulties that result from the disorder) (Clarkin, Haas, & Glick, 1988). Until recently, the principal objective of psychosocial intervention was to increase compliance with medication regimens such as lithium (Cochran, 1984). We noted before that the "pleasures" of a manic state make refusal to take lithium a major therapeutic obstacle. Giving up drugs between episodes or skipping dosages during an episode significantly undermines treatment. Therefore, a careful integration of psychosocial and lithium treatments is very important (F. K. Goodwin & Jamison, 1990; Scott, 1995). I. W. Miller and his colleagues, in a small pilot study, added family therapy to a drug regimen and reported a significant increase in the percentage of patients with bipolar disorder who fully recovered (56%) over those who had drug treatment alone (20%) (see Figure 7.9). During a 2-year follow-up, patients who received psychosocial treatment had less than half the recidivism of those who had drug treatment alone (I. W. Miller, Keitner, Epstein, Bishop, & Ryan, 1991). David Miklowitz and his colleagues found that family tension is associated with relapse in bipolar disorder; preliminary studies indicate that psychosocial treatment directed at helping families understand symptoms and develop new coping skills prevents relapse (Miklowitz & Goldstein, 1990; Miklowitz, Simoneau, Sachs-Ericsson, Warner, & Suddath, 1996). Similarly, Clarkin, Carpenter, Hull, Wilner, & Glick (in press) evaluated the advantages of adding psychosocial treatment to medication in inpatients, and found that it improved adherence to medication for all

with long-term use of medication and women of childbearing age may feel free to conceive. But continuing the full therapeutic dosages of medication may well be effective if psychosocial strategies alone are ineffective.

Because psychosocial treatments affect biological aspects of disorders, and drug treatments affect psychological components, the integrative model of mood disorders is helpful in studying the effects of treatment. There is evidence that psychological treatments alter neurochemical correlates of depression. McKnight, Nelson-Gray, and Barnhill (1992) used either cognitive therapy or tricyclic medication to treat groups of patients with major depressive disorder. They found that an abnormal pretreatment response to the dexamethasone suppression test (DST) of cortisol secretion did *not* predict which treatment would be more effective, and both produced a normalization of posttreatment DST responses. Similarly, successful cognitive therapy and tricyclic medication both decrease thyroid hormone levels (Joffe, Segal, & Singer, 1996).

An interesting finding is that patients with higher levels of a metabolite (by-product) of norepinephrine, specifically, *3-methoxy-4-hydroxyphenylglycol* (MHPG) *do not* respond as well to tricyclic antidepressants as do those with lower levels of MHPG (Garvey, Hollon, DeRubeis, & Evans, 1990a, 1990b; Mooney, Schatzberg, Cole, & Samson, 1991). Why might this be important? Samson and colleagues (1992) reported that the higher the level of MHPG, the higher the subject's score on a measure of learned helplessness. It is possible, therefore, that cognitive therapy, which addresses learned helplessness and hopelessness, might be more effective with this type of depression than medication. This assumption remains to be demonstrated, but it illustrates another strategy for discovering meaningful subtypes of depression. On the other hand, as noted above, abnormal sleep profiles may predict a poor response to psychosocial treatment (Thase, Simons, & Reynolds, 1996). All of these results are at the forefront

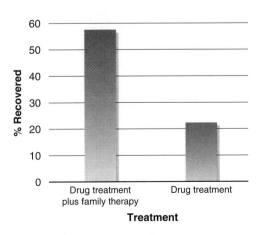

figure 7.9 Percentage of patients with bipolar disorder recovered after standard drug treatment or drug treatment plus family therapy (adapted from Miller et al., 1991).

patients and resulted in better overall outcomes for the most severe patients compared to medication alone. More advanced studies are underway (Craighead, Miklowitz, Vajk, & Frank, 1998). For example, Ellen Frank and her colleagues are testing a psychosocial treatment that regulates circadian rhythms by helping patients regulate their sleep cycles and other daily schedules (Frank et al., 1997).

Let us now return to Katie, who, you will remember, had made a serious suicide attempt in the midst of a major depressive episode.

Katie
The Triumph of the Self

Like the overwhelming majority of people with serious psychological disorders, Katie had never received an adequate course of treatment, although she was evaluated from time to time by various mental health professionals. She lived in a rural area where competent professional help was not readily available. Her life ebbed and flowed with her struggle to subdue anxiety and depression. When she could manage her emotions sufficiently, she took an occasional course in the high school independent study program. Katie discovered that she was fascinated by learning. She enrolled in a local community college at the age of 19 and did extremely well, despite the fact that she had not progressed beyond her freshman year in high school. At the college she earned a high school equivalency degree. She went to work in a local factory. But she continued to drink heavily and to take Valium; on occasion, anxiety and depression would return and disrupt her life.

Finally, Katie left home, attended college full time, and fell in love. But the romance was one-sided, and she was rejected.

One night after a phone conversation with him, I nearly drank myself to death. I lived in a single room alone in the dorm. I drank as much vodka as quickly as I could. I fell asleep. When I awoke, I was covered in vomit and couldn't recall falling asleep or being sick. I was drunk for much of the next day. When I awoke the following morning, I realized I could have killed myself by choking on my own vomit. More importantly, I wasn't sure if I fully wanted to die. That was the last of my drinking.

Katie decided to make some changes. Taking advantage of what she had learned in the little treatment she had received, she began looking at life and herself differently. Instead of dwelling on how inadequate and evil she was, she began to pay attention to her strengths. "But I now realized that I needed to accept myself as is, and work with any stumbling blocks that I faced. I needed to get myself through the world as happily and as comfortably as I could. I had a right to that." Other lessons learned in treatment now became valuable, and Katie became more aware of her mood swings:

I learned to objectify periods of depression as [simply] periods of "feeling." They are a part of who I am, but not the whole. I recognize when I feel that way, and I check my perceptions with someone that I trust when I feel

uncertain of them. I try to hold on to the belief that these periods are only temporary.

Katie developed other strategies for coping successfully with life:

I try to stay focused on my goals and what is important to me. I have learned that if one strategy to achieve some goal doesn't work there are other strategies that probably will. My endurance is one of my blessings. Patience, dedication, and discipline are also important. None of the changes that I have been through occurred instantly or automatically. Most of what I have achieved has required time, effort, and persistence.

Katie dreamed that if she worked hard enough she could help other people who had problems similar to her own. Katie pursued that dream and earned her Ph.D. in psychology.

Katie is a remarkable person who demonstrates the great strengths of human character. Very few people who suffer from severe psychological disorders, particularly mood disorders, are able to pull themselves together on a relatively permanent basis. Psychologists hope to learn more about what helps people like Katie that overcome emotional disorders and achieve their goals, so we can develop better treatments and, perhaps, prevent emotional disorders from occurring in the first place.

Suicide

Statistics

Most days we are confronted with news about the war on cancer or the frantic race to find a cure for AIDS. We also hear never-ending admonitions to improve our diet and exercise more to prevent heart disease. But another cause of death ranks right up there with the most frightening and dangerous medical conditions. This is the inexplicable decision to kill themselves made by more than 30,000 people a year in the United States alone. Suicide is officially the eighth leading cause of death in the United States, and most epidemiologists agree that the actual number of suicides may be two to three times higher. Many of these unreported suicides occur when people purposefully drive into a bridge or off a cliff (Blumenthal, 1990).

Suicide is overwhelmingly a white phenomenon. Most minority groups, including African-Americans and Hispanics, seldom resort to this violent alternative, as is evident in Figure 7.10. As you might expect from the incidence of depression in Native Americans, however, their suicide rate is extremely high, although there is great variability across tribes (among the Apache, the rates are nearly four times the national average) (Berlin, 1987). Even more frightening is

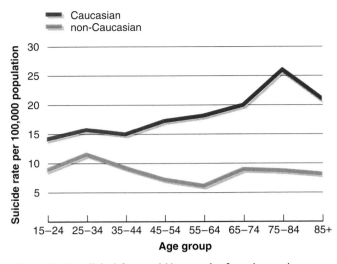

figure 7.10 United States suicide rates for Caucasians and non-Caucasians by age group, sexes combined (data from the National Center for Health Statistics, Vital Statistics of the United States 1987) (from Buda & Tsuang, 1990).

In fact, in 1990, when approximately 12.5% of the population was 65 or over, this age group accounted for 20.6% of the suicides. In every country studied, the elderly, particularly elderly males, have the highest suicide rate (Gallagher-Thompson & Osgood, 1997; National Center for Health Statistics, 1993). Suicide is not attempted only by adolescents and adults: P. A. Rosenthal and Rosenthal (1984) described 16 children 2 to 5 years of age who had attempted suicide at least once, many injuring themselves severely.

Regardless of age, males are four to five times more likely to *commit* suicide than females. This startling fact seems to be related in part to gender differences in the types of suicide *attempts*. Males generally choose far more violent methods, such as guns and hanging; females tend to rely on less violent options, such as drug overdose (Buda & Tsuang, 1990; Gallagher-Thompson & Osgood, 1997). More men commit suicide during old age and more women during middle age, in part because most attempts by older women are unsuccessful. The suicide rate for young men in the United States is now the highest in the world, even surpassing rates in Japan and Sweden, countries long known for high rates of suicide (Blumenthal, 1990). But, as noted above, older men (over 65) in all countries are most at risk for completing suicide worldwide, with white men at highest risk (McIntosh, Santos, Hubbard, & Overholser, 1994).

In China, and in this country alone, more women commit suicide than men, particularly in rural settings (Murray, 1996; Murray & Lopez, 1996). What accounts for this culturally determined reversal? Chinese scientists agree that China's suicide rates, probably the highest in the world, are due to an absence of stigma. In fact, suicide, particularly among women, is often portrayed in classical Chinese literature as a reasonable solution to problems. A rural Chinese woman's family is her entire world, and suicide is an honorable solution if the family collapses. Fur-

the dramatic *increase* in death by suicide in recent years, most evident among adolescents. Figure 7.11 presents suicide rates for the population as a whole as well as the rates for teenagers. As you can see, between 1960 and 1988 the suicide rate in adolescents rose from 3.6 to 11.3 per 100,000 population, an increase of 200% compared with a general population increase of 17%. For teenagers, suicide is the *third* leading cause of death. Note also the dramatic increase in suicide rates among the elderly in Figure 7.10. This rise has been connected to the growing incidence of medical illness in our oldest citizens and to their increasing loss of social support. As we have noted, a strong relationship exists between illness or infirmity and hopelessness or depression.

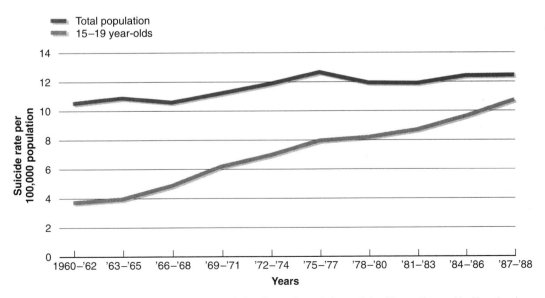

figure 7.11 Suicide rates per 100,000 in population for total population and for 15- to 19-year-olds (data for the years 1966–1988 from *Vital Statistics of the United States: Volume II. Mortality—Part A.* National Center for Health Statistics, 1968–1991, Washington, DC: U.S. Government Printing Office. In the public domain) (from Buda & Tsuang, 1990).

Men often choose violent methods of committing suicide. Nirvana's Curt Cobain shot himself.

thermore, highly toxic farm pesticides are readily available and it is possible that many women who did not necessarily intend to kill themselves die after accidentally swallowing poison.

In addition to "successful" suicides, two other important indices of suicidal behavior are **suicidal attempts** (the person survives) and **suicidal ideation** (thinking seriously about suicide). Although males *commit* suicide more often than females in most of the world, females *attempt* suicide at least three times as often (Berman & Jobes, 1991). This high incidence may reflect the fact that more women than men are depressed, and that depression is strongly related to suicide attempts (R. Frances, Franklin, & Flavin, 1986). Some estimates place the ratio of attempted to completed suicides at 50:1 or higher (Garland & Zigler, 1993). In addition, results from another study (Kovacs, Goldston, & Gatsonis, 1993) suggested that among adolescents the ratio of *thoughts* about suicide to *attempts* is between 3:1 and 6:1. In other words, between 16% and 30% of adolescents in this study who had thought about killing themselves actually attempted it. "Thoughts" in this context does not refer to a fleeting philosophical type of consideration but rather to a serious contemplation of the act. The first step down the dangerous road to suicide is thinking about it.

In a study of college students (whose rate of suicide is only about half that of the general population), approximately 25% had thought about suicide during the past 12 months (Meehan, Lamb, Saltzman, & O'Carroll, 1992; A. J. Schwartz & Whitaker, 1990). Only a minority of these college students with thoughts of suicide (perhaps around 15%) will attempt to kill themselves, and only a few will succeed (Kovacs et al., 1993). Nevertheless, given the enormity of the problem, suicidal thoughts are taken very seriously by mental health professionals.

Causes

PAST CONCEPTIONS

The great sociologist Emile Durkheim (1951) defined a number of suicide types, based on the social or cultural conditions in which they occurred. One type is "formalized" suicides that were approved of, such as the ancient custom of *hara-kiri* in Japan, in which an individual who brought dishonor to himself or his family was expected to impale himself on a sword. Durkheim referred to this as *altruistic suicide*. Durkheim also recognized the loss of social supports as an important provocation for suicide; he called this *egoistic suicide*. (Elderly citizens who kill themselves after losing touch with their friends or family fit into this category.) Magne-Ingvar, Ojehagen, and Traskman-Bendz (1992) found that only 13% of 75 individuals who had seriously attempted suicide had an adequate social network of friends and relationships. *Anomic suicides* are the result of marked disruptions, such as the sudden loss of a high-prestige job. ("Anomie" is feeling lost and confused.) Finally, *fatalistic suicides* result from a loss of control over one's own destiny. The recent mass suicide of 39 Heaven's Gate cult members is an example of this type because the lives of those people were largely in the hands of Marshall Applewhite, a supreme and charismatic leader. Durkheim's work was important in alerting us to the social contribution to suicide. Freud (1917/1957) believed that suicide (and depression, to some extent) indicated unconscious hostility directed *inward* to the self rather than *outward* to the person or situation causing the anger. Indeed, suicide victims often seem to be psychologically "punishing" others who may have rejected them or caused some other personal hurt. Current thinking considers social and psychological factors but also highlights the potential importance of biological contributions.

Risk Factors

Edward Shneidman pioneered the study of risk factors for suicide (Shneidman, 1989; Shneidman, Farberow, & Litman, 1970). Among the methods he and others have used to study those conditions and events that make a person vulnerable is **psychological autopsy**. The psychological profile of the person who committed suicide is reconstructed through extensive interviews with friends and family members who are likely to know what the individual was thinking and doing in the period before death. This and other methods have allowed researchers to identify a number of risk factors for suicide.

FAMILY HISTORY

If a family member committed suicide, there is an increased risk that someone else in the family will also (Kety, 1990). This may not be surprising, because so many people who kill themselves are depressed, and depression runs in families. Nevertheless, the question remains: Are people who kill themselves simply adopting a familiar solution or does an inherited trait, such as impulsivity, account for increased suicidal behavior in families? The possibility that something is inherited is supported by several adoption studies. One found an increased rate of suicide in the biological relatives of adopted individuals who had committed suicide, compared to a control group of adoptees who had not committed suicide (Schulsinger, Kety, & Rosenthal, 1979; Wender et al., 1986). In a recent small study of people whose twins had committed suicide, 10 out of 26 surviving monozygotic co-twins, and *none* of nine surviving dizygotic co-twins had themselves attempted suicide (Roy, Segal, & Sarchiapone, 1995). This suggests that there is *some* biological (genetic) contribution to suicide, even if it is relatively small.

■ **concept check 7.3**

Check your understanding of types of suicides by matching the following summaries with the correct suicide type. Choose from: (a) altruistic, (b) egoistic, (c) anomic, (d) fatalistic.

1. Ralph's wife left him and took the children. He is a well-known TV personality but, due to a conflict with the new station owners, he was recently fired. If Ralph kills himself, his suicide would be considered _____.

2. Sam killed himself while a prisoner of war in Vietnam. _____

3. Sheiba lives in a remote village in Africa. She was recently caught in an adulterous affair with a man in a nearby village. Her husband wants to kill her, but won't have to because of a tribal custom that requires her to kill herself. She leaps from the nearby "sinful woman's cliff." _____

4. Mabel lived in a nursing home for many years. At first, her family and friends visited her often; now they come only at Christmas. Her two closest friends in the nursing home died recently. She has no hobbies or other interests. Mabel's suicide would be identified as what type? _____

NEUROBIOLOGY

A variety of evidence suggests that low levels of serotonin may be associated with suicide and with violent suicide attempts (Asberg, Nordstrom, & Traskman-Bendz, 1986; Winchel, Stanley, & Stanley, 1990). As we have noted, extremely low levels of serotonin are associated with impulsivity, instability, and the tendency to overreact to situations (Spoont, 1992). It is very possible, then, that low levels of serotonin may contribute to creating a vulnerability to act impulsively. This may include killing oneself, which is sometimes a very impulsive act.

EXISTING PSYCHOLOGICAL DISORDERS

More than 90% of people who kill themselves suffer from a psychological disorder (Black & Winokur, 1990; Brent &

Kolko, 1990; Conwell et al., 1996; Garland & Zigler, 1993). Suicide is often associated with mood disorders, and for good reason. As many as 60% of suicides (75% of adolescent suicides) are associated with an existing mood disorder (Brent & Kolko, 1990; R. Frances et al., 1986). Lewinsohn, Rohde, and Seeley (1993) concluded that in adolescents suicidal behavior is in large part an expression of severe depression. But many people with mood disorders do not attempt suicide and, conversely, many people who attempt suicide do not have mood disorders. Therefore, depression and suicide, while very strongly related, are still independent. Looking more closely at the relationship of mood disorder and suicide, some investigators have isolated hopelessness, a specific component of depression, as strongly predicting suicide (A. T. Beck, 1986; A. T. Beck, Steer, Kovacs, & Garrison, 1985; Kazdin, 1983).

Alcohol use and abuse are associated with approximately 25% to 50% of suicides (for example, R. Frances et al., 1986) and are particularly evident in adolescent suicides (Conwell et al., 1996; Woods et al., 1997). Brent and colleagues (1988) found that about one-third of adolescents who commit suicide were intoxicated when they died, and that many more might have been under the influence of drugs. Combinations of disorders, such as substance abuse and mood disorders in adults or mood disorders and conduct disorder in children and adolescents, seem to create a stronger vulnerability than any one disorder alone (Conwell et al., 1996; Woods et al., 1997). In fact, Woods et al. (1997) found that substance abuse combined with other risk-taking behaviors such as getting into fights, carrying a gun, or smoking were predictive of teenage suicide, possibly reflecting impulsivity in these troubled adolescents. Past suicide attempts are another strong risk factor, and must be taken very seriously.

A disorder characterized more by impulsivity than depression is borderline personality disorder (see Chapter 12). A. Frances and Blumenthal (1989) suggest that these individuals, known for making manipulative and impulsive suicidal gestures without necessarily wanting to destroy themselves, sometimes kill themselves by mistake in as many as 10% of the cases.

The association of suicide with severe psychological disorders, especially depression, belies the myth that it is a response to disappointment in people who are otherwise healthy.

STRESSFUL LIFE EVENTS

Perhaps the most important risk factor for suicide is a severe, stressful event that is experienced as shameful or humiliating, such as a failure (real or imagined) in school or at work, an unexpected arrest, or rejection by a loved one (Blumenthal, 1990; Brent et al., 1988; Shaffer, Garland, Gould, Fisher, & Trautmen, 1988). Physical and sexual abuse are also important sources of stress (Wagner, 1997). New evidence now confirms that the stress and disruption of natural disasters increase the likelihood of suicide

(Krug et al., 1998). Based on data from 337 countries experiencing natural disasters in the 1980s, the authors concluded that the rates of suicide increased 13.8% in the 4 years after severe floods, 31% in the 2 years after hurricanes, and 62.9% in the first year after an earthquake. Given preexisting vulnerabilities—including psychological disorders, traits of impulsiveness, and lack of social support—a stressful event can often put a person over the edge. An integrated model of the causes of suicidal behavior is presented in Figure 7.12.

Is Suicide Contagious?

We hear all too often of the suicide of a teenager or celebrity. Most people react with sadness and curiosity. Some people react by attempting suicide themselves, often by the same method they have just heard about. Gould (1990) reported an increase in suicides during a 9-day period after widespread publicity about a suicide. Clusters of suicides (several people copying one person) seem to predominate among teenagers, with as many as 5% of all teenage suicides reflecting an imitation (Gould, 1990).

Why would anyone want to copy a suicide? First, suicides are often romanticized in the media: An attractive young person under unbearable pressure commits suicide and becomes something of a martyr to friends and peers by getting even with the (adult) world for creating such a difficult situation. Also, media accounts often describe in detail the methods used in the suicide, thereby providing a guide to potential victims. Little is reported about the paralysis, brain damage, and other tragic consequences of the incomplete or failed suicide or about the fact that suicide is almost always associated with a severe psychological disorder. More important, even less is said about the futility of this method of solving problems (Gould, 1990; O'Carroll, 1990). To prevent these tragedies, the media should not inadvertently glorify suicides in any way, and mental health professionals must intervene immediately in schools and other locations with people who might be depressed or otherwise vulnerable to the contagion of suicide.

Treatment

Despite the identification of important risk factors, predicting suicide is still an uncertain art. Individuals with very few precipitating factors unexpectedly kill themselves, and many who live with seemingly insurmountable stress and illness and have little social support or guidance somehow survive and overcome their difficulties.

Mental health professionals are very thoroughly trained in assessing for possible suicidal ideation. Others might be reluctant to ask leading questions for fear of putting the idea in someone's head. However, we know that it is far more important to check for these "secrets" than to do nothing, because the risk of inspiring suicidal thoughts is very small and the risk of leaving them undiscovered is enormous. Therefore, if there is any indication whatsoever that someone is suicidal, the mental health professional will inquire: "Has there been any time recently when you've had some thoughts about hurting yourself or possibly killing yourself?"

The mental health professional will also check for possible humiliations and determine whether any of the factors are present that might indicate a high probability of suicide. For example, does a person who is thinking of suicide have a detailed plan or just a vague fantasy? If a plan is discovered that includes a specific time, place, and method, the risk is obviously high. Does the detailed plan include putting all personal affairs in order, giving away possessions, and other final acts? If so, the risk is higher still. What specific method is the person considering? Generally, the more lethal and violent the method (guns, hanging, poison, and so on), the greater the risk that it will be used. Does the person really

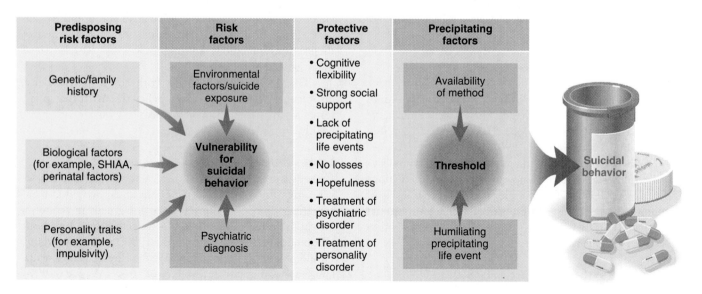

figure 7.12 Threshold model for suicidal behavior (from Blumenthal & Kupfer, 1988).

understand what might actually happen? Many people do not understand the effects of the pills on which they might overdose. Finally, has the person taken any precautions against being discovered? If so, the risk is extreme.

If a risk is present, clinicians attempt to get the individual to agree to or even sign a "no-suicide contract." Usually this includes a promise not to do anything remotely connected with suicide without contacting the mental health professional first. If the person at risk refuses a contract (or the clinician has serious doubts about the patient's sincerity) and the suicidal risk is judged to be high, immediate hospitalization is indicated, even against the will of the patient. Whether the person is hospitalized or not, treatment aimed at resolving underlying life stressors and treating existing psychological disorders should be initiated immediately.

In view of the public health consequences of suicide, a number of programs have been implemented to reduce the rates of suicide. They include curriculum-based programs in which teams of professionals go into schools or other organizations to educate people about suicide and provide information on handling life stress. In fact, the United Kingdom has targeted reducing suicide rates by 15% by the year 2000, and policy makers and mental health professionals are determining the best methods for achieving this goal (Lewis, Hawton, & Jones, 1997). Unfortunately, most research indicates that such programs are not effective (Garland & Zigler, 1993; Shaffer, Garland, Vieland, Underwood, & Busner, 1991).

More helpful are programs targeted to at-risk individuals including adolescents in schools where a student has committed suicide. The Centers for Disease Control (1988) recommend making services available immediately to friends and relatives of victims. An important step is limiting access to lethal weapons for anyone at risk for suicide. In an important study following a suicide in a high school, Brent and colleagues (1989) identified 16 students as strongly at risk and referred them for treatment. Telephone hotlines and other crisis intervention services also seem to be useful. Nevertheless, as Garland and Zigler point out, it is important that hotline volunteers be backed up by competent mental health professionals who can identify potentially serious risks.

Specific treatments for people at risk have also been developed. For example, Salkovskis, Atha, and Storer (1990) treated 20 patients at high risk for *repeated* suicide attempts with a cognitive–behavioral problem-solving approach. Results indicated that they were significantly less likely to attempt suicide in the 6 months following treatment. Marsha Linehan and her colleagues (for example, Linehan & Kehrer, 1993) have developed a noteworthy treatment for the type of impulsive suicidal behavior associated with borderline personality disorder (see Chapter 12).

In an important study, David Rudd and colleagues developed a brief psychological treatment targeting young adults who were at risk for suicide due to the presence of suicidal ideation accompanied by previous suicidal attempts and/or mood or substance use disorders (Rudd et al., 1996).

from the inside

An Unquiet Mind
By Kay Redfield Jamison

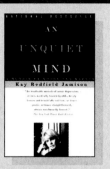

Kay Jamison, who makes a point of calling her illness "manic-depressive" instead of "bipolar," was a teenager when she suffered her first terrifying episode: "Looking back I am amazed I survived . . . and that high school contained such complicated life and palpable death" (p. 40). Confiding in no one, she ambitiously pursued high academic goals and earned a doctorate in psychology; however "within three months of becoming a professor I was ravingly psychotic" (p. 63). Jamison became an internationally respected authority on mood disorders, revealing her own chronic illness only with the publication of this gripping memoir.

Jamison's early response to her condition was to feel betrayed by her own mind, which had always been her "best friend." A depressive episode made daily life almost unendurable: "My thinking . . . was tortuous . . . Nothing made sense. I could not begin to follow the material presented in my classes. . . . It was very frightening" (p. 37). The euphoria of mania felt inexhaustible and empowering: "My mind seemed clear, fabulously focused, and able to make intuitive mathematical leaps that had up to that point entirely eluded me. Indeed, they elude me still" (p. 36).

Jamison combines a scientist's detachment with a novelist's involvement in the dual subject of herself and the disorder that is part of her. Her insights are sometimes even funny: "Suicidal depression, I decided in the midst of my indescribably awful, eighteen-month bout of it, is God's way of keeping maniacs in their place" (p. 114). Her willingness to cast light on every aspect of her experience results in passages that are chilling in their honesty:

> I have, in my psychotic, seizurelike attacks—my black, agitated manias—destroyed things I cherish, pushed to the utter edge people I love, and survived to think I could never recover from the shame. I have been physically restrained by terrible, brute force; kicked and pushed to the floor; thrown on my stomach with my hands pinned behind my back; and heavily medicated against my will. (p. 120)

Because this is, after all, a memoir, we know as we read that the writer survives, yet the extremes of manic depression push her so close to the edge of existence (she survives a suicide attempt) that it is almost with surprise, as well as with relief, that we come to the end, where we find Kay Jamison happily married, adjusted to the lifesaving lithium she once rejected, and continuing her active professional life. Brilliant achievement and unimaginable suffering entwine through the years described in this account, which affirms life even as it horrifies: "It is true that I wanted to die," writes Jamison, "but that is peculiarly different from regretting having been born" (p. 192).

They randomly assigned 264 young people to either a new treatment or to treatment as usual in the community. Patients spent approximately 9 hours each day for 2 weeks at a hospital treatment facility. Treatment consisted of problem solving, the development of social competence, coping more adaptively with life's problems, and recognizing emotional and life experiences that may have precipitated the suicide attempt or ideation. Patients were assessed up to 2 years following treatment and results indicated reductions in suicidal ideation and behavior as well as marked improvement in problem-solving ability. Furthermore, the brief experimental treatment was significantly more effective at retaining the highest risk young adults in the program.

With the increased rate of suicide, particularly in adolescents, the tragic and paradoxical act is receiving increased scrutiny from public health authorities. The quest will go on to determine more effective and efficient ways of preventing the most serious consequence of any psychological disorder, the taking of one's own life.

 # Summary

Mood Disorders: An Overview
- Mood disorders are among the most common psychological disorders, and the risk of developing them is increasing worldwide, particularly in younger people.
- Two fundamental experiences can contribute either singly or in combination to all the specific mood disorders: a major depressive episode and mania. A less severe episode of mania that does not cause impairment in social or occupational functioning is known as a hypomanic episode. An episode of mania coupled with anxiety or depression at the same time is known as a dysphoric manic or a mixed episode.
- An individual who suffers from episodes of depression only is said to have a *unipolar disorder*. An individual who alternates between depression and mania has a *bipolar disorder*.

Clinical Descriptions of Mood Disorders
- Major depressive disorder may be a single episode or recurrent, but it is always time-limited; in another form of depression, dysthymic disorder, the symptoms are somewhat milder but remain relatively unchanged over long periods of time. In cases of double depression, an individual experiences both depressive episodes and dysthymic disorder.
- The key identifying feature of bipolar disorders is an alternation of manic episodes and major depressive episodes. Cyclothymic disorder is a milder but more chronic version of bipolar disorder.
- Patterns of additional features that sometimes accompany mood disorders, called *specifiers*, may predict the course or patient response to treatment, as does the temporal patterning or course of mood disorders. One pattern, seasonal affective disorder, often occurs in winter.

Additional Statistics and Course for Mood Disorders
- Approximately 20% of bereaved individuals may experience pathological grief reaction, in which the normal grief response develops into a full-blown mood disorder.
- Mood disorders in children are fundamentally similar to mood disorders in adults.
- Symptoms of depression are increasing dramatically in our elderly population.
- The experience of anxiety across cultures varies, and it can be difficult to make comparisons, especially, for example, when we attempt to compare subjective feelings of depression.

The Relationship of Anxiety and Depression
- Some of the latest theories on the causes of depression are based, in part, on research into the relationship of anxiety and depression. Anxiety almost always precedes depression, and everyone with depression is also anxious.

Causes of Mood Disorders
- The causes of mood disorders lie in a complex interaction of biological, psychological, and social factors. From a biological perspective, researchers are particularly interested in the role of neurohormones. Psychological theories of depression focus on learned helplessness and the depressive cognitive schemas as well as interpersonal disruptions.

Treatment of Mood Disorders
- A variety of treatments, both biological and psychological, have proven effectiveness for the mood disorders, at least in the short term. For those individuals who do not respond to antidepressant drugs or psychosocial treatments, a more dramatic physical treatment, electroconvulsive therapy (ECT) is sometimes used. Two psychosocial treatments—cognitive therapy and interpersonal therapy (IPT)—seem effective in treating depressive disorders.
- Relapse and recurrence of mood disorders are common in the long term, and treatment efforts must focus as well on maintenance treatment; that is, on preventing relapse or recurrence.

Suicide
- Suicide is often associated with mood disorders but can occur in their absence. In any case, the incidence of suicide has been increasing in recent years, particularly among adolescents, for whom it is the third leading cause of death.
- In understanding suicidal behavior, two indices are important: suicidal attempts (that are not successful) and suicidal ideation (serious thoughts about committing suicide). Important, too, in learning about risk factors for suicides is the psychological autopsy, in which the psychological profile of an individual who has committed suicide is reconstructed and examined for clues.

Key Terms

mood disorders
major depressive episode

mania
hypomanic episode
dysphoric manic or mixed episode
major depressive disorder, single or recurrent episode
dysthymic disorder
double depression
pathological or impacted grief reaction
bipolar disorders
cyclothymic disorders
bipolar I disorder
bipolar II disorder
catalepsy
hallucinations
delusions
seasonal affective disorder (SAD)
neurohormones
learned helplessness theory of depression
depressive cognitive triad
electroconvulsive therapy (ECT)
cognitive therapy
interpersonal therapy (IPT)
maintenance treatment
suicidal attempts

suicidal ideation
psychological autopsy

Answers to Concept Checks

7.1
1. f
2. a
3. c
4. d
5. b

7.2
1. b
2. c
3. a
4. d
5. e

7.3
1. c
2. d
3. a
4. b

EXPLORING MOOD DISORDERS

People with mood disorders experience one or both of the following:
• **Mania:** a frantic "high" with extreme overconfidence and energy, often leading to reckless behavior
• **Depression:** a devastating "low" with extreme lack of energy, interest, confidence, and enjoyment of life

Trigger
• Negative or positive life change (death of a loved one, promotion, etc.)
• Physical illness

Biological Influences
• Inherited vulnerability
• Altered neurotransmitters and neurohormonal systems
• Sleep deprivation
• Circadian rhythm disturbances

Social Influences
• Women and minorities
  –social inequality and oppression
  –socialization toward passivity
• Women
  –socializiation toward seeking help
• Men
  –socialization against seeking help
• Social support can reduce symptoms.
• Lack of social support can aggravate symptoms.

Behavioral Influences
Depression
• General slowing down
• Neglect of responsibilities and appearance
• Irritability; complaints about matters that used to be taken in stride
Mania
• Hyperactivity
• Reckless or otherwise unusual behavior

Emotional and Cognitive Influences
Depression
• Emotional flatness or emptiness
• Inability to feel pleasure
• Poor memory
• Inability to concentrate
• Hopelessness and/or learned helplessness
• Loss of sexual desire
• Loss of warm feelings for family and friends
• Exaggerated self-blame or guilt
• Overgeneralization
• Loss of self-esteem
• Suicidal thoughts or actions
Mania
• Exaggerated feelings of euphoria and excitement

DEPRESSIVE DISORDERS

Major Depressive Disorder
Symptoms of major depressive disorder:
- begin suddenly, often triggered by a crisis, change, or loss
- are extremely severe, interfering with normal functioning
- can be long-term, lasting months or years if untreated

Some people have only one episode but the pattern usually involves repeated episodes or lasting symptoms.

Dysthymia
Long-term unchanging symptoms of mild depression, sometimes lasting 20 to 30 years if untreated. Daily functioning not as severely affected, but over time impairment is cumulative

Double Depression
Alternating periods of major depression and dysthymia

BIPOLAR DISORDERS

PEOPLE WHO HAVE A BIPOLAR DISORDER LIVE ON AN UNENDING EMOTIONAL ROLLER COASTER.

During the **Depressive Phase** the person may:
- feel tired all the time
- feel worthless, helpless, and hopeless
- Have trouble concentrating
- lose or gain weight without trying
- have trouble sleeping, or sleep more than usual
- lose all interest in pleasurable activities and friends
- feel physical aches and pains that have no medical cause
- think about death or attempt suicide

During the **Manic Phase** the person may:
- feel extreme pleasure and joy from every activity
- be extraordinarily active, planning excessive daily activities
- sleep very little without getting tired
- develop grandiose plans leading to reckless behavior: unrestrained buying sprees, sexual indiscretions, foolish business investments, etc.
- have "racing thoughts" and talk on and on very fast
- be easily irritated and distracted

TYPES OF BIPOLAR DISORDERS
- **Bipolar I**: major depression and full mania
- **Bipolar II**: major depression and mild mania
- **Cyclothymia**: mild depression with mild mania, chronic and long term

TREATMENT OF MOOD DISORDERS
Treatment for mood disorders is most effective and easiest when it's started early. Most people are treated with a combination of these methods.

Medication
Antidepressants can help to control symptoms and restore neurotransmitter functioning. Common types of antidepressants:
- Tricyclics (Tofranil, Elavil)
- Monamine oxidase inhibitors MAOIs (Nardil, Parnate). MAOIs can have severe side effects, especially when combined with certain foods or over-the-counter medications.
- Selective serotonergic reuptake inhibitors or SSRIs (Prozac, Zoloft) are newer and cause fewer side effects than tricyclics or MAOIs.

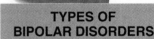

Cognitive–Behavioral Therapy
helps depressed people:
- learn to replace negative depressive thoughts and attributions with more positive ones
- develop more effective coping behaviors and skills

Interpersonal Psychotherapy
helps depressed people:
- focus on the social and interpersonal triggers for their depression (such as the loss of a loved one)
- develop skills to resolve interpersonal conflicts and build new relationships

Light Therapy
- For seasonal affective disorder

ECT (Electroconvulsive Therapy)
- For severe depression, used when other treatments have been ineffective. Usually has temporary side effects such as memory loss and lethargy. In some patients, certain intellectual and/or memory functions may be permanently lost.

8

Eating and Sleep Disorders

I saw that I needed to work from the "inside out," from my feelings, my dreams, my angers, rather than from the "outside in," which began with my body.

Geneen Roth
Feeding the Hungry Heart: The Experience of Compulsive Eating

We now begin a series of three chapters on the interaction of psychological and social factors and physical functioning. Most of us take our bodies for granted. We wake up in the morning assuming we will be alert enough to handle our required daily activities; we eat two or three meals a day and perhaps a number of snacks in between; we may engage in some vigorous exercise; and, on some days, in sexual activity. We don't focus on our functioning to any great degree unless it is disrupted by illness or disease. And yet, psychological and social factors can significantly disrupt these "activities of survival."

At school the syndrome is called scarf 'n' barf, although none of us will admit their problem. . . . *

In this chapter we talk about psychological disruptions of two of our relatively automatic behaviors, eating and sleeping, which have substantial impact on the rest of our behavior. In Chapter 9 we discuss the psychological factors involved in physical malfunctioning: specifically, illness and disease. Finally, in Chapter 10 we discuss disordered sexual behavior.

Eating Disorders: An Overview

Although some of the disorders we discuss in this chapter can be deadly, many of us are not aware that they are widespread among us. They began to increase during the 1950s or early 1960s and have spread insidiously over the ensuing decades. In **bulimia nervosa,** out-of-control eating episodes, or **binges,** are followed by self-induced vomiting, excessive use of laxatives, or other attempts to "purge" (get rid of) the food. In **anorexia nervosa,** the person eats nothing beyond minimal amounts of food, so that body weight sometimes drops dangerously. The chief characteristic of these related disorders is an overwhelming, all-encompassing drive to be thin. Of the people with anorexia nervosa who are followed over a sufficient period of time, up to 20% die as a result of their disorder with slightly over

5% dying within 10 years (for example, Ratnasuriya, Eisler, Szmuhter, & Russell, 1991; Sullivan, 1995; Theander, 1985). As many as half the deaths are suicides (Agras, 1987; Sullivan, 1995).

A growing number of studies in different countries indicate that eating disorders are widespread. In Switzerland, from 1956 to 1958 the number of new cases of anorexia nervosa under treatment among females between the ages of 12 and 25 was 3.98 per 100,000. There were 16.76 new cases per 100,000 during the 1973 to 1975 period, a fourfold increase (Willi & Grossman, 1983). Similar results were found in Scotland by Eagles, Johnston, Hunter, Lobban, and Millar (1995) between 1965 and 1991; by Lucas, Beard, O'Fallon, and Kurlan (1991) in Minnesota, over a 50-year period; and by Moller-Madsen and Nystrup (1992) in Denmark, between 1970 and 1989. Eagles et al. (1995) documented a steady increase of over 5% per year in Scotland.

Even more dramatic are the data for bulimia nervosa. Garner and Fairburn (1988) reviewed rates of referral to a major eating disorder center in Canada. Between 1975 and 1986, the referral rates for anorexia rose slowly, but the rates for bulimia rose dramatically—from virtually none to over 140 (see Figure 8.1). Similar findings have been reported from other parts of the world (Hay & Hall, 1991; Lacey, 1992). Other studies estimate a sixfold increase in death rates in this group compared to the normal population (Crisp, Callender, Halek, & Hsu, 1992; Patton, 1988). Eating disorders are included for the first time as a separate group of disorders in DSM-IV.

The increase in eating disorders would be puzzling enough if they were occurring across the population as a whole. What makes them even more intriguing is that they tend to be culturally specific. Until recently, eating disorders were not found in developing countries, where access to sufficient food is so often a daily struggle; only in the West, where food is generally plentiful, have they been rampant. Now this is changing; there is evidence that eating disorders are going global. Unsystematic interviews with health professionals in Asia (Efon, 1997) show estimates of prevalence in those countries, particularly Japan, are approaching those in the United States and other Western countries.

Not everyone in the world is at risk. In fact, eating disorders tend to occur in a relatively small segment of the population. More than 90% of the severe cases are young females, mostly in families with upper socioeconomic status, who live in a socially competitive environment. Perhaps the most visible example is the late Diana, Princess of Wales, who recounted her 7-year battle with bulimia (Morton, 1992). She reported bingeing and vomiting four or more times a day during her honeymoon.

---

*Featured quotations in this chapter are from Geneen Roth, *Feeding the Hungry Heart: The Experience of Compulsive Eating* (Plume, 1993).

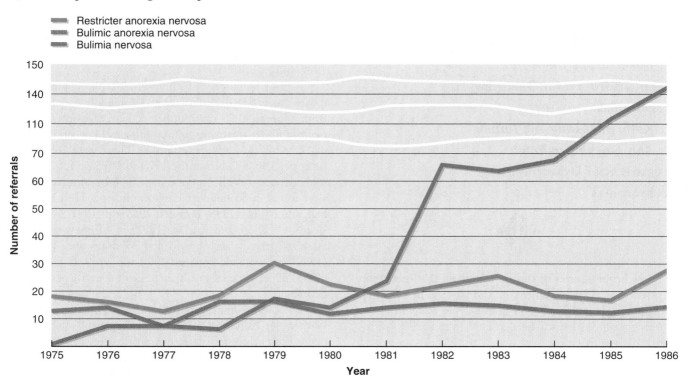

figure 8.1   Rates of referral for eating disorders (from Garner & Fairburn, 1988).

The very specificity of these disorders in terms of sex, age, and social class is unparalleled, and makes the search for causes all the more interesting. In these disorders, unlike almost any other, the strongest contributions to etiology seem to be sociocultural rather than psychological or biological factors. We will look in some detail at bulimia nervosa and anorexia nervosa, and examine briefly other eating disorders that are more common in infancy or among people with mental retardation.

Bulimia Nervosa

You are probably familiar with bulimia nervosa from your own experience or a friend's. It is one of the most common psychological disorders on college campuses. Consider the following case.

The late Princess of Wales spoke candidly about her battle against bulimia.

Phoebe
Apparently Perfect

Phoebe was a classic all-American girl: popular, attractive, intelligent, and talented, and by the time she was a senior in high school, she had accomplished a great deal. She was a class officer throughout high school, homecoming princess her sophomore year, and junior prom queen. She dated the captain of the football team. Phoebe had many talents, among them a beautiful singing voice and marked ability in ballet. Each year at Christmas time, her ballet company performed the *Nutcracker Suite,* and Phoebe attracted much attention with her poised performance in a lead role. She played on several of the school athletic teams. Phoebe maintained an A-minus average, was considered a model student, and was headed for a top-ranked university.

But Phoebe had a secret: She was haunted by her belief that she was fat and ugly. Every single bite of food that she put in her mouth was, in her mind, another step down the inexorable path that led to the end of her success and popularity. Phoebe had been concerned about her weight since she was 11. Ever the perfectionist, she began regulating her eating in junior high school. She would skip breakfast (over the protestations of her mother), eat a small bowl of pretzels at noon, and allow herself one-half of whatever she was served for dinner.

This behavior continued into high school, as Phoebe struggled to restrict her eating to occasional binges on junk food. Sometimes she stuck her fingers down her throat after a binge (she even tried a toothbrush once), but this tactic was unsuccessful. During her sophomore year in high school, Phoebe reached her full adult height of 5′ 2″ and weighed 110 pounds; she continued to fluctuate between 105 and 110 pounds throughout high school. By the time she was a senior, Phoebe's was obsessed with what she would eat and when. She used every bit of her willpower attempting to restrict her eating, but occasionally she failed. One day during the fall of her senior year, she came home after school, and alone in front of the TV, she ate two big boxes of candy. Depressed, guilty, and absolutely desperate, she went to the bathroom and stuck her fingers further down her throat than she had ever before dared. She vomited. And she kept vomiting. Although so physically exhausted that she had to lie down for half an hour, Phoebe had never in her life felt such an overwhelming sense of relief from the anxiety, guilt, and tension that always accompanied her binges. She realized that she had actually gotten to eat all that candy and now her stomach was empty. It was the perfect solution to her problems.

Phoebe learned very quickly what foods she could easily vomit. And she always drank lots of water. She began to restrict her eating even more. She ate almost nothing until after school, but then the results of her dreaming and scheming and planning all morning would be realized. Although the food sometimes varied, the routine did not. She might pick up a dozen doughnuts and a box of cookies. When she got home, she might make a bowl of popcorn.

And then she ate and ate, forcing down the doughnuts, cookies, and popcorn until her stomach actually hurt. Finally, with a mixture of revulsion and relief, she purged, forcing herself to vomit. When she was done, she stepped on the scale to make sure she had not gained any weight and then collapsed into bed and slept for about half an hour.

This routine went on for about 6 months, until April of her senior year in high school. By this time Phoebe had lost much of her energy, and her school work was deteriorating. Her teachers noticed this, and also saw that she looked bad. She was continually tired, her skin was broken out, and her face puffed up, particularly around her mouth. Her teachers and mother suspected that she might have an eating problem. When they confronted her, she was relieved that her problem was finally out in the open.

In an effort to eliminate opportunities to binge and purge, her mother rearranged her schedule to be home in the afternoon when Phoebe got there; in general, her parents minimized the occasions when Phoebe was left alone, particularly after eating. This tactic worked for about a month. Mortally afraid of gaining weight and losing her popularity, Phoebe resumed her pattern, but she was now much better at hiding it. For 6 months, Phoebe binged and purged approximately 15 times a week.

When Phoebe went away to college that fall, things became more difficult. Now she had a roommate to contend with, and she was more determined than ever to keep her problem a secret. Although the student health service offered workshops and seminars on eating disorders for the freshman women, Phoebe knew that she could not break her cycle without the risk of gaining weight. To avoid the communal bathroom, she went to a deserted place behind a nearby building to vomit. Social life at college often involved drinking beer and eating fattening foods, so she vomited more often. Nevertheless, she gained 10 pounds and weighed 120 pounds. Gaining weight was common among freshmen, but her mother commented without thinking one day that Phoebe seemed to be putting on weight. This remark was devastating to Phoebe.

She kept her secret until the beginning of her sophomore year, when her world fell apart. One night, after drinking a lot of beer at a party, Phoebe and her friends went to Kentucky Fried Chicken. Although Phoebe did not truly binge because she was with friends, she did eat a lot of fried chicken, the most forbidden food on her list. Her guilt, anxiety, and tension increased to new heights. Her stomach throbbed with pain, but when she tried to vomit, her gag reflex seemed to be gone. Breaking into hysterics, she called her boyfriend and told him she was ready to kill herself. Her loud sobbing and crying attracted the attention of her friends in her dormitory, who attempted to comfort her. She confessed her problem to them. She also called her parents. At this point, Phoebe realized that her life was totally out of control and that she needed professional help.

Clinical Description

The hallmark of bulimia nervosa is eating a larger amount of food—typically, more junk food than fruits and vegetables—than most people would eat under similar circumstances (Fairburn & Cooper, 1993). Patients with bulimia readily identify with this description, even though the actual caloric intake for binges varies significantly from person to person. Just as important as the *amount* of food eaten is the fact that the eating is experienced as *out of control* (Fairburn, Cooper, & Cooper, 1986), a criterion that is an integral part of the definition of binge eating. Both criteria characterized Phoebe.

Another important criterion is that the individual attempts to *compensate* for the binge eating and potential weight gain, almost always by **purging techniques**. Techniques include self-induced vomiting immediately after eating, as in the case of Phoebe, and using laxatives (drugs that relieve constipation) and diuretics (drugs that result in loss of fluids through greatly increased frequency of urination). Some people use both methods; others attempt to compensate in other ways. Some exercise excessively (although rigorous exercising is more usually a characteristic of anorexia nervosa; in fact, Davis et al. (1997) found that 57% of a group of patients with bulimia nervosa exercised excessively, but fully 81% of a group with anorexia did). Others fast for long periods between binges. Bulimia nervosa is subtyped in DSM-IV into *purging type* and *nonpurging type.* Approximately two-thirds of bulimics are purgers; the remaining third are nonpurgers (Hsu, 1990). McCann, Rossiter, King, and Agras (1991) and

Harold Leitenberg has studied the nature and treatment of purging in people with bulimia.

Willmuth, Leitenberg, Rosen, and Cado (1988) compared purging versus nonpurging bulimics. In both studies, purging bulimics evidence more severe psychopathology than nonpurging bulimics, including more frequent binge episodes, higher lifetime prevalence of major depression and panic disorder, and higher scores on measures of disordered eating attitudes and behaviors.

Purging is not a particularly efficient method of reducing caloric intake. Vomiting reduces approximately 50% of the calories that were just consumed, less if it is delayed at all (Kaye, Weltzin, Hsu, McConaha, & Bolton, 1993); laxatives and related procedures have very little effect, acting, as they do, so long after the binge.

One of the more important additions to the DSM-IV criteria is the specification of a psychological characteristic clearly present in Phoebe. Despite her accomplishments and success, she felt that her continuing popularity and self-esteem would be determined, to a large extent, by the weight and shape of her body. Garfinkel (1992) noted that, of 107 women seeking treatment for bulimia nervosa, only 3% did not share this attitude.

MEDICAL CONSEQUENCES

Chronic bulimia with purging has a number of medical consequences. One is salivary gland enlargement caused by repeated vomiting, which gives the face a chubby appearance. This was very noticeable with Phoebe. Repeated vomiting also may erode the dental enamel on the inner surface of the front teeth. More important, continued vomiting may upset the chemical balance of bodily fluids, including sodium and potassium levels. This condition, called an *electrolyte imbalance,* can result in serious medical complications if unattended, including cardiac arrhythmia (disrupted heartbeat) and renal (kidney) failure, both of which can be fatal. Normalization of eating habits will quickly reverse the imbalance. Intestinal problems resulting from laxative abuse are also potentially serious; they can include severe constipation or permanent colon damage. Finally, some individuals with

bulimia have marked calluses on their fingers or the backs of their hands caused by the friction of contact with the teeth and throat when repeatedly sticking their fingers down their throats to stimulate the gag reflex.

ASSOCIATED PSYCHOLOGICAL DISORDERS

An individual with bulimia usually presents with additional psychological disorders, particularly anxiety and mood disorders. We compared 20 patients with bulimia nervosa to 20 individuals with panic disorder and another 20 with social phobia (Schwalburg, Barlow, Alger & Howard, 1992). The most striking finding was that fully 75% of the patients with bulimia also presented with an anxiety disorder such as social phobia or generalized anxiety disorder; patients with anxiety disorders, on the other hand, did not necessarily have an elevated rate of eating disorders. Mood disorders, particularly depression, also commonly co-occur with eating disorders. For a number of years, one prominent theory suggested that eating disorders were simply a way of expressing depression. But almost all evidence indicates that depression *follows* bulimia and may be a reaction to it (Hsu, 1990; Brownell & Fairburn, 1995). Finally, substance abuse commonly accompanies bulimia nervosa. For example, Kendler et al. (1991) surveyed more than 2,000 twins who were not necessarily seeking treatment and found an elevated rate of alcoholism (15.5%) in subjects with bulimia. Thus, bulimia seems strongly related to anxiety disorders, and somewhat less so to mood and substance use disorders.

Anorexia Nervosa

Like Phoebe, the overwhelming majority of individuals with bulimia are within 10% of their normal weight (Hsu, 1990). In contrast, individuals with anorexia nervosa (which literally means a "nervous loss of appetite," an incorrect definition because appetite often remains healthy) differ in one important way from individuals with bulimia. They are so successful at losing weight that they put their lives in considerable danger. Both anorexia and bulimia, are characterized by a morbid fear of gaining weight and losing control over eating. The major difference seems to be whether the individual is successful at losing weight. People with anorexia are proud of both their diets and their extraordinary control. People with bulimia are ashamed of both the problem itself and their lack of control (Brownell & Fairburn, 1995). Consider the following case.

Julie
The Thinner the Better

Julie was 17 years old when she first came for help. If you looked hard enough past her sunken eyes and pasty skin, you could see that she had once been attractive. But at present, she looked emaciated and unwell. Eighteen months earlier she had been overweight, weighing 140 pounds at 5′ 1″. Her mother, a well-meaning but overbearing and demanding woman, nagged Julie incessantly about her appearance. Her friends were kinder but no less relentless. Julie, who had never had a date, was told by a friend that she was really cute and would have no trouble at all getting dates if she lost some weight. So she did! After many previous unsuccessful attempts, she was determined to succeed this time.

After several weeks on a strict diet, Julie noticed she was losing weight. She felt a control and mastery that she had never known before. It wasn't long before she received positive comments, not only from her friends but from her mother. Julie began to feel good about herself. The difficulty was that she was losing weight too fast. She stopped menstruating. But now nothing could stop her from dieting. By the time she reached our clinic, she weighed 75 pounds but she thought she looked fine and, perhaps, could even stand to lose a bit more weight. Her parents had just begun to worry about her. In fact, Julie did not initially seek treatment for her eating behavior. Rather, she had developed a numbness in her left lower leg and a left foot drop that a neurologist determined was caused by peritoneal nerve paralysis believed to be related to inadequate nutrition. The neurologist referred her to our clinic.

Like most people with anorexia, Julie said she probably should put on a little weight, but she didn't mean it. She thought she looked fine but she had "lost all taste for food," a report that may not have been true because most people with anorexia crave food at least some of the time but control their cravings. Nevertheless, she was participating in most of her usual activities and continued to do extremely well in school and in her extracurricular pursuits. Her parents were happy to buy her most of the workout videotapes available, and she began doing one every day, and then two. When her parents suggested she was really exercising enough, perhaps too much, she worked out when no one was around. After every meal, she exercised with a workout tape until, in her mind, she burned up all the calories she had just taken in.

Responses to the current physical fitness and exercise craze can become extreme for female athletes. Perhaps the best-known recent example is the world-class gymnast Christy Henrich, who died of kidney failure at the age of 22. Christy weighed approximately 95 pounds at the peak of her career. Later, during repeated hospitalizations for anorexia, Christy had to be physically restrained to prevent excessive exercise; like Julie, she exercised to the point of exhaustion if given half a chance. When she died in 1994, Christy weighed 64 pounds.

Clinical Description

Bulimia nervosa is more common than anorexia, but there is a great deal of overlap. For example, many bulimics have a history of anorexia; that is, they once used fasting to reduce their body weight below desirable levels (Mitchell & Pyle, 1988).

Although decreased body weight is the most notable feature of anorexia nervosa, it is not the core of the disorder. Many people lose weight because of a medical condition, but people with anorexia have an intense fear of obesity and relentlessly pursue thinness (Bruch, 1986; Garfinkel & Garner, 1982; Hsu, 1990; Schlundt & Johnson, 1990). As with Julie, the disorder most commonly begins in an adolescent who is actually overweight or who perceives herself to be. She then starts a diet that escalates into an obsessive preoccupation with being thin. As noted above, severe, almost punishing exercise is common, as with Julie (Davis et al., 1997). Dramatic weight loss is achieved through severe caloric restriction or by combining caloric restriction and purging.

DSM-IV specifies two subtypes of anorexia nervosa. In the *restricting type*, individuals diet to limit calorie intake; in the *binge-eating–purging type*, they rely on purging. Unlike individuals with bulimia, the binge-eating–purging anorexic binges on relatively small amounts of food and purges more consistently, in some cases each time she eats. Approximately half the individuals who meet criteria for anorexia engage in binge eating and purging (Agras, 1987; Garfinkel, Moldofsky, & Garner, 1979). Binge–purge anorexics engage in such impulsive behavior as stealing, alcohol and drug use, and self-mutilation more than restricting anorexics, and their moods are more variable (labile); in this way they resemble normal-weight bulimics. Individuals who binge and purge, whether they suffer from anorexia or not, are also

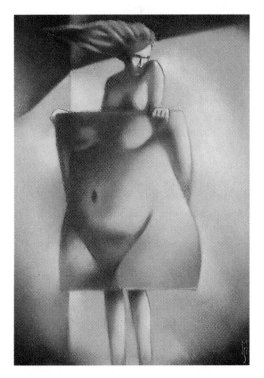

Many women with anorexia are overweight when they develop an obsessive preoccupation with being thin.

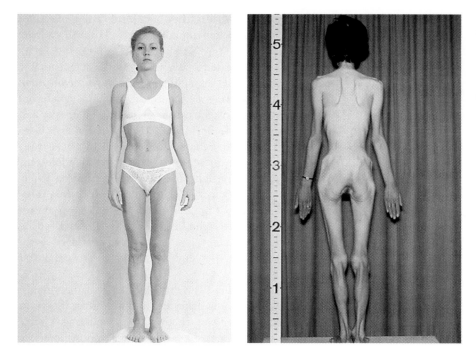

These women are at different stages of anorexia.

more likely to have been obese as children and to have a history of obesity in their families (Garner, Garfinkel, & O'Shaughnessy, 1985).

A girl with anorexia is never satisfied with her weight loss. Staying the same weight from one day to the next or gaining any weight at all is likely to cause intense panic, anxiety, and depression. Only continued weight loss every day for weeks on end is satisfactory. Although DSM-IV criteria specify body weight 15% below that expected, the average is approximately 25% to 30% below normal by the time treatment is sought (Hsu, 1990). Another key criterion of anorexia is a marked disturbance in body image. When Julie looked at herself in the mirror, she saw something very different from what others saw. They saw an emaciated, sickly, frail girl in the throes of semistarvation. Julie saw a girl who needed to lose at least a few pounds from some parts of her body. For Julie, her face and buttocks were the problems. Other girls might focus on other parts, such as the arms or legs or stomach.

After seeing numerous doctors, people like Julie become good at mouthing what others expect to hear. They may agree that they are underweight and need to gain a few pounds—but they don't believe it. Question further and they will tell you that the girl in the mirror is fat. For this reason, individuals with anorexia seldom seek treatment on their own. Usually pressure from somebody in the family leads to the initial visit, as in Julie's case (Agras, 1987; Sibley & Blinder, 1988). Perhaps as a demonstration of absolute control over their eating, some anorexic individuals show increased interest in cooking and food. Some have become expert chefs, preparing all the food for the family. Others hoard food in their rooms, looking at it from time to time. We will review research that seems to explain these curious behaviors.

MEDICAL CONSEQUENCES

The most common medical complication of anorexia nervosa is cessation of menstruation (amenorrhea), which also occurs occasionally in bulimia. This defining feature is an objective physical index of the degree of food restriction. In fact, studies have demonstrated a strong correlation between ovulation and resulting menstruation and weight (Pirke, Schweiger, & Fichter, 1987), but overwhelming evidence indicates that alterations in endocrine levels resulting in amenorrhea are a consequence of semistarvation rather than a cause. Other medical signs and symptoms of anorexia include dry skin, brittle hair or nails, and sensitivity to or intolerance of cold temperatures. Also it is relatively common to see *lanugo*, downy hair on the limbs and cheeks. Cardiovascular problems, such as chronically low blood pressure and heart rate, can also result. If vomiting is part of the anorexia, electrolyte imbalance and resulting cardiac and kidney problems can result, as in bulimia.

ASSOCIATED PSYCHOLOGICAL DISORDERS

Like bulimia nervosa, anxiety disorders and mood disorders are often present in individuals with anorexia (Kaye, Weltzin, & Hsu, 1993). Interestingly, one that seems to co-occur frequently is obsessive–compulsive disorder (OCD) (see Chapter 5). In anorexia nervosa, unpleasant thoughts are focused on gaining weight and the individual engages in a variety of behaviors, some of them ritualistic, to rid themselves of such thoughts. Future research will determine whether anorexia and OCD are truly similar, or simply resemble each other. Substance abuse is also common in individuals with anorexia nervosa (Wilson, 1993).

■ concept check 8.1

Decide if the following are characteristics of (a) anorexia nervosa or (b) bulimia nervosa.

1. The major component of this disorder is binge eating. _____

2. Often leads to electrolyte imbalance, resulting in serious medical problems. _____

3. Individuals with this disorder are successful at losing weight. _____

4. In DSM-IV this disorder is divided into two subtypes, restricting and binge-eating–purge type. _____

5. Amenorrhea, the absence of at least three consecutive menstrual cycles, frequently occurs. _____

Binge-Eating Disorder

Recent research has focused on a group of individuals who experience marked distress due to binge eating but do *not* engage in extreme compensatory behaviors and therefore cannot be diagnosed with bulimia (Castonguay, Eldredge, & Agras, 1995; Spitzer et al., 1991). These individuals have **binge-eating disorder (BED)**. Currently, BED is in the appendix of DSM-IV as a potential new disorder requiring further study. Many investigators are beginning to conclude that it should be included as a full-fledged disorder in future editions of the DSM, or at least combined with existing disorders. For example, Castonguay et al. (1995) suggest that bulimia and binge-eating disorder could be combined, because bingeing is a prominent feature of both disorders; individuals could then be subtyped as to whether they purge or not and whether they are obese or not. Further research will determine if this designation would be useful (Fairburn, Hay, & Welch, 1993; Fairburn & Wilson, 1993).

Individuals who meet preliminary criteria for BED are often found in weight-control programs. For example, Brody, Walsh and Devlin (1994) studied mildly obese subjects in a weight-control program and identified 18.8% who met criteria for BED. In other programs, with the full range of obese subjects, close to 30% meet criteria (e.g., Spitzer et al., 1993); and among Overeaters Anonymous the figure is 70% (Spitzer et al., 1992). People who have binge-eating disorder seem to differ in a variety of ways from people with other eating disorders and from obese people who don't binge. For example, the gender difference is not as dramatic in BED, with the female-to-male ratio at 3:1 in weight-control samples and no more than 2:1 in community surveys (Bruce & Agras, 1992; Spitzer et al., 1993), compared to 9:1 for bulimia and anorexia (see below). Tanofsky, Wilfly, Spurrel, Welch, and Brownell (1997) found no significant differences in concerns about shape or weight, measures of eating disturbance, interpersonal difficulties, or self-esteem when comparing men and women with BED. Men, however, did seem to have a greater number of other diagnoses, such as anxiety and substance abuse disorders, whereas women reported bingeing in response to anxiety, anger, frustration, or depression more than men. Individuals with BED who seek treatment are typically in their 40s, older on average than individuals with anorexia or bulimia (Arnow, Kenardy, & Agras, 1992; Schwalberg, Barlow, Alger, & Howard, 1992; Telch & Agras, 1994). But, since age of onset seems to be from 19 to 25, it simply may be that people with BED wait longer before seeking treatment. They show an increased frequency of additional psychological disorders and more psychopathology in general than obese people who don't binge. Marcus and colleagues (1990) reported significant rates of mood and anxiety disorders and psychosexual dysfunction among obese binge eaters. Schwalberg and colleagues (1992) also reported roughly equal rates of anxiety and mood disorders among normal-weight bulimics and obese binge eaters. Other studies have found similar results (Castonguay et al., 1995; Kirkley, Kolotkin, Hernandez, & Gallagher, 1992; Marcus, Smith, Santelli, & Kaye, 1992). Again, higher rates of psychopathology among individuals with BED, compared to obese individuals who don't binge, underscore differences in degree of psychological disturbance.

About half try dieting before bingeing, while half start with bingeing; those who begin bingeing first become more severely affected and more likely to have additional disorders (Spurrell, Wilfley, Tanofsky, & Brownell, 1997). It's also increasingly clear that individuals with BED have some of the same concerns about shape and weight as people with anorexia and bulimia (Eldredge & Agras, 1996).

Statistics

Clear cases of bulimia have been described for thousands of years (Parry-Jones & Parry-Jones, 1994), but bulimia nervosa was recognized as a distinct psychological disorder only in the 1970s (Boskind-Lodahl, 1976; Russell, 1979). Therefore, information on prevalence has been acquired quite recently.

We have already noted that the overwhelming majority (90% to 95%) of individuals with bulimia are women; most are white and middle to upper-middle class. The 5% to 10% of cases who are male have a slightly later age of onset and a large minority are predominately homosexual or bisexual. For example, Carlat, Camargo, and Herzog (1997) accumulated information on 135 male patients with eating disorders who were seen over 13 years and found that 42% were either homosexual or bisexual. Male athletes in sports that require weight regulation, such as wrestling, are another large group of males with eating disorders. During 1998, stories were widely published about the deaths of 3 wrestlers from complications of eating disorders. Interestingly, the gender imbalance in bulimia was not always present. Historians of psychopathology note that for hundreds of years the vast majority of (unsystematically) recorded cases were male (Parry-Jones & Parry-Jones, 1994). Because women with bulimia are overwhelmingly preponderant today, most of our examples are women.

Age of onset is typically 16 to 19 years of age (Garfinkel et al., 1995; Mitchell & Pyle, 1988), although signs of impending bulimic behavior can occur much earlier, as in Phoebe's case. Schlundt and Johnson (1990), summarizing a large number of surveys, suggest that between 6% and 8% of young women, especially on college campuses, meet criteria for bulimia nervosa. J. Gross and Rosen (1988) reported that as many as 9% of high school girls would meet criteria, although only about 2% were purging at that age. Most people who seek treatment are in the purging subtype.

> *The problem with bingeing is that the relief is only temporary.*

A somewhat different view of the prevalence of bulimia comes from studies of the population as a whole rather than of specific groups of adolescents. In one of the better studies, sampling over 8,000 individuals in the Province of Ontario, the lifetime prevalence was 1.1% for females and 0.1% for males (Garfinkel et al., 1995). This very low prevalence rate for males is consistent with earlier reports (Carlat & Camargo, 1991). In careful study in New Zealand (Bushnell, Wells, Hornblow, Oakley-Browne, & Joyce, 1990), the lifetime prevalence of bulimia nervosa among women age 18 to 44 years was 1.6%. However, the rate was substantially higher among younger women. For instance, among women age 18 to 24, the prevalence was 4.5%. Among women aged 25 to 44, the prevalence was 2%, but it was only 0.4% among women age 45 to 64. Numbers seem to be highest in urban areas (Hoek et al., 1995).

Perhaps the most important study of prevalence was reported by Kendler and colleagues (1991). In this study, 2,163 twins (more than 1,000 sets of twins) were interviewed and the lifetime prevalence of bulimia nervosa was found to be 2.8%, increasing to 5.3% when marked bulimic symptoms that did not meet full criteria for the disorder were included. Once again, the prevalence was greatest in younger women. As is evident in Figure 8.2, the risk was much higher for females born from 1960 onward than for females born before 1960. Nevertheless, as pointed out by Fairburn and his colleagues (Fairburn & Beglin, 1990; Fairburn, Hay, & Welch, 1993), estimates are probably low, because many individuals with eating disorders refuse to participate in studies. Therefore, the percentages represent only those individuals who consented to participate in the survey. Once bulimia develops, it tends to be chronic if untreated (Keel & Mitchell, 1997); one study shows the "drive for thinness" and accompanying symptoms still present in a group of women 10 years after diagnosis (Joiner, Heatherton, & Keel, 1997).

The same high percentage (90% to 95%) of individuals with anorexia are female, with onset also in adolescence, usually around the age of 13 (Herzog, 1988). Studies cited in the beginning of this chapter noted the increase in rates of anorexia, particularly in the 1960s and 1970s. Walters and Kendler (1995) have now analyzed data from the same 2,163 twins mentioned above to determine the prevalence of anorexia nervosa. The results indicate that 1.62% met criteria for lifetime prevalence and that this figure increased to 3.70% with the inclusion of marked anorexic symptoms that did not meet full criteria for the disorder. These results are in agreement with data in Figure 8.1, suggesting that bulimia is somewhat more common than anorexia.

Cross-Cultural Considerations

We have already discussed the highly culturally specific nature of anorexia and bulimia. A particularly striking finding is that these disorders develop in immigrants who have recently moved to Western countries (Nasser, 1988). One of the more interesting studies is Nasser's (1986) survey of 50 Egyptian women in London universities and 60 Egyptian women in Cairo universities. There were no instances of eating disorders in Cairo, but 12% of the Egyptian women in England had developed eating disorders. Mumford, Whitehouse, and Platts (1991) found the same result with Asian women living in the U.S. The prevalence of eating disorders varies among most North American minority populations, including African-Americans, Hispanics, Native Americans, and Asians. The prevalence of eating disorders among African-American and Asian-American females is lower than among Caucasians, but they are equally common among Hispanic females and more frequent among Native Americans (Crago, Shisslak, & Estes, 1996). Generally, surveys reveal that African-American adolescent girls have less body dissatisfaction, fewer weight concerns, a positive self-image, and perceive themselves to be thinner than they actually are compared to Caucasian adolescent girls. Major risk factors for eating disorders in all groups include overweight, higher social class, and acculturation to the majority (A. Anderson & Hay, 1985; Crago, Shisslak, & Estes, 1997; Raich et al., 1992; J. E. Smith & Krejci, 1991).

There is a relatively high incidence of purging behavior in some minority groups. In most cases, the purging seems to be associated with obesity. L. W. Rosen and colleagues (1988) found widespread purging and related behaviors in a group of Chippewa women. Among this group, 74% had dieted and 55% had used harmful weight-loss techniques such as fasting or purging; 12% had vomited, and 6% reported use of laxatives or diuretics.

One culturally determined difference in criteria for eating disorders has been reported by S. Lee and colleagues (1991). In traditional Chinese cultures, being slightly plump is highly valued. Ideals of beauty focus on the face rather than the body. Therefore, in this group, acne was more often

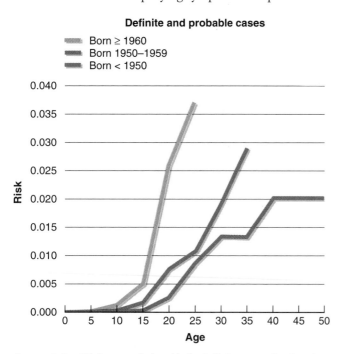

figure 8.2 Lifetime cumulative risk for bulimia among female twins (from Kendler et al., 1991).

Anorexia seldom occurs among North American black women.

reported as a precipitant for anorexia nervosa than a fear of being fat, and body image disturbance is rare (S. Lee, Hsu, & Wing, 1992). Patients said they refused to eat because of feelings of fullness or pain, although it is possible that they related food intake to their skin conditions. Beyond that, they met all criteria for anorexia.

In Japan, the prevalence of anorexia nervosa among teenage girls is still lower than the rate in North America but, as mentioned above, it seems to be increasing. The need to be thin or the fear of becoming overweight has not been as important in Japanese culture as it is in North America, although this may be changing as cultures around the world become more westernized. Body image distortion and denial that a problem exists are clearly present in patients who have the disorder (Ritenbaugh, Shisstak, Teufel, Leonard-Green, & Prince, 1994).

In conclusion, anorexia and bulimia are relatively homogeneous and, until recently, overwhelmingly associated with Western cultures. In addition, the frequency and pattern of occurrence among minority Western cultures differs somewhat, but is associated with closer identification with Caucasian middle class values.

Developmental Considerations

Because the overwhelming majority of cases begin in adolescence, it is very clear that anorexia and bulimia are strongly related to development. As pointed out by Striegal-Moore, Silberstein, and Rodin (1986) and Attie and Brooks-Gunn (1995), differential patterns of physical development in girls and boys interact with cultural influences to create eating disorders. After puberty, girls gain weight primarily in fat tissue, whereas boys develop muscle and lean tissue. As the ideal look is tall and muscular for men and thin and prepubertal for women, physical development brings boys closer to the ideal and takes girls further away.

Eating disorders, particularly anorexia nervosa, occasionally occur in children under the age of 11. In those rare cases of young children developing anorexia, they are very likely to restrict fluid intake as well as food intake, perhaps not understanding the difference (Gislason, 1988). This, of course, is particularly dangerous. Concerns about weight are less common in young children, but many have experienced severe stress such as the death of a loved one, parental divorce, or the birth of a sibling.

Both bulimia and anorexia occur in later years, particularly after the age of 55. Hsu and Zimmer (1988) reported that most of these individuals had had an eating disorder for decades with very little change in their behavior. However, in a few cases onset did not occur until later years, and it is not yet clear what factors were involved.

 **Causes**

As with all the disorders discussed in this book, biological, psychological, and social factors contribute to the development of these serious eating disorders, but the evidence is increasingly clear that the most dramatic factors are social and cultural.

Social Dimensions

Remember that anorexia and bulimia are the most culturally specific psychological disorders yet diagnosed. What drives so many young people into a punishing and life-threatening routine of semistarvation or purging? For many young Western women, looking good is more important than being healthy. In fact, for young females in middle- to upper-class competitive environments, self-worth, happiness, and success are determined to a large extent by body measurements and percentage of body fat, factors that have little or no correlation with personal happiness and success in the long run. The cultural imperative for thinness directly results in dieting, the first dangerous step down the slippery slope to anorexia and bulimia.

What makes the modern emphasis on thinness in women even more puzzling is that standards of desirable body sizes change much like fashion styles in clothes, if not as quickly. Several groups of investigators have documented this phenomenon in some interesting ways. Garner, Garfinkel, Schwartz, and Thompson (1980) collected data from *Playboy* magazine centerfolds and from Miss America pageants from 1959 to 1978. Over the years, both *Playboy* centerfolds and Miss America contestants became significantly thinner after 1960. Bust and hip measurements be-

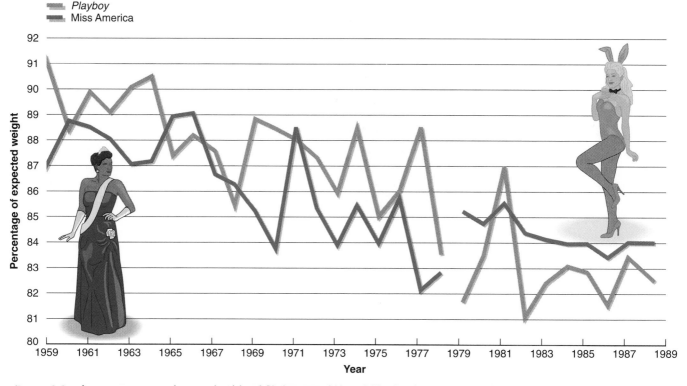

figure 8.3   Average percentage of expected weight of Playboy centerfolds and Miss America contestants, 1959–1988 (from Wiseman et al., 1992).

came smaller, although waists became somewhat larger, suggesting a change in what is considered desirable in the *shape* of the body in addition to weight. The preferred shape during the 1960s and 1970s was thinner and more tubular than before (Agras & Kirkley, 1986). More recently, Wiseman, Gray, Mosimann, and Ahrens (1992) updated the research, collecting data from 1979 to 1988. They reported that Miss America contestants continued to decrease in weight significantly, while *Playboy* centerfolds remained at a relatively low level of body weight. In fact, 69% of the *Playboy* centerfolds and 60% of the Miss America contestants weighed 15% or more below normal for their age and height, actually meeting one of the criteria for anorexia. Data from both studies are presented in Figure 8.3. Just as important, when Wiseman and colleagues (1992) counted diet and exercise articles in six women's magazines from 1959 to 1988, they found a significant increase in both, with articles on exercise increasing dramatically over the past 8 years, surpassing the number on diet. Levine and Smolak (1996) refer to "the glorification of slenderness" in magazines and on television, where the vast majority of females are thinner than average American women. Because overweight men are two to five times more common as television characters than overweight women, the message from the media to be thin

is clearly aimed at women. Stice, Schupak-Neuberg, Shaw, and Stein (1994) established a strong relationship between amount of media exposure and eating disorder symptomatology in college women. In another study, girls who watched eight or more hours of TV per week reported significantly greater body dissatisfaction than girls who watched less TV (Gonzalez-Lavin and Smolak, 1995; Levine and Smolak, 1996).

Pictures of Marilyn Monroe, the popular movie star and pinup of the 1950s, reflect the standard of beauty at that

Changing concepts of ideal weight are evident in a turn-of-the-20th-century painting by Auguste Renoir and in a 1990s photograph of a fashion model.

time, which was much thinner than some of the beauties depicted in famous Renaissance paintings several hundred years ago. Rubens and Botticelli depicted women who were considered gorgeous in their day but would be quite overweight in the present (Brownell, 1991).

An emphasis on thinness that increased steadily over the centuries would be a source of substantial concern for future generations, but this has not been the case. During the 1920s, the ideal female body was similar in shape to the ideal today (Agras & Kirkley, 1986); however, this shape was achieved through fashion (for instance, binding of the breasts) rather than dieting. In fact, no diet articles appeared in the magazines of the period that were sampled, whereas today we see what Brownell and Rodin (1994) have called "the dieting maelstrom," in which health professionals, the media, and a powerful diet and food industry all have stakes.

The problem with today's standards is that they are increasingly difficult to achieve, since the size and weight of the average woman has increased over the years with improved nutrition; there is also a general increase in size throughout history (Brownell, 1991; Brownell & Rodin, 1994). Whatever the cause, the collision between our culture and our physiology (Brownell, 1991; Brownell & Fairburn, 1995) has had some very negative effects, one of which is that women are no longer satisfied with their bodies. A second clear effect is the dramatic increase, especially among women, in dieting and exercise in order to achieve what may in fact be an impossible goal. Look at the increase in dieting since the 1950s. Dwyer, Feldman, Seltzer, and Mayer reported in 1969 that more than 80% of female high school seniors wished to lose weight and that 30% were dieting. Among their male counterparts, fewer than 20% wished to lose weight and only 6% were dieting. More recently, Hunnicut and Newman (1993) surveyed a national sample of 3,632 eighth- and tenth-grade students and found that 60.6% of females and 28.4% of males were dieting. Although these studies are not directly comparable, younger girls typically diet less than older girls, which suggests that the increase is even more dramatic.

Fallon and Rozin (1985), studying male and female undergraduates, found that men rated their current size, their ideal size, and the size they figured would be most attractive to the opposite sex as approximately equal; indeed, they rated their ideal body weight as *heavier* than the weight females thought most attractive in men (see Figure 8.4). Women, however, rated their current figures as much heavier than the most attractive, which, in turn, was rated as heavier than the ideal. In addition, women's judgment of ideal female body weight was *less* than the weight men thought most attractive. This conflict between reality and fashion seems most closely related to the current epidemic of eating disorders. Greenberg and LaPorte (1996) observed in an experiment that young white males preferred somewhat thinner figures in women

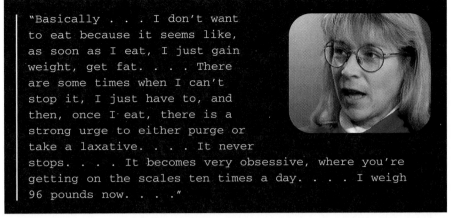

"Basically . . . I don't want to eat because it seems like, as soon as I eat, I just gain weight, get fat. . . . There are some times when I can't stop it, I just have to, and then, once I eat, there is a strong urge to either purge or take a laxative. . . . It never stops. . . . It becomes very obsessive, where you're getting on the scales ten times a day. . . . I weigh 96 pounds now. . . ."

Kelly Brownell documented the collision between culture and physiology that results in overwhelming pressure to be thinner.

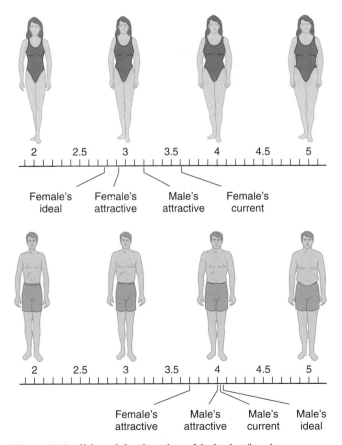

figure 8.4 Male and female ratings of body size (based on Stunkard, Sorensen, & Schulsinger, 1980).

than African-American males, which may contribute to the somewhat lower incidence of eating disorders in African-American women. The efforts of some people to maintain thin, athletic shapes are almost superhuman. Miss America contestants work out an average of 14 hours per week, with some exercising 35 hours per week (Trebbe, 1979).

The abhorrence of fat can have tragic consequences. Remember the case of failure to thrive or psychosocial dwarfism mentioned in Chapter 2? The individual's growth was severely stunted by inadequate nutrition and severely abusive or neglectful parenting. A number of toddlers with affluent parents appeared at hospitals with the same syndrome, but in each case the parents had put their young, healthy, but somewhat chubby infants on diets in the hope of preventing obesity at a later date (Pugliese, Weyman-Daun, Moses, & Lifshitz, 1987). Of course, most people who diet don't develop eating disorders, but Patton, Johnson-Sabine, Wood, Mann, and Wakeling (1990) determined in a prospective study that adolescent girls who dieted were eight times more likely to develop an eating disorder 1 year later than those who weren't dieting. More recently, C. F. Telch and Agras (1993) noted marked increases in bingeing during and after rigorous dieting in 201 obese women. It is not yet entirely clear why dieting leads to bingeing in some people but not all (Polivy & Herman, 1993), but the relationship is strong.

The conflict over body image would be bad enough if size were infinitely malleable, but it is not. Increasing evidence indicates a strong genetic contribution to body size; that is, some of us are born to be heavier than others and we are all shaped differently. Although most of us can be physically fit, very few can achieve the levels of fitness and shape so highly valued today. It is biologically nearly impossible (Brownell, 1991). Nevertheless, many young people in our society fight biology to the point of starvation. In adolescence, cultural standards are often experienced as peer pressure, and are much more influential than reason and fact. The high number of males who are homosexual among the relatively small numbers of males with eating disorders has also been attributed to pressures in the gay culture to be physically trim (Carlat et al., 1997).

Dietary Restraint

During World War II, in what has become a classic study, Keys and his colleagues (Keys, Brozek, Henschel, Michelson, & Taylor, 1950) conducted a semistarvation experiment involving 36 conscientious objectors who volunteered for the study as an alternative to military service. For 6 months, these healthy men were given about half their former full intake of food. This period was followed by a 3-month rehabilitation phase, during which food was gradually increased. During the diet, the subjects lost an average of 25% of their body weight. The results were carefully documented, particularly the psychological effects.

The investigators found that the subjects became preoccupied with food and eating. Conversations, reading, and daydreams revolved around food. Many began to collect recipes and to hoard food-related items. Some men never lost their obsession with food. The bizarre behavior of individu-

als with anorexia who become chefs for their families and hoard food could be an effect of dieting or starvation alone.

If cultural pressures to be thin are as important as they seem to be in triggering eating disorders, then such disorders would be expected to occur where these pressures are particularly severe, which is just what happens to ballet dancers, who are under extraordinary pressures to be thin. In an important study, Szmukler, Eisler, Gillis, and Haywood (1985) examined 100 adolescent female ballet students in London. Fully 7% were diagnosed with anorexia nervosa, and an additional 3% were borderline cases. Another 20% had lost a significant amount of weight, and 30% were clearly afraid of becoming fat, although they were actually below normal weight (Garner & Garfinkel, 1985). All these figures are much higher than in the population as a whole. In another study, Garner, Garfinkel, Rockert, and Olmsted (1987) followed a group of 11- to 14-year-old female students in ballet school. Their conservative estimate was that at least 25% of these girls developed eating disorders during the 2 years of the study. Very similar results are apparent among athletes, particularly females, such as gymnasts.

What exactly goes on in ballet classes that has such a devastating effect on girls?

Phoebe
Dancing to Destruction

Phoebe remembered very clearly that during her early years in ballet the older girls talked incessantly about their weight. Phoebe performed very well and looked forward to the rare compliment. In fact, the ballet mistress seemed to comment more on weight than on dance technique, often remarking, "You'd dance better if you lost weight." If one little girl managed to lose a few pounds through heroic dieting, the instructor always pointed it out: "You've done well working on your weight; the rest of you had better follow this example." One day, without warning, the instructor said to Phoebe, "You need to lose 5 pounds before the next class." At that time Phoebe was 5' 2" tall and weighed 98 pounds. The next class was in 2 days. After one of these admonitions and several days of restrictive eating, Phoebe experienced her first uncontrollable binge.

Early in high school, Phoebe gave up the rigors of ballet to pursue a variety of other interests. She did not forget the glory of her starring roles as a young dancer or how to perform the steps. She still danced from time to time by herself and retained the grace that serious dancers effortlessly display. But in college, as she stuck her head in the toilet bowl, vomiting her guts out for perhaps the third time that day, she realized that there was one lesson she had learned in ballet class more deeply and thoroughly than any other—the life-or-death importance of being thin at all costs.

Family Influences

Much has been made of the possible significance of family interaction patterns in cases of eating disorders. A number of investigators (for example, Attie & Brooks-Gunn, 1995; Bruch, 1985; Humphrey, 1986, 1988, 1989; Minuchin, Rosman, & Baker, 1978) have found that the "typical" anorexic's family is successful, hard-driving, concerned about external appearances, and eager to maintain harmony. To accomplish these goals, family members often deny or ignore conflicts or negative feelings and tend to attribute their problems to other people at the expense of frank communication among themselves (Hsu, 1990).

Pike and Rodin (1991) confirmed the differences in interactions within the families of girls with disordered eating in comparison with control families. Basically, mothers of girls with disordered eating seemed to act as "society's messengers" in wanting their daughters to be thin. They were very likely to be dieting themselves and, generally, were more perfectionistic than control mothers in that they were less satisfied with their families and family cohesion.

> *When I was eleven, my mother told me I couldn't have two Good Humor ice creams in one day because I was getting fat.*

Whatever the preexisting relationships, after the onset of an eating disorder, particularly anorexia, family relationships can deteriorate quickly. Nothing is more frustrating than watching your daughter starve herself at a dinner table where food is plentiful. Educated and knowledgeable parents, including psychologists and psychiatrists with full understanding of the disorder at hand, have reported resorting to physical violence (for instance, hitting or slapping) in moments of extreme frustration, in a vain attempt to get their daughters to put some food, however little, in their mouths. The parents' guilt and anguish often exceed the levels of anxiety and depression present in the children with the disorder.

Biological Dimensions

Like most psychological disorders, eating disorders run in families and thus seem to have a genetic component. Although completed studies are only preliminary, they suggest that relatives of patients with eating disorders are four to five times more likely than the general population to develop eating disorders themselves (for instance, Hudson, Pope, Jonas, & Yurgelun-Todd, 1983; Strober & Humphrey, 1987). In important twin studies of bulimia by Kendler and colleagues (1991) and of anorexia by Walten and Kendler (1995), researchers used structured interviews to ascertain the prevalence of the disorders among 2,163 female twins. In 23% of monozygotic twin pairs, both twins had bulimia, as compared to 9% of dizygotic twins. Because no adoption studies have yet been reported, strong sociocultural influences cannot be ruled out. But the results from this study, if replicated, would certainly suggest a genetic contribution to bulimia. For anorexia, numbers were too small for precise estimates, but the disorder in one twin conferred a significant risk for both anorexia and bulimia in the co-twin. However, once again, there is no clear agreement on just *what* (if anything) is inherited. Hsu (1990) speculates that nonspecific personality traits such as emotional instability and, perhaps, poor impulse control might be inherited. In other words, a person might inherit a tendency to be emotionally respon-

sive to stressful life events and, as one consequence, might eat impulsively in an attempt to relieve stress and anxiety. This biological vulnerability might then interact with social and psychological factors to produce an eating disorder.

Obviously, biological processes are quite active in the regulation of eating and thus of eating disorders, and substantial evidence points to the hypothalamus as playing an important role. Investigators have studied the hypothalamus and the major neurotransmitter systems—including norepinephrine, dopamine, and, particularly, serotonin—that pass through it to determine whether something is misfunctioning when eating disorders occur. Low levels of serotonergic activity are associated with impulsivity in general and binge eating specifically (see Chapter 2). Thus, most drugs currently under study as bulimia treatments target the serotonin system (e.g., Walsh et al., 1997).

If investigators do find a strong association between neurobiological functions and eating disorders, the question of cause or effect remains. At present, the consensus is that some neurobiological abnormalities do exist in people with eating disorders, but they are a *result* of semistarvation or a binge–purge cycle rather than a cause, although they may well contribute to the *maintenance* of the disorder once it is established.

Psychological Dimensions

Clinical observations indicate that many young women with eating disorders have a diminished sense of personal control and confidence in their own abilities and talents (Bruch, 1973, 1985; Striegal-Moore, Silberstein, & Rodin, 1993; Walters & Kendler, 1995). Women with eating disorders are intensely preoccupied with how they appear to others. They also perceive themselves as frauds, considering false any impressions they make of being adequate, self-sufficient, or worthwhile. In this sense they feel like impostors in their social groups and experience heightened levels of social anxiety (Smolak & Levine, 1996). Striegal-Moore and colleagues (1993) suggest that these social self-deficits are likely to increase as a consequence of the eating disorder, further isolating the woman from the social world.

Specific distortions in perception of body shape change frequently, depending on day-to-day experience. McKenzie, William-

Judith Rodin and her colleagues have made important discoveries about the social influences on people with eating disorders.

son, and Cubic (1993) found that bulimic women judged their body size to be larger and their ideal weight to be less than same-size controls. Indeed women with bulimia judged that their bodies were larger after they ate a candy bar and soft drink, whereas the judgments of women in control groups were unaffected by snacks. Thus, rather minor events related to eating may activate fear of gaining weight, further distortions in body image, and corrective schemes such as purging.

J. C. Rosen and Leitenberg (1985) observed substantial anxiety before and during snacks, which they theorized is *relieved* by purging. They suggested that the state of relief strongly reinforces the purging, in that we tend to repeat behavior that gives us pleasure or relief from anxiety. This seemed to be true for Phoebe. However, other evidence suggests that in treating bulimia, reducing the anxiety associated with eating is less important than countering the tendency to overly restrict food intake and the associated

negative attitudes about body image that lead to bingeing and purging (for example, Agras, Schneider, Arnow, Raeburn, & Telch, 1989; Fairburn, Agras, & Wilson, 1992).

An Integrative Model

In putting together what we know about eating disorders, it is important to remember, once again, that no one factor seems sufficient to cause them (see Figure 8.5). Individuals with eating disorders may have some of the same biological vulnerabilities (such as being highly responsive to stressful life events) as individuals with anxiety disorders. Anxiety and mood disorders are also common in the families of individuals with eating disorders (Schwalberg et al., 1992). In addition, as we will see, drug and psychosocial treatments with proven effectiveness for anxiety disorders are also the treatments of choice for eating disorders. Indeed, we could

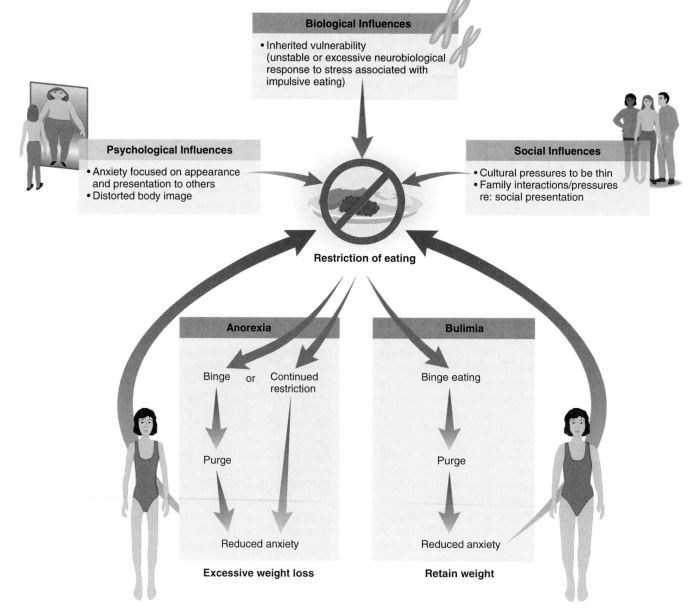

figure 8.5 An integrative causal model of eating disorders.

conceptualize eating disorders as anxiety disorders focused exclusively on becoming overweight.

In any case, it is clear that social and cultural pressures to be thin motivate significant restriction of eating, usually through severe dieting. Remember, however, that many people go on strict diets, including adolescent females, but only a small minority develop eating disorders, so dieting alone does not account for the disorders. It is also important to note that the interactions in high-income, high-achieving families may well be a factor. An emphasis on looks and achievement may help establish very strong attitudes about the overriding importance of physical appearance to popularity and success. Finally, there is the question of why a small minority of individuals with eating disorders can successfully control their intake, resulting in alarming weight loss, while the majority are unsuccessful at losing weight and compensate in a cycle of bingeing and purging. These differences may be determined by biology or physiology, such as a genetically determined disposition to be somewhat thinner to begin with. Then again, perhaps preexisting personality characteristics, such as a tendency to be overcontrolling, are important determinants of which disorder a girl develops.

Treatment of Eating Disorders

Only since the 1980s have there been treatments for bulimia; treatments for anorexia have been around much longer but were not well developed. Rapidly accumulating evidence indicates that at least one, possibly two psychosocial treatments are effective, particularly for bulimia nervosa. Certain drugs may also help, although the evidence is not so strong.

Drug Treatments

At present, drug treatments have not been found to be effective in the treatment of anorexia nervosa (for example, Agras, 1987; Garner & Needleman, 1996; Hsu, 1990). The drugs generally considered the most effective for bulimia are the same antidepressant medications proven effective for mood disorders and anxiety disorders (Craighead & Agras, 1991; Fairburn, Agras, & Wilson, 1992; Walsh, et al., 1997; Wilson, 1993). In fact, the Food and Drug Administration (FDA) in 1996 approved Prozac as effective for eating disorders. Effectiveness is usually mea-

Tim Walsh has made significant scientific contributions to our understanding of eating disorders.

sured by reductions in the frequency of binge eating as well as by the percentage of patients who stop binge eating and purging altogether, at least for a period of time. In two studies, one of tricyclic antidepressant drugs and the other of fluoxetine (Prozac), researchers found the average *reduction* in binge eating and purging was, respectively, 47% and 65% (Walsh, 1991; Walsh, Hadigan, Devlin, Gladis, & Roose, 1991). However, although antidepressants are more effective than placebo in the short term, the available evidence suggests that, pending further evaluation, antidepressant drugs alone do not have substantial long-lasting effects on bulimia nervosa (Walsh, 1995), although they may enhance the effects of psychosocial treatment.

Psychosocial Treatments

Until recently, psychosocial treatments were directed at the patient's low self-esteem and difficulties in developing an individual identity. Disordered patterns of family interaction and communication were also targeted for treatment. However, these treatments alone have not had the effectiveness that clinicians hoped they might (for instance, Minuchin et al., 1978; Russell, Szmukler, Dare, & Eisler, 1987). Short-term cognitive-behavioral treatments target problem eating behavior and associated attitudes about the overriding importance and significance of body weight and shape.

BULIMIA NERVOSA

In the cognitive–behavioral treatment approach pioneered by Christopher Fairburn (1985), the first stage is teaching the patient the physical consequences of binge eating and purging, as well as the ineffectiveness of vomiting and laxative abuse for weight control. The adverse effects of dieting are also described, and patients are scheduled to eat small, manageable amounts of food five or six times per day with no more than a 3-hour interval between any planned meals and snacks, which eliminates the alternating periods of overeating and dietary restriction that are hallmarks of bulimia. In later stages of treatment, cognitive therapy focuses on altering dysfunctional thoughts and attitudes about body shape, weight, and eating. Coping strategies for resisting the impulse to binge and purge are also developed, including arranging activities so that the individual will not spend time alone after eating during the early stages of treatment (Fairburn, Marcus, & Wilson, 1993; Wilson & Pike, 1993). Evaluations of short-term (approximately 3 months) cognitive–behavioral treatments for bulimia have been good, showing a mean reduction in purging of 79%;

Christopher Fairburn developed an effective psychosocial treatment for bulimia nervosa.

57% of the patients eliminated bingeing and purging altogether (Craighead & Agras, 1991). Furthermore, these results seem to last.

In a thorough, carefully conducted study, Fairburn, Jones, Peveler, Hope, and O'Connor (1993) evaluated three different treatments. *Cognitive–behavioral therapy* (CBT) focused on changing eating habits *and* changing attitudes about weight and shape; *behavior therapy* (BT) focused only on changing eating habits; and *interpersonal psychotherapy* (IPT) focused on improving interpersonal functioning. For patients receiving CBT, both binge eating and purging declined by more than 90% at a 1-year follow-up. In addition, 36% of the patients had ceased all binge eating and purging; the others had occasional episodes. Attitudes toward body shape and weight also improved. These results were significantly better than the results from BT. Even more interesting was the finding that IPT did as well as CBT at the 1-year follow-up, although CBT was more effective at the assessment immediately after treatment was completed. This result indicates that IPT caught up with CBT in terms of effectiveness by the end of the 1-year follow-up. This is particularly interesting because IPT does not concentrate directly on disordered eating patterns or dysfunctional attitudes about eating but rather on improving interpersonal functioning, a focus that may, in turn, promote changes in eating habits and attitudes. Both treatments were more effective than BT. Fairburn et al. (1995) combined patients from this study with those in another very similar study and followed them up to 6 years. Some patients received a slightly different form of interpersonal therapy (that achieved almost identical results), which the authors called "focal interpersonal therapy" (FIT). Combined results of these two studies and the follow-up period are presented in Figure 8.6. Remarkably, at a 6-year follow-up patients had

retained their gains in the two effective treatments. Clearly, we need to understand much more about how to improve such treatments to deal more successfully with the growing number of patients with eating disorders.

Phoebe
Taking Control

During her sophomore year in college, Phoebe entered the short-term cognitive-behavior therapy program outlined here. She made good progress during the first several months and worked carefully to eat regularly and gain control over her eating. She also made sure that she was with somebody during her high-risk times and planned alternative activities that would reduce her temptation to purge if she felt she had eaten too much at a restaurant or drunk too much beer at a party. During the first 2 months Phoebe had three slips, and she and her therapist discussed what led to her temporary relapse. Much to Phoebe's surprise, she did not gain weight on this program, even though she did not have time to increase her exercise. Nevertheless, she still was preoccupied with food, was concerned about her weight and appearance, and had strong urges to vomit if she thought she had overeaten the slightest amount.

During the 9 months following treatment, Phoebe reported that her urges seemed to decrease somewhat, although she had one major slip after eating a big pizza and drinking a lot of beer. She reported that she was thoroughly disgusted with herself for purging, and was quite careful to return to her program after this episode. Two years after finishing treatment, Phoebe reported that her urges to vomit had disappeared, a report confirmed by her parents. All that remained of her problem were some very bad but increasingly vague and distant memories.

Short-term treatments for eating disorders, although clearly effective for many, are no panacea. Indeed, some people do not benefit at all from short-term cognitive–behavioral treatments. There is now evidence that combining drugs with psychosocial treatments might boost the overall outcome, at least in the short term (Agras et al., 1992). In the largest study to date (Walsh et al., 1997), cognitive–behavioral therapy was significantly superior to supportive psychotherapy in the treatment of bulimia nervosa; and, adding two antidepressant medications to CBT, including an SSRI, modestly increased the benefit of CBT. But CBT remains the preferred treatment for bulimia. There is also evidence that people who do not respond to CBT might benefit from interpersonal psychotherapeutic methods (Fairburn et al., 1993; Klerman, Weissman, Rounsaville, & Chevron, 1984).

BINGE EATING DISORDER

D. E. Smith, Marcus, and Kaye (1992) have adapted cognitive–behavioral treatments for bulimia to obese binge eaters, and the preliminary results look very promising. In their study, the frequency of binge eating was reduced by an aver-

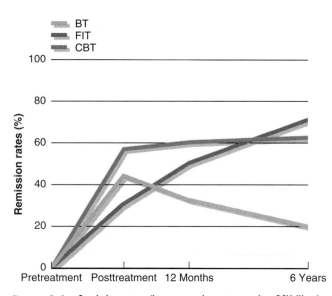

figure 8.6 Remission rates (i.e., proportion not meeting DSM-IV criteria for eating disorder) in patients who received cognitive behavior therapy (CBT) (*n* = 35), behavior therapy (BT) (*n* = 22), or focal interpersonal therapy (FIT) (*n* = 32). Mean (±SD) length of follow-up was 5.8 ± 2.0 years (from Fairburn et al., 1995)

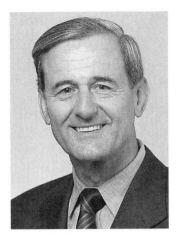

Stewart Agras has made many important contributions to our understanding of eating disorders.

age of 81%, with 50% of the subjects totally abstinent from bingeing by the end of treatment. Agras, Telch, Arnow, Eldredge, and Marnell (1997) followed 93 obese individuals with binge eating disorder for 1 year and found that immediately after treatment 41% of the participants abstained from bingeing and 72% binged less frequently. After 1 year binge eating was reduced by 64% and 33% of the group remained abstinent. Importantly, those who had stopped binge eating during CBT maintained a weight loss of approximately 9 pounds over the follow-up period, while those who continued to binge gained approximately 8 pounds. Thus, stopping binge eating is critical to sustaining weight loss in obese patients, a finding consistent with other studies of weight loss procedures (Marcus, Wing, & Hopkins, 1988; Marcus et al., 1990; C. F. Telch, Agras, & Rossiter, 1988).

ANOREXIA NERVOSA

In anorexia, of course, the most important initial goal is to restore the patient's weight to a point that is at least within the low-normal range (American Psychiatric Association, 1993). If body weight is below 70% of the average or if weight has been lost very rapidly, inpatient treatment would be recommended (American Psychiatric Association, 1993; Casper, 1982) because severe medical complications, particularly acute cardiac failure, could occur if weight restoration is not begun immediately. If the weight loss has been more gradual and seems to have stabilized, weight restoration can be accomplished on an outpatient basis.

Restoring weight is probably the easiest part of treatment. Clinicians who treat patients in different settings, as reported in a variety of studies, find that at least 85% will be able to gain weight. The gain is often as much as a half-pound to a pound a day until weight is within the normal range. Typical strategies used with inpatients are outlined in Table 8.1. In fact, knowing they can leave the hospital when their weight gain is adequate is often sufficient to motivate young women (Agras, Barlow, Chapin, Abel, & Leitenberg, 1974). A chart of Julie's weight gain while she was in the hospital for 6 weeks is shown in Figure 8.7.

Then the difficult stage begins. As Hsu (1988) and others have demonstrated, initial weight gain is a poor predictor of long-term outcome in anorexia. Without attention to the patient's underlying dysfunctional attitudes about body shape, she will almost always relapse. For restricting anorexics, the focus of treatment must shift to their marked anxiety over becoming obese and losing control of eating, as well as to their undue emphasis on thinness as a determinant of self-worth, happiness, and success. In this regard, effective treatments for restricting anorexics are similar to those for patients with bulimia nervosa (Pike, Loeb, & Vitousek, 1996).

In addition, every effort is made to include the family in order to accomplish two goals. First, the negative and dysfunctional communication regarding food and eating must be eliminated and meals made more structured and reinforcing. Second, attitudes toward body shape and image distortion are discussed at some length in family sessions. Unless the therapist attends to these attitudes, individuals with anorexia are likely to face a lifetime preoccupation with weight and body shape, struggle to maintain marginal weight and social adjustment, and be subject to repeated hospitalization. Family therapy seems effective, particularly with young girls with a short history of the disorder. Under

---

table 8.1   Strategies to Attain Weight Gain

1. Weight restoration occurs in conjunction with other treatments, such as individual and family therapy, so that the patient does not feel that eating and weight gain are the only goals of treatment.
2. The patient trusts the treatment team and believes that she will not be allowed to become overweight.
3. The patient's fear of loss of control is contained; this may be accomplished by having her eat frequent, smaller meals (e.g., four to six times per day, with 400 to 500 calories per meal) so as to produce a gradual but steady weight gain (e.g., an average of 0.2 kg/day).
4. A member of the nursing staff is present during mealtimes to encourage the patient to eat and to discuss her fears and anxiety about eating and weight gain.
5. Gradual weight gain rather than the amount of food eaten is regularly monitored, and the result is made known to the patient; thus the patient should be weighed at regular intervals, and she should know whether she has gained or lost weight.
6. Some negative and positive reinforcements exist, such as the use of graduated level of activity and bedrest, whether or not these reinforcements are formally conceptualized as behavior modification techniques, so that the patient may thereby learn that she can control not only her behavior but also the consequence of her behavior.
7. The patient's self-defeating behavior, such as surreptitious vomiting or purging, is confronted and controlled.
8. The dysfunctional conflict between the patient and the family about eating and food is not reenacted in the hospital; or if the pattern is to be reenacted in a therapeutic lunch session, the purpose is clearly defined.

Source: Hsu, 1990

● Weight

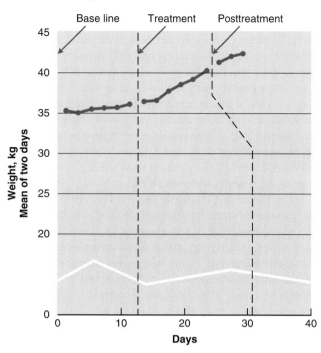

figure 8.7   Julie's weight gain during her hospital stay (from Agras et al., 1974).

---

table 8.2   **Weight Concerns**

1. How much *more or less* do you feel you worry about your weight and body shape than other girls your age?

   1. I worry a lot less than other girls (4)*
   2. I worry a little less than other girls (8)
   3. I worry about the same as other girls (12)
   4. I worry a little more than other girls (16)
   5. I worry a lot more than other girls (20)

2. How afraid are you of gaining 3 pounds?

   1. Not afraid of gaining (4)
   2. Slightly afraid of gaining (8)
   3. Moderately afraid of gaining (12)
   4. Very afraid of gaining (16)
   5. Terrified of gaining (20)

3. When was the last time you went on a diet?

   1. I've never been on a diet (3)
   2. I was on a diet about one year ago (6)
   3. I was on a diet about 6 months ago (9)
   4. I was on a diet about 3 months ago (12)
   5. I was on a diet about 1 month ago (15)
   6. I was on a diet less than 1 month ago (18)
   7. I'm now on a diet (21)

4. How important is your weight to you?

   1. My weight is not important compared to other things in my life (5)
   2. My weight is a little more important than some other things (10)
   3. My weight is more important than most, but not all, things in my life (15)
   4. My weight is the most important thing in my life (20)

5. Do you ever feel fat?

   1. Never (4)
   2. Rarely (8)
   3. Sometimes (12)
   4. Often (16)
   5. Always (20)

*Value assigned to each answer is in parentheses. Thus, if you chose an answer worth 12 in questions 1, 2, 3, and 5, and an answer worth 10 in question 4, your score would be 60. (Remember that the prediction from this scale worked for girls aged 11–13 but hasn't been evaluated in college students. *Source:* Killen, 1996.

---

these circumstances, Eisler et al. (1997) found that 90% of a small group maintained substantial benefits for 5 years, and that family therapy was superior to individual therapy.

PREVENTING EATING DISORDERS

Attempts are being made to prevent the development of eating disorders. If successful methods are confirmed they will be very important, since many cases of eating disorders are resistant to treatment and most individuals who do not receive treatment suffer for many years, in some cases all of their lives (Killen, 1996). Before implementing a prevention program, however, it is necessary to target specific behaviors to change. Killen et al. (1994) conducted a prospective analysis on a sample of 887 young adolescent girls. Over a three-year interval 32 girls, or 3.6% of the sample, developed symptoms of eating disorders. Early concern about being overweight was the most powerful predictive factor of later symptoms. The instrument used to measure weight concerns is presented in Table 8.2. Girls who scored high on this scale (an average score of 58) were at substantial risk for developing serious symptoms. Killen et al. (1996) then evaluated a prevention program on 967 sixth- and seventh-grade girls from 11 to 13 years of age. Half the girls were put on the intervention program and the other half were not. The program emphasized the normality of female weight gain after puberty and that excessive caloric restriction could actually cause increased gain. The interesting results were that the intervention had relatively little effect on the treatment group as a whole compared to the control group. But for those girls at high risk for developing eating disorders (as reflected by a high score on the scale in Table

8.2), the program significantly reduced weight concerns (Killen, 1996; Killen et al., 1993). The authors conclude from this preliminary study that the most cost-effective preventive approach would be to carefully screen 11- and 12-year-old girls who are at high risk for developing eating disorders and to apply the program selectively to them (Killen, 1996). Our best hope for dealing effectively with eating disorders may lie with preventive approaches such as this.

Other Eating Disorders

The following eating disorders differ from those covered thus far in that they are often associated with mental retardation and involve rather bizarre eating patterns. However, as with other eating disorders, if they are not treated there is a substantially increased risk of illness or death.

Rumination Disorder

Rumination is the process of regurgitating and then reswallowing partially digested food, which is normal in ruminant animals who chew the cud, such as cattle and deer. In centuries past the term *mercyism* (from the Greek word for abnormal regurgitation) was often used (Parry-Jones, 1994). When this process interferes with appropriate nutritional intake or weight gain, **rumination disorder** is present. Rumination usually seems to be as enjoyable to those engaging in it as eating the food initially. Consider the following case.

> ### Sandra
> #### The Baby Who Faded
>
> Sandra was born in September to an economically marginal rural family after an unplanned, uncomplicated pregnancy. She was delivered at home by a nurse-midwife and weighed 8 pounds. The next day she was admitted to University Hospital for feeding difficulties associated with a cleft palate and lip. These difficulties were rectified with gastric tube feedings, and Sandra was discharged to her aunt 9 days after admission. During the next 4 months, weight gain was below average, although neither mother nor aunt reported any further feeding difficulties. There were, however, indications of neglect, and Sandra was cared for during this period by a number of different individuals, including neighborhood children.
>
> Sandra was taken back to University Hospital by her aunt in February of the following year, at the age of about 6 months, because of a failure to gain weight associated with rumination. On examination, she was emaciated and unresponsive to her environment. There was very little grasping of objects, no smiling, no babbling, no gross movements, and some crying. She was primarily lethargic and lay passively in her crib. Exhaustive medical examinations and laboratory analyses revealed no organic cause for her difficulties. Her weight, however, fell rapidly below her birth weight, and below the third percentile for infant girls. Malnutrition and dehydration were pressing problems and death was a distinct possibility.
>
> Sandra was fed a commercially prepared formula every 4 hours. Immediately after each feeding, Sandra opened her mouth, elevated and folded her tongue, and then vigorously thrust her tongue forward and backward. Within a few seconds, formula appeared at the back of her mouth and then slowly flowed out. This behavior continued for 20 to 40 minutes until she apparently lost all the formula she had previously consumed. No crying or evidence of pain or discomfort was observed by nurses. Rumination could be interrupted by touches, pokes, or mild slaps, but would resume immediately (Sajwaj, Libet, & Agras, 1974, p. 558).

Rumination is classified as a disorder of infancy, childhood, or adolescence in DSM-IV, and it affects approximately 10% of adults who have mental retardation. Little is known about this disorder, but many investigators believe that the causes are in a combination of biological and psychological variables (Blinder, Goodman, & Goldstein, 1988). Direct behavioral treatment of rumination seems to be successful, based on single-case studies. Small amounts of lemon juice were squirted into Sandra's mouth by a nurse as soon as her tongue movements began. After several days all rumination had stopped and 1 year later Sandra was developing normally. Considering that the mortality rate for infants approaches 25%, quick and effective treatments can be lifesaving.

Rumination can also occur with bulimia. Fairburn and Cooper (1984) reported 7 such cases out of 35 patients. These individuals would regurgitate small quantities of food shortly after eating and chew on it, sometimes repeating the pattern for several hours. Most described the process as soothing, and four reported that the taste of food was improved by a period of "marination" in the stomach. Successful treatment for bulimia also eliminated rumination in these patients, a finding reported in other studies as well (Murray, Keele, & McCarver, 1976; Singh, Manning, & Angell, 1982), and in historical accounts (Parry-Jones, 1994).

 Pica

Pica is characterized by the repeated eating of non-nutritive substances and occurs in infants and people with mental retardation or dementia. Individuals typically eat paint, plaster, string, hair, or cloth. Older children may eat animal droppings, sand, insects, leaves, or pebbles. Most cases involve individuals with severe or profound intellectual disabilities (K. E. Bell & Stein, 1992; Singh & Winton, 1984). Consider the case of Mike.

> ### Mike
> #### Tasting the World
>
> Mike was a 17-year-old who lived in an institution for people with mental retardation. (This was before the current practice of placing people like Mike in their own communities.) Mike had a variety of behavior problems, the most serious of which was his habit of eating anything that was available. If left alone for any period of time, he would secretly pick up small pieces of paper, string, or cardboard and eat them. Unfortunately, his appetite often went beyond such relatively harmless objects to more dangerous things. Once, when he was in the hospital for an appendectomy, an X-ray of his stomach revealed paper clips, thumbtacks, and what appeared to be a metal spring.

(continued)

> The people who worked with Mike made every effort to lock up any objects that might be dangerous for him to eat. However, despite his mental retardation. Mike was ingenious at finding inedible objects to ingest. One day as I showed a group of people the bedroom where Mike and his roommate lived, someone asked to see the closets. When I opened the large door to Mike's closet, it fell off its hinges and crashed to the floor. When we looked more closely, we saw that the wood around the hinges had been chipped away, bit by bit. Mike had eaten large parts of his closet door!

Pica poses serious health problems. There is a danger of lead poisoning and roundworm infection; sometimes surgery is required to remove ingested objects (for instance, Foxx & Martin, 1975). The risk of death is quite high (Fisher et al., 1994). Occasionally, the eating of non-nutritive substances is culturally sanctioned. For example, in certain African societies and during the early history of the United States, pregnant women ate clay to facilitate child-bearing (M. Cooper, 1957), a practice still encountered today. Culturally approved pica is not considered a disorder.

Other causes of pica are largely unknown, although certain mineral deficiencies may be involved. Psychosocial factors such as stress are an important contribution to the behavior (Blinder et al., 1988). Psychological factors are usually associated with substantial neglect or abuse (Singhi, Singhi, & Adwani, 1981). In addition, pica seems in some cases to be maintained by reinforcing consequences, such as flavor or other forms of sensory reinforcement, although this is hard to imagine for people without the disorder. Because many people who eat inedibles spend considerable time in institutions, pica may reduce the boredom that so often afflicts people in these settings.

Operant conditioning procedures have been used with pica, primarily the systematic reinforcement of appropriate eating and mild punishment or withholding of reinforcement when the behavior occurs (Foxx & Martin, 1975). Although there is not yet a standard treatment (K. E. Bell & Stein, 1992), recent efforts have produced more encouraging long-term results (Fisher et al., 1994).

Feeding Disorder

In Chapter 2 we mentioned *feeding disorder of infancy or early childhood*, which may result in a "failure to thrive syndrome"; that is, failure to eat adequately results in insufficient weight gain. "Insufficient" indicates a growth rate below the third percentile in weight or height (Budd et al., 1992). This condition accounts for up to 5% of all admissions to pediatric units. Older children who fail to thrive may be found in a disorganized, chaotic family, exhibit oppositional behavior, or, most likely, have a conflicted relationship with a caregiver. Treatment always involves regulating eating in the hospital and attempting to improve family functioning. Re-

sults are mixed, depending on the severity of family disorganization. (Attie & Brooks-Gunn, 1995).

■ **concept check 8.2**

Check your understanding by identifying the proper eating disorder in the following scenarios. Choose your answers from (a) bulimia nervosa, (b) anorexia nervosa, (c) pica, and (d) binge-eating disorder.

1. Jason has been having episodes lately when he eats prodigious amounts of food. He's been putting on a lot of weight because of it. _____

2. I noticed Sally eating a whole pie, a cake, and two bags of potato chips the other day when she didn't know I was there. She ran to the bathroom when she was finished and it sounded like she was vomiting. _____

3. Kirsten wants to lose some weight though she is already slim. She counts her calories religiously and keeps her daily intake at about 400 calories. She exercises for about 4 hours every day. _____

4. Pam eats large quantities of food in a short time. She then takes laxatives and exercises for long periods to prevent weight gain. She has been doing this almost daily for several months and feels she will become worthless and ugly if she gains even an ounce. _____

5. Mary has lost several pounds and now weighs less than 90 pounds. She eats only a small portion of the food her mother serves her and fears that intake above her current 500 calories daily will make her fat. Since losing the weight, Mary has stopped having periods. She sees a fat person in the mirror. _____

Most of us recognize that eating is essential to our survival. Equally important is sleep, a still relatively mysterious process that is crucial to everyday functioning and strongly implicated in many psychological disorders. We turn our attention to this additional survival activity in an effort to better understand how and why we can be harmed by sleep disturbances.

Sleep Disorders: An Overview

We spend about one-third of our lives asleep. That means most of us sleep nearly 3,000 hours per *year*. A question that arises frequently is, "What is a normal amount of sleep?" Most of us think we need 8 hours of sleep in a 24-hour period, but the ideal amount varies considerably from person to person: 5 to 6 hours per night is enough for some people to feel fully rested; others may need 9 hours. Our sleep patterns change as we age. Infants sleep as much as 16 hours per day, and college-age students average 7 to 8 hours per day. When people pass the age of 50, their total sleep per day can drop below 6 hours.

For many of us, sleep is energizing, both mentally and physically. However, you or someone you know may have a problem with sleeping. Most of us know what it's like to have a bad night's sleep. The next day we're a little groggy, and as the day wears on we may become irritable. Imagine, if you can, that it has been years since you've had a good night's sleep. Your relationships suffer, it is difficult to do your schoolwork, and your efficiency and productivity at work are diminished. Lack of sleep might also affect you physically. People who do not get enough sleep report more health problems and are more often hospitalized than people who sleep normally (Morin, 1993), perhaps because immune system functioning is reduced with the loss of even a few hours of sleep (Irwin et al., 1994). Sleep problems in the United States are estimated to cost from 30 to 35 billion dollars per year in lost worker productivity, absenteeism, and related outcomes (Chilcott & Shapiro, 1996).

Here you might ask yourself how sleep disorders fit into a textbook on abnormal psychology. Different variations of disturbed sleep clearly have physiological bases and therefore could be considered purely medical concerns. However, like other physical disorders, sleep problems interact in important ways with psychological factors.

The study of sleep has long influenced concepts of abnormal psychology. Moral treatment, used in the 19th century for people with severe mental illness, included adequate amounts of sleep as part of therapy (Armstrong, 1993). Sigmund Freud greatly emphasized dreams and discussed them with patients as a way of better understanding their emotional lives (Anch, Browman, Mitler, & Walsh, 1988). Researchers who prevented people from sleeping for prolonged periods of time found that chronic sleep deprivation often had profound effects. An early study in this area looked at the effects of keeping 350 volunteers awake for 112 hours (Tyler, 1955). Seven volunteers engaged in bizarre behavior that seemed psychotic. Subsequent research suggested that interfering with the sleep of people with preexisting psychological problems can create these disturbing results (Brauchi & West, 1959). A number of the disorders covered in this book are frequently associated with sleep complaints, including schizophrenia, major depression, bipolar disorder, and anxiety-related disorders. Individuals with developmental disorders (see Chapter 14) are also at greater risk for having sleep disorders (Durand, 1998). You may think at first that a sleep problem is the result of a psychological disorder. For example, how many of you have been anxious about a future event (for example, an upcoming exam) and not been able to fall asleep? However, the relationship between sleep disturbances and mental health is more complex. Sleep problems may cause the difficulties people experience in everyday life (Balter & Bauer, 1975), or they may result from some disturbance common to a psychological disorder.

In Chapter 5 we explained how a brain circuit in the limbic system may be involved with anxiety. We know that

This man is participating in a polysomnograph, an overnight electronic evaluation of his sleep patterns.

this region of the brain is also involved with our dream sleep, which is called **rapid eye movement (REM) sleep** (Ware, 1988). This mutual neurobiological connection suggests that anxiety and sleep may be interrelated in important ways, although the exact nature of the relationship is still unknown. Similarly, REM sleep seems related to depression, as noted in Chapter 7 (Emslie, Rush, Weinberg, Rintelmann, & Roffwarg, 1994). One study, for example, indicates that sleep abnormalities are preceding signs of serious clinical depression, which may suggest that sleep problems can help predict who is at risk for later mood disorders (Giles, Kupfer, Rush, & Roffwarg, 1998). In an intriguing recent study, researchers found that cognitive–behavior therapy improved symptoms among a group of depressed men and also normalized REM sleep patterns (Nofzinger et al., 1994). Furthermore, sleep deprivation has temporary antidepressant effects on some people (Hillman, Kripke, & Gillin, 1990), although in people who are not already depressed sleep deprivation may bring on a depressed mood (Boivin et al., 1997). We do not fully understand how psychological disorders are related to sleep, yet accumulating research points to the importance of understanding sleep if we are to complete the broader picture of abnormal behavior.

Sleep disorders are divided into two major categories: **dyssomnias** and **parasomnias.** Dyssomnias involve difficulties in getting enough sleep, problems with sleeping when you want to—not being able to fall asleep until 2 A.M. when you have a 9 A.M. class—and complaints about the quality of sleep, such as not feeling refreshed even though you have slept the whole night. The parasomnias are characterized by abnormal behavioral or physiological events that occur during sleep, such as nightmares and sleepwalking.

The clearest and most comprehensive picture of your sleep habits can be determined only by a **polysomnographic (PSG) evaluation.** The patient spends one or more nights sleeping in a sleep laboratory, being monitored on a number of measures that include respiration and oxygen desaturation (a measure of airflow); leg movements; brain wave activity, measured by an *electroencephalograph* (EEG); eye movements, measured by an *electrooculograph* (EOG); muscle movements, measured by an *electromyograph* (EMG); and heart activity, measured by an *electrocardiogram*. Daytime behavior and typical sleep patterns are also noted; for example, whether the person uses drugs or alcohol, is anxious about work or interpersonal problems, takes afternoon naps, or has a psychological disorder. Collecting all these data can be both timely and costly, but it is important to ensure an accurate diagnosis and treatment plan.

In addition, clinicians and researchers find it helpful to know the average number of hours the individual sleeps each day, taking into account **sleep efficiency (SE),** the percentage of time actually spent asleep, not just lying in bed trying to sleep. Sleep efficiency is calculated by dividing the amount of time sleeping by the amount of time in bed. An SE of 100% would mean that you fall asleep as soon as your head hits the pillow and do not awake at all during the night. In contrast, an SE of 50% would mean that half your time in bed is spent trying to fall asleep; that is, you are awake half the time. Such measurements help the clinician determine objectively how well you sleep.

One way to determine whether a person has a problem with sleep is to observe his or her *daytime sequelae*, or behavior while awake. For example, if it takes you 90 minutes to fall asleep at night, but this doesn't bother you and you feel rested during the day, then you do not have a problem. A friend who also takes 90 minutes to fall asleep but finds this delay anxiety provoking and is fatigued the next day might be considered to have a sleep problem. It is to some degree a subjective decision, dependent in part on how the person perceives the situation and reacts to it.

Dyssomnias

Primary Insomnia

Insomnia is one of the most common sleep disorders. You may picture someone with insomnia as being awake all the time. However, it isn't possible to go completely without sleep. For example, after being awake for about 40 hours, a person begins having **microsleeps** that last several seconds or longer (Anch et al., 1988). In the very rare occurrences of *fatal familial insomnia* (a degenerative brain disorder), total lack of sleep eventually leads to death (Fiorino, 1996). Despite the common use of the term *insomnia* to mean "not sleeping," it actually applies to a number of complaints. People are considered to have insomnia if they have trouble falling asleep at night (difficulty initiating sleep), if they wake up frequently or too early and can't go back to sleep (difficulty maintaining sleep), or even if they sleep a reasonable number of hours but are still not rested the next day (nonrestorative sleep). Consider the following case.

Kathryn
Tossing and Turning

Kathryn, who was 73, reported having serious sleep problems ever since her husband died 19 years earlier. She could not fall asleep until she had lain in bed for several hours, and she awakened a number of times each night. She had an average of 4 to 5 hours of broken sleep per night. It is not surprising that she was chronically tired throughout the day and complained that fatigue interfered with her friendships. She no longer enjoyed going out with her friends because she fell asleep in public, which was very embarrassing to her.

Kathryn used nonprescription sleeping pills on and off over the years, sometimes she just lay in bed listening to the radio and nodding off occasionally. When her sleep problems started, Kathryn recognized that her distress over her husband's death was probably to blame. As the years passed, she assumed that poor sleep was normal for a person her age and that her fatigue was also part of the aging process. However, during the past months she began to realize that she wasn't playing with her grandchildren or leaving her house because she was too tired. On the advice of a friend, she decided to get some help.

We will return to Kathryn later in this chapter.

CLINICAL DESCRIPTION

Kathryn's symptoms meet the DSM-IV criteria for **primary insomnia,** with *primary* indicating that the complaint is not related to other medical or psychiatric problems. Looking at sleep disorders as primary recalls the overlap of sleep problems with psychological disorders such as anxiety and depression. Because not sleeping makes you anxious and anxiety further interrupts your sleep, which makes you more anxious, and so on, it is uncommon to find a person with a simple sleep disorder and no related problems.

Kathryn's is a typical case of insomnia. She had trouble both initiating and maintaining sleep. Other people sleep all night but still feel as if they've been awake for hours. Although most people can carry out necessary day-to-day activities, their inability to concentrate can have serious consequences, such as debilitating accidents when they attempt to drive long distances (like bus drivers) or handle dangerous material (like electricians). Kathryn wouldn't drive her car on the highway because she feared falling asleep at the wheel. Students with insomnia may do poorly in school because of difficulty concentrating.

STATISTICS

Almost a third of the general population report some symptoms of insomnia during any given year, and 17% indicate that their problems with sleeping are severe (Gillin, 1993). In one study, 31% of the people who expressed concern about sleep continued to experience difficulties a year later (D. E. Ford & Kamerow, 1989), a result showing that sleep problems may become chronic. Approximately 20% of elderly persons report excessive daytime sleepiness, with older black men reporting the most problems (Whitney et al., 1998).

A number of psychological disorders are associated with insomnia (Benca, Obermeyer, Thisted, & Gillin, 1992). Total sleep time often decreases with depression, substance use disorders, anxiety disorders, and dementia of the Alzheimer's type. The interrelationship between alcohol use and sleep disorders can be particularly troubling. Alcohol is often used to initiate sleep (Gillin, 1993). In small amounts it may work, but it also interrupts ongoing sleep. Interrupted sleep causes anxiety, which often leads to repeated alcohol use and an obviously vicious cycle.

Women report insomnia twice as often as men. Does this mean that men sleep better than women? Not necessarily. Remember, a sleep problem is considered a disorder only *if you experience discomfort* about it. Women may be more frequently diagnosed as having insomnia because they more often report the problem, not necessarily because their sleep is disrupted more. Women may be more aware of their sleep patterns than men or may be more comfortable acknowledging and seeking help for problems.

Just as normal sleep needs change over time, complaints of insomnia differ in frequency among people of different ages. Children who have difficulty falling asleep usually throw bedtime tantrums or do not want to go to bed. Many children cry when they wake up in the middle of the night. Estimates of insomnia among young children range from 25% to more than 40% (Mindell, 1993). This percentage goes down in adolescence and early adulthood but rises to more than 25% again for people over the age of 65 (Mellinger, Balter, & Uhlenhuth, 1985). This increase in reports of sleeping problems among older people makes sense when you remember that the number of hours we sleep decreases as we age. It is not uncommon for someone over 65 to sleep fewer than 6 hours and wake up several times each night.

CAUSES

Insomnia accompanies many medical and psychological disorders, including pain and physical discomfort, physical inactivity during the day, and respiratory problems.

Sometimes insomnia is related to problems with the biological clock and its control of temperature. People who can't fall asleep at night may have a delayed temperature rhythm: Their body temperature doesn't drop and they don't become drowsy until later at night (M. Morris, Lack, & Dawson, 1990). As a group, people with insomnia seem to have higher body temperatures than good sleepers, and their body temperatures seem to vary less; this lack of fluctuation may interfere with sleep (Monk & Moline, 1989).

Among the other factors that can interfere with sleeping are drug use and a variety of environmental influences such as changes in light, noise, or temperature. People ad-

mitted to hospitals often have difficulty sleeping because the noises and routines differ from those at home. Other sleep disorders, such as sleep apnea (a disorder that involves obstructed nighttime breathing) or periodic limb movement disorder (excessive jerky leg movements) can cause interrupted sleep and may seem similar to insomnia.

Finally, various psychological stresses can also disrupt your sleep (Morin, 1993). Poll your friends around finals time to see how many of them are having trouble falling asleep or are not sleeping through the night. The stress that you experience during such times may interfere with your sleep, at least temporarily. R. T. Gross and Borkovec (1982), for example, found that if good sleepers were told that they would have to present a speech the next day, they took longer to fall asleep than did control subjects.

Research shows that people with insomnia may have unrealistic expectations about how much sleep they need (I need a full 8 hours) and about how disruptive disturbed sleep will be (I won't be able to think or do my job if I sleep for only 5 hours) (Morin, Stone, Trinkle, Mercer, & Remsberg, 1993). These studies illuminate the role of cognition in insomnia, proving that our thoughts alone may disrupt our sleep.

Is poor sleeping a learned behavior? It is generally accepted that people associate the bedroom and bed with the frustration and anxiety that go with insomnia. Eventually, the arrival of bedtime itself may cause anxiety (Bootzin & Nicassio, 1978). Interactions associated with sleep may contribute to children's sleep problems. For example, one study found that when a parent was present when the child fell asleep the child was more likely to wake during the night (Adair, Bauchner, Philipp, Levenson, & Zuckerman, 1991). Researchers think that some children learn to fall asleep only with a parent present; if they wake up at night, they are frightened at finding themselves alone and their sleep is disrupted. Despite widespread acceptance of the role of learning in insomnia, there is relatively little research on this phenomenon, perhaps in part because this type of research would involve going into homes and bedrooms at an especially private time.

Cross-cultural sleep research has focused primarily on children. In the predominant culture in the United States, infants are expected to sleep on their own, in a separate bed, and, if possible, in a separate room. However, in many other cultures as diverse as rural Guatemala and Korea and urban Japan, the child spends the first few years of life in the same room and sometimes the same bed as the mother (Mosko, Richard, & McKenna, 1997). In many cultures mothers report that they do not ignore the cries of their children (K. Lee, 1992; Morelli, Rogoff, Oppenheim, & Goldsmith, 1992), in stark contrast to the United States, where most pediatricians recommend that parents ignore the cries of their infants at night (Ferber, 1985). One conclusion from this research is that sleep can be negatively impacted by cultural norms, as in the United States. Unmet demands can result in stress that negatively affects the ultimate sleep outcome

She'd tried everything to bring the smothering blanket of sleep. . . .

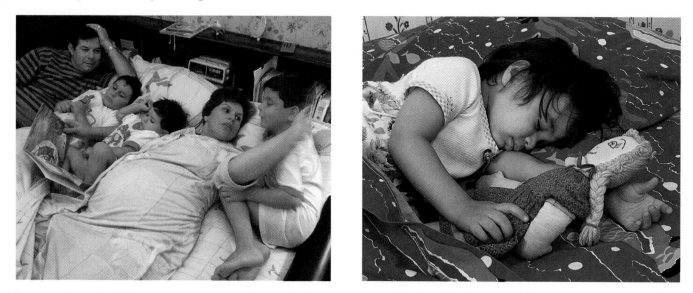

In many cultures, all family members share the same bed (left). In the United States, children usually sleep alone (right).

for children (Durand, Mindell, Mapstone, & Gernert-Dott, 1995).

As we noted in our discussion of assessment issues, biology interacts with cognitive, behavioral, and even cultural dimensions to create problems. A multidimensional view of sleep disorders includes several assumptions. The first is that at some level, both *biological and psychological factors* are present in most cases. A second assumption is that these multiple factors are *reciprocally related*. This can be seen in the study we just noted. Adair and colleagues (1991) observed that children who woke frequently at night often fell asleep in the presence of parents. However, they also noted that child temperament (or personality) may have played a role in this arrangement, because these children had comparatively difficult temperaments, and their parents were presumably present in order to attend to sleep initiation difficulties. In other words, personality characteristics, sleep difficulties, and parental reaction interact in a reciprocal manner to produce and maintain sleep problems.

People may be biologically vulnerable to disturbed sleep. This vulnerability differs from person to person and can range from mild to more severe disturbances. For example, a person may be a light sleeper (easily aroused at night), or have a family history of insomnia, narcolepsy, or obstructed breathing. All these factors can lead to eventual sleeping problems. Such influences have been referred to as *predisposing conditions* (Spielman & Glovinsky, 1991); they may not, by themselves, always cause problems, but they may combine with other factors to interfere with sleep (see Figure 8.8).

Biological vulnerability may in turn interact with *sleep stress* (Durand et al., 1995), which includes a number of events that can negatively affect sleep. For example, poor bedtime habits (such as having too much alcohol or caffeine) can interfere with falling asleep (Hauri, 1991). It is important to point out that biological vulnerability and sleep stress influence each other (see the double arrows in the integrative model of sleep disturbance in Figure 8.8). Although we

may intuitively assume that biological factors come first, extrinsic influences such as poor sleep hygiene (the daily activities that affect how we sleep) can affect the physiological activity of sleep. One of the most striking examples of this phenomenon is jet lag, in which people's sleep patterns are disrupted, sometimes seriously, when they fly across several different time zones. Whether disturbances continue or become more severe may depend on how they are managed. For example, many people react to disrupted sleep by taking over-the-counter sleeping pills. Unfortunately, most people are not aware that **rebound insomnia** may occur when the medication is withdrawn. This rebound leads people to think they still have a sleep problem, readminister the med-

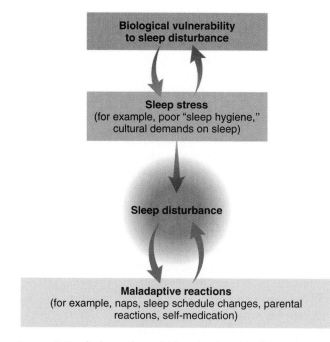

figure 8.8   An integrative multidimensional model of sleep disturbance.

icine, and go through the cycle over and over again. In other words, taking sleep aids can perpetuate sleep problems.

Other ways of reacting to poor sleep can also prolong problems. It seems reasonable that a person who hasn't had enough sleep can make up for this loss by napping during the day. Unfortunately, naps that alleviate fatigue during the day will also disrupt sleep the next night. Anxiety can also extend the problem. Lying in bed worrying about school, family problems, or even about not being able to sleep will interfere with your sleep (Morin, 1993). The behavior of parents can also help to maintain these problems in children. Children who receive a great deal of positive attention at night when they wake up may wake up during the night more often (Durand & Mindell, 1990). Such maladaptive reactions, when combined with a biological predisposition to sleep problems and sleep stress, may account for continuing problems.

Primary Hypersomnia

Insomnia involves not getting enough sleep (the prefix *in* means "lacking" or "without"), and **hypersomnia** is a problem of sleeping too much (*hyper* means in great amount or abnormal excess). Many people who sleep all night find themselves falling asleep several times the next day. Consider the following case.

Excessive sleepiness can be very disruptive.

> ## Ann
> ### Sleeping in Public
>
> Ann, a college student, came to my office to discuss her progress in class. We talked about several questions that she got wrong on the last exam, and as she was about to leave she said that she never fell asleep during my class. This seemed like faint praise, but I thanked her for the feedback. "No," she said, "you don't understand. I usually fall asleep in *all* of my classes, but not in yours." Again, I didn't quite understand what she was trying to tell me and joked that she must pick her professors more carefully. She laughed. "That's probably true. But I also have this problem with sleeping too much."
>
> As we talked more seriously, Ann told me that excessive sleeping had been a problem since her teenage years. In situations that were monotonous or boring, or when she couldn't be active, she fell asleep. This could happen several times a day, depending on what she was doing. Recently, large lecture classes had become a problem unless the lecturer was particularly interesting or animated. Watching television and driving long distances were also problematic.
>
> Ann reported that her father had a similar problem. He had recently been diagnosed with *narcolepsy* (which we will discuss next) and was now getting help at a clinic. Both she and her brother had been diagnosed with hypersomnia. Ann had been prescribed Ritalin (a stimulant medication) about 4 years ago and said that it was only somewhat effective in keeping her awake during the day. She said the drug helped to reduce the sleep attacks but did not eliminate them altogether.

The DSM-IV diagnostic criteria for hypersomnia include not only the excessive sleepiness that Ann described but also the subjective impression of this problem. Remember that whether insomnia is a problem depends on how it affects each person individually. Ann found her disorder very disruptive because it interfered with driving and paying attention in class. Hypersomnia caused her to be less successful academically and also upset her personally, both of which are defining features of this disorder. She slept approximately 8 hours each night, so her daytime sleepiness couldn't be attributed to insufficient sleep.

Several factors that can cause excessive sleepiness would not be considered hypersomnia. For example, people with insomnia (who get inadequate amounts of sleep) often report being tired during the day. In contrast, people with hypersomnia sleep through the night and appear rested upon awakening, but still complain of being excessively tired throughout the day. Another sleep problem that can cause a similar excessive sleepiness is a breathing-related sleep disorder called **sleep apnea.** People with this problem have difficulty breathing at night. They often snore loudly, pause between breaths, and wake in the morning with a dry mouth and headache. In identifying hypersomnia, you need to rule out insomnia, sleep apnea, or other reasons for sleepiness during the day (Gillin, 1993).

We are just beginning to understand the nature of hypersomnia, so there has been relatively little research on its causes. Genetic influences seem to be involved in a portion of cases, as 39% of people with hypersomnia also have a family history of the disorder (Parkes & Block, 1989). An excess of serotonin has been implicated as one influence, although researchers generally believe that there are several biological causes (Anch et al., 1988), including the infectious disease mononucleosis, which has been found in about one-sixth of patients with hypersomnia (Guilleminault & Mondini, 1986).

Narcolepsy

Ann described her father as having **narcolepsy,** a different form of the sleeping problem she and her brother shared (Bassetti & Aldrich, 1996). In addition to daytime sleepiness, people with narcolepsy experience *cataplexy,* a sudden loss of muscle tone. Cataplexy occurs while the person is awake and can range from slight weakness in the facial muscles to complete physical collapse. Cataplexy lasts from several seconds to several minutes; it is usually preceded by strong emotion such as anger or happiness. Imagine that while cheering for your favorite team, you suddenly fall asleep; while arguing with a friend, you collapse to the floor in a sound sleep. You can imagine how disruptive this disorder can be!

Cataplexy appears to result from a sudden onset of REM sleep. Instead of falling asleep normally and going through the four NREM stages that typically precede REM sleep, people with narcolepsy periodically progress right to this dream sleep stage almost directly from the state of being awake. One outcome of REM sleep is the inhibition of input to the muscles, and this seems to be the process that leads to cataplexy.

Two other characteristics distinguish people who have narcolepsy (American Sleep Disorders Association, 1990). They commonly report *sleep paralysis,* a brief period after awakening when they can't move or speak that is often frightening to those who go through it. The last characteristic of narcolepsy is *hypnagogic hallucinations,* vivid and often terrifying experiences that begin at the start of sleep and are said to be unbelievably realistic because they include not only visual aspects but also touch, hearing, and even the sensation of body movement. Examples of hypnagogic hallucinations, which, like sleep paralysis, can be quite terrifying, include the vivid illusion of being caught in a fire or flying through the air. Narcolepsy is relatively rare, occurring in 0.03% to 0.16% of the population, with the numbers approximately equal among males and females. Although some cases have been reported in young children, the problems associated with narcolepsy usually are first seen during the teenage years. Excessive sleepiness usually occurs first, with cataplexy appearing either at the same time or with a delay of up to 30 years. Fortunately, the cataplexy, hypnagogic hallucinations, and sleep paralysis often decrease in frequency over time, although sleepiness during the day does not seem to diminish with age.

Specific genetic models of narcolepsy are just now being studied. Previous research with Doberman pinschers and Labrador retrievers, who also inherit this disorder, suggests that narcolepsy is associated with a cluster of genes on chromosome number 6, and that it may be an autosomal recessive trait. Advances in understanding the etiology and treatment of such disorders can be credited to the help of "man's best friend."

Breathing-Related Sleep Disorders

For some people, sleepiness during the day or disrupted sleep at night has a physical origin; namely, problems with breathing while asleep. In DSM-IV these problems are diagnosed as **breathing-related sleep disorders.** People whose breathing is interrupted during their sleep experience numerous brief arousals throughout the night and do not feel rested even after 8 or 9 hours asleep (Bootzin, Manber, Perlis, Salvio, & Wyatt, 1993). For all of us, the muscles in the upper airway relax during sleep, constricting the passageway somewhat and making breathing a little more difficult. For some, unfortunately, breathing is constricted a great deal, and may be very labored (*hypoventilation*) or, in the extreme, there may be short periods (10 to 30 seconds) when they stop breathing altogether, called **sleep apnea.** Often the affected person is only minimally aware of breathing difficulties and doesn't attribute the sleep problems to the breathing. However, a bed partner usually notices loud snoring (which is one sign of this problem) or will have noticed frightening episodes of interrupted breathing. Other signs that a person has breathing difficulties are heavy sweating during the night, morning headaches, and episodes of falling asleep during the day *(sleep attacks)* with no resulting feeling of being rested (Hauri, 1982).

There are three types of apnea, each with different causes, daytime complaints, and treatment: *obstructive, central,* and *mixed sleep apnea.* Obstructive sleep apnea (OSA) occurs when airflow stops despite continued activity by the respiratory system. In some people, the airway is too narrow; in others, some abnormality or damage interferes with the ongoing effort to breathe. One hundred percent of a group of people with OSA reported snoring at night (Guilleminault, 1989). Obesity is sometimes associated with this problem, as is increasing age. Sleep apnea is most common in males and is thought to occur in 1% to 2% of the population (American Sleep Disorders Association, 1990).

The second type, central sleep apnea, involves the complete cessation of respiratory activity for brief periods of time and is often associated with certain central nervous system disorders such as cerebral vascular disease, head trauma, and degenerative disorders (Wooten, 1990). Unlike people with obstructive sleep apnea, those with central sleep apnea wake up frequently during the night, but they tend not to report excessive daytime sleepiness and often are not aware of having a serious breathing problem. Because of the lack of daytime symptoms, people tend not to seek treatment, so we know relatively little about its prevalence or course. The third breathing disorder, mixed sleep apnea, is a combination of both obstructive and central sleep apneas. All these breathing difficulties interrupt sleep and result in symptoms similar to those of insomnia.

Circadian Rhythm Sleep Disorders

"Spring ahead; fall back": People in most of the United States use this mnemonic device to remind themselves to turn the clocks ahead 1 hour in the spring and back again 1 hour in the fall. Most of us consider the shift to daylight saving time a minor inconvenience (although getting worse with so many watches and clocks to change!) and are thus

■ **concept check 8.3**

Check your understanding of sleep disorders. Match the following descriptions of sleeping problems with the correct term: (a) cataplexy, (b) hypersomnia, (c) insomnia, (d) sleep apnea, (e) sleep paralysis, and (f) stimulant somnia.

1. Judy averages only 3 to 4 hours of sleep per night. She has trouble functioning at work and occasionally falls asleep while driving. _____

2. It seems like all Fred ever does is sleep. He averages 12 hours per night and takes at least two naps every day. _____

3. Sometimes when Trudy awakens, she cannot move or speak. This is terrifying. _____

4. Bob sometimes experiences sudden loss of muscle tone in his arms when he is under extreme stress. It usually lasts only a couple of minutes. _____

5. Susan's husband is extremely overweight. He snores every night and often wakes up exhausted as though he never slept. Susan suspects that he may be suffering from _____ and makes an appointment at the local clinic.

surprised to see how disruptive this time change can be. For at least a day or two, we may be sleepy during the day and have difficulty falling asleep at night, almost as if we had jet lag. The reason for this disruption is not just that we gain or lose 1 hour of sleep; our bodies adjust to this fairly easily. The difficulty has to do with how our biological clocks adjust to this change in time. Convention says to go to sleep at this new time while our brains are saying something different. If the struggle continues for any length of time, you may have what is called a **circadian rhythm sleep disorder.** This disorder is characterized by disturbed sleep (either insomnia or excessive sleepiness during the day) brought on by the brain's inability to synchronize its sleep patterns with the current patterns of day and night.

In the 1960s, German and French scientists identified several bodily rhythms that seem to persist without cues from the environment, rhythms that are self-regulated (Aschoff & Wever, 1962; Siffre, 1964). Because these rhythms don't exactly match our 24-hour day; they are called "circadian" (from *circa* meaning "about" and *dian* meaning "day"). If our circadian rhythms don't match the 24-hour day, why isn't our sleep completely disrupted over time?

Fortunately, our brains have a mechanism that keeps us in synch with the outside world. Our biological clock is in the *suprachiasmatic nucleus* in the hypothalamus. Connected to the suprachiasmatic nucleus is a pathway that comes from our eyes. The light we see in the morning and the decreasing light at night signal the brain to reset the biological clock each day. Unfortunately, some people have trouble sleeping when they want to because of problems with their circadian rhythms. The causes may be outside the person (for example, crossing several time zones in a short amount of time) or internal.

Not being synchronized with the normal wake and sleep cycles causes people to be interrupted when they do try to sleep and to be tired during the day. There are several different types of circadian rhythm sleep disorders. *Jet lag type* is, as its name implies, caused by rapidly crossing multiple time zones. People with jet lag usually report difficulty going to sleep at the proper time and feeling fatigued during the day. Interestingly, older people, introverts (loners), and early risers (morning people) are most likely to be negatively affected by these time zone changes (Gillin, 1993). *Shift work type* sleep problems are associated with work schedules. Many people, such as hospital employees, police, or emergency personnel, work at night or must work irregular hours; as a result, they may have problems sleeping or experience excessive sleepiness during waking hours. Unfortunately, the problems of working (and thus staying awake) at unusual times can go beyond sleep and include gastrointestinal symptoms, increased potential for alcohol abuse, low worker morale, the disruption of family and social life, and feelings of depression (Boivin et al., 1997). Recent research suggests that people with circadian rhythm disorders are at greater risk of having one or more of the personality disorders (Dagan, Dela, Omer, Hallis, & Dar, 1996). About 36% of working men and 26% of working women in the United States work at times other than the typical 9 to 5 and are therefore at risk for having shift work sleep problems (Czeisler & Allan, 1989).

In contrast with jet lag and shift work sleep-related problems, which have external causes such as long-distance travel and job selection, several circadian rhythm sleep disorders seem to arise from within the person experiencing the problems. Extreme "night owls," people who stay up late and sleep late, may have a problem known as *delayed sleep phase type.* Sleep is delayed or later than normal bedtime. At the other end of the extreme, people with an *advanced sleep phase type* of circadian rhythm disorder are "early to bed and early to rise." Here, sleep is advanced or earlier than normal bedtime. In part because of our general lack of knowledge about them, DSM-IV does not include these sleep phases as circadian rhythm sleep disorders.

Research on why our sleep rhythms are disrupted is advancing at a great pace, and we are now beginning to understand the circadian rhythm process. Scientists believe that the hormone *melatonin* contributes to the setting of our biological clocks that tell us when to sleep. This hormone is produced by the pineal gland, in the center of the brain. Melatonin (which shouldn't be confused with melanin, the chemical that determines skin color) has been nicknamed the "Dracula hormone" because its production is stimulated by darkness and ceases in daylight. When our eyes see it is nighttime, this information is passed on to the pineal gland, which, in turn, begins producing melatonin. Researchers believe that both light and melatonin help set the biological clock (see Figure 8.9). Recent work suggests that light can affect the biological clock in ways other than through our eyes. Researchers have found that if the skin is exposed to

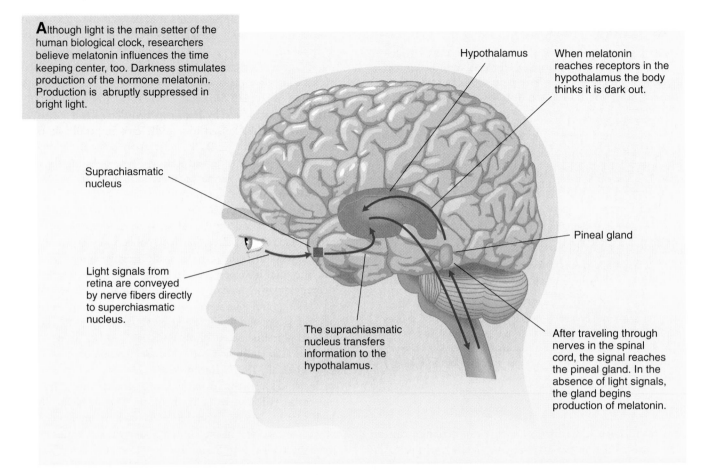

Although light is the main setter of the human biological clock, researchers believe melatonin influences the time keeping center, too. Darkness stimulates production of the hormone melatonin. Production is abruptly suppressed in bright light.

Hypothalamus

When melatonin reaches receptors in the hypothalamus the body thinks it is dark out.

Suprachiasmatic nucleus

Pineal gland

Light signals from retina are conveyed by nerve fibers directly to superchiasmatic nucleus.

The suprachiasmatic nucleus transfers information to the hypothalamus.

After traveling through nerves in the spinal cord, the signal reaches the pineal gland. In the absence of light signals, the gland begins production of melatonin.

figure 8.9   Understanding the hormone of darkness (based on *New York Times,* 1992, November 3).

light, it can have an effect on our biological clock, perhaps working through the blood stream to signal the brain (Campbell & Murphy, 1998).

People who study sleep are interested in melatonin because it helps to explain the sleep mechanism in our bodies. In addition, this hormone may help us treat some of the sleep problems people experience. People who are blind are a sort of natural circadian rhythm experiment because, as you would expect, without cues from the sun, their clocks continually run out of phase, resulting in a chronic form of jet lag. Researchers can reset their circadian rhythms by giving them melatonin (Sack & Lewy, 1993), which tells their brains it is nighttime even though their eyes cannot. Melatonin may be used as a treatment for people who experience severe jet lag and other sleep problems associated with circadian rhythm disruption.

 Treatment of Dyssomnias

When we can't fall asleep or we awaken frequently, or when sleep does not restore our energy and vitality, we need help. A number of biological and psychological interventions have been designed and evaluated to help people regain the benefits of normal sleep.

Medical Treatments

Perhaps the most common treatments for insomnia are medical. Researchers have estimated that during any given year, 2.7% of men and 5.5% of women in the general population use prescription drugs for sleep problems, and about 3% of men and women use over-the-counter medications (Mellinger et al., 1985). People who complain of insomnia to a medical professional will most likely be prescribed one of several *benzodiazepine* medications, which include short-acting drugs such as *triazolam* (Halcion) and long-acting drugs such as *flurazepam* (Dalmane). Short-acting drugs (those that cause only brief drowsiness) are preferred because the longer-acting drugs sometimes do not stop working by morning, and people report more daytime sleepiness. The longer-acting benzodiazepines are sometimes preferred when negative effects such as daytime anxiety are observed in people taking the short-acting drugs (Gillin, 1993). People over the age of 65 are most likely to use medication to help them sleep, although people of all ages, including young children (Mindell, 1993), have been prescribed medications for insomnia.

There are several drawbacks to medical treatments for insomnia. First, benzodiazepine medications can cause excessive sleepiness. Second, people can easily become dependent on them and rather easily misuse them, deliberately or not. Third, these medications are meant for short-term treatment and are not recommended for use longer than 4 weeks.

concept check 8.4

The term *dyssomnia* refers to conditions in which there are disturbances in the amount, quality, and timing of sleep. There are a number of different types of dyssomnia. Match the type with the situations given: (a) primary insomnia; (b) primary hypersomnia; (c) narcolepsy; (d) breathing-related sleep disorder; and (e) circadian rhythm sleep disorder.

1. Suzy can hardly make it through a full day of work if she doesn't take a nap during her lunch hour. No matter how early she goes to bed in the evening, she still sleeps as late as she possibly can in the morning. _____

2. Jerod wakes up several times each evening because he feels he is about to hyperventilate. He can't seem to get enough air, and often his wife will wake him to tell him to quit snoring. _____

3. Charlie has had considerable trouble sleeping since he started a new job that requires him to change shifts every 3 weeks. Sometimes he works during the day and sleeps at night, and other times he works at night and sleeps during the day. _____

4. Jill has problems staying awake throughout the day. Even while talking on the phone or riding the bus across town, she often loses muscle tone and falls asleep for a while. _____

5. Tommy can rarely fall asleep at a decent hour anymore. Every evening he reads, or drinks warm milk, or watches television until he can sleep. When he does fall asleep, he wakes up two or three times during the night, and each time it takes him a while to fall into a deep sleep again. _____

William C. Dement is a pioneering sleep researcher and director of the Sleep Disorders Center at Stanford University.

cal device that improves breathing. Medications include those that help stimulate respiration (for example, *medroxyprogesterone*) or the *tricyclic antidepressants*, which are thought to act on the locus ceruleus, which affects REM sleep. These drugs seem to reduce the muscle tone loss usually seen during REM sleep, which means that the respiratory muscles do not relax as much as usual at this time, thereby improving the person's breathing (Guilleminault & Dement, 1988). Certain mechanical devices have also been used to reposition either the tongue or the jaw during sleep to help improve breathing, but people tend to resist them because of discomfort. Severe breathing problems may require surgery to help remove blockages in parts of the airways.

Behavioral Treatments

Because medication as a primary treatment isn't usually recommended (Czeisler & Allan, 1989), other ways of getting people back in step with their sleep rhythms are usually tried. One general principle for treating circadian rhythm disorders is that *phase delays* (moving the bedtime later) are easier than *phase advances* (moving bedtime earlier). In other words, it is easier to stay up several hours later than usual than to force yourself to go to sleep several hours earlier. Scheduling shift changes in a clockwise direction (going from day to evening schedule) seems to help workers adjust better. People can best readjust their sleep patterns by going to bed several hours later each night, until bedtime is at the desired hour (Czeisler et al., 1981). A drawback of this approach is that it requires the person to sleep during the day for several days, which is obviously difficult for people with regularly scheduled responsibilities.

Another recent effort to help people with sleep problems involves using *bright light* to trick the brain into readjusting the biological clock. (In Chapter 7 we described light therapy for *seasonal affective disorder*.) Recent research indicates that very bright light may help people with circadian rhythm problems readjust their sleep patterns (Czeisler et al., 1986). People typically sit in front of a bank of fluorescent lamps that generate light greater than 2,500 lux, an amount significantly different from normal indoor light (250 lux). Several hours of exposure to this bright light have successfully reset the circadian rhythms of a number of individuals (Czeisler & Allan, 1989). Although this type of treatment is still new and relatively untested, it provides some hope for people with sleep problems.

Longer use can cause dependence and **rebound insomnia.** Therefore, although medications may be helpful for sleep problems that will correct themselves in a short period (for example, insomnia due to anxiety related to hospitalization), they are not intended for long-term, chronic problems.

To help people with hypersomnia or narcolepsy, physicians usually prescribe a stimulant such as *methylphenidate* (Ritalin, the medication Ann was taking) or *amphetamine* (Gillin, 1993). Cataplexy, or loss of muscle tone, is usually addressed with antidepressant medication, not because people with narcolepsy are depressed but because antidepressants suppress REM (or dream) sleep. Cataplexy seems to be related to the sudden onset of REM sleep, and therefore the antidepressant medication can be helpful in reducing these attacks.

Treatment of breathing-related sleep disorders focuses on helping the person breathe better during sleep. For some, this means recommending weight loss. In some people who are obese, the neck's soft tissue compresses the airways. Unfortunately, as we have seen earlier in this chapter, voluntary weight loss is rarely successful in the long term; as a result, this treatment has not proven to be very successful for breathing-related sleep disorders (Guilleminault & Dement, 1988).

For mild or moderate cases of obstructive sleep apnea, treatment usually involves either medication or a mechani-

Psychological Treatments

As you can imagine, the limitations of using drugs to help people sleep better has led to psychological treatments. Table 8.3 lists and briefly describes some of the psychological approaches to insomnia. Different treatments help people with different kinds of sleep problems. For example, relaxation treatments reduce the physical tension that seems to prevent some people from falling asleep at night. Some people report that their anxiety about work, relationships, or other situations prevents them from sleeping or wakes them up in the middle of the night. To address this problem, *cognitive treatments* are used.

Research shows that some psychological treatments for insomnia may be more effective than others. For adult sleep problems, *stimulus control* may be recommended. People are instructed to use the bedroom only for sleeping and for sex and *not* for work or other anxiety-provoking activities (for example, watching the news on television). *Progressive relaxation* or *sleep hygiene* (changing daily habits that may interfere with sleep) alone may not be as effective as stimulus control alone for some people (Lacks & Morin, 1992).

Kathryn's sleep problems were addressed with several techniques. She was instructed to limit her time in bed to about 4 hours of sleep time (*sleep restriction*), about the amount of time she actually slept each night. The period was lengthened when she began to sleep through the night. Kathryn was also asked not to listen to the radio while in bed and to get out of bed if she couldn't fall asleep (stimulus control). Finally, therapy involved confronting her unrealistic expectations about how much sleep was enough for a person of her age (cognitive therapy). Within about 3 weeks of treatment, Kathryn was sleeping longer (6 to 7 hours per night as opposed to 4 to 5 hours previously) and had fewer interruptions in her sleep. Also, she felt more refreshed in the morning and had more energy during the day. Kathryn's results mirror those of a recent study that found combined treatments to be effective in older adults with insomnia (Morin, Kowatch, Barry, & Walton, 1993).

For young children, some of the cognitive treatments may not be possible. Instead, treatment often includes setting up bedtime routines such as a bath, followed by a parent's reading a story, to help children go to sleep at night. Graduated extinction (described in Table 8.2) has been used with some success for bedtime problems as well as for waking up at night (Durand & Mindell, 1990). Integrating both medical and behavioral treatments seems especially important for insomnia. Research suggests that short-term use of medication in combination with other types of interventions may prove to be a quick and lasting treatment for insomnia (Milby et al., 1993; Morin & Azrin, 1988).

Psychological treatment research for the other dyssomnias is virtually nonexistent. For the most part, counseling or support groups assist in managing the psychological and social effects of disturbed sleep, and are especially helpful for people who suffer from feelings of low self-esteem and depression (Bootzin et al., 1993).

Parasomnias

Have you ever been told that you walk in your sleep? Talk in your sleep? Have you ever had troublesome nightmares? Do you grind your teeth in your sleep? If you answered yes to one or more of these questions (and it's likely that you did), you have experienced sleep problems in the category of parasomnia. Parasomnias are not problems with sleep itself, but abnormal events that occur either during sleep or during that twilight time between sleeping and waking. Some of the events that are associated with parasomnia are not unusual if they happen while you are awake (walking to the kitchen to look into the refrigerator) but can be distressing if they take place while you are sleeping.

Parasomnias are of two types: those that occur during rapid eye movement (REM) sleep, and those that occur during non-rapid eye movement sleep (NREM). As you might

table 8.3	**Psychological Treatments for Insomnia**
Sleep Treatment	*Description*
Cognitive	This approach focuses on changing the sleepers' unrealistic expectations and beliefs about sleep ("I must have 8 hours of sleep each night"; "If I get less than 8 hours of sleep it will make me ill"). Therapist attempts to alter beliefs and attitudes about sleeping by providing information on topics such as normal amounts of sleep and a person's ability to compensate for lost sleep.
Cognitive relaxation	Because some people become anxious when they have difficulty sleeping, this approach uses meditation or imagery to help with relaxation at bedtime or after a night waking.
Graduated extinction	Used for children who have tantrums at bedtime or wake up crying at night, this treatment instructs the parent to check on the child after progressively longer periods of time, until the child falls asleep on his or her own.
Paradoxical intention	This technique involves instructing individuals in the opposite behavior from the desired outcome. Telling poor sleepers to lie in bed and try to stay awake as long as they can is used to try to relieve the performance anxiety surrounding efforts to try to fall asleep.
Progressive relaxation	This technique involves relaxing the muscles of your body in an effort to introduce drowsiness.

A nightmare is distressing for both child and parent.

have guessed, **nightmares** occur during REM or dream sleep. About 20% of children and 5% to 10% of adults experience them (Buysse, Reynolds, & Kupfer, 1993). To qualify as a nightmare disorder, according to DSM-IV criteria, these experiences must be so distressful that they impair a person's ability to carry on normal activities. Because nightmares are so common, you would expect that a great deal of research would have focused on their causes and treatment. Unfortunately, this is not so, and we still know little about why people have nightmares and about how to treat them. Fortunately, they tend to decrease with age.

Sleep terrors, which most commonly afflict children, usually begin with a piercing scream. The child is extremely upset, is often sweating, and frequently has a rapid heartbeat. On the surface, sleep terrors appear to resemble nightmares—the child cries and appears frightened—but they occur during NREM sleep and therefore are not caused by frightening dreams. During sleep terrors children cannot be easily awakened and comforted, as they can during a nightmare. Children do not remember sleep terrors, despite their often dramatic effect on the observer. Approximately 5% of children (more boys than girls) may experience sleep terrors; for adults, the prevalence rate is less than 1% (Buysse et al., 1993). As with nightmares, we know relatively little about sleep terrors, although several theories have been proposed, including the possibility of a genetic component because the disorder tends to occur in families (Mindell, 1993). Treatment for sleep terrors usually begins with a recommendation to wait and see if they disappear on their own. If the problem is frequent or continues a long time, sometimes antidepressants (imipramine) or benzodiazepines are recommended, although their effectiveness has not yet been clearly demonstrated (Mindell, 1993). To date, there is not much evidence for a good and lasting treatment of sleep terrors.

It might surprise you to learn that **sleepwalking** (also called *somnambulism*) occurs during NREM sleep. This means that when people walk in their sleep they are probably not acting out a dream. This parasomnia typically occurs during the first few hours while a person is in the deep stages of sleep. The DSM-IV criteria for sleepwalking require that the person leave the bed, although less active episodes can involve small motor behaviors such as sitting up in bed and picking at the blanket or gesturing. Because sleepwalking occurs during the deepest stages of sleep, waking someone during an episode is difficult; if the person is wakened, he or she typically will not remember what has happened. It is not true, however, that waking a sleepwalker is somehow dangerous.

Sleepwalking is primarily a problem during childhood, although a small proportion of adults are affected. A relatively large number of children—from 15% to 30%—have at least one episode of sleepwalking, with about 2% reported to have multiple incidents (Thorpy & Glovinsky, 1987). For the most part, the course of sleepwalking is short, and few people over the age of 15 continue to exhibit this parasomnia. When sleepwalking occurs among adults, it is often associated with other psychological disorders (Kales, Soldatos, Caldwell, et al., 1980).

We do not yet clearly understand why some people sleepwalk, although factors such as extreme fatigue, previous sleep deprivation, the use of sedative or hypnotic drugs, and stress have been implicated (Anch et al., 1988). There also seems to be a genetic component to sleepwalking, with a higher incidence observed among identical twins and within families (Kales, Soldatos, Bixler, et al., 1980). A related disorder, *nocturnal eating syndrome*, where individuals rise from their beds and eat although they are still asleep, may be more frequent than previously thought, being found in almost 6% of individuals in one study who were referred because of insomnia complaints (Manni, Ratti, & Tartara, 1997).

■ **concept check 8.5**

Diagnose the following sleep problems: (a) primary hypersomnia; (b) narcolepsy; (c) sleep terrors; (d) primary insomnia.

1. Ashley wakes up screaming nearly every night. Her parents rush to comfort her, but she doesn't respond. Her heart rate is elevated during these episodes, and her pajamas are soaked in sweat. The next day, Ashley has no memory of the experience. _____

2. Rick has been having difficulty falling asleep at night for a month. He also feels exhausted in the morning even after nights when he thought he had slept well. He is chronically tired at work, and his supervisors have reprimanded him for inattention. _____

3. Eddie sleeps 10 to 12 hours per night yet still feels sleepy at work after dragging himself out of bed. He finds himself napping on his lunch hour. He has been sleeping excessively for 2 months. _____

from the inside

Feeding the Hungry Heart:
The Experience of Compulsive Eating
By Geneen Roth*

Geneen Roth says her book is "about recognizing, dealing with, and resolving compulsive eating. It is also about the agony, the frustration, and the disillusionment of feeling and being fat" (p. 5). Her own compulsive eating began with her childhood fear that she was the cause of her parents' unhappiness. She also includes poignant descriptions by women who have attended her Breaking Free workshops, in which people learn what to do about compulsive eating.

Roth explains why bingeing never leads to satisfaction, why women feel fat even when their body image may not be the issue that is really bothering them, how eating becomes a metaphor, and how to break the cycle of compulsive eating and purging to satisfy needs that are unrelated to food.

Roth sees binges as valuable messages that are worth attending to: "Binges are purposeful acts, not demented journeys. . . . a binge can actually be an urgent attempt to care for yourself when you feel uncared for" (p. 16) She helps us understand that we may eat not to overcome hunger but to satisfy our desire for things that are missing from our lives: "Every time you reach out for food when you're not hungry, you are getting a signal of need. If you recognize that, you're lucky; you've found a way of getting your own attention" (129).

In the final section, Roth quotes a workshop participant: "We want to change in order to love ourselves, but we've got to love ourselves in order to change" (p. 159). Roth herself concludes:

> In the end, you break free from the illusion that your hunger has to do with food and that the answer to it is being thin. You begin answering the call of a hunger that has never before been satisfied. You begin realizing your potential as the irreplaceable human being that you are, instead of using food to postpone that recognition. (167)

Part memoir, part self-help manual, *Feeding the Hungry Heart* was clearly inspired by a warm and intimate concern for people who suffer from eating disorders. Geneen Roth kindly and firmly motivates her readers, who are likely to be as enthusiastic about her message as are the many who benefit from her workshops.

*Geneen Roth, *Feeding the Hungry Heart: The Experience of Compulsive Eating* (Plume, 1993).

Summary

- The prevalence of eating disorders has increased rapidly over the last half century. As a result, they are included for the first time as a separate group of disorders in DSM-IV.

Bulimia Nervosa and Anorexia Nervosa
- There are two prevalent eating disorders. In bulimia nervosa, dieting results in out-of-control binge-eating episodes that are often followed by purging the food through vomiting or other means. Anorexia nervosa, in which food intake is cut down dramatically, results in substantial weight loss and sometimes dangerously low body weight.

Additional Eating Disorders
- In binge-eating disorder, a pattern of binge eating is *not* followed by purging; in rumination disorder, food is regurgitated, chewed, and reswallowing to the point of interfering with nutritional intake or weight gain; in pica, infants and young children ingest non-nutritive substances.

Statistics and Course for Eating Disorders
- Bulimia nervosa and anorexia nervosa are largely confined to young, middle- to upper-class women in Western cultures who are pursuing a thin body shape that is culturally mandated and biologically inappropriate, making it extremely difficult to achieve.
- Without treatment, eating disorders become chronic and can, on occasion, result in death.

Causes
- In addition to sociocultural pressures, causal factors include possible biological and genetic vulnerabilities (the disorders tend to run in families), psychological factors (low self-esteem), social anxiety (fears of rejection), and distorted body image (relatively normal-weight individuals view themselves as fat and ugly).

Treatment
- Several psychosocial treatments are effective, including cognitive–behavioral approaches combined with family therapy and interpersonal psychotherapy. Drug treatments are less effective at the current time.

Sleep Disorders
- Sleep disorders are highly prevalent in the general population and are of two types: dyssomnias (disturbances of sleep) and parasomnias (abnormal events such as nightmares and sleepwalking that occur during sleep).

- Of the dyssomnias, the most common disorder, primary insomnia, involves the inability to initiate sleep, problems maintaining sleep, or failure to feel refreshed after a full night's sleep. Other dyssomnias include primary hypersomnia (excessive sleep), narcolepsy (sudden and irresistible sleep attacks), circadian rhythm sleep disorders (sleepiness or insomnia caused by the body's inability to synchronize its sleep patterns with day and night), and breathing-related sleep disorders (disruptions that have a physical origin, such as sleep apnea, that leads to excessive sleepiness or insomnia).

- The formal assessment of sleep disorders, a polysomnographic (PSG) evaluation, is typically done by monitoring the heart, muscles, respiration, brain waves, and other functions of a sleeping client in the lab. In addition to such monitoring, it is helpful to determine the individual's sleep efficiency (SE), a percentage based on the time the individual *actually* sleeps as opposed to time spent in bed trying to sleep.

- Benzodiazepine medications have been helpful for short-term treatment of many of the dyssomnias, but they must be used carefully, or they might cause rebound insomnia, a withdrawal experience that can cause worse sleep problems after the medication is stopped. Any long-term treatment of sleep problems should include psychological interventions such as stimulus control and sleep hygiene.

- Parasomnias such as nightmares occur during REM (or dream) sleep, and sleep terrors and sleepwalking during NREM sleep.

Key Terms

bulimia nervosa
binge
anorexia nervosa
purging techniques
binge-eating disorder (BED)
rumination disorder
pica
rapid eye movement (REM) sleep
dyssomnias
parasomnias
polysomnographic (PSG) evaluation
sleep efficiency (SE)

microsleeps
primary insomnia
hypersomnia
narcolepsy
breathing-related sleep disorders
sleep apnea
circadian rhythm sleep disorders
rebound insomnia
nightmares
sleep terrors
sleepwalking

Answers

8.1
1. b
2. b
3. a
4. a
5. a

8.2
1. d
2. a
3. b
4. a
5. b

8.3
1. c
2. b
3. e
4. a
5. d

8.4
1. b
2. d
3. e
4. c
5. a

8.5
1. c
2. d
3. a

EXPLORING EATING DISORDERS

Eating disorders are a modern phenomenon that until recently were widespread only in the West.
• Overwhelmingly an affliction of young females
• Primary characteristic is all-encompassing drive to be thin.

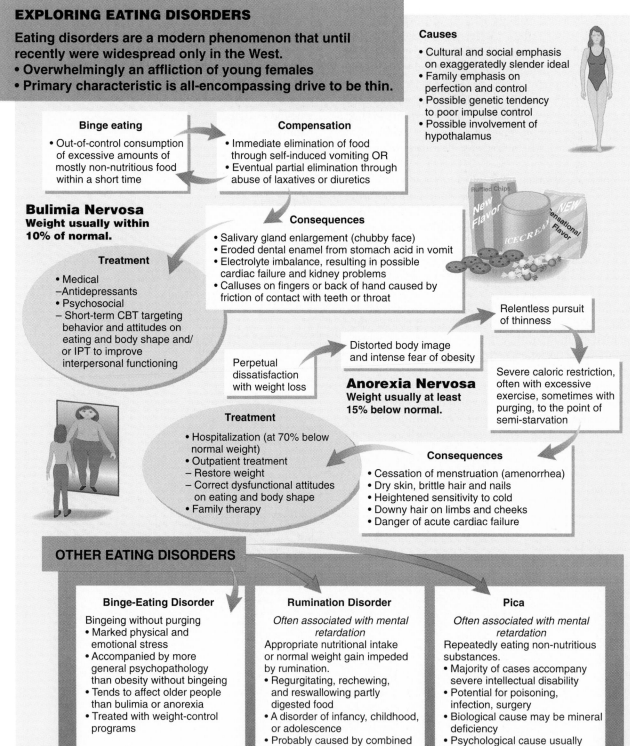

Causes

• Cultural and social emphasis on exaggeratedly slender ideal
• Family emphasis on perfection and control
• Possible genetic tendency to poor impulse control
• Possible involvement of hypothalamus

Binge eating

• Out-of-control consumption of excessive amounts of mostly non-nutritious food within a short time

Compensation

• Immediate elimination of food through self-induced vomiting OR
• Eventual partial elimination through abuse of laxatives or diuretics

Bulimia Nervosa
Weight usually within 10% of normal.

Consequences

• Salivary gland enlargement (chubby face)
• Eroded dental enamel from stomach acid in vomit
• Electrolyte imbalance, resulting in possible cardiac failure and kidney problems
• Calluses on fingers or back of hand caused by friction of contact with teeth or throat

Treatment

• Medical
 –Antidepressants
• Psychosocial
 – Short-term CBT targeting behavior and attitudes on eating and body shape and/ or IPT to improve interpersonal functioning

Perpetual dissatisfaction with weight loss

Distorted body image and intense fear of obesity

Relentless pursuit of thinness

Severe caloric restriction, often with excessive exercise, sometimes with purging, to the point of semi-starvation

Anorexia Nervosa
Weight usually at least 15% below normal.

Treatment

• Hospitalization (at 70% below normal weight)
• Outpatient treatment
 – Restore weight
 – Correct dysfunctional attitudes on eating and body shape
• Family therapy

Consequences

• Cessation of menstruation (amenorrhea)
• Dry skin, brittle hair and nails
• Heightened sensitivity to cold
• Downy hair on limbs and cheeks
• Danger of acute cardiac failure

OTHER EATING DISORDERS

Binge-Eating Disorder

Bingeing without purging
• Marked physical and emotional stress
• Accompanied by more general psychopathology than obesity without bingeing
• Tends to affect older people than bulimia or anorexia
• Treated with weight-control programs

Rumination Disorder

Often associated with mental retardation
Appropriate nutritional intake or normal weight gain impeded by rumination.
• Regurgitating, rechewing, and reswallowing partly digested food
• A disorder of infancy, childhood, or adolescence
• Probably caused by combined biological and psychological factors
• Direct behavioral treatment

Pica

Often associated with mental retardation
Repeatedly eating non-nutritious substances.
• Majority of cases accompany severe intellectual disability
• Potential for poisoning, infection, surgery
• Biological cause may be mineral deficiency
• Psychological cause usually neglect or abuse
• Treated with operant conditioning procedures (reinforcing appropriate eating, punishing mildly for pica)

EXPLORING SLEEP DISORDERS

Sleep disorders can be extremely disruptive to affected individuals and are an important factor in many psychological disorders. Understanding sleep is important to understanding behavior.
- **Physiological mechanisms and cognitive, behavioral, and cultural factors are reciprocally related in the etiology of sleep disorders.**

In diagnosing sleep disorders, assessment is made through a polysomnographic (PSG) evaluation. Various electronic tests measure brain activity, eye movements, muscle movements, and heart activity. Results are weighed with a measure of sleep efficiency (SE), the percentage of time spent asleep.

DYSSOMNIAS
Disturbances in the timing, amount, or quality of sleep

Primary Insomnia

Difficulty initiating or maintaining sleep; non-restorative sleep
- Causes include pain, insufficient exercise, drug use, environmental influences, anxiety, biological vulnerability.
- Treatment may be medical (benzodiazepines) or psychological (anxiety reduction, progressive relaxation, improved sleep hygiene); combined approach is usually most effective.

Narcolepsy

Sudden daytime onset of REM sleep combined with cataplexy, a rapid loss of muscle tone that can be quite mild or result in complete collapse. Often accompanied by sleep paralysis and/or hypnagogic hallucinations.
- Causes are likely to be genetic.
- Treatment is medical (stimulant drugs).

Primary Hypersomnia

Abnormally excessive sleep; involuntary daytime sleeping; classified as a disorder only when it's subjectively perceived as disruptive.
- Causes may involve genetic link and/or excess serotonin.
- Treatment is usually medical (stimulant drugs).

PARASOMNIAS

Nightmares

Frightening REM dreams stressful enough to impair normal functioning.
Causes unknown; decrease with age.

Sleep terrors

Sleeping child screams, cries, sweats, sometimes walks, has rapid heartbeat, cannot easily be awakened or comforted. Possible genetic link. May subside naturally.

Sleepwalking

Occurs at least once during non-REM (non-dreaming) sleep in 15% to 30% of children under age 15. Causes may include sedative or hypnotic drugs and stress. Adult sleepwalking is usually associated with other psychological disorders.

Breathing-Related Sleep Disorder

Disturbed sleep and daytime fatigue result from hypoventilation (labored breathing) or sleep apnea (suspension of breathing).
- Causes may include narrow or obstructed airway, obesity, aging, or CNS disorders.
- Treatments to improve breathing are medical or mechanical.

Circadian Rhythm Sleep Disorder

Sleepiness or insomnia that is
- Caused by inability to synchronize sleep patterns with current pattern of day and night due to
- jet lag, shift work, delayed or advanced sleep phases
- Treatment includes phase delays to adjust bedtime and bright light to readjust biological clock.

9

Physical Disorders and Health Psychology

The story I want to tell is about heroism and sacrifice and love, but I will not be avoiding the anger.

Paul Monette
Borrowed Time: An AIDS Memoir

The U.S. Surgeon General and others have pointed out that at the beginning of this century, the leading causes of death were influenza, pneumonia, diphtheria, tuberculosis, and gastrointestinal infections. Since then, the yearly death rate from these diseases has been reduced greatly, from 623 to 50 per one hundred thousand people (see Table 9.1). This reduction represents a revolution in public health that eliminated many infectious diseases and mastered many more. But the enormous success of our health care system in reducing mortality from disease has revealed a more complex and challenging problem: At present, some major contributing factors to illness and death in this country are *psychological and behavioral.* Consider for example, the relationship between genital herpes and stress.

There's a chance that someone you know has *genital herpes,* and hasn't told you about it. It's not difficult to understand why. Genital herpes is an incurable sexually transmitted disease. Recent estimates indicate that 30 million or more Americans—between 10% and 15% of the entire population—have been infected by the herpes simplex virus II (R. E. Johnson et al., 1989). Because the disease is concentrated in young adults, the percentage in that group is much higher.

The virus remains dormant until it is reactivated periodically. When it recurs, infected individuals usually experience any of a number of symptoms including pain, itching, vaginal or urethral discharge and, most commonly, ulcerative lesions (open sores) in the genital area. Lesions recur approximately four times each year, but can appear much more frequently. Cases of genital herpes have increased dramatically during the past 20 years, for reasons that are as much psychological and behavioral as biological. Although genital herpes is a biological disease, it spreads so rapidly because

people choose not to change their behavior by simply using a condom.

There is increasing evidence that stress plays a role in triggering recurrences (for instance, Glaser, Kiecolt-Glaser, Speicher, & Holliday, 1985; Hoon et al., 1991; Stout & Bloom, 1986) by suppressing the immune system (Kemeny, Cohen, Zegans, & Conant, 1989). Stress-control procedures, particularly relaxation, may decrease recurrences of genital herpes as well as the duration of each episode. Burnette, Koehn, Kenyon-Jump, Hutton, and Stark (1991) treated seven women and one man using a single-case, multiple baseline, across-subjects design (see Chapter 4) in which treatment is introduced at a different time for each subject. If changes in the disorder do not occur *until* treatment is introduced, we can be fairly confident that the change is caused by the treatment and not some other factor, such as attention from the therapist. Data from five individuals who responded well to treatment are represented in Figure 9.1. The data reflect the number of days per week that each person had a recurrence of genital herpes. On the horizontal line is the average number of recurrences before and after treatment. Note the response of subject #7. During some weeks she had outbreaks almost every day, but after stress-reduction treatment they were almost eliminated.

Four other patients responded reasonably well to treatment (see Figure 9.1), but three others did not respond in a clinically significant way. At least one reported not practicing relaxation, which might account for the lack of progress; the other two, evidently, just did not benefit. Although these data are only preliminary, the findings strongly suggest that for some people there is a relationship between psychological factors and viral infections.

table 9.1 The Ten Leading Causes of Death in the United States in 1900 and in 1993 (rates per 100,000 population)

1900	Rate	1993	Rate
1. Cardiovascular diseases (heart disease, stroke)	345	1. Cardiovascular diseases (heart disease, stroke)	366
2. Influenza and pneumonia	202	2. Cancer	206
3. Tuberculosis	194	3. Chronic obstructive pulmonary diseases	39
4. Gastritis, duodenitis, enteritis, and colitis	143	4. Accidents	34
5. Accidents	72	5. Influenza and pneumonia	32
6. Cancer	64	6. Diabetes	21
7. Diphtheria	40	7. Other infectious and parasitic diseases	18
8. Typhoid fever	31	8. Suicide	12
9. Measles	13	9. Homicide and legal intervention	9.9
10. Chronic liver diseases and cirrhosis	*	10. Chronic liver diseases and cirrhosis	9.6

*data unavailable
Source: Figures for 1900 from *Historical Statistics of the United States: Colonial Times to 1970, Pt. 1* by U.S. Bureau of the Census, 1975, Washington, DC: U.S. Government Printing Office. Figures for 1993 from *Statistical Abstracts of the United States* by U.S. Bureau of the Census, 1995, Washington, DC: U.S. Government Printing Office.

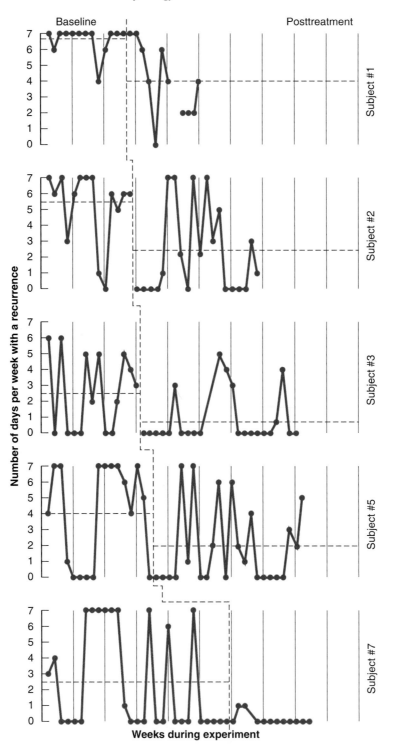

figure 9.1   Measures of genital herpes outbreaks. The graphs show before- and after-treatment measures of genital herpes outbreaks for 5 subjects who received stress reduction treatment. The horizontal broken lines—representing the average number of outbreaks during baseline and posttreatment periods—show that these subjects experienced a significant decrease in outbreaks after treatment (adapted from Burnette et al., 1991).

In Chapter 2 we described the profound effects of psychological and social factors on brain structure and function. These factors seem to influence neurotransmitter activity, the secretion of neurohormones in the endocrine system and, at a more fundamental level, gene expression. We have repeatedly looked at the complex interplay of biological, psychological, and social factors in the production and maintenance of psychological disorders. It will come as no surprise that psychological and social factors are very important to a number of additional disorders, including endocrinological disorders such as diabetes and disorders of the immune system such as AIDS. The difference between these and the other disorders discussed in this chapter is that they are clearly *physical disorders.* They have known (or strongly inferred) physical causes and, for the most part, observable physical pathology (for example, genital herpes, damaged heart muscle, malignant tumors, measurable hypertension). Contrast this with the somatoform disorders discussed in Chapter 6: In conversion disorders, for example, clients complain of physical damage or disease but show no physical pathology. In DSM-IV, physical disorders such as hypertension and diabetes are coded separately on Axis III. However, there is a provision for recognizing *psychological factors affecting medical condition.*

The study of how psychological and social factors affect physical disorders used to be distinct and somewhat separate from the remainder of psychopathology. Early on, the field was called *psychosomatic medicine* (Alexander, 1950), which meant that *psychological* factors affected *somatic* (physical) function. *Psychophysiological disorders* was a label used to communicate a similar idea. Such terms are less often used today because they are misleading. Describing as psychosomatic disorder with an obvious physical component gave the impression that psychological ("mental") disorders of mood and anxiety did not have a strong biological component. As we now know, this assumption is not viable. Dividing the *causes* of mental disorders and physical disorders is not at all supported by current evidence. Biological, psychological, and social factors are implicated in the cause and maintenance of every disorder.

The contribution of psychosocial factors to the etiology and treatment of physical disorders is widely studied. Some of the discoveries are among the more exciting findings in all of psychology and biology. For example, in Chapter 2, we described briefly the specific harmful influences of anger on heart function. The tentative conclusion from that research was that the pumping efficiency of an angry person's heart is reduced, risking dangerous disturbances of heart rhythms (Ironson et al., 1992). We also discussed recent studies demonstrating that psychological factors, including psycho-

> *The party was going to have to stop. The evidence was too ominous:* We were making ourselves sick.*

logical treatment, increase survival time in patients with cancer (Spiegel, Bloom, & Kramer, 1989). Remember, too, the tragic physical and mental deterioration among elderly people who are removed from social networks of family and friends (Broadhead, Kaplan, & James, 1983; Grant, Patterson, & Yager, 1988). Finally, long-term unemployment among men who previously held steady jobs doubles the risk of death over the following 5 years compared to men who continued working (Morris, Cook, & Shaper, 1994).

The shift in focus from infectious disease to psychological factors has been called the second revolution in public health. Two closely related new fields of study have developed. In the first, **behavioral medicine** (Agras, 1982; Meyers, 1991), knowledge derived from behavioral science is applied to the prevention, diagnosis, and treatment of medical problems. This is an interdisciplinary field in which psychologists, physicians, and other health professionals work closely together to develop new treatments and preventive strategies (G. E. Schwartz & Weiss, 1978). A second field, **health psychology,** is not interdisciplinary and is usually considered a subfield of behavioral medicine. Practitioners study psychological factors that are important to the promotion and maintenance of health; they also analyze and recommend improvements of health care systems and health policy formation within the discipline of psychology (Feuerstein, Labbe, & Kuczmierczyk, 1986; G. Stone, 1987).

Psychological and social factors influence health and physical problems in *two* distinct ways (see Figure 9.2). First, they can affect the basic biological processes that lead to illness and disease. Second, long-standing behavior patterns may put people at risk to develop certain physical disorders. Sometimes both of these avenues contribute to the etiology or maintenance of disease (Taylor & Repetti, 1997; Uchino, Cacioppo, & Kiecolt-Glaser, 1995). Consider the tragic example of AIDS. AIDS is a disease of the immune system, which is directly affected by stress (Cohen & Herbert, 1996), so stress may promote the deadly progression of AIDS (a conclusion that is pending confirmation from additional studies). This is an example of how psychological factors may directly influence biological processes. We also know that a variety of things we may choose to *do* put us at risk for AIDS; for example, having unprotected sex or sharing dirty needles. Because there is no medical cure for AIDS yet, our best weapon is large-scale behavior modification to *prevent acquisition* of the disease.

Other behavioral patterns contribute to disease. Fully 50% of deaths from the 10 leading causes of death in the United States can be traced to behaviors common to certain life-styles (N. E. Miller, 1987). Smoking has been estimated to cause 19% of all deaths (McGinnis & Foege, 1993; Brannon & Feist, 1997). Behavioral patterns subsumed under unhealthy life-styles also include poor eating

*Featured quotations in this chapter are from Paul Monette, *Borrowed Time: An AIDS Memoir* (Avon, 1990).

1 Psychosocial factors (such as negative emotions and stress) disrupt basic biological processes, which may lead to physical disorders and disease.

Stress

Lack of control

2 "Risky" behaviors cause or contribute to a variety of physical disorders and disease.

Smoking
Drinking
Poor eating habits
No exercise

figure 9.2   Psychosocial factors directly affect physical health

habits, lack of exercise, and insufficient injury control (not wearing seatbelts, and so on). These behaviors are grouped under the label *life-style* because they are, for the most part, enduring habits that are an integral part of a person's daily living pattern (Faden, 1987; Oyama & Andrasik, 1992). We will return to life-styles in the closing pages of this chapter when we look at efforts to modify them and promote health.

Psychological and Social Factors That Influence Biology

We have much to learn about how psychological factors affect physical disorders and disease. Available evidence suggests that the same kinds of causal factors active in psychological disorders—social, psychological, and biological—play a role in some physical disorders (Taylor & Repetti, 1997). But the factor attracting the most attention is stress, particularly the neurobiological components of the stress response.

The Nature of Stress

In 1936, a young scientist in Montreal named Hans Selye noticed that one group of rats he injected with a certain chemical extract developed ulcers and other physiological problems, including atrophy of immune system tissues. But a control group of rats who received a daily saline (salty water) injection that should not have had any effect developed the *same* physical problems. Selye pursued this unexpected finding and discovered that the daily injections themselves seemed to be the culprit rather than the injected substance. Furthermore, many different types of environmental changes produced the same results. Borrowing a term from engineering, he decided that the cause of this nonspecific reaction was *stress*. As so often happens in science, an accidental or "serendipitous" observation led to a new area of study; in this case, *stress physiology* (Selye, 1936).

Selye theorized that the body went through several stages in response to *sustained* stress. The first phase was a type of *alarm* response to immediate danger or threat. With continuing stress, we seem to pass into a stage of *resistance,* in which we mobilize various coping mechanisms to respond to the stress. Finally, if the stress is too intense or lasts too long, we may enter a stage of *exhaustion,* in which our bodies suffer permanent damage or death (Selye, 1936, 1950). Selye called this sequence the **general adaptation syndrome (GAS).** The idea that chronic stress may inflict permanent bodily damage or contribute to disease has been confirmed and elaborated on in recent years (McEwen & Stellar, 1993; Sapolsky, 1990).

The word "stress" means many things in modern life. In engineering, stress is the strain on a bridge when a heavy truck drives across it; stress is the *response* of the bridge to the truck's weight. But stress is also a *stimulus.* The truck is a "stressor" for the bridge, just as being fired from a job or facing a difficult final exam is a stimulus or stressor for a person. These varied meanings can create some confusion, but we will concentrate on **stress** as the physiological response of the individual to a stressor.

The Physiology of Stress

In Chapter 2, we described the physiological effects of the early stages of stress, noting in particular its activating effect on the sympathetic nervous system, which mobilizes our resources during times of threat or danger by activating internal organs to prepare the body for immediate action, either fight or flight. These changes increase our strength and mental activ-

Hans Selye suggested in 1936 that stress contributes to certain physical problems.

A human under stress is like a bridge bearing a heavy weight.

ity. We also noted in Chapter 2 that the activity of the endocrine system increases when we are stressed, primarily through activation of the HYPAC axis. Although a variety of neurotransmitters begin flowing in the nervous system, much attention has focused on the endocrine system's neuromodulators or neuropeptides, hormones affecting the nervous system that are secreted by the glands directly into the bloodstream (Krishnan, Doraiswamy, Venkataraman, Reed, & Richie, 1991; Owens, Mulchachy, Stout, & Plotsky, 1997). These neuromodulating hormones act very much like neurotransmitters in carrying the brain's messages to various parts of the body. One of the neurohormones, *corticotropin releasing factor* (CRF), is secreted by the hypothalamus and stimulates the pituitary gland. Farther down the chain of the HYPAC axis, the pituitary gland (along with the autonomic nervous system) activates the adrenal gland, which secretes, among other things, the hormone *cortisol*. Because of their very close relationship to the stress response, cortisol and other related hormones are known as the *stress hormones*.

Remember that the HYPAC axis is closely related to the limbic system. The hypothalamus, at the very top of the brain stem, is right next to the limbic system, which contains the hippocampus and which seems to control our emotional memories. The hippocampus is very responsive to cortisol. When stimulated by this hormone during HYPAC axis activity, the hippocampus helps to *turn off* the stress response, completing a feedback loop between the limbic system and the various parts of the HYPAC axis.

This loop may be important for a number of reasons. Working with primates, Robert Sapolsky and his colleagues (for instance, Sapolsky & Meaney, 1986) showed that increased levels of cortisol in response to chronic stress may kill nerve cells in the hip-

pocampus. If hippocampal activity is thus compromised, excessive cortisol is secreted and, over time, the ability to turn off the stress response decreases, which leads to further aging of the hippocampus. These findings indicate that chronic stress leading to chronic secretion of cortisol may have long-lasting effects on physical function, including brain damage. Cell death may, in turn, lead to deficient problem-solving abilities among the aged and, ultimately, dementia. This physiological process may also affect our susceptibility to infectious disease and our recovery from it in other pathophysiological systems. Sapolsky's work is important because we now know that hippocampal cell death as a result of chronic stress and anxiety occurs in humans with, for example, posttraumatic stress disorder (see Chapter 5). The long-term effects of this cell death are not yet known.

Contributions to the Stress Response

Stress physiology is profoundly influenced by psychological and social factors (Taylor & Repetti, 1997). This link has been demonstrated by Sapolsky (1990), who is studying baboons living freely in a national reserve in Kenya. He is studying baboons because their primary sources of stress, like humans', are psychological rather than physical. As with many species, baboons arrange themselves in a social hierarchy with dominant members at the top and submissive members at the bottom. And life is tough at the bottom! The lives of subordinate animals are made difficult (Sapolsky calls it "stressful") by continual bullying from the dominant animals, and they have less access to food, preferred resting places, and sexual partners.

Baboons at the top of the social hierarchy have a sense of predictability and control that allows them to cope with problems and maintain physical health; baboons at the bottom of the hierarchy suffer the symptoms of stress because they have little control over access to food, resting places, and mates.

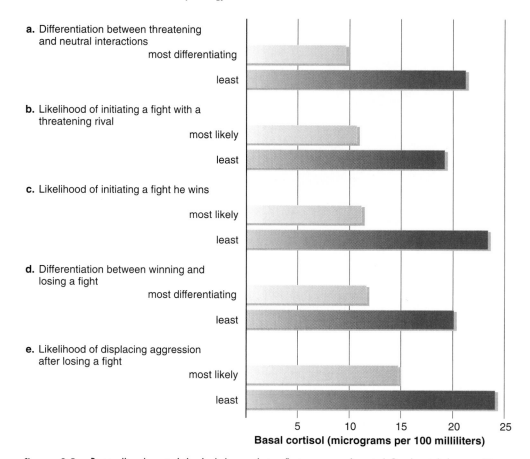

figure 9.3   Personality characteristics in baboons that reflect a sense of control. Dominant baboons with certain personality traits (light bar) have lower base levels of cortisol than do other dominant males (dark bar), which suggests that attitude is a more important mediator of physiology than is rank alone. Dominant males who can distinguish between the threatening and neutral actions of a rival have cortisol levels that are about half as high as those of other dominant males (a). Similarly, low cortisol levels are found in males who start a fight with a threatening rival instead of waiting to be attacked (b); who know which fights to pick, and so are likely to win fights they initiate (c); who distinguish between having won and lost a fight (d); or who, when they do lose, take out their frustration on subordinates (e) (from Sapolsky & Ray, 1989).

Particularly interesting are Sapolsky's findings on levels of cortisol in the baboons as a function of their social rank in a dominance hierarchy. Remember from our description of the HYPAC axis that the secretion of cortisol from the adrenal glands is the final step in a cascade of hormone secretion that originates in the limbic system in the brain during periods of stress. The secretion of cortisol contributes to our arousal and mobilization in the short run but, if produced chronically, it can damage the hippocampus. In addition, muscles atrophy, fertility is affected by declining testosterone, hypertension develops in the cardiovascular system, and the immune response is impaired. Sapolsky discovered that dominant males in the baboon hierarchy ordinarily had *lower* resting levels of cortisol than subordinate males. When an emergency occurred, however, cortisol levels rose more quickly in the dominant males than in the subordinate males.

Sapolsky and his colleagues sought the causes of these differences by working backward up the HYPAC axis. They found an excess secretion of corticotropin releasing factor by the hypothalamus in subordinate animals, combined with a diminished sensitivity of the pituitary gland (which is stimulated by CRF). Therefore, subordinate animals, unlike dominant animals, continually secrete cortisol, probably because their lives are so stressful. In addition, their HYPAC system is less sensitive to the effects of cortisol and therefore less efficient in turning off the stress response.

Sapolsky also discovered that subordinate males have fewer circulating lymphocytes (white blood cells) than dominant males, a sign of immune system suppression. In addition, subordinate males evidence less circulating HDL (high density lipoprotein) cholesterol, which puts them at higher risk for atherosclerosis and coronary heart disease, a subject we discuss later in this chapter.

What is it about being on top that produces positive effects? Sapolsky concluded that it is primarily the psychological benefits of having *predictability and controllability*. Parts of his data were gathered during years in which a number of male baboons were at the top of the hierarchy, with no clear "winner." Although these males dominated the rest of the animals in the group, they constantly attacked each other. Under these conditions they displayed hormonal profiles

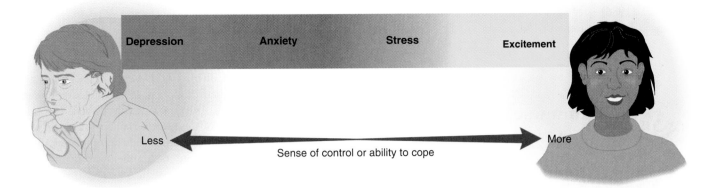

figure 9.4 Responses to threats and challenges. Our feelings range along a continuum from depression to anxiety to stress to excitement, depending in part on our sense of control and ability to cope (after Barlow & Rapee, 1991).

more like those of subordinate males. Thus, dominance combined with stability produced optimal stress hormone profiles. But the most important factor in regulating stress physiology seems to be a sense of control (Sapolsky & Ray, 1989). Control of social situations and the ability to cope with any tension that arises go a long way toward blunting the long-term effects of stress. "Personality characteristics" in baboons that reflect a sense of control are shown in Figure 9.3. Dominant males with these characteristics have lower basal levels of cortisol than dominant males without the characteristics.

Stress, Anxiety, Depression, and Excitement

If you have read the chapters on anxiety, mood, and related psychological disorders, you might conclude, correctly, that stressful life events combined with psychological vulnerabilities such as an inadequate sense of control are a factor in psychological and physical disorders. Is there any relationship between emotional and physical disorders? There seems to be a very strong one. George Vaillant (1979) studied more than 200 Harvard University sophomore men between 1942 and 1944 who were mentally and physically healthy. He followed these men closely for more than 30 years. Those who developed psychological disorders or who were highly stressed became chronically ill or died at a significantly higher rate than men who remained well adjusted and free from psychological disorders. This suggests that the same types of stress-related psychological factors that contribute to psychological disorders may also contribute to the later development of physical disorders and that stress, anxiety, and depression are closely related.

Can you tell the difference between feelings of stress, anxiety, depression, and excitement? You might say, "No problem," but these four states have a lot in common. Which one you experience may depend on your *sense of*

control at the moment or how well you think you can cope with the threat or challenge you are facing (Barlow, Chorpita, & Turovsky, 1996; Barlow & Rapee, 1991). This continuum of feelings from excitement to stress to anxiety to depression is shown in Figure 9.4.

Consider how you feel when you are excited. You might experience a rapid heartbeat, a sudden burst of energy, or a jumpy stomach. But if you're well prepared for the challenge—for example, if you're an athlete, really up for the game and confident in your abilities, or a musician, sure you are going to give an outstanding performance—these feelings of *excitement* can actually be pleasurable.

Sometimes when you face a challenging task you feel that you could handle it if you only had the time or help you need, but because you don't have these resources, you feel pressured. In response, you may work harder to do better and be perfect, even though you think you will be all right in the end. If you are under too much pressure, you may become tense and irritable or develop a headache or an upset stomach. This is what stress feels like. If something really is threatening and you believe there is little you can do about it, you may feel anxiety. The threatening situation could be anything from a physical attack to making a fool of yourself in front of someone. As your body prepares for the challenge you worry about it incessantly. Your sense of control is considerably less than if you were stressed. In some cases, there may not be any difficult situation out there at all. Sometimes we are anxious for no reason except that we feel certain aspects of our lives are out of control. Finally, individuals who always perceive life as threatening may lose hope about ever having control and slip into a state of *depression,* no longer trying to cope.

To sum up, the underlying physiology of these particular emotional states is relatively similar. This is why we refer to the activation of specific neurotransmitters and neurohormones in discussing anxiety, depression, and stress-related physical disorders. But psychological factors—specifically a sense of control and confidence that we

These three years have taught me that fear . . . is equal parts rage and despair.

can cope with stress or challenges called **self-efficacy** by Bandura (1986)—seem to differ and thus lead to different feelings (Taylor & Repetti, 1997).

The Immune System and Physical Disorders

Have you had a cold during the past several months? How did you pick it up? Did you spend the day with someone else who had a cold? Did someone sneeze nearby while you were sitting in class? Exposure to cold viruses is a necessary factor in developing a cold, but the level of stress you are experiencing at the time seems to play a major role in whether the exposure results in a cold. Sheldon Cohen and his associates (Cohen, 1996; Cohen, Tyrrell, & Smith, 1991, 1993) exposed volunteer subjects to a specific dosage of a cold virus and followed them very closely. They found that the chance that a subject would get sick was directly related to how much stress the person had experienced during the past year. In a later study, Cohen et al. (1995) linked the intensity of stress and negative affect at the time of exposure to the later *severity* of the cold, as measured by mucous production. These are among the first well-controlled studies to demonstrate that stress actually increases the risk of infection.

Think back to your last exam. Did you (or your roommate) have a cold? Exam periods are stressors that have been shown to produce increased infections, particularly of the upper respiratory tract (Glaser et al., 1987, 1990). Therefore, if you are susceptible to colds, maybe you should skip final exams! A better solution is to learn how to control your stress before and during exams. Almost certainly, the effect of stress on susceptibility to infections is mediated through the **immune system,** which protects the body from any foreign materials that may enter it.

Research dating back to the original reports of Hans Selye (1936) demonstrates the detrimental effects of stress on immune system functioning. Humans under stress show clearly increased rates of infectious diseases, including colds, herpes, and mononucleosis (for instance, Cohen & Herbert, 1996; Vander Plate, Aral, & Magder, 1988). Direct evidence links a number of stressful situations to lowered immune system functioning, including marital discord or relationship difficulties (Kiecolt-Glaser et al., 1994), job loss, and the death of a loved one (Irwin, Daniels, Smith, Bloom, & Weiner, 1987; Morris, Cook, & Shaper, 1994; Pavalko, Elder, & Clipp, 1993). Furthermore, these stressful events affect the immune system very rapidly. Studies in laboratories have demonstrated weakened immune system response within 2 hours of exposure to stress (Kiecolt-Glaser & Glaser, 1992; Weisse, Pato, McAllister, Littman, & Breier, 1990; Zakowski, McAllister, Deal, & Baum, 1992). It is therefore possible that stress contributes to physical illness, although this last link has not been firmly established.

We have already noted that emotional disorders seem to make us more susceptible to developing physical disorders (Vaillant, 1979). We had assumed this was due to the effect of emotional disorders on the immune system. Now there is direct evidence that depression lowers immune system functioning (Herbert & Cohen, 1993; Weisse, 1992), particularly in the aged (Herbert & Cohen, 1993; Schleifer, Keller, Bond, Cohen, & Stein, 1989). Carol Silvia Weisse (1992) suggests that the level of depression (and perhaps the underlying sense of uncontrollability that accompanies most depressions) is a more potent factor in lowering immune system functioning than are specific stressful life events, such as job loss. Depression can also lead to poor self-care and a tendency to engage in more risky behaviors. For humans, like Sapolsky's baboons, the ability to retain a sense of control over events in our lives may be one of the most important psychological contributions to good health.

Most studies concerning stress and the immune system have examined a sudden or acute stressor. But *chronic stress* may be more problematic because the effects are, by definition, longer lasting. In the 1970s, at Three Mile Island near Harrisburg, Pennsylvania, the nuclear power plant leaked. Many residents feared that any exposure to radiation they might have sustained would lead to cancer or other illnesses, and they lived with this fear for years. More than 6 years after the explosion, some individuals who had been in the area during the crisis still had lowered immune system functioning (McKinnon, Weisse, Reynolds, Bowles, & Baum, 1989). A similar finding has been reported for people who care for chronically ill family members, such as Alzheimer's disease patients (Kiecolt-Glaser & Glaser, 1987).

To understand how the immune system protects us, we must first understand how it works. We will take a brief tour of the immune system, using Figure 9.5 as a visual guide, and then examine psychological contributions to the biology of two diseases strongly related to immune system functioning: AIDS and cancer.

A Brief Overview

The immune system identifies and eliminates foreign materials, called **antigens,** in the body. Antigens can be any of a number of substances, usually bacteria, viruses, or parasites. But the immune system also targets the body's own cells that have become aberrant or damaged in some way, perhaps as part of a malignant tumor. Donated organs are foreign, and so the immune system attacks them after surgical transplant; consequently, it is necessary to suppress the immune system temporarily after surgery.

The immune system has two main parts: the *humoral* and the *cellular.* Specific types of cells function as agents of both. White blood cells, called *leukocytes,* do most of the work. There are several different types of leukocytes. *Macrophages* might be considered one of the body's first lines of defense: They surround identifiable antigens and destroy them. They also signal *lymphocytes,* which consist of two groups, B cells and T cells.

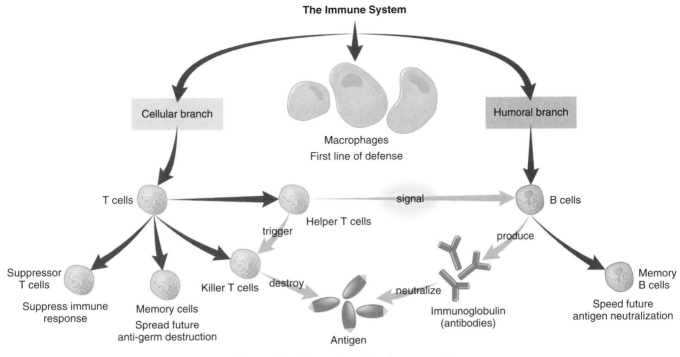

The Immune System

Cellular branch

Humoral branch

Macrophages
First line of defense

T cells

Helper T cells

signal

B cells

trigger

produce

Suppressor
T cells

Killer T cells

destroy

neutralize

Memory
B cells

Suppress immune
response

Memory cells

Spread future
anti-germ destruction

Antigen

Immunoglobulin
(antibodies)

Speed future
antigen neutralization

figure 9.5 An overview of the immune system

The *B cells* operate within the humoral part of the immune system, releasing molecules that seek out antigens in blood and other bodily fluids with the purpose of neutralizing them. The B cells produce highly specific molecules called *immunoglobulins* that act as *antibodies,* which combine with the antigens to neutralize them. After the antigens are neutralized, a subgroup called *memory B cells* are created so that the next time that antigen is encountered, the immune system response will be even faster. This action accounts for the success of inoculations you may have received for mumps or measles as a child. An inoculation actually contains small amounts of the targeted organism, but not enough to make you sick. Your immune system then "remembers" this antigen and prevents you from coming down with the full disease when you are exposed to it.

The second group of lymphocytes, called *T cells,* operate in the cellular branch of the immune system. These cells don't produce antibodies. Instead, one subgroup, *killer T cells,* directly destroys viral infections and cancerous processes (Borysenko, 1987; O'Leary, 1990; Roitt, 1988). When the process is complete, *memory T cells* are created to speed future responses to the same antigen. Other subgroups of T cells help regulate the immune system. For example, *T4 cells* are called *helper T cells* because they *enhance* the immune system response by signaling B cells to produce antibodies and telling other T cells to destroy the antigen. *Suppressor T cells* suppress the production of antibodies by B cells when they are no longer needed.

We should have twice as many T4 (helper) cells as suppressor T cells. With too many T4 cells, the immune system is overreactive and may attack the body's normal cells rather than antigens. When this happens, we have what is called an **autoimmune disease,** such as **rheumatoid arthritis.** With too many suppressor T cells, the body is subject to invasion by a number of antigens. The human immunodeficiency virus (HIV) directly attacks the T helper cells, lymphocytes that are crucial to both humoral and cellular immunity, thereby severely weakening the immune system and causing AIDS.

Until the mid-1970s, most scientists believed that the brain and the immune system operated independently of each other. However, in 1974 Robert Ader and his colleagues

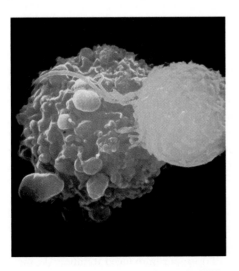

This colored scanning electron micrograph (SEM) shows a killer T-cell (yellow) attacking a cancer cell (pink).

Robert Ader demonstrated that the immune system is responsive to environmental cues.

(for instance, Ader & Cohen, 1975, 1993) made a startling discovery. Working with a classical conditioning paradigm, they gave sugar-flavored water to rats, together with a drug that suppresses the immune system. Ader and Cohen then demonstrated that giving the same rats only the sweet-tasting water produced similar changes in the immune system. In other words, the rats had "learned" (through classical conditioning) to respond to the water by suppressing their immune systems. We now know that there are many connections between the nervous system and the immune system. For example, nerve endings exist in many immune system tissues, including the thymus, the lymph nodes, and bone marrow. These findings have generated a new field known as **psychoneuroimmunology** or **PNI** (Ader & Cohen, 1993), which simply means that the object of study is *psycho*logical influences on the *neuro*logical responding implicated in our *immune* response.

Cohen and Herbert (1996) illustrate pathways through which psychological and social factors may influence immune system functioning. Direct connections between the brain (CNS) and HYPAC axis (hormonal) and the immune system have already been described. Behavioral changes in response to stressful events, such as increased smoking or poor eating habits may also suppress the immune system (Figure 9.6).

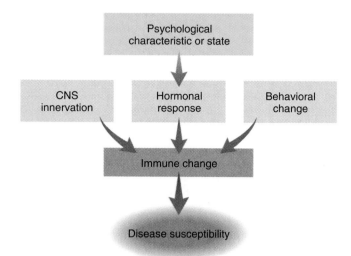

figure 9.6 Pathways through which psychological factors might influence onset and progression of immune system-mediated disease. For simplicity, arrows are drawn in only one direction, from psychological characteristics to disease. No lack of alternative paths is implied (from Cohen & Herbert, 1996).

■ **concept check 9.1**

The immune system protects the body from foreign bodies that may enter it. Sometimes stress has such an effect on the immune system that the body becomes susceptible to infections. Assess your knowledge of the immune system by matching components of the system with their function in the body: (a) macrophages, (b) B cells, (c) immunoglobins, (d) killer T cells, (e) suppressor T cells, (f) memory cells.

1. This subgroup targets viral infections within the cells by directly destroying the antigens. _____

2. A type of leukocyte that surrounds identifiable antigens and destroys them. _____

3. Highly specific molecules that act as antibodies. They combine with antigens to neutralize them. _____

4. Lymphocytes that operate within the humoral part of the system and circulate in the blood and bodily fluids. _____

5. These are created so that when a specific antigen is encountered in the future, the immune response will be faster. _____

6. These T cells stop the production of antibodies by B cells when they are no longer needed. _____

AIDS

The ravages of the AIDS epidemic have made this disease the highest priority of our public health system. In the absence of a cure, or more effective prevention or treatment, it

was projected in 1993 (Chesney, 1993) that the world could expect 30 to 40 million new cases by the year 2000 (Merson, cited in Cohen, 1993; Mann, 1991). These projections are on track or are proving to be underestimates, particularly in developing nations. In 1996 new HIV infections amounted to 5.3 million and were over 6 million in 1997, bringing the total number of people living with HIV to 30 million by the end of 1997. In the hardest hit regions in southern Africa, 25 to 30% of the adult population are believed to be HIV positive. Furthermore, the United Nations suspects that the worst is yet to come (Holden, 1997).

Once a person is infected with HIV, the course of the disease is quite variable. After several months to several years with no symptoms, patients may develop minor health problems such as weight loss, fever, and night sweats, symptoms that make up the condition known as **AIDS-related complex (ARC)**. A diagnosis of AIDS itself is not made until one of several serious diseases appears, such as pneumocystis pneumonia, cancer, dementia, or a wasting syndrome in which the body literally withers away. The median time from initial infection to the development of full-blown AIDS has been estimated to range from 7.3 to 10 years or more (Moss & Bacchetti, 1989; Pantaleo, Graziosi, & Fauci, 1993). Although most people with AIDS die within 1 year of diagnosis, as many as 15% survive 5 years or longer (Kertzner & Gorman, 1992). Recently, clinical scientists have developed powerful new combinations of drugs that seem to suppress the virus in those infected with HIV, thereby delaying onset of AIDS. Although this is a hopeful development, it does not seem to be a cure, since the most recent evidence suggests that the virus is seldom if ever eliminated, but rather lies dormant in reduced numbers (Cohen, 1997).

Because AIDS is a relatively new disease, with a very long latency to development, we are still learning about the factors, including possible psychological factors, that extend survival. Investigators identified a group of people who have been exposed repeatedly to the AIDS virus but have not contracted the disease. A major distinction of these people is that their immune systems, particularly the cellular branch, are very robust and strong (Ezzel, 1993). Therefore, efforts to boost the immune system may contribute to the prevention of AIDS.

> *Once you have your arms around your friend with his terrible news, your eyes are too shut to cry.*

Can psychological factors affect the progression of AIDS? Learning we have an incurable terminal illness is extremely stressful for anyone. This happens every day to individuals stricken with HIV. The stress of learning that you are carrying the AIDS virus can be devastating. Antoni et al. (1991) studied the effects of administering a psychosocial stress-reduction treatment to a group of individuals who believed that they might have the HIV virus, during the weeks before they were tested for HIV-1. Half of the group received the stress-reduction program; the other half received the usual medical and psychological care. Unfortunately, many individuals in this group turned out to be HIV-positive. However, those who had undergone the psychosocial stress-reduction procedures, unlike their counterparts, did *not* show substantial increases in anxiety and depression. Furthermore—and more important—they actually demonstrated *increases* in their immune system functioning as measured by such indices as T-helper, inducer (CD4), and natural killer (NK) cells. In addition, participants in the stress-reduction program showed significant decreases in antibodies to two herpes viruses, suggesting improved functioning of the immune system (Esterling et al., 1992). This is important because herpes viruses are very closely related to HIV and seem to promote further activation of HIV-infected cells, resulting in a faster and more deadly spread of HIV. What was most encouraging about this study, however, was that a follow-up showed less disease progression in the stress-reduction group 2 years later (Ironson et al., 1994).

Remember, though, that the subjects in these studies had just learned that they were infected with HIV and therefore were in a very early asymptomatic stage of the disease. Now a very important new study suggests that the same cognitive–behavioral stress management program may have positive effects on the immune systems of individuals who are already symptomatic (Lutgendorf et al., 1997). Specifically, the intervention program significantly decreased depression and anxiety compared to a control group that did not receive the treatment. More importantly, there was a significant reduction in antibodies to the herpes simplex virus II (HSV–II) in the treatment group compared to the control group, which reflects the greater ability of the cellular component of the immune system to control the virus. These results are shown in Figure 9.7. Thus, even in progressed symptomatic HIV disease, psychosocial interventions may not only enhance psychological adjustment but also influence immune system functioning.

It is too early to tell whether these results will be strong or persistent enough to translate into increased survival time for AIDS patients, although earlier results from Ironson et al. (1994) suggest they might. It is also important to note that some earlier studies of stress-reduction procedures on AIDS patients found no effect on other aspects of the immune system (for example, Coates, McKusick, Kuno, & Stites, 1989). If stress and related variables are clinically significant to immune response in HIV-infected patients, as suggested by Ironson et al. (1994), then it is possible that psychosocial interventions to bolster the immune system might increase survival rates and, in the most optimistic scenario, prevent the slow deterioration of the immune system (Kiecolt-Glaser & Glaser, 1992). These interventions would be particularly important for women and minorities, who often are faced with numerous stressors in their environments and who possess fewer means of coping (Schneiderman, Antoni, Ironson, LaPerriere, & Fletcher, 1992).

If stress-reduction procedures do affect the disease process directly, perhaps through the immune system, it is not clear why they are effective. Among the possibilities are that stress-reduction procedures may give patients a greater sense of control, decrease their hopelessness, build active coping responses, change negative cognitions, help them use social support networks more effectively, or some combination of these factors (Uchino, Cacioppo, & Kiecolt-Glaser, 1996). We don't know the answer, but few areas of

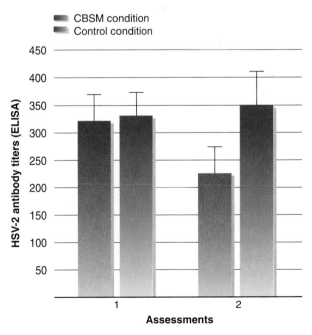

figure 9.7   Means (and standard error of the means) for immunoglobulin G antibody titers to herpes simplex virus-Type 2 (HSV-2) for the cognitive-behavioral stress management (CBSM) and control conditions preintervention (1) and postintervention (2). ELISA = enzyme-linked immunosorbent assay (from Lutgendorf et al., 1997)

study in behavioral medicine and health psychology are more urgent.

Cancer

Among the more mind-boggling developments in the study of illness and disease is the discovery that the development and course of different varieties of **cancer** are also subject to psychosocial influences. This has resulted in a new field of study called **psychoncology** (Andersen, 1992; Antoni & Goodkin, 1991). *Oncology* means the study of cancer. In Chapter 2, we reviewed the landmark studies by Spiegel, Fawzy, and their colleagues, demonstrating that relatively brief psychosocial treatments aimed at reducing stress, increasing coping and control, and maximizing social support reduced cancer symptoms and psychosocial distress, bolstered immune system functioning, and prolonged life. Results from the landmark study by Spiegel et al. (1989) showing survival rates of patients with advanced breast cancer who received psychosocial treatment compared to those who did not are presented in Figure 9.8. Once again, those who received therapy lived twice as long on the average (approximately 3 years) as the control group (approximately 18 months). Four years after the study began, one-third of the therapy patients were still alive, and all of the patients receiving the best medical care without therapy had died. David Spiegel and his colleagues (Spiegel et al., 1996) later demonstrated that their treatment can be implemented relatively easily in oncology clinics everywhere, which is necessary if the treatment is going to be truly useful. Clinical trials involving large numbers of patients with cancer are in

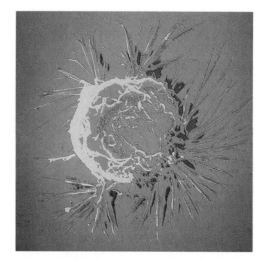

Breast cancer cell

progress to evaluate more thoroughly the life prolonging and life enhancing effects of psychosocial treatments for cancer.

The initial success of these treatments has generated a great deal of interest in exactly how they work. Possibilities include better health habits, closer adherence to medical treatment, and improved endocrine functioning and response to stress, all of which may improve immune function (Classen, Diamond, & Spiegel, in press). Andersen, Kiecolt-Glaser, and Glazer (1994) have suggested similar factors as important, but also stress the benefits of enhanced social adjustment and coping. There is even preliminary evidence that psychological factors may contribute not only to the *course* but also to the *development* of cancer and other diseases (for example, Stam & Steggles, 1987). Perceived lack

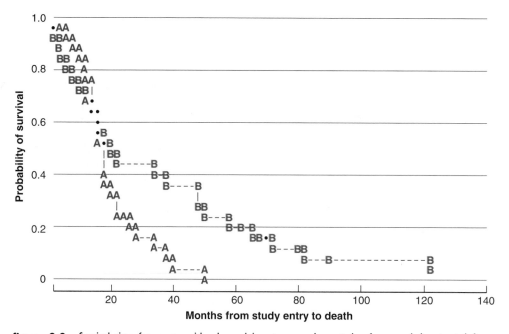

figure 9.8 Survival time for women with advanced breast cancer. In a study of women being treated for advanced breast cancer, researchers found that women in a treatment group (*N* = 50) who received psychosocial intervention survived significantly longer than did women who were in a control group (*N* = 36) with no psychosocial treatment. A = control, B = psychosocial intervention (adapted from Spiegel et al., 1989).

David Spiegel found that psychosocial interventions helped prolong the lives of women with advanced breast cancer.

of control, inadequate coping responses, overwhelmingly stressful life events, or the use of inappropriate coping responses (such as denial) may all contribute to the development of cancer (Antoni & Goodkin, 1991; Schneiderman et al., 1992). However, most studies on which these conclusions are based involve retrospective psychological tests of people who have cancer; much stronger evidence is required to demonstrate that psychological factors may contribute to the onset of cancer.

Psychological factors are implicated in other aspects of cancer and its treatment. Many people who undergo chemotherapy experience the negative side effects of nausea and vomiting. These reactions are so powerful that they become "conditioned" or learned, and may occur at times other than treatment. For some patients, conditioned nausea and vomiting are associated with a wide variety of stimuli that evoke chemotherapy, such as nurses' uniforms or even the sight of a hospital itself (Jacobsen et al., 1993, 1995). The problem with this reaction is that many people will refuse the chemotherapy treatments altogether, thinking the cure worse than the disease. Others stop eating because of the nausea, or generally just feel miserable. These reactions usually begin after the fourth or fifth treatment and slowly escalate in severity. Between 18% and 50% of patients experience conditioned nausea (Morrow & Dobkin, 1988). Morrow (1986) reported that 23% of 1,480 patients suffered from these reactions. Psychological treatments focusing on relaxation and a gradual exposure to the cues triggering the conditioned nausea can diminish or eliminate the response. This facilitates compliance with chemotherapy and generally improves a patient's overall physical and mental health (Burish, Carey, Krozely, & Greco, 1987; Carey & Burish, 1988; Morrow, 1986; Redd, Andreason, & Minagawa, 1982).

Psychological factors are also very prominent in treatment and recovery from cancer in children (Koocher, 1996). Many different types of cancer require invasive and painful medical procedures; the suffering can be very difficult to bear, not only for the children but also for parents and health care providers. Children usually struggle and cry hysterically, so in order to complete many of the procedures, they must be physically restrained. Not only does their behavior interfere with successful completion, but the stress and anxiety associated with repeated painful procedures may have their own detrimental effect on the disease process. Psychological procedures designed to reduce pain and stress in these children include breathing exercises, watching films of exactly what happens in order to take the uncertainty out of the procedure, and rehearsal of the procedure with dolls, all of which make the interventions much more tolerable and therefore more successful for young patients (Hubert, Jay, Saltoun, & Hayes, 1988; Jay, Elliott, Ozolins, Olson, & Pruitt, 1985; McGrath & DeVeber, 1986). Much of this work is based on the pioneering efforts of Barbara Melamed and her colleagues, who demonstrated the importance of incorporating psychological procedures into children's medical care, particularly children about to undergo surgery (for ex-

Psychological preparation reduces suffering and facilitates recovery in children who undergo surgery.

ample, Melamed & Siegel, 1975). In any case, pediatric psychologists are making more routine use of these procedures.

 ## Cardiovascular Problems

The *cardiovascular system* comprises the heart, blood vessels, and complex control mechanisms for regulating their function. Many things can go wrong with this system and lead to **cardiovascular disease.** For example, many individuals, particularly older individuals, suffer strokes, also called *cerebral vascular accidents (CVA),* which are temporary blockages of blood vessels leading to the brain or a rupture of blood vessels in the brain that results in temporary or permanent brain damage and loss of functioning. People with Raynaud's disease lose circulation to peripheral parts of their bodies such as their fingers and toes, suffering some pain and continual sensations of cold in their hands and feet. The cardiovascular problems that are receiving the most attention these days are hypertension and coronary heart disease, and we will look at both. First, let's consider a case.

John
The Human Volcano

John is a 55-year-old business executive, married, with two teenage children. For most his adult life, John has smoked about a pack of cigarettes each day. Although he maintains a busy and active schedule, John is mildly obese, partly from regular meals with business partners and colleagues. He has been taking several medications for high blood pressure since age 42. John's doctor has warned him repeatedly to cut down on his smoking and to exercise more frequently, especially because John's father died of a heart attack. Although John has episodes of chest pain, he continues his busy and stressful life-style. It is difficult for John to slow down, as his business has been doing extremely well during the past 10 years.

Moreover, John believes that life is too short, that there is no time to slow down. He sees relatively little of his family and works late most evenings. Even when he's at home, John typically works into the night. It is very difficult for him to relax; he feels a constant urgency to get as many things done as possible and prefers to work on several tasks simultaneously. For instance, John often proofreads a document, engages in a phone conversation, and eats lunch all at the same time. He attributes much of the success of his business to his working style. Despite his success, John is not well liked by his peers. His co-workers and employees often find him to be overbearing, easily frustrated and, at times, even hostile. His subordinates in particular claim he is overly impatient and critical of their performance.

Do you think John has a problem? Today most people would recognize that his behaviors and attitudes make his life unpleasant and also possibly lethal. Some of these behaviors and attitudes appear to operate directly on the cardiovascular system and may result in hypertension and coronary heart disease.

Hypertension

Hypertension (high blood pressure) is a major risk factor not only for stroke and heart disease but also for kidney disease. This makes hypertension an extremely serious medical condition. Blood pressure increases when the blood vessels leading to organs and peripheral areas constrict, (become narrower), forcing more and more blood to muscles in central parts of the body. Because so many blood vessels have constricted, the heart muscles must work much harder to force the blood to all parts of the body, which causes the increased pressure. These factors produce wear and tear on the ever-shrinking blood vessels and lead to cardiovascular disease. A small percentage of cases of hypertension can be traced to specific physical abnormalities such as kidney disease or tumors on the adrenal glands (Papillo & Shapiro, 1990), but the overwhelming majority have no specific verifiable physical cause and are considered **essential hypertension.** Blood pressure is defined as high by the World Health Organization if it exceeds 160 over 95 (Papillo & Shapiro, 1990), although measures of 140/90 or above are borderline and cause for concern. The first value is called the *systolic blood pressure,* the pressure when the heart is pumping blood. The second value is the *diastolic blood pressure,* the pressure between beats when the heart is at rest. Elevations in diastolic pressure seem to be more worrisome in terms of risk of disease.

As many as 20% of adults between the ages of 25 and 74 suffer from essential hypertension (Johnston, 1997; Roberts & Rowland, 1981)—extraordinary numbers when you consider that hypertension, contributing to as many fatal diseases as it does, has been called the "silent killer." These numbers are much higher than for any single psychological disorder. Even more striking is the fact that African-Americans are approximately *twice* as likely to develop hypertension as whites (Anderson & Jackson, 1987; Brannon & Feist, 1997). The rate is approximately 18 per 100 for white men ages 25 to 74 and 35 per 100 for African-American men in the same age range. For women, the figures are approximately 15 per 100 for whites and 30 per 100 for African-Americans (Roberts & Rowland, 1981). More important, African-Americans have hypertensive vascular diseases at a rate 5 to 10 times greater than whites. This makes hypertension a principal disorder of concern among our African-American population. Saab and colleagues (1992) demonstrated that during laboratory stress tests, African-Americans without high blood pressure show greater vascular responsiveness, including heightened blood pressure. Thus, African-Americans in general may be at greater risk to develop hypertension.

You will not be surprised to learn that there are biological, psychological, and social contributions to the develop-

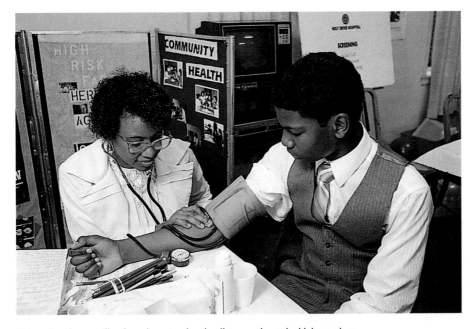

African-Americans suffer from hypertension in disproportionately high numbers.

ment of this potentially deadly condition. It has long been clear that hypertension runs in families and very likely is subject to marked genetic influences (Papillo & Shapiro, 1990). When stressed in the laboratory, even individuals with *normal* blood pressure show greater reactivity in their blood pressure if their parents have high blood pressure than individuals with normal blood pressure whose parents also had normal blood pressure (Fredrikson & Matthews, 1990). In other words, it doesn't take much to activate an inherited vulnerability to hypertension. In fact, the offspring of hypertensives are at twice the risk of developing hypertension than children of parents with normal blood pressure (N. M. Kaplan, 1980; Brannon & Feist, 1997). Elevated blood pressure is evident even during the first few weeks of life in babies of hypertensive parents (Turk, Meichenbaum, & Genest, 1987).

Studies examining neurobiological causes of hypertension have centered on two factors that are central to the regulation of blood pressure: autonomic nervous system activity and mechanisms regulating sodium in the kidneys. When the sympathetic branch of the autonomic nervous system becomes active, one consequence is the constriction of blood vessels, which produces greater resistance against circulation; that is, blood pressure is elevated (Guyton, 1981). Because the sympathetic nervous system is very responsive to stress, many investigators have long assumed that stress is a major contributor to essential hypertension. Sodium and water regulation, one of the functions of the kidneys, is also important in regulating blood pressure. Retaining too much salt increases blood volume and heightens blood pressure. This is one reason that people with hypertension are often told to restrict their intake of salt.

Psychological factors, such as personality, coping style and, again, level of stress, have been used to explain individual differences in blood pressure. For example, in a review of

28 studies Uchino et al. (1996) found a strong relationship between levels of social support and blood pressure. Loneliness, depression, and uncontrollability are psychological mechanisms that may contribute to the association between hypertension and social support. Also, both anger and hostility have been associated with increases in blood pressure in the laboratory setting (Jamner, Shapiro, Goldstein, & Hug, 1991; A. C. King, Taylor, Albright, & Haskell, 1990; Miller, Smith, Turner, Guijarro, & Hallet, 1996). The notion that hostility or repressed hostility predicts hypertension (and other cardiovascular problems) can be traced back to Alexander (1939), who suggested that an inability to express anger could result in hypertension and other cardiovascular problems. What may be more important is not whether anger is suppressed but rather how frequently anger and hostility are experienced (Ironson et al., 1992; Miller et al., 1996). Let's return to the case of John for a moment. John clearly suffered from hypertension. Do you detect any anger in John's case study? John's hypertension may well be related to his stressful life-style, frustration levels, and hostility.

Coronary Heart Disease

It may not surprise you that psychological and social factors contribute to high blood pressure, but can changes in behavior and attitudes prevent heart attacks? The answers are still not entirely clear, but increasing evidence indicates that psychological and social factors are implicated in coronary heart disease. Why is this important? Heart disease is the number one cause of death in Western cultures.

Coronary heart disease (CHD) is, quite simply, a blockage of the arteries supplying blood to the heart muscle (the *myocardium*). A number of terms describe heart disease. Chest pain resulting from partial obstruction of the arteries is called *angina pectoris* or, usually, just *angina. Atherosclerosis* occurs when a fatty substance or plaque builds up inside the arteries and causes an obstruction. *Ischemia* is the name for deficiency of blood to a body part caused by the narrowing of the arteries by too much plaque. And *myocardial infarction,* or *heart attack,* is the death of heart tissue when a specific artery becomes completely clogged with plaque. Arteries can constrict or become blocked for a variety of reasons other than plaque. For example, a blood clot might lodge in the artery.

It seems clear that we inherit a vulnerability to CHD (and to many other physical disorders) and that other factors such as diet, exercise, and culture make very important con-

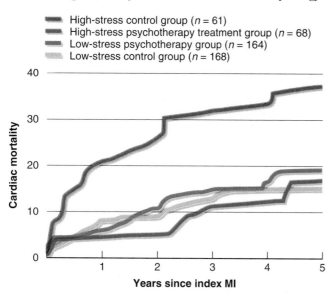

figure 9.9 Cardiac mortality. For patients in low-stress situations, stress-reduction training seems to make little difference in cardiac deaths; however, for patients in high-stress situations, cardiac mortality was dramatically reduced for those who received stress-reduction training (adapted from Frasure-Smith, 1991).

tributions to our cardiovascular status (Thoresen & Powell, 1992). But what sort of psychological factors contribute to coronary heart disease?

Nancy Frasure-Smith (1991) studied 461 men who were hospitalized after acute myocardial infarctions (heart attacks) and followed their progress for 5 years. Psychological stress was measured on a clinical rating scale on the basis of symptoms obtained during periodic telephone interviews. Approximately half the men received stress-reduction treatments whenever they reported high levels of stress during the 5-year period. Control patients received routine medical care. Men in both groups modified their risk factors for heart disease by improving their diet or increasing their exercise to approximately the same extent. Of patients who experienced high stress at some time after their discharge from the hospital, approximately three times as many in the control group died than in the stress-reduction group. In addition, men in the control group were at greater risk for another heart attack over the same period than men in the treatment group. Among those individuals in either group who *did not* experience high levels of stress, the stress-reduction program was of little benefit, as might be expected. The data for deaths in both groups are displayed in Figure 9.9. These results replicate and extend an earlier study by M. Friedman and colleagues (1984), and certainly suggest, pending further replication, that psychological factors are implicated directly in the process of heart disease, a finding confirmed in more recent studies (Johnston, 1997). Some studies indicate that even *healthy* men who experience stress are later more likely to experience coronary heart disease than low-stress groups (Rosengren, Tibblin, & Wilhelmsen, 1991). For such individuals, stress-reduction procedures may prove to be an important preventive technique. This brings us to an important

question: Can we identify, before an attack, people who are under a great deal of stress that might make them susceptible to a first heart attack? The answer seems to be yes, but the answer is more complex than we first thought.

Clinical investigators reported several decades ago that certain groups of people engage in a cluster of behaviors in stressful situations that seem to put them at considerable risk for coronary heart disease. These behaviors include excessive competitive drive, a sense of always being pressured for time, impatience, incredible amounts of energy that may show up in accelerated speech and motor activity, and angry outbursts. This set of behaviors came to be called the **type A behavior pattern** and was first identified by two cardiologists, Meyer Friedman and Ray Rosenman (1959, 1974). The **type B behavior pattern,** also described by these clinicians, applies to people who basically do not have type A attributes. In other words, the type B individual is more relaxed, less concerned about deadlines, and seldom feels the pressure or, perhaps, the excitement of challenges or overriding ambition.

The concept of the type A personality or behavior pattern is widely accepted in our hard-driving, goal-oriented culture. Indeed, some early studies supported the concept of type A behavior as putting people at risk for coronary heart disease (Friedman & Rosenman, 1974). But the most convincing evidence came from two large prospective studies that followed thousands of patients over a long period of time to determine the relationship of their behavior to heart disease. The first study was the Western Collaborative Group Study (WCGS). In this project 3,154 healthy men, aged 39 to 59, were interviewed at the beginning of the study to determine their typical behavioral patterns. They were then followed for 8 years. The basic finding was that the men who displayed a type A behavior pattern at the beginning of the study were at least twice as likely to develop coronary heart disease as the men with a type B behavior pattern. When the investigators analyzed the data for the younger men in the study (aged 39 to 49) the results were even more striking, with coronary heart disease developing approximately six times more frequently in the type A group than in the type B group (Rosenman et al., 1975).

A second major study is the Framingham Heart Study that has been ongoing for more than 40 years (Haynes, Feinleib, & Kannel, 1980) and has taught us much of what we know about the development and course of coronary heart disease. In this study, 1,674 healthy men and women were categorized by type A or type B behavior pattern and followed for 8 years. Once again, both men and women with a type A pattern were more than twice as likely to develop coronary heart disease as their type B counterparts (in men, the risk was nearly three times as great). But, in the male group, the results were evident only in those individuals in higher-status white collar occupations, not in individuals with blue collar socioeconomic status and occupations. For women, the results were strongest for those with a low level of education (Eaker, Pinsky, & Castelli, 1992).

Both type A behavior and coronary heart disease seem to be culturally determined.

Population-based studies in Europe essentially replicated these results (DeBacker, Kittel, Kornitzer, & Dramaix, 1983; French-Belgian Collaborative Group, 1982). It is interesting that a large study of Japanese men conducted in Hawaii *did not* replicate these findings (J. Cohen & Reed, 1985). In fact, the prevalence of type A behavior among Japanese men is much lower than among men in the United States (18.7% versus approximately 50%). Similarly, the prevalence of coronary heart disease is equally low (Japanese men 4%, American men in the Framingham study 13%) (Haynes & Matthews, 1988). In a study that illustrates the effects of culture more dramatically, 3,809 Japanese-Americans were classified into groups according to how "traditionally Japanese" they were. In other words, did they speak Japanese at home, retain traditional Japanese values and behaviors, and so on. Japanese-Americans who were the "most Japanese" had the lowest incidence of coronary heart disease, not significantly different than Japanese men in Japan. In contrast, the group that was the "least Japanese" had a three to five times greater incidence of coronary heart disease levels (Marmot & Syme, 1976; Matsumoto, 1996). Clearly, sociocultural differences are important.

Despite these positive results, at least in Western cultures, the type A concept has proven much more complex and elusive than scientists had hoped. First, it is very difficult to determine whether someone is type A from structured interviews, questionnaires, or other measures of this construct, because the measures often do not agree with one another. Many people have *some* of the characteristics of type A but not all of them, and others present with a mixture of types A and B. The notion that we can divide the world into two types of people—an assumption underlying the early work in this area—has long since been discarded. As a result, more recent studies have not necessarily supported the relationship of type A behavior to coronary heart disease (Dembroski & Costa, 1987; Hollis, Connett, Stevens, & Greenlick, 1990).

The Role of Chronic Negative Emotions

At this point, investigators decided that something might be wrong with the type A construct itself (Matthews, 1988; Rodin & Salovey, 1989). A general consensus developed that some behaviors and emotions representative of the type A personality might be very important in the development of coronary heart disease, but not all of them. The primary factor that seems to be responsible for much of the relationship is anger, which will come as no surprise if you read the study in Chapter 2 (Miller et al., 1996). As you may remember, Ironson and her colleagues (1992) compared increased heart rate when they instructed individuals with heart disease to imagine situations or events in their own lives that made them angry with heart rates when they imagined other situations, such as exercise. They found that anger actually impaired the pumping efficiency of the heart, putting these individuals at risk for dangerous disturbances in heart rhythm (arrhythmias). This study confirms earlier findings relating the frequent experience of anger to later coronary heart disease (Dembrosky, MacDougall, Costa, & Grandits, 1989; Houston, Chesney, Black, Cates, & Hecker, 1992; T. W. Smith, 1992).

Is type A irrelevant to the development of heart disease? Most investigators conclude that some components of the type A construct are important determinants of CHD, with a chronically high level of negative affect, such as anger, one of the prime candidates (Thoresen & Powell, 1992). Recall again the case of John who had all the type A behaviors but also had frequent angry outbursts. But what about people who experience closely related varieties of negative affect on a chronic basis? Look back to Figure 9.4 and notice the very close relationship between stress, anxiety, and depression. There is some evidence that the physiological components of these emotions and their effects on the cardiovascular system may be identical, or at least very similar. We also know that the emotion of anger, so commonly associated with stress, is very closely related to the emotion of fear as evidenced in the fight/flight syndrome. Fight is the typical behavioral action tendency associated with anger and flight or escape is associated with fear. But our bodily alarm response, activated by an immediate danger or threat, is associated with both emotions. Some investigators, after reviewing the literature, have concluded that anxiety and depression are as important as anger in the development of CHD (Barlow, 1988; Booth-Kewley & Friedman, 1987; Brannon & Feist, 1997; Carney et al., 1995; Frasure-Smith, Lesperance, & Talajic, 1993). Thus, it may be that the chronic experience of the negative emotions of stress (anger), anxiety (fear), and depression (ongoing) and the neurobiological activation that accompanies these emotions provide the most important psychosocial contributions to CHD and perhaps to other physical disorders as well. On the other hand, in the Ironson et al. (1992) study, subjects who were asked to imagine being in situations producing performance anxiety (having to give a speech or take a difficult test) *did not* experience the same effect on their hearts as those who imagined anger—

at least, not in those individuals with existing CHD. We still have much to learn about these relationships.

Chronic Pain

Pain is not in itself a disorder, yet for most of us it is the fundamental signal of injury, illness, or disease. The importance of pain in our lives cannot be underestimated. Without low levels of pain providing feedback on the functioning of the body and its various systems, we would incur substantially more injuries. For example, you might lie out in the hot sun a lot longer. You might not roll over while sleeping or shift your posture while sitting, thereby affecting your circulation in a way that might be harmful. Reactions to this kind of pain are mostly automatic; that is, we are not aware of the discomfort. When pain crosses the threshold of awareness, which varies a great deal from one person to another, we are forced to take action. If we can't relieve the pain ourselves or we are not sure of its cause, we usually seek medical help. Americans spend at least $100 billion annually on over-the-counter medication to reduce temporary pain from headaches, colds, and other minor disorders. Worldwide, 20 million tons of aspirin are consumed each year by headache sufferers alone (S. Taylor, 1991). In fact, 80% of all visits to physicians are due to pain (Gatchel & Turk, 1996).

There are two kinds of clinical pain: acute and chronic. **Acute pain** typically follows an injury and disappears once the injury heals or is effectively treated, often within a month (Philips & Grant, 1991). **Chronic pain,** by contrast, may begin with an acute episode but *does not decrease* over time, even when the injury has healed or effective treatments have been administered. Typically, chronic pain is in the muscles, joints, or tendons, particularly in the lower back. Vascular pain due to enlarged blood vessels may be chronic, as may headaches, and pain caused by the slow degeneration of tissue, as in some terminal diseases, and by the growth of cancerous tumors that impinge on pain receptors (Melzack & Wall, 1982; S. Taylor, 1991). In this country alone, estimates of the number of affected people have reached 65 million (S. Taylor, 1991), yet most researchers now agree that the cause of chronic pain and the resulting enormous drain on our health care system *are substantially psychological and social* (Turk, 1996).

To better understand the experience of pain, clinicians and researchers generally make a clear distinction between the subjective experience termed "pain," reported by the patient, and the overt manifestations of this experience, termed "pain behaviors." Pain behaviors include changing the way one sits or walks, continually complaining about pain to others, grimacing and, most important, avoiding various activities, particularly those involving work or leisure. Finally, an emotional component of pain called "suffering" sometimes accompanies pain and sometimes does not (Fordyce, 1988; Liebeskind, 1991). Because they are so important, we will first review psychological and social contributions to pain.

Psychological and Social Aspects

In mild forms, chronic pain can be an annoyance that eventually wears you down and takes the pleasure out of your life. Severe chronic pain may cause you to lose your job, withdraw from your family, give up the fun in your life, and focus your entire awareness on seeking relief. What is interesting for our purposes is that the *severity* of the pain does not seem to predict the *reaction* to it. Some individuals experience intense pain frequently and yet continue to work productively, rarely seek out medical services, and lead reasonably normal lives; others become invalids. These differences appear to be due primarily to psychological factors (Gatchel, 1996; M. P. Jensen, Turner, Romano, & Karoly, 1991; Keefe, Dunsmore, & Burnett, 1992; Turk, 1996). It will come as no surprise that these factors are the same as those implicated in the stress response and other negative emotional states, such as anxiety and depression (see Chapters 5 and 7). The determining fac-

Some people with chronic pain or disability cope extremely well and become high achievers.

It is not uncommon for people to feel specific pain in limbs that are no longer part of them.

tor seems to be the individual's general sense of control over the situation: whether or not he or she can deal with the pain and its consequences in an effective and meaningful way. When a positive sense of control is combined with a generally optimistic outlook about the future, there is substantially less distress and disability (Bandura, O'Leary, Taylor, Gauthier, & Gossard, 1987; Flor & Turk, 1988; M. P. Jensen et al., 1991; Keefe et al., 1992). Positive psychological factors are also associated with active attempts to cope, such as exercise and other regimens, as opposed to suffering passively (G. K. Brown & Nicassio, 1987; Gatchel, 1996; R. A. Lazarus & Folkman, 1984; Turk, 1996).

To take one example, Philips and Grant (1991) studied 117 patients who suffered from back and neck pain after an injury. Almost all were expected to recover very quickly, but fully 40% of them still reported substantial pain at 6 months, thereby qualifying for "chronic pain" status. Of the 60% who reported no pain at the 6-month point, most had been pain free since approximately 1 month after the accident. Furthermore, Philips and Grant report that the relationship between the experience of pain and subsequent disability was *not* as strongly related to the intensity of the pain as other factors, such as personality and socioeconomic differences and whether the person planned to initiate a lawsuit concerning the injury. More recently, Gatchel, Polatin, and Kinney (1995) found that preexisting anxiety and personality problems predicted who would suffer chronic pain.

That the experience of pain can be largely disconnected from disease or injury is perhaps best exemplified by *phantom limb pain*. In this not uncommon condition, people who have lost an arm or leg feel excruciating pain in the limb that is no longer there. Furthermore, they can describe in exquisite de-

tail the exact location of the pain and its type, such as a dull ache or a sharp cutting pain. The fact that they are fully aware that the limb is amputated does nothing to relieve the pain. Evidence suggests that changes in the sensory cortex of the brain may contribute to this phenomenon (Flor et al., 1995; Ramachandran, 1993). Generally, someone who thinks that pain is disastrous, uncontrollable, or reflective of personal failure experiences more intense pain and greater psychological distress than someone who does not feel this way (Gil, Williams, Keefe, & Beckham, 1990). Thus, treatment programs for chronic pain concentrate on psychological factors.

Other examples of psychological influences on the experience of pain are encountered every day. Athletes with significant tissue damage frequently continue to perform and report relatively little pain. In an important study, 65% of war veterans wounded in combat reported feeling no pain. Presumably, their attention was focused externally on what they had to do to survive rather than internally on the experience of pain (Melzack & Wall, 1982).

Social factors also influence how we experience pain. Fordyce (1976, 1988; see also Turk, 1996) has studied social forms of pain behavior such as verbal complaints, facial expressions, and obvious limps or other symptoms that may reflect strong social contingencies. For example, family members who were formerly critical and demanding may become caring and sympathetic (Kerns et al., 1991). This phenomenon is referred to as "operant" control of pain behavior because the behavior clearly seems under the control of social consequences. But these consequences have an uncertain relation to the amount of pain actually being experienced.

By contrast, a strong network of social support may reduce pain. Jamison and Virts (1990) studied 521 chronic pain patients (with back, abdominal, and chest conditions) and discovered that those who lacked social support from their families reported more pain sites and showed more pain behavior, such as staying in bed. These patients also exhibited more emotional distress *without* rating their pain as any more intense than subjects with strong socially supportive families. The subjects with strong support returned to work earlier, showed less reliance on medications, and increased their activity levels more quickly than the others.

Although these results may seem to contradict studies on the operant control of pain, different mechanisms may be at work. General social support may reduce the stress associated with pain and injury and promote more adaptive coping procedures and control. However, specifically reinforcing pain behaviors, particularly in the absence of social supports, may powerfully increase such behavior. These very complex issues have not yet been entirely sorted out.

Biological Aspects

GATE CONTROL THEORY

No one thinks that pain is entirely psychological, just as no one thinks that it is entirely physical. The *gate control theory* (Melzack & Wall, 1965, 1982) accommodates both psychological and physical factors. According to this theory, nerve impulses from painful stimuli make their way to the spinal column, and from there to the brain. An area called the *dorsal horns of the spinal column* acts as a "gate" and may open and transmit sensations of pain if the stimulation is sufficiently intense. Specific nerve fibers referred to as *small fibers* (A-delta and C fibers) and *large fibers* (A-beta fibers) determine the pattern as well as the intensity of the stimulation. Small fibers tend to open the gate, thereby increasing the transmission of painful stimuli, whereas large fibers tend to close the gate.

Most important for our purpose is that the brain sends signals back down the spinal cord that may affect the gating mechanism. For example, a person with negative emotions such as fear or anxiety may experience pain more intensely because the basic message from the brain is to be vigilant against possible danger or threat. Then again, in a person whose emotions are more positive or who is totally absorbed in an activity (such as a runner intent on finishing a long race), the brain sends down an inhibitory signal that closes the gate. Although many think that the gate control theory is overly simplistic, its basic elements have held up, particularly as it describes the complex interaction of psychological and biological factors in the experience of pain (Turk, 1996).

ENDOGENOUS OPIOIDS

The neurochemical means by which the brain inhibits pain is a very important discovery. Drugs such as heroin and morphine are manufactured from opioid substances. It now turns out that there are **endogenous** (natural) **opioids** within the body. Called *endorphins* or *enkephalins*, they act very much like neurotransmitters. The brain uses them to shut down pain, even in the presence of marked tissue damage or injury. Because endogenous opioids are distributed widely throughout the body, they may be implicated in a variety of psychopathological conditions, including eating disorders and, more commonly, the "runners' high" that accompanies the release of endogenous opioids after intense (and sometimes painful) physical activity. Bandura and colleagues (1987) found that people with a greater sense of self-efficacy and control had a higher tolerance for pain than individuals with low self-efficacy and they actually increased their production of endogenous opioids when they were confronted with a painful stimulus.

Gender Differences in Pain

Most animal and human studies have been conducted on males to avoid the complications of hormonal variation. But men and women seem to experience different types of pain. On the one hand, in addition to menstrual cramps and labor pains, women suffer more frequently than men from migraine headaches and arthritis. Men, on the other hand, have more cardiac pain and backache. Both males and females have endogenous opioid systems, although in males it may be more powerful. But both sexes seem to have additional pain-regulating mechanisms that may be different. The female neurochemistry may be based on an estrogen-dependent neuronal system that may have evolved to cope with the pain associated with reproductive activity (Mogil, Sternberg, Kest, Marek, & Liebeskind, 1993). It is an "extra" pain-regulating pathway in females that, if taken away by removing hormones, has no implications for the remaining pathways, which continue to work as well. One implication of this finding is that males and females may benefit from different kinds of drugs, different kinds of psychosocial interventions, or unique combinations of these treatments to best manage and control pain.

Chronic Fatigue Syndrome

In the mid-19th century, a rapidly growing number of patients suffered from lack of energy, marked fatigue, a variety of aches and pains and, on occasion, low-grade fever. No physical pathology could be discovered, and George Beard (1869) labeled the condition *neurasthenia*, literally, lack of nerve strength (Abbey & Garfinkel, 1991; Costa e Silva & DeGirolamo, 1990; Morey & Kurtz, 1989). The disease was attributed to the demands of the time, including a preoccupation with material success, a strong emphasis on hard work, and the changing role of women. Neurasthenia disappeared in the early 20th century in Western cultures but remains the most prevalent form of psychopathology in China (Good & Kleinman, 1985; Kleinman, 1986).

Now **chronic fatigue syndrome (CFS)** is spreading rapidly throughout the Western world. The symptoms of CFS, listed in Table 9.2, are almost identical to those of neurasthenia and, until recently, were attributed to viral infection, specifically the Epstein-Barr virus (Straus et al., 1985), immune system dysfunction (Straus, 1988), exposure

---

table 9.2   Definition of Chronic Fatigue Syndrome

Inclusion criteria

1. Clinically evaluated, medically unexplained fatigue of at least 6 months duration that is:
   - of new onset (not life-long)
   - not resulting from ongoing exertion
   - not substantially alleviated by rest
   - a substantial reduction in previous level of activities
2. The occurrence of four or more of the following symptoms:
   - Subjective memory impairment
   - Sore throat
   - Tender lymph nodes
   - Muscle pain
   - Joint pain
   - Headache
   - Unrefreshing sleep
   - Post-exertional malaise lasting more than 24 hours

Source: Adapted from Fukuda et al., 1995

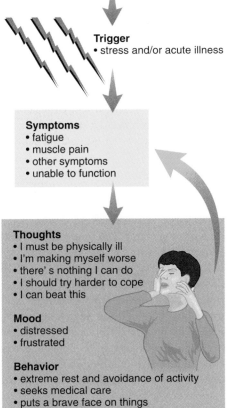

Core beliefs
• I am inadequate (?)

Beliefs
• I must always perform perfectly
• I must always cope
• I must never show weakness
• depression is evidence of weakness

Lifestyle
• achievement-oriented and hard working
• puts on a brave face
• doesn' t ask for help

Trigger
• stress and/or acute illness

Symptoms
• fatigue
• muscle pain
• other symptoms
• unable to function

Thoughts
• I must be physically ill
• I'm making myself worse
• there' s nothing I can do
• I should try harder to cope
• I can beat this

Mood
• distressed
• frustrated

Behavior
• extreme rest and avoidance of activity
• seeks medical care
• puts a brave face on things
• episodic bursts of activity

Physiology
• effects of inactivity and emotional distress
• other processes (?)

figure 9.10 A complex specific model of chronic fatigue syndrome (from Sharpe, 1997).

possibility suggested by Abbey and Garfinkel (1991) is that the condition represents a rather nonspecific response to stress. But it is not clear why certain individuals respond with chronic fatigue instead of some other psychological or physical disorder. Michael Sharpe (1997) has developed the first model of the causes of CFS that accounts for all of its features (see Figure 9.10). Sharpe theorizes that individuals with particularly achievement-orientated life-styles (driven, perhaps, by a basic sense of inadequacy) undergo a period of extreme stress or acute illness. They misinterpret the lingering symptoms of fatigue, pain, and inability to function at their usual very high levels as a continuing disease that is worsened by activity and improved by rest. This results in behavioral avoidance, helplessness, depression, and frustration. They think they should be able to conquer the problem and cope with its symptoms. Chronic inactivity, of course, leads to lack of stamina, weakness, and increased feelings of depression and helplessness that in turn result in episodic bursts of long activity followed by further fatigue.

Pharmacological treatment has not proven to be effective for CFS (Sharpe, 1992), but Michael Sharpe in Oxford has developed a cognitive–behavioral program that includes procedures to increase activity, regulate periods of rest, and direct cognitive therapy at the cognitions specified in Figure 9.10. This treatment also includes relaxation, breathing exercises, and general stress-reduction procedures, interventions we will describe in the next section (Sharpe, 1992, 1993, 1997). Time will tell if Sharpe's approach to CFS is correct in whole or in part, but it is the first comprehensive model and it does have treatment implications. Now results are in from the first large-scale evaluation of a similar cognitive–behavioral approach to CFS (Deale, Chalder, Marks, & Wessely, 1997). In a clinical trial, 60 patients with CFS were randomly assigned to cognitive–behavioral therapy or relaxation exercises alone. The results indicated that fatigue diminished and overall functioning improved significantly more in the group that received cognitive–behavioral therapy. As is evident in Table 9.3, 70% of individuals who completed cognitive–behavioral therapy achieved substantial improvement in physical functioning at a 6-month follow-up compared to only 19% of those in the relaxation-only group. This study is yet to be replicated, but the results are very encouraging.

to toxins, or to clinical depression (Costa e Silva & DiGirolamo, 1990). No evidence has yet to support any of these hypothetical physical causes (Sharpe, 1997).

People with CFS suffer considerably and often must give up their careers. As Abbey and Garfinkel (1991) and Sharpe (1997) point out, both neurasthenia in the last century and CFS in the present have been attributed to an extremely stressful environment, the changing role of women, and the rapid dissemination of new technology and information. Both disorders are most common in women. It is possible, of course, that a virus or a specific immune system dysfunction will be found to account for CFS. Another

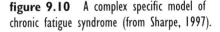

■ **concept check 9.3**

Which of the following is not considered to be a part of the experience of pain?

1. The subjective impression of pain as reported by the patient

2. Pain behaviors or overt manifestations of pain

3. Cuts, bruises, and other injuries

4. An emotional component called *suffering*

table 9.3	Patients with Chronic Fatigue Syndrome Who Had Good Outcomes at 6-Month Follow-up		
		*Good Outcomes**	
Study Group		N	%
Treatment Completers			
Cognitive–behavioral therapy (N = 27)		19	70
Relaxation (N = 26)		5	19
Completers plus dropouts			
Cognitive–behavioral therapy (N = 30)		19	63
Relaxation (N = 30)		5	17

*An increase of 50 or more, from pretreatment to 6-month follow-up, or an end score of 83 or more on the physical functioning scale of the Medical Outcomes Study Short-Form General Health Survey.
Source: Adapted from Deale et al. (1997)

Psychosocial Treatment of Physical Disorders

Recent experiments suggest that pain is not only bad for you but that it may kill you. John Liebeskind and his colleagues (Page, Ben-Eliyahu, Yirmiya, & Liebeskind, 1993) demonstrated that postsurgical pain in rats doubles the rate at which a certain cancer metastasizes (spreads) to the lungs. Rats undergoing abdominal surgery *without* morphine developed twice the number of lung metastases than rats who were given morphine for the same surgery. In fact, the rats undergoing surgery with the pain-killing drug had even lower rates of metastases than rats that did not have surgery.

This effect may result from the interaction of pain with the immune system. Pain may reduce the number of natural killer (NK) cells in the immune system, perhaps because of the general stress reaction to the pain. Thus, if a rat is in *extreme* pain, the associated stress may further enhance the pain, completing a vicious circle. If this finding is found to apply to humans it is important, because the general consensus is that we are very reluctant to use pain-killing medication in chronic diseases such as cancer. Some estimates suggest that fewer than half of all cancer patients in the United States receive sufficient pain relief. Adequate pain-management procedures, either medical or psychological, are an essential part of the management of chronic disease.

A variety of psychosocial treatments have been developed for physical disorders and pain, including biofeedback, relaxation procedures, and hypnosis. But because of the overriding role of stress in the etiology and maintenance of many physical disorders, comprehensive stress-management programs are increasingly incorporated into medical centers where such disorders are treated. We will briefly review specific psychosocial approaches to physical disorders and describe a typical comprehensive stress-management program.

BIOFEEDBACK

Biofeedback is a process of making patients aware of specific physiological functions that, ordinarily, they would not notice consciously, such as heart rate, blood pressure, muscle tension in specific areas of the body, EEG rhythms (brain waves), and patterns of blood flow. This is the first step, but the second step is more remarkable. In the 1960s, Neal Miller reported that rats could *learn to directly control* many of these responses. He used a variation of operant conditioning procedures in which the animals were reinforced for increases or decreases in their physiological responses (N. E. Miller, 1969). Although it was subsequently difficult to replicate these findings with animals, clinicians applied the procedures with some success to humans who suffered from various physical disorders or stress-related conditions, such as hypertension and headache.

Clinicians use physiological monitoring equipment to make the response, such as heart rate, visible or audible to the patient. The patient then works with the therapist to learn to control the response. A successful response produces some type of signal. For example, if the patient is successful in lowering his or her blood pressure by a certain amount, the pressure reading will be visible on a gauge and a tone will sound. It wasn't long before researchers discovered that humans could discriminate changes in autonomic nervous system activity with a high degree of accuracy (Blanchard & Epstein, 1977). The question then became this: Why are people ordinarily so poor at discriminating their internal states? Zillmann (1983) suggests that our abilities have always been highly developed in this regard,

In biofeedback, the patient learns to control physiological responses that are visible on a screen.

Edward Blanchard was a pioneer in the development and testing of biofeedback.

but that we have simply lost our skills through lack of practice. Shapiro (1974) suggests that, in an evolutionary sense, it might have been very adaptive to turn our attention away from precise monitoring of our internal responses. He proposes that whether humans function as hunter-gatherers or in the home or office, they would be far less efficient if they were continually distracted by a turmoil of internal stimuli. In other words, to focus successfully on the task at hand, we may have found it necessary to ignore our internal functioning and leave it to the more automatic and less aware parts of the brain. Of course, internal sensations often take control of our consciousness and make us fully aware of our needs. Consider for example, the compelling sensations that signal the need to urinate or the insistence of hunger pangs. In any case, it does seem that through precise physiological feedback we can learn to control our responses, although the mechanisms by which we do so are not yet clearly known.

One goal of biofeedback has been to reduce tension in the muscles of the head and scalp, thereby relieving headaches. Pioneers in the area, such as Ed Blanchard, Ken Holroyd, and Frank Andrasik, found that biofeedback was successful in this area (Holroyd, Andrasik, & Noble, 1980), although no more successful than deep muscle relaxation procedures (Blanchard & Andrasik, 1982; Blanchard, Andrasik, Ahles, Teders, & O'Keefe, 1980; Holroyd & Penzien, 1986). Because of these results, some have thought that biofeedback might achieve its effects with tension headaches by simply teaching people to relax. However, Holroyd and colleagues (1984) concluded instead that the success of biofeedback, at least for headaches, may depend not on reducing tension but on the extent to which the procedures instill a sense of *control* over the pain (How do you think this relates to the study of stress in baboons described in the beginning of the chapter?) Whatever the mechanism, biofeedback and relaxation are more effective treatments than, for example, placebo medication interventions. Several reviews have found that 38% to 63% of patients undergoing relaxation or biofeedback achieve significant reductions in headaches compared to approximately 35% who receive placebo medication (Blanchard, 1992; Blanchard et al., 1980; Holroyd & Penzien, 1986). Furthermore, the effects of biofeedback and relaxation seem to be long-lasting (Blanchard, 1987; Lisspers & Öst, 1990).

RELAXATION AND MEDITATION

Various types of relaxation and meditation procedures have also been used, either alone or in combination with other procedures, to treat physical disorder and pain patients. In *progressive muscle relaxation,* devised by Edwin Jacobson in 1938, people become acutely aware of any tension in their bodies and counteract it by relaxing specific muscle groups. In Jacobson's original conception, learning the art of relaxation was a structured procedure that took months or even years to master. In most clinics today, however, the procedure is usually taught in a matter of weeks, and is very seldom used as the sole treatment (Bernstein & Borkovec, 1973). There are a number of procedures to focus attention either on a specific part of the body or on a single thought or image. This attentional focus is often accompanied by regular slowed breathing. In *transcendental meditation* (TM), attention is focused solely on a repeated syllable, or the *mantra.*

Herbert Benson stripped transcendental meditation of what he considered its nonessentials and developed a brief procedure he calls the **relaxation response,** in which a person silently repeats a mantra to minimize distraction by closing the mind to intruding thoughts. Although Benson suggested focusing on the word *one,* any neutral word or phrase would do. Individuals who meditate for 10 or 20 minutes a day report feeling calmer or more relaxed throughout the day. These brief, simple procedures can be very powerful in actually reducing the flow of certain neurotransmitters and stress hormones, an effect that may be mediated by an increased sense of control and mastery (Benson, 1975, 1984). Benson's ideas are very popular and are taught in 60% of U.S. medical schools and offered by many major hospitals (Roush, 1997).

Relaxation has generally positive effects on headaches, hypertension, and acute and chronic pain, although the results are relatively modest (S. Taylor, 1991). Nonetheless, relaxation and meditation are almost always part of a comprehensive pain-management program.

A COMPREHENSIVE STRESS- AND PAIN-REDUCTION PROGRAM

In our own stress-management program (Barlow & Rapee, 1991, 1997), individuals practice a variety of stress-management procedures presented to them in a workbook. First, they learn to monitor their stress very closely and to identify the stressful events in their daily lives. (Samples of a stressful events record and a daily stress record are in Figure 9.11). Note that clients are taught to be very specific about recording the times they experience stress, the intensity of the stress, and what seems to trigger the stress. They also note the somatic symptoms and thoughts that occur when they are stressed. All this monitoring becomes important in carrying through with the program, but it can be very helpful in itself, as it reveals precise patterns and causes of stress and helps clients learn what changes to make in order to cope better.

After learning to monitor stress, clients are taught deep muscle relaxation, which involves, first, tensing various muscles to identify the location of different muscle groups.

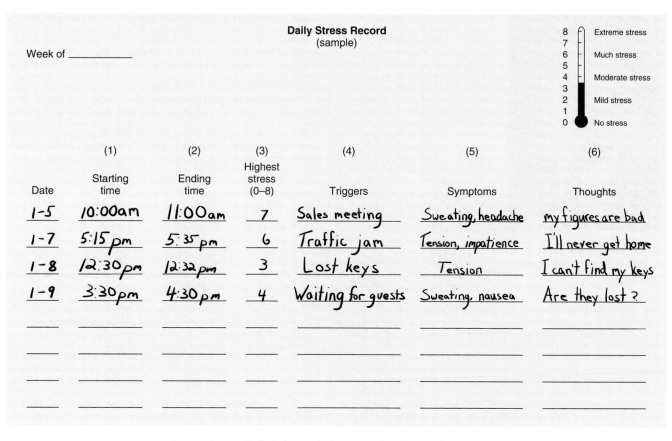

figure 9.11   Methods for monitoring stress (from Barlow & Rapee, 1991)

table 9.4   Suggestions for Tensing Muscles

	12 Muscle Groups
Lower arm	Make fist, palm down, and pull wrist toward upper arm.
Upper arm	Tense biceps; with arms by side, pull upper arm toward side without touching. (Try not to tense the lower arm while doing this; let the lower arm hang loosely.)
Lower leg and foot	Point toes upward to knees.
Thighs	Push feet hard against floor.
Abdomen	Pull in stomach toward back.
Chest and breathing	Take a deep breath and hold it about 10 seconds, then release.
Shoulders and lower neck	Shrug shoulders, bring shoulders up until they almost touch ears.
Back of neck	Put head back and press against back of chair.
Lips	Press lips together; don't clench teeth or jaw.
Eyes	Close eyes tightly but don't close too hard (be careful if you have contacts).
Lower forehead	Pull eyebrows down and in (try to get them to meet).
Upper forehead	Raise eyebrows and wrinkle your forehead.

Source: Barlow & Rapee, 1991

(Instructions for tensing specific muscle groups are included in Table 9.4.) Clients are then systematically taught to relax the muscle groups beyond the point of inactivity; that is, to actively "let go" of the muscle so that no tension remains in it.

Appraisals and attitudes are an important part of stress, and clients learn how they exaggerate the negative impact of events in their day-to-day lives. In the program, therapist and client use cognitive therapy to develop more realistic appraisals and attitudes, as exemplified in the case of Sally.

Sally

Improving Her Perception

(Sally is a 45-year-old real estate agent.)

Sally: My mother is always calling just when I'm in the middle of doing something important and it makes me so angry, I find that I get short with her.

Therapist: Let's try and look at what you just said in another way. When you say that she *always* phones in the middle of something, it implies 100% of the time. Is that true? How likely is it really that she will call when you are doing something important?

Sally: Well, I suppose that when I think back over the last ten times she's called, most of the times I was just watching TV or reading. There was once when I was making dinner and it burned because she interrupted me. Another time, I was busy with some work I had brought home from the office, and she called. I guess that makes it 20% of the time.

Therapist: OK, great; now let's go a bit further. So what if she calls at an inconvenient time?

Sally: Well, I know that one of my first thoughts is that she doesn't think anything I do is important. But before you say anything, I know that is a major overestimation since she obviously doesn't know what I'm doing when she calls. However, I suppose I also think that it's a major interruption and inconvenience to have to stop at that point.

Therapist: Go on. What is the chance that it is a major inconvenience?

Sally: When I was doing my work, I forgot what I was up to and it took me 10 minutes to work it out again. I guess that's not so bad; it's only 10 minutes. And when the dinner burned, it was really not too bad, just a little burned. Part of that was my fault anyway, because I could have turned the stove down before I went to the phone.

Therapist: So, it sounds like quite a small chance that it would be a major inconvenience, even if your mother does interrupt you.

Sally: True. And I know what you are going to say next. Even if it is a major inconvenience, it's not the end of the world. I have handled plenty of bigger problems than this at work.

In this program individuals work hard to identify unrealistic negative thoughts and to develop new appraisals and attitudes almost instantaneously when negative thoughts occur. Such assessment is often the most difficult part of the program. After the session just related, Sally began using what she had learned in cognitive therapy to reappraise stressful situations.

Finally, clients in *stress-reduction* programs develop new coping strategies, such as *time management* and *assertiveness training*. During time-management training, patients are taught to prioritize their activities and pay less attention to nonessential demands. During assertiveness training, they learn to stand up for themselves in an appropriate way.

Clients also learn other procedures for managing everyday problems.

A number of studies have evaluated some version of this comprehensive program. The results suggest that it is generally more effective than individual components alone, such as relaxation or biofeedback, for chronic pain (Keefe, Crisson, Urban, & Williams, 1990; Keefe et al., 1992), chronic fatigue syndrome (Deale et al., 1997), tension headaches (Blanchard et al., 1990; Murphy, Lehrer, & Jurish, 1990), hypertension (Ward, Swan, & Chesney, 1987), and cancer pain (Fawzy, Cousins, et al., 1990).

■ concept check 9.4

Check your understanding by matching the treatments to the scenarios: (a) biofeedback, (b) meditation and relaxation response, (c) cognitive coping procedure.

1. Mary is often upset by the stupid things other people are always doing. Her doctor wants her to realize her exaggeration of these events. _____

2 Karl can't seem to focus on anything at work. He feels too stressed. He needs a way of minimizing intruding thoughts that he can do at work in a short amount of time. _____

3. Harry's blood pressure soars when he feels stressed. His doctor showed him how to become aware of his body processes in order to better control them. _____

DRUGS AND STRESS-REDUCTION PROGRAMS

We have already noted the enormous nationwide reliance on over-the-counter analgesic medication for pain, particularly headaches. There is some evidence that *chronic* reliance on these medications lessens the efficacy of comprehensive programs in the treatment of headache. Michultka, Blanchard, Appelbaum, Jaccard, and Dentinger (1989) matched high analgesic users to low analgesic users in terms of age, duration of headache activity, and response to comprehensive treatment. Only 29% of high users versus 55% of low users achieved at least a 50% reduction in headache activity. In addition, Holroyd, Nash, Pingel, Cordingley, and Jerome (1991) compared a comprehensive cognitive–behavioral treatment to an antidepressant drug, amitriptyline, in the treatment of tension headache. The psychological treatment produced at least a 50% reduction in headache activity in 56% of the patients, whereas the drug produced a comparable reduction in only 27% of users. It is important that psychological treatment also seems to reduce drug consumption fairly consistently (Radnitz, Appelbaum, Blanchard, Elliott, & Andrasik, 1988) not only for headaches but also for severe hypertension.

DENIAL AS A MEANS OF COPING

We have emphasized the importance of confronting and working through one's feelings, particularly after stressful or traumatic events. Beginning with Freud, mental health professionals have recognized the importance of reliving or processing intense emotional experiences in order to put them behind you and to develop better coping responses. For example, individuals undergoing coronary artery bypass surgery who were optimistic recovered more quickly, returned to normal activities more rapidly, and reported a stronger quality of life 6 months after surgery than those who were not optimistic (Scheier et al., 1989). Scheier et al. also discovered that optimistic people are less likely to use denial as a means of coping with a severe stressor such as surgery. Most mental health professionals work to eliminate denial because it has many negative effects. For example, people who deny the severe pain connected with disease may not notice meaningful variations in their symptoms, and they typically avoid treatment regimens or rehabilitation programs.

But is denial always harmful? The well-known health psychologist, Shelley Taylor (1991), points out that most individuals who are functioning well deny the implications of a potentially serious condition, at least initially. A common reaction is to assume that what they have is not serious or that it will go away quickly. Most people with serious diseases react this way, including those with cancer (Meyerowitz, 1983) and coronary heart disease (Krantz & Deckel, 1983). Several groups of investigators (for example, Hackett & Cassem, 1973; Meyerowitz, 1983) have found that during that extremely stressful period when a person is first diagnosed, denial of the general implications and of anxiety and depression may help the patient endure the shock more easily. He or she is then more able to develop coping responses later. In one study, high initial denial resulted in less time in the intensive care section of the hospital (Levine et al., 1988) although, after discharge, the same patients were not as good at doing what they had to do to enhance their rehabilitation. Other studies show lower levels of corticosteroids and other stress-related responses among deniers during the most stressful phase of the illness (Katz, Weiner, Gallagher, & Hellman, 1970). Thus, the value of denial as a coping mechanism may depend more on timing than on anything else. In the long run though, all the evidence indicates that at some point we must face the situation, process our emotions, and come to terms with what is happening.

Modifying Behaviors to Promote Health

In the beginning of the chapter, we talked of psychological and social factors influencing health and physical problems in two distinct ways: by directly affecting biological processes, and through unhealthy lifestyles. In this section, we consider the effects of unhealthy lifestyle.

In 1991 the director of the National Institutes of Health said, "Our research is teaching us that many common diseases can be prevented and others can be postponed or controlled simply by making possible life-style changes" (U.S. Department of Health and Human Services, 1991). Unhealthy eating habits, lack of exercise, and smoking are three of the most common behaviors that put us at risk in

table 9.5	Areas for Health-Risk Behavior Modification

Smoking
Hyperlipidemia
High blood pressure
Dietary habits related to disease
High sodium; low calcium, magnesium, potassium—*high blood pressure*
High fat—cardiovascular disease and cancer of the prostate, breast, colon, and pancreas
High simple carbohydrates—diabetes mellitus
Low fiber—diabetes mellitus, digestive diseases, cardiovascular disease, colon cancer
Low intake of Vitamins A and C—cancer
Sedentary life-style
Obesity
Substance abuse (alcohol and drug)
Nonuse of seatbelts
High-risk sexual behavior
Nonadherence to recommended immunization and screening procedures
High stress levels and type A personality
High-risk situations for childhood accidents, neglect, abuse
Poor dental hygiene/infrequent care
Sun exposure
Poor-quality relationships/supports
Occupational risks

Source: Johns et al., 1987

the long term for a number of physical disorders. High-risk behaviors and conditions are listed in Table 9.5. Many of these behaviors contribute to diseases and physical disorders that are among the leading causes of death, including not only coronary heart disease and cancer, but also accidents of various kinds (related to consumption of alcohol and the nonuse of safety restraints), cirrhosis of the liver (related to excessive consumption of alcohol), and a variety of respiratory diseases, including influenza and pneumonia (related to smoking and stress) (Sexton, 1979). Considerable work is ongoing to develop effective behavior modification procedures to improve diet, increase adherence to drug and medical treatment programs, and develop optimal exercise programs. Here we review briefly four areas of interest: injury control, the prevention of AIDS, efforts to reduce smoking in China, and a major community intervention known as the Stanford Three Community Study.

INJURY CONTROL

Injuries are the leading cause of death for people age 1 to 45. Furthermore, the loss of productivity to the individual and society from injuries is far greater than from the other three leading causes of death: heart disease, cancer, and stroke (Rice & MacKenzie, 1989). For this reason our government has become very interested in methods for reducing injury. Spielberger and Frank (1992) point out that psychological variables are crucial in mediating virtually all the factors that lead to injury. The psychological contributors have been un-

Lizette Peterson developed important behavior-change procedures for preventing injuries in children.

derstudied until recently, but they are now beginning to receive attention. A good example is the work of Lizette Peterson and her colleagues (for instance, Peterson & Roberts, 1992). Peterson is particularly interested in preventing accidents in children. Injuries kill more children than the next six causes of childhood death combined (Dershewitz & Williamson, 1977), and yet most people, including parents, don't think too much about prevention, even in their own children, because they usually consider injuries to be due to fate and, therefore, out of their hands (Peterson, Farmer, & Kashani, 1990; Peterson & Roberts, 1992). However, there are a variety of programs with proven effectiveness for preventing injuries in children. For example, children have been systematically and successfully taught to escape fires (R. T. Jones & Haney, 1984), identify and report emergencies (R. T. Jones & Kazdin, 1980), safely cross streets (Yeaton & Bailey, 1978), ride bicycles safely, and deal with injuries such as serious cuts (Peterson & Thiele, 1988). In many of these programs, the participating children maintained the safety skills they had learned for months after the intervention—as long as assessments were continued, in most cases. Because there is little evidence that repeated warnings are effective in preventing injuries, programmatic efforts to change behavior are very important, and yet such programs are nonexistent in most communities.

AIDS Prevention

Earlier we documented the horrifying spread of AIDS, particularly in developing countries. Table 9.6 illustrates modes of transmission of AIDS in the United States. In developing countries, in Africa for instance, the development of AIDS is almost exclusively linked to heterosexual intercourse with an infected partner (Center for Disease Control, 1994). There is no vaccine for the disease. *Changing high-risk behavior is the only effective prevention strategy.*

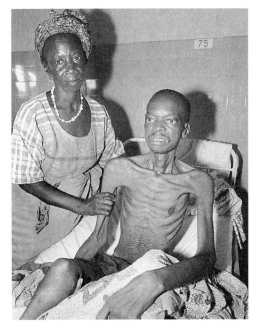

The prevalence of AIDS is high in Africa, where this woman cares for her dying husband.

Comprehensive programs are particularly important because testing alone to learn whether one is HIV positive or HIV negative does little to change behavior (for example, Landis, Earp, & Koch, 1992). Even educating at-risk individuals is generally ineffective in changing high-risk behavior (Helweg-Larsen & Collins, 1997). One of the most successful behavior change programs was carried out in San Francisco. Table 9.7 shows what behaviors were specifically targeted and what methods were used to achieve behavior change in various groups. Before this program was introduced, frequent unprotected sex was reported by 37.4% of one sample of gay men and 33.9% of another sample (Stall, McKusick, Wiley, Coates, & Ostrow, 1986). At a follow-up point in 1988 the incidence had dropped to 1.7% and 4.2%, respectively, in the same two samples (Ekstrand & Coates, 1990). These changes did not occur in comparable groups where a program of this type had not been instituted. In a similar large community-based program in eight small cities, Kelly et al. (1997) trained popular and well liked members of the gay community to provide information and education.

table 9.6   Distribution of Adult and Adolescent AIDS Cases in the United States

Exposure Category	Percentage
Male homosexual or bisexual contact history	54
Injection drug use history	24
Injection drug use and male homosexual or bisexual contact history	7
Heterosexual contact history	6
Receipt of blood transfusion	2
Hemophilia/coagulation disorder	1
Undetermined	6

Source: From Center for Disease Control (1994)

table 9.7   The San Francisco Model: Coordinated Community-Level Program to Reduce New HIV Infection

Information	*Skills*
Intervention: Media Educate about how HIV is and is not transmitted.	Model how to clean needles and use condoms and spermicides. Model skills for safer sex/needle negotiation. Provide classes and videos to demonstrate safe sex skills.
Health Care Establishments and Providers Provide educational materials and classes about HIV transmission.	Provide classes and models for safe sex/drug injection skills. Instruct and rehearse safer sex/drug injection skills during medical and counseling encounters. Provide classes and videos for AIDS risk-reduction skills.
Schools Distribute materials about HIV transmission and prevention.	*Norms*
Worksites Distribute materials about HIV transmission and prevention.	Publicize the low prevalence of high-risk behaviors. Publicize public desirability of safer sex classes and condom advertisements.
STD, Family Planning, and Drug Abuse Treatment Centers Distribute materials and video models about HIV transmission.	Advise patients about prevalent community norms. Create a climate of acceptance for HIV-infected students and teachers.
Community Organizations (Churches, Clubs) Make guest speakers, materials, videos available.	Publicize student perceptions about desirability of safe sex. Create a climate of acceptance for HIV-infected persons.
Antibody Testing Centers Distribute materials and instruction about HIV transmission.	Provide classes and videos for AIDS risk-reduction skills.
Motivation	*Policy/Legislation*
Provide examples of different kinds of individuals who have become HIV infected.	Generate concern and action about policy. Advocate policies and laws that will prevent spread of HIV.
Ask all patients about risk factors for HIV transmission. Advise high-risk patients to be tested for HIV antibodies. Provide models of teens who became infected with HIV. Provide examples of co-workers who became infected with HIV. Make detailed assessment of HIV risk. Advise about testing for antibodies to HIV. Provide examples that HIV-infected individuals are similar to club/organization membership.	Mobilize students and faculty to work to allow sex education to take place in the schools. Install condom machines in public bathrooms. Allow HIV-infected persons to work. Mobilize clients to request additional treatment slots and facilities. Advocate beneficial laws and policies. Advocate policy changes and laws suggesting AIDS risk reduction. Advocate confidentiality and nondiscrimination.

Note: HIV = human immunodeficiency virus; STD = sexually transmitted disease.
Source: Based on Coates, 1990

Risky sexual practices were substantially reduced in the four cities where the program occurred, compared to four cities where only educational pamphlets were distributed.

Careful evaluation of smaller at-risk groups or individuals demonstrates that high-risk sexual practices are reduced substantially by a comprehensive program of *cognitive–behavioral self-management training* and the development of an effective *social support network*. Kelly (1995) has developed an up-to-date program that is adjustable to the individual, either young or old, woman or man, inner city or rural, and that emphasizes helping each one assess personal risk and change risky behavior (Kelly, 1995). Analysis of factors that predict the adoption of safe sex practices indicates that treatment programs should focus on instilling in participants a sense of self-efficacy and control over their own sexual practices (Aspinwall, Kemeny, Taylor, Schneider, & Dudley, 1991; Kelly, 1995; O'Leary, 1992).

It is crucial that these programs be extended to minorities and women, who frequently do not consider themselves at risk, probably because most media coverage has focused

Women are increasingly at risk for AIDS.

on gay white males (Mays & Cochran, 1988). Indeed, most research on the epidemiology and natural history of AIDS has largely ignored the disease in women (Ickovics & Rodin, 1992). In 1992 women accounted for 14% of AIDS cases, and the proportion is steadily rising. A report from the Centers for Disease Control and Prevention indicates that women are contracting AIDS at a rate four times faster than men (Center for Disease Control, 1994). Furthermore, the highest age of risk for women is between ages 15 and 25; the peak risk for men is during their late 20s and early 30s. In view of the very different circumstances in which women put themselves at risk for HIV infection—for example, prostitution in response to economic deprivation—effective behavior change programs for them must be very different from those developed for men. Yet, we have barely begun to attend to this pressing need.

SMOKING IN CHINA

Despite efforts by the government to reduce smoking among its citizens, China has one of the most tobacco-addicted populations in the world. Approximately 250 million people in China are habitual smokers, 90% of them male, a number that equals the entire population of the United States. In an attempt to reach these individuals, health professionals took advantage of the strong family ties in China and decided to persuade the *children* of smokers to intervene with their fathers. In so doing, they conducted the largest study yet reported of attempted behavior modification to promote health. In 1989, they developed an antismoking campaign in 23 primary schools in Hangzhou, capital of Zhejiang Province. Children took home antismoking literature and questionnaires to almost 10,000 fathers. They then wrote letters to their fathers asking them to quit smoking, and they submitted monthly reports on their fathers' smoking habits to the schools. Approximately 9 months later, the results were assessed. Indeed, the children's intervention had some effect. Almost 12% of the fathers in the intervention group had quit smoking for at least 6 months. By contrast, in a control group of another 10,000 males, the quit rate was only 0.2% ("Somber News," 1993).

STANFORD THREE COMMUNITY STUDY

One of the best-known and most successful efforts to reduce risk factors for disease in the community is the *Stanford Three Community Study* (A. Meyer, Nash, McAlister, Maccoby, & Farquhar, 1980). Rather than assemble three groups of people, these investigators studied three entire communities in central California that were reasonably alike in size and type of residents between 1972 and 1975. The target was reduction of risk factors for coronary heart disease (CHD). The positive behaviors that were introduced focused on smoking, high blood pressure, diet, and weight reduction. In

If everyone doesn't stop and face the calamity, hand in hand with the sick till it can't break through anymore, then it will claim the millennium for its own.

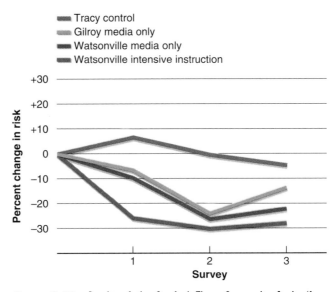

figure 9.12 Results of the Stanford Three Community Study (from Meyer et al., 1980)

Tracy, the first community, no interventions were conducted, but detailed information was collected from a random sample of adults to assess any increases in their knowledge of risk factors as well as any changes in risk factors over time. In addition, participants in Tracy received a medical assessment of their cardiovascular factors. The residents of Gilroy and part of Watsonville were subjected to a media blitz on the dangers of behavioral risk factors for CHD, the importance of reducing these factors, and helpful hints for doing so. Most residents of Watsonville also had a face-to-face intervention in which behavioral counselors worked with the townspeople judged to be at particularly high risk for CHD. Subjects in all three communities were surveyed once a year for a 3-year period following the intervention. Results indicate that the interventions were markedly successful at reducing risk factors for coronary heart disease in these communities (see Figure 9.12). Furthermore, for the residents of Watsonville who also received individual counseling, risk factors were substantially lower than for people in Tracy, or even in Gilroy and people in the part of Watsonville that received only the media blitz, and their knowledge of risk factors was substantially higher.

Interventions such as the Stanford study cost money, although in many communities the media are willing to donate time to such a worthy effort. Results show that mounting an effort like this is worthwhile to individuals, to the community, and to public health officials because many lives will be saved, and disability leave will be decreased to an extent that will more than cover the original cost of the program.

from the inside

Borrowed Time: An AIDS Memoir
by Paul Monette*

"How do I speak of the person who's my life's best reason?" (p. 9) asks Paul Monette at the beginning of his always eloquent, often heartbreaking chronicle of the 2 years he spent caring for Roger Horwitz, his partner of 12 years, who became sick with AIDS and died 18 months after the diagnosis.

Part love story, part historical document of the "plague years" of the early 1980s, Monette's memoir describes first the strong wall of denial he built against this catastrophe in his community, then his gradual facing of the crisis as first one friend, then another, falls ill: "It comes like a slowly dawning horror. At first you are equipped with a hundred different amulets to keep it far away. Then someone you know goes into the hospital, and suddenly you are at high noon in full battle gear" (p. 2).

Partly owing to denial and partly to the fact that they are so busy and happy, the couple doesn't immediately notice Roger's nightly two-note cough and his gathering weariness. "Besides, the particular indignities of AIDS are so grotesque . . . that the general aura of fatigue and accelerated aging are so much more difficult to pin down" (p. 130). The last brick crumbles when Roger is taken to the hospital for tests and is diagnosed with pneumocystis, a lung infection and a sure indicator of AIDS. "Was there a pause for the world to stop? There must have been because I remember the crack of silence, Roger staring. . . . Then he simply shut his eyes, and only I, who was the rest of him, could see how stricken was the stillness in his face" (p. 77).

From this world-stopping moment on, the memoir charts the couple's gradual heroic coming to terms with Roger's illness, their search for medical information, their roller-coaster ride as they wait for and try new drugs, some of which were not yet legally available ("all this AZT optimism was better than a Currier & Ives snowfall"), and their struggle against despair.

At first they conceal Roger's illness, so as not to worry parents and friends: "I still have such conflicted feelings about hiding the diagnosis. What's privacy and what's denial? How much is guilt and the lingering self-hatred of the closet?" (p. 81), but as Roger's condition worsens, they must tell the truth. Indeed, toward the end, it was impossible to hide: "It was the most emaciated he ever got: only ten or fifteen pounds below his normal weight, yet his face was so thin you could see the skull beneath" (p. 212). The outpouring of love and support is overwhelming, and it is enormously clear that along with Roger's inborn calm, the support from his social network, and most of all, Paul's love for him, kept him fighting and holding onto his health for almost 2 years after his diagnosis.

Monette didn't set out to write a memoir, but he finds that "writing about AIDS was a small measure of power over the nightmare" (p. 178), a way to reclaim control and grapple with the tumble of emotions: fear, despair, and plenty of anger, at both the illness and the indifference of the media and the government. And although Roger does die, and although Monette himself discovers that "the virus ticks" in him (he died of AIDS in 1995), his chronicle serves as a lasting testimony to the love and courage sustained by the two men, who remained side by side, sometimes literally 24 hours a day. By the time the memoir ends, more research on AIDS and the immune system is being conducted and more drugs are available. Monette tells us, even in his mourning and in illness ("I don't know if I will live to finish this") (p. 1) that all of us, the sick and the well, must continue to learn and to fight: "We cannot go down to defeat and darkness, we have to say we have been here" (p. 129).

*Paul Monette, *Borrowed Time: An AIDS Memoir* (Avon, 1990).

Summary

Psychological and Social Factors Influencing Biological Processes

• Psychological and social factors play a major role in the development and maintenance of a number of physical disorders.

• Two fields of study have emerged as a result of a growing interest in psychological factors contributing to illness. Behavioral medicine involves the application of behavioral science techniques to prevent, diagnose, and treat medical problems. Health psychology is a subfield that focuses on psychological factors involved in the promotion of health and well-being.

• Psychological and social factors may contribute directly to illness and disease through the psychological effects of stress on the immune system and other physical functioning. If the immune system is compromised, it may no longer be able to attack and eliminate antigens from the body effec-

tively, or it may even begin to attack the body's normal tissue instead, a process known as autoimmune disease.

• Growing awareness of the many connections between the nervous system and the immune system has resulted in the new field of psychoneuroimmunology.

• Diseases that may be related in part to the effects of stress on the immune system include AIDS, rheumatoid arthritis, and cancer.

• Long-standing patterns of behavior or life-style may put people at risk for developing certain physical disorders. For example, unhealthy sexual practices can lead to AIDS and other sexually transmitted diseases, and unhealthy behavioral patterns, such as poor eating habits, lack of exercise, or type A behavior pattern may contribute to cardiovascular diseases such as stroke, hypertension, and coronary heart disease.

• Of the 10 leading causes of death in the United States, fully 50% of deaths can be traced to life-style behaviors.

• Psychological and social factors also contribute to chronic pain. The brain inhibits pain through naturally occurring endogenous opioids, which may also be implicated in a variety of psychological disorders.

• Chronic fatigue syndrome is a relatively new disorder that is attributed at least in part to stress but may also have a viral or immune system dysfunction component.

Psychosocial Treatment of Physical Disorders

• A variety of psychosocial treatments have been developed with the goal of either treating or preventing physical disorders. Among these are biofeedback and the relaxation response.

A Comprehensive Stress- and Pain-Reduction Program

• Comprehensive stress- and pain-reduction programs include not only relaxation and related techniques but also new methods to encourage effective coping, including stress-management, realistic appraisals, and improved attitudes through cognitive therapy.

• Comprehensive programs are generally more effective than individual components delivered singly.

Modifying Behaviors and Life-Styles to Promote Health

• Other interventions aim to modify such behaviors as unsafe sexual practices, smoking, and unhealthy dietary habits. Such efforts have been made in a variety of areas, including injury control, AIDS prevention, smoking cessation campaigns in China, and the Stanford Three Community Study to reduce risk factors for disease.

Key Terms

behavioral medicine
health psychology
general adaptation syndrome (GAS)
stress
self-efficacy
immune system
antigens
autoimmune disease
rheumatoid arthritis
psychoneuroimmunology (PNI)
AIDS-related complex (ARC)
cancer
psychoncology
cardiovascular disease
stroke (cerebral vascular accident/CVA)
hypertension
essential hypertension
coronary heart disease (CHD)
type A behavior pattern
type B behavior pattern
acute pain
chronic pain
endogenous opioids
chronic fatigue syndrome (CFS)
biofeedback
relaxation response

Answers to Concept Checks

9.1
1. d
2. a
3. c
4. b
5. f
6. e

9.2
1. d
2. b
3. c
4. a

9.3
3

9.4
1. c
2. b
3. a

EXPLORING PHYSICAL DISORDERS AND HEALTH PSYCHOLOGY

- Psychological and behavioral factors are major contributors to illness and death.
- Behavioral science is applied to medical problems in *behavioral medicine*.
- The study of psychological influences on health and health care is known as *health psychology*.

Psychological and Social Factors Influence Biology

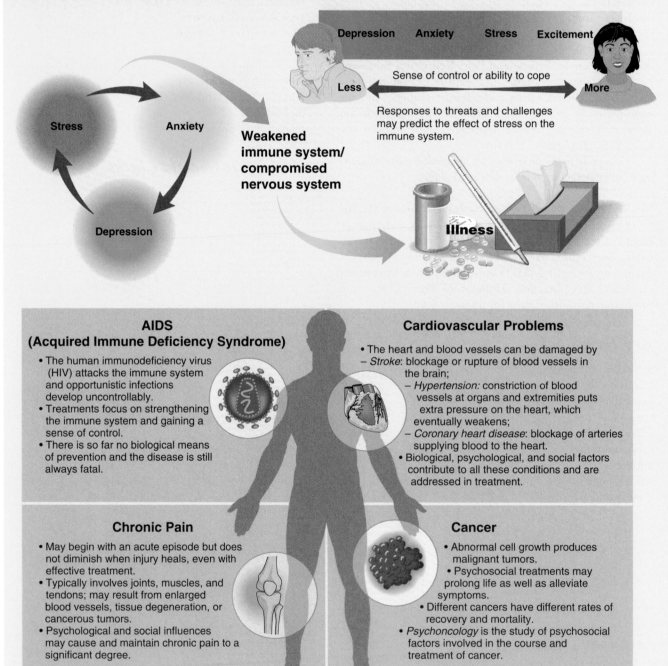

Depression   Anxiety   Stress   Excitement

Less ◄── Sense of control or ability to cope ──► More

Responses to threats and challenges may predict the effect of stress on the immune system.

Stress   Anxiety

Depression

Weakened immune system/ compromised nervous system

Illness

AIDS (Acquired Immune Deficiency Syndrome)

- The human immunodeficiency virus (HIV) attacks the immune system and opportunistic infections develop uncontrollably.
- Treatments focus on strengthening the immune system and gaining a sense of control.
- There is so far no biological means of prevention and the disease is still always fatal.

Cardiovascular Problems

- The heart and blood vessels can be damaged by
  - *Stroke*: blockage or rupture of blood vessels in the brain;
    - *Hypertension*: constriction of blood vessels at organs and extremities puts extra pressure on the heart, which eventually weakens;
    - *Coronary heart disease*: blockage of arteries supplying blood to the heart.
- Biological, psychological, and social factors contribute to all these conditions and are addressed in treatment.

Chronic Pain

- May begin with an acute episode but does not diminish when injury heals, even with effective treatment.
- Typically involves joints, muscles, and tendons; may result from enlarged blood vessels, tissue degeneration, or cancerous tumors.
- Psychological and social influences may cause and maintain chronic pain to a significant degree.

Cancer

- Abnormal cell growth produces malignant tumors.
- Psychosocial treatments may prolong life as well as alleviate symptoms.
- Different cancers have different rates of recovery and mortality.
- *Psychoncology* is the study of psychosocial factors involved in the course and treatment of cancer.

PSYCHOSOCIAL TREATMENTS FOR PHYSICAL DISORDERS

The stress reaction associated with pain may reduce the number of natural killer (NK) cells in the immune system:

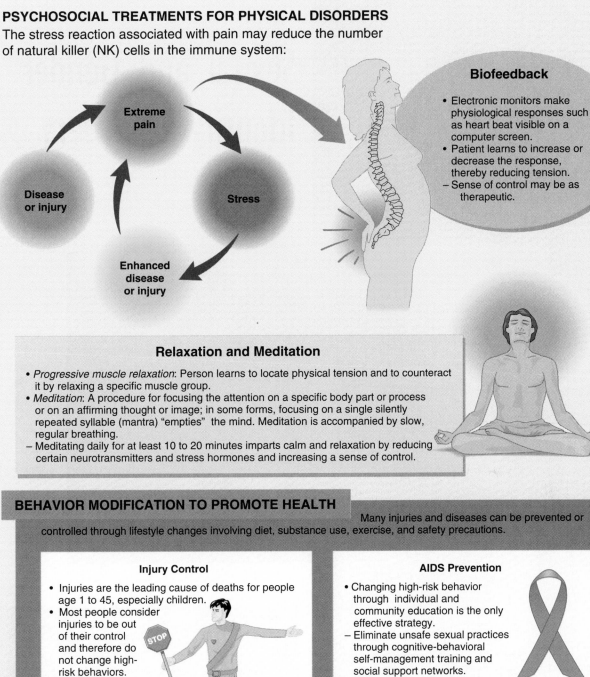

Extreme pain

Disease or injury

Stress

Enhanced disease or injury

Biofeedback

- Electronic monitors make physiological responses such as heart beat visible on a computer screen.
- Patient learns to increase or decrease the response, thereby reducing tension.
- Sense of control may be as therapeutic.

Relaxation and Meditation

- *Progressive muscle relaxation*: Person learns to locate physical tension and to counteract it by relaxing a specific muscle group.
- *Meditation*: A procedure for focusing the attention on a specific body part or process or on an affirming thought or image; in some forms, focusing on a single silently repeated syllable (mantra) "empties" the mind. Meditation is accompanied by slow, regular breathing.
- Meditating daily for at least 10 to 20 minutes imparts calm and relaxation by reducing certain neurotransmitters and stress hormones and increasing a sense of control.

BEHAVIOR MODIFICATION TO PROMOTE HEALTH

Many injuries and diseases can be prevented or controlled through lifestyle changes involving diet, substance use, exercise, and safety precautions.

Injury Control

- Injuries are the leading cause of deaths for people age 1 to 45, especially children.
- Most people consider injuries to be out of their control and therefore do not change high-risk behaviors.
- Prevention focuses on
  - escaping fires
  - crossing streets
  - using car seats, seat belts, and bicycle helmets
  - first aid

AIDS Prevention

- Changing high-risk behavior through individual and community education is the only effective strategy.
- Eliminate unsafe sexual practices through cognitive-behavioral self-management training and social support networks.
- Show drug abusers how to clean needles and make safe injections.
- Target minorities and women, groups that do not perceive themselves to be at risk.
- Media coverage focuses on gay white males.
- More women are infected through heterosexual interactions than by IV drug use.

10

Sexual and Gender Identity Disorders

Man, dominated by drives, has no power over himself. . . . We are in bondage in proportion as we are dominated by drives.
Benedict de Spinoza

You have all read magazine surveys reporting sensational information on sexual practices. According to one, men can reach orgasm 15 or more times a day (in reality, such ability is very rare) and women fantasize about being raped (this is even rarer). Surveys like this fail us on two counts: First, they claim to reveal sexual norms when they are really, for the most part, distorted half-truths. Second, the facts they present typically are not based on any scientific methodology that would make them reliable, although they do sell magazines.

What is normal sexual behavior? As we will see, it depends. By contrast, when is sexual behavior somewhat different from the norm a disorder? Again, it depends. Current views tend to be quite tolerant of a variety of sexual expressions, even if they are unusual, unless the behavior is associated with a substantial impairment in functioning. Three kinds of sexual behavior meet this definition. In *gender identity disorders,* there is psychological dissatisfaction with one's biological sex. The disorder is not specifically sexual, but rather a disturbance in the person's sense of identity as a male or a female. But these disorders are often grouped with sexual disorders, as in DSM–IV. Individuals with *sexual dysfunction* find it difficult to function adequately while having sex, for example, they may not become aroused or achieve orgasm. *Paraphilia,* the relatively new term for sexual deviation, includes disorders in which sexual arousal occurs primarily in the context of inappropriate objects or individuals. "Philia" means a strong attraction or liking, and "para" indicates that the attraction is abnormal. Paraphilic arousal patterns tend to be focused rather narrowly, often precluding mutually consenting adult patterns, even if desired. Before describing these three types of disorders, we'll return to our initial question, "What is normal sexual behavior?" to gain an important perspective.

What Is Normal?

Determining the prevalence of sexual practices accurately requires careful surveys that randomly sample the population. In a scientifically sound survey, Billy, Tanfer, Grady, and Klepinger (1993) reported data from 3,321 men in the United States aged 20 to 39. The participants were interviewed, which is more reliable than having them fill out a questionnaire, and the responses were analyzed in detail. The purpose of this survey was to ascertain risk factors for sexually transmitted diseases, including AIDS. Some of the data are presented in Figure 10.1.

Virtually all men studied were sexually experienced, with vaginal intercourse a nearly universal experience, even for those who had never been married. Three-fourths of the men also engaged in oral sex but only one-fifth had ever engaged in anal sex, a particularly high-risk behavior for AIDS transmission, and half of these had not had anal sex in the previous year and a half. Slightly more troublesome is the finding that 23.3% had had sex with 20 or more partners, another high-risk behavior. Then again, more than 70% had had only

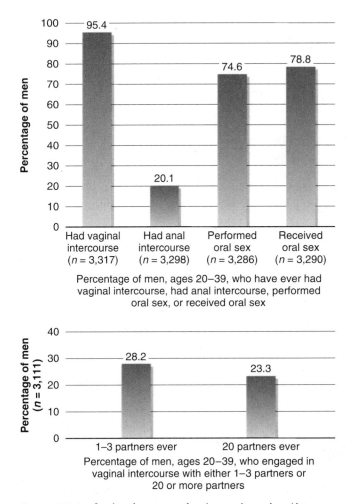

figure 10.1   Results of a survey of male sexual practices (data from Billy et al., 1993).

one sexual partner during the previous year, and fewer than 10% had had four or more partners during the same period.

A surprising finding is that the overwhelming majority of the men had engaged exclusively in **heterosexual sex** (sex with the opposite sex). Only 2.3% had engaged in **homosexual sex** (sex with the same sex), and only 1.1% engaged exclusively in homosexual activity. These results require some rethinking of our assumptions, because for over 40 years sex researchers and public health officials have relied on the comprehensive survey of sexual behaviors and attitudes by a pioneer investigator into sexual behavior, Alfred Kinsey. Kinsey and his colleagues (Kinsey, Pomeroy, & Martin, 1948; Kinsey, Pomeroy, Martin, & Gebhard, 1953) reported a figure of about 10% for any same-gender sexual activity. Since sampling procedures were not nearly so sophisticated in Kinsey's day as now, his data are presumed to be inaccurate, particularly in light of the additional surveys reported below.

One study from Britain (A. M. Johnson, Wadsworth, Wellings, Bradshaw, & Field, 1992) and one from France (Spira et al., 1992) surveyed sexual behavior and practices among more than 20,000 men *and women* in each country. The results were surprisingly similar to those reported for American men. More than 70% of the respondents from all age groups in the British and French studies reported no more than one sexual partner during the past year. Women were somewhat more likely than men to have had fewer than two partners. Only 4.1% of French men and 3.6% of British men reported ever having had a male sexual partner. Almost certainly, the percentage of males engaging exclusively in homosexual behavior would be considerably lower. The consistency of these data across three countries suggests strongly that the results represent something close to the norm, at least for Western countries. This has been confirmed in additional similar surveys (Seidman & Rieder, 1994).

Nevertheless, the sexual risks taken by college students and other young adults remain alarmingly high despite the well-publicized AIDS epidemic and the recent increase in other sexually transmitted diseases. DeBuono, Zinner, Daamen, and McCormack (1990) surveyed college women in 1975, in 1986, and again in 1989. They found very little change in the number of *male sexual partners,* the frequency of oral sex, and the frequency of *anal intercourse* (see Table 10.1). Regular condom use increased from 12% in 1975 to 41% in 1989. This is an improvement, but more than half the sexually active college-age women still practiced unprotected sex.

Another interesting set of data counters the many views we have of sexuality among elderly individuals. Sexual behavior can continue well into old age, even past 80 for some people. Table 10.2 presents the percentage by age group of married individuals in a community sample who were sexually active and continuing to have sexual intercourse (Diokno, Brown, & Herzog, 1990). Notably, 50% of men and 36% of women aged 75 to 79 were sexually active. Reasons for the discrepancy between men and women are not clear, although given the earlier mortality of men, many older women lack a suitable partner; it is also possible that some women are married to men in an older age bracket. The

Sexual behavior often continues well into old age.

sample of individuals over the age of 80 is too small to allow meaningful conclusions, although many remained sexually active. Decreases in sexual activity are correlated, for the most part, with decreases in general mobility, various disease processes and consequent medication, which may reduce arousal; furthermore, the speed and intensity of various vasocongestive responses decrease with age.

Gender Differences

Although both men and women tend toward a monogamous (one partner) pattern of sexual relationships, gender differences in sexual behavior do exist, and some of them are quite dramatic. One common finding among sexual surveys is that a much higher percentage of men than women report that they masturbate (self-stimulate to orgasm) (Oliver & Hyde, 1993). When Leitenberg, Detzer, and Srebnik (1993) surveyed 280 university students, they found that this discrepancy remained (81% of men versus only 45% of women reported ever masturbating) despite the fact that for 25 years women had been encouraged to take more responsibility for their own sexual fulfillment and to engage in more sexual self-exploration.

Among those who did masturbate, the frequency was about three times greater for men than for women, and had been throughout adolescence. Masturbation was not related in any way to later sexual functioning; that is, whether individuals masturbated or not during adolescence had no influence on whether they had experienced intercourse, the frequency of intercourse, the number of partners, or other factors reflecting sexual adjustment.

Why women masturbate less frequently than men puzzles sex researchers, particularly when other long-standing

table 10.1 Percentages of College Women Who Participated in Various Sexual Activities in 1975, 1986, and 1989

Number of Male Sexual Partners Ever	1975 (n = 486)	1986 (n = 161)	1989 (n = 132)
0	12.1	13.0	12.9
1	25.1	24.8	12.1
2–5	40.5	42.2	52.3
≥6	22.2	19.9	21.2
No answer	0	0	1.5
Fellatio (female oral contact with male genitals)			
Never	17.9	16.8	12.9
Occasionally	47.3	45.3	43.9
Regularly	32.5	33.5	42.4
No answer	2.3	4.3	0.8
Cunnilingus (male oral contact with female genitals)			
Never	33.1	34.8	33.3
Occasionally	38.9	37.3	36.4
Regularly	24.3	23.6	28.8
No answer	3.7	4.3	1.5
Anal intercourse			
Never	87.4	89.4	90.2
Occasionally	9.7	7.5	8.3
Regularly	0.6	0	0.8
No answer	2.3	3.1	0.8

Frequency of condom use during sexual intercourse in college women in 1975, 1986, and 1989

	% of Women		
	1975 (n = 427)	1986 (n = 140)	1989 (n = 113)
Frequency			
Always or almost always	12	21	41
Seldom or never	87	71	58
Uncertain	1	8	1

Source: DeBuono et al., 1990

table 10.2 Sexual Activity of Elderly Married Respondents Classified by Age and Sex

	Males			Females		
Age	Yes	%	Total	Yes	%	Total
60–64	83	87.4	95	57	64.0	89
65–69	64	79.0	81	49	63.6	77
70–74	18	58.1	31	13	43.3	30
75–79	13	50.0	26	9	36.0	25
80+	4	28.6	14	1	25.0	4
Total	182	73.7	247	129	57.3	225

Source: Diokno, Brown, & Herzog, 1990

gender differences in sexual behavior, such as the probability of engaging in premarital intercourse, have virtually disappeared (Clement, 1990). One traditional view accounting for differences in masturbatory behavior is that women have been taught to associate sex with romance and emotional in-timacy whereas men are more interested in physical gratification. But the discrepancy continues despite decreases in gen-der-specific attitudes toward sexuality. A more likely reason is anatomical. Because of the nature of the erectile response in men and their relative ease in providing sufficient stimulation to reach orgasm, masturbation may simply be more convenient for men than for women. This may explain why gender differences in masturbation are also evident in primates and other animals further down the phylogenetic scale (C. Ford & Beach, 1951). In any case, incidence of masturbation continues to be the largest gender difference in sexuality.

Another continuing gender difference is reflected in attitudes toward *casual* premarital sex, with men expressing a far more permissive attitude than women, although this gap is becoming much smaller. By contrast, results from a large number of studies suggest that *no* gender differences are apparent at the current time in attitudes about homosexuality (generally acceptable), the experience of sexual satisfaction (important for both), or attitudes toward masturbation (generally accepting). Small to moderate gender differences were evident in attitudes toward premarital intercourse when the couple was engaged or in a committed relationship (with men more approving than women); and in attitudes toward extramarital sex. As in the British and French studies, the number of sexual partners and the frequency of intercourse were slightly greater for men, and men were slightly younger at age of first sexual intercourse. Examining trends from the 1960s to the 1980s, we see that almost all existing gender differences became smaller over time, especially in regard to attitudes toward premarital sex.

Nevertheless, although they are decreasing, differences still exist in attitudes toward sexuality between men and women. Hatfield and colleagues (1988) assessed young, unmarried female undergraduates as well as a sample of newly married couples (age 17 to 46 years) to determine what parts of the sexual relationship contributed most substantially to their satisfaction. Consistent with long-standing gender differences, women desired more demonstrations of love and intimacy during sex, and men were more interested in focusing on the arousal aspects. Although these attitudes may not correlate perfectly with actual behavior during sexual relations, they probably represent something basically different in the way men and women feel about sexual relations.

What happened to the sexual revolution? Where are the effects of the "anything goes" attitude toward sexual expression and fulfillment that supposedly began in the 1960s and 1970s? Clearly there has been some change. The "double standard" has disappeared, in that women no longer feel constrained by a stricter and more conservative social standard of sexual conduct. The sexes are definitely drawing together in their attitudes and behavior. Regardless, the overwhelming majority of individuals engage in heterosexual, vaginal intercourse in the context of a relationship with one partner. Based on these data, the sexual revolution may be largely a creation of the media, focusing as it does on extreme or sensational cases.

Cultural Differences

What is normal in the year 2000 in Western countries may not necessarily be normal in other parts of the world. The Sambia in New Guinea believe that semen is an essential substance for growth and development in young boys

John Bancroft was one of the first researchers to describe the interaction of biology and psychology as determinants of sexual behavior.

of the tribe. They also believe that semen is *not* produced naturally; that is, the body is incapable of producing it spontaneously. Therefore, all young boys in the tribe, beginning at approximately age 7, become semen recipients by engaging exclusively in homosexual oral sex with teenage boys. Only oral sexual practices are permitted; masturbation is forbidden and totally absent. Early in adolescence the boys switch roles and become semen providers to younger boys. Heterosexual relations and even contact with the opposite sex are prohibited until the boys become teenagers. Late in adolescence, the boys are expected to marry and begin exclusive heterosexual activity. And they do, with no exceptions (Herdt, 1987; Herdt & Stoller, 1989). By contrast, the Munda of Northeast India also require adolescents and children to live together. But in this group both male and female children live in the same setting, and the sexual activity, consisting mostly of petting and mutual masturbation, is all heterosexual (Bancroft, 1989).

Even within Western cultures, there are some variations. I. M. Schwartz (1993) surveyed attitudes surrounding the first premarital experience of sexual intercourse in nearly 200 female undergraduates in the United States and compared them to a similar sample in Sweden, where attitudes toward sexuality are somewhat more permissive. The average age at the time of first intercourse for the woman and the age of her partner are presented in Table 10.3, as well as the age the women thought it would be socially acceptable in their culture for them to have sexual intercourse. Acceptable perceived ages for both men and women were significantly younger in Sweden, but few other differences existed, with one striking exception: 73.7% of Swedish women and only 56.7% of American women used some form of contraception during their first sexual intercourse, a significant difference. In about half of more than 100 societies surveyed worldwide, premarital sexual behavior is culturally accepted and encouraged; in the remaining half, premarital sex is unacceptable and discouraged (Bancroft, 1989; Broude & Greene, 1980). Thus, what is normal sexual behavior in one culture is not necessarily normal in another, and the wide range of sexual expression must be considered in diagnosing the presence of a disorder.

The Development of Sexual Orientation

Reports suggest that homosexuality runs in families (Bailey & Benishay, 1993), and concordance for homosexuality is more common among monozygotic twins than among dizy-

table 10.3 Group Differences Between U.S. and Swedish Female Undergraduates Regarding Premarital Sex

Variable	United States Mean/(SD)	Sweden Mean/(SD)
Age at first coitus	16.97 (1.83)	16.80 (1.92)
Age of first coital partner	18.77 (2.88)	19.10 (2.96)
Perceived age of social acceptance for *females* to engage in premarital coitus	18.76 (2.57)	15.88 (1.43)
Perceived age of social acceptance for *males* to engage in premarital coitus	16.33 (2.13)	15.58 (1.20)

Source: I. M. Schwartz, 1993

gotic twins or natural siblings (Bailey & Pillard, 1991; Bailey, Pillard, Neale, & Agyei, 1993; Whitnam, Diamond, & Martin, 1993), is associated with differential exposure to hormones early in life, perhaps before birth (Ehrhardt et al., 1985; Gladue, Green, & Hellman, 1984), and that the actual structure of the brain might be different in homosexuals and heterosexuals (Allen & Gorski, 1992; LeVay, 1991). A report has located a possible gene (or genes) for homosexuality on the X chromosome (Hamer, Hu, Magnuson, Hu, & Pattatucci, 1993). In two excellent twin studies (Bailey & Pillard, 1991; Bailey et al., 1993), homosexual orientation was shared in approximately 50% of monozygotic twins compared with 16% to 22% of dizygotic twins. Approximately the same or a slightly lower percentage of nontwin brothers or sisters were homosexual.

The principal conclusion drawn in the media is that sexual orientation has a biological cause. Gay rights activists are decidedly split on the significance of these findings. Some are pleased with the biological interpretation, because people can no longer assume that homosexuals have made a morally depraved choice of "deviant" arousal patterns. Others, however, note how quickly the public has pounced on the implication that there is something biologically wrong with individuals with homosexual arousal patterns, assuming that someday the abnormality will be detected in the fetus and prevented, perhaps through genetic engineering.

Do such arguments over biological causes sound familiar? Think back to studies described in Chapter 2 that attempted to link complex behavior to particular genes. In almost every case, these studies could not be replicated, and investigators fell back on a model in which genetic contributions to behavioral traits and psychological disorders come from many genes, each making a relatively small contribution to a *vulnerability*. This biological vulnerability then interacts in a complex way with various environmental conditions, personality traits, and other contributors to determine behavioral patterns. We also discussed gene–environment interactions in which certain learning experiences and environmental events may affect brain structure and function and genetic expression.

Most theoretical models outlining these complex interactions for sexual orientation imply that there may be

many pathways to the development of heterosexuality or homosexuality, and that no one factor, biological or psychological, can predict the outcome (Bancroft, 1994; Byne & Parsons, 1993). It is likely, too, that different types of homosexuality (and, perhaps, heterosexuality), with different patterns of etiology, may be discovered. Daryl Bem (1996) refers to his model as "exotic becomes erotic," a phrase that summarizes the principals of the theory nicely. Bem proposes that we inherit a temperament to behave in certain ways that later interacts with environmental factors to produce sexual orientation. For example, if a boy prefers active and aggressive or "boy typical" behaviors, he will feel very similar to his same-sex peers. A young boy who feels less aggressive may avoid rough and tumble play in favor of "girl typical" activities. Their activities, whether typical or atypical, lead children to feel different from either their opposite or their same-sex peers. A young boy with boy typical activities will feel more different from girls than he does from boys, making the opposite sex more "exotic." Sexual attraction in later years will be to the group of more exotic individuals. A young boy who engages in girl typical activities is likely to feel more different from other boys than he does from girls (or other boys with atypical activities). Therefore, what is exotic to this boy, is other boys. Sexual attraction later follows. Bem has some evidence that gay men and women feel more different from their same-sex peers than heterosexual men and women, but there is little direct evidence that this feeling, in turn, determines sexual attraction. There is some evidence from other sources, however, regarding the attractiveness of novel or exotic stimuli. What is important for our purposes is that this theory combines biological and psychological or environmental variables, and suggests how they interact to form sexual orientation (Figure 10.2). Almost certainly, in our view, scientists will pin down biological contributions to the formation of sexual orientation, both heterosexual and homosexual. And just as certainly, the environment and experience will be found to powerfully influence how these patterns of potential sexual arousal develop.

One of the more intriguing findings from the twin studies of Bailey and his colleagues is that approximately 50% of the monozygotic twins with *exactly* the *same genetic*

Michael Bailey and his colleagues are among the pioneer researchers into genetic contributions to sexual orientation.

structure as well as the *same environment* (growing up in the same house) *did not* have the same sexual orientation (Bailey & Pillard, 1991). Also intriguing is the finding in a study of 302 homosexual men that males growing up with older brothers are more likely to be homosexual, whereas having older sisters, or younger brothers or sisters, is not correlated with later sexual orientation. In fact, each additional older brother increased the odds of homosexuality by one-third! This may suggest the importance of environmental influences, although the mechanism has not been identified. (Blanchard & Bogart, 1996).

In any case, the simple, one-dimensional claims that homosexuality is caused by a gene or that heterosexuality is

caused by healthy early developmental experiences will continue to appeal to the general populace. Although we could be wrong, neither explanation is likely to be proven correct. Almost certainly, biology sets certain limits within which social and psychological factors affect development (Diamond, 1995).

Gender Identity Disorders

What is it that makes you think you are a man? Or a woman? Clearly, it's more than your sexual arousal patterns or your anatomy. It's also more than the reactions and expectations of your family and society at large. The essence of your masculinity or femininity is a deep-seated personal sense called *gender identity*. **Gender identity disorder** is present if a person's physical gender is not consistent with the person's sense of identity. People with this disorder feel trapped in a body of the wrong sex. Consider the following case.

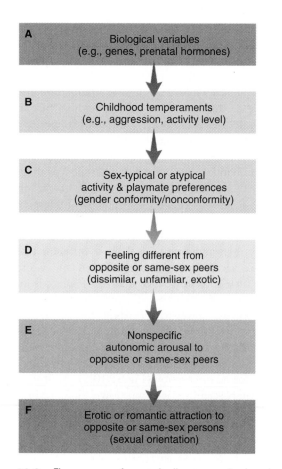

figure 10.2   The sequence of events leading to sexual orientation for most men and women in a gender-polarizing culture. (from Bem, 1996).

Joe
Trapped in the Wrong Body

Joe was a 17-year-old male and the last of five children. Although his mother had wanted a girl, he became her favorite child. His father worked long hours and had little contact with the boy. For as long as Joe could remember, he had thought of himself as a girl. He began dressing in girls' clothes totally of his own accord before he was 5 years old and continued cross-dressing into junior high school. He developed interests in cooking, knitting, crocheting, and embroidering, skills he acquired by reading an encyclopedia. His older brother often scorned him for his distaste of such "masculine" activities such as hunting. Joe associated mostly with girls during this period, although he remembered being strongly attached to a boy in the first grade. In his sexual fantasies, which developed at about 12 years of age, he pictured himself as a female having intercourse with a male. His extremely effeminate behavior made him the object of scorn and ridicule when he entered high school at age 15. Usually passive and unassertive, he ran away from home and attempted suicide. Unable to continue in high school, he attended secretarial school, where he was the only boy in his class. During his first interview with a therapist he reported, "I am a woman trapped in a man's body and I would like to have surgery to become a woman."

We'll return to Joe in our discussion of treatment.

Gender identity disorder (or *transsexualism*, as it used to be called) must be distinguished from *transvestic fetishism*, a paraphilic disorder (discussed later) in which individuals, usually males, are sexually aroused by wearing articles of clothing associated with the opposite sex. There is an occasional preference on the part of the male for the fe-

RuPaul Andre Charles (left) is famous as drag queen RuPaul (right). Also a recording artist, television personality, and gay media star, RuPaul says, "If it was just drag I was about I would've already disappeared."

male role, but the primary purpose of cross-dressing is sexual gratification. In the case of gender identity disorder, the primary goal is not sexual but rather the desire to live one's whole life openly in a manner consistent with that of the other gender.

Gender identity disorder must also be distinguished from *intersex individuals (hermaphrodites),* who are actually born with ambiguous genitalia associated with documented hormonal or other physical abnormalities. Depending on their particular mix of characteristics, they are "assigned" to a specific sex at birth, sometimes requiring surgery as well as hormonal treatments to alter their sexual anatomy. Individuals with gender identity disorder, by contrast, have *no* demonstrated physical abnormalities.

Finally, gender identity disorder must be distinguished from the homosexual arousal patterns of a male who sometimes behaves effeminately or a woman with masculine gestures. Such an individual does not feel like a woman trapped in a man's body or have any desire to be a woman. Note also, as the DSM-IV criteria do, that gender identity is *independent* of sexual arousal patterns. For example, a male-to-female transsexual (a male with a feminine gender identity) may be sexually attracted to females, which, technically, makes his arousal homosexual. Recently Eli Coleman and his associates (Coleman, Bockting, & Gooren, 1993) reported on nine female-to-male cases who were sexually attracted to men. Thus, heterosexual women before surgery were gay men after surgery.

Gender identity disorder is relatively rare. The estimated incidence based on studies in Sweden and Australia is 1 in 37,000 in Sweden and 1 in 24,000 in Australia for biological males compared to 1 in 103,000 and 1 in 150,000 for biological females (M. W. Ross, Walinder, Lundstrom, & Thuwe, 1981). Many countries now allow a series of legal steps to change one's gender identity. In Germany, between 2.1 and 2.4 per 100,000 in the population took at least the first legal steps of changing their first names. Here again the male–female ratio is 2.3:1 (Weitze & Osburg, 1996).

In some cultures individuals with mistaken gender identity are often accorded the status of "shaman" or "seer" and treated as wisdom figures. A shaman is almost always a male adopting a female role (for example, Coleman, Colgan, & Gooren, 1992). Stoller (1976) reported on two contemporary feminized Native American men who were not only accepted but also esteemed by their tribes for their expertise in healing rituals. Contrary to the respect accorded these individuals in some cultures, social tolerance for them is relatively low in Western cultures, where they are the objects of curiosity at best and derision at worst.

Causes

Research has yet to uncover any specific biological contributions to gender identity disorder, although it seems very likely that a biological predisposition will ultimately be discovered. Early research suggests that, as with sexual orientation, slightly higher levels of testosterone or estrogen at certain critical periods of development might masculinize a female fetus or feminize a male fetus (for instance, Gladue et al., 1984; Imperato-McGinley, Peterson, Gautier, & Sturla, 1979). Variations in hormonal levels could occur naturally or because of medication that a pregnant mother is taking. However, scientists have yet to establish a link between prenatal hormonal influence and later gender identity, although it is still possible that one exists. Recently, structural differences in the area of the brain that controls male sex hormones have been observed in individuals with male and female gender identity disorder (Zhou et al., 1995), with the result that the brains are comparatively more feminine. But it isn't clear whether this is a cause or an effect. There is at least some evidence that gender identity firms up between 18 months and 3 years of age (Ehrhardt & Meyer-Bahlburg, 1981; Money & Ehrhardt, 1972) and is relatively fixed after that. But studies suggest that preexisting biological factors have had their impact. One interesting case illustrating this phenomenon was originally reported by R. Green and Money (1969), who described the following sequence of events.

John/Joan

A set of male identical twins was born into a well-adjusted family. Several weeks later, an unfortunate accident occurred. Although circumcision went routinely for one of the boys, the physician's hand slipped so that the electric current in the device burned off the penis of the second baby. After working through their hostility to the physician, the parents consulted specialists in children with intersexual problems and were faced with a choice. The specialists pointed out that the easiest solution would be to reassign their son John as a girl, and the parents agreed. At the age of several months, John became "Joan." The parents purchased a new wardrobe and treated the child in every way possible as a girl. These twins were followed through childhood and, upon reaching puberty, the young girl was given hormonal replacement therapy. After 6 years the doctors lost track of the case but assumed she had adjusted well. In fact, Joan endured almost intolerable inner turmoil. We know this because two clinical scientists found this individual and recently reported a long-term follow-up (Diamond & Sigmundson, 1997). Joan never adjusted to her assigned gender. As a child she preferred rough and tumble play and resisted wearing girls' clothes. In public bathrooms she often insisted on urinating while standing up, which usually made a mess. By early adolescence Joan was pretty sure she was a boy, but her doctors pressed her to act more feminine. When she was 14 she confronted her parents, telling them she was so miserable she was considering suicide. At that point they told her the true story and the muddy waters of her mind began to clear. Shortly thereafter, Joan had additional surgery changing her back to John, and is now the happily married father of three adopted children.

Of course there are other case studies of children whose gender was reassigned at birth who adapted successfully (e.g., Gearhart, 1989). But it certainly seems that biology expressed itself in John's case.

Richard Green, a pioneering researcher in this area, has studied feminine boys and masculine girls, investigating what makes them that way, and following what happens to them (Green, 1987). He discovered that when most young boys spontaneously display "feminine" interests and behaviors, they are typically discouraged by most families. However, boys who consistently display these behaviors are not discouraged and are sometimes encouraged, as seemed to be the case with Joe. Other factors, such as excessive attention and physical contact on the part of the mother, *may* also play some role, as may a lack of male playmates during the early years of socialization. These are just some of the factors identified by Green as characteristic of effeminate boys. Remember that as yet undiscovered biological factors may also contribute to the spontaneous display of cross-gender behaviors and interests. However, in following up these boys, Green discovered that very few seem to develop the "wrong" gender identity, although he is not sure how many do so because follow-ups are continuing. The most likely outcome is

the development of homosexual preferences, but even this particular sexual arousal pattern seems to occur exclusively in only approximately 40% of the feminine boys. Another 32% show some degree of *bisexuality*, sexual attraction to both their own and the opposite sex. Looking at it from the other side, 60% were functioning heterosexually. We can safely say that the causes of mistaken gender identity are still something of a mystery.

Treatment

Treatment is available for gender identity disorder in a few specialty clinics around the world, although much controversy surrounds treatment. At present the most common decision is to physically alter the anatomy to be consistent with the identity through **sex reassignment surgery.** Recently, psychosocial treatments to directly alter mistaken gender identity itself have been attempted in a few cases.

SEX REASSIGNMENT SURGERY

To qualify for surgery at a reputable clinic, individuals must live in the opposite-sex role for 18 months to 2 years so they can be sure they want to change sex. They also must be stable psychologically, financially, and socially. In male-to-female candidates, hormones are administered to promote *gynecomastia* (the growth of breasts) and the development of other secondary sex characteristics. Facial hair is typically removed through electrolysis. If the individual is satisfied with the events of the trial period, the genitals are removed and a vagina is constructed.

For female-to-male transsexuals, an artificial penis is typically constructed through plastic surgery, using sections of skin and muscle from elsewhere in the body, such as the

Physician Renee Richards played competitive tennis when she was a man, Richard Raskin, and after sex-reassignment surgery.

thigh. Breasts are surgically removed. Genital surgery is a more difficult and complex in biological females.

Estimates of transsexuals' satisfaction with surgery indicate predominantly successful adjustment (approximately 75% improved) among those who could be reached for follow-ups, with female-to-male conversions adjusting better than male-to-female (Bancroft, 1989; R. Blanchard & Steiner, 1992; Bodlund & Kullgren, 1996; R. Green & Fleming, 1990; Kuiper & Cohen-Kettenis, 1988). However, many people were lost to follow-up. Approximately 7% of sex reassignment cases later regret surgery (Bancroft, 1989; Lundstrom, Pauly, & Walinder, 1984). This is unfortunate, because the surgery is irreversible. Nevertheless, surgery has made life worth living for some people who suffered the effects of existing in what they felt to be the wrong body.

Psychosocial Treatment

In some clinics, therapists attempt to change gender identity itself before considering surgery. Most adult clients cannot conceive of changing their basic identity. However, some individuals request psychosocial treatment prior to embarking on a treatment course leading to surgery, usually because they are in great psychological distress or because surgery is immediately unavailable. The first successful effort to change gender identity was reported from our sexuality clinic (Barlow, Reynolds, & Agras, 1973). Joe, described earlier, was extremely depressed and suicidal; because surgery was not possible at his age without parental consent, which was not forthcoming, he agreed to a course of psychosocial treatment.

Joe's greatest difficulty was the ridicule and scorn heaped on him for his extremely effeminate gestures. We developed a behavioral rating scale for gender-specific motor behavior (Barlow et al., 1979; J. G. Beck & Barlow, 1984) to help Joe identify the precise ways he sat, stood, and walked that were stereotypically masculine or feminine. Through behavioral rehearsal and modeling, we taught him to act in a more typically masculine manner when he so chose. Very soon he reported enormous satisfaction in avoiding ridicule by simply choosing to behave differently in some situations. What followed was more extensive role playing and rehearsal for social skills as he learned to make better eye contact and converse more positively and confidently. After this phase of therapy he was better adjusted, but he still felt he was really a woman and he was strongly sexually attracted to males.

During the next phase, a female therapist worked directly on his fantasies in an intense, almost hypnotic way, encouraging him to imagine himself in sexual situations with a woman and to generate more characteristically masculine fantasies as he went about his day-to-day business. After several months of intensive training, Joe's gender identity began to change, slowly at first and then more rapidly. At the end of this phase, much to his delight, he reported that he now felt like a 17-year-old boy in addition to behaving like one, although he was still sexually attracted to males.

Because he expressed a strong desire to become sexually attracted to females, procedures were implemented to alter his patterns of sexual arousal, and at a 5-year follow-up Joe had made a very successful adjustment.

Two additional cases were treated in a similar fashion (Barlow, Abel, & Blanchard, 1979) and also resulted in altered gender identity. These two individuals, who were somewhat older than Joe, wished to retain their homosexual arousal patterns, and they were assisted in adjusting to a standard homosexual life-style without the burden of mistaken gender identity. Similar efforts to treat gender identity disturbance in prepubescent boys have been successful in a larger number of cases with follow-ups of 4 years or more (Rekers, Kilgus, & Rosen, 1990).

Sexual Dysfunctions: Clinical Descriptions

Before describing **sexual dysfunctions,** we should note that the problems that arise in the context of sexual interactions may occur in both heterosexual and homosexual relationships. Inability to become aroused or reach orgasm seem to be as common in homosexual as in heterosexual relationships, but we discuss them in the context of heterosexual relationships, which are the majority of cases we see in our clinic. The three stages of the sexual response cycle—desire, arousal, and orgasm (see Figure 10.3)—are each associated with specific sexual dysfunctions. In addition, pain can become associated with sexual functioning, which leads to additional dysfunctions.

An overview of the DSM-IV categories of the sexual dysfunctions we'll examine is in Table 10.4. As you can see, both males and females can experience parallel versions of most disorders, which take on specific forms determined by anatomy and other gender-specific characteristics. However, two disorders are sex specific: Premature ejaculation obviously occurs only in males, and vaginismus, painful contractions of the vagina during attempted penetration, appears only in females. Sexual dysfunctions can be either *lifelong* or *acquired.* "Lifelong" refers to a chronic condition that is present during a person's entire sexual life; "acquired" refers to a disorder that begins after sexual activity has been relatively normal. In addition, disorders can either be *generalized*, occurring every time the individual attempts sex, or they can be *situational*, occurring only with some partners or at certain times, but not with other partners or at other times. Finally, sexual dysfunctions are further specified as (a) due to psychological factors or (b) due to psychological factors combined with a general medical condition. The latter specification occurs when there is a demonstrable vascular, hormonal, or associated physical condition that is known to contribute to the sexual dysfunction.

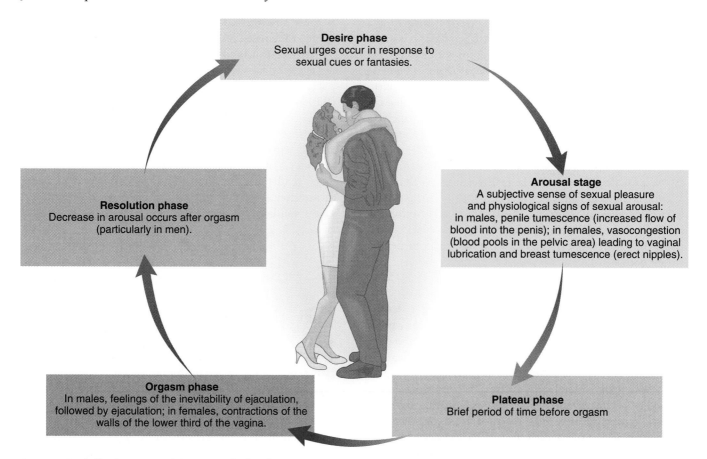

figure 10.3   The human sexual response cycle (based on Kaplan, 1979, and Masters & Johnson, 1966).

table 10.4   Categories of Sexual Dysfunction Among Men and Women

	Sexual Dysfunction	
Type of Disorder	*Men*	*Women*
Desire	Hypoactive sexual desire disorder (little or no desire to have sex)	Hypoactive sexual desire disorder (little or no desire to have sex)
	Sexual aversion disorder (aversion to and avoidance of sex)	Sexual aversion disorder (aversion to and avoidance of sex)
Arousal	Male erectile disorder (difficulty attaining or maintaining erections)	Female sexual arousal disorder (difficulty attaining or maintaining lubrication or swelling response)
Orgasm	Inhibited male orgasm	Inhibited female orgasm
	Premature ejaculation	
Pain	Dyspareunia (pain associated with sexual activity)	Dyspareunia (pain associated with sexual activity)
		Vaginismus (muscle spasms in the vagina that interfere with penetration)

Source: Wincze & Carey, 1991

Sexual Desire Disorders

HYPOACTIVE SEXUAL DESIRE DISORDER

A person with **hypoactive sexual desire disorder** has no interest in any type of sexual activity. It is very difficult to as-

sess low sexual desire, and a great deal of clinical judgment is required (Leiblum & Rosen, 1988; Segraves & Althof, 1998; Wincze & Barlow, 1997a, 1997b). You might gauge it by frequency of sexual activity—say, less than twice a month for a married couple. Or you might determine whether someone ever *thinks* about sex or has sexual fantasies. Then there is the person who has sex twice a week but really doesn't want to and thinks about it only because "his wife is on his case to live up to his end of the marriage and have sex more often." This individual might, in fact, have no desire whatsoever, despite having frequent sex. Consider the following cases.

Judy and Ira
A Loving Marriage?

Judy, a married woman in her late 20s, reached a clinic staff member on the phone and reported that she thought her husband, Ira, was having an affair and that she was very upset about it. The reason for her assumptions? He had demonstrated no interest whatsoever in sex during the past 3 years, and they had not had sex at all for 9 months. However, Ira was willing to come into the clinic.

When he was interviewed, it became clear that Ira was not having an affair. In fact, he did not masturbate and hardly ever thought about sex. He noted that he loved his wife very much but that he had not been concerned about the issue until she raised it because he had too many other things to think about and he assumed they would eventually get back to having sex. He now realized that his wife was quite distressed about the situation, particularly because they were thinking about having children.

Although Ira did not have extensive sexual experience, he had engaged in several very erotic relationships before his marriage, which Judy knew. During a separate interview, Ira confided that during his premarital affairs he would get a "hard on" just thinking about his lovers, each of whom was quite promiscuous. His wife, in contrast, was a pillar of the community and otherwise very unlike these women, although attractive. Because he did not become aroused by thinking about his wife, he did not initiate sex.

Mr. and Mrs. C.
Getting Started

Mrs. C., a 31-year-old, very successful businesswoman, was married to a 32-year-old lawyer. They had two children, ages 2 and 5, and had been married 8 years when they entered therapy. The presenting problem was Mrs. C.'s lack of sexual desire. Mr. and Mrs. C. were interviewed separately during the initial assessment and both professed attraction to and love for their partner. Mrs. C. reported that she could enjoy sex once she got involved and almost always was orgasmic. The problem was her total lack of desire to get involved in the first place. She avoided her husband's sexual advances and looked on his affection and romanticism with great skepticism and, usually, anger and tears.

Mrs. C. was raised in an upper-middle-class family that was supportive and loving. However, from age 6 to age 12 she had been repeatedly pressured into sexual activity by a male cousin who was 5 years her senior. This sexual activity was always initiated by the cousin, always against her

will. She did not tell her parents because she felt guilty, as the boy did not use physical force to make her comply. It appeared that romantic advances by Mr. C. triggered memories of abuse by her cousin.

The treatment of Mr. and Mrs. C. is discussed later in the chapter.

Problems of hypoactive sexual desire disorder used to be presented as marital rather than sexual difficulties. Since the recognition in the late 1980s of hypoactive sexual desire as a distinct disorder, however, more and more couples present to sex therapy clinics with one of the partners reporting this problem (Hawton, 1995; Leiblum & Rosen, 1988). Best estimates suggest that something over 50% of patients who come to sexuality clinics for help complain of hypoactive sexual desire (H. S. Kaplan, 1979; LoPiccolo & Friedman, 1988). In many clinics it is the most frequent presenting complaint of women; men present more often with erectile dysfunction (Hawton, 1995). Although no community studies have been reported recently, earlier studies (for example, Frank, Anderson, & Rubinstein, 1978) suggested that approximately 25% of individuals might have hypoactive sexual desire. Schreiner-Engel and Schiavi (1986) noted that their patients with the disorder rarely have sexual fantasies, seldom masturbate (35% of the women and 52% of the men never masturbate and most of the rest masturbate no more than once a month), and attempt intercourse once a month or less.

SEXUAL AVERSION DISORDER

On a continuum with hypoactive sexual desire disorder is **sexual aversion disorder,** in which even the thought of sex or a brief casual touch may evoke fear, panic, or disgust (H. S. Kaplan, 1987). In some cases, the principal problem might actually be panic disorder (see Chapter 5), in which the fear or alarm response is associated with the physical sensations of sex. In other cases, sexual acts and fantasies may trigger traumatic images or memories similar to but perhaps not as severe as those experienced by people with posttraumatic stress disorder (see Chapter 5). Consider the following case from one of our clinics.

Lisa
The Terror of Sex

Lisa was 36, had been married for 3 years, and was a full-time student working on an associate degree. She had been married once before. Lisa reported that sexual problems had begun 9 months earlier. She complained of poor lubrication during intercourse and of having "anxiety attacks" during sex. She had not attempted intercourse in 2 months and had tried only intermittently during the past 9 months. Despite their sexual difficulties, Lisa had a loving and close relationship with her husband. She could not remember precisely what happened 9 months ago except that she had been under a great deal of stress and experienced an anxiety attack during sex. Even her husband's touch was becoming increasingly intolerable because she was afraid it might bring on the scary feelings again. Her primary fear was of having a heart attack and dying during sex.

Among male patients presenting for sexual aversion disorder, 10% experienced panic attacks during attempted sexual activity. H. S. Kaplan (1987) reports that 25% of 106 patients presenting with sexual aversion disorder also met criteria for panic disorder. In such cases, treating the panic may be a necessary first step.

Sexual Arousal Disorders

Disorders of arousal are called **male erectile disorder** and **female sexual arousal disorder.** The problem here is not desire. Many individuals with arousal disorders have frequent sexual urges and fantasies and a strong desire to have sex. Their problem is in becoming aroused: A male has difficulty achieving or maintaining an erection, and a female cannot achieve or maintain adequate lubrication (Segraves & Althof, 1998; Wincze & Barlow, 1997a, 1997b). Consider the following case of male erectile disorder.

Bill

Long Marriage, New Problem

Bill, a 58-year-old white man, was referred to our clinic by his urologist. He was a retired accountant who had been married for 29 years to his 57-year-old wife, a retired nutritionist. They had no children. For the past several years, Bill had had difficulties obtaining and maintaining an erection. He reported a rather rigid routine he and his wife had developed to deal with the problem. They scheduled sex for Sunday mornings. However, Bill had to do a number of chores first, including letting the dog out, washing the dishes, and shaving. The couple's current behavior consisted of mutual hand stimulation. Bill was "not allowed" to attempt insertion until after his wife had climaxed. Bill's wife was adamant that she was not going to change her sexual behavior and "become a whore," as she put it. This included refusing to try K–Y jelly as a lubricant appropriate to her postmenopausal decrease in lubrication. She described their behavior as "lesbian sex."

Bill and his wife agreed that despite marital problems over the years, they had always maintained a good sexual relationship until the onset of the current problem and that sex had kept them together during their earlier difficulties. Useful information was obtained in separate interviews. Bill masturbated on Saturday night in an attempt to control his erection the following morning; his wife was unaware of this. In addition, he quickly and easily achieved a full erection when viewing erotica in the privacy of the sex-

uality clinic laboratory (surprising the assessor). Bill's wife privately acknowledged being very angry at her husband for an affair that he had had 20 years earlier.

At the final session, three specific recommendations were made: for Bill to cease masturbating the evening before sex, for the couple to use a lubricant, and for them to delay the morning routine until after they had had sexual relations. The couple called back 1 month later to report that their sexual activity was much improved.

The old and somewhat pejorative terms for male erectile disorder and female arousal disorder are *impotence* and *frigidity,* but these are imprecise labels that do not specify the specific phase of the sexual response where the problems are localized. The man typically feels more impaired by his problem than the woman does by her own. Inability to achieve and maintain an erection makes intercourse difficult or impossible. Women who are unable to achieve vaginal lubrication, however, may be able to compensate by using a commercial lubricant (Schover & Jensen, 1988). In women, arousal and lubrication may decrease at any time but, as in men, such problems tend to accompany ageing (Morokoff, 1993). In addition, until relatively recently, some women were not as concerned as men about experiencing intense pleasure during sex as long as they could consummate the act; this is generally no longer the case (Morokoff, 1993; Wincze & Carey, 1991). It is unusual for a man to be completely unable to achieve an erection. More typical is a situation like Bill's, where full erections are possible during masturbation and partial erections during attempted intercourse, but with insufficient rigidity to allow penetration.

Before we describe the prevalence of arousal disorders and other sexual dysfunctions, we need to note an important study by Ellen Frank and her colleagues, who carefully interviewed 100 well-educated, happily married couples who were *not* seeking treatment (Frank et al., 1978). More than 80% of these couples reported that their marital and sexual relations were happy and satisfying. Surprisingly, 40% of the men reported occasional erectile and ejaculatory difficulties, and 63% of the women reported occasional dysfunctions of arousal or orgasm. But the crucial finding was that these dysfunctions did not detract from the respondents' overall sexual satisfaction. This study indicates that sexual satisfaction and occasional sexual dysfunction are not mutually exclusive categories. In the context of a healthy relationship, occasional or partial sexual dysfunctions are easily accommodated.

The prevalence of erectile dysfunction is startlingly high, and increases with age. Data from a recent study (shown in Figure 10.4) suggest that at least some impairment is present in approximately 40% of men in their 40s and 70% of men in their 70s (Feldman et al., 1994; Kim & Lipshultz, 1997). Male erectile disorder is easily the most common problem for which men seek help, accounting for 50% or more of the men referred to specialists for sexual problems (Hawton, 1995). The prevalence of female arousal disorders is somewhat more difficult to estimate because

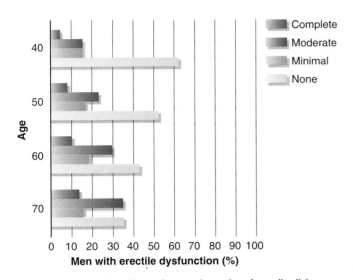

figure 10.4 Estimated prevalence and severity of erectile disfunction in a sample of 1290 men between 40 and 70 years of age (adapted from Feldman et al., 1994)

interested. She had progressed from initiating sex occasionally early in their marriage to almost never doing so, except for an occasional spurt every 6 months or so, when she would initiate two or three times in a week. But Greta noted that it was the physical closeness she wanted most during these times rather than sexual pleasure. Further inquiry revealed that she did, in fact, become sexually aroused on occasion but had never in her life reached orgasm, even during several attempts at masturbation mostly before her marriage. Both Greta and Will reported that the sexual problem was a concern to them because everything else about their marriage was very positive.

Greta had been brought up in a strict but loving and supportive Catholic family that more or less ignored sexuality. The parents were always very careful not to display their affections in front of Greta and when her mother caught Greta touching her genital area, she was cautioned rather severely to avoid that kind of activity.

We discuss Greta and Will's treatment later.

many women still do not consider absence of arousal to be a problem, let alone a disorder. In community studies, disorders of arousal in women have been estimated to occur in 11% (Levine & Yost, 1976) to 48% of the population (Frank et al., 1978). Because disorders of desire, arousal, and orgasm often overlap, it is difficult to estimate precisely how many women with specific arousal disorders present to sex clinics (Segraves & Althof, 1998; Wincze & Carey, 1991).

Orgasm Disorders

INHIBITED ORGASM

An inability to achieve an orgasm despite adequate sexual desire and arousal is commonly seen in women (Stock, 1993; Wincze & Barlow, 1997a, 1997b) but **inhibited orgasm** is relatively rare in men. Consider the following case.

Greta and Will
Loving Disunion

Greta, a teacher, and Will, an engineer, were a very attractive couple who came together to the first interview and entered the office clearly showing affection for each other. They had been married for 5 years and were in their late 20s. When asked about the problems that had brought them to the office, Greta quickly reported that she didn't think she had ever had an orgasm—"didn't think" because she wasn't really sure what an orgasm was! She loved Will very much and on occasion would initiate lovemaking, although with decreased frequency over the past several years.

Will certainly didn't think Greta was reaching orgasm. In any case, he reported, they were clearly going in "different directions" sexually, in that Greta was less and less

An inability to reach orgasm is the most common complaint among women who seek therapy for sexual problems. In community samples, estimates from a number of studies suggest that 5% to 10% of women may experience **female orgasmic disorder** and *never* or *almost never* reach orgasm (Wincze & Carey, 1991). This distinction is important because only approximately 50% of all women experience reasonably regular orgasms during sexual intercourse (Lo-Piccolo & Stock, 1987). Therefore, approximately 50% do not achieve orgasm with every sexual encounter, unlike most men, who tend to experience orgasm more consistently. Thus, the "never or almost never" inquiry is important, along with establishing the extent of the couple's distress, in diagnosing orgasmic dysfunction. Community samples also suggest that somewhere between 1% and 10% of men have delayed orgasms or none at all during sexual interactions, although they seldom seek treatment for this condition. It is quite possible that in many cases some men reach climax through alternative forms of stimulation and that **male orgasmic disorder** is accommodated by the couple.

Some men who are unable to ejaculate with their partners can obtain an erection and ejaculate during masturbation. In the most usual pattern ejaculation is delayed; this is called *retarded ejaculation*. Occasionally men suffer from *retrograde ejaculation*, in which ejaculatory fluids travel backward into the bladder rather than forward. This phenomenon is almost always due to the effects of certain drugs or a coexisting medical condition and should not be confused with male orgasmic disorder.

PREMATURE EJACULATION

A far more common male orgasmic disorder is **premature ejaculation**, ejaculation that occurs well before the man and his partner wish it to (Weiner, 1996). A rather typical case follows.

Gary
Running Scared

Gary, a 31-year-old salesman, engaged in sexual activity with his wife three or four times a month. He noted that he would have liked to have had sex more often but his very busy schedule kept him working about 80 hours a week. His primary difficulty was an inability to control the timing of his ejaculation. Approximately 70% to 80% of the time he ejaculated within seconds of penetration. This pattern had been constant since he met his wife approximately 13 years earlier. Previous experience with other women, although limited, was not characterized by premature ejaculation. In an attempt to delay his ejaculation, Gary distracted himself by thinking of nonsexual things (scores of ball games or work-related issues) and sometimes attempted sex soon after a previous attempt because he seemed not to climax as quickly under these circumstances. Gary reported masturbating very seldom (three or four times a year at most). When he did masturbate, he usually attempted to reach orgasm quickly, a habit he acquired during his teens to avoid being caught by a family member.

One of his greatest concerns was that he was not pleasing his wife, and under no circumstances did he want her told that he was seeking treatment. Further inquiry revealed that he made many extravagant purchases at his wife's request, even though it strained their finances, since he wished to please her. He felt that if they had met recently his wife probably would not even accept a date with him since he had lost much of his hair and she had lost weight and was more attractive than she used to be.

Treatment for Gary and his wife is described shortly.

The frequency of premature ejaculation seems to be quite high, with a prevalence of 36% to 38% in community samples (Spector & Carey, 1990). This difficulty is also a presenting complaint in as many as 60% of men who seek treatment (Malatesta & Adams, 1984). (Many men also present with erectile dysfunction as the major problem.) In one clinic, premature ejaculation was the principal complaint of 16% of men seeking treatment (Hawton, 1995).

It is very difficult to define "premature." An adequate length of time before ejaculation varies from individual to individual. Some surveys indicate that men who complain of premature ejaculation typically climax no more than 1 or 2 minutes after penetration, compared with 7 to 10 minutes in individuals without this complaint (Strassberg, Kelly, Carroll, & Kircher, 1987). A perception of lack of control over orgasm, however, may be the more important psychological determinant of this complaint.

Although occasional early ejaculation is perfectly normal, serious and consistent premature ejaculation appears to occur primarily in young men, particularly inexperienced ones, and to decline with age (Masters & Johnson, 1970). The contrast in ages between men with erectile disorder and those complaining of premature ejaculation is striking.

Sexual Pain Disorders

In the **sexual pain disorders,** intercourse is associated with marked pain. For some men and women, sexual desire is present, and arousal and orgasm are easily attained, but the pain of intercourse is so severe that sexual behavior is disrupted. This subtype is named **dyspareunia,** which, in its original Greek, means "unhappily mated as bedfellows" (Wincze & Carey, 1991). Obviously this is not a very accurate or descriptive name, but it has been used for decades and is accepted. Dyspareunia is diagnosed only if no medical reasons for pain can be found. It can be very tricky to make this assessment. Several years ago a patient described having sharp pains in his head like a migraine headache that began during ejaculation and lasted for several minutes. This man, in his 50s at the time, had had a healthy sexual relationship with his wife until a severe fall approximately 2 years earlier that left him partially disabled and with a severe limp. The pain during ejaculation developed shortly thereafter. Extensive medical examination from a number of specialists revealed no physical reason for the pain. Thus, he met the criteria for dyspareunia, and psychosocial interventions were administered—in this case, without benefit. He subsequently engaged in manual stimulation of his wife and, occasionally, intercourse, but he avoided ejaculation.

Dyspareunia is rarely seen in clinics, with estimates ranging from 1% to 5% of men (Bancroft, 1989; Spector & Carey, 1990; Wincze & Carey, 1991) and a more substantial 10% to 15% of women (Hawton, 1995; Rosen & Leiblum, 1995). Community samples provide estimates ranging from 8% (Schover, 1981) to 33.5% (Glatt, Zinner, & McCormack, 1990). Glatt and colleagues report that many women experience pain occasionally, but it either resolves or is not sufficient to motivate them to seek treatment.

In the commoner **vaginismus,** the pelvic muscles in the outer third of the vagina undergo involuntary spasms when intercourse is attempted (Bancroft, 1997). The spasm reaction of vaginismus may occur during any attempted penetration, including a gynecological exam or insertion of a tampon (J. Beck, 1993). Women report sensations of "ripping, burning, or tearing during attempted intercourse" (J. Beck, 1993, p. 384). Consider the following case.

Jill
No Way In

Jill was referred to our clinic by another therapist because she had not consummated her marriage of 1 year. At 23 years of age, she was an attractive and loving wife who managed a motel while her husband worked as an accountant. Despite numerous attempts in a variety of positions to engage in intercourse, Jill's severe vaginal spasms prevented penetration of any kind. Jill was also unable to use tampons. With great reluctance, she submitted to gynecological exams at infrequent intervals. Sexual behavior with her husband consisted of mutual masturbation or, on occasion, Jill had him rub his penis against her breasts to the point of ejaculation. She refused to engage in oral sex.

Jill, a very anxious young woman, came from a family in which sexual matters were seldom discussed and sexual contact between the parents had ceased some years before. Although she enjoyed petting, Jill's general attitude was that intercourse was disgusting. Furthermore, she expressed some fears of becoming pregnant despite taking adequate contraceptive measures. She also thought that she would perform poorly when she did engage in intercourse, therefore embarrassing herself with her new husband.

Although we have no data on the prevalence of vaginismus in community samples, best estimates are that it affects well over 5% of women who seek treatment in North America and 10% to 15% in Britain (J. Beck, 1993; Hawton, 1995). The prevalence of this condition in cultures with very conservative views of sexuality, such as Ireland, may be much higher—as high as 42% to 55% in at least two clinic samples (Barnes, Bowman, & Cullen, 1984; O'Sullivan, 1979). (Of course, results from any one clinic may not be applicable even to other clinics, let alone to the population of Ireland.)

■ concept check 10.1

Diagnose the following sexual and gender identity disorders.

1. Gina has always dressed in masculine clothing and prefers male friends. She identifies with males and wishes to be treated as one. She binds her breasts to hide them and feels trapped in the wrong body. She is considering surgery to become her "true" self. She is attracted only to women. Her situation indicates (a) gender identity disorder, (b) fetishism, (c) sexual aversion disorder, or (d) transvestism. _____

2. Kay is in a serious relationship and is quite content. Lately, though, the thought of her boyfriend's touch disgusts her. Kay has no idea what is causing this. She could be suffering from (a) panic disorder, (b) sexual arousal disorder, (c) sexual aversion disorder, or (d) both a and b.

_____

3. After Bob was injured playing football, he started having pain in his arm during sex. All medical reasons for the pain have been ruled out. Bob is probably displaying (a) dyspareunia, (b) vaginismus, (c) penile strain gauge, or (d) male orgasmic disorder. _____

4. Kelly has no real desire for sex. She has sex only because she feels that otherwise her husband may leave her. Kelly suffers from (a) sexual aversion disorder, (b) hypoactive sexual desire, (c) boredom, or (d) female sexual arousal disorder. _____

✥ Assessing Sexual Behavior

There are three major aspects to the assessment of sexual behavior:

1. *interviewing,* usually supported by numerous questionnaires because patients may provide more information on paper than in a verbal interview;
2. *a thorough medical evaluation,* to rule out the variety of medical conditions that can contribute to sexual problems; and
3. *psychophysiological assessment,* to directly measure the physiological aspects of sexual arousal.

Interviews

All clinicians who conduct interviews for sexual problems should be aware of several useful assumptions (Wincze & Barlow, 1997a, 1997b; Wincze & Carey, 1991). For example, they must demonstrate to the patient through their actions and interviewing style that they are perfectly comfortable talking about these issues. Since many patients do not know the various clinical terms professionals use to describe the sexual response cycle and various aspects of sexual behavior, clinicians must always be prepared to use the vernacular of the patient, realizing also that idiomatic terms vary from person to person.

The following are examples of the questions asked in semistructured interviews in our sexuality clinic.

> How would you describe your current interest in sex?
> Do you avoid engaging in sexual behavior with a partner?
> Do you have sexual fantasies?
> How often do you currently masturbate?
> How frequently do you engage in sexual intercourse?
> How often do you engage in mutual caressing or cuddling without intercourse?
> Have you ever been sexually abused, raped, or had a very negative experience associated with sex?
> Do you have problems attaining an erection? [or] Do you have problems achieving or maintaining vaginal lubrication?
> Do you ever have problems reaching orgasm?
> Do you ever experience pain associated with sexual activity?

A clinician must be very careful to ask these questions in a manner that puts the patient at ease. During an interview lasting approximately 2 hours, the clinician also covers nonsexual relationship issues and physical health, and screens for the presence of additional psychological disorders. When possible, the partner is interviewed concurrently.

Patients may volunteer in writing information that they are not ready to talk about, so they are usually given a vari-

John Wincze (left) and Michael Carey (right) developed new approaches for treating sexual dysfunction.

ety of questionnaires that help reveal sexual activity and attitudes toward sexuality.

Medical Examination

Any human sexuality clinician routinely inquires about medical conditions that impact sexual functioning. A variety of drugs, including some that are commonly prescribed for hypertension, anxiety, and depression often disrupt sexual arousal and functioning. Recent surgery or concurrent medical conditions must be evaluated for their impact on sexual functioning; often the surgeon or treating physician will not have described possible side effects, or the patient may not have told the physician that a medical procedure or drug has affected sexual functioning. Most males with specific sexual dysfunctions such as erectile disorder have already visited a urologist—a physician specializing in disorders of the genitals, bladder, and associated structures—before coming to a sexuality clinic, and, many females already have visited a gynecologist. These specialists may check levels of sexual hormones necessary for adequate sexual functioning and, in the case of males, evaluate vascular functioning necessary for an erectile response.

Psychophysiological Assessment

Many clinicians assess the ability of individuals to become sexually aroused under a variety of conditions by taking psychophysiological measurements while the patient is either awake or asleep. In men, penile erection is measured directly, using, for example, a *penile strain gauge* developed in our clinic (Barlow, Becker, Leitenberg, & Agras, 1970). As the penis expands, the strain gauge picks up the changes and records them on a polygraph. It is interesting to note that subjects are often not aware of these more objective measures of their arousal; their awareness differs as a function of the type of problem they have.

The comparable device for women is a *vaginal photoplethysmograph*, developed by James Geer and his associates (Geer, Morokoff, & Greenwood, 1974). This device, which is smaller than a tampon, is inserted by the woman into her vagina. A light source at the tip of the instrument and two light-sensitive photoreceptors on the sides of the instrument measure the amount of light reflected back from the vaginal walls. Because blood flows to the vaginal walls during arousal, the amount of light passing through them decreases with increasing arousal. Ray Rosen and Gayle Beck (1988) have described these measures in great detail.

Typically in our clinic, individuals undergoing physiological assessment view an erotic videotape for 2 to 5 minutes or, on occasion, listen to an erotic audiotape (Bach, Brown, & Barlow, in press). The patient's sexual responsivity during this time is assessed psychophysiologically. Patients also report subjectively on the amount of sexual arousal they experience. This assessment allows the clinician to observe carefully the conditions under which arousal is possible for the patient. For example, many individuals with psychologically based sexual dysfunctions may achieve strong arousal in a laboratory but be unable to become aroused with a partner (Bancroft, 1997; Sakheim, Barlow, Abrahamson, & Beck, 1987).

Because erections may occur during REM sleep in physically healthy men, psychophysiological measurement of *nocturnal penile tumescence (NPT)* was in the past used frequently to determine a man's ability to obtain normal erectile response. If he could attain normal erections while he was asleep, the reasoning went, then the causes of his dysfunction were psychological. An inexpensive way to monitor nocturnal erections is for the clinician to provide a simple "snap gauge" that the patient fastens around his penis each night before he goes to sleep. If the snap gauge has come undone he has probably had a nocturnal erection. But this is a crude and often inaccurate screening device that should never supplant medical and psychological evaluation (Carey, Wincze, & Meisler, 1993; Mohr & Beutler, 1990). Finally, we now know that lack of NPT could also be due to psy-

Ray Rosen (left) and Gayle Beck (right) pioneered research on the psychophysiological measurement of sexual arousal.

chological problems, such as depression, or to a variety of medical difficulties that have nothing to do with physiological problems preventing erections.

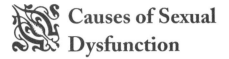

Causes of Sexual Dysfunction

Individual sexual dysfunctions seldom present in isolation. Usually a patient referred to a sexuality clinic complains of a wide assortment of sexual problems, although one may be of most concern (Hawton, 1995; Wincze & Barlow, 1997a, 1997b). A 45-year-old man recently referred to our clinic had been free of problems until 10 years earlier, when he was under a great deal of pressure at work and was preparing to take a major career-related licensing examination. He began experiencing erectile dysfunction about 50% of the time, a condition that had now progressed to approximately 80% of the time. In addition, he reported that he had no control over ejaculation, often ejaculating prior to penetration with only a semierect penis. Over the past 5 years, he had lost most interest in sex and was coming to treatment only at his wife's insistence. Thus, this man suffered simultaneously from erectile dysfunction, premature ejaculation, and low sexual desire. Because of the frequency of such combinations, we will discuss the causes of various sexual dysfunctions together, reviewing briefly the biological, psychological, and social contributions and specifying causal factors thought to be associated exclusively and specifically with one or another dysfunction.

Biological Contributions

A number of physical and medical conditions contribute to sexual dysfunction (Carey et al., 1993; Kim & Lipshultz, 1997). Although this is not surprising, most patients and even many health professionals are unfortunately unaware of the connection.

Neurological diseases and other conditions that affect the nervous system, such as diabetes and kidney disease, may directly interfere with sexual functioning by reducing sensitivity in the genital area, and are a common cause of erectile dysfunction in males (Schover & Jensen, 1988; Wincze & Barlow, 1997a, 1997b), as is *vascular disease.* The two relevant vascular problems are *arterial insufficiency* (constricted arteries), which makes it difficult for blood to reach the penis, and *venous leakage* (blood flows out too quickly for an erection to be maintained) (Carey et al., 1993).

Chronic illness can also indirectly affect sexual functioning. For example, it is not uncommon for individuals who have had heart attacks to be wary of the physical exercise involved in sexual activity to the point of preoccupation. They often become unable to achieve arousal despite being assured by their physicians that sexual activity is safe for them (A. J. Cooper, 1988).

A major physical cause of sexual dysfunction is *prescription medication.* Antihypertensive medications, in the class known as beta blockers, including propranolol, may contribute to sexual dysfunction. Tricyclic antidepressant medications and other antidepressant and anti-anxiety drugs may also interfere with sexual desire and arousal in both men and women (Segraves & Althof, 1998). A number of these drugs, particularly the psychoactive drugs, may dampen sexual desire and arousal by altering levels of certain subtypes of serotonin in the brain. Sexual dysfunction is the most widespread side effect of SSRIs, such as Prozac, specifically low sexual desire and arousal difficulties. Informal consensus estimates suggest that as many as 75% of individuals who take these medications experience some degree of sexual dysfunction. Some people are aware that *alcohol* suppresses sexual arousal, but they may not know that most *other drugs of abuse* such as cocaine and heroin also produce widespread sexual dysfunction in frequent users and abusers, both male and female. Cocores, Miller, Pottash, and Gold (1988) and Macdonald, Waldorf, Reinarman, and Murphy (1988) reported that more than 60% of a large number of cocaine users had a sexual dysfunction. In the Cocores group's study, some of the patients also abused alcohol.

There is also the misconception that alcohol facilitates sexual arousal and behavior. What actually happens is that alcohol at low and moderate levels reduces social inhibitions so that people feel more like having sex (and perhaps more willing to request it) (Crowe & George, 1989). In fact, people's expectation that arousal will increase when they drink alcohol may have more effect than any disinhibition that does occur because of the effects of the alcohol itself, at least at low doses (Roehrich & Kinder, 1991; Wilson, 1977). Physically, alcohol is a central nervous system *suppressant,* and for men to achieve erection and women to achieve lu-

> "In the process of becoming aroused, all of a sudden it would be over. And I didn't understand that at all. So then everything is coupled with a bunch of depressing thoughts, like fear of failure. And so I begin to say, is this happening to me because I'm afraid I'm going to fail, and I don't want to be embarrassed by that? It's really very difficult to deal with emotionally. . . . The worse I feel about myself, the slower I am sexually, and sometimes I describe it as the fear of losing masculinity."

brication is much more difficult when the central nervous system is suppressed (Schiavi, 1990). Chronic alcohol abuse may cause permanent neurological damage and may virtually eliminate the sexual response cycle. Such abuse may lead to liver and testicular damage, resulting in decreased testosterone levels and concomitant decreases in sexual desire and arousal. This dual effect of alcohol (social disinhibition and physical suppression) has been recognized since the time of Shakespeare: "[I]t provokes the desire, but it takes away the performance; therefore much drink may be said to be an equivocator with lechery: it makes him and it mars him; it sets him on and it takes him off; it persuades him and disheartens him; makes him stand to and not stand to; in conclusion, equivocates him in a sleep, and giving him the lie, leaves him" (*Macbeth*, II, iii, 29).

Chronic alcoholism can also cause fertility problems in both men and women. Fahrner (1987) examined the prevalence of sexual dysfunction among male alcoholics and found that 75% had erectile dysfunction, low sexual desire, and premature or delayed ejaculation.

Many people report that cocaine or marijuana enhances sexual pleasure. Although little is known about the effects of marijuana across the wide range of use, it is unlikely that chemical effects increase pleasure. Rather, in those individuals who report some enhancement of sexual pleasure (and many don't), the effect may be psychological in that their attention is focused more completely and fully on sensory stimulation (Buffum, 1982), a factor that seems to be an important part of healthy sexual functioning. If so, imagery and attentional focus can be enhanced with nondrug procedures such as meditation, in which a person practices concentrating on something with as few distractions as possible.

Psychological Contributions

For years, most sex researchers and therapists thought the principal cause of sexual dysfunctions was anxiety, pure and simple (e.g., H. S. Kaplan, 1979; Masters & Johnson, 1970). While evaluating the role of anxiety and sexual functioning in our own laboratory, we discovered that it was not all that simple. In certain circumstances, anxiety *increases* sexual arousal (Barlow, Sackeim, & Beck, 1983). We designed an experiment in which young, sexually functional men viewed erotic films under three different conditions. In one condition we attempted to replicate the kinds of performance anxiety that males might experience during a sexual interaction. Prior to viewing an erotic film, all subjects were exposed to a harmless but somewhat painful electric shock to the forearm. During one condition subjects were told to relax and enjoy the film and that there was no chance of shock. This served as a control condition. In the second condition, subjects were told that there was a 60% chance that they would receive the shock at some time while they were watching the erotic film no matter what they did (noncontingent shock threat). In the third condition, most closely paralleling the types of performance anxiety that some individuals might experience, subjects were told that there was a

60% chance that they would receive a shock if they did not achieve the average level of erection achieved by the previous subjects (contingent shock threat). In fact, no shocks were delivered during the viewing of the erotic films in any of the conditions, although subjects really believed that they might be administered. The results, presented in Figure 10.5, indicate that the noncontingent shock threat condition *increased* sexual arousal compared with the no-shock threat control condition. However, in an even more surprising development, the contingent shock threat condition (in which subjects were told there was a 60% chance they would be shocked if they did not achieve adequate arousal) increased sexual response *even more significantly* than the no-shock threat control condition. Similar results for women were reported by Hoon, Wincze, and Hoon (1977), Palace (1995), and Palace and Gorzalka (1990), who developed slightly different experimental paradigms, using the vaginal photoplethysmograph.

These counterintuitive findings have some parallels outside the laboratory. In one unusual and startling report, Sarrel and Masters (1982) described the ability of men to perform sexually under threat of physical harm. These men, the victims of gang rape by women, reported later that they had been able to achieve erections and repeatedly engage in intercourse despite being constantly threatened with knives and other weapons if they failed. Certainly they experienced extreme levels of anxiety, and yet they reported that their sexual performance was not impaired.

If anxiety does not necessarily decrease sexual arousal and performance, what does? A partial answer is *distraction*. In one experiment, subjects were asked to listen to a narrative through earphones while they watched an erotic film, and told that they would later have to report on the narrative to make sure they were listening. Sexually functional males demonstrated significantly less arousal based on penile strain gauge measurements when they were distracted by the narrative than when they were not distracted (Abrahamson, Barlow, Sakheim, Beck, & Athanasiou, 1985). To any male who has tried to concentrate on baseball scores or some other nonsexual event to reduce unwanted arousal, this result will come as no surprise. Males with erectile dysfunction in whom physical disease processes had been ruled out reacted somewhat differently from functional men to both shock threat and distraction conditions. Anxiety induced by shock threat ("You'll be shocked if you don't get aroused") *did* seem to reduce sexual arousal in males who were dysfunctional. Remember that the reverse was true for the normally functioning males. By contrast, the kind of neutral distracting conditions present in the Abrahamson and colleagues (1985) experiment *did not* reduce arousal in those males who were dysfunctional. This discovery is puzzling.

Two other findings from different experiments are important. One revealed that patients with erectile dysfunction consistently *underreport* their actual levels of arousal; that is, at the same level of erectile response (as measured by the penile strain gauge), men who are dysfunctional report far less sexual arousal than do sexually functional men (Sakheim et al., 1987). This result seems to be true for dysfunctional

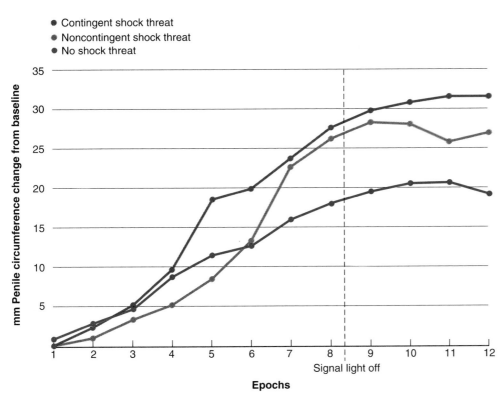

figure 10.5 Performance anxiety and sexual arousal in males. Shown here are the average changes in male sexual arousal (penile circumference change) during each of three conditions (from Barlow, Sakheim, & Beck, 1983). (*Note:* An epoch is a period of 10 seconds.)

also may distract themselves with negative thoughts, such as, "I'm going to make a fool of myself; I'll never be able to get aroused; she [or he] will think I'm stupid." We know that as arousal increases a person's attention focuses more intently and consistently. But the person who is focusing on negative thoughts will find it impossible to become sexually aroused.

People with normal sexual functioning react to a sexual situation very positively. They focus their attention on the erotic cues and do not become distracted. When they become aroused, they focus even more strongly on the sexual and erotic cues, allowing themselves to become more and more sexually aroused. The model presented in Figure 10.6 illustrates both functional and dysfunctional sexual arousal (Barlow, 1986; Barlow, Chorpita, & Turovsky, 1996; Sbrocco & Barlow, 1994). These experiments demonstrate that sexual arousal is strongly determined by psychological factors, particularly cognitive and emotional factors, that are powerful enough to determine whether blood flows to the appropriate areas of the body, such as the genitals, confirming once again the strong interaction of psychological and biological factors in most of our functioning.

We know little about the psychological (or biological) factors associated with premature ejaculation (Ertekin, Colakoglu, & Altay, 1995; Weiner, 1996). We do know that the condition is most prevalent in young men and that excessive physiological arousal in the sympathetic nervous system may lead to rapid ejaculation. These observations suggest that some men may have a naturally lower threshold for ejaculation; that is, they require less stimulation and arousal to ejaculate. Unfortunately, the psychological factor of anxiety also increases sympathetic arousal. Thus, when a man becomes anxiously aroused about ejaculating too quickly, his concern only makes the problem worse. We will return to the role of anxiety in sexual dysfunctions later.

women as well (Meston & Gorzalka, 1995; Morokoff & Heiman, 1980). Another finding showed that inducing positive or negative mood by playing joyful or sad music directly affected sexual arousal, at least in normals, with sad music decreasing sexual arousal (Mitchell, DiBartolo, Brown, & Barlow, 1998).

In summary, normally functioning men show increased sexual arousal during "performance demand" conditions, experience positive affect, are distracted by nonsexual stimuli, and have a pretty good idea of how aroused they are. Men with sexual problems such as erectile dysfunction show decreased arousal during performance demand, experience negative affect, are not distracted by nonsexual stimuli, and *do not* have an accurate sense of how aroused they are. This process seems to apply to most sexual dysfunctions which, you will remember, tend to occur together, but it is particularly applicable to sexual arousal disorders.

How do we interpret this complex series of experiments to account for sexual dysfunction from a psychological perspective? Basically, we have to break the concept of "performance anxiety" into several components. One component is *arousal*, another is *cognitive processes*, and third is *negative affect*.

When confronted with the possibility of having sexual relations, individuals who are dysfunctional tend to expect the worst and find the situation to be relatively negative and unpleasant. As far as possible, they avoid becoming aware of any sexual cues (and therefore are not aware of how aroused they are physically, thus underreporting their arousal). They

Social and Cultural Contributions

The model of sexual dysfunction displayed in Figure 10.6 helps explain why some individuals may be dysfunctional *at the present time* but not how they *became* that way in the first place. Although we do not know for sure why some people develop problems, many people learn early that sexuality can

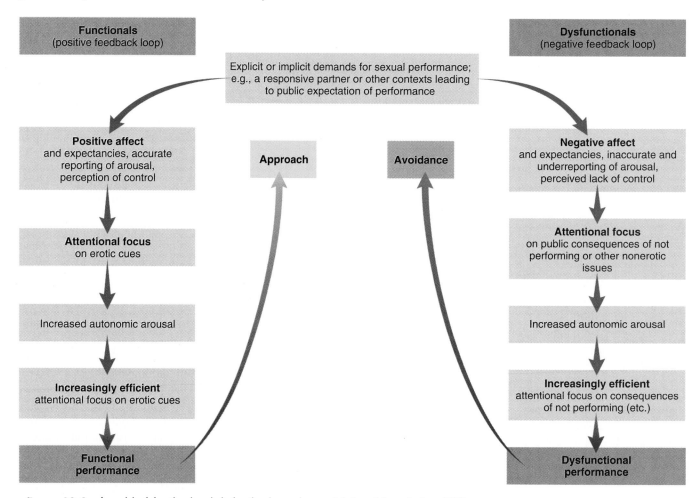

figure 10.6   A model of functional and dysfunctional sexual arousal (adapted from Barlow, 1986)

be negative and somewhat threatening, and the responses they develop reflect this belief. Donn Byrne and his colleagues call this negative cognitive set *erotophobia*. They have demonstrated that erotophobia, presumably learned early in childhood from families, religious authorities, or others, seems to predict sexual difficulties later in life (Byrne & Schulte, 1990). Thus, for some individuals, sexual cues become associated early with negative affect. In other cases, both men and women may experience specific negative or traumatic events after a period of relatively well-adjusted sexuality. These negative events might include sudden failure to become aroused or actual sexual trauma such as rape. We have already spoken about the potentially tragic effects on sexual functioning of early sexual abuse (p. 309). Such stressful events may initiate negative affect, in which individuals experience a loss of control over their sexual response cycle, throwing them into the kind of dysfunctional pattern depicted in Figure 10.6. It is common for people who experience erectile failure during a particularly stressful time to continue sexual dysfunction long after the stressful situation has ended.

In addition to generally negative attitudes or experiences associated with sexual interactions, a number of other factors may contribute to sexual dysfunction. Among these,

the most common is a marked deterioration in close interpersonal relationships. It is difficult to have a satisfactory sexual relationship in the context of growing dislike for one's partner. Occasionally, the partner may no longer seem physically attractive. M. P. Kelly, Strassberg, and Kircher (1990) found that anorgasmic women, in addition to displaying more negative attitudes toward masturbation, greater sex guilt, and greater endorsement of sex myths, reported discomfort in telling their partners what sexual activities might increase their arousal or lead to orgasm, such as direct clitoral stimulation. Poor sexual skills might also lead to frequent sexual failure and, ultimately, lack of desire.

Thus, social and cultural factors seem to affect later sexual functioning. John Gagnon has studied this phenomenon and constructed an important concept called *script theory* of sexual functioning, according to which, we all operate according to "scripts" that reflect social and cultural expectations and guide our behavior (Gagnon, 1990; Laumann, Gagnon, Michael, & Michaels, 1994). Discovering these scripts, both in individuals and across cultures, will tell us much about sexual functioning. For example, a person who learns that sexuality is potentially dangerous, dirty, or forbidden is more vulnerable to developing sexual dysfunction later on in life. This pattern is most evident in cul-

table 10.5   Myths of Sexuality

Heiman and LoPiccolo's Myths of Female Sexuality (1988)	*Zilbergeld's Myths of Male Sexuality (1992)*
1. Sex is only for women under 30. 2. Normal women have an orgasm every time they have sex. 3. All women can have multiple orgasms. 4. Pregnancy and delivery reduce women's sexual responsiveness. 5 A woman's sex life ends with menopause. 6. There are different kinds of orgasm related to a woman's personality. Vaginal orgasms are more feminine and mature than clitoral orgasms. 7. A sexually responsive woman can always be turned on by her partner. 8. Nice women aren't aroused by erotic books or films. 9. You are frigid if you don't like the more exotic forms of sex. 10. If you can't have an orgasm quickly and easily, there's something wrong with you. 11. Feminine women don't initiate sex or become wild and unrestrained during sex. 12. Double jeopardy: You're frigid if you don't have sexual fantasies and wanton if you do. 13. Contraception is a woman's responsibility, and she's just making up excuses if she says contraceptive issues are inhibiting her sexually.	1. We're liberated folks who are very comfortable with sex. 2. A real man isn't into sissy stuff like feelings and communicating. 3. All touching is sexual or should lead to sex. 4. A man is always interested in and always ready for sex. 5. A real man performs in sex. 6. Sex is centered on a hard penis and what's done with it. 7. Sex equals intercourse. 8. A man should be able to make the earth move for his partner, or at the very least knock her socks off. 9. Good sex requires orgasm. 10. Men don't have to listen to women in sex. 11. Good sex is spontaneous, with no planning and no talking. 12. Real men don't have sex problems.

tures with very restrictive attitudes toward sex. For example, vaginismus is relatively rare in North America but is the most common cause of unconsummated marriages in Ireland (Barnes, 1981; O'Sullivan, 1979). Even in our own culture, certain socially communicated expectations and attitudes may stay with us despite our relatively enlightened and permissive attitude toward sex. Zilbergeld (1992), one of the foremost authorities on male sexuality, has elaborated a number of myths about sex believed by many men, and Heiman and LoPiccolo (1988) have done the same for women. These myths are listed in Table 10.5. Baker and DeSilva (1988) converted an earlier version of Zilbergeld's male myths into a questionnaire and presented it to groups of sexually functional and dysfunctional men. They found that men with dysfunctions showed significantly greater belief in the myths than did men who were sexually functional. We explore such myths further in our discussion of treatment.

The Interaction of Psychological and Physical Factors

Having reviewed the various causes, we must now say that seldom is any sexual dysfunction associated exclusively with either psychological or physical factors (Bancroft, 1997). More often there is a subtle combination of factors. To take a typical example, a young man, vulnerable to developing anxiety and holding to a certain number of sexual

myths (the social contribution), may experience erectile failure unexpectedly after using drugs or alcohol, as many men do (the biological contribution). He will anticipate the next sexual encounter with anxiety, wondering if the failure might happen again. This combination of experience and apprehension activates the psychological sequence depicted in Figure 10.6, regardless of whether he's had a few drinks.

In summary, socially transmitted negative attitudes about sex may interact with a person's relationship difficulties and predispositions to develop performance anxiety and, ultimately, lead to sexual dysfunction. From a psychological point of view, we don't know why some individuals develop one dysfunction and not another, although it is common for several dysfunctions to occur in the same patient. Very possibly, an individual's specific biological predispositions interact with psychological factors to produce a specific sexual dysfunction.

Treatment of Sexual Dysfunction

Unlike other disorders discussed in this book, one surprisingly simple treatment is effective for a large number of individuals who experience sexual dysfunction: education. Ignorance of the most basic aspects of the sexual response cycle and intercourse often leads to long-lasting dysfunctions. Consider the case of Carl, who recently came to our sexuality clinic.

Carl

Never Too Late

Carl, a 55-year-old white man, was referred to our clinic by his urologist because he had difficulty maintaining an erection. Although he had never been married, he was at present involved in an intimate relationship with a 50-year-old woman. This was only his second sexual relationship. He was reluctant to ask his partner to come to the clinic because of his embarrassment in discussing sexual issues. A careful interview revealed that Carl engaged in sex twice a week, but requests by the clinician for a step-by-step description of his sexual activities revealed a very unusual pattern: Carl skipped foreplay and immediately proceeded to intercourse! Unfortunately, because his partner was not aroused and lubricated, he was unable to penetrate her. His valiant efforts sometimes resulted in painful abrasions for both of them. Two sessions of extensive sex education, including very specific step-by-step instructions for carrying out foreplay, provided Carl with a whole new outlook on sex. For the first time in his life he had successful, satisfying intercourse, much to his delight and his partner's.

In the case of hypoactive sexual desire disorder, one common presentation is a marked difference *within* a couple that leads to one partner's being labeled as having low desire. For example, if one partner is quite happy with sexual relations once a week but the other partner desires sex every day, the latter partner may accuse the former of having low desire and, unfortunately, the former partner might agree. Facilitating better conditions often resolves these misunderstandings. Fortunately, for people with this and more complex sexual dysfunctions, treatments are now available, both psychosocial and biological (medical). Advances in medical treatments, particularly for erectile dysfunction, have been dramatic in just the last few years. We will look first at psychosocial treatments; then we'll examine the latest medical procedures.

Psychosocial Treatments

Among the many advances in our knowledge of sexual behavior, none was more dramatic than the publication in 1970 by William Masters and Virginia Johnson of *Human Sexual Inadequacy*. The procedures outlined in this book literally revolutionized sex therapy by providing a brief, direct, and reasonably successful therapeutic program for sexual dysfunctions. Underscoring once again the common basis of most sexual dysfunctions, a very similar approach to therapy is taken with all patients, male and female, with some slight variations depending on the specific sexual problem (for instance, premature ejaculation or orgasmic disorder). This intensive program involves a male and a female therapist to facilitate communication between the dysfunctional partners. (Masters and Johnson were the original male and female therapists.) Therapy is conducted daily over a 2-week period.

The actual program is quite straightforward. In addition to providing basic education about sexual functioning, altering deep-seated myths, and increasing communication, the clinicians' primary goal is to eliminate psychologically based performance anxiety (refer back to Figure 10.6). To accomplish this, Masters and Johnson introduced *sensate focus* and *nondemand pleasuring*. In this exercise, couples are instructed to refrain from intercourse or genital caressing and simply to explore and enjoy each other's body through touching, kissing, hugging, massaging, or similar kinds of behavior. In the first phase, *nongenital pleasuring*, breasts and genitals are excluded from the exercises. After successfully accomplishing this phase, the couple moves to genital pleasuring but with a ban on orgasm and intercourse and clear instructions to the man that achieving an erection is not the goal.

At this point, arousal should be reestablished and the couple should be ready to attempt intercourse. So as not to proceed too quickly, this stage is also broken down into parts. For example, a couple might be instructed to attempt *the beginnings* of penetration; that is, the depth of penetration and the time it lasts are only very gradually built up, and both genital and nongenital pleasuring continue. Eventually, full intercourse and thrusting are accomplished.

After this 2-week intensive program, recovery was reported by Masters and Johnson for the vast majority of more than 790 sexually dysfunctional patients, with some differences in the rate of recovery depending on the disorder. Close to 100% of individuals with premature ejaculation recovered, whereas the rate for more difficult cases of lifelong generalized erectile dysfunction was closer to 60%.

Specialty sexuality clinics based on the pioneering work of Masters and Johnson were established around the country to administer these new treatment techniques. Subsequent research revealed that many of the structural aspects of the program did not seem necessary. For example, one therapist seems to be as effective as two (LoPiccolo, Heiman, Hogan, & Roberts, 1985), and seeing patients once a week seems to be as effective as seeing them every day (Heiman & LoPiccolo, 1983). It has also become clear in the succeeding decades that the results achieved by Masters and Johnson were much better than those achieved in clinics around the world using similar procedures. Reasons for this are not entirely clear. One possibility is that because patients had to take at least 2 weeks off and fly to St. Louis to meet with Masters and Johnson, they were very highly motivated to begin with.

Sex therapists have expanded on and modified these procedures over the years to take advantage of recent advances in knowledge (for example, Bancroft, 1997; Wincze & Barlow, 1997a, 1997b). Recent results with sex therapy for erectile dysfunction indicate that as many as 60% to 70% of the cases show a positive treatment outcome for at least several years, although there may be some slipping after that (Segraves & Althof, 1998). For better treatment of *specific*

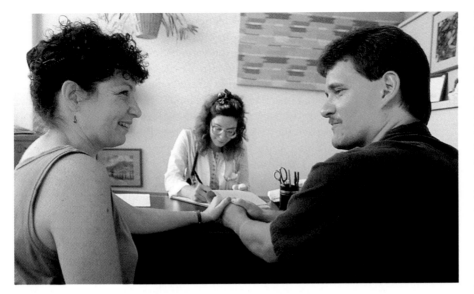

A therapist usually treats a dysfunction in one partner by seeing the couple together.

sexual dysfunctions, sex therapists integrate specific procedures into the context of general sex therapy. For example, to treat premature ejaculation, most sex therapists use a procedure developed by Semans (1956), sometimes called the *squeeze* technique, in which the penis is stimulated, usually by the partner, to nearly full erection. At this point the partner firmly squeezes the penis near the top where the head of the penis joins the shaft, which quickly reduces arousal. These steps are repeated until (for heterosexual partners), eventually the penis is briefly inserted in the vagina without thrusting. If arousal occurs too quickly, the penis is withdrawn and the squeeze technique is employed again. In this way the man develops a sense of control over arousal and ejaculation. Reports of success with this approach over the past 20 years suggest that 60% to 90% of men benefit, but the success rates drop to about 25% after 3 years or more of follow-up (Segraves & Althof, 1998). Gary, the 31-year-old salesman, was treated with this method, and his wife was very cooperative during the procedures. Brief marital therapy also persuaded Gary that his insecurity over his perception that his wife no longer found him attractive was unfounded. After treatment, he reduced his work hours somewhat, and the couple's marital and sexual relations improved.

Lifelong female orgasmic disorder may be treated with explicit training in masturbatory procedures. For example, Greta was still unable to achieve orgasm with manual stimulation by her husband, even after proceeding through the basic steps of sex therapy. At this point, following certain standardized treatment programs for this problem (for instance, Heiman & LoPiccolo, 1988), Greta and Will purchased a vibrator and Greta was taught to let go of her inhibitions by talking out loud about how she felt during sexual arousal, even shouting or screaming if she wanted to. In the context of appropriate genital pleasuring and disinhibition exercises, the vibrator brought on Greta's first orgasm. With practice and good communication, the couple eventually learned how to bring on Greta's orgasm without the vi-

brator. Although Will and Greta were both delighted with her progress, Will was concerned that Greta's screams during orgasm would attract the attention of the neighbors. When they planned a vacation at a lake, they were concerned about whether the cabin had electricity to power the vibrator in case they needed it! Summaries of results from a number of studies suggests that 70% to 90% of women will benefit from treatment, and that these gains are stable and even improve further over time (Segraves & Althof, 1998).

To treat vaginismus, the woman and, eventually, the partner gradually insert larger and larger dilators at the woman's own pace. After the woman (and then the partner) can insert the largest dilator, in a heterosexual couple the woman gradually inserts the man's penis. These exercises are carried out in the context of genital and nongenital pleasuring so as to retain arousal. Of course, close attention must be accorded to any increased fear and anxiety that may be associated with the process, which may trigger memories of early sexual abuse that may have contributed to the onset of the condition. These procedures are highly successful, with a large majority of women (80% to 100%) overcoming vaginismus in a relatively short period of time (J. G. Beck, 1993; Segraves & Althof, 1998).

A variety of treatment procedures have also been developed for low sexual desire (for instance, LoPiccolo & Friedman, 1988; Wincze & Barlow, 1997a, 1997b; Wincze & Carey, 1991). At the heart of these are the standard reeducation and communication phases of traditional sex therapy with, possibly, the addition of masturbatory training and exposure to erotic material. Of course, each case may require individual strategies. Remember Mrs. C., who was sexually abused by her cousin? Therapy involved helping the couple understand the impact of the repeated, unwanted sexual experiences in Mrs. C.'s past and to approach sex so that Mrs. C. was much more comfortable with foreplay. She gradually lost the idea that once sex was started she had no control. She and her husband worked on starting and stopping sexual encounters. Cognitive restructuring was used to help Mrs. C. interpret her husband's amorousness in a positive rather than a skeptical light. In general, approximately 50% to 70% of individuals with low sexual desire benefit from sex therapy, at least initially (Hawton, 1995; Segraves & Althof, 1998).

Medical Treatments

A variety of pharmacological and surgical techniques have been developed in recent years to treat sexual dysfunction, almost all focusing on male erectile disorder. But the introduction of the drug Viagra in 1998 may make other approaches obsolete. We will look at the four most popular

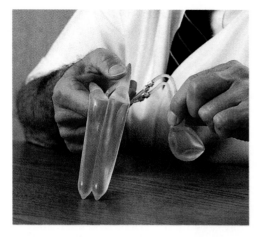

An inflatable penile implant may be used for men with inadequate sexual functioning.

procedures: oral medication, injection of vasoactive substances directly into the penis, surgery, and vacuum device therapy. It is important to combine any medical treatment with a comprehensive educational and sex therapy program to ensure maximum benefit.

Several "wonder drugs" for various disorders have been introduced with a flourish, including Prozac for depression and Redux for obesity. As noted in Chapter 2, the usual course is initial overwhelming enthusiasm that the drug is a cure-all followed by a period of profound disappointment as people realize that the drug is not what it's cracked up to be and may even be harmful in some cases. Finally, rationality sets in and the drug, if it has been proven effective in a number of studies, usually is found to be of a moderate benefit to some people and becomes a useful part of a treatment plan. The wonder drug of 1998 is Sildenafil (tradename Viagra) for erectile dysfunction. Approval from the Food and Drug Administration (FDA) occurred early in 1998, and preliminary trials suggest that between 50% and 80% of a large number of men benefit from this treatment (Goldstein et al., 1998). However, as many as 30% may suffer severe headaches as a side effect, particularly at higher doses. Only time will tell how effective the treatment really is, but its reception is following the same course as other wonder drugs. For example, almost 37,000 prescriptions were written in the first 2 weeks, and 10,000 a day by late spring of 1998, making it one of the most popular new drugs in history, despite a cost of approximately $10 a pill. For some time, Yohimbine (Carey & Johnson, 1996) and testosterone (Schiavi, White, Mandeli, & Levine, 1997) have been used to treat erectile dysfunction. But although they are safe and have relatively few side effects, they have only negligible effects on erectile dysfunction (Mann et al., 1996).

Some urologists teach patients to inject vasodilating drugs such as *papaverine* or *prostaglandin* directly into the penis when they want to have sexual intercourse. These drugs dilate the blood vessels, allowing blood to flow to the penis and thereby producing an erection within 15 minutes that can last from 1 to 4 hours (Kim & Lipshultz, 1997; Segraves & Althof, 1998). Because this procedure is a bit painful (although not as much as you might think), a sub-

stantial number of men, usually 50% to 60%, stop using it after a short time. In one study 50 of 100 patients discontinued papaverine for various reasons (Lakin, Montague, Vanderbrug, Medendorp, Tesar, & Schover, 1990; Segraves & Althof, 1998). Side effects include bruising and, with repeated injections, the development of fibrosis nodules in the penis (Gregoire, 1992). Although some patients have found papaverine very helpful, it needs more study, and scientists are attempting to develop more palatable ways to deliver the drug. A soft capsule that contains the drug, called MUSE, can be inserted directly into the urethra, but this is somewhat painful, and less effective than injections.

Insertion of *penile prostheses* or implants has been a surgical option for almost 100 years; only recently are they good enough to approximate normal sexual functioning. One procedure involves the implantation of a semirigid silicone rod that can be bent by the male into correct position for intercourse and maneuvered out of the way at other times. In a more popular procedure, the male squeezes a small pump that is surgically implanted into the scrotum, forcing fluid into an inflatable cylinder and thus producing an erection. The newest model of penile prosthetic device is an inflatable rod that contains the pumping device, which is more convenient than having the pump outside the rod. However, surgical implants fall short of restoring presurgical sexual functioning or assuring satisfaction in most patients (Gregoire, 1992; Kim & Lipshultz, 1997) and are now generally used only if other approaches don't work. More recently, *vascular surgery* to correct arterial or venous malfunctions has been attempted (for example, Bennett, 1988). Although the initial results are often successful, follow-up evaluations reveal a high failure rate.

Another approach is *vacuum device therapy,* which works by creating a vacuum in a cylinder placed over the penis. The vacuum draws blood into the penis, which is then trapped by a specially designed ring placed around the base of the penis. Although using the vacuum device is rather awkward, between 70% and 100% of users report satisfactory erections, particularly if psychosocial sex therapy is ineffective (Segraves & Althof, 1998; Witherington, 1988). The procedure is also less intrusive than surgery or injections.

Summary

Treatment programs, both psychosocial and medical, offer hope to most people who suffer from sexual dysfunctions. Unfortunately, such programs are not readily available in many locations because few health and mental health professionals are trained to apply them, although the availability of Viagra for male erectile disfunction is widespread. Psychosocial treatment of sexual arousal disorders requires further improvement, and treatments for low sexual desire are largely untested. New medical developments appear yearly, but most are still intrusive and clumsy, although new drugs such as Viagra appear promising.

Unfortunately, most health professionals tend to ignore the issue of sexuality in the aging. Along with the usual emphasis on communication, education, and sensate focus, appropriate lubricants for women and a discussion of methods to maximize the erectile response in men should be a part of any sexual counseling for older couples. More important, even with reduced physical capabilities, continued sexual relations, not necessarily including intercourse, should be a very enjoyable and important part of an aging couple's relationship. Further research and development in the treatment of sexual dysfunction must address all these issues.

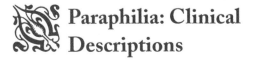 Paraphilia: Clinical Descriptions

If you are like most people, your sexual interest is directed to other physically mature adults (or late adolescents), all of whom are capable of freely offering or withholding their consent. But what if you are sexually attracted to something or somebody other than another adult? What if you are attracted to a vacuum cleaner? (Yes, it does happen!) Or what if your only means of obtaining sexual satisfaction is to commit a brutal murder? Such patterns of sexual arousal and countless others exist in a large number of individuals, causing untold human suffering both for them and, if their behavior involves other people, for their victims. As noted in the beginning of the chapter, these disorders of sexual arousal are called "paraphilias."

Over the years, we have assessed and treated a large number of these individuals, ranging from the slightly eccentric and sometimes pitiful case to some of the most dangerous killer–rapists encountered anywhere. We will begin by describing briefly the major types of paraphilia, using in all instances cases from our own files. As with sexual dys-

functions, it is unusual for an individual to have just one paraphilic pattern of sexual arousal. Many of our cases may present with two, three, or more patterns, although one is usually dominant (Abel et al., 1987; Abel, Becker, Cunningham-Rathner, Mittelman, & Rouleau, 1988; Brownell, Hayes, & Barlow, 1977).

Although paraphilias are not widely prevalent and estimates of their frequency are hard to come by, some disorders, such as transvestic fetishism, seem relatively common (Bancroft, 1989; Mason, 1997). You may have been the victim of *frotteurism* in a large city, typically on a crowded subway or bus. (We mean really crowded, with people packed in like sardines.) In this situation women have been known to experience more than the usual jostling and pushing from behind. What they discover, much to their horror, is a male with a frotteuristic arousal pattern rubbing against them until he is stimulated to the point of ejaculation. Because the victims cannot escape easily, the frotteuristic act is usually successful.

Paraphilia is seldom seen in females. Occasionally a female is heavily involved in sadomasochism, but even these cases are relatively rare. Women may sexually abuse children, usually while babysitting, but much less frequently than men, a topic we touch on when we discuss causes of paraphilia.

Fetishism

In **fetishism,** a person is sexually attracted to nonliving objects. There are almost as many different types of fetishes as there are objects, although women's undergarments and shoes are very popular. Fetishistic arousal is associated with two different classes of objects or activities: (a) an inanimate

A crowded subway car is a typical setting for frotteuristic activity, in which a person takes advantage of forced physical contact with strangers to become aroused.

object or (b) a source of specific tactile stimulation, such as rubber, particularly clothing made out of rubber. Shiny black plastic is also used (Bancroft, 1989; Junginger, 1997). Most, if not all, of the person's sexual fantasies, urges, and desires focus on this object. A third source of attraction (sometimes called *partialism*) is a part of the body, such as the foot, buttocks, or hair, but this attraction is no longer technically classified as a fetish because distinguishing it from more normal patterns of arousal is often difficult.

For a period of several months, bras hung out on a woman's backyard clothesline disappeared. The women in the neighborhood soon began talking to each other and discovered that bras were missing from every clothesline for blocks around. A police stakeout caught the perpetrator, who turned out to have a strong fetish for brassieres. A male former employee of the celebrity Marla Maples was caught on video surveillance stealing her shoes; he had stolen hundreds of pairs and confessed to a severe fetish. It is relatively common for a urologist to be called to the emergency room to surgically remove a long thin object, like a pencil or the arm of an eyeglass frame, from the urethra. Men who insert such objects think that partially blocking the urethra in this way can increase the intensity of ejaculation during masturbation. However, if the entire object slips into the penis, major medical intervention is required.

Voyeurism and Exhibitionism

Voyeurism is the practice of observing an unsuspecting individual undressing or naked in order to become aroused. **Exhibitionism,** by contrast, is achieving sexual arousal and gratification by exposing one's genitals to unsuspecting strangers. Consider the following case.

Robert
Outside the Curtains

Robert, a 31-year-old married blue-collar worker, reported that he first started "peeping" into windows when he was 14. He rode around the neighborhood on his bike at night, and when he spotted a female through a window he stopped and stared. During one of these episodes, he felt the first pangs of sexual arousal. Eventually he began masturbating while watching, thereby exposing his genitals, although out of sight. When he was older, he drove around until he spotted some prepubescent girls. He parked his car near them, unzipped his fly, called them over, and attempted to carry on a nonsexual conversation. Later he was sometimes able to talk a girl into mutual masturbation and fellatio. Although he was arrested several times, paradoxically the threat of arrest *increased* his arousal (Barlow & Wincze, 1980).

Remember that anxiety actually *increases* arousal under some circumstances. Many voyeurs just don't get the same satisfaction from attending readily available strip shows at a local bar. Although paraphilias may occur separately, it is not

The Lawyer
Who Needed the Bus

Several years ago a distinguished lawyer reported that he needed help and that his career was on the line. An intelligent, good-looking single man, he noted, without bragging, that he could have sex with any number of beautiful women in the course of his law practice. However, the only way he could become aroused was to leave his office, go down to the bus stop, ride around the city until a reasonably attractive young woman got on, expose himself just before the next stop, and then run off the bus, often with people chasing after him. To achieve maximal arousal, the bus could not be full or empty; there had to be just a few people sitting on the bus, and the woman getting on had to be the right age. Sometimes hours would pass before these circumstances lined up correctly. The lawyer observed that if he was not fired for exhibitionism he would be fired for all the time he was missing from work. On several occasions he had requested a girlfriend to role play sitting on a bus in his apartment. Although he exposed himself to her he could not achieve sexual arousal and gratification because the activity just wasn't exciting.

unusual to find them co-occurring. Exhibitionism is not always associated with lower-class uneducated people.

Note again that the thrilling element of risk is an important part of exhibitionism.

Transvestic Fetishism

In **transvestic fetishism,** sexual arousal is strongly associated with the act of dressing in clothes of the opposite sex, or cross-dressing. Consider the following case.

Mr. M.
Strong Man in a Dress

Mr. M., a 31-year-old married police officer, came to our clinic seeking treatment for uncontrollable urges to dress in women's clothing and appear in public. He had been doing this for 16 years and had been discharged from the Marine Corps for cross-dressing. Since then, he had risked public disclosure on several occasions. Mr. M.'s wife had threatened to divorce him because of the cross-dressing, and yet she frequently purchased women's clothing for him and was "compassionate" while he wore them.

Note that Mr. M. was in the Marine Corps before he joined the police force. It is not unusual for males who are strongly inclined to dress in female clothes to compensate by associating with "macho" organizations. Some of our cross-dressing patients have been associated with various paramilitary organizations. Nevertheless, most individuals with this disorder do not seem to display any compensatory behaviors.

Interestingly, the wives of many men who cross-dress have accepted their husbands' behavior and can be quite supportive if it is a private matter between them. Docter and Prince (1997) reported that 60% of over 1,000 cases of transvestic fetishism were married at the time of the survey. Some people, both married and single, join cross-dressing clubs that meet periodically or subscribe to newsletters devoted to the topic. Recent research suggests that transvestic fetishism is indistinguishable from other fetishes in most respects (Freund, Seto, & Kuban, 1996).

Sexual Sadism and Sexual Masochism

Both **sexual sadism** and **sexual masochism** are associated with either inflicting pain or humiliation (sadism) or suffering pain or humiliation (masochism). Although Mr. M. was extremely concerned about his cross-dressing, he was also disturbed by another problem. To maximize his sexual pleasure during intercourse with his wife, he had her wear a collar and leash, tied her to the bed, and handcuffed her. He sometimes tied himself with ropes, chains, handcuffs, and wires, all while he was cross-dressed. Mr. M. was concerned he might injure himself seriously. As a member of the police force he had heard of cases and even investigated one himself in which an individual was found dead, very tightly and completely bound up in harnesses, handcuffs, and ropes. In many such cases something goes wrong and the individual accidentally hangs himself, an event that should be distinguished from the closely related condition called "hypoxiphilia," which involves self-strangulation to reduce the flow of oxygen to the brain and enhance the sensation of orgasm. It may

Murderer Jeffrey Dahmer obtained sexual gratification from acts of sadism and cannibalism. (In prison, he was killed by fellow inmates.)

seem paradoxical that one has to either inflict or receive pain to become sexually aroused, but these types of cases are not uncommon. On many occasions, the behaviors themselves are quite mild and harmless, but they can become dangerous and costly. It was not unusual that Mr. M. presented with three different patterns of deviant arousal, in his case sexual masochism, sexual sadism, and transvestic fetishism.

■ **concept check 10.2**

People have a wide range of sexual preferences. Check your understanding of some sexual paraphilias: (a) exhibitionism; (b) voyeurism; (c) fetishism. This is a story about Peeping Tom.

1. Peeping Tom loves to look through Susie's bedroom window and watch her undress. He gets extremely excited as she slowly exposes her voluptuous body. He is practicing _____ .

2. What Peeping Tom does not realize is that Susie knows that he is watching. She is aroused by slowly undressing while Tom is watching, and fantasizes about what he is thinking. Susie is suffering from _____ .

3. Peeping Tom also loves to look at Susie's shoes while she is undressing, especially her 6-inch black pumps. This is a form of _____ .

4. What Peeping Tom would be shocked to find out is that Susie is really not "Susie"; she is actually Scott, who can become aroused only if he wears feminine clothing. Scott's problem is _____ .

SADISTIC RAPE

After murder, rape is the most devastating assault one person can make on another. It is not classified as a paraphilia because most instances of rape are better characterized as an assault by a male (or, quite rarely, a female) whose patterns of sexual arousal are not paraphilic. Instead, many rapists meet criteria for antisocial personality disorder (see Chapter 12) and may engage in a variety of antisocial and aggressive acts. In fact, many rapes could be described as opportunistic, in that an aggressive or antisocial individual spontaneously took advantage of a vulnerable and unsuspecting woman. These unplanned assaults often occur during robberies or other criminal events. Knight and Prentky (1990) describe rapes that are motivated by anger and vindictiveness against specific women and that may have been planned in advance (Hucker, 1997).

Several years ago, we determined in our sexuality clinic that certain rapists do, in fact, fit definitions of paraphilia closely and could probably better be described as *sadists*. We constructed two audiotapes on which were described (a) mutually enjoyable sexual intercourse and (b) sexual intercourse involving force on the part of the male (rape). Each tape was played twice for selected listeners. Response differences between rapists and nonrapists are presented in Figure 10.7 (Abel, Barlow, Blanchard, & Guild, 1977). As you can see, the nonrapists became sexually aroused to descriptions of mutually consenting intercourse, but not to those involving force. Rapists, however, became aroused to both types of descriptions.

Among the rapists we were evaluating, a subgroup seemed to be particularly aroused when force and acts of cruelty were involved. To assess this reaction more completely, we put together a third audiotape consisting of aggression and assault without any sexual content. A number of individuals displayed strong sexual arousal to nonsexual aggressive themes as well as to rape, and little or no arousal to mutually enjoyable intercourse, as depicted by the data from one individual in Figure 10.8. In fact, this man was the most brutal rapist we have ever encountered. By his own report he had raped, well over 100 times. His last victim spent 2 weeks in the hospital recovering from various injuries. He would bite his victim's breasts, burn her with cigarettes, beat her with belts and switches, and pull out her pubic hair while shoving objects in her vagina. Although there was some evidence that

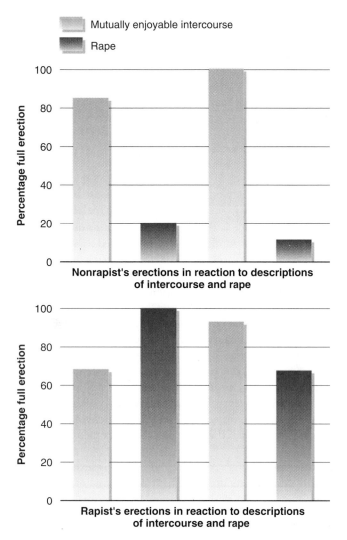

figure 10.7 Erectile arousal differences between rapists and nonrapists. Nonrapists became aroused to descriptions of mutually enjoyable intercourse but not to descriptions of rape; rapists experienced significant arousal to both types of descriptions (from Abel et al., 1977).

he had killed at least three of his victims, it was not sufficient to convict him. Nevertheless, he was convicted of multiple assaults and rapes and was about to begin a life sentence in a closely guarded area of the maximum-security state prison. Realizing that his behavior was hopelessly out of control, he himself was eager to get there. He reported that all his waking hours were spent ruminating uncontrollably on sadistic fantasies. He knew he was going to spend the rest of his life in prison, probably in solitary confinement, but hoped there was something we could do to relieve him of his obsession. By any definition, this man met criteria for sexual sadism.

Pedophilia and Incest

Perhaps the most tragic sexual deviance is a sexual attraction to children (or very young adolescents), called **pedophilia.** Individuals with this pattern of arousal may be attracted to male children, female children, or both. If the children are the person's relatives, the pedophilia takes the form of **incest.** Although pedophilia and incest have much in common, victims of pedophilia tend to be young children, and victims of incest tend to be girls who are beginning to mature physically. Marshall, Barbaree, and Christophe (1986; Marshall, 1997) demonstrated by using penile strain gauge measures that incestuous males are, in general, more aroused to adult women than are males with pedophilia, who tend to focus exclusively on children. Thus, incestuous relations may have more to do with availability and interpersonal issues ongoing in the family than pedophilia, as in the following case from our files.

Tony
More and Less a Father

Tony, a 52-year-old married television repairman, came in very depressed. About 10 years earlier he had begun sexual activity with his 12-year-old daughter. Light kissing and some fondling gradually escalated to heavy petting and, finally, mutual masturbation. When his daughter was 16 years old, his wife discovered the ongoing incestuous relationship. She separated from her husband and eventually divorced him, taking her daughter with her. Soon, Tony remarried. Just before his initial visit to our clinic, Tony visited his daughter, then 22 years old, who was living alone in a different city. They had not seen each other for 5 years. A second visit, shortly after the first, led to a recurrence of the incestuous behavior. At this point, Tony became extremely depressed and told his new wife the whole story. She contacted our clinic with his full cooperation, while his daughter sought treatment in her own city.

We will return to the case of Tony later, but there are several features worth noting. First, Tony loved his daughter very much and was bitterly disappointed and depressed over his behavior. On occasion, a child molester is abusive and aggressive, sometimes killing the victims; in these cases, the disorder is often both sexual sadism and pedophilia. But

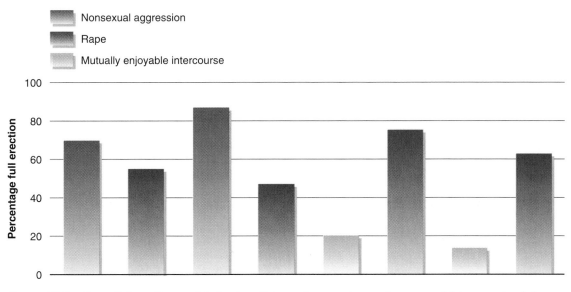

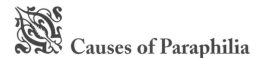

figure 10.8 One sadist's erections on listening to audiotapes of nonsexual aggression, rape, and intercourse descriptions (from Abel et al., 1977).

most child molesters are *not* physically abusive. Very rarely is a child actually physically forced or injured. From the molester's perspective, no harm is done because there is no physical force or threats. In fact, child molesters often rationalize their behavior as "loving" the child or teaching the child useful lessons about sexuality. The child molester almost never considers the psychological damage the victim suffers, and yet these interactions often destroy the child's trust and ability to share intimacy. Child molesters can rarely gauge their power over the children, who may participate in the molestation without protest, yet be very frightened and

unwilling. Often children feel responsible for the abuse because no outward force or threat was used by the adult, and only after the abused children grow up are they able to understand that they were powerless to protect themselves and not responsible for what was done to them.

Causes of Paraphilia

Although no substitute for scientific inquiry, case histories often provide hypotheses that can then be tested by controlled scientific observations. Let's return to the cases of Robert and Tony to see if their histories contain any clues.

Elementary school teacher Mary Kay LeTourneau, 35, pleaded guilty to rape of a child after having a baby by a 13-year-old former student. LeTourneau, who lost custody of her four other children, said of the boy, "He was my best friend. We just walked together in the same rhythm." On her release from prison she violated probation, saw the boy again, again became pregnant, and was returned to prison.

Robert
Revenge on Repression

Robert (who sought help for exhibitionism) was raised by a very stern authoritarian father and a passive mother in a small Texas town. His father, who was a firm believer in old-time religion, often preached the evils of sexual intercourse to his family. Robert learned little about sex from his father except that it was bad, so he suppressed any emerging heterosexual urges and fantasies, and as an adolescent felt very uneasy around girls his own age. By accident, he discovered a private source of sexual gratification: staring at attractive and unsuspecting females through the window. This led to his first masturbatory experience.

Robert reported in retrospect that being arrested was not so bad because it disgraced his father, which was his only way of getting back at him. In fact, the courts treated him lightly (which is not unusual), and his father was publicly humiliated, forcing the family to move away from their small Texas town (Barlow & Wincze, 1980).

Tony
Trained Too Young

Tony, who sought help because of an incestuous relationship with his daughter, reported an early sexual history that contained a number of interesting events. Although he was brought up in a reasonably loving and outwardly normal Catholic family, he had an uncle who did not fit the family pattern. When he was 9 or 10, Tony was encouraged by his uncle to observe a game of strip poker that the uncle was playing with a neighbor's wife. During this period, he also observed his uncle fondling a waitress at a drive-in restaurant and shortly thereafter was instructed by his uncle to fondle his young female cousin. Thus, he had an early model for mutual fondling and masturbation and obtained some pleasure from interacting in this way with young girls. Although the uncle never touched Tony, his behavior was clearly abusive. When Tony was about 13, he engaged in mutual manipulation with a sister and her girlfriend, which he remembers as pleasurable. Later, when Tony was 18, a brother-in-law took him to a prostitute and he first experienced sexual intercourse. He remembered this visit as unsatisfactory because, on that and subsequent visits to prostitutes, he ejaculated prematurely—a sharp contrast to his early experience with young girls. Other experiences with adult women were also unsatisfactory. When he joined the service and was sent overseas, he sought out prostitutes who were often as young as 12.

These cases remind us that deviant patterns of sexual arousal often occur in the context of other sexual and social problems. Undesired kinds of arousal may be associated with deficiencies in levels of "desired" arousal with consensual adults; this was certainly true for both Tony and Robert, whose sexual relationships with adults were incomplete. In many cases, an inability to develop adequate social relations with the appropriate people for sexual relationships seems to be associated with developing inappropriate sexual outlets (Barlow & Wincze, 1980; Marshall, 1997). However, many people with deficient sexual and social skills do *not* develop deviant patterns of arousal.

Early experience seems to have an effect that may be quite accidental. Tony's early sexual experiences just happened to be of the type he later found sexually arousing. Robert's first erotic experience occurred while he was "peeping." But many of us do not find our early experiences reflected in our sexual patterns.

Another factor may be the nature of the person's early sexual fantasies. For example, Rachman and Hodgson (1968; see also Bancroft, 1989) demonstrated that sexual arousal could become associated with a neutral object—a boot, for example—if the boot was repeatedly presented while the individual was sexually aroused. One of the most powerful engines for the development of unwanted arousal may be *early sexual fantasies that are repeatedly reinforced through the very strong sexual pleasure associated with mastur-*

bation. Before a pedophile or sadist ever acts on his behavior, he may fantasize about it thousands of times while masturbating. Expressed as a clinical or operant conditioning paradigm, this is another example of a learning process in which a behavior (sexual arousal to a specific object or activity) is repeatedly reinforced through association with a pleasurable consequence (orgasm). This mechanism may explain why paraphilias are almost exclusively male disorders. The basic differences in frequency of masturbation between men and women that exist across cultures may contribute to the differential development of paraphilias. Still, many women masturbate, and many of them do so quite frequently, so one would think that at least occasionally a woman would present with a paraphilic arousal pattern if this mechanism were contributory. On rare occasions, cases of women with paraphilia do turn up (Hunter & Mathews, 1997; Stoller, 1982).

However, if early experiences contribute strongly to later sexual arousal patterns, then what about the Sambia males who practice exclusive homosexual behavior during childhood and early adolescence and yet are exclusively heterosexual as adults? Of course, in such cohesive societies, the social demands or "scripts" for sexual interactions are much stronger and more rigid than in our culture and thus may override the effects of early experiences (Baldwin & Baldwin, 1989).

In addition, therapists and sex researchers who work with paraphilics have observed what seems to be an incredibly strong sex drive. It is not uncommon for some paraphilics to masturbate three or four times a day. In one case seen in our clinic, a sadistic rapist masturbated approximately every half hour all day long, just as often as it was physiologically possible. We have speculated elsewhere that activity this consuming may be related to the obsessional processes of obsessive–compulsive disorder (Barlow, 1988). In both instances, the very act of trying to suppress unwanted emotionally charged thoughts and fantasies seems to have the paradoxical effect of *increasing* their frequency and intensity (see Chapter 5). This process is also ongoing in eating disorders and addictions, when attempts to restrict strong addictive cravings lead to uncontrollable *increases* in the undesired behaviors. Psychopathologists are becoming interested in the phenomenon of weak inhibitory control across these disorders, which may indicate a weak biologically based behavioral inhibition system (BIS) in the brain (Fowles, 1993; Kafka, 1997) that might repress serotonergic functioning. (You may remember from Chapter 5 that the BIS is a brain circuit associated with anxiety and inhibition.)

The model shown in Figure 10.9 incorporates the factors that are thought to contribute to the development of paraphilia. Nevertheless, all speculations, including the hypotheses we have described, have little scientific support at this time. For example, this model does not include the biological dimension. Excess arousal in paraphilics could be biologically based. Before we can make any steadfast conclusions here, more research is needed.

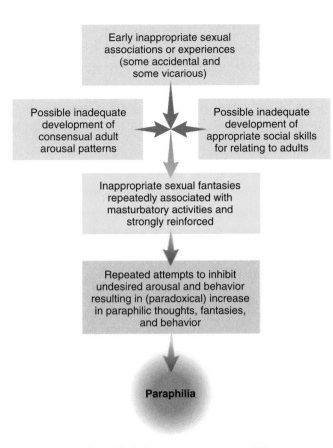

Early inappropriate sexual associations or experiences (some accidental and some vicarious)

Possible inadequate development of consensual adult arousal patterns

Possible inadequate development of appropriate social skills for relating to adults

Inappropriate sexual fantasies repeatedly associated with masturbatory activities and strongly reinforced

Repeated attempts to inhibit undesired arousal and behavior resulting in (paradoxical) increase in paraphilic thoughts, fantasies, and behavior

Paraphilia

figure 10.9 A model of the development of paraphilia

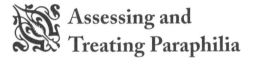

Assessing and Treating Paraphilia

Assessment

In recent years we have developed sophisticated methods for assessing specific patterns of sexual arousal (Maletzky, 1998). This is important in studying paraphilia because sometimes even the individual presenting with the problem is not fully aware of what caused arousal. An individual once came in complaining of uncontrollable arousal to open-toed white sandals worn by women. He noted that he was irresistibly drawn to any woman wearing open-toed white sandals and would follow her for miles. These urges occupied much of his summer. Subsequent assessment revealed that the sandal itself had no erotic value for this individual; rather, he had a strong sexual attraction to women's feet, particularly moving in a certain way.

Using the model of paraphilia described previously, we assess each patient not only for the presence of deviant arousal but also for levels of appropriate arousal to adults, for social skills, and for the ability to form relationships. Tony had no problems with social skills: He was 52 years old, reasonably happily married, and generally compatible with his second wife. His major difficulty was his continuing strong incestuous attraction to his daughter. Nevertheless, he loved

his daughter very much and wished strongly to interact in a normal fatherly way with her.

Psychosocial Treatment

There are a number of treatment procedures for decreasing unwanted arousal. Most are behavior therapy procedures directed at changing the associations and context from arousing and pleasurable to neutral. One procedure, carried out entirely in the imagination of the patient, called **covert sensitization,** was first described by Joseph Cautela (1967; see also Barlow, 1993). Sexually arousing images are associated with the very consequences of the behavior that bring the patient to treatment in the first place. The notion here is that the patient's arousal patterns are undesirable because of their long-term consequences, but the immediate pleasure and thus strong reinforcement they provide more than overcome any thoughts of possible harm or danger that might arise in the future. This model also applies to much unwanted addictive behavior, including bulimia.

In imagination, harmful or dangerous consequences can be associated quite directly with the unwanted behavior and arousal in a very powerful and emotionally meaningful way. One of the most powerful negative aspects of Tony's behavior was his embarrassment over the thought of being discovered by his current wife, other family members, or, most important, the family priest. Therefore, he was guided through the following fantasy.

Tony

Imagining the Worst

You are alone with your daughter in your trailer. You realize that you want to caress her breasts. So you put your arm around her, slip your hand inside her blouse, and begin to caress her breasts. Unexpectedly the door to the trailer opens and in walks your wife with Father X. Your daughter immediately jumps up and runs out the door. Your wife follows her. You are left alone with Father X. He is looking at you as if waiting for an explanation of what he has just seen. Seconds pass, but they seem like hours. You know what Father X must be thinking as he stands there staring at you. You are very embarrassed and want to say something, but you can't seem to find the right words. You realize that Father X can no longer respect you as he once did. Father X finally says, "I don't understand this; this is not like you." You both begin to cry. You realize that you may have lost the love and respect of both Father X and your wife, who are very important to you. Father X asks, "Do you realize what this has done to your daughter?" You think about this and you hear your daughter crying; she is hysterical. You want to run, but you can't. You are miserable and disgusted with yourself. You don't know if you will ever regain the love and respect of your wife and Father X. (Adapted from Harbert, Barlow, Hersen, & Austin, 1974, p. 82)

During six or eight sessions, the therapist narrates such scenes dramatically, and, the patient is then instructed to imagine them on a daily basis until all arousal disappears.

The results of Tony's treatment are presented in Figure 10.10. "Card-sort scores" are a measure of how much Tony wanted sexual interactions with his daughter in comparison with his wish for nonsexual fatherly interactions. His incestuous arousal was largely eliminated after 3 to 4 weeks, but the treatment did not affect his desire to interact with his daughter in a healthier manner. These results were confirmed by psychophysiological measurement of his arousal response. A return of some arousal at a 3-month follow-up prompted us to ask Tony if anything unusual was happening in his life. He confessed that his marriage had taken a turn for the worse and that sexual relations with his wife had all but ceased. A period of marital therapy restored the therapeutic gains (see Figure 10.10). Several years later, after his daughter's therapist decided she was ready, she and Tony resumed a nonsexual relationship, which they both wanted.

Two major areas in Tony's life needed treatment: deviant (incestuous) sexual arousal and marital problems. Most individuals with paraphilic arousal patterns need a great deal of attention to family functioning or other interpersonal systems in which they operate (Barabee & Seto, 1997). In addition, many require intervention to help strengthen appropriate patterns of arousal. In **orgasmic reconditioning,** patients are instructed to masturbate to their usual fantasies but to substitute more desirable ones just before ejaculation. With repeated practice, subjects should be able to begin the desired fantasy earlier in the masturbatory process and still retain their arousal. This technique, first described by Gerald Davison (1968), has been used with some success in a variety of different settings (Brownell, Hayes, & Barlow, 1997; Maletzky, 1998). Finally, as with most strongly pleasurable but undesirable behaviors (including addiction), care must be taken to provide the patient with coping skills to prevent slips

table 10.6   Treatment Outcome for Paraphilias (N = 7, 186)

Category	N	Percentage Meeting Criteria for Success
Situational pedophilia, heterosexual	3,012	95.6
Predatory pedophilia, heterosexual	864	88.3
Situational pedophilia, homosexual	717	91.8
Predatory pedophilia, homosexual	596	80.1
Exhibitionism	1,130	95.4
Rape	543	75.5
Voyeurism	83	93.9
Public masturbation	77	94.8
Frotteurism	65	89.3
Fetishism	33	94.0
Transvestic fetishism	14	78.6
Telephone scatologia	29	93.1
Zoophilia	23	95.6

[a]A treatment success was defined as an offender who:
1. Completed all treatment sessions.*
2. Reported no covert or overt deviant sexual behavior at the end of treatment or at any follow-up session.†
3. Demonstrated no deviant sexual arousal, defined as greater than 20% on the penile plethysmograph, at the end of treatment or at any follow-up session.†
4. Had no repeat legal charges for any sexual crime at the end of treatment or at any follow-up session.†

*Any offender who dropped out of treatment, even if the offender met other criteria for success, was counted as a treatment failure.
†Follow-up sessions occurred at 6, 12, 24, 36, 48, and 60 months after the end of active treatment.
Source: From Maletzky, 1998

or relapses. **Relapse prevention** treatment created for addictons (Laws, 1989; Laws & O'Donohue, 1997) does just that. Patients are taught to recognize the early signs of temptation and to institute a variety of self-control procedures before their urges become too strong.

The success of treatment with this rich arrray of procedures is surprisingly high when carried out by an experienced professional. Barry Maletzky, a psychiatrist at the University of Oregon Medical School, and his staff reported on the treament over 17 years of some 7,000 sexual offenders of numerous types. A variety of procedures were used in a program of 3 to 4 months in a clinic devoted exclusively to this type of treatment. The numbers of people successfully treated are presented in parentheses after each category in Table 10.6 (Maletzky, 1998). These are truly astounding numbers. What makes them even more impressive is that Maletzky collected objective physiological outcome measures on almost every case, in addition to patients' reports of progress. In many cases, he also obtained corroborating information from families and legal authorities.

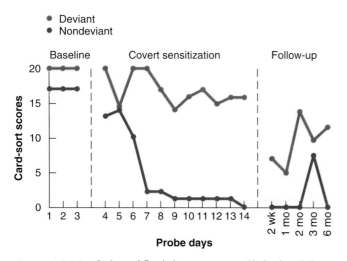

figure 10.10 Ratings of Tony's incestuous urges (deviant) and desire for normal interactions with daughter (nondeviant) during covert sensitization treatment (from Harbert et al., 1974).

In his follow-up of these patients, Maletzky defined a treatment as successful when someone had (a) completed all treatment sessions, (b) demonstrated no deviant sexual arousal on plethysmograph testing at any annual follow-up testing session, (c) reported no deviant arousal or behavior at any time since treatment ended, and (d) had no legal record of any charges of deviant sexual activity, even if unsubstantiated. He defined as a treatment failure anyone who was not a success. Any offender who did not complete treatment for any reason was counted as a failure, even though some may well have benefited from the partial treatment and gone on to recover.

Although these results are extremely good overall, Maletzky points out that men who rape have the lowest success rate among all offenders with a *single* diagnosis, and that individuals with multiple paraphilias have the lowest success rate of any group. Maletzky also examined factors associated with failure. Among the strongest predictors were a history of unstable social relationships, an unstable employment history, strong denial that the problem exists, a history of multiple victims, and a situation in which the offender continues to live with a victim (as might be typical in cases of incest).

Other groups using similar treatment procedures have achieved comparable success rates (Abel, 1989; Becker, 1990; Pithers, Martin, & Cummings, 1989). In general, results are less satisfactory when general summaries of the outcomes from all studies are evaluated, including programs that do not always incorporate these approaches (e.g., Nagayama Hall, 1995). Thus, therapist knowledge and expertise seem to be important. Judith Becker uses the procedures in a program for adolescent sexual offenders in an inner city setting (for example, Becker, 1990; Morenz & Becker, 1995). Preliminary results indicate that 10% of those who completed treatment had committed further sex crimes. If these results hold up, the findings will be important both because many adolescent offenders carry the AIDS virus and literally are putting their victims' lives in danger and because the recidivism rate of sexual offenders without treatment is very high (for instance, Hanson, Steffy, & Gauthier, 1993; Nagayama Hall, 1995), just as it is for all pleasurable but undesirable behavior, including substance abuse.

Drug Treatments

The most popular drug used to treat paraphilics (Bradford, 1997) is an anti-androgen called *cyproterone acetate.* This drug eliminates sexual desire and fantasy by reducing testosterone levels dramatically, but fantasies and arousal return as soon as the drug is removed. This is the "chemical castration" treatment you may have read about in the news. A second drug is *medroxyprogesterone acetate* (Depo-Provera is the injectable form), a hormonal agent that reduces testosterone. These drugs may be useful for dangerous sexual offenders who do not respond to alternative treatments or to temporarily suppress sexual arousal in patients who require it, but in an earlier report of the Maletzky series (Maltezky, 1991) it was necessary to administer the drug to only 8 of approximately 5,000 patients.

Summary

Based on evidence from a number of clinics, the psychosocial treatment of paraphilia is surprisingly effective. Success rates ranging from 70% to 100% with follow-ups for longer than 10 years in some cases seem to make this one of the more treatable psychological disorders. However, most results are from a small number of clinical research centers, and it seems that they are not so good in other clinics and offices. In any case, like treatment for sexual dysfunctions, psychosocial approaches to paraphilia are not readily available outside of specialized treatment centers. In the meantime, the outlook for most individuals with this disorder is bleak because paraphilias run a very chronic course and recurrence is common.

■ **concept check 10.3**

Check your understanding of paraphilias by matching the scenarios with the correct label: (a) fetishism, (b) voyeurism, (c) exhibitionism, or (d) sexual masochism.

1. Jane enjoys being slapped with leather whips during foreplay. _____

2. Bryan often watches through dorm windows with his binoculars in hopes of seeing women undress. _____

3. Michael has a collection of women's panties that arouse him. _____

4. Sam finds arousal in walking up to strangers in the park and showing them his genitals. _____

 ## Summary

What Is "Normal"?

• Patterns of sexual behavior, both heterosexual and homosexual, vary around the world, in terms of both behavior and risks. Approximately 20% of individuals who have been surveyed engage in sex with numerous partners, which puts them at risk for sexually transmitted diseases such as AIDS. Recent surveys also suggest that as many as 60% of American college females practice unsafe sex by not using appropriate condoms.

• Three different types of disorders are associated with sexual functioning and gender identity: *gender identity disorders, sexual dysfunctions,* and *paraphilias.*

Gender Identity Disorders

• Gender identity disorder is a dissatisfaction with one's biological sex and the sense that one is really the opposite gender (for instance, a woman trapped in a man's body). A person develops gender identity between 18 months and 3 years of age, and it seems that both appropriate gender identity and mistaken gender identity have biological roots that are influenced by learning.

• Treatment includes both psychosocial approaches, which have been attempted on only a few cases thus far, and sex reassignment surgery.

Sexual Dysfunctions: Clinical Descriptions

• Sexual dysfunction includes a variety of disorders in which people find it difficult to function adequately during sexual relations.

• Specific sexual dysfunctions include disorders of sexual *desire*—hypoactive sexual desire disorder and sexual aversion disorder—in which interest in sexual relations is extremely low or nonexistent; disorders of sexual *arousal*—male erectile disorder and female sexual arousal disorder—in which achieving or maintaining adequate penile erection or vaginal lubrication is problematic; and *orgasmic disorders*—female orgasmic disorder and male orgasmic disorder—in which orgasm occurs too quickly or not at all. The most common disorder in this category is premature ejaculation, which occurs in males; *inhibited orgasm* is commonly seen in females.

• Sexual pain disorders, in which unbearable pain is associated with sexual relations, include dyspareunia and vaginismus.

Assessing Sexual Behavior

• The three components of assessment are interviewing, a complete medical evaluation, and psychophysiological assessment.

Causes of Sexual Dysfunctions

• Sexual dysfunction is associated with socially transmitted negative attitudes about sex, interacting with current relationship difficulties, and anxiety focused on sexual activity.

Treatment of Sexual Dysfunctions

• Psychosocial treatment of sexual dysfunctions is generally successful but not readily available. In recent years, various medical approaches have become available, including the drug Viagra. These treatments focus mostly on male erectile dysfunction and are promising.

Paraphilia: Clinical Descriptions

• Paraphilia is sexual attraction to inappropriate people, such as children, or to inappropriate objects, such as articles of clothing.

• The paraphilias include fetishism, in which sexual arousal occurs almost exclusively in the context of inappropriate objects or individuals; exhibitionism, in which sexual gratification is attained by exposing one's genitals to unsuspecting strangers; voyeurism, in which sexual arousal is derived from observing unsuspecting individuals undressing or naked; transvestic fetishism, in which individuals are sexually aroused by wearing clothing of the opposite sex; sexual sadism, in which sexual arousal is associated with inflicting pain or humiliation; sexual masochism, in which sexual arousal is associated with experiencing pain or humiliation; and pedophilia, in which there is a strong sexual attraction toward children. Incest is a type of pedophilia in which someone typically focuses on a child who is beginning to mature physically.

Causes of Paraphilia

• The development of paraphilia is associated with deficiencies in consensual adult sexual arousal, deficiencies in consensual adult social skills, deviant sexual fantasies that may develop before or during puberty, and attempts by the individual to suppress thoughts associated with these arousal patterns.

Assessment and Treatment of Paraphilia

• Psychosocial treatments of paraphilia, including covert sensitization, orgasmic reconditioning, and relapse prevention, seem highly successful but are available only in specialized clinics.

Key Terms

heterosexual sex
homosexual sex
gender identity disorders
sex reassignment surgery
sexual dysfunction
hypoactive sexual desire disorder
sexual aversion disorder
male erectile disorder
female sexual arousal disorder
inhibited orgasm
female orgasmic disorder
male orgasmic disorder
premature ejaculation
sexual pain disorders
dyspareunia
vaginismus
paraphilias
fetishism
voyeurism
exhibitionism
transvestic fetishism
sexual sadism
sexual masochism
pedophilia
incest
covert sensitization
orgasmic reconditioning
relapse prevention

Answers to Concept Checks

10.1
1. a
2. c
3. a
4. b

10.2
1. b
2. a

3. c
4. c

10.3
1. d
2. b
3. a
4. c

EXPLORING SEXUAL AND GENDER IDENTITY DISORDERS

- Sexual behavior is considered normal in our culture unless it is associated with one of three kinds of impaired functioning.
- Sexual orientation probably has a strong biological basis that is influenced by environmental and social factors.

GENDER IDENTITY DISORDERS

Present when a person feels trapped in a body that is the "wrong" sex, that does not match his or her innate sense of personal identity. (Gender identity is independent of sexual arousal patterns.)

Biological Influences

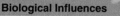

- Not yet confirmed, although likely to involve prenatal exposure to hormones.
- Hormonal variations may be natural or result from medication.

Psychosocial Influences

- Gender identity develops between 1 ½ and 3 years of age.
- "Masculine" behaviors in girls and "feminine" behaviors in boys evoke different responses in different families.

Treatment

- Sex reassignment surgery: removal of breasts or penis; genital reconstruction
- Requires rigorous psychological preparation and financial and social stability
- Psychosocial intervention to change gender identity
- Usually unsuccessful except as temporary relief until surgery

PARAPHILIAS

Sexual arousal occurs almost exclusively in the context of inappropriate objects or individuals.

Causes

- Preexisting deficiencies
- In levels of arousal with consensual adults
- In consensual adult social skills
- Treatment received from adults during childhood
- Early sexual fantasies reinforced by masturbation
- Extremely strong sex drive combined with uncontrollable thought processes

Treatment

- *Covert sensitization:* Repeated mental reviewing of aversive consequences to establish negative associations with behavior
- *Orgasmic reconditioning:* Pairing appropriate stimuli with masturbation to create positive arousal patterns
- *Relapse prevention:* Therapeutic preparation for coping with future situations

Fetishism: Sexual attraction to non-living objects

Voyeurism: Sexual arousal achieved by viewing unsuspecting person undressing or naked

Exhibitionism: Sexual gratification from exposing one's genitals to unsuspecting strangers

Transvestite fetishism: Sexual arousal from wearing opposite-sex clothing

Sexual sadism: Sexual arousal associated with inflicting pain or humiliation

Sexual masochism: Sexual arousal associated with experiencing pain or humiliation

Pedophilia: Strong sexual attraction to children

Incest: Sexual attraction to family member

SEXUAL DYSFUNCTIONS

Sexual dysfunctions can be
- *Lifelong:* Present during entire sexual history
- *Acquired:* Interrupts normal sexual pattern
- *Generalized:* Present in every encounter
- *Situational:* Present only with certain partners or at certain times

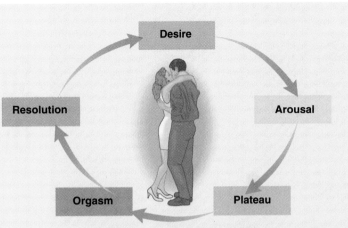

The human sexual response cycle
A dysfunction is an impairment in one of the highlighted stages.

Sexual Desire Disorders	Sexual Arousal Disorders	Orgasm Disorders	Sexual Pain Disorders
Hypoactive sexual desire disorder: Apparent lack of interest in sexual activity or fantasy *Sexual aversion disorder:* Extreme persistent dislike of sexual contact	*Male erectile disorder:* Recurring inability to achieve or maintain adequate erection *Female sexual arousal disorder:* Recurring inability to achieve or maintain adequate lubrication	*Inhibited orgasm:* Inability to achieve orgasm despite adequate desire and arousal *Premature ejaculation:* Ejaculation before it is desired, with minimal stimulation	*Dyspareunia:* Marked pain associated with intercourse for which there is no medical cause. Occurs in males and females. *Vaginismus:* Involuntary muscle spasms in the front of the vagina that prevent or interfere with intercourse

Psychological Contributions
- Distraction
- Underestimates of arousal
- Negative thought processes

Psychological and Physical Interactions
- A combination of influences is almost always present.
  - Specific biological predisposition *and* psychological factors may produce a particular disorder.

Sociocultural Contributions
- Erotophobia, caused by formative experiences of sexual cues as alarming
- Negative experiences, such as rape
- Deterioration of relationship

Biological Contributions
- Neurological or other nervous system problems
- Vascular disease
- Chronic illness
- Prescription medication
- Drugs of abuse

Treatment

Psychosocial: Therapeutic program to facilitate communication, improve sexual education, and eliminate anxiety. Both partners participate fully.
Medical: Almost all interventions focus on male erectile disorder, including drugs, prostheses, and surgery.

II

Substance-Related Disorders

For a long time, when it's working, the drink feels like a path to self–enlightenment, something that turns us into the person we wish to be, or the person we think we really are.

In some ways the dynamic is this simple: alcohol makes everything better until it makes everything worse.

Caroline Knapp
Drinking: A Love Story

Would you be surprised if we told you that a group of psychological disorders cost U.S. citizens hundreds of billions of dollars each year, kill 500,000 Americans annually, and are implicated in street crime, homelessness, and gang violence? Would you be even more surprised to learn that most of us have behaved in ways that are characteristic of these disorders at some point in our lives? You shouldn't. Smoking cigarettes, drinking alcohol, and using illegal drugs are all related to these disorders, and are responsible for astronomical financial costs and the tragic waste of hundreds of thousands of human lives each year. In this chapter we explore the **substance-related disorders,** which are associated with the abuse of drugs such as alcohol, cocaine, and heroin and with a variety of other substances people take to alter the way they think, feel, and behave. These disorders represent a problem that has cursed us for millennia and that continues to affect how we live, work, and play.

The cost in lives, money, and emotional turmoil has made the issue of drug abuse a major concern worldwide. Many presidential administrations in this country have declared various "wars on drugs," but the problem remains. In 1992 the Roman Catholic church issued a new universal catechism, officially declaring that drug abuse and drunk driving are sins (Riding, 1992). Yet, from the deaths of rock stars Jimi Hendrix and Janis Joplin in 1970 to the drug involvement of contemporary celebrities such as Robert Downey, Jr.—who was arrested three times in 1996 in drug-related incidents—illicit drug use occupies the lives of many. And stories such as these are not only about the rich and famous, but are retold in every corner of our society.

Fortunately, drug use in the United States has declined in recent years. A 20-year survey found that recreational drug use among college students rose between 1969 and 1978 but declined substantially by 1989 (Pope, Ionescu-Pioggia, Aizley, & Varma, 1990). More recent surveys have found that drug use increased somewhat in the early 1990s, and current estimates indicate a leveling off during the past few years (Office of Applied Studies, 1997). For example, it is estimated that approximately 13 million Americans used illicit drugs in 1996, down from 25 million in 1979. These findings are encouraging; nonetheless, a significant number of people continue to use illicit drugs on a regular basis. Heroin use has increased (141,000 users in 1995), as have the number of Americans between the ages of 18 and 25 who have used illicit drugs in general and cocaine specifi-

cally (Office of Applied Studies, 1997). Consider the case of Danny, who has the disturbing but common habit of **polysubstance use,** using multiple substances. (We will cover this issue in more detail later in the chapter.)

Danny
Multiple Dependencies

At the age of 35, Danny was in jail, awaiting trial on charges that he broke into a gas station and stole money. Danny's story illustrates the lifelong pattern that characterizes the behavior of many people who are affected by substance-related disorders.

Danny grew up in the suburban United States, the youngest of three children. He was well liked in school and was an average student. Like many of his friends, he smoked cigarettes in his early teens and drank beer with his friends at night behind his high school. Unlike most of his friends, however, Danny almost always drank until he was obviously drunk; he also experimented with many other drugs, including cocaine, heroin, "speed" (amphetamines), and "downers" (barbiturates).

After high school, Danny attended a local community college for one semester, but he dropped out after failing most of his courses. His dismal performance in school seemed to be related to his missing most classes rather than to an inability to learn and understand the material. He had difficulty getting up for classes after partying most of the night, which he did with increasing frequency. His moods were highly variable, and he was often unpleasant. Danny's family knew he occasionally drank too much, but they didn't know (or didn't want to know) about his other drug use. He had for years forbidden anyone to go into his room, after his mother found little packets of white powder (probably cocaine) in his sock drawer. He said he was keeping them for a friend and that he would return them immediately. He was furious that his family might suspect him of using drugs. Money was sometimes missing from the house, and once some stereo equipment "disappeared," but if anyone in his family suspected Danny they never admitted it.

After high school, Danny held a series of low-paying jobs, and when he was working his family reassured themselves that he was back on track and things would be fine. Unfortunately, he rarely held a job for more than a few months. The money he earned had a magical way of turning into drugs, and he was usually fired for poor job attendance and performance. Because he continued to live at home, Danny could survive despite frequent periods of unemployment.

When he was in his late 20s, Danny seemed to have a personal revelation. He announced that he needed help and planned to check into an alcohol rehabilitation center; he still would not admit to using other drugs. His family's joy and relief were overwhelming, and no one questioned his request for several thousand dollars to help pay for the private program he said he wanted to attend. Danny disappeared for several weeks, presumably because he was in the rehabilitation program. However, a call from the local police station put an end to this fantasy: Danny had been found quite high, living in an abandoned building. As with many of these incidents, we never learned all the details, but it appears that Danny spent his family's money on drugs and had a 3-week binge with some friends.

Danny's deceptiveness and financial irresponsibility greatly strained his relationship with his family. He was allowed to continue living at home, but his parents and siblings excluded him from their emotional lives. Danny seemed to straighten out, and he held a job at a gas station for almost 2 years. He became friendly with the station owner and his son, and frequently went hunting with them during the season. However, without any obvious warning, Danny resumed drinking and using drugs and was arrested for robbing the very place that had kept him employed for many months.

Why did Danny become dependent on drugs when many of his friends and siblings did not? Why did he steal from his family and friends? What ultimately became of him? We will return to Danny's frustrating story when we look at the causes and treatment of substance-related disorders.

Perspectives on Substance-Related Disorders

Although each drug described in this chapter has unique effects, there are similarities in the ways they are used and how people who abuse them are treated. We first survey some concepts that apply to substance-related disorders in general, noting important terminology and addressing several diagnostic issues.

Can you use drugs and not abuse them? Can you abuse drugs and not become addicted to them? To answer these important questions, we first need to outline what we mean by *substance use, substance intoxication, substance abuse,* and *dependence.* The term *substance* refers to chemical compounds that are ingested in order to alter mood or behavior. Although you might first think of drugs such as cocaine and heroin, this definition also includes more commonplace legal drugs such as alcohol, the nicotine found in tobacco, and the caffeine in coffee, soft drinks, and chocolate. As we will see, these "safe" drugs also affect mood and behavior; they can be addictive, and they account for more health problems and mortality than all the illegal drugs combined. You could make a good argument for directing the war on drugs to cigarette smoking (nicotine use) because of its addictive properties and negative health consequences.

Levels of Involvement

To understand substance-related disorders, we must first know what it means to ingest **psychoactive substances**—which alter mood and/or behavior—to become intoxicated or high, to abuse these substances, and to become dependent on or addicted to them.

Comic actor Chris Farley died in December 1997 at the age of 33, from what the medical examiner described as "one drug binge too many." At 5'6" tall and 296 pounds, Farley was suffering from advanced heart disease when he took morphine and cocaine and accidentally died. Although no alcohol was found in his system, his liver was heavily scarred by heavy drinking.

Use

Substance use is the ingestion of psychoactive substances in moderate amounts that does not significantly interfere with social, educational, or occupational functioning. Most of you reading this chapter probably use some sort of psychoactive substance on occasion. Drinking a cup of coffee in the morning in order to wake up or smoking a cigarette and having a drink with a friend in order to relax are examples of substance use, as is the occasional ingestion of illegal drugs such as marijuana, cocaine, amphetamines, or barbiturates.

Intoxication

Our physiological reaction to ingested substances—drunkenness, or getting high—is referred to as **substance intoxication.** For a person to become intoxicated depends on which drug he or she takes, how much is ingested, and the person's individual biological reaction. For many of the substances we discuss here, intoxication is experienced as impaired judgment, mood changes, and lowered motor ability (for example, problems walking or talking).

Abuse

Defining **substance abuse** by how much of a substance is ingested is problematic. For example, is drinking two glasses of wine in an hour abuse? Three glasses? Six? Is taking one injection of heroin considered abuse? DSM-IV defines substance abuse in terms of how significantly the substances interfere with the user's life. If substances disrupt your education, job, or relationships with others, and put you in

Substance use

Intoxication

Substance abuse

Substance dependence

physically dangerous situations (e.g., while driving), and if you have related legal problems, you would be considered a drug abuser.

Danny seems to fit this definition of abuse. His inability to complete a semester of community college was a direct result of drug use. Danny often drove while drunk or under the influence of other drugs, and he had already been arrested twice. In fact, Danny's use of multiple substances was so relentless and pervasive that he would probably be diagnosed as drug dependent, which indicates a severe form of the disorder.

SUBSTANCE DEPENDENCE

Drug dependence is usually described as addiction. Although we use the term "addiction" routinely when we describe people who seem to be enslaved by drugs, there is some disagreement about how to define addiction, or **substance dependence** (Woody & Cacciola, 1997). In one definition, the person is physiologically dependent on the drug or drugs, requires greater and greater amounts of the drug to experi-

ence the same effect **(tolerance),** and will respond physically in a negative way when the substance is no longer ingested **(withdrawal)** (Kalant, 1989). Tolerance and withdrawal are physiological reactions to the chemicals being ingested. How many of you have experienced headaches when you didn't get your morning coffee? You were probably going through caffeine withdrawal. In a more extreme example, withdrawal from alcohol can cause *alcohol withdrawal delirium* (or *delirium tremens*—the "DTs"), in which a person can experience frightening hallucinations and body tremors. Withdrawal from many substances can bring on chills, fever, diarrhea, nausea and vomiting, and aches and pains. This physiological response can be observed in laboratory animals under the same conditions (Goode, 1993). However, not all substances are physiologically addicting. For example, you do not go through severe physical withdrawal when you stop taking LSD or marijuana. Cocaine withdrawal has a pattern that includes anxiety, lack of motivation, and boredom (Gold & Miller, 1997). We return to the ways drugs act on our bodies when we examine the causes of abuse and dependence.

Another view of substance dependence uses the "drug-seeking behaviors" themselves as a measure of dependence. The repeated use of a drug, a desperate need to ingest more of the substance (stealing money to buy drugs, standing outside in the cold to smoke), and the likelihood that use will resume after a period of abstinence are behaviors that define the extent of drug dependence. Such behavioral reactions are different from the physiological responses to drugs we described before, and are sometimes referred to in terms of *psychological dependence*. The DSM-IV definition of substance dependence combines the physiological aspects of tolerance and withdrawal with the

ACCORDING TO THE STANDARD psychiatric definition, any drug user who passes three of the nine tests below is hooked. Several researchers were asked to apply the tests not only to drugs but also to other substances and activities—chocolate, sex, shopping. Their responses show it's possible to become addicted to all sorts of things. For example, serious runners could pass three of the tests by spending more time running than originally intended, covering increasing distances, and experiencing withdrawal symptoms (a devoted runner forced to stop because of an injury, say, might become anxious and irritable). Of course, that sort of dependency isn't necessarily destructive. Conversely, a drug that fails the addictiveness test—LSD, for instance—may be harmful just the same. That so many things are potentially addictive suggests the addiction's cause is not confined to the substance or activity—our culture may play a large role, too.

	Nicotine	Alcohol	Caffeine	Cocaine	Crack	Heroin	Ice*	LSD	Marijuana	PCP	Valium, Xanax, etc.†	Steroids	Chocolate	Running	Gambling	Shopping	Sex	Work	Driving	Television	Mountain climbing
TAKES substance or does activity more than originally intended	✓	✓	✓	✓	✓	✓	✓		✓	✓	✓	✓	✓	✓	✓	✓	✓	✓		✓	✓
WANTS to cut back or has tried to cut back but failed	✓	✓	✓	✓	✓	✓	✓		✓	✓	✓	✓	✓	✓	✓	✓	✓	✓		✓	✓
SPENDS lots of time trying to get substance or set up activity, taking substance or doing activity, or recovering	✓	✓		✓	✓	✓	✓	✓	✓	✓	✓			✓	✓		✓	✓		✓	✓
IS OFTEN intoxicated or suffers withdrawal symptoms when expected to fulfill obligations at work, school, or home		✓		✓	✓	✓	✓		✓	✓	✓										
CURTAILS or gives up important social, occupational, or recreational activities because of substance or activity		✓		✓	✓	✓	✓		✓	✓	✓			✓	✓	✓	✓	✓		✓	✓
USES substance or does activity despite persistent social, psychological, or physical problems caused by substance or activity	✓	✓	✓	✓	✓	✓	✓	✓	✓	✓	✓	✓	✓	✓	✓	✓	✓	✓		✓	✓
NEEDS more and more of substance or activity to achieve the same effect (tolerance)	✓	✓	✓	✓	✓	✓	✓				✓										
SUFFERS characteristic withdrawal symptoms when activity or substance is discontinued (cravings, anxiety, depression, jitters)	✓	✓	✓	✓	✓	✓	✓				✓			✓	✓	✓	✓	✓		✓	✓
TAKES substance or does activity to relieve or avoid withdrawal symptoms	✓	✓	✓	✓	✓	✓	✓				✓										

* Methamphetamine
† Benzodiazepines

Research by Valerie Fahey

figure 11.1 Ice, LSD, chocolate, TV: Is everything addictive? (from Franklin, 1990) behavioral and psychological aspects (American Psychiatric Association, 1994).

This definition of dependence must be seen as a "work in progress." By these criteria, many people can be considered dependent on such activities as sex, work, or even eating chocolate. Figure 11.1 shows the results of applying the DSM-IV definition of dependence to a variety of daily activities, including substance use (Franklin, 1990). Is your own behavior on this list? Obviously, what most people consider serious addiction to drugs is qualitatively different from dependence on shopping or television. The physiological and behavioral patterns may need to be further refined before we can separate the truly serious phenomenon of substance dependence from less debilitating "addictions."

Let's go back to the questions we started with: "Can you use drugs and not abuse them?" "Can you abuse drugs and not become addicted to or dependent on them?" The answer to the first question is yes. Obviously, some people drink wine or beer on a pretty regular basis without drinking to excess. Although it is not commonly believed, some people use drugs such as heroin, cocaine, or "crack" (a form of cocaine) on an occasional basis (for instance, several times a year) without abusing them (M. S. Goldman & Rather, 1993). What is disturbing is that we do not know ahead of time who might be likely to lose control and abuse these drugs, and who is likely to become dependent with even a passing use of a substance.

It may be counterintuitive, but dependence can be present without abuse. For example, cancer patients who take morphine for pain may become dependent on the drug—build up a tolerance, and go through withdrawal if it is stopped—without abusing it (Portenoy & Payne, 1997). Later in this chapter we discuss biological and psychosocial theories of the causes of substance-related disorders and of why we have individualized reactions to these substances.

Expert professionals in the substance use field were asked about the relative "addictiveness" of various drugs (Franklin, 1990). The survey results are shown in Figure 11.2. You may be surprised to see nicotine placed just ahead of methamphetamine and crack cocaine as the most addictive of drugs. Although this is only a subjective rating by these experts, it shows that our society sanctions or proscribes drugs based on factors other than their addictiveness.

Diagnostic Issues

In early editions of the DSM, alcoholism and drug abuse weren't treated as disorders in and of themselves. Instead, they were categorized as *sociopathic personality disturbances* (a forerunner of the current "antisocial personality disorder," which we'll discuss in Chapter 12), because substance use was seen as a symptom of other problems. In fact, it was considered a sign of "moral weakness," and the influence of genetics and biology was hardly acknowledged. A separate category was created in DSM-III, in 1980, and since then we have acknowledged the complex biological and psychological nature of the problem.

The DSM-IV term *substance-related disorders* indicates several subtypes of diagnoses for each substance, including

TO RANK today's commonly used drugs by their addictiveness, experts were asked to consider two questions: How easy is it to get hooked on these substances, and how hard is it to stop using them? Although a person's vulnerability to a drug also depends on individual traits—physiology, psychology, and social and economic pressures—these rankings reflect only the addictive potential inherent in the drug. The numbers below are relative rankings, based on the experts' scores for each substance.

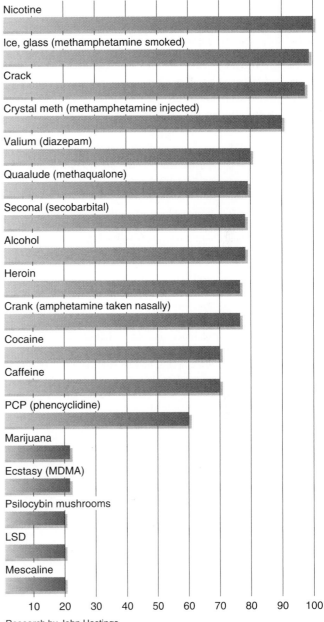

Research by John Hastings

figure 11.2   Easy to get hooked on, hard to get off (from Franklin, 1990)

dependence, abuse, intoxication, and/or withdrawal. These distinctions help clarify the problem and focus treatment on the appropriate aspect of the disorder. Danny received the diagnosis "cocaine dependence" because of the tolerance he showed for the drug, his use of larger amounts than he intended, his unsuccessful attempts to stop using it, and the activities he gave up in order to buy it. His pattern of use was more pervasive than simple abuse, and the

■ concept check 11.1

To check your understanding of substance-related definitions, read the following case summaries and then state whether they describe (a) use, (b) intoxication, (c) abuse, or (d) dependence.

1. Joe is a member of the high school football team and is out celebrating a big win. Joe doesn't believe in drinking alcohol, but doesn't mind taking a hit of marijuana every now and then. Because Joe had such a good game, he decides to smoke marijuana to celebrate. Despite his great performance in the game, Joe is easily irritated, laughing one minute and yelling the next. During a game of darts, at which he usually excels, Joe barely hits the target. And the more Joe boasts about his stats, the more difficult it is to understand him. _____

2. Jill routinely drinks diet cola. Instead of having coffee in the morning, she heads straight for the fridge. Another habit of Jill's is having a cigarette immediately after dinner. If for some reason Jill is unable to have her diet cola in the morning or her cigarette in the evening, she is not dependent upon them and can still function normally. Jill also smokes marijuana with her friends every few weeks to escape the "real world." _____

3. Steve is a 23-year-old college student who started drinking heavily when he was 16. Instead of getting drunk at weekend parties, Steve drinks a moderate amount every night. In high school Steve would become drunk after about 6 beers; now his tolerance has more than doubled. Steve claims alcohol relieves the pressures of college life. He once attempted to quit drinking, but he had chills, fever, diarrhea, nausea and vomiting, and body aches and pains. At one point, he even experienced scary hallucinations and tremors. _____

4. Jan is 32 and has just been fired from her third job in 1 year. She has been absent from work 2 days a week for the past 3 weeks. Not only did her boss telephone her and find her speech slurred, but she was also seen at a local pub in a drunken state during regular office hours. On one occasion as Jan returned to work on her lunch hour, she was pulled over by police and found to be intoxicated. During her previous job, she came to work with alcohol on her breath and was unable to conduct herself in an orderly fashion. When confronted about her problem, Jan went home and tried to forget the situation by drinking more.

_____

diagnosis of dependence provided a clear picture of his need for help.

Symptoms of other disorders can complicate the substance-abuse picture significantly. For example, do some people drink to excess because they are depressed, or do drinking and its consequences (for example, loss of friends, job) create depression? Some researchers have estimated that more than half the people with alcohol disorders have an additional psychiatric disorder, such as antisocial personality disorder, schizophrenia, or bipolar disorder (Goodwin & Gabrielli, 1997).

Substance use might occur concurrently with other disorders for several reasons (Schuckit, 1993). Substance-related disorders and anxiety and the mood disorders are highly prevalent in our society and may occur together so often just by chance. Drug intoxication and withdrawal can cause symptoms of anxiety, depression, and psychosis. Disorders such as schizophrenia and antisocial personality disorder are highly likely to include a secondary problem of substance use.

Because substance-related disorders can be so complicated, the DSM-IV tries to define when a symptom is a result of substance use and when it is not. Basically, if symptoms seen in schizophrenia or in extreme states of anxiety appear during intoxication or within 6 weeks after withdrawal from drugs, they aren't considered signs of a separate psychiatric disorder. So, for example, individuals who show signs of severe depression just after they have stopped taking heavy doses of stimulants would not be diagnosed with a major mood disorder. However, individuals who were severely depressed before they used stimulants and those whose symptoms persist more than 6 weeks after they stop might have a separate disorder (Schuckit, 1993).

We now turn to the individual substances themselves, their effects on our brains and bodies, and how they are used in our society. We have grouped the substances into four categories, depending on their effect.

- **Depressants**—These substances result in behavioral sedation. They include alcohol (ethyl alcohol) and the sedative, hypnotic, and anxiolytic drugs in the families of barbiturates (for example, Seconal) and benzodiazepines (for instance, Valium, Halcion).
- **Stimulants**—These substances cause us to be more active and alert, and can elevate mood. Included in this group are amphetamines, cocaine, nicotine, and caffeine.
- **Opiates**—The major effect of these substances is to temporarily produce analgesia (reduce pain) and euphoria. Heroin, opium, codeine, and morphine are included in this group.
- **Hallucinogens**—These substances alter sensory perception and can produce delusions, paranoia, and hallucinations. Marijuana and LSD are included in this category.

Depressants

The depressants primarily *decrease* central nervous system activity. Their principal effect is to reduce our levels of physiological arousal and help us relax. Included in this group are alcohol and the sedative, hypnotic, and anxiolytic drugs such as those prescribed for insomnia (see Chapter 8). These substances are among those most likely to produce symptoms of physical dependence, tolerance, and withdrawal. We first look at the most commonly used of these substances—alcohol—and the **alcohol use disorders** that can result.

Alcohol Use Disorders

Danny's substance abuse began when he drank beer with friends, a rite of passage for many teenagers. Alcohol has been widely used throughout history. Recently, for example, scientists found evidence of wine or beer in pottery jars at the site of a Sumerian trading post in western Iran that dates back 6,000 years (Goodwin & Gabrielli, 1997). For hundreds of years, Europeans drank large amounts of beer, wine, and hard liquor. When they came to North America in the early 1600s, they brought their considerable thirst for alcohol with them. In the United States during the early 1800s, consumption of alcohol (mostly whiskey) was over seven gallons per year for every person older than 15. This is more than three times the current rate of alcohol use in this country (Goodwin & Gabrielli, 1997; Rorabaugh, 1991).

Alcohol is produced when certain yeasts react with sugar and water and *fermentation* takes place. Historically, we have been very creative about fermenting alcohol from just about any fruit or vegetable, in part because many foods contain sugar. Alcoholic drinks have included mead from honey, sake from rice, wine from palm, mezcal and pulque from agave and cactus, liquor from maple syrup, liquor from South American jungle fruits, wine from grapes, and beer from grains (Lazare, 1989).

Clinical Description

Although alcohol is a depressant, its initial effect is an apparent stimulation. We generally experience a feeling of well-being, our inhibitions are reduced, and we become more outgoing. This is because what is initially depressed—or slowed down—are the inhibitory centers in the brain. With continued drinking, however, alcohol depresses more areas of the brain, which impedes the ability to function properly. Motor coordination is impaired (staggering, slurred speech), reaction time is slowed, we become confused, our ability to make judgments is reduced, even vision and hearing can be negatively affected, all of which help to explain why driving while intoxicated is clearly very dangerous.

Effects

Alcohol affects many parts of the body (see Figure 11.3). After it is ingested, it passes through the esophagus (1) and into the stomach (2), where small amounts are absorbed. From there most of it travels to the small intestine (3), where it is easily absorbed into the bloodstream. The circulatory system distributes the alcohol throughout the body, where it contacts every major organ, including the heart (4). Some of the alcohol goes to the lungs, where it vaporizes and is exhaled, a phenomenon that is the basis for the *breath analyzer* test that measures levels of intoxication. As alcohol passes through the liver (5) it is broken down or metabolized into carbon dioxide and water by enzymes (Maher, 1997). An average-size person is able to metabolize about 7 to 10 grams of alcohol per hour, an amount comparable to about one glass of beer or 1 ounce of 90-proof spirits (P. E. Nathan, 1993).

Most of the substances we describe in this chapter, including marijuana, the opiates, and tranquilizers, interact with specific receptors in the brain cells. The effects of alcohol, however, are much more complex. Alcohol influences a number of different neuroreceptor systems, which makes it difficult to study. For example, the **gamma-aminobutyric acid (GABA) system,** which we discussed in Chapter 2 and Chapter 5, seems to be particularly sensitive to alcohol. GABA, as you will recall, is an inhibitory neurotransmitter. Its major role is to interfere with the firing of the neuron it attaches to. When GABA attaches to its receptor, chloride ions enter the cell and make it less sensitive to the effects of other neurotransmitters. Alcohol seems to reinforce the movement of these chloride ions; as a result, the neurons have difficulty firing. In other words, although alcohol seems to loosen our tongues and make us more sociable, it makes it difficult for neurons to communicate with each other (Oscar-Berman, Shagrin, Evert, & Epstein, 1997). Because the GABA system seems to act on our feelings of anxiety, alcohol's anti-anxiety properties may result from its interaction with the GABA system.

The *glutamate system* is currently under study for its role in the effects of alcohol. In contrast to the GABA system, the glutamate system is excitatory, helping neurons to fire. It is suspected to involve learning and memory, and it may be the avenue through which alcohol affects our cognitive abilities. Blackouts, the loss of memory for what happens during intoxication, may result from the interaction of alcohol with the glutamate system. The *serotonin system* also appears to be sensitive to alcohol. This neurotransmitter system affects mood, sleep, and eating behavior and is thought to be responsible for alcoholic cravings (Oscar-Berman et al., 1997). Because alcohol affects so many neurotransmitter systems, we should not be surprised that it has such widespread and complex effects.

The long-term effects of heavy drinking are often severe. Withdrawal from chronic alcohol use typically includes hand tremors and, within several hours, nausea or vomiting, anxiety, transient hallucinations, agitation, insomnia, and, at its most extreme, **withdrawal delirium** (or **delirium tremens**—the **"DTs"**), a condition that can produce frightening hallucinations and body tremors. The devastating ex-

"When I drink, I don't care about anything, as long as I'm drinking. Nothing bothers me. The world doesn't bother me. So when I'm not drinking, the problems come back, so you drink again. The problems will always be there. You just don't realize it when you're drinking. That's why people tend to drink a lot."

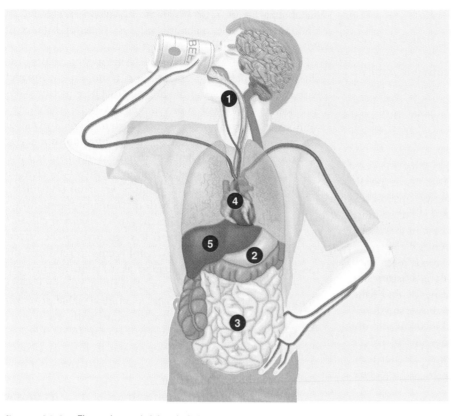

figure 11.3   The path traveled by alcohol throughout the body (see text for complete description)

experiences of people who are alcohol dependent and experience blackouts, seizures, and hallucinations. Memory and the ability to perform certain tasks may also be impaired. More seriously, two types of organic brain syndromes may result from long-term heavy alcohol use: dementia and Wernicke's disease. Dementia, which we discuss more fully in Chapter 15, involves the general loss of intellectual abilities, and can be a direct result of neurotoxicity or "poisoning of the brain" by excessive amounts of alcohol (P. E. Nathan, 1993). *Wernicke's disease* results in confusion, loss of muscle coordination, and unintelligible speech (Gordis, 1991); it is believed to be caused by a deficiency of thiamine, a vitamin that is metabolized poorly by heavy drinkers.

In spite of such damaging results, some research suggests that the neurological effects of heavy drinking are not all permanent. By painstakingly counting the neurons in the brains of deceased alcoholics and nonalcoholics, researchers in Denmark found that chronic alcohol use may not permanently damage the neurons in the cortex (the outer area of the brain). Instead, the damage may be to the connections between the neurons, which may be able to regenerate (G. B. Jensen & Pakkenberg, 1993). This finding suggests that a heavy drinker's cognitive ability may improve if the person successfully stops drinking.

The effects of alcohol abuse extend beyond the health and well-being of the drinker. Although alcohol was suspected for years to negatively affect prenatal development, this connection has been studied in earnest only a short time (K. L. Jones & Smith, 1973; Lemoine, Harousseau, Borteyru, & Menuet, 1968). **Fetal alcohol syndrome (FAS)**

perience of delirium tremens can be reduced with adequate medical treatment (McCreery & Walker, 1993).

Whether alcohol will cause organic damage depends on genetic vulnerability, frequency of use, the length of drinking binges, the blood alcohol levels attained during the drinking periods, and whether the body is given time to recover between binges (Gordis, 1991). Consequences of long-term excessive drinking include liver disease, pancreatitis, cardiovascular disorders, and brain damage (see Figures 11.4 and 11.5).

Part of the folklore concerning alcohol is that it permanently kills brain cells (neurons). As we see below, this may not be true. Some evidence for brain damage comes from the

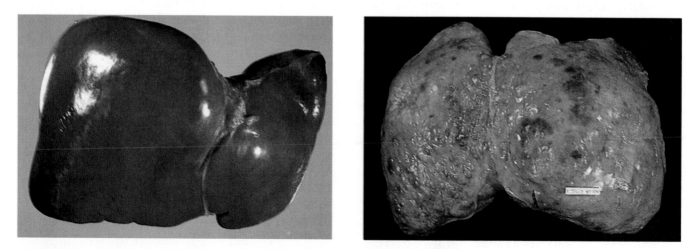

figure 11.4   A healthy liver (left) and a cirrhotic liver scarred by years of alcohol abuse (right)

is now generally recognized as a combination of problems that can occur in a child whose mother drank while she was pregnant. These problems include fetal growth retardation, cognitive deficits, behavior problems, and learning difficulties (Finnegan & Kandall, 1997). In addition, children with fetal alcohol syndrome often have characteristic facial features.

It is interesting that not all women who drink during pregnancy are at equal risk for having children with FAS. African-Americans and the Apache and Ute Indian tribes of the American Southwest appear to be at greater risk for having children with FAS (Gordis, 1991; May & Hymbaugh, 1983) than Caucasian women. We metabolize alcohol with the help of an enzyme called *alcohol dehydrogenase* (ADH) (Gordis, 1991). Three different forms of this enzyme have been identified (beta 1, beta 2, and beta 3 ADH); one form (beta 3 ADH) is found most frequently in African-Americans. Initial work also shows that beta 3 ADH may be prevalent among children with fetal alcohol syndrome. What these two findings suggest is that, in addition to the drinking habits of the mother, the likelihood that a child will have FAS may depend on whether there is a genetic tendency to have certain enzymes. Children from certain racial groups may thus be more susceptible to fetal alcohol syndrome than others. If this research is confirmed, we may have a way of identifying parents who might put their children at risk for FAS.

STATISTICS ON USE

Because alcohol consumption is legal in this country, we know more about it than about most of the other psychoactive substances we discuss in this chapter (with the possible exception of nicotine and caffeine, also legal here). Despite a national history of heavy alcohol use, most adults in the U.S. characterize themselves as light drinkers or abstainers. In fact, most alcohol is consumed by about 11% of the population (Goodwin & Gabrielli, 1997). Alcohol use has diminished during the past 20 years (U.S. Department of Health and Human Services, 1990); although this decline may be temporary, it is paralleled in many other major industrialized countries (Horgan, Sparrow, & Brazeau, 1986). Figure 11.6 shows the change in alcohol consumption in 25 countries between 1979 and 1984. Reduced consumption may reflect increased public awareness of the health risks associated with alcohol use and abuse. A change in demographics may also partly account for the decline, as the proportion of the over-60 population has increased, and alcohol use among people in this age group is historically low (U.S. Department of Health and Human Services, 1990).

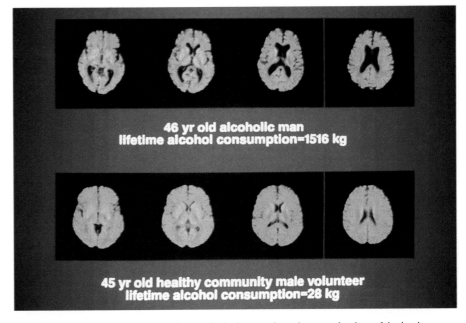

**46 yr old alcoholic man
lifetime alcohol consumption=1516 kg**

**45 yr old healthy community male volunteer
lifetime alcohol consumption=28 kg**

figure 11.5 The dark areas in the top brain images show the extensive loss of brain tissue that result from heavy alcohol use.

Alcohol use is highest among white Americans (56%), and somewhat lower among Hispanics (45%) and African-Americans (41%) (Office of Applied Studies, 1997). Binge drinking (five or more drinks on the same occasion at least once in the past month) is lower among African-Americans (11.2%) than among whites (16.6%) or Hispanics (17.2%). And, in a pattern that is the reverse of the trend for illicit drug use, education is positively correlated with recent alcohol use: People with college degrees are more likely to drink than people with less than a high school education (Office of Applied Studies, 1997).

Men are more likely than women to drink alcohol and are also more likely to drink heavily (Office of Applied Studies,

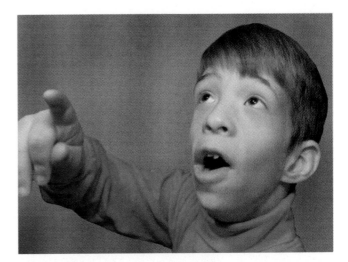

Physical characteristics of fetal alcohol syndrome include skin folds at the corners of the eyes, low nasal bridge, short nose, groove between nose and upper lip, small head circumference, small eye opening, small midface, and thin upper lip.

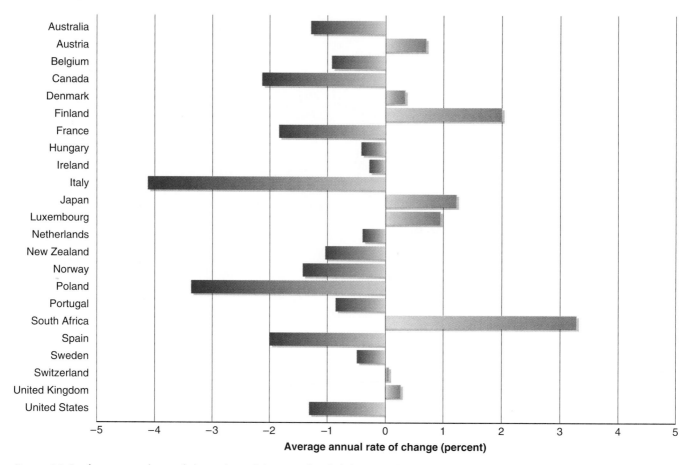

figure 11.6   Average annual rate of change (percent) in per capita alcohol consumption for 25 countries, 1979-1984 (from Brazeau & Burr, 1992)

1997; U.S. Department of Health and Human Services, 1990). In a large survey among college-age men and women, about 42% of respondents said they had gone on a binge of heavy drinking once in the preceding 2 weeks (Presley & Meil-

Males of 18 to 29 years of age are most vulnerable to drinking problems.

man, 1992). Men, however, were more likely to report several binges in the 2-week period. The same survey found that students with a grade-point average of "A" had no more than three drinks per week, whereas "D" and "F" students averaged 11 alcoholic drinks per week (Presley & Meilman, 1992). Overall, these data point to the popularity and pervasiveness of drinking in our society.

STATISTICS ON ABUSE AND DEPENDENCE

Our everyday experience tells us that not everyone who drinks becomes dependent on alcohol or abuses it. However, researchers estimate that about 10% of Americans experience some level of problem with alcohol, with about 10.5 million adults thought to be alcohol dependent (McCreery & Walker, 1993). Males seem to be most vulnerable to drinking problems when they are between the ages of 18 and 29. Approximately 14% report symptoms of dependence during this period, and 20% report some negative drinking-related consequences (U.S. Department of Health and Human

Services, 1990). This number decreases with age to about 5% reporting dependence and 7% reporting drinking-related consequences by age 60 and older. The picture for women is not so clear. The number of women reporting symptoms of dependence stays at a low and stable rate of about 5% to 6% through age 49, and then decreases to around 1%. Drinking-related consequences start out higher than for men, at around 12%, but they quickly decline almost to nonexistence after age 60. In short, among the general population, young (18–29), single males are most likely to be heavy drinkers and to have alcohol use problems (U.S. Department of Health and Human Services, 1990).

This picture of a heavy drinking, young, single male doesn't fit the stereotype of a skid row drunk, does it? It is true, however, that homelessness is associated with alcohol use and dependence. Unlike the general population, 20% to 45% of homeless people experience their highest level of alcohol abuse and dependence during the middle years. Over their lifetime, some 63% of this group will experience drinking problems (U.S. Department of Health and Human Services, 1990). Some may drink through mid-life to help cope with the frustration and desperation of being homeless. It is probably also true that, for some, homelessness is in part a consequence of drinking or of a combination of substance abuse and other mental health problems.

Outside the United States, rates of alcohol abuse and dependence vary widely. Compared to the U.S. average of 10%, the prevalence of alcohol dependence in Peru is about 35%; in South Korea it is approximately 22%; it is about 3.5% in Taipei and as low as 0.45% in Shanghai (Helzer & Canino, 1992; Yamamoto, Silva, Sasao, Wang, & Nguyen, 1993). Such cultural differences can be accounted for by different attitudes toward drinking, the availability of alcohol, physiological reactions, and family norms and patterns. For example, the high drinking rates in Korea may reflect the cultural expectation that men drink heavily on some social occasions (C. K. Lee, 1992).

PROGRESSION

Remember that Danny went through periods of heavy alcohol and drug use, but also had times when he was relatively "straight" and did not use drugs. Similarly, many people who abuse alcohol or are dependent on it fluctuate between drinking heavily, drinking "socially" without negative effects, and being abstinent, not drinking at all (Schuckit, Smith, Anthenelli, & Irwin, 1993; Vaillant, 1983). It seems that about 20% of people with severe alcohol dependence have a spontaneous remission and do not reexperience problems with drinking (Ludwig, 1985; Vaillant, 1983).

It used to be thought that once problems arose with drinking, they would become steadily worse, following a predictable downward pattern so long as the person kept drinking (Sobell & Sobell, 1993). In other words, like a disease that isn't treated properly, alcoholism will get progressively worse if left unchecked. First championed by Jellinek more than 50 years ago, this view continues to influence the way people view and treat the disorder (Jellinek, 1946, 1952, 1960). Unfortunately, Jellinek based his model of the pro-

Intoxication is often involved in cases of domestic violence.

gression of alcohol use on a now famous but faulty study (Jellinek, 1946), which we will briefly review.

In 1945, the newly formed self-help organization Alcoholics Anonymous (AA) sent out some 1,600 surveys to its members asking them to describe symptoms related to drinking, such as feelings of guilt or remorse, and rationalizations about their actions, and to note when these reactions first occurred. Only 98 of the almost 1,600 surveys were returned, however. As you know, such a small response could seriously affect data interpretation. Obviously, a group of 98 may be very different from the group as a whole, so they may not represent the typical person with alcohol problems. Also, because the responses were retrospective (participants were recalling past events), their reports may be inaccurate. Despite these and other problems, Jellinek agreed to analyze the data and he developed a four-stage model for the progression of alcoholism based on this limited information (Jellinek, 1952). According to his model, individuals go through a *prealcoholic stage* (drinking occasionally with few serious consequences), a *prodromal stage* (drinking heavily but with few outward signs of a problem), a *crucial stage* (loss of control, with occasional binges), and a *chronic stage* (the primary daily activities involve getting and drinking alcohol). A number of attempts by other researchers to confirm this progression of stages has not been successful (Schuckit et al., 1993).

It appears instead that the course of *alcohol dependence* may be progressive for most people, although the course of *alcohol abuse* may be more variable. For example, a recent study followed 636 male inpatients in an alcohol rehabilitation center (Schuckit et al., 1993). Among these chronically alcohol-dependent men, a general progression of alcohol-related life problems did emerge, although not in the specific pattern proposed by Jellinek. Three-quarters of the men reported moderate consequences of their drinking, such as demotions at work, in their 20s. During their 30s, the men had more serious problems, such as regular blackouts and signs of alcohol withdrawal. By their late 30s and early 40s, these men demonstrated long-term serious consequences of their drinking, which included hallucinations, withdrawal convulsions, and hepatitis or pancreatitis. This study suggests a common pattern among people with chronic alcohol abuse and dependence, one with increasingly severe consequences. This progressive pattern is not inevitable for everyone who abuses alcohol, although we do not as yet understand what distinguishes those who are and those who are not susceptible (Sobell & Sobell, 1993; Vaillant & Hiller–Sturmhöfel, 1997).

Finally, statistics frequently link alcohol with violent behavior. Numerous studies have found that many people who commit such violent acts as murder, rape, and assault are often intoxicated at the time of the crime (Murdoch, Pihl, & Ross, 1990). We hope that you are skeptical of this type of correlation. Just because drunkenness and violence overlap does not mean that alcohol will necessarily make you violent. Laboratory studies show that alcohol does make subjects more aggressive (Bushman, 1993). However, whether a person behaves aggressively outside the laboratory probably involves a number of interrelated factors, such as the quantity and timing of alcohol consumed, the person's history of violence, his or her expectations about drinking, and what happens to the individual while intoxicated. Alcohol does not *cause* aggression, but it may reduce the fear associated with being punished, and it may impair the ability to consider the consequences of acting impulsively (Ito, Miller, & Pollock, 1996). Given the right circumstances, such impaired rational thinking may increase a person's risk of behaving aggressively (Pihl, Peterson, & Lau, 1993).

Sedative, Hypnotic, or Anxiolytic Substance Use Disorders

The general group of depressants also includes *sedative* (calming), *hypnotic* (sleep-inducing), and *anxiolytic* (anxiety-reducing) drugs (Wesson, Smith, Ling, & Seymour, 1997). These drugs include the barbiturates and the benzodiazepines. **Barbiturates** (which include Amytal, Seconal, and Nembutal) are a family of sedative drugs first synthesized in Germany in 1882 (McKim, 1991). They were prescribed to help people sleep and replaced such drugs as alcohol and opium. Barbiturates were widely prescribed by physicians during the 1930s and 1940s, before their addictive properties were fully understood. By the 1950s they were among the drugs most abused by adults in the United States (Abadinsky, 1993).

The **benzodiazepines** (which today include Valium, Xanax, Rohypnol, and Halcion) have been used since the 1960s, primarily to reduce anxiety. These drugs were originally touted as a miracle cure for the anxieties of living in our highly pressured technological society. Although in 1980 the Food and Drug Administration ruled that they are not appropriate for reducing the tension and anxiety resulting from everyday stresses and strains, an estimated 3.7 billion doses of benzodiazepines are consumed by Americans each year (Shabecoff, 1987). In general, benzodiazepines are considered much safer than barbiturates, with less risk of abuse and dependence (Warneke, 1991). Recent reports on the misuse of Rohypnol, however, show how dangerous these drugs can be. Rohypnol (otherwise known as "roofies") gained a following among teenagers in the 1990s because it has the same effect as alcohol without the telltale odor. However, there are disturbing reports of men giving the drug to women without their knowledge, making it easier for them to engage in date rape (Wesson, Smith, Ling, & Seymour, 1997).

CLINICAL DESCRIPTION

At low doses, barbiturates relax the muscles and can produce a mild feeling of well-being. However, larger doses can have results similar to those of heavy drinking: slurred speech, and problems walking, concentrating, and working. At extremely high doses the diaphragm muscles can relax so much as to cause death by suffocation. In fact, overdosing on barbiturates is a common means of suicide.

Like the barbiturates, benzodiazepines are used to calm an individual and induce sleep. In addition, drugs in this class are prescribed as muscle relaxants and anticonvulsants (antiseizure medications) (Wesson et al., 1997). People who use them for nonmedical reasons report first feeling a pleasant high and a reduction of inhibition, similar to the effects of drinking alcohol. However, with continued use, tolerance and dependence can develop. Users who try to stop taking the drug experience symptoms like those of alcohol withdrawal (anxiety, insomnia, tremors, and delirium).

The DSM-IV criteria for sedative, hypnotic, and anxiolytic drug use disorders do not differ substantially from those for alcohol disorders. Both include maladaptive behavioral changes such as inappropriate sexual or aggressive behavior, variable moods, impaired judgment, impaired social or occupational functioning, slurred speech, motor coordination problems, and unsteady gait.

Like alcohol, sedative, hypnotic, and anxiolytic drugs affect the brain by impacting the GABA neurotransmitter system (Gardner, 1997), though by slightly different mechanisms; as a result, when people combine alcohol with any of these drugs, there can be synergistic effects (Fils-Aime, 1993). In other words, if you drink alcohol after taking a benzodiazepine or barbiturate, the total effects can reach dangerous levels. One theory about actress Marilyn Monroe's death in 1962 is that she combined alcohol with too many barbiturates and unintentionally killed herself.

STATISTICS

Barbiturate use has declined and benzodiazepines use has increased since 1960 (Warneke, 1991). Recent surveys to learn the annual extent of benzodiazepine use, other than for sleep or medical uses, estimate that approximately 11.1% of Americans use them, 7.4% of the Dutch, and 17% of Belgians, with females being twice as likely to report their use as males (Warneke, 1991). Physicians increasingly prescribe benzodiazepines instead of barbiturates, because they provide similar beneficial effects with fewer of the harmful effects. Benzodiazepines may be misused less because they have an upper limit of effectiveness—in other words, there is a point at which taking more of the drug has no additional effect (McKim, 1991).

Stimulants

Of all the psychoactive drugs used in this country, the most commonly consumed are the stimulants. Included in this group are caffeine (in coffee, chocolate, and many soft drinks), nicotine (in tobacco products such as cigarettes), amphetamines, and cocaine. You probably used caffeine when you got up this morning. In contrast to the depressant drugs, stimulants—as their name suggests—make you more alert and energetic. They have a long history of use. Chinese physicians, for example, have used an amphetamine compound called Ma-huang for more than 5,000 years (King & Ellinwood, 1997). We will describe several stimulants and their effects on behavior, mood, and cognition.

Amphetamine Use Disorders

At low doses, amphetamines can induce feelings of elation and vigor, and can reduce fatigue. You literally feel "up." However, after a period of elevation you come back down and "crash," feeling depressed or tired. In sufficient quantities, stimulants can lead to **amphetamine use disorders.**

Amphetamines are manufactured in the laboratory; they were first synthesized in 1887 and later used as a treatment for asthma and as a nasal decongestant (King & Ellinwood, 1997). Because amphetamines also reduce appetite, some people take them to lose weight. In 1987 Kitty Dukakis, wife of Massachusetts governor Michael Dukakis, revealed that she had been addicted for 26 years to amphetamines that were originally prescribed for weight control. Long-haul truck drivers, pilots, and some college students trying to "pull all-nighters" use amphetamines to get that extra energy boost and stay awake. Amphetamines are prescribed for people with *narcolepsy*, a sleep disorder characterized by excessive sleepiness. Some of these drugs (Ritalin, Cylert) are even given to children with *attention deficit/hyperactivity disorder*, which we discuss in Chapter 14.

DSM-IV diagnostic criteria for amphetamine intoxication include significant behavioral symptoms, such as euphoria or affective blunting, changes in sociability, interpersonal sensitivity, anxiety, tension, anger, stereotyped behaviors, impaired judgment, and impaired social or occupational functioning. In addition, physiological symptoms occur during or shortly after amphetamine or related substances are ingested, and can include heart rate or blood pressure changes, perspiration or chills, nausea or vomiting, weight loss, muscular weakness, respiratory depression, chest pain, seizures, or coma. The danger in amphetamines and the other stimulants

Designer drugs, especially Ecstasy, are popular among young people.

we discuss is their negative effects. Severe intoxication or overdose can cause hallucinations, panic, agitation, and paranoid delusions (R. M. Stein & Ellinwood, 1993). Amphetamine tolerance builds quickly, making it doubly dangerous. Withdrawal often results in apathy, prolonged periods of sleep, irritability, and depression.

Periodically, certain "designer drugs" appear in local mini-epidemics (Morgan, 1997). An amphetamine called methylene-dioxymethamphetamine (MDMA), first synthesized in 1912 in Germany, was used as an appetite suppressant (Grob & Poland, 1997). Recreational use of this drug, now commonly called Ecstasy, rose sharply in the late 1980s, and one poll estimates that 2% of all college students used it during the previous school year (NIDA, 1993). Its effects are best described by a user: "just like speed but without the comedown, and you feel warm and trippy like acid, but without the possibility of a major freak-out" (O'Hagan, 1992, p. 10). A purified crystallized form of amphetamine, called "ice," is ingested through smoking. This drug causes marked aggressive tendencies and stays in the system longer than cocaine, making it particularly dangerous (R. M. Stein & Ellinwood, 1993). However enjoyable these new amphetamines may be in the short term, the potential for users to become dependent on them is extremely high, with great risk for long-term difficulties.

Amphetamines stimulate the central nervous system by enhancing the activity of norepinephrine and dopamine. Specifically, amphetamines help the release of these neurotransmitters and block their reuptake, thereby making more of them available throughout the system (R. M. Stein & Ellinwood, 1993). Too much amphetamine—and therefore too much dopamine and norepinephrine—can lead to hallucinations and delusions. As we will see in Chapter 13, this effect has stimulated theories on the causes of schizophrenia, which can also include hallucinations and delusions.

Cocaine Use Disorders

The use and misuse of drugs, such as those leading to **cocaine use disorders,** wax and wane according to societal fashion, moods, and sanctions (Uddo, Malow, & Sutker, 1993). Cocaine replaced amphetamines as the stimulant of choice in the 1970s (R. M. Stein & Ellinwood, 1993). Cocaine is derived from the leaves of the coca plant, a flowering bush indigenous to South America. In his essay "On Coca" (1885/1974), a young Sigmund Freud wrote of cocaine's magical properties: "I have tested [the] effect of coca, which wards off hunger, sleep, and fatigue and steels one to intellectual effort, some dozen times on myself" (p. 60).

Latin Americans have chewed coca leaves for centuries to get relief from hunger and fatigue (Musto, 1992). Cocaine was introduced into the United States in the late 19th century; it was widely used from then until the 1920s. In 1885, Parke, Davis & Co. manufactured coca and cocaine in 15 different forms, including coca-leaf cigarettes and cigars, inhalants, and crystals. For people who couldn't afford these products, a cheaper way to get cocaine was in Coca-Cola, which up until 1903 contained 60 mg of cocaine per 8-ounce serving (Gold, 1997).

CLINICAL DESCRIPTION

Like the amphetamines, in small amounts cocaine increases alertness, produces euphoria, increases blood pressure and pulse, and causes insomnia and loss of appetite. Remember that Danny snorted (inhaled) cocaine when he partied through the night with his friends. He later said the drug made him feel powerful and invincible—the only way he really felt self-confident. The effects of cocaine are short-lived; for Danny they lasted less than an hour, and he had to snort repeatedly to keep himself up. During these binges he often became paranoid, experiencing exaggerated fears

For centuries, Latin Americans have chewed coca leaves to get relief from hunger and fatigue.

This little girl's mother used crack cocaine during her pregnancy. Research continues into the effects of the drug on children of dependent mothers.

that he would be caught or that someone would steal his cocaine. Such paranoia is common among cocaine abusers, occurring in two-thirds or more (Satel, 1992). Cocaine also makes the heart beat more rapidly and irregularly, and it can have fatal consequences, depending on a person's physical condition and the amount of the drug ingested. It is now believed that the outstanding college basketball player Len Bias died from cardiac irregularities after using only a moderate amount of cocaine.

We saw that alcohol can damage the developing fetus. It has also been suspected that the use of cocaine (especially crack) by pregnant women *may* adversely affect their babies. Nationally, some estimates suggest that as many as 250,000 children may have been exposed to cocaine prenatally (Phibbs, Bateman, & Schwartz, 1991). "Crack babies" appear at birth to be more irritable than normal babies and have long bouts of high-pitched crying. They were originally thought to have permanent brain damage. All these symptoms were initially attributed to the mother's cocaine use. However, a closer look at these children suggests that we may have been too quick to blame cocaine exclusively. Recent work suggests that many children born to mothers who have used cocaine during pregnancy may have decreased birth weight and decreased head circumference, but they show no evidence of problems with cognitive or motor skills at birth or 1 month later (Gold, 1997; N. S. Woods, Eyler, Behnke, & Conlon, 1992). The problem with evaluating most children born to mothers who used cocaine is that their mothers almost always used other substances as well, including alcohol and nicotine. Many of these children are raised in disrupted home environments, which further complicates the picture. It may be that damage once attributed only to cocaine results from a combination of drugs and/or inadequate parenting.

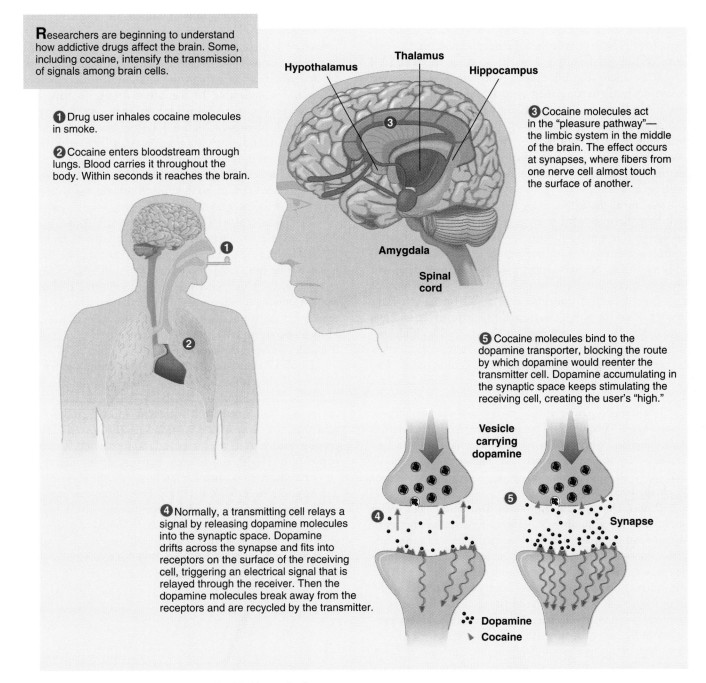

Researchers are beginning to understand how addictive drugs affect the brain. Some, including cocaine, intensify the transmission of signals among brain cells.

1 Drug user inhales cocaine molecules in smoke.

2 Cocaine enters bloodstream through lungs. Blood carries it throughout the body. Within seconds it reaches the brain.

Hypothalamus   Thalamus   Hippocampus

3 Cocaine molecules act in the "pleasure pathway"— the limbic system in the middle of the brain. The effect occurs at synapses, where fibers from one nerve cell almost touch the surface of another.

Amygdala

Spinal cord

5 Cocaine molecules bind to the dopamine transporter, blocking the route by which dopamine would reenter the transmitter cell. Dopamine accumulating in the synaptic space keeps stimulating the receiving cell, creating the user's "high."

Vesicle carrying dopamine

Synapse

4 Normally, a transmitting cell relays a signal by releasing dopamine molecules into the synaptic space. Dopamine drifts across the synapse and fits into receptors on the surface of the receiving cell, triggering an electrical signal that is relayed through the receiver. Then the dopamine molecules break away from the receptors and are recycled by the transmitter.

Dopamine
Cocaine

figure 11.7 Anatomy of a high (from *The Washington Post*)

Continuing research should help us better understand the negative effects of cocaine on children. One recent study suggests that prenatal cocaine exposure may affect the fetus's "biological clock"—the suprachiasmatic nucleus (Weaver, Rivkees, & Reppert, 1992), which would cause a reaction similar to jet lag that might contribute to the irritability and other problems experienced by the newborn.

STATISTICS

Cocaine use across most age groups has decreased during the past decade and a half, from approximately 2.5% in 1979 to less than 1.0% in 1995 (National Institute on Drug Abuse, 1991; Office of Applied Studies, 1997). Approximately 17% of cocaine users have also used crack cocaine

(a crystallized form of cocaine that is smoked) (Closser, 1992). In 1991, one estimate was that about 0.2% of Americans had tried crack, and that an increasing proportion of the abusers seeking treatment were young, unemployed adults living in urban areas (Closser, 1992). Cocaine use by high school seniors was at its highest level in 1985 and has been decreasing since that time, with 3.4% of seniors in 1988 saying that they had used cocaine in the past month (R. M. Stein & Ellinwood, 1993).

Cocaine is in the same group of stimulants as amphetamines because it has similar effects on the brain. The "up" seems to come primarily from the effect of cocaine on the dopamine system. If you look at Figure 11.7 you will see how this action occurs. Cocaine enters the bloodstream and is carried to the brain. There the cocaine molecules block the reuptake of dopamine. As you know, neurotransmitters released at the synapse stimulate the next neuron and then are recycled back to the original neuron. Cocaine seems to bind to places where dopamine neurotransmitters reenter their home neuron, blocking their reuptake by the neuron. The dopamine that cannot be taken in by the neuron remains in the synapse, causing repeated stimulation of the next neuron. This stimulation of the dopamine neurons in the "pleasure pathway" (the site in the brain that seems to be involved in the experience of pleasure) causes the high associated with cocaine use.

As late as the 1980s, many felt that cocaine was a wonder drug that produced feelings of euphoria without being addictive (Gawin & Kleber, 1992). Such a conservative source as the *Comprehensive Textbook of Psychiatry* in 1980 indicated that, "taken no more than two or three times per week, cocaine creates no serious problems" (Grinspoon & Bakalar, 1980). Just imagine—a drug that gives you extra energy, helps you think clearly and more creatively, and lets you accomplish more throughout the day, all without any negative side effects! In our highly competitive and complex technological society, this would be a dream come true. But, as you probably realize, such temporary benefits have a high cost. Cocaine fooled us. Dependence comes on slowly, not becoming apparent until 2 to 5 years after use begins (Gawin & Kleber, 1992). Few negative effects are noted at first; however, with continued use, sleep is disrupted, increased tolerance causes a need for higher doses, paranoia and other negative symptoms set in, and the cocaine user gradually becomes socially isolated.

Again, Danny's case illustrates this pattern. He was a social user for a number of years, using cocaine only with friends and only occasionally. Eventually he had more frequent episodes of excessive use or binges, and he found himself craving the drug more and more between binges. After the binges, Danny would crash and sleep. Cocaine withdrawal isn't like that of alcohol. Instead of rapid heart beat, tremors, or nausea, withdrawal from cocaine produces pronounced feelings of apathy and boredom. Think for a minute how dangerous this type of withdrawal is. First, you're bored with everything and find little pleasure from the everyday activities of work or relationships. The one thing that can "bring you back to life" is cocaine. As you can imagine, a particularly vicious cycle develops: Cocaine is abused, withdrawal causes apathy, cocaine abuse resumes. The atypical withdrawal pattern misled people into believing that cocaine was not addictive. We now know that cocaine abusers go through patterns of tolerance and withdrawal comparable to those experienced by abusers of other psychoactive drugs (Gawin & Kleber, 1992).

Nicotine Use Disorders

When you think of "addicts," what image comes to mind? Do you see dirty and disheveled people huddled on an old mattress in an abandoned building, waiting for the next fix?

Do you picture businesspeople huddled outside a city building on a rainy afternoon furtively smoking cigarettes? Of course, both these images are accurate, because the nicotine in tobacco is a psychoactive substance that produces patterns of dependence, tolerance, and withdrawal—**nicotine use disorders**—comparable to the other drugs we have discussed so far (Schmitz, Schneider, & Jarvik, 1997). In 1942, the Scottish physician Lennox Johnson "shot up" nicotine extract and found after 80 injections that he liked it more than cigarettes and felt deprived without it (Kanigel, 1988). This colorless, oily liquid—called nicotine after Jean Nicot, who introduced tobacco to the French court in the 16th century—was what gave smoking its pleasurable qualities.

The tobacco plant is indigenous to North America, and Native Americans cultivated and smoked the leaves centuries ago. Today, almost a quarter of all Americans smoke, which is down from the 42.4% who were smokers in 1965 (Schmitz et al., 1997). Unfortunately, there has not been a decline in smoking among teenagers, and 17% of all high school seniors report that they smoke daily (U.S. Department of Health and Human Services, 1989); overall, approximately 2.2 million teenagers between the ages of 12 and 17 smoke.

DSM-IV does not describe an intoxication pattern for nicotine. Rather, it lists withdrawal symptoms, which include depressed mood, insomnia, irritability, anxiety, difficulty concentrating, restlessness, and increased appetite and weight gain. Nicotine in small doses stimulates the central nervous system; it can also relieve stress and improve mood (U.S. Department of Health and Human Services, 1988). But it can also cause high blood pressure and increase the risk of heart disease and cancer (McKim, 1991). High doses can blur your vision, cause confusion, lead to convulsions, and sometimes even cause death. Once smokers are dependent on nicotine, going without it causes these withdrawal symptoms (Hughes, Gust, Skoog, Keenan, & Fenwick, 1991). If you doubt the addictive power of nicotine, consider that the rate of relapse

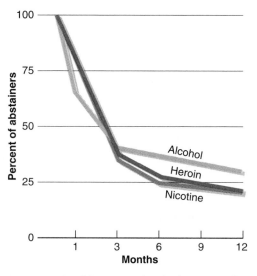

figure 11.8 Relapse rates for nicotine compared to alcohol and heroin. Smokers trying to give up cigarettes backslide about as frequently as alcoholics and heroin addicts (adapted from Kanigel, 1988).

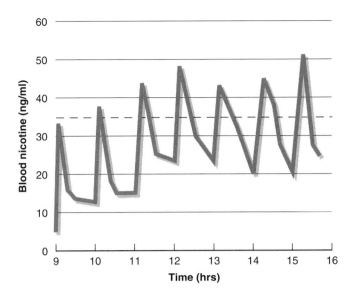

figure 11.9 Smoking patterns and nicotine levels. This subject smoked one cigarette an hour, illustrating how smokers inhale more or less deeply or often, to get the desired blood levels of nicotine—on average 35 nanograms per milliliter (adapted from Kanigel, 1988).

among people trying to give up drugs is equivalent among those using alcohol, heroin, and cigarettes (see Figure 11.8).

Nicotine is inhaled into the lungs, where it enters the bloodstream. Only 7 to 19 seconds after a person inhales the smoke, the nicotine reaches the brain (Benowitz, 1992). Nicotine appears to stimulate specific receptors—*nicotinic acetylcholine receptors (nAChRs)*—in the midbrain reticular formation and the limbic system, the site of the "pleasure pathway" mentioned before (McGehee, Heath, Gelber, Devay, & Role, 1995). Recent evidence also suggests that nicotine may affect the fetal brain, and may increase the likelihood that children of mothers who smoke during pregnancy will smoke later in life (Kandel, Wu, & Davies, 1994). Smokers actually dose themselves throughout the day, in an effort to keep nicotine at a steady level in the bloodstream (10 to 50 nanograms per milliliter) (see Figure 11.9) (Dalack, Glassman, & Covey, 1993).

Smoking has been linked with signs of negative affect, such as depression, anxiety, and anger (Hall, Muñoz, Reus, & Sees, 1993). For example, many people who quit smoking but later resume report that feelings of depression or anxiety were responsible for the relapse (Marlatt & Gordon, 1980). This finding suggests that nicotine may help improve mood.

More recently, however, two studies have examined the complex relationship between cigarette smoking and negative affect. In one, severe depression was found to occur significantly more often among people with nicotine dependence (Breslau, Kilbey, & Andreski, 1993). This was true whether they continued smoking or tried to quit during the study period. In other words, people dependent on nicotine may be more likely than others to be depressed, whether or not they are trying to quit. The second study further explored the relationship between depression and smoking. Kenneth Kendler, whose large-scale twin study of depression among women was discussed in Chapter 4, found that

among identical twins there was a relationship between smoking and depression only if both pairs of identical twins had a history of depression or smoking (Kendler, Neale, MacLean, et al., 1993). In other words, if only one of the pair had a history of depression then there was no relationship between depression and smoking. What does this mean? It suggests that in some women there may be a genetic vulnerability that, combined with personal experiences, may lead to both depression and smoking, not that depression causes smoking or smoking causes depression. (We discuss evidence for the genetics of smoking when we cover the causes of substance abuse later in this chapter.)

Caffeine Use Disorders

Caffeine is the most common of the psychoactive substances, used regularly by 90% of all Americans (A. Goldstein, 1994). Called the "gentle stimulant" because it is thought to be the least harmful of all the addictive drugs, caffeine can still lead to **caffeine use disorders.** This drug is found in tea, coffee, many of the cola drinks sold today, and in cocoa products.

As most of you have experienced firsthand, caffeine in small doses can elevate your mood and decrease fatigue. In larger doses, it can make you feel jittery and can cause insomnia. Because caffeine takes a relatively long time to leave our bodies (it has a blood half-life of about 6 hours), sleep can be disturbed if the caffeine is ingested in the hours close to bedtime (Bootzin, Manber, Perlis, Salvio, & Wyatt, 1993). As with the other psychoactive drugs, people react variously to caffeine; some are very sensitive to it and others can consume relatively large amounts with little effect. Recent research suggests that moderate use of caffeine (a cup of coffee per day) by pregnant women does not harm the developing fetus (Mills et al., 1993).

As with other stimulants, regular caffeine use can result in tolerance and dependence on the drug (Strain, Mumford, Silverman, & Griffiths, 1994). Those of you who have experienced headaches, drowsiness, and a generally unpleasant mood when denied your morning coffee have had the withdrawal symptoms characteristic of this drug (Silverman, Evans, Strain, & Griffiths, 1992). Caffeine's effect on the brain seems to involve the neurotransmitters *adenosine* and, to a lesser extent, *serotonin* (Greden & Walters, 1997). Caffeine seems to block adenosine reuptake. However, we do not yet know the role of adenosine in brain function, nor whether the interruption of the adenosine system is responsible for the elation and increased energy that come with caffeine use.

 **Opioids**

The word *opiate* refers to the natural chemicals in the opium poppy that have a *narcotic* effect (they relieve pain and induce sleep). In some circumstances they can cause **opioid**

Opium poppies

use disorders. The broader term *opioids* refers to the family of substances that includes natural opiates, synthetic variations (methadone, pethidine), and the comparable substances that occur naturally in the brain (enkephalins, beta-endorphins, and dynorphins) (Jaffe, Knapp, & Ciraulo, 1997). In *The Wizard of Oz,* the Wicked Witch of the West puts Dorothy, Toto, and their companions to sleep by making them walk through a field of poppies, a literary allusion to the opium poppies that are used to produce morphine, codeine, and heroin.

Just as the poppies lull the Tin Man, the Scarecrow, Dorothy, the Cowardly Lion, and Toto, opiates induce euphoria, drowsiness, and slowed breathing. High doses can lead to death if respiration is completely depressed. Opiates are also *analgesics,* substances that help relieve pain. People are sometimes given morphine before and after surgery to calm them and help block pain.

Withdrawal from opioids can be so unpleasant that people may continue to use these drugs despite a sincere desire to stop. However, barbiturate and alcohol withdrawal can be even more distressing. The perception among many people that opioid withdrawal can be life-threatening stems from the experiences of heroin addicts in the 1920s and 1930s. These users had access to cheaper and purer forms of the drug than are available today and withdrawal had more serious side effects than withdrawal from the weaker versions currently in use (McKim, 1991). Even so, people who cease or reduce their opioid intake begin to experience symptoms within 6 to 12 hours; these include excessive yawning, nausea and vomiting, chills, muscle aches, diarrhea, and insomnia—temporarily disrupting work, school, and social relationships. The symptoms can persist for 1 to 3 days, and the process is completed in about a week.

Because opiate users tend to be secretive, estimates of the exact number of people who use, abuse, or are dependent on these drugs are difficult to come by, but one estimate placed the users in the United States at about a million (A. Goldstein, 1994). We noted before that there

are trends in drug use. Opiate use, in particular heroin, was popular in the early to mid-1970s, and has since been replaced by cocaine and its derivatives as the drug of choice (Uddo et al., 1993). Unfortunately, there is some indication that opiates may be making a comeback, with a steady increase in abuse of "speedballs," a dangerous combination of both heroin and cocaine (M. H. Pollack, Brotman, & Rosenbaum, 1989). Advertising that glamorizes the physical symptoms of these drugs—a gaunt and haunted look known as "heroin chic"—may also increase their popularity. People who use opiates face risks beyond addiction and the threat of overdose. Because these drugs are usually injected intravenously, users are at increased risk for HIV infection, and therefore AIDS.

The life of an opiate addict is bleak. Recently, results were published from a 24-year follow-up study of more than 500 addicts in California (Hser, Anglin, & Powers, 1993). Figure 11.10 illustrates their history. At the follow-up in 1985–1986, 27.7% addicts had died, and the mean age at death was only about 40 years. Almost half the deaths were the results of homicide, suicide, or accident, and about a third were from drug overdose. There is a fairly stable pattern of daily narcotic use in 7%–8% of the group.

The high or "rush" experienced by users comes from activation of the body's natural opioid system. In other words, the brain already has its own opioids—called enkephalins and endorphins—that provide narcotic effects (Simon, 1997). Heroin, opium, morphine, and other opiates activate this system. The discovery of the natural opioid system was a major breakthrough in the field of psychopharmacology: Not only does it allow us to study the effects of addictive drugs on the brain, but it has led to important discoveries that may help us treat people dependent on these drugs.

Hallucinogens

The substances we have examined so far affect people by making them feel "up" if they are stimulants such as cocaine, caffeine, and nicotine, or "down" if they are depressants such as alcohol and the barbiturates. Next we explore the substances that can lead to **hallucinogen use disorder.** They essentially change the way the user perceives the world. Sight, sound, feelings, taste, and even smell are distorted, sometimes in dramatic ways, when a person is under the influence of drugs such as marijuana and LSD.

Marijuana

Marijuana was the drug of choice in the 1960s and early 1970s. Although it has decreased in popularity, it is still the most routinely used illegal substance, with 66.5 million Americans reporting they have tried marijuana and 5.5 million saying they smoke it at least once a week (Roffman &

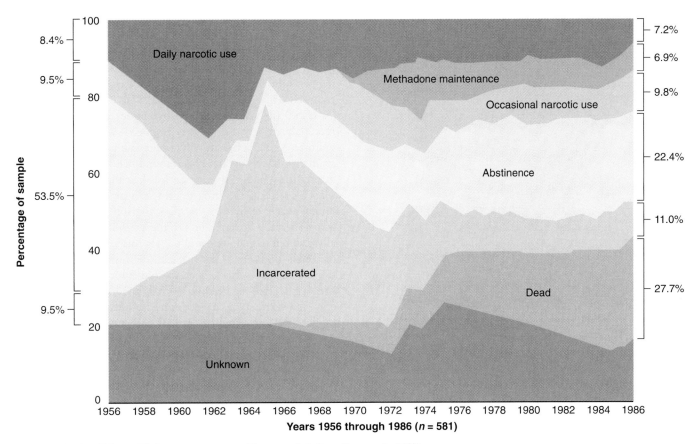

figure 11.10 Opiate addiction patterns over a 30-year period (from Hser et al., 1993).

Stephens, 1993). Marijuana is the name given to the dried parts of the *cannabis* or hemp plant (its full scientific name is *Cannabis sativa*). Cannabis grows wild throughout the tropical and temperate regions of the world, which accounts for one of its nicknames, "weed."

> Three men, so the story goes, arrived one night at the closed gates of a Persian city. One was intoxicated by alcohol, another was under the spell of opium, and the third was steeped in marihuana.
>
> The first blustered: "Let's break the gates down."
>
> "Nay," yawned the opium eater, "let us rest until morning, when we may enter through the wide-flung portals."
>
> "Do as you like," was the announcement of the marihuana addict. "But I shall stroll in through the keyhole!" (Rowell & Rowell, 1939)

As demonstrated by this parable, people who smoke marijuana often experience altered perceptions of the world.

Reactions to marijuana usually include mood swings. Otherwise normal experiences seem extremely funny, or the person might enter a dreamlike state where time seems to stand still. Users often report heightened sensory experiences, seeing vivid colors, or appreciating the subtleties of music. Perhaps more than any other drug, however, marijuana can produce very different reactions in people. It is not uncommon for someone to report having no reaction to the first use of the drug; it also appears that people can "turn

off" the high if they are sufficiently motivated (McKim, 1991). The feelings of well-being produced by small doses can change to paranoia, hallucinations, and dizziness when larger doses are taken. Research on frequent marijuana users suggests that impairments of memory, concentration, motivation, self-esteem, relationships with others, and employment are common negative outcomes of long-term use (Haas & Hendin, 1987; Roffman & Barnhart, 1987). The impairment in motivation—apathy, or unwillingness to carry out long-term plans—has sometimes been called *amotivational syndrome,* although how prevalent this problem is remains unclear (McKim, 1991).

The evidence for marijuana tolerance is contradictory. Chronic and heavy users report tolerance, especially to the euphoric high (B. A. Johnson, 1991); they are unable to reach the levels of pleasure they experienced earlier. However, there is also evidence of "reverse tolerance," when regular users experience more pleasure from the drug after repeated use. Major signs of withdrawal do not usually occur with marijuana. Chronic users who stop taking the drug report a period of irritability, restlessness, appetite loss, nausea, and difficulty sleeping (B. A. Johnson, 1991); but there is no evidence that they go through the craving and psychological dependence characteristic of other substances (Grinspoon & Bakalar, 1997).

Controversy surrounds the use of marijuana for medicinal purposes. The popular media frequently describe individuals who illegally use marijuana to help ward off the

Marijuana

nausea associated with chemotherapy or to ease the symptoms of other illnesses such as glaucoma, and the medical benefits of this drug may be promising (Grinspoon & Bakalar, 1997). Unfortunately, there is also evidence that marijuana smoke may contain as many carcinogens as tobacco smoke, and long-term use may contribute to diseases such as lung cancer. Obviously this potential health risk should be weighed against the benefits of using marijuana under certain medical circumstances.

Most marijuana users inhale the drug by smoking the dried leaves in marijuana cigarettes; others use preparations such as hashish, which is the dried form of the resin in the leaves of the female plant. Marijuana contains over 80 varieties of the chemicals called *cannabinoids,* which are believed to alter mood and behavior. The most common of these chemicals includes the *tetrahydrocannabinols,* otherwise known as THC. An exciting finding in the area of marijuana research is that the brain makes its own version of THC, a neurochemical called *anandamide* after the Sanskrit word *ananda,* which means bliss (Fackelmann, 1993). Because work in this area is so new, scientists are only beginning to explore how this neurochemical affects the brain and this behavior.

LSD and Other Hallucinogens

On a Monday afternoon in April, 1943, Albert Hoffmann, a scientist at a large Swiss chemical company, prepared to test a newly synthesized compound. He had been studying derivatives of ergot, a fungus that grows on diseased kernels of grain, and sensed that he had missed something important in the 25th compound of the lysergic acid series. Ingesting what he thought was an infinitesimally small amount of this drug, which he referred to in his notes as LSD-25, he waited to see what subtle changes might come over him as a result. Thirty minutes later he reported no change; but some 40 minutes

after taking the drug he began to feel dizzy and had a noticeable desire to laugh. Riding his bicycle home, he hallucinated that the buildings he passed were moving and melting. By the time he arrived home, he was terrified that he was losing his mind. Albert Hoffmann was experiencing the first recorded "trip" on LSD (Stevens, 1987).

LSD (d-lysergic acid diethylamide) is the most common hallucinogenic drug. It is produced synthetically in laboratories, although naturally occurring derivatives of this grain fungus (ergot) have been found historically. In Europe during the Middle Ages, an outbreak of illnesses occurred as a result of people's eating grain that was infected with the fungus. One version of this illness—later called *ergotism*—constricted the flow of blood to the arms or legs and eventually resulted in gangrene and the loss of limbs. Another type of illness resulted in convulsions, delirium, and hallucinations. Years later, scientists connected ergot with the illnesses and began studying versions of this fungus for possible benefits. This is the type of work Albert Hoffmann was engaged in when he discovered LSD's hallucinogenic properties.

LSD remained in the laboratory until the 1960s, when it was first produced illegally for recreational use. The mind-altering effects of the drug suited the social effort to reject established culture and enhanced the search for enlightenment that characterized the mood and behavior of many people during that decade. The late Timothy Leary, at the time a Harvard research professor, first used LSD in 1961 and immediately began a movement to have every child and adult try the drug and "turn on, tune in, and drop out."

There are a number of other hallucinogens, some occurring naturally in a variety of plants: *psilocybin* (found in certain species of mushrooms); *lysergic acid amide* (found in the seeds of the morning glory plant); *dimethyltryptamine* (DMT) (found in the bark of the Virola tree which grows in South and Central America); *mescaline* (found in the peyote cactus plant); and *phencyclidine* (PCP) (processed synthetically).

The DSM-IV diagnostic criteria for hallucinogen intoxication are similar to those for marijuana: perceptual changes such as the subjective intensification of perceptions, depersonalization, and hallucinations. Physical symptoms include pupillary dilation, rapid heartbeat, sweating, and blurred vision (American Psychiatric Association, 1994). Many users have written about hallucinogens, and they describe a variety of experiences. The kinds of sensory distortions reported by Hoffmann are characteristic reactions. People tell of watching intently as a friend's ear grows and bends in beautiful spirals or of looking at the bark of a tree and seeing little civilizations living there. These people will tell you that they usually know what they are seeing isn't real, but that it looks as real as anything they have ever seen. But many also recount experiences that are more intense than hallucinations, with an emotional content that sometimes takes on religious proportions.

Tolerance develops quickly to a number of the hallucinogens, including LSD, psilocybin, and mescaline (Pechnick & Ungerleider, 1997). If taken repeatedly over a period of days, these drugs completely lose their effectiveness. However, sensitivity returns after about a week of abstinence. For most of the hallucinogens, no withdrawal symptoms are reported. Even so, a number of concerns have been expressed about their use. One is the possibility of psychotic reactions. Stories in the popular press about people who jumped out of windows because they believed they could fly or who stepped into moving traffic with the mistaken idea that they couldn't be hurt have provided for sensational reading, but there is little evidence that using hallucinogens produces a greater risk than being drunk or under the influence of any other drug. People do report having "bad trips"; these are the sort of frightening episodes in which clouds turn into threatening monsters or deep feelings of paranoia take over. Usually someone on a bad trip can be "talked down" by supportive people who provide constant reassurance that the experience is the temporary effect of the drug, and that it will wear off in a few hours.

We still do not fully understand how LSD and the other hallucinogens affect the brain. Most of these drugs bear some resemblance to neurotransmitters; LSD, psilocybin, lysergic acid amide, and DMT (dimethyltryptamine) are chemically similar to serotonin; mescaline resembles norepinephrine; and a number of other hallucinogens that we have not discussed are similar to acetylcholine. However, the mechanisms responsible for the hallucinations and other perceptual changes users experience remain unknown.

The psychedelic art of the 1960s reflects the visual distortions that result from taking hallucinogens.

concept check 11.2

Identify the terms relating to substance abuse from the descriptions below.

1. These drugs influence perception, distorting feelings, sights, sounds, and smells. _____

2. Greater and greater amounts of a substance are required to achieve the same effect. _____

3. These substances affect behavior, cognition, and mood. Many accepted, commonly used substances are in this category. _____

4. An unpleasant physical response occurs when a dependent user stops taking a substance. _____

5. Substances that include alcohol reduce arousal and cause relaxation. _____

Causes

People continue to use psychoactive drugs for their effects on mood, perception, and behavior despite the obvious negative consequences of abuse and dependence. We saw that despite his clear potential as an individual, Danny continued to use drugs to his detriment. Various factors help explain why people like Danny persist in using drugs. Drug abuse and dependence, once thought to be the result of "moral weakness," are now believed to be influenced by a combination of biological and psychosocial factors.

Why do some people use psychoactive drugs without abusing or becoming dependent on them? Why do some people stop using these drugs or use them in moderate amounts after being dependent on them, and others continue a lifelong pattern of dependence despite their efforts to stop? These questions continue to occupy the time and attention of numerous researchers throughout the world.

Biological Dimensions

FAMILIAL AND GENETIC INFLUENCES

In 1994, famed baseball player Mickey Mantle suffered the greatest tragedy that can befall a parent: the death of his child. His son died in a rehabilitation center where he had been fighting his addiction to drugs. Mickey Mantle himself had just finished treatment for his own, years-long addiction to alcohol. He later died of liver disease. Did the son inherit a vulnerability to addiction from the father? Did he pick up Mickey's habits from living with him over the years? Is it just a coincidence that both father and son were dependent on drugs?

Students often think that a genetic vulnerability to a certain disorder means that the disorder is inevitable. However, especially in the case of substance abuse, even for a person with an inherited vulnerability, abuse and dependence are not inevitable, but require the presence of several factors.

- First, the drug has to be available, which is the rationale for outlawing many drugs: If you can't get it, you can't become addicted. When the People's Republic of China was established in the late 1940s, the government virtually eliminated access to opium, thus creating significant reductions in abuse and dependence.
- Second, the genetically vulnerable person must decide to use the drug, and many choose not to, even when the drug is legal and accessible, like alcohol. If you never drink, you can't become addicted to alcohol. People whose parents have serious addictions may never use certain drug, even on a one-time basis, because they fear becoming dependent.
- Third, a genetic vulnerability does not automatically lead from use to dependence.

A great deal of animal research confirms the importance of genetic influences on substance abuse (Crabbe, Belknap, & Buck, 1994). In work with humans, twin and adoption studies indicate that certain people may be genetically vulnerable to drug abuse (Anthenelli & Schuckit, 1997). One twin study of smoking, for example, found a moderate genetic influence among male smokers (Carmelli, Swan, Robinette, & Fabsitz, 1992). However, most genetic data on substance abuse come from research on alcoholism, which is widely studied because alcohol use is legal and because a great many people are dependent on it. Among men, both twin and adoption studies suggest genetic factors play a role in alcoholism (Bohman, Sigvardsson, & Cloninger, 1981; Cloninger, Bohman, & Sigvardsson, 1981; Cook & Gurling, 1991; D. S. Goodwin, 1979). The research on women, however, is sometimes contradictory. Several studies suggest that genetics has relatively little influence on alcoholism in women (for instance, McGue, Pickens, & Svikis, 1992), and others suggest that the disorder may be inherited in some form (for example, Pickens et al., 1991).

To try to resolve these discrepancies, Kenneth Kendler and his fellow researchers surveyed a large number of female twins—1033 pairs—about their drinking habits (Kendler, Heath, Neale, Kessler, & Eaves, 1992). This was a much larger sample than had been examined in any previous twin studies, and the researchers also had the advantage of surveying women from the general population rather than in psychiatric facilities or alcohol treatment centers. Kendler found that, like men, women seem to inherit a vulnerability to alcoholism (see Table 11.1). Kendler wisely used several definitions of alcoholism, ranging from problem drinking to both tolerance and dependence, and still found that the range of influence that could be explained by genetics was comparable to that among men regardless of which definition was used (Kendler et al., 1992). Follow-up analyses confirmed that vulnerability to alcoholism among women could be attributed to genetic factors (Kendler, Neale, Heath, Kessler, & Eaves, 1994).

An interesting question remains: Why did Kendler's study find a strong relationship between genetics and substance abuse among women whereas other studies have not?

table 11.1	Alcohol Problems in Female Twin Pairs	
Definition of Alcoholism	*Concordance, MZ Twins*	*Concordance, DZ Twins*
Narrow	26.2	11.9
Intermediate	31.6	24.4
Broad	46.9	31.5

Narrow = Only alcoholism with dependence-tolerance.
Intermediate = Alcoholism with or without dependence-tolerance (the DSM-III-R definition of alcohol dependence).
Broad = Alcoholism with or without dependence-tolerance or problem drinking.

Source: Adapted from Kendler et al., 1992.

In addition to the methodological differences in his studies (size of the sample of twins, the nature of the study population), the women tended to be younger than in previous studies. Kendler believes that, as societal attitudes about women drinking have become more permissive over the years, more women drink, and therefore more women are exposed to their genetic vulnerabilities to dependence. In the past, women may not have had drinking problems because they lacked access to alcohol rather than because they weren't genetically vulnerable. A negative side effect of a more egalitarian social attitude toward women may be the increased expression of genetic vulnerabilities to substance abuse.

Knowledge about the influence of genetic vulnerability has increased rapidly. In 1990, a study suggested that alcoholism may be related to a particular gene, DRD2, on chromosome 11 (Blum et al., 1990). This gene appears to regulate the sensitivity of D_2 receptor sites to dopamine. Blum and colleagues found that about two-thirds of the alcoholics they examined carried the DRD2 gene, whereas only about one-fifth of the nonalcoholics did. Several studies have since replicated parts of this finding (Cloninger, 1991). Does this mean that the DRD2 gene causes people to be alcoholic? Not exactly. The research suggests that the DRD2 gene interacts with other factors to increase susceptibility to alcoholism. In other words, just having the DRD2 gene does not by itself cause alcoholism (one-fifth of Blum's nonalcoholics also had this gene), and *not* having the gene is no guarantee that you are protected from drinking problems (one-third of Blum's alcoholics did not have the DRD2 gene). As we will see later in this chapter, the dopamine system affects the ability of drugs to provide pleasurable experiences or block unpleasant ones, and the DRD2 gene may increase the positive quality of these experiences. This hypothesis seems to be supported by evidence that abuse of drugs in addition to alcohol is also affected by the DRD2 gene (S. S. Smith et al., 1992).

One genetic factor that appears to be involved in alcoholism involves the body's ability to metabolize alcohol. We previously described how the liver produces an enzyme called aldehyde dehydrogenase that breaks down a by-product of alcohol, a chemical called acetaldehyde. If acetaldehyde is not broken down but is allowed to build up in the body, the person becomes very ill. Drugs such as disulfiram (Antabuse) help people stop drinking by chemically preventing the breakdown of acetaldehyde so that people feel sick when they drink. In some people of Asian descent, the enzyme that breaks down acetaldehyde seems to be absent naturally. It appears that the gene that produces the enzyme is altered or mutated in many Asians, who therefore have difficulty metabolizing alcohol (Goedde & Agarwal, 1987; Yoshida, Huang, & Ikawa, 1984). The result is a physiological response, known as the alcohol-flush syndrome or skin-flushing response, characterized by reddening and warmth of the face, dizziness, and nausea; it is experienced by 30% to 50% of Asians and is thought to contribute to the relatively low rates of alcohol use among people in this group (Newlin, 1989).

Genetic research to date tells us that substance abuse is affected by our genes, but, no one gene causes substance abuse or dependence. Research suggests that genetic factors may affect how people experience certain drugs, which in turn may partly determine who will or will not become abusers.

NEUROBIOLOGICAL INFLUENCES

For the most part, the pleasurable experiences reported by people who use psychoactive substances partly explain why people continue to use them (Gardner, 1997). In behavioral terms, people are *positively reinforced* for using drugs. But what mechanism is responsible for such experiences? Complex and fascinating studies indicate that the brain appears to have a natural "pleasure pathway" that mediates our experience of reward. All abused substances seem to affect this internal reward center. In other words, what psychoactive drugs may have in common is their ability to activate this reward center and provide the user with a pleasurable experience, at least for a time.

The pleasure center was discovered over 40 years ago by James Olds, who studied the effects of electrical stimulation of rat brains (Olds, 1956; Olds & Milner, 1954). If certain areas were stimulated with very small amounts of electricity, the rats behaved as if they had received something very pleasant, such as food. The exact location of the area in the human brain is still subject to debate, although it is believed to include the *dopaminergic system* and its *opioid-releasing neurons,* which begin in the midbrain *ventral tegmental area,* and then work their way forward through the *nucleus accumbens* and on to the *frontal cortex* (Korenman & Barchas, 1993).

How do different drugs that affect different neurotransmitter systems all converge to activate the pleasure pathway, which is primarily made up of dopamine-sensitive neurons? Researchers are only beginning to sort out the answers to this question, but some surprising findings have emerged in recent years. For example, we know that amphetamines and co-

*Many of us drink in order . . . to pour ourselves, literally, into new personalities: uncap the bottle, pop the cork, slide into someone else's skin. A liquid makeover, from the inside out.**

caine act directly on the dopamine system. Other drugs, however, appear to increase the availability of dopamine in more roundabout and intricate ways. For example, the neurons in the ventral tegmental area are kept from continuous firing by GABA neurons. (Remember that the GABA system is an inhibitory neurotransmitter system that blocks other neurons from sending information.) One thing that keeps us from being on an unending high is the presence of these GABA neurons, which act as the "brain police" or superegos of the reward neurotransmitter system. The opiates (opium, morphine, heroin) inhibit GABA, which in turn stops the GABA neurons from inhibiting dopamine, which makes more dopamine available in the reward center. Drugs that stimulate the reward center directly or indirectly include not only amphetamine, cocaine, and the opiates, but also nicotine and alcohol (A. Goldstein, 1994; Koob, 1992).

This complicated picture is far from complete. There may be other pleasure pathways in the brain (Wise, 1988). The coming years should yield even more interesting insights into the interaction of drugs and the brain. One aspect that awaits explanation is how drugs not only provide pleasurable experiences (positive reinforcement) but also how they help remove unpleasant experiences such as pain, feelings of illness, or anxiety (negative reinforcement). Aspirin is a negative reinforcer: We take it not because it makes us feel good, but because it stops us from feeling bad. In much the same way, one property of the psychoactive drugs is that they stop people from feeling bad, an effect that is as powerful as making them feel good.

With several drugs, negative reinforcement is related to the anxiolytic effect, the ability to reduce anxiety (discussed briefly in the section on the sedative, hypnotic, and anxiolytic drugs). Alcohol has an anxiolytic effect. The neurobiology of how these drugs reduce anxiety seems to involve the septal/hippocampal system (Gray, 1987), which includes a large number of GABA sensitive neurons. Certain drugs may reduce anxiety by enhancing the activity of GABA in this region, thereby inhibiting the brain's normal reaction (anxiety/fear) to anxiety-producing situations (Pihl et al., 1993).

Researchers have identified individual differences in the way people respond to alcohol. Understanding these response differences is important because they may help explain why some people continue to use drugs until they acquire a dependence on them, whereas others stop before this happens. Newlin and Thomson (1990) reviewed numerous studies comparing individuals with and without a family history of alcoholism. They concluded that, compared to the sons of nonalcoholics, the sons of alcoholics may be more sensitive to alcohol when it is first ingested, and then become less

*Featured quotations in this chapter are from Caroline Knapp, *Drinking: A Love Story* (The Dial Press, 1996).

sensitive to its effects as the hours pass after drinking. This finding is significant because the euphoric effects of alcohol occur just after drinking, but the experience after several hours is often sadness and depression. People who are at risk for developing alcoholism (in this case, the sons of alcoholics) may be better able to appreciate the initial highs of drinking and be less sensitive to the lows that come later, making them ideal candidates for continued drinking. In support of this observation, a recent study followed sons of alcoholics and sons of nonalcoholics for 10 years and found that those men who tended to be less sensitive to alcohol also tended to drink more heavily and more often (Schuckit, 1994).

One line of research involves studying the brain wave patterns of people who are at risk for developing alcoholism. The sons of people with alcohol problems are recruited to participate, because of their own increased likelihood of having alcohol problems. Participants are asked to sit quietly and listen for a particular tone. When they hear the tone, they are to signal the researcher. During this time, their brain waves are monitored and a particular pattern emerges called the *P300 amplitude.* At approximately 300 milliseconds (the origin of the "P300" designation) after the tone is presented, a characteristic spike in brain waves occurs that indicates that the brain is processing this information. In general, researchers find that this spike is lower among males with a family history of alcoholism (Polich, Pollock, & Bloom, 1994).

Is this brain wave difference somehow connected to the reasons people later develop a dependence on alcohol, or is it just a marker or sign that these individuals have in common but that is not related to their drinking? One piece of evidence that argues against the P300 difference as a marker for alcoholism is that individuals with a variety of other psychological disorders (for example, schizophrenia and depression) also show lower P300 amplitude than control subjects (Polich et al., 1994). Researchers continue trying to understand this interesting but puzzling phenomenon.

Psychological Dimensions

POSITIVE REINFORCEMENT

We have shown that the substances people use to alter mood and behavior have unique effects. The high from heroin differs substantially from the experience of smoking a cigarette, which in turn differs from the effects of amphetamines or LSD. Nevertheless, it is important to point out the similarities in the way people react to most of these substances. The feelings that result from using them are pleasurable in some way, and people will continue to take the drugs in order to recapture the pleasure. Research shows quite clearly that many of the drugs used and abused by humans also seem to

be pleasurable to animals (Young & Herling, 1986). Laboratory animals will work to have injected into their bodies drugs such as cocaine, amphetamines, opiates, sedatives, and alcohol, which demonstrates that even without social and cultural influences these drugs are pleasurable.

Human research also indicates that to some extent all the psychoactive drugs provide a pleasurable experience (A. Goldstein, 1994). People are often very inventive in how they administer these drugs in order to maximize their euphoric effects. For example, individuals who are dependent on heroin sometimes combine it with benzodiazepines (such as Valium) to intensify their pleasure (American Psychiatric Association, 1990). Cocaine users may heat the drug and inhale the fumes in a process known as "freebasing," or use the highly concentrated form known as "crack" to obtain a more rapid and intense experience. Such activities tend to increase as tolerance increases and more of the substance is needed to produce the high that is the hallmark of drug use.

NEGATIVE REINFORCEMENT

Most researchers have looked at how drugs help reduce unpleasant feelings through negative reinforcement. Many people are likely to initiate and continue drug use to escape from unpleasantness in their lives. In addition to the initial euphoria, many drugs provide escape from physical pain (opiates), from stress (alcohol), or from panic and anxiety (benzodiazepines). This phenomenon has been explored under a number of different names, including *tension reduction, negative affect,* and *self-medication,* each of which has a somewhat different focus (Cappell & Greeley, 1987).

Basic to many views of abuse and dependence is the premise that substance use becomes a way for users to cope with the unpleasant feelings that go along with life circumstances (Cooper, Russell, & George, 1988). Drug use by soldiers in Vietnam is one tragic example of this phenomenon. Almost 42% of these mostly young men experimented with heroin, half of whom became dependent, because the drug was readily available and because of the extreme stress of the war (Jaffe, Knapp, & Ciraulo, 1997). It is interesting that only 12% of these soldiers were still using heroin 3 years after their return to the United States (L. N. Robins, Helzer, & Davis, 1975), which suggests that once the stressors were removed they no longer needed the drug to relieve their pain. People who experience trauma such as sexual abuse are more likely to abuse alcohol (Stewart, 1996). This observation emphasizes the important role played by each aspect of abuse and dependence—biological, psychological, social, and cultural—in determining who will and who will not have difficulties with these substances.

In a study that examined substance use among adolescents as a way to reduce stress (Chassin, Pillow, Curran, Molina, & Barrera, 1993), researchers compared a group of

You hide behind the professional persona all day; then you leave the office and hide behind the drink.

adolescents with alcoholic parents with a group whose parents did not have drinking problems. The average age of the adolescents was 12.7 years. The researchers found that just having a parent with alcohol dependence was a major factor in predicting who would use alcohol and other drugs. However, they also found that children who reported negative affect, such as feeling lonely, crying a lot, or being tense, were more likely than others to use drugs. The researchers further determined that the adolescents tended to use drugs as a way to cope with unpleasant feelings. Although this study has yet to be replicated by other researchers, it suggests that one contributing factor to children's drug use is the desire to escape from unpleasantness. It also suggests that to prevent people from using drugs we may need to address influences such as stress and anxiety, a strategy that we discuss in our section on treatment.

Many people who use psychoactive substances experience a crash after being high. If people reliably crash, why don't they just stop taking drugs? One explanation is given by Solomon and Corbit in an interesting integration of both the positive and negative reinforcement processes (R. L. Solomon, 1980; R. L. Solomon & Corbit, 1974). The *opponent-process theory* holds that an increase in positive feelings will be followed by an increase in negative feelings a short time later. Similarly, an increase in negative feelings will be followed by a period of positive feelings. Athletes often report feeling depressed after finally attaining a long-sought goal. The opponent-process theory claims that this mechanism is strengthened with use and weakened by disuse. So, a person who has been using a drug for some time will need more of it to achieve the same results (tolerance). At the same time, the negative feelings that follow drug use tend to intensify. For many people, this is the point at which the motivation for drug taking shifts from desiring the euphoric high to alleviating the increasingly unpleasant crash. Unfortunately, the best remedy is more of the same drug. People who are hungover after drinking too much alcohol are often advised to have "the hair of the dog that bit you." The sad irony here is that the very drug that can make you feel so bad is also the one thing that can take away your pain. You can see why people can become enslaved by this insidious cycle.

Researchers have also looked at substance abuse as a way of self-medicating for other problems. If people have difficulties with anxiety, for example, they may be attracted to barbiturates or alcohol because of their anxiety-reducing qualities. In one study, researchers were successful in treating a small group of cocaine addicts who had attention deficit disorder with methylphenidate (Ritalin) (Khantzian, Gawin, Kleber, & Riordan, 1984). They had hypothesized that these individuals used cocaine to help focus their attention. Once their ability to concentrate improved with the methylphenidate, the users stopped ingesting cocaine. Research is just beginning to outline the complex interplay among stressors, negative feelings, other psychological disorders, and negative reactions to the drugs themselves as causative factors in psychoactive drug use.

Cognitive Factors

What people expect to experience when they use drugs influences how they react to them. A person who expects to be less inhibited when she drinks alcohol will act less inhibited whether she actually drinks alcohol or a placebo that she thinks is alcohol (M. L. Cooper, Russell, Skinner, Frone, & Mudar, 1992; Wilson, 1987). This observation about the influence of how we think about drug use has been labeled an *expectancy effect* and has received considerable research attention.

Expectancies develop before people actually use drugs, perhaps as a result of parents' and peers' drug use, advertising, and media figures who model drug use (P. M. Miller, Smith, & Goldman, 1990). In one study, a large group of seventh and eighth graders were given questionnaires that focused on their expectations about drinking. The researchers reexamined the students 1 year later to see how their expectancies predicted their later drinking (Christiansen et al., 1989). One surprising finding was the marked increase in drinking among the students only 1 year later. When researchers first questioned them, about 10% of the students reported getting drunk two to four times per year. This number had risen to 25% by the next year. The students' expectations of drinking did predict who would later have drinking problems. Students who thought that drinking would improve their social behavior and their cognitive and motor abilities (despite all evidence to the contrary) were more likely to have drinking problems 1 year later. These results suggest that children may begin drinking partly because they believe that drinking will have positive effects.

Expectations appear to change as people have more experience with drugs, although their expectations are similar for alcohol, nicotine (T. H. Brandon & Baker, 1992; Wetter et al., 1994), marijuana, and cocaine (Schafer & Brown, 1991). One theory about why abusers *relapse* (fail in their efforts to abstain from using drugs and go back to using them) is that their expectations about the positive effects of the drug create powerful "urges" (T. B. Baker, Morse, & Sherman, 1987; Tiffany, 1990). If you've ever tried to give up ice cream, and then found yourself compelled to have some, you have a limited idea of what it might be like to crave a drug. These urges seem to be triggered by factors such as the availability of the drug, contact with things that are associated with drug taking (for example, sitting in a bar), specific moods (for example, being depressed), or by having a small dose of the drug; any one may motivate the person to "fall off the wagon" and reabuse drugs (Cooney, Litt, Morse, Bauer, & Gaupp, 1997; Rubonis et al., 1994; Stacy, 1995).

A factor studied so far only in people who drink alcohol is a cognitive phenomenon called *alcohol myopia*. This condition has been defined as "a state of shortsightedness in which superficially understood, immediate aspects of experience have a disproportionate influence on behavior and emotion" (Steele & Josephs, 1990, p. 923).

Picture someone who is drunk, carefully and methodically placing one foot in front of the other as he walks so as not to fall, walking straight into the path of an oncoming truck. Although alcohol myopia may not explain why people drink in the first place, it may help us understand why they continue to drink when they know that excessive drinking can have severe negative consequences. People under the influence of alcohol may not be able to evaluate properly the risks involved in their continued drinking.

Social Dimensions

Previously we pointed out the importance of exposure to psychoactive substances as a necessary prerequisite to their use and possible abuse. You could probably list a number of ways people are exposed to these substances—through friends, through the media, and so on. For example, recent research on the consequences of cigarette advertising suggests that the effects of media exposure may be more influential than peer pressure in determining whether teens smoke (Pierce & Gilpin, 1995). One study looked at how, besides advertising, very young children might be introduced to drugs (Noll, Zucker, & Greenberg, 1990). Children between the ages of 3 and 6 were given a smelling task at school. They were told to close their eyes and try to tell just by smelling what was in a jar. Nine different substances were presented to them: apple juice, Play-Doh, popcorn, coffee, perfume, beer, whiskey, wine, and cigarettes. Of the older children in this group, more than half could already recognize either beer, wine, or whiskey, while 20% of the youngest children were able to identify alcohol. The importance of this study is in its suggestion that many children are

exposed to alcohol as preschoolers; it seems that they learn about alcohol from relatives and acquaintances rather than from television alone.

Research suggests that drug-addicted parents spend less time monitoring their children than parents without drug problems (Dishion, Patterson, & Reid, 1988), and that this is an important contribution to early adolescent substance use (Chassin et al., 1993). When parents did not provide appropriate supervision, their children developed friendships with peers who supported drug use. Children who are influenced by drug use at home may be exposed to peers who use drugs as well. There seems to be a self-perpetuating pattern associated with drug use that extends beyond the genetic influences we discussed previously.

How does our society view people who are dependent on drugs? This issue is of tremendous importance because it affects efforts to legislate the sale, manufacture, possession, and use of these substances. It also dictates how drug-dependent individuals are treated. Two views of substance abuse and dependence characterize contemporary thought: *moral weakness* and *the disease model of dependence*. According to the moral weakness view, drug use is seen as a failure of self-control in the face of temptation; this is a psychosocial perspective. Drug users lack the character or "moral fiber" to resist the lure of drugs. We saw earlier, for example, that the Catholic church recently made drug abuse an official sin—an indication of its disdain. The disease model, on the other hand, assumes that drug dependence is caused by an underlying physiological disorder; this is a biological perspective. Just as diabetes or asthma can't be blamed on the afflicted individuals, neither should drug dependence. Alcoholics Anonymous and similar organizations see drug dependence as an incurable disease over which you have no control (Marlatt, 1985).

Obviously, neither perspective in itself does justice to the complex interrelationship between the psychosocial and biological influences that affect substance disorders. Viewing drug use as moral weakness leads to punishing those afflicted with the disorder, whereas a disease model includes seeking treatment for a medical problem. On the other hand, people certainly help determine the outcome of treatment for drug abuse and dependence, and messages that the disorder is out of their control can at times be counterproductive. A comprehensive view of substance-related disorders that includes both psychosocial and biological influences is needed for this important societal concern to be addressed adequately.

Cultural Dimensions

When you examine a behavior as it appears in different cultures, it is necessary to reexamine what is considered abnormal (Matsumoto, 1994). Each culture has its own preferences for psychoactive drugs as well as its own proscriptions for substances it finds unacceptable. Keep in mind that in addition to defining what is or is not acceptable, cul-

Many young children are exposed to drug use.

In many cultures, alcohol is used ceremonially.

As yet we do not know whether biological differences across cultures contribute to the varying use and abuse rates. Looking ahead to what we may find through future research, it is important for us to consider that biological factors may interact with cultural norms in a complex way. For example, it seems logical that cultural norms may develop over time as a consequence of biological difference. Certain cultures may adapt their drug use (for instance, condoning substance use only in "safe" social surroundings) to ethnically idiosyncratic reactions (for example, a tendency to react aggressively). On the other hand, we have seen in looking at other disorders that behavior can also affect biology, and we may discover that the norms established by a society affect the biology of its people. Research on the cultural dimensions of substance abuse is in its infancy, but it holds great promise for helping to unravel the mysteries of this disorder.

tural norms affect the rates of substance abuse and dependence in important ways. For example, in certain cultures, including Korea, members are expected to drink alcohol heavily on certain social occasions (C. K. Lee, 1992). As we have seen before, exposure to these substances in addition to social pressure for heavy and frequent use may facilitate their abuse, and this may explain the high abuse rates in countries like Korea. On the other hand, poor economic conditions in certain parts of the world limit the availability of drugs, which appears in part to account for the relatively low prevalence of substance abuse in Mexico and Brazil (de Almeidia-Filho, Santana, Pinto, & de Carvalho-Neto, 1991; Ortiz & Medicna-Mora, 1988).

Cultural factors not only influence the rates of substance abuse but also determine how it is manifest. Research indicates that alcohol consumption in Poland and Finland is relatively low, yet conflicts related to drinking and arrests for drunkenness in those countries are high compared to those in the Netherlands, which has about the same rate of alcohol consumption (Osterberg, 1986). Our discussion of expectancies may provide some insight into how the same amount of drinking can have different behavioral outcomes. Expectancies about the effects of alcohol use differ across cultures (for example, "Drinking makes me more aggressive" versus "Drinking makes me more withdrawn"); these differing expectancies may partially account for the variations in the consequences of drinking in Poland, Finland, and the Netherlands. Whether substance use is considered a harmful dysfunction often depends on the assumptions of the cultural group.

An Integrative Model

Any explanation of substance use, abuse, and dependence must account for the basic issue raised earlier in this chapter: "Why do some people use drugs, but not abuse them or become dependent?" Figure 11.11 illustrates how the multiple influences we have discussed may interact to account for this process. Access to a drug is a necessary but obviously not sufficient condition for abuse or dependence. Exposure has many sources, including the media, parents, peers and, indirectly, lack of supervision. Whether people use a drug depends also on social and cultural expectations, some encouraging and some discouraging, such as laws against possession or sale of the drug.

The path from drug use to abuse and dependence is more complicated (see Figure 11.11). As major stressors aggravate many of the disorders we have discussed, so do they increase the risk of abuse and dependence on psychoactive substances. Genetic influences may be of several different types. Some individuals may inherit a greater sensitivity to the effects of certain drugs; others may inherit an ability to metabolize substances more quickly, and are thereby able to tolerate higher (and more dangerous) levels. Other psychiatric conditions may indirectly put someone at risk for substance abuse. Antisocial personality disorder, which is characterized by the frequent violation of social norms (see Chapter 12) is thought to include a lowered rate of arousal; this may account for the increased prevalence of substance abuse in this group. People with mood disor-

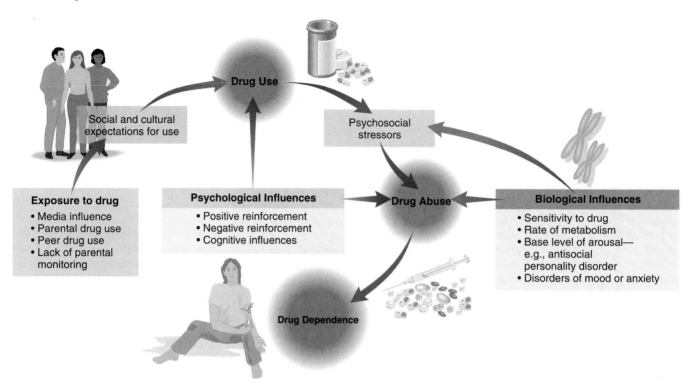

figure 11.11 An integrative model of substance related disorders

ders or anxiety disorders may self-medicate by using drugs to relieve the negative symptoms of their disorder, and this may account for the high rates of substance abuse in this group.

Equifinality, the concept that a particular disorder may arise from multiple and different paths, is particularly appropriate to substance disorders. It is clear that abuse and dependence cannot be predicted from one factor, be it genetic, neurobiological, psychological, or cultural. We saw, for example, that *some* people with the DRD2 gene common to many with substance abuse problems do not become abusers. Many people who experience the most crushing stressors, such as abject poverty or bigotry and violence, cope without resorting to drug use. There are different pathways to abuse, and we are only now beginning to identify their basic outlines.

Once a drug has been used repeatedly, biology and cognition conspire to create dependence. Continual use of most drugs causes tolerance, which requires the user to ingest more of the drug to produce the same effect. Conditioning is also a factor. If pleasurable drug experiences are associated with certain settings, a return to such a setting will later cause urges to develop, even if the drugs themselves are not available.

This obviously complex picture still does not convey the intricate lives of people who develop substance-related disorders (Wills, Vaccaro, McNamara, & Hirky, 1996). Each person has his or her own story and path to abuse and dependence. We have only begun to discover the commonalities of substance disorders; we need to understand a great deal more about how all the factors interact to produce them.

 **Treatment**

When we left Danny, he was in jail, awaiting the legal outcome of being arrested for robbery. At this point in his life Danny needs more than legal help; he needs to free himself from his addiction to alcohol and cocaine. And the first step in his recovery has to come from him. Danny must admit he needs help, that he does indeed have a problem with drugs, and that he needs others to help him overcome his chronic dependence. The personal motivation to work on a drug problem appears to be essential in the treatment of substance abuse (W. R. Miller, 1985). A therapist cannot help someone who doesn't want to change, and this can be a problem in treating substance abuse just as it is for people with disorders such as anorexia nervosa and antisocial personality disorder. Fortunately (and at last), Danny's arrest seemed to shock him into realizing how serious his problems had become, and he was now ready to confront them head-on.

Treating people who have substance-related disorders is a difficult task. Perhaps because of the combination of influences that often work together to keep people hooked, the outlook for those who are dependent on drugs is often not very positive. We will see in the case of heroin dependence, for example, that a best-case scenario is often just trading one addiction (heroin) for another (methadone). And even people who successfully cease taking drugs may feel the urge to resume drug use all their lives.

Treatment for substance-related disorders focuses on several areas. Sometimes the first step is to help someone through the withdrawal process; typically, the ultimate goal is abstinence. In other situations the goal is to get a person to maintain a certain level of drug use without escalating its intake, and sometimes it is geared toward preventing exposure to drugs. Because substance abuse arises from so many influences, it should not be surprising that treating people with substance-related disorders is not a simple matter of finding just the right drug or the best way to change thoughts or behavior.

We discuss the treatment of substance-related disorders as a group because treatments have so much in common. For example, many programs that treat people for dependence on a variety of substances also teach skills for coping with life stressors. Biological treatments focus on how to mask the effects of the ingested substances. We discuss the obvious differences among substances as they arise.

Biological Treatments

AGONIST SUBSTITUTION

Increased knowledge about how psychoactive drugs work on the brain has led researchers to explore ways of changing how they are experienced by people who are dependent on them. One method, **agonist substitution,** involves providing the person with a safe drug that has a chemical makeup similar to the addictive drug (therefore the name *agonist*). *Methadone* is an opiate agonist that is often given as a heroin substitute. Methadone is a synthetic narcotic that was developed in Germany during World War II when morphine was not available for pain control; it was originally called *adolphine* after Adolph Hitler (Bellis, 1981). Although it does not give the quick high of heroin, methadone initially provides the same analgesic (pain reducing) and sedative effects. However, when users develop a tolerance for methadone it loses its analgesic and sedative qualities. Because heroin and methadone are *cross-tolerant*, acting on the same neurotransmitter receptors, a heroin addict who takes methadone may become addicted to the methadone instead (O'Brien, 1996). Research suggests that when addicts combine methadone with counseling, many reduce their use of heroin and engage in less criminal activity (Ball & Ross, 1991). All the news is not good, however. A proportion of people under methadone treatment continue to abuse other substances such as cocaine (Condelli, Fairbank, Dennis, & Rachal, 1991) and benzodiazepines (Iguchi et al., 1990). Research suggests that some people who use methadone as a substitute for heroin benefit significantly, but they may be dependent on methadone for the rest of their lives (O'Brien, 1996).

Addiction to cigarette smoking is also treated by a substitution process. The drug is provided to smokers by prescription, in the form of nicotine gum or a nicotine patch, which lack the carcinogens included in cigarette smoke; the dose is later tapered off to lessen withdrawal from the drug. In general, nicotine gum has been successful in helping people stop smoking, although it works best in combination with supportive psychological therapy (Cepeda-Benito, 1993; Hall et al., 1996; Hughes, 1993). People must be taught how to use the gum properly, and about 20% of people who successfully quit smoking become dependent on the gum itself (Hughes et al., 1991). The nicotine patch, which requires less effort and provides a steadier nicotine replacement, may be somewhat more effective in helping people quit smoking (Hughes, 1993). However, if either treatment is used without a comprehensive psychological treatment program (see below), a substantial number of smokers relapse after they stop using the gum or patch (Cepeda-Benito, 1993).

ANTAGONIST TREATMENTS

We described how many of the psychoactive drugs produce euphoric effects through their interaction with the neurotransmitter systems in the brain. What would happen if the effects of these drugs were blocked, so that the drugs no longer produced the pleasant results? Would people stop using the drugs? **Antagonist drugs** block or counteract the effects of psychoactive drugs, and a variety of drugs that seem to cancel out the effects of opiates have been used with people dependent on a variety of substances. The most often prescribed opiate-antagonist drug, *naltrexone*, has had only limited success (A. Goldstein, 1994). When it is given to a person who is dependent on opiates, it produces immediate withdrawal symptoms, an extremely unpleasant effect. A person must be withdrawn from the opiate completely before starting naltrexone, and because it removes the euphoric effects of the opiates, the user must be highly motivated to continue treatment.

Naltrexone has also been evaluated as a treatment for alcohol dependence. Joseph Volpicelli and his colleagues at the University of Pennsylvania in Philadelphia studied 70 men who had an average of 20 years of heavy alcohol use (Volpicelli, Alterman, Hayashida, & O'Brien, 1992). Each man was required to attend group therapy sessions, individual counseling, and sessions focusing on health and exercise. In addition, half the men were given naltrexone and the other half received a placebo pill. After 3 months, about one-quarter of the men in the naltrexone group were again drinking heavily, and one-half of the group receiving the placebo had relapsed. These results, which have been replicated by other investigators, suggest that naltrexone may enhance an overall treatment approach that includes therapy (O'Malley et al., 1992). Overall, naltrexone is not the magic bullet that would shut off the addict's response to psychoactive drugs and put an end to dependence. It does appear to help some drug abusers handle withdrawal symptoms and the craving that accompanies attempts to abstain from drug use; antagonists may therefore be a useful addition to other therapeutic efforts.

AVERSIVE TREATMENTS

In addition to looking for ways to block the euphoric effects of psychoactive drugs, workers in this area may prescribe drugs that make ingesting the abused substances extremely unpleasant. The expectation is that a person who associates the drug with feelings of illness will avoid using the drug. The most commonly known aversive treatment uses *disulfiram (Antabuse)* with people who are alcohol dependent. Antabuse prevents the breakdown of acetaldehyde, a by-product of alcohol, and the resulting buildup of acetaldehyde causes feelings of illness. People who drink alcohol after taking Antabuse will experience nausea, vomiting, and elevated heart rate and respiration. Ideally, Antabuse is taken each morning, before the desire to drink wins out (P. E. Nathan, 1993). Unfortunately, noncompliance is a major concern, and a person who skips the Antabuse for a few days is able to resume drinking.

Efforts to make smoking aversive have included the use of *silver nitrate* in lozenges or gum. This chemical combines with the saliva of a smoker to produce a bad taste in the mouth. Research has not shown it to be particularly effective (E. J. Jensen, Schmidt, Pedersen, & Dahl, 1991). Both Antabuse for alcohol abuse and silver nitrate for cigarette smoking have generally been less than successful as treatment strategies on their own, primarily because they require that people be extremely motivated to continue taking them outside the supervision of a mental health professional (Leccese, 1991).

OTHER BIOLOGICAL TREATMENTS

Medication is frequently prescribed to help people deal with the often very disturbing symptoms of withdrawal. *Clonidine*, developed to treat hypertension, has been given to people withdrawing from opiates. Because withdrawal from certain prescribed medications such as the sedatives can cause cardiac arrest or seizures, these drugs are gradually tapered off to minimize dangerous reactions. In addition, sedative drugs (benzodiazepines) are often prescribed to help minimize discomfort for people withdrawing from other drugs such as alcohol (McCreery & Walker, 1993).

One of the few controlled studies of the use of medication to treat cocaine abuse (Gawin et al., 1989) found that *desipramine*, one of the antidepressant drugs, was more effective in increasing abstinence rates among cocaine users

than lithium or a placebo. However, 41% of those receiving the medication were unable to achieve even a month of continuous cocaine abstinence, suggesting that it may not be helpful for a large subgroup of users.

A recently developed enzyme, not yet used on humans, may hold some promise for the treatment of cocaine addiction. This enzyme seems to cut cocaine molecules into two parts, neither of which has any narcotic effect (Landry, Zhao, Yang, Glickman, & Georgiadis, 1993). Because it breaks down the cocaine so fast, the brain would not be affected by the drug. We do not know whether the enzyme will be helpful to people addicted to cocaine, but it offers some hope that we may be able to "immunize" people against the euphoric effects of such drugs.

Psychosocial Treatments

Most of the biological treatments for substance abuse show some promise with people who are trying to eliminate their drug habit. However, none of these treatments alone is successful for most people. Most research indicates a need for social support or therapeutic intervention. Because so many people need help to overcome their substance disorder, a number of models and programs have been developed. Unfortunately, in no other area of psychology have unvalidated and untested methods of treatment been so widely accepted. A reminder: Just because a program has not been subject to the scrutiny of research does not mean it doesn't work, but the sheer number of people receiving services of unknown value is cause for concern. We next review several therapeutic approaches that *have* been evaluated.

INPATIENT FACILITIES

The first specialized facility for people with substance abuse problems was established in 1935, when the first federal narcotic "farm" was built in Lexington, Kentucky. Now mostly privately run, such facilities are designed to help people get through the initial withdrawal period and to provide supportive therapy so they can go back to their communities (Morgan, 1981). Inpatient care can be extremely expensive, often exceeding $15,000 (W. R. Miller & Hester, 1986). The question arises, then, as to how effective this type of care is compared to outpatient therapy that can cost 90% less. Research suggests that there may be no difference between intensive residential setting programs and quality outpatient care in the outcomes for alcoholic patients (W. R. Miller & Hester, 1986). Although some people do improve as inpatients, they may not need this expensive care.

ALCOHOLICS ANONYMOUS AND ITS VARIATIONS

Without question, the most popular model for the treatment of substance abuse is a variation of the Twelve-Step program first developed by Alcoholics Anonymous (AA). Established in 1935 by two alcoholic professionals, William "Bill W." Wilson and Robert "Dr. Bob" Holbrook Smith, the foundation of AA is the notion that alcoholism is a dis-

---

■ **concept check 11.3**

Substance-related disorders are difficult to treat. See if you understand how these treatments work. Read the examples and match them with the following terms: (a) dependent, (b) cross-tolerant, (c) agonist substitution, (d) antagonist.

1. Methadone is used to help heroin addicts kick their habit in a method called _____ .

2. Heroin and methadone are _____ , which means they affect the same neurotransmitter receptors.

3. Unfortunately, the heroin addict may become permanently _____ on methadone.

4. _____ drugs block or counteract the effects of psychoactive drugs and are sometimes effective in treating addicts.

table 11.2 Twelve Suggested Steps of Alcoholics Anonymous

1. We admitted we were powerless over alcohol—that our lives had become unmanageable.
2. Came to believe that a power greater than ourselves could restore us to sanity.
3. Made a decision to turn our will and our lives over to the care of God *as we understood Him.*
4. Made a searching and fearless moral inventory of ourselves.
5. Admitted to God, to ourselves, and to another human being the exact nature of our wrongs.
6. Were entirely ready to have God remove all these defects of character.
7. Humbly asked Him to remove our shortcomings.
8. Made a list of all persons we had harmed, and became willing to make amends to them all.
9. Made direct amends to such people wherever possible, except when to do so would injure them or others.
10. Continued to take personal inventory and, when we were wrong, promptly admitted it.
11. Sought through prayer and meditation to improve our conscious contact with God *as we understood Him,* praying only for knowledge of His will for us and the power to carry that out.
12. Having had a spiritual awakening as the result of these steps, we tried to carry this message to alcoholics and to practice these principles in all our affairs.

Source: Alcoholics Anonymous World Services, Inc.

ease and that alcoholics must acknowledge their addiction to alcohol and its destructive power over them. The addiction is seen as more powerful than any individual, and therefore they must look to a Higher Power to help them overcome their shortcomings. Central to the design of AA is its independence from the established medical community and the freedom it offers from the stigmatization of alcoholism (Denzin, 1987; Robertson, 1988). An important component is the social support it provides through group meetings.

Since 1935, Alcoholics Anonymous has steadily expanded to include over 20,000 groups holding more than 25,000 meetings each week all over the world (P. E. Nathan, 1993). In a recent survey, over 3% of the adult population in the United States reported that they had at one time attended an AA meeting (Room, 1993). The Twelve Steps of AA are the basis of its philosophy (see Table 11.2). In them you can see the reliance on prayer and a belief in God.

Reaction is rarely neutral to AA and similar organizations, like Cocaine Anonymous and Narcotics Anonymous (N. S. Miller, Gold, & Pottash, 1989). Many people credit the approach with saving their lives, whereas others object that its reliance on spirituality and adoption of a disease model foster dependence. Because participants attend meetings anonymously and only when they feel the need to, conducting systematic research on its effectiveness has been unusually difficult (W. R. Miller & McCrady, 1993). There have been numerous attempts, however, to evaluate AA's effect on alcoholism (Emrick, Tonigan, Montgomery, & Little, 1993). Although there are not enough data to show what percentage of people abstain from using alcohol as a result of participating in AA, Emrick and his colleagues found that those people who regularly participate in AA activities and follow its guidelines carefully are more likely to have a positive outcome. Other more recent studies suggest that persons who fully participate in AA do as well as those receiving cognitive-behavioral treatments (Ouimette, Finney, & Moos, 1997). On the other hand, a very large number of people who initially contact AA for their drinking problems seem to drop out, 50% after 4 months, and 75% after 12 months (Alcoholics Anonymous, 1990). AA is clearly an effective treatment for *some* people with alcohol dependence. We do not yet know, however, who is likely to succeed and who is likely to fail in AA. Other treatments are needed for the large numbers of people who do not respond to AA's approach.

CONTROLLED USE

One of the tenets of Alcoholics Anonymous is total abstinence; recovering alcoholics who have just one sip of alcohol are believed to have "slipped" until they again achieve abstinence. However, some researchers question this assumption and believe that at least a portion of abusers of several substances (notably alcohol and nicotine) may be capable of becoming social users without resuming their abuse of these drugs. Some people who smoke only occasionally are thought to react differently to nicotine than heavy users (A. Goldstein, 1994).

In the alcoholism treatment field, the notion of teaching people **controlled drinking** is extremely controversial, in part because of a study showing partial success in teaching severe abusers to drink in a limited way (Sobell & Sobell, 1978). The subjects were 40 male alcoholics in an alcoholism treatment program at a state hospital who were thought to have a good prognosis. The men were assigned either to a program that taught them how to drink in moderation (experimental group) or to a group that was abstinence oriented (control group). The researchers, Mark and Linda Sobell, followed the men for over 2 years, maintaining contact with 98% of them. During the second year after treatment, those who participated in the controlled drinking group were functioning well 85% of the time, whereas the men in the abstinence group were reported to be doing well only 42% of the time. Although results in the two groups differed significantly, some of the men in both groups suffered serious relapses and required rehospitalization, and some were incarcerated. The results of this study suggest that controlled drinking may be a viable alternative to abstinence for some alcohol abusers, although it clearly isn't a cure.

The controversy over this study began with a paper published in the prestigious journal *Science* (Pendery, Maltzman, & West, 1982). The authors reported that they had contacted the men in the Sobell study after 10 years and found that only one of the twenty men in the experimental group maintained a pattern of controlled drinking. Although this reevaluation made headlines and was the subject of a segment on the *60 Minutes* television show, it had a number of flaws (Marlatt, Larimer, Baer, & Quigley, 1993). Most serious was the lack of data on the abstinence group over the same 10-year follow-up period. Because no treatment study on substance abuse pretends to help everyone who participates, control groups are added to compare progress. In this case, we obviously need to know how well the controlled drinking group fared compared to the abstinence group.

The controversy over the Sobell study still had a chilling effect on controlled drinking as a treatment of alcohol abuse in the United States. In contrast, controlled drinking is widely accepted as a treatment for alcoholism in the United Kingdom (Rosenberg, 1993). Despite opposition, research on this approach has been conducted in the ensuing years (Marlatt et al., 1993), and the results seem to show that controlled drinking is at least as effective as abstinence, but that neither treatment is successful for 70%–80% of patients over the long term—a rather bleak outlook for people with alcohol dependence problems.

COMPONENT TREATMENT

Most comprehensive treatment programs aimed at helping people with substance abuse and dependence problems have a number of different components thought to boost the effectiveness of the "treatment package." We saw in our review of biological treatments that their effectiveness is increased when psychologically based therapy is added. In *aversion therapy*, which uses a conditioning model, substance use is paired with something extremely unpleasant, such as a brief electric shock or feelings of nausea. For example, a person might be offered a drink of alcohol, and receive a painful shock when the glass reaches his lips. The goal is to counteract the positive associations with substance use with negative associations. The negative associations can also be made by imagining unpleasant scenes in a technique called *covert sensitization* (Cautela, 1966); the person might picture herself beginning to snort cocaine and be interrupted with visions of herself becoming violently ill.

One component that seems to be a valuable part of therapy for substance use is *contingency management.* Here, the clinician and client together select the behaviors that the client needs to change and decide on the reinforcers that will reward reaching certain goals, perhaps money, or small retail items like CDs. In a recent study of cocaine abusers, clients received things like lottery tickets for having cocaine-negative urine specimens (Higgins et al., 1993). This study found greater abstinence rates among cocaine-dependent users with the contingency management approach and other skills training than among users in a more traditional counseling program that included a Twelve-Step approach to treatment.

One of the first things you hear in AA—one of the first things that makes core, gut-level sense—is that in some deep and important personal respects you stop growing when you start drinking alcoholically.

Another package of treatments is the *community reinforcement approach* (Sisson & Azrin, 1989). In keeping with the multiple influences that affect substance use, several different facets of the drug problem are addressed, to help identify and correct aspects of the person's life that might contribute to substance use, or interfere with efforts to abstain. First, a spouse, friend, or relative who is not a substance user is recruited to participate in relationship therapy in order to help the abuser improve his or her relationships with other important people. Second, clients are taught how to identify the antecedents and consequences that influence their drug taking. For example, if they are likely to use cocaine with certain friends, clients are taught to recognize the relationship and encouraged to avoid the associations. Third, clients are given assistance with employment, education, finances, or other social service areas that may help reduce their stress. Fourth, new recreational options help the person replace substance use with new activities. Preliminary studies of the community reinforcement approach with alcohol and cocaine abusers appear encouraging, although more research is needed to assess its long-term effectiveness.

Because people present such different challenges to substance abuse treatment, a "shotgun-like" effort, using a variety of approaches, is often required to cover the wide range of problems influencing substance use. In an example of the individualized approach, a study recently reported on the treatment of smokers who had a history of major depressive disorder (Hall, Muñoz, & Reus, 1994). The researchers creatively combined education on smoking cessation, nicotine gum, and cognitive-behavioral intervention for the mood disorder; they found that the addition of the mood disorder treatment increased participants' rates of abstinence.

This type of treatment matching has received increased attention from workers in the area of substance abuse. For example, the National Institute on Alcohol Abuse and Alcoholism initiated Project MATCH (Matching Alcoholism Treatment to Client Heterogeneity) to assess whether people with differing characteristics (having little hope for improvement versus searching for spiritual meaning) would respond better or worse to different treatments (Project MATCH Research Group, 1993). Initial reports suggest that well-run programs of various types can be effective with a range of people with substance use problems (Project MATCH Research Group, 1997). Although no exact matches are yet recommended, research is ongoing to help clinicians tailor their treatments to the particular needs of their clients (Jaffe et al., 1996). By identifying the factors that support a person's substance

from the inside

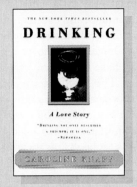
Caroline Knapp, a professional writer, describes her 20-year experience with alcohol abuse, the most common of all the substance-related disorders. She describes the conflicting emotions that accompanied her alcoholism. She knew that " . . . drinking could ruin my mind and my future. It could eat its way through my life in exactly the same way a physical cancer eats its way through bones and blood and tissue, destroying everything" (p. 5). At the same time, "I loved the way drink made me feel, and I loved its . . . ability to shift my focus away from my own awareness of self and onto something else, something less painful than my own feelings" (p. 7).

Knapp chronicles her gradual and insidious transformation into a "functional" alcoholic:

I wrote a book during my last, most active year of alcoholism. I wrote several award-winning columns. I spent my days in a bustle of focused, highly concentrated activity—editing stories, working with designers, meeting with writers and editors—and only a very particular sort of person (probably another alcoholic) could have peered into that cubicle and realized that, in fact, I was clicking away at my computer with a pounding hangover, or sitting there at the end of the day, my body screaming for a drink. (p. 14)

Knapp confides that smoking and anorexia were cross-addictions related to her alcoholism, and considers the function such dependencies served: "The parallels between anorexia and alcoholism astonish me today, the way they both served to refract emotion and keep me at a distance from my own feelings, one through food and one through drink" (p. 130).

In the end, with great fortitude, Knapp manages to stop drinking. Now:

I find joy these days in the oddest places, the smallest ways. I set out my recycling bin every Tuesday night with an odd, quiet delight. Nothing in there these days but plastic milk cartons and empty water bottles. I go out to dinner with a friend and I take note of the fact that we are communicating without booze, that at last I am the chemically unaltered version of myself, and that, in fact, I can almost say I like that person. I relish the understanding that I'll drive home safely, and wake up remembering where my car is, how I got from the driveway to my bed. (p. 247)

Drinking: A Love Story, a fearless and generous account of a frighteningly ordinary and destructive relationship with alcohol, is a compelling and inspirational story.

*Caroline Knapp, *Drinking: A Love Story* (The Dial Press, 1996).

abuse and treating them in an integrated fashion, clinicians may improve the success rates of the various approaches we have discussed.

RELAPSE PREVENTION

Another kind of treatment directly addresses the problem of relapse. Marlatt and Gordon's (1985) **relapse prevention** treatment model looks at the learned aspects of dependence and sees relapse as a failure of cognitive and behavioral coping skills. Therapy involves helping people remove any ambivalence about stopping their drug use by examining their beliefs about the positive aspects of the drug ("There's nothing like a cocaine high") and confronting the negative consequences of its use ("I fight with my wife when I'm high"). High-risk situations are identified ("having extra money in my pocket") and strategies are developed to deal with potentially problematic situations as well as with the craving that arises from abstinence. Incidents of relapse are dealt with as occurrences from which the person can recover; instead of looking on these episodes as inevitably leading to more drug use, people in treatment are encouraged to see them as episodes brought on by temporary stress or a situation that can be changed. Research on this technique suggests that it may be useful in treating marijuana dependence (Stephens, Roffman, & Simpson, 1994), smoking (Gruder et al., 1993; Shiffman et al., 1996), cocaine abuse (Carroll, 1992), and alcohol dependence (J. S. Baer et al., 1992).

Sociocultural Intervention

It seems particularly appropriate that we end this chapter by looking at the potential for sociocultural intervention in substance-related disorders. We noted in the beginning of the chapter that the rates of substance use are declining in the United States. Although treatment efforts have improved in recent years, the decline in use is probably not directly attributable to treatment. It may be that the major cause of this reduced use of drugs is cultural. Over the past 25 years or so, we have gone from a "turn on, tune in, drop out," "if it feels good, do it," and "I get by with a little help from my friends" society to one that champions statements like "Just say no to drugs." The social unacceptability of drinking, smoking, and other drug use is probably responsible for this change. The sociocultural disapproval of cigarette smoking, for example, is readily apparent in the following description by a former smoker:

I began smoking (in Boy Scouts!) at age 11. By the time I was a college freshman, freed from the restrictions of school and home, my smoking had increased to a pack a day. The seminal Surgeon General's Report *Smoking and Health* was issued that year (1964), but I didn't notice. The warnings that began appearing on cigarette packs a couple of years later were also easy to ignore, since I had grown up knowing that smoking was unhealthy. As a graduate student and young professor I often smoked while leading class discussions, as had some of my favorite teachers. That ended in 1980, when an undergraduate student, no doubt empowered by the anti-smoking movement, asked me to stop because smoke bothered him. A few years later there were hardly any social situations left in which it was acceptable to smoke. Even my home was no longer a refuge, since my children were pestering me to quit. And so I did. Now my status as former smoker puts me in company with fully half of all those who have ever smoked regularly and are alive today. For many of us the deteriorating social environment for smoking made it easier to quit. (Cook, 1993, p. 1750)

Implementing this sort of intervention is obviously beyond the scope of one research investigator or even a consortium of researchers collaborating across many sites. It requires the cooperation of governmental, educational, and even religious institutions. Many states, for example, have school-based education programs to try to deter students from using drugs. The widely used DARE program (Drug Abuse Resistance Education) encourages a "no drug use" message through fear of consequences, rewards for commitments not to use drugs, and strategies for refusing offers of drugs. Unfortunately, a recent large survey study suggests that this type of program is often rejected by students and therefore may not have its intended effects (Brown, D'Emidio-Caston, & Pollard, 1997). We may need to rethink our approach to preventing drug use and abuse. It is, however, premature to discount the potential of prevention-based interventions since they may be more effective than any treatment-oriented approach we can ever envision.

 **Summary**

• In DSM-IV, substance-related disorders are divided into the depressants (alcohol, barbiturates, and benzodiazepines), stimulants (amphetamine, cocaine, nicotine, and caffeine), opiates (heroin, codeine, and morphine), and hallucinogens (marijuana and LSD).

• Specific diagnoses are further categorized as substance dependence, substance abuse, substance intoxication, and substance withdrawal.

• Nonmedical drug use in the United States has declined in recent times, although it continues to cost billions of dollars and seriously impairs the lives of millions of people each year.

• Depressants are a group of drugs that decrease central nervous system activity. The primary effect is to reduce our levels of physiological arousal and help us relax. Included in this group are alcohol and the sedative, hypnotic, and anxiolytic drugs such as those prescribed for insomnia.

• Stimulants, the most commonly consumed psychoactive drugs, include caffeine (in coffee, chocolate, and many soft drinks), nicotine (in tobacco products such as cigarettes), amphetamines, and cocaine. In contrast to the depressant drugs, stimulants make you more alert and energetic.

• Opiates include *opium, morphine, codeine,* and *heroin;* they have a *narcotic* effect—relieving pain and inducing sleep. The broader term *opioids* is used to refer to the family of substances that includes these opiates as well as synthetic variations created by chemists (methadone, pethidine) and the similarly acting substances that occur naturally in our brains (enkephalins, beta-endorphins, and dynorphins).

• Hallucinogens essentially change the way the user perceives the world. Sight, sound, feelings, and even smell are distorted, sometimes in dramatic ways, in a person under the influence of drugs such as marijuana and LSD.

• Most psychotropic drugs seem to produce positive effects by acting directly or indirectly on the dopaminergic mesolimbic system (the "pleasure pathway"). In addition, psychosocial factors such as expectations, stress, and cultural practices interact with the biological influences to influence drug use.

• Substance dependence is treated successful only with a minority of those affected, and the best results reflect the motivation of the drug user and a combination of biological and psychosocial treatments.

• Programs aimed at preventing drug use may have the greatest chance of significantly affecting the drug problem.

Key Terms

substance-related disorders
polysubstance use
psychoactive substances
substance intoxication
substance abuse
substance dependence
tolerance
withdrawal
depressants
stimulants
opiates
hallucinogens
alcohol use disorders
GABA system
withdrawal delirium (delirium tremens/"DTs")
fetal alcohol syndrome (FAS)
barbiturates
benzodiazepines
amphetamine use disorders
cocaine use disorders
nicotine use disorders
caffeine use disorders
opioid use disorders
hallucinogen use disorder
marijuana (cannabis)
LSD (d-lysergic acid diethylamide)
agonist substitution

antagonist drugs
controlled drinking
relapse prevention

Answers to Concept Checks

11.1
1. B
2. A
3. D
4. C

11.2
1. Hallucinogens
2. Tolerance
3. Psychoactive
4. Withdrawal
5. Depressants

11.3
1. C
2. B
3. A
4. D

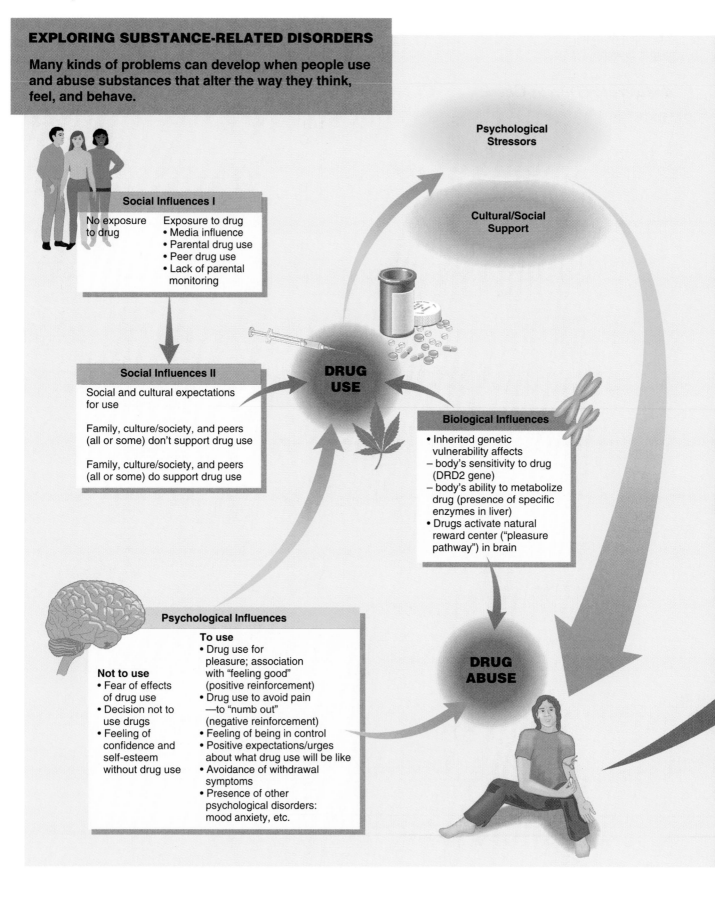

EXPLORING SUBSTANCE-RELATED DISORDERS

Many kinds of problems can develop when people use and abuse substances that alter the way they think, feel, and behave.

Psychological Stressors

Cultural/Social Support

Social Influences I

No exposure to drug

Exposure to drug
• Media influence
• Parental drug use
• Peer drug use
• Lack of parental monitoring

Social Influences II

Social and cultural expectations for use

Family, culture/society, and peers (all or some) don't support drug use

Family, culture/society, and peers (all or some) do support drug use

DRUG USE

Biological Influences

• Inherited genetic vulnerability affects
 – body's sensitivity to drug (DRD2 gene)
 – body's ability to metabolize drug (presence of specific enzymes in liver)
• Drugs activate natural reward center ("pleasure pathway") in brain

Psychological Influences

Not to use
• Fear of effects of drug use
• Decision not to use drugs
• Feeling of confidence and self-esteem without drug use

To use
• Drug use for pleasure; association with "feeling good" (positive reinforcement)
• Drug use to avoid pain —to "numb out" (negative reinforcement)
• Feeling of being in control
• Positive expectations/urges about what drug use will be like
• Avoidance of withdrawal symptoms
• Presence of other psychological disorders: mood anxiety, etc.

DRUG ABUSE

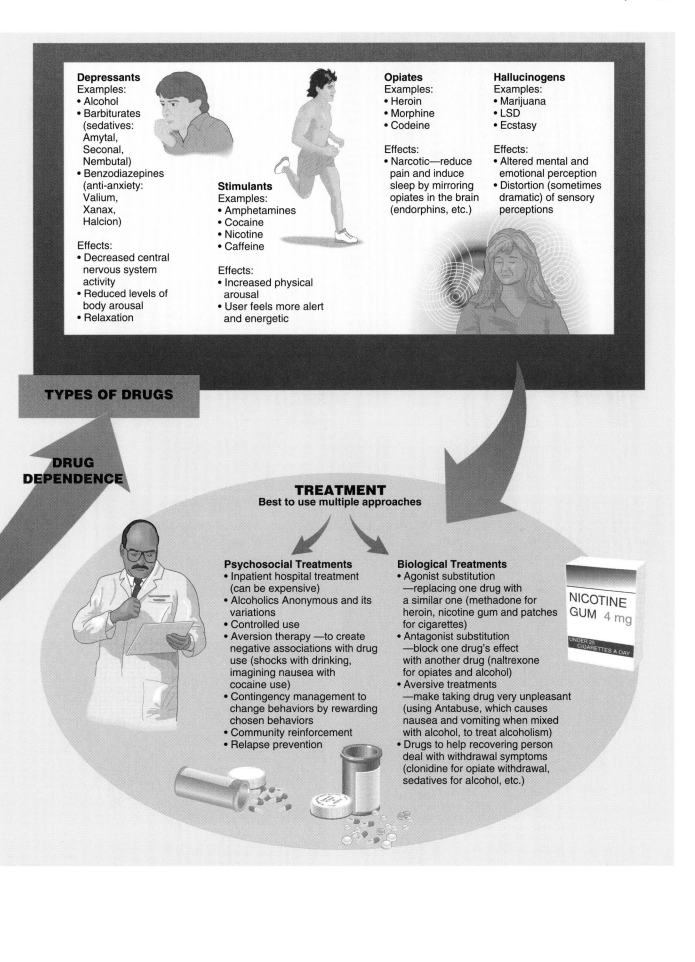

Depressants
Examples:
• Alcohol
• Barbiturates
 (sedatives:
 Amytal,
 Seconal,
 Nembutal)
• Benzodiazepines
 (anti-anxiety:
 Valium,
 Xanax,
 Halcion)

Effects:
• Decreased central
 nervous system
 activity
• Reduced levels of
 body arousal
• Relaxation

Stimulants
Examples:
• Amphetamines
• Cocaine
• Nicotine
• Caffeine

Effects:
• Increased physical
 arousal
• User feels more alert
 and energetic

Opiates
Examples:
• Heroin
• Morphine
• Codeine

Effects:
• Narcotic—reduce
 pain and induce
 sleep by mirroring
 opiates in the brain
 (endorphins, etc.)

Hallucinogens
Examples:
• Marijuana
• LSD
• Ecstasy

Effects:
• Altered mental and
 emotional perception
• Distortion (sometimes
 dramatic) of sensory
 perceptions

TYPES OF DRUGS

**DRUG
DEPENDENCE**

TREATMENT
Best to use multiple approaches

Psychosocial Treatments
• Inpatient hospital treatment
 (can be expensive)
• Alcoholics Anonymous and its
 variations
• Controlled use
• Aversion therapy —to create
 negative associations with drug
 use (shocks with drinking,
 imagining nausea with
 cocaine use)
• Contingency management to
 change behaviors by rewarding
 chosen behaviors
• Community reinforcement
• Relapse prevention

Biological Treatments
• Agonist substitution
 —replacing one drug with
 a similar one (methadone for
 heroin, nicotine gum and patches
 for cigarettes)
• Antagonist substitution
 —block one drug's effect
 with another drug (naltrexone
 for opiates and alcohol)
• Aversive treatments
 —make taking drug very unpleasant
 (using Antabuse, which causes
 nausea and vomiting when mixed
 with alcohol, to treat alcoholism)
• Drugs to help recovering person
 deal with withdrawal symptoms
 (clonidine for opiate withdrawal,
 sedatives for alcohol, etc.)

NICOTINE
GUM 4 mg

UNDER 25
CIGARETTES A DAY

12

Personality Disorders

When I was supposed to be awake, I was asleep; when I was supposed to speak, I was silent; when a pleasure offered itself to me, I avoided it.

Susanna Kaysen
Girl, Interrupted

Karen: Whatever You Say
Daniel: Getting It Exactly Right
Personality Disorders Under Study

According to DSM-IV, **personality disorders** are "enduring patterns of perceiving, relating to, and thinking about the environment and oneself" that "are exhibited in a wide range of important social and personal contexts," and "are inflexible and maladaptive, and cause either significant functional impairment or subjective distress" (p. 630). Now that you have taken out your yellow marker and highlighted this definition of personality disorders, what do you think it means?

We all think we know what a "personality" is. It's all the characteristic ways a person *behaves* and *thinks:* "Michael tends to be shy"; "Mindy likes to be very dramatic"; "Juan is always suspicious of others"; "Annette is very outgoing"; "Bruce seems to be very sensitive and gets upset very easily over minor things"; "Sean has the personality of an eggplant!" We tend to "type" people as behaving in one way in many different situations. For example, like Michael, many of us are shy with people we don't know, but we wouldn't be shy around our friends. A truly shy person is shy even among people he has known for some time. His shyness is part of the way he behaves in most situations. We have all probably behaved in all the ways noted above ("dramatic," "suspicious," "outgoing," "easily upset"). However, we usually consider a way of behaving part of a person's personality only if it occurs in many times and places. In this chapter we look at characteristic ways of behaving in relation to personality disorders. First we examine in some detail how we conceptualize personality disorders and the issues related to them; then we describe the disorders themselves.

An Overview

What if a person's characteristic ways of thinking and behaving cause significant distress to the self or others? What if the person can't change this way of relating to the world and is unhappy? We might consider this person to have a "personality disorder." The DSM-IV definition notes that these personality characteristics are "inflexible and maladaptive, and cause either significant functional impairment or subjective distress." Unlike many of the disorders we have already discussed, personality disorders are chronic; they do not come and go but originate in childhood and continue throughout adulthood. Because they affect personality, these chronic problems pervade every aspect of a person's life. If a man is overly suspicious, for example (a sign of a possible paranoid personality disorder), this trait will affect almost everything he does, including his employment (he may have to change jobs frequently if he believes co-workers conspire against him), his relationships (he may not be able to sustain a lasting relationship if he can't trust anyone), and even where he lives (he may have to move often if he suspects his landlord is out to get him).

DSM-IV notes that having this disorder *may* distress the affected person. However, individuals with personality disorders may not feel any subjective distress; indeed, it may be acutely felt by others because of the actions of the person with the disorder. This is particularly common with antisocial personality disorder, because the individual may show a blatant disregard for the rights of others yet exhibit no remorse (Hare, 1993). In certain cases, someone other than the person with the personality disorder must decide whether the disorder is causing significant functional impairment, because the affected person often cannot make such a judgment.

DSM-IV lists 10 specific personality disorders and several others that are being studied for future consideration; we review them all. Unfortunately, as we will see later, people who have personality disorders along with other psychological problems tend to do poorly in treatment. Data from several studies show that people who are depressed have a worse outcome in treatment if they also have a personality disorder (Sanderson & Clarkin, 1994; Shea et al., 1990).

Most of the disorders we discuss in this book are in Axis I of the DSM-IV, which includes the standard traditional disorders. The personality disorders are included in a separate axis, Axis II, because as a group they are distinct. The characteristic traits are more ingrained and inflexible in people who have personality disorders, and the disorders themselves are less likely to be successfully modified.

Having personality disorders on a separate axis requires the clinician to consider in each assessment whether the person has a personality disorder. In the axis system, a patient can receive a diagnosis on only Axis I, only Axis II, or on both axes. A diagnosis on both Axis I and Axis II indicates that a person has both a current disorder (Axis I) and a more chronic problem (for instance, personality disorder). As you will see, it is not unusual for one person to be diagnosed on both axes.

You may be surprised to learn that the category of personality disorders is controversial, because it involves a number of unresolved issues. Examining these issues can help us understand all the disorders described in this book.

Categorical and Dimensional Models

Most of us are sometimes suspicious of others and a little paranoid, or overly dramatic, or too self-involved, or reclusive. Fortunately, these characteristics have not lasted for too long or been overly intense, and they haven't significantly impaired how we live and work. People with personality disorders, however, display problem characteristics over extended periods of time and in many situations, which can cause great emotional pain for themselves and/or others. Their difficulty, then, can be seen as one of *degree* rather than *kind;* in other words, the problems of people with personality disorders may just be extreme versions of the problems many of us experience on a temporary basis, such as being shy or suspicious.

The distinction between problems of *degree* and problems of *kind* is usually described in terms of *dimensions* instead of *categories*. The issue that continues to be debated in the field is whether personality disorders are extreme versions of otherwise normal personality variations ("dimensions") or ways of relating that are different from psychologically healthy behavior ("categories") (Costa & Widiger, 1994; Gunderson, 1992; Livesley, Schroeder, Jackson, & Jang, 1994). We can see the difference between dimensions and categories in everyday life. For example, we tend to look at gender categorically. Our society views us as being in one category—"female"—or the other—"male". Yet we could also look at gender in terms of dimensions. For example, we know that "maleness" and "femaleness" are in part determined by hormones. We could identify people along testosterone and/or estrogen dimensions and rate them on a continuum of "maleness" and "femaleness" rather than in the absolute categories of "male" or "female." We also often label people's size categorically, as "tall," "medium," or "short." But height too can be viewed dimensionally, in inches or centimeters.

Most people in the field see personality disorders as extremes on one or more personality dimensions. Yet because of the way people are diagnosed with the DSM, the personality disorders—like most of the other disorders—end up being viewed in categories. You have two choices—either you do ("yes") or you do not ("no") have a disorder. For example, either you have antisocial personality disorder or you don't. The DSM doesn't rate how obsessive or compulsive you are; if you meet the criteria, you are labeled as having obsessive–compulsive personality disorder. There is no in-between when it comes to personality disorders.

There are advantages to using categorical models of behavior, the most important being their convenience. With simplification, however, come problems. One is that the mere act of using categories leads clinicians to "reify" them; that is, to view disorders as real "things," comparable to the realness of an infection or a broken arm. Some argue that personality disorders are not things that exist but points at which society decides that a particular way of relating to the world has become a problem. There is the important unresolved issue again: Are personality disorders just an extreme variant of normal personality, or are they distinctly different disorders?

Many researchers believe that many or all of the personality disorders represent extremes on one or more personality dimensions. Consequently, some have proposed that the DSM-IV personality disorders section be replaced or at least supplemented by a dimensional model (Widiger, 1991; Widiger & Frances, 1985) in which individuals would not only be given categorical diagnoses but also would be rated on a series of personality dimensions. Widiger (1991) believes that such a system would have at least three advantages over a purely categorical system: (a) It would retain more information about each individual, (b) it would be more flexible because it would permit both categorical and dimensional differentiations among individuals, and (c) it would avoid the often arbitrary decisions involved in assigning a person to a diagnostic category.

Although there is no general consensus about what the basic personality dimensions might be, there are several contenders (Eysenck & Eysenck, 1975; Tellegen, 1978; Watson, Clark, & Harkness, 1994). The most widely accepted is called the *five factor model* or the "Big Five" and is taken from work on normal personality (Costa & McCrae, 1990; Costa & Widiger, 1994; Goldberg, 1993; Tupes & Christal, 1992). In this model, people can be rated on a series of personality dimensions, and the combination of five components describe why people are so different. The five factors or dimensions are *extraversion* (talkative, assertive, and active versus silent, passive, and reserved), *agreeableness* (kind, trusting, and warm versus hostile, selfish, and mistrustful), *conscientiousness* (organized, thorough, and reliable versus careless, negligent, and unreliable), *emotional stability* (even-tempered versus nervous, moody, and temperamental), and *openness to experience* (imaginative, curious, and creative versus shallow and imperceptive) (Goldberg, 1993). On each dimension, people are rated high, low, or somewhere in-between.

Recent work establishes the universal nature of the five dimensions. In German, Portuguese, Hebrew, Chinese, Korean, and Japanese samples, individuals have personality trait structures similar to American samples (McCrae & Costa, 1997). A number of researchers are trying to determine whether people with personality disorders can also be rated in a meaningful way along these dimensions and whether the system will help us better understand these disorders (L. A. Clark, 1993; Krueger, Caspi, Moffitt, Silva, & McGee, 1996; Schroeder, Wormworth, & Livesley, 1993). Again, the major obstacle to the adoption of a dimensional approach to personality disorders is the lack of consensus regarding the most appropriate framework (Widiger, 1991). The DSM-IV thus continues to use categories.

Personality Disorder Clusters

DSM-IV divides the personality disorders into three groups or "clusters"; this will probably continue until there is a strong scientific basis for viewing them differently. The cluster division is based on resemblance. Cluster A is called the "odd" or "eccentric" cluster; it includes paranoid, schizoid, and schizotypal personality disorders. Cluster B is the "dramatic," "emotional," or "erratic" cluster; it consists of antisocial, borderline, histrionic, and narcissistic personality disorders. Cluster C is the "anxious" or "fearful" cluster; it includes avoidant, dependent, and obsessive–compulsive personality disorders. We follow this order in our review.

Statistics and Development

Personality disorders are found in 10% to 13% of the general population (Weissman, 1993), which makes them fairly common. As you can see from Table 12.1, schizoid, narcis-

table 12.1 Statistics and Development of Personality Disorders

Disorder	Prevalence	Gender Differences	Course
Paranoid personality disorder	.5% to 2.5% (Bernstein, Useda, & Siever, 1993)	More common in males (O'Brien, Trestman, & Siever, 1993)	Insufficient information
Schizoid personality disorder	Less than 1% in United States, Canada, New Zealand, Taiwan (Weissman, 1993)	More common in males (O'Brien et al., 1993)	Insufficient information
Schizotypal personality disorder	3% to 5% (Weissman, 1993)	More common in males (Kotsaftis & Neale, 1993)	Chronic: some go on to develop schizophrenia
Antisocial personality disorder	3% in males; less than 1% in females (Sutker et al., 1993)	More common in males (Dulit, Marin, & Frances, 1993)	Dissipates after age 40 (Hare, McPherson, & Forth, 1988)
Borderline personality disorder	1% to 3% (Widiger & Weissman, 1991)	Females make up 75% of cases (Dulit et al., 1993)	Symptoms gradually improve if individuals survive into their 30s (Dulit et al., 1993). Approximately 6% die by suicide (Perry, 1993).
Histrionic personality disorder	2% (Nestadt et al., 1990)	Equal numbers of males and females (Nestadt et al., 1990)	Chronic
Narcissistic personality disorder	Less than 1% (Zimmerman & Coryell, 1990)	More prevalent among men	May improve over time (Cooper & Ronningstam, 1992; Gunderson, Ronningstam, & Smith, 1991)
Avoidant personality disorder	Less than 1% (Reich, Yates, & Nduaguba, 1989; Zimmerman & Coryell, 1990)	Equal numbers of males and females (Millon, 1986)	Insufficient information
Dependent personality disorder	2% (Zimmerman & Coryell, 1989)	May be equal numbers of males and females (Reich, 1987)	Insufficient information
Obsessive-compulsive personality disorder	4% (Weissman, 1993)	More common in males (M. H. Stone, 1993)	Insufficient information

sistic, and avoidant personality disorders are relatively rare, occurring in less than 1% of the general population. In addition, some of the disorders are gender-related; for example, borderline personality disorder is relatively rare among men (Widiger & Weissman, 1991) and antisocial personality disorder is uncommon among women (Sutker, Bugg, & West, 1993). Paranoid, schizotypal, histrionic, dependent, and obsessive–compulsive personality disorders are found in 1% to 4% of the general population.

Personality disorders are thought to originate in childhood and continue into the adult years (Krueger et al., 1996) and to be so ingrained that it is difficult to pinpoint an onset. Maladaptive personality characteristics develop over time into the maladaptive behavior patterns that create distress for the affected person and draw the attention of others. Our relative lack of information about such important features of personality disorders as their developmental course is a repeating theme. The gaps in our knowledge of the course of about half these disorders are visible in Table 12.1. One reason for this dearth of research is that many individuals do not seek treatment in the early developmental phases of their disorder, but only after years of distress. This makes it difficult to study people with personality disorders from the beginning, although a few research studies have helped us understand the development of several disorders.

People with borderline personality disorder are characterized by their volatile and unstable relationships; they tend to have persistent problems in early adulthood, with frequent hospitalizations, unstable personal relationships, severe depression, and suicidal gestures. Approximately 6% succeed in their suicidal attempts (Perry, 1993; M. H. Stone, 1989). On the bright side, their symptoms gradually improve if they survive into their 30s (Dulit, Marin, & Frances, 1993), although elderly individuals may have difficulty making plans and may be disruptive in nursing homes (Rosowsky & Gurian, 1992). People with antisocial personality disorder display a characteristic disregard for the rights and feelings of others; they tend to continue their destructive behaviors of lying and manipulation through adulthood. Fortunately, some tend to "burn out" after the age of about 40 and engage in fewer criminal activities (Hare, McPherson, & Forth, 1988). As a group, however, the problems of people with personality disorders continue, as shown when researchers follow their progress over several years. This pes-

Personality disorders tend to begin in childhood.

simistic prognosis appears to hold even when significant treatment efforts are made (Perry, 1993).

Gender Differences

Borderline personality disorder is diagnosed much more frequently in females, who make up about 75% of the identified cases (Dulit et al., 1993) (see Table 12.1). Historically, histrionic and dependent personality were identified by clinicians more often in women (Dulit et al., 1993; M. H. Stone, 1993), but according to recent studies of their prevalence in the general population, there may be equal numbers of males and females with histrionic and dependent personality disorders (Lilienfeld, VanValkenburg, Larntz, & Akiskal, 1986; Nestadt et al., 1990; Reich, 1987). If this observation holds up in future studies, why have these disorders been predominantly diagnosed among females in general clinical practice and in other studies (Dulit et al., 1993)?

Do the disparities indicate differences between men and women in certain basic genetic and/or sociocultural experience, or do they represent biases on the part of the clinicians who make the diagnoses? Take, for example, a study by Maureen Ford and Thomas Widiger (1989), who sent fictitious case histories to clinical psychologists for diagnosis. One case described a person with *antisocial personality disorder,* which is characterized by irresponsible and reckless behavior and is usually diagnosed in males; the other case described a person with *histrionic personality disorder,* which is characterized by excessive emotionality and attention seeking and is more often diagnosed in females. The subject was identified as male in some versions of each case, and as female in others, although everything else was identical. As the graph in Figure 12.1 shows, when the antisocial personality disorder case was labeled male, most psychologists gave the correct diagnosis. However, when the same case

was labeled female, most psychologists diagnosed it as histrionic personality disorder rather than antisocial personality disorder. In the case of histrionic personality disorder, being labeled a woman increased the likelihood of that diagnosis. Ford and Widiger (1989) concluded that the psychologists incorrectly diagnosed more women as having histrionic personality disorder.

This gender difference in diagnosis has also been criticized by other authors (for example, M. Kaplan, 1983) on the grounds that histrionic personality disorder, like several of the other personality disorders, is biased against females. As Kaplan (1983) points out, many of the features of histrionic personality disorder, such as overdramatization, vanity, seductiveness, and overconcern with physical appearance, are characteristic of the Western "stereotypical female." This disorder may simply be the embodiment of extremely "feminine" traits (Chodoff, 1982); branding such an individual mentally ill, according to Kaplan, reflects society's inherent bias against females. Interestingly, the "macho" personality (Mosher & Sirkin, 1984), in which the individual possesses stereotypically masculine traits, is nowhere to be found in the DSM.

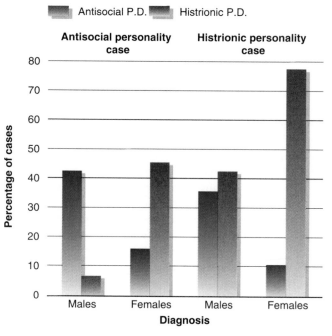

figure 12.1 Gender bias in diagnosing personality disorders. Data are shown for the percentage of cases clinicians rated as antisocial personality disorder or histrionic personality disorder, depending on whether the case was described as a male or a female (from Ford & Widiger, 1989).

The issue of gender bias in diagnosing personality disorder remains highly controversial. It is important to remember, however, that just because certain disorders are observed more in men or women doesn't necessarily indicate bias (Lilienfeld et al., 1986). When it is present, bias can occur at different stages of the diagnostic process. Widiger and Spitzer (1991) point out that the criteria for the disorder may themselves be biased *(criterion gender bias)*, or the assessment measures and the way they are used may be biased *(assessment gender bias)*. For example, Westen (1997) found that although clinicians use the behaviors outlined in the DSM-IV for Axis I disorders, for the personality disorders in Axis II they tend to use subjective impressions based on their interpersonal interactions with the client. This may well allow more bias, including gender bias, to influence diagnoses of personality disorders. As research efforts continue, we will try to make the diagnosis of personality disorders more accurate with respect to gender, and more useful to clinicians.

Gender bias may affect the diagnoses of clinicians who associate certain behavioral characteristics with one sex or the other.

Comorbidity

A reader looking at Table 12.1 who added up the prevalence rates across the personality disorders might conclude that between 20% and 30% of all people are affected. In fact, the percentage of people in the general population with a personality disorder is estimated to be between 10% and 13% (Weissman, 1993). What accounts for this discrepancy? A major concern with the personality disorders is that people tend to be diagnosed with more than one. The term *comorbidity* historically describes the condition in which a person has multiple diseases (Caron & Rutter, 1991). There is a fair amount of disagreement about whether the term should be used with psychological disorders because of the frequent overlap of different disorders (for example, Nurnberg et al., 1991). In just one example, Morey (1988) conducted a study of 291 persons who were diagnosed with personality disorder and found considerable overlap (see Table 12.2). In the far left column is the primary diagnosis, and across the table are the percentages of people who also meet the criteria for other disorders. For example, a person who is identified with borderline personality disorder is also likely to fit the definition of another supposedly different disorder. In general, about half the people who are diagnosed meet the criteria for at least one additional personality disorder (Grove & Tellegen, 1991).

table 12.2 Diagnostic Overlap of Personality Disorders

Diagnosis	Paranoid	Schizoid	Schizotypal	Antisocial	Borderline	Histrionic	Narcissistic	Avoidant	Dependent	Obsessive–compulsive
				Percentage of People Qualifying for Other Personality Disorder Diagnoses						
Paranoid		23.4	25.0	7.8	48.4	28.1	35.9	48.4	29.7	7.8
Schizoid	46.9		37.5	3.1	18.8	9.4	28.1	53.1	18.8	15.6
Schizotypal	59.3	44.4		3.7	33.3	18.5	33.3	59.3	29.6	11.1
Antisocial	27.8	5.6	5.6		44.4	33.3	55.6	16.7	11.1	0.0
Borderline	32.0	6.2	9.3	8.2		36.1	30.9	36.1	34.0	2.1
Histrionic	28.6	4.8	7.9	9.5	55.6		54.0	31.7	30.2	4.8
Narcissistic	35.9	14.1	14.1	15.6	46.9	53.1		35.9	26.6	10.9
Avoidant	39.2	21.5	20.3	3.8	44.3	25.3	29.1		40.5	16.5
Dependent	29.2	9.2	12.3	3.1	50.8	29.2	26.2	49.2		9.2
Obsessive–compulsive	21.7	21.7	13.0	0.0	8.7	13.0	30.4	56.5	26.1	

Source: Adapted from Morey, 1988

Do people really tend to have more than one personality disorder? Are the ways we define these disorders inaccurate, and do we need to improve our definitions so they do not overlap? Or did we divide the disorders in the wrong way to begin with, and need to rethink the categories? Such questions about comorbidity are just a few of the important issues faced by researchers who study personality disorders.

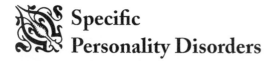

Specific Personality Disorders

We now review the personality disorders that are currently in DSM-IV, 10 in all. Then we will look briefly at a few categories that are being considered for inclusion.

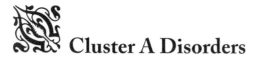

Cluster A Disorders

Paranoid Personality Disorder

Although it is probably very adaptive to be a little wary of other people and their motives, being too distrustful can interfere with making friends, working with others and, in general, getting through daily interactions in a functional way. People with **paranoid personality disorder** are excessively mistrustful and suspicious of others, without any justification. They tend not to confide in others and to think other people want to harm them. Consider the following case from the Quality Assurance Project (1990), a commission that studied psychological disorders under the auspices of the Royal Australian and New Zealand College of Psychiatrists.

Mr. P.
Nobody's Friend

Mr. P. was a 41-year-old man with paranoid personality disorder, who had been seen repeatedly over an 8-year period. Mr. P. grew up in a family with a psychotic father, and at high school was noted to be suspicious, a troublemaker, and a fighter. He enlisted and went to Vietnam where his suspiciousness and attacks on Vietnamese civilians caused him to be reprimanded. Returning to Australia he remained unsettled, moving from job to job because coworkers used to "gang up on me." He came to attention because he was imprisoned for assault on a girl who had rejected his advances. [It was] reported that although Mr. P. has continued to work he has remained arrogant, suspicious, and very difficult to help apart from the rare occasion when he would accept help for feelings of depression. (pp. 341–342)

CLINICAL DESCRIPTION

The defining characteristic of people with paranoid personality disorder is a pervasive unjustified distrust. Certainly there may be times when someone is deceitful and "out to get you"; however, people with paranoid personality disorder are suspicious in situations where most other people would agree that their suspicions are unfounded. Even events that have nothing to do with them are interpreted as personal attacks: These people would view a neighbor's barking dog or a delayed airline flight as a deliberate attempt to annoy them. Unfortunately, such mistrust often extends to people close to them, and makes meaningful relationships very difficult. Imagine what a lonely existence this must be! Suspiciousness and mistrust can show themselves in a number of ways. People with paranoid personality disorder may be argumentative, may complain, or may be quiet, but they are obviously hostile toward others. They often appear tense and are "ready to pounce" when they think they've been slighted by someone. These individuals are very sensitive to criticism and have an excessive need for autonomy (Bernstein, Useda, & Siever, 1993).

CAUSES

Evidence for biological contributions to paranoid personality disorder is limited. Some research suggests the disorder may be slightly more common among the relatives of people who have schizophrenia, although the association does not seem to be strong (Bernstein et al., 1993; Coryell & Zimmerman, 1989; Kendler & Gruenberg, 1982). In other words, relatives of individuals with schizophrenia *may* be more likely to have paranoid personality disorder than people who do not have a relative with schizophrenia. As we will see with the other "odd" or "eccentric" personality disorders in Cluster A, there seems to be some relationship with schizophrenia although its exact nature is not yet clear (Siever, 1992).

Psychological contributions to this disorder are even less certain, although some interesting speculations have been made. Some psychologists point directly to the thoughts of people with paranoid personality disorder as a way of explaining their behavior. One view is that people with this disorder have the following basic mistaken assumptions about others: "People are malevolent and deceptive," "They'll attack you if they get the chance," and "You can be OK only if you stay on your toes" (Freeman, Pretzer, Fleming, & Simon, 1990). This is a maladaptive way to view the world, yet it seems to pervade every aspect of the lives of these individuals. Although we don't know why they develop these perceptions, there is some speculation that the roots are in their early upbringing. Their parents may teach them to be careful about making mistakes and to impress on them that they are different from other people (Turkat & Maisto, 1985). This vigilance causes them to see signs that other people are deceptive and malicious (A. T. Beck & Freeman, 1990). It is certainly true that people are not always benevolent and sincere, and our interactions are sometimes ambiguous enough to make other people's intentions unclear. Looking too closely at what other people say and do can sometimes lead you to misinterpret them.

Cultural factors have also been implicated in paranoid personality disorder. Certain groups of people such as prisoners, refugees, people with hearing impairments, and the elderly are thought to be particularly susceptible because of their unique experiences (Christenson & Blazer, 1984; O'Brien, Trestman, & Siever, 1993). Imagine how you might view other people if you were an immigrant who had difficulty with the language and the customs of your new culture. Such innocuous things as other people laughing or talking quietly might be interpreted as somehow directed at you. The late musician Jim Morrison of The Doors described this phenomenon in his song "People Are Strange" (The Doors, 1967):

> People are strange,
> When you're a stranger,
> Faces look ugly,
> When you're alone.

We have seen how someone could misinterpret ambiguous situations as malevolent. Thus, cognitive and cultural factors may interact to produce the suspiciousness observed in some people with paranoid personality disorder.

TREATMENT

Because people with paranoid personality disorder are mistrustful of everyone, they are unlikely to seek professional help when they need it and also have difficulty developing the trusting relationships necessary for successful therapy (Quality Assurance Project, 1990). When they do seek therapy, the trigger is usually a crisis in their lives or other problems such as anxiety or depression, and not necessarily their personality disorder.

Therapists try to provide an atmosphere that is conducive to developing a sense of trust (Freeman et al., 1990). They often use cognitive therapy to counter the person's mistaken assumptions about others (Turkat & Maisto, 1985), focusing on changing the person's beliefs that all people are malevolent and that most people cannot be trusted. Be forewarned, however, that to date there are no confirmed demonstrations that any form of treatment can significantly improve the lives of people with paranoid personality disorder. In fact, a survey of mental health professionals indicated that only 11% of therapists who treat paranoid personality disorder thought that these individuals would continue in therapy long enough to be helped (Quality Assurance Project, 1990).

People with paranoid personality disorder often believe that impersonal situations exist specifically to annoy or otherwise disturb them.

Schizoid Personality Disorder

Do you know someone who is a "loner"? Someone who would choose a solitary walk over an invitation to a party? A person who comes to class alone, sits alone, and leaves alone? Now, magnify this preference for isolation many times over and you can begin to grasp the impact of **schizoid personality disorder** (Kalus et al., 1995). People with this personality disorder show a pattern of detachment from social relationships and a very limited range of emotions in interpersonal situations. They seem "aloof," "cold," and "indifferent" to other people. The term *schizoid* is relatively old, having been used by Bleuler (1924) to describe people who have a tendency to turn inward and away from the outside world. These people were said to lack emotional expressiveness and pursued vague interests. Consider the following case.

Mr. Z.
All on His Own

A 39-year-old scientist referred after his return from a tour of duty in Antarctica where he had stopped cooperating with others, had withdrawn to his room and begun drinking on his own. Mr. Z. was orphaned at 4 years, raised by an aunt until 9, and subsequently looked after by an aloof housekeeper. At university he excelled at physics, but chess was his only contact with others. Throughout his subsequent life he made no close friends and engaged primarily in solitary activities. Until the tour of duty in Antarctica he had been quite successful in his research work in physics. He was now, some months after his return, drinking at least a bottle of Schnapps each day and his work had continued to deteriorate. He presented as self-contained, unobtrusive, and was difficult to engage effectively. He was at a loss to explain his colleagues' anger at his aloofness in Antarctica and appeared indifferent to their opinion of him. He did not appear to require any interpersonal relations although he did complain of some tedium in his life and at one point during the interview became sad, expressing longing to see his uncle in Germany, his only living relation. (Quality Assurance Project, 1990, p. 346)

CLINICAL DESCRIPTION

Individuals with schizoid personality disorder seem neither to desire nor enjoy closeness with others, including romantic or sexual relationships. As a result they appear cold and detached and do not seem affected by praise or criticism. One of the changes in DSM-IV from previous versions is the recognition that at least some people with schizoid personality disorder are sensitive to the opinions of others but are unwilling or unable to express this emotion. For them, social isolation may be extremely painful.

The social deficiencies of people with schizoid personality disorder are similar to those of people with paranoid personality disorder, although they are more extreme. As A. T. Beck and Freeman (1990) put it, they "consider themselves to be observers rather than participants in the world around them" (p. 125). They do not seem to have the very unusual thought processes that characterize the other disorders in Cluster A (Kalus et al., 1993) (see Table 12.3). For example, people with paranoid and schizotypal personality disorders often have ideas of reference, mistaken beliefs that meaningless events relate just to them. In contrast, those with schizoid personality disorder share the social isolation, poor rapport, and constricted affect (showing neither positive nor negative emotion) seen in people with paranoid personality disorder. We see in Chapter 13 that this distinction among psychotic-like symptoms is important to understanding people with schizophrenia, some of whom show the "positive" symptoms (actively unusual behaviors such as ideas of reference) and others have only the "negative" symptoms (the more passive manifestations of social isolation or poor rapport with others).

CAUSES AND TREATMENT

Research on the genetic neurobiological, and psychosocial contributions to schizoid personality disorder remains to be conducted (Siever, 1992). It is interesting to note, however, that the preference for social isolation resembles aspects of autism. As we explain more fully in Chapter 14, autistic disorder is characterized by a pervasive impairment in social interaction. People with autism either ignore others or respond to them unemotionally. Although their significant difficulties with language are not a problem among those with schizoid personality disorder, they have a strikingly similar indifference to interactions with others. Research over the past several decades has pointed to biological causes of autism, and it is possible that a similar biological

dysfunction combines with early learning or early problems with interpersonal relationships to produce the social deficits that define schizoid personality disorder. For example, research on the neurochemical dopamine suggests that people with a lower density of dopamine receptors scored higher on a measure of "detachment" (Farde, Gustavsson, & Jonsson, 1997). It may be that dopamine (which seems to be involved with schizophrenia as well) may contribute to the social aloofness of people with schizoid personality disorder.

It is rare for a person with this disorder to request treatment except in response to a crisis such as extreme depression or losing a job (Kalus et al., 1995). Therapists often begin treatment by pointing out the value in social relationships. The person with the disorder may even need to be taught the emotions felt by others in order to learn empathy (A. T. Beck & Freeman, 1990). Because their social skills were never established or have atrophied through lack of use, people with schizoid personality disorder often receive social skills training. The therapist takes the part of a friend or significant other in a technique known as *role playing*, and helps the patient practice establishing and maintaining social relationships (A. T. Beck & Freeman, 1990).

Unfortunately, the treatment prospects for people with schizoid personality disorder are not good. The Quality Assurance Project (1990) received responses from 360 mental health professionals about the case of Mr. Z. Seventy-five percent reported that they saw individuals like him about twice a year. Almost half of them either felt they couldn't provide therapy to such people or believed they were untreatable. The half who thought they could treat them believed that therapy would be complicated because the patients probably wouldn't follow treatment recommendations. Even one of the more optimistic replies rings of pessimism about Mr. Z.:

This man has a severe personality disorder and the issues are: Does he want help and is he able to persist in

table 12.3   Grouping Schema for Cluster A Disorders

	Psychotic-like Symptoms	
Cluster A Personality Disorder	*"Positive" (e.g., ideas of reference, magical thinking, and perceptual distortions)*	*"Negative" (e.g., social isolation, poor rapport, and constricted affect)*
Paranoid	Yes	Yes
Schizoid	No	Yes
Schizotypal	Yes	No

Source: Adapted from Siever, 1992

seeking it despite difficulties in himself and the difficulties of treatment; will he be able to develop trust and decrease intellectual-distancing defences; can the therapist understand and soothe him rather than have him continue to use work and alcohol; and it will take 12 months before it is clear if supportive psychotherapy will help him. (p. 346)

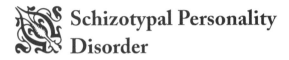

Schizotypal Personality Disorder

People with **schizotypal personality disorder** are typically socially isolated, like those with schizoid personality disorder. In addition, however, they also behave in ways that would seem unusual to many of us (Siever et al., 1995), and they tend to be suspicious and to have odd beliefs (Kotsaftis & Neale, 1993). Consider the following case.

Mr. S.
Man with a Mission

Mr. S. was a 35-year-old chronically unemployed man who had been referred by a physician because of a vitamin deficiency. This was thought to have eventuated because Mr. S. avoided any foods that "could have been contaminated by machine." He had begun to develop alternative ideas about diet in his twenties, and soon left his family and begun to study an eastern religion. "It opened my third eye, corruption is all about," he said.

He now lived by himself on a small farm, attempting to grow his own food, bartering for items he could not grow himself. He spent his days and evenings researching the origins and mechanisms of food contamination and, because of this knowledge, had developed a small band who followed his ideas. He had never married and maintained little contact with his family: "I've never been close to my father. I'm a vegetarian."

He said he intended to do a herbalism course to improve his diet before returning to his life on the farm. He had refused medication from the physician and became uneasy when the facts of his deficiency were discussed with him. (Quality Assurance Project, 1990, p. 344)

CLINICAL DESCRIPTION

People who are given a diagnosis of schizotypal personality disorder are often considered "odd" or "bizarre" because of how they relate to other people, how they think and behave, and even how they dress. They have *ideas of reference,* which means they think insignificant events relate directly to them. For example, they may believe that somehow everyone on a passing city bus is talking about them, yet they may be able to acknowledge that this is unlikely. Again, as we will see in

Chapter 13, some people with schizophrenia also have ideas of reference, but they are usually not able to "test reality" or see the illogic of their ideas.

Individuals with schizotypal personality disorder also have odd beliefs or engage in "magical thinking," believing, for example, that they are clairvoyant or telepathic. In addition, they report unusual perceptual experiences, including such *illusions* as feeling the presence of another person when they are alone. You should notice the subtle but important difference between *feeling* as if someone else is in the room, and the more extreme perceptual distortion in people with schizophrenia who might report that there is someone else in the room when there isn't. Only a small proportion of individuals with schizotypal personality disorder go on to develop schizophrenia (Wolff, Townshed, McGuire, & Weeks, 1991). Unlike people who simply have unusual interests or beliefs, those with schizotypal personality disorder tend to be suspicious and have paranoid thoughts, express little emotion, and may dress or behave in unusual ways (for example, wear many layers of clothing in the summertime or mumble to themselves) (Siever, Bernstein, & Silverman, 1991). Recent prospective research on children who later develop schizotypal personality disorder found that they tend to be passive and unengaged and are hypersensitive to criticism (Olin et al., 1997).

CAUSES

Historically, the word *schizotype* was used to describe people who were predisposed to develop schizophrenia (Meehl, 1962; Rado, 1962). Schizotypal personality disorder is viewed by some to be one phenotype of a schizophrenia genotype. You will recall that a phenotype is one way a person's genetics is expressed. Your genotype is the gene or genes that make up a particular disorder. However, depending on a variety of other influences, the way you turn out, your *phenotype,* may vary from other people with a similar genetic makeup. Some people are thought to have "schizophrenia genes" (the genotype) and yet, because of the relative lack of biological influences (for instance, prenatal illnesses) or environmental stresses (for example, poverty), some will have the less severe schizotypal personality disorder (the phenotype).

The idea of a relationship between schizotypal personality disorder and schizophrenia arises in part from the way people with the disorders behave. Many characteristics of schizotypal personality disorder, including ideas of reference, illusions, and paranoid thinking, are similar but milder forms of behaviors observed among people with schizophrenia. Genetic research also seems to support a relationship. Family, twin, and adoption studies have shown an increased prevalence of schizotypal personality disorder among relatives of people with schizophrenia who do not also have schizophrenia themselves (Dahl, 1993; Torgersen, Onstad, Skre, Edvardsen, & Kringlen, 1993). However, these studies also tell us that the environment can strongly influence schizotypal personality disorder. For example, recent research suggests that a woman's exposure to influenza in pregnancy may increase the chance of schizotypal personality disorder in her children (Venables, 1996). It may be that a subgroup of people with schizotypal personality disorder is related to people with schizophrenia.

TREATMENT

There are some estimates that between 30% and 50% of the people with this disorder who request clinical help also meet the criteria for major depressive disorder. Treatment will obviously include some of the medical and psychological treatments for depression (Goldberg, Schultz, Resnick, Hamer, & Schultz, 1987).

Controlled studies of attempts to treat groups of people with schizotypal personality disorder are few and, unfortunately, the results are modest at best. One general approach has been to teach social skills to help them reduce their isolation from and suspicion of others (Bellack & Hersen, 1985; O'Brien et al., 1993). A rather unusual tactic used by some therapists is not to encourage major changes at all; instead, the goal is to help the person accept and adjust to a solitary life-style (M. Stone, 1983).

Not surprisingly, medical treatment has been similar to that for people who have schizophrenia. In one study, haloperidol, often used with schizophrenia, was given to 17 people with schizotypal personality disorder (Hymowitz, Frances, Jacobsberg, Sickles, & Hoyt, 1986). There were some improvements in the group, especially with ideas of reference, odd communication, and social isolation. Unfortunately, because of the negative side effects of the medication, including drowsiness, many stopped taking their medication and dropped out of the study. About half the subjects persevered through treatment but showed only mild improvement.

Further research on the treatment of people with this disorder is important for a variety of reasons. They tend not to improve over time and there is some evidence that some will go on to develop the more severe characteristics of schizophrenia.

Cluster B Disorders

Antisocial Personality Disorder

People with **antisocial personality disorder** have a history of failing to comply with social norms. They perform actions most of us would find unacceptable, such as stealing from friends and family. They also tend to be irresponsible, impulsive, and deceitful (Widiger & Corbitt, 1995). Dr. Robert Hare describes them as "social predators who charm, manipulate, and ruthlessly plow their way through life, leaving a broad trail of broken hearts, shattered expectations, and empty wallets. Completely lacking in conscience and empathy, they selfishly take what they want and do as they please, violating social norms and expectations without the slightest sense of guilt or regret" (Hare, 1993, p. xi). Just who are these people with antisocial personality disorder? Consider the following case.

Ryan
The Thrill Seeker

I first met Ryan on his 17th birthday. Unfortunately, he was celebrating the event in a psychiatric hospital. He had been truant from school for several months and had gotten into some trouble; the local judge who heard his case had recommended psychiatric evaluation one more time, though Ryan had been hospitalized six previous times, all for problems related to drug use and truancy. He was a veteran of the system and already knew most of the staff. I interviewed him to assess why he was admitted this time, and to recommend treatment.

My first impression was that Ryan was cooperative and pleasant. He pointed out a tattoo on his arm that he had made himself, saying that it was a "stupid" thing to have done, and that he now regretted it. In fact, he regretted many things and was looking forward to moving on with his life. I later found out that he was never truly remorseful for anything.

Our second interview was quite different. During those 48 hours, Ryan had done a number of things that showed why he needed a great deal of help. The most serious incident involved a 15-year-old girl named Ann who attended class with Ryan in the hospital school. Ryan had told her that he was going to get himself discharged, get in trouble, and be sent to the same prison Ann's father was in, where he would rape her father. Ryan's threat so upset Ann that she hit her teacher and several of the staff. When I spoke to Ryan about this, he smiled slightly and said he was bored and that it was fun to upset Ann. When I asked whether it bothered him that his behavior might extend her stay in the hospital, he looked puzzled and said, "Why should it bother me? She's the one who'll have to stay in this hell hole!"

Just before Ryan's admittance, a teenager in his town was murdered. A group of teens went to the local cemetery at night to perform satanic rituals and a young man was stabbed to death, apparently over a drug purchase. Ryan was in the group, although he did not stab the boy. He told me that they occasionally dug up graves to get skulls for their parties; not because they really believed in the devil, but because it was fun and it scared the younger kids. I asked, "What if this were the grave of someone you knew, a relative or a friend? Would it bother you that strangers were digging up the remains?" He shook his head, "They're *dead,* man; they don't care. Why should I?"

Ryan told me he loved PCP, or "angel dust," and that he would rather be dusted than anything else. He routinely made the 2-hour trip to New York City to buy drugs in a particularly dangerous neighborhood. He denied that he was ever nervous. This wasn't machismo; he really seemed unconcerned.

Ryan made little progress. I discussed his future in family therapy sessions and we talked about his pattern of showing supposed regret and remorse, and then stealing money from his parents and going back onto the street. In fact, most of our discussions centered on trying to give his parents the courage to say no to him and not to believe his lies.

One evening, after many sessions, Ryan said that he had seen the "error of his ways" and that he felt bad that he had hurt his parents. If they would only take him home this one last time, he would be the son that he should have been all these years. His speech moved his parents to tears, and they looked at me gratefully as if to thank me for curing their son. When Ryan finished talking, I smiled, applauded, told him it was the best performance I had ever seen. His parents turned on me in anger. Ryan paused for a second, then he too smiled and said, "It was worth a shot!" Ryan's parents were astounded that he had once again tricked them into believing him; he hadn't meant a word of what he had just said.

Ryan was eventually discharged to a drug rehabilitation program. Within 4 weeks, he had convinced his parents to take him home, and within 2 days he had stolen all their cash and disappeared; he apparently went back to his friends and to drugs.

When he was in his 20s, after one of his many arrests for theft, he was diagnosed as having antisocial personality disorder. His parents never summoned the courage to turn him out or refuse him money, and he continues to con them into providing him with a means of buying more drugs.

CLINICAL DESCRIPTION

Individuals with antisocial personality disorder tend to have long histories of violating the rights of others (Widiger & Corbitt, 1995). They are often described as being aggressive because they take what they want, indifferent to the concerns of other people. Lying and cheating seem to be second nature to them, and often they appear unable to tell the difference between the truth and the lies they make up to further their own goals. They show no remorse or concern over the sometimes devastating effects of their actions. Substance abuse is common, occurring in 83% of people with antisocial personality disorder (Dulit et al., 1993; S. S. Smith & Newman, 1990).

Antisocial personality disorder has had a number of names over the years. Phillipe Pinel (1801/1962) identified what he called *manie sans délire* (mania without delirium) to describe people with unusual emotional responses and impulsive rages but no deficits in reasoning ability (Sutker et al., 1993). Other labels have included "moral insanity," "egopathy," "sociopathy," and "psychopathy." A great deal has been written about these labels; we will focus on the two that have figured most prominently in psychological research: **psychopathy** and DSM-IV's *antisocial personality disorder*. As you will see, there are important differences between the two.

Hervey Cleckley (1941, 1982), a psychiatrist who spent much of his career working with the "psychopathic personality," identified a constellation of 16 major characteristics,

Robert Hare has made extensive studies of people with psychopathic personalities.

most of which are personality traits and are sometimes referred to as the "Cleckley criteria." They include superficial charm and good intelligence; absence of delusions and other signs of irrational thinking; absence of "nervousness" and other psychoneurotic manifestations; unreliability; untruthfulness and insincerity; lack of remorse or shame; inadequately motivated antisocial behavior; poor judgment and failure to learn by experience; pathologic egocentricity and incapacity for love; general poverty in major affective reactions; specific loss of insight; unresponsiveness in general interpersonal relations; fantastic and uninviting behavior, with and without; suicide rarely carried out; sex life impersonal, trivial, and poorly integrated; failure to follow any life plan (Cleckley, 1982, p. 204).

Robert Hare and his colleagues, building on the descriptive work of Cleckley, researched the nature of psychopathy (for example, Hare, 1970; Harpur, Hare, & Hakstian, 1989) and developed a 20-item checklist that serves as an assessment tool. Six of the criteria that Hare (1991) includes in his Revised Psychopathy Checklist-PCL-R are

1. Glibness/superficial charm
2. Grandiose sense of self-worth
3. Proneness to boredom/need for stimulation
4. Pathological lying
5. Conning/manipulative
6. Lack of remorse

With some training, clinicians are able to gather information from interviews with a person, along with material from significant others or institutional files (for example, prison records), and assign the person scores on the checklist, with high scores indicating psychopathy (Hare, 1990).

The DSM-IV criteria for antisocial personality focus almost entirely on observable *behaviors* (for instance, "impulsively and repeatedly changes employment, residence or sexual partners"). In contrast, the Cleckley/Hare criteria focus primarily on underlying *personality traits* (for instance, being self-centered or manipulative). DSM-IV and previous versions chose to use only observable behaviors so that clinicians could reliably agree on a diagnosis.

*Lisa had run away again. We were sad, because she kept our spirits up. She was funny.**

*Featured quotations in this chapter are from Susanna Kaysen, *Girl, Interrupted* (Vintage Books, 1993).

The framers of the criteria felt that trying to assess a personality trait—for example, whether someone was manipulative—would be more difficult than determining whether the person engaged in certain behaviors, such as repeated fighting.

Although Cleckley did not deny that many psychopaths are at greatly elevated risk for criminal and antisocial behaviors, he did emphasize that some have few or no legal or interpersonal difficulties. In other words, some psychopaths are not criminals and some do not display the aggressiveness that is a DSM-IV criterion for antisocial personality disorder. Although the relationship between psychopathic personality and antisocial personality disorder is uncertain, the two syndromes clearly do not overlap perfectly (Figure 12.2) (Hare, 1983). Figure 12.2 illustrates the relative overlap among the characteristics of *psychopathy* as described by Cleckley and Hare, *antisocial personality disorder* as outlined in DSM-IV, and *criminality,* which includes all people who get into trouble with the law.

Dyssocial psychopathy may be included with antisocial personality disorder but *not* psychopathy (McNeil, 1970). Their antisocial behavior is thought to originate in allegiance to a culturally deviant subgroup. Many former gang delinquents may fall into this category, as may some members of the Cosa Nostra and some ghetto guerrillas in South Africa. Unlike Cleckley psychopaths, dyssocial psychopaths are presumed to have the capacity for guilt and loyalty.

As you can see in the diagram, not everyone who has psychopathy or antisocial personality disorder becomes involved with the legal system. What separates many in this group from those who get into trouble with the law may be IQ. In a prospective, longitudinal study, White, Moffit, and Silva (1989) followed almost 1,000 children, beginning at age 5, to see what predicted antisocial behavior at age 15. They found that of the 5-year-olds who were determined to be at high risk for later delinquent behavior, by the age of 15

16% did indeed have run-ins with the law, and 84% did not. What distinguished these two groups? In general, the at-risk children with lower IQs were the ones who got in trouble. This suggests that having a higher IQ may help protect some people from developing more serious problems, or may at least prevent them from getting caught!

Some psychopaths function quite successfully in certain segments of society (for example, politics, business, entertainment). Because of the difficulty in identifying these people, such "successful" or "subclinical" psychopaths (who meet some but not all the criteria for psychopathy) have not been the focus of much research. In a clever exception, Widom (1977) recruited a sample of subclinical psychopaths through advertisements in underground newspapers that invited many of the major personality characteristics of psychopathy. For example, one of the advertisements read:

> Wanted: charming, aggressive, carefree people who are impulsively irresponsible but are good at handling people and at looking after number one.

Widom found that her sample appeared to possess many of the same characteristics as imprisoned psychopaths; for example, a large percentage of them received low scores on questionnaire measures of empathy and socialization and had high rates of parental psychopathology, including alcoholism. Moreover, many of these individuals had stable occupations and had managed to stay out of prison. Widom's study, although lacking a control group, shows that at least some individuals with psychopathic personality traits avoid repeated contact with the legal system and may even function successfully in society.

Identifying psychopaths among the criminal population seems to have important implications for predicting their future criminal behavior. One study found that criminals who scored high on Hare's Psychopathy Checklist (PCL–R) put in less effort and showed fewer improvements in a therapy program than did criminals who were not psychopaths (Ogloff, Wong, & Greenwood, 1990). Other studies have shown that psychopaths are more likely than nonpsychopathic criminals to repeat their criminal offenses, especially those that are violent and/or sexual in nature (Rice, Harris, & Quinsey, 1990).

As we review the literature on antisocial personality disorder, we should note that the people included in the research may be members of only one of the three groups we have described. For example, genetic research is usually conducted with criminals because they and their families are easier to identify than members of the other groups. As you now know, the criminal group may include people other than those with antisocial personality disorder or psychopathy. Keep this in mind as you read on.

Before we discuss causal factors, it is important to note the developmental nature of antisocial behavior. DSM-IV provides a separate diagnosis for children who engage in behaviors that violate societal norms: *conduct disorder.* Many children with conduct disorder become juvenile offenders (Eppright, Kashani, Robison, & Reid, 1993) and tend to be-

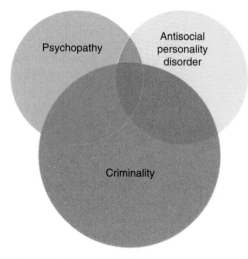

figure 12.2 Overlap and lack of overlap among antisocial personality disorder, psychopathy, and criminality.

come involved with drugs (VanKammen, Loeber, & Southamer-Loeber, 1991). Ryan fit into this category. More important, the lifelong pattern of antisocial behavior is evident in the fact that young children who display antisocial behavior are likely to continue these behaviors as they grow older (Charlebois, LeBlanc, Gagnon, Larivée, & Tremblay, 1993; Loeber, 1982). Data from long-term follow-up research indicate that many adults with antisocial personality disorder or psychopathy had conduct disorder as children (Robins, 1978); the likelihood increases if the child has both conduct disorder and attention deficit-hyperactivity disorder (Lynam, 1996).

"I have hatred inside me. I don't care how much I be somebody. . . . The more I hear somebody, the more anger I get inside me. . . . I used drugs when I was . . . probably 9 or 10 years old . . . smoked marijuana. . . . First time I drank some alcohol I think I was probably about 3 years old. . . . I assaulted a woman. . . . I had so much anger. . . . I was just like a bomb . . . it's just ticking . . . and the way I'm going, that bomb was going to blow up in me. I wouldn't be able to get away from it . . . going to be a lot of people hurt. . . . I'm not going out without taking somebody with me. . . ."

In many cases, the types of norm violations that an adult would engage in—irresponsibility regarding work or family—appear as younger versions in conduct disorder: truant from school, running away from home. A major difference is that lack of remorse is included under antisocial personality disorder but not in the conduct disorder criteria.

Obviously there is a tremendous amount of interest in studying a group that causes a great deal of harm to society. Research has been conducted for a number of years, and so we know a great deal more about antisocial personality disorder than about the other personality disorders.

GENETIC INFLUENCES

Family, twin, and adoption studies all suggest a genetic influence on both antisocial personality disorder and criminality (Bock & Goode, 1996; DiLalla & Gottesman, 1991). For example, Crowe (1974) examined adopted-away children of mothers who were felons and compared them with adopted-away children of normal mothers. All were separated from their mothers as newborns, minimizing the possibility that environmental factors from their biological families were responsible for the results. Crowe found that the adopted-away offspring of felons had significantly higher rates of arrests, conviction, and antisocial personality than did the adopted-away offspring of normal mothers, which suggests at least some genetic influence on criminality and antisocial behavior.

However, Crowe also found something else quite interesting: The adopted children of felons who themselves later became criminals had spent more time in interim orphanages than either the adopted children of felons who did not become criminals or the adopted children of normal mothers. As Crowe points out, this suggests a *gene–environment interaction;* in other words, genetic factors may be important *only* in the presence of certain environmental influences (alternatively, certain environmental influences are important only in the presence of certain genetic predispositions). Ge-

"We are very rare . . . and mostly we are men."

netic factors may present a vulnerability, but actual development of criminality may require environmental factors, such as a deficit in early, high-quality contact with parents or parent-surrogates.

This gene–environment interaction was demonstrated most clearly by Cadoret, Yates, Troughton, Woodworth, and Stewart (1995), who studied adopted children and their likelihood of developing conduct problems. If the childrens' biological parents had a history of antisocial personality disorder *and* their adoptive families exposed them to chronic stress through marital, legal, or psychiatric problems, the children were at greater risk for conduct problems. Once again, research shows that genetic influence does not necessarily mean that certain disorders are inevitable.

Data from twin studies generally support those of adoption studies. In a review of the major twin studies of criminality, Eysenck and Eysenck (1978) found that the average concordance rate for criminality among monozygotic (MZ) twins was 55%, whereas among dizygotic (DZ) twins it was only 13%. It is important to remember several limitations when you interpret findings on the genetics of criminality. First, "criminality" is an extremely heterogeneous category that includes people with and without antisocial personality disorder and psychopathy. Genetics may influence one or more subtypes of criminality. Second, it is clear that environmental factors play a substantial role in many, if not all, cases of criminality. In the studies reviewed by Eysenck and Eysenck (1978), for example, the concordance rate of criminality among identical twins would be 100% if criminality were caused entirely by genetic factors. Third and finally, the interaction between genes and environment may be important in the genesis of criminality (see Crowe, for example). Genetic factors may substantially contribute to criminal behavior only in the presence of certain environmental factors (Rutter, 1997). Recent research on twins with conduct disorder supports the role of genetic and en-

Many prisons allow visits between inmates and their children, in part to help reduce later problems in these children.

vironmental influences on this disorder (Slutske et al., 1997).

NEUROBIOLOGICAL INFLUENCES

A great deal of research has focused on neurobiological influences that may be specific to antisocial personality disorder. One thing seems clear: General brain damage does not explain why people become psychopaths or criminals; they appear to score as well on neuropsychological tests as the rest of us (Hart, Forth, & Hare, 1990). However, such tests are designed to detect significant damage in the brain and will not pick up subtle changes in chemistry or structure that could affect behavior. Two major theories have attracted a great deal of attention: (a) the *underarousal hypothesis* and (b) the *fearlessness hypothesis*.

According to the underarousal hypothesis, psychopaths have abnormally low levels of *cortical arousal* (Quay, 1965). There appears to be an inverted U-shaped relation between arousal and performance. The *Yerkes-Dodson curve* suggests that people with *either* very high or very low levels of arousal tend to experience negative affect and perform poorly in many situations, whereas individuals with intermediate levels of arousal tend to be relatively content and perform satisfactorily in most situations.

According to the underarousal hypothesis, the abnormally low levels of cortical arousal characteristic of psychopaths are the primary cause of their antisocial and risk-taking behaviors; they seek stimulation in order to boost their chronically low levels of arousal. This means that Ryan lied, took drugs, and dug up graves to achieve the same level of arousal we might get from talking on the phone with a good friend or watching television. Several researchers have examined childhood and adolescent psychophysiological predictors of adult antisocial behavior and criminality.

Raine, Venables, and Williams (1990), for example, assessed a sample of 15-year-olds on a variety of autonomic and central nervous system variables. They found that future criminals had lower skin conductance activity, lower heart rate during rest periods, and more slow-frequency brain wave activity, all indicative of low arousal.

Low-frequency *theta waves* are found in brain wave measures of children and largely disappear in adulthood; their specific purpose is as yet unknown. There is evidence that many psychopaths have excessive theta waves when they are awake. This finding has generated another theory related to arousal levels that is sometimes referred to as the *cortical immaturity hypothesis* of psychopathy (Hare, 1970) which holds that the cerebral cortex of psychopaths is at a relatively primitive stage of development. This hypothesis may help to explain why the behavior of psychopaths is often childlike and impulsive: Their cerebral cortices, which play such a key role in the inhibition and control of impulses, may be insufficiently developed.

The data on theta waves are open to an alternative and perhaps simpler explanation. Because theta waves also indicate states such as drowsiness or boredom, psychopaths' higher levels of theta waves may simply reflect their relative lack of concern regarding being hooked up to psychophysiological equipment! Picture yourself having your brain waves measured. You sit next to the intimidating polygraph machine, attached to a number of electrodes and wires. How will you react? As a nonpsychopath, you will probably feel anxiety and apprehension. In contrast, a psychopath, who is low in anxiety, will probably be bored, apathetic, and unresponsive. The excessive theta waves of psychopaths may simply reflect their relative absence of anxiety.

According to the *fearlessness hypothesis,* psychopaths possess a higher threshold for experiencing fear than most other individuals (Lykken, 1957, 1982). In other words, things that greatly frighten the rest of us have little or no effect on the psychopath. Remember that Ryan was unafraid of going alone to dangerous neighborhoods to buy drugs. According to proponents of this hypothesis, the fearlessness of the psychopath gives rise to all the other major features of the syndrome.

Early evidence for the fearlessness hypothesis came from a series of studies by Lykken (1957) using prison inmates. For the first study, Lykken developed a questionnaire (later termed the Activity Preference Questionnaire) consisting of a number of items, each with two options. There was one catch, however: both options referred to activities that most people would find unpleasant and prefer not to do.

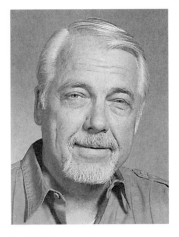

David Lykken conducted early research on the nature of psychopathy.

Lykken's test is essentially a "lesser of two evils" questionnaire. In each case, one option was boring or demanding (for example, "standing in a long line for something," "shoveling the walks after a snowstorm") and the other option was frightening or embarrassing (for instance, "being given an electric shock as part of a medical experiment," "belching in church during a prayer"). Lykken thought that if the fearlessness hypothesis were correct psychopaths would choose the more frightening option more often because they would be less distressed by potentially frightening activities. Indeed, this is precisely what happened.

In a second study, Lykken constructed a classical conditioning task involving painful electric shock. His primary dependent measure was galvanic skin response (GSR), a reaction marked by an increase in palmar sweating and typically interpreted as a sign of autonomic arousal. Lykken repeatedly paired a tone (the conditioned stimulus) with electric shock to the subjects' fingertips (the unconditioned stimulus). Then, he presented the tone (conditioned stimulus) alone on multiple occasions. Nonpsychopaths showed a predictable and understandable pattern: When they heard the tone, their palms began to sweat, signaling that they expected the shock to come next. Moreover, their GSRs were quite slow to extinguish. In contrast, psychopaths showed a striking pattern: In most cases, they exhibited very weak GSRs to the tones alone, and their GSRs tended to extinguish rapidly.

This study by Lykken has important implications, suggesting that psychopaths may have difficulty associating certain cues or signals with impending punishment or danger, much as children are socialized to inhibit their behavior. Most parents do not punish their children directly on every occasion for harmful or inappropriate behavior, but instead rely on cues such as "No" or even a threatening stare to inhibit inappropriate behavior. Largely because of classical conditioning, such cues tend to be quite effective substitutes for direct punishment. But if they have little or no impact on the prepsychopathic child, he or she will probably not acquire a well-developed capacity for impulse control.

Theorists have tried to connect what we know about the workings of the brain with clinical observations of people with antisocial personality disorder, especially those with psychopathy. Several theorists have applied Jeffrey Gray's (1987) model of brain functioning to this population (Fowles, 1988; Quay, 1993). According to Gray, three major brain systems influence learning and emotional behavior: the behavioral inhibition system (BIS), the reward system

(REW), and the fight/flight system (F/F). Box 12.1 illustrates the possible role of the fight/flight system in psychopathic behavior. The BIS is responsible for our ability to stop or slow down when we are faced with impending punishment, nonreward, or novel situations, which leads to anxiety and frustration. The BIS is thought to be located in the septohippocampal system and involves the noradrenergic and serotonergic neurotransmitter systems. The reward system is responsible for our approach behaviors—in particular, our approach to positive rewards—and is associated with hope and relief. This system probably involves the dopaminergic system in the mesolimbic area of the brain, which we previously noted as the "pleasure pathway" for its role in substance use and abuse (Chapter 11).

If you think about the behavior of psychopaths, the possible malfunctioning of these systems is clear. An imbalance between the BIS and REW may make the fear and anxiety produced by the BIS less apparent, and the positive feelings associated with the REW more prominent (Fowles, 1988; Quay, 1993). Theorists have proposed that this type of neurobiological dysfunction may explain why psychopaths aren't anxious about committing the antisocial acts that characterize their disorder.

PSYCHOLOGICAL AND SOCIAL DIMENSIONS

What goes on in the mind of a psychopath? In one of several studies of how psychopaths process reward and punishment, Newman, Patterson, and Kosson (1987) set up a card-playing task on a computer; they provided five-cent rewards and fines for correct and incorrect answers to psychopathic and nonpsychopathic criminal offenders. The game was constructed so that at first they were rewarded about 90% of the time and fined only about 10% of the time. Gradually, the odds changed until the probability of getting a reward was 0%. Despite feedback that reward was no longer forthcoming, the psychopaths continued to play and lose. As a result of this and other studies, the researchers hypothesized that once psychopaths set their sights on a reward goal, they are less likely than nonpsychopaths to be deterred despite signs that the goal is no longer achievable (Newman & Wallace, 1993). Again, considering the reckless and daring behavior of some psychopaths (robbing banks without a mask and getting caught immediately) failure to abandon an unattainable goal fits the overall picture.

Remember our discussion in Chapter 4 of Gerald Patterson's studies of aggressive children, who may develop antisocial personality disorder or psychopathy (Robins, 1978). Patterson's influential work suggests that aggression in such children may escalate, in part as a result of their interactions with their parents (Patterson, 1982). He found that the parents often give in to the problems displayed by their children. For example, parents ask their son to make his bed and he refuses. One parent yells at the boy. He yells back and becomes abusive. At some point this interchange becomes so aversive that the parent stops fighting and walks away, thereby ending the fight but also letting the son not make his bed. Giving in to these problems results in short-

box 12.1   *Is There an "Aggression" Gene?*

Researchers in the Netherlands are cautiously optimistic after discovering that a gene mutation found in a large Dutch family may cause aggression (Brunner et al., 1993). Their study is important because it may tell us more about how genes affect behavior.

Hans G. Brunner and his colleagues at the university hospital in Nijmegen have tracked the males of one family since 1978. Some of the men are prone to particularly violent outbursts. One raped his sister, two others were arsonists, and still another tried to run over his boss after being told his work wasn't good enough. All these men also have mild levels of mental retardation. None of the women in the family are given to violent outbursts, nor do they exhibit mental retardation.

The evidence for a genetic explanation of these behaviors is impressive. The observation that the condition occurs only in the males indicates that the gene is probably on the X chromosome. Because men have only one X chromosome, any "bad" or mutated

gene will show up. On the other hand, because women have two X chromosomes, they tend to have a "good" or normal gene to balance out the bad one.

To further narrow down the location of the mutated gene, Brunner and his colleagues conducted a linkage study. As you may remember from Chapter 4, such studies try to identify marker genes that are inherited along with the gene you are trying to locate. Because we already know where the marker genes are, we can get a good idea of the approximate location of the mutated gene.

On the basis of the linkage study and biochemical analyses, Brunner and his fellow researchers believe the defect involves the gene that produces monoamine oxidase A or MAOA. MAOA is an enzyme that helps break down neurotransmitters, specifically those that are involved in our "fight or flight" responses to threats and other stresses; they include serotonin, dopamine, and noradrenaline. If the

MAOA enzyme isn't working properly, these neurotransmitters may build up and the affected people will have trouble handling stressful situations. For example, after the deaths of close relatives, the two arsonists in the Dutch family set fires. A subsequent study confirms that MAOA is deficient only in the affected males (Brunner, Nelen, Breakefield, Ropers, & van Oost, 1993).

The possible genetic vulnerability to react violently, in combination with certain stressors, may result in aggression. It is important to remember that this defect, to date, has been found only in one family. It is unlikely that all or even most aggressive behavior will be traced to the same cause. Finally, social, economic, and cultural factors determine the type and severity of stresses. What this research suggests, however, is that just the right (or wrong!) combination of genetic, neurobiological, and psychosocial contributions came together to create devastating outcomes in one Dutch family.

---

term gains for both the parent (calm is restored in the house) and the child (he gets what he wants), but it results in continuing problems. The child has learned to continue fighting and not give up, and the parent learns that the only way to "win" is to withdraw all demands. This "coercive family process" combines with other factors, such as parents' inept monitoring of their child's activities and less parental involvement, to help maintain the aggressive behaviors (Patterson, DeBaryshe, & Ramsey, 1989; Sansbury & Wahler, 1992).

Although little is known about which environmental factors play a direct role in causing antisocial personality disorder and psychopathy (as opposed to childhood conduct disorders), evidence from adoption studies strongly suggests that shared environmental factors—that tend to make family members similar—are important to the etiology of criminality and perhaps antisocial personality disorder. For example, in the adoption study by Sigvardsson, Cloninger, Bohman, and von-Knorring (1982), low social status of the adoptive parents increased the risk of nonviolent criminality among females. Like children with conduct disorders, individuals with antisocial personality disorder come from homes with inconsistent parental discipline (for example, Robins, 1966). It is not known for certain, however, whether inconsistent discipline directly causes antisocial personality

disorder; it is conceivable, for example, that parents have a genetic vulnerability to antisocial personality disorder that they pass on to their children but that also causes them to be inadequate parents.

One interesting study looked at the social environment and attitudes of neighborhoods and their effect on violent crime. Sampson, Raudenbush, and Earls (1997) asked members of city neighborhoods in Chicago questions about the willingness of local residents to intervene for the common good; for example, whether neighbors would intervene if children were skipping school and hanging out on the street. The researchers found that the degree of mutual trust and solidarity in a neighborhood was inversely related to violent crime. This study points out that factors outside the family can influence behaviors associated with antisocial personality disorder.

A final factor that has been implicated in antisocial personality disorder is the role of stress. One study found that trauma associated with combat may increase the likelihood of antisocial behavior. Barrett and colleagues studied over 2,000 Army veterans of the Vietnam War (Barrett et al., 1996). Even after adjusting for histories of childhood problems, the researchers found that those who had been exposed to the most traumatic events were most likely to engage in violence, illegal activities, lying, and using aliases.

DEVELOPMENTAL INFLUENCES

The forms that antisocial behaviors take changes as children move into adulthood, from truancy and stealing from friends to extortion, assaults, armed robbery, or other crimes. Fortunately, clinical lore, as well as scattered empirical reports (Robins, 1966), suggest that rates of antisocial behavior begin to decline rather markedly around the age of 40. Hare et al., (1988) provided empirical support for this phenomenon. They examined the conviction rates of male psychopaths and male nonpsychopaths who had been incarcerated for a variety of crimes. The researchers found that between the ages of 16 and 45 the conviction rates of nonpsychopaths remained relatively constant. In contrast, the conviction rates of psychopaths remained relatively constant up until about 40, at which time they decreased markedly (see Figure 12.3). Why antisocial behavior often declines around middle age remains unanswered.

Children with conduct disorder may become adults with antisocial personality disorder.

AN INTEGRATIVE MODEL

How can we put all this information together to get a better understanding of people with antisocial personality disorder? It is important to remember that research in each area may involve people labeled as having antisocial personality disorder, people labeled as psychopathic, or criminals. Whatever the label, it appears that these people have a genetic vulnerability to antisocial behaviors and personality traits. Perhaps this vulnerability results in underarousal and/or fearlessness. The genetic inheritance might be the propensity for weak inhibition systems (BIS) and overactive reward systems (REW) that could partially account for the differences in cognitive set we saw in the research by Newman and his colleagues (Newman & Wallace, 1993).

In a family that may already be under stress because of divorce or substance abuse (Hetherington, Stanley-Hagan, & Anderson, 1989; Patterson et al., 1989), there may be an interaction style that actually encourages antisocial behavior on the part of the child (Wooton, Frick, Shelton, & Silverthorn, 1997). The child's antisocial and impulsive behavior alienates other children who might be good role models and attracts others who encourage antisocial behavior (Vuchinich, Bank, & Patterson, 1992). These behaviors may also result in the child's dropping out of school and a poor occupational history in adulthood, which help create increasingly frustrating life circumstances that further incite acts against society (Caspi, Elder, & Bem, 1987).

This is, admittedly, an abbreviated version of a complex scenario. The important element is that in this integrative model of antisocial behavior, biological, psychological, and cultural factors combine in intricate ways to create someone like Ryan.

TREATMENT

One of the major problems with treating people in this group is typical of numerous personality disorders: They rarely identify themselves as needing treatment. Because of this, and because they can be very manipulative even with their therapists, most clinicians are pessimistic about the outcome of treatment for adults who have antisocial personality disorder, and there are few documented success stories. Antisocial behavior is predictive of poor prognosis even in childhood (Kazdin & Mazurick, 1994). In general, therapists agree with incarcerating these people to deter future antisocial acts. Clinicians encourage identification of high-

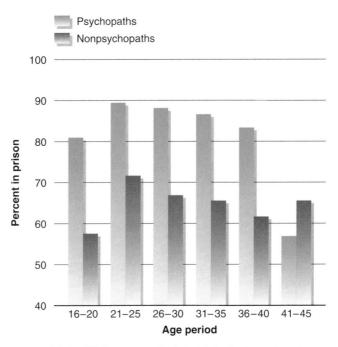

figure 12.3 Lifetime course of criminal behavior in psychopaths and nonpsychopaths (based on Hare, McPherson, & Forth, 1988).

risk children so treatment can be attempted before they become adults (Patterson, 1982).

The most common treatment strategy for children involves parent training (Patterson, 1986; Sanders, 1992). Parents are taught to recognize behavior problems early and how to use praise and privileges to reduce problem behavior and encourage prosocial behaviors. Treatment studies typically show that these types of programs can significantly improve the behaviors of many children who display antisocial behaviors (Fleischman, 1981; Patterson, Chamberlain, & Reid, 1982; Webster-Stratton & Hammond, 1997). A number of factors, however, put families at risk for either not succeeding in treatment or for dropping out early; these include cases with a high degree of family dysfunction, socioeconomic disadvantage, high family stress, parent's history of antisocial behavior, and severe conduct disorder on the part of the child (Dumas & Wahler, 1983; Kazdin, Mazurick, & Bass, 1993).

Some programs address these problems even earlier, in an attempt to *prevent* problems from arising. Typically preschool programs, they combine teaching good parenting skills with a variety of supports for families with social and economic disadvantages (Zigler, Taussig, & Black, 1992). It is too soon to assess the success of such programs in preventing the types of adult antisocial behaviors typically observed among people with this personality disorder. However, given the ineffectiveness of treatment for adults, prevention may be the best approach to this problem.

Borderline Personality Disorder

People with *borderline personality disorder* lead tumultuous lives. Their moods and relationships are unstable, and usually they have a very poor self-image. These people often feel empty and are at great risk of dying by their own hands. Consider the following case.

Claire

A Stranger Among Us

I have known Claire for over 25 years and have watched her through the good but mostly bad times of her often shaky and erratic life as a person with borderline personality disorder. Claire and I went to school together from the eighth grade through high school, and we've kept in touch periodically. My earliest memory of her is of her hair, which was cut short and rather unevenly. She told me that when things were not going well she cut her own hair severely, which helped to "fill the void." I later found out that the long sleeves she usually wore hid scars and cuts that she had made herself.

Claire was the first of our friends to smoke. What was unusual about this and her later drug use was not that they occurred (this was in the 1960s when "If it feels good, do it!" hadn't been replaced by "Just say no!") or that they began early; it was that she didn't seem to use them to get at-

tention, like everyone else. Claire was also one of the first whose parents divorced, and both of them seemed to abandon her emotionally. She later told me that her father was an alcoholic who had regularly beaten her and her mother. She did poorly in school and had very low self-esteem. She frequently said she was stupid and ugly, yet she was obviously neither.

Throughout our school years, Claire left town periodically, without any explanation. I learned many years later that she was in psychiatric facilities to get help with her suicidal depression. She often threatened to kill herself, although we didn't guess that she was serious.

In our later teens we all drifted away from Claire. She had become more and more unpredictable, sometimes berating us for a perceived slight ("You're walking too fast. You don't want to be seen with me!"), and at other times desperate to be around us. We were obviously confused by her behavior. With some people, emotional outbursts can bring you closer together. Unfortunately for Claire, these incidents and her overall demeanor made us feel that we didn't know her at all. As we all grew older, the "void" she described in herself became overwhelming and eventually shut us all out.

Claire married twice, and both times had very passionate but stormy relationships interrupted by hospitalizations. She tried to stab her first husband during a particularly violent rage. She tried a number of drugs, but mainly used alcohol to "deaden the pain."

Now, in her mid-40s, things have calmed down some. Although she says she is rarely happy, Claire does feel a little better about herself and is doing well as a travel agent. Although she is seeing someone, she is reluctant to become very involved because of her personal history. Claire was ultimately diagnosed with depression and borderline personality disorder.

CLINICAL DESCRIPTION

Borderline personality disorder is one of the more common personality disorders; in psychiatric settings, it accounts for about 15% of the population and about 50% of the patients with personality disorders (Widiger & Weissman, 1991). Claire's life illustrates the instability characteristic of people with borderline personality disorder. They tend to have very turbulent relationships, fearing abandonment but lacking control over their emotions (Gunderson, Zanarini, & Kisiel, 1995). They frequently engage in suicidal and/or self-mutilative behaviors, cutting or burning or punching themselves. Claire sometimes used her cigarette to burn her palm or forearm, and carved her initials in her arm. A significant proportion—about 6%—succeed at suicide (M. H. Stone, 1989; Widiger & Trull, 1993).

People with this personality disorder are often very intense, going from anger to deep depression in a short time. They also are characterized by impulsivity, which can be seen in their drug abuse and self-mutilation. Claire's empty feeling is also common; these people are sometimes described as chronically bored. The mood disorders that we discussed in Chapter 7 are common among people with borderline personality disorder, with 24% to 74% having major

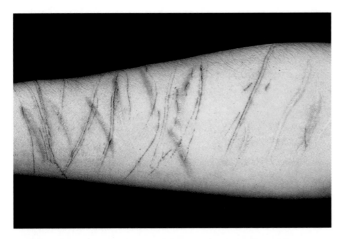

Borderline personality disorder is often accompanied by self-mutilation.

depression, and 4% to 20% having bipolar disorder (Widiger & Rogers, 1989). Eating disorders are also common, particularly bulimia (see Chapter 8): Almost 25% of bulimics also have borderline personality disorder (Levin & Hyler, 1986). Up to 67% of the people with this disorder are also diagnosed with at least one substance use disorder (Dulit et al., 1993). As with antisocial personality disorder, people with borderline personality disorder tend to improve during their 30s and 40s, although they may continue to have difficulties into old age (Rosowsky & Gurian, 1992).

CAUSES

The results from almost 20 family studies suggest that borderline personality disorder is more prevalent in families with the disorder, and is somehow linked with mood disorders (for example, Baron, Gruen, Asnis, & Lord, 1985; Links, Steiner, & Huxley, 1988; Zanarini, Gunderson, Marino, Schwartz, & Frankenburg, 1988). Just as schizotypal personality disorder seems to share a familial association with schizophrenia, borderline personality disorder may have a similar connection to mood disorders (Widiger & Trull, 1993). Although some traits may be inherited (for instance, impulsivity), there appears to be a great deal of room for environmental influences.

One psychosocial influence that has received a great deal of attention is the possible contribution of early trauma, especially sexual and physical abuse. Several studies have shown that people with this disorder are more likely to report abuse than are individuals with other psychiatric conditions (for example, Goldman, D'Angelo, DeMaso, & Mezzacappa, 1992; Ogata et al., 1990). Wagner and Linehan (1994) found that among women with both borderline personality disorder and parasuicidal behavior (which includes both serious and minor suicide attempts) 76% reported some type of childhood sexual abuse and had made the most serious attempts to commit suicide. In a large study, researchers found an even higher rate of abuse histories in individuals with borderline personal-

I spent hours in my butterfly chair banging my wrist.

ity disorder with 91% reporting abuse and 92% reporting being neglected before the age of 18 (Zanarini et al., 1997). Although we obviously do not know whether abuse and neglect cause later borderline personality disorder (data are based on recollection and a correlation between the two phenomena), they may be predisposing factors in at least some cases. If childhood abuse or neglect does lead to most cases of borderline personality disorder, the connection may well explain why women are affected more often than men. Girls are two to three times more likely to be sexually abused than boys (Herman, Perry, & van der Kolk, 1989).

Building on the possible link to abuse, Gunderson and Sabo (1993) argued that borderline personality disorder is similar to posttraumatic stress disorder (PTSD); they see many resemblances in the two behavior patterns. Herman et al. (1989) have drawn similar parallels; for example, difficulties in the regulation of mood, impulse control, and interpersonal relationships. These observations all seem to support the hypothesis that borderline personality disorder may be caused by early trauma.

Borderline personality disorder has been observed among people who have gone through rapid cultural changes. The problems of identity, emptiness, fears of abandonment, and low anxiety threshold have been found in child and adult immigrants (Laxenaire, Ganne-Vevonec, & Streiff, 1982; Skhiri, Annabi, Bi, & Allani, 1982). These observations further support the possibility that early trauma may, in some individuals, lead to borderline personality disorder.

Remember, however, that a history of childhood trauma, including sexual and physical abuse, occurs in a number of other disorders such as somatoform disorder (Chapter 6), panic disorder (Chapter 5), and multiple personality disorder (Chapter 6). In addition, 20% to 40% of individuals with borderline personality disorder have no apparent history of such abuse (Gunderson & Sabo, 1993).

Although childhood sexual and physical abuse seems to play some role in the etiology of borderline personality disorder, neither appears to be necessary or sufficient to produce the syndrome.

Zanarini and Frankenberg (1997) attempt to integrate the different aspects of etiology in borderline personality disorder. They suggest that childhood trauma combines with a predisposing temperament or personality and a stressful triggering event causes the unstable behaviors. The individuals abused as children who do not develop the disorder may lack the biological predisposition which, in this case, may be a volatile or impulsive personality style (Figueroa & Silk, 1997).

TREATMENT

In contrast to the extensive research on the nature of borderline personality disorder, there are relatively few studies that examine the effects of treatment. Many people appear to respond positively to a variety of medications, including tricyclic antidepressants (Soloff et al., 1989; M. H. Stone,

1986), and lithium (Links, Steiner, Boiago, & Irwin, 1990). However, efforts to provide successful treatment are complicated by problems with drug abuse, compliance with treatment, and suicide attempts. As a result, many clinicians are reluctant to work with people who have borderline personality disorder.

Research on psychological treatment is limited. In one exception, Linehan (1987) used an approach she called *dialectical behavior therapy* (DBT), which involves helping people cope with the stressors that seem to trigger suicidal behaviors. Weekly individual sessions provide support and patients are taught how to identify and regulate their emotions. Problem solving is emphasized, so they can handle difficulties more effectively. In addition, they receive treatment similar to that used for people with posttraumatic stress disorder, in which prior traumatic events are reexperienced to help extinguish the fear associated with them (see Chapter 5). In the final stage of therapy, clients learn to trust their own responses rather than depend on the validation of others, sometimes by visualizing themselves not reacting to criticism.

Preliminary results suggest that DBT may help reduce suicide attempts, dropouts from treatment, and hospitalizations (Linehan, Armstrong, Suarez, Allmon, & Heard, 1991; Linehan, Heard, & Armstrong, 1992). A follow-up of 39 women who received either dialectic behavior therapy or general therapeutic support (called "treatment as usual") for 1 year showed that, during the first 6 months of follow-up, the women in the DBT group were less suicidal, less angry, and better adjusted socially (Linehan & Kehrer, 1993). This type of treatment therefore appears promising.

■ **concept check 12.1**

Which personality disorders are the following people displaying?

1. Homer, who seems eccentric, never shows much emotion. He does not have any close personal relationships and does not seek interactions with people. _____

2. Matt is 19 and has been in trouble with the law since he was 14. He lies to his parents, vandalizes buildings in his community and, when caught, shows no remorse. He frequently fights with others and doesn't care whom he injures. _____

3. Russell trusts no one and incorrectly believes other people want to harm him or spoil his plans. He is sure his wife is having an affair. He no longer confides in friends for fear that the information will be used against him. He dwells for hours on harmless comments by co-workers.
_____

4. Alan is involved in drugs and has casual sexual encounters. He feels empty unless he does dangerous and exciting things. He threatens to commit suicide if his girlfriend suggests getting help or if she talks about leaving him. He alternates between loving her and hating her. He has low self-esteem and has recently experienced high levels of stress. _____

Histrionic Personality Disorder

Individuals with *histrionic personality disorder* tend to be overly dramatic and often seem almost to be acting, which is why the term *histrionic*, which means theatrical in manner, is used. Consider the following case.

Pat
Always Onstage

When we first met, Pat seemed to radiate enjoyment of life. She was single, in her mid-30s, and was going to night school for her master's degree. She often dressed very flamboyantly. During the day she taught children with disabilities, and when she didn't have class she was often out late on a date. When I first spoke with her, she enthusiastically told me how impressed she was with my work in the field of developmental disabilities and that she had been extremely successful in using some of my techniques with her students. She was clearly overdoing the praise, but who wouldn't appreciate such flattering comments?

Because some of our research included children in her classroom, I saw Pat frequently. Over a period of weeks, however, our interactions grew strained. She frequently complained of various illnesses and injuries (falling in the parking lot, twisting her neck looking out a window) that interfered with her work. She was very disorganized, often leaving to the very last minute tasks that required considerable planning. Pat made promises to other people that were impossible to keep but that seemed to be aimed at winning their approval; when she broke the promise, she usually made up a story that was designed to elicit sympathy and compassion. For example, she promised the mother of one of her students that she would put on a "massive and unique" birthday party for her daughter, but completely forgot about it until the mother showed up with cake and juice. Upon seeing her, Pat flew into a rage and blamed the principal for keeping her late after school, although there was no truth to this accusation.

Pat often interrupted meetings about research to talk about her latest boyfriend. The boyfriends changed almost weekly, but her enthusiasm ("Like no other man I have ever met!") and optimism about the future ("He's the guy I want to spend the rest of my life with!") remained high for each of them. Wedding plans were seriously discussed with almost every one, despite their brief acquaintance. Pat was very ingratiating, especially to the male teachers, who often helped her out of trouble she got into because of her disorganization.

When it became clear that she would probably lose her teaching job because of her poor performance, Pat managed to manipulate several of the male teachers and the assistant principal into recommending her for a new job in a nearby school district. A year later she was still at the new school, but had been moved twice to different classrooms. According to teachers she worked with, Pat still lacked close interpersonal relationships, although she described her current relationship as "deeply involved." After a rather long period of depression, Pat sought help from a psychologist, who diagnosed her as also having histrionic personality disorder.

CLINICAL DESCRIPTION

People with histrionic personality disorder are inclined to express their emotions in an exaggerated fashion; for example, hugging someone they have just met or crying uncontrollably during a sad movie (Pfohl, 1995). They also tend to be vain and self-centered, and to be uncomfortable when they are not in the limelight. They are often seductive in appearance and behavior, and they are typically very concerned about their looks. (Pat, for example, spent a great deal of money on unusual jewelry and was sure to point it out to anyone who would listen.) In addition, they seek reassurance and approval constantly and may become upset or angry when others do not attend to them or praise them. People with histrionic personality disorder also tend to be impulsive and have great difficulty delaying gratification.

The cognitive style associated with histrionic personality disorder is impressionistic (Shapiro, 1965), characterized by a tendency to view situations in very global, black-and-white terms. Speech is often vague, lacking in detail, and characterized by hyperbole (Pfohl, 1991). For example, when Pat was asked about a date she had had the night before, she might say it was "way cool" but fail to provide more detailed information.

CAUSES

Despite its long history, very little research has been done on the causes or treatment of histrionic personality disorder. The ancient Greek philosophers believed that many unexplainable problems of women were caused by the uterus *(hystera)* migrating within the body (Abse, 1987). As we have seen, however, histrionic personality disorder also occurs among men.

One hypothesis involves a possible relationship with antisocial personality disorder. There is evidence that histrionic personality and antisocial personality co-occur much more often than chance would account for. Lilienfeld and his colleagues (1986), for example, found that roughly two-thirds of people with histrionic personality also met criteria for antisocial personality disorder. The evidence for this association has led to the suggestion (for example, Cloninger, 1978; Lilienfeld, 1992) that histrionic personality and antisocial personality may be sex-typed alternative expressions of the same unidentified underlying condition. Females with the underlying condition may be predisposed to exhibit a predominantly histrionic pattern, whereas males with the underlying condition may be predisposed to exhibit a predominantly antisocial pattern.

TREATMENT

Although a great deal has been written about ways of helping people with this disorder, very little research demonstrates success (Dulit et al., 1993). Some therapists have tried to modify the attention-getting behavior. Kass, Silvers, and Abrams (1972) worked with five women, four of whom had been hospitalized for suicide attempts and all of whom were later diagnosed with histrionic personality disorder. The women were rewarded for appropriate interactions and were fined for attention-getting behavior. The

People with histrionic personality disorder tend to be vain, extravagant, and seductive.

therapists noted improvement after an 18-month follow-up, but they did not collect scientific data to confirm their observation.

A large part of therapy for these individuals usually focuses on the problematic interpersonal relationships. They often manipulate others through emotional crises, using charm, sex, seductiveness, or complaining (A. T. Beck & Freeman, 1990). People with histrionic personality disorder often need to be shown how the short-term gains derived from this interactional style result in long-term costs, and they need to be taught more appropriate ways of negotiating their wants and needs.

Narcissistic Personality Disorder

We all know people who think highly of themselves—perhaps exaggerating their real abilities. They consider themselves somehow different from others and deserving of special treatment. In **narcissistic personality disorder,** this tendency is taken to its extreme. In Greek mythology, Narcissus was a youth who spurned the love of Echo, so enamored was he of his own beauty. He spent his days admiring his own image reflected in a pool of water. Psychoanalysts, including Sigmund Freud, used the term *narcissistic* to describe people who show an exaggerated sense of self-importance and are preoccupied with receiving attention (Cooper & Ronningstam, 1992). Consider the following case.

David
Taking Care of Number One

David was an attorney in his early 40s when he sought treatment for depressed mood. He appeared to be an outgoing man who paid meticulous attention to his appearance. He made a point of asking for the therapist's admiration of his new designer suit, his winter tan, and his new foreign convertible. He also asked the therapist what kind of car he drove and how many VIP clients he dealt with. David wanted to make sure that he was dealing with someone who was the best in the business. David spoke of being an "ace" student and a "super" athlete, but could not provide any details that would validate a superior performance in these areas.

During law school, David became a workaholic, fueled by fantasies of brilliant work and international recognition. He spent minimal time with his wife, and after their son was born, even less time with either of them. He waited until he felt reasonably secure in his first job so that he could let go of her financial support, and then he sought a divorce.

After his divorce, David decided that he was totally free to just please himself. He loved spending all his money on himself, and he lavishly decorated his condominium and bought an attention-getting wardrobe. He constantly sought the companionship of different, attractive women.

David felt better when someone flattered him; when he was in a group social situation where he could easily grab the center of attention; and when he could fantasize about obtaining a high-level position, being honored for his great talent, or just being fabulously wealthy. (Beck & Freeman, 1990, pp. 245–246)

CLINICAL DESCRIPTION

People with narcissistic personality disorder have an unreasonable sense of self-importance and are so preoccupied with themselves that they lack sensitivity and compassion for other people (Gunderson, Ronningstam, & Smith, 1995). They aren't comfortable unless someone is admiring them. Their exaggerated feelings and their fantasies of greatness, called "grandiosity," create a number of negative attributes. They require and expect a great deal of special attention—the best table in the restaurant, the illegal parking space in front of the movie theater. They also tend to use or exploit others for their own interests and show little empathy. When confronted with other successful people, they can be extremely envious and arrogant. And because they often fail to live up to their own expectations, they are frequently depressed.

CAUSES AND TREATMENT

We start out as infants being self-centered and demanding, which is part of our struggle for survival. However, part of the socialization process involves teaching children empathy and altruism. Some writers, including Kohut (1971, 1977), believe that narcissistic personality disorder arises largely from a profound failure of empathic "mirroring" by the parents very early in a child's development. As a consequence, the child remains fixated at a self-centered, grandiose stage of development. In addition, the child (and later the adult) becomes involved in an essentially endless and fruitless search for the ideal person who will meet their unfulfilled empathic needs.

In a sociological view, Christopher Lasch (1978) wrote in his popular book *The Culture of Narcissism* that this personality disorder is increasing in prevalence in most Western societies, primarily as a consequence of large-scale social changes, including greater emphasis on short-term hedonism, individualism, competitiveness, and success. According to Lasch, the "me generation" has produced more than its share of individuals with narcissistic personality disorder. Indeed, reports confirm that narcissistic personality disorder is increasing in prevalence (Cooper & Ronningstam, 1992). However, this apparent rise may be a consequence of increased interest in and research on the disorder.

Treatment research is extremely limited in both number of studies and reports of success (Turkat & Maisto, 1985). When therapy is attempted with these individuals it often focuses on their grandiosity their hypersensitivity to evaluation, and their lack of empathy toward others (A.T. Beck & Freeman, 1990). Cognitive therapy aims at replacing their fantasies with a focus on the day-to-day pleasurable experiences that are truly attainable. Coping strategies such as relaxation training are used to help them face and accept criticism. Helping them focus on the feelings of others is also a goal. Because individuals with this disorder are vulnerable to severe depressive episodes, particularly in middle age, treatment is often initiated for the depression. However, it is impossible to draw any conclusions about the impact of such treatment on the actual narcissistic personality disorder.

Cluster C Disorders

Avoidant Personality Disorder

As the name suggests, people with **avoidant personality disorder** are extremely sensitive to the opinions of others and therefore avoid most relationships. Their extremely low self-esteem, coupled with a fear of rejection, causes them to be limited in their friendships and very dependent on those they feel comfortable with. Consider the following case.

Jane
Not Worth Noticing

Jane was raised by an alcoholic mother who had borderline personality disorder and who abused her verbally and physically. As a child she made sense of her mother's abusive treatment by believing that she (Jane) must be an intrinsically unworthy person to be treated so badly. As an adult in her late 20s, Jane still expected to be rejected when others found out that she was inherently unworthy and bad.

Jane was highly self-critical and predicted that she would not be accepted. She thought that people would not like her, that they would see she was a loser, and that she would not have anything to say. She became upset if she perceived that someone in even the most fleeting encounter was reacting negatively or neutrally. If a newspaper vendor failed to smile at her, or a sales clerk was slightly curt, Jane automatically thought it must be because she (Jane) was somehow unworthy or unlikable. She then felt quite sad. Even when she was receiving positive feedback from a friend, she discounted it. As a result, Jane had few friends and certainly no close ones. (Beck & Freeman, 1990, p. 263)

CLINICAL DESCRIPTION

Theodore Millon (1981), who initially proposed this diagnosis, notes that it is important to distinguish between individuals who are asocial because they are apathetic, affectively flat, and relatively uninterested in interpersonal relationships (comparable to what DSM-IV terms schizoid personality disorder) and individuals who are asocial because they are interpersonally anxious and fearful of rejection. It is the latter who fit the criteria of avoidant personality disorder (Millon & Martinez, 1995).

CAUSES

A number of theories have been proposed that integrate biological and psychosocial influences as the cause of avoidant personality disorder. Millon (1981), for example, suggests that these individuals may be born with a difficult temperament or personality characteristics. As a result, their parents may reject them, or at least not provide them with enough early, uncritical love. This rejection, in turn, may result in low self-esteem and social alienation, conditions that persist into adulthood. Limited support does exist for psychosocial influences. Stravynski, Elie, and Franche (1989) questioned a group of people with avoidant personality disorder and a group of control subjects about their early treatment by their parents. Those with the disorder remembered their parents as more rejecting, more guilt engendering, and less affectionate than the control group.

In interpreting the results of this study some caution is in order. You probably noticed that it was a *retrospective study,* because it relied on the subjects' memories for a report of what had happened. The differences in the reports of the two groups could be a consequence of differences in their ability to remember their childhoods rather than actual differences in the ways they were treated. Also, it could be that people with avoidant personality disorder are more sensitive to the way they are treated, and therefore their memories are different

from what actually happened. The findings are intriguing nonetheless, and should be followed up as a possible contributor to our understanding of this disorder.

TREATMENT

In contrast to the scarcity of research into most of the other personality disorders, there are a number of well-controlled studies on approaches to therapy for people with avoidant personality disorder. Behavioral intervention techniques for anxiety and social skills problems have had some success (Alden, 1989; Alden & Capreol, 1993; Renneberg, Goldstein, Phillips, & Chambless, 1990; Stravynski, Lesage, Marcouiller, & Elie, 1989). Because the problems experienced by people with avoidant personality disorder resemble those of people with social phobia, many of the same treatments are used for both groups (see Chapter 5).

Renneberg et al. (1990) identified areas that caused anxiety in a group of 17 people with avoidant personality disorder, including a fear of rejection, a fear of criticism, and anxiety about their appearance. In groups of five or six patients, they used *systematic desensitization,* which involves relaxing in the presence of feared situations (for example, "You speak to a group of people at work, and you realize that your voice is not powerful enough. Your voice is childish,") and *behavioral rehearsal,* in which patients act out situations that cause anxiety. As a group, these people improved in such areas as fear of negative evaluation and social avoidance and distress. The improvements tended to be modest, although, given the usually poor outcomes found among people with personality disorders, even moderate improvement is encouraging.

Dependent Personality Disorder

We all know what it means to be dependent on another person. People with **dependent personality disorder,** however, rely on others to make ordinary decisions as well as impor-

In Greek mythology, Narcissus was so in love with his own image that he pined away and died of longing.

tant ones, which results in an unreasonable fear of abandonment. Consider the following case.

Karen
Whatever You Say

Karen was a 45-year-old married woman who was referred for treatment by her physician for problems with panic attacks. During the evaluation, she appeared to be very worried, sensitive, and naive. She was easily overcome with emotion and cried on and off throughout the session. She was self-critical at every opportunity throughout the evaluation. For example, when asked how she got along with other people, she reported that "others think I'm dumb and inadequate," although she could give no evidence as to what made her think that. She reported that she didn't like school because "I was dumb," and that she always felt that she was not good enough.

Karen described staying in her first marriage for 10 years, even though "it was hell." Her husband had affairs with many other women and was verbally abusive. She tried to leave him many times, but gave in to his repeated requests to return. She was finally able to divorce him, and shortly afterwards she met and married her current husband, whom she described as kind, sensitive, and supportive.

Karen stated that she preferred to have others make important decisions, and agreed with other people in order to avoid conflict. She worried about being left alone without anyone to take care of her, and reported feeling lost without other people's reassurance. She also reported that her feelings were easily hurt, so she worked hard not to do anything that might lead to criticism. (Beck & Freeman, 1990, pp. 288–289)

CLINICAL DESCRIPTION

Individuals with dependent personality disorder sometimes agree with other people when their own opinion differs, so as not to be rejected (Hirschfeld, Shea, & Weise, 1995). Their desire to obtain and maintain supportive and nurturant relationships may lead to their other behavioral characteristics (Bornstein, 1997), including submissiveness, timidity, and passivity. People with this disorder are similar to those with *avoidant personality disorder* in their feelings of inadequacy, sensitivity to criticism, and need for reassurance. However, people with avoidant personality disorder respond to these feelings by avoiding relationships, whereas those with dependent personality disorder respond by clinging to relationships (Hirschfeld, Shea, & Weise, 1991). (For a somewhat different point of view, see Box 12-2).

CAUSES AND TREATMENT

We are all born dependent on other people for food, physical protection, and nurturance. Part of the socialization process involves helping us live independently (Bornstein, 1992). It is thought such disruptions as the early death of a parent or neglect or rejection by caregivers may cause people to grow up fearing abandonment (M.H. Stone, 1993). This view comes from work in child development on "attachment," or how children learn to bond with their parents and other people who are important in their lives (Bowlby,

1977). If early bonding is interrupted, individuals may be constantly anxious that they will lose people close to them.

The treatment literature for this disorder is mostly descriptive; very little research exists to show whether a particular treatment is effective. On the surface, because of their attentiveness and eagerness to give responsibility for their problems to the therapist, people with dependent personality disorder can appear to be ideal patients. However, their submissiveness negates one of the major goals of therapy, which is to make the person more independent and personally responsible. Therapy therefore progresses gradually, as the patient develops confidence in his or her ability to make decisions independently (A.T. Beck & Freeman, 1990). There is a particular need for care that the patient does not become overly dependent on the therapist.

■ concept check 12.2

Review your ability to differentiate among the personality disorders.

1. John is very reluctant to talk to anyone, not to mention a therapist. His reluctance and mistrust of others seem to be unlimited. John gives the impression that everyone is out to get him. _____

2. The therapist immediately notices that Joan displays extreme emotional behavior a great deal when she speaks, so much so that she seems to be acting. _____

3. Susan was brought in by her parents because they found her uncontrollable. She has been stealing from her parents and friends and she's so impulsive her parents don't know what she might try next. Some people call her a "psychopath." _____

4. Jeffery is especially anxious at even the thought of social interactions. He reacts excessively to criticism, which only feeds his pervasive feelings of inadequacy. _____

Obsessive-Compulsive Personality Disorder

People who have **obsessive-compulsive personality disorder** are characterized by a fixation on things being done "the right way." Although many might envy their persistence and dedication, this preoccupation with details prevents them from actually completing much of anything. Consider the following case.

Daniel
Getting It Exactly Right

Each day at exactly 8 a.m., Daniel arrived at his office at the university where he was a graduate student in psychology. On his way, he always stopped at the 7–11 for coffee and the *New York Times*. From 8 to 9:15 a.m. he drank his coffee and read the paper. At 9:15 he reorganized the files that held the hundreds of papers related to his doctoral dissertation, now several years overdue. From 10 a.m. until noon he read one of these papers, highlighting relevant passages. Then he took the paper bag that held his lunch (always a peanut butter and jelly sandwich and an apple) and went to the cafeteria to purchase a soda and eat by himself. From 1 p.m. until 5 p.m. he held meetings, organized his desk, made lists of things to do, and entered his references into a new database program on his computer. At home, Daniel had dinner with his wife, then worked on his dissertation until after 11 p.m., although much of the time was spent trying out new features of his home computer.

Daniel was no closer to completing his dissertation than he had been 4½ years ago. His wife was threatening to leave him because he was equally rigid about everything at home and she didn't want to remain in this limbo of graduate school forever. When Daniel eventually sought help from a therapist for his anxiety over his deteriorating marriage, he was diagnosed as having obsessive-compulsive personality disorder.

CLINICAL DESCRIPTION

Like many with this personality disorder, Daniel is very work-oriented, spending little time going to movies or parties, or doing anything that isn't related to psychology. Because of their general rigidity, these people tend to have poor interpersonal relationships (Pfohl & Blum, 1995).

This personality disorder seems to be only distantly related to obsessive-compulsive disorder, one of the anxiety disorders we described in Chapter 5. People like Daniel tend not to have the obsessive thoughts and the compulsive behaviors seen in the like-named obsessive-compulsive disorder (OCD). Although people with the anxiety disorder sometimes show characteristics of the personality disorder, they also show the characteristics of other personality disorders as well (for example, avoidant, histrionic, dependent) (M.H. Stone, 1993).

CAUSES AND TREATMENT

There seems to be a weak genetic contribution to this disorder (McKeon & Murray, 1987; M.H. Stone, 1993). Some people may be predisposed to favor structure in their lives, but to reach the level it did in Daniel may require parental reinforcement of conformity and neatness.

■ concept check 12.3

Check your understanding of these additional personality disorders by identifying the patterns described next as (a) dependent; (b) narcissistic; (c) obsessive-compulsive; (d) schizoid; or (e) histrionic.

1. Katherine thinks she is the best candidate for any job, thinks her performance is always excellent, and looks for admiration from others. _____

2. Lynn is afraid to be left alone and seeks constant reassurance from her family. She won't make decisions or do things on her own. She thinks that if she shows any resolve or initiative she will be abandoned and have to take care of herself. _____

3. The therapist discovers that Tim has yet to fill out the information form, although he was given at least 15 minutes. Tim says he first had to resharpen the pencil, then clean it of debris, then he noticed that the pencil sharpener wasn't very clean. The paper also wasn't properly placed on the clipboard. _____

4. George is overly dramatic about everyday occurrences and thinks the world revolves around him.

_____

We do not have much information on the successful treatment of individuals with this disorder. Therapy often attacks the fears that seem to underlie the need for orderliness. These individuals are often afraid that what they do will be inadequate, so they procrastinate and excessively ruminate about important issues and minor details. Therapists help the individual relax or use distraction techniques to redirect the compulsive thoughts.

Personality Disorders Under Study

We started this chapter by noting difficulties in categorizing personality disorders; for example, there is much overlap of the different categories, which suggests that there

---

box 12.2 *Should There Be a Diagnosis of "Independent" Personality Disorder?*

We have pointed out the possibility that sexism is relevant to several personality disorders. Marcie Kaplan (1983) facetiously uses a fictitious diagnosis to illustrate her case. Should we identify a new personality disorder in accord with the following criteria? What do you think the sex ratio would be for this disorder? Do you know anyone who fits this description, and who it affects with sig-

nificant functional impairment or subjective distress?

Diagnostic Criteria for "Independent" Personality Disorder (Kaplan, 1983)
A. Puts work (career) above relationships with loved ones (e.g., travels a lot on business, works late at night and on weekends).
B. Is reluctant to take into account others' needs when making deci-

sions, especially concerning the individual's career or use of leisure time, e.g., expects spouse and children to relocate to another city because of individual's career plans.
C. Passively allows others to assume responsibility for major areas of social life because of inability to express necessary emotion (e.g., lets spouse assume most child-care responsibilities).

from the inside

Girl, Interrupted
by Susanna Kaysen*

In 1967, 18-year-old Susanna Kaysen agreed to enter a psychiatric hospital. Although she did not have hallucinations or delusions, depression and distress made her feel "crazy," and she had attempted suicide:

> My motives were weak: an American history paper I didn't want to write and the question I'd asked myself earlier, Why not kill myself? Dead, I wouldn't have to write the paper. Nor would I have to keep debating the question (p. 36).

When she entered the hospital, Kaysen felt exposed and vulnerable to uncontrollable sensations and perceptions:

> . . . anything might be something else. Once I'd accepted that, it followed that I might be mad, or that someone might think me mad. How could I say for certain that I wasn't, if I couldn't say for certain that a curtain wasn't a mountain range? (p. 42)

In spare, often humorous prose, Kaysen describes her fellow inmates, the daily routines of their life on the ward, and her own condition:

> I began scratching at the back of my hand. My plan was to get hold of a flap of skin and peel it away, just to have a look. I wanted to see that my hand was a normal human hand, with bones. My hand got red and white . . . but I couldn't get the skin to open up and let me in.

In the end, Kaysen studies the DSM and diagnoses her own condition as borderline personality disorder. To supplement her searing recollections of the 2 years in treatment that "interrupted" her life, she reproduces copies of her medical records; in the last one, the box marked "outcome" contains the single word "recovered." Susanna Kaysen went on to write two novels before attempting the self-exposure of this memoir, which is all the more compelling because every word is true.

*Susanna Kaysen, *Girl Interrupted* (Vintage Books, 1993).

may be other ways to arrange these pervasive difficulties of character. It shouldn't surprise you to learn that other personality disorders have been proposed for inclusion in the DSM; for example, sadistic personality disorder, which included people who receive pleasure by inflicting pain on others (Fiester & Gay, 1995), and self-defeating personality disorder, which included people who are overly passive and accept the pain and suffering imposed by others (Fiester, 1995). However, few studies supported the existence of these disorders, so they were not included in the DSM-IV (Pfohl, 1993). Two new categories of personality disorder are under study. *Depressive personality disorder* includes self-criticism, dejection, a judgmental stance toward others, and a tendency to feel guilt. *Negativistic personality disorder* is characterized by a passive-aggression in which people adopt a negativistic attitude to resist routine demands and expectations. This category is an expansion of a previous DSM-III-R category, *passive-aggressive personality disorder*. Neither of these categories has yet had enough research attention to warrant inclusion as additional personality disorders in the DSM.

 Summary

An Overview

- The personality disorders represent long-standing and ingrained ways of thinking, feeling, and behaving that can cause significant distress. Because people may display two or more of these maladaptive ways of interacting with the world, considerable disagreement remains over how to categorize the personality disorders.
- DSM-IV includes 10 personality disorders that are divided into three "clusters": Cluster A ("odd or eccentric") includes paranoid, schizoid, and schizotypal personality disorders; Cluster B ("dramatic, emotional, or erratic") includes antisocial, borderline, histrionic, and narcissistic personality disorders; Cluster C ("anxious or fearful") includes avoidant, dependent, and obsessive-compulsive personality disorders.

Specific Personality Disorders
- People with paranoid personality disorder are excessively mistrustful and suspicious of other people, without any justification. They tend not to confide in others and expect other people to do them harm.
- People with schizoid personality disorder show a pattern of detachment from social relationships and a very limited range of emotions in interpersonal situations. They seem aloof, cold, and indifferent to other people.
- People with schizotypal personality disorder are typically socially isolated and behave in ways that would seem unusual to most of us. Additionally, they tend to be suspicious and have odd beliefs about the world.
- People with antisocial personality disorder have a history of failing to comply with social norms. They perform actions most of us would find unacceptable, such as stealing from friends and family. They also tend to be irresponsible, impulsive, and deceitful.
- In contrast to the DSM-IV criteria for antisocial personality, which focuses almost entirely on observable behaviors (for example, impulsively and repeatedly changing employment, residence, or sexual partners), the related concept of psychopathy primarily reflects underlying personality traits (for instance, self-centeredness, manipulativeness).
- People with borderline personality disorder lack stability in their moods and in their relationships with other people, and usually have very poor self-esteem. These individuals often feel empty and are at great risk of suicide.

- Individuals with histrionic personality disorder tend to be overly dramatic and often appear almost to be acting.
- People with narcissistic personality disorder think highly of themselves—beyond their real abilities. They consider themselves somehow different from others and deserving of special treatment.
- People with avoidant personality disorder are extremely sensitive to the opinions of others and therefore avoid social relationships. Their extremely low self-esteem, coupled with a fear of rejection, causes them to reject the attention others crave.
- Individuals with dependent personality disorder rely on others to the extent of letting them make everyday decisions as well as major ones; this results in an unreasonable fear of being abandoned.
- People who have obsessive-compulsive personality disorder are characterized by a fixation on things being done "the right way." This preoccupation with details prevents them from actually completing much of anything.
- Treating people with personality disorders is often difficult because they usually do not see that their difficulties are a result of the way they relate to others.
- Personality disorders are important for the clinician to consider because they may interfere with efforts to treat more specific problems such as anxiety, depression, or substance abuse. Unfortunately, the presence of one or more personality disorder is associated with a poor treatment outcome and a generally negative prognosis.

Key Terms

personality disorders
paranoid personality disorder
schizoid personality disorder
schizotypal personality disorder
antisocial personality disorder
psychopathy
borderline personality disorder
histrionic personality disorder
narcissistic personality disorder
avoidant personality disorder
dependent personality disorder
obsessive-compulsive personality disorder

Answers to Concept Checks

12.1
1. schizoid personality disorder
2. antisocial personality disorder
3. paranoid personality disorder
4. borderline personality disorder

12.2
1. paranoid personality disorder
2. histrionic personality disorder
3. antisocial personality disorder
4. avoidant personality disorder

12.3
1. b
2. a
3. c
4. e

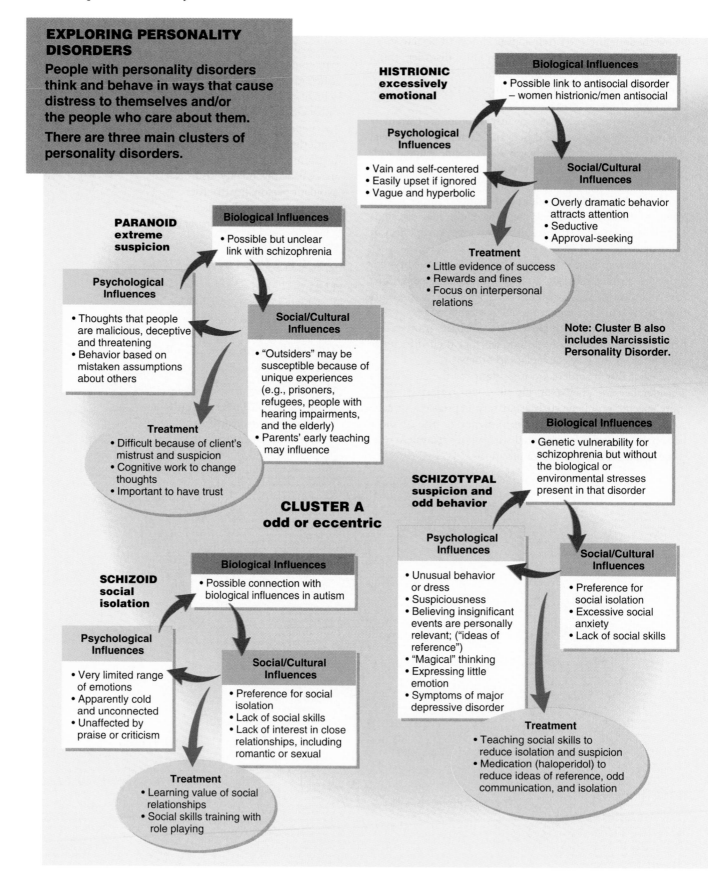

EXPLORING PERSONALITY DISORDERS

People with personality disorders think and behave in ways that cause distress to themselves and/or the people who care about them.

There are three main clusters of personality disorders.

HISTRIONIC excessively emotional

Biological Influences
• Possible link to antisocial disorder – women histrionic/men antisocial

Psychological Influences
• Vain and self-centered
• Easily upset if ignored
• Vague and hyperbolic

Social/Cultural Influences
• Overly dramatic behavior attracts attention
• Seductive
• Approval-seeking

Treatment
• Little evidence of success
• Rewards and fines
• Focus on interpersonal relations

Note: Cluster B also includes Narcissistic Personality Disorder.

PARANOID extreme suspicion

Biological Influences
• Possible but unclear link with schizophrenia

Psychological Influences
• Thoughts that people are malicious, deceptive and threatening
• Behavior based on mistaken assumptions about others

Social/Cultural Influences
• "Outsiders" may be susceptible because of unique experiences (e.g., prisoners, refugees, people with hearing impairments, and the elderly)
• Parents' early teaching may influence

Treatment
• Difficult because of client's mistrust and suspicion
• Cognitive work to change thoughts
• Important to have trust

CLUSTER A odd or eccentric

SCHIZOTYPAL suspicion and odd behavior

Biological Influences
• Genetic vulnerability for schizophrenia but without the biological or environmental stresses present in that disorder

Psychological Influences
• Unusual behavior or dress
• Suspiciousness
• Believing insignificant events are personally relevant; ("ideas of reference")
• "Magical" thinking
• Expressing little emotion
• Symptoms of major depressive disorder

Social/Cultural Influences
• Preference for social isolation
• Excessive social anxiety
• Lack of social skills

Treatment
• Teaching social skills to reduce isolation and suspicion
• Medication (haloperidol) to reduce ideas of reference, odd communication, and isolation

SCHIZOID social isolation

Biological Influences
• Possible connection with biological influences in autism

Psychological Influences
• Very limited range of emotions
• Apparently cold and unconnected
• Unaffected by praise or criticism

Social/Cultural Influences
• Preference for social isolation
• Lack of social skills
• Lack of interest in close relationships, including romantic or sexual

Treatment
• Learning value of social relationships
• Social skills training with role playing

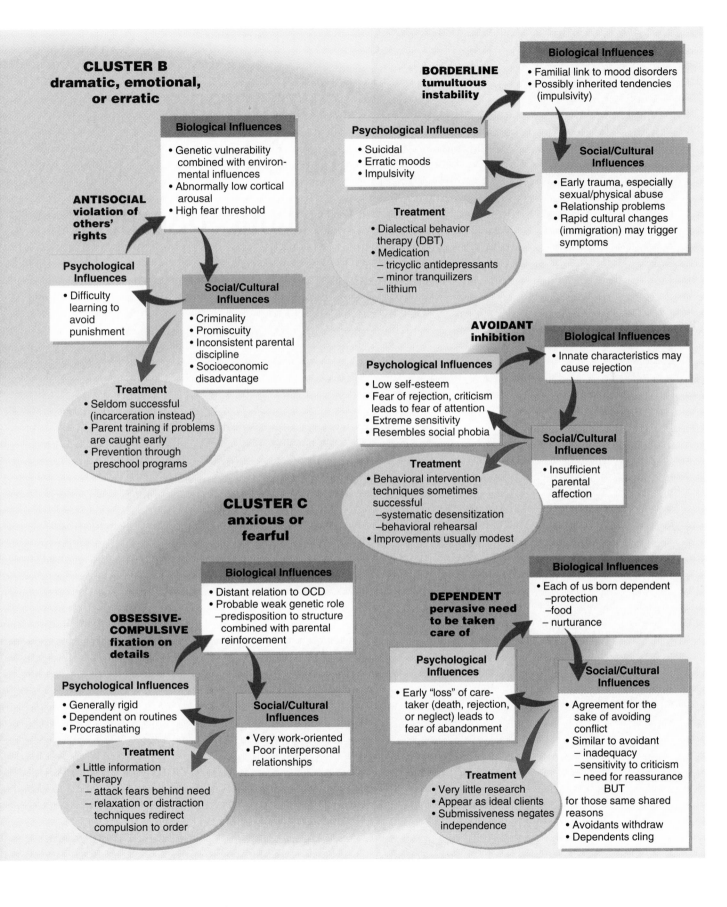

CLUSTER B
dramatic, emotional,
or erratic

ANTISOCIAL
violation of
others'
rights

Biological Influences
- Genetic vulnerability combined with environmental influences
- Abnormally low cortical arousal
- High fear threshold

Psychological Influences
- Difficulty learning to avoid punishment

Social/Cultural Influences
- Criminality
- Promiscuity
- Inconsistent parental discipline
- Socioeconomic disadvantage

Treatment
- Seldom successful (incarceration instead)
- Parent training if problems are caught early
- Prevention through preschool programs

BORDERLINE
tumultuous
instability

Biological Influences
- Familial link to mood disorders
- Possibly inherited tendencies (impulsivity)

Psychological Influences
- Suicidal
- Erratic moods
- Impulsivity

Social/Cultural Influences
- Early trauma, especially sexual/physical abuse
- Relationship problems
- Rapid cultural changes (immigration) may trigger symptoms

Treatment
- Dialectical behavior therapy (DBT)
- Medication
  – tricyclic antidepressants
  – minor tranquilizers
  – lithium

AVOIDANT
inhibition

Biological Influences
- Innate characteristics may cause rejection

Psychological Influences
- Low self-esteem
- Fear of rejection, criticism leads to fear of attention
- Extreme sensitivity
- Resembles social phobia

Social/Cultural Influences
- Insufficient parental affection

Treatment
- Behavioral intervention techniques sometimes successful
  –systematic desensitization
  –behavioral rehearsal
- Improvements usually modest

CLUSTER C
anxious or
fearful

OBSESSIVE-
COMPULSIVE
fixation on
details

Biological Influences
- Distant relation to OCD
- Probable weak genetic role
  –predisposition to structure combined with parental reinforcement

Psychological Influences
- Generally rigid
- Dependent on routines
- Procrastinating

Social/Cultural Influences
- Very work-oriented
- Poor interpersonal relationships

Treatment
- Little information
- Therapy
  – attack fears behind need
  – relaxation or distraction techniques redirect compulsion to order

DEPENDENT
pervasive need
to be taken
care of

Biological Influences
- Each of us born dependent
  –protection
  –food
  – nurturance

Psychological Influences
- Early "loss" of caretaker (death, rejection, or neglect) leads to fear of abandonment

Social/Cultural Influences
- Agreement for the sake of avoiding conflict
- Similar to avoidant
  – inadequacy
  –sensitivity to criticism
  – need for reassurance
  BUT
  for those same shared reasons
- Avoidants withdraw
- Dependents cling

Treatment
- Very little research
- Appear as ideal clients
- Submissiveness negates independence

13

Schizophrenia and Other Psychotic Disorders

I filled in the emptiness in my mind by picking up pieces of scattered conversation. They thought I was an idiot, a goose, a clown, and they would talk this way until they drove

me from the group, and then make snide comments behind my back. They were all looking at me. I had to face the tension of the great dream. I was hated. I am the inventor of rock and roll. I am not a star but a discus, a sorcerer.

Ross David Burke
When the Music's Over: My Journey Into Schizophrenia

A middle-aged man walks the streets of New York City with aluminum foil on the inside of his hat so that Martians can't read his mind. A young woman sits in her college classroom and hears the voice of God telling her that she is a vile and disgusting person. You try to strike up a conversation with the supermarket bagger, but he stares at you vacantly and will say only one or two words in a flat, toneless voice. Each of these people may have **schizophrenia,** the startling disorder that is characterized by a broad spectrum of cognitive and emotional dysfunctions including delusions and hallucinations, disorganized speech and behavior, and inappropriate emotions.

Schizophrenia is a complex syndrome that inevitably has a devastating effect on the lives of the person affected and on family members. This disorder can disrupt a person's perception, thought, speech, and movement: almost every aspect of daily functioning. And despite important advances in treatment, complete recovery from schizophrenia is rare. Obviously, this catastrophic disorder takes a tremendous emotional toll on everyone involved. In addition to the emotional costs, the financial drain is considerable. The cost of caring for people with schizophrenia in the U.S. was estimated to be between $16 and $19 billion for 1990 alone, which was 2.5% of total health care expenditures in the U.S. that year (Rupp & Keith, 1993). Because schizophrenia is so widespread, affecting approximately one out of every hundred persons at some point in their lives, and because its consequences are so severe, research on its causes and treatment has proliferated. Given the attention it has received, you would think that the question, "What is schizophrenia?" would by now be answered easily. It is not.

In this chapter we explore this intriguing disorder and review efforts to determine whether schizophrenia is distinct in itself or a combination of disorders. The search is complicated by the presence of subtypes: different presentations and combinations of symptoms such as hallucinations, delusions, and disorders of speech, emotion, and socialization. After discussing the characteristics of people with schizophrenia, we describe research into its causes and treatment.

Perspectives on the Concept of Schizophrenia

The history of schizophrenia as it has evolved over the years is unparalleled by any other disorder covered in this book. Knowing something about it will help you understand that the nature of the disorder itself is multifaceted and that treatment is correspondingly complex.

In *Observations on Madness and Melancholy*, published in 1809, John Haslam eloquently portrayed what he called "a form of insanity." In the following passage, Haslam mentions some (though not all) of the symptoms that inform our current conception of schizophrenia.

> The attack is almost imperceptible; some months usually elapse before it becomes the subject of particular notice; and fond relatives are frequently deceived by the hope that it is only an abatement of excessive vivacity, conducting to a prudent reserve, and steadiness of character. A degree of apparent thoughtfulness and inactivity precede, together with a diminution of the ordinary curiosity, concerning that which is passing before them; and they therefore neglect those objects and pursuits which formerly proved courses of delight and instruction. The sensibility appears to be considerably blunted: they do not bear the same affection towards their parents and relations: they become unfeeling to kindness, and careless of reproof. . . . I have painfully witnessed this hopeless and degrading change, which in a short time has transformed the most promising and vigorous intellect into a slavering and bloated idiot. (Haslam, 1809, pp. 64–67)

At about the same time Haslam was writing his description in England, the French physician Philippe Pinel was writing about people whom we would describe as having schizophrenia (Pinel, 1801, 1809). Some 50 years later another physician, Benedict Morel, used the French term *démence* (loss of mind) *précoce* (early, premature), because the onset of the disorder is often during adolescence.

Toward the end of the 19th century, the German psychiatrist Emil Kraepelin (1899) built on the writings of Haslam, Pinel, and Morel (among others) to give us what stands today as the most enduring description and categorization of schizophrenia. Two of Kraepelin's accomplishments are especially important. First, he combined several symptoms of insanity that had usually been viewed as reflecting separate and distinct disorders: **catatonia** (alternating immobility and excited agitation), **hebephrenia** (silly and immature emotionality), and **paranoia** (delusions of grandeur or persecution). Kraepelin thought these symptoms shared similar underlying features and included them under the Latin term *dementia praecox*. Although the clinical manifestation might differ from person to person, Kraepelin believed an early onset at the heart of each disorder ultimately developed into "mental weakness."

In a second important contribution, Kraepelin (1898) distinguished dementia praecox from manic-depressive illness (bipolar disorder). For people with dementia praecox, an

Eugen Bleuler (1857–1939), a Swiss psychiatrist, introduced the term *schizophrenia* and was a pioneer in the field.

early age of onset and a poor outcome were characteristic; in contrast, these patterns were not essential to manic depression (Peters, 1991). Kraepelin also noted the numerous symptoms in people with dementia praecox, including hallucinations, delusions, negativism, and stereotyped behavior.

A second major figure in the history of schizophrenia was Kraeplin's contemporary, Eugen Bleuler (1908), a Swiss psychiatrist who introduced the term *schizophrenia*. The label was significant because it signaled Bleuler's departure from Kraepelin on what he thought was the core problem. "Schizophrenia," which comes from the combination of the Greek words for split *(skhizein)* and mind *(phren)*, reflected Bleuler's belief that underlying all the unusual behaviors shown by people with this disorder was an **associative splitting** of the basic functions of personality. This concept emphasized the "breaking of associative threads," or the destruction of the forces that connect one function to the next. Furthermore, Bleuler believed that a difficulty keeping a consistent train of thought that was characteristic of all persons with this disorder led to the many and diverse symptoms they displayed. Whereas Kraepelin focused on early onset and poor outcomes, Bleuler highlighted what he believed to be the universal underlying problem. Unfortunately, the concept of "split mind" inspired the common but incorrect use of the term *schizophrenia* to mean split or multiple personality. For a summary of the early contributors to the concept of schizophrenia, see Table 13.1.

Identifying Symptoms

It is not easy to point to one thing that makes a person "schizophrenic." As you read about different disorders in this book, you have learned that a particular behavior, way of thinking, or emotion usually defines or is characteristic of each disorder. For example, depression always includes feelings of sadness, and panic disorder is always accompanied by intense feelings of anxiety. Surprisingly, this isn't the case for schizophrenia. Schizophrenia is actually a number of behaviors or symptoms that aren't necessarily shared by all the people who are given this diagnosis. Kraepelin described the situation when he outlined his view of dementia praecox in the late 1800s.

> The complexity of the conditions which we observe in the domain of dementia praecox is very great, so that their inner connection is at first recognizable only by their occurring one after the other in the course of the same disease. In any case certain fundamental disturbances, even though they cannot for the most part be regarded as characteristic, yet return frequently in the same form, but in the most diverse combinations. (Kraepelin, 1919, p. 5)

This heterogeneity was also highlighted by Bleuler in the title of his 1911 book, *Dementia Praecox or the Group of Schizophrenias*, which emphasizes the complexity of the disorder. The varied nature of schizophrenia is something we will come back to throughout this chapter. Individuals who have schizophrenia have varying symptoms, and we will ultimately find that the causes vary as well.

Despite these complexities, researchers have identified clusters of symptoms that make up the disorder of schizophrenia. Later, we describe these very dramatic symptoms, such as seeing or hearing things that others do not (hallucinations) or having beliefs that are unrealistic, bizarre, and not shared by others in the same culture (delusions). But first, consider the following cases of individuals we have worked with.

David
Missing Uncle Bill

David was 25 years old when I met him; he had been living in a psychiatric hospital for about 3 years. He was a little overweight and of average height; he typically dressed in a T-shirt and jeans and tended to be active. I first encountered

---

table 13.1   Early Figures in the History of Schizophrenia

Date	Historical Figure	Contribution
1809	John Haslam (1764–1844)	Superintendent of a British hospital. In *Observations on Madness and Melancholy*, he outlined a description of the symptoms of schizophrenia.
1801/1809	Philippe Pinel (1745–1826)	A French physician who described cases of schizophrenia.
1852	Benedict Morel (1809–1873)	Physician at a French institution who used the term *démence précoce* (in Latin, *dementia praecox*), meaning early or premature (précoce) loss of mind (démence) to describe schizophrenia.
1898/1899	Emil Kraepelin (1856–1926)	A German psychiatrist who unified the distinct categories of schizophrenia (hebephrenic, catatonic, and paranoid) under the name *dementia praecox*.
1908	Eugen Bleuler (1857–1939)	A Swiss psychiatrist who introduced the term *schizophrenia*, meaning splitting of the mind.

him while I was talking to another man who lived on the same floor. David interrupted us by pulling on my shoulder. "My Uncle Bill is a good man. He treats me well." Not wanting to be impolite, I said, "I'm sure he is. Maybe after I've finished talking to Michael here, we can talk about your uncle." David persisted, "He can kill fish with a knife. Things can get awfully sharp in your mind, when you go down the river. I could kill you with my bare hands—taking things into my own hands....I know you know!" He was now speaking very quickly, and had gained emotionality along with speed as he spoke. I talked to him quietly until he calmed down for the moment; later I looked into David's file for some information about his background.

David was brought up on a farm by his Aunt Katie and Uncle Bill. His father's identity is unknown and his mother, who had mental retardation, couldn't care for him. David too was diagnosed as having mental retardation, although his functioning was only mildly impaired, and he attended school. The year David's Uncle Bill died, his high school teachers first reported unusual behavior. David occasionally talked to his deceased Uncle Bill in class. Later, he became increasingly agitated and verbally aggressive toward others and was diagnosed as having schizophrenia. He managed to graduate from high school but never obtained a job after that; he lived at home with his aunt for several years. Although his aunt really wanted him to stay with her, his threatening behavior escalated to the point that she requested he be seen at the local psychiatric hospital.

I spoke with David again and had a chance to ask him a few questions. "Why are you here in the hospital, David?" "I really don't want to be here," he told me. "I've got other things to do. The time is right, and you know, when opportunity knocks ..." He continued for a few minutes until I interrupted him. "I was sorry to hear that your Uncle Bill died a few years ago. How are you feeling about him these days?" "Yes, he died. He was sick and now he's gone. He likes to fish with me, down at the river. He's going to take me hunting. I have guns. I can shoot you and you'd be dead in a minute."

David's conversational speech resembled a ball rolling down a rocky hill. Like an accelerating object, his speech gained momentum the longer he went on and, as if bouncing off obstacles, the topics almost always went in unpredictable directions. If he continued for too long, he often became agitated and spoke of harming others. David also told me that his uncle's voice spoke to him repeatedly. He heard other voices also, but he couldn't identify them or tell me what they said. We will return to David's case later in this chapter when we discuss causes and treatments.

Arthur
Saving the Children

We first met 22-year-old Arthur at an outpatient clinic in a psychiatric hospital. Arthur's family was extremely concerned and upset by his unusual behavior, and was desperately seeking help for him. They said that he was "sick" and "talking like a crazy man," and they were afraid he might harm himself.

Arthur had a normal childhood in a middle-class suburban neighborhood. His parents had been happily married

until his father's death several years earlier. Arthur was an average student throughout school and had completed an associate's degree in junior college. His family seemed to think he regretted not continuing on to receive a bachelor's degree. Arthur had worked in a series of temporary jobs, and his mother reported that he seemed satisfied with what he was doing. He lived and worked in a major city, some 15 minutes away from his mother and his married brother and sister.

Arthur's family said that about 3 weeks before he came to the clinic he had started speaking strangely. He had been laid off from his job a few days before due to cutbacks and hadn't communicated with any of his family members for several days. When they next spoke with him, his behavior startled them. Although he had always been idealistic and anxious to help other people, he now talked about saving all the starving children in the world with his "secret plan." At first his family assumed this was just an example of Arthur's sarcastic wit, but his demeanor changed to one of extreme concern, and he spoke nonstop about his plans. He began carrying several spiral notebooks that he claimed contained his scheme for helping starving children; he said he would reveal it only at the right time to the right person. Suspecting that Arthur might be taking drugs, which could explain the sudden and dramatic change in his behavior, his family searched his apartment. Although they didn't find any evidence of drug use, they did find his checkbook and noticed a number of strange entries. Over the past several weeks, Arthur's handwriting had deteriorated, and he had written notes instead of the usual check information ("Start to begin now"; "This is important!" "They must be saved"). He had also made unusual notes in several of his most prized books, a particularly alarming development given his reverence for these books.

As the days went on, Arthur showed dramatic changes in emotion, often crying and acting very apprehensive. He stopped wearing socks and underwear and, despite the extremely cold weather, wouldn't wear a jacket when he went outdoors. At the family's insistence, he moved into his mother's apartment. He slept little, and kept the family up until the early morning. His mother said it was like being in a living nightmare. Each morning she would wake up with a knot in her stomach, not wanting to get out of bed because she felt so helpless to do anything to rescue Arthur from his obvious distress.

The family's sense of alarm grew as Arthur revealed more details of his plan. He said that he was going to the German embassy because that was the only place people would listen to him. He would climb the fence at night when everyone was asleep and present his plan to the German ambassador. Fearing that Arthur would be hurt trying to enter the embassy grounds, his family contacted a local psychiatric hospital, described Arthur's condition, and asked that he be admitted. Much to their surprise and disappointment, they were told that Arthur could commit himself, but that they couldn't bring him in involuntarily unless he was in danger of doing harm to himself or others. The fear that Arthur might be harmed wasn't sufficient reason to admit him involuntarily.

His family finally talked Arthur into meeting the staff at the outpatient clinic. In our interview, it was clear that he was delusional, firmly believing in his ability to help all starving children. After some cajoling, I finally convinced him to let me see his books. He had written random thoughts (for example, "The poor, starving souls"; "The moon is the only place") and made drawings of rocket ships. Parts of his plan involved building a rocket ship that would go to the moon, where he would create a community for all malnourished children, a place where they could live and be helped. After a few brief comments on his plan, I began to ask him about his health.

"You look tired; are you getting enough sleep?"
"Sleep isn't really needed," he noted. "My plans will take me through, and then they can all rest."
"Your family is worried about you," I said. "Do you understand their concern?"
"It's important for all concerned to get together, to join together," he replied.

With that, he got up and walked out of the room and out of the building, after telling his family that he would be right back. After 5 minutes they went to look for him, but he had disappeared. He was missing for 2 days, which caused his family a great deal of concern about his health and safety. In an almost miraculous sequence of events, they found him walking the streets of the city. He acted as if nothing had happened. Gone were his notebooks and the talk of his secret plan.

What caused Arthur to act so strangely? Was it being fired from his job? Was it the death of his father? Was it a genetic predisposition to have schizophrenia or another disorder that kicked in during a period of stress? Unfortunately, we will never know exactly what happened to Arthur to make him behave so bizarrely and then recover so quickly and completely. However, research that we discuss next may shed some light on schizophrenia and potentially help other Arthurs and their families.

 **Clinical Description**

The cases of David and Arthur show the range of problems experienced by people with schizophrenia or other psychotic disorders. The term **psychotic** has been used to characterize many unusual behaviors, although in its strictest sense it usually involves delusions (irrational beliefs) and/or hallucinations (sensory experiences in the absence of external events). Schizophrenia is one of the disorders that involve psychotic behavior; others are described in more detail later.

Schizophrenia can affect all the functions we rely on each day. Before we describe the symptoms, it is important to look carefully at the specific characteristics of people who exhibit these behaviors, partly because we constantly see distorted images of people with schizophrenia. Headlines such as "Ex-Mental Patient Kills Family" falsely imply that everyone with schizophrenia is dangerous and violent. Pop-

ular authors also contribute to this misinformation. In *The Eden Express*, Mark Vonnegut describes what he calls his entry into schizophrenia, although the cycles of depression and manic behavior suggest that he actually had bipolar affective disorder. The central character in *I Never Promised You a Rose Garden* is often thought to have schizophrenia, although her dramatic periods of blindness, deafness, and hallucinations are more characteristic of somatoform disorder. Like mistakenly assuming that "schizophrenia" means "split personality," the popular press misrepresents abnormal psychology to the detriment of people who experience these debilitating disorders.

DSM-IV has a multiple-part process for determining whether or not someone has schizophrenia. Below we discuss the symptoms the person experiences during the disorder *(active phase symptoms)*, the course of the disorder, and the subtypes of schizophrenia currently in use.

Mental health workers typically distinguish between *positive* and *negative* symptoms of schizophrenia. Recently, *disorganized*, a third distinct category of symptoms, has been added (Andreasen, Arndt, Alliger, Miller, & Flaum, 1995; Arndt, Andreasen, Flaum, Miller, & Nopoulos, 1995; Docherty, DeRosa, & Andreasen, 1996). There is not yet universal agreement about which symptoms should be included in these categories. Positive symptoms generally include the more active manifestations of abnormal behavior, or an excess or distortion of normal behavior; these include delusions and hallucinations (American Psychiatric Association, 1994). Negative symptoms involve deficits in normal behavior in such areas as speech and motivation (Carpenter, 1994; Earnst & Kring, 1997). Disorganized symptoms include rambling speech, erratic behavior, and inappropriate affect (Andreasen et al., 1995). A diagnosis of schizophrenia requires that two or more positive, negative, and/or disorganized symptoms be present for at least 1 month. A great deal of research has focused on the different symptoms of schizophrenia, each of which is described here in some detail.

Positive Symptoms

DELUSIONS

A belief that would be seen by most members of a society as a misrepresentation of reality is called a *disorder of thought content*, or a **delusion**. Because of its importance in schizophrenia, delusion has been called "the basic characteristic of madness" (Jaspers, 1963). If, for example, you believe that squirrels really are aliens sent to earth on a reconnaissance mission, you would be considered delusional. The media often portray people with schizophrenia as believing that they are famous or important people (such as Napoleon or Jesus Christ). Arthur's belief that he could end starvation for all the world's children is also a *delusion of grandeur*.

A common delusion in people with schizophrenia is that others are "out to get them." Called *delusions of persecution*, these beliefs can be most disturbing. One of us worked with a world-class cyclist who was on her way to making the Olympic team. Tragically, however, she believed that other competitors were determined to sabotage her efforts, which forced her to stop riding for years. She believed that opponents would spray her bicycle with chemicals that would take her strength away, and that they would slow her down by putting small pebbles in the road that only she would ride over. These thoughts created a great deal of anxiety, and she refused even to go near her bicycle for some time.

A man recovering from schizophrenia frankly described his delusional experiences (Fleshner, 1995).

> I would like to describe the few delusions I've had in the past to help others understand how frightening and real these thoughts can be. . . . The sign from Clinton stems from my uncertainty about whether to vote for the Governor. I was wavering between Clinton and Perot. On the morning of the vote, as I drove to the polls, I decided to vote for Clinton . . . When I went to the polls, voting was not by machine but rather by ballot. After receiving instructions on how to fill out the ballot I thought I heard the registrar say to initial it in the lower right-hand corner. I wondered why I would have to initial a ballot. It was supposed to be a secret ballot. Immediately I suspected that my vote and my vote alone would determine the destiny of the presidency for election year 1992 . . . I thought Clinton was the power boss who controlled everything including his "evil empire." So later, while watching TV, I saw what I perceived to be a rather sheepish, maybe slightly devilish glance from Clinton and a thumbs up (presumably at me) for having cast my vote the way I did. You see I had an additional delusion that while watching TV the subject being televised can peer right into your living room . . . In my deluded mind, the thumbs up was for me personally for voting as I did. (pp. 704–705)

An intriguing possibility is that delusions may serve a purpose for people with schizophrenia who are otherwise quite upset by the changes taking place within themselves. For example, G. A. Roberts (1991) studied 17 people who had elaborate delusions about themselves and the world, and compared them to a matched group of people who previously had delusions but were now improving. The "deluded" individuals expressed a much stronger sense of purpose and meaning in life *and less depression,* all of which seemed related to their delusional belief systems. Compare this with the opposite situation we discussed in Chapter 7, where we found that people who were depressed seemed sadder but wiser. That delusions may serve an adaptive function is at present just a theory with little support, but it may help us understand the phenomenon and its effect on those who experience it.

HALLUCINATIONS

Did you ever think someone called your name, only to discover that no one was there? Did you ever think you saw something move by you, yet nothing did? We all have fleeting moments when we think we see or hear something that isn't there. However, for many people with schizophrenia, these perceptions are very real and occur on a regular basis. The experience of sensory events without any input from the surrounding environment is called an **hallucination.**

Hallucinations can involve any of the senses, although hearing things that aren't there, or *auditory hallucination,* is the most common form experienced by people with schizophrenia. David had frequent auditory hallucinations, usually of his uncle's voice. When David heard a voice that belonged to his Uncle Bill, he often couldn't understand what his uncle was saying; on other occasions the voice was clearer. "He told me to turn off the TV. He said, 'It's too damn loud, turn it down, turn it down.' Other times he talks about fishing. 'Good day for fishing. Got to go fishing.'" You could tell when David was hearing voices. He was usually unoccupied, and he sat and smiled as if listening to someone next to him, but no one was there. This behavior is consistent with research, which suggests that people tend to experience hallucinations more frequently when they are unoccupied or restricted from sensory input (for example, Margo, Hemsley, & Slade, 1981).

Exciting new research on hallucinations uses sophisticated brain-imaging techniques to try to localize these phenomena in the brain. Using single photon emission computed tomography (SPECT) to study the cerebral blood flow of men with schizophrenia who also had auditory hallucinations, researchers in London made a surprising discovery (McGuire, Shah, & Murray, 1993). The researchers used the brain-imaging technique while the men were experiencing hallucinations and while they were not, and found that the part of the brain most active during hallucinations was *Broca's area* (see Figure 13.1). This is surprising because Broca's area is known to be involved in speech production. Because auditory hallucinations usually involve understanding the "speech" of others, you might expect more activity in *Wernicke's area,* which involves language comprehension. However, this study supports an

"If anyone gets into the house, they say I'd get shot. . . . [Who said?] That's the eagle. . . . The eagle works through General Motors. They have something to do with my General Motors check I get every month . . . when you do the 25 of the clock, it means that you leave the house 25 after 1 to mail letters so that they can check on you . . . and they know where you're at. That's the eagle. . . . If you don't do something they tell you to do, Jesus makes the shotgun sound, and then . . . not to answer the phone or the doorbell . . . because you'd get shot [by the] eagle."

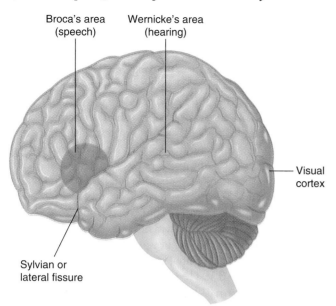

Broca's area (speech)
Wernicke's area (hearing)
Visual cortex
Sylvian or lateral fissure

figure 13.1 Some major language areas of the cerebral cortex. In most people, only the left hemisphere is specialized for language.

earlier finding by a different group of researchers who also found that Broca's area was more active than Wernicke's area during hallucinations (Cleghorn et al., 1992). These observations support a theory that people who are hallucinating are in fact *not* hearing the voices of others, but are listening to their own thoughts or their own voices and cannot recognize the difference. More advanced imaging technology is allowing researchers to get a better view of just what is going on inside the brain during hallucinations, and should help identify the role of the brain in the symptoms observed among people with schizophrenia (e.g., Silbersweig et al., 1995).

Negative Symptoms

In contrast to the active presentations that characterize the positive symptoms of schizophrenia, the negative symptoms usually indicate the absence or insufficiency of normal behavior. They include emotional and social withdrawal, apathy, and poverty of thought or speech (Carpenter, 1992).

AVOLITION

Combining the prefix *a*, meaning "without," and *volition*, which means "an act of willing, choosing, or deciding," **avolition** is the inability to initiate and persist in activities. People with this symptom (also referred to as apathy) show little interest in performing even the most basic day-to-day functions, including those associated with personal hygiene.

ALOGIA

Derived from the combination of *a* (without) and *logos* (words), **alogia** refers to the relative absence of speech. A person with alogia may respond to questions with very brief replies that have little content, and may appear uninterested in the conversation. For example, to the question, "Do you have any children?" most parents might reply, "Oh yes, I

have two beautiful children, a boy and a girl. My son is 6 and my daughter is 12." In the following exchange, someone with alogia responds to the same question:

Interviewer: Do you have any children?
Client: Yes.
Interviewer: How many children do you have?
Client: Two.
Interviewer: How old are they?
Client: Six and twelve.

Such deficiency in communication is believed to reflect a negative thought disorder rather than inadequate communication skills. Recent research, for example, suggests that people with alogia may have trouble finding the right words formulating their thoughts (Alpert, Clark, & Pouget, 1994). Sometimes alogia takes the form of delayed comments or slow responses to questions. Talking with individuals who manifest this symptom can be extremely frustrating, making you feel as if you are "pulling teeth" to get them to respond.

ANHEDONIA

A related symptom is called **anhedonia,** which derives from the word *hedonic*, pertaining to pleasure. Anhedonia is the presumed lack of pleasure experienced by some people with schizophrenia. Like some of the mood disorders, anhedonia signals an indifference to activities that would typically be considered pleasurable, including eating, social interactions, and sexual relations.

AFFECTIVE FLATTENING

Imagine that people wore masks at all times: You could communicate with them but you wouldn't be able to see their emotional reactions. Approximately two-thirds of the people with schizophrenia exhibit what is called **flat affect** (World Health Organization, 1973). They are similar to people wearing masks because they do not show emotions when you would normally expect them to. They may stare at you vacantly, speak in a flat and toneless manner, and seem unaffected by things going on around them. However, although they do not react openly to emotional situations, they may indeed be responding on the inside.

Howard Berenbaum and Thomas Oltmanns (1992) compared people with schizophrenia who had flat (or "blunted") affect with those who did not. The two groups were shown clips from films selected to create emotional reactions in the viewer (for instance, *Chinatown, Marathon Man, Bill Cosby: Himself*). Berenbaum and Oltmanns found that the people with flat affect showed little change in facial expression, although they reported experiencing the appropriate emotions. The authors concluded that the flat affect in schizophrenia may represent difficulty expressing emotion, not a lack of feeling. In a replication of this type of research, Kring and Neale (1996) also observed people with flat affect who reported appropriate emotional reactions, and they also confirmed the emotional responses through physiological recordings.

The expression of affect—or the lack of this expression—may be an important symptom of the development

Negative symptoms of schizophrenia include social withdrawal and apathy.

of schizophrenia. In a creative research study, Elaine Walker and her colleagues examined the facial expressions of children who later developed schizophrenia and compared them with the expressions of brothers and sisters who did not develop the disorder (Walker, Grimes, Davis, & Smith, 1993). They identified adults who already showed other signs of schizophrenia, and looked at home movies taken when they were children. The researchers were able to show that children who later went on to develop schizophrenia typically displayed less positive and more negative affect than their siblings. This suggests that emotional expression may be one way to identify potential schizophrenia in children.

Disorganized Symptoms

Disorganized Speech

A conversation with someone who has schizophrenia can be particularly frustrating. If you want to understand what is bothering or upsetting this person, eliciting relevant information is especially difficult. For one thing, people with schizophrenia often lack *insight,* an awareness that they have a problem. In addition, they experience what Bleuler called "associative splitting" and what Paul Meehl calls "cognitive

slippage" (Bleuler, 1908; Meehl, 1962). These phrases help describe the speech problems of people with schizophrenia: Sometimes they jump from topic to topic and at other times they talk illogically. DSM-IV uses the term **disorganized speech** to describe such communication problems. Let's go back to our conversation with David to demonstrate the symptom.

VMD: Why are you here in the hospital, David?
David: I really don't want to be here. I've got other things to do. The time is right, and you know, when opportunity knocks . . .

David didn't really answer the question he was asked. This type of response is called *tangentiality*—that is, going off on a tangent instead of answering a specific question (Andreasen, 1979). David also abruptly changed the topic of conversation to unrelated areas, a behavior that has variously been called *loose association* or *derailment* (Cutting, 1985).

VMD: I was sorry to hear that your Uncle Bill died a few years ago. How are you feeling about him these days?
David: Yes, he died. He was sick, and now he's gone. He likes to fish with me, down at the river. He's going to take me hunting. I have guns. I can shoot you and you'd be dead in a minute.

Again, David didn't answer my question. I could not tell whether he didn't understand the question, couldn't focus his attention, or found it too difficult to talk about his uncle. You can see why people spend a great deal of time trying to interpret all the hidden meanings behind this type of conversation. Unfortunately, however, such analyses have yet to provide us with useful information about the nature of schizophrenia or its treatment.

Inappropriate Affect and Disorganized Behavior

Occasionally, people with schizophrenia display **inappropriate affect,** laughing or crying at improper times. Sometimes they exhibit bizarre behaviors such as hoarding objects or acting in unusual ways in public. People with schizophrenia engage in a number of other "active" behaviors that are usually viewed as unusual. For example, **catatonia** is one of the most curious symptoms in some individuals with schizophrenia; it involves motor dysfunctions that range from wild agitation to immobility. On the active side of the continuum, some people pace excitedly or move their fingers or arms in stereotyped ways. At the other end of the extreme, people hold unusual postures, as if they were fearful of something terrible happening if they move **(catatonic immobility).** This manifestation can also involve waxy flexibility, or the tendency to keep their bodies and limbs in the position they are put in by someone else.

Again, to receive a diagnosis of schizophrenia, a person must display two or more positive, negative, and/or disorganized symptoms for a major portion of at least 1 month. Depending on the combination of symptoms displayed, two people could receive the same diagnosis but behave very differently, one having marked hallucinations and delusions and the other displaying disorganized speech and some of the negative symptoms. Proper treatment depends on differentiating individuals in terms of their varying symptoms.

■ concept check 13.1

Identify the following terms associated with schizophrenia: affective flattening, avolition, delusions, hallucinations.

1. Beliefs that most people would describe as a misrepresentation of reality, called a disorder of thought content. _____

2. Apathy, or an inability to initiate or persist in important activities. _____

3. Lack of visible emotional response or reactivity. _____

4. Perceptions of sensory events that do not originate in the surrounding environment. _____

Schizophrenia Subtypes

As we noted earlier, the search for subtypes of schizophrenia began before Kraepelin described his concept of schizophrenia. Three divisions have persisted: *catatonic* (alternate immobility and excited agitation), *hebephrenic* (disorganization; silly and immature emotionality), and *paranoid* (delusions of grandeur or persecution). Research supports dividing schizophrenia into these categories, because differences among them are identifiable (Andreasen & Flaum, 1990). For example, the prognosis for individuals with the hebephrenic subtype is more pessimistic than for people with the other subtypes. People with the catatonic subtype have a distinctive course and treatment response. Because of their usefulness, DSM-IV has integrated all three subtypes into its revised classification system for schizophrenia.

PARANOID TYPE

People with the **paranoid type of schizophrenia** stand out because of their delusions or hallucinations; at the same time, their cognitive skills and affect are relatively intact. They generally do not have disorganized speech or flat affect, and they typically have a better prognosis than people with other forms of schizophrenia. The delusions and hallucinations usually have a theme, such as grandeur or persecution. The DSM-IV criteria for inclusion in this subtype specify preoccupation with one or more delusions or frequent auditory hallucinations but without a marked display of disorganized speech, disorganized or catatonic behavior, or flat or inappropriate affect (American Psychiatric Association, 1994).

DISORGANIZED TYPE

In contrast to the paranoid type of schizophrenia, people with the **disorganized type of schizophrenia** show marked disruption in their speech and behavior; they also show flat or inappropriate affect, such as laughing in a silly way at the wrong times (American Psychiatric Association, 1994). If delusions or hallucinations are present, they tend not to be organized around a central theme, as in the paranoid type,

but are more fragmented. This subtype was previously called hebephrenic. Individuals with this diagnosis tend to show signs of difficulty early, and their problems are often chronic, lacking the remissions (improvement of symptoms) that characterize other forms of the disorder (McGlashan & Fenton, 1991).

CATATONIC TYPE

In addition to the unusual motor responses of remaining in fixed positions (waxy flexibility), engaging in excessive activity, and being oppositional by remaining rigid, individuals with the **catatonic type of schizophrenia** sometimes display odd mannerisms with their bodies and faces, including grimacing (American Psychiatric Association, 1994). They often repeat or mimic the words of others (*echolalia*) or the movements of others (*echopraxia*). This cluster of behaviors is relatively rare and there is some debate about whether it should remain classified as a separate subtype of schizophrenia (McGlashan & Fenton, 1991). Its infrequency may be due partly to the success of neuroleptic medications.

UNDIFFERENTIATED TYPE

People who do not fit neatly into these subtypes are classified as having an **undifferentiated type of schizophrenia;** they include people who have the major symptoms of schizophrenia but who do not meet the criteria for paranoid, disorganized, or catatonic types.

RESIDUAL TYPE

People who have had at least one episode of schizophrenia but who no longer manifest major symptoms are diagnosed as having the **residual type of schizophrenia.** Although they may not suffer from bizarre delusions or hallucinations,

This homeless man suffers from paranoid schizophrenia. His persecutory delusions interfere with efforts to help him.

they may display residual or "leftover" symptoms, such as negative beliefs, or they may still have unusual ideas that are not fully delusional. Residual symptoms can include social withdrawal, bizarre thoughts, inactivity, and flat affect. All the versions of the DSM (from DSM-I through DSM-IV) have included a residual type to describe the condition of individuals who have less severe problems associated with an episode of schizophrenia.

Research suggests that the paranoid subtype may have a stronger familial link than the others and that these people may function better before and after episodes of schizophrenia than people diagnosed with other subtypes (McGlashan & Fenton, 1991). More work will determine whether dividing schizophrenia into five subtypes helps us understand and treat people. Several other disorders that are also characterized by psychotic behaviors such as hallucinations and delusions do not manifest in the same way as schizophrenia. In the next section they are first distinguished from schizophrenia, and then described in greater detail.

■ concept check 13.2

Subtypes have been used for years to diagnose schizophrenia according to varying symptoms. Check your understanding by labeling each situation according to subtype.

1. Gary often has delusions and hallucinations that convince him enemies are out to persecute him.
   _____

2. Sally displays motor immobility, and often repeats words said by others around her. _____

3. Carrie had an episode of schizophrenia in the past, but she no longer displays the major symptoms of the disorder. She does, however, still have some negative, unusual ideas and displays flat affect on occasion. _____

4. Tim suffers from a type of schizophrenia that is identified by disruption and incoherence in his speech and behavior. He also shows inappropriate affect, often laughing in sad or upsetting situations. _____

5. As a psych intern, you are assigned to interview a rather unremarkable-looking gentleman. He is quite pleasant and talkative. After exchanging a few pleasantries, he mentions something about someone listening in on the conversation. You see no one nearby. When you ask the man what he means, he reluctantly explains that spies with hidden cameras follow him constantly. He attributes this to the fact that he has developed a plan to move the earth's population to the planet Pluto. _____

6. You sit down next to a gentleman who suddenly giggles. When you ask what he's laughing at, he answers, but you can't make sense of what he says. _____

7. Your next client is a woman who has been diagnosed as schizophrenic, but her behavior patterns do not fit any of the identified subtypes. _____

8. As you enter the room of the institution, you see your patient in the opposite corner, standing in a fixed karate-like pose with a grimace on his face. _____

SCHIZOPHRENIFORM DISORDER

Some people experience the symptoms of schizophrenia for a few months only; they can usually resume normal lives. The symptoms sometimes disappear as the result of successful treatment, but often for reasons unknown, and are classified under the label **schizophreniform disorder.** As there are relatively few studies on this disorder, data on important aspects of it are sparse. It appears, however, that the lifetime prevalence is approximately 0.2% (American Psychiatric Association, 1994). The DSM-IV diagnostic criteria for schizophreniform disorder include onset of psychotic symptoms within 4 weeks of the first noticeable change in usual behavior, confusion at the height of the psychotic episode, good premorbid social and occupational functioning, and the absence of blunted or flat affect (American Psychiatric Association, 1994).

SCHIZOAFFECTIVE DISORDER

Historically, people who had symptoms of schizophrenia and who also exhibited the characteristics of mood disorders (for example, depression or bipolar affective disorder) were lumped together in the category of schizophrenia (Siris, 1993). Now, however, this mixed bag of problems is diagnosed as **schizoaffective disorder.** The prognosis is similar to the prognosis for people with schizophrenia—that is, individuals tend not to get better on their own and are likely to continue experiencing major life difficulties for many years (Tsuang & Coryell, 1993). DSM-IV criteria for schizoaffective disorder require that in addition to the presence of a mood disorder there have been delusions or hallucinations for at least 2 weeks in the absence of prominent mood symptoms (American Psychiatric Association, 1994).

DELUSIONAL DISORDER

Delusions are beliefs that are not generally held by other members of a society. The major feature of **delusional disorder** is a persistent belief that is contrary to reality, in the absence of other characteristics of schizophrenia. For example, a woman who believes without any evidence that co-workers are tormenting her by putting poison in her food and spraying her apartment with harmful gases has a delusional disorder. This disorder is characterized by a persistent delusion that is not the result of an organic factor such as brain seizures or of any severe psychosis. Individuals tend not to have flat affect, anhedonia, or other negative symptoms of schizophrenia; importantly, however, they may become socially isolated because they are suspicious of others. The delusions are often long-standing, sometimes persisting over several years (Breier, 1993).

DSM-IV recognizes the following delusional subtypes: *erotomanic, grandiose, jealous, persecutory,* and *somatic.* An erotomanic delusion is the irrational belief that one is loved by another person, usually of higher status. Some of the individuals who stalk celebrities appear to have erotomanic delusional disorder. The grandiose type of delusion involves believing in one's inflated worth, power, knowledge, identity, or special relationship to a deity or famous person. A person with the jealous type of delusion believes that the sexual partner is unfaithful. The persecutory type of delusion involves believing oneself (or someone close) is being malevolently treated in some way. Finally, with the somatic type of delusion the person feels afflicted by a physical defect or general medical condition. These delusions differ from the more bizarre types often found in people with schizophrenia because in delusional disorder *the imagined events could be happening but aren't* (for example, mistakenly believing you are being followed); in schizophrenia, on the other hand, *the imagined events aren't possible* (for example, believing that your brain waves broadcast your thoughts to other people around the world).

Delusional disorder seems to be relatively rare, affecting 24 to 30 people out of every 100,000 in the general population. Among those people with identified psychological disorders, between 1% and 4% are thought to have delusional disorder (Kendler, 1982). Researchers can't be confident about the percentages because they know that many of these individuals have no contact with the mental health system.

The onset of delusional disorder is relatively late: The average age of first admission to a psychiatric facility is between 40 and 49 (Kendler, 1982). However, because many people with this disorder can lead relatively normal lives, they may not seek treatment until their symptoms become most disruptive. Delusional disorder seems to afflict more females than males (55% and 45%, respectively, of the affected population).

In a longitudinal study, Opjordsmoen (1989) followed 53 people with delusional disorder for an average of 30 years and found that they tended to fare better in life than people with schizophrenia, but not as well as those with some other psychotic disorders, such as schizoaffective disorder. About 80% of the 53 individuals had been married at some time, and half were employed, which demonstrates an ability to function relatively well despite delusions.

We know relatively little about either the biological or the psychosocial influences on delusional disorder (Breier, 1993). Research on families suggests that the characteristics of suspiciousness, jealousy, and secretiveness may occur more often among the relatives of people with delusional disorder than among the population at large, suggesting that some aspect of this disorder may be inherited (Winokur, 1985).

A number of other disorders can cause delusions and their presence should be ruled out before diagnosing delusional disorder. For example, abuse of amphetamines, alcohol, and cocaine can cause delusions, as can brain tumors, Huntington's disease, and Alzheimer's disease (Breier, 1993).

BRIEF PSYCHOTIC DISORDER

Recall the puzzling case of Arthur, who suddenly experienced the delusion that he could save the world and whose intense emotional swings lasted for only a few days. He would receive the DSM-IV diagnosis of **brief psychotic disorder,** which is characterized by the presence of one or more positive symptoms such as delusions, hallucinations, or disorganized speech or behavior within a month. Individuals like Arthur regain their previous ability to function well in day-to-day activities. Brief psychotic disorder is often precipitated by extremely stressful situations.

SHARED PSYCHOTIC DISORDER (FOLIE À DEUX)

Relatively little is known about **shared psychotic disorder (folie à deux),** the condition in which an individual develops delusions simply as a result of a close relationship with a delusional individual. The content and nature of the delusion originate with the partner and can range from the relatively bizarre, such as believing that enemies are sending harmful gamma rays through your house, to the fairly ordinary, such as believing that you are about to receive a major promotion despite evidence to the contrary.

Other Psychotic Disorders

Schizotypal personality disorder, which was discussed in Chapter 12, is a related psychotic disorder. As you may recall, the characteristics are similar to those experienced by people with schizophrenia, but less severe. There is also some evidence that schizophrenia and schizotypal personality disorder may be genetically related as part of a "schizophrenia spectrum."

It is important to remember that although people with related psychotic disorders display many of the characteristics of schizophrenia, these disorders differ significantly. We now examine the nature of schizophrenia itself, and learn how researchers have attempted to understand and treat people who have it.

Statistics

Schizophrenia sometimes defies our desire for simplicity. We have seen how very different symptoms can be displayed by individuals who would all be considered to have the disorder; in some people they develop slowly and in others they occur suddenly. Schizophrenia is generally chronic, and most people with the disorder have a very difficult time functioning in society. This is especially true of their ability to relate to others; they tend not to establish or maintain significant relationships, and therefore many people with schizophrenia never marry or have children. Unlike the delusions of people with other psychotic disorders, the delusions of people with schizophrenia are likely to be outside the realm of possibility. Finally, even when individuals with schizophrenia improve with treatment, they are likely to experience difficulties throughout their lives.

Worldwide, the lifetime prevalence rate of schizophrenia is roughly equivalent for men and women, and is estimated at 0.2% to 1.5% in the general population (Jablensky, 1995), which means that the disorder will affect around 1% of the population at some point. Life expectancy is slightly less than average, partly due to the higher rate of suicide among people with schizophrenia (Potkin, Albers, & Richmond, 1993).

Although there is some disagreement about the distribution of schizophrenia between men and women, the difference between the sexes in age of onset is clear. As you can see in Figure 13.2, the onset of schizophrenia among a group of 470 patients was highest in early adulthood (ages 16–25) (Howard, Castle, Wessely, & Murray, 1993). For men, the likelihood of onset diminishes with age, but it can still first occur after the age of 75. The onset for women is lower than for men until age 36, when the relative risk for onset switches, with more women than men being affected later in life.

Other Classification Systems

An approach that focused on onset and received considerable attention for a time was to distinguish between *process* and *reactive* subtypes (Carson & Sanislow, 1993). **Process schizophrenia,** which is similar to Kraepelin's dementia praecox, was thought to come on slowly, without any obvious stressful event as trigger, leaving a person withdrawn and apparently emotionless. In contrast, **reactive schizophrenia** was thought to be a response to an extremely stressful set of situations, coming on suddenly and producing behavior that was highly social, volatile, and intense. Process schizophrenia was believed to be physiologically based and to have a poor prognosis, whereas reactive schizophrenia was attributed to stress and thought to have a good outcome.

Despite the simplicity that the process–reactive distinction seems to bring to the concept of schizophrenia, the categories do not apply neatly to many people. There is also another problem: Some people with "reactive" schizophrenia eventually show many of the characteristics of "process" schizophrenia. In fact, the changing nature of schizophre-nia—that people have different forms of the disorder at different times in their lives—continues to perplex experts, defying their efforts to categorize people. Because of these limitations, the process–reactive distinction for schizophrenia is no longer accepted by most workers in the field. A similar division, **poor premorbid** versus **good premorbid,** terms that refer to the social functioning of the person just before the major symptoms of schizophrenia are observed, was also adopted for a time, but it too has been abandoned as a useful distinction.

An alternate classification system, introduced in the mid-1970s by Strauss, Carpenter, and Bartko (1974), emphasizes the positive, negative, and, more recently, disorganized symptoms. Timothy Crow elaborated on this approach, suggesting that schizophrenia can be dichotomized into two types (Crow, 1980, 1985), based on a variety of characteristics, including symptoms, response to medication, outcome, and the presence or absence of intellectual impairment. Type I is associated with the **positive symptoms** of hallucinations and delusions, a good response to medication, an optimistic prognosis, and the absence of intellectual impairment. In contrast, Type II includes people with the **negative symptoms** of flat affect and poverty of speech, who show a poor response to medication, a pessimistic prognosis, and intellectual impairments. Although not without its critics (Andreasen & Carpenter, 1993), Crow's model has influenced current thinking regarding the nature of schizophrenia.

Development

Increasing attention has been paid to the developmental course of schizophrenia (Asarnow, 1994; Walker, 1991), which may shed some light on its causes. Research suggests

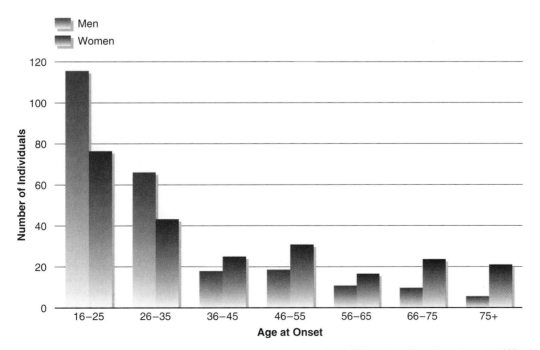

figure 13.2   Gender differences in onset of schizophrenia in a sample of 470 patients (from Howard et al., 1993)

that children who later develop schizophrenia show some abnormal signs before they display the characteristic symptoms (Fish, 1987). Their emotional reactions may be abnormal, with less positive and more negative affect than their unaffected siblings (Walker et al., 1993). Remember that although the age of onset varies, schizophrenia is generally seen by early adulthood. If the causative factors are present very early on, why does the disorder show itself only later in life?

It may be that brain damage very early in the developmental period causes later schizophrenia (Weinberger, 1987). However, instead of resulting in an immediate progressive deterioration, the damage may lie dormant until later in development when the signs of schizophrenia first appear. Supporting evidence comes from an animal study showing that damage to a rat hippocampus becomes apparent only when the rat matures (Lipska, Jaskiw, & Weinberger, 1993). A study found that people with schizophrenia who demonstrated early signs of abnormality at birth and during early childhood tended to fare better than people who did not (Torrey, Bowler, Taylor, & Gottesman, 1994). One interpretation of these results is that the earlier the damage occurs, the more time the brain has to compensate for it, which results in milder symptoms.

A life-span perspective may at least partly reveal the development of schizophrenia (Belitsky & McGlashan, 1993). In one of the few studies that have followed people with schizophrenia into late life, researchers tracked 52 people over a 40-year period (Winokur, Pfohl, & Tsuang, 1987). Their general finding was that older adults tended to display fewer of the positive symptoms, such as delusions and hallucinations, and more of the negative symptoms, such as speech and cognitive difficulties. In other words, people with schizophrenia may show improvement during later adulthood.

The relapse rate must also be considered in discussing the course of schizophrenia. Unfortunately, a great many people who improve after an episode of schizophrenia later experience the symptoms again. In fact, most people with schizophrenia fluctuate between severe and moderate levels of impairment throughout their lives (Harrow, Sands, Silverstein, & Goldberg, 1997). Figure 13.3 illustrates the data from one study that show the course of schizophrenia among four prototypical groups (Zubin, Steinhauer, & Condray, 1992). As you can see, about 22% of the group had one episode of schizophrenia and improved without lasting impairment. However, the remaining 78% experienced several episodes, with differing degrees of impairment between them. Relapses are an important subject in the field of schizophrenia; we will return to this phenomenon when we discuss causes and treatment.

Cultural Factors

Because schizophrenia is so complex, the diagnosis itself can be controversial. Some have argued that "schizophre-

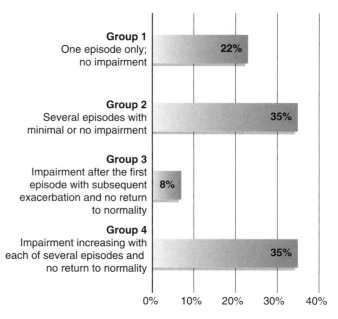

figure 13.3 The natural history of schizophrenia: a 5-year follow-up (from Zubin et al., 1989)

nia" does not really exist but is a pejorative label for people who behave in ways that are outside the cultural norm (for instance, Laing, 1967; Sarbin & Mancuso, 1980; Szasz, 1961). Although the idea that schizophrenia exists only in the minds of mental health professionals is certainly provocative, this extreme view is contradicted by experience. We have both had a great deal of contact with people who have this disorder and with their families and friends, and the tremendous amount of emotional pain resulting from schizophrenia gives definite credence to its existence. In addition, many people in extremely diverse cultures have the symptoms of schizophrenia, which supports the notion that it is a reality for many people worldwide (Wyatt, Alexander, Egan, & Kirch, 1988). Schizophrenia is thus universal, affecting all racial and cultural groups studied so far (Jablensky, 1995).

However, the course and outcome of schizophrenia vary from culture to culture. For example, in Colombia, India, and Nigeria, more people improve significantly or recover than in other countries (Leff, Sartorius, Jablensky, Korten, & Ernberg, 1992). These differences may be due to cultural variations or prevalent biological influences such as immunization, but we cannot yet explain these differences in outcomes.

In the United States, proportionately more African-Americans receive the diagnosis of schizophrenia than whites (Lindsey & Paul, 1989). Research from both England and the United States suggests that people from devalued ethnic minority groups (Afro-Caribbean in England, and African-Americans and Puerto Ricans in the United States) may be victims of bias and stereotyping (B. E. Jones & Gray, 1986; Lewis, Croft-Jeffreys, & Anthony, 1990); in other words, they may be more likely to receive a diagnosis of schizophrenia than members of a dominant group. The differing rates of schizophrenia,

Schizophrenia has been known throughout the ages all over the world. In this scene, Shakespeare's King Lear descends into "madness."

therefore, appear to be due to *misdiagnosis* rather than to any real cultural distinctions.

 Causes

Studying schizophrenia reveals the many levels on which we must decipher what makes us behave the way we do. As we survey the work of many specialists, we will examine many state-of-the-art techniques for studying both biological and psychosocial influences, a process that may be slow going at times, but will bring new insight to your understanding of psychopathology.

Genetic Influences

We could argue that no other area of abnormal psychology so clearly illustrates the enormous complexity and intriguing mystery of genetic influences on behavior as does the phenomenon of schizophrenia. Despite the possibility that schizophrenia may be several different disorders, we can safely make one generalization: *Genes are responsible for making some individuals vulnerable to schizophrenia.* We will look at a range of research findings from family, twin, adoptee, offspring of twins, and linkage and association studies (Sherman et al., 1997). We conclude by discussing the compelling reasons that no one gene is responsible for schizophrenia; rather, multiple genes combine to produce vulnerability. Readers who want a more detailed but highly readable discussion of this research should refer to *Schizophrenia Genesis: The Origins of Madness* by Irving Gottesman (1991).

FAMILY STUDIES

In 1938, Franz Kallmann published a major study of the families of people with schizophrenia (Kallmann, 1938).

Kallmann examined family members of over 1,000 persons diagnosed with schizophrenia in a Berlin psychiatric hospital. Several of his observations continue to guide research on schizophrenia. Kallmann showed that the severity of the parent's disorder influenced the likelihood of the child's having schizophrenia: The more severe the parent's schizophrenia, the more likely the children were to develop it also. Another observation was important: All forms of schizophrenia (for instance, catatonic, paranoid) were seen within the families. In other words, it does not appear that you inherit a predisposition for, say, paranoid schizophrenia. Instead, you may inherit a general predisposition for schizophrenia that manifests in the same form or differently from that of your parent.

A more recent study, in the west of Ireland, used sophisticated research methodologies to study the risk to the relatives of people with schizophrenia (Kendler et al., 1993). Consistent with the Kallmann study, the newer research found that families in which a member had schizophrenia were more likely to have other members with schizophrenia or other related psychotic disorders (such as schizoaffective disorder and schizotypal personality disorder). That is, families who have a member with schizophrenia are at risk not just for schizophrenia alone, nor for all psychological disorders; instead, there appears to be some familial risk for a spectrum of psychotic disorders related to schizophrenia.

Gottesman (1991) summarized the data from about 40 studies of schizophrenia, as shown in Figure 13.4. The

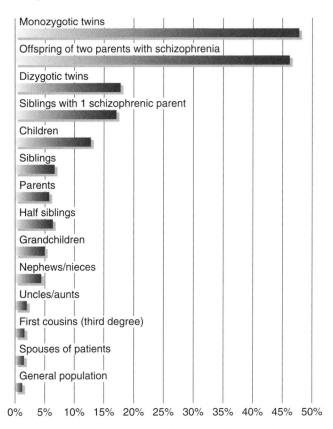

figure 13.4 Risk of developing schizophrenia (based on Gottesman, 1991)

most striking feature of this graph is its orderly demonstration that the risk of having schizophrenia varies according to how many genes an individual shares with someone who has the disorder. For example, you have the greatest chance (approximately 48%) of having schizophrenia if it has affected your identical (monozygotic) twin, a person who shares 100% of your genetic information. Your risk drops to about 17% with a fraternal (dizygotic) twin, who shares about 50% of your genetic information. And having any relative with schizophrenia makes you more likely to have the disorder than someone in the general population without such a relative (about 1%). Because family studies can't separate genetic influence from the impact of the environment, we use twin and adoption studies to help us evaluate the role of shared experiences in the cause of schizophrenia.

TWIN STUDIES

If they are raised together, identical twins share 100% of their genes and 100% of their environment, whereas fraternal twins share only about 50% of their genes and 100% of their environment. If the environment is solely responsible for schizophrenia, we would expect little difference between identical and fraternal twins with regard to this disorder. If only genetic factors are relevant, both identical twins would always have schizophrenia (be concordant) and the fraternal twins would both have it about 50% of the time. Research from twin studies indicates that the truth is somewhere in the middle (Fowles, 1992b; Gottesman, McGuffin, & Farmer, 1987; Kendler & Diehl, 1993; Sherman et al., 1997).

In a Norwegian study, the concordance rate for identical twins was 48.4% and the concordance rate for fraternal twins was only 3.6% (Onstad, Skre, Torgersen, & Kringlen, 1991). Referring to Figure 13.4, you see that this percentage resembles Gottesman's summary of the concordance rates of 48% and 17%, respectively, which suggests that the shared genes of the identical twins may account for their higher rates of schizophrenia.

In one of the most fascinating of "nature's experiments," identical quadruplets, all of whom have schizophrenia, have been studied extensively. Nicknamed the "Genain" quadruplets (from the Greek, meaning "dreadful gene"), these women have been followed by David Rosenthal and his colleagues at the National Institute of Mental Health for a number of years (Rosenthal, 1963). In a sense, the women represent the complex interac-

Irving Gottesman, a psychologist at the University of Virginia, has contributed significantly to our understanding of schizophrenia.

The Genain quadruplets (shown here at age 4) all had schizophrenia but exhibited different symptoms over the years.

tion between genetics and the environment. All four shared the same genetic predisposition, and all were brought up in the same particularly dysfunctional household; yet the time of onset for schizophrenia, the symptoms and diagnoses, the course of the disorder and, ultimately, their outcomes, differed significantly from sister to sister.

The case of the Genain quadruplets reveals an important consideration in studying genetic influences on behavior— *unshared environments* (Plomin, 1990). We tend to think that siblings, and especially identical multiples, are brought up the same way. The impression is that "good" parents expose their children to favorable environments, and "bad" parents give them unstable experiences. However, even identical siblings can have very different prenatal and family experiences and therefore be exposed to varying degrees of biological and environmental stress. For example, Hester, one of the Genain sisters, was described by her disturbed parents as a habitual masturbator, and she had more social problems than her sisters as she grew up. Hester was the first to experience severe symptoms of schizophrenia, at age 18, but her sister Myra was not hospitalized until 6 years later. This very unusual case demonstrates that even siblings who are very close in every aspect of their lives can still have considerably different experiences physically and socially as they grow up, which may result in vastly different outcomes.

ADOPTION STUDIES

Several adoption studies have distinguished the roles of the environment and genetics as they affect schizophrenia. These studies often span many years; because people often do not show the first signs of schizophrenia until middle age, researchers need to be sure that all the offspring reach that point before drawing conclusions. Many schizophrenia studies are conducted in Europe, primarily because of the extensive and comprehensive records that are kept in countries where socialized medicine is practiced.

Figure 13.5 illustrates the two primary strategies for studying the effects of adoption on children: the *adoptees'*

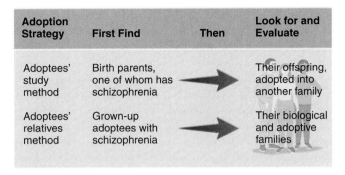

figure 13.5 Two adoption research strategies that can be applied to the study of schizophrenia (adapted from Tienari, 1992)

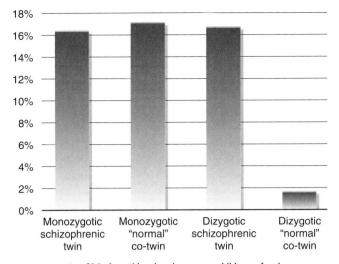

figure 13.6 Risk for schizophrenia among children of twins

study method and the *adoptees' relatives method* (Tienari, 1992). The largest and most recent adoption study, currently being conducted in Finland (Tienari, 1991), is an example of the adoptees' study method. From a sample of almost 20,000 women with schizophrenia, the researchers found 164 mothers who gave up children for adoption. To date, 155 offspring of mothers with schizophrenia and 185 children of control mothers without schizophrenia have been studied. As of 1991, researchers identified 16 children with schizophrenia or other psychotic disorders (for example, delusional disorder, schizophreniform disorder) who had mothers with schizophrenia (16/155 = 10.3%), and only 2 children with schizophrenia or other psychotic disorders with nonschizophrenic mothers have been found (2/185 = 1.1%). Even when raised away from their biological parents, children of parents with schizophrenia have a much higher chance of having the disorder themselves.

The adoptees' relatives method is exemplified in a study by a team of researchers from the United States and Denmark. They searched the national register of Denmark for people with schizophrenia who had been adopted (Kety, Rosenthal, Wender, Schulsinger, & Jacobsen, 1978; Lowing, Mirsky, & Pereira, 1983; D. Rosenthal et al., 1968). They then examined these adoptees and compared them to adoptees without schizophrenia. Although this study has been analyzed in a number of different ways, the general conclusion is that children of people with schizophrenia who are adopted into families without schizophrenia still have a higher than average rate of having schizophrenia themselves. Something other than living in the home of a person with schizophrenia must account for this disorder.

THE OFFSPRING OF TWINS

Twin and adoption studies strongly suggest a genetic component for schizophrenia, but what about children who develop schizophrenia even though their parents do not? For example, the Tienari (1991) study we just discussed found that 1.1% of the children with nonschizophrenic parents developed schizophrenia. Does this mean that you can develop schizophrenia without "schizophrenic genes"? Or are some people carriers, having the genes for schizophrenia but for some reason not showing the disorder themselves? An important clue to this question comes from research on the children of twins with schizophrenia.

In a study begun in 1971 by Margit Fischer and later continued by Irving Gottesman and Aksel Bertelsen, 21 identical twin pairs and 41 fraternal twin pairs with a history of schizophrenia were identified along with their children (Fischer, 1971; Gottesman & Bertelsen, 1989). The researchers wanted to determine the relative likelihood that a child would have schizophrenia if his or her parent did, and if the parent's twin had schizophrenia but the parent did not. Figure 13.6 illustrates the findings from this study. For example, if your parent is an identical (monozygotic) twin with schizophrenia, you have about a 17% chance of having the disorder yourself, a figure that holds if you are the child of an unaffected identical twin whose co-twin has the disorder.

On the other hand, look at the risks for the child of a fraternal (dizygotic) twin. If your parent has schizophrenia, you too have about a 17% chance of having schizophrenia. However, if your parent does not have schizophrenia but your parent's fraternal twin does, your risk is only about 2%. The only way to explain this finding is through genetics. The data clearly indicate that you can have genes that predispose you to schizophrenia, not show the disorder yourself, but still pass on the genes to your children. In other words, you can be a "carrier" for schizophrenia. This is some of the strongest evidence yet that people are genetically vulnerable to schizophrenia. Remember, however, that there is only a 17% chance of inheritance, meaning that other factors help determine who will have this disorder.

LINKAGE AND ASSOCIATION STUDIES

If genes are involved in schizophrenia, where are they? One report brought the astonishing news that a gene responsible for the disorder had been found on the fifth chromosome (Bassett, 1989; McGillivray, Bassett, Langlois, Pantzar, & Wood, 1990). A young man and his uncle were identified who had schizophrenia and the same unusual facial features. An analysis showed that they both had the same anomaly involving the fifth chromosome, so researchers concluded that both their facial features and their schizophrenia were due to their unusual fifth chromosome. This startling finding was rapidly refuted by other studies. Within 3 years, more than 10 linkage studies found little evidence for a schizophrenia gene on the fifth chromosome (Kendler & Diehl, 1993).

Recall from Chapter 4 that genetic linkage and association studies rely on traits such as blood types (whose exact location on the chromosome is already known) that are inherited in families along with the disorder you are looking for—in this case, schizophrenia. Because we know the location of the genes for these traits (called *marker genes*), we can make a rough guess about the location of the disorder genes that are inherited along with them. To date, researchers have looked at several sites for genes that may be responsible for schizophrenia. For example, because there is some evidence that siblings who have schizophrenia tend to be of the same gender (Crow, 1988), researchers have examined the X and Y sex chromosomes for a gene for schizophrenia. Again, there was initial evidence that it had been located (d'Amato et al., 1992), but the finding could not be replicated (Asherson et al., 1992).

One line of this genetic linkage research relates to a topic we discuss shortly: neurobiological influences in schizophrenia. Because one long-standing theory about the cause of schizophrenia is that it involves the neurotransmitter *dopamine*, researchers have understandably been interested in the genes responsible for dopamine functioning and their relationship to schizophrenia. Instead of looking for a "schizophrenia gene" or genes, they seek the location of the dopamine genes and attempt to determine whether they are related to schizophrenia. Linkage studies to establish a link between dopamine sites (referred to as D_1, D_2, D_3, and D_4 loci) and the presence of schizophrenia have not yet turned up strong evidence (Byerly et al., 1991; Su et al., 1993).

THE SEARCH FOR MARKERS

We learned from the genetic linkage studies that one way to conduct genetic research is to identify markers that are inherited along with a disorder. If a certain blood type is common to family members who also have schizophrenia, for example, and we know where the gene for this blood type is located, we can guess that a gene influencing schizophrenia might be nearby. Researchers thus look for common traits other than the symptoms of the disorder itself. If some people have the positive symptoms of schizophrenia, others have the negative symptoms, and still others have a mixture of these symptoms, yet they all have a particular problem completing a certain task, the skill deficit would be very useful for identifying what else these people may have in common.

Several potential markers for schizophrenia have been studied over the years. One of the more highly researched is called *smooth-pursuit eye movement* or eye-tracking. Keeping your head still, you must be able to track a moving pendulum, back and forth, with your eyes. The ability to track objects smoothly across the visual field is deficient in many people who also have schizophrenia (Clementz & Sweeney, 1990; Holzman & Levy, 1977; Iacono, 1988); it does not appear to be the result of drug treatment or institutionalization (Lieberman et al., 1993). It also seems to be a problem for

relatives of these people (Kuechenmeister, Linton, Mueller, & White, 1977) and is observed more frequently among people with schizophrenia than in others who do not have the disorder (Clementz & Sweeney, 1990). Finally, recent genetic research suggests that deficient eye-tracking may be the result of a single gene defect that is inherited along with the gene or genes involved in schizophrenia (Grove, Clementz, Iacono, & Katsanis, 1992). When all these observations are combined, they suggest that an eye-tracking deficit may be a marker for schizophrenia that could be used in further study.

EVIDENCE FOR MULTIPLE GENES

Because identical twins can be discordant for schizophrenia (when only one has it) despite their identical genetic material, something about their different environments must contribute to their ultimate outcomes. However, that both the affected and unaffected twin have the same likelihood of passing on schizophrenia to their children seems to be overwhelming evidence for a genetic component.

It may be that schizophrenia involves more than one gene, a phenomenon referred to as *quantitative trait loci* (QTL) (Plomin, Owen, & McGuffin, 1994). The schizophrenia we see most often is probably caused by several genes located at different sites throughout the chromosomes. This would also clarify why there can be gradations of severity in people with the disorder (from mild to severe), and why the risk of having schizophrenia increases with the number of affected relatives in the family. It is likely that the QTL model is not unique to schizophrenia and that many of the disorders people experience are caused by more than one gene.

■ concept check 13.3

Genes are responsible for making some individuals vulnerable to schizophrenia. Check your understanding of genetic vulnerability by filling in the blanks of the following sentences associated with family, twin, and adoption studies. You may choose from the following words: (a) higher, (b) lower, (c) equal, (d) severity, (e) type, (f) identical twin, (g) specific, (h) fraternal twin, (i) general.

1. The likelihood of a child's having schizophrenia is influenced by the _____ of the parent's disorder. One may inherit a _____ predisposition for schizophrenia that is the same or different from that of the parent.

2. The greatest risk of having schizophrenia is in those who have a(n) _____ with schizophrenia. The chances drop considerably for those who have a(n) _____ with schizophrenia. Any relative with schizophrenia will make your chances (a) greater than, (b) less than, or (c) the same as the general population.

3. Raised in a home other than that of their biological parents, adopted children of parents with schizophrenia have a(n) _____ chance of having the disorder themselves. Children of people with schizophrenia adopted into families without schizophrenia have a _____ than average chance of having schizophrenia.

Neurobiological Influences

A parent of someone with schizophrenia wrote the following statement:

> Many of us who have a son, daughter, or other relative with schizophrenia have observed so great a change in the person's behavior with the onset of the psychosis that we know intuitively that the cause had to be something basic, such as an alteration of the brain's functioning. (D. L. Johnson, 1989, p. 553)

The belief that schizophrenia involves a malfunctioning brain goes back as far as the writings of Emil Kraepelin (1856–1926). It is therefore not surprising that a great deal of research has focused on the brain. Before we discuss some of this work, however, be forewarned: To study abnormalities in the brain for clues to the cause of schizophrenia is to face all the classic problems of doing correlational research that were discussed in Chapter 4. For example, if a person has schizophrenia and too much of a neurotransmitter, (a) does too much neurotransmitter cause schizophrenia, (b) does schizophrenia create too much of the neurotransmitter, or (c) does something else cause both the schizophrenia and the chemical imbalance? Keep this caveat in mind as you review the following research.

DOPAMINE

One of the most enduring yet still controversial theories of the cause of schizophrenia involves the neurotransmitter *dopamine* (Carlsson, 1995; Maas et al., 1997). Before we consider the research, however, we need to review briefly how neurotransmitters operate in the brain and how they are affected by neuroleptic medications. In Chapter 2 we discussed the sensitivity of specific neurons to specific neurotransmitters, and described how they cluster throughout the brain. The top of Figure 13.7 shows two neurons and the important synaptic gap that separates them. Neurotransmitters are released from the storage vessels (synaptic vesicles) at the end of the axon, cross the gap, and are taken up by receptors in the dendrite of the next axon. Chemical "messages" are transported in this way from neuron to neuron throughout the brain.

This process can be influenced in a number of ways, and the rest of Figure 13.7 illustrates some of them. The chemical messages can be increased by *agonistic agents* or decreased by *antagonistic agents*. (You should recognize the word "antagonistic" as meaning hostile or unfriendly; in some way this is the effect of antagonistic agents on the chemical messenger service.) *Antagonistic effects* slow down or stop messages from being transmitted by preventing the release of the neurotransmitter, blocking uptake at the level of the dendrite, or causing leaks that reduce the amount of neurotransmitter that is ultimately released. On the other hand, *agonistic effects* assist with the transference of chemical messages and, if extreme, can produce too much neurotransmitter activity by increasing production or release of the neurotransmitter, and by affecting more receptors at the dendrites.

What we've learned about antipsychotic medications points to the possibility that the dopamine system is too active in persons with schizophrenia. The simplified picture in Figure 13.7 does not show that there are actually different receptor sites and that a chemical such as dopamine produces different results depending on which of those sites it affects. In schizophrenia, attention has focused on four dopamine sites, referred to simply as D_1, D_2, D_3, and D_4 loci. As we will see, D_2 is of particular interest to researchers in this field.

In a story that resembles a mystery plot, several pieces of "circumstantial evidence" are clues to the role of dopamine in schizophrenia:

1. Antipsychotic drugs *(neuroleptics)* that are often effective in treating people with schizophrenia are dopamine antagonists, partially blocking the brain's use of dopamine (Creese, Burt, & Snyder, 1976; Seeman, Lee, Chau Wong, & Wong, 1976).
2. These drugs can produce negative side effects similar to those in Parkinson's disease, a disorder that is known to be due to insufficient dopamine.
3. The drug L-dopa, a dopamine agonist that is used to treat people with Parkinson's disease, produces schizophrenia-like symptoms in some people (M. Davidson et al., 1987).

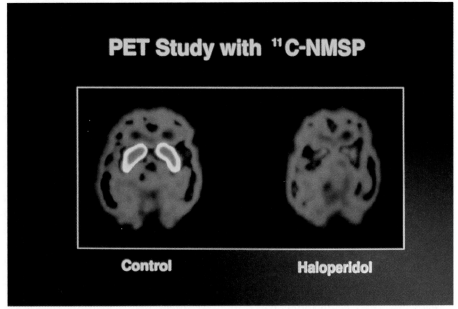

These PET images show the brain of a man with schizophrenia who had never been medicated (left) and after he received halperidol (right). The red and yellow areas indicate activity in the D2 receptors; halperidol evidently reduced dopamine activity.

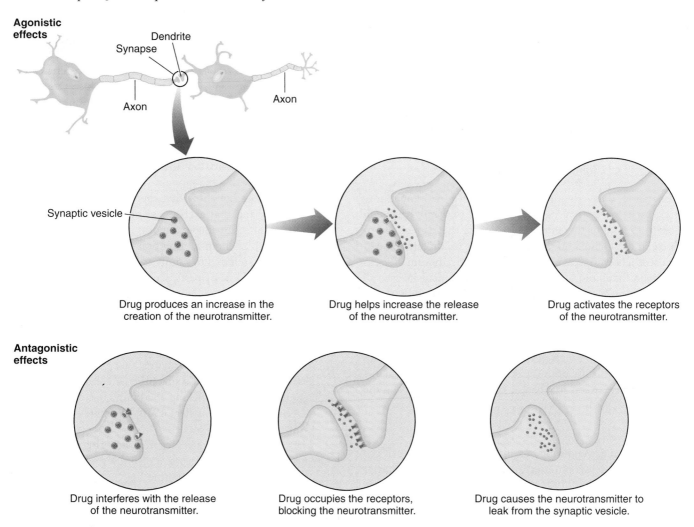

figure 13.7   Some ways drugs affect neurotransmission

4. Amphetamines, which also activate dopamine, can make psychotic symptoms worse in some people with schizophrenia (van Kammen, Docherty, & Bunney, 1982).

In other words, when drugs are administered that are known to increase dopamine (agonists), there is an increase in schizophrenic behavior; when drugs that are known to decrease dopamine activity (antagonists) are used, schizophrenic symptoms tend to diminish. Specifically, the neuroleptic drugs (antagonistic agents) appear to work primarily by blocking one group of dopamine receptors: the D_2 receptors (Bates, Gingrich, Senogles, Falardeau, & Caron, 1991; Carlsson, 1978). Taking these observations together, researchers theorized that schizophrenia in some people was attributable to excessive dopamine activity at the D_2 receptors.

Despite these observations, some evidence contradicts the dopamine theory (Carson & Sanislow, 1993; Davis, Kahn, Ko, & Davidson, 1991):

1. A significant number of people with schizophrenia are not helped by the use of dopamine antagonists.
2. Although the neuroleptics block the reception of dopamine quite quickly, the relevant symptoms subside only after several days or weeks, much more slowly than one would expect.

3. These drugs are only partly helpful in reducing the negative symptoms (for instance, flat affect, anhedonia) of schizophrenia.
4. There is conflicting evidence about whether people with schizophrenia have more D_2 receptors than other people (Crow et al., 1981; Farde et al., 1990).
5. Genetic linkage studies are inconclusive about the connection between schizophrenia and the gene region for D_2 receptors (Su et al., 1993).

In addition to these concerns, there is evidence of a "double-edged sword" with respect to schizophrenia. A medication called *clozapine* is effective with many people who were not helped with traditional neuroleptic medications (Kane, Honigfeld, Singer, & Meltzer, 1988). That's the good news. The bad news for the dopamine theory is that clozapine is one of the weakest dopamine antagonists by far, much less able to block the D_2 sites than other drugs (Creese et al., 1976). Why would a medication that is inefficient at blocking dopamine be effective as a treatment for schizophrenia if schizophrenia is caused by excessive dopamine activity?

The answer may be that although dopamine is involved in the symptoms of schizophrenia, the relationship is more complicated than we once thought (Potter & Manji, 1993).

Several recent studies suggest that two neurotransmitters, *serotonin* and dopamine, and their relationship to each other may account for some of the symptoms of schizophrenia, especially positive ones such as hallucinations and delusions. To describe the complex interaction between these two neurotransmitters and the daunting task of disentangling their effects, we will use a rather unusual analogy—the mail system in the United States.

When neuroscientists study the amount of a neurotransmitter in the brain of a living person they use indirect methods. Because they can't ethically probe the living brain, researchers measure metabolites, the by-products of neurotransmitters, *homovanillic acid (HVA)* for dopamine and *5-hydroxyindoleacetic acid (5-HIAA)* for serotonin, in the cerebrospinal fluid (within the brain and spinal cord). To use our analogy, that's like trying to guess the productivity of the mail system by rummaging through garbage cans in search of empty envelopes and packages. As you can imagine, estimating postal production and effectiveness from the by-products of mail may not yield very accurate results. For example, although the U.S. Postal Service might stop delivery of the mail briefly, this wouldn't necessarily stop the production of garbage because some people temporarily keep envelopes and packages, and dispose of them later. Similarly, neurotransmitters "pool" at the nerve endings. Therefore, even if the production of dopamine or serotonin were interrupted, there might be no decrease in the amounts of HVA and 5-HIAA in cerebrospinal fluid because of the extra reserves.

Dopamine and serotonin are made in relative amounts. Let's call dopamine the U.S. Postal Service and serotonin can be Federal Express. A major snowstorm might slow down both services or temporarily prevent them from delivering mail in that area. In fact, you could complicate the situation even further by supposing that interruption in U.S. mail processing hampers Federal Express, which relies on the U.S. Postal Service. Like it or not, what one delivery service does affects the other. In a comparable way, dopamine and serotonin interact with each other and both are affected by mixed antagonists (snowstorms). Again, trying to learn whether the dopamine system is overactive in people with schizophrenia by studying the HVA metabolite is comparable to looking through garbage cans for mail-related trash. Although they are certainly related, metabolite amounts can't give you a completely accurate measure of dopamine production.

Two recent studies suggest that the dopamine–serotonin relationship may better explain the effects of neuroleptic drugs than looking at the levels of dopamine alone (Hsiao et al., 1993; Kahn et al., 1993). The interaction of these neurotransmitters seems confirmed by research on clozapine, which is effective with difficult cases of schizophrenia but does not block as much dopamine as other neuroleptic medications (Breier et al., 1994). Like the snowstorm, clozapine affects several systems at the same time, so its success may depend on its ability to affect both dopamine and serotonin in just the right combination (T. Lee & Tang, 1984; Peroutka & Snyder, 1980).

Sophisticated research methods like those described in Box 13.1 (see page 424) allows us to refine our understanding of the complex relationship between the neurotransmit-ter systems and schizophrenia by improving our ability to monitor neurotransmitters directly instead of measuring their by-products. New technologies such as in vivo brain receptor imaging and metabolic brain activity mapping involve positron emission tomography and will clarify how these brain chemicals interact and may help us identify more meaningful subtypes (Potter & Manji, 1993).

BRAIN STRUCTURE

Evidence for neurological damage in people with schizophrenia comes from a number of observations (Andreasen, 1997). A child with a parent who has the disorder, and who is thus at risk, tends to show subtle but observable neurological problems such as abnormal reflexes and inattentiveness (Fish, 1977; Hans & Marcus, 1991). These difficulties are persistent: Adults who have schizophrenia show deficits in their ability to perform certain tasks and to attend during reaction time exercises (Cleghorn & Albert, 1990). Such findings suggest that brain damage or dysfunction may cause or accompany schizophrenia, although it is likely that no one site is responsible for the whole range of symptoms (Andreasen, 1997).

One of the most reliable observations about the brain in people with schizophrenia involves the size of the ventricles (see Figure 13.8). As early as 1927, these liquid-filled cavities showed enlargement (see Figure 13.8) in some but not all of the brains that were examined in people with schizophrenia (Jacobi & Winkler, 1927). Since then, more sophisticated techniques have been developed for observing the brain, and in the almost 50 studies that have been conducted on ventricle size, the great majority show abnormally large lateral ventricles in people with schizophrenia (Pahl,

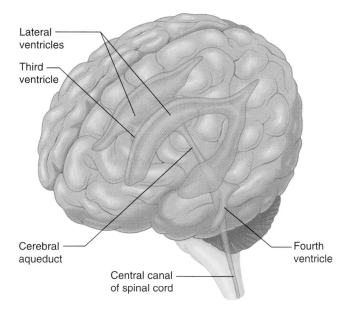

figure 13.8 Location of the cerebrospinal fluid in the human brain. This extracellular fluid surrounds and cushions the brain and spinal cord. It also fills the four interconnected cavities (cerebral ventricles) within the brain and the central canal of the spinal cord.

box 13.1   *The Complexities of Neurotransmitter Research*

Researchers have come a long way in a short time toward understanding the chemistry of schizophrenia. Although we still have many questions, research technology is becoming quite advanced. Researchers at the Bronx Veterans Affairs Hospital recruited 19 male inpatients with schizophrenia to participate in a study (Kahn et al., 1993). The patients agreed to take a neuroleptic medication called Haldol (haloperidol) to learn whether—and how—it helped them. The researchers wanted to study the way the medication worked in the brain to affect dopamine and serotonin levels.

The subjects who were selected for the study, who had shown symptoms of schizophrenia for at least 5 years, had not ingested alcohol or nonprescribed drugs for at least 6 months. The researchers controlled the patients' diets and had them fast for approximately 12 hours before sampling their cerebrospinal fluid, to ensure that their levels of HVA (a metabolite of dopamine) and 5-HIAA (a metabolite of serotonin) would not be affected by food.

A sample of cerebrospinal fluid was extracted from each patient by means of a lumbar puncture. The fluid was used to assess HVA and 5-HIAA levels, which gave researchers the baseline measure of the two metabolites that they would later compare with the metabolite levels after the patients had received neuroleptic medication. Both before and after they were given the Haldol, the patients' schizophrenic symptoms were assessed with the *Brief Psychiatric Rating Scale* so researchers could determine whether changed metabolite levels predicted behavioral improvements.

Two weeks after the symptom assessments (during which time they received no neuroleptic medication), the patients were started on a course of Haldol; 5 weeks later they again had a lumbar puncture and were assessed with the rating scale. HVA and 5-HIAA levels in the cerebrospinal fluid were measured by a machine called a high-performance liquid chromograph, which uses light to identify certain chemicals.

Results showed that Haldol did affect the metabolites, increasing HVA concentrations in the cerebrospinal fluid. This means that dopamine was produced, but that it was prevented by the Haldol from going to the receptors—as if you blocked your mailbox and the mail carrier threw your mail directly into the garbage! However, the researchers found improvements in schizophrenic symptoms only in patients who had more HVA than 5-HIAA. This suggests that blocking dopamine may not by itself reduce schizophrenic symptoms. Rather, you may need to block both dopamine and serotonin, but *you may need to block more dopamine than serotonin.*

Although this study does not answer every question about neurotransmitters and schizophrenia, you should now have an idea of how difficult, but ultimately rewarding (many of the patients improved!), research can be in this highly technical area of schizophrenia.

Swayze, & Andreasen, 1990). Ventricle size in itself may not be a problem, but the dilation (enlargement) of the ventricles indicates that adjacent parts of the brain have either not developed fully or atrophied, thus allowing the ventricles to become larger.

Ventricle enlargement is not seen in everyone who has schizophrenia. Several factors seem to be associated with this finding. For example, enlarged ventricles are observed more often in men than in women (Andreasen et al., 1990). Also, ventricles seem to enlarge in proportion to age and to the duration of the schizophrenia. A recent study found that individuals with schizophrenia who were exposed to influenza prenatally may be more likely to have enlarged ventricles (Takei, Lewis, Jones, Harvey, & Murray, 1996). (We describe the possible role of prenatal exposure to influenza and schizophrenia in the next section.)

In a study of ventricle size, researchers investigating the possible interaction between genes and the physical environment (Suddath, Christison, Torrey, Casanova, & Weinberger, 1990) found 15 pairs of identical twins who were discordant for schizophrenia (only one of each pair had the disorder). Using a brain-imaging technique, magnetic resonance imaging (MRI), researchers showed that in most of the affected twins, the ventricles were enlarged and the an-

terior hippocampus was reduced, but not in the unaffected twins.

We touched on the concept of unshared environments in the section on genetics (Plomin, 1990). Although twins are identical genetically, they can experience a number of environmental differences, even before they are born. For instance, in the intrauterine environment twins must compete for nutrients, and they may not be equally successful. In addition, birth complications, such as the loss of oxygen (anoxia), could affect only one of the twins (Carson & Sanislow, 1993). In fact, obstetrical complications appear often among twins with schizophrenia in discordant identical pairs, and among the more severely affected if both twins have schizophrenia (McNeil, 1987). Different experiences among twins who are already predisposed to the disorder could damage the brain and cause the types of symptoms we associate with schizophrenia.

The frontal lobes of the brain have also interested people looking for structural problems associated with schizophrenia (Gur & Pearlson, 1993). This area may be less active in people with schizophrenia than in people without the disorder, a phenomenon known as *hypofrontality* ("hypo" means less active, or deficient). Research by Weinberger and other scientists at the National Institute of Mental Health further refined this observation, suggesting that deficient activity in a particular area of the frontal lobes, the dorsolateral prefrontal cortex (DLPFC), may be implicated in schizophrenia (Berman & Weinberger, 1990; Weinberger, Berman, & Chase, 1988). When people with and without schizophrenia are given tasks that involve the DLPFC, less activity (measured by cerebral blood flow) is recorded in the brains of those with schizophrenia. Researchers measured DLPFC activity among the 15 twin pairs discussed in the previous section and found that brain activity in all the twins with schizophrenia was lower than in the healthy twins (Weinberger, Berman, Suddath, & Torrey, 1992). Hypofrontality also seems to be associated with the negative symptoms of schizophrenia (Andreasen et al., 1992; Wolkin et al., 1992).

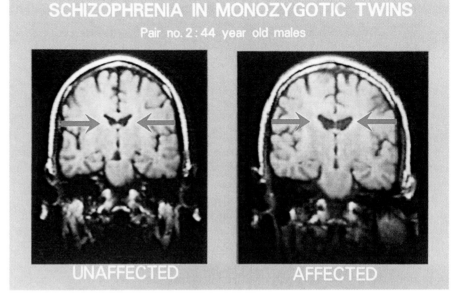

The arrows point to the ventricles, which are normal in the unaffected twin and enlarged in the twin with schizophrenia.

Kenneth Davis and his colleagues integrated research on structural anomalies with research on neurotransmitters (Davis et al., 1991). They note that the prefrontal area that seems less active among many people with schizophrenia is also one site of a major dopamine pathway. They hypothesize that inactivity here activates points on the dopamine pathway that are deeper in the brain (the mesolimbic area). They suggest that the relative inactivity causes the negative symptoms of schizophrenia, and that the excessive activity deeper in the brain accounts for the positive symptoms. Changes in activity at different sites over a number of years would help explain why some people have positive and negative symptoms at different times. This possibility remains theoretical, but it can be tested and may help us put together in a meaningful way apparently disparate observations about the neurobiology of people with schizophrenia.

It appears that several brain sites are implicated in the cognitive dysfunction observed among people with schizophrenia, especially the prefrontal cortex, various other related cortical regions, and subcortical circuits including the thalmus and the stratum (Andreasen, 1997). It is important to remember that this dysfunction seems to occur *prior to the onset* of schizophrenia. In other words, brain damage may develop progressively, beginning before the symptoms of the disorder are apparent, perhaps prenatally (Weinberger, 1995).

VIRAL INFECTION

A curious fact about schizophrenia is that, according to some authors, no adequate descriptions of people having this disorder appear earlier than about 1800 (for example, Gottesman, 1991). If you look at historic records or read ancient literature, you can find people with such disorders as mental retardation, mania, depression, and senile dementia. Even William Shakespeare, who describes most human

conditions, mentions nothing that resembles our current image of schizophrenia. Historically, such an obvious aberration of behavior is puzzlingly absent.

One intriguing hypothesis is that schizophrenia is a recent phenomenon, appearing only during the past 200 years and that, like AIDS, it may involve some newly introduced virus (Gottesman, 1991). In other words, a "schizo-virus" could have caused some cases of this debilitating disorder (Torrey, 1988b). In fact, there is evidence that a virus-like disease may account for some cases (Kirch, 1993). The higher prevalence of schizophrenia among men living in urban areas (Lewis, David, Andreasson, & Allbeck, 1992) implies that they are more likely to have been exposed to infectious agents than their peers in less-populated areas.

Several studies have shown that schizophrenia may be associated with prenatal exposure to influenza. For example, Sarnoff Mednick and his colleagues followed a large number of people after a severe Type A2 influenza epidemic in Helsinki, Finland, and found that those whose mothers were exposed to influenza during the second trimester of pregnancy were much more likely to have schizophrenia than others (T. D. Cannon, Barr, & Mednick, 1991). This observation has been confirmed by some researchers (for instance, O'Callaghan, Sham, Takei, Glover, & Murray, 1991; Venables, 1996) but not by others (for example, Torrey, Rawlings, & Waldman, 1988).

More direct evidence of a link between schizophrenia and influenza comes from research on the brains of deceased people. One group of researchers found, deep in the brains of people with schizophrenia, a certain type of brain cell containing an enzyme called nicotinamide-adenide dinucleotide phosphate-diaphorase (NADPH-d, for short) (Akbarian, Bunney et al., 1993; Akbarian, Vinuela et al.,

1993). Normally, cells containing NADPH-d migrate during mid-pregnancy from inner portions of the brain to the cortex. The observation that in people with schizophrenia the cells have not made this migration suggests a problem during fetal development, perhaps the presence of a viral disease. Another group of researchers studying a different type of brain cell found similar developmental problems in the brains of people with schizophrenia (Scheibel & Conrad, 1993). They note that influenza is one of the few viruses known to disrupt the developmental migration of neurons.

Evidence that second-trimester developmental problems may be associated with schizophrenia has led researchers to look further into this area. Among the types of cells that normally migrate to the cortex during this period are the fingertip dermal cells, which are responsible for the number of fingerprint ridges. Although there is no such thing as an abnormal number of ridges, identical twins generally have the same number. However, if some interruption in second-trimester fetal development resulted in schizophrenia (when, according to the viral theory, a virus may have had its effect), it would also affect the fingertip dermal cells. Recently, researchers compared the fingerprint ridges of identical twins who were discordant for schizophrenia with those of identical twins without schizophrenia (Bracha, Torrey, Gottesman, Bigelow, & Cunniff, 1992). They found that the number of ridges on the fingertips of the twins without schizophrenia differed very little from each other; however, they differed a great deal among about one-third of the twin pairs who were discordant for schizophrenia. This study suggests that ridge count may be a marker of prenatal brain damage. Although there is no characteristic fingerprint for schizophrenia, this physical sign may add to our understanding of the second-trimester conditions that can trigger the genetic predisposition for schizophrenia (Weinberger, 1995).

The indications that virus-like diseases may cause damage to the fetal brain, which later may cause the symptoms of schizophrenia, are, like the circumstantial evidence for the excessive dopamine hypothesis, interesting, and they may help explain why some people with schizophrenia behave the way they do. However, there is not yet enough evidence to show convincingly that there is a "schizo-virus."

Psychological and Social Influences

That one identical twin may develop schizophrenia and the other may not suggests that schizophrenia involves something in addition to genes. We know that early brain trauma, perhaps resulting from a second-trimester virus-like attack or obstetrical complications, may generate physical stress that contributes to schizophrenia. All these observations show clearly that schizophrenia does not fall neatly into a few simple causal packages. For instance, not all people with schizophrenia have enlarged ventricles, nor do they all have a hypofrontality or excessive activity in their dopamine systems. The causal picture may be further complicated by psy-

chological and social factors. We next look at research into psychosocial factors. Do emotional stressors or family interaction patterns *initiate* the symptoms of schizophrenia? If so, how might those factors cause people to relapse after a period of improvement?

HIGH-RISK CHILDREN

In our discussion of genetics, we noted that approximately 13% of the children born to parents who have schizophrenia are likely themselves to develop the disorder. These high-risk children have been the focus of several studies, both *prospective* (before and during an expected situation) and *longitudinal* (over long periods of time).

A classic at-risk study was initiated in the 1960s by Sarnoff Mednick and Fini Schulsinger (Mednick & Schulsinger, 1965, 1968). They identified 207 Danish children of mothers who had severe cases of schizophrenia and 104 control children born to mothers who had no history of the disorder. The average age of these children was about 15 when they were first identified, and the researchers followed them for 10 more years to determine whether any factors had predicted who would and would not develop schizophrenia. We have already discussed pregnancy and delivery-related complications. Mednick and Schulsinger also identified *instability of early family rearing environment,* which suggests that environmental influences may trigger the onset of schizophrenia (Cannon et al., 1991). Poor parenting may place additional strain on a vulnerable person who is already at risk. When the at-risk children in the Danish study enter middle age, we will know the eventual outcomes for all of them; until then we cannot draw strong conclusions from the study (Mirsky, 1995).

It is important to learn how much and what kind of stress makes a person with a predisposition for schizophrenia develop the disorder itself. Think back to the two cases we presented at the beginning of this chapter. Did you notice any precipitating events? Arthur's father had died several years earlier, and he was laid off from his job right around the time his symptoms first appeared. David's uncle had died the same year he began acting strangely. Were these stressful events just coincidences, or did they contribute to the men's later problems?

Researchers have studied the effects of a variety of stressors on schizophrenia. B. P. Dohrenwend and Egri (1981), for instance, observed that otherwise healthy people who engage in combat during a war often display temporary symptoms that resemble those of schizophrenia. In an early study, G. W. Brown and Birley (1968; Birley & Brown, 1970) examined people whose onset of schizophrenia could be dated within a week. These individuals had experienced a high number of stressful life events in the 3 weeks just before they started showing signs of the disorder. In a large-scale study sponsored by the World Health Organization, researchers also looked at the role of life events in the onset of schizophrenia (Day et al., 1987). This cross-national study confirmed the findings of Brown and Birley across eight different research centers.

The *retrospective* nature of such research creates problems. Each study relies on after-the-fact reports, collected after the person showed signs of schizophrenia. One always wonders whether such reports are biased in some way and therefore misleading (Hirsch, Cramer, & Bowen, 1992). One recent study used a *prospective* approach to examine the impact of stress on relapse.

Ventura, Nuechterlein, Lukoff, and Hardesty (1989) identified 30 people with recent-onset schizophrenia and followed them for a 1-year period. The researchers interviewed the subjects every 2 weeks to learn whether they had experienced any stressful life events and whether their symptoms had changed. Notice that, unlike the previous studies, this research examines the factors that predict the recurrence of schizophrenic symptoms after a period of improvement. During the 1-year assessment period, 11 of the 30 people had a significant relapse, in that their symptoms returned or worsened. Like Brown and Birley, Ventura et al. found that relapses occurred when stressful life events increased during the previous month. An important finding is that, although the people experienced more stressful events *as a group* just before their relapse, 55% *did not* have a major life event during the previous month. Other factors must account for the return of symptoms among these people (Bebbington et al., 1993; Ventura, Nuechterlein, Hardesty, & Gitlin, 1992).

FAMILIES AND RELAPSE

There has been a great deal of research on how interactions within the family affect people who have schizophrenia. For example, the term **schizophrenogenic** was used for a time to describe a mother whose cold, dominant, and rejecting nature was thought to cause schizophrenia in her children (Fromm-Reichmann, 1948). In addition, the term **double bind** was used to portray a type of communication style that produced conflicting messages, which, in turn, caused schizophrenia to develop (Bateson, 1959). Here, the parent presumably communicates messages that have two conflicting meanings; for example, a mother responds coolly to her child's embrace, but says, "Don't you love me anymore?" when the child withdraws. Although these theories are no longer supported, they have been—and in some cases continue to be—destructive, producing guilt in parents who are persuaded that their early mistakes caused devastating consequences.

Recent work has focused more on how family interactions contribute, not to the onset of schizophrenia itself, but to relapse after initial symptoms are observed. Research has focused on a particular emotional communication style that is known as **expressed emotion (EE)**. This concept was formulated by George W. Brown and his colleagues in London. Following a sample of people who had been discharged from the hospital after an episode of schizophrenic symptoms, the researchers found that former patients who had limited contact with their relatives did better than the patients who spent longer periods of time with their families (G. W. Brown, 1959). Additional research results indicated that if the level of *criticism* (disapproval), *hostility* (animosity), and *emotional overinvolvement* (intrusiveness) expressed by the families was high, patients tended to relapse (G. W. Brown, Monck, Carstairs, & Wing, 1962).

Other researchers have since found that ratings of high expressed emotion in a family are a good predictor of relapse among people with chronic schizophrenia (Bebbington, Bowen, Hirsch, & Kuipers, 1995). In fact, if you have schizophrenia and live in a family with high expressed emotion, you are 3.7 times more likely to relapse than if you lived in a family with low expressed emotion (Kavanagh, 1992; Parker & Hadzi-Pavlovic, 1990). Below are examples of interviews that show how families of people with schizophrenia might communicate expressed emotion (Hooley, 1985).

High Expressed Emotion
I always say, "Why don't you pick up a book, do a crossword or something like that to keep your mind off it." That's even too much trouble.
I've tried to jolly him out of it and pestered him into doing things. Maybe I've overdone it, I don't know.

Low Expressed Emotion
I know it's better for her to be on her own, to get away from me and try to do things on her own.
Whatever she does suits me.
I just tend to let it go because I know that when she wants to speak she will speak. (Hooley, 1985, pp. 148–149)

The literature on expressed emotion is valuable to our understanding of why symptoms of schizophrenia recur. It may also show us how to treat people with this disorder so that they do not experience further psychotic episodes (Mueser et al., 1993).

An interesting issue that arises when you study family influences is whether what you see is unique to our culture or universal. Looking at expressed emotion across different cultures may help us learn whether it is a *cause* of schizophrenia. Remember that schizophrenia is observed at about the same rate worldwide, with a prevalence of about 1% in the global population. If a factor like high expressed emotion in families is a causal agent, we should see the same rates in families across cultures; in fact, however, they differ, as you can see in Figure 13.9. These data come from an analysis of the concept of expressed emotion in several studies, from India, Mexico, Great Britain, and the United

Jill Hooley of Harvard University is a noted researcher of expressed emotion in families with schizophrenia.

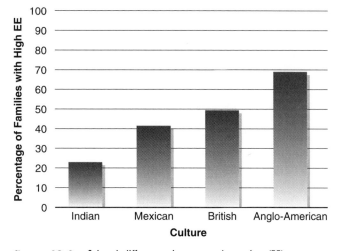

figure 13.9   Cultural differences in expressed emotion (EE)

States (J. H. Jenkins & Karno, 1992). The differences suggest that there are cultural variations in how families react to someone with schizophrenia, and that their reactions do not cause the disorder. However, it seems clear that critical and hostile environments provide additional stressors that can in turn lead to more relapses.

 **Treatment**

If you remember our descriptions of Arthur and David, you will recall their families' concern for them. Arthur's mother spoke of the "living nightmare" and David's aunt expressed concern for both her safety and David's. There is little doubt that in each case there was a desperate desire on the family's part to help, but what do you do for someone who has delusions, hears his dead uncle's voice, or can't communicate complete thoughts? The search for help has taken many paths, sometimes down some very disturbing roads; for example, in the 1500s primitive surgery was conducted to remove the "stone of madness," which was thought to cause disturbed behavior. As barbaric as this practice may seem today, it is not very different from the prefrontal lobotomies performed on people with schizophrenia as late as the 1950s. This procedure severed the frontal lobes from the lower portion of the brain, which sometimes calmed the patient but also caused cognitive and emotional deficits. Even today, some societies use crude surgical procedures to eliminate the symptoms of schizophrenia. In Kenya, for instance, Kisii tribal doctors listen to their patients to find the location of the noises in their heads (hallucinations), then get them drunk, cut out a piece of scalp, and scrape the skull in the area of the voices (Mustafa, 1990).

In the Western world today, treatment usually begins with one of the neuroleptic drugs that are invaluable in re-

ducing the symptoms of schizophrenia for many people. They are typically used in combination with a variety of psychosocial treatments to reduce relapse, compensate for skills deficits, and improve cooperation for taking the medications (Liberman, Kopelowicz, & Young, 1994).

Biological Interventions

Researchers have assumed for over a hundred years that schizophrenia required some form of biological intervention. Emil Kraepelin, who so eloquently described dementia praecox in the late 19th century, saw the disorder as a brain disease. Lacking a biological treatment, he routinely recommended that the physician use "good patience, kindly disposition, and self-control" to calm excited patients (Nagel, 1991). This approach was seen as only a temporary way of helping the person through disturbing times and was not thought to be an actual treatment.

During the 1930s, several novel biological treatments were tried. One approach was to inject massive doses of insulin—the drug used to treat diabetes—to induce comas in people suffering from schizophrenia. *Insulin coma therapy* was thought for a time to be helpful, but closer examination showed that it carried great risk of serious illness and death. During this time *psychosurgery,* including prefrontal lobotomies, was introduced; and in the late 1930s, electroconvulsive therapy (ECT) was advanced as a treatment for schizophrenia. As with earlier drastic treatments, initial enthusiasm for ECT faded as it was found not to be beneficial for most people with schizophrenia—although it is still used with a limited number of people today (Fink & Sackeim, 1996). As we explained in Chapter 7, ECT is sometimes recommended for people who experience very severe episodes of depression.

An early 16th-century painting of psychosurgery, in which part of the brain is removed to treat mental illness.

table 13.2　Antipsychotic Medications

Class	Example*	Degree of Extrapyramidal Side Effects
Conventional Antipsychotics Phenothiazines		
	Fluphenazine/*Prolixin*	high
	Trifluoperazine/*Stelazine*	high
	Perphenazine/*Trilafon*	high
	Mesoridazine/*Serentil*	low
	Chlorpromazine/*Thorazine*	moderate
	Thioridazine/*Mellaril*	low
Butyrophenone		
	Haloperidol/*Haldol*	high
Others		
	Thiothixene/*Navane*	high
	Molindone/*Moban*	low
	Loxapine/*Loxitane*	high
New Antipsychotics		
	Clozapine/*Clozaril*	low
	Risperidone/*Risperdal*	low
	Olanzapine/*Zyprexa*	low
	Sertindole/*Serlect*	low
	Quetiapine/*Seroquel*	low

Adapted from a table in American Psychiatric Association (1997). Practice guidelines for the treatment of patients with schizophrenia. *The American Journal of Psychiatry, 154 (4) Supplement,* 1-63. (pg. 10)
*The trade name is in italics.

A breakthrough in the treatment of schizophrenia came during the 1950s with the introduction of several drugs that relieved symptoms in many people (Potkin et al., 1993). Called *neuroleptics* (meaning "taking hold of the nerves"), these medications provided the first real hope that help was available for people with schizophrenia. When they are effective, neuroleptics help people think more clearly and reduce or eliminate hallucinations and delusions. They work by affecting the positive symptoms (delusions, hallucinations, agitation) and to a lesser extent the negative and disorganized ones, such as social deficits. Table 13.2 shows the classes of these drugs (based on their chemical structure) and their trade names (Potkin et al., 1993).

Recall from our discussion of the dopamine theory of schizophrenia that the neuroleptics are dopamine antagonists. One of their major actions in the brain is to interfere with the dopamine neurotransmitter system. However, they can also affect other systems, such as the serotonergic system. We are just beginning to understand the mechanisms by which these drugs work.

In general, each drug is effective with some people and not with others. Clinicians and patients often must go through a trial and error process to find the medication that works best, and some individuals do not benefit significantly from any of them. The earliest neuroleptic drugs, called conventional antipsychotics, are effective with approximately 60% of persons who try them (American Psychiatric Association, 1997). However, many people are not helped by antipsychotics or have unpleasant side effects. Fortunately, some people respond well to newer medications; the most common are clozapine and risperidone. First marketed in 1990, clozapine is now used widely, and riperidone and other newer drugs hold promise for helping patients who were previously unresponsive to medications (American Psychiatric Association, 1997; Meltzer, 1995). These medications tend to have fewer serious side effects than the conventional antipsychotics (Umbricht & Kane, 1996).

Despite the optimism generated by the effectiveness of antipsychotics, they work only when they are taken properly, and many people with schizophrenia do not routinely take their medication. David frequently "cheeked" the Haldol pills that were helpful in reducing his hallucinations, holding them in his mouth until he was alone, then spitting them out. Approximately 7% of the people prescribed antipsychotic medication refuse to take it at all (Hoge et al., 1990). Research on the prevalence of occasional noncompliance suggests that a majority of people with schizophrenia stop taking their medication from time to time. A recent follow-up study, for example, found that over a 2-year period of time three out of four patients studied refused to take their antipsychotic medication for at least 1 week (Weiden et al., 1991).

A number of factors seem to be related to patients' noncompliance with a medication regimen, including negative doctor–patient relationships, cost of the medication, and poor social support (Weiden et al., 1991). Not

Josh is schizo-affective most of the time. "It's no fun being on meds," he says. "It's like a coffeepot boiling over."

surprisingly, negative side effects are a major factor in patient refusal. Antipsychotics can produce a number of unwanted physical symptoms, such as grogginess, blurred vision, and dryness of the mouth. Because the drugs affect neurotransmitter systems, more serious side effects, called *extrapyramidal symptoms,* can also result (Umbricht & Kane, 1996). These symptoms include the motor difficulties similar to those experienced by people with Parkinson's disease that are sometimes called parkinsonian symptoms. *Akinesia* is one of the most common; it includes an expressionless face, slow motor activity, and monotonous speech (Blanchard & Neale, 1992). Another extrapyramidal symptom is *tardive dyskinesia,* which involves involuntary movements of the tongue, face, mouth, or jaw, and can include protrusions of the tongue, puffing of the cheeks, puckering of the mouth, and chewing movements. Tardive dyskinesia seems to result from long-term use of high doses of antipsychotic medication, is often irreversible, and may occur in as many as 20% of people who take the medications over long periods of time (Morgenstern & Glazer, 1993). Obviously, these very serious negative side effects have justifiably concerned people who otherwise benefit from the drugs.

To learn what patients themselves say, Windgassen (1992) questioned 61 people who had had recent onsets of schizophrenia. About half reported the feeling of sedation or grogginess as an unpleasant side effect: "I always have to fight to keep my eyes open," "I felt as though I was on drugs . . . drowsy, and yet really wound up" (p. 407). Other complaints included deterioration in the ability to think or concentrate (18%), problems with salivation (16%), and blurred vision (16%). Although a third

of the patients felt that the medications were beneficial, about 25% had a negative attitude toward them. A significant proportion of people who could benefit from antipsychotic medications find them unacceptable as a treatment, which may explain the relatively high rates of refusal and noncompliance.

Recently, researchers have made this a major treatment issue in schizophrenia, realizing that medications can't be successful if they aren't taken regularly. Clinicians hoped that the new antipsychotics such as clozapine, which produce fewer negative side effects, would allay some legitimate concerns. However, even clozapine produces undesirable effects, and its use must be monitored closely to avoid rare effects that are potentially life-threatening (Umbricht & Kane, 1996). Researchers hoped compliance rates would improve with the introduction of injectable medications. Instead of taking an oral antipsychotic every day, patients can have their medications injected every few weeks. Unfortunately, noncompliance remains an issue, primarily because patients do not return to the hospital or clinic for repeated doses (Weiden et al., 1991). Psychosocial interventions are now used not only to treat schizophrenia but also to increase medication-taking compliance by helping patients communicate better with professionals about their concerns.

■ concept check 13.4

Read the descriptions and then match them to the following words: (a) clozapine, (b) extrapyramidal symptoms, (c) serotonin, (d) dopamine, and (e) metabolites.

1. Recent studies sometimes indicate that the relationship of the neurotransmitters _____ and _____ may explain some of the positive symptoms of schizophrenia.

2. Spinal fluid from people with schizophrenia can be analyzed for the level of neurotransmitter by-products, which indicates the levels of the neurotransmitters. Such by-products are called _____.

3. Difficult cases of schizophrenia seem to improve with a serotonin and dopamine antagonist called _____.

4. Because antipsychotic medication may cause serious side effects, some patients stop taking them. One serious side effect is called _____, which may have parkinsonian symptoms.

Psychosocial Interventions

Historically, a number of psychosocial treatments have been tried for schizophrenia, reflecting the belief that the disorder results from problems in adapting to the world due to early experiences (Nagel, 1991). Many therapists have thought that individuals who could achieve insight into the presumed role of their personal histories could be safely led to deal with their existing situations. Although clinicians who take a psychodynamic or psychoanalytic approach to therapy continue to use this type of treatment, research suggests that their efforts at best may not be beneficial and at worst may be harmful (Mueser & Berenbaum, 1990; Scott & Dixon, 1995b).

Today, few believe that psychological factors cause people to have schizophrenia or that traditional psychotherapeutic approaches will cure them. We will see, however, that psychological methods do have an important role (Bellack & Mueser, 1993). Despite the great promise of drug treatment, the problems with ineffectiveness, consistent use, and relapse suggest that by themselves drugs may not be effective with many people. As with a number of the disorders discussed in this text, recent work in the area of psychosocial intervention has suggested the value of an approach that uses both kinds of treatment (Liberman, Spaulding, & Corrigan, 1995).

Until relatively recently, most people with severe and chronic cases of schizophrenia were treated in hospital settings. During the 19th century, inpatient care involved "moral treatment," which emphasized improving patients' socialization, helping them establish routines for self-control, and showing them the value of work and religion (Armstrong, 1993). Various types of such "milieu" treatment have been popular but, with one important exception, none seems to have helped people with schizophrenia (Tucker, Ferrell, & Price, 1984).

Gordon Paul and Robert Lentz conducted pioneering work in the 1970s at a mental health center in Illinois (Paul & Lentz, 1977). Borrowing from the behavioral approaches used by Ted Ayllon and Nate Azrin (Ayllon & Azrin, 1968), Paul and Lentz designed an environment for inpatients that encouraged appropriate socialization, participation in group sessions, and self-care such as bed making, while discouraging violent outbursts. They set up an elaborate **token economy,** in which residents could earn access to meals and small luxuries by behaving appropriately. A patient could, for example, buy cigarettes with the tokens he earned for keeping his room neat. On the other hand, a patient would be fined (lose tokens) for being disruptive or otherwise acting inappropriately. This incentive system was combined with a full schedule of daily activities. Paul and Lentz compared the effectiveness of applied behavioral (or *social learning*) principles to traditional inpatient environments. In general, they found that patients who went through their program did better than others on social, self-care, and vocational skills, and more of them could be discharged from the hospital. This study was one of the first to show that people suffering from the debilitating effects of schizophrenia can learn to perform some of the skills they need to live more independently.

During the years since 1955, many efforts have combined to halt the routine institutionalization of people with schizophrenia in the United States (Talbott, 1990). This trend has occurred in part because of court rulings that limit involuntary hospitalization (as we saw in Arthur's case) and in part because of the relative success of antipsychotic medication. The bad news is that policies of deinstitutionalization have often been ill conceived, so that many people who have schizophrenia or other serious psychological disorders are homeless. The good news is that more attention is being focused on supporting these people in their communities, among their friends and families. The trend is away from creating better hospital environments and toward the perhaps more difficult task of addressing complex problems in the less-predictable and insecure world outside. So far, only a small fraction of the growing number of homeless individuals with mental disorders are being helped.

One of the more insidious effects of schizophrenia is its negative impact on a person's ability to relate to other people. Although not as dramatic as hallucinations and delusions, this problem can be the most visible impairment displayed by people with schizophrenia and can prevent them from getting and keeping jobs and making friends. Clinicians attempt to re-teach social skills such as basic conversation, assertiveness, and relationship building to people with schizophrenia (Smith, Bellack & Liberman, 1996).

Therapists divide complex social skills into their component parts, which they model. Then the clients do role playing and ultimately practice their new skills in the "real world," all the while receiving feedback and encouragement at signs of progress. This isn't as easy as it may sound. For

Marsha is excited to have her son home from a psychiatric hospital, but acknowledges that "Now the real struggle begins."

example, how would you teach someone to make a friend? Many skills are involved, such as maintaining eye contact when you talk to someone and providing the prospective friend with some (but not too much!) positive feedback on his or her own behavior ("I really enjoy talking to you"). Such individual skills are practiced and then combined until they can be used naturally (Liberman, DeRisi, & Mueser, 1989). Basic skills can be taught to people with schizophrenia, but there is some disagreement about how ultimately successful the treatment is (Bellack & Mueser, 1992; Hogarty et al., 1992). The problem is that the positive results of social skills training may fade after the training is over (Scott & Dixon, 1995b). The challenge of teaching social skills, as with all therapies, is to maintain the effects over a long period of time.

In addition to social skills, programs often teach a range of ways people can adapt to their disorder yet still live in the community. At the Independent Living Skills Program at the University of California, Los Angeles, for example, the focus is on helping people take charge of their own care by such methods as identifying signs that warn of a relapse and learning how to manage their medication (see Table 13.3) (Corrigan, Wallace, Schade, & Green, 1994; Eckman et al., 1992). Preliminary evidence indicates that this type of training may help prevent relapses by people with schizophrenia,

although longer-term outcome research is needed to see how long the effects last. To address some of the obstacles to this much-desired maintenance, such programs combine skills training with the support of a multidisciplinary team that provides services directly in the community, which seems to reduce hospitalization (Scott & Dixon, 1995a). The more time and effort given to these services, the more likely the improvement (Brekke, Long, Nesbitt, & Sobell, 1997).

In our discussion of the psychosocial influences on schizophrenia we reviewed some of the work linking the person's social and emotional environments to the recurrence of schizophrenic episodes (Bebbington, Bowen, Hirsch, & Kuipers, 1995; Hooley, 1985). It is logical to ask whether families could be helped by learning to reduce their level of expressed emotion, and whether this would result in fewer relapses and better overall functioning for people with schizophrenia. Several studies have addressed these issues in a variety of ways (Falloon et al., 1985; Hogarty et al., 1986; Hogarty et al., 1991), and behavioral family therapy has been used to teach the families of persons with schizophrenia to be more supportive (Dixon & Lehman, 1995; Mueser, Liberman, & Glynn, 1990).

In contrast to traditional therapy, behavioral family therapy resembles classroom education (Falloon et al.,

table 13.3   Independent Living Skills Program at UCLA

Module	Skill Areas	Learning Objectives
Symptom management	Identifying warning signs of relapse	To identify personal warning signs To monitor personal warning signs with assistance from other people
	Managing warning signs	To obtain assistance from health care providers in differentiating personal warning signs from persistent symptoms, medication side effects, and variations in mood; to develop an emergency plan for responding to warning signs
	Coping with persistent symptoms	To recognize and monitor persistent personal symptoms: to obtain assistance from health care providers in differentiating persistent symptoms from warning signs, medication side effects, and variations in mood; to use specific techniques for coping with persistent symptoms To monitor persistent symptoms daily
	Avoiding alcohol and street drugs	To identify the adverse effects of alcohol and illicit drugs and the benefits of avoiding them; to refuse offers of alcohol and street drugs; to know how to resist using these substances in coping with anxiety, low self-esteem, or depression; to discuss openly use of alcohol and drugs with health care providers
Medication management	Obtaining information about antipsychotic medication	To understand how these drugs work, why maintenance drug therapy is used, and the benefits of taking medication
	Knowing correct self-administration and evaluation	To follow the appropriate procedures for taking medication; to evaluate responses to medication daily
	Identifying side effects of medication	To know the specific side effects that sometimes result from taking medication and what to do when these problems occur
	Negotiating medication issues with health care providers	To practice ways of obtaining assistance when problems occur with medication

Source: Eckman et al., 1992.

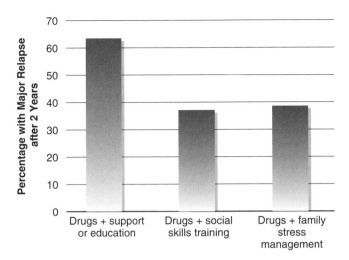

figure 13.10 Studies on treatment of schizophrenia from 1980 to 1992 (from Falloon, Brooker, & Graham-Hole, 1992)

1985). Family members are informed about schizophrenia and its treatment, relieved of the myth that they caused the disorder, and taught practical facts about antipsychotic medications and their side effects. They are also helped with communication skills so they can become more empathic listeners, and they learn constructive ways of expressing negative feelings to replace the harsh criticism that characterizes some family interactions. In addition, they learn problem-solving skills to help them resolve conflicts that arise. Like the research on social skills training, outcome research suggests that the effects of behavioral family therapy are significant during the first year, but less robust 2 years after intervention (Hogarty et al., 1991). This type of therapy, therefore, must be ongoing if patients and their families are to benefit from it (Mueser & Glynn, in press).

Adults with schizophrenia face great obstacles to maintaining gainful employment. Their social skills deficits make reliable job performance and adequate employee relationships a struggle. To address these difficulties, some programs focus on vocational rehabilitation, such as supportive-employment. Providing coaches who give on-the-job training may help some people with schizophrenia maintain meaningful jobs (Bond, Drake, Mueser, & Becker, 1997; Drake, McHugo, Becker, Anthony, & Clark, 1996; Lehman, 1995).

Research suggests that individual social skills training, family intervention, and vocational rehabilitation may be helpful additions to biological treatment for schizophrenia. Significant relapses may be avoided or delayed by such psychosocial interventions. Figure 13.10 illustrates the studies reviewed by one group (Falloon, Brooker, & Graham-Hole, 1992), which show that multilevel treatments reduce the number of relapses among persons receiving drug therapy in comparison with simple social support or educational efforts.

The locus of treatment has expanded over the years from locked wards in large mental hospitals to family homes to local communities. In addition, the services have expanded to include self-advocacy and self-help groups. Former patients have organized programs such as Fountain House in New York City to provide mutual support (Beard, Propst, & Malamud, 1982). Psychosocial clubs have differing models, but all are "person centered" and focus on obtaining positive experiences through employment opportunities, friendship, and empowerment. In just one example, 25,000 New Yorkers over the past 20 years have participated in clubhouses sponsored by the New York Association of Psychiatric Rehabilitation Services. Some research indicates that participation may help reduce relapses (Beard, Malamud, & Rossman, 1978), but as it is also possible that those who participate may be a special group of individuals, it is difficult to interpret improvements (Mueser et al., 1990).

Treatment Across Cultures

Treatment of schizophrenia and its delivery differ from one country to another and across cultures within countries. Hispanics, for example, may be less likely than other groups to seek help in institutional settings, relying instead on family support (Dassori, Miller, & Saldana, 1995). In China, the most frequently used treatment is antipsychotic medication, although 7% to 9% of patients also receive traditional herbal medicine and acupuncture (Mingdao & Zhenyi, 1990). For financial and cultural reasons, more people in China are treated outside the hospital than in Western societies. In many countries in Africa, people with schizophrenia are kept in prisons, primarily because of the lack of adequate alternatives (Mustafa, 1990). In general, the movement away from housing people in large institutional settings to community care is ongoing in most Western countries.

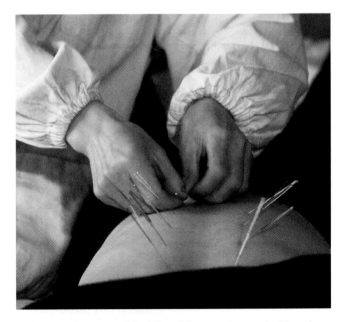

In China, acupuncture and herbal medicine are often used with antipsychotic medications for schizophrenia.

from the inside

When the Music's Over: My Journey into Schizophrenia
By Ross David Burke*

"I'm a paranoid schizophrenic and for us life is a living hell." With these words, Ross David Burke completed his first-person account of his ten-year journey into madness, then took his own life.

Burke began writing *The Truth Effect,* the memoir that forms the core of *When the Music's Over,* as a form of therapy while serving a prison sentence for armed robbery. Published by his psychiatrist at Burke's own request, this harrowing and courageous memoir provides a rare glimpse into the mind of the schizophrenic. "I live in a psychiatric hospital. . . . Society is out to kill me and already my thoughts have begun to hallucinate about this place. . . . My dream is going to take you to a delicate, sensitive world. In my psychosis I am going to take you on a little trip of confusion. A trip into insanity" (p. 26).

With remarkable candor, Burke describes the onset of his illness. "I was out of control, lost in my world of confusion. I realized that something was going wrong with my reasoning. . . . My thoughts jumped" (p. 25). He recounts his delusions and hallucinations. "I believe that I invented rock and roll" (p. 139). "I have a transmitter in my tooth . . ." (p. 162). "I tried to kill my father. I went insane and thought he ruled the world before me and caused World War Two . . ." (p. 198). His account of a psychotic episode in a barber's chair is astoundingly detailed and vivid: "Balls of lightning appeared and disappeared. . . . My mind was in a razzle-dazzle peak of a black and red swirling anxiety attack. . . . I was ashamed of imperfections in myself as the mirror went psychedelic. My reflections broke up into squares and my mind was disassembled, as I flew outward into the square of my mind" (p. 31).

Burke's narrative is frank, and often shocking and disturbing. He depicts his twin obsessions with drugs (LSD, psylocibin mushrooms, marijuana, and heroin) and sexuality in graphic—sometimes pornographic—detail. "We lusted after the flesh. We dug sexual abuse till it burned" (p. 48). "Timing it right, the LSD special came on strong and overtook the confusion of marijuana. . . ." (p. 77). However, his first-hand description of his illness and treatment offer an unusual perspective on the effects of both biological and psychosocial interventions. "Did you know they have medication that can stop you thinking? They are little white pills that take everything away and leave you as a vegetable" (p. 137).

Although in the end Ross Burke lost his battle with schizophrenia, his courage, his unflinching honesty, and his generosity of spirit have provided us with an unprecedented and invaluable insight into this devastating illness.

*Ross David Burke, *When the Music's Over: My Journey into Schizophrenia* (Plume/Penguin, 1995).

Summary

Successful treatment for people with schizophrenia rarely includes complete recovery. However, the quality of life for these individuals can be meaningfully affected by combining antipsychotic medications with psychosocial approaches, employment support, and community-based and family interventions.

- Schizophrenia is characterized by a broad spectrum of cognitive and emotional dysfunctions that include delusions and hallucinations, disorganized speech and behavior, and inappropriate emotions.
- The symptoms of schizophrenia can be divided into "positive," "negative," and "disorganized." Positive symptoms are active manifestations of abnormal behavior, or an excess or distortion of normal behavior, and include delusions and hallucinations. Negative symptoms involve deficits in normal behavior on such dimensions as affect, speech, and motivation. Disorganized symptoms include rambling speech, erratic behavior, and inappropriate affect.
- DSM-IV divides schizophrenia into five subtypes. People with the paranoid type of schizophrenia have prominent delusions or hallucinations while their cognitive skills and affect remain relatively intact. People with the disorganized type of schizophrenia tend to show marked disruption in their speech and behavior; they also show flat or inappropriate affect. People with the catatonic type of schizophrenia have unusual motor responses, such as remaining in fixed positions (waxy flexibility), excessive activity, and being oppositional by remaining rigid. In addition, they display odd mannerisms with their bodies and faces, including grimacing. People who do not fit neatly into these subtypes are classified as having an undifferentiated type of schizophrenia. Some people who have had at least one episode of schizophrenia, but who no longer have major symptoms, are diagnosed as having the residual type of schizophrenia.
- Several other disorders are characterized by psychotic behaviors such as hallucinations and delusions; these include schizophreniform disorder (which includes people who experience the symptoms of schizophrenia for less than 6 months); schizoaffective disorder (which includes people who have symptoms of schizophrenia and who also exhibit the characteristics of mood disorders such as depression and bipolar affective disorder); delusional disorder (which includes people with a persistent belief that is contrary to reality, in the absence of the other characteristics of schizophrenia); brief psychotic disorder (which includes people with one or more positive symptoms such as delusions, hallucinations, or disorganized speech or behavior over the course of less than a month); and shared psychotic disorder (which includes individuals who develop delusions simply as a result of a close relationship with a delusional individual).
- A number of causative factors have been implicated for schizophrenia, including genetic influences, neurotransmit-

ter imbalances, structural damage to the brain caused by a prenatal viral infection or birth injury, and psychological stressors.

• Relapse appears to be triggered by hostile and critical family environments characterized by high expressed emotion.

• Treatment typically involves antipsychotic drugs that are usually administered in combination with a variety of psychosocial treatments, with the goal of reducing relapse and improving skills deficits and compliance in taking the medications. The effectiveness of treatment is limited, as schizophrenia is typically a chronic disorder.

Answers to Concept Checks

13.1
1. delusions
2. avolition
3. affective flattening
4. hallucinations

13.2
1. paranoid
2. catatonic
3. residual
4. disorganized
5. paranoid
6. disorganized
7. undifferentiated
8. catatonic

13.3
1. d, i
2. f, h, greater than
3. a, a

13.4
1. c, d
2. e
3. a
4. b

Key Terms

schizophrenia
catatonia
hebephrenia
paranoia
associative splitting
psychotic
delusion
hallucination
avolition
alogia
anhedonia
flat affect
disorganized speech
inappropriate affect
catatonic immobility
paranoid type of schizophrenia
disorganized type of schizophrenia
catatonic type of schizophrenia
undifferentiated type of schizophrenia
residual type of schizophrenia
schizotypal personality disorder
schizophreniform disorder
schizoaffective disorder
delusional disorder
brief psychotic disorder
shared psychotic disorder (folie à deux)
process schizophrenia
reactive schizophrenia
poor premorbid
good premorbid
positive symptoms
negative symptoms
schizophrenogenic
double bind
expressed emotion (EE)
token economy

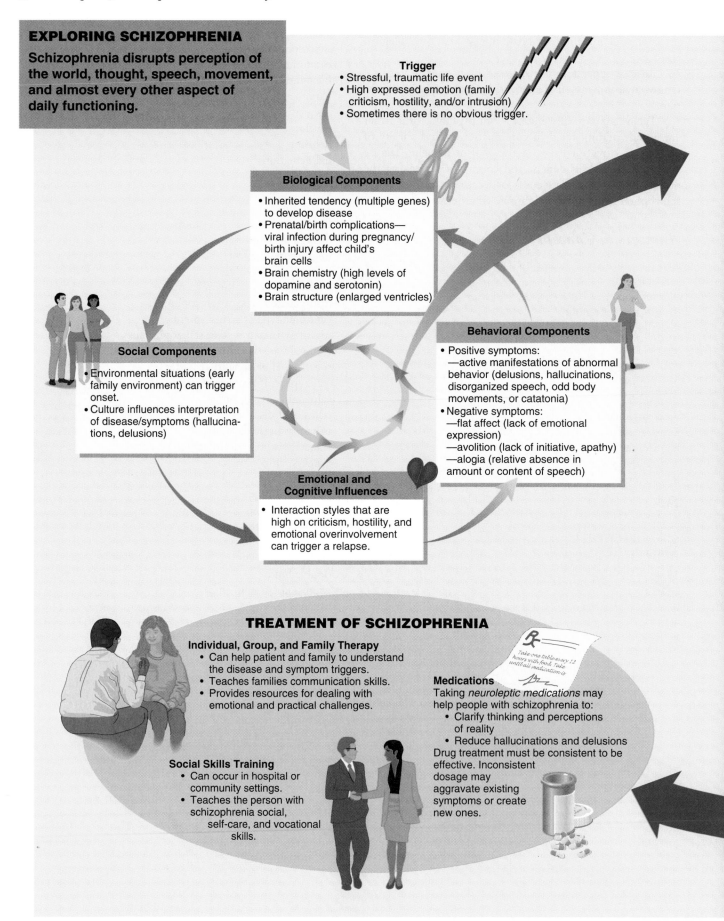

EXPLORING SCHIZOPHRENIA

Schizophrenia disrupts perception of the world, thought, speech, movement, and almost every other aspect of daily functioning.

Trigger
- Stressful, traumatic life event
- High expressed emotion (family criticism, hostility, and/or intrusion)
- Sometimes there is no obvious trigger.

Biological Components
- Inherited tendency (multiple genes) to develop disease
- Prenatal/birth complications— viral infection during pregnancy/ birth injury affect child's brain cells
- Brain chemistry (high levels of dopamine and serotonin)
- Brain structure (enlarged ventricles)

Social Components
- Environmental situations (early family environment) can trigger onset.
- Culture influences interpretation of disease/symptoms (hallucinations, delusions)

Behavioral Components
- Positive symptoms:
  —active manifestations of abnormal behavior (delusions, hallucinations, disorganized speech, odd body movements, or catatonia)
- Negative symptoms:
  —flat affect (lack of emotional expression)
  —avolition (lack of initiative, apathy)
  —alogia (relative absence in amount or content of speech)

Emotional and Cognitive Influences
- Interaction styles that are high on criticism, hostility, and emotional overinvolvement can trigger a relapse.

TREATMENT OF SCHIZOPHRENIA

Individual, Group, and Family Therapy
- Can help patient and family to understand the disease and symptom triggers.
- Teaches families communication skills.
- Provides resources for dealing with emotional and practical challenges.

Medications
Taking *neuroleptic medications* may help people with schizophrenia to:
- Clarify thinking and perceptions of reality
- Reduce hallucinations and delusions

Drug treatment must be consistent to be effective. Inconsistent dosage may aggravate existing symptoms or create new ones.

Social Skills Training
- Can occur in hospital or community settings.
- Teaches the person with schizophrenia social, self-care, and vocational skills.

SYMPTOMS OF SCHIZOPHRENIA

People with schizophrenia do not all show the same kinds of symptoms. Symptoms vary from person to person and may be cyclical. Common symptoms include:

Delusions
- Unrealistic and bizarre beliefs not shared by others in the culture
- May be delusions of grandeur (that you are really Mother Teresa or Napoleon) or delusions of persecution (the cyclist who believed her competitors were sabotaging her by putting pebbles in the road)

Hallucinations
- Sensory events that aren't based on any external event: hearing voices, seeing people who have died
- Many have *auditory hallucinations* (David hears his dead uncle talking to him)

Disorganized Speech
- Jumping from topic to topic
- Talking illogically: not answering direct questions, going off on tangents
- Speaking in unintelligible words and sentences

Behavioral Problems
- Pacing excitably, wild agitation
- Catatonic immobility
- Waxy flexibility: keeping body parts in the same position when they are moved by someone else
- Inappropriate dress: coats in the summer, shorts in the winter
- Ignoring personal hygiene

Withdrawal
- Lack of emotional response: flat speech, little change in facial expressions
- Apathy: little interest in day-to-day activities
- Delayed and very brief responses in conversation
- Loss of enjoyment in pleasurable activities (eating, socializing, sex)

TYPES OF SCHIZOPHRENIA

Paranoid

- Delusions of grandeur or persecution
- Hallucinations (especially auditory)
- Higher level of functioning between episodes

Disorganized
- Disorganized speech and/or behavior
- Immature emotionality (inappropriate affect)
- Chronic and lacking in remissions

Catatonic
- Alternating immobility and excited agitiation
- Unusual motor responses (waxy flexibility, rigidity)
- Odd facial or body mannerisms (often mimicking others)
- Rare

Residual
- Person has had at least one schizophrenic episode but no longer shows major symptoms.
- Still shows "leftover" symptoms: social withdrawal, bizarre thoughts, inactivity, flat affect.

Undifferentiated
- Symptoms of several types that taken together do not neatly fall into one specific category

14

Developmental Disorders

Staring into nothingness since time began,
There and yet not there she stood.
In a world of dreams, shadows, and fantasy,
Nothing more complex than

color and indiscernible sound.
With the look of an angel no doubt,
But also without the ability to love or
Feel anything more complex than the
sensation of cat's fur
Against her face.

Donna Williams
Nobody Nowhere: The Extraordinary
Autobiography of an Autistic

Perspectives

Almost all of the disorders described in this book are developmental disorders in the sense that they change over time. Most disorders originate in childhood, although the full presentation of the problem may not manifest itself until much later. Disorders that show themselves early in life often persist as the person grows older, so the term *childhood disorder* may be a misnomer. In this chapter we cover those disorders that are revealed in a clinically significant way during a child's developing years and are of concern to families and the educational system. Remember, however, that these difficulties often persist through adulthood and are typically lifelong problems, not unique to children.

Again, a number of difficulties and, indeed, distinct disorders begin in childhood. In certain disorders, some children are fine except for difficulties with talking. Others have problems relating to their peers. Still other children have a combination of conditions that significantly hinder their development, as illustrated by the following case.

Timmy
The Boy Who Looked Right Through You

Timmy, a beautiful blonde baby, was born with the umbilical cord wrapped around his neck, so he had been without oxygen for an unknown period of time. Nonetheless, he appeared to be a healthy little boy. His mother later related that he was a very good baby who rarely cried, although she was concerned that he didn't like to be picked up and cuddled. His family became worried about his development when he was 2 years old and didn't talk (his older sister had at that age). They also noticed that he didn't play with other children; he spent most of his time alone, spinning plates on the floor, waving his hands in front of his face, and lining up blocks in a certain order.

The family's pediatrician assured them that Timmy was just developing at a different rate and that he would grow out of it. When, at age 3, Timmy's behavior persisted, his parents consulted a second pediatrician. Neurological examinations revealed nothing unusual but suggested, on the basis of Timmy's delay in learning such basic skills as talking and feeding himself, that he had mild mental retardation.

Timmy's mother did not accept this diagnosis, and over the next few years she consulted numerous other professionals and received numerous diagnoses (including childhood schizophrenia, childhood psychosis, and developmental delay). By age 7, Timmy still didn't speak or play with other children, and he was developing aggressive and self-injurious behaviors. His parents brought him to a clinic for children with severe disabilities. Here, Timmy was diagnosed as having autism.

The clinic specialists recommended a comprehensive educational program of intensive behavioral intervention to help Timmy with language and socialization and to counter his increasing tendency to engage in tantrums. The work continued for approximately 10 years on a daily basis, both at the clinic and at home. During this time Timmy learned to say only three words: "soda," "cookie," and "Mama." Socially, he appeared to like other people (especially adults), but his interest seemed to center on their ability to get him something he wanted, such as a favorite food or drink. If his surroundings were changed in even a minor way, Timmy became disruptive and violent to the point of hurting himself; to minimize his self-injurious behavior, the family took care to ensure that his surroundings stayed the same as much as possible. However, no real progress was made toward eliminating his violent behavior and, as he grew bigger and stronger, he became increasingly difficult to work with; he physically hurt his mother on several occasions. With great reluctance, she institutionalized Timmy when he was 17.

As clinicians have grown to appreciate the far-reaching effects of childhood problems and the importance of early intervention in treating most disorders, they have become more interested in understanding the diversity of severe problems experienced in early life. Timmy was diagnosed with autism in the early 1970s. Two decades later, we know more—though still not enough—about how to help children who have autism. Who can say what the prognosis for Timmy might be today, especially if he were diagnosed correctly at age 2 instead of at age 7?

What Is Normal? What Is Abnormal?

Before we discuss specific disorders, we need to address the broad topic of development in relation to disorders usually first diagnosed in infancy, childhood, or adolescence. What can we learn from such people as Timmy, and what effect do the very early disruptions in their skills have on their later lives? Does it matter when in the developmental period certain problems arise? Are disruptions in development permanent, thus making any hope for treatment doubtful?

Recall that in Chapter 2 we described developmental psychopathology as the study of how disorders arise and how they change with time. Childhood is considered to be particularly important because the brain changes significantly for several years after birth; this is also when critical developments occur in social, emotional, cognitive, and other important competency areas. For the most part, these changes follow a pattern: The child develops one skill before acquiring the next. Although this pattern of change is only one aspect of development, it is an important concept for us at this point because it implies that any disruption in the development of early skills will, by the very nature of this sequential process, disrupt the development of later skills. For example, some researchers believe that people with autism suffer from a disruption in early social development, which prevents them from developing important social relationships, even with their parents. From a developmental perspective, the absence of early and meaningful social relationships has serious consequences. Children whose motivation to interact with others is disrupted may have a more difficult time learning to communicate; that is, they may not want to learn to speak if other people are not important to them. We don't know whether a disruption in communication skills is a direct outcome of the disorder or a by-product of disrupted early social development.

Understanding this type of developmental relationship is important for several reasons. Knowing what skills are disrupted will help us understand the disorder better and may lead to more appropriate intervention strategies. It may be important to identify children with autism at an early age, for example, so their social deficits can be addressed before they affect other skill domains, such as language and communication. Too often, people see early and pervasive disruptions in developmental skills (such as we saw with Timmy), and expect a negative prognosis, with the problems predetermined and permanent. However, it is important to remember that biological and psychosocial influences continuously interact with each other. Therefore, even for disorders such as autism that have clear biological bases, the presentation of the disorder is different for each individual. Changes at the biological or the psychosocial level may reduce the impact of the disorder.

One note of caution is appropriate here. There is real concern in the profession, especially among developmental psychologists, that some workers in the field may view aspects of normal development as symptoms of abnormality. For example, *echolalia*, which involves repeating the speech of others, was once thought to be a sign of autism. However, when you study the development of speech in children without disorders, you find that repeating what someone else says is an intermediate step in language development. In children with autism, therefore, echolalia is just a sign of relatively delayed language skills and not a symptom of their disorder (Durand & Carr, 1988). Here again, knowledge of development is important for understanding the nature of psychological disorders. With that caveat in mind, we now examine several of the disorders usually diagnosed first in infancy, childhood, or adolescence, including *attention deficit/hyperactivity disorder (ADHD)*, which involves characteristics of inattention or hyperactivity and impulsivity, and *learning disorders*, which are characterized by one or more difficulties in areas such as reading and writing. We then focus on *autism*, a more severe disability, in which the

child shows significant impairment in social interactions and communication and restricted patterns of behavior, interest, and activities. Finally, we examine *mental retardation*, which involves significant deficits in cognitive abilities.

Attention Deficit/ Hyperactivity Disorder

Do you know people who flit from activity to activity, who start many tasks but seldom finish one, who have trouble concentrating, and who don't seem to pay attention when others speak? These people may have attention deficit/hyperactivity disorder, one of the most common reasons children are referred for mental health services in the United States (Frick, Strauss, Lahey, & Christ, 1993). The primary characteristics of such people include a pattern of inattention, such as not paying attention to school- or work-related tasks, or of hyperactivity and impulsivity. These deficits can significantly disrupt academic efforts as well as social relationships. Consider the following case.

Danny
The Boy Who Couldn't Sit Still

Danny, a handsome 9-year-old boy, was referred to us because of his difficulties at school and at home. Danny had a great deal of energy and loved playing most sports, especially baseball. Academically his work was adequate, although his teacher reported that his performance was diminishing and she believed he would do better if he paid more attention in class. Danny rarely spent more than a few minutes on a task without some interruption: He would get up out of his seat, rifle through his desk, or constantly ask questions. His peers were frustrated with him because he was equally impulsive during their interactions: He never finished a game and, in sports, he tried to play *all* the positions simultaneously.

At home, Danny was considered a handful. His room was in a constant mess because he became engaged in a game or activity only to drop it and initiate something else. Danny's parents reported that they often scolded him for not carrying out some task, although the reason seemed to be that he forgot what he was doing rather than that he deliberately tried to defy them. They also said that, out of their own frustration, they sometimes grabbed him by the shoulders and yelled "Slow down!" because his hyperactivity drove them crazy.

Clinical Description

Danny has many of the characteristics of attention deficit/hyperactivity disorder. Like Danny, people with this disorder have a great deal of difficulty sustaining their attention on a task or activity (Barkley, 1997). As a result, their tasks are frequently unfinished and they often seem not to be listening when someone else is speaking. In addition to this serious disruption in attention, some people with ADHD also display motor hyperactivity (Mariani & Barkley, 1997). Children with this disorder are often described as fidgety in school, unable to sit still for more than a few minutes. Danny's restlessness in his classroom was a considerable source of concern for his teacher and peers, who were frustrated by his impatience. In addition to hyperactivity and problems sustaining attention, impulsivity—acting apparently without thinking—is a common complaint made about people with ADHD. For instance, during meetings of his baseball team, Danny often shouted out responses to the coach's questions even before the coach had a chance to finish his sentence.

For ADHD, DSM-IV differentiates two clusters of symptoms. The first includes problems of *inattention*. People may appear not to listen to others; they may lose necessary school assignments, books, or tools; and they may not pay enough attention to details, making careless mistakes. The second cluster of symptoms includes *hyperactivity*, which includes fidgeting, having trouble sitting for any length of time, always being on the go, and *impulsivity*, which includes blurting out answers before questions have been completed and having trouble waiting turns. Either the first (inattention) or the second (hyperactivity and impulsivity) cluster must be present for someone to be diagnosed with ADHD.

Inattention, hyperactivity, and impulsivity often cause other problems that appear secondary to ADHD. Academic performance tends to suffer, especially as the child progresses in school. The cause of this poor performance is not known. It could be a result of the problems with attention and impulsivity characteristic of ADHD, or it might be caused by factors such as brain impairment that may be responsible for the disorder itself (Frick et al., 1993). Children with ADHD are likely to be unpopular and rejected by their peers (Carlson, Lahey, & Neeper, 1984; Erhardt & Hinshaw, 1994). Here, however, the difficulty appears to be directly related to the behaviors symptomatic of ADHD, as inattention, impulsivity, and hyperactivity get in the way of establishing and maintaining friendships. Problems with peers combined with frequent negative feedback from parents and teachers often result in low self-esteem among these children (Johnston, Pelham, & Murphy, 1985).

A child with ADHD is likely to behave inappropriately regardless of the setting.

Statistics

Attention deficit/hyperactivity disorder is estimated to occur in 3% to 5% of all children (Cantwell, 1996), with boys outnumbering girls roughly 4 to 1 (Baumgaertel, Wolraich, & Dietrich, 1995). The reason for this large gender difference is unknown. It may be that adults are more tolerant of hyperactivity among girls, who tend to be less active than boys with ADHD. Whether ADHD has a different presentation in girls is as yet unknown, but this may account for the different prevalence rates for girls and boys. Children with ADHD are first identified as different from their peers around age 3 or 4; their parents describe them as very active, mischievous, slow to toilet train, and oppositional (Barkley, 1989). The symptoms of inattention, impulsivity, and hyperactivity become increasingly obvious during the school years. Despite the perception that children grow out of ADHD, their problems usually continue: 75% of adolescents with ADHD have ongoing difficulties at school and at home (G. Weiss & Hechtman, 1986). Over time, children with ADHD seem to be less impulsive, although inattention persists (Hart, Lahey, Loeber, Applegate, & Frick, 1995). Although little research on adults with ADHD is currently available, it appears that 10% of children diagnosed with ADHD will have a clinically significant form of the disorder as adults (Mannuzza, Klein, Bessler, Malloy, & LaPadula, 1993), and that as many as 60% will as adults have such symptoms as difficulties concentrating (Barkley, 1989). One study found that young adults with

> *... I participated too much, but never in the right ways. I chatted incessantly to myself, annoying everyone else.**

*Featured quotations in this chapter are from Donna Williams, *Nobody Nowhere: The Extraordinary Autobiography of an Autistic* (Avon Books, 1992).

ADHD were more likely than individuals without ADHD to have driving difficulties such as crashes, and were more likely to be cited for speeding and have their licenses suspended (Barkley, Murphy, & Kwasnik, 1996). In short, although the manifestations of ADHD change as people grow older, many of their problems persist.

Causes

Numerous theories about the causes of ADHD have been suggested over the years, but only recently has hard evidence become available on the etiology of this disorder. As with many other disorders, we are just beginning to explore the genetics of ADHD. What research we have, however, is suggestive of a hereditary factor. For example, the relatives of children with ADHD have been found to be more likely to have ADHD themselves than would be expected in the general population (Biederman et al., 1992).

For several decades, ADHD has been thought to involve brain damage, and this notion is reflected in the previous use of labels such as "minimal brain damage" or "minimal brain dysfunction" (A. Ross & Pelham, 1981). In recent years, our scanning technology has permitted a sophisticated assessment of the validity of this assumption. Two areas of the brain, the frontal cortex (in the outer portion of the brain) and the basal ganglia (deep within the brain), recently have been associated with ADHD; specifically, a relative lack of activity in these areas has been observed in people with ADHD (Zametkin et al., 1990). Other evidence suggests that portions of the right hemisphere may be malfunctioning (Riccio, Hynd, Cohen, & Gonzalez, 1993), and that frontal lobe development and functioning also may be abnormal (Giedd et al., 1994). Researchers have yet to outline precisely the neurological mechanisms underlying the basic symptoms of ADHD, so we await further breakthroughs in this area.

A variety of such toxins as allergens and food additives have been considered as possible causes of ADHD over the years, although very little evidence supports the association. The theory that food additives such as artificial colors, flavorings, and preservatives are responsible for the symptoms of ADHD has had a substantial impact. Feingold (1975) presented this view along with recommendations for eliminating these substances as a treatment for ADHD. Hundreds of thousands of families have put their children on the Feingold diet, despite evidence that it has little or no effect on the symptoms of ADHD (Barkley, 1990; Kavale & Forness, 1983).

Psychological and social dimensions of ADHD further influence the disorder itself. Negative responses by parents, teachers, and peers to the affected child's impulsivity and hyperactivity may contribute to his or her feelings of low self-esteem (Barkley, 1989). Years of constant reminders by teachers and parents to behave, sit quietly, and pay attention may create a negative self-image in these children, which, in turn, can have a negative impact on their ability to make friends. Thus, the possible biological influences on impulsivity, hyperactivity, and attention, combined with attempts to control these children, may lead to their being rejected and to consequent poor self-image. Research on the psychological and social dimensions of ADHD is currently in its infancy.

Treatment

Treatment for ADHD has proceeded on two fronts: biological and psychosocial interventions. Typically, the goal of biological treatments is to reduce the children's impulsivity and hyperactivity and to improve their attentional skills. Psychosocial treatments generally focus on broader issues such as improving academic performance, decreasing disruptive behavior, and improving social skills. Although these two kinds of approaches have typically developed independently, recent efforts combine them in order to have a broader impact on people with ADHD.

Since the use of stimulant medication with children with ADHD was first described (W. Bradley, 1937), hundreds of studies have documented the effectiveness of this kind of medication in reducing the core symptoms of the disorder. Drugs such as methylphenidate (Ritalin), D-amphetamine (Dexedrine), and pemoline (Cylert) have proven to be helpful for approximately 70% of cases in at least temporarily reducing hyperactivity and impulsivity and improving concentration on tasks (Cantwell, 1996; Swanson et al., 1993). More recent work suggests that other drugs, such as one of the antidepressants (imipramine) and a drug used for treating high blood pressure (clonidine), may have similar effects on people with ADHD (Cantwell, 1996). All these drugs seem to improve compliance and decrease negative behaviors in many children, but they do not appear to produce substantial improvement in learning and academic performance, and their effects do not usually last over the long term.

Originally, it seemed paradoxical or contrary to expectation that children would calm down after taking a stimulant. However, on the same low doses,

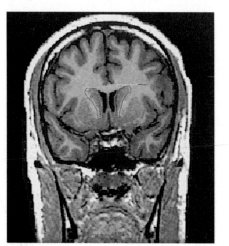
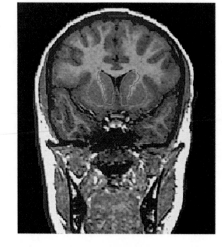

Thanks to brain scan technology we are beginning to understand the neurological aspects of ADHD.

children and adults with and without ADHD react in the same way. It appears that stimulant medications reinforce the brain's ability to focus attention during problem-solving tasks (Mattay, Berman, Ostrem, Esposito, Van-Horn, Bigelow, & Weinberger, 1996). Although the use of stimulant medications remains controversial, especially for children, most clinicians recommend them temporarily, in combination with psychosocial interventions, to help improve children's social and academic skills.

Some portion of children with ADHD do not respond to medications, and most children who do respond do not show gains in the important areas of academics and social skills (Pelham & Milich, 1991). In addition, the medications often result in unpleasant side effects such as insomnia, drowsiness, or irritability (DuPaul, Anastopoulos, Kwasnik, Barkley, & McMurray, 1996). Because of these findings, researchers have applied various behavioral interventions to help these children at home and in school (Fiore, Becker, & Nero, 1993; Garber, Garber, & Spizman, 1996). In general, the programs set such goals as increasing the amount of time the child remains seated, the number of math papers completed, or appropriate play with peers. Reinforcement programs reward the child for improvements and, at times, punish misbehavior with loss of rewards (Braswell & Bloomquist, 1994). Although many children have benefited from these types of programs, others have not, and there is no way to predict which children will respond positively (Fiore et al., 1993). In sum, both medication and behavioral interventions have shortcomings. Most clinicians typically recommend a combination of approaches designed to individualize treatments for children with ADHD, targeting both short-term management issues (decreasing hyperactivity and impulsivity) and long-term concerns (preventing and reversing academic decline and improving social skills). Currently, however, children with ADHD continue to pose a considerable challenge to their families and to the educational system.

■ concept check 14.1

Check your understanding of the different clusters of symptoms that can accompany a diagnosis of attention deficit/hyperactivity disorder. Assign a label of (a) ADHD or (b) ADHD without hyperactivity to each of the following cases.

1. Ten-year-old Michael is frequently off-task in school. He often forgets to bring his homework to school and typically comes home without an important book. He works quickly and makes careless mistakes. _____

2. Nine-year-old Evan can be very frustrating to his parents, teachers, and friends. He often calls out answers in school, sometimes before the complete question is asked. He has trouble waiting his turn during games, and will do things seemingly without thinking. _____

3. Nine-year-old Cathy is described by everyone as a "handful." She fidgets constantly in class, drumming her fingers on the desk, squirming around in her chair, and getting up and down. She has trouble waiting her turn at work or at play, and sometimes has violent outbursts. _____

Learning Disorders

Academic achievement is highly valued in our society. We often compare the performance of our schoolchildren with that of children in other cultures to estimate whether we are succeeding or failing as a world leader and economic force. On a personal level, because parents often invest a great deal of time and emotional energy to assure their children's academic success, it can be extremely upsetting when a child with no obvious intellectual deficits does not achieve as expected. In this section we describe **learning disorders** in reading, mathematics, and written expression—all characterized by performance that is substantially below what would be expected given the person's age, IQ, and education. We also look briefly at disorders that involve how we communicate. Consider the following case.

Alice
Taking a Reading Disorder to College

Alice, a 20-year-old college student, sought help because of her difficulty in several of her classes. She reported that she had enjoyed school and had been a good student up until about the sixth grade, when her grades suffered significantly. Her teacher informed her parents that she wasn't working up to her potential and that she needed to be better motivated. Alice had always worked hard in school but promised to try harder. However, with each report card her mediocre grades made her feel worse about herself. She managed to graduate from high school, but by that time she felt she was not as bright as her friends.

Alice enrolled in the local community college and again found herself struggling with the work. Over the years, she had learned several tricks that seemed to help her study and at least get passing grades. She read the material in her textbooks aloud to herself; she had earlier discovered that she could recall this material much better this way than if she just read silently to herself. In fact, reading silently, she could barely remember any of the details just minutes later.

After her sophomore year, Alice transferred to the university, which she found even more demanding and where she failed most of her classes. After our first meeting, I suggested that she be formally assessed to identify the source of her difficulty. As suspected, Alice had a learning disability. Scores from an IQ test placed her slightly above average, but she was assessed to have significant difficulties with reading. Her comprehension was poor, and she could not remember most of the content of what she read. We recommended that she continue with her trick of reading aloud, because her comprehension for what she heard was adequate. In addition, Alice was taught how to analyze her reading—that is, how to outline and take notes. She was even encouraged to audiotape her lectures and play them back to herself as she drove around in her car. Although Alice did not become an A student, she was able to graduate from the university and she now works with young children who themselves have learning disabilities.

Clinical Description

According to DSM-IV criteria, Alice would be diagnosed as having a **reading disorder,** which is defined as a significant discrepancy between a person's reading achievement and what would be expected for someone of the same age. More specifically, the criteria require that the person read at a level significantly below that of a typical person of the same age, cognitive ability (as measured on an IQ test), and educational background. In addition, this disability cannot be caused by a sensory difficulty such as trouble with sight or hearing. Similarly, DSM-IV defines a **mathematics disorder** as achievement below expected performance in mathematics and a **disorder of written expression** as achievement below expected performance in writing. In each of these disorders, the difficulties are sufficient to interfere with the students' academic achievement and to disrupt their daily activities.

Statistics

Because definitions of learning disorders vary considerably, their incidence and prevalence are difficult to estimate (see Figure 14.1). Very conservatively, there is a 1% to 3% incidence of learning disorders in the United States (Reeve & Kauffman, 1988), although the frequency of this diagnosis appears to increase in wealthier regions of the country (see Figure 14.2). Among school-age children, the prevalence rate is estimated at 10% to 15% (Heaton, 1988), currently believed to include nearly 4 million children in the U.S. alone (NIMH, 1993). Boys are more often identified as having a learning disorder than are girls, and the ratio probably falls between 2:1 and 6:1 boys to girls (Rubin & Balow, 1971). A learning disorder can lead to a number of different outcomes, depending on the extent of the disability and the extent of available support. A recent study found that about 32% of students with learning

disabilities dropped out of school (M. Wagner, 1990). In addition, employment rates for students with learning disorders tend to be discouragingly low, ranging from 60% to 70% (E. Shapiro & Lentz, 1991). The low figure may be due in part to the students' low expectations; one study reported that only 50% of students with learning disabilities had postgraduation plans (E. Shapiro & Lentz, 1991). Some individuals with learning disorders attain their education or career goals; however, this appears to be more difficult for people with severe learning disorders (Spreen, 1988).

Interviews with adults who have learning disabilities reveal that their school experiences were generally negative, and that the effects often lasted beyond graduation. One man who did not have special assistance during school reports:

> I faked my way through school because I was very bright. I resent most that no one picked up my weaknesses. Essentially I judge myself on my failures. . . . [I] have always had low self-esteem. In hindsight I feel that I had low self-esteem in college. . . . I was afraid to know myself. A blow to my self-esteem when I was in school was that I could not write a poem or a story. . . . I could not write with a pen or pencil. The computer has changed my life. I do everything on my computer. It acts as my memory. I use it to structure my life and for all of my writing since my handwriting and written expression has always been so poor. (Polloway, Schewel, & Patton, 1992, p. 521)

A group of disorders that are loosely identified as verbal or communication disorders seem closely related to learning disorders. These disorders can appear deceptively benign, yet their presence early in life can cause wide-ranging problems later on. For a brief overview of these disorders, which include **stuttering, expressive language disorder, selective mutism,** and **tic disorders,** see Box 14.1 on page 446.

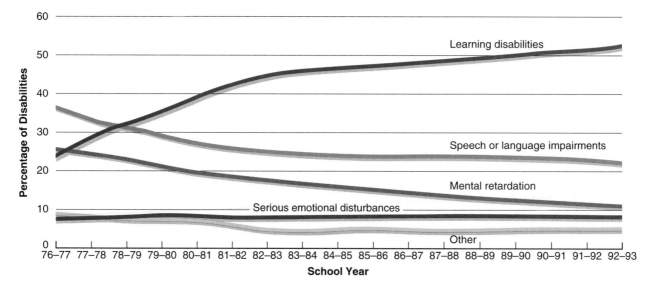

figure 14.1   Growth area. More than half of all schoolchildren classified as disabled have learning disabilities. Twenty-one years ago, the proportion was around 25%.

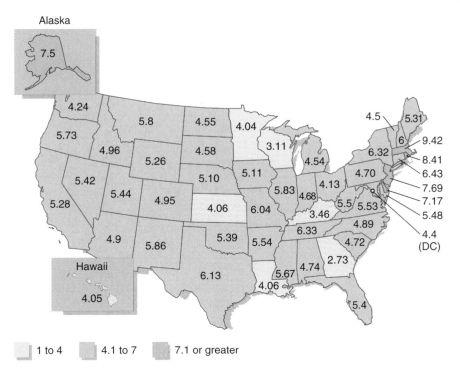

figure 14.2 Uneven distribution. The highest percentages of schoolchildren with learning disabilities are in the wealthiest states.

Causes

Theories about the etiology of learning disorders assume a diverse and complex origin, and include genetic, neurobiological, and environmental factors. For example, *some* disorders of reading may have a genetic basis; the parents and siblings of people with reading disorders are more likely to display these disorders than are relatives of people without reading problems (Reeve & Kauffman, 1988). Pennington and Smith (1988) reported several studies supporting the notion that some aspect of this disorder is inherited, although the exact mechanism may differ across families. Recent research indicates a possible link between reading disorders and genetic material on chromosome 6 (Cardon, Smith, Fulker, Kimberling, Pennington, & Defries, 1994). It is important to remember, however, that problems in learning are extremely diverse, and undoubtably are influenced by both biological and psychosocial influences.

Various forms of subtle brain damage have also been thought to be responsible for learning disabilities; some of the earliest theories involve a neurological explanation (Hinshelwood, 1896). Research suggests structural as well as functional differences in the brains of people with learning disabilities. For example, a recent study looked at children who are delayed in mastering language or reading skills because they are not able to distinguish certain sounds (for example, the difference between "da" and "ga") (Kraus, McGee, Carrell, Zecker, Nicol, & Koch, 1996). The researchers found that the children's brains simply did not register the difference between the sounds, which implies a neuropsychological deficit that interferes with the processing of certain essential language sounds. Such physiological

deficits are not consistent across individuals (Hynd & Semrud-Clikeman, 1989), which is not surprising, given that people with learning disorders display very different types of cognitive problems and therefore probably represent a number of etiological subgroups (NIMH, 1993).

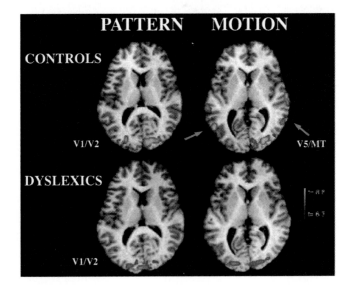

These functional MRI scans of composite data from 6 dyslexic adults and 8 controls show a horizontal slice through the brain, with the face at the top. Imaging shows atypical brain activity associated with dyslexia. The scans were performed while subjects tracked a pattern of moving dots on a computer screen. A brain area (V5/MT) normally active during such motion tasks did not switch on in dyslexic subjects (right). Their brain activity was more similar to that of controls during a pattern recognition task (left).

box 14.1 *Communication and Related Disorders*

STUTTERING
Clinical Description
A disturbance in speech fluency that includes a number of problems with speech, such as repeating syllables or words, prolonging certain sounds, making obvious pauses, or substituting words to replace ones that are difficult to articulate.

Statistics
Occurs twice as frequently among boys as among girls; begins most often in children under the age of 3 (Yairi & Ambrose, 1992); 98% of cases occur before the age of 10 (Mahr & Leith, 1992); approximately 80% of children who stutter before they enter school will no longer stutter after they have been in school a year or so (Yairi & Ambrose, 1992).

Causes
Rather than anxiety causing stuttering, stuttering makes people anxious (S. Miller & Watson, 1992); multiple brain pathways appear to be involved (Fox, Ingham, Ingham, Hirsch, Downs, Martin, Jerabek, Glass, & Lancaster, 1996); genetic influences also may be a factor (Andrews, Morris-Yates, Howie, & Martin, 1991).

Treatment
Psychological: Parents are counseled about how to talk to their children; *regulated-breathing method* is a promising behavioral treatment in which the person is instructed to stop speaking when a stuttering episode occurs and then to take a deep breath (exhale, then inhale) before proceeding (Gagnon & Ladouceur, 1992).
Pharmacological: The serious side effects of haloperidol outweigh any benefit it may offer; verapamil may decrease the severity of stuttering in some individuals (Brady, 1991).

EXPRESSIVE LANGUAGE DISORDERS
Clinical Description
Very limited speech in *all* situations; *expressive language* (what is said) is significantly below their usually average *receptive language* (what is understood).

Statistics
2.2% of 3-year-olds experience this disorder (Silva, 1980); boys are almost five times as likely as girls to be affected (Whitehurst et al., 1988).

Causes
An unfounded psychological explanation is that the children's parents may not speak to them enough; a biological theory is that middle ear infection is a contributory cause.

Treatment
May be self-correcting and may not require special intervention.

SELECTIVE MUTISM
Clinical Description
Persistent failure to speak in very specific situations—such as school—despite the ability to do so.

Statistics
Less than 1% of children; more prevalent among girls than boys; most often between the ages of 5 and 7.

Causes
Not much is known; anxiety is one possible cause (Wilkins, 1985).

Treatment
Contingency management: giving children praise and reinforcers for speaking while at the same time ignoring their attempts to communicate in other ways.

TIC DISORDERS
Clinical Description
Involuntary motor movements *(tics)*, such as head twitching, or vocalizations, such as grunts, that often occur in rapid succession, come on suddenly, and happen in very idiosyncratic or stereotyped ways. In one type, *Tourette's disorder*, vocal tics often include the involuntary repetition of obscenities.

Statistics
Of all children, 12% to 24% show some tics during their growing years (Ollendick & Ollendick, 1990); 2–8 children out of every 10,000 have Tourette's disorder (Leckman, Peterson, Anderson, Arnstein, Pauls, & Cohen, 1997); usually develops before the age of 14. High comorbidity between tics and obsessive–compulsive behavior.

Causes
Inheritance may be through a dominant gene or genes (Bowman & Nurnberger, 1993; Wolf, Jones, Knable, Gorey, Lee, Hyde, Coppola, & Weinberger, 1996).

Treatment
Psychological: self-monitoring, relaxation training, and habit reversal.
Pharmacological: haloperidol and more recently pimozide and clonidine.

We saw that Alice persisted despite the obstacles caused by her learning disorder, as well as by the reactions of teachers and others. What helped her to continue toward her goal when others choose, instead, to drop out of school? Psychological and motivational factors that have been reinforced by others seem to play an important role in the eventual outcome of people with learning disorders. Factors such as socioeconomic status, cultural expectations, parental interactions and expectations, and child management practices, together with existing neurological deficits and the types of support provided in the school, seem to determine outcome (H. Taylor, 1988).

Specially designed computer games may help children with learning disorders improve their language skills.

Treatment

As we will see in the case of mental retardation, learning disorders primarily require educational intervention. Biological treatment is typically restricted to those individuals who may also have attention deficit/hyperactivity disorder, which we have seen involves impulsivity and an inability to sustain attention, and can be helped with certain stimulant medications such as methylphenidate (Ritalin). Educational efforts can be broadly categorized into (a) efforts to directly remediate the underlying basic *processing* of problems (for instance, by teaching students visual and auditory perception skills); (b) efforts to improve *cognitive* skills through general instruction in listening, comprehension, and memory; and (c) targeting the *behavioral* skills needed to compensate for specific problems the student may have with reading, mathematics, or written expression—such as those we discussed in the case of Alice (Reeve & Kauffman, 1988).

We saw in the previous section that some children with learning disorders have difficulties processing language—such as distinguishing certain sounds (for example, the difference between "da" and "ga") (Kraus et al., 1996). Treatment using exercises such as specially designed computer games that help children distinguish among sounds appears to be helpful (Merzenich, Jenkins, Johnston,

Schreiner, Miller, & Tallal, 1996). Considerable research supports the usefulness of teaching the behavioral skills necessary to improve academic skills (Hammill, 1993). For example, children with specific reading problems are taught to re-read material and ask questions about what they read, and are given points or reinforcers for working and improving. Although the prospects of long-term success for any of these approaches await further study, there appears to be room for optimism when it comes to helping children with learning disorders improve their academic abilities (Hammill, 1993).

Autistic Disorder

Autistic disorder, or autism, is a rare childhood disorder that is characterized by significant impairment in social interactions and communication and by restricted patterns of behavior, interest, and activities. Individuals have a puzzling array of symptoms. Consider the following case.

Amy
In Her Own World

Amy, 3 years old, spends much of her day picking up pieces of lint. She drops the lint in the air, and then watches intently as it falls to the floor. She also licks the back of her hands and stares at the saliva. She hasn't spoken yet and can't feed or dress herself. Several times a day she screams so loudly that the neighbors at first thought she was being abused. She doesn't seem to be interested in her mother's love and affection but will take her mother's hand to lead her to the refrigerator. Amy likes to eat butter—whole pats of it, several at a time. Her mother uses the pats of butter that you get at some restaurants to help Amy learn and to keep her well behaved. If Amy helps with dressing herself, or if she sits quietly for several minutes, her mother gives her some butter. Amy's mother knows that the butter isn't good for her, but it is the only thing that seems to get through to the child. The family's pediatrician has been concerned about Amy's developmental delays for some time and has recently suggested that she be evaluated by specialists. The pediatrician feels that Amy may have autism and that the child and her family will probably need extensive support.

Clinical Description

Three major characteristics of autism are expressed in DSM-IV: impairment in social interactions, impairment in communication, and restricted behavior, interests, and activities.

A child with autism is likely to focus away from other people, even parents.

Notice that this child with autism continues to play with a stick he picked up even while he is being helped with his gymnastic moves.

IMPAIRMENT IN SOCIAL INTERACTIONS

One of the defining characteristics of people with autistic disorder is that they do not develop the types of social relationships expected for their age (Waterhouse, Morris, Allen, Dunn, Fein, Feinstein, Rapin, & Wing, 1996). Timmy (whom we discussed at the beginning of this chapter) and Amy never made any friends among their peers and often limited their contact with adults to using them as tools; for example, taking the adult's hand to reach for something they wanted. For many people with autism, the problems they experience with social interactions may be more *qualitative* than *quantitative*. They may have about the same rate of exposure to others as you or your friends, but the way they make contact is unusual. Timmy, for instance, seemed to enjoy sitting on his mother's lap, but he always sat facing away from her rather than taking the face-to-face position that is typical of most children. Although they do not make eye contact and smile at their mothers like children without autism, they still recognize the difference between their mothers and strangers and prefer to be near their mothers in stressful situations (Dissanayake & Crossley, 1996; Sigman & Ungerer, 1984); for example, they will sit near their mothers rather than near strangers after being left alone for a short period of time. This research suggests that people with autism are not totally unaware of others, as we once thought; however, for some reason we do not yet fully understand, they may not enjoy meaningful relationships with others or have the ability to develop them.

. . . although I mimicked everything, it appeared that I was deaf. My parents would stand behind me and make sudden loud noises without my so much as blinking in response. The "world" simply wasn't getting in.

IMPAIRMENT IN COMMUNICATION

People with autism nearly always have severe problems with communicating (Mundy, Sigman, & Kasari, 1990). About 50% are like Timmy, never acquiring useful speech (Rutter, 1978; Volkmar, Klin, Siegel, Szatmari, et al., 1994). In those with some speech, much of their communication is unusual. Some repeat the speech of others, a pattern called *echolalia* we referred to before as a sign of delayed speech development. If you say, "My name is Eileen, what's yours?" they will repeat all or part of what you said: "Eileen, what's yours?" And often, not only are your words repeated, but so is your intonation. Some who can speak are unable or unwilling to carry on conversations with others.

RESTRICTED BEHAVIOR, INTERESTS, AND ACTIVITIES

The more striking characteristics of autism include *restricted patterns of behavior, interests,* and *activities.* Timmy appeared to like things to stay the same; he became extremely upset if even a small change was introduced (such as moving a living room chair a few inches). This intense preference for the status quo has been called *maintenance of sameness.* One parent related that her son with autism liked one particular helicopter from a toy set, and that she had contacted the manufacturer and obtained more than 50 identical helicopters for her son. He would spend hours lining them up, and his mother reported that he could immediately tell if even 1 of the 50 was removed.

In a pose typical of autism, a boy's gaze is fixed on an overhead light.

Temple Grandin has a Ph.D. in animal science and a successful career designing humane equipment for handling livestock. She also has autism.

Often, people with autism spend countless hours in *stereotyped and ritualistic behaviors,* making such stereotyped movements as spinning around in circles, waving their hands in front of their eyes with their heads cocked to one side, or biting their hands. Amy spent hours watching lint fall to the floor. The rituals are often complex: Some people must touch each door as they walk down a hall; others touch each desk in a classroom. If they are interrupted or prevented from completing the ritual, they may have a severe tantrum.

What must it be like to have autism? Is it an exquisite solitude, divorced from the stressors of modern life? Or is it an oppressive state of anxiety, filled with the need to try constantly to maintain sameness in a chaotic world? Such fundamental questions have led some researchers to interview the few rare individuals who have both autism and good verbal abilities, hoping to gain a better understanding of autism in order to aid those who have it.

One such firsthand account is an extensive interview with a 27-year-old man named Jim, who was diagnosed with autism during his preschool years (Cesaroni & Garber, 1991). Jim showed all the typical characteristics, including stereotypic movements, resistance to

At the table, I was looking at a plate of colors, a knife and fork in my hands. I looked through the plate of colors, and everything faded out. Hands disturbed my vision—a silver knife, a silver fork, cutting up color.

change, repetitive play, and social impairments. Because of these unusual behaviors, a psychiatrist had recommended that he be placed in an institution when he was about 9 years old. Despite these obstacles, Jim acquired sufficient skills to complete high school, and at the time the interview was published he was completing graduate studies in developmental psychology! During his interview, Jim explained how he views the world and talked about his own behavior. In describing his sensory impressions, he noted that his processing often gets mixed up: "Sometimes the channels get confused, as when sounds come through as color. Sometimes I know that something is coming in somewhere, but I can't tell right away what sense it's coming through" (Cesaroni & Garber, 1991, p. 305). He observed that not only do his senses sometimes become switched (hearing sounds and interpreting them as seeing colors) but that sometimes they overlap and become distracting: "I have caught myself turning off the car radio while trying to read a road sign, or turning off the kitchen appliances so that I could taste something" (Cesaroni & Garber, 1991, p. 306).

As he was growing up, Jim's stereotyped behaviors included rocking back and forth, twirling around, and swinging his limbs from side to side. He continued to behave this way on a limited basis even into adulthood. He has difficulty explaining why he does these things:

Stereotyped movements aren't things I decide to do for a reason; they're things that happen by themselves when I'm not paying attention to my body. If I'm not monitoring them because I'm worn out, distracted, overwhelmed, intensely focused on something else, or just relaxed and off-guard, then stereotyped movements will occur.

People who are close enough for me to be relaxed and off-guard with can expect to see me acting "weird," while people who only see me in my "public display" mode don't see such behavior. (Cesaroni & Garber, 1991, p. 309)

Social relationships seem to have given Jim the most trouble, and he reports putting in a tremendous amount of effort to improve them. He felt that he had succeeded in establishing meaningful relationships with others, but at great cost. For example, it wasn't until he was 23 that he allowed people to touch him.

Jim's description of his disorder may illustrate what autism is like for most people or only what is unique to him. However, to hear about such experiences is enlightening and helps us gain some insight into the disorder. Jim's account makes us wonder whether the abnormal sensory experiences are responsible for the disrupted social development, for instance. As we gain access to more of these accounts, our understanding of autism should grow, allowing us to offer greater assistance to those with this disorder.

Statistics

Autism is relatively rare, although exact estimates of its occurrence vary. Early research placed the prevalence of this condition at approximately 2 to 5 per 10,000 people (Lotter, 1966). Recent estimates, using contemporary definitions of autistic disorder, have lowered the rate to about 2 per 10,000 people (Gillberg, 1984). Gender differences for autism vary depending on the IQ level of the person affected. For people with IQs under 35, autism is more prevalent among females; in the higher IQ range, it is more prevalent among males. We do not know the reason for these differences (Volkmar, Szatmari, & Sparrow, 1993). Autistic disorder appears to be a universal phenomenon, identified in every part of the world including Sweden (Gillberg, 1984), Japan (Sugiyama & Abe, 1989), Russia (Lebedinskaya & Nikolskaya, 1993), and China (Chung, Luk, & Lee, 1990). The vast majority of people with autism develop the associated symptoms before the age of 36 months (American Psychiatric Association, 1994).

There are people with autism along the continuum of IQ scores. Timmy showed all the classic signs of autism but also seemed to have the cognitive delays characteristic of people with mental retardation, as do three of every four people with autism. Almost half are in the severe to profound range of mental retardation (IQ less than 50), about a quarter test in the mild to moderate range (IQ of 50 to 70), and the remaining people display abilities in the borderline to average range (IQ greater than 70) (Waterhouse, Wing, & Fein, 1989).

IQ measures are used to determine prognosis: The higher children score on IQ tests, the less likely they are to need extensive support by family members or people in the helping professions. Conversely, young children with autistic disorder who score poorly on IQ tests are more likely to be severely delayed in acquiring communication skills and to need a great deal of educational and social support as they grow older. Usually, language abilities and IQ scores are reliable predictors of how children with autistic disorder will fare later in life: The better the language skills and IQ test performance, the better the prognosis.

Timothy plays violin and piano as well as baseball. Autistic disorder occurs in all cultures and races.

I didn't like anyone coming too close to me, let alone touching me. I felt that all touching was pain, and I was frightened.

Autistic disorder is considered a type of **pervasive developmental disorder,** of which there are three other types: **Asperger's disorder, Rett's disorder, and childhood disintegrative disorder.** We are focusing on autistic disorder, on which the most research has been conducted. The other three disorders are highlighted in Box 14.2. People with pervasive developmental disorders all experience problems with language, socialization, and cognition. The word *pervasive* means that these problems are not relatively minor (as in learning disabilities), but significantly affect individuals throughout their lives. There is general agreement children with a pervasive developmental disorder can be identified fairly easily because of the delays in their daily functioning. Picking Timmy out from his nondisabled peers didn't require a great deal of diagnostic sophistication. His lack of speech and his problems interacting with others were obvious by the age of 3. What is not so easily agreed on, however, is how we should define specific subdivisions of the general category of pervasive developmental disorders (Waterhouse, Wing, Spitzer, & Siegel, 1992).

Most specialists agree that autism should remain a separate category. There is less agreement, however, on whether Asperger's disorder, Rett's disorder, or childhood disintegrative disorder are distinctly different conditions. Some believe that they are at different points on an autistic continuum, especially Asperger's disorder. Others believe that there are important differences, and that the disorders should be con-

box 14.2 *Additional Pervasive Developmental Disorders*

ASPERGER'S DISORDER

Clinical Description

Impaired social relationships and restricted or unusual behaviors or activities (such as following airline schedules or memorizing ZIP codes), but without the language delays associated with autism. Individuals show few cognitive impairments and usually have IQ scores within the average range. They often exhibit clumsiness and poor coordination. Some researchers think Asperger's may be a milder form of autism rather than a separate disorder.

Statistics

Prevalence is estimated at 1 per 10,000, which is even less than the rate for autism; it occurs more often in boys than in girls (Volkmar & Cohen, 1991).

Causes

Little causal research exists, though a possible genetic contribution is suspected.

Treatment

Similar to that for autism, though with less need to work on communication and academic skills.

RETT'S DISORDER

Clinical Description

A progressive neurological disorder that primarily affects girls. It is characterized by constant handwringing, increasingly severe mental retardation, and impaired motor skills, all of which appear *after* an apparently normal start in development (Van Acker, 1991). Motor skills seem to deteriorate progressively over time; social skills, however, develop normally at first, decline between the ages of 1 and 3, and then partially improve.

Statistics

Rett's disorder is relatively rare, occurring in approximately 1 per 12,000–15,000 live female births.

Causes

It is unlikely that psychological factors play a role in causation; more likely, it is a genetic disorder involving the X chromosome.

Treatment

Focuses on teaching self-help and communication skills and on efforts to reduce problem behaviors.

CHILDHOOD DISINTEGRATIVE DISORDER

Clinical Description

Involves severe regression in language, adaptive behavior, and motor skills after a 2- to 4-year period of normal development.

Statistics

Very rare, occurring once in approximately every 100,000 births (Kurita, Kita, & Miyake, 1992).

Causes

Though no specific cause has been identified, several factors suggest a neurological origin, with abnormal brain activity in almost half the cases; incidence of seizures is about 10% and may rise to nearly 25% in teenagers (Hill & Rosenbloom, 1986).

Treatment

Typically involves behavioral interventions to regain lost skills and behavioral and pharmacological treatments to help reduce behavioral problems.

---

sidered separately in order to improve research on each one (Rutter & Schopler, 1992).

Causes

Much research has been done on the causes of autism, but to date it has provided little conclusive data. Autism is a puzzling condition, so we should not be surprised to find numerous theories of why it develops. One generalization is that autistic disorder probably does not have a single cause (Rutter, 1978). Instead, there may be a number of biological contributions that combine with psychosocial influences to result in the unusual behaviors of people with autism. Because historical context is important to research, it is helpful to examine past as well as more recent theories of autism. (In doing this, we are departing from our usual format of providing biological dimensions first.)

PSYCHOLOGICAL AND SOCIAL DIMENSIONS

Historically, autistic disorder was seen as the result of failed parenting (Bettelheim, 1967; Ferster, 1961; Tinbergen &

Tinbergen, 1972). Mothers and fathers of children with autism were characterized as perfectionistic, cold, and aloof (Kanner, 1949), with relatively high socioeconomic status (Allen, DeMyer, Norton, Pontius, & Yang, 1971; Cox, Rutter, Newman, & Bartak, 1975), and higher IQs than the general population (Kanner, 1943). Descriptions such as these have inspired theories holding parents responsible for their children's unusual behaviors. These views were devastating to a generation of parents, who felt guilty and responsible for their children's problems. Imagine being accused of such coldness toward your own child as to cause serious and permanent disabilities! More recent research contradicts these studies, suggesting that on a variety of personality measures the parents of individuals with autism may not differ substantially from parents of children without disabilities (Koegel, Schreibman, O'Neill, & Burke, 1983; McAdoo & DeMyer, 1978).

Other theories about the origins of autism were based on the unusual speech patterns of some individuals—namely, their tendency to avoid first-person pronouns such as *I* and *me* and to use *he* and *she* instead. For example, if you ask a child with autism, "Do you want something to drink?"

Many disorders and abnormalities appear during childhood. Some children develop well in all areas except communication. Others have difficulties in social relations. Still others have a combination of deficits that hinder their development significantly. Determine how well you are able to diagnose the disorder in each of the following situations by labeling them autistic disorder, Asperger's disorder, Rett's disorder, Tourette's disorder, selective mutism, or attention deficit/hyperactivity disorder.

1. Five-year-old Sally has a low IQ and enjoys sitting in a corner by herself, where she arranges her blocks in little lines or watches the pump in the fish tank bubble. She cannot communicate verbally, but she throws temper tantrums when her parents try to get her to do something she doesn't want to do. _____

2. Mike's developmental disorder is characterized by uncontrollable yelps, sniffs, and grunting noises. _____

3. Three-year-old Abby has severe mental retardation and trouble walking on her own. One of the characteristics of her disorder is constant handwringing. _____

4. Aaron started the crossword puzzle. Before getting very far, he turned on the TV and flipped through all the channels a few times. Then he pulled out the model he had started a few weeks ago. After a few minutes, he decided to go for a walk. _____

5. Brad's parents first noticed when he was an infant that he did not like to play with the other children, or to be touched or held. He spent most of his time in his playpen by himself. His speech development, however, was not delayed. _____

6. At home, 8-year-old Hanna has been excitedly telling her cousins about a recent trip to a theme park. This would surprise her teachers, who have never heard her speak.

_____

he might say, "He wants something to drink" (meaning "I want something to drink"). This observation led some theorists to wonder whether autism involves a lack of self-awareness (Goldfarb, 1963; M. Mahler, 1952). Imagine, if you can, not understanding that your existence is distinct. There is no "you," only "them"! Such a debilitating view of the world was used to explain the unusual ways people with autism behaved. Theorists suggested that the withdrawal seen among people with autistic disorder reflected a lack of awareness of their own existence.

However, later research has shown that some people with autistic disorder do seem to have self-awareness (Dawson & McKissick, 1984; Spiker & Ricks, 1984), and that it follows a developmental progression. Just like children without a disability, those with cognitive abilities below the level expected for a child of 18 to 24 months show little or no self-recognition, but people with more advanced abilities do demonstrate self-awareness. Self-concept may be lacking when people with autism also have cognitive disabilities or

delays, and not because of autism in itself. Both self-awareness and the affected person's possible lack of attachment to others point to the importance of studying disorders from a developmental perspective. Knowing more about how people *without* autism change over time will help us better understand the people *with* this disorder.

A mythology about people with autism is encouraged when the idiosyncracies of the disorder are highlighted. These perceptions are furthered by portrayals such as Dustin Hoffman's *Rain Man*—his character could, for instance, instantaneously and accurately count hundreds of toothpicks falling to the floor. This type of ability is just not typical with autism. It is important always to separate myth from reality and to be aware that such portrayals do not accurately represent the full range of manifestations of this very complex disorder.

It is also important to distinguish between problems that are a result of delays in development and problems that are a result of autism. For example, we've seen that individuals with autism do acquire some form of attachment to others, although the way it is expressed may be different from the way a typical child would show it.

Another phenomenon that was once thought to be unique to autism is known as *stimulus overselectivity* (Rosenblatt, Bloom, & Koegel, 1995). Some people with autism will respond to a small number of sometimes irrelevant cues when they are learning. It would not be unusual for a child with autism to learn to point to a picture of food to communicate hunger, then later to stop pointing to the picture if it is placed on the right side of the table rather than on the left. In this case, the child seems to overselect the cue of position (left side versus right side) rather than focus on the image in the picture, as if to the child the particular side of the table means "hungry" and not the picture itself. Only after comparing this type of learning in younger normal children and children with mental retardation did researchers realize that it was common among children at an early stage of cognitive development and not an oddity unique to autism (Schover & Newsom, 1976).

The phenomenon of *echolalia,* repeating a word or phrase spoken by another person, was once believed to be an unusual characteristic of this disorder. Subsequent work in developmental psychopathology, however, has demonstrated that repeating the speech of others is part of the normally developing language skills observed in most young children (L. K. Koegel, 1995; Prizant & Wetherby, 1989). Even a behavior as disturbing as the self-injurious behavior sometimes seen in people with autism is observed in milder forms, such as head banging, among typically developing infants (de Lissovoy, 1961). This type of research has helped workers isolate the facts from the myths about autism and clarify the role of development in the disorder. Primarily, it appears that what clearly distinguish people with autism from others are social deficiencies.

At present, few workers in the field of autism believe that psychological or social influences play a major role in the development of this disorder. To the relief of many families, it is now clear that poor parenting is not responsible for autism. Deficits in such skills as socialization and communication appear to be biological in origin. Biological theories about the origins of autism, examined next, have received much empirical support.

BIOLOGICAL DIMENSIONS

A number of different medical conditions have been associated with autism, including congenital rubella (German measles), hypsarhythmia, tuberous sclerosis, cytomegalovirus, and difficulties during pregnancy and labor. However, although a small percentage of mothers exposed to the rubella virus have children with autism, most often no autism is present. We still don't know why certain conditions result in autism sometimes but not always.

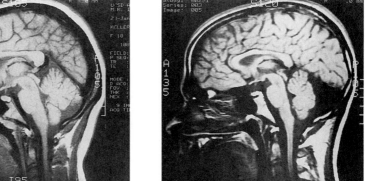

MRIs of two different brains: The person on the left has no neurological disorders, and the person on the right has autism. Note (lower right) that the cerebellum is smaller in the person with autism.

Genetic influences. It is now clear that autism has a *genetic component* (Smalley, 1991). We know that families who have one child with autism have a 3% to 5% risk of having another child with the disorder. When compared to the incidence rate of approximately 0.0002% to 0.0005% in the general population, this rate is evidence of a genetic component in the disorder (Falconer, 1965).

Twin studies have been conducted to assess genetic influences on autistic disorder, although autism is so rare that finding enough people for valid research is extremely difficult. Susan Folstein and Michael Rutter (1977) studied 11 people with autism who had identical (or monozygotic) twins and 10 people with autism who had fraternal (or dizygotic) twins. They found a concordance rate of 36% for the monozygotic twins: In 4 of the 11 twin pairs, both twins had autism. In contrast, they found that none of the dizygotic twin pairs were concordant for autism. Folstein and Rutter also examined the twins for the presence of other developmental and cognitive problems and found that the concordance rate increased to 82% for the monozygotic group and to 10% for the dizygotic group. In other words, when they looked at developmental disorders in general, they found that, if one of the monozygotic twins had autism, the other twin was highly likely to have autism or some other cognitive or developmental problem. This study and others (Herault, Petit, Buchler, Martineau, Cherpi, Perrot, Sauvage, Barthelemy, Muh, & Lelord, 1994; Ritvo, Freeman, Mason-Brothers, Mo, & Ritvo, 1985; Steffenburg et al., 1989) are important because they strongly suggest that autism is inherited. As with so many of the disorders we have examined, the exact nature of the genetic influence on autism is not yet clear to researchers. Current thinking suggests an *autosomal recessive inheritance* (Smalley, 1991).

Neurobiological influences. Evidence that autism is associated with some form of organic (brain) damage comes most obviously from the prevalence of data showing that three of every four people with autism also have some level of mental retardation. In addition, it has been estimated that between 30% and 75% of these people display some neurological abnormality such as clumsiness and abnormal posture or gait (Tsai & Ghaziuddin, 1992). These observations provide suggestive but only correlational evidence that autism is physical in origin. With modern brain-imaging and scanning technologies, a clearer picture is evolving of the possible neurological dysfunctions in people with autism (B. S. Peterson, 1995). Researchers using computerized axial tomography and magnetic resonance imaging technologies have found abnormalities of the cerebellum, including reduced size, among people with autism. Eric Courchesne and his colleagues at the University of California at San Diego examined the brain of a 21-year-old man who had a diagnosis of autism but no other neurological disorders and a tested IQ score in the average range (Courchesne, Hesselink, Jernigan, & Yeung-Courchesne, 1987). He was selected as a subject because he did not have the severe cognitive deficits seen in three-quarters of people with autism. Hence, the researchers could presume that he was free of any brain damage associated with mental retardation but not necessarily with autism. After obtaining the informed consent of this man and his parents, they conducted an MRI scan of his brain. In the MRI scans of a person without autism on the left and of Courchesne's subject on the right, the most striking finding was that the cerebellum of the subject was abnormally small compared with that of a person without autism. Although this kind of abnormality has not been found in every study using brain imaging, it appears to be one of the more reliable findings of brain involvement in autism to date (Courchesne, 1991), and may point out an important subtype of people with autism.

The study of autism is a relatively young field and still awaits an integrative theory. It is likely, however, that further research will identify the biological mechanisms that may ultimately explain the social aversion experienced by many people with the disorder. Also to be outlined are the psychological and social factors that interact very early with the biological influences, producing deficits in socialization and communication as well as the characteristic unusual behaviors.

Treatment

One generalization that can be made about autism is that there is no effective treatment. We have not been successful in eliminating the social problems experienced by people with this disorder. Rather, like the approach to individuals with mental retardation, most efforts at treating people with autism focus on enhancing their communication and daily living skills and on reducing problem behaviors such as tantrums and self-injury (Durand, in press). Some of these approaches are described next, including new work on early intervention for young children with autism.

Psychosocial Treatments

Early psychodynamic treatments were based on the belief that autism was the result of improper parenting, and encouraged ego development (Bettelheim, 1967). Given our current understanding about the nature of the disorder, we should not be surprised to learn that treatments based solely on ego development have not had a positive impact on the lives of people with autism (Kanner & Eisenberg, 1955). Greater success has been achieved with behavioral approaches that focus on skill building and behavioral treatment of problem behaviors. This approach is based on the early work of Charles Ferster and Ivar Lovaas.

Although Ferster's view of the origins of autism is now generally discounted, he provided a valuable perspective by showing that children with this disorder respond to simple behavioral procedures (Ferster & DeMyer, 1961). Ferster used basic, single-case experimental designs, modeling his work after the pigeon and rat learning experiments of B. F. Skinner. He found that he could teach children with autism very simple responses, such as putting coins in the proper slots, by reinforcing them with food (Ferster, 1961). Ivar Lovaas at UCLA took Ferster's findings further by demonstrating their clinical importance. He reasoned that if people with autism responded to reinforcers and punishers in the same way as everyone else, we should be able to use these techniques to help them communicate with us, to help them become more social, and to help them with their behavior problems. Although the work of Ferster and Lovaas has been greatly refined over the past 30 years, the basic premise—that people with autism can learn and that they can be taught some of the skills they lack—remains central. There is a great deal of overlap between the treatment of autism and the treatment of mental retardation. With that in mind, we highlight several treatment areas that are particularly important for people with autism, including communication and socialization.

I could say words but I wanted to communicate. *I wanted to express something. I wanted to let something out. . . . I began to hit myself in frustration—slapping my own face, biting myself, and pulling out my hair.*

Communication.   Problems with communication and language are among the defining characteristics of this dis-

order. As we saw in Timmy's case, people with autism often do not acquire meaningful speech; they tend to have either very limited speech or use unusual speech such as echolalia. Teaching people to speak in a useful way is difficult. Think about how we teach languages: It mostly involves imitation. Imagine how you would teach a young girl to say the word *spaghetti*. You could wait for several days until she said a word that sounded something like "spaghetti" (maybe "confetti"), then reinforce her. You could then spend several weeks trying to shape "confetti" into something closer to "spaghetti." Or you could just prompt, "Say 'spaghetti.'" Fortunately, most children can imitate and learn to communicate very efficiently. But a child who has autism can't or won't imitate.

In the mid-1960s, Lovaas and his colleagues took a monumental first step toward addressing the difficulty of getting children with autism to respond. They used the basic behavioral procedures of *shaping* and *discrimination training* to teach these nonspeaking children to imitate others verbally (Lovaas, Berberich, Perloff, & Schaeffer, 1966). The first skill the researchers taught them was to imitate other people's speech. They began by reinforcing a child with food and praise for making any sound while watching the teacher. After the child mastered that step, they reinforced the child only if she or he made a sound after the teacher made a request—such as the phrase, "Say 'ball'" (a procedure known as discrimination training). Once the child reliably made some sound after the teacher's request, the teacher used shaping to reinforce only approximations of the requested sound, such as the sound of the letter "b." Sometimes the teacher helped the child with physical prompting—in this case, by gently holding the lips together to help the child make the sound of "b." Once the child responded successfully, a second word was introduced—such as "mama"—and the procedure was repeated. This continued until the child could correctly respond to multiple requests, demonstrating imitation by copying the words or phrases made by the teacher. Once the children could imitate, speech was easier, and progress was made in teaching some of them to use labels, plurals, sentences, and other more complex forms of language (Lovaas, 1977). Despite the success of some children in learning speech, other children do not respond to this training, and workers sometimes use alternatives to vocal speech such as sign language and devices that have vocal output and can literally "speak" for the child (Johnson, Baumgart, Helmstetter, & Curry, 1996).

Socialization.   One of the most striking features of people with autism is their unusual reactions to other people. One study compared rates of adolescent interaction among children with autism, those with Down syndrome, and those developing normally; the adolescents with autism

The communication deficits that are typical of autism often lead to social isolation.

showed significantly fewer interactions with their peers (Attwood, Frith, & Hermelin, 1988). Although social deficits are among the more obvious problems experienced by people with autism, limited progress has been achieved toward developing social skills. Behavioral procedures have increased behaviors such as playing with toys or with peers, although the *quality* of these interactions appears to remain limited (Durand & Carr, 1988). In other words, behavioral clinicians have not found a way of teaching people with autism the subtle social skills that are important for interactions with peers—including how to initiate and maintain social interactions that lead to meaningful friendships.

Timing and settings for treatment.   Lovaas and his colleagues at UCLA reported on their early intervention efforts with very young children (Lovaas, 1987). They used intensive behavioral treatment for communication and social skills problems for 40 hours or more per week, which seemed to improve intellectual and educational functioning. Follow-up suggests that these improvements are long-lasting (McEachin, Smith, & Lovaas, 1993). These studies created considerable interest as well as controversy. Some critics question the research on practical as well as experimental grounds, claiming that one-on-one therapy for 40 hours per week was too expensive and time-consuming; they also criticized the studies for having no proper control group. Nevertheless, the results from this important study and a number of replications around the world suggest that early intervention is promising for children with autism (Anderson, Avery, DiPietro, Edwards, & Christian, 1987; Fenske, Zalenski, Krantz, & McClannahan, 1985; Harris, Handleman, Kristoff, Bass, & Gordon, 1990; Hoyson, Jamieson, & Strain, 1984; Rogers & DiLalla, 1991; Rogers & Lewis, 1989; Rogers, Lewis, & Reis, 1987).

Lovaas found that the children who improved most had been placed in regular classrooms, and children who did not do well were placed in separate special education classes. As we will see in our discussion of mental retardation, children

with even the most severe disabilities are now being taught in regular classrooms. In addition, *inclusion*—helping children fully participate in the social and academic life of their peers—applies not only to school but to all aspects of life. Many different models are being used to integrate people with autism in order to normalize their experiences (Durand, in press). For instance, community homes are being recommended over separate residential settings, including special foster care programs (M. D. Smith, 1992), and supported employment options are being tested that would let individuals with autism have regular jobs. The behavioral interventions discussed are essential to easing this transition to fully integrated settings.

BIOLOGICAL TREATMENTS

No one medical treatment has been found to cure autism. In fact, medical intervention has had little success. A variety of pharmacological treatments have been tried, and some medical treatments have been heralded as effective before research has validated them. Although vitamins and dietary changes have been promoted as one approach to treating autism and initial reports were very optimistic, research to date has found little support that they significantly help children with autism (Holm & Varley, 1989).

Because autism may result from a variety of different deficits, it is unlikely that one drug will work for everyone with this disorder. Much current work is focused on finding pharmacological treatments for specific behaviors or symptoms.

INTEGRATING TREATMENTS

The treatment of choice for people with autism combines various approaches to the many facets of this disorder. For children, most therapy consists of school education combined with special psychological supports for problems with communication and socialization. Behavioral approaches have been most clearly documented as benefiting children in this area. Pharmacological treatments can help some of them on a temporary basis. Parents also need support because of the great demands and stressors involved in living with and caring for such children. As children with autism grow older, intervention focuses on efforts to integrate them into the community, often with supported living arrangements and work settings. Because the range of abilities of people with autism is so great, however, these efforts differ dramatically. Some people are able to live in their own apartments with only minimal support from family members. Others, with more severe forms of mental retardation, require more extensive efforts to support them in their communities.

Mental Retardation

Mental retardation is a disorder that is evident in childhood as significantly below-average intellectual and adaptive functioning (Luckasson et al., 1992). People with mental re-

Actor Chris Burke, who has Down syndrome, plays an angel with Down syndrome on the TV show *Touched by an Angel*.

tardation experience difficulties with day-to-day activities, to an extent that reflects both the severity of their cognitive deficits and the type and amount of assistance they receive. Perhaps more than any other group we have studied, people with mental retardation have throughout history received treatment that can best be described as shameful (Scheerenberger, 1983). With notable exceptions, societies throughout the ages have devalued individuals whose intellectual abilities are deemed less than adequate.

The field of mental retardation has undergone dramatic and fundamental changes during the past decade. What it means to have mental retardation, how to define it, and how people with this disorder are treated have been scrutinized, debated, and fought over by a variety of concerned groups. We describe the disorder in the context of these important changes, explaining both the status of people who have mental retardation and our current understanding of how best to understand its causes and treatment.

The manifestations of mental retardation are varied. Some individuals function quite well, even independently, in our complex society, one example being the actor Chris Burke, who starred in the television series *Life Goes On* and appears on *Touched by an Angel*, in which he plays an angel with Down syndrome! Others with mental retardation have significant cognitive and physical impairments and require considerable assistance to carry on day-to-day activities. Consider the case of James.

James
Up to the Challenge

James's mother contacted us because he was disruptive at school and at work. James was 17 and attended the local high school. He had Down syndrome and was described as very likable and, at times, mischievous. He enjoyed skiing,

bike riding, and many other activities common among teenage boys. In fact, his desire to participate was a source of some conflict between him and his mother: He wanted to take the driver's education course at school, which his mother felt would set him up for failure; and he had a girlfriend whom he wanted to date, a prospect that also caused his mother concern.

School administrators complained because James didn't participate in activities such as physical education, and at the work site that was part of his school program he was often sullen, sometimes lashing out at the supervisors. They were considering moving him to a program with more supervision and less independence.

James's family had moved frequently during his youth, and they experienced striking differences in the way each community they lived in responded to James and his mental retardation. In some school districts, he was immediately placed in classes with other children his age and his teachers were provided with additional assistance and consultation. In others, it was just as quickly recommended that he be taught separately. Sometimes the school district had a special classroom in the local school for children with mental retardation. Other districts had programs in other towns, and James would have to travel an hour to and from school each day. Every time he was assessed in a new school, the evaluation was similar to earlier ones. He received scores on his IQ tests in the range of 40 to 50, which placed him in the moderate range of mental retardation. Each school gave him the same diagnosis: Down syndrome with moderate mental retardation. At each school, the teachers and other professionals were competent and caring individuals who wanted the best for James and his mother. Yet some believed that in order to learn skills James needed a separate program with specialized staff. Others felt they could provide a program with specialized staff. Others felt they could provide a comparable education in a regular classroom and that to have peers without disabilities would be an added benefit.

In high school, James had several academic classes in a separate classroom for children with learning problems, but he participated in some classes, such as gym, with students who did not have mental retardation. His current difficulties in gym (not participating) and at work (being oppositional) were jeopardizing his placement in both programs. When I spoke with James's mother, she expressed frustration that the work program was beneath him because he was asked to do boring, repetitive work such as folding paper. James expressed a similar frustration, saying that he was treated like a baby. He could communicate fairly well when he wanted to, although he sometimes would get confused about what he wanted to say, and it was difficult to understand everything he tried to articulate. On observing him at school and at work, and after speaking with his teachers, we realized that a common paradox had developed. James resisted work he thought was too easy. His teachers interpreted his resistance to mean that the work was too hard for him, and they gave him even simpler tasks. He resisted or protested more vigorously, and they responded with even more supervision and structure.

Later, when we discuss treatment, we will return to James, showing how we intervened at school and work to help him progress and become more independent.

Clinical Description

People with mental retardation display a broad range of abilities and personalities. Individuals like James, who have mild or moderate impairments, can, with proper preparation, carry out most of the day-to-day activities expected of any of us. Many can learn to use mass transportation, purchase groceries, and hold a variety of jobs. Those with more severe impairments may need help to eat, bathe, and dress themselves, although with proper training and support they can achieve a degree of independence. These individuals experience impairments that affect most areas of functioning. Language and communication skills are often the most obvious. James was only mildly impaired in this area, needing help with articulation. In contrast, people with more severe forms of mental retardation may never learn to use speech as a form of communication, requiring alternatives such as sign language or special communication devices to express even their most basic needs. Because many cognitive processes are adversely affected, individuals with mental retardation have difficulty learning, the level of challenge depending on how extensive the cognitive disability is.

Before examining the specific criteria for mental retardation, note that, like the personality disorders we described in Chapter 12, mental retardation is included on Axis II of DSM-IV. Remember that separating disorders by axes serves two purposes: first, indicating that disorders on Axis II tend to be more chronic and less amenable to treatment, and second, reminding clinicians to consider whether these disorders, if present, are affecting an Axis I disorder. People can be diagnosed on both Axis I (for instance, generalized anxiety disorder) and Axis II (for example, mild mental retardation).

The DSM-IV criteria for mental retardation are in three groups. First, a person must have *significantly subaverage intellectual functioning,* a determination made with one of several IQ tests with the cutoff score set by DSM-IV at approximately 70 or below. Roughly 2% to 3% of the population score at 70 or below on these tests. The American Association on Mental Retardation (AAMR), which has its own, very similar definition of mental retardation, has a cutoff score of approximately 70 to 75 or below (Luckasson et al., 1992).

The second criterion of both the DSM-IV and AAMR definitions for mental retardation calls for *concurrent deficits or impairments in adaptive functioning.* In other words, scoring "approximately 70 or below" on an IQ test is not sufficient for a diagnosis of mental retardation; a person must also have significant difficulty in at least two of the following areas: communication, self-care, home living, social and interpersonal skills, use of community resources, self-direction, functional academic skills, work, leisure, health, and safety. To illustrate, although James had many strengths, such as his ability to communicate and his social and interpersonal skills (he had several good friends), he was not as proficient as other teenagers at caring for himself in areas such as home living, health, and safety, or in academic areas. This aspect of the definition is important because it excludes people who can function quite well in society but for various reasons do poorly on IQ tests. For instance, someone whose primary language is not English may do poorly on an IQ test but may still function at a level comparable to his or her peers. This person would not be considered to have mental retardation even if he or she scored below 70 on the IQ test.

The final criterion for mental retardation is the *age of onset.* The characteristic below-average intellectual and adaptive abilities must be evident before the person is 18. This cutoff is designed to identify affected individuals during the developmental period, when the brain is developing and therefore when any problems should become evident. The age criterion rules out the diagnosis of mental retardation for adults who suffer from brain trauma or forms of dementia that impair their abilities. The age of 18 is somewhat arbitrary, but it is the age at which most children leave school, when our society considers a person an adult.

The imprecise definition of mental retardation points up an important issue: Mental retardation, perhaps more than any of the other disorders, is defined by society. The cutoff score of 70 or 75 is based on a statistical concept

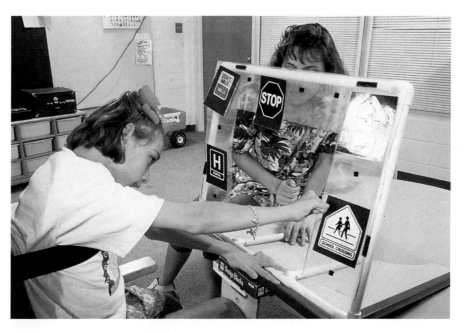

Although she cannot speak, this girl is learning to communicate with an eye-gaze board, pointing to or simply looking at the image that conveys her message.

(two or more standard deviations from the mean) and not on qualities inherent in people who supposedly have mental retardation. There is little disagreement about the diagnosis for people with the most severe disabilities; however, the majority of people diagnosed with mental retardation are in the mild range of cognitive impairment. They need some support and assistance, but it is important to remember that the criteria for using the label of "mental retardation" are based partly on a somewhat arbitrary cutoff score for IQ that can (and does) change with changing social expectations.

People with mental retardation differ significantly in their degree of disability. Almost all classification systems have differentiated these individuals in terms of their ability or on the etiology of the mental retardation (Hodapp & Dykens, 1994). Traditionally (and still evident in the DSM-IV), classification systems have identified four levels of mental retardation: *mild*, which is identified by an IQ score between 50 or 55 and 70; *moderate*, with a range of 35–40 to 50–55; *severe*, ranging from 20–25 up to 35–40; and *profound*, which includes people with IQ scores below 20–25. It is difficult to categorize each level of mental retardation according to "average" individual achievements by people at each level. A person with severe or profound mental retardation tends to have extremely limited formal communication skills (no spoken speech or only one or two words) and may require great or even total assistance in dressing, bathing, and eating. Yet people with these diagnoses have a wide range of skills that depend on training and the availability of other supports. Similarly, people like James, who have mild or moderate mental retardation, should be able to live independently or with minimal supervision; again, however, their achievement depends in part on their education and the community support available to them.

Perhaps the most controversial change in the AAMR definition of mental retardation is its description of different levels of this disorder, which are based on the level of support or assistance people need: *intermittent, limited, extensive,* or *pervasive* (Luckasson et al., 1992). You may recognize parallels with the DSM-IV levels of mental retardation, including the use of four categories. Thus, someone who needs only intermittent support is in AAMR terms similar to a person labeled by DSM-IV as having mild mental retardation. Similarly, the categories of limited, extensive, and pervasive support may be analogous to the levels of moderate, severe, and profound mental retardation. The important difference is that the AAMR system identifies the role of "needed supports" in determining level of functioning, whereas DSM-IV implies that the ability of the person is the sole determining factor. The AAMR system focuses on specific areas of assistance that a person needs that can then be translated into training goals. Whereas his DSM-IV diagnosis might be "moderate mental retardation," James might receive the following AAMR diagnosis: "a person with mental retardation who needs limited supports in home living, health and safety, and in academic skills." The AAMR definition emphasizes the types of support James and others require, and it highlights the

need to identify what assistance is available when considering a person's abilities and potential. However, at this writing, the AAMR system has not been assessed empirically to determine whether it has greater value than traditional systems.

An additional method of classification has been used in the educational system to identify the abilities of students with mental retardation. It relies on three categories: *educable mental retardation* (based on an IQ of 50 to approximately 70–75), *trainable mental retardation* (IQ of 30 to 50), and *severe mental retardation* (IQ below 30) (Cipani, 1991). The assumption was that students with educable mental retardation (comparable to mild mental retardation) could learn basic academic skills; students with trainable mental retardation (comparable to moderate mental retardation) could not master academic skills but could learn rudimentary vocational skills; and students with severe mental retardation (comparable to severe and profound mental retardation) would not benefit from academic or vocational instruction. Built into this categorization system is the automatic negative assumption that certain individuals cannot benefit from certain types of training. This system and the potentially stigmatizing and limiting DSM-IV categories (mild, moderate, severe, and profound mental retardation) inspired the AAMR categorization of needed supports. Current trends are away from the educational system of classification, because it inappropriately creates negative expectations in teachers. Clinicians continue to use the DSM-IV system; we have yet to see whether the AAMR categories will be widely adopted.

■ concept check 14.3

Different degrees of mental retardation are identified in DSM-IV, each one determined by the level of intellectual impairment. Different IQ levels require different amounts of support (as determined by the AAMR). In the following situations, label each level of mental retardation as either mild, moderate, severe, or profound. Also label the corresponding levels of necessary support: intermittent, limited, extensive, or pervasive.

1. Bobby received an IQ score of 45. He lives in a fully staffed group home, and needs a great deal of help with many tasks. He is beginning to receive training for a job in the community. _____ / _____

2. James received an IQ score of 20. He needs help with all his basic needs, including dressing, bathing, and eating. _____ / _____

3. Robin received an IQ score of 65. He lives at home, goes to school, and is preparing to work when he is through with school. _____ / _____

4. Katie received an IQ score of 30. She lives in a fully staffed group home where she is trained in basic adaptive skills and communication. She is improving over time and can communicate by pointing or using her eye-gaze board. _____ / _____

Mental retardation can be defined in terms of the level of support people need.

Statistics

Prevalence rates for mild mental retardation (IQ of 50 to 70) are about 3 to 4 per 1,000 people, with a comparable combined prevalence for those with moderate, severe, and profound mental retardation (IQ below 50)—a total of 6 to 8 per 1,000, or less than 1% of the population (McLaren & Bryson, 1987).

The course of mental retardation is chronic, meaning that people do not recover. However, the prognosis for people with this disorder varies considerably. Given appropriate training and support, individuals with less severe forms can live relatively independent and productive lives. People with more severe impairments require more assistance in order to participate in work and community life. Mental retardation is observed more often among males, with a male-to-female ratio of about 1.6 to 1 (Laxova, Ridler, & Bowen-Bravery, 1977). This difference may be present mainly among people with mild mental retardation; no gender differences are found among people with severe forms (Richardson, Katz, & Koller, 1986).

Causes

There are literally hundreds of known causes of mental retardation, including the following.

> *Environmental:* for example, deprivation, abuse, and neglect

> *Prenatal:* for instance, exposure to disease or drugs while still in the womb
> *Perinatal:* such as difficulties during labor and delivery
> *Postnatal:* for example, infections, head injury

As we mentioned in Chapter 11, heavy use of alcohol among pregnant women can produce a disorder in their children called *fetal alcohol syndrome,* a condition that can lead to severe learning disabilities. Other prenatal factors that can produce mental retardation include the pregnant woman's exposure to disease and chemicals, and poor nutrition. In addition, lack of oxygen (anoxia) during birth, and insults such as malnutrition and head injuries during the developmental period, can lead to severe cognitive impairments. Despite the rather large number of known causes of mental retardation, one fact must be kept in mind: Nearly 75% of cases either cannot be attributed to any known cause or are thought to be the result of social and environmental influences (Zigler & Hodapp, 1986). Most of the affected individuals have mild mental retardation and are sometimes referred to as having cultural–familial mental retardation (see page 462).

BIOLOGICAL DIMENSIONS

Genetic influences. Most researchers believe that people with mental retardation probably are affected by multiple gene disorders in addition to environmental influences (Abuelo, 1991). However, a portion of the people with more severe mental retardation have identifiable single-gene disorders, involving genes that are *dominant* (expresses itself when paired with a normal gene), *recessive* (expresses itself only when paired with another copy of itself), or *X-linked* (present on the X or sex chromosome).

Only a few dominant genes result in mental retardation, probably as a result of natural selection: Someone who carries a dominant gene that results in mental retardation is less likely to have children and thus less likely to pass the gene to offspring. Therefore, this gene becomes less likely to continue in the population. However, some people, especially those with mild mental retardation, do marry and have children, thus passing on their genes. One example of a dominant gene disorder, *tuberous sclerosis,* is relatively rare, occurring in 1 of approximately every 30,000 births. About 60% of the people with this disorder have mental retardation (Vinken & Bruyn, 1972), and most have seizures (uncontrolled electrical discharges in the brain) and characteristic bumps in their skin that during adolescence resemble acne.

The next time you drink a diet soda, notice the warning, "Phenylketonurics: Contains Phenylalanine." This is a caution for people with the recessive disorder called *phenylketonuria* or PKU, which affects 1 of every 14,000 newborns and is characterized by an inability to break down a chemical in our diets called *phenylalanine.* Until the mid-1960s, the majority of people with this disorder had mental retardation, seizures, and behavior problems, resulting from high levels of this chemical. However, researchers developed a screening technique that identifies the existence of PKU; infants are now routinely tested at birth, and any individuals identified with PKU can be successfully treated with a special diet that avoids the chemical phenylalanine. This is a rare example of the successful prevention of one form of mental retardation.

Ironically, successful early identification and treatment of people with PKU during the past three decades has some worried that an outbreak of PKU-related mental retardation will recur. The special diet to prevent symptoms is necessary only until the person reaches age 6 or 7. At this point, people tend to become lax and eat a regular diet—fortunately, with no harmful consequences for themselves. Because untreated maternal PKU can harm the developing fetus (Lenke & Levy, 1980), there is concern now that women with PKU who are of childbearing age may not stick to their diets and inadvertently cause PKU-related mental retardation in their children before birth. Many physicians now recommend dietary restriction through the childbearing period—thus the warnings on products with phenylalanine (Abuelo, 1991).

Lesch-Nyhan syndrome, an X-linked disorder, is characterized by mental retardation, signs of cerebral palsy (spasticity or tightening of the muscles), and self-injurious behavior, including finger and lip biting (Nyhan, 1978). Only males are affected, because a recessive gene is responsible; when it is on the X chromosome in males it does not have a normal gene to balance it because males do not have a second X chromosome. Women with this gene are carriers and do not show any of the symptoms.

As our ability to detect genetic defects improves, more disorders will be identified genetically. The hope is that our

An adult with Down syndrome.

increased knowledge will be accompanied by improvements in our ability to treat or, as in the case of PKU, prevent mental retardation and other negative outcomes.

Chromosomal influences.   It was only about 40 years ago that the number of chromosomes—46—was correctly identified in human cells (Tjio & Levan, 1956). Three years later, researchers found that people with Down syndrome (the disorder James displayed) had an additional small chromosome (Lejeune, Gauthier, & Turpin, 1959). Since that time, a number of other chromosomal aberrations that result in mental retardation have been identified. We describe Down syndrome and fragile X syndrome in some detail, but there are hundreds of other ways in which abnormalities among the chromosomes can lead to mental retardation.

Down syndrome, the most common chromosomal form of mental retardation, was first identified by the British physician Langdon Down in 1866. Down had tried to develop a classification system for people with mental retardation based on their resemblance to people of other races; he described individuals with this particular disorder as "mongoloid" because they resembled people from Mongolia (Scheerenberger, 1983). The term *mongoloidism* was used for some time but has been replaced with the term *Down syndrome.* The disorder is caused by the presence of an extra 21st chromosome and is therefore sometimes referred to as *trisomy 21.* For reasons we don't completely understand, during cell division two of the 21st chromosomes stick together (a condition called *nondisjunction*), creating one cell with one copy that dies, and one cell with three copies that divide to create a person with Down syndrome.

People with Down syndrome have characteristic facial features, including folds in the corners of their upwardly slanting eyes, a flat nose, and a small mouth with a flat roof that makes the tongue protrude somewhat. Like James, they tend to have congenital heart malformations. Tragically, nearly *all* adults with Down syndrome past the age of 40 show signs of dementia of the Alzheimer's type, a degenerative brain disorder that causes impairments in memory, and other cognitive disorders (Visser, Aldenkamp, van Huffelen, Kuilman, Overweg, & van Wijk, 1997). This disorder among people with Down syndrome occurs earlier than

Rates of Down Syndrome Births

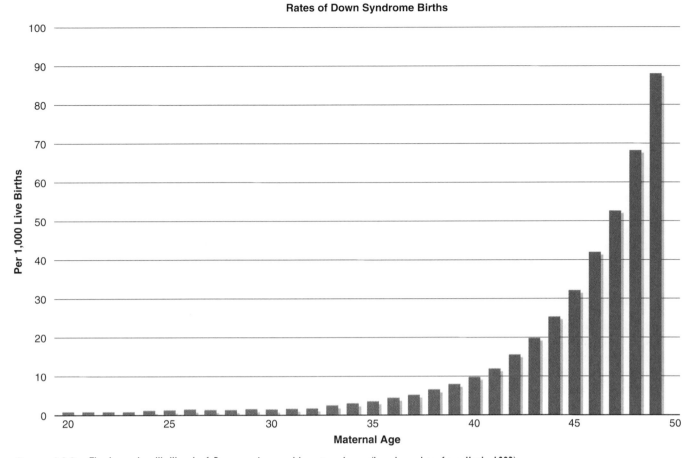

figure 14.3   The increasing likelihood of Down syndrome with maternal age (based on data from Hook, 1982)

usual (sometimes in their early 20s) and has led to the finding that at least one form of Alzheimer's disease is attributable to a gene on the 21st chromosome.

The incidence of children born with Down syndrome has been tied to maternal age: As the age of the mother increases, so does her chance of having a child with this disorder (Figure 14.3). A woman at age 20 has a 1 in 2,000 chance of having a child with Down syndrome; at the age of 35 this risk increases to 1 in 500, and at the age of 45 it increases again to 1 in 18 births (J. A. Evans & Hammerton, 1985; Hook, 1982). Despite these numbers, many more children with Down syndrome are born to younger mothers because, as women get older, they tend to have fewer children. The reason for the rise in incidence with maternal age is not clear. Some suggest that because a woman's ova (eggs) are all produced in youth, the older ones have been exposed to toxins, radiation, and other harmful substances over longer periods of time. This exposure may interfere with the normal meiosis (division) of the chromosomes, creating an extra 21st chromosome (Pueschel & Goldstein, 1991). Others believe that the hormonal changes that occur as women age are responsible for this error in cell division (Crowley, Hayden, & Gulati, 1982).

For some time it has been possible to detect the presence of Down syndrome—but not the degree of mental retardation—through **amniocentesis,** a procedure that involves removing and testing a sample of the fluid that surrounds the fetus in the amniotic sac. Down syndrome and a number of other disorders can be detected through amniocentesis.

Fragile X syndrome is a second common chromosomally related cause of mental retardation (Dykens, Leckman, Paul, & Watson, 1988). As its name suggests, this disorder is caused by an abnormality on the X chromosome, a muta-

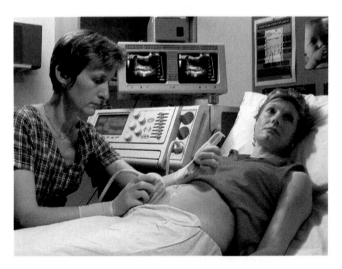

Amniocentesis can detect the presence of Down syndrome in a fetus. Guided by an ultrasound image, the doctor withdraws amniotic fluid for analysis.

tion that makes the tip of the chromosome look as though it were hanging from a thread, giving it the appearance of fragility (Sutherland & Richards, 1994). As with Lesch-Nyhan syndrome, which also involves the X chromosome, fragile X primarily affects males because they do not have a second X chromosome with a normal gene to balance out the mutation. Unlike Lesch-Nyhan carriers, however, women who carry fragile X syndrome commonly display mild to severe learning disabilities (S. E. Smith, 1993). Men with the disorder display moderate to severe levels of mental retardation and also have higher rates of hyperactivity, short attention spans, gaze avoidance, and perseverative speech. In addition, such physical characteristics as large ears, testicles, and head circumference are also common. Estimates are that 1 of every 2,000 males is born with fragile X syndrome (Dykens et al., 1988).

Psychological and Social Dimensions

Cultural–familial retardation is the presumed cause of up to 75% of the cases of mental retardation and is perhaps the least understood (Scott & Carran, 1987). Individuals with cultural–familial retardation tend to score in the mild mental retardation range on IQ tests and have relatively good adaptive skills (Zigler & Cascione, 1984). Their mental retardation is thought to result from a combination of psychosocial and biological influences, although the specific mechanisms that lead to this type of mental retardation are not yet understood. The cultural influences that may contribute to this condition include abuse, neglect, and social deprivation.

It is sometimes useful to consider people with mental retardation in two distinct groups: those with cultural–familial retardation, and those with biological (or "organic") forms of mental retardation. People in the latter group have more severe forms of mental retardation that are usually traceable to known causes such as fragile X syndrome. Figure 14.4 shows that the cultural–familial group is composed primarily of individuals at the lower end of the IQ continuum, whereas in the organic group genetic, chromosomal, and other factors affect intellectual performance. The organic group increases the number of people at the lower end of the IQ continuum so that it exceeds the expected rate for a normal distribution (Zigler & Hodapp, 1986).

Two views of cultural–familial retardation further our understanding of this phenomenon. The *difference view* holds that those with cultural–familial retardation have a subset of deficits, such as attentional (Fisher & Zeaman, 1973) or memory problems (Ellis, 1970), that represents a limited portion of the larger set of deficiencies experienced by people with more severe forms of mental retardation. In other words, these individuals *differ* from people without mental retardation in terms of specific damage, and they are similar to people with more severe retardation. In contrast, the *developmental view* sees the mild mental retardation of people with cultural–familial retardation as simply a difference in the rate and ultimate ceiling of an otherwise

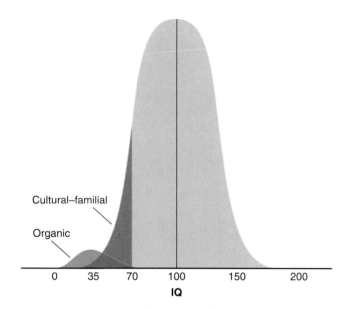

figure 14.4 The actual distribution of IQ scores for individuals with cultural-familial retardation and organic retardation. Note that the cultural-familial group represents the normal expected lower end of the continuum, but the organic group is a separate and overlapping group (adapted from Zigler & Hodapp, 1986).

normal developmental sequence (Zigler & Balla, 1982). Put another way, as children these individuals go through the same developmental stages as people without mental retardation, but they do so at a slower pace and do not attain all the skills they probably would have developed in a more supportive environment (Zigler & Stevenson, 1993). Support is mixed for both these views of the nature of cultural–familial retardation. Much is still not understood about people with cultural–familial retardation; future work may reveal important subgroups among them.

Treatment

Direct biological treatment of mental retardation is currently not a viable option. However, given recent advances in genetic screening and technology, it may someday be possible to detect and ultimately correct genetic and chromosomal abnormalities. For example, a recent study used mice with a disease similar to an inherited enzyme deficiency (Sly disease) found in some individuals with mental retardation. Researchers found that they could transplant healthy brain cells into the diseased young mice to correct the disease (Snyder, Taylor, & Wolfe, 1995). Someday it may be possible for similar research to be performed prenatally on children identified as having syndromes associated with mental retardation (Simonoff, Bolton, & Rutter, 1996).

Generally, the treatment of individuals with mental retardation parallels that of people with autism, attempting to teach them the skills they need to become more productive and independent. For individuals with mild mental retardation, intervention is similar to that for people with learning disorders. Specific learning deficits are identified and addressed to help the student improve such skills as reading and writing. At the same time, these individuals often need additional support to live in the community. For people with more severe disabilities, the general goals are the same; however, the level of assistance they need is frequently more extensive. Remember that the expectation for all people with mental retardation is that they will in some way participate in community life, attend school and later hold a job, and have the opportunity for meaningful social relationships. Advances in electronic and educational technologies have made this goal realistic even for people with profound mental retardation.

Early intervention can target and assist children who, because of inadequate environments, are at risk for developing cultural–familial retardation (Fewell & Glick, 1996; Ramey & Ramey, 1992). The national Head Start program is one such effort at early intervention; it combines educational, medical, and social supports for these children and their families. One project identified a group of children shortly after birth and provided them with an intensive preschool program along with medical and nutritional supports. This intervention continued until the children began formal education in kindergarten (Martin, Ramey, & Ramey, 1990). The authors of this study found that for all but one of the children in a control group who received medical and nutritional support but not the intensive educational experiences, each had IQ scores below 85 at age 3, but 3-year-olds in the experimental group all tested above 85. Obviously, such findings are important because they show the potential for creating a lasting impact on the lives of these children and their families. Other prevention strategies include genetic counseling services, prenatal care, biological screening methods such as amniocentesis, and drug prevention and treatment programs for women of childbearing age (Crocker, 1992).

People with mental retardation can acquire skills through the many behavioral innovations first introduced in the early 1960s to teach such basic self-care as dressing, bathing, feeding, and toileting to persons with even the most severe disabilities (Reid, Wilson, & Faw, 1991). The skill is broken into its component parts (a procedure called a *task analysis*) and the person is taught each part in succession until he or she can perform the whole skill. Performance on each step is encouraged by praise and by access to objects or activities the person desires (reinforcers). Success in teaching these skills is usually measured by the level of independence the person can attain by using them. Typically, most individuals, regardless of their disability, can be taught to perform some skills.

Communication training is very important for people with mental retardation. Making their needs and wants known is essential for personal satisfaction and for participation in most social activities. The goals of communication training differ, depending on the existing skills. For people with mild levels of mental retardation, the goals may be relatively minor (for instance, improving articulation) or more extensive (for instance, organizing a conversation) (Abbeduto & Rosenberg, 1992). Some, like James, have communication skills that are already adequate for day-to-day needs.

For individuals with the most severe disabilities, this type of training can be particularly challenging, as they may have multiple physical or cognitive deficits that make spoken communication difficult or impossible (Warren & Reichle, 1992). Creative researchers, however, use alternative systems that may be easier for these individuals, including the sign language used primarily by people with hearing disabilities and *augmentative communication strategies*. Augmentative strategies may use picture books, teaching the person to make a request by pointing to a picture—for instance, pointing to a picture of a cup to request a drink (Reichle, Mirenda, Locke, Piche, & Johnston, 1992). A variety of computer-assisted devices can be programmed so that the individual presses a button to produce complete spoken sentences (for example, "Would you come here? I need your help."). People with very limited communication skills can be taught to use these devices, which helps them reduce the frustration of not being able to relate their feelings and experiences to other people (Durand, 1993).

Concern is often expressed by parents, teachers, and employers that some people with mental retardation can be physically or verbally aggressive or may hurt themselves. Considerable debate has ensued over the proper way to reduce these behavior problems; the most heated discussions

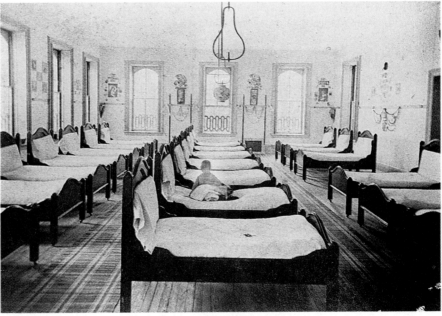

The Illinois Asylum for Feeble-Minded Children, about 1880. Today, great efforts are made to keep children with mental retardation in their homes and communities.

involve whether to use painful punishers (Repp & Singh, 1990). Alternatives to punishment that may be equally effective in reducing behavior problems such as aggression and self-injury (Durand, 1990) include teaching people how to communicate their need or desire for such things as attention that they seem to be getting with their problem behaviors. To date, however, no treatment or treatment package has proven successful in all cases, although important advances are being made in significantly reducing even severe behavior problems for some people.

In addition to ensuring that people with mental retardation are taught specific skills, caretakers also focus on the important task of supporting them in their communities. "Supported employment" involves helping an individual find and satisfactorily participate in a competitive job (Bellamy, Rhodes, Mank, & Albin, 1988). Research has shown that not only can people with mental retardation be placed in meaningful jobs but that, despite the costs associated with supported employment, it can ultimately be cost-effective. One study found that for every dollar invested in supported employment, $2.21 was returned in taxes (McCaughrin, 1988). The benefits to people who achieve the satisfaction of being a productive part of society are incalculable.

There is general agreement about *what* should be taught to people with mental retardation. The controversy in recent years has been over *where* this teaching should take place. Should people with mental retardation especially the severe forms, be taught in specially designed separate classrooms or workshops, or should they attend their neighborhood public schools and work at local businesses? More and more, teaching strategies to help these students learn are being used in regular classrooms and in preparing them to work at jobs in the community (L. Meyer, Peck, & Brown, 1991). There is at present no cure for mental retardation, but the current prevention and treatment efforts suggest that meaningful changes can be achieved in the lives of these people.

Summary

Normal and Abnormal Development
- Developmental psychopathology is the study of how disorders arise and change with time. These changes usually follow a pattern, with the child mastering one skill before acquiring the next. This aspect of development is important because it implies that any disruption in the acquisition of early skills will, by the very nature of the developmental process, also disrupt the development of later skills.

Attention Deficit/Hyperactivity Disorder
- The primary characteristics of people with attention deficit/hyperactivity disorder are a pattern of inattention (such as not paying attention to school- or work-related tasks) or hyperactivity–impulsivity, or both. These deficits can significantly disrupt academic efforts and social relationships.

Learning Disorders
- DSM-IV groups the learning disorders as reading disorder, mathematics disorder, and disorder of written expression. All are defined by performance that falls far short of expectations based on intelligence and school preparation.
- Verbal or communication disorders seem closely related to learning disorders. They include stuttering, a disturbance in speech fluency; expressive language disorder, very limited speech in all situations but without the types of cognitive

deficits that lead to language problems in people with mental retardation or one of the pervasive developmental disorders; selective mutism, refusal to speak despite having the ability to do so; and tic disorders, which include involuntary motor movements such as head twitching, and vocalizations such as grunts, that occur suddenly, in rapid succession, and in very idiosyncratic or stereotyped ways.

Pervasive Developmental Disorder

• People with pervasive developmental disorder all experience trouble progressing in language, socialization, and cognition. The use of the word *pervasive* means that these are not relatively minor problems (like learning disabilities) but conditions that significantly affect how individuals live. Included in this group are *autistic disorder, Rett's disorder, Asperger's disorder,* and *childhood disintegrative disorder.*

• Autistic disorder, or autism, is a childhood disorder characterized by significant impairment in social interactions, gross and significant impairment in communication, and restricted patterns of behavior, interest, and activities. It probably does not have a single cause; instead, a number of biological conditions may contribute, and these, in combination with psychosocial influences, result in the unusual behaviors displayed by people with autism.

• Asperger's disorder is characterized by impairments in social relationships and restricted or unusual behaviors or activities, but it does not present the language delays observed in people with autism.

• Rett's disorder, almost exclusively observed in females, is a progressive neurological disorder that is characterized by constant handwringing, mental retardation, and impaired motor skills.

• Childhood disintegrative disorder involves severe regression in language, adaptive behavior, and motor skills after a period of normal development for approximately 2 to 4 years.

Mental Retardation

• The definition of mental retardation has three parts: significantly subaverage intellectual functioning, concurrent deficits or impairments in present adaptive functioning, and an onset before the age of 18.

• Down syndrome is a type of mental retardation caused by the presence of an extra 21st chromosome. It is possible to detect the presence of Down syndrome in utero through a process known as amniocentesis.

• Two other types of mental retardation are common: fragile X syndrome, which is caused by a chromosomal abnormality of the tip of the X chromosome, and cultural–familial retardation, the presumed cause of up to 75% of mental retardation, which is thought to be caused by a combination of psychosocial and biological factors.

Answers to Concept Checks

14.1
1. ADHD without hyperactivity
2. ADHD
3. ADHD

14.2
1. autistic disorder
2. Tourette's disorder
3. Rett's disorder
4. attention deficit/hyperactivity disorder
5. Asperger's disorder
6. selective mutism

14.3
1. Moderate/limited support
2. Profound/pervasive support
3. Mild/intermittent support
4. Severe/extensive support

Key Terms

attention deficit/hyperactivity disorder (ADHD)
learning disorders
reading disorder
mathematics disorder
disorder of written expression
stuttering
expressive language disorder
selective mutism
tic disorder
autistic disorder
pervasive developmental disorder
Asperger's disorder
Rett's disorder
childhood disintegrative disorder
mental retardation
Down syndrome
amniocentesis
fragile X syndrome
cultural–familial retardation

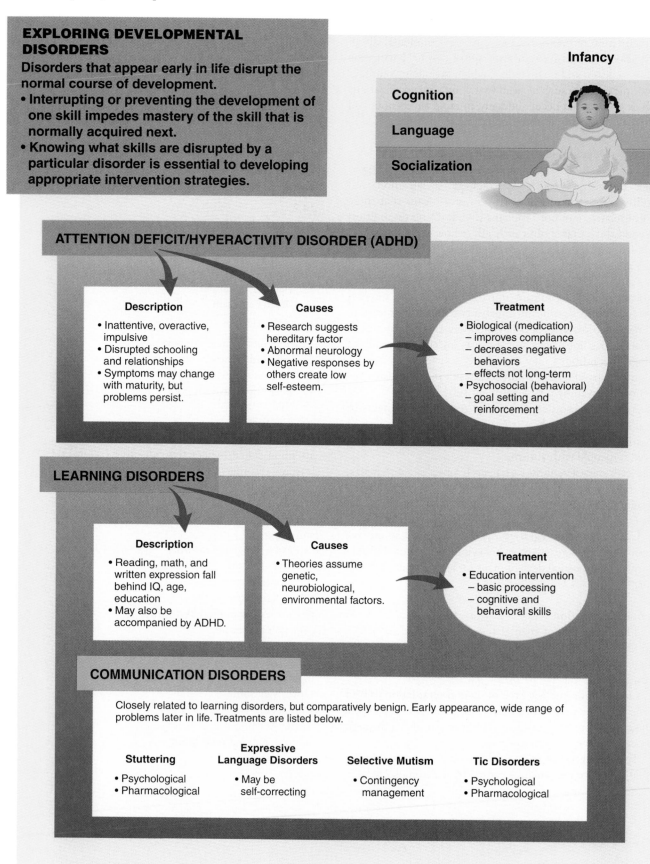

EXPLORING DEVELOPMENTAL DISORDERS

Disorders that appear early in life disrupt the normal course of development.

- Interrupting or preventing the development of one skill impedes mastery of the skill that is normally acquired next.
- Knowing what skills are disrupted by a particular disorder is essential to developing appropriate intervention strategies.

Infancy

Cognition

Language

Socialization

ATTENTION DEFICIT/HYPERACTIVITY DISORDER (ADHD)

Description
- Inattentive, overactive, impulsive
- Disrupted schooling and relationships
- Symptoms may change with maturity, but problems persist.

Causes
- Research suggests hereditary factor
- Abnormal neurology
- Negative responses by others create low self-esteem.

Treatment
- Biological (medication)
  - improves compliance
  - decreases negative behaviors
  - effects not long-term
- Psychosocial (behavioral)
  - goal setting and reinforcement

LEARNING DISORDERS

Description
- Reading, math, and written expression fall behind IQ, age, education
- May also be accompanied by ADHD.

Causes
- Theories assume genetic, neurobiological, environmental factors.

Treatment
- Education intervention
  - basic processing
  - cognitive and behavioral skills

COMMUNICATION DISORDERS

Closely related to learning disorders, but comparatively benign. Early appearance, wide range of problems later in life. Treatments are listed below.

Stuttering	Expressive Language Disorders	Selective Mutism	Tic Disorders
• Psychological • Pharmacological	• May be self-correcting	• Contingency management	• Psychological • Pharmacological

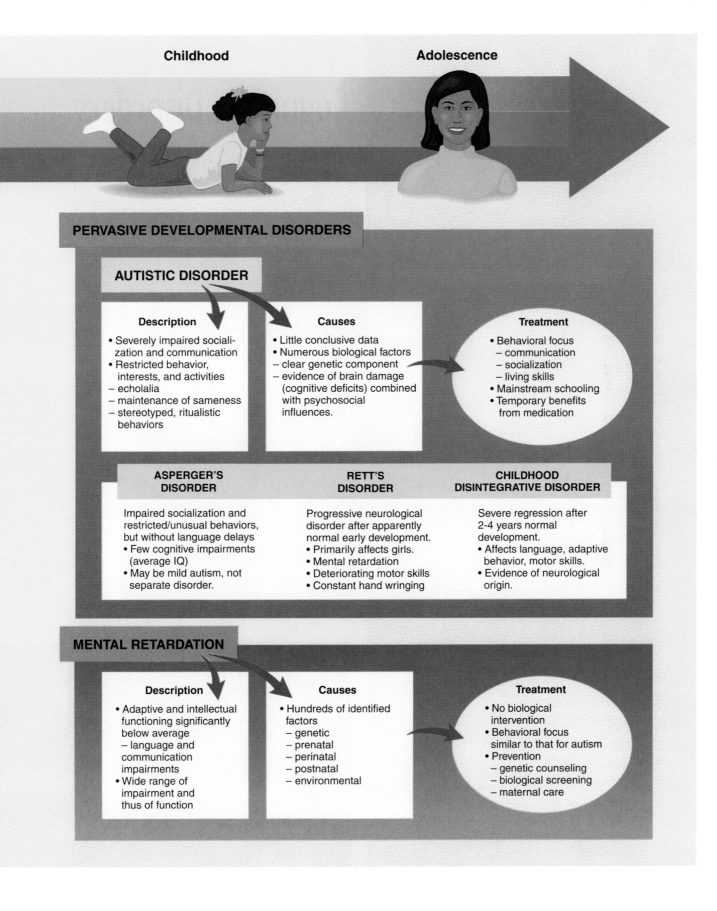

Childhood

Adolescence

PERVASIVE DEVELOPMENTAL DISORDERS

AUTISTIC DISORDER

Description

- Severely impaired socialization and communication
- Restricted behavior,
  interests, and activities
  – echolalia
  – maintenance of sameness
  – stereotyped, ritualistic
    behaviors

Causes

- Little conclusive data
- Numerous biological factors
  – clear genetic component
  – evidence of brain damage
    (cognitive deficits) combined
    with psychosocial
    influences.

Treatment

- Behavioral focus
  – communication
  – socialization
  – living skills
- Mainstream schooling
- Temporary benefits
  from medication

ASPERGER'S DISORDER	**RETT'S DISORDER**	**CHILDHOOD DISINTEGRATIVE DISORDER**
Impaired socialization and restricted/unusual behaviors, but without language delays • Few cognitive impairments (average IQ) • May be mild autism, not separate disorder.	Progressive neurological disorder after apparently normal early development. • Primarily affects girls. • Mental retardation • Deteriorating motor skills • Constant hand wringing	Severe regression after 2-4 years normal development. • Affects language, adaptive behavior, motor skills. • Evidence of neurological origin.

MENTAL RETARDATION

Description

- Adaptive and intellectual
  functioning significantly
  below average
  – language and
    communication
    impairments
- Wide range of
  impairment and
  thus of function

Causes

- Hundreds of identified
  factors
  – genetic
  – prenatal
  – perinatal
  – postnatal
  – environmental

Treatment

- No biological
  intervention
- Behavioral focus
  similar to that for autism
- Prevention
  – genetic counseling
  – biological screening
  – maternal care

Cognitive Disorders

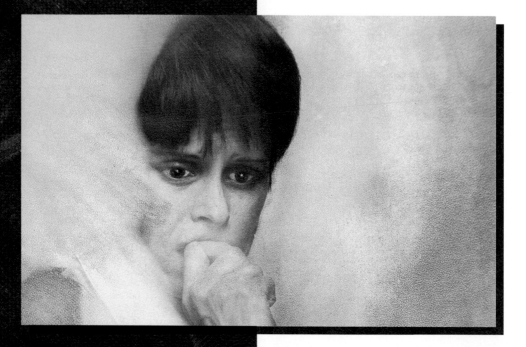

As my grip upon the present slips, more and more comfort is found within my memories of the past. Childhood nostalgia is so keen I can actually

smell the aroma of the small town library where I spent so many childhood hours.

Diana Friel McGowin
Living in the Labyrinth: A Personal Journey Through the Maze of Alzheimer's

Perspectives

Research on the brain and its role in psychopathology has increased in recent years, and we have described many of the latest advances throughout this book. All the disorders we have reviewed are in some way influenced by the brain. We have seen, for example, that relatively subtle changes in neurotransmitter systems can significantly affect mood, cognition, and behavior. Unfortunately, the brain is sometimes affected profoundly and, when this happens, drastic changes occur. It is important to remember that neurons do not regenerate when they are injured and die. Any such damage is irreversible, usually accumulating until certain symptoms appear. In this chapter we examine the brain disorders that affect cognitive processes such as learning, memory, and consciousness.

Whereas mental retardation and other learning disorders are believed to be present from birth (see Chapter 14), most cognitive disorders develop much later in life. In this section we review three classes of cognitive disorders: *delirium,* an often temporary condition that is displayed as confusion and disorientation; *dementia,* a progressive condition marked by gradual deterioration of a broad range of cognitive abilities; and *amnestic disorders,* dysfunctions of memory due to a medical condition or a drug or toxin.

The DSM-IV label "cognitive disorders" reflects a shift in the way these disorders are viewed (Tucker, Popkin, Caine, Folstein, & Grant, 1990). In previous editions of the DSM they were defined as "organic mental disorders," along with mood, anxiety, personality, hallucinosis, and delusional disorders. The word "organic" indicated that brain damage or dysfunction was believed to be involved. Although brain dysfunction is still thought to be the primary cause, we now know that some dysfunction in the brain is involved in most of the disorders described in DSM-IV (Tucker, 1993).

We have repeatedly emphasized the complex relationship between neurological and psychosocial influences in many, if not all, psychological disorders. Few people would disagree, for example, that schizophrenia involves some damage to the brain. In one sense then, most disorders are "organic." This fundamental shift in perspective immediately affected the categorizing of disorders. Obviously, the term *organic mental disorders* now covered so many as to make any distinction meaningless. Consequently, the traditional organic disorders—delirium, de-

mentia, and amnestic disorders—were kept together, and the others—organic mood, anxiety, personality, hallucinosis, and delusional disorders—were categorized with disorders that shared their symptoms (such as anxiety and mood disorders).

Once the term *organic* was dropped, attention moved to developing a better label for delirium, dementia, and the amnestic disorders. The term *cognitive disorders* signifies that their predominant feature is the impairment of such cognitive abilities as memory, attention, perception, and thinking. Although disorders such as schizophrenia and depression also involve cognitive problems, they are not believed to be primary characteristics (Tucker et al., 1990). Problems still exist with this term, however, because although the cognitive disorders usually first appear in older adults, mental retardation and learning disorders, which are apparent early, also have cognitive impairment as a predominant characteristic. Forthcoming research may provide a more useful way of distinguishing among disorders. Figure 15.1 illustrates the incidence of several different disorders in people of varying ages. Schizophrenia, alcoholism, and the personality disorders tend to appear first in adolescence or early adulthood. In contrast, the cognitive disorders (which are given the older label of "brain syndromes" in this figure) generally first appear during the patient's 50s or 60s and accelerate after the age of 70. As our life expectancy increases, these disorders are more prevalent and have become a major concern for mental health professionals.

As with certain other disorders, it may be useful to clarify why cognitive disorders are discussed in a textbook on abnormal psychology. Because they so clearly have organic causes, one could argue that they are purely medical concerns. We will see, however, that the consequences of a cognitive disorder often include profound changes in a person's behavior and personality. Intense anxiety and/or depression are common, especially among people with dementia. In addition, paranoia is frequently reported, as are extreme agitation and aggression. Families and friends are also profoundly affected by such changes. Imagine your emotional distress as a loved one is transformed into a different person, often one who no longer remembers who you are or your history together. The deterioration of cognitive ability, behavior, and personality and the effects on others are a major concern for mental health professionals.

Delirium

The disorder known as **delirium** is characterized by impaired consciousness and cognition during the course of several hours or days (Trzepacz, 1996). Delirium is one of the earliest recognized mental disorders: Descriptions of people with these symptoms were written more than 2,500 years ago (Lipowski, 1990). Consider the following case.

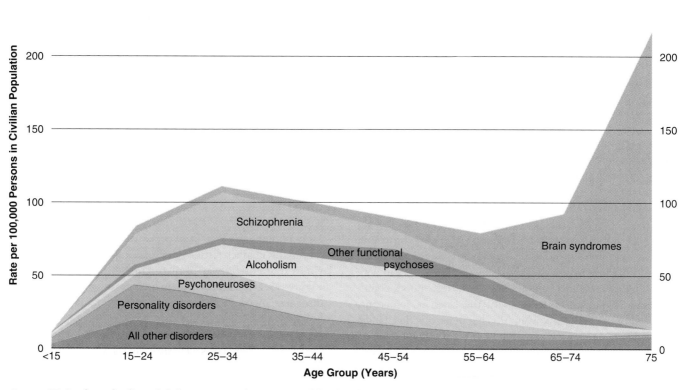

figure 15.1   Rates for first admission to state and county mental hospitals in the United States in 1965, specific for age and mental disorder (from Kramer, 1969)

Mr. J.
Sudden Distress

Mr. J., an older gentleman, was brought to the hospital emergency room. He didn't know his own name and at times he didn't seem to recognize his daughter, who was with him. Mr. J. appeared confused, disoriented, and a little agitated. He had difficulty speaking clearly, and could not focus his attention to answer even the most basic questions. Mr. J.'s daughter reported that he had begun acting this way the night before, had been awake most of the time since then, was frightened, and seemed even more confused today. She told the nurse that this behavior was not normal for him and she was worried that he was becoming senile. She mentioned that his doctor had just changed his hypertension medication and wondered whether the new medication could be causing her father's distress. Mr. J. was ultimately diagnosed as having substance-induced delirium (a reaction to his new medication); once the medication was stopped, he improved significantly over the course of the next 2 days. This scenario is played out on a daily basis in most major metropolitan hospital emergency rooms.

Clinical Description and Statistics

People with delirium appear confused, disoriented, and out of touch with their surroundings. They cannot focus and sustain their attention on even the simplest tasks. There are marked impairments in memory and language. Mr. J. had trouble speaking; he was not only confused but couldn't remember basic facts such as his own name. As we saw, the symptoms of delirium do not come on gradually, but develop over hours or a few days, and they can vary over the course of a day.

Delirium is estimated to be present in as many as 10% to 15% of the people who come into acute care facilities, such as emergency rooms (I. R. Katz, 1993). It is most prevalent among older adults, people undergoing medical procedures, cancer patients, and people with acquired immunodeficiency syndrome (AIDS) (Adams, 1988; Fernandez, Levy, & Mansell, 1989). Delirium subsides relatively quickly, with full recovery expected in most cases within several weeks. A minority of individuals will continue to have problems on and off; some even lapse into a coma and may die.

Many medical conditions that impair brain function have been linked to delirium, including intoxication by drugs and poisons; withdrawal from drugs such as alcohol and sedative, hypnotic, and anxiolytic drugs; infections; head injury; and various other types of brain trauma (Lipowski, 1990). DSM-IV recognizes several causes of delirium among its subtypes. The criteria for *delirium due to a general medical condition* include a disturbance of consciousness (reduced awareness of the environment) and a change in cognitive abilities such as memory and language skills, occurring over a short period of time and brought about by a general medical condition. Other subtypes include the diagnosis received by Mr. J.—*substance-induced delirium*—as well as *delirium due to multiple etiologies*, and *delirium not otherwise specified*. The last two categories indicate the often complex nature of delirium.

That delirium can be brought on by the improper use of medication can be a particular problem for older adults, because they tend to use prescription medications more than any other age group (U.S. General Accounting Office, 1995). The risk of problems among the elderly is increased further because they tend to eliminate drugs from their systems less efficiently than younger individuals. It is not surprising, then, that adverse drug reactions resulting in hospitalization are almost six times higher among elderly people than in other age groups (Col, Fanale, & Kronholm, 1990). And it is believed that delirium brought on by improper use of medications contributes to the 32,000 hip fractures that result annually from falls by older adults (Ray, Griffin, Schaffner, Baugh, & Melton, 1987), and the 16,000 serious car accidents that occur each year in the U.S. among elderly drivers (Ray, Fought, & Decker, 1992). Although there has been some improvement in the use of medication among older adults, improper use continues to produce serious side effects, including symptoms of delirium (U.S. General Accounting Office, 1995). Because possible combinations of illnesses and medications are so numerous, determining the cause of delirium is extremely difficult (J. Francis, Martin, & Kapoor, 1990).

Delirium may be experienced by children who have high fevers or who are taking certain medications and is often mistaken for noncompliance. It often occurs during the course of dementia; as many as 44% of people with dementia suffer at least one episode of delirium (Purdie, Hareginan, & Rosen, 1981). Because many of the primary medical conditions can be treated, delirium is often reversed within a relatively short time.

Factors other than medical conditions can trigger delirium. Age itself is an important factor; older adults are more susceptible to developing delirium as a result of mild infections or medication changes (Lipowski, 1983). Sleep deprivation, immobility, and excessive stress can also cause delirium (Wolanin & Phillips, 1981).

Treatment

Delirium brought on by withdrawal from alcohol or other drugs is usually treated with benzodiazepines, which are calming and sleep-inducing medications (I. R. Katz, 1993). Infections, brain injury, and tumors are given the necessary and appropriate medical intervention. The antipsychotic drug Haloperidol is often prescribed for individuals in acute delirium (Trzepacz, 1996).

Psychosocial interventions may also be beneficial (Richeimer, 1987). The goal of nonmedical treatment is to reassure the person in order to help him or her deal with the agitation, anxiety, and hallucinations of delirium. A person in the hospital may be comforted by familiar personal belongings such as family photographs (Trzepacz, 1996). Also, a patient who is included in all treatment decisions re-

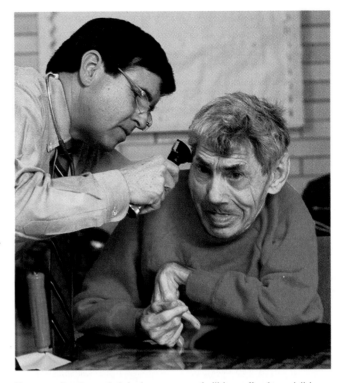

Many people who seek help in acute-care facilities suffer from delirium.

tains a sense of control (I. R. Katz, 1993). This type of psychosocial treatment can help the person manage during this disruptive period until the medical causes are identified and addressed.

Preventive efforts may be most successful in assisting people who are susceptible to delirium. Proper medical care for illnesses and therapeutic drug monitoring can play a significant role in preventing delirium. For example, the increased number of older adults involved in managed care and patient counseling on drug use appear to have led to more appropriate use of prescription drugs among the elderly (U.S. General Accounting Office, 1995).

 # Dementia

Few things are more frightening than the possibility that you will one day not recognize those you love, that you will not be able to perform the most basic of tasks and, worse yet, that you will be acutely aware of this failure of your mind. **Dementia** is the cognitive disorder that makes these fears real: a gradual deterioration of brain functioning that affects judgment, memory, language, and other advanced cognitive processes. Dementia is caused by several medical conditions and by the abuse of drugs or alcohol that cause negative changes in cognitive functioning. Some of these conditions—for instance, infection or depression—can cause dementia, although it is often reversible through treatment of the primary condition. Some forms of the disorder, such as Alzheimer's disease, are at present irreversible. Although delirium and dementia can occur together; dementia has a gradual progression as opposed to delirium's acute onset; people with dementia are not disoriented or confused in the early stages, unlike people with delirium. Like delirium, however, dementia has many causes, including a variety of insults to the brain such as stroke (which destroys blood vessels), the infectious diseases of syphilis and HIV, severe head injury, the introduction of certain toxic or poisonous substances, and diseases such as Parkinson's, Huntington's, and the most common cause of dementia, Alzheimer's disease. Consider the following rare personal account by a woman who poignantly writes of her experiences with this disorder (McGowin, 1993).

Diana
Humiliation and Fear

At the age of 45, Diana Friel McGowin was a successful legal assistant, wife, and mother; but she was beginning to experience "lapses." She writes about developing these problems just before a party she was planning for her family.

> Nervously, I checked off the table appointments on a list retrieved from my jumpsuit pocket. Such a list had never been necessary before, but lately I noticed frequent little episodes of confusion and memory lapses.
>
> I had decided to "cheat" on this family buffet and have the meal prepared on a carry-out basis. Cooking was also becoming increasingly difficult, due to what my children and my husband Jack teasingly referred to as my "absentmindedness." (pp. 1–2)

In addition to memory difficulties, other problems began at this time, including brief dizzy spells. Diana wrote of her family's growing awareness of the additional symptoms.

> Shaun walked past me on his way to the kitchen, and paused. "Mom, what's up? You look ragged," he commented sleepily. "Late night last night, plenty of excitement, and then up early to get your father off to work," I answered. Shaun laughed disconcertingly. I glanced up at him ruefully. "What is so funny?" I demanded. "You, Mom! You are talking as though you are drunk or something! You must really be tired!" (pp. 4–5)

In the early stages of her dementia, Diana tended to explain these changes in herself as temporary, with such causes as tension at work. However, the extent of her dysfunction continued to increase, and she had more frightening experiences. In one episode, she describes an attempt to drive home from a brief errand.

> Suddenly, I was aware of car horns blowing. Glancing around, nothing was familiar. I was stopped at an intersection and the traffic light was green. Cars honked impatiently, so I pulled straight ahead, trying to get my bearings. I could not read the street sign, but there

was another sign ahead; perhaps it would shed some light on my location.

> A few yards ahead, there was a park ranger building. Trembling, I wiped my eyes, and breathing deeply, tried to calm myself. Finally, feeling ready to speak, I started the car again and approached the ranger station. The guard smiled and inquired how he could assist me. "I appear to be lost," I began, making a great effort to keep my voice level, despite my emotional state. "Where do you need to go?" the guard asked politely. A cold chill enveloped me as I realized I could not remember the name of my street. Tears began to flow down my cheeks. I did not know where I wanted to go. (pp. 7–8)

Diana's difficulties continued. She sometimes forgot the names of her children, and once astounded her nephew when she didn't recognize him. If she left home, she almost invariably got lost. She learned to introduce herself as a tourist from out of town, because people would give her better directions. She felt as if there "was less of me every day than there was the day before."

During initial medical examinations, Diana didn't recall this type of problem in her family history. However, a look through some of her late mother's belongings revealed that she was not the first to experience symptoms of dementia.

> Then I noticed the maps. After mother's death I had found mysterious hand drawn maps and bits of directions scribbled on note papers all over her home. They were in her purses, in bureau drawers, in the desks, seemingly everywhere. Too distraught at the time to figure out their purpose, I simply packed them all away with other articles in the box.
>
> Now I smoothed out each map and scrawled note, and placed them side by side. They covered the bedroom floor. There were maps to every place my mother went about town, even to my home and my brother's home. As I deciphered each note and map, I began recollecting my mother's other eccentric habits. She would not drive out of her neighborhood. She would not drive at night. She was teased by both myself and my brother about "memory goofs" and would become irate with both of her children over their loving teasing.
>
> Then with a chill, I recalled one day when I approached my mother to tell her something, and she did not recognize me. (p. 52)

After several evaluations, which included an MRI showing some damage in several parts of her brain, Diana's neurologist concluded that she had dementia. The cause could be a stroke she had several years before that damaged several small areas of her brain by breaking or blocking several blood vessels. The dementia could also indicate Alzheimer's disease. As of this writing, Diana Friel McGowin is still alive, but her condition will continue to deteriorate and eventually she may die from complications of her disorder.

Clinical Description and Statistics

Depending on the individual and the cause of the disorder, the gradual progression of dementia may have somewhat different symptoms, although all aspects of cognitive functioning are eventually affected. In the initial stages, memory impairment is typically seen as an inability to register ongoing events. In other words, a person can remember how to talk, and may remember events from many years ago, but have trouble remembering what happened in the past hour. For example, Diana still knew how to use the stove, but couldn't remember whether she had turned it on or off.

Diana couldn't find her way home because *visuospatial* skills are impaired among people with dementia. *Agnosia,* the inability to recognize and name objects, is one of the most familiar symptoms. *Facial agnosia,* the inability to recognize even familiar faces, can be extremely distressing to family members. Diana failed to recognize not only her nephew but also co-workers whom she had seen on a daily basis for years. A general deterioration of intellectual function results from impairment in memory, planning, and abstract reasoning.

Perhaps because victims of dementia are aware that they are deteriorating mentally, emotional changes often occur as well. Common side effects are delusions (irrational beliefs), depression, agitation, aggression, and apathy (Sultzer, Levin, Mahler, High, & Cummings, 1993). Again, it is difficult to establish the cause-and-effect relationship. We don't know how much behavioral change is due to progressive brain deterioration directly and how much is a result of the frustration and discouragement that inevitably accompany the loss of function and the isolation of "losing" loved ones. Cognitive functioning continues to deteriorate until the person requires almost total support to carry out day-to-day activities. Ultimately, death occurs as the result of inactivity combined with the onset of other illnesses such as pneumonia.

Dementia can occur at almost any age, although the incidence of this disorder is highest in older adults. In one large representative study, researchers found a prevalence of a little over 1% in people between the ages of 65 and 74; this rate increased to almost 4% in those aged 75 to 84, and to more than 10% in people 85 and older (see Figure 15.2) (George, Landoman, Blazer, & Anthony, 1991). The actual rate may be considerably higher, however, especially among older adults. Some researchers have estimated that as many as 47% of adults over the age of 85 may have dementia of the Alzheimer's type (D. A. Evans et al., 1989). The discrepancy in estimates may result from the difficulty in identifying people with dementia, especially in its early stages. Dementia of the Alzheimer's type rarely occurs in people under 45 years of age (Ernst & Hay, 1994).

People with facial agnosia, a common symptom of dementia, are unable to recognize faces, even of their closest friends and relatives.

"What is the doctor saying? That you are going to become a babbling idiot?" His words cut through my heart and mind like a knife. My worst fear had been put into words.*

An additional problem with confirming prevalence figures for dementia is that survival rates alter the outcomes. Incidence studies, which count the number of new cases in a year, may thus be the most reliable method for assessing the frequency of dementia, especially among the elderly. In one study, the annual incidence rates for dementia were 2.3% for people 75–79 years of age, 4.6% for people 80–84 years of age, and 8.5% for those 85 and older (Paykel et al., 1994). The research showed that the rate for new cases doubled with every 5 years of age. In addition, the rate for dementia was comparable for men and women and was equivalent across educational level and social class. Many other studies, however, find greater increases of dementia among women (for example, Rorsman, Hagnell, & Lanke, 1986), although this may be due to the tendency of women to live longer. Dementia of the Alzheimer's type may, as we discuss later, be more prevalent among women. Together, results suggest that dementia is a relatively common disorder among older adults, and that the chances of developing it increase rapidly after the age of 75. Keep in mind, however, that approximately 85% of all

*Featured quotations in this chapter are from Diana Friel McGowin, *Living in the Labyrinth: A Personal Journey Through the Maze of Alzheimer's* (Delta Books, 1994).

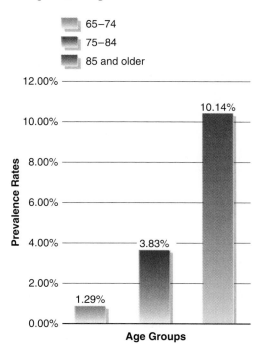

figure 15.2 Prevalence of dementia (adapted from George, Landoman, Blazer, & Anthony, 1991)

individuals over the age of 65 are not cognitively impaired; such disorders are not an inevitable consequence of aging (see Figure 15.2).

In addition to the human costs of dementia, the financial costs are staggering. It was estimated, for example, that the Medicaid cost for people with dementia of the Alzheimer's type was $5.7 billion in 1991, $1.5 billion more than the cost for all persons with AIDS that same year (Ernst & Hay, 1994). But medical costs are only a fraction of the total financial burden of caring for a person with dementia on a 24-hour basis. Yearly nursing home care averages approximately $40,000 per patient. Many times family members care for an afflicted person round-the-clock, which is an inestimable personal and financial commitment (Ernst & Hay, 1994).

The statistics on prevalence and incidence cover dementias that arise from a variety of etiologies. DSM-IV groups are based on presumed cause, but determining the cause of dementia is an inexact process. Sometimes, as with dementia of the Alzheimer's type, clinicians rely on ruling out alternative explanations—identifying all the things that are *not* the cause—instead of determining the precise origin.

Five classes of dementia based on etiology have been identified: (1) *dementia of the Alzheimer's type;* (2) *vascular dementia;* (3) *dementia due to other general medical conditions;* (4) *substance-induced persisting dementia;* and (5) *dementia due to multiple etiologies.* A sixth, *dementia not otherwise specified,* is

included when etiology cannot be determined. We emphasize dementia of the Alzheimer's type because of its prevalence (almost half of those with dementia exhibit this type) and the relatively large amount of research conducted on its etiology and treatment.

Dementia of the Alzheimer's Type

DESCRIPTION AND STATISTICS

The German psychiatrist Alois Alzheimer first described the disorder that bears his name in 1906. He wrote of a 51-year-old woman who had a "strange disease of the cerebral cortex" that manifested as a progressive memory impairment and other behavioral and cognitive problems including suspiciousness (Bogerts, 1993; Loebel, Dager, & Kitchell, 1993). He called the disorder an "atypical form of senile dementia," and thereafter it was referred to as **Alzheimer's disease.**

The DSM-IV diagnostic criteria for **dementia of the Alzheimer's type** include multiple cognitive deficits that develop gradually and steadily. Predominant is the impairment of memory. The inability to integrate new information results in failure to learn new associations. Individuals with Alzheimer's disease forget important events and lose objects. Their interest in nonroutine activities narrows. It is difficult, however, to determine the extent to which social isolation is the direct result of the progressive brain damage and how much reflects embarrassment over failing abilities.

People with dementia of the Alzheimer's type also display one or more other cognitive disturbances, including *aphasia* (difficulty with language), *apraxia* (impaired motor functioning), *agnosia* (failure to recognize objects), or difficulty with activities such as planning, organizing, sequencing, or abstracting information. These cognitive impairments also have a serious negative impact on social and occupational functioning, and represent a significant decline from previous abilities.

A definitive diagnosis of Alzheimer's disease can be made only after an autopsy determines that certain characteristic types of damage are present in the brain, although clinicians are accurate in identifying this condition in living patients 75% to 90% of the time (Jobst, Hindley, King, & Smith, 1994). To make a diagnosis without direct examination of the brain, a simplified version of a mental status exam is used to assess language and memory problems (see Table 15.1).

In an interesting recent, somewhat controversial study, the writings of a group of Catholic nuns that were collected over several decades appeared to indicate early in life which women were most likely to later develop Alzheimer's disease (Massie et al., 1996). Researchers observed that samples from the nun's journals over the years differed in the number of ideas each contained, which the scientists called "idea

> *My behavior was often repetitive as I checked and rechecked the date, the time of day, the location of my purse and other belongings. I was rapidly developing fetishes or mannerisms indicative of slipping capacities.*

density." In other words, some of the sisters described events in their lives very simply: "I was born in Eau Claire, Wis, on May 24, 1913 and was baptized in St. James Church." Others were more elaborate in their prose: "The happiest day of my life so far was my First Communion Day which was in June nineteen hundred and twenty when I was but eight years of age, and four years later in the same month I was confirmed by Bishop D. D. McGavich." When findings of autopsies on fourteen of the nuns were correlated with idea density, the very simple writing (low idea density) occurred among all five of the nuns with Alzheimer's disease (Massie et al., 1996). This is a very elegant research study because the daily lives of the nuns were similar on a day-to-day basis, which ruled out many other possible causes. However, it is helpful to be cautious in depending on this study, because only a small number of people were examined. It is not yet clear that dementia of the Alzheimer's type has such early signs, but research continues in the hope of early detection so early intervention can be developed.

Cognitive deterioration of the Alzheimer's type is slow during the early and later stages but more rapid during the middle stages (Y. Stern et al., 1994). The average survival time is estimated to be about 8 years (Trèves, 1991), although many individuals live very dependently for more

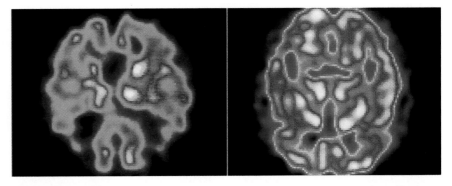

The PET scan of a brain afflicted with Alzheimer's disease (left) shows significant tissue deterioration in comparison with a normal brain (right).

than 10 years (Report of the Advisory Panel on Alzheimer's Disease, 1995). In some forms, the disease can occur relatively early, during the 40s or 50s (sometimes referred to as presenile dementia), but it usually appears during the 60s or 70s (Trèves, 1991). Approximately 50% of the cases of dementia are ultimately found to be the result of Alzheimer's disease (Loebel et al., 1993), which is believed to afflict more than 4 million Americans (Report of the Advisory Panel on Alzheimer's Disease, 1995).

Some research on prevalence suggests that Alzheimer's disease may occur most often in people who are poorly educated (Fratiglioni et al., 1991; Korczyn, Kahana, & Galper, 1991). Greater impairment among uneducated people might indicate a much earlier onset, suggesting that Alzheimer's

---

table 15.1   Testing for Dementia of the Alzheimer's Type

One part of the diagnosis of the dementia of Alzheimer's disease uses a relatively simple test of the patient's mental state and abilities, like this one, called the Mini Mental State Inpatient Consultation Form. A low score on such a test does not necessarily indicate a medical diagnosis of dementia.

Type	Maximum Score	Question
Orientation	5	What is the (year) (season) (date) (day) (month)?
	5	Where are we (state) (country) (town) (hospital) (floor)?
Registration	3	(Name three objects, using 1 second to say each. Then ask the patient all three after you have said them. Give one point for each correct answer. Then repeat them until the patient learns all three. Count and record the number of trials.)
Attention and Calculation	5	Count backward from given number (like 100) by subtracting 7's. (Give one point for each correct answer; stop after five answers.) Alternatively, spell "world" backwards.
Recall	3	Name the three objects learned above. (Give one point for each correct answer.)
Language	9	(Have a patient name a pencil and a watch.) (1 point) Repeat the following: "No ifs, ands, or buts." (1 point) Follow a three-stage command: "Take a piece of paper in your right hand, fold it in half, and put it on the floor." (3 points) Read and obey the following: "Close your eyes." (1 point) Write a sentence. (1 point) Copy this design. (1 point)

The examination also includes an assessment of the patient's level of consciousness: Alert   Drowsy   Stupor   Coma
Total maximum score is 30.
Adapted from the Mini Mental State examination form, Folstein, Folstein, and McHugh, reprinted in *The Merck Manual of Geriatrics*

Alzheimer's disease affects more women than men, only in part because women usually live longer.

disease causes intellectual dysfunction that in turn hampers educational efforts. Or there could be something about intellectual achievement that prevents or delays the onset or symptoms of the disorder. To address these issues, Stern, Gurland, and others (1994) examined the incidence of Alzheimer's-type dementia to learn whether educational levels affected who would and who would not later be diagnosed with the disorder. They found that those with the least amount of formal education were more likely to develop dementia than those with more education. It is important that the researchers were able to study living subjects before they could be identified as having dementia; such a prospective study rules out many alternative explanations for the results, such as a possible bias toward identifying one group over another. Stern and his colleagues concluded that educational attainment may somehow create a mental "reserve," a learned set of skills that help one cope longer with the cognitive deterioration that marks the beginning of dementia. Like Diana's mother, who made copious notes and maps to help her function despite her cognitive deterioration, some people may adapt more successfully than others and thus escape detection longer. Brain deterioration may thus be comparable for both groups, but better-educated individuals may be able to function successfully on a day-to-day basis for a longer period of time. This tentative hypothesis may prove useful in designing treatment strategies, especially during the early stages of the disorder.

At one time, I had managed a law office. At one time, I had an IQ of 137.

Recent research suggests that Alzheimer's disease may be more prevalent among women (Report of the Advisory Panel on Alzheimer's Disease, 1995), even when women's higher survival rate is factored into the statistics. In other words, because women live longer than men on average, they are more likely to experience Alzheimer's and other diseases, but longevity alone does not account for the higher prevalence of the disorder among women. A tentative explanation involves the hormone estrogen. Women lose estrogen as they grow older, so perhaps it is protective against the disease. Research that supports this hypothesis found that women who participate in estrogen replacement therapy after menopause may have a late onset or reduced incidence of Alzheimer's disease (Larson, 1993).

Finally, there appear to be differences in the prevalence of Alzheimer's disease according to racial identity. Populations that seem to be less likely to be affected include people with Japanese, Nigerian, certain Native American, and Amish backgrounds. For example, one study found that the greater the genetic degree of Cherokee ancestry, the lower the likelihood of having Alzheimer's disease (Rosenberg et al., 1996). Similarly, the prevalence of late-onset Alzheimer's disease is low among the Amish, which suggests the absence of certain genetic factors in this group (Pericak-Vance et al., 1996). As we will see, findings like these help bring us closer to understanding the causes of this devastating disease.

Vascular Dementia

DESCRIPTION AND STATISTICS

Each year, 500,000 people die from strokes (any diseases or insults to the brain that result in restriction or cessation of blood flow). Although stroke is the third leading cause of death in the United States (Hademenos, 1997), many people survive, but one potential long-term consequence can be severely debilitating. **Vascular dementia** is a progressive brain disorder that is second only to Alzheimer's disease as a cause of dementia (Stuss & Cummings, 1990). The word *vascular* refers to blood vessels. When the blood vessels in the brain are blocked or damaged and no longer carry oxygen and other nutrients to certain areas of brain tissue, damage results. MRI scans of Diana Friel McGowin's brain showed a number of damaged areas, or *multiple infarctions,* left by a stroke several years earlier; this was one probable cause of her dementia. Because multiple sites in the brain can be damaged, the profile of degeneration—the particular skills that are impaired—differs from person to person. DSM-IV lists as criteria for vascular dementia memory and other cognitive disturbances that are identical to those for dementia of the Alzheimer's type. However, certain neurological signs of brain tissue damage, such as abnormalities in walking and weakness in the limbs, are observed in many people with vascular dementia but not in people in the early stages of dementia of the Alzheimer's type.

In comparison with research on dementia of the Alzheimer's type, there are fewer studies on vascular dementia, perhaps because of its lower incidence rates. One study, of people living in a Swedish city, suggests that the lifetime risk of having vascular dementia is 4.7% among men and 3.8% among women (Hagnell et al., 1992). The higher risk for men is typical for this disorder, in contrast with the higher risk among women for Alzheimer's type dementia (Report of the Advisory Panel on Alzheimer's Disease, 1995). The relatively high rate of cardiovascular disease among men in general may account for their increased risk of vascular dementia. The onset of vascular dementia is typically more sudden than for the Alzheimer's type, probably because the disorder is the result of a stroke, which inflicts brain damage immediately. The outcome, however, is similar for people with both types: Ultimately, they will require formal nursing care until they succumb to an infectious disease such as pneumonia.

Dementia Due to Other General Medical Conditions

DESCRIPTIONS AND STATISTICS

In addition to Alzheimer's disease and vascular damage, a number of other neurological and biochemical processes can lead to dementia. DSM-IV lists several other types with specific causes, including *dementia due to HIV disease, dementia due to head trauma, dementia due to Parkinson's disease, dementia due to Huntington's disease, dementia due to Pick's disease,* and *dementia due to Creutzfeldt-Jakob disease.* Each of these is discussed here. Other medical conditions that can lead to dementia include normal pressure hydrocephalus (excessive water in the cranium, due to brain shrinkage), hypothyroidism (an underactive thyroid gland), brain tumor, and vitamin B_{12} deficiency. In their affect on cognitive ability, these disorders are comparable to the other forms of dementia we have discussed so far.

The human immunodeficiency virus-type-1 **(HIV-1),** which causes AIDS (acquired immunodeficiency syndrome), can also cause dementia (S. Perry, 1993). This impairment seems to be independent of the other infections that accompany HIV; in other words, the HIV infection itself seems to be responsible for the neurological impairment (Price & Brew, 1988). The early symptoms of dementia due to HIV are cognitive slowness, impaired attention, and forgetfulness. Affected individuals also tend to be clumsy, to show repetitive movements such as tremors and leg weakness, and to become apathetic and socially withdrawn (Navia, 1990).

People with HIV seem particularly susceptible to cognitive impairments in the later stages of HIV infection, although significant impairment of cognitive abilities may occur earlier (Heaton et al., 1994). Cognitive impairments are observed in 29% to 87% of people with AIDS, and ap-

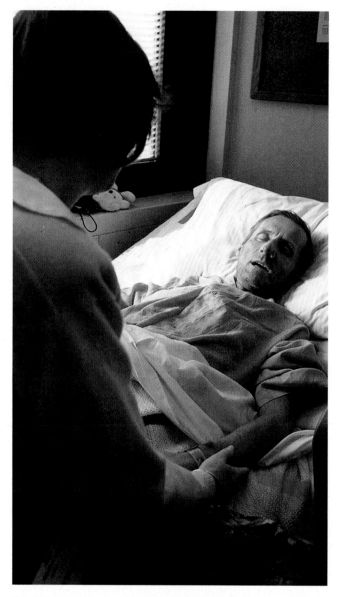

The AIDS virus may cause dementia in the later stages.

presence complicates an already devastating and ultimately fatal set of conditions.

Like dementia from Parkinson's disease, Huntington's disease, and several other causes, dementia resulting from HIV is sometimes referred to as *subcortical dementia,* because it affects primarily the inner areas of the brain, below the outer layer called the *cortex* (Cummings, 1990). The distinction between "cortical" (including dementia of the Alzheimer's type) and "subcortical" is important because of the different expressions of dementia in these two categories (see Table 15.2). *Aphasia,* which involves impaired language skills, occurs among people with dementia of the Alzheimer's type, but not among people with subcortical dementia. In contrast, people with subcortical dementia are more likely to experience severe depression and anxiety than those with dementia of the Alzheimer's type. In general, motor skills including speed and coordination are impaired early on among those with subcortical dementia. The differing patterns of impairment can be attributed to the different areas of the brain affected by the disorders.

Head trauma, injury to the head and therefore to the brain, is typically caused by accidents, and can lead to cognitive impairments in both children and adults. Memory loss is the most common symptom (Capruso & Levin, 1992).

Parkinson's disease is a degenerative brain disorder that affects about 1 out of every 1,000 people worldwide (Freedman, 1990). Motor problems are characteristic among people with Parkinson's disease, who tend to have stooped posture, slow body movements (called *bradykinesia*), tremors, and jerkiness in walking. The voice is also affected; afflicted individuals speak in a very soft monotone. The changes in motor movements are the result of damage to dopamine pathways. Because dopamine is involved in complex movement, a reduction in this neurotransmitter makes affected individuals increasingly unable to control their muscle movements, which leads to tremors and muscle weakness.

Some people with Parkinson's develop dementia (La Rue, 1992); conservative estimates place the rate at twice that found in the general population (Gibb, 1989). The pattern of impairments for these individuals fits the general pattern of subcortical dementia (Table 15.2).

Huntington's disease is a genetic disorder that initially affects motor movements, typically in the form of *chorea,* in-

proximately one-third of the infected people will ultimately meet the criteria for dementia due to HIV disease (Day et al., 1992; Price & Brew, 1988). HIV disease accounts for a relatively small percentage of people with dementia compared to Alzheimer's disease and vascular causes, but its

table 15.2   Characteristics of Dementias

Characteristic	Dementia of the Alzheimer's Type	Subcortical Dementias
Language	Aphasia (difficulties with articulating speech)	No aphasia
Memory	Both recall and recognition are impaired	Impaired recall; normal or less impaired recognition
Visuospatial skills	Impaired	Impaired
Mood	Less severe depression and anxiety	More severe depression and anxiety
Motor speed	Normal	Slowed
Coordination	Normal until late in the progression	Impaired

Adapted from: Cummings, J. L. (1990). Introduction. In J. L. Cummings (Ed.), *Subcortical dementia.* New York: Oxford University Press. (p. 7)

Nancy Wexler headed the team of scientists who found the gene for Huntington's disease.

voluntary limb movements (Folstein, Brandt, & Folstein, 1990). People with Huntington's can live for 20 years after the first signs of the disease appear, although skilled nursing care is often required during the last stages. Just as with Parkinson's disease, only a portion of persons with Huntington's disease go on to display dementia—somewhere between 20% and 80%—although some researchers believe that all Huntington's patients would eventually display dementia if they lived long enough (Edwards, 1994). Dementia due to Huntington's disease also follows the subcortical pattern.

The search for the gene that is responsible for Huntington's disease is like a detective story. For some time researchers have known that the disease is inherited as an autosomal dominant disorder, meaning that approximately 50% of the offspring of an adult with Huntington's will develop the disease. Since 1979, behavioral scientist Nancy Wexler and a team of researchers have been studying the largest known extended family in the world afflicted by Huntington's disease, in small villages in Venezuela. The villagers have cooperated with the research, in part because Wexler herself lost her mother, three uncles, and her maternal grandfather to Huntington's, and she too may have the disorder (Turkington, 1994). Using genetic linkage analysis techniques (see Chapter 4), these researchers first mapped the deficit to an area on chromosome 4 (Gusella et al., 1983), and then identified the elusive gene (Huntington's Disease Collaborative Research Group, 1993). Finding that one gene causes a disease is exceptional; research on other inherited mental disorders typically points to multiple gene (polygenic) influences.

Pick's disease is a very rare neurological condition that produces a cortical dementia similar to that of Alzheimer's disease. The course of this disease is believed to last from 5 to 10 years, although its cause is as yet unknown (McDaniel, 1990). Like Huntington's disease, Pick's disease usually occurs relatively early in life—during a person's 40s or 50s—and is therefore considered an example of presenile dementia. An even rarer condition, **Creutzfeldt-Jakob disease,** is believed to affect only one in every million individuals (Edwards, 1994). An alarming development in the study of Creutzfeldt-Jacob disease is the recent finding of 10 cases of a new variant that may be linked to bovine spongiform encephalopathy (BSE), more commonly referred to as "mad cow disease" (Smith & Cousens, 1996). This discovery led to a ban on exporting beef from the United Kingdom because the disease might be transmitted from infected cattle to humans. We do not yet have definitive information about the link between mad cow disease and the new form of Creutzfeldt-Jacob disease.

Substance-Induced Persisting Dementia

DESCRIPTION AND STATISTICS

Prolonged drug use, especially in combination with poor diet, can damage the brain and, in some circumstances, can also lead to dementia. As many as 10% of individuals who are dependent on alcohol meet the criteria for dementia (Horvath, 1975). DSM-IV identifies several drugs that can lead to symptoms of dementia, including alcohol, inhalants such as glue or gasoline (which some people inhale for the euphoric feeling they produce), and the sedative, hypnotic, and anxiolytic drugs (see Chapter 11). These drugs pose a threat because they create dependence, making it difficult for a user to stop ingesting them. The resulting brain damage can be permanent and can cause the same symptoms seen in dementia of the Alzheimer's type (Parsons & Nixon, 1993). The DSM-IV criteria for substance-induced persisting dementia are essentially the same as for the other forms of dementia; they include memory impairment and at least one of the following cognitive disturbances: aphasia (language disturbance), apraxia (inability to carry out motor activities despite intact motor function), agnosia (failure to recognize or identify objects despite intact sensory function), or a disturbance in executive functioning (such as planning, organizing, sequencing, and abstracting).

Causes

BIOLOGICAL INFLUENCES

Cognitive abilities can be adversely compromised in many ways. As we have seen, dementia can be caused by a number of processes: Alzheimer's disease, Huntington's disease, Parkinson's disease, head trauma, substance abuse, and others. The most common cause of dementia, Alzheimer's disease, is also the most mysterious. Because of its prevalence and our relative ignorance about the factors responsible for it, Alzheimer's disease has held the attention of a great many researchers who are trying to find the cause and ultimately a treatment or cure for this devastating condition.

Findings from Alzheimer's research seem to appear almost daily. We should be cautious when interpreting the output of this fast-paced and competitive field; too often, as we have seen in other areas, findings are heralded prematurely as conclusive and important. Remember that "discoveries" of a single gene for bipolar disorder, schizophrenia, and alcoholism were later shown to be based on overly simplistic accounts. Similarly, findings from Alzheimer's research are sometimes too quickly sanctioned as accepted truths before they have been replicated, an essential validation process. Several recent examples illustrate this tendency to accept conclusions too quickly.

In 1991, several papers were published by scientists who claimed to have found strains of mice that developed brain abnormalities similar to those in patients with Alzheimer's disease (Kawabata, Higgins, & Gordon, 1991; Wirak et al., 1991). If true, this would be an important advance because researchers could study the degenerative process directly, without having to wait to examine the brains of people with Alzheimer's who had died. In less than a year, however, two of the reports were retracted by their authors because errors were found that threatened the validity of their results (Rennie, 1992). They had been too quick to declare a major discovery. Researchers are still trying to develop a strain of mice with relevant brain abnormalities for the sake of research; as yet, however, they have not been successful (Mar, 1993; Quon et al., 1991).

In a more influential effort, a number of researchers have for over a decade studied the link between aluminum and Alzheimer's disease. Several studies have reported elevated levels of aluminum in the brains of people with Alzheimer's disease and researchers have hypothesized that the metal may be one cause of the disorder (for example, Candy et al., 1986). On the other hand, others have argued that the presence of aluminum may be a consequence of the disease and not its cause (Alfrey, 1986). The concern about aluminum was reported in the popular press and, as a result, many people became fearful that aluminum in the water they drank, the food they ate, their pots and pans, or even their antacids and antiperspirants could be putting them at risk for Alzheimer's disease (Edwards, 1994; Kolata, 1992). Another study suggested that the aluminum observed in the neuritic plaques—small areas of damaged nerve terminals—in the brains of people with Alzheimer's disease may simply be a lab contaminant: metal from the air and from the chemicals used to prepare the tissue for observation (Landsberg, McDonald, & Watt, 1992). Of course, this is only one study and we must be careful about accepting its findings prematurely. It reminds us, however, of the importance of confirming every research result in order to avoid false conclusions.

Although I had tried for years to determine what was happening to me, I was not prepared for the truth I was so frantically seeking.

Finally, one more lesson in scientific caution comes from research that demonstrates a negative correlation between cigarette smoking and Alzheimer's disease (Brenner et al., 1993). In other words, the study found that smokers are less likely than nonsmokers to develop Alzheimer's disease. Does this mean smoking has a protective effect, shielding a person against the development of this disease? On close examination, the finding may instead be the result of the differential survival rates of those who smoke and those who do not. In general, nonsmokers tend to live longer, and are thereby more likely to develop Alzheimer's disease, which appears later in life. In fact, some believe that the relative inability of cells to repair themselves, a factor that may be more pronounced among people with Alzheimer's disease, may interact with cigarette smoking to shorten the lives of smokers who are at risk for Alzheimer's (J. E. Riggs, 1993). Put another way, smoking may exacerbate the degenerative process of Alzheimer's disease, causing people with the disease who also smoke to die much earlier than nonsmokers who have Alzheimer's. These types of studies and the conclusions drawn from them should make us sensitive to the complicated nature of the disorders we study.

What do we know about Alzheimer's disease, the most common cause of dementia? After the death of the patient he described as having a "strange disease of the cerebral cortex," Alois Alzheimer performed an autopsy. He found that the brain contained large numbers of tangled, strandlike filaments (referred to as *neurofibrillary tangles*). This type of damage occurs in everyone with Alzheimer's disease, although we do not know what causes it. A second type of degeneration involves the dendrites, or branches, of the neurons, which deteriorate to the point that the neuron itself can no longer function properly. These dead neurons cluster in *neuritic plaques* (also referred to as *senile* or *amyloid plaques*). Neuritic plaques are also found in older adults who do not have symptoms of dementia, but they have far fewer of them than individuals with Alzheimer's disease (Dewji & Singer, 1996). Both forms of damage—neurofibrillary tangles and neuritic plaques—accumulate over the years and are believed to produce the characteristic cognitive disorders we have been describing.

These two types of degeneration affect extremely small areas and can be detected only by a microscopic examination of the brain. Even sophisticated brain-scan techniques are not powerful enough to observe these changes in the living brain, which is why a definitive diagnosis of Alzheimer's disease requires an autopsy. In addition to having neurofibrillary tangles and neuritic plaques, over time the brains of many people with Alzheimer's disease atrophy (shrink) to a greater extent than would be expected through normal aging (La Rue, 1992). Because brain shrinkage has many causes, however, only by observing the tangles and plaques can a diagnosis of Alzheimer's be properly made.

Rapid advances are being made toward uncovering the genetic bases of Alzheimer's disease. Because important discoveries happen almost daily, we cannot speak conclusively; however, certain overall themes have arisen from genetic research. As with most of the other behavioral disorders we have examined, multiple genes seem to be involved in the development of Alzheimer's disease. Table 15.3 illustrates what we know so far. Genes on chromosomes 21, 19, 14, and 1 have all been linked to certain forms of Alzheimer's disease (Barinaga, 1995; Selkoe, 1997). The link to chromosome 21 was discovered first, and resulted from the unfortunate observation that individuals with Down syndrome, who have three copies of chromosome 21 instead of the usual two, developed the disease at an unusually high rate (Report of the Advisory Panel on Alzheimer's Disease, 1995). More recent work has located relevant genes on three other chromosomes. These discoveries indicate that there is more than one genetic cause of Alzheimer's disease. Some forms, including the one associated with chromosome 14, have an early onset. Diana Friel McGowin may have an early-onset form, because she started noting symptoms at the age of 45. In contrast, Alzheimer's disease associated with chromosome 19 seems to be a late-onset form of the disease that has an effect only after the age of about 60.

Although discovering the genetic origins of Alzheimer's has not brought immediate treatment implications, researchers are closer to understanding how the disease develops, which may result in medical interventions. Genetic research has advanced our knowledge of how the neuritic plaques develop in the brains of people with Alzheimer's disease and may hold a clue to its origins. In the core of the plaques is a solid waxy substance called amyloid protein. Just as cholesterol buildup on the walls of blood vessels chokes the blood supply, deposits of amyloid proteins are believed by some researchers to cause the cell death associated with Alzheimer's (Hardy, Mann, Wester, & Winblad, 1986). An important question, then, is why does this protein accumulate in the brain cells of some people but not others?

Two mechanisms that may account for amyloid protein buildup are currently being studied. The first involves *amyloid precursor protein* (APP), a large protein that is eventually broken down into the amyloid protein found in the neuritic plaques. Important work resulted in identifying the gene responsible for producing APP, on chromosome 21 (Tanzi et al., 1987). This finding may help to integrate two observations about Alzheimer's disease: (a) APP produces the amyloid protein found in the neuritic plaques; (b) Down syndrome, which is associated with an extra 21st chromosome, also results in a higher incidence of the disease. The gene responsible for producing APP and, ultimately, amyloid protein, may be responsible for the relatively infrequent early-onset form of the disease, and its location could explain why people with Down syndrome—who have an extra 21st chromosome and therefore an extra APP gene—are much more likely than the general population to develop Alzheimer's disease.

A second, more indirect way that amyloid protein may build up in brain cells is through *apolipoprotein E* (apoE),

table 15.3	**Genetic Factors in Alzheimer's Disease**
Chromosomal Location	*Age of Onset*
21	45-65
19	60-
14	30-60
1	40-70

Adapted from Barinaga (1995) and Selkoe (1997).

which normally helps transport cholesterols, including amyloid protein, through the bloodstream. There are at least three different forms of this transporter protein: apoE-2, apoE-3, and apoE-4. Individuals who have late-onset Alzheimer's, the most common form, are likely to carry the gene associated with apoE-4, located on chromosome 19. Researchers have found that about 80% of people with Alzheimer's who also have a family history of the disease will have at least one gene for apoE-4 (Saunders et al., 1993; Strittmatter et al., 1993). In contrast, of the individuals with Alzheimer's who have no family history of the disease, approximately 64% have at least one gene for apoE-4, and only 31% of nonaffected individuals have the gene. Having two genes for apoE-4 (one on each of the pairs of chromosome 19) increases one's risk for Alzheimer's: One study found that as many as 90% of people with both genes developed Alzheimer's disease (Corder et al., 1993). In addition, having two of the apoE-4 genes also seemed to decrease the mean age of onset from 84 years of age to 68 years. These results suggest that apoE-4 may be responsible for late-onset Alzheimer's disease and that a gene on chromosome 19 is responsible for synthesizing the transporter. What is still not completely understood is how apoE-4 causes amyloid proteins to build up in the neurons of people who ultimately exhibit Alzheimer's disease and whether this process is responsible for the disease itself.

Another intriguing question is how amyloid protein causes brain cell death. In a potentially important study, a group of researchers found that amyloid protein may induce these cells to self-destruct through a natural process called *apoptosis* (Loo et al., 1993). The brain of a developing fetus has more cells than it needs. The brain eventually improves its efficiency by killing off unnecessary cells through the process known as apoptosis. Loo and his colleagues found that when they added amyloid protein to central nervous system neurons cultured in the laboratory, the neurons died in a manner resembling the self-destructive process of apoptosis. The researchers hypothesized that this process may produce Alzheimer's disease in two ways.

First, cell death and the resulting neuritic plaques occur when amyloid protein comes in contact with the neurons. In a sense, the amyloid protein signals the neuron that it is no longer useful. Second, even when amyloid protein occurs in nonlethal doses, its presence may still weaken cells and make them more susceptible to other stressors that occur in the brain, such as glucose deprivation. This theory has intuitive appeal because it could explain why some individuals display Alzheimer's disease and others do not, even though they may both have factors (such as the apoE-4 gene) that would make them vulnerable. Psychological and biological stressors may interact with physiological processes to produce Alzheimer's disease.

We opened the section with a word of caution, which it is appropriate at this point to repeat. Some of the findings just reviewed are considered controversial. It is possible, for example, that neuritic plaques may be a by-product of the deterioration caused by other processes, and not its cause. The apoE-4 gene on chromosome 19 may be only a marker for a nearby gene that contributes to the condition. We are clearly learning, but many questions remain to be answered about this destructive condition.

PSYCHOLOGICAL AND SOCIAL INFLUENCES

For the most part, research has focused on the biological conditions that produce dementia. Although few would claim that psychosocial influences *directly* cause the type of brain deterioration seen in people with dementia, they may help determine onset and course. For example, a person's life-style may involve contact with factors that can cause dementia. We saw, for instance, that substance abuse can lead to dementia and, as we discussed previously (see Chapter 11), whether a person abuses drugs is determined by a combination of biological and psychosocial factors. In the case of vascular dementia, a person's biological vulnerability to vascular disease will influence the chances of strokes that can lead to this form of dementia. Life-style issues such as diet, exercise, and stress influence cardiovascular disease, and therefore help determine who ultimately experiences vascular dementia.

Cultural factors may also affect this process. For example, hypertension and strokes are prevalent among African-Americans and certain Asian-Americans (Cruickshank & Beevers, 1989), which may explain why vascular dementia is most often observed in members of these groups (de la Monte, Hutchins, & Moore, 1989). In an extreme example, exposure to a viral infection can lead to dementia similar in form to Creutzfeldt-Jakob disease through a condition known as kuru. This virus is passed on through a ritual form of cannibalism that is practiced in Papua New Guinea as a part of mourning (Gajdusek, 1977). Dementia caused by head trauma and malnutrition are relatively prevalent in preindustrial rural societies (Lin, 1986; Westermeyer, 1989), which suggests that social engineering in the form of occupational safety and economic conditions influencing diet also affect the prevalence of certain forms of dementia. It is apparent that psychosocial factors help influence who does and who does not develop certain forms of dementia. Brain deterioration is a biological process but, as we have seen throughout this text, even biological processes are influenced by psychosocial factors.

Psychosocial factors also influence the course of dementia. Recall that educational attainment may affect the onset of dementia (Fratiglioni et al., 1991; Korczyn et al., 1991). Having certain skills may help some people cope better than others with the early stages of dementia. As we saw earlier, Diana Friel McGowin's mother was able to carry on her day-to-day activities by making maps and using other tricks to help compensate for her failing abilities. The early stages of confusion and memory loss may be better tolerated in cultures with lowered expectations of older adults. In certain cultures, including the Chinese, younger people are expected to take the demands of work and care from older adults after a certain age (Ikels, 1991). Dementia may go undetected for years in these societies.

Much remains to be learned about the cause and course of most types of dementia. As we saw in Alzheimer's and Huntington's disease, certain genetic factors make some individuals vulnerable to progressive cognitive deterioration. In addition, brain trauma, some diseases, and exposure to certain drugs such as alcohol, inhalants, and the sedative, hypnotic, and anxiolytic drugs can cause the characteristic decline in cognitive abilities. We also noticed that psychosocial factors can help determine who is subject to these causes, and how they cope with the condition. Looking at dementia from this integrative perspective should help us view treatment approaches in a more optimistic light. It may be possible to protect people from conditions that lead to dementia, and to support them in dealing with the devastating consequences of having it. We next review attempts to help from both biological and psychosocial perspectives.

Treatment: An Overview

For many of the disorders we have considered, treatment prospects are fairly good. Clinicians can combine various strategies to reduce suffering significantly. Even when treatment does not bring expected improvements, mental health professionals have usually been able to stop problems from progressing. This is not the case in the treatment of dementia.

One factor preventing major advances in the treatment of dementia is the nature of the damage caused by this disorder. The brain contains billions of neurons, many more than are used. Damage to some can be compensated for by others, due to *plasticity*. However, there is a limit to where and how many neurons can be destroyed before vital functioning is disrupted. Neurons are currently irreplaceable, although researchers are closing in on this previously insurmountable obstacle as well (Kirschenbaum et al., 1994). Therefore, with extensive brain damage, no known treatment can restore lost abilities. The goals of treatment therefore become (a) trying to prevent certain conditions, such as substance abuse, that may bring on dementia, (b) trying to stop the brain damage from spreading and becoming worse, and (c) attempting to help these individuals and their caregivers cope with the advancing deterioration. Most of the efforts in treating dementia have focused on the second and third goals, with biological treatments aimed at stopping the cerebral deterioration and psychosocial treatments directed at helping patients and caregivers cope.

Simple signs and labels can help people with memory loss.

A troubling statistic further clouds the tragic circumstances of dementia: More than half the caregivers of people with dementia—usually relatives—eventually become clinically depressed (D. Cohen & Eisdorfer, 1988). Compared with the general public, these caregivers use more psychotropic medications and report stress symptoms at three times the normal rate (George, 1984). Caring for people with dementia, especially in its later stages, is clearly an especially trying experience.

BIOLOGICAL TREATMENTS

Dementia due to known infectious diseases, nutritional deficiencies, and depression can be treated if it is caught early. Unfortunately, however, there is no known treatment for most of the different types of dementia that are responsible for the vast majority of cases. Dementia due to stroke, HIV, Parkinson's disease, and Huntington's disease is not currently treatable because there is no effective treatment for the primary disorder. However, exciting new research in several related areas has brought us closer to helping individuals with these forms of dementia. Substances that may help preserve and perhaps restore neurons—called *glial cell-derived neurotrophic factor* or *GDNF*—may someday be used to help reduce or reverse the progression of degenerative brain diseases (Tomac et al., 1995). Researchers are also looking into the possible benefits of transplanting fetal brain tissue (taking from aborted fetuses) into the brains of people with such diseases. Preliminary results from these studies appear promising (e.g., Kopyov, Jacques, Lieberman, Duma,

& Rogers, 1996). Dementia brought on by strokes may now be more preventable by new drugs that help prevent much of the damage inflicted by the blood clots that are characteristic of stroke (Barinaga, 1996). Most current attention is on a treatment for dementia of the Alzheimer's type, because it affects so many people. Here too, however, success has been modest at best.

Much work has been directed at developing drugs that will enhance the cognitive abilities of people with dementia of the Alzheimer's type. Many seem to be effective initially, but long-term improvements have not been observed in placebo-controlled studies (Loebel et al., 1993). Two drugs that have had a modest impact on cognitive abilities in some patients, *tacrine hydrochloride* (Cognex) and *donepezil* (Aricept) are the first to receive Food and Drug Administration approval for use with Alzheimer's disease. Tacrine and donepezil prevent the breakdown of the neurotransmitter acetylcholine, which is deficient in people with Alzheimer's disease, thus making more acetylcholine available to the brain. Research suggests that people's cognitive abilities improve to the point where they were 6 months earlier (Knapp et al., 1994; Rogers & Friedhoff, 1996; Samuels & Davis, 1997). But the gain is not permanent. Even people who respond positively do not stabilize but continue to experience the cognitive decline associated with Alzheimer's disease. In addition, if they stop taking the drug—as almost three-quarters of the patients do because of negative side effects such as liver damage and nausea—they lose even that 6-month gain (Winker, 1994). The drugs and required testing can cost over $250 per month, so the affected person and the family must decide whether the cost is worth the temporary benefit.

Several other medical approaches appear to hold promise in slowing the course of Alzheimer's disease. For example, the effects of vitamin E recently have been evaluated. One large study found that among individuals with moderately severe impairment, high doses of the vitamin (2,000 IU per day) delayed progression compared to a placebo (Sano et al., 1997). Several findings point to the beneficial effects of estrogen replacement therapy (prescribed for some women following menopause) on Alzheimer's disease (e.g., Tang et al., 1996). Finally, aspirin and other nonsteroidal anti-inflammatory drugs (NSAIDs) have also been demonstrated to be helpful in slowing the onset of the disease (Stewart, Kawas, Corrada, & Metter, 1997). To date, however, no drugs are available that directly treat and therefore completely stop the progression of the conditions that cause the cerebral damage in Alzheimer's disease.

Psychosocial treatments focus on enhancing the lives of people with dementia and their families. People with dementia can be taught skills to compensate for their lost abilities. Recall that Diana's mother learned on her own to make maps to help her get from place to place. Diana herself began making lists so she would not forget important things. Some researchers have evaluated more formal adaptations to help people in the early stages of dementia. Bourgeois (1992, 1993) created "memory wallets" to help people with dementia carry on conversations. On white index cards inserted into a plastic wallet are printed declarative statements such as "My husband John and I have 3 children," or "I was born on January 6, 1911, in Pittsburgh." In one of her studies, Bourgeois (1992) found that six adults with dementia could, with minimal training, use this memory aid to improve their conversations with others. Three of the adults used their memory wallets with people who had initially not been involved in the training, such as children and grandchildren. (One participant withdrew from the training after several weeks, which seemed to coincide with a substantial decline in her cognitive abilities during that time.) Other researchers have used similar devices to help people orient themselves in time and place, another ability that is disrupted by dementia (Hanley, 1986; Hanley & Lusty, 1984). Adaptations such as these help people communicate with others and remain aware of their surroundings, and can also reduce the frustration that comes with the awareness of their own decline.

Individuals with advanced dementia are not able to feed, bathe, or dress themselves. They cannot communicate with or recognize even familiar family members. They may wander away from home and become lost. Because they are no longer aware of social stigma, they may engage in public displays of sexual behavior such as masturbation. They may be frequently agitated or even physically violent. To help both the person with dementia and the caregiver, researchers have explored interventions for dealing with these consequences of the disorder (Fisher & Carstensen, 1990).

Of great concern is the tendency of people with dementia to wander. Sometimes they wind up in places or situations that may be dangerous (for instance, stairwells, the street). Often, the person is tied to a chair or bed, or sedated, to prevent roaming. Unfortunately, physical and medical restraint has its own risks, including additional medical complications; it also adds greatly to the loss of control and independence that already plague the person with dementia. Psychological treatment as an alternative to restraint sometimes involves providing cues for people to help them safely navigate around their home or other areas (Hussian & Brown, 1987). Colored arrows and grids on the floor indicate "safe" and "dangerous" areas, allowing people more freedom to ambulate; they also relieve caregivers of the necessity of constant monitoring.

Someone with dementia can become agitated and is sometimes verbally and physically aggressive. This behavior is understandably very stressful for people trying to provide care. In these situations, medical intervention is often used, although frequently with only modest results (Loebel et al., 1993). Caregivers are often given assertiveness training to help them deal with hostile behaviors (see Table 15.4). Otherwise, caregivers may either passively accept all the criticism inflicted by the person with dementia, which increases stress, or become angry and aggressive in return. This last response is of particular concern because of the potential for *elder abuse*. Withholding food or medication or inflicting physical abuse is most common among caregivers of elderly people who have cognitive deficits (Sachs & Cassel, 1989). It is important to teach caregivers how to handle stressful circumstances so that they do not escalate into abusive situations. There is not a great deal of objective evidence supporting the usefulness of assertiveness training for reducing caregiver stress, and we await research to guide future efforts.

In general, families of people with dementia can benefit from supportive counseling to help them cope with the frustration, depression, guilt, and loss that take a heavy emotional toll. However, clinicians must first recognize that the

table 15.4   Sample Assertive Responses

Patient Behavior	Assertive Response
	Calmly but firmly say:
1. The patient refuses to eat, bathe, or change clothes.	"We agreed to do this at this time so that we will be able to (give specific activity or reward)."
2. The patient says she/he wants to go home.	"I know you miss some of the places we used to be. This is our home now and together we are safe and happy here."
3. The patient demands immediate gratification.	"It's not possible to have everything we want. As soon as I've finished (describe your task or actions), we can discuss other things we want to do."
4. The patient accuses the caregiver of taking his or her possessions.	"We both enjoy our own things. I'll help you look for (specific item missing) so you can enjoy it just as soon as I have finished (describe specific task or action)."
5. The patient is angry and/or rebellious.	"I like to be treated fairly just as you do. Let's discuss what's bothering you so we can go back to our usual good relationship."

Source: Adapted from Edwards, 1994.

ability to adapt to stressors differs among people. One study found cultural differences in the appraisal of psychological distress associated with the role of caregiver. Black caregivers reported less depression and had better coping responses than white caregivers (Haley et al., 1996). One group, which conducted a large-scale study of 555 principal caregivers over a 3-year period, identified a number of steps that can be taken to support caregivers through this difficult time (Aneshensel, Pearlin, Mullan, Zarit, & Whitlatch, 1995). Early on, caregivers need basic information on the causes and treatment of dementia, as well as on financial and legal issues, and on locating help for the patient and the family. As the dementia progresses, and the affected person requires more and more assistance, caregivers will need help managing behavioral difficulties (wandering away, violent outbursts) and developing effective ways to communicate with the patient. Clinicians also assist the family with decisions about hospitalization and, finally, help them adjust during bereavement (Aneshensel et al., 1995).

Overall, the outlook for stopping the cognitive decline characteristic of dementia is not good, and we have no sense that a research breakthrough is imminent. The best available medications provide some recovery of function, but they do not stop the progressive deterioration. Psychological interventions may help people cope more effectively with the loss of cognitive abilities, especially in the earlier stages of this disorder but, for now, the emphasis is on helping caregivers—the other victims of dementia—as the person they care for continues to decline.

Amnestic Disorder

Say these three words to yourself: apple, bird, roof. Try to remember them, then count backward from 100 by 3s. After about 15 seconds of counting, can you still recall the three words? Probably so. However, people with amnestic disorder will not remember them, even after such a short period of time (Butters & Cermak, 1980). The loss of this type of memory, which we described as a primary characteristic of dementia, can occur without the loss of other high-level cognitive functions. The main deficit of **amnestic disorder** appears to be the inability to transfer information like the list we just described into long-term memory, which can cover minutes, hours, or years. This disturbance in memory is due either to the physiological effects of a medical condition, such as head trauma,

"I still have a pretty major memory problems, which has since brought about a divorce and which I now have a new girlfriend, which helps very much. I even call her . . . my new brain or my new memory. . . . If I want to know something, besides on relying on this so-called memory notebook, which I jot notes down in constantly and have it every day dated, so I know what's coming up or what's for that day. She also helps me very much with the memory. My mother types up the pages for this notebook, which has each half hour down and the date, the day and the date, which anything coming within an hour or two or the next day or the next week, I can make a note of it so that when that morning comes, and I wake up, I right away, one of the first things, is look at the notebook. What have I got to do today?"

or to the long-term effects of a drug. Consider the following case.

S.T.
Remembering Fragments

S.T., a 67-year-old white woman, suddenly fell, without loss of consciousness. She appeared bewildered and anxious but oriented to person and place yet not to time. Language functioning was normal. She was unable to recall her birthplace, the ages of her children, or any recent presidents of the United States. She could not remember 3 objects for 1 minute, nor recall what she had eaten for her last meal. She could not name the color of any object shown to her but could correctly name the color related to certain words—for example, "grass," "sky." Object naming was normal. Examined one year later, she could repeat 5 digits forward and backward but could not recall her wedding day, the cause of her husband's death, or her children's ages. She did not know her current address or phone number and remembered 0 out of 3 objects after 5 minutes. While she was described by her family as extremely hard-working prior to her illness, after hospitalization she spent most of her time sitting and watching television. She was fully oriented, displayed normal language function, and performed simple calculations without error. (Cole, Winkelman, Morris, Simon, & Boyd, 1992, pp. 63–64)

The DSM-IV criteria for amnestic disorder describe the inability to learn new information or to recall previously learned information. As with all cognitive disorders, memory disturbance causes significant impairment in social and occupational functioning. The woman we just described was diagnosed with a type of amnestic disorder called *Wernicke-Korsakoff syndrome*, which is caused by damage to

from the inside

Living in the Labyrinth: A Personal Journey Through the Maze of Alzheimer's
By Diana Friel McGowin*

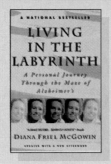

In what may be the first autobiographical account of Alzheimer's, Diana Friel McGowin frankly shares what her life was like when she learned the devastating fact of her condition: "When I first received my diagnosis of Alzheimer's disease, I closed myself up in one room of my darkened and tightly locked house, and refused to answer the telephone or door bell" (p. viii). She describes her early denial of memory loss, close friends' and relatives' reactions to her worsening condition, and how she ultimately acknowledged and adjusted to her deteriorating cognitive ability: "I knew he was my son, my baby—just could not remember what in blazes his name was!" (p. 108). She presents each stage of her condition with fearless clarity:

> At home, meals, pot holders, dishcloths and my arms were being burned. . . . I had lost weight I could ill afford to lose, and was beginning to suffer from insomnia. I sometimes lost my thread of thought in mid-sentence. Memories of childhood and long ago events were quite clear, yet I could not remember if I ate that day. On more than one occasion when my grandchildren were visiting, I forgot they were present and left them to their own devices. Moreover, on occasions when I had picked them up to come play at my house, the small children had to direct me home. (pp. 64–65)

Readers will appreciate this rare glimpse into the heart and mind of a person facing a steady decline with her eyes open and her dignity intact. As she makes her way through the labyrinth of Alzheimer's, McGowin becomes a dedicated activist, working hard to educate the public about this disease that strikes so many and has been so little understood. Although she freely admits her despair, she never gives up hope. Citing a 1993 research report that "the smile is the last to go," McGowin states firmly, "I don't believe that is an accident. I do believe it is significant" (p. 139).

* Diana Friel McGowin, *Living in the Labyrinth: A Personal Journey Through the Maze of Alzheimer's* (Delta Books, 1994).

earlier. As with other people with amnestic disorder, despite these obvious deficits with her memory her language command was fine and she could perform simple chores. Yet these individuals are often significantly impaired in social or vocational functioning because of the importance of memory to such activities.

As we saw with the other cognitive impairments, a wide range of insults to the brain can cause permanent amnestic disorders. Recent research has focused on attempting to *prevent* the damage associated with Wernicke-Korsakoff syndrome. Specifically, a deficiency in thiamine (vitamin B-1) due to alcohol abuse in persons developing Wernicke-Korsakoff syndrome is leading researchers to try supplementing this vitamin, especially for very heavy drinkers (e.g., Bowden, Bardenhagen, Ambrose, & Whelan, 1994; Martin, Pekovich, McCool, Whetsell, & Singleton, 1994). To date, however, there is little research pointing to long-term assistance in treating people with amnestic disorders.

concept check 15.3

Identify the cognitive disorders described.

1. Decline in cognitive functioning that is gradual and continuous and has been associated with neurofibrillary tangles and neuritic plaques. _____

2. The apparent loss of ability to transfer information to long-term memory without loss of other high-level cognitive functions. _____

3. José is a recovering alcoholic. Ask him about his wild partying days, and his stories usually end quickly because he can't remember the whole tale. He even has to write down things he has to do in a notebook; otherwise, he's likely to forget. _____

4. Grandpa has suffered from a number of strokes, but can still care for himself. However, his ability to remember important things has been declining steadily for the past few years. _____

Summary

- Delirium is a temporary state of confusion and disorientation that can be caused by brain trauma, intoxication by drugs or poisons, surgery, and a variety of other stressful conditions, especially among older adults.
- Dementia is a progressive and degenerative condition marked by gradual deterioration of a broad range of cognitive abilities including memory; language; and planning, organizing, sequencing, and abstracting information.
- Alzheimer's disease is the leading cause of dementia, affecting approximately 4 million Americans; there is currently no known cause or cure.

the thalamus, a small region deep inside the brain that acts as a relay station for information from many other parts of the brain. In her case, the damage to the thalamus was believed due to a stroke that caused vascular damage. Another common cause of Wernicke-Korsakoff syndrome is chronic heavy alcohol use. As you saw, S. T. had pronounced difficulty recalling information presented just minutes before. Although she could repeat a series of numbers, she couldn't remember three objects that were presented to her moments

- To date, there is no effective treatment for the irreversible dementias caused by Alzheimer's disease, Parkinson's disease, Huntington's disease, and the various other less common conditions that produce this progressive cognitive impairment. Treatment often focuses on helping the patient cope with the continuing loss of cognitive skills, and helping caregivers deal with the stress of caring for the affected individuals.

- Amnestic disorders involve a dysfunction in the ability to recall recent and past events. The most common is Wernicke-Korsakoff syndrome, a memory disorder usually associated with chronic alcohol abuse.

Key Terms

delirium
dementia
Alzheimer's disease
dementia of the Alzheimer's type
vascular dementia
HIV-1 disease
head trauma
Parkinson's disease
Huntington's disease
Pick's disease
Creutzfeldt-Jakob disease
amnestic disorder

Answers to Concept Checks

15.1
1. dementia (a)
2. delirium (b)
3. dementia (a)

15.2
1. aphasia (c)
2. agnosia (b)
3. facial agnosia (a)

15.3
1. dementia of the Alzheimer's type
2. amnestic disorder
3. Wernicke-Korsakoff syndrome
4. vascular dementia

EXPLORING COGNITIVE DISORDERS

- When the brain is damaged, the effects are irreversible, accumulating until learning, memory, or consciousness are obviously impaired.
- Cognitive disorders develop much later than mental retardation and other learning disorders, which are believed to be present at birth.

DELIRIUM

Description

- Impaired consciousness and cognition for several hours or days.
  - confusion, disorientation, inability to focus
- Most prevalent among older adults, people with AIDS, patients on medication

Causes (subtypes)

- Delirium due to a general medical condition
- Substance-induced delirium
- Delirium due to multiple etiologies
- Delirium not otherwise specified

Treatment

- Pharmacological
  - benzodiazepines
  - antipsychotics
- Psychosocial
  - reassurance
  - presence of personal objects
  - inclusion in treatment decisions

AMNESTIC DISORDER

Description

- Permanent short-term memory loss without impairment of other cognitive functions
  - inability to learn new information or recall previously learned information
  - significant impairment in social and occupational functioning

Causes

- Medical condition such as head trauma
- Lasting effects of a drug, even after the substance is no longer ingested

Treatment

- Prevention: proper medical care and drug monitoring
- No long-term success at combating damage

Subtype: Wernicke/Korsakoff Syndrome

Caused by damage to the thalamus from injury (stroke) or chronic heavy alcohol use (thiamine depletion).

DEMENTIA

- Gradual deterioration of brain functioning that affects judgment, memory, language, and other advanced cognitive processes.
- Caused by medical condition or drug abuse
- Some forms irreversible, some resolved by treatment of primary condition

DEMENTIA OF THE ALZHEIMER'S TYPE

Description

- Increasing memory impairment and other multiple behavioral and cognitive deficits, affecting language, motor functioning, ability to recognize people or things, and/or planning.
- Most prevalent dementia
- Subject of most research

Causes

Progressive brain damage, evident in neurofibrillary tangles and neuritic plaque, confirmed by autopsy but assessed by simplified mental status exam. Involves multiple genes.

Treatment

No cure so far, but hope lies in genetic research and amyloid protein in neurine plaques. Management may include lists, maps, notes to help maintain orientation. New medications that prevent acetylocholine breakdown and vitamin therapy show promise.

VASCULAR DEMENTIA

Permanent deterioration due to blocked or damaged blood vessels in the brain (stroke); symptoms identical to Alzheimer's and may also include problems with walking and weakness of limbs.
- Treatment focuses on coping.

DEMENTIA DUE TO OTHER GENERAL MEDICAL CONDITIONS

Similar in effect to other cognitive disorders, but caused by
– head trauma
– HIV, Parkinson's, Huntington's, Pick's, or Creutzfeldt-Jakob disease
– hydrocephalus, hypothyroidism, brain tumor, and vitamin B_{12} deficiency.
- Treatment of primary condition is sometimes possible

SUBSTANCE–INDUCED PERSISTING DEMENTIA

Caused by brain damage due to prolonged drug use, especially in combination with poor diet, as in alcohol dependency; substances may also include inhalants, and the sedative, hypnotic, and anxiolytic drugs.
- Treatment focuses on prevention.

16

Mental Health Services: Legal and Ethical Issues

Mind is the great lever of all things; human thought is the process by which human ends are ultimately answered.
Daniel Webster

We begin this chapter with a return to Arthur, who we described in Chapter 13 as having psychotic symptoms. Revisiting the case from his family's perspective reveals the complexities of mental health law and the ethical aspects of working with people who have psychological disorders.

Arthur
A Family's Dilemma

As you remember, Arthur was brought to our clinic by family members because he was speaking and acting strangely. He talked incessantly about his "secret plan" to save all the starving children in the world. His family's concern intensified when Arthur said that he was planning to break into the German embassy and present his plan to the German ambassador. Alarmed by his increasingly inappropriate behavior and fearing that he would be hurt, the family was astounded to learn that they could not force him into a psychiatric hospital. Arthur could admit himself—which was not likely, given his belief that nothing was wrong with him—but they had no power to involuntarily admit him unless he was in danger of doing harm to himself or others. Even if they sincerely believed some harm might be forthcoming, this wasn't sufficient reason to admit him involuntarily. The family coped with this emergency as best they could for several weeks until the worst of Arthur's behaviors began to diminish.

Arthur suffered from what is known as brief psychotic disorder (see Chapter 13). Fortunately for him, this is one of the few psychotic disorders that is not chronic. What is important here is to see how the mental health system responded. Because Arthur had not in actuality hurt himself or someone else, he had to seek help on his own before the hospital would assist him, even though everyone involved realized that such action on his part was very unlikely. This response by the mental health system added one more layer of helplessness to the family's already desperate emotional state. Why wouldn't the mental health facility admit Arthur, who was clearly out of touch with reality and in need of help? Why couldn't his own family authorize the mental health facility to act? What would have happened if Arthur had entered the German embassy and hurt or, worse, killed someone? Would he have gone to jail, or would he have finally received help from the mental health community? Would Arthur have been held responsible if he hurt other people while he was delusional? These are just a few of the many issues that surface when you try to balance the rights of people who have psychological disorders with the responsibilities of society to provide care.

Mental health professionals daily face such questions. They must both diagnose and treat people and also consider individual and societal rights and responsibilities. As we describe how systems of ethics and legal concepts have developed, remember they change with time and with shifting societal and political perspectives on mental illness. How we treat people with psychological disorders is in part a function of how society views them. For example, do people with mental illness need help and protection, or does society need protection from them? As public opinion of people with mental illness changes, so do the laws affecting them, and legal and ethical issues have an effect on both research and practice. As you will see, the issues affecting research and practice are often complementary. For one example, confidentiality is required to protect the identity of a participant in a research study and of a patient seeking help for a psychological disorder. Because people who receive mental health services often simultaneously participate in research studies, we must consider the concerns of both constituencies.

People with mental illness are treated differently in different cultures.

Civil Commitment

The legal system exercises significant influence over the mental health system, for better or for worse. Laws have been designed to protect people who display abnormal behavior and society. Often, achieving this protection is a delicate balancing act, with the scales sometimes thought to be tipped in favor of the rights of individuals and at other times in favor of society as a whole. For example, each state has **civil commitment laws** that detail when a person can be legally declared to have a mental illness and be placed in a hospital for treatment (La Fond, 1996). When Arthur's family tried to have him involuntarily committed to a mental health facility, hospital officials decided that because he was not in imminent danger of hurting himself or others he could not be committed against his will. In this case, the laws protected Arthur from involuntary commitment, but they also put him and others at potential risk by not compelling him to get help. La Fond and Durham (1992) argue that two clear trends in mental health law are evident in the recent history of the United States. According to these authors, a "liberal era" from 1960 to 1980 was characterized by a commitment to individual rights and fairness. In contrast, 1980 to the present has been a "neoconservative era," partly in reaction to the liberal reforms of the 1960s and 1970s, that has focused on majority concerns including law and order. In the liberal era, the rights of people with mental illness dominated; in the neoconservative era, these rights have been limited to provide greater protection to society.

Civil commitment laws in the United States date back to the late 19th century. Before this time, almost all people with severe mental illness were cared for by family members or the community at large or were left to care for themselves. With the development of a large public hospital system devoted to treating such individuals came an alarming trend: involuntary commitment of people for reasons that were unrelated to mental illness (La Fond & Durham, 1992). There were even instances in which women were committed to psychiatric hospitals by their husbands simply for holding differing personal or political views. Mrs. E. P. W. Packard crusaded for better civil commitment laws after being involuntarily confined to a psychiatric hospital for 3 years (Weiner & Wettstein, 1993).

Criteria for Civil Commitment

Historically, states have permitted commitment when several conditions have been met: (a) The person has a "mental illness" and is in need of treatment, (b) the person is dangerous to himself or herself or others, or (c) the person is unable to care for himself or herself, a situation considered a "grave disability." How these conditions are interpreted has varied over the years and has always been controversial. It is important to see that the government justifies its right to act against the wishes of an individual—in this case, to commit someone to a mental health facility—under two types of authority: police power and *parens patriae* ("state or country as the parent") power. Under police power, the government takes responsibility for protecting the public health, safety, and welfare and can create laws and regulations to ensure this protection. Criminal offenders are held in custody if they are a threat to society. The state applies parens patriae power in circumstances in which citizens are not likely to act in their own best interest, for example, to assume custody of children who have no living parents. Similarly, it is used to commit individuals with severe mental illness to mental health facilities when it is believed that they might be harmed because they are unable to secure the basic necessities of life, such as food and shelter (grave disability), or because they do not recognize their need for treatment (Brakel, Parry, & Weiner, 1985). Under parens patriae power, the state acts as a surrogate parent, presumably in the best interests of a person who needs help.

A person in need of help can always voluntarily request admission to a mental health facility; after an evaluation by a mental health professional, he or she may be accepted for treatment. However, when an individual does not voluntarily seek help, but others feel that treatment or protection is necessary, the formal process of civil commitment can be initiated. The specifics of this process differ from state to state, but it usually begins with a petition by a relative or mental health professional to a judge. The court may then request an examination to assess psychological status, ability for self-care, need for treatment, and potential for harm. The judge considers this information and decides whether commitment is appropriate. This process is similar to other legal proceedings, and the person under question has all the rights and protections provided by the law. In most states, the person can even request that a jury hear the evidence and make a determination. In all cases, the person must be notified that the civil commitment proceedings are taking place, must be present during the trial, must have representation by an attorney, and can examine the witnesses and request an independent evaluation. These safeguards are built into the civil commitment process to guarantee the rights of the person being examined and to ensure that no one is involuntarily committed to a psychiatric facility for other than legitimate reasons.

In emergency situations, when there is clearly immediate danger, a short-term commitment can be made without the formal proceedings required of a civil commitment. Family members or sometimes police officers certify that the person presents a "clear and present danger" to self or to others (Weiner & Wettstein, 1993). Arthur's family was unsuccessful in having him admitted on an emergency basis because it was not clear that anyone was in immediate danger, only that someone *might* be hurt. Again, deciding what is a clear and present danger sometimes requires a great deal of subjective judgment from the court and from mental health professionals.

Defining Mental Illness

The concept of mental illness figures prominently in civil commitment, and it is important to understand how it is

A woman facing an unplanned pregnancy contemplates suicide.

defined. **Mental illness** is a legal concept, typically meaning severe emotional or thought disturbances that negatively affect an individual's health and safety. Each state has its own definition. For example, in New York, "'Mental illness' means an affliction with a mental disease or mental condition which is manifested by a disorder or disturbance in behavior, feeling, thinking, or judgment to such an extent that the person afflicted requires care, treatment and rehabilitation" (New York Mental Hygiene Law, 1992). In contrast, in Connecticut, a "'Mentally ill person' means a person who has a mental or emotional condition that has substantial adverse effects on his or her ability to function and who requires care and treatment, and specifically excludes a person who is an alcohol-dependent person or a drug-dependent person" (Connecticut Gen. Stat. Ann., 1992). Many states, in fact, exclude mental retardation or substance-related disorders from the definition of mental illness.

Mental illness is *not* synonymous with psychological disorder; in other words, receiving a DSM-IV diagnosis does not necessarily mean that a person fits the legal definition of mental illness. Although the DSM is quite specific about criteria that must be met for diagnosis, there is considerable ambiguity about what constitutes a "mental condition" or what are "adverse effects on his or her ability to function." This allows for flexibility in making decisions on an individual basis, but it also maintains the possibility of subjective impression and bias as influences on these decisions.

Dangerousness

Assessing whether someone is a danger to self or others is a critical determinant of the civil commitment process. **Dangerousness** is a particularly controversial concept for the mentally ill: Popular opinion tends to be that people who are mentally ill are more dangerous than those who are not. Though this conclusion is questionable, it is still widespread, in part because of sensational media reports. Such views are important to the process of civil commitment if they bias a determination of *dangerousness* and unfairly link it with severe mental illness.

The results of research on dangerousness and mental illness are mixed. Some studies show no unusual association between mental illness and violence (Steadman & Ribner, 1980; Teplin, 1985); others find a slightly greater risk for violence among people with mental illness (Lindquist & Allebeck, 1990). In one study, researchers found that although having a mental illness in general did not increase the likelihood of future violence (defined as re-arrest for a violent crime), specific symptoms (such as hallucinations and delusions) did slightly increase the rate of violence (Teplin, Abram, & McClelland, 1994). This study suggests that even previously violent individuals with mental illness are not necessarily going to commit violent crimes after they are released, although the presence of certain symptoms may increase the risk.

Unfortunately, the widely held misperception that people with mental illness are more dangerous may differentially affect ethnic minorities and women. Women, for example, are likely to be viewed as more dangerous than men when they engage in similar aggressive behaviors (Coughlin, 1994). Homeless women are more likely to be involuntarily committed even in warm climates because they are perceived to be less capable than men of caring for themselves, and thus at greater risk of harming themselves (Stefan, 1996). Black males are often perceived as dangerous, even when they don't exhibit any violent behavior (Bond, DeCandia, & McKinnon, 1988), which may partly explain why blacks are overrepresented among those who are involuntarily committed to state psychiatric institutions (Lawson, Hepler, Holladay, & Cuffel, 1994).

To return to the general issue, how do you determine whether a person is dangerous to others? How accurate are mental health professionals at predicting who will and who will not later be violent? The answers bear directly on the process of civil commitment as well as on protection for society. If we can't accurately predict dangerousness, how can we justify involuntary commitment?

Research suggests that we are better at assessing the relative risk required of the legal system than determining dangerousness on a case-by-case basis (Grisso & Appelbaum, 1992). Stated in another way, mental health professionals can identify groups of people who are at greater risk than the general population for being violent—such as having both a previous history of violence and drug or alcohol dependence—and can so advise the court. What we cannot yet do

Larry Hogue was involuntarily committed to a psychiatric hospital because, homeless and under the influence of drugs (left), he terrorized residents of a New York City neighborhood for years. Once off drugs (right) Hogue was able to control himself.

is predict with certainty whether a particular person will or will not become violent.

Changes Affecting Civil Commitment

Clearly, there are significant problems with the process of civil commitment. In particular, deciding whether a person has a mental illness or is dangerous requires considerable subjective judgment and, because of varying legal language, this determination can differ from state to state. These problems have resulted in a number of significant legal developments. We will look next at how changes in civil commitment procedures have resulted in significant economic and social consequences, including an impact on one of our more important social problems: homelessness.

The Supreme Court and Civil Commitment

In 1957, the parents of Kenneth Donaldson had him committed to the Florida State Hospital for treatment of paranoid schizophrenia. Donaldson was not considered dangerous, yet, despite repeated offers of placement in a halfway house or with a friend, Dr. O'Connor, the superintendent of the hospital, refused to release him for almost 15 years, during which Donaldson received virtually no treatment (Donaldson, 1976). Donaldson successfully sued Dr. O'Connor for damages, winning $48,500. In deciding the case, the Supreme Court found that "a State cannot constitutionally confine . . . a non-dangerous individual who is capable of surviving safely in freedom by himself or with the help of willing and responsible family and friends" (*O'Connor v. Donaldson*, 1975).

Here and in a subsequent decision known as *Addington v. Texas* (1979), the Supreme Court said that more than just a promise of improving one's quality of life is required to commit someone involuntarily. If non-dangerous persons can survive in the community with the help of others, they should not be detained against their will. Needing treatment or having a grave disability was not sufficient to involuntar-

ily commit someone with a mental illness. The effect of this decision was to limit substantially the government's ability to commit individuals unless they were dangerous (La Fond & Durham, 1992).

Criminalization

Because of the tightened restrictions on involuntary commitment that prevailed in the 1970s and 1980s, many people who would normally have been committed to mental health facilities for treatment were instead being handled by the criminal justice system. In other words, people with severe mental illness were now living in the community, but many were not receiving the mental health services they needed and would eventually run afoul of the legal system because of their behavior. This "criminalization" of the mentally ill was of great concern because the criminal justice system was not prepared to care for these individuals (Cohen, 1996; Teplin, 1984). Family members were increasingly frustrated that they couldn't obtain treatment for their loved ones, who were instead languishing in jail without help.

Deinstitutionalization and Homelessness

In addition to criminalization, two other trends emerged at this time: the increase in the number of people who were homeless and **deinstitutionalization,** the movement of people with severe mental illness out of institutions. Homelessness, although not exclusively a problem of the mentally ill, is largely determined by social views of people with mental illness. Rough estimates place the numbers of homeless people at between 250,000 and 3 million in the United States alone (Morse, 1992). About 25% have a previous history of hospitalization for mental health problems (M. Robertson, 1986), and about 30% are considered severely mentally ill (Koegl, Burnam, & Farr, 1988). One recent study found that as many as 15% of people experiencing severe psychiatric disturbances for the first time had been homeless prior to their psychological difficulties (Herman, Susser, Jandorf, Lavelle, & Bromet, 1998).

Information on the characteristics of people who are homeless is important because it provides us with clues about why people become homeless, and it dispels the notion that all homeless people have mental health problems. For a time, homelessness was blamed on strict civil commitment criteria and deinstitutionalization (Perlin, 1996; Torrey, 1988a); that is, policies to severely limit who can be involuntarily committed, the limits placed on the stays of people with severe mental illness, and the concurrent closing of large psychiatric hospitals were held responsible for the substantial increase in homelessness during the 1980s. Al-

People become homeless because of many factors, including economic conditions, mental health status, and drug use.

though a sizable percentage of homeless people do have mental illness, the rise in homelessness is also due to such economic factors as increased unemployment and a shortage of low-income housing (Morse, 1992). Yet the perception that civil commitment restrictions and deinstitutionalization caused homelessness resulted in movements to change commitment procedures.

Reforms in civil commitment that made it more difficult to commit someone involuntarily occurred at the same time the policy of deinstitutionalization was closing large psychiatric hospitals (Turkheimer & Parry, 1992). Deinstitutionalization had two goals: (a) to close the large state mental hospitals and (b) to create a network of community mental health centers where the released individuals could be treated. Although the first goal appears to have been substantially accomplished, with about a 75% decrease in the number of hospitalized patients (Kiesler & Sibulkin, 1987), the essential goal of providing alternative community care appears not to have been attained. Instead, there was **transinstitutionalization,** or the movement of people with severe mental illness from large psychiatric hospitals to nursing homes or other group residences, including jails and prisons, many of which provide only marginal services (Bachrach, 1987; Sharfstein, 1987). Because of the deterioration in care for many people who had previously been served by the mental hospital system, deinstitutionalization is largely considered a failure. Although many praise the ideal of providing community care for people with severe mental illness, the support needed to provide this type of care has been severely deficient.

Reactions to Strict Commitment Procedures

Arthur's psychotic reaction and his family's travails in trying to get help occurred during the mid-1970s, a time that was characterized by greater concern for individual freedom than for society's rights and by the belief that people with mental illness were not properly served by being forced into treatment. Others, however, especially relatives of afflicted people, felt that by not coercing some individuals into treatment, the system was sanctioning their mental decline and placing them at grave risk of harm. The culmination of a number of factors—such as the lack of success with deinstitutionalization, the rise in homelessness, and the criminalization of people with severe mental illness—gave rise to a backlash against their perceived causes, including the strict civil commitment laws. The case of Joyce Brown captures this clash of concerns between individual freedoms for people with mental illness and society's responsibility to treat them.

Joyce Brown
Homeless but Not Helpless

During a 1988 winter emergency in New York City, Mayor Ed Koch ordered that all homeless people who appeared to be mentally ill should be involuntarily committed to a mental health facility for their protection. He used the legal principle of parens patriae to justify this action, citing the need to protect these individuals from the cold and from themselves. One of the people who was taken off the streets, 40-year-old Joyce Brown, was picked up against her will and admitted to Bellevue Hospital, where she received a diagnosis of paranoid schizophrenia. She had been homeless for some time, swearing at people as they walked by; at one point she adopted the name Billie Boggs after a New York television personality with whom she fantasized a relationship. Supported by the New York Civil Liberties Union, Joyce Brown contested her commitment and was released after 3 months (Kasindorf, 1988).

Homeless parents and their children are given job training and day care at this Florida facility.

This case is important because it illustrates the conflicting interests over civil commitment. Joyce Brown's family had for some time been concerned over her well-being and had tried unsuccessfully to have her involuntarily committed. Although she had never hurt anyone or tried to commit suicide, they felt that living on the streets of New York City was too hazardous, and they feared for her welfare. City officials expressed concern for Brown and others like her, especially during the dangerously cold winter, although some suspected that this was an excuse to remove people with disturbing behavior from the streets of affluent sections (Kasindorf, 1988). Brown chose not to seek treatment and resisted efforts to place her in alternative settings. At times, she could be quite articulate in making a case for her freedom of choice. Only weeks after she was released from the hospital, she was again living on the streets. Brown was involuntarily committed to a mental health facility again in early 1994, and by February she was once more attempting to be released from the hospital (*New York Times*, 1994).

Rulings such as *O'Connor v. Donaldson* and *Addington v. Texas* had argued that mental illness and dangerousness should be criteria for involuntary commitment. However, because of cases like Joyce Brown's and concerns about homelessness and criminalization, a movement has emerged that calls for a return to broader civil procedures that would permit commitment not only of those who showed dangerousness to self or others but also of individuals who were not dangerous but were in need of treatment and of those with grave disability. Groups such as the National Alliance for the Mentally Ill (NAMI), a coalition of family members of people with mental illness, argued for legal reform to make involuntary commitment easier—an emotional response like that of Arthur's family. Several states in the late 1970s and early 1980s changed their civil commitment laws in an attempt to address these concerns. For example, the state of Washington revised its laws in 1979 to allow commitment of people who were judged to be in need of treatment, which produced a 91% increase in the number of involuntary commitments in the first year it was in effect (Durham & La Fond, 1985). There was essentially no change in the size of the hospital population at this time, only in the status under which patients were committed (La Fond & Durham, 1992). Whereas people were previously detained because of violence, they were now admitted under parens patriae powers; also, whereas most admissions had been voluntary, they were now involuntary. Hospitals began to fill up because of longer stays and repeated admissions and accepted only involuntary admissions; therefore, the result of easing the procedure for involuntarily committing people with mental illness was only to change the authority under which they were admitted.

The special case of sex offenders has attracted public attention in recent years, and the issue of how to treat repeat offenders is at the heart of the concerns over civil commitment. In the years between 1930 and 1960, some states passed "sexual psychopath laws" that provided hospitalization instead of incarceration, but for an indefinite period of time (Zonana, 1997). Sex offenders (rapists, pedophiles) could be civilly committed until they demonstrated that treatment was effective. However, because treatment is often unsuccessful when attempted with uncooperative clients (see Chapter 10) and because public opinion moved from a priority to treat to a priority to punish, these laws were repealed or went unused. Recent efforts have focused on incarcerating sex offenders for their crimes and, if they are judged still dangerous at the end of their sentences, civilly committing them. Such "sexual predator" laws were first enacted in 1990 and the Kansas version was recently upheld as constitutional by the U.S. Supreme Court (*Kansas v. Hendricks*, 1997). Confinement of this type was viewed by the court as acceptable because it was seen as treatment, even though the justices conceded that such treatment is often ineffective (Zonana, 1997).

An Overview of Civil Commitment

What should the criteria be for involuntarily committing someone with severe mental illness to a mental health facility? Should imminent danger to self or others be the only justification, or should society paternalistically coerce people who appear to be in distress and in need of asylum or safety? How do we address the concerns of families like Arthur's who see their loved ones overcome by psychological problems? And what of our need not to be harassed by people like Joyce Brown? When do these rights take precedence over the rights of an individual to be free from unwanted incarceration? It is tempting to conclude that the legal system has failed to address these issues, and reacts only to the political whims of the times.

However, from another point of view, the periodic change in laws is a sign of a healthy system that responds to the limitations of previous decisions. The reactions by the Supreme Court in the 1970s to the coercive and arbitrary nature of civil commitment were as understandable as more recent attempts to make it easier to commit people in obvious need of help. As the consequences of these changes become apparent, the system responds to correct injustices. Although improvements may seem excruciatingly slow and may not always correctly address the issues in need of reform, the fact that laws can be changed should make us optimistic that the needs of individuals and of society can ultimately be addressed through the courts.

 Criminal Commitment

What would have happened if Arthur had been arrested for trespassing on embassy grounds or, worse yet, if he had hurt or killed someone in his effort to present his plan for saving the world? Would he have been held responsible for his actions, given his obvious disturbed mental state? How would a jury have responded to him when he seemed fine just several days later? If he was not responsible for his behavior then, why does he seem so normal now?

These questions are of enormous importance as we debate whether people should be held responsible for their criminal behavior despite the possible presence of mental illness. Cases such as that of Lyle and Eric Menendez, who admit to murdering their parents but who claim they were driven to it by their father's abuse, make us wonder whether the laws have gone too far. **Criminal commitment** is the process by which people are held because (a) they have been accused of committing a crime and are detained in a mental health facility until they can be assessed as fit or unfit to participate in legal proceedings against them, or (b) they have been found not guilty of a crime by reason of insanity.

The Insanity Defense

The purpose of our criminal justice system is to protect our lives, our liberty, and our pursuit of happiness, but not all people are punished for criminal behavior. The law recognizes that, under certain circumstances, people are not responsible for their behavior and that it would be unfair and perhaps ineffective to punish them. Current views originate from a case recorded over 150 years ago in England. Daniel M'Naghten today might receive the diagnosis of paranoid schizophrenia. He held the delusion that the English Tory party was persecuting him, and he set out to kill the British prime minister. He mistook the man's secretary for the prime minister himself and killed the secretary instead. In what has become known as the M'Naghten rule, the English court decreed that people are not responsible for their criminal behavior if they do not know what they are doing or if they don't know that what they are doing is wrong. This ruling was, in essence, the beginning of the insanity defense, the highlights of which are summarized in Table 16.1. For more than 100 years, this rule was used to determine culpability when a person's mental state was in question.

In the intervening years, other standards have been introduced to modify the M'Naghten rule because many critics felt that simply relying on an accused person's knowledge of right or wrong was too limiting and that a broader definition was needed (Guttmacher & Weihofen, 1952). Mental illness alters not only a person's cognitive abilities but also emotional functioning, and mental health professionals believed that the entire range of functioning should be taken into account when a person's responsibility was determined. One influential decision, known as the Durham rule, was initiated in 1954 by Judge David Bazelon of the Federal Circuit Court of Appeals for the District of Columbia and based on the case *Durham v. United States*. The Durham rule broadened the criteria for responsibility from a knowledge of right or wrong to include the presence of a "mental disease or defect" (see Table 16.1). This decision was initially hailed by mental health professionals because it allowed them to present to a judge or jury a complete picture of the person with mental illness. Unfortunately, it was soon apparent that mental health professionals did not have the expertise to reliably assess whether a person's mental illness caused the criminal behavior in question and therefore that decisions were being based on unscientific opinions (Arens, 1974). Although the Durham rule is no longer used, its effect was to cause a reexamination of the criteria used in the insanity defense.

An influential study of this question was conducted around the same time as the Durham decision by a group of attorneys, judges, and law scholars who belonged to the American Law Institute (ALI). Their challenge was to develop criteria for determining whether a person's mental competence makes him or her answerable for criminal behavior. The ALI first reaffirmed the importance of distinguishing the behavior of people with mental illness from that of people without mental disorders. They pointed out that the threat of punishment was unlikely to deter someone who had severe mental illness; their position was that these individuals should instead be treated until they improve and then

table 16.1   Important Factors in the Evolution of the Insanity Defense

The *M'Naghten* Rule	1843	[I]t must be clearly proved that at the time of committing the act, the party accused was labouring under such a defect of reason, from disease of the mind, as not to know the nature and quality of the act he was doing; or if he did know it, that he did not know he was doing what was wrong. [101 Cl. & F. 200, 8 Eng. Rep. 718 (H.L. 1843)]
The *Durham* Rule	1954	An accused is not criminally responsible if his unlawful act was the product of mental disease or mental defect. [*Durham v. United States*, 214 F.2d 862, 876 (D.C. Cir. 1954)]
American Law Institute (ALI) Rule	1962	1. A person is not responsible for criminal conduct if at the time of such conduct as a result of mental disease or defect he lacks substantial capacity either to appreciate the criminality (wrongfulness) of his conduct or to conform his conduct to the requirements of law. 2. As used in the Article, the terms "mental disease or defect" do not include an abnormality manifested only by repeated criminal or otherwise antisocial conduct. [American Law Institute (1962). *Model penal code: Proposed official draft*. Philadelphia: Author.]
Diminished Capacity	1978	Evidence of abnormal mental condition would be admissible to affect the degree of crime for which an accused could be convicted. Specifically, those offenses requiring intent or knowledge could be reduced to lesser included offenses requiring only reckless or criminal neglect. [New York State Department of Mental Hygiene (1978). *The insanity defense in New York*. New York: New York Department of Mental Hygiene.]
Insanity Defense Reform Act	1984	A person charged with a criminal offense should be found not guilty by reason of insanity if it is shown that, as a result of mental disease or mental retardation, he was unable to appreciate the wrongfulness of his conduct at the time of his offense. (American Psychiatric Association, 1982, p. 685)

released. (This recommendation is discussed further when we examine recent developments and criticisms of the insanity defense.) The ALI concluded that people were not responsible for their criminal behavior if, because of their mental illness, they could not recognize the inappropriateness of their behavior or control it (American Law Institute, 1962). The criteria shown in Table 16.1, which are known as the ALI test, stipulate that a person must either be unable to distinguish right from wrong—as set forth in the M'Naghten rule—or be incapable of self-control to be shielded from legal consequences.

The ALI also included provisions for the concept of **diminished capacity** (see Table 16.1), which held that people's ability to understand the nature of their behavior and therefore their criminal intent could be diminished by their mental illness. The theory of criminal intent—otherwise called *mens rea* or having a "guilty mind"—is important legally because to convict someone of a crime, there must be proof of the physical act (actus rea) and the mental state (mens rea) of the person committing the act (Weiner & Wettstein, 1993). For example, if a woman accidentally hits someone who steps in front of her car and the person subsequently dies, the woman would not be held criminally responsible; although a person was killed, there was no criminal intent— the driver didn't deliberately hit the person and attempt murder. The diminished capacity concept proposes that a person with mental illness who commits a criminal offense may not, because of the illness, have criminal intent and therefore cannot be held responsible. By the mid-1970s, ap-

proximately 25 states had adopted the concept of diminished capacity as a way to assess the responsibility of persons with mental illness, in part because it softens the strict requirements of the M'Naghten rule (Lewin, 1975).

■ **concept check 16.1**

Commitment laws determine the conditions under which a person is certified to have a mental disorder and therefore placed in a hospital, sometimes in conflict with the person's own wishes. The following paragraph is about civil commitment, criminal commitment, and the two types of authority by which the state takes control of its citizens. Check your understanding by filling in the blanks.

Several conditions must be met before the state is permitted to commit a person involuntarily: The person has a (1) _____ and is in need of treatment; the person is considered (2) _____ to herself or himself or others, and the person is unable to care for himself or herself, otherwise known as a (3) _____ .

In the case of criminal commitment, people are held for two reasons: (4) _____ or (5) _____ .

Reactions to the Insanity Defense

Judicial rulings through the 1960s and 1970s regarding criminal responsibility parallel the course of civil commit-

James Brady, Ronald Reagan's press secretary, was wounded in 1981 by a gunman attempting to assassinate the president. In 1994, Brady and his wife Sarah celebrated the passage of the Brady Law, which imposed stricter controls on the possession of hand guns.

ment. An effort was made to focus on the needs of people with mental illness who also broke the law, providing mental health treatment instead of punishment. However, the successful use of concepts such as insanity or diminished capacity in criminal cases alarmed large segments of the population. For instance, in 1979 a man successfully pleaded not guilty by reason of insanity after being arrested for writing bad checks. His case was based on the testimony of an expert witness who said that he suffered from pathological gambling disorder and he therefore could not distinguish right from wrong (*State v. Campanaro*, 1980). Other successful defenses were based on disorders in the DSM, such as posttraumatic stress disorder, and on disorders not in this system, including "battered wife syndrome."

Without question, the case that prompted the strongest outrage against the insanity defense and the most calls for its abolition is that of John W. Hinckley, Jr. (Simon & Aaronson, 1988). On March 31, 1981, as President Ronald Reagan walked out of the Washington Hilton Hotel, Hinckley fired several shots, hitting and seriously wounding the president, a Secret Service agent, and James Brady, the president's press secretary. In an instant, Secret Service agents tackled and disarmed Hinckley. Hinckley was obsessed with actress Jodie Foster; he claimed he tried to kill the president to impress her. Hinckley was judged by a jury to be not guilty by reason of insanity (NGRI), using the American Law Institute standard. The verdict sent shockwaves throughout the country and legal community (R. Rogers, 1987). One of the many consequences of this event was that James Brady and his wife Sarah became advocates for stricter gun control laws and saw the ultimate passage of the Brady Law in 1994.

Although there was already criticism of the insanity defense, one study found that after Hinckley's verdict more than half the states considered abolishing it (Keilitz &

Fulton, 1984). As we have seen before, such impulses often are based more on emotion than on fact. Highly publicized cases such as those of Hinckley, Charles Manson, Jeffrey Dahmer, and Ted Kaczynski, with the media characterization of people with mental illness as excessively violent, have created an unfavorable public perception of the insanity defense. One telephone survey study found that 91% of people who responded agreed with the statement that "judges and juries have a hard time telling whether the defendants are really sane or insane" (V. Hans, 1986). Almost 90% agreed that the "insanity plea is a loophole that allows too many guilty people to go free." In a similar study, 90% of people agreed that "the insanity plea is used too much. Too many people escape responsibilities for crimes by pleading insanity" (Pasewark & Seidenzahl, 1979). Is there hard evidence that the insanity defense is used too often?

A recent study of the public's impression of the insanity defense compared it to the actual use of the defense and its outcomes (Silver, Cirincione, & Steadman, 1994). As Table 16.2 shows, the public's perception that this defense is used in 37% of all felony cases is a gross overestimate; the actual figure is less than 1%. The public also overestimates how often the defense is successful as well as how often people judged NGRI are set free. People tend to *under*estimate the length of hospitalization of those who are acquitted. This last issue is important: In contrast to the perceptions of the general public, the length of time a person is confined to a hospital after being judged NGRI may exceed the time the

table 16.2 Comparison of Public Perceptions with the Actual Operation of the Insanity Defense

	Public	*Actual*
A. *Use of the insanity defense*		
Percentage of felony indictments resulting in an insanity plea	37	0.9
Percentage of insanity pleas resulting in acquittal	44	26
B. *Disposition of insanity acquittees*		
Percentage of insanity acquittees sent to a mental hospital	50.6	84.7
Percentage of insanity acquittees set free	25.6	15.3
Conditional Release		11.6
Outpatient		2.6
Release		1.1
C. *Length of confinement of insanity acquittees* (in months)		
All crimes	21.8	32.5
Murder		76.4

Source: Silver, Cirincione, & Steadman, 1994

Theodore Kaczynski, once a promising mathematician (left), became a notorious terrorist who killed three people and injured 23 more with handmade bombs sent through the mail. Awaiting trial as the Unabomber (right), Kaczynski refused to cooperate with his lawyers, who fought to have him declared mentally ill in order to save his life. Ironically, the prosecution, in pressing for the death penalty, supported his claim of sanity. (In the end, Kaczynski pleaded guilty and accepted a life sentence.)

person would have spent in jail had he or she been convicted of the crime (Steadman, 1985). John Hinckley, for example, has been a patient in St. Elizabeth's Hospital for more than 15 years. People with mental illness apparently do not often "beat the rap" as a result of being judged NGRI.

Despite sound evidence that it is not used excessively and does not result in widespread early release of dangerous individuals, major changes were made in the criteria for the insanity defense after the Hinckley verdict. Both the American Psychiatric Association (1983) and the American Bar Association (1984) recommended modifications, moving back toward M'Naghten-like definitions. Shortly afterward, Congress passed the Insanity Defense Reform Act of 1984, which incorporated these suggestions and made successful use of the insanity defense more difficult.

Another attempt at reforming the insanity plea has been to replace the verdict "not guilty by reason of insanity" (NGRI) with "guilty but mentally ill" (GBMI) (Callahan, McGreevy, Cirincione, & Steadman, 1992). Although there are several versions of the GBMI verdict, the shared premise is that the consequences for a person ruled GBMI are different from those for a person who is NGRI. People who are found to be NGRI are not sent to prison but are evaluated. A person who is found to be mentally ill is sent to a psychiatric facility until such time as he or she is judged ready for release. A person who is determined to be no longer mentally ill must be released. If Arthur had committed a crime and was found NGRI, because his brief psychotic disorder was quickly resolved he would probably have been released immediately. In contrast, one version of the GBMI verdict in theory allows the system both to treat and to punish the

individual. The person who is found guilty is given a prison term just as if there were no question of mental illness. Whether the person is incarcerated in prison or in a mental health facility is decided by legal authorities. If the person recovers from mental illness before the sentence has passed, he or she can be confined in prison for the maximum length of the term. If Arthur were found GBMI under this system, he could serve a full prison sentence, even though his mental illness was resolved. This version of GBMI has, as of 1992, been adopted by 11 states (La Fond & Durham, 1992).

The second version of GBMI is even harsher for the mentally ill offender. Convicted individuals are imprisoned, and the prison authorities may provide mental health services if they are available. The verdict itself is simply a declaration by the jury that the person was mentally ill at the time the crime was committed and does not result in differential treatment for the perpetrator. Currently, Idaho, Montana, and Utah have abandoned the insanity defense altogether and have adopted this version of GBMI (La Fond & Durham, 1992). The Supreme Court upheld the constitutionality of Montana's abolition of the insanity defense in Cowan v. Montana (De Angelis, 1994).

As noted, the GBMI verdict was a reaction to the perceived loophole provided by the insanity defense. It has been used in several states for more than 15 years, and its effects have been investigated by researchers. Two studies have shown that persons who receive the GBMI verdict are more likely to be imprisoned and to receive longer sentences than people pleading not guilty by reason of insanity (Callahan et al., 1992; Keilitz, 1987). Research also indicates that individuals receiving GBMI verdicts are no more likely to receive treatment than other prisoners who have mental illness (Keilitz, 1987; G. A. Smith & Hall, 1982).

Society has long recognized the need to identify criminals who may not be in control of their behavior and who may not benefit from simple incarceration. The challenge is in trying to do what may be impossible: determining whether the person knew what he or she was doing, knew right from wrong, and could control his or her behavior. Mental health professionals cannot assess mental health retrospectively. An additional dilemma is the desire, on the one hand, to provide care to people with mental illness and, on the other, to treat them as responsible individuals. Finally, we must resolve the simultaneous and conflicting interests of wanting to assist people with mental illness and wanting to be protected from them. By evaluating the effects of various consequences, science may be able to help resolve some of these issues. We must reach a national consensus about the basic value of people with mental illness in order to decide how they should be dealt with legally. We hope that the recent trend of favoring law and order over the rights of people with mental illness can be mitigated to provide attention to both concerns.

Competence to Stand Trial

Before people can be tried for a criminal offense, they must be able to understand the charges against them and to assist with their own defense, criteria outlined by the Supreme Court in *Dusky v. United States* (1960). Thus, in addition to interpreting a person's state of mind during the criminal act, experts must also anticipate his or her state of mind during the subsequent legal proceedings. A person could be ruled not guilty by reason of insanity because of his or her mental illness at the time of the criminal act yet still be competent to stand trial, a situation that would have occurred in Arthur's case had he committed a crime.

A person who is determined to be incompetent to stand trial typically loses the authority to make decisions and faces commitment. Because a trial requires a determination of **competence,** most people with obvious and severe impairments who commit crimes are never tried. Some observers estimate that for every person who receives a verdict of NGRI, 45 others are committed to a mental health facility with a diagnosis of severe mental illness (Steadman, 1979). The length of stay is the time it takes the committed person to regain competence. Because this period can be protracted, the courts have ruled that it cannot be indefinite and that, after a reasonable amount of time, the person must be found competent, set free, or committed under civil law (*Jackson v. Indiana*, 1972). Laws are often not precise in their language, and the phrase "reasonable amount of time" is open to a great deal of interpretation.

A final issue relates to the legal concept of burden of proof, the weight of evidence needed to win a case. In decisions of competence to stand trial, a recent ruling placed responsibility on the defendant to provide the burden of proof, in this case, that he or she is incompetent to stand trial (*Medina v. California,* 1992). Again, public concern that dangerous individuals with mental illness are routinely acquitted and let loose on society after committing multiple violent offenses flies in the face of the facts. More realistically, a person with mental illness commits a nonviolent crime and receives treatment through legal actions, such as the competence proceedings.

Duty to Warn

Do mental health professionals have any responsibility for the actions of the people they serve? This is especially important when you consider the dangerous behavior exhibited by a minority of people with severe mental illness. What are the responsibilities of professionals who suspect that someone with whom they are working may hurt or even kill another person? Must they contact the appropriate authority

---

■ concept check 16.2

The legal system has evolved to incorporate the idea that some people cannot be held responsible for their criminal actions due to mental disorder. Check your understanding of this evolution by identifying the following concepts. Pick your answers from (a) competence to stand trial, (b) diminished capacity, (c) American Law Institute rule, (d) the Durham rule, and (e) the M'Naughton rule.

1. The person could not distinguish between right and wrong at the time of the crime. _____

2. The person is not criminally responsible if the crime was due to "mental disease or mental defect." _____

3. The person is not responsible for the crime if he or she is not able to appreciate wrongfulness of behavior due to mental disease or defect. _____

4. A mental disorder could lessen a person's ability to understand criminal behavior and to form criminal intent. _____

5. The defendant does not go to trial because he or she is unable to understand the proceedings and assist in the defense. _____

---

or the person who may be harmed, or are they forbidden to discuss information disclosed during therapy sessions?

These issues are the subject of a tragic case known as *Tarasoff v. Regents of the University of California* (1974, 1976). In 1969, Prosenjit Poddar, a graduate student at the University of California, killed a fellow student, Tatiana Tarasoff, who had previously rejected his romantic advances. At the time of the murder he was being seen by two therapists at the University Health Center and had received a diagnosis of paranoid schizophrenia. At his last session, Poddar hinted that he was going to kill Tarasoff. His therapist believed this threat was serious and contacted the campus police, who investigated the allegation and received assurances from Poddar that he would leave Tarasoff alone. Weeks later, after repeated attempts to contact her, Poddar shot and stabbed Tarasoff until she died.

After learning of the therapists' role in the case, Tatiana Tarasoff's family sued the university, the therapists, and the university police, saying that they should have warned Tatiana that she was in danger. The court agreed, and the Tarasoff case has been used ever since as a standard for therapists concerning their **duty to warn** a client's potential victims. Related cases have further defined the role of the therapist in warning others (Kermani & Drob, 1987; La Fond, 1996). Courts have generally ruled that the threats must be specific. In *Thompson v. County of Alameda* (1980), the California Supreme Court ruled that a therapist does not have a duty to warn when a person makes nonspecific threats against nonspecific people. It is difficult for therapists to know their exact responsibilities for protecting third parties from their clients. Good clinical practice dictates that

Pamela Bozanich (left), deputy district attorney, discusses evidence in the Lyle and Erik Menendez double-murder trial with mental health expert Ann Wolpert Burgess (right).

any time they are in doubt they should consult with colleagues. A second opinion can be just as helpful to a therapist as to a client.

Mental Health Professionals as Expert Witnesses

Judges and juries often have to rely on **expert witnesses,** individuals who have specialized knowledge, to assist them in making decisions (Melton, Petrila, Poythress, & Slobogin, 1987; O'Connor, Sales, & Shuman, 1996). We have alluded to several instances in which mental health professionals serve in such a capacity, providing information about a person's dangerousness or ability to understand and participate in the defense. The public's perception of expert witnesses is characterized by ambivalence. On one hand, they see the value of persuasive expert testimony in educating a jury; on the other, they see expert witnesses as "hired guns" whose opinions suit the side that pays their bills (Hollien, 1990). How reliable are the judgments of mental health professionals who act as expert witnesses?

To take one example, in deciding whether someone should be civilly committed, the assessor must determine the person's potential for future violence. Research suggests that mental health professionals can make reliable predictions of dangerousness over the short term, for a period of 2 to 20 days after the evaluation (Lidz, Mulvey, Appelbaum, & Cleveland, 1989; McNiel & Binder, 1991). However, they have not been able to make reliable predictions of violence after longer periods of time (Monahan, 1984). A second area in which mental health professionals are frequently asked to provide consultation is in assigning a diagnosis. In Chapter 3, we discussed the development of systems to ensure the reliability of diagnoses. Recent revisions of diagnostic criteria, most notably DSM-III-R and the current DSM-IV, have

addressed this issue directly, thus helping clinicians make diagnoses that are generally reliable. Remember, however, that the legal definition of mental illness is not matched by a comparable disorder in DSM-IV. Therefore, statements about whether someone has a "mental illness" reflect determinations made by the court and not by mental health professionals.

Mental health professionals do appear to have expertise in identifying **malingering** and in assessing competence. Remember that to malinger is to fake or grossly exaggerate symptoms, usually in order to be absolved from blame. For example, a person might claim to have been actively hallucinating at the time of the crime and therefore not responsible. Research indicates that the Minnesota Multiphasic Personality Inventory (MMPI) test is almost 90% accurate in revealing malingering in people claiming to have posttraumatic stress disorder (PTSD) (McCaffrey & Bellamy-Campbell, 1989). Mental health professionals also appear capable of providing reliable information about a person's competence, or ability to understand and assist with a defense (Melton et al., 1987). Overall, mental health professionals can provide judges and juries with reliable and useful information in certain specific areas (Garb, 1992).

The research described here does not indicate how accurate expert testimony actually is under everyday conditions. In other words, under the right circumstances, experts can make accurate determinations of the short-term risks that a person will commit an act of violence, is faking certain symptoms, or is competent to stand trial, and of what diagnosis should be made. Yet, other factors conspire to influence expert testimony. Personal and professional opinions that exceed the competence of the expert witness can influence what information is or is not presented, as well as how it is relayed to the court (Hollien, 1990). For instance, if the expert witness believes in general that people should not be involuntarily committed to mental health facilities, this opinion will likely influence how the witness presents clinical information in civil commitment court proceedings.

 **Patients' Rights**

Until about 20 years ago, people in mental health facilities were accorded few rights. What treatment they received, whether they could make phone calls, send and receive mail, or have visitors were typically decided by hospital personnel who rarely consulted with the patient. However, abuses of this authority led to legal action and subsequent rulings by the courts concerning the rights of people in these facilities.

The Right to Treatment

One of the most fundamental rights of people in mental health facilities is, obviously, the right to treatment. For too many and for too long, conditions were poor and treatment was lacking in numerous large mental health facilities. Starting in the early 1970s, a series of class action lawsuits (filed on behalf of many individuals) helped establish the rights of people with mental illness and mental retardation. A landmark case, *Wyatt v. Stickney* (1972), grew out of a lawsuit filed by the employees of large institutions in Alabama who were fired because of funding difficulties and established for the first time the minimum standards that facilities had to meet in relation to the people who were hospitalized. Among the standards set by *Wyatt v. Stickney* were minimum staff–patient ratios and physical requirements, such as a certain number of showers and toilets for a given number of residents. The case also mandated that facilities make positive efforts to attain treatment goals for their patients.

Wyatt v. Stickney went further and expanded on a concept called the "least restrictive alternative," indicating that, wherever possible, people should be provided with care and treatment in the least confining and limiting environment. For example, the court noted the following for those with mental retardation:

> Residents shall have a right to the least restrictive conditions necessary to achieve the purpose of habilitation. To this end the institution shall make every attempt to move residents from (1) more to less structured living; (2) large to smaller facilities; (3) large to smaller living units; (4) group to individual residences; (5) segregated from the community to integrated into the community; (6) dependent living to independent living.

Despite this movement to secure treatment for people in mental health facilities, a gap was left as to what constituted proper treatment. The case of *Youngberg v. Romeo* (1982) reaffirmed the need to treat people in nonrestrictive settings but essentially left to professionals the decision about the type of treatment to be provided. This concerned patient advocates because, historically, leaving treatment to professional judgment has not always resulted in the intended end for the people in need of help. In 1986, Congress provided a number of safeguards by passage of the Protection and Advocacy for Mentally Ill Individuals Act (Woodside & Legg, 1990), which established a series of protection and advocacy agencies in each state to investigate allegations of abuse and neglect and to act as legal advocates. This layer of protection has resulted in a balance between professional concerns and the needs and rights of patients in mental health facilities.

The Right to Refuse Treatment

One of the most controversial issues in mental health today is the right of people, especially those with severe mental illness, to refuse treatment (Winick, 1997). In recent times,

the argument has centered on the use of antipsychotic medications. On one side of this issue is the mental health professional who believes that, under certain circumstances, people with severe mental illness are not capable of making a decision in their own best interest and that the clinician is therefore responsible for providing treatment despite the protestations of the affected person. On the other side, patients and their advocates argue that all people have a fundamental right to make decisions about their own treatment, even if doing so is not in their own best medical interests.

Although this controversy is not yet completely resolved, one court case has responded to a related question: Can people be "forced" to become competent to stand trial? This is an interesting dilemma: If people facing criminal charges are delusional or have such frequent severe hallucinations that they cannot fully participate in the legal proceedings, can they be forced against their will to take medication to reduce these symptoms, thereby making them competent to stand trial? A Supreme Court ruling, *Riggins v. Nevada* (1992), stated that because of the potential for negative side effects (such as tardive dyskinesia), people cannot be forced to take antipsychotic medication. Although this decision does not settle the issue of refusing treatment, it does indicate the high court's wish to honor individual choice (Perlin & Dorfman, 1993; Winick, 1997).

Research Participants' Rights

Throughout this text we have described research conducted worldwide with people who have psychological disorders; and we touched briefly in Chapter 4 on the issue of the rights of these individuals. In general, people who participate in psychological research have the following rights:

1. The right to be informed about the purpose of the research study
2. The right to privacy
3. The right to be treated with respect and dignity
4. The right to be protected from physical and mental harm
5. The right to choose to participate or to refuse to participate without prejudice or reprisals
6. The right to anonymity in the reporting of results
7. The right to the safeguarding of their records (American Psychological Association, 1992)

These rights are particularly important for people with psychological disorders who may not be able to understand them fully. One of the most important concepts in research is that those who participate must be fully informed about the risks and benefits of the study. Simple consent is not sufficient; it must be informed consent, or formal agreement by the subject to participate after being fully apprised of all important aspects of the study, including any possibility of harm. A recent case underlines the importance of **informed consent** and the sometimes gray areas that exist in applied research.

Greg Aller
Concerned about Rights

In 1988, 23-year-old Greg Aller signed a consent form agreeing to participate in a treatment study at the University of California at Los Angeles (UCLA) Neuropsychiatric Institute (Willwerth, 1993). Since the previous year, Greg had experienced vivid and frightening hallucinations and delusions about space aliens. His parents had contacted UCLA for assistance. They learned that the university was initiating a new study to evaluate people in the early stages of schizophrenia and to assess the effects of the withdrawal of medication. If Greg participated he could receive extremely expensive drug therapy and counseling free. After taking the drug Prolixin for 3 months as part of the study, he improved dramatically; the hallucinations and delusions were gone. He was now able to enroll in college and he made the dean's list.

Although overjoyed with the results, Greg's parents were concerned about the second phase of the study, which involved taking him off the medication. They were reassured by the researchers that this was an important and normal part of treatment for people with schizophrenia and that the potential for negative side effects of taking the drug for too long was great. They were also told that the researchers would put Greg back on the medication if he grew considerably worse without it.

Toward the end of 1989, Greg was slowly taken off the drug, and he soon started having delusions about Ronald Reagan and space aliens. Although his deterioration was obvious to his parents, Greg did not indicate to the researchers that he needed the medication or tell them of his now continuous hallucinations and delusions. Greg continued to deteriorate, at one point threatening to kill his parents. After several more months, Greg's parents persuaded him to ask for more medication. Although better than he was earlier, Greg has still not returned to the much-improved state he achieved following his first round of medication.

This case highlights the conflicts that can arise when researchers attempt to study important questions in psychopathology. Administrators at the National Institutes of Health reported that the UCLA researchers did not give Greg and his family all the information about the risks of treatment and the possibility of other approaches (Hilts, 1994). Critics claim that informed consent in this and similar situations is too often not fully met and that information is frequently colored to assure participation. However, the UCLA researchers note that what they did was no different from what would have happened outside the research study: They attempted to remove Greg from potentially dangerous antipsychotic medication. The controversy emerging from this case should be an added warning to researchers about their responsibilities to people who participate in their studies and their obligation to design added safeguards to protect the welfare of their study subjects.

■ concept check 16.3

Psychological professionals assume many roles and responsibilities. Identify the following situations using one of these terms: (a) informed consent; (b) duty to warn; (c) expert witness; (d) deinstitutionalization; (e) malingering.

1. Dr. X testified in court that the defendant was faking and exaggerating symptoms to evade responsibility. Dr. X is acting as a(n) _____ and the defendant is _____ .

2. The therapist has learned he is required to release more mentally ill patients from the hospital. He is worried that many of them will end up homeless and without continuing treatment as a result of _____ .

3. One of my clients threatened his mother's life during his session today. Now I must decide whether I have a _____ .

4. The clinical researcher knows the potential for harm of the participants is very slight, but is nevertheless careful to tell them about it and asks them whether they agree to give their _____ .

Clinical Practice Guidelines

The Food and Drug Administration (FDA) is one of the toughest drug regulatory agencies in the world, but it is uncertain if we will see a similar watchdog for psychosocial interventions soon because of the inherent differences between such treatments and medication. Drugs are manufactured in a factory to preset specifications. The job of the clinician is to monitor the effects very closely. Psychosocial treatments, by contrast, are delivered in the context of a continual interplay between the clinician and patient and therefore require more flexibility and less structure than drug treatments. Nevertheless, recognizing the wide differences in treating the same disorder and the increasing demand of managed-care companies for knowledge of appropriate and effective treatments, the government has stepped in. In 1989, legislation established a new branch of the federal government called the Agency for Health Care Policy and Research (AHCPR). The purpose of this agency is to establish uniformity in the delivery of effective health and mental health care and to communicate to practitioners throughout the country the latest developments in treating certain disorders effectively. The agency is also responsible for research into improving systems for the delivery of health and mental health services.

To accomplish its goals, the AHCPR published some clinical practice guidelines for specific disorders, including sickle cell disease, management of cancer pain, unstable angina, and depression in primary care settings. The AHCPR also facilitates guideline construction by other agencies. The government hopes not only to reduce costs by eliminating unnecessary or ineffective treatments but also to

Greg Aller (right, with his parents) participated in a drug study at UCLA and suffered a severe relapse of psychotic symptoms when medication was withdrawn. He and his family subsequently raised the issue of informed consent for such research.

facilitate the dissemination of effective interventions based on the latest research evidence. Treating people effectively—alleviating their pain and distress—is ultimately the most important way to reduce health care costs because these individuals will no longer request one treatment after another in an unending search for relief.

Recognizing the importance of this trend and the necessity that clinical practice guidelines be sound and valid, a task force of the American Psychological Association composed a template, or set, of principles for constructing and evaluating guidelines for clinical interventions for both psychological disorders and psychosocial aspects of physical disorders. These principles were published in 1995. They are necessary to ensure that future clinical practice guidelines will be comprehensive and consistent. As envisioned by the task force creating the template, the guidelines developed from it should help both the practitioner and the patient make decisions about appropriate treatment interventions for cognitive, emotional, and behavioral disorders and dysfunctions as well as psychosocial aspects of physical disorders. The guidelines will also ideally restrain administrators of health care plans from sacrificing or proscribing effective treatment, or limiting the amount of clinician time necessary to deliver treatment, in order to cut costs. The task force also felt that guidelines for psychosocial interventions could never be inflexible, since they must allow for the individual issues that arise in treating people with psychological disorders.

The task force decided that clinical practice guidelines for specific disorders should be constructed on the basis of two simultaneous considerations, or axes. The **clinical efficacy** axis is a thorough consideration of the scientific evidence to determine whether the intervention in question is effective. This evidence would answer the question, "Is the treatment effective when compared to an alternative treatment or to no treatment in a controlled clinical research context?" In Chapter 4, we reviewed the various research strategies used to determine whether an intervention is effective. As you will remember, for many reasons a treatment might seem effective when it is not effective at all. For instance, if patients improve on their own while being treated simply because of the passage of time or the natural healing process, the treatment had little to do with the improvement. It is possible that nonspecific effects of the treatment—perhaps just meeting with a caring health professional—are enough to make someone feel better without any contribution from the particular treatment technique. To determine clinical efficacy, experiments must establish whether the intervention in question is better than no therapy, better than a nonspecific therapy, or better than an alternative therapy. (The latter finding provides the highest level of evidence for a treatment's effectiveness.) We might also rely on information collected from various clinics where a large number of practitioners are treating the disorder in question. If these clinicians collect systematic data on the outcomes of their patients, they can ascertain how many are "cured," how many improve somewhat without recovering totally, and how many fail to respond to the intervention. Such data are referred to as *quantified clinical observations* or *clinical replication series*. Finally, a clinical consensus of leading experts is also a valuable source of information, although not as valuable as data from quantified clinical observations or randomized control trials.

The **clinical utility** axis is concerned with the effectiveness of the intervention in the practice setting in which it is to be applied, regardless of research evidence on its efficacy; in other words, will an intervention with proven efficacy in a research setting also be effective in the various frontline clinical settings in which it will be most frequently applied? Also, is application of the intervention in the settings where it is needed feasible and cost-effective? This axis is concerned with external validity, the extent to which an internally valid intervention is effective in different settings or under different circumstances from those where it was tested.

The first major issue to consider on the clinical utility axis is feasibility. Will patients accept the intervention and comply with its requirements, and is it relatively easy to administer? As noted in Chapter 7, electroconvulsive therapy (ECT) is an effective treatment for very severe depression in many cases, but it is extremely frightening to patients, many of whom refuse it. The treatment also requires sophisticated procedures and close supervision by medical personnel, usually in a hospital setting. Therefore, it is not particularly feasible.

A second issue on the clinical utility axis is generalizability, which refers to the extent to which an intervention is effective with patients of differing backgrounds—ethnicity, age, or sex—as well as in different settings—inpatient, outpatient, community—or with different therapists. Once

table 16.3   Overview of Template for Constructing Psychological Intervention Guidelines

Clinical Efficacy (Internal Validity)
1. Better than alternative therapy (randomized controlled trials/RCTs)
2. Better than nonspecific therapy (RCTs)
3. Better than no therapy (RCTs)
4. Quantified clinical observations
5. Clinical consensus
   Strongly positive
   Mixed
   Strongly negative
6. Contradictory evidence

Note: Confidence in treatment efficacy is based on both (a) the absolute and relative efficacy of the treatment and (b) the quality and replicability of the studies in which this judgment is made.

Clinical Utility (External Validity)
1. Feasibility
   A. Patient acceptability (cost, pain, duration, side effects, etc.)
   B. Patient choice in face of relatively equal efficacy
   C. Probability of compliance
   D. Ease of dissemination—number of practitioners with competence, requirements for training, opportunities for training, need for costly technologies or additional support personnel, etc.
2. Generalizability
   A. Patient characteristics
      (1) Cultural background issues
      (2) Gender issues
      (3) Developmental level issues
      (4) Other relevant patient characteristics
   B. Therapist characteristics
   C. Issues of robustness when applied in practice settings with different time frames, etc.
   D. Contextual factors regarding setting in which treatment is delivered
3. Costs and benefits
   A. Costs of delivering intervention to individual and society
   B. Costs to individual and society of withholding intervention

Note: Confidence in clinical utility as reflected on these three dimensions should be based on systematic and objective methods and strategies for assessing these characteristics of treatment as they are applied in actual practice. In some cases, randomized controlled trials will exist. More often, data will be in the form of quantified clinical observations (clinical replication series) or other strategies such as health economic calculations.

Source: American Psychological Association, 1995.

again an intervention could be very effective in a research setting with one group of patients but generalize very poorly across different ethnic groups. A summary of these two axes is presented in Table 16.3.

In reading the disorder chapters, you will have noted that there are now a number of effective treatments, both psychosocial and medical. However, most treatments are still in a preliminary stage of development. In the future, we will see a great deal of research to establish both the clinical efficacy and the clinical utility of various interventions for psychological disorders.

In Chapter 1, we reviewed various activities that make up the role of scientist–practitioners in the mental health professions, who take a scientific approach to their clinical work in order to provide the most effective assessment procedures and interventions. Changes in the delivery of mental health services are likely to be accompanied by considerable disruption, because this is a major system that affects millions of people. But the change will also bring opportunities. Scientist–practitioners will contribute to the process of guidelines development in several ways. For example, as attempts are made to assess the clinical utility or external validity of interventions, the collected experience of

thousands of mental health professionals will be immensely valuable. In fact, most of the information relevant to clinical utility or external validity will be collected by these clinicians in the course of their practice. Thus they will truly fulfill the scientist–practitioner role to the benefit of patients in our field.

 **Conclusions**

Therapy and scientific progress do not occur in a vacuum. People who study and treat abnormal behavior are responsible not only for mastering the wealth of information we have only touched on in this book but also for understanding and appreciating their role in society and in the world at large. Every facet of life—from the biological to the social, political, and legal—interacts with every other; if we are to help people, we must appreciate this complexity.

We hope we have given you a good sense of the challenges faced by workers in the field of mental health and have spurred some of you to join us in this rewarding work.

Summary

- Societal views of people with mental illness, and of relevant laws, do not remain static; they change with time. Often these changes are responses to perceived problems with the laws, and are intended to improve them. According to La Fond and Durham (1992), two trends in mental health law are evident in the recent history of the United States. A "liberal era" between 1960 and 1980 was characterized by a commitment to individual rights and fairness; a "neoconservative era," which began in 1980, focuses on majority concerns and on law and order.

Civil Commitment

- Civil commitment laws determine the conditions under which a person may be certified legally to have a mental illness and therefore to be placed in a hospital, sometimes in conflict with the person's own wishes.
- Historically, states have permitted commitment when several conditions have been met: (a) when the person has a mental illness and is in need of treatment, (b) when the person is dangerous to himself or herself or to others, or (c) when the person is unable to care for himself or herself.
- "Mental illness" as used in legal system language is not synonymous with "psychological disorder"; each state has its own definition of mental illness, usually meant to include people with very severe disturbances that negatively impact on their health and safety.
- Having a mental illness does not seem to increase the likelihood of dangerousness, that is, that a person will commit violent acts in the future, although having symptoms of hallucinations and delusions does seem to indicate more risk for behaving violently.
- The combination of the lack of success with deinstitutionalization, which has resulted instead in transinstitutionalization, the rise in homelessness, and the criminalization of people with severe mental illness, led to a backlash against the perceived causes of these factors, including the strict civil commitment laws.

Criminal Commitment

- Criminal commitment is the process by which people are held for one of two reasons: (a) They have been accused of committing a crime and are detained in a mental health facility until they can be determined as fit or unfit to participate in legal proceedings against them, or (b) they have been found not guilty of a crime by reason of insanity.
- The insanity defense is defined by a number of legal rulings: The M'Naghten rule states that people are not responsible for criminal behavior if they do not know what they are doing, or if they do know and they don't know it is wrong. The Durham rule broadened the criteria for responsibility from a knowledge of right or wrong to the presence of a "mental disease or defect." The American Law Institute (ALI) criteria concluded that people were not responsible for their criminal behavior if, because of their mental illness, they lacked either the cognitive ability to recognize the inappropriateness of their behavior or the ability to control their behavior.
- The concept of diminished capacity holds that people's ability to understand the nature of their behavior and therefore their criminal intent could be lessened by their mental illness.
- A determination of competence must be made before an individual can be tried for a criminal offense: To stand trial, people must be competent—able to understand the charges against them and to assist with their own defense.

A Duty to Warn

- Duty to warn is a standard that sets forth the responsibility of the therapist to warn potential victims that a client may attempt to hurt or kill them.

Mental Health Professionals as Expert Witnesses

- Individuals who have specialized knowledge and who assist judges and juries in making decisions, especially about such issues as competence and malingering, are called expert witnesses.

Patients' Rights

- One of the more fundamental rights of patients in mental facilities is their right to treatment; that is, they have a legal right to some sort of ongoing effort to both define and strive toward treatment goals. By contrast, a great deal of controversy exists over whether all patients are capable of making a decision to refuse treatment; this is an especially difficult dilemma in the case of antipsychotic medications that may improve a patients' symptoms but also bring with them severe negative side effects.

Research Participants' Rights

- Subjects who participate in any research study must be fully informed of the risks and benefits and formally give their informed consent to indicate so.

Clinical Practice Guidelines

- Clinical practice guidelines can play a major role in providing information about types of interventions that are likely to be effective for a specific disorder. Critical to such a determination are measures of clinical efficacy (internal validity) and clinical utility (external validity); in other words, the former is a measure of whether a treatment works, and the latter is a measure of whether the treatment is effective in a variety of settings.

Key Terms

civil commitment laws
mental illness
dangerousness
deinstitutionalization
transinstitutionalization
criminal commitment
diminished capacity
competence

duty to warn
expert witnesses
malingering
informed consent
clinical efficacy
clinical utility

Answers to Concept Checks

16.1
(a) mental disorder
(b) dangerous
(c) grave disability
(d) They have been accused of committing crimes and their mental competence to stand trial has being assessed.
(e) They have been found not guilty by reason of insanity.

16.2
1. e
2. d
3. c
4. b
5. a

16.3
1. c; e
2. d
3. b
4. a

Appendix A

DSM-IV Diagnostic Criteria

Proposed Axes for Further Study

Three additional axes have been placed in the appendix of DSM-IV for further study for possible inclusion in subsequent editions of the DSM. Research on the usefulness of these axes will continue for the next several years.

Defensive Functioning Scale

As described in Chapter 1, defense mechanisms (or coping styles) are conceptualized as psychological processes that protect the individual from emotional conflicts as well as internal or external stressors. These defense mechanisms are automatic or unconscious in that the individual may not be aware of their use. Some examples of adaptive and unadaptive defense mechanisms are provided on Table 1.1. With this axis clinicians should use up to seven specific defense mechanisms, starting with the most prominent—meaning the coping style used most frequently—and then indicate whether the defenses are adaptive or unadaptive.

Social and Occupational Functioning Assessment Scale (SOFAS)

Social and occupational functioning is a very important part of any individual's life and must be considered in the clinical formulation of any psychological disorder. In addition, it is important to note changes in social and occupational functioning as a result of treatment. In other words, changes in features of the disorder itself, such as panic attacks and panic disorder, would be less important if the changes did not result in a general relief from the impairment in social and occupational functioning associated with the onset of the disorder. Social and occupational functioning will be rated by the clinician on a 0–100 scale, where a score of 100 indicates superior functioning in a wide range of activities while a score of 1 would reflect an inability to maintain even minimal personal hygiene.

Global Assessment of Relational Functioning (GARF) Scale

Just as social and occupational functioning is an important consideration, so is functioning in a network of interpersonal relationships including family, friends, and significant others. In this scale, the clinician will rate, also on a 0–100 scale, the degree to which the family or other personal relationships provide the necessary social and emotional support for the individual.

Barlow and Durand, second edition, p. 82
Durand and Barlow, second edition, —

Panic Attack

The predominant complaint is a discrete period of intense fear or discomfort, in which at least four (or more) of the following symptoms developed abruptly and reached a peak within 10 minutes:

1. Palpitations, pounding heart, or accelerated heart rate

2. Sweating

3. Trembling or shaking

4. Sensations of shortness of breath or smothering

5. Feeling of choking

6. Chest pain or discomfort

7. Nausea or abdominal distress

8. Feeling dizzy, unsteady, lightheaded, or faint

9. Derealization (feelings of unreality) or depersonalization (being detached from oneself)

10. Fear of losing control or going crazy

11. Fear of dying

12. Paresthesias (numbness or tingling sensations)

13. Chills or hot flushes

Barlow and Durand, second edition, p. 112
Durand and Barlow, second edition, p. 108

Panic Disorder with Agoraphobia

A. Both 1 and 2:

1. Recurrent unexpected panic attacks are present.
2. At least one of the attacks has been followed by 1 month (or more) of one (or more) of the following: (a) persistent concern about having additional attacks, (b) worry about the implications of the attack or its consequences (e.g., losing control, having a heart attack, "going crazy"), or (c) a significant change in behavior related to the attacks.

B. The presence of agoraphobia in which the predominant complaint is anxiety about being in places or situations from which escape might be difficult or embarrassing, or in which help may not be available in the event of an unexpected or situationally predisposed panic attack or panic-like symptoms. Agoraphobic fears typically involve characteristic clusters of situations that include being outside the home alone; being in a crowd or standing in a line; being on a bridge; and traveling in a bus, train, or automobile.

C. The panic attacks are not due to the direct physiological effects of a substance (e.g., drug of abuse, medication) or a general medical condition (e.g., hyperthyroidism).

D. The panic attacks are not better accounted for by another mental disorder, such as social phobia (e.g., occurring on exposure to feared social situations), specific phobia (e.g., on exposure to a specific social situation), obsessive-compulsive disorder (e.g., on exposure to dirt, in someone with an obsession about contamination), posttraumatic stress disorder (e.g., in response to stimuli associated with a severe stressor), or separation anxiety disorder (e.g., in response to being away from home or close relatives).

Barlow and Durand, second edition, p. 120
Durand and Barlow, second edition, p. 115

Specific Phobia

A. Marked and persistent fear that is excessive or unreasonable, cued by the presence or anticipation of a specific object or situation (e.g., flying, heights, animals, receiving an injection, seeing blood).

B. Exposure to the phobic stimulus almost invariably provokes an immediate anxiety response, which may take the form of a situationally bound or situationally predisposed panic attack. Note: in children, the anxiety may be expressed by crying, tantrums, freezing, or clinging.

C. The person recognizes that the fear is excessive or unreasonable. Note: In children, this feature may be absent.

D. The phobic situation(s) is avoided or else is endured with intense anxiety or distress.

E. The avoidance, anxious anticipation, or distress in the feared situations interferes significantly with the person's normal routine, occupational (or academic) functioning, or social activities or relationships, or there is marked distress about having the phobia.

F. In individuals under age 18, the duration is at least 6 months.

G. The anxiety, panic attacks, or phobic avoidance associated with the specific object or situation are not better accounted for by another mental disorder, such as obsessive-compulsive disorder (e.g., fear of dirt, in someone with an obsession about contamination), posttraumatic stress disorder (e.g., avoidance of stimuli associated with a severe stressor), separation anxiety disorder (e.g., avoidance of school), social phobia (e.g., avoidance of social situations because of fear of embarrassment), panic disorder with agoraphobia, or agoraphobia without history of panic disorder.

Specify type:

Animal Type
Natural Environment Type (e.g., heights, storms, and water)
Blood-Injection-Injury Type
Situational Type (e.g., planes, elevators, or enclosed places)
Other Type (e.g., phobic avoidance of situations that may lead to choking, vomiting, or contracting an illness; or in children, avoidance of loud sounds or costumed characters)

Barlow and Durand, second edition, p. 128
Durand and Barlow, second edition, p. 122

Social Phobia

A. A marked and persistent fear of one or more social or performance situations in which the person is exposed to unfamiliar people or to possible scrutiny by others. The individual fears that he or she will act in a way (or show anxiety symptoms) that will be humiliating or embarrassing. Note: In children, there must be evidence of the capacity for age-appropriate social relationships with familiar people, and the anxiety must occur in peer settings, not just in interactions with adults.

B. Exposure to the feared social situation almost invariably provokes anxiety, which may take the form of a situationally bound or situationally predisposed panic attack. Note: In children, the anxiety may be expressed by crying, tantrums, freezing, or shrinking from social situations with unfamiliar people.

C. The person recognizes that the fear is excessive or unreasonable. Note: In children, this feature may be absent.

D. The feared social or performance situations are avoided or are endured with intense anxiety or distress.

E. The avoidance, anxious anticipation, or distress in the feared social or performance situation(s) interferes significantly with the person's normal routine, occupational (academic) functioning, or social activities or relationships, or there is marked distress about having the phobia.

F. In individuals under age 18, duration is at least 6 months.

G. The fear or avoidance is not due to the direct physiological effects of a substance (e.g., a drug of abuse, medication) or a general medical condition, and is not better accounted for by another mental disorder (e.g., panic disorder with or without agoraphobia, separation anxiety disorder, body dysmorphic disorder, a pervasive developmental disorder, or schizoid personality disorder).

H. If a general medical condition or another mental disorder is present, the fear in criterion A is unrelated to it; e.g., the fear is not of stuttering, trembling in Parkinson's disease, or exhibiting abnormal eating behavior in anorexia nervosa or bulimia nervosa.

Specify if **Generalized:** if the fears include most social situations (also consider the additional diagnosis of avoidant personality disorder).

Barlow and Durand, second edition, p. 136
Durand and Barlow, second edition, p. 129

Posttraumatic Stress Disorder

A. The person has been exposed to a traumatic event in which both of the following were present:

1. The person experienced, witnessed, or was confronted with an event or events that involve actual or threatened death or serious injury, or a threat to the physical integrity of himself or herself or others
2. The person's response involved intense fear, helplessness, or horror. Note: In children, it may be expressed instead by disorganized or agitated behavior

B. The traumatic event is persistently reexperienced in one (or more) of the following ways:

1. Recurrent and intrusive distressing recollections of the event, including images, thoughts, or perceptions. Note: In young children, repetitive play may occur in which themes or aspects of the trauma are expressed
2. Recurrent distressing dreams of the event. Note: In children, there may be frightening dreams without recognizable content
3. Acting or feeling as if the traumatic event were recurring (includes a sense of reliving the experience, illusions, hallucinations, and dissociative flashback episodes, including those that occur on awakening or when intoxicated). Note: In young children, trauma-specific reenactment may occur
4. Intense psychological distress at exposure to internal or external cues that symbolize or resemble an aspect of the traumatic event
5. Physiologic reactivity on exposure to internal or external cues that symbolize or resemble an aspect of the traumatic event

C. Persistent avoidance of stimuli associated with the trauma and numbing of general responsiveness (not present before the trauma), as indicated by three (or more) of the following:

1. Efforts to avoid thoughts, feelings, or conversations associated with the trauma
2. Efforts to avoid activities, places, or people that arouse recollections of the trauma
3. Inability to recall an important aspect of the trauma
4. Markedly diminished interest or participation in significant activities
5. Feeling of detachment or estrangement from others
6. Restricted range of affect (e.g., unable to have loving feelings)
7. Sense of a foreshortened future (e.g., does not expect to have a career, marriage, children, or a normal life span)

D. Persistent symptoms of increased arousal (not present before the trauma), as indicated by two (or more) of the following:

1. Difficulty falling or staying asleep
2. Irritability or outbursts of anger
3. Difficulty concentrating
4. Hypervigilance
5. Exaggerated startle response

E. Duration of the disturbance (symptoms in B, C, and D) is more than one month.

F. The disturbance causes clinically significant distress or impairment in social, occupational, or other important areas of functioning.

Specify if:
   Acute: if duration of symptoms is less than 3 months
   Chronic: if duration of symptoms is 3 months or more

Specify if:
   With Delayed Onset: if onset of symptoms is at least 6 months after the stressor

---

Barlow and Durand, second edition, p. 138
Durand and Barlow, second edition, p. 131

Obsessive-Compulsive Disorder

A. Either obsessions or compulsions:

Obsessions as defined by 1, 2, 3, and 4:

1. Recurrent and persistent thoughts, impulses, or images that are experienced, at some time during the disturbance, as intrusive and inappropriate, and cause marked anxiety or distress
2. The thoughts, impulses, or images are not simply excessive worries about real-life problems
3. The person attempts to ignore or suppress such thoughts, impulses, or images, or to neutralize them with some other thought or action
4. The person recognizes that the obsessional thoughts, impulses, or images are a product of his or her own mind (not imposed from without as in thought insertion)

Compulsions as defined by 1 and 2:

1. Repetitive behaviors (e.g., handwashing, ordering, checking) or mental acts (e.g., praying, counting, repeating words silently) that the person feels driven to perform in response to an obsession, or according to rules that must be applied rigidly
2. The behaviors or mental acts are aimed at preventing or reducing distress or preventing some dreaded event or situation; however, these behaviors or mental acts either are not connected in a realistic way with what they are designed to neutralize or prevent, or are clearly excessive

B. At some point during the course of the disorder, the person has recognized that the obsessions or compulsions are excessive or unreasonable. Note: This does not apply to children.

C. The obsessions or compulsions cause marked distress, are time-consuming (take more than 1 hour a day), or significantly interfere with the person's normal routine, occupational (or academic) functioning, or usual social activities or relationships.

D. If another Axis I disorder is present, the content of the obsessions or compulsions is not restricted to it (e.g., preoccupation with food in the presence of an eating disorder; hair pulling in the presence of trichotillomania; concern with appearance in the presence of body dysmorphic disorder; preoccupation with drugs in the presence of a substance use disorder; preoccupation with having a serious illness in the presence of hypochondriasis; preoccupation with sexual urges or fantasies in the presence of a paraphilia; or guilty ruminations in the presence of major depressive disorder).

E. The disturbance is not due to the direct effects of a substance (e.g., drugs of abuse, medication) or a general medical condition.

Specify if: **With Poor Insight:** if, for most of the time during the current episode, the person does not recognize that the obsessions and compulsions are excessive or unreasonable

---

Barlow and Durand, second edition, p. 144
Durand and Barlow, second edition, p. 137

Hypochondriasis

A. Preoccupation with fears of having, or the idea that one has, a serious disease based on the person's misinterpretation of bodily symptoms.

B. The preoccupation persists despite appropriate medical evaluation and reassurance.

C. The belief in Criterion A is not of delusional intensity (as in Delusional Disorder, Somatic Type) and is not restricted to a circumscribed concern about appearance (as in Body Dysmorphic Disorder).

D. The preoccupation causes clinically significant distress or impairment in social, occupational, or other important areas of functioning.

E. The duration of the disturbance is at least 6 months.

F. The preoccupation is not better accounted for by Generalized Anxiety Disorder, Obsessive-Compulsive Disorder, Panic Disorder, a Major Depressive Episode, Separation Anxiety, or another Somatoform Disorder.

Specify if:

With Poor Insight: if, for most of the time during the current episode, the person does not recognize that the concern about having a serious illness is excessive or unreasonable

Barlow and Durand, second edition, p. 153
Durand and Barlow, second edition, p. 145

Somatization Disorder

A. A history of many physical complaints beginning before age 30 that occur over a period of several years and result in treatment being sought or significant impairment in social, occupational, or other important areas of functioning.

B. Each of the following criteria must have been met, with individual symptoms occurring at any time during the course of disturbance.

   1. Four pain symptoms: A history of pain related to at least four different sites or functions (such as head, abdomen, back, joints, extremities, chest, rectum, during sexual intercourse, during menstruation, or during urination)
   2. Two gastrointestinal symptoms: A history of at least two gastrointestinal symptoms other than pain (such as nausea, diarrhea, bloating, vomiting other than during pregnancy, or intolerance of several different foods)
   3. One sexual symptom: A history of at least one sexual or reproductive symptom other than pain (such as sexual indifference, erectile or ejaculatory dysfunction, irregular menses, excessive menstrual bleeding, vomiting throughout pregnancy)
   4. One pseudoneurologic symptom: A history of at least one symptom or deficit suggesting a neurological disorder not limited to pain (conversion symptoms such as blindness, double vision, deafness, loss of touch or pain sensation, hallucinations, aphonia, impaired coordination or balance, paralysis or localized weakness, difficulty swallowing, difficulty breathing, urinary retention, seizures; dissociative symptoms such as amnesia; or loss of consciousness other than fainting)

Barlow and Durand, second edition, p. 157
Durand and Barlow, second edition, p. 149

Conversion Disorder

A. One or more symptoms or deficits affecting voluntary motor or sensory function that suggest a neurological or general medical condition.

B. Psychological factors are judged to be associated with the symptom or deficit because the initiation or exacerbation of the symptom or deficit is preceded by conflicts or other stressors.

C. The symptom or deficit is not intentionally produced or feigned (as in factitious disorder or malingering).

D. The symptom or deficit cannot, after appropriate investigation, be fully explained by a general medical condition, or by the direct effects of a substance, or as a culturally sanctioned behavior or experience.

E. The symptom or deficit causes clinically significant distress or impairment in social, occupational, or other important areas of functioning or warrants medical evaluation.

F. The symptom or deficit is not limited to pain or sexual dysfunction, does not occur exclusively during the course of somatization disorder, and is not better accounted for by another mental disorder.

Barlow and Durand, second edition, p. 160
Durand and Barlow, second edition, p. 151

Factitious Disorder

A. Intentional production or feigning of physical or psychological signs or symptoms.

B. The motivation for the behavior is to assume the sick role.

C. External incentives for the behavior (such as economic gain, avoiding legal responsibility, or improving physical well-being, as in malingering) are absent.

Specify Type:
With Predominantly Psychological Signs and Symptoms if psychological signs and symptoms predominate in the clinical presentation.
With Predominantly Physical Signs and Symptoms if physical signs and symptoms predominate in the clinical presentation.
With Combined Psychological and Physical Signs and Symptoms if neither psychological nor physical signs and symptoms predominate in the clinical presentation.

Barlow and Durand, second edition, p. 161
Durand and Barlow, second edition, p. 152

Pain Disorder

A. Pain in one or more anatomical sites is the predominant focus of the clinical presentation and is of sufficient severity to warrant clinical attention.

B. The pain causes clinically significant distress or impairment in social, occupational, or other important areas of functioning.

C. Psychological factors are judged to have an important role in the onset, severity, exacerbation, or maintenance of the pain.

D. The symptom or deficit is not intentionally produced or feigned (as in factitious disorder or malingering).

E. The pain is not better acounted for by a mood, anxiety, or psychotic disorder and does not meet criteria for dyspareunia.

Specify if:
Acute (duration of less than 6 months)
Chronic (duration of 6 months or more)

Barlow and Durand, second edition, p. 163
Durand and Barlow, second edition, p. 155

Body Dysmorphic Disorder

A. Preoccupation with an imagined defect in appearance. If a slight physical anomaly is present, the person's concern is markedly excessive.

B. The preoccupation causes significant distress or impairment in social, occupational, or other important areas of functioning.

C. The preoccupation is not better accounted for by another mental disorder (e.g., dissatisfaction with body shape and size in anorexia nervosa).

Barlow and Durand, second edition, p. 164
Durand and Barlow, second edition, p. 155

Depersonalization Disorder

A. Persistent or recurrent experiences of feeling detached from, and as if one is an outside observer of, one's mental processes or body (e.g., feeling like one is in a dream).

B. During the depersonalization experience, reality testing remains intact.

C. The depersonalization causes clinically significant distress or impairment in social, occupational, or other important areas of functioning.

D. The depersonalization experience does not occur exclusively during the course of another mental disorder, such as schizophrenia, panic disorder, acute stress disorder, or another dissociative disorder, and is not due to the direct physiological effects of a substance (e.g., a drug of abuse, a medication) or a general medical condition (e.g., temporal lobe epilepsy).

Barlow and Durand, second edition, p. 168
Durand and Barlow, second edition, p. 159

Trance and Possession Disorder

A. Either (1) or (2):
   1. Trance, i.e., temporary marked alteration in the state of consciousness or loss of customary sense of personal identity without replacement by an alternate identity, associated with at least one of the following;
      (a) narrowing of awareness of immediate surroundings, or unusually narrow and selective focusing on environmental stimuli
      (b) stereotyped behaviors or movements that are experienced as being beyond one's control
   2. Possession trance, a single or episodic alteration in the state of consciousness characterized by the replacement of customary sense of personal identity by a new identity. This is attributed to the influence of a spirit, power, deity, or other person, as evidenced by one (or more) of the following:
      (a) stereotyped and culturally determined behaviors or movements that are experienced as being controlled by the possessing agent
      (b) full or partial amnesia for the event

B. The trance or possession state is not accepted as a normal part of a collective cultural or religious practice.

C. The trance or possession state causes clinically significant distress or impairment in social, occupational, or other important areas of functioning.

D. The trance or possession trance state does not occur exclusively during the course of a Psychotic Disorder (including Mood Disorder With Psychotic Features and Brief Reactive Psychosis) or Dissociative Identity Disorder and is not due to the direct physiological effects of a substance or a general medical condition.

Barlow and Durand, second edition, p. 170
Durand and Barlow, second edition, p. 161

Dissociative Amnesia

A. The predominant disturbance is one or more episodes of inability to recall important personal information, usually of a traumatic or stressful nature, that is too extensive to be explained by ordinary forgetfulness.

B. The disturbance does not occur exclusively during the course of dissociative identity disorder, dissociative fugue, posttraumatic stress disorder, acute stress disorder, or somatization disorder and is not due to the direct physiological effects of a substance (e.g., a drug of abuse, a medication) or a neurological or other general medical condition (e.g., amnestic disorder due to head trauma).

C. The symptoms cause clinically significant distress or impairment in social, occupational, or other important areas of functioning.

Barlow and Durand, second edition, p. 168
Durand and Barlow, second edition, p. 159

Dissociative Fugue

A. The predominant disturbance is sudden, unexpected travel away from home or one's customary place of work, with inability to recall one's past.

B. Confusion about personal identity or assumption of new identity (partial or complete).

C. The disturbance does not occur exclusively during the course of dissociative identity disorder and is not due to the direct physiological effects of a substance (e.g., a drug of abuse, a medication) or a general medical condition (e.g., temporal lobe epilepsy).

D. The symptoms cause clinically significant distress or impairment in social, occupational, or other important areas of functioning.

Barlow and Durand, second edition, p. 169
Durand and Barlow, second edition, p. 160

Dissociative Identity Disorder

A. The presence of two or more distinct identities or personality states (each with its own relatively enduring pattern of perceiving, relating to, and thinking about the environment and self).

B. At least two of these identities or personality states recurrently take control of the person's behavior.

C. Inability to recall important personal information that is too extensive to be explained by ordinary forgetfulness.

D. The disturbance is not due to the direct physiological effects of a substance (e.g., blackouts or chaotic behavior during alcohol intoxication) or a general medical condition (e.g., complex partial seizures). Note: In children, the symptoms are not attributable to imaginary playmates or other fantasy play.

Barlow and Durand, second edition, p. 170
Durand and Barlow, second edition, p. 161

Major Depressive Episode

A. Five (or more) of the following symptoms have been present during the same 2-week period and represent a change from previous functioning; at least one of the symptoms is either (1) depressed mood or (2) loss of interest or pleasure.

Note: Do not include symptoms that are clearly due to a general medical condition, or mood-incongruent delusions or hallucinations.

  1. depressed mood most of the day, nearly every day, as indicated by either subjective report (e.g., feels sad or empty) or observation made by others (e.g., appears tearful). Note: In children and adolescents can be irritable mood.
  2. markedly diminished interest or pleasure in all, or almost all, activities most of the day, nearly every day (as indicated by either subjective account or observation made by others)
  3. significant weight loss when not dieting or weight gain (e.g., a change of more than 5% of body weight in a month), or decrease or increase in appetite nearly every day. Note: In children, consider failure to make expected weight gains.
  4. insomnia or hypersomnia nearly every day
  5. psychomotor agitation or retardation nearly every day (observable by others, not merely subjective feelings of restlessness or being slowed down)
  6. fatigue or loss of energy nearly every day
  7. feelings of worthlessness or excessive or inappropriate guilt (which may be delusional) nearly every day (not merely self-reproach or guilt about being sick)
  8. diminished ability to think or concentrate, or indecisiveness, nearly every day (either by subjective account or as observed by others)
  9. recurrent thoughts of death (not just fear of dying), recurrent suicidal ideation without a specific plan, or a suicide attempt or a specific plan for committing suicide

B. The symptoms do not meet criteria for a Mixed Episode.

C. The symptoms cause clinically significant distress or impairment in social, occupational, or other important areas of functioning.

D. The symptoms are not due to the direct physiological effects of a substance (e.g., a drug of abuse, a medication) or a general medical condition (e.g., hypothyroidism).

E. The symptoms are not better accounted for by Bereavement, i.e., after the loss of a loved one, and persist for longer than 2 months or are characterized by marked functional impairment, morbid preoccupation with worthlessness, suicidal ideation, psychotic symptoms, or psychomotor retardation.

Barlow and Durand, second edition, p. 184
Durand and Barlow, second edition, p. 175

Manic Episode

A. A distinct period of abnormally and persistently elevated, expansive, or irritable mood, lasting at least 1 week (or any duration if hospitalization is necessary).

B. During the period of mood disturbance, three (or more) of the following symptoms have persisted (four if the mood is only irritable) and have been present to a significant degree:

  1. inflated self-esteem or grandiosity
  2. decreased need for sleep (e.g., feels rested after only 3 hours of sleep)
  3. more talkative than usual or pressure to keep talking
  4. flight of ideas or subjective experience that thoughts are racing
  5. distractibility (i.e., attention too easily drawn to unimportant or irrelevant external stimuli)
  6. increase in goal-directed activity (either socially, at work or school, or sexually) or psychomotor agitation
  7. excessive involvement in pleasurable activities that have a high potential for painful consequences (e.g., engaging in unrestrained buying sprees, sexual indiscretions, or foolish business investments)

C. The symptoms do not meet criteria for a Mixed Episode.

D. The mood disturbance is sufficiently severe to cause marked impairment in occupational functioning or in usual social activities or relationships with others, or to necessitate hospitalization to prevent harm to self or others, or there are psychotic features.

E. The symptoms are not due to the direct physiological effects of a substance (e.g., a drug of abuse, a medication, or other treatment) or a general medical condition (e.g., hyperthyroidism).

Note: Manic-like episodes that are clearly caused by somatic antidepressant treatment (e.g., medication, electroconvulsive therapy, light therapy) should not count toward a diagnosis of Bipolar I Disorder.

Barlow and Durand, second edition, p. 184
Durand and Barlow, second edition, p. 174

Major Depressive Disorder, Single Episode

A. Presence of a single Major Depressive Episode

B. The Major Depressive Episode is not better accounted for by Schizoaffective Disorder and is not superimposed on Schizophrenia, Schizophreniform Disorder, Delusional Disorder, or Psychotic Disorder Not Otherwise Specified.

C. There has never been a Manic Episode, a Mixed Episode, or a Hypomanic Episode. Note: This exclusion does not apply if all of the manic-like, mixed-like, or hypomanic-like episodes are substance or treatment induced or are due to the direct physiological effects of a general medical condition.

Specify (for current or most recent episode):
  Severity/Psychotic/Remission Specifiers
  Chronic
  With Catatonic Features
  With Melancholic Features
  With Atypical Features
  With Postpartum Onset

Barlow and Durand, second edition, p. 185
Durand and Barlow, second edition, p. 175

Dysthymic Disorder

A. Depressed mood for most of the day, for more days than not, as indicated either by subjective account or observation by others, for at least 2 years. Note: In children and adolescents, mood can be irritable and duration must be at least 1 year.

B. Presence, while depressed, of two (or more) of the following:

  1. Poor appetite or overeating
  2. Insomnia or hypersomnia
  3. Low energy or fatigue
  4. Low self-esteem
  5. Poor concentration or difficulty making decisions
  6. Feelings of hopelessness

C. During the 2-year period (1 year for children or adolescents) of the disturbance, the person has never been without the symptoms in Criteria A and B for more than 2 months at a time.

D. No Major Depressive Episode has been present during the first 2 years of the disturbance (1 year for children and adolescents); i.e., the disturbance is not better accounted for by chronic Major Depressive Disorder, or Major Depressive Disorder, In Partial Remission.

Note: There may have been a previous Major Depressive Episode provided there was a full remission (no significant signs or symptoms for 2 months) before development of the Dysthymic Disorder. In addition, after the initial 2 years (1 year in children or adolescents) of Dysthymic Disorder, there may be superimposed episodes of Major Depressive Disorder, in which case both diagnoses may be given when the criteria are met for a Major Depressive Episode.

E. There has never been a Manic Episode, a Mixed Episode, or a Hypomanic Episode, and criteria have never been met for Cyclothymic Disorder.

F. The disturbance does not occur exclusively during the course of a chronic Psychotic Disorder, such as Schizophrenia or Delusional Disorder.

G. The symptoms are not due to the direct physiological effects of a substance (e.g., a drug of abuse, a medication) or a general medical condition (e.g., hypothyroidism).

H. The symptoms cause clinically significant distress or impairment in social, occupational, or other important areas of functioning.

Specify if:
Early Onset: if onset is before age 21 years
Late Onset: if onset is age 21 years or older

Specify (for most recent 2 years of Dysthymic Disorder):
With Atypical Features

Barlow and Durand, second edition, p. 186
Durand and Barlow, second edition, p. 176

Bipolar II Disorder

A. Presence (or history) of one or more Major Depressive Episodes.

B. Presence (or history) of at least one Hypomanic Episode.

C. There has never been a Manic Episode or a Mixed Episode.

D. The mood symptoms in Criteria A and B are not better accounted for by Schizoaffective Disorder and are not superimposed on Schizophrenia, Schizophreniform Disorder, Delusional Disorder, or Psychotic Disorder Not Otherwise Specified.

E. The symptoms cause clinically significant distress or impairment in social, occupational, or other important areas of functioning.

Specify current or most recent episode:
Hypomanic: if currently (or most recently) in a Hypomanic Episode
Depressed: if currently (or most recently) in a Major Depressive Episode

Specify (for current or most recent Major Depressive Episode only if it is the most recent type of mood episode):
Severity/Psychotic/Remission Specifiers—Note: Fifth-digit codes specified cannot be used here because the code for Bipolar II Disorder already uses the fifth digit.
Chronic
With Catatonic Features
With Melancholic Features
With Atypical Features
With Postpartum Onset

Specify:
Longitudinal Course Specifiers (With and Without Interepisode Recovery)
With Seasonal Pattern (applies only to the pattern of Major Depressive Episodes)
With Rapid Cycling

Barlow and Durand, second edition, p. 188
Durand and Barlow, second edition, p. 178

Cyclothymic Disorder

A. For at least 2 years, the presence of numerous periods with hypomanic symptoms and numerous periods with depressive symptoms that do not meet criteria for a Major Depressive Episode. **Note:** In children and adolescents, the duration must be at least 1 year.

B. During the above 2-year period (1 year in children and adolescents), the person has not been without the symptoms in Criterion A for more than 2 months at a time.

C. No Major Depression Episode, Manic Episode, or Mixed Episode has been present during the first 2 years of the disturbance.

   Note: After the initial 2 years (1 year in children and adolescents) of Cyclothymic Disorder, there may be superimposed Manic or Mixed Episodes (in which case both Bipolar I Disorder and Cyclothymic Disorder may be diagnosed) or Major Depressive Episodes (in which case both Bipolar II Disorder and Cyclothymic Disorder may be diagnosed).

D. The symptoms in Criterion A are not better accounted for by Schizoaffective Disorder and are not superimposed on Schizophrenia, Schizophreniform Disorder, Delusional Disorder, or Psychotic Disorder Not Otherwise Specified.

E. The symptoms are not due to the direct physiological effects of a substance (e.g., a drug of abuse, a medication) or a general medical condition (e.g., hyperthyroidism).

F. The symptoms cause clinically significant distress or impairment in social, occupational, or other important areas of functioning.

Barlow and Durand, second edition, p. 190
Durand and Barlow, second edition, p. 179

Bulimia Nervosa

A. Recurrent episodes of binge eating. An episode of binge eating is characterized by both of the following:

   1. Eating, in a discrete period of time (e.g., within any 2-hour period), an amount of food that is definitely larger than most people would eat during a similar period of time and under similar circumstances
   2. A sense of lack of control over eating during the episode (e.g., a feeling that one cannot stop eating or control what or how much one is eating)

B. Recurrent inappropriate compensatory behavior in order to prevent weight gain, such as self-induced vomiting; misuse of laxatives, diuretics or other medications; fasting; or excessive exercise.

C. The binge eating and inappropriate compensatory behaviors both occur, on average, at least twice a week for 3 months.

D. Self-evaluation is unduly influenced by body shape and weight.

E. The disturbance does not occur exclusively during episodes of anorexia nervosa.

Specify type:
   Purging Type: During the current episode of bulimia nervosa, the person has regularly engaged in self-induced vomiting or the misuse of laxatives, diuretics, or enemas
   Nonpurging Type: During the current episode of bulimia nervosa, the person has used other inappropriate compensatory behaviors, such as fasting or exercise, but has not regularly engaged in self-induced vomiting or the misuse of laxatives, diuretics, or enemas

Barlow and Durand, second edition, p. 230
Durand and Barlow, second edition, p. 247

Sleep Disorders

Sleep Disorder	Description
Dyssomnias	(Disturbances in the amount, timing, or quality of sleep.)
Primary Insomnia	Difficulty initiating or maintaining sleep, or sleep that is not restorative (person not feeling rested even after normal amounts of sleep).
Primary Hypersomnia	Complaint of excessive sleepiness that is displayed as either prolonged sleep episodes or daytime sleep episodes.
Narcolepsy	Irresistible attacks of refreshing sleep occurring daily, accompanied by episodes of brief loss of muscle tone (cataplexy).
Breathing-Related Sleep Disorder	Sleep disruption leading to excessive sleepiness or insomnia that is caused by sleep-related breathing difficulties.
Circadian Rhythm Sleep Disorder (Sleep-Wake Schedule Disorder)	Persistent or recurrent sleep disruption leading to excessive sleepiness or insomnia that is due to a mismatch between the sleep-wake schedule required by a person's environment and his or her circadian sleep-wake pattern.
Parasomnias	(Disturbances in arousal and sleep stage transition that intrude into the sleep process.)
Nightmare Disorder (Dream Anxiety Disorder)	Repeated awakenings with detailed recall of extended and extremely frightening dreams, usually involving threats to survival, security, or self-esteem. The awakenings generally occur during the second half of the sleep period.
Sleep Terror Disorder	Recurrent episodes of abrupt awakening from sleep, usually occurring during the first third of the major sleep episode and beginning with a panicky scream.
Sleepwalking Disorder	Repeated episodes of arising from bed during sleep and walkingabout, usually occurring during the first third of the major sleep episode

Barlow and Durand, second edition, p. 248
Durand and Barlow, second edition, p. 262

Primary Insomnia

A. The predominant complaint is difficulty initiating or maintaining sleep, or nonrestorative sleep, for at least 1 month.

B. The sleep disturbance (or associated daytime fatigue) causes clinically significant distress or impairment in social, occupational, or other important areas of functioning.

C. The sleep disturbance does not occur exclusively during the course of Narcolepsy, Breathing-Related Sleep Disorder, Circadian Rhythm Sleep Disorder, or a Parasomnia.

D. The disturbance does not occur exclusively during the course of another mental disorder (e.g., Major Depressive Disorder, Generalized Anxiety Disorder, a delirium).

E. The disturbance is not due to the direct physiological effects of a substance (e.g, a drug of abuse, a medication) or a general medical condition.

Barlow and Durand, second edition, p. 250
Durand and Barlow, second edition, p. 263

Primary Hypersomnia

A. The predominant complaint is excessive sleepiness for at least 1 month (or less if recurrent) as evidenced by either prolonged sleep episodes or daytime sleep episodes that occur almost daily.

B. The excessive sleepiness causes clinically significant distress or impairment in social, occupational, or other important areas of functioning.

C. The excessive sleepiness is not better accounted for by insomnia and does not occur exclusively during the course of another Sleep Disorder (e.g., Narcolepsy, Breathing-Related Sleep Disorder, Circadian Rhythm Sleep Disorder, or a Parasomnia) and cannot be accounted for by an inadequate amount of sleep.

D. The disturbance does not occur exclusively during the course of another mental disorder.

E. The disturbance is not due to the direct physiological effects of a substance (e.g., a drug of abuse, a medication) or a general medical condition.

Specify if:
   Recurrent: if there are periods of excessive sleepiness that last at least 3 days occurring several times a year for at least 2 years.

Barlow and Durand, second edition, p. 253
Durand and Barlow, second edition, p. 265

Narcolepsy

A. Irresistible attacks of refreshing sleep that occur daily over at least 3 months.

B. The presence of one or both of the following:
   1. Cataplexy (i.e., brief episodes of sudden bilateral loss of muscle tone, most often in association with intense emotion)
   2. Recurrent intrusions of elements of rapid eye movement (REM) sleep into the transition between sleep and wakefulness, as manifested by either hypnopompic or hypnagogic hallucinations or sleep paralysis at the beginning or end of sleep episodes

C. The disturbance is not due to the direct physiological effects of a substance (e.g., a drug of abuse, a medication) or another general medical condition.

Barlow and Durand, second edition, p. 254
Durand and Barlow, second edition, p. 266

Breathing-Related Sleep Disorder

A. Sleep disruption, leading to excessive sleepiness or insomnia, that is judged to be due to a sleep-related breathing condition (e.g., obstructive or central sleep apnea syndrome or central alveolar hypoventilation syndrome).

B. The disruption is not better accounted for by another mental disorder and is not due to the direct physiological effects of a substance (e.g., a drug of abuse, a medication) or another general medical condition (other than a breathing-related disorder).

Barlow and Durand, second edition, p. 254
Durand and Barlow, second edition, p. 267

Circadian Rhythm Sleep Disorder

A. A persistent or recurrent pattern of sleep disruption leading to excessive sleepiness or insomnia that is due to a mismatch between the sleep-wake schedule required by a person's environment and his or her circadian sleep-wake pattern.

B. The sleep disturbance causes clinically significant distress or impairment in social, occupational, or other important areas of functioning.

C. The disturbance does not occur exclusively during the course of another Sleep Disorder or other mental disorder.

D. The disturbance is not due to the direct physiological effects of a substance (e.g., a drug of abuse, a medication) or a general medical condition.

Specify type:
Delayed Sleep Phase Type: a persistent pattern of late sleep onset and late awakening times, with an inability to fall asleep and awaken at a desired earlier time
Jet Lag Type: sleepiness and alertness that occur at an inappropriate time of day relative to local time, occurring after repeated travel across more than one time zone
Shift Work Type: insomnia during major sleep period or excessive sleepiness during major awake period associated with night shift work or frequently changing shift work
Unspecified Type

Barlow and Durand, second edition, p. 254
Durand and Barlow, second edition, p. 267

Nightmare Disorder

A. Repeated awakenings from the major sleep period or naps with detailed recall of extended and extremely frightening dreams, usually involving threats to survival, security, or self-esteem. The awakenings generally occur during the second half of the sleep period.

B. On awakening from the frightening dreams, the person rapidly becomes oriented and alert (in contrast to the confusion and disorientation seen in Sleep Terror Disorder and some forms of epilepsy).

C. The dream experience, or the sleep disturbance resulting from the awakening, causes significant distress or impairment in social, occupational, or other important areas of functioning.

D. The nightmares do not occur exclusively during the course of another mental disorder (e.g., a delirium, Posttraumatic Stress Disorder) and are not due to the direct physiological effects of a substance (e.g., a drug of abuse, a medication) or a general medical condition.

Barlow and Durand, second edition, p. 259
Durand and Barlow, second edition, p. 271

Sleep Terror Disorder

A. Recurrent episodes of abrupt awakening from sleep, usually occurring during the first third of the major sleep episode and beginning with a panicky scream.

B. Intense fear and signs of autonomic arousal, such as tachycardia, rapid breathing, and sweating, during each episode.

C. Relative unresponsiveness to efforts of others to comfort the person during the episode.

D. No detailed dream is recalled and there is amnesia for the episode.

E. The episodes cause clinically significant distress or impairment in social, occupational, or other important areas of functioning.

F. The disturbance is not due to the direct physiological effects of a substance (e.g., a drug of abuse, a medication) or a general medical condition.

Barlow and Durand, second edition, p. 259
Durand and Barlow, second edition, p. 272

Sleepwalking Disorder

A. Repeated episodes of rising from bed during sleep and walking about, usually occurring during the first third of the major sleep episode.

B. While sleepwalking, the person has a blank, staring face, is relatively unresponsive to the efforts of others to communicate with him or her, and can be awakened only with great difficulty.

C. On awakening (either from the sleepwalking episode or the next morning), the person has amnesia for the episode.

D. Within several minutes after awakening from the sleepwalking episode, there is no impairment of mental activity or behavior (although there may initially be a short period of confusion or disorientation).

E. The sleepwalking causes clinically significant distress or impairment in social, occupational, or other important areas of functioning.

F. The disturbance is not due to the direct physiological effects of a substance (e.g., a drug of abuse, a medication) or a general medical condition.

Barlow and Durand, second edition, p. 259
Durand and Barlow, second edition, p. 272

Gender Identity Disorders

A. A strong and persistent cross-gender identification (not merely a desire for any perceived cultural advantages of being the other sex).
   In children, the disturbance is manifested by four (or more) of the following:

   1. Repeatedly stated desire to be, or insistence that he or she is, the other sex
   2. In boys, preference for cross-dressing or simulating female attire; in girls, insistence on wearing only stereotypical masculine clothing
   3. Strong and persistent preferences for cross-sex roles in make-believe play or persistent fantasies of being the other sex
   4. Intense desire to participate in the stereotypical games and pastimes of the other sex
   5. Strong preference for playmates of the other sex

   In adolescents and adults, the disturbance is manifested by symptoms such as a stated desire to be the other sex, frequent passing as the other sex, desire to live or be treated as the other sex, or the conviction that he or she has the typical feelings and reactions of the other sex.

B. Persistent discomfort with his or her sex or sense of inappropriateness in the gender role of that sex.

   In children, the disturbance is manifested by any of the following: in boys, assertion that his penis or testes are disgusting or will disappear or assertion that it would be better not to have a penis, or aversion toward rough-and-tumble play and rejection of male stereotypical toys, games, and activities; in girls, rejection of urinating in a sitting position, assertion that she has or will grow a penis, or assertion that she does not want to grow breasts or menstruate, or marked aversion toward normative feminine clothing.

   In adolescents and adults, the disturbance is manifested by symptoms such as preoccupation with getting rid of primary and secondary sex characteristics (e.g., request for hormones, surgery, or other procedures to physically alter sexual characteristics to simulate the other sex) or belief that he or she was born the wrong sex.

C. The disturbance is not concurrent with a physical intersex condition.

D. The disturbance causes clinically significant distress or impairment in social, occupational, or other important areas of functioning.

Code based on current age:
302.6 Gender Identity Disorder in Children
302.85 Gender Identity Disorder in Adolescents or Adults

Specify if (for sexually mature individuals):
Sexually Attracted to Males
Sexually Attracted to Females
Sexually Attracted to Both
Sexually Attracted to Neither

Barlow and Durand, second edition, p. 304
Durand and Barlow, second edition, p. 281

Hypoactive Sexual Desire Disorder

A. Persistently or recurrently deficient (or absent) sexual fantasies and desire for sexual activity. The judgment of deficiency or absence is made by the clinician, taking into account factors that affect sexual functioning, such as age and the context of the person's life.

B. The disturbance causes marked distress or interpersonal difficulty.

C. The sexual dysfunction is not better accounted for by another Axis I disorder (except another Sexual Dysfunction) and is not due exclusively to the direct physiological effects of a substance (e.g., a drug of abuse, a medication) or a general medical condition.

Specify type:
Lifelong Type
Acquired Type

Specify type:
Generalized Type
Situational Type

Specify:
Due to Psychological Factors
Due to Combined Factors

Barlow and Durand, second edition, p. 308
Durand and Barlow, second edition, p. 285

Sexual Aversion Disorder

A. Persistent or recurrent extreme aversion to, and avoidance of, all (or almost all) genital sexual contact with a sexual partner.

B. The disturbance causes marked distress or interpersonal difficulty.

C. The sexual dysfunction is not better accounted for by another Axis I disorder (except another Sexual Dysfunction).

Specify type:
   Lifelong Type
   Acquired Type

Specify type:
   Generalized Type
   Situational Type

Specify:
   Due to Psychological Factors
   Due to Combined Factors

Barlow and Durand, second edition, p. 309
Durand and Barlow, second edition, p. 286

Sexual Arousal Disorders

Female

A. Persistent or recurrent inability to attain, or to maintain until completion of the sexual activity, an adequate lubrication-swelling response of sexual excitement.

B. The disturbance causes marked distress or interpersonal difficulty.

C. The sexual dysfunction is not better accounted for by another Axis I disorder (except another Sexual Dysfunction) and is not due exclusively to the direct physiological effects of a substance (e.g., a drug of abuse, a medication) or a general medical condition.

Specify type:
   Lifelong Type
   Acquired Type

Specify type:
   Generalized Type
   Situational Type

Specify:
   Due to Psychological Factors
   Due to Combined Factors

Male

A. Persistent or recurrent inability to attain, or to maintain until completion of the sexual activity, an adequate erection.

B. The disturbance causes marked distress or interpersonal difficulty.

C. The erectile dysfunction is not better accounted for by another Axis I disorder (other than a Sexual Dysfunction) and is not due exclusively to the direct physiological effects of a substance (e.g., a drug of abuse, a medication) or a general medical condition.

Specify type:
   Lifelong Type
   Acquired Type

Specify type:
Generalized Type
Situational Type

Specify:
Due to Psychological Factors
Due to Combined Factors

Barlow and Durand, second edition, p. 310
Durand and Barlow, second edition, p. 287

Orgasmic Disorder

Female

A. Persistent or recurrent delay in, or absence of, orgasm following a normal sexual excitement phase. Women exhibit wide variability in the type or intensity of stimulation that triggers orgasm. The diagnosis of Female Orgasmic Disorder should be based on the clinician's judgment that the woman's orgasmic capacity is less than would be reasonable for her age, sexual experience, and the adequacy of sexual stimulation she receives.

B. The disturbance causes marked distress or interpersonal difficulty.

C. The orgasmic dysfunction is not better accounted for by another Axis I disorder (except another Sexual Dysfunction) and is not due exclusively to the direct physiological effects of a substance (e.g., a drug of abuse, a medication) or a general medical condition.

Specify type:
Lifelong Type
Acquired Type

Specify type:
Generalized Type
Situational Type

Specify:
Due to Psychological Factors
Due to Combined Factors

Male

A. Persistent or recurrent delay in, or absence of, orgasm following a normal sexual excitement phase during sexual activity that the clinician, taking into account the person's age, judges to be adequate in focus, intensity, and duration.

B. The disturbance causes marked distress or interpersonal difficulty.

C. The orgasmic dysfunction is not better accounted for by another Axis I disorder (except another Sexual Dysfunction) and is not due exclusively to the direct physiological effects of a substance (e.g., a drug of abuse, a medication) or a general medical condition.

Specify type:
Lifelong Type
Acquired Type

Specify type:
Generalized Type
Situational Type

Specify:
Due to Psychological Factors
Due to Combined Factors

Barlow and Durand, second edition, p. 311
Durand and Barlow, second edition, p. 288

Premature Ejaculation

A. Persistent or recurrent ejaculation with minimal sexual stimulation before, on, or shortly after penetration and before the person wishes it. The clinician must take into account factors that affect duration of the excitement phase, such as age, novelty of the sexual partner or situation, and recent frequency of sexual activity.

B. The disturbance causes marked distress or interpersonal difficulty.

C. The premature ejaculation is not due exclusively to the direct effects of a substance (e.g., withdrawal from opioids).

Specify type:
   Lifelong Type
   Acquired Type

Specify type:
   Generalized Type
   Situational Type

Specify:
   Due to Psychological Factors
   Due to Combined Factors

Barlow and Durand, second edition, p. 311
Durand and Barlow, second edition, p. 288

Sexual Pain Disorders

Dyspareunia

A. Recurrent or persistent genital pain associated with sexual intercourse in either a male or a female.

B. The disturbance causes marked distress or interpersonal difficulty.

C. The disturbance is not caused exclusively by Vaginismus or lack of lubrication, is not better accounted for by another Axis I disorder (except another Sexual Dysfunction), and is not due exclusively to the direct physiological effects of a substance (e.g., a drug of abuse, a medication) or a general medical condition.

Specify type:
   Lifelong Type
   Acquired Type

Specify type:
   Generalized Type
   Situational Type

Specify:
   Due to Psychological Factors
   Due to Combined Factors

Vaginismus

A. Recurrent or persistent involuntary spasm of the musculature of the outer third of the vagina that interferes with sexual intercourse.

B. The disturbance causes marked distress or interpersonal difficulty.

C. The disturbance is not better accounted for by another Axis I disorder (e.g., Somatization Disorder) and is not due exclusively to the direct physiological effects of a general medical condition.

Specify type:
  Lifelong Type
  Acquired Type

Specify type:
  Generalized Type
  Situational Type

Specify:
  Due to Psychological Factors
  Due to Combined Factors

Barlow and Durand, second edition, p. 312
Durand and Barlow, second edition, p. 289

Fetishism

A. Over a period of at least 6 months, recurrent, intense sexually arousing fantasies, sexual urges, or behaviors involving the use of nonliving objects (e.g., female undergarments).
B. The fantasies, sexual urges, or behaviors cause clinically significant distress or impairment in social, occupational, or other important areas of functioning.
C. The fetish objects are not limited to articles of female clothing used in cross-dressing (as in Transvestic Fetishism) or devices designed for the purpose of tactile genital stimulation (e.g., a vibrator).

Barlow and Durand, second edition, p. 323
Durand and Barlow, second edition, p. 300

Voyeurism and Exhibitionism

Voyeurism

A. Over a period of at least 6 months, recurrent, intense sexually arousing fantasies, sexual urges, or behaviors involving the act of observing an unsuspecting person who is naked, in the process of disrobing, or engaging in sexual activity.

B. The fantasies, sexual urges, or behaviors cause clinically significant distress or impairment in social, occupational, or other important areas of functioning.

Exhibitionism

A. Over a period of at least 6 months, recurrent, intense sexually arousing fantasies, sexual urges, or behaviors involving the exposure of one's genitals to an unsuspecting stranger.

B. The fantasies, sexual urges, or behaviors cause clinically significant distress or impairment in social, occupational, or other important areas of functioning.

Barlow and Durand, second edition, p. 324
Durand and Barlow, second edition, p. 300

Transvestic Fetishism

A. Over a period of at least 6 months, in a heterosexual male, recurrent, intense sexually arousing fantasies, sexual urges, or behaviors involving cross-dressing.

B. The fantasies, sexual urges, or behaviors cause clinically significant distress or impairment in social, occupational, or other important areas of functioning.

Specify if:
With Gender Dysphoria: if the person has persistent discomfort with gender role or identity

---

Barlow and Durand, second edition, p. 324
Durand and Barlow, second edition, p. 300

Sexual Sadism and Sexual Masochism

Sexual Sadism

A. Over a period of at least 6 months, recurrent, intense sexually arousing fantasies, sexual urges, or behaviors involving acts (real, not simulated) in which the psychological or physical suffering (including humiliation) of the victim is sexually exciting to the person.

B. The fantasies, sexual urges, or behaviors cause clinically significant distress or impairment in social, occupational, or other important areas of functioning.

Sexual Masochism

A. Over a period of at least 6 months, recurrent, intense sexually arousing fantasies, sexual urges, or behaviors involving the act (real, not simulated) of being humiliated, beaten, bound, or otherwise made to suffer.

B. The fantasies, sexual urges, or behaviors cause clinically significant distress or impairment in social, occupational, or other important areas of functioning.

Barlow and Durand, second edition, p. 325
Durand and Barlow, second edition, p. 301

Pedophilia

A. Over a period of at least 6 months, recurrent, intense sexually arousing fantasies, sexual urges, or behaviors involving sexual activity with a prepubescent child or children (generally age 13 years or younger).

B. The fantasies, sexual urges, or behaviors cause clinically significant distress or impairment in social, occupational, or other important areas of functioning.

C. The person is at least age 16 years and at least 5 years older than the child or children in Criterion A.

   Note: Do not include an individual in late adolescence involved in an ongoing sexual relationship with a 12- or 13-year-old.

Specify if:
   Sexually Attracted to Males
   Sexually Attracted to Females
   Sexually Attracted to Both

Specify if:
   Limited to Incest

Specify type:
Exclusive Type (attracted only to children)
Nonexclusive Type

Barlow and Durand, second edition, p. 326
Durand and Barlow, second edition, p. 302

Paraphilia Not Otherwise Specified

This category is included for coding paraphilias that do not meet the criteria for any of the specific categories. Examples include, but are not limited to, telephone scatologia (obscene phone calls), necrophilia (corpses), partialism (exclusive focus on part of body), zoophilia (animals), coprophilia (feces), klismaphilia (enemas), and urophilia (urine).

Barlow and Durand, second edition, p. 323
Durand and Barlow, second edition, p. 299

Substance Abuse Intoxication

A. The development of a reversible substance-specific syndrome due to recent ingestion of (or exposure to) a substance. *Note:* Different substances may produce similar or identical syndromes.

B. Clinically significant maladaptive behavioral or psychological changes that are due to the effect of the substance on the central nervous system (e.g., belligerence, mood lability, cognitive impairment, impaired judgment, impaired social or occupational functioning) and develop during or shortly after use of the substance.

C. The symptoms are not due to a general medical condition and are not better accounted for by another mental disorder.

Barlow and Durand, second edition, p. 338
Durand and Barlow, second edition, p. 314

Substance Abuse

A. A maladaptive pattern of substance use leading to clinically significant impairment or distress, as manifested by one (or more) of the following, during the same 12-month period:

1. Recurrent substance use resulting in a failure to fulfill major role obligations at work, school, or home (e.g., repeated absences or poor work performance related to substance use; substance-related absences, suspensions, or expulsions from school; neglect of children or household)
2. Recurrent substance use in situations in which it is physically hazardous (e.g., driving an automobile or operating a machine when impaired by substance use)
3. Recurrent substance-related legal problems (e.g., arrests for substance-related disorderly conduct)
4. Continued substance use despite having persistent or recurrent social or interpersonal problems caused or exacerbated by the effects of the substance (e.g., arguments with spouse about consequences of intoxication, physical fights)

B. The symptoms have never met the criteria for Substance Dependence for this class of substance.

Barlow and Durand, second edition, p. 338
Durand and Barlow, second edition, p. 314

Substance Dependence

A maladaptive pattern of substance use, leading to clinically significant impairment or distress, as manifested by three (or more) of the following, occurring at any time in the same 12-month period:

1. Tolerance, as defined by either of the following:
   a. a need for markedly increased amounts of the substance to achieve intoxication or desired effect
   b. markedly diminished effect with continued use of the same amount of the substance
2. Withdrawal, as manifested by either of the following:
   a. the characteristic withdrawal syndrome for the substance (refer to Criteria A and B of the criteria sets for Withdrawal from the specific substances)
   b. the same (or a closely related) substance is taken to relieve or avoid withdrawal symptoms
3. The substance is often taken in larger amounts or over a longer period than was intended
4. There is a persistent desire or unsuccessful efforts to cut down or control substance use
5. A great deal of time is spent in activities necessary to obtain the substance (e.g., visiting multiple doctors or driving long distances), use the substance (e.g., chain-smoking), or recover from its effects
6. Important social, occupational, or recreational activities are given up or reduced because of substance use
7. The substance use is continued despite knowledge of having a persistent or recurrent physical or psychological problem that is likely to have been caused or exacerbated by the substance (e.g., current cocaine use despite recognition of cocaine-induced depression, or continued drinking despite recognition that an ulcer was made worse by alcohol consumption)

Specify if:
   With Physiological Dependence: evidence of tolerance or withdrawal (i.e., either Item 1 or 2 is present)
   Without Physiological Dependence: no evidence of tolerance or withdrawal (i.e., neither Item 1 nor 2 is present)

Barlow and Durand, second edition, p. 339
Durand and Barlow, second edition, p. 315

Alcohol Intoxication

A. Recent ingestion of alcohol.

B. Clinically significant maladaptive behavioral or psychological changes (e.g., inappropriate sexual or aggressive behavior, mood lability, impaired judgment, impaired social or occupational functioning) that developed during, or shortly after, alcohol use.

C. One or more of the following signs, developing during, or shortly after, alcohol use:

   1. Slurred speech
   2. Incoordination
   3. Unsteady gait
   4. Hystagmus
   5. Impairment in attention or memory
   6. Stupor or coma

D. The symptoms are not due to a general medical condition and are not better accounted for by another mental disorder.

Barlow and Durand, second edition, p. 343
Durand and Barlow, second edition, p. 318

Sedative, Hypnotic, or Anxiolytic Intoxication

A. Recent use of a sedative, hypnotic, or anxiolytic drug.

B. Clinically significant maladaptive behavioral or psychological changes (e.g., inappropriate sexual or aggressive behavior, mood lability, impaired judgment, impaired social or occupational functioning) that developed during, or shortly after, sedative, hypnotic, or anxiolytic use.

C. One or more of the following signs, developing during, or shortly after, sedative, hypnotic, or anxiolytic use:

1. Slurred speech
2. Incoordination
3. Unsteady gait
4. Hystagmus
5. Impairment in attention or memory
6. Stupor or coma

D. The symptoms are not due to a general medical condition and are not better accounted for by another mental disorder.

Barlow and Durand, second edition, p. 348
Durand and Barlow, second edition, p. 323

Amphetamine (or Related Substance) Intoxication

A. Use of amphetamine or a related substance (e.g., methylphenidate).

B. Clinically significant maladaptive behavioral or psychological changes (e.g., euphoria or affective blunting; changes in sociability; hypervigilance; interpersonal sensitivity, anxiety, tension, or anger; stereotyped behaviors; impaired judgment or impaired social or occupational functioning) that developed during, or shortly after, use of amphetamine or a related substance.

C. Two (or more) of the following, developing during, or shortly after, use of amphetamine or a related substance:

1. Tachycardia or bradycardia
2. Pupillary dilation
3. Elevated or lowered blood pressure
4. Perspiration or chills
5. Nausea or vomiting
6. Evidence of weight loss
7. Psychomotor agitation or retardation
8. Muscular weakness, respiratory depression, chest pain, or cardiac arrhythmias
9. Confusion, seizures, dyskinesias, dystonias, or coma

D. The symptoms are not due to a general medical condition and are not better accounted for by another mental disorder.

Specify if:
   With perceptual disturbances

Barlow and Durand, second edition, p. 349
Durand and Barlow, second edition, p. 324

Cocaine Intoxication

A. Recent use of cocaine.

B. Clinically significant maladaptive behavioral or psychological changes (e.g., euphoria or affective blunting; changes in sociability; hypervigilance; interpersonal sensitivity; anxiety, tension, or anger; stereotyped behaviors; impaired judgment or impaired social or occupational functioning) that developed during, or shortly after, use of cocaine.

C. Two (or more) of the following, developing during, or shortly after, cocaine use:

1. Tachycardia or bradycardia
2. Pupillary dilation
3. Elevated or lowered blood pressure
4. Perspiration or chills
5. Nausea or vomiting
6. Evidence of weight loss
7. Psychomotor agitation or retardation
8. Muscular weakness, respiratory depression, chest pain, or cardiac arrhythmias
9. Confusion, seizures, dyskinesias, dystonias, or coma

D. The symptoms are not due to a general medical condition and are not better accounted for by another mental disorder.

Specify if:
With perceptual disturbances

Barlow and Durand, second edition, p. 350
Durand and Barlow, second edition, p. 325

Nicotine Withdrawal

A. Daily use of nicotine for at least several weeks.

B. Abrupt cessation of nicotine use, or reduction in the amount of nicotine used, followed within 24 hours by four (or more) of the following signs:

1. Dysphoric or depressed mood
2. Insomnia
3. Irritability, frustration, or anger
4. Anxiety
5. Difficulty concentrating
6. Restlessness
7. Decreased heart rate
8. Increased appetite or weight gain

C. The symptoms in Criterion B cause clinically significant distress or impairment in social, occupational, or other important areas of functioning.

D. The symptoms are not due to a general medical condition and are not better accounted for by another mental disorder.

Barlow and Durand, second edition, p. 352
Durand and Barlow, second edition, p. 326

Caffeine Intoxication

A. Recent consumption of caffeine, usually in excess of 250 mg (e.g., more than 2-3 cups of brewed coffee).

B. Five (or more) of the following signs, developing during, or shortly after, caffeine use:

1. Restlessness
2. Nervousness
3. Excitement
4. Insomnia
5. Flushed face
6. Diuresis
7. Gastrointestinal disturbance
8. Muscle twitching
9. Rambling flow of thought and speech
10. Tachycardia or cardiac arrhythmia
11. Periods of inexhaustibility
12. Psychomotor agitation

C. The symptoms in Criterion B cause clinically significant distress or impairment in social, occupational, or other important areas of functioning.

D. The symptoms are not due to a general medical condition and are not better accounted for by another mental disorder (e.g., Anxiety Disorder).

Barlow and Durand, second edition, p. 353
Durand and Barlow, second edition, p. 328

Opioid Intoxication

A. Recent use of an opioid.

B. Clinically significant maladaptive behavioral or psychological changes (e.g., initial euphoria followed by apathy, dysphoria, psychomotor agitation or retardation, impaired judgment, or impaired social or occupational functioning) that developed during, or shortly after, opioid use.

C. Pupillary constriction (or pupillary dilation due to anoxia from severe overdose) and one (or more) of the following signs, developing during, or shortly after, opioid use:

1. Drowsiness or coma
2. Slurred speech
3. Impairment in attention or memory

D. The symptoms are not due to a general medical condition and are not better accounted for by another mental disorder.

Specify if:
With Perceptual Disturbances

Barlow and Durand, second edition, p. 353
Durand and Barlow, second edition, p. 329

Cannabis Intoxication

A. Recent use of cannabis.

B. Clinically significant maladaptive behavioral or psychological changes (e.g., impaired motor coordination, euphoria, anxiety, sensation of slowed time, impaired judgment, social withdrawal) that developed during, or shortly after, cannabis use.

C. Two (or more) of the following signs, developing within 2 hours of cannabis use:

1. Conjunctival injection
2. Increased appetite
3. Dry mouth
4. Tachycardia

D. The symptoms are not due to a general medical condition and are not better accounted for by another mental disorder.

Specify if:
With Perceptual Disturbances

Barlow and Durand, second edition, p. 354
Durand and Barlow, second edition, p. 330

Hallucinogen Intoxication

A. Recent use of a hallucinogen.

B. Clinically significant maladaptive behavioral or psychological changes (e.g., marked anxiety or depression, ideas of reference, fear of losing one's mind, paranoid ideation, impaired judgment, or impaired social or occupational functioning) that developed during, or shortly after, hallucinogen use.

C. Perceptual changes occurring in a state of full wakefulness and alertness (e.g., subjective intensification of perceptions, depersonalization, derealization, illusions, hallucinations, synesthesia) that developed during, or shortly after, hallucinogen use.

D. Two (or more) of the following signs developing during, or shortly after, hallucinogen use:

1. Pupillary dilation
2. Tachycardia
3. Sweating
4. Palpitations
5. Blurring of vision
6. Tremors
7. Incoordination

D. The symptoms are not due to a general medical condition and are not better accounted for by another mental disorder.

Barlow and Durand, second edition, p. 356
Durand and Barlow, second edition, p. 331

Schizoid Personality Disorder

A. A pervasive pattern of detachment from social relationships and a restricted range of expression of emotions in interpersonal settings, beginning by early adulthood and present in a variety of contexts, as indicated by four (or more) of the following:

1. Neither desires nor enjoys close relationships, including being part of a family
2. Almost always chooses solitary activities
3. Has little, if any, interest in having sexual experiences with another person
4. Takes pleasure in few, if any, activities
5. Lacks close friends or confidants other than first-degree relatives
6. Appears indifferent to the praise or criticism of others
7. Shows emotional coldness, detachment, or flattened affectivity

B. Does not occur exclusively during the course of Schizophrenia, a Mood Disorder with Psychotic Features, another Psychotic Disorder, or a Pervasive Developmental Disorder and is not due to the direct physiological effects of a general medical condition.

Note: If criteria are met prior to the onset of Schizophrenia, add "Premorbid," e.g., "Schizoid Personality Disorder (Premorbid)."

Barlow and Durand, second edition, p. 381
Durand and Barlow, second edition, p. 353

Borderline Personality Disorder

A pervasive pattern of instability of interpersonal relationships, self-image, and affects, and marked impulsivity beginning by early adulthood and present in a variety of contexts, as indicated by five (or more) of the following:

1. Frantic efforts to avoid real or imagined abandonment. **Note:** Do not include suicidal or self-mutilating behavior covered in Criterion 5.
2. A pattern of unstable and intense interpersonal relationships characterized by alternating between extremes of idealization and devaluation
3. Identity disturbance: markedly and persistently unstable self-image or sense of self
4. Impulsivity in at least two areas that are potentially self-damaging (e.g., spending, sex, substance abuse, reckless driving, binge eating). Note: Do not include suicidal or self-mutilating behavior covered in Criterion 5.
5. Recurrent suicidal behavior, gestures, or threats, or self-mutilating behavior
6. Affective instability due to a marked reactivity of mood (e.g., intense episodic dysphoria, irritability, or anxiety usually lasting a few hours and only rarely more than a few days)
7. Chronic feelings of emptiness
8. Inappropriate, intense anger or difficulty controlling anger (e.g., frequent displays of temper, constant anger, recurrent physical fights)
9. Transient, stress-related paranoid ideation or severe dissociative symptoms

Barlow and Durand, second edition, p. 392
Durand and Barlow, second edition, p. 362

Histrionic Personality Disorder

A pervasive pattern of excessive emotionality and attention seeking, beginning by early adulthood and present in a variety of contexts, as indicated by five (or more) of the following:

1. Is uncomfortable in situations in which he or she is not the center of attention
2. Interaction with others is often characterized by inappropriate sexually seductive or provocative behavior
3. Displays rapidly shifting and shallow expression of emotions
4. Consistently uses physical appearance to draw attention to self
5. Has a style of speech that is excessively impressionistic and lacking in detail
6. Shows self-dramatization, theatricality, and exaggerated expression of emotion
7. Is suggestible, i.e., easily influenced by others or circumstances
8. Considers relationships to be more intimate than they actually are

Barlow and Durand, second edition, p. 394
Durand and Barlow, second edition, p. 364

Narcissistic Personality Disorder

A pervasive pattern of grandiosity (in fantasy or behavior), need for admiration, and lack of empathy, beginning by early adulthood and present in a variety of contexts, as indicated by five (or more) of the following:

1. Has a grandiose sense of self-importance (e.g., exaggerates achievements and talents, expects to be recognized as superior without commensurate achievements)
2. Is preoccupied with fantasies of unlimited success, power, brilliance, beauty, or ideal love

3. Believes that he or she is "special" and unique and can only be understood by, or should associate with, other special or high-status people (or institutions)
4. Requires excessive admiration
5. Has a sense of entitlement, i.e., unreasonable expectations of especially favorable treatment or automatic compliance with his or her expectations
6. Is interpersonally exploitative, i.e., takes advantage of others to achieve his or her own ends
7. Lacks empathy: is unwilling to recognize or identify with the feelings and needs of others
8. Is often envious of others or believes that others are envious of him or her
9. Shows arrogant, haughty behaviors or attitudes

Barlow and Durand, second edition, p. 395
Durand and Barlow, second edition, p. 365

Avoidant Personality Disorder

A pervasive pattern of social inhibition, feelings of inadequacy, and hypersensitivity to negative evaluation, beginning by early adulthood and present in a variety of contexts, as indicated by four (or more) of the following:

1. Avoids occupational activities that involve significant interpersonal contact, because of fears of criticism, disapproval, or rejection
2. Is unwilling to get involved with people unless certain of being liked
3. Shows restraint within intimate relationships because of the fear of being shamed or ridiculed
4. Is preoccupied with being criticized or rejected in social situations
5. Is inhibited in new interpersonal situations because of feelings of inadequacy
6. Views self as socially inept, personally unappealing, or inferior to others
7. Is unusually reluctant to take personal risks or to engage in any new activities because they may prove embarrassing

Barlow and Durand, second edition, p. 396
Durand and Barlow, second edition, p. 367

Dependent Personality Disorder

A pervasive and excessive need to be taken care of that leads to submissive and clinging behavior and fears of separation, beginning by early adulthood and present in a variety of contexts, as indicated by five (or more) of the following:

1. Has difficulty making everyday decisions without an excessive amount of advice and reassurance from others
2. Needs others to assume responsibility for most major areas of his or her life
3. Has difficulty expressing disagreement with others because of fear of loss of support or approval. Note: Do not include realistic fears of retribution.
4. Has difficulty initiating projects or doing things on his or her own (because of a lack of self-confidence in judgment or abilities rather than a lack of motivation or energy)
5. Goes to excessive lengths to obtain nurturance and support from others, to the point of volunteering to do things that are unpleasant
6. Feels uncomfortable or helpless when alone because of exaggerated fears of being unable to care for himself or herself
7. Urgently seeks another relationship as a source of care and support when a close relationship ends
8. Is unrealistically preoccupied with fears of being left to take care of himself or herself

Barlow and Durand, second edition, p. 397
Durand and Barlow, second edition, p. 368

Obsessive-Compulsive Personality Disorder

A pervasive pattern of preoccupation with orderliness, perfectionism, and mental and interpersonal control, at the expense of flexibility, openness, and efficiency, beginning by early adulthood and present in a variety of contexts, as indicated by four (or more) of the following:

1. Is preoccupied with details, rules, lists, order, organization, or schedules to the extent that the major point of the activity is lost
2. Shows perfectionism that interferes with task completion (e.g., is unable to complete a project because his or her own overly strict standards are not met)
3. Is excessively devoted to work and productivity to the exclusion of leisure activities and friendships (not accounted for by obvious economic necessity)
4. Is overconscientious, scrupulous, and inflexible about matters of morality, ethics, or values (not accounted for by cultural or religious identification)
5. Is unable to discard worn-out or worthless objects even when they have no sentimental value
6. Is reluctant to delegate tasks or to work with others unless they submit to exactly his or her way of doing things
7. Adopts a miserly spending style toward both self and others; money is viewed as something to be hoarded for future catastrophes
8. Shows rigidity and stubbornness

Barlow and Durand, second edition, p. 398
Durand and Barlow, second edition, p. 368

Schizophrenia

A. *Characteristic symptoms:* Two (or more) of the following, each present for a significant portion of time during a 1-month period (or less if successfully treated):

1. Delusions
2. Hallucinations
3. Disorganized speech (e.g., frequent derailment or incoherence)
4. Grossly disorganized or catatonic behavior
5. Negative symptoms, i.e., affective flattening, alogia, or avolition

Note: Only one Criterion A symptom is required if delusions are bizarre, or hallucinations consist of a voice keeping up a running commentary on the person's behavior or thoughts or two or more voices conversing with each other.

B. *Social/occupational dysfunction:* For a significant portion of the time since the onset of the disturbance, one or more major areas of functioning such as work, interpersonal relations, or self-care are markedly below the level achieved prior to the onset (or when the onset is in childhood or adolescence, failure to achieve expected level of interpersonal, academic, or occupational achievement).

C. *Duration:* Continuous signs of the disturbance persist for at least 6 months. This 6-month period must include at least 1 month of symptoms (or less if successfully treated) that meet Criterion A (i.e., active-phase symptoms) and may include periods of prodromal or residual symptoms. During these prodromal or residual periods, the signs of the disturbance may be manifested by only negative symptoms or two or more symptoms listed in Criterion A present in an attenuated form (e.g., odd beliefs, unusual perceptual experiences).

D. *Schizoaffective and mood disorder exclusion:* Schizoaffective Disorder and Mood Disorder with Psychotic Features have been ruled out because either (1) no Major Depressive, Manic, or Mixed Episodes have occurred concurrently with the active-phase symptoms; or (2) if mood episodes have occurred during active-phase symptoms, their total duration has been brief relative to the duration of the active and residual periods.

E. *Substance/general medical condition exclusion:* The disturbance is not due to the direct physiological effects of a substance (e.g., a drug of abuse, a medication) or a general medical condition.

F. *Relationship to a pervasive developmental disorder:* If there is a history of Autistic Disorder or another Pervasive Developmental Disorder, the additional diagnosis of Schizophrenia is made only if prominent delusions or hallucinations are also present for at least a month (or less if successfully treated).

Classification of longitudinal course (can be applied only after at least 1 year has elapsed since the initial onset of active-phase symptoms):

Episodic with Interepisode Residual Symptoms (episodes are defined by the reemergence of prominent psychotic symptoms); *also specify if:* **with Prominent Negative Symptoms**

Episodic with No Interepisode Residual Symptoms

Continuous (prominent psychotic symptoms are present throughout the period of observation); *also specify if:* **with Prominent Negative Symptoms**

Single Episode in Partial Remission; *also specify if:* **with Prominent Negative Symptoms**

Single Episode in Full Remission

Other or Unspecified Pattern

Barlow and Durand, second edition, p. 405
Durand and Barlow, second edition, p. 375

Paranoid Type

A type of Schizophrenia in which the following criteria are met:

A. Preoccupation with one or more delusions or frequent auditory hallucinations.

B. None of the following is prominent: disorganized speech, disorganized or catatonic behavior, or flat or inappropriate affect.

Barlow and Durand, second edition, p. 412
Durand and Barlow, second edition, p. 381

Catatonic Type

A type of Schizophrenia in which the clinical picture is dominated by at least two of the following:

1. Motoric immobility as evidenced by catalepsy (including waxy flexibility) or stupor

2. Excessive motor activity (that is apparently purposeless and not influenced by external stimuli)

3. Extreme negativism (an apparently motiveless resistance to all instructions or maintenance of a rigid posture against attempts to be moved) or mutism

4. Peculiarities of voluntary movement as evidenced by posturing (voluntary assumption of inappropriate or bizarre postures), stereotyped movements, prominent mannerisms, or prominent grimacing

5. Echolalia or echopraxia

Barlow and Durand, second edition, p. 412
Durand and Barlow, second edition, p. 382

Disorganized Type

A type of Schizophrenia in which the following criteria are met:

A. All the following are prominent:

    1. Disorganized speech
    2. Disorganized behavior
    3. Flat or inappropriate affect

B. The criteria are not met for Catatonic Type.

Barlow and Durand, second edition, p. 412
Durand and Barlow, second edition, p. 381

Residual Type

A type of Schizophrenia in which the following criteria are met:

A. Absence of prominent delusions, hallucinations, disorganized speech, and grossly disorganized or catatonic behavior.

B. There is continuing evidence of the disturbance, as indicated by the presence of negative symptoms or two or more symptoms listed in Criterion A for Schizophrenia, present in an attenuated form (e.g., odd beliefs, unusual perceptual experiences).

Barlow and Durand, second edition, p. 412
Durand and Barlow, second edition, p. 382

Schizophreniform Disorder

A. Criteria A, D, and E of Schizophrenia are met.

B. An episode of the disorder (including prodromal, active, and residual phases) lasts at least 1 month but less than 6 months. (When the diagnosis must be made without waiting for recovery, it should be qualified as "Provisional.")

Specify if:
    Without Good Prognostic Features
    With Good Prognostic Features: as evidenced by two (or more) of the following:

    1. Onset of prominent psychotic symptoms within 4 weeks of the first noticeable change in usual behavior or functioning
    2. Confusion or perplexity at the height of the psychotic episode
    3. Good premorbid social and occupational functioning
    4. Absence of blunted or flat affect

Barlow and Durand, second edition, p. 413
Durand and Barlow, second edition, p. 382

Schizoaffective Disorder

A. An uninterrupted period of illness during which, at some time, there is either a Major Depressive Episode, a Manic Episode, or a Mixed Episode concurrent with symptoms that meet Criterion A for Schizophrenia.

    Note: The Major Depressive Episode must include Criterion A1: depressed mood.

B. During the same period of illness, there have been delusions or hallucinations for at least 2 weeks in the absence of prominent mood symptoms.

C. Symptoms that meet criteria for a mood episode are present for a substantial portion of the total duration of the active and residual periods of the illness.

D. The disturbance is not due to the direct physiological effects of a substance (e.g., a drug of abuse, a medication) or a general medical condition.

Specify type:
Bipolar Type: if the disturbance includes a Manic or a Mixed Episode (or a Manic or a Mixed Episode and Major Depressive Episodes)
Depressive Type: if the disturbance only includes Major Depressive Episodes

Barlow and Durand, second edition, p. 413
Durand and Barlow, second edition, p. 383

Delusional Disorder

A. Nonbizarre delusions (i.e., involving situations that occur in real life, such as being followed, poisoned, infected, loved at a distance, or deceived by spouse or lover, or having a disease) of at least 1 month's duration.

B. Criterion A for Schizophrenia has never been met. Note: Tactile and olfactory hallucinations may be present in Delusional Disorder if they are related to the delusional theme.

C. Apart from the impact of the delusion(s) or its ramifications, functioning is not markedly impaired and behavior is not obviously odd or bizarre.

D. If mood episodes have occurred concurrently with delusions, their total duration has been brief relative to the duration of the delusional periods.

E. The disturbance is not due to the direct physiological effects of a substance (e.g., a drug of abuse, a medication) or a general medical condition.

Specify type (the following types are assigned based on the predominant delusional theme):
Erotomanic Type: delusions that another person, usually of higher status, is in love with the individual
Grandiose Type: delusions of inflated worth, power, knowledge, identity, or special relationship to a deity or famous person
Jealous Type: delusions that the individual's sexual partner is unfaithful
Persecutory Type: delusions that the person (or someone to whom the person is close) is being malevolently treated in some way
Somatic Type: delusions that the person has some physical defect or general medical condition
Mixed Type: delusions characteristic of more than one of the above types but no one theme predominates
Unspecified Type

Barlow and Durand, second edition, p. 413
Durand and Barlow, second edition, p. 383

Brief Psychotic Disorder

A. Presence of one (or more) of the following symptoms:

1. Delusions
2. Hallucinations
3. Disorganized speech (e.g., frequent derailment or incoherence)
4. Grossly disorganized or catatonic behavior

Note: Do not include a symptom if it is a culturally sanctioned response pattern.

B. Duration of an episode of the disturbance is at least 1 day but less than 1 month, with eventual full return to premorbid level of functioning.

C. The disturbance is not better accounted for by a Mood Disorder with Psychotic Features, Schizoaffective Disorder, or Schizophrenia and is not due to the direct physiological effects of a substance (e.g., a drug of abuse, a medication) or a general medical condition.

Specify if:

With Marked Stressor(s) (brief reactive psychosis): if symptoms occur shortly after and apparently in response to events that, singly or together, would be markedly stressful to almost anyone in similar circumstances in the person's culture

Without Marked Stressor(s): if psychotic symptoms do not occur shortly after, or are not apparently in response to events that, singly or together, would be markedly stressful to almost anyone in similar circumstances in the person's culture

With Postpartum Onset: if onset within 4 weeks postpartum

Barlow and Durand, second edition, p. 414
Durand and Barlow, second edition, p. 383

Shared Psychotic Disorder

A. A delusion develops in an individual in the context of a close relationship with another person(s), who has an already-established delusion.

B. The delusion is similar in content to that of the person who already has the established delusion.

C. The disturbance is not better accounted for by another Psychotic Disorder (e.g., Schizophrenia) or a Mood Disorder with Psychotic Features and is not due to the direct physiological effects of a substance (e.g., a drug of abuse, a medication) or a general medical condition.

Barlow and Durand, second edition, p. 414
Durand and Barlow, second edition, p. 383

Mental Retardation

A. Significantly subaverage intellectual functioning: an IQ of approximately 70 or below on an individually administered IQ test (for infants, a clinical judgment of significantly subaverage intellectual functioning).

B. Concurrent deficits or impairments in present adaptive functioning (i.e., the person's effectiveness in meeting the standards expected for his or her age by his or her cultural group) in at least two of the following areas: communication, self-care, home living, social/interpersonal skills, use of community resources, self-direction, functional academic skills, work, leisure, health, and safety.

C. The onset is before age 18 years.

Code based on degree of severity reflecting level of intellectual impairment:

Mild Mental Retardation: IQ level 50-55 to approximately 70
Moderate Mental Retardation: IQ level 35-40 to 50-55
Severe Mental Retardation: IQ level 20-25 to 35-40
Profound Mental Retardation: IQ level below 20 or 25
Mental Retardation, Severity Unspecified: when there is strong presumption of Mental Retardation but the person's intelligence is untestable by standard tests

Barlow and Durand, second edition, p. 455
Durand and Barlow, second edition, p. 423

Learning Disorders* for Reading Disorder (Developmental Reading Disorder), Mathematics Disorder (Developmental Arithmetic Disorder), and Disorder of Written Expression (Developmental Expressive Writing Disorder)

A. [Reading achievement]
   [Mathematical ability]
   [Writing skill], as measured by individually administered standardized tests, is substantially below that expected given the person's chronological age, measured intelligence, and age-appropriate education.

B. The disturbance in Criterion A significantly interferes with academic achievement or activities of daily living that require [reading skills] [mathematical ability] [composition of written texts].

C. If a sensory deficit is present, the learning difficulties are in excess of those usually associated with it.

*The three separate learning disorders are combined here because the basic criteria are identical with the exception of the specific ability that is affected.

Barlow and Durand, second edition, p. 443
Durand and Barlow, second edition, p. 411

Delirium Due to . . . [Indicate the General Medical Condition]

A. Disturbance of consciousness (i.e., reduced clarity of awareness of the environment) with reduced ability to focus, sustain, or shift attention.

B. A change in cognition (such as memory deficit, disorientation, language disturbance) or the development of a perceptual disturbance that is not better accounted for by a preexisting, established, or evolving dementia.

C. The disturbance develops over a short period of time (usually hours to days) and tends to fluctuate during the course of the day.

D. There is evidence from the history, physical examination, or laboratory findings that the disturbance is caused by the direct physiological consequences of a general medical condition.

Barlow and Durand, second edition, p. 469
Durand and Barlow, second edition, p. 431

Dementia of the Alzheimer's Type

A. The development of multiple cognitive deficits manifested by both
   1. Memory impairment (impaired ability to learn new information or to recall previously learned information)
   2. One (or more) of the following cognitive disturbances:
      a. aphasia (language disturbance)
      b. apraxia (impaired ability to carry out motor activities despite intact motor function)
      c. agnosia (failure to recognize or identify objects despite intact sensory function)
      d. disturbance in executive functioning (i.e., planning, organizing, sequencing, abstracting)

B. The cognitive deficits in Criteria A1 and A2 each cause significant impairment in social or occupational functioning and represent a significant decline from a previous level of functioning.

C. The course is characterized by gradual onset and continuing cognitive decline.

D. The cognitive deficits in Criteria A1 and A2 are not due to any of the following:
1. Other central nervous system conditions that cause progressive deficits in memory and cognition (e.g., cerebrovascular disease, Parkinson's disease, Huntington's disease, subdural hematoma, normal-pressure hydrocephalus, brain tumor)
2. Systemic conditions that are known to cause dementia (e.g., hypothyroidism, vitamin B12 or folic acid deficiency, niacin deficiency, hypercalcemia, neurosyphilis, HIV infection)
3. Substance-induced conditions

E. The deficits do not occur exclusively during the course of a delirium.

F. The disturbance is not better accounted for by another Axis I disorder (e.g., Major Depressive Disorder, Schizophrenia).

With Early Onset: if onset is at age 65 years or below
   With Delirium: if delirium is superimposed on the dementia
   With Delusions: if delusions are the predominant feature
   With Depressed Mood: if depressed mood (including presentations that meet full symptom criteria for a Major Depressive Episode) is the predominant feature. A separate diagnosis of Mood Disorder Due to a General Medical Condition is not given.
   Uncomplicated: if none of the above predominates in the current clinical presentation

With Late Onset: if onset is after age 65 years
   With Delirium: if delirium is superimposed on the dementia
   With Delusions: if delusions are the predominant feature
   With Depressed Mood: if depressed mood (including presentations that meet full symptom criteria for a Major Depressive Episode) is the predominant feature. A separate diagnosis of Mood Disorder Due to a General Medical Condition is not given.
   Uncomplicated: if none of the above predominates in the current clinical presentation

Specify if:
With Behavioral Disturbance

Barlow and Durand, second edition, p. 474
Durand and Barlow, second edition, p. 434

Vascular Dementia

A. The development of multiple cognitive deficits manifested by both
1. Memory impairment (impaired ability to learn new information or to recall previously learned information)
2. One (or more) of the following cognitive disturbances:
   a. aphasia (language disturbance)
   b. apraxia (impaired ability to carry out motor activities despite intact motor function)
   c. agnosia (failure to recognize or identify objects despite intact sensory function)
   d. disturbance in executive functioning (i.e., planning, organizing, sequencing, abstracting)

B. The cognitive deficits in Criteria A1 and A2 each cause significant impairment in social or occupational functioning and represent a significant decline from a previous level of functioning.

C. Focal neurological signs and symptoms (e.g., exaggeration of deep tendon reflexes, extensor plantar response, pseudobulbar palsy, gait abnormalities, weakness of an extremity) or laboratory evidence indicative of cerebrovascular disease (e.g., multiple infarctions involving cortex and underlying white matter) that are judged to be etiologically related to the disturbance.

D. The deficits do not occur exclusively during the course of a delirium.

With Delirium: if delirium is superimposed on the dementia
With Delusions: if delusions are the predominant feature
With Depressed Mood: if depressed mood (including presentations that meet full symptom criteria for a Major Depressive Episode) is the predominant feature. A separate diagnosis of Mood Disorder Due to a General Medical Condition is not given.

Uncomplicated: if none of the above predominates in the current clinical presentation

Specify if:
With Behavioral Disturbance

Barlow and Durand, second edition, p. 477
Durand and Barlow, second edition, p. 437

Dementia Due to Other General Medical Conditions

A. The development of multiple cognitive deficits manifested by both
1. Memory impairment (impaired ability to learn new information or to recall previously learned information)
2. One (or more) of the following cognitive disturbances:
   a. aphasia (language disturbance)
   b. apraxia (impaired ability to carry out motor activities despite intact motor function)
   c. agnosia (failure to recognize or identify objects despite intact sensory function)
   d. disturbance in executive functioning (i.e., planning, organizing, sequencing, abstracting)

B. The cognitive deficits in Criteria A1 and A2 each cause significant impairment in social or occupational functioning and represent a significant decline from a previous level of functioning.

C. There is evidence from the history, physical examination, or laboratory findings that the disturbance is the direct physiological consequence of one of the general medical conditions listed below.

D. The deficits do not occur exclusively during the course of a delirium.

Dementia Due to HIV Disease
Dementia Due to Head Trauma
Dementia Due to Parkinson's Disease
Dementia Due to Huntington's Disease
Dementia Due to Pick's Disease
Dementia Due to Creutzfeldt-Jakob Disease
Dementia Due to *[Indicate the General Medical Condition not listed above]*
   For example, normal-pressure hydrocephalus, hypothyroidism, brain tumor, vitamin B12 deficiency, intracranial radiation

---

Barlow and Durand, second edition, p. 477
Durand and Barlow, second edition, p. 438

Substance-Induced Persisting Dementia

A. The development of multiple cognitive deficits manifested by both
1. Memory impairment (impaired ability to learn new information or to recall previously learned information)
2. One (or more) of the following cognitive disturbances:
   a. aphasia (language disturbance)
   b. apraxia (impaired ability to carry out motor activities despite intact motor function)
   c. agnosia (failure to recognize or identify objects despite intact sensory function)
   d. disturbance in executive functioning (i.e., planning, organizing, sequencing, abstracting)

B. The cognitive deficits in Criteria A1 and A2 each cause significant impairment in social or occupational functioning and represent a significant decline from a previous level of functioning.

C. The deficits do not occur exclusively during the course of a delirium and persist beyond the usual duration of Substance Intoxication or Withdrawal.

D. There is evidence from the history, physical examination, or laboratory findings that the deficits are etiologically related to the persisting effects of substance use (e.g., a drug of abuse, a medication).

Barlow and Durand, second edition, p. 479
Durand and Barlow, second edition, p. 440

Autistic Disorder

A. A total of six (or more) items from (1), (2), and (3), with at least two from (1), and one each from (2) and (3):

1. Qualitative impairment in social interaction, as manifested by at least two of the following:

   a. marked impairment in the use of multiple nonverbal behaviors such as eye-to-eye gaze, facial expression, body postures, and gestures to regulate social interaction
   b. failure to develop peer relationships appropriate to developmental level
   c. a lack of spontaneous seeking to share enjoyment, interests, or achievements with other people (e.g., by a lack of showing, bringing, or pointing out objects of interest)
   d. lack of social or emotional reciprocity

2. Qualitative impairments in communication as manifested by at least one of the following:

   a. delay in, or total lack of, the development of spoken language (not accompanied by an attempt to compensate through alternative modes of communication such as gesture or mime)
   b. in individuals with adequate speech, marked impairment in the ability to initiate or sustain a conversation with others
   c. stereotyped and repetitive use of language or idiosyncratic language
   d. lack of varied, spontaneous make-believe play or social imitative play appropriate to developmental level

3. Restricted repetitive and stereotyped patterns of behavior, interests, and activities, as manifested by at least one of the following:

   a. encompassing preoccupation with one or more stereotyped and restricted patterns of interest that is abnormal either in intensity or focus
   b. apparently inflexible adherence to specific, nonfunctional routines or rituals
   c. stereotyped and repetitive motor mannerisms (e.g., hand or finger flapping or twisting, or complex whole-body movements)
   d. persistent preoccupation with parts of objects

B. Delays or abnormal functioning in at least one of the following areas, with onset prior to age 3 years: (1) social interaction, (2) language as used in social communication, or (3) symbolic or imaginative play.

C. The disturbance is not better accounted for by Rett's Disorder or Childhood Disintegrative Disorder.

Barlow and Durand, second edition, p. 447
Durand and Barlow, second edition, p. 415

Asperger's Disorder

A. Qualitative impairment in social interaction, as manifested by at least two of the following:

1. Marked impairment in the use of multiple nonverbal behaviors such as eye-to-eye gaze, facial expression, body postures, and gestures to regulate social interaction
2. Failure to develop peer relationships appropriate to developmental level
3. A lack of spontaneous seeking to share enjoyment, interests, or achievements with other people (e.g., by a lack of showing, bringing, or pointing out objects of interest to other people)
4. Lack of social or emotional reciprocity

B. Restricted repetitive and stereotyped patterns of behavior, interests, and activities, as manifested by at least one of the following:

1. Encompassing preoccupation with one or more stereotyped and restricted patterns of interest that is abnormal either in intensity or focus
2. Apparently inflexible adherence to specific, nonfunctional routines or rituals
3. Stereotyped and repetitive motor mannerisms (e.g., hand or finger flapping or twisting, or complex whole-body movements)
4. Persistent preoccupation with parts of objects

C. The disturbance causes clinically significant impairment in social, occupational, or other important areas of functioning.

D. There is no clinically significant general delay in language (e.g., single words used by age 2 years, communicative phrases used by age 3 years).

E. There is no clinically significant delay in cognitive development or in the development of age-appropriate self-help skills, adaptive behavior (other than in social interaction), and curiosity about the environment in childhood.

F. Criteria are not met for another specific Pervasive Developmental Disorder or Schizophrenia.

Barlow and Durand, second edition, p. 451
Durand and Barlow, second edition, p. 418

Rett's Disorder

A. All of the following:

1. Apparently normal prenatal and perinatal development
2. Apparently normal psychomotor development through the first 5 months after birth
3. Normal head circumference at birth

B. Onset of all of the following after the period of normal development:

1. Deceleration of head growth between ages 5 and 48 months
2. Loss of previously acquired purposeful hand skills between ages 5 and 30 months with the subsequent development of stereotyped hand movements (e.g., handwringing or hand washing)
3. Loss of social engagement early in the course (although often social interaction develops later)
4. Appearance of poorly coordinated gait or trunk movements
5. Severely impaired expressive and receptive language development with severe psychomotor retardation

Barlow and Durand, second edition, p. 451
Durand and Barlow, second edition, p. 418

Childhood Disintegrative Disorder

A. Apparently normal development for at least the first 2 years after birth as manifested by the presence of age-appropriate verbal and nonverbal communication, social relationships, play, and adaptive behavior.

B. Clinically significant loss of previously acquired skills (before age 10 years) in at least two of the following areas:

1. Expressive or receptive language
2. Social skills or adaptive behavior
3. Bowel or bladder control
4. Play
5. Motor skills

C. Abnormalities of functioning in at least two of the following areas:

1. Qualitative impairment in social interaction (e.g., impairment in nonverbal behaviors, failure to develop peer relationships, lack of social or emotional reciprocity)
2. Qualitative impairments in communication (e.g., delay or lack of spoken language, inability to initiate or sustain a conversation, stereotyped and repetitive use of language, lack of varied make-believe play)
3. Restricted, repetitive, and stereotyped patterns of behavior, interests, and activities, including motor stereotypes and mannerisms

D. The disturbance is not better accounted for by another specific Pervasive Developmental Disorder or by Schizophrenia.

Barlow and Durand, second edition, p. 451
Durand and Barlow, second edition, p. 418

Attention Deficit/Hyperactivity Disorder

A. Either (1) or (2):

1. Six (or more) of the following symptoms of inattention have persisted for at least 6 months to a degree that is maladaptive and inconsistent with developmental level:

   Inattention
   a. often fails to give close attention to details or makes careless mistakes in schoolwork, work, or other activities
   b. often has difficulty sustaining attention in tasks or play activities
   c. often does not seem to listen when spoken to directly
   d. often does not follow through on instructions and fails to finish schoolwork, chores, or duties in the workplace (not due to oppositional behavior or failure to understand instructions)
   e. often has difficulty organizing tasks and activities
   f. often avoids, dislikes, or is reluctant to engage in tasks that require sustained mental effort (such as schoolwork or homework)
   g. often loses things necessary for tasks or activities (e.g., toys, school assignments, pencils, books, or tools)
   h. is often easily distracted by extraneous stimuli
   i. is often forgetful in daily activities

2. Six (or more) of the following symptoms of hyperactivity/impulsivity have persisted for at least 6 months to a degree that is maladaptive and inconsistent with developmental level:

   Hyperactivity
   a. often fidgets with hands or feet or squirms in seat
   b. often leaves seat in classroom or in other situations in which remaining seated is expected
   c. often runs about or climbs excessively in situations in which it is inappropriate (in adolescents or adults, may be limited to subjective feelings of restlessness)
   d. often has difficulty playing or engaging in leisure activities quietly
   e. is often "on the go" or often acts as if "driven by a motor"
   f. often talks excessively

   Impulsivity
   g. often blurts out answers before questions have been completed
   h. often has difficulty awaiting turn
   i. often interrupts or intrudes on others (e.g., butts into conversations or games)

B. Some hyperactive-impulsive or inattentive symptoms that caused impairment were present before age 7 years.

C. Some impairment from the symptoms is present in two or more settings (e.g., at school [or work] and at home).

D. There must be clear evidence of clinically significant impairment in social, academic, or occupational functioning.

E. The symptoms do not occur exclusively during the course of a Pervasive Developmental Disorder, Schizophrenia, or other Psychotic Disorder and are not better accounted for by another mental disorder (e.g., Mood Disorder, Anxiety Disorder, Dissociative Disorder, or a Personality Disorder).

Barlow and Durand, second edition, p. 440
Durand and Barlow, second edition, p. 408

Tourette's Disorder

A. Both multiple motor and one or more vocal tics have been present at some time during the illness, although not necessarily concurrently. (A tic is a sudden, rapid, recurrent, nonrhythmic, stereotyped motor movement or vocalization.)

B. The tics occur many times a day (usually in bouts) nearly every day or intermittently throughout a period of more than 1 year, and during this period there is never a tic-free period of more than 3 consecutive months.

C. The disturbance causes marked distress or significant impairment in social, occupational, or other important areas of functioning.

D. The onset is before age 18 years.

E. The disturbance is not due to the direct physiological effects of a substance (e.g., stimulants) or a general medical condition (e.g., Huntington's disease or postviral encephalitis).

Barlow and Durand, second edition, p. 446
Durand and Barlow, second edition, p. 414

Selective Mutism

A. Consistent failure to speak in specific social situations (in which there is an expectation for speaking, such as at school) despite speaking in other situations.

B. The disturbance interferes with educational or occupational achievement or with social communication.

C. The duration of the disturbance is at least 1 month (not limited to the first month of school).

D. The failure to speak is not due to a lack of knowledge of, or comfort with, the spoken language required in the social situation.

E. The disturbance is not better accounted for by a Communication Disorder (e.g., Stuttering) and does not occur exclusively during the course of a Pervasive Developmental Disorder, Schizophrenia, or other Psychotic Disorder.

Barlow and Durand, second edition, p. 446
Durand and Barlow, second edition, p. 414

Stuttering

A. Disturbance in the normal fluency and time patterning of speech (inappropriate for the individual's age), characterized by frequent occurrences of one or more of the following:

1. Sound and syllable repetitions
2. Sound prolongations
3. Interjections
4. Broken words (e.g., pauses within a word)

    5. Audible or silent blocking (filled or unfilled pauses in speech)
    6. Circumlocutions (word substitutions to avoid problematic words)
    7. Words produced with an excess of physical tension
    8. Monosyllabic whole-word repetitions (e.g., "I-I-I-I see him")

B. The disturbance in fluency interferes with academic or occupational achievement or with social communication.

C. If a speech-motor or sensory deficit is present, the speech difficulties are in excess of those usually associated with these problems.

Barlow and Durand, second edition, p. 446
Durand and Barlow, second edition, p. 414

Expressive Language Disorder

A. The scores obtained from standardized individually administered measures of expressive language development are substantially below those obtained from standardized measures of both nonverbal intellectual capacity and receptive language development. The disturbance may be manifest clinically by symptoms that include having a markedly limited vocabulary, making errors in tense, or having difficulty recalling words or producing sentences with developmentally appropriate length or complexity.

B. The difficulties with expressive language interfere with academic or occupational achievement or with social communication.

C. Criteria are not met for Mixed Receptive-Expressive Language Disorder or a Pervasive Developmental Disorder.

D. If Mental Retardation, a speech-motor or sensory deficit, or environmental deprivation is present, the language difficulties are in excess of those usually associated with these problems.

Barlow and Durand, second edition, p. 446
Durand and Barlow, second edition, p. 414

Glossary

Note: Many familiar words have specialized meanings and usage in psychology. A number of these, used in the text, are defined here.

3-methoxy-4-hydroxy-phenylglycol (MHPG) By-product of **norepinephrine.** Depressed patients with lower levels of MHPG respond better to tricyclic antidepressants than those with higher levels.

5-hydroxyindoleacetic acid (5-HIAA) By-product of the **neurotransmitter serotonin** in the cerebrospinal fluid, which serves as an indirect measure of serotonin.

abnormal behavior Actions that are unexpected and often evaluated negatively because they differ from typical or usual behavior.

abnormality Deviation from the average or the usual.

acetylcholine (ACh) Neurotransmitter, pervasive throughout the nervous system, that contributes to movement, attention, arousal, and memory. A deficiency of ACh is found in people with Alzheimer's disease.

acute onset Sudden beginning of a disease or disorder.

acute pain Pain that typically follows an injury and that disappears once the injury heals or is effectively treated.

acute PTSD Posttraumatic stress disorder that is diagnosed one to three months following the traumatic event.

acute stress disorder Severe reaction immediately following a terrifying event, often including amnesia about the event, emotional numbing, and derealization. Many victims later develop **posttraumatic stress disorder.**

addiction Informal term for **substance dependence.**

adoptees' relatives method In genetics research, the evaluation and study of the biological and adoptive families of individuals who display the disorder being investigated. The purpose is to assess genetic and environmental contributions to the disorder.

adoptees' study method In genetics research, the evaluation and study of children who have been adopted by another family and who have a biological parent displaying the disorder in question. The purpose is to assess genetic and environmental contributions to the disorder.

adoption studies In genetics research, the study of first-degree relatives reared in different families and environments. If they share common characteristics, such as a disorder, this finding suggests

that those characteristics have a genetic component.

advanced sleep phase type Type of circadian rhythm problem, not a DSM-IV disorder, involving a persistent pattern of early sleep onset and awakening times.

affect Conscious, subjective aspect of an emotion that accompanies an action at a given time.

age normed Standardized by age level; used for test scores.

age of onset Person's age when he or she develops or exhibits symptoms of a disease or condition.

agnosia Inability to recognize and name objects; may be a symptom of dementia or other brain disorders.

agonist Chemical substance that effectively increases the activity of a **neurotransmitter** by imitating its effects.

agonist substitution Replacement of a drug on which a person is dependent with one having a similar chemical makeup, an agonist. Used as a treatment for substance dependence.

agoraphobia Anxiety about being in places or situations from which escape might be difficult.

agreeableness One of the dimensions of the five-factor model of personality and individual differences, involving being warm, kind, and trusting as opposed to hostile, selfish, and mistrustful.

AIDS-related complex (ARC) Group of minor health problems such as weight loss, fever, and night sweats that appears after HIV infection, but prior to development of full-blown AIDS.

akinesia Extrapyramidal symptom involving slow motor activity, an expressionless face, and emotionless speech (see also **extrapyramidal symptoms**).

alcohol By-product of the fermentation of yeasts, sugar, and water; the most commonly used and abused depressant substance.

alcohol dehydrogenase (ADH) Enzyme that helps humans metabolize alcohol. Different levels of its subtypes may account for different susceptibilities to disorders such as **fetal alcohol syndrome.**

alcohol myopia Condition in which a person under the influence of alcohol ignores the long-range consequences of his or her behavior and responds only to the poorly thought-out immediate aspects of a situation.

alcohol use disorders Cognitive, biological, behavioral, and social problems associated with alcohol use and abuse.

alcohol withdrawal delirium Set of symptoms including body tremors and frightening hallucinations that may result during withdrawal from extended alcohol use. Also known as delirium tremens or the "DTs."

alogia Deficiency in the amount or content of speech, a disturbance often seen in people with schizophrenia.

alpha adrenergic receptors One group of nervous system receptors stimulated by the neurotransmitter norepinephrine.

alpha waves Regular pattern of brainwave voltage changes typical of calm relaxation.

alprazolam High-potency **benzodiazepine** medication (trade-name Xanax) for panic disorder that is fast acting but may lead to dependence and addiction.

alters Shorthand term for alter egos, the different personalities or identities in **dissociative identity disorder.**

altruistic suicide Formalized suicide approved and even expected by some cultures.

Alzheimer's disease The "strange disease of the cerebral cortex" that caused an "atypical form of senile dementia," discovered in 1906 by the German psychiatrist Alois Alzheimer.

ambulatory polysomnography Assessment of sleep disorders with portable electronic metering devices that allow clients sleeping in their natural home environments to be monitored for heart, muscle, respiration, brain wave, and other functions.

amnestic disorder Deterioration in the ability to transfer information from short- to long-term memory, in the absence of other dementia symptoms, as a result of head trauma or drug abuse.

amniocentesis Prenatal medical procedure that allows the detection of abnormalities (e.g., Down syndrome) in the developing fetus. It involves removal and analysis of amniotic fluid from the mother.

amok One of several running disorders seen in non-Western cultures—as in "running amok"—in which the individual enters a trancelike state and may commit violent acts; later he or she will have amnesia about the episode.

amotivational syndrome Impairment reported among heavy marijuana users involving apathy or an unwillingness to carry out long-term plans. Its actual prevalence level is controversial.

amphetamine Stimulant medication used to treat hypersomnia by keeping the person awake during the day, and to treat narcolepsy by suppressing REM sleep, including sudden onset episodes.

amphetamine use disorders Psychological, biological, behavioral, and social problems associated with amphetamine use and abuse.

amygdala Part of the brain's limbic system that regulates emotions and the ability to learn and control impulses; figures prominently in some psychopathology.

amyloid precursor protein Large protein, controlled by a gene on chromosome 21, that breaks down to contribute to the neuritic plaque characteristic of people with Alzheimer's disease.

amyloid protein Solid waxy substance forming the core of the neuritic plaque characteristic of people with Alzheimer's disease.

analgesic rebound headache Headache, more severe than the original one, that occurs after the medication used to treat headache pain has "worn off."

analog model Approach to research employing subjects who are similar to clinical clients, allowing replication of a clinical problem under controlled conditions.

anandamide Neurochemical that seems to be a naturally occurring version of the active chemical in marijuana.

angina pectoris Chest pain caused by partial blockage of the arteries that supply blood to the heart.

angulate gyrus Part of the brain's limbic system that regulates emotions and the ability to learn and control impulses; figures prominently in some psychopathology.

anhedonia Inability to experience pleasure, associated with some mood and schizophrenic disorders.

animal phobia Unreasonable, enduring fear of animals or insects that usually develops early in life.

anomic suicide Suicide motivated by loss and confusion caused by a major life disruption.

anorexia nervosa Eating disorder characterized by recurrent food refusal leading to dangerously low body weight.

Antabuse See **disulfiram.**

antagonist In neuroscience, a chemical substance that decreases or blocks the effects of a **neurotransmitter.**

antagonist drugs Medications that block or counteract the effects of psychoactive drugs.

antibodies Highly specific molecules called *immunoglobulins* produced by B cells to combine with and neutralize antigens.

antigens Foreign materials that enter the body, including bacteria and parasites.

antisocial personality disorder Cluster B (dramatic, emotional, or erratic) **personality disorder** involving a pervasive pattern of disregard for and violation of the rights of others. Similar to the non-DSM label psychopathy but with greater emphasis on overt behavior rather than personality traits.

anxiety Mood state characterized by marked negative affect and bodily symptoms of tension in which a person apprehensively anticipates future danger or misfortune. Anxiety may involve feelings, behaviors, and physiological responses.

Anxiety Disorders Interview Schedule-IV (ADIS-IV) Specialized, structured interview protocol to assess anxiety and related disorders.

aphasia Impairment or loss of language skills resulting from brain damage caused by stroke, Alzheimer's disease, or other illness or trauma.

apnea Brief interruption in breathing, sometimes occurring during sleep.

apolipoprotein E (apoE) Protein involved in the transport of cholesterol. High concentration of one subtype, controlled by a gene on chromosome 19, is associated with Alzheimer's disease.

apoptosis Naturally occurring process that kills unnecessary nerve cells. It may be induced to occur excessively by amyloid protein and is associated with Alzheimer's disease.

arousal stage Phase of sexual activity featuring sensations of pleasure and physiological changes including erection of the penis in males and the nipples in females. Women also experience vaginal lubrication and blood pooling in the pelvic region.

arrhythmia Irregular heart beat.

Asperger's disorder Pervasive developmental disorder characterized by impairments in social relationships and restricted or unusual behaviors, but without language delays seen in autism.

assertiveness training Instruction in which an individual learns to cope with stress by rehearsing ways to protect his or her time and personal rights in appropriate ways to avoid being exploited and feeling used. For example, caregivers of people with Alzheimer's disease learn assertion to prevent them from resorting to abuse in frustration.

assessment gender bias Possibility that gender differences in the reported prevalence or diagnosis of certain diagnostic categories may be due to prejudice in the assessment measures or the ways they are used.

association studies Research strategies for comparing genetic markers in groups of people with and without a particular disorder.

associative splitting Separation among basic functions of human personality (e.g., cognition, emotion, perception) that is seen by some as the defining characteristic of schizophrenia.

asylum Safe refuge; specifically, an institution to house mentally disordered people.

atherosclerosis Process by which a fatty substance or plaque builds up inside arteries to form obstructions.

attention-deficit/hyperactivity disorder (ADHD) Developmental disorder featuring maladaptive levels of inattention, excessive activity, and impulsiveness.

atypical depressive episode Depressive episode characterized by some ability to experience interest and pleasure, increased anxiety, overeating, and oversleeping.

auditory hallucinations Psychotic disturbance in perception in which person hears sounds or voices although these are not real or actually present. The voices are often critical, accusatory, or demanding.

augmentative communication strategies Pictures or computer aids to assist people with communication deficits to communicate.

autistic disorder (autism) Pervasive developmental disorder characterized by significant impairment in social interactions and communication, and restricted patterns of behavior, interest, and activity.

autogenic relaxation training Instruction that teaches clients to relax by focusing attention on blood flow and tense muscle groups, and by suggesting to themselves that they are feeling warm and relaxed.

autoimmune disease Condition in which the body's immune system attacks healthy tissue rather than antigens.

autonomic nervous system Part of the **peripheral nervous system** that regulates cardiovascular (heart, blood vessel), endocrine (hormone), and digestive functions. Includes the **sympathetic** and **parasympathetic** nervous systems.

autonomic restrictors Term for people with **generalized anxiety disorder (GAD)** because they show lower heart rate, blood pressure, skin conductance, and respiration rate activity than do people with other anxiety disorders.

avoidant personality disorder Cluster C (anxious or fearful) personality disorder featuring a pervasive pattern of social inhibition, feelings of inadequacy, and hypersensitivity to criticism.

avolition Apathy, or the inability to initiate or persist in important activities.

axes Several dimensions for which information is provided in DSM-IV diagnosis protocols—for example, clinical disorders and medical conditions.

axon Nerve cell branches that transmit outgoing electrochemical impulses to other neurons.

B cells Special type of white blood cells produced in bone marrow. They release molecules in the humoral branch of the immune system that circulate in the blood to seek out, identify, and neutralize antigens.

barbiturates Sedative (and addictive) drugs including Amytal, Seconal, and Nembutal that are used as sleep aids.

basal ganglia Brain area at the base of the telencephalon that seems to control motor behavior and to be involved in obsessive-compulsive disorder.

baseline Measured rate of a behavior before introduction of an intervention that allows comparison and assessment of the effects of the intervention.

behavioral assessment Measuring, observing, and systematically evaluating (rather than inferring) the client's thoughts, feelings and behavior in the actual problem situation or context.

behavioral inhibition system (BIS) Brain circuit in the **limbic system** that responds to threat signals by inhibiting activity and causing anxiety.

behavioral medicine Interdisciplinary approach applying behavioral science to the prevention, diagnosis, and treatment of medical problems.

behavioral model Explanation of human behavior, including dysfunction, based on principles of learning and adaptation derived from experimental psychology.

behavioral rehearsal Behavior therapy technique in which the client practices coping with troublesome or anxiety-arousing situations in a safe and supervised situation.

behaviorism Explanation of human behavior, including dysfunction, based on principles of learning and adaptation derived from experimental psychology.

behavior rating scales Structured assessment instruments used before and during treatment to evaluate the frequency and severity of specific behaviors.

behavior therapy Array of therapy methods based on the principles of behavioral and cognitive science as well as principles of learning as applied to clinical problems. It considers specific behaviors rather than inferred conflict as legitimate targets for change.

Bender Visual-Motor Gestalt Test Neuropsychological test for children in which they copy a variety of lines and shapes.

benzodiazepine-GABA system Chemical benzodiazepines (minor tranquilizers) that facilitate the effects of the **neurotransmitter gamma-aminobutyric acid (GABA)** in reducing anxiety. Such a system suggests the existence of natural benzodiazepines in the nervous system that have not yet been discovered.

benzodiazepines Anti-anxiety drugs including Valium, Xanax, Dalmane, and Halcion also used to treat insomnia. Effective against anxiety (and, at high potency, panic disorder), they show some side effects, such as some cognitive and motor impairment, and may result in dependence and addiction. Relapse rates are extremely high when the drug is discontinued.

beta adrenergic receptors Group of nervous system receptors stimulated by the neurotransmitter norepinephrine to increase blood pressure and heart rate. Drugs called beta blockers act at this level to control high blood pressure.

binge Relatively brief episode of uncontrolled, excessive consumption, usually of food or alcohol.

binge-eating disorder (BED) Pattern of eating involving distress-inducing binges not followed by purging behaviors; being considered as a new DSM diagnostic category.

biofeedback Use of physiological monitoring equipment to make individuals aware of their own bodily functions, such as blood pressure or brain waves, that they cannot normally access, with the purpose of controlling these functions.

biological model Explanation of psychological dysfunction that primarily emphasizes brain disorder or illness as the cause.

bipolar I disorder The alternation of major depressive episodes with full manic episodes.

bipolar II disorder The alternation of major depressive episodes with hypomanic (not full manic) episodes.

bisexuality Attraction to both same- and opposite-sex sexual partners.

black box Concept of the inner workings of the organism, such as thoughts and feelings that cannot be observed directly.

blind sight Also called **unconscious vision;** phenomenon in which a person is able to perform visual functions while having no awareness or memory of these abilities.

blood-injury-injection phobia Unreasonable fear and avoidance of exposure to blood, injury, or the possibility of an injection. Victims experience fainting and a drop in blood pressure.

body dysmorphic disorder (BDD) Somatoform disorder featuring a disruptive preoccupation with some imagined defect in appearance ("imagined ugliness").

borderline personality disorder Cluster B (dramatic, emotional, or erratic) personality disorder involving a pervasive pattern of instability of interpersonal relationships, self-image, affects, and control over impulses.

bradykinesia Slowed body movements, as occur in **Parkinson's disease.**

brain circuits **Neurotransmitter** currents or neural pathways in the brain.

brain stem Ancient lower part of the brain responsible for many life-sustaining automatic functions such as breathing and coordinated movement.

breathalyzer test Measure of alcohol intoxication that uses a breath sample because some consumed alcohol is vaporized in the lungs and exhaled.

breathing-related sleep disorders Sleep disruption leading to excessive sleepiness or insomnia, caused by a breathing problem such as interrupted **(apnea)** or labored **(hypoventilation)** breathing.

Brief Psychiatric Rating Scale Behavior rating scale used to assess the severity of patient problem areas such as guilt feelings and preoccupation with health.

brief psychotic disorder Psychotic disturbance involving delusions, hallucinations, or disorganized speech or behavior, but lasting less than one month; often occurs in reaction to a stressor.

Briquet's syndrome Obsolete term for **somatization disorder.**

bulimia nervosa Eating disorder involving recurrent episodes of uncontrolled excessive (binge) eating followed by compensatory actions to remove the food (e.g., deliberate vomiting, laxative abuse, excessive exercise).

caffeine use disorders Cognitive, biological, behavioral, and social problems associated with the use and abuse of caffeine.

cancer Category of often-fatal medical conditions involving abnormal cell growth and malignancy.

cannabinoids Family of chemicals in marijuana believed to be responsible for its mood- and behavior-altering ability.

carbamazepine Antiseizure medication sometimes effective in treating bipolar disorder.

cardiovascular disease Afflictions in the mechanisms, including the heart, blood vessels, and their controllers, that are responsible for transporting blood to the body's tissues and organs. Psychological factors may play important roles in such diseases and their treatments.

cardiovascular system Heart, blood vessels, and their controlling mechanisms, all of which serve to transport blood and nutrients to the tissues of the body.

case study method Research procedure in which a single person or small group is studied in detail. The method does not allow conclusions about cause and effect relationships, and findings can be generalized only with great caution.

castration anxiety In psychoanalysis, the fear in young boys that they will be mutilated genitally because of their lust for their mothers.

catalepsy Motor movement disturbance seen in people with some psychoses and mood disorders in which body postures are waxy and can be "sculpted," to remain fixed for long periods of time.

cataplexy Sudden loss of muscle tone that accompanies **narcolepsy** (sudden sleep attacks).

catatonia Disorder of movement involving immobility or excited agitation.

catatonic depressive episode (depressive stupor) Rare but severe mood disorder depressive episode usually featuring substantial reduction in spontaneous motor movement or, on occasion, agitation or odd mannerisms.

catatonic immobility Disturbance of motor behavior in which the person remains motionless, sometimes in an awkward posture, for extended periods of time.

catatonic type of schizophrenia Type of **schizophrenia** in which motor disturbances (rigidity, agitation, odd mannerisms) predominate.

catecholamine hypothesis Outdated, simplistic theory of mood disorder etiology stating that norepinephrine (a catecholamine) excess causes mania, and that low levels of it cause some forms of depression.

catharsis Rapid or sudden release of emotional tension thought to be an important factor in psychoanalytic therapy.

caudate nucleus Brain structure; part of the basal ganglia that controls motor behavior and is implicated in **obsessive-compulsive disorder.**

cellular branch Branch of the immune system using specialized cells to protect the body cells against viral and parasite infections.

central nervous system Brain and spinal cord.

central sleep apnea Brief periods of complete cessation in respiratory activity during sleep that may be associated with central nervous system disorders. Most clients awaken often as a result but do not report sleepiness and may be unaware of any problem.

cerebellum Part of the **hindbrain** in the **brain stem** that controls motor coordination and may be involved in **autism.**

cerebral cortex Largest part of the **forebrain,** divided into two hemispheres; responsible for human functions such as perceiving, reasoning, planning, creating, and remembering.

chemical imbalance Relative excess or deficit in brain chemicals, such as neurotransmitters, that may be implicated in some psychological disorders.

Child Behavior Checklist Behavior rating scale completed by parents and teachers to assess the frequency and severity of a range of possible childhood behavior problems.

childhood disintegrative disorder Pervasive developmental disorder involving severe regression in language, adaptive behavior, and motor skills after a two- to four-year period of normal development.

choking phobia Also known as *hypersensitive gag reflex* or *globus hystericus;* the fear and avoidance of swallowing pills, foods, and fluids, which may lead to significant weight loss.

chorea Motor problems characterized by involuntary limb movements.

chronic fatigue syndrome Incapacitating exhaustion following only minimal exertion, accompanied by fever, headaches, muscle and joint pain, depression, and anxiety.

chronic pain Enduring pain that does not decrease over time; may occur in muscles, joints, and the lower back, and may be due to enlarged blood vessels, or degenerating or cancerous tissue. Other significant factors are social and psychological.

chronic PTSD **Posttraumatic stress disorder** that endures longer than three months and is associated with greater avoidance and a higher likelihood of **comorbidity** with additional disorders.

chronic stage Final of Jellinek's four stages identified in the progression of alcoholism, where the individual's primary daily activities revolve around obtaining and drinking alcohol.

chronological age Person's age in calendar years.

chronotherapy Treatment for circadian rhythm sleep disorders that systematically moves bedtime later in intervals (phase delays) until it approaches the desired bedtime.

circadian rhythm sleep disorder Sleep disturbance resulting in sleepiness or insomnia, caused by the body's inability to synchronize its sleep patterns with the current pattern of day and night.

civil commitment laws Legal proceedings that determine a person is mentally disordered and may be hospitalized, even involuntarily.

classical categorical approach Classification method founded on the assumption of clear-cut differences among disorders, each with a different known cause.

classical conditioning Fundamental learning process first described by Ivan Pavlov. An event that automatically elicits a response is paired with another stimulus event that does not (a neutral stimulus). After repeated pairings, the neutral stimulus becomes a conditioned stimulus that by itself can elicit the desired response.

classification Assignment of objects or people to categories on the basis of shared characteristics.

clinical assessment Systematic evaluation and measurement of psychological, biological, and social factors in a person presenting with a possible psychological disorder.

clinical efficacy (axis) One of a proposed set of guidelines for evaluating clinical interventions on the evidence of their effectiveness.

clinical description Details of the combination of behaviors, thoughts, and feelings of an individual that make up a particular disorder.

clinical psychologist Person who has earned a Ph.D. or related degree (e.g., Psy.D.) in psychology and is trained to conduct research into the causes and treatment of severe psychological disorders as well as to diagnose, assess, and treat them.

clinical significance Degree to which research findings have useful and meaningful applications to real problems.

clinical utility (axis) One of a proposed set of guidelines for evaluating clinical interventions by whether they can be applied effectively and cost effectively in real clinical settings.

clonidine Medical treatment for hypertension that is often used to reduce the negative symptoms of withdrawal from **opiates.**

clozapine One of the newer medications for **schizophrenia,** trade name Clozaril, a weak **dopamine antagonist** that seems effective in some previously untreatable cases and with fewer serious side effects.

cocaine Derivative of coca leaves used medically as a local anesthetic and narcotic; often a substance of abuse.

cocaine use disorders Cognitive, biological, behavioral, and social problems associated with the use and abuse of **cocaine.**

codeine Opiate; a mild, medical narcotic derived from morphine.

cognitive-behavioral therapy Group of treatment procedures aimed at identifying and modifying faulty thought processes, attitudes and attributions, and problem behaviors; often used synonymously with **cognitive therapy.**

cognitive relaxation Use of meditation or imagery to combat anxiety that may result from sleeplessness.

cognitive restructuring Cognitive therapy procedure used to change negative or unrealistic thoughts or attributions.

cognitive science Field of study that examines how humans and other animals acquire, process, store, and retrieve information.

cognitive therapy Treatment approach that involves identifying and altering negative thinking styles related to psychological disorders such as depression and anxiety and replacing them with more positive beliefs and attitudes—and, ultimately, more adaptive behavior and coping styles.

cohort Participants in each age group of a cross-sectional research study.

cohort effect Observation that people of different age groups also differ in their values and experiences.

collective unconscious Accumulated wisdom of a culture collected and remembered across generations, a psychodynamic concept introduced by Carl Jung.

communication disorders Problems in transmitting or conveying information, including stuttering, **selective mutism,** and expressive language disorder.

community intervention Approach to treating and preventing disorders by directing action at the organizational, agency, and community levels rather than at individuals.

comorbidity The presence of two or more disorders in an individual at the same time.

comparative treatment research Outcome research that contrasts two or more treatment methods to determine which is most effective.

competency Ability of legal defendants to participate in their own defense and understand the charges and the roles of the trial participants.

Comprehensive System Standardized system of administering and scoring the Rorschach inkblot test that seeks to improve its reliability and validity.

compulsions Repetitive, ritualistic, time-consuming behaviors or mental acts a person feels driven to perform.

computerized axial tomography (CAT) scan Noninvasive imaging procedure useful in identifying abnormalities in the structure or shape of the brain.

concurrent (descriptive) validity Condition of testing in which the results from one test correspond to the results of other measures of the same phenomenon.

conditioned response (CR) Learned reaction, similar to the unconditioned response, that is elicited by a conditioned stimulus following classical conditioning.

conditioned stimulus (CS) Environmental event that acquires the ability to elicit a learned response as a result of classical conditioning associated with an unconditioned stimulus.

conditioning Process by which behaviors can be learned or modified through interaction with the environment. See **classical** and **operant** conditioning.

confound Any factor occurring in a research study that makes the results uninterpretable because its effects cannot be separated from those of the variables being studied.

confusional arousals Sleep disturbance characterized by bewildered reactions of the sleeper on awakening that may last for several minutes.

conscientiousness One of the dimensions of the five-factor model of personality and individual differences involving being organized, thorough, and reliable as opposed to careless, negligent, and unreliable.

construct validity Degree to which signs and symbols used to categorize a disorder relate to each other while differing from those for other disorders.

content validity Degree to which the characteristics of a disorder are a true sample of the phenomenon in question.

contingency management Encouragement of reinforcers to promote and maintain desired behaviors, and the removal of those reinforcers that maintain undesired behaviors.

control group Group of individuals in a research study who are similar to the experimental subjects in every way but are not exposed to the treatment received by the experimental group; their presence allows for a comparison of the differential effects of the treatment.

controlled drinking An extremely controversial treatment approach to alcohol dependence, in which severe abusers are taught to drink in moderation.

conversion disorder Physical malfunctioning, such as blindness or paralysis, suggesting neurological impairment, but with no organic pathology to account for it.

conversion hysteria Obsolete term for **conversion disorder** derived from the Freudian notion that physical symptoms represented a conversion of unconscious conflicts into a more acceptable form.

coping procedure Another term for **defense mechanism,** a pattern of behavior for dealing with anxiety-arousing situations.

coprolalia Vocal tic characterized by the involuntary repetition of obscenities.

coronary heart disease Blockage of the arteries supplying blood to the heart muscle, the major cause of death in Western culture, with social and psychological factors involved.

correlation Degree to which two variables are associated. In a **positive correlation,** the two variables increase or decrease together; in a **negative correlation,** one variable decreases as the other increases.

correlational coefficient Computed statistic reflecting the strength and direction of any association between two variables. It can range from +1.00 through zero (indicating no association) to −1.00, with the absolute value indicating the strength, and the sign reflecting the direction.

correlational method Research procedure in which variables are measured and compared to detect any association but are not manipulated. Conclusions about cause-and-effect relationships are not permissible.

cortical immaturity hypothesis Theory that the behavior and arousal levels of psychopaths result from incomplete development of the cerebral cortex.

corticosteroids Hormones, including cortisol, released by the adrenal gland in response to stressors to activate and, later, to turn off the body's stress response. Also called **stress hormones.**

corticotropin releasing factor (CRF) Neuromodulator hormone secreted into the blood by the hypothalamus. It stimulates the pituitary gland as part of a reaction chain called the stress response. It may be implicated in mood disorders as well as physical problems.

cortisol Stress hormone **(corticosteroid)** secreted by the cortex of the adrenal glands as part of the stress response.

counseling psychologist Person who has earned a Ph.D. or related degree in psychology and is trained to study and treat adjustment and vocational issues in relatively healthy people.

countertransference Psychoanalytic concept involving personal issues the therapist brings to professional relationships with clients.

course Pattern of development and change of a disorder over time.

course modifiers Patterns of development in a disorder that help predict its future course. These include recurrence, time sequences, and seasonal patterns.

covert sensitization Cognitive-behavioral intervention to reduce unwanted behaviors by having clients imagine the extremely aversive consequences of the behaviors and establish negative rather than positive associations with them.

crack Cocaine in a highly potent, solid, rocklike form.

crack babies Infants who were exposed to cocaine prenatally because of their mothers' use. Their characteristic irritability and high-pitched crying may in fact be due to other abuse or neglect in addition to the cocaine itself.

Creutzfeldt-Jakob disease Extremely rare condition that causes **dementia.**

criminal commitment Legal procedure by which a person who is found not guilty of a crime by reason of insanity must be confined in a psychiatric hospital.

criterion gender bias Possibility that gender differences in the reported prevalence or diagnosis of certain diagnostic categories may be due to prejudice in the defining criteria for the disorder.

criterion validity Extent to which categorization accurately predicts the future course of a disorder, whether treated or untreated; also known as predictive validity.

cross-generational effect Limit to the generalizability of longitudinal research because the group under study may differ from others in culture and experience.

cross-sectional design Methodology to examine a characteristic by comparing different individuals of different ages. Contrast with **longitudinal research design.**

cross-tolerance Condition in which a person may replace addiction to one drug with addiction to the other when the two drugs have similar chemical makeup and act on the same **neurotransmitter receptors.**

crucial stage Third of four of Jellinek's stages identified in the progression of alcoholism, involving a loss of control of drinking and occasional binges of heavy drinking.

cued, or situationally bound, panic attack Panic attack for which the triggering circumstances are known to the client.

cultural-familial retardation Mild mental retardation which may be caused largely by environmental influences.

cyclothymic disorder Chronic (at least two years) mood disorder characterized by alternating mood elevation and depression levels that are not as severe as manic or major depressive episodes.

dangerousness Tendency to violence which, contrary to popular opinion, is not more likely among mental patients.

deep sleep Sleep stage characterized by slow (**delta**) brain wave patterns. A person in deep sleep is difficult to rouse and slow to become alert.

defense mechanisms Common patterns of behavior, often adaptive coping styles when they occur in moderation, observed in response to particular situations. In psychoanalysis, these are thought to be unconscious processes originating in the **ego.**

deinstitutionalization Systematic removal of people with severe mental illness or mental retardation out of institutions like psychiatric hospitals.

delayed-onset PTSD **Posttraumatic stress disorder** with onset more than six months after the traumatic event.

delayed sleep phase type of circadian rhythm sleep disorder A persistent pattern of late sleep onset and awakening time.

delirium Rapid-onset reduced clarity of consciousness and cognition, with confusion, disorientation, and deficits in memory and language.

delta waves Relatively slow and irregular pattern of brain waves typical of the deepest, most relaxed stage of sleep; this is the time when sleeping panic attacks may occur. Delta activity during wakefulness may indicate brain dysfunction.

delusion Psychotic symptom involving disorder of thought content and presence of strong beliefs that are misrepresentations of reality.

delusional disorder Psychotic disorder featuring a persistent belief contrary to reality (delusion) but no other symptoms of **schizophrenia.**

delusion of grandeur Psychotic symptom, a person's unfounded belief that he or she is more famous or important than is true.

delusion of persecution Person's unfounded belief that others seek to harm him or her.

demence precoce French-language form of **dementia praecox.**

dementia Gradual-onset deterioration of brain functioning, involving memory loss, inability to recognize objects or faces, and problems in planning and abstract reasoning. These are associated with frustration and discouragement.

dementia of the Alzheimer's type Gradual onset of cognitive deficits caused by Alzheimer's disease, principally identified by person's inability to recall newly or previously learned material. The most common form of dementia.

dementia praecox Latin term meaning "premature loss of mind," an early label for what is now called schizophrenia, emphasizing the disorder's frequent appearance during adolescence.

dendrite Nerve cell branches that receive incoming electrochemical information for transmission along the neuron.

dependent personality disorder Cluster C (anxious or fearful) personality disorder characterized by a person's pervasive and excessive need to be taken care of, a condition that leads to submissive and clinging behavior and fears of separation.

dependent variable In an experimental research study, the phenomenon that is measured and expected to be influenced.

depersonalization Altering of perception that causes a person temporarily to lose a sense of his or her own reality; most prevalent in people with the dissociative disorders. There is often a feeling of being an outside observer of one's own behavior.

depersonalization disorder Dissociative disorder in which feelings of depersonalization are so severe they dominate the client's life and prevent normal functioning.

depressants Psychoactive substances that result in behavioral sedation, including alcohol and the sedative, hypnotic, and anxiolytic drugs.

depressive cognitive triad Thinking errors in depressed people negatively focused in three areas: themselves, their immediate world, and their future.

depressive personality disorder Pervasive pattern dominated by dejection, self-criticism, and a judgmental stance toward other people; under consideration as a future DSM category.

derailment See **loose associations.**

derealization Situation in which the individual loses his or her sense of the reality of the external world.

desipramine Antidepressant medication that has shown some effectiveness in increasing abstinence rates among cocaine users.

desire phase First stage of sexual activity, when sexual urges, thoughts, or fantasies occur, either in reaction to or even in the absence of a stimulating cue.

developmental psychology Study of changes in behavior that occur over time.

developmental psychopathology Study of changes in abnormal behavior that occur over time.

deviation IQ Intelligence test score that estimates how much a child's school performance will deviate from the average performance of others of the same age.

dexamethasone suppression test (DST) Proposed biological test for depression; the test failed to discriminate depression from other disorders, however.

diagnosis Process of determining whether a presenting problem meets the established criteria for a specific psychological disorder.

Diagnostic and Statistical Manual, Fourth Edition (DSM-IV) Current version of the official classification system for psychological disorders, published by the American Psychiatric Association.

dialectical behavioral therapy Promising treatment for borderline personality disorder that involves exposing the client to stressors in a controlled situation as well as helping the client regulate emotions and cope with stressors that might trigger suicidal behavior.

diastolic blood pressure Blood pressure level when the heart is at rest or between heartbeats.

diathesis-stress model Hypothesis that both an inherited tendency (a vulnerability) and specific stressful conditions are required to produce a disorder.

diencephalon Brain structure containing the **thalamus** and hypothalamus that serves as a relay between the forebrain and the **brain stem.**

dimensional approach Method of categorizing characteristics on a continuum rather than on a binary, either-or, or all-or-none basis.

dimethyltryptamine (DMT)   Natural hallucinogen from the bark of trees that grow in Central and South America.

diminished capacity   Evidence of an abnormal mental condition in a person that causes criminal charges against him or her requiring intent or knowledge to be reduced to lesser offenses requiring only reckless or criminal neglect.

directionality   The possibility that, when two variables A and B are correlated, variable A causes variable B, or that B causes A.

discrimination training   Arrangement of experiences in which the person or animal learns to respond under certain conditions and not to respond under other conditions.

disease conviction   Core feature of **hypochondriasis**, the firm belief that one currently has a disease, based on the misinterpretation of one's own symptoms and sensations.

disease model of dependence   View that drug dependence is caused by a physiological disorder. This implies that the user is a blameless victim of an illness.

disorder of written expression   Condition in which one's writing performance is significantly below age norms.

disorganized speech   Style of talking often seen in people with **schizophrenia**, involving incoherence and a lack of typical logic patterns.

disorganized type of schizophrenia   Type of schizophrenia featuring disrupted speech and behavior, disjointed delusions and hallucinations, and flat or silly affect.

displacement   Defense mechanism in which a person directs a problem impulse toward a safe substitute.

dispositional optimism   Cognitive style involving expectations of positive outcomes; seems to influence physical health in a positive way.

dissociation   Detachment or loss of integration between identity or reality and consciousness.

dissociative amnesia   Dissociative disorder featuring the inability to recall personal information, usually of a stressful or traumatic nature.

dissociative disorders   Disorder in which individuals feel detached from themselves or their surroundings, and reality, experience, and identity may disintegrate.

dissociative fugue   Dissociative disorder featuring sudden, unexpected travel away from home, along with an inability to recall one's past, sometimes with assumption of a new identity.

dissociative identity disorder (DID)   Formerly known as **multiple personality disorder**, a disorder in which as many as 100 personalities or fragments of personalities coexist within one body and mind.

dissociative trance disorder (DTD)   Altered state of consciousness in which the person believes firmly that he or she is possessed by spirits; considered a disorder only where there is distress and dysfunction.

disulfiram (Antabuse)   Chemical used as an aversion treatment for heavy drinking because it causes a buildup in the body of an alcohol by-product, making the person vomit after drinking. Clients must continue taking it for the chemical to remain effective.

dominant gene   The one gene of any pair of genes that determines a particular trait.

dopamine   Neurotransmitter whose generalized function is to activate other neurotransmitters and to aid in exploratory and pleasure-seeking behaviors (thus balancing **serotonin**). A relative excess of dopamine is implicated in **schizophrenia** (though contradictory evidence suggest the connection is not simple) and its deficit is involved in **Parkinson's disease.**

dopaminergic system   Parts of the nervous system activated by the **neurotransmitter dopamine;** involved in many functions including the experience of reward.

dorsal horns of the spinal cord   Sections of the spinal cord responsible for transmitting sensory input to the brain. They function as a "gate" that allows transmission of pain sensations if the stimulation is sufficiently intense.

double bind communication   According to an obsolete, unsupported theory, the practice of transmitting conflicting messages that was thought to cause schizophrenia.

double-blind control   Procedure in outcome studies that prevents bias by ensuring that neither the subjects nor the providers of the experimental treatment know who is receiving treatment and who is receiving placebo.

double depression   Severe mood disorder typified by major depressive episodes superimposed over a background of **dysthymic disorder.**

Down syndrome   Type of mental retardation caused by a chromosomal aberration (chromosome 21) and involving characteristic physical appearance.

dream analysis   Psychoanalytic therapy method in which dream contents are examined as symbolic of **id** impulses and intrapsychic conflicts.

duty to warn   Mental health professional's responsibility to break confidentiality and notify the potential victim whom a client has specifically threatened.

dysfunctional attitudes   Cognitive errors seen in depressed individuals, who may automatically assume the worst, draw negative conclusions arbitrarily, and treat minor problems as major ones.

dyslexia   Learning disability involving problems in reading.

dysmorphophobia   Literally, "fear of ugliness," an obsolete term for **body dysmorphic disorder.**

dysphoric manic or mixed episode   See **mixed manic episode.**

dyssomnias   Problems in getting to sleep or in obtaining sufficient quality sleep.

dysthymic disorder   Mood disorder involving persistently depressed mood, with low self-esteem, withdrawal, pessimism or despair, present for at least two years, with no absence of symptoms for more than two months.

echolalia   Repetition or echoing of the speech of others, a normal intermediate step in the development of speech skills. Originally thought to be a unique symptom of **autism,** it is now seen as evidence of developmental delay involved in that disorder.

echo planar magnetic resonance imaging   Experimental version of magnetic resonance imaging that can make rapid multiple sequential images of the brain as it functions.

educable mental retardation   Obsolete term referring to level of retardation comparable to the DSM "mild" designation that assumes the individual can learn basic academic skills.

ego   In psychoanalysis, the psychical entity responsible for finding realistic and practical ways to satisfy **id** drives.

egoistic suicide   Suicide that occurs in the context of diminished social supports, as in the case of some elderly persons who have lost friends and family contacts.

ego psychology   Derived from psychoanalysis, this theory emphasizes the role of the ego in development and attributes psychological disorders to failure of the ego to manage impulses and internal conflicts.

Electra complex   In psychoanalysis, a young girl's intrapsychic desire to replace her mother, possess her father, and acquire a penis. The resolution of this complex results in development of the **superego.**

electrocardiogram   Measure of electrical activity generated by heart muscle exertion used to detect and evaluate heart diseases.

electroconvulsive therapy (ECT)   Biological treatment for severe, chronic depression involving the application of electrical impulses through the brain to produce seizures. The reasons for its effectiveness are unknown.

electrodermal responding Psychophysiological assessment of skin conductance and sweat gland activity as a measure of **autonomic nervous system** responses to stress.

electroencephalogram (EEG) Measure of electrical activity patterns in the brain, taken through electrodes placed on the scalp.

electromyogram (EMG) Measure of muscle movement.

electrooculogram (EOG) Measure of eye muscle movement particularly relevant to detecting dream stages during sleep.

emotion Pattern of action elicited by an external event and a feeling state, accompanied by a characteristic physiological response.

emotional stability One of the dimensions of the five-factor model of personality and individual differences, involving being even-tempered as opposed to nervous, moody, and temperamental.

emotion contagion Situation in which an emotional reaction spreads from one individual to others nearby.

empathy Condition of sharing and understanding the emotions of another person.

empirical criterion keying Selection of test items by their ability to identify people with known characteristics.

endocrine system Network of glands that affect bodily functions by releasing hormones into the bloodstream. Some endocrine activity is implicated in psychological disorders.

endogenous Having internal causes or sources.

endogenous opioids Substances occurring naturally throughout the body that function like **neurotransmitters** to shut down pain sensation even in the presence of marked tissue damage. These may contribute to psychological problems such as eating disorders. Also known as endorphins or enkephalins.

endorphins See **endogenous opioids.**

enkephalins See **endogenous opioids.**

epidemiology Psychopathology research method examining the prevalence, distribution, and consequences of disorders in populations.

episodic course Pattern of a disorder alternating between recovery and recurrence.

equifinality Developmental psychopathology principle that a behavior or disorder may have several different causes.

erotomanic type Type of delusional disorder featuring belief that another person, usually of higher status, is in love with the individual.

erotophobia Learned negative reaction to or attitude about sexual activity, perhaps developed as a result of a negative or even traumatic event such as rape.

essential hypertension High blood pressure with no verifiable physical cause, which makes up the overwhelming majority of high blood pressure cases.

etiology Cause or source of a disorder.

event-related potential (ERP) Also known as **evoked potential;** the brain's electrical reaction to a psychologically meaningful environment event, as measured by the **EEG.**

exhibitionism Sexual gratification attained by exposing one's genitals to unsuspecting strangers.

exorcism Religious ritual that, attributing disordered behavior to possession by demons, seeks to treat the individual by driving the demons from his or her body.

expectancy effect People's response to a substance on the basis of their beliefs about it, even if it contains no active ingredient. This phenomenon demonstrates that cognitive as well as physiological factors are involved in drug reaction and dependence.

experiment Research method that can establish causation by manipulating the variables in question and controlling for other alternative explanations of any observed effects.

expert witness Person who because of special training and experience is allowed to offer opinion testimony in legal trials.

explicit memory Good recollection of actual events. Contrast with **implicit memory.**

expressed emotion (EE) The hostility, criticism, and overinvolvement demonstrated by some families toward a family member with a psychological disorder; this can often contribute to the person's relapse.

expressive language Communication with words.

expressive language disorder An individual's problems in spoken communication, as measured by significantly low scores on standardized tests of expressive language relative to nonverbal intelligence test scores. Symptoms may include a markedly limited vocabulary or errors in verb tense.

extensive support retardation Retardation level characterized by the long-term and regular care required for individuals with this degree of disability.

external validity Extent to which research study findings generalize, or apply, to people and settings not involved in the study.

extinction Learning process in which a response maintained by reinforcement in operant conditioning or pairing in **classical conditioning** decreases when that reinforcement or pairing is removed. The procedure of removing that reinforcement or pairing is also called **extinction.**

extrapyramidal symptoms Serious side effects of **neuroleptic** medications resembling the motor difficulties of **Parkinson's disease.** Also called parkinsonian symptoms, they include **akinesia** and **tardive dyskinesia.**

extraversion One of the dimensions of the five-factor model of personality and individual differences, involving being talkative, assertive, and active, as opposed to silent, passive, and reserved.

face validity Condition of testing in which test items appear plausible for their intended purposes, even if they are not truly valid discriminators.

facial agnosia Type of **agnosia** characterized by a person's inability to recognize even familiar faces.

facilitated communication Method claimed by proponents to allow autistic individuals to communicate when a facilitator supports their arms and provides encouragement while they type messages on a keyboard. Objective attempts to validate the procedures often find that the communication actually originates with the facilitator.

factitious disorder Nonexistent physical or psychological disorder deliberately faked for no apparent gain except possibly sympathy and attention.

failure to thrive Stunted physical growth and maturation in children, often associated with psychosocial factors such as lack of love and nurturing.

false negative Assessment error in which no pathology is noted (i.e., test results are negative) when it is actually present.

false positive Assessment error in which pathology is reported (i.e., test results are positive) when none is actually present.

family studies Genetic studies that examine patterns of traits and behaviors among relatives.

fatalistic suicide Suicide in the context of a person's hopelessness and loss of the feeling of control over his or her own destiny.

fear Emotion of an immediate alarm reaction to present danger or life-threatening emergencies.

fearlessness hypothesis One of the major theories of the etiology of antisocial personality disorder, stating that psychopaths are less prone to fear and, thus, less inhibited from dangerous or illicit activities.

female orgasmic disorder Recurring delay or absence of orgasm in some women following a normal sexual excitement phase, relative to their prior experience and current stimulation. Also known as **inhibited female orgasm.**

female sexual arousal disorder Recurrent inability in some women to attain or maintain adequate lubrication and swelling sexual excitement responses until completion of sexual activity.

fermentation The decomposition process by which yeasts, water, and sugar form alcohol.

fetal alcohol syndrome (FAS) Pattern of problems including learning difficulties, behavior deficits, and characteristic physical flaws, resulting from heavy drinking by the victim's mother when she was pregnant with the victim.

fetishism Long-term, recurring, intense sexually arousing urges, fantasies, or behavior involving the use of nonliving, unusual objects, which cause distress or impairment in life functioning.

fixation In psychoanalysis, stopping or concentrating at a psychosexual stage because of a lack of appropriate gratification at that stage.

flashback Sudden, intense reexperiencing of a previous, usually traumatic, event.

flat affect Apparently emotionless demeanor (including toneless speech and vacant gaze) when a reaction would be expected.

flight/fight system (FFS) Brain circuit in animals that when stimulated causes an immediate alarm and escape response resembling human panic.

flight or fight response Biological reaction to alarming stressors that musters the body's resources (e.g., blood flow, respiration) to resist or flee the threat.

fluoxetine Trade name *Prozac;* a selective **serotonin reuptake blocker,** that acts on the serotonergic system as a treatment for depression, **obsessive-compulsive disorder,** and bulimia.

flurazepam Trade name *Dalmane;* a long-acting medication for insomnia that may cause daytime sleepiness.

forebrain Top section of the brain, also called the **telencephalon,** that includes the **limbic system, basal ganglia, caudate nucleus,** and **cerebral cortex.**

formal observation Structured recording of behaviors that are measurable and well defined.

fragile X syndrome Pattern of abnormality caused by a defect in the **X chromosome** resulting in mental retardation, learning problems, and unusual physical characteristics.

free association Psychoanalytic therapy technique intended to explore threatening material repressed into the unconscious. The patient is instructed to say whatever comes to mind without censoring.

frenzy witchcraft Running frenzy disorder among the Navajo tribe that seems equivalent to dissociative fugue.

frontal lobe Forward section of each cerebral hemisphere, most responsible for thinking, reasoning, memory, the experience of reward, and social behavior and, thus, most likely to be involved in a wide range of psychopathology.

frotteurism **Paraphilia** in which the person gains sexual gratification by rubbing against unwilling victims in crowds from which they cannot escape.

functional analysis Careful study of behaviors and the environmental variables that cause or maintain them.

functional communication training Teaching of speech or nonspeech communication skills to replace undesired behavior. The new skills are useful to the person and will be maintained because of the effects they have on others.

gamma aminobutyric acid (GABA) A neurotransmitter that reduces activity across the synapse and thus inhibits a range of behaviors and emotions, especially generalized anxiety.

gate control theory of pain View that psychological factors can enhance or diminish the sensation and perception of pain by influencing the transmission of pain impulses through the section of the spinal cord that acts as a "gate."

gender identity disorder Psychological dissatisfaction with one's own biological gender, a disturbance in the sense of one's identity as a male or female. The primary goal is not sexual arousal but rather to live the life of the opposite gender.

General adaptation syndrome (GAS) Sequence of reactions to sustained stress described by Hans Selye. These stages are alarm, resistance, and exhaustion, which may lead to death.

generalizability Extent to which research results apply to a range of individuals not included in the study.

generalized amnesia Condition in which one loses memory of all personal information, including one's own identity.

generalized anxiety disorder (GAD) Anxiety disorder characterized by intense, uncontrollable, unfocused, chronic, and continuous worry that is distressing and unproductive accompanied by physical symptoms of tenseness, irritability, and restlessness.

genes Long deoxyribonucleic acid (DNA) molecules, the basic physical units of heredity that appear as locations on chromosomes.

genetic linkage studies Studies that seek to match the inheritance pattern of a disorder to that of a genetic marker; this helps researchers establish the location of the gene responsible for the disorder.

genetic marker Inherited characteristic for which the chromosomal location of the responsible gene is known.

genital herpes Incurable sexually transmitted viral disease with alternating periods of dormancy and activity. The active periods involve pain, liquid discharge, itching, and ulcerative lesions, and their recurrence may be influenced by stress.

genotype Specific genetic makeup of an individual.

gila Disorder reported in Malaysia, similar to **schizophrenia** but different in important ways that may illuminate details of both disorders.

globus hystericus Sensation of a lump in the throat causing the person difficulty in swallowing, eating, and talking. A **conversion** symptom or part of **choking phobia.**

glutamate system Excitatory neurotransmitter system that may be the avenue by which alcohol affects cognitive abilities.

good premorbid Outdated classification for **schizophrenia,** referring to the quality of social functioning of the individual just prior to the emergence of the disorder.

graduated extinction Monitoring of a desired behavior, such as sleeping or compliance by children, less and less frequently to encourage independence.

grandiose type Type of delusional disorder featuring beliefs of inflated worth, power, knowledge, identity, or special relationship to a deity or famous person.

habit reversal Treatment for tics that requires the person to practice a competing response to replace the tic when it occurs.

hallucinations Psychotic symptoms of perceptual disturbance in which things are seen or heard or otherwise sensed although they are not real or actually present.

hallucinogen Any psychoactive substance such as **LSD** or marijuana that can produce delusions, hallucinations, paranoia, and altered sensory perception.

hallucinogen use disorders Cognitive, biological, behavioral, and social problems associated with the use and abuse of hallucinogenic substances.

Halstead-Reitan Neuropsychological Battery Relatively precise instrument that helps identify and locate organic damage by testing various skills, including rhythm, grip, and tactile performance.

head trauma Injury to the head and therefore to the brain, typically caused by accidents; can lead to cognitive impairments, including memory loss.

health psychology Subfield of behavioral medicine that studies psychological factors important in health promotion and maintenance.

hebephrenia Silly and immature emotionality, a characteristic of some types of schizophrenia.

helper T cells T-type of lymphocyte that enhances the immune system response by signaling B cells to produce **antibodies** and other T cells to destroy **antigens.**

hermaphrodite See **intersex individual.**

heterosexual behavior Sexual activity with members of the opposite gender.

hierarchy of needs   Ranking of human necessities from basic food to self-actualization, proposed by Abraham Maslow.

hindbrain   Lowest part of the **brain stem;** regulates many automatic bodily functions such as breathing and digestion; includes the **medulla, pons,** and **cerebellum.**

hippocampus   Part of the brain's **limbic system** that regulates emotions and the ability to learn and control impulses; figures prominently in some psychopathology.

histrionic personality disorder   Cluster B (dramatic, emotional, or erratic) personality disorder involving a pervasive pattern of excessive emotionality and attention seeking.

HIV-1 disease   The human immunodeficiency virus-type-1 that causes AIDS.

homosexual behavior   Sexual activity with members of the same gender.

Homovanillic acid (HVA)   By-product of the **neurotransmitter dopamine** in the cerebrospinal fluid that serves as an indirect measure of dopamine.

hormone   A chemical messenger produced by the endocrine glands.

human genome project   Ongoing scientific attempt to develop a comprehensive map of all human genes.

humoral branch   One of two main branches of the **immune system;** operates in the blood and other bodily fluids to develop **antibodies** and neutralize **antigens.**

humoral theory   Ancient belief that psychological disorders were caused by imbalances in bodily humors or fluids.

humors   Bodily fluids (blood, black and yellow bile, and phlegm) that early theorists believed controlled normal and abnormal functioning.

Huntington's disease   Genetic disorder marked by involuntary limb movements and progressing to dementia.

hypersomnia   Abnormally excessive sleep; a person with this condition will fall asleep several times a day.

hypertension   Also known as **high blood pressure;** a major risk factor for stroke and heart and kidney disease that is intimately related to psychological factors.

hypnagogic hallucinations   Characteristic of **narcolepsy** involving frightening and vivid experiences during sleep that are visual, tactile, aural, and mobile.

hypoactive sexual desire disorder   Apparent lack of interest in sexual activity or fantasy that would be expected considering the person's age and life situation.

hypochondriasis Somatoform disorder involving severe anxiety over the belief that one has a disease process without any evident physical cause.

hypofrontality   Relative deficiency in activity in the **frontal lobes** of the brains of people with **schizophrenia;** associated with the negative symptoms of the disorder.

hypomanic episode   Less severe and less disruptive version of a **manic episode** that is one of the criteria for several mood disorders.

hypothalamic-pituitary-adrenalcortical (HYPAC) axis   Brain-endocrine system connection implicated in some psychological disorders.

hypothalamus   Part of the **diencephalon** of the brain broadly involved in the regulation of behavior and emotion.

hypothesis   Educated guess or statement to be tested by research.

hypoventilation   Reduced or labored breathing—for example, during sleep.

id   In psychoanalysis, the unconscious psychical entity present at birth representing basic drives.

ideas of reference   Person's delusion that the actions, thoughts, laughter, and meaningless activities of others are directed toward or refer to him or her.

idiographic strategy   Close and detailed investigation of one individual emphasizing what makes him or her unique (compare with **nomothetic strategy**).

illness phobia   Extreme fear of the possibility of contracting a disease (as opposed to the belief that one already has it), combined with irrational behaviors to avoid contracting it.

imaginal exposure   Presentation or **systematic exposure** of emotions or fearful or traumatic experiences in the imagination.

imipramine   One of the **tricyclic antidepressant** drugs affecting the serotonergic and noradrenergic neurotransmitter systems. It blocks panic attacks but not more generalized anxiety and causes side effects such as dry mouth, dizziness, and, occasionally, sexual dysfunction; effective in some mood and anxiety disorders, as well as other disorders.

immune system   Body's means of identifying and eliminating any foreign materials (e.g., bacteria, parasites, even transplanted organs) that enter.

implicit memory   Condition of memory in which a person cannot recall past events even though he or she acts in response to them.

inappropriate affect   Emotional displays that are improper for the situation.

incest   Deviant sexual attraction (**pedophilia**) directed toward one's own family member; often the attraction of a father toward a daughter who is maturing physically.

incidence   Number of new cases of a disorder appearing during a specific time period (compare with **prevalence**).

independent variable   Phenomenon that is manipulated by the experimenter in a research study and that is expected to influence the dependent variable.

index disorder   In genetics research family studies, the particular disorder being investigated.

indoleamine hypothesis   Outdated, simplistic theory that low levels of **serotonin** (one of the indoleamines) might cause depression.

inferiority complex   Feeling of being inferior to others while striving for superiority.

informal observation   Attention paid to behavior but without defining or recording it in any systematic fashion.

information transmission   Warnings about the feared object repeated so often that the person develops a phobia solely on the basis of hearing them.

informed consent   Ethical requirement whereby research subjects agree to participate in a research study only after they receive full disclosure about the nature of the study and their own role in it.

inhibited orgasm   An inability to achieve orgasm despite adequate sexual desire and arousal; commonly seen in women but relatively rare in men.

insanity   Legal rather than psychological or medical concept involving both mental disorder and an inability to know or appreciate the wrongfulness of criminal acts.

insanity defense   Legal plea that a defendant should not be held responsible for a crime because he or she was mentally ill at the time of the offense.

insidious onset   Development of a disorder that occurs gradually over an extended period of time. Contrast with **acute onset.**

insight   In psychoanalysis, recognition of the causes of emotional distress.

insomnia, primary   Difficulty falling asleep, staying asleep, or feeling rested where there is no apparent medical or psychological cause.

insulin shock therapy   A dangerous biological treatment involving the administration of large doses of insulin to induce seizures.

intelligence quotient (IQ)   Score on an intelligence test, abbreviated IQ, estimating a person's deviation from average test performance.

intermittent support retardation   Retardation level characterized by the need for only episodic special care—for example, during crises and difficult life changes.

internal validity   Extent to which the results of a research study can be attributed to the independent variable after confounding alternative explanations have been ruled out.

interoceptive avoidance   Avoidance of situations or activities, such as exercise, that produce internal physical arousal similar to the beginnings of a panic attack.

interpersonal psychotherapy (IPT) Newer brief treatment approach that emphasizes resolution of interpersonal problems and stressors such as role disputes in marital conflict, or forming relationships in marriage or a new job. It has demonstrated effectiveness for such problems as depression.

interpersonal therapy Brief, structured treatment that focuses on teaching a person skills to improve existing relationships or develop new ones.

interrater reliability Degree to which two or more observers make the same ratings or measurements.

intersex individuals (hermaphrodites) People born with ambiguous genitalia and hormonal abnormalities. They are assigned a gender at birth and then often provided hormones and surgery to complete the correspondence.

intrapsychic conflict In psychoanalysis, the struggles among the **id, ego,** and **superego.**

introjection In object relations theory, the process of incorporating memories and values of individuals who are important and close to the person.

introspection Early, nonscientific approach to the study of psychology involving systematic attempts to report thoughts and feelings that specific stimuli evoked.

introversion Tendency to be shy and withdrawn.

inverse agonist Chemical substance that produces effects opposite those of a particular neurotransmitter.

ischemia Narrowing of arteries caused by plaque buildup within the arteries.

jealous type Type of delusional disorder featuring delusions that the individual's sexual partner is unfaithful.

jet lag type of circadian rhythm sleep disorder Disorder in which sleepiness and alertness patterns conflict with local time and occur after recent or repeated travel across time zones.

K complexes Brain wave pattern of high-amplitude spikes typical of Stage 2 sleep.

Klinefelter's syndrome Disorder among males caused by an extra **X chromosome,** resulting in physical deformities, infertility, and sometimes mental retardation.

koro In Singapore, a condition of mass hysteria or group delusion in which people believe their genitals are retracting into their bodies.

Korsakoff syndrome Amnestic disorder caused by damage to the **thalamus** resulting from stroke or chronic and heavy alcohol use.

labeling Applying a name to a phenomenon or a pattern of behavior. The label may acquire negative connotations or be applied erroneously to the person rather than his or her behaviors.

la belle indifférence Lack of distress shown by some individuals presenting **conversion, somatization,** or **amnestic disorders.**

large fibers Nerve fibers in the **dorsal horns of the spinal cord** that regulate the pattern and intensity of pain sensations. They close the gate, decreasing the transmission of painful stimuli.

lateral ventricles Naturally occurring cavities in the brain filled with cerebrospinal fluid. Some individuals with **schizophrenia** have enlarged ventricles, probably resulting from insufficient development or atrophy of surrounding tissue.

law of effect Thorndike's principle that behaviors are strengthened or weakened by the environmental events that follow them.

learned helplessness theory of depression Seligman's theory that people become anxious and depressed when they make an *attribution* that they have no control over the stress in their lives (whether in reality they do or not).

learning disorders Reading, mathematics, or written expression performance substantially below levels expected relative to the person's age, IQ, and education.

Lesch-Nyhan syndrome X-linked disorder characterized by **mental retardation,** signs of cerebral palsy, and **self-injurious behavior.**

leukocytes White blood cells of varying types that play specialized roles in the immune system to fight viral and parasitic infections.

libido In psychoanalysis, the energy within the **id** that drives people toward life and fulfillment.

life-span developmental psychopathology The study of psychological disorders over the entire age range.

limbic system Part of the **forebrain** involved in emotion, the ability to learn and to control impulses, and the regulation of sex, hunger, thirst, and aggression drives. This system figures prominently in much of psychopathology.

limited support retardation Retardation level characterized by the special care needed on a consistent though time-limited basis—for example, during employment training.

lithium carbonate Common salt used in substantial doses to treat bipolar disorder. Clients often discontinue its use because they enjoy the manic periods, and relapse rates are high. The mechanism for its effects is unknown.

lobotomy Neurosurgery procedure intended to eliminate undesirable behaviors by severing the connections between the **thalamus/hypothalamus** and the **frontal lobes** of the brain.

localized or selective amnesia Memory loss limited to specific times and events, particularly traumatic events.

locus coeruleus Area in the **hindbrain** that is part of a noradrenergic (norepinephrine-sensitive) circuit. It is involved in emergency and alarm reactions and may be related to panic states.

longitudinal course specifiers Time patterns among mood disorders (e.g., prior dysthymia or cyclothymia rapid cycling, seasonal patterns) that may suggest their course, treatment, and prognosis.

longitudinal design Systematic study of changes in the same individual or group examined over time.

loose associations Deficits in logical continuity of speech, with abrupt movement between ideas. A characteristic of **schizophrenia** also called derailment.

LSD (d-lysergic acid diethylamide) Most common hallucinogenic drug; a synthetic version of the grain fungus ergot.

Luria-Nebraska Neuropsychological Battery Relatively precise instrument that helps identify and locate organic damage by testing various skills.

lysergic acid amide A naturally occurring hallucinogen found in the seeds of the morning glory plant.

madhouses Perjorative, negative term for asylums, the institutions of refuge for the mentally disordered.

magnetic resonance imaging (MRI) Procedure using radio signals generated in a strong magnetic field and passed through body tissue to produce detailed, even layered, images of its structure.

maintenance of sameness Necessity among people with **autism** that their familiar environments remain unchanged; they become upset when changes are introduced.

maintenance treatment Combination of continued psychosocial treatment and/or medication designed to prevent relapse following therapy.

major depressive disorder, single or recurrent episode Mood disorder involving one **(single episode)** or more (separated by at least two months without depression—**recurrent**) major depressive episodes.

major depressive episode Most common and severe experience of depression, including feelings of worthlessness, disturbances in bodily activities such as sleep, loss of interest, and the inability to experience pleasure, persisting at least two weeks.

male erectile disorder Recurring inability in some men to attain or maintain adequate penile erection until completion of sexual activity.

male orgasmic disorder Recurring delay in or absence of orgasm in some men following a normal sexual excitement phase, relative to age and current stimulation. Also known as **inhibited male orgasm.**

malingering Deliberate faking of a physical or psychological disorder motivated by gain.

mania Period of abnormally excessive elation or euphoria, associated with some **mood disorders.**

manic episode Period of abnormally elevated or irritable mood that may include inflated self-esteem, decreased need for sleep, pressured speech, flight of ideas, agitation, or self-destructive behavior.

marijuana (cannabis sativa) Dried part of the hemp plant, a hallucinogen that is the most widely used illegal substance.

marital therapy Interventions for the relationship problems of couples, whether married or not.

mass hysteria Phenomenon in which people in groups share the same fear, delusion, abnormal behavior, or even physical symptoms as a result of psychological processes and suggestion.

mathematics disorder Mathematics performance significantly below age norms.

medroxyprogesterone Medication that helps stimulate respiration and is used in treatment of **obstructive sleep apnea.**

medulla Part of the **hindbrain,** which regulates such automatic bodily functions as breathing and digestion.

melancholic (endogenous) depressive episode Mood disorder depressive episode associated with more severe somatic disturbances such as **anhedonia,** loss of sex drive, or weight loss.

melatonin Hormone produced by the pineal gland that is activated by darkness to control the body's biological clock and to induce sleep. It is implicated in **seasonal affective disorder** and may be used in treatments for **circadian rhythm sleep disorders.**

memory B cells Specialized lymphocytes created after **antigens** are neutralized to help the **immune system** fight off new invasions by those antigens more rapidly. These account for the effectiveness of inoculations.

mental age (MA) Score a person achieves on an intelligence test representing the highest age-equivalent items he or she passed.

mental disorder Psychological disorder.

mental hygiene movement Mid-19th-century effort to improve care of the mentally disordered by informing the public of their mistreatment.

mental illness Term formerly used to mean psychological disorder but less preferred because it implies that the causes of the disorder can be found in a medical disease process.

mental retardation Significantly subaverage intellectual functioning paired with deficits in adaptive functioning such as self-care or occupational activities, appearing prior to age 18.

mental status exam Relatively coarse preliminary test of a client's judgment, orientation to time and place, and emotional and mental state; typically conducted during an initial interview.

mescaline Naturally occurring hallucinogen found in the peyote cactus plant.

metabolites By-products of **neurotransmitter** activity; their measurement allows study of that activity.

methadone **Opiate agonist** used as a treatment for heroin addiction. It initially provides the analgesic and sedative effects of heroin. After extended use, these effects diminish and tolerance develops. An effective treatment for some when combined with counseling.

methylphenidate Stimulant medication known as Ritalin used to treat hypersomnia by keeping the person awake during the day, narcolepsy by suppressing REM sleep including that with sudden onset, and attention deficit hyperactivity disorder.

microsleeps Short, seconds-long periods of sleep that occur in people who have been deprived of sleep.

midbrain Section of the brain that coordinates movement with sensory input and contributes to the processes of arousal and tension.

migraine headache Debilitating, throbbing, or pulsing head pain with rapid onset, usually occurring on one side of the head.

mild mental retardation Level of retardation defined by IQ scores between 55 and 70.

Millon Multiaxial Clinical Inventory (MMCI) Standardized measure to identify and assess personality disorders.

Minnesota Multiphasic Personality Inventory (MMPI) Empirically derived standardized personality test that provides scales for assessing such abnormal functioning as depression and paranoia. One of the most widely used and heavily researched assessment instruments.

mixed manic episode Condition in which the individual experiences both elation and depression or anxiety at the same time. Also known as **dysphoric manic episode.**

mixed sleep apnea Combination of obstructive and central sleep apnea, such as brief interruptions in breathing during sleep caused by a blocked air passage and by cessation in respiratory activity.

modeling Learning through observation and imitation of the behavior of other

individuals and the consequences of that behavior.

moderate mental retardation Level of retardation defined by IQ scores between 40 and 55.

monoamine oxidase (MAO) inhibitors Medications that treat depression and severe social anxiety by blocking an enzyme that breaks down the **neurotransmitters norepinephrine** and **serotonin.**

mood Enduring period of emotionality.

mood congruent Consistent with the person's emotional level. Hallucinations and delusions may be congruent or incongruent with a depressed person's mood.

mood disorders Group of disorders involving severe and enduring disturbances in emotionality ranging from elation to severe depression.

mood incongruent Not consistent with the person's emotional level. Psychotic symptoms associated with mood disorders may not be congruent with the person's mood.

moral therapy 19th-century psychosocial approach to treatment that involved treating patients as normally as possible in normal environments.

moral weakness model of chemical dependence View that substance abusers should be blamed because their behavior results from lack of self-control, character, or moral fiber.

morphine Opiate medication used as an analgesic (pain reliever) and narcotic that is sometimes a substance of abuse.

multiaxial classification Categorization system, such as in DSM-IV, employing several dimensions or axes, each used for differentiating among the categories.

Multidimensional integrative approach An approach to the study of psychopathology that holds that psychological disorders are always the products of multiple interacting causal factors.

multiple baseline Single-case experimental research design in which measures are taken on two or more behaviors, or on a single behavior in two or more situations. A particular intervention is introduced for each at different times. If behavior change is coincident with each introduction, this is strong evidence the intervention caused the change.

multiple infarctions More than one area or incident of death to tissue (e.g., in the brain or heart) due to blockage of blood flow.

myocardial infarction Death of heart tissue when its blood supply artery is blocked by plaque or a blood clot.

myocardium Heart muscle.

naltrexone Most widely used **opiate-antagonist** drug; it produces immediate withdrawal and, thus, a great deal of discomfort. It may also contribute to the treatment of alcohol abuse, but is not as successful for either substance as was originally hoped.

narcissistic personality disorder Cluster B (dramatic, emotional, or erratic) **personality disorder** involving a pervasive pattern of grandiosity in fantasy or behavior, need for admiration, and lack of empathy.

narcolepsy Sleep disorder involving sudden and irresistible sleep attacks.

natural environment phobia Fear of situations or events in nature, especially heights, storms, and water.

necessary condition Circumstance required for a particular phenomenon to occur.

negative affect Emotional symptoms that are part of the definition of both anxiety and depression but are not specific to either of these. Also, the fact that substance abuse may be maintained because the substance causes an escape from unpleasant circumstances, responsibilities, or especially, feelings.

negative correlation An association between two variables in which one increases as the other decreases.

negative schema Automatic, enduring, and stable negative cognitive bias or belief system about some aspect of life.

negative symptoms Less outgoing symptoms, such as flat affect and poverty of speech, displayed by some people with schizophrenia.

negativistic personality disorder Pervasive pattern of resisting routine requests and expectations and adopting a contrary attitude; considered for but not included in DSM-IV. Corresponds to former category known as passive-aggressive personality disorder.

nervous breakdown Lay term for a severe psychological upset that actually has no meaning in scientific or professional psychopathology.

neurasthenia Disorder common in the United States in the mid-1800s, although the label is no longer used here (though still prevalent in China). Its symptoms include a lack of energy, a variety of aches and pains, and sometimes fever. This disorder is similar to present-day **chronic fatigue syndrome.**

neuritic plaque Clusters of dead neurons found during autopsy in the brains of people with Alzheimer's disease.

neurofibrillary tangles Brain damage in the form of large numbers of strand-like filaments found during autopsy in people with Alzheimer's disease.

neurohormones Hormones that affect the brain and are increasingly the focus of study in psychopathology.

neuroimaging Sophisticated computer-aided procedures that allow nonintrusive examination of nervous system structure and function.

neuroleptics Major antipsychotic medications, dopamine antagonists, that diminish delusions, hallucinations, and aggressive behavior in psychotic patients but that may also cause serious side effects.

neuromodulators Hormones secreted into the blood to transmit brain messages throughout the body; also known as **neuropeptides.**

neuron Individual nerve cell; responsible for transmitting information.

neuropsychological testing Assessment of brain and nervous system functioning by testing an individual's performance on behavioral tasks.

neuroscience Study of the nervous system and its role in behavior, thoughts, and emotions.

neurosis Obsolete psychodynamic term for psychological disorder thought to result from unconscious conflicts and the anxiety they cause. Plural is *neuroses.*

neurotransmitters Chemicals that cross the **synaptic cleft** between nerve cells to transmit impulses from one **neuron** to the next. Their relative excess or deficiency is involved in several psychological disorders.

nicotine Toxic and addictive substance found in tobacco leaves.

nicotine gum Chewing gum that delivers nicotine to smokers without the carcinogens in cigarette smoke. This substitute may help people stop smoking, especially when combined with counseling.

nicotine patch Patch placed on the skin that delivers nicotine to smokers without the carcinogens in cigarette smoke. Somewhat more successful than nicotine gum because it requires less effort by the user and delivers the drug more consistently; should be coupled with counseling to stop smoking and avoid relapse.

nicotine use disorders Cognitive, biological, behavioral, and social problems associated with the use and abuse of nicotine.

nightmares Frightening and anxiety-provoking dreams occurring during rapid eye movement (REM) sleep. The individual recalls the bad dreams and recovers alertness and orientation quickly.

nocturnal myoclonus Periodic jerky arm and leg motions occurring during sleep.

nocturnal penile tumescence (NPT) Erection of the penis during sleep, usually **REM-stage sleep.** If this normal reaction occurs in a man with erectile problems in the waking state, his problems may be assumed to have psychological origins.

nomenclature In a naming system or **nosology,** the actual labels or names that are applied. In psychopathology

these include, for example, mood disorders or eating disorders.

nomothetic strategy Identification and examination of large groups of people with the same disorder to note similarities and develop general laws (compare with **idiographic**).

nondemand pleasuring Procedure to reestablish sexual arousal involving fondling and caressing while intercourse is forbidden. This method avoids the anxiety provoked by the need to perform sexually.

nondisjunction In Down syndrome, the fusing of two of the 21st chromosomes to create one cell with one copy that dies and one cell with three copies that continue to divide.

non-rapid eye movement (NREM) sleep Periods in the sleep cycle, divided into four substages, when the body may be active while the brain is relatively less active and dreaming does not occur.

non-24-hour sleep-wake syndrome Disruptive circadian rhythm problem, not a DSM-IV disorder, in which the person's biological clock does not correspond to a 24-hour cycle, forcing the sleep-wake pattern out of synchrony with this cycle.

Norepinephrine (also noradrenaline) Neurotransmitter also known as noradrenaline that is active in the central and peripheral nervous systems controlling heart rate, blood pressure, and respiration, among other functions. Because of its role in the body's alarm reaction, it may also contribute in general and indirectly to panic attacks and other disorders.

nosology Classification and naming system for medical and psychological phenomena.

nucleus accumbens A complex of neurons that is part of the brain's "pleasure pathway" responsible for the experience of reward.

object relations A modern development in psychodynamic theory involving the study of how children incorporate the memories and values of people who are close and important to them.

obsessions Recurrent intrusive thoughts or impulses the client seeks to suppress or neutralize while recognizing they are not imposed by outside forces.

obsessive-compulsive disorder (OCD) Anxiety disorder involving unwanted, persistent, intrusive thoughts and impulses as well as repetitive actions intended to suppress them.

obsessive-compulsive personality disorder Cluster C (anxious or fearful) **personality disorder** featuring a pervasive pattern of preoccupation with orderliness, perfectionism, and mental and interpersonal control at the expense of flexibility, openness, and efficiency.

obstructive sleep apnea Snoring and brief interruptions in breathing during sleep caused by blockage of the airway.

occipital lobe Section of each cerebral hemisphere that integrates and makes sense of visual inputs.

Oedipus complex In psychoanalysis, the intrapsychic struggle within a young boy between his lust for his mother and his fear of castration because of it. The resolution of this complex results in development of the **superego.**

operant conditioning Fundamental behavioral learning process in which responses are modified by their consequences (reinforcers, punishers, extinction, and so on).

operational definition Delineation of a concept on the basis of the operation used to measure it.

opiates Addictive psychoactive substances such as **heroin, opium,** and **morphine** that cause temporary euphoria and analgesia (pain reduction).

opioid-releasing neurons Nerve cells that release **endogenous opioids** and that play a role in the brain's pleasure pathway controlling the experience of reward.

opioids Family of substances including **opiates** and **endorphins** as well as synthetic variants such as **methadone** that have a narcotic effect.

opioid use disorders Cognitive, biological, behavioral, and social problems associated with the use and abuse of **opiates** and their synthetic variants.

opium Naturally occurring compound from the poppy plant that is a strong narcotic, having pain-relieving and sleep- and euphoria-inducing effects. Its derivatives include morphine and heroin.

opponent-process theory Explanation of drug tolerance and dependence suggesting that when a person experiences positive feelings these will be followed shortly by negative feelings, and vice versa. Eventually, the motivation for drug taking shifts from a desire for the euphoric high to a need to relieve the increasingly unpleasant feelings that follow drug use. A vicious cycle develops in that the drug that makes a person feel terrible is the one thing that can eliminate the pain.

orgasmic reconditioning Learning procedure to help clients strengthen appropriate patterns of sexual arousal by pairing appropriate stimuli with the pleasurable sensations of masturbation.

orgasm phase Stage of sexual activity involving ejaculation in men and vaginal wall contractions in women. Women are able to experience orgasm again immediately while men are unable to form an erection for a time interval called a refractory period.

oriented times three Patient is aware of, or oriented to, his or her identity, location, and time (person, place, and time).

otitis media Infection of the middle ear, an extremely common childhood problem; the attendant temporary or chronic hearing loss may lead to language development delays.

outcome research Studies examining the effectiveness and results, positive or negative, of treatment procedures.

pain behaviors Observable manifestations of the private experience of pain. These may include wincing or other facial expressions, verbal complaints of distress, and avoidance of activities that increase pain sensations.

pain disorder **Somatoform disorder** featuring true pain but for which psychological factors play an important role in onset, severity, or maintenance.

panic Sudden overwhelming fright or terror.

panic attack Abrupt experience of intense fear or discomfort accompanied by a number of physical symptoms, such as dizziness or heart palpitations.

panic control treatment (PCT) Cognitive-behavioral treatment for panic attacks, involving gradual exposure to feared somatic sensations and modification of perceptions and attitudes about them.

panic disorder with agoraphobia (PDA) Fear and avoidance of situations the person believes might induce a dreaded panic attack.

panic disorder without agoraphobia (PD) Panic attacks experienced without development of agoraphobia.

papaverine Vasodilating medication used to treat male erectile disorder by dilating blood vessels, increasing blood flow to the penis to form an erection. The medication must be injected and the procedure can be painful; it is also so intrusive it is often declined or discontinued by patients.

paradoxical intention Instructing clients to do the opposite of the desired behavior. Telling an impotent man not to have sex or an insomniac not to sleep reduces anxiety to perform.

paranoia Person's irrational beliefs that he or she is especially important (delusions of grandeur) or that other people are seeking to do him or her harm.

paranoid personality disorder Cluster A (odd or eccentric) **personality disorder** involving pervasive distrust and suspiciousness of others such that their motives are interpreted as malevolent.

paranoid type of schizophrenia Type of schizophrenia in which symptoms primarily involve delusions and hallucinations, while speech, and motor and emotional behavior are relatively intact.

paraphilias Sexual disorders and deviations in which sexual arousal occurs almost exclusively in the context of inappropriate objects or individuals.

parasomnias Abnormal behaviors such as nightmares or sleepwalking that occur during sleep.

parasympathetic nervous system Part of the **autonomic nervous system** that regulates bodily systems (e.g., digestion) while activity level is low and that balances sympathetic nervous system activity.

parietal lobe Section of each cerebral hemisphere responsible for recognizing touch sensations.

Parkinson's disease Degenerative brain disorder principally affecting motor performance (e.g., tremors, stooped posture) associated with reduction in dopamine. Dementia may be a result as well.

passive-aggressive personality disorder Former diagnostic category not included in DSM-IV for lack of sufficient research. See a similar category **negativistic personality disorder.**

pathological or impacted grief reaction Extreme reaction to the death of a loved one that involves psychotic features, suicidal ideation, or severe loss of weight or energy, or that persists more than two months.

patient uniformity myth Tendency to consider all members of a category as more similar than they are, ignoring their individual differences.

pedophilia **Paraphilia** (sexual deviation) involving strong sexual attraction toward children.

penile implant Surgical treatment for **male erectile disorder** involving the insertion of a prosthesis that may be a semirigid silicone rod or an inflatable tube.

penile strain gauge Psychophysiological monitoring device that measures male sexual arousal by changes in penis circumference.

performance scales In the Wechsler group of intelligence tests, subtests that assess psychomotor and nonverbal reasoning skills and the ability to learn new relationships.

peripheral nervous system Neural networks outside the brain and spinal cord, including the somatic nervous system, which controls muscle movement, and the **autonomic nervous system,** which regulates cardiovascular, endocrine, digestion, and regulation functions.

permissive hypothesis Theory that **neurotransmitter systems** contribute to mood irregularities when low **serotonin** levels permit them to range widely and become unregulated.

personality disorders Enduring maladaptive patterns for relating to the environment and oneself, exhibited in a wide range of contexts that cause significant functional impairment or subjective distress.

personality inventories Self-report questionnaires that assess personal traits by asking respondents to identify descriptions that apply to them.

personality trait Enduring tendency to behave in particular predisposed ways across situations.

person-centered therapy Therapy method in which the client, rather than the counselor, primarily directs the course of discussion, seeking self-discovery and self-responsibility.

pervasive developmental disorders Wide-ranging, significant, and long-lasting dysfunctions that appear before the age of eighteen.

pervasive support retardation Retardation level characterized by the constant, intensive care needed by the individual in all environments.

phantom limb pain Perception of pain in a limb that actually is absent due to amputation. This phenomenon suggests pain is not entirely a physical experience.

phencyclidine (PCP) Dangerous synthetic hallucinogen, also called angel dust, that may cause agitated or violent behavior, disorientation, convulsions, coma, and even death.

phenotype Observable characteristics or behaviors of an individual.

phenylketonuria (PKU) Recessive disorder involving the inability to break down a food chemical whose buildup causes retardation, seizures, and behavior problems. PKU can be detected by infant screening and prevented by a specialized diet.

phii pob Thailand's version of **dissociative trance** states.

phobia A psychological disorder characterized by marked and persistent fear of an object or situation.

phobic avoidance Extreme shunning of feared objects or situations displayed by people with phobias.

phototherapy Treatment of seasonal affective disorder with large doses of exposure to bright light.

pica Eating disorder in infants or individuals with mental retardation characterized by ingesting non-nutritive substances such as paint, dirt, or insects.

Pick's disease Very rare neurological disorder that results in **presenile** (early onset) **dementia.**

pivloktoq Running frenzy disorder among native peoples of the Arctic that seems equivalent to **dissociative fugue.**

placebo control group In an outcome experiment, a control group that does not receive the experimental manipulation but is given a similar procedure with an

identical expectation of change, allowing the researcher to assess any placebo effect.

placebo effect Behavior change resulting from the person's expectation of change rather than from the experimental manipulation itself.

plasticity Phenomenon by which damage to neurons sometimes can be compensated for by the action of other neurons.

plateau phase Brief time period immediately before orgasm.

pleasure principle Tendency to seek pleasure and minimize discomfort.

polygenetic abnormality Abnormality whose causes include action by several genes located at different chromosome sites.

polysomnographic (PSG) evaluation Assessment of sleep disorders in which a client sleeping in the lab is monitored for heart, muscle, respiration, brain wave, and other functions.

polysubstance use Use of multiple mind- and behavior-altering substances, such as drugs.

pons Part of the hindbrain that controls such automatic bodily functions as breathing and digestion.

poor premorbid Outdated classification for schizophrenia, referring to the quality of social functioning of the individual just prior to the emergence of the disorder.

positive correlation Association between two variables in which one increases as the other increases.

positive symptoms More overt symptoms, such as delusions and hallucinations, displayed by some people with schizophrenia.

positron emission tomography (PET) scan Imaging procedure in which a radioactive tracer that binds to blood glucose is detected as the glucose is metabolized during brain activity. This allows nonintrusive localization and observation of brain activity.

postpartum onset Disorder that first appears in mothers during the time immediately following childbirth.

posttraumatic stress disorder (PTSD) Enduring, distressing emotional disorder that follows exposure to a severe helplessness- or fear-inducing threat. The victim reexperiences the trauma, avoids stimuli associated with it, and develops a numbing of responsiveness and an increased vigilance and arousal.

prealcoholic stage First of Jellinek's four stages identified in the progression of alcoholism, involving occasional drinking with few serious consequences.

predictive validity Degree to which an assessment instrument accurately predicts a person's future behavior. See **criterion validity.**

premature ejaculation Recurring ejaculation before the person wishes it, with minimal sexual stimulation.

premorbid Individual's level of functioning prior to the development of a disorder. Good and poor premorbid are no longer considered useful distinguishing categories of schizophrenia.

prepared learning Certain associations can be learned more readily than others because this ability has been adaptive for evolution.

presenile dementia Dementia that appears before old age, between ages 40 and 60.

presenting problem Original complaint reported by the client to the therapist. The actual treated problem may sometimes be a modification derived from the presenting problem.

prevalence Number of people displaying a disorder in the total population at any given time (compare with **incidence**).

primary gain Freudian notion that anxiety reduction is the principal reinforcement obtained for the display of psychological symptoms.

primary insomnia Difficulty in initiating, maintaining or gaining from sleep; not related to other medical or psychological problems.

primary process In psychodynamic theory, the **id**'s characteristic mode of thinking, which is emotional, irrational, and preoccupied with sex, aggression, and envy.

proband In genetics research, the individual displaying the trait or characteristic being studied. Also known as **index case.**

process schizophrenia Means of grouping schizophrenia on the basis of slow onset, lack of a precipitating stressor, with associated social skill deficits and flat affect.

prodromal stage Second of Jellinek's four stages identified in the progression of alcoholism, featuring heavy drinking but with few outward signs of a problem.

profound mental retardation Level of retardation defined by IQ scores below 20 and extremely limited communication and self-help skills.

prognosis Predicted future development of a disorder over time.

progressive muscle relaxation Set of exercises to teach people to become aware of and actively counteract muscle tension to induce relaxation or drowsiness.

projective tests Psychoanalytically based measures that present ambiguous stimuli to clients on the assumption that their responses will reveal their unconscious conflicts. Such tests are very inferential and lack high reliability and validity.

prototypal approach System for categorizing disorders using both essential, defining characteristics and a range of variation on other characteristics.

psilocybin Naturally occurring hallucinogen found in certain species of mushrooms.

psychiatric nurse Person with nursing training who specializes in care and treatment of psychiatric patients, usually in a hospital setting.

psychiatric social worker Person who has earned a Master of Social Work (MSW) degree or, occasionally, a Doctor of Social Work (DSW) and is trained to work with social agencies to help psychologically disordered clients and their families.

psychiatrist Person who has earned an M.D. degree and then has specialized in psychiatry during residency training. Psychiatrists are trained to investigate primarily the biological nature and causes of psychiatric disorders, and to diagnose and treat them as well.

psychoactive substances Substances, such as drugs, that alter mood or behavior.

psychoanalysis Psychoanalytic assessment and therapy, which emphasizes exploration of, and insight into, unconscious processes and conflicts, pioneered by Sigmund Freud.

psychoanalyst Therapist who practices psychoanalysis after earning either an M.D. or Ph.D. degree and then receiving additional specialized postdoctoral training.

psychoanalytic model Complex and comprehensive theory originally advanced by Sigmund Freud that seeks to account for the development and structure of personality, as well as the origin of abnormal behavior, based primarily on inferred inner entities and forces.

psychodynamic psychotherapy Contemporary version of psychoanalysis that still emphasizes unconscious processes and conflicts but is briefer and more focused on specific problems.

psychological autopsy Postmortem psychological profile of a suicide victim constructed from interviews with people who knew the person before death.

psychological disorder Psychological dysfunction associated with distress or impairment in functioning that is not a typical or culturally expected response.

psychological model Explanation of human behavior and its dysfunction that emphasizes the influence of the social environment and early experience.

psychomotor retardation Deficits in motor activity and coordination development.

psychoncology Study of psychological factors involved in the course and treatment of cancer.

psychoneuroimmunology (PNI) Study of psychological influences on the neurological responding involved in the body's immune response.

psychopathology Scientific study of psychological disorders.

psychopathy Non-DSM category similar to **antisocial personality disorder** but with less emphasis on overt behavior; indicators include superficial charm, lack of remorse, and other personality characteristics.

psychophysiological assessment Measurement of changes in the nervous system reflecting psychological or emotional events such as anxiety, stress, and sexual arousal.

psychophysiological disorders Outdated term, similar to **psychosomatic medicine,** for the study of psychological and social factors influencing physical disorders. The term is misleading because it falsely implies that other psychological problems such as mood disorders do not also have significant biological components.

psychosexual stages of development In psychoanalysis, the sequence of phases a person passes through during development. Each stage is named for the location on the body where **id** gratification is maximal at that time.

psychosis Group of severe psychological disorders, including **schizophrenia,** featuring **delusions** and **hallucinations.**

psychosocial treatment Treatment practices that focus on social and cultural factors (such as family experience) as well as psychological influences. These approaches include cognitive, behavioral, and interpersonal methods.

psychosomatic medicine See **behavioral medicine.**

psychosurgery Biological treatment involving neurosurgery, such as **lobotomy,** for a psychological disorder. For example, a specific surgical lesion to the cingulate bundle may be an effective last-resort treatment for **obsessive-compulsive disorder.**

psychotic behavior Severe psychological disorder category characterized by hallucinations and loss of contact with reality.

psychotic depressive episode Condition in which psychotic symptoms such as delusions and hallucinations accompany depressive episodes.

psychotic symptoms Delusions and hallucinations that may appear during depressive or manic episodes.

purging techniques In the eating disorder **bulimia nervosa,** the self-induced vomiting or laxative abuse used to compensate for excessive food ingestion.

Purkinje cells Cells in the **cerebellum** that may inhibit the action of other cells and may be sensitive to a major inhibitory neurotransmitter, GABA. A deficit of these cells has been noted in some people with **autism.**

quantitative genetics Method of genetics research that examines patterns of genetic control over a wide range of genes, each of which may contribute only a small effect.

randomization Method for placing individuals into research groups that assures each one of an equal chance of being assigned to any group, to eliminate any systematic differences across groups.

rapid cycling pattern Temporal course of a **bipolar disorder** when transitions between mania and depression are quick, occurring four or more times in one year.

rapid eye movement (REM) sleep Periodic intervals of sleep during which the eyes move rapidly from side to side, and dreams occur, but the body is inactive.

rational-emotive therapy Cognitive-behavioral treatment approach that seeks to identify and eliminate irrational beliefs that may cause maladaptive emotions and behavior.

rauwolfia serpentina More commonly known as reserpine, an early medication derived from the snakeroot plant that helps control the agitation and aggressiveness of some psychotic patients.

Raynaud's disease Cardiovascular disease involving blockage of blood circulation to the extremities, with resultant pain and cold sensations in the hands and feet.

reactive schizophrenia Means of grouping schizophrenia on the basis of rapid onset, presence of a precipitating stressor, with associated social adequacy and volatile and intense emotional expression.

reactivity Changes in one person's behavior as a result of observing the behavior in another.

reading disorder Reading performance significantly below age norms.

reality principle In psychodynamic theory, the logical reasoning style of the **ego** that ensures that actions are practical and realistic.

rebound insomnia In a person with insomnia, the worsened sleep problems that can occur when medications are used to treat insomnia and then withdrawn.

receptive language Communicated material that is understood.

receptors Locations on nerve cell **dendrites** that receive chemical impulses for transmission through the **neuron.**

recessive gene Gene that must be paired with another recessive gene to determine a trait.

reciprocal gene-environment model Hypothesis that people with a genetic predisposition for a disorder may also have a genetic tendency to create environmental risk factors that promote the disorder.

reexperiencing Careful and systematic visualizing and reliving of traumatic life events to diminish their power and emotional effects as a means of treating **dissociative identity disorder** or **post-traumatic stress disorder.**

regulated breathing Intervention for **stuttering** in which the person is instructed to stop and take a deep breath whenever a stuttering episode begins.

reinforcement In **operant conditioning,** consequences for behavior that strengthen it or increase its frequency. **Positive** reinforcement involves the contingent delivery of a desired consequence, while **negative** reinforcement is the contingent escape from an aversive consequence. Unwanted behaviors may result from their reinforcement, or the failure to reinforce desired behaviors.

relapse Reappearance of or return to problem behaviors after treatment or recovery.

relapse prevention Extending therapeutic progress by teaching the client how to cope with future troubling situations.

relaxation response Active components of meditation methods, including repetitive thoughts of a sound to reduce distracting thoughts, and closing the mind to other intruding thoughts, that decrease the flow of stress hormones and **neurotransmitters** and cause a feeling of calm.

relaxation training Intervention for tics in which the person is taught to relax the muscles involved in the tics.

reliability Degree to which a measurement is consistent—for example, over time or among different raters.

replication Confirming the results of a research study by repeating it, often by a separate, independent researcher.

repressed memories Concept involving recollections of traumatic events actively eliminated from memory. Controversy surrounds whether recall that seems to occur years later is real or accurate.

repression In psychoanalytic theory, a process that forces unwanted material from the conscious to the unconscious.

research design Plan of experimentation used to test a hypothesis.

reserpine See **rauwolfia serpentina.**

residual type of schizophrenia Diagnostic category for people who have experienced at least one episode of schizophrenia, and who no longer display its major symptoms but still show some bizarre thoughts or social withdrawal.

resolution phase Decrease in sexual arousal after orgasm, particularly in men. This phase is not involved in sexual dysfunctions.

response prevention Behavioral therapy method to diminish compulsive behavior by prohibiting that behavior in its usual circumstance while the individual learns the dreaded outcome will not occur.

retarded ejaculation Male orgasmic disorder in which ejaculation is delayed so the patient is unable to reach orgasm with his partner, though he is able to ejaculate during masturbation.

reticular activating system (RAS) Section of the **midbrain** responsible for tension and arousal processes, including sleep and wakefulness.

retrograde ejaculation Condition in which ejaculatory fluids travel backward into the bladder, usually as a result of certain drugs or a medical condition. This is not considered a DSM-IV male orgasmic disorder.

retrospective information Literally "the view back," data collected by examining records or recollections of the past. It is limited by the accuracy, validity, and thoroughness of the sources.

retrospective study Research that utilizes retrospective information and shares its limitations.

Rett's disorder Progressive neurological developmental disorder featuring constant hand-wringing, mental retardation, and impaired motor skills.

reuptake Action by which a neurotransmitter is quickly drawn back into the discharging neuron after being released into a synaptic cleft.

reversal design See **withdrawal design.**

rheumatoid arthritis Painful, degenerative disease in which the immune system essentially attacks itself, resulting in stiffness, swelling, and even destruction of the joints. Cognitive-behavioral treatments can help relieve pain and stiffness.

Rhythm Test Subtest of the **Halstead-Reitan Neuropsychological Battery** that asks respondents to compare rhythmic beats to assess sound recognition, attention, and concentration.

Rorschach inkblot test Projective test that uses irregular patterns of ink as its ambiguous stimuli.

rumination disorder Regurgitation and reswallowing of partially digested food, interfering with nutritional intake or weight gain.

sadistic personality disorder Pervasive pattern of deriving pleasure by inflicting pain on others; proposed as a category for DSM-III-R but not included in DSM-IV for lack of research.

Saint Vitus's Dance Instance of mass hysteria in which groups of people experienced a simultaneous compulsion to dance and shout in the streets.

scheduled awakening For children who wake frequently at night, awakening them about an hour before and from a deeper sleep than their usual times to help them learn to fall asleep on their own.

Schedule for Affective Disorders and Schizophrenia (SADS) Specialized semistructured interview protocol that specifically assesses mood and schizophrenic disorders.

schedules of reinforcement In operant conditioning, the pattern of consequences following a behavior, based on the number of responses emitted or the time intervals between them.

schizoaffective disorder Psychotic disorder featuring symptoms of both schizophrenia and major mood disorder.

schizoid personality disorder Cluster A (odd or eccentric) **personality disorder** featuring a pervasive pattern of detachment from social relationships and a restricted range of expression of emotions.

schizophrenia Devastating psychotic disorder that may involve characteristic disturbances in thinking (delusions), perception (hallucinations), speech, emotions, and behavior.

schizophrenia, childhood type Outdated, global category formerly used to cover all severe childhood disorders. It included problems in communication, learning, and social interaction, but ignored the wide variety of needs and disorders of children.

schizophreniform disorder Psychotic disorder involving the symptoms of schizophrenia but lasting less than six months.

schizophrenogenic mother According to an obsolete, unsupported theory, a cold, dominating, and rejecting parent who was thought to cause schizophrenia in her offspring.

schizotypal personality disorder Cluster A (odd or eccentric) **personality disorder** involving a pervasive pattern of interpersonal deficits featuring acute discomfort with, and reduced capacity for, close relationships, as well as by cognitive or perceptual distortions and eccentricities of behavior.

scientist-practitioner model Expectation that mental health professionals will apply scientific methods to their work. They must keep current in the latest research on diagnosis and treatment, they must evaluate their own methods for effectiveness, and they may generate their own research to discover new knowledge of disorders and their treatment.

script theory Theory of sexual functioning that suggests people's sexual behavior and attitudes are guided by scripts reflecting social and cultural expectations.

Negative scripts may increase vulnerability to the development of sexual dysfunction.

seasonal affective disorder (SAD) Mood disorder involving a cycling of episodes corresponding to the seasons of the year, typically with depression occurring during winter.

seasonal patterning Temporal course of bipolar or recurrent major depressive disorders in which episodes occur during particular seasons of the year.

secondary gain Additional reinforcers beyond *primary gain* that a person may obtain by the display of symptoms. These may include attention, sympathy, and avoidance of unwanted responsibilities.

selective mutism Developmental disorder characterized by the individual's consistent failure to speak in specific social situations despite speaking in other situations.

selective serotonergic reuptake inhibitors (SSRIs) Class of medications for depression (including *Prozac*) that act on the serotonergic system by inhibiting the **reuptake** of the **neurotransmitter serotonin.**

self-actualizing Process emphasized in humanistic psychology in which people strive to achieve their highest potential against difficult life experiences.

self-defeating personality disorder Pervasive pattern of being overly passive and accepting the pain and suffering imposed by others. A category proposed for DSM-III-R but not included in DSM-IV for lack of research.

self-efficacy Perception that one has the ability to cope with stress or challenges.

self-injurious behavior Dangerous actions, including head-banging and hitting and biting oneself, seen in many children with **autism.**

self-medication Process by which some individuals may abuse substances in attempting to use them to relieve other problems such as anxiety, pain, or sleeplessness.

self-monitoring Action by which clients observe and record their own behaviors as either an assessment of a problem and its change, or a treatment procedure that makes them more aware of their responses.

self-psychology See **ego psychology.**

semistructured interviews Interviews that employ preplanned, standardized questions to elicit information in a consistent way.

sensate focus Sex therapy in which couples concentrate on pleasurable sensations from caressing and fondling. Intercourse is forbidden to prevent focus on sexual performance and the anxiety it may provoke.

sensorium Person's general awareness of the surroundings, including time and place.

sentence-completion method Projective test in which the person is asked to finish a series of incomplete sentences.

separation anxiety disorder Excessive enduring fear in some children that harm will come to them or their parents while they are apart.

septum Part of the **limbic system** that regulates emotions and the ability to learn and control impulses as well as such drives as sex, hunger, thirst, and aggression.

sequential design Combination of the cross-sectional and longitudinal research methods involving repeated study of different cohorts over time.

serotonin Neurotransmitter involved in processing information and coordination of movement as well as inhibition and restraint; it also assists in the regulation of eating, sexual, and aggressive behaviors, all of which may be involved in different psychological disorders. Its interaction with **dopamine** is implicated in schizophrenia.

serotonin reuptake blockers See **selective serotonergic reuptake inhibitors.**

severe mental retardation Level of retardation defined by IQ scores between 20 and 40 and with somewhat limited communication, self-help, social, and vocational skills.

sex ratio Percentage of people with a disorder who are male and female.

sex reassignment surgery Surgical procedures to alter a person's physical anatomy to conform to that person's psychological gender identity.

sexual aversion disorder Extreme and persistent dislike of sexual contact or similar activities.

sexual dysfunction Sexual disorder in which the client finds it difficult to function adequately while having sex.

sexual masochism Paraphilia in which sexual arousal is associated with experiencing pain or humiliation.

sexual pain disorder (dyspareunia) Recurring genital pain in either males or females before, during, or after sexual intercourse.

sexual sadism Paraphilia in which sexual arousal is associated with inflicting pain or humiliation.

shaping In operant conditioning, the development of a new response by reinforcing successively more similar versions of that response. Both desirable and undesirable behaviors may be learned in this manner.

shared psychotic disorder (folie à deux) Psychotic disturbance in which an individual develops a delusion similar to that of a person with whom he or she shares a close relationship.

shift work type Circadian rhythm sleep disorder characterized by insomnia during sleep time and sleepiness during wake time due to late-shift work or frequent work shift changes.

silver nitrate Chemical that can be used in gum or lozenges to make subsequent smoking aversive by producing a bad taste in the mouth. Research indicates this treatment approach is not particularly effective.

single-case experimental design Research tactic in which an independent variable is manipulated for a single individual, allowing cause-and-effect conclusions, but with limited generalizability (contrast with **case study method**).

single photon emission computed tomography (SPECT) Neuroimaging procedure similar to PET scanning, though less accurate, less complex, and less costly.

sinoaortic baroreflex arc Body's mechanism to compensate for sudden blood pressure increases by decreasing pressure. This reaction causes some people to faint and may lead them to develop phobias.

situationally predisposed panic attack Circumstance that increases the likelihood that a panic attack may be triggered.

situational phobia Anxiety involving enclosed places (e.g., claustrophobia) or public transportation (e.g., fear of flying).

sleepwalking (or *somnambulism*) A parasomnia that involves leaving the bed during NREM—deep, nondreaming—sleep.

sleep apnea Disorder involving brief periods when breathing ceases during sleep.

sleep attacks Unexpected episodes of falling asleep during the day.

sleep efficiency (SE) Percentage of time actually spent sleeping of the total time spent in bed.

sleep enuresis Urination while sleeping.

sleep hygiene Psychological treatment for insomnia that teaches clients to recognize and eliminate environmental obstacles to sleep. These include the use of nicotine, caffeine, certain medications, and alcohol as well as ill-timed exercise.

sleep paralysis Brief and frightening period at the beginning or end of sleep when the individual cannot move or speak; sometimes mistaken for nocturnal panic attack.

sleep restriction Treatment for insomnia that involves limiting time in bed to the actual amount spent sleeping so that the bed is associated with sleep and no other competing activities.

sleep spindles Brief spurts of rapid brain wave activity during Stage 2 sleep.

sleep starts Brief muscle contractions, usually in the legs, just as sleep begins.

sleep state misperception (SSM) Under- or overestimating the amount or quality of sleep one is experiencing.

sleep stress Environmental events, such as ingesting excess caffeine, that can affect sleep negatively.

sleep terrors Episodes of apparent awakening from sleep, accompanied by signs of panic, followed by disorientation and amnesia for the incident. These occur during NREM sleep and so do not involve frightening dreams.

slow wave/delta sleep Slow brain wave activity that characterizes deep sleep.

small fibers Nerve fibers in the **dorsal horns of the spinal cord** that regulate the pattern and intensity of pain sensations. They open the gate, increasing the transmission of painful stimuli.

smooth-pursuit eye movement Also called **eye-tracking;** the ability to follow moving targets visually. Deficits in this skill can be caused by a single gene whose location is known. This problem is associated with schizophrenia and, thus, may serve as a genetic marker for this disorder.

social phobia Extreme, enduring, irrational fear and avoidance of social or performance situations.

sociopathic personality disturbances Obsolete term corresponding to the current category **antisocial personality disorder;** it included alcohol and drug abuse because these were considered merely symptoms of other problems.

somatic delusions False and unfounded beliefs about the body—for example, that parts are rotting or turning to stone.

somatic nervous system Part of the **peripheral nervous system** that controls muscle movement.

somatic treatments Biological interventions that include medication, electroconvulsive (shock) therapy, and psychosurgery.

somatization disorder **Somatoform disorder** involving extreme and long-lasting focus on multiple physical symptoms for which no medical cause is evident.

somatoform disorders Pathological concern of individuals with the appearance or functioning of their bodies, usually in the absence of any identifiable medical condition.

somnambulism Repeated sleepwalking that occurs during NREM sleep and so is not the acting out of a dream. The person is difficult to waken and does not recall the experience.

specific phobia Unreasonable fear of a specific object or situation that markedly interferes with daily life functioning.

specifiers in mood disorders Patterns of characteristics that sometimes accompany major depressive or manic episodes and may help predict their course and prognosis. These include psychotic, melancholic, atypical, catatonic, chronic, and with postpartum onset.

standardization Process of establishing specific norms and requirements for a measurement technique to ensure that it is used consistently across measurement occasions. This includes instructions for administering the measure, evaluating its findings, and comparing these to data for large numbers of people.

Stanford-Binet Early standardized intelligence test designed to identify children who will experience academic difficulties by assessing their attention, perception, reasoning, and comprehension.

statistical significance Probability that obtaining the observed research findings merely by chance is small.

statistics Branch of mathematics concerned with gathering, analyzing, and interpreting data from research.

stimulants Psychoactive substances that elevate mood, activity, and alertness, including amphetamines, caffeine, cocaine, and nicotine.

stimulus control Deliberate arrangement of the environment so that it encourages desired behaviors and discourages problem behaviors. For example, insomnia may be combatted by limiting time in, and associations with, the bed.

stimulus overselectivity Failure to generalize a learned behavior to other stimulus situations. Originally thought to be a characteristic of people with autism, it is now seen as a normal early stage of cognitive development, indicating the delays involved in autism.

Strength of Grip Test Subtest of the Halstead-Reitan Neuropsychological Battery that compares the grip strength of the client's right and left hands.

stress Body's physiological response to a stressor, which is any event or change that requires adaptation.

stress hormones Group of hormones including corticosteroids, that are involved in the body's physiological stress response.

stress physiology Study of the body's response to stressful events.

stroke/cerebral vascular accident (CVA) Temporary blockage of blood vessels supplying the brain, or a rupture of vessels in the brain, resulting in temporary or permanent loss of brain functioning.

Structured Clinical Interview for DSM-III-R (SCID) General, semistructured interview for assessing a wide range of disorders by examining a minimal sample of information about each of the major disorders.

stuttering Disturbance in the fluency and time patterning of speech (e.g., sound and syllable repetitions or prolongations).

subcortical dementia Disease affecting the inner areas of the brain below the cortex that differs from dementia of the Alzheimer's type in that it involves impaired recall but normal recognition, more severe depression and anxiety, slowed motions and impaired coordination, but no aphasia.

sublimation Psychodynamic defense mechanism in which the person redirects energy from conflict and anxiety into more constructive outlets, such as work.

substance abuse Pattern of psychoactive substance use leading to significant distress or impairment in social and occupational roles, and in hazardous situations.

substance dependence Maladaptive pattern of substance use characterized by the need for increased amounts to achieve the desired effect, negative physical effects when the substance is withdrawn, unsuccessful efforts to control its use, and substantial effort expended to seek it or recover from its effects.

substance intoxication Physiological reactions, such as impaired judgment and motor ability as well as mood changes, resulting from the ingestion of psychoactive substances.

substance-related disorders Range of problems associated with the use and abuse of drugs such as alcohol, cocaine, heroin, and other substances people use to alter the way they think, feel, and behave. These are extremely costly in human and financial terms.

sufficient condition Circumstance that, by itself, is enough to cause or allow for a particular phenomenon to occur.

suicidal ideation Serious thoughts about committing suicide.

suicidal attempts Efforts made to kill oneself.

superego In psychoanalysis, the psychical entity representing the internalized moral standards of parents and society.

supernatural model Explanation of human behavior and its dysfunction that posits important roles for spirits, demons, grace, sin, and so on.

sympathetic nervous system Part of the **autonomic nervous system** that prepares the body for activity or to respond to stressors—by increasing heart rate and blood flow to muscles, for instance.

Symptom Check List-90 Revised (SCL-90 R) Self-report measure in which respondents indicate their degree of distress on 90 physical and psychological symptoms.

symptom substitution Psychodynamic assertion that if overt problem behavior (the "symptom") is treated without eliminating the underlying conflict thought to be causing it, that conflict will reemerge in the form of new, perhaps worse, symptoms.

synaptic cleft Space between nerve cells where chemical transmitters act to move impulses from one neuron to the next.

systematic desensitization Behavioral therapy technique to diminish excessive fears, involving gradual exposure to the feared stimulus paired with a positive coping experience, usually relaxation.

systematic exposure Behavioral therapy method to reduce excessive fears by gradually presenting the feared stimulus until the fear reaction extinguishes.

systemic perspective View that the many contributing causes of abnormal behavior form a system involving biology, behavior, cognition, emotion, culture, and society. Each component of the system affects all the others.

systolic blood pressure blood pressure generated when the heart is at work pumping blood.

T cells Lymphocytes produced in bone marrow, developed in the thymus gland, and operating in the cellular branch of the **immune system.** Some attack **antigens** directly while others help regulate the system.

tacrine hydrochloride Medication for patients with Alzheimer's disease that prevents the breakdown of **acetylcholine,** keeping it available for use by the brain. Improvements are small and the drug is expensive and causes serious side effects.

Tactile Performance Test Subtest of the **Halstead-Reitan Neuropsychological Battery** that asks the respondent to insert wooden shapes into a hidden form board, allowing the examiner to assess the subject's learning and memory skills.

taijin **phobia** Japanese variant of **social phobia.** In many cases individuals avoid social interaction believing they have terrible body or breath odor.

tangentiality Characteristic of the loose cognitive and verbal associations seen in schizophrenia in which the person fails to answer questions and quickly moves the conversation to unrelated topics.

Tarantism See **St. Vitus's Dance.**

tardive dyskinesia **Extrapyramidal symptom** and sometimes irreversible side effect of long-term **neuroleptic** medication, involving involuntary motor movements, especially in the face and tongue.

task analysis Method for evaluating a skill to be learned, breaking it down into its component parts.

taxonomy System of naming and classification (e.g., of specimens) in science.

telencephalon See **forebrain.**

telephone scatologia **Paraphilia** in which the person gains sexual gratification by making obscene phone calls, usually while masturbating.

temporal lobe Section of each cerebral hemisphere associated primarily with sight and sound recognition and with long-term memory storage.

temporal patterning Course modifier for mood disorders describing their time sequences, including recurrence, recovery, and alternation.

tension headaches Bilateral head pain characterized by a dull ache, usually starting at the front or back of the head.

tension reduction Negative reinforcement motivation account for substance abuse, suggesting it is maintained because it allows people to escape anxiety.

testability Ability of a hypothesis, for example, to be subjected to scientific scrutiny and to be accepted or rejected, a necessary condition for the hypothesis to be useful.

test-retest reliability Degree to which results of two administrations of a test to the same person are similar.

tetrahydrocannabinols (THC) Most common active chemicals in **marijuana (cannabis sativa)** responsible for its ability to alter mood and behavior.

thalamus Part of the **diencephalon** of the brain, broadly associated with regulation of behavior and emotion.

thanatos Freudian concept of a human drive toward death and destruction.

Thematic Apperception Test Projective test in which the respondent is asked to tell stories about a series of ambiguous drawings.

tic disorder Disruption in early development involving involuntary motor movements or vocalizations.

tics Sudden, rapid, and recurrent involuntary motor movements or vocalizations.

time-limited course Condition in which a disorder improves on its own in a relatively brief period of time.

time-management training Instruction that teaches one to deal with stress by establishing priorities among activities and demands, and paying less attention to the less important ones.

token economy Social learning behavior modification system in which individuals earn items they can exchange for desired rewards by displaying appropriate behaviors.

tolerance Need for increased amounts of a substance to achieve the desired effect, and a diminished effect with continued use of the same amount.

total sleep time (TST) Actual combined time a person spends sleeping each day.

Tourette's disorder Developmental disorder featuring multiple dysfunctional motor and vocal tics.

trainable mental retardation Obsolete term referring to level of retardation comparable to the DSM "moderate" designation that suggests the individual can learn rudimentary vocational but not academic skills.

transcendental meditation Technique for focusing attention by softly repeating a single syllable (mantra); often accompanied by slow and regular breathing.

transference Psychoanalytic concept suggesting that clients may seek to relate to the therapist as they do to important authority figures, particularly their parents.

transinstitutionalization Movement of people with severe mental illness from large psychiatric hospitals to smaller group residences.

transsexualism Obsolete term for **gender identity disorder.**

transvestic fetishism **Paraphilia** in which individuals, usually males, are sexually aroused or receive gratification by wearing clothing of the opposite sex.

treatment outcome Effects, including success or failure, of clinical interventions.

treatment outcome research Studies of the effectiveness of clinical interventions, including the comparison of competing treatments.

triazolam Short-acting benzodiazepine medication known as Halcion used to treat insomnia. Possible negative side effects include drowsiness, dependence, short-term memory loss, or rebound.

tricyclic antidepressants Most common treatment for depression, a group of medications including imipramine and amitriptyline that block the **reuptake of neurotransmitters,** principally **serotonin** and **norepinephrine,** at the synapse. The drugs are effective for some anxiety disorders and mood disorders. They are also used to treat **obstructive sleep apnea** because they help maintain respiratory muscle tone to assist breathing during REM sleep. Positive effects are delayed, and negative side effects may include dizziness and even death, so close monitoring is required. Relapse rates range from 20% to 50% when the drug is stopped.

tuberous sclerosis Rare dominant gene disorder characterized by bumps on the skin and sometime mental retardation and seizures.

Turner's syndrome Pattern of abnormality involving a missing X chromosome in females that causes mental retardation and physical deformities.

twin studies In genetics research, the comparison of twins with unrelated or less closely related individuals. If twins, particularly monozygotic twins who share identical genotypes, share common characteristics such as a disorder, even if they were reared in different environments, this is strong evidence of genetic involvement in those characteristics.

type A behavior pattern Cluster of behaviors including excessive competitiveness, time-pressured impatience, accelerated speech and anger, originally thought to promote high risk for heart disease.

type B behavior pattern Cluster of behaviors including a relaxed attitude, indifference to time pressure, and less forceful ambition; originally thought to cause low risk for heart disease.

unconditional positive regard Acceptance by the counselor of the client's feelings and actions without judgment or condemnation.

unconditioned response (UCR) In classical conditioning, the natural or unlearned reaction to the unconditioned stimulus.

unconditioned stimulus (UCS) Environmental event that would elicit a response in almost anyone and requires no learning. In classical conditioning, it is paired with a neutral stimulus that, after training, may become a conditioned stimulus.

unconscious Part of the psychic make-up that is outside the awareness of the person.

unconscious vision Also called **blind sight;** a phenomenon in which a person is able to perform visual functions while having no awareness or memory of these abilities.

underarousal hypothesis Theory of the etiology of **antisocial personality disorder** suggesting psychopaths engage in dangerous or illicit behavior to stimulate the underaroused cerebral cortex in their brains.

undifferentiated somatoform disorder Somatization disorder with fewer than eight symptoms but still causing distress and impaired functioning.

undifferentiated type of schizophrenia Category for individuals who meet the criteria for schizophrenia but not for any one of the defined subtypes.

unexpected or uncued panic attack Panic attack that has no identified triggering circumstance.

unipolar mood disorder Mood disorder characterized by depression or mania, but not both. Most cases involve unipolar depression.

unshared environments Term indicating that even identical twins living in the same home may have different prenatal and family experiences.

vacuum device therapy Mechanical treatment for male erectile disorder that employs a vacuum cylinder to draw blood into the penis, where it is held by a ring placed at the base of the penis.

vaginal photoplethysmograph Light-sensitive psychophysiological monitoring device that measures female sexual arousal reflected by blood flow to the vagina.

vaginismus Recurring involuntary muscle spasms in the outer third of the vagina that interfere with sexual intercourse.

validity Degree to which a technique actually measures what it purports to measure.

variability Degree of change in a phenomenon over time.

vascular Pertaining to the vessels that transport blood and other fluids in the body.

vascular dementia Progressive brain disorder involving loss of cognitive functioning, caused by blockage of blood flow to the brain, that appears concurrently with other neurological signs and symptoms.

vasovagal syncope Fainting due to low blood pressure in the head and brain.

ventral tegmental area The **midbrain** region that includes part of the "pleasure pathway" responsible for the experience of reward.

verbal scales Sections of the Wechsler series of intelligence tests that assess vocabulary, memory, reasoning skills, and information facts.

vinvuza Nigerian variant of **dissociative trance** states.

visuospatial skills Ability to see, recognize, orient within, and negotiate between objects in space.

voyeurism **Paraphilia** in which sexual arousal is derived from observing unsuspecting individuals undressing or naked.

vulnerability Susceptibility or tendency to develop a disorder.

waxy flexibility Characteristic of **catatonia** in which the person remains in bodily postures positioned by another person.

Wechsler Adult Intelligence Scale-Revised (WAIS-R) IQ test for adults, assessing a range of verbal and performance abilities.

Wechsler Intelligence Scale for Children—3rd Edition (WISC-III) IQ test for children assessing a range of verbal and performance abilities.

Wechsler Preschool and Primary Scale of Intelligence—Revised (WPPSI-R) IQ test for young children that measures a range of performance, verbal, and preverbal abilities.

Wernicke's disease Organic brain syndrome resulting from prolonged heavy alcohol use, involving confusion, unintelligible speech, and loss of motor coordination. It may be caused by a deficiency of thiamine, a vitamin that is metabolized poorly by heavy drinkers.

withdrawal Severely negative physiological reaction to removal of a psychoactive substance, which can be alleviated by the same or a similar substance.

withdrawal delirium (delirium tremens/ DTs) Frightening hallucinations and body tremors that result when a heavy drinker withdraws from alcohol.

withdrawal design Removing a treatment to note whether it has been effective. In single-case experimental designs, a behavior is measured (baseline), an independent variable is introduced *(intervention)*, and then the intervention is withdrawn. Because the behavior continues to be measured throughout *(repeated measurement)*, any effects of the intervention can be noted. Also called **reversal design.**

X chromosome One of the two sex chromosomes that determine gender; females have two and males have one, contributed by the mother. X chromosome abnormalities are implicated in some physical and cognitive problems.

Y chromosome One of the two sex chromosomes that determine gender; its presence, contributed by the father, determines the offspring will be male.

Yerkes-Dodson curve Inverted U-shaped graphical relationship between arousal and performance. Optimal performance occurs at intermediate levels of arousal. Psychopaths may engage in stimulus-seeking behavior to increase their low arousal to more useful levels.

references

Abadinsky, H. (1993). *Drug abuse: An introduction* (2nd ed). Chicago: Nelson-Hall Publishers. **(Chap 11)**

Abbeduto, L., & Rosenberg, S. (1992). Linguistic communication in persons with mental retardation. In S. F. Warren & J. Reichle (Eds.), *Causes and effects in communication and language intervention* (pp. 331–359). Baltimore: Paul H. Brookes. **(Chap 14)**

Abbey, S. E., & Garfinkel, P. E. (1991). Neurasthenia and chronic fatigue syndrome: The role of culture in the making of a diagnosis. *American Journal of Psychiatry, 148,* 1638–1646. **(Chap 9)**

Abel, G. G. (1989). Behavioral treatment of child molesters. In A. J. Stunkard & A. Baum (Eds.), *Perspectives in behavioral medicine: Eating, sleeping and sex.* Hillsdale, NJ: Lawrence Erlbaum. **(Chap 10)**

Abel, G. G., Barlow, D. H., Blanchard, E. B., & Guild, D. (1977). The components of rapists' sexual arousal. *Archives of General Psychiatry, 34,* 895–903. **(Chap 10)**

Abel, G. G., Becker, J. V., Cunningham-Rathner, J., Mittelman, M., & Rouleau, J. L. (1988). Multiple paraphilic diagnoses among sex offenders. *Bulletin of the American Academy of Psychiatry and Law, 16,* 153–168. **(Chap 10)**

Abel, G. G., Becker, J. V., Mittelman, M., Cunningham-Rathner, J., Rouleau, J. L., & Murphy, W. E. (1987). Self-reported sex crimes of nonincarcerated paraphiliacs. *Journal of Interpersonal Violence, 2,* 3–25. **(Chap 10)**

Abrahamson, D. J., Barlow, D. H., Sakheim, D. K., Beck, J. G., & Athanasiou, R. (1985). Effects of distraction on sexual responding in functional and dysfunctional men. *Behavior Therapy, 16,* 503–515. **(Chap 10)**

Abramson, L. Y., Alloy, L. B., & Metalsky, J. I. (1995). Hopelessness depression. In J. N. Buchanan & M. E. P. Seligman (Eds.), *Explanatory style* (pp. 113–134). Hillsdale, NJ: Erlbaum. **(Chap 7)**

Abramson, L. Y., Metalsky, G. I., & Alloy, L. B. (1989). Hopelessness depression: A theory-based subtype of depression. *Psychological Review, 96*(2), 358–372. **(Chaps 4, 7)**

Abramson, L. Y., Seligman, M. E. P., & Teasdale, J. D. (1978). Learned helplessness in humans: Critique and reformulation. *Journal of Abnormal Psychology, 87,* 49–74. **(Chaps 2, 7)**

Abse, D. W. (1987). *Hysteria and related mental disorders: An approach to psychological medicine.* Bristol: Wright. **(Chap 12)**

Abuelo, D. N. (1991). Genetic disorders. In J. L. Matson & J. A. Mulick (Eds.), *Handbook of mental retardation* (2nd ed.), pp. 97–114. Elmsford, NY: Pergamon Press. **(Chap 14)**

Acklin, M. W., McDowell, C. J., & Orndoff, S. (1992). Statistical power and the Rorschach: 1975–1991. *Journal of Personality Assessment, 59,* 366–379. **(Chap 3)**

Adair, R., Bauchner, H., Philipp, B., Levenson, S., & Zuckerman, B. (1991). Night waking during infancy: Role of parent presence at bedtime. *Pediatrics, 87,* 500–504. **(Chap 8)**

Adams, F. (1988). Neuropsychiatric evaluation and treatment of delirium in cancer patients. *Advanced Psychosomatic Medicine, 18,* 26–36. **(Chap 15)**

Addington v. Texas, 99 S. Ct. 1804. (1979). **(Chap 16)**

Ader, R., & Cohen, N. (1975). Behaviorally conditioned immunosuppression. *Psychosomatic Medicine, 37,* 333–340. **(Chap 9)**

Ader, R., & Cohen, N. (1993). Psychoneuroimmunology: Conditioning and stress. *Annual Review of Psychology, 44,* 53–85. **(Chap 9)**

Adler, C. M., Côte, G., Barlow, D. H., & Hillhouse, J. J. (1994). *Phenomenological relationships between somatoform, anxiety, and psychophysiological disorders.* Unpublished manuscript. **(Chap 6)**

Agbayewa, M. O., & Cossette, P. (1990). A psychiatric clinic within a geriatric medical day hospital: Descriptive study. *Canadian Journal on Aging, 9*(1), 5–12. **(Chap 7)**

Agras, W. S. (1982). Behavioral medicine in the 1980s: Nonrandom connections. *Journal of Consulting and Clinical Psychology, 50,* 797–803. **(Chap 9)**

Agras, W. S. (1987). *Eating disorders: Management of obesity, bulimia, and anorexia nervosa.* Elmsford, NY: Pergamon Press. **(Chap 8)**

Agras, W. S., Barlow, D. H., Chapin, H. N., Abel, G. G., & Leitenberg, H. (1974). Behavior modification of anorexia nervosa. *Archives of General Psychiatry, 30,* 279–286. **(Chap 8)**

Agras, W. S., & Kirkley, B. G. (1986). Bulimia: Theories of etiology. In K. D. Brownell & J. P. Foreyt (Eds.), *Handbook of eating disorders: Physiology, psychology, and treatment of obesity, anorexia, and bulimia* (pp. 367–378). New York: Basic Books. **(Chap 8)**

Agras, W. S., Rossiter, E. M., Arnow, B., Schneider, J. A., Telch, C. F., Raeburn, S. D., Bruce, B., Perl, M., & Koran, L. M. (1992). Pharmacologic and cognitive-behavioral treatment for bulimia-nervosa: A controlled comparison. *American Journal of Psychiatry, 149,* 82–87. **(Chap 8)**

Agras, W. S., Schneider, J. A., Arnow, B., Raeburn, S. D., & Telch, C. F. (1989). Cognitive-behavioral and response-prevention treatments for bulimia nervosa. *Journal of Consulting and Clinical Psychology, 57,* 215–221. **(Chap 8)**

Agras, W. S., Sylvester, D., & Oliveau, D. (1969). The epidemiology of common fears and phobia. *Comprehensive Psychiatry, 10,* 151–156. **(Chap 5)**

Agras, W. S., Telch, C. F., Arnow, B., Eldredge, K., & Marnell, M. (1997). One year follow-up of cognitive-behavioral therapy of obese individuals with binge eating disorder. *Journal of Consulting and Clinical Psychology, 65,* 343–347. **(Chap 8)**

Akbarian, S., Bunney, W. E., Potkin, S. G., Wigal, S. B., Hagman, J. O., Sandman, C. A., & Jones, E. G. (1993). Altered distribution of nicotinamide-adenine dinucleotide phosphate-diaphorase cells in frontal lobe of schizophrenics implies disturbances of cortical development. *Archives of General Psychiatry, 50,* 169–177. **(Chap 13)**

Akbarian, S., Vinuela, A., Kim, J. J., Potkin, S. G., Bunney, W. E., & Jones, E. G. (1993). Distorted distribution of nicotinamide-adenine dinucleotide phosphate-diaphorase neurons in temporal lobe of schizophrenics implies anomalous cortical development. *Archives of General Psychiatry, 50,* 178–187. **(Chap 13)**

Akiskal, H. S. (1997). Overview of chronic depressions and their clinical management. In H. S. Akiskal & G. B. Cassano (Eds.), *Dysthymia and the spectrum of chronic depressions* (pp. 1–34). New York: Guilford Press. **(Chap 7)**

Akiskal, H. S., & Cassano, G. B. (Eds.). (1997). *Dysthymia and the spectrum of chronic depressions.* New York: Guilford Press. **(Chap 7)**

Akiskal, H. S., Khani, M. K., & Scott-Strauss, A. (1979). Cyclothymic temperamental disorders. *Psychiatric Clinics of North America, 2,* 527–554. **(Chap 7)**

Aktar, S., & Brenner, I. (1979). Differential diagnosis of fugue-like states. *Journal of Clinical Psychiatry, 40,* 381–385. **(Chap 6)**

Albano, A. M., & Barlow, D. H. (1996). Breaking the vicious cycle: Cognitive-behavioral group treatment for socially anxious youth. In E. D. Hibbs & P. S. Jensen (Eds.), *Psychosocial treatment research and adolescent disorders* (pp. 43–62). Washington, DC: APA Press. **(Chap 5)**

Albano, A. M., Chorpita, B. F., & Barlow, D. H. (1996). Childhood anxiety disorders. In E. J. Mash & R. A. Barkley (Eds.), *Child psychopathology* (pp. 196–241). New York: Guilford Press. **(Chap 5)**

Albano, A. M., DiBartolo, P. M., Heimberg, R. G., & Barlow, D. H. (1995). Children and adolescents: Assessment and treatment. In. R. G. Heimberg, M. R. Liebowitz, D. A. Hope, & F. Schneier (Eds.), *Social phobia: Diagnosis, assessment and treatment.* New York: Guilford Press. **(Chap 5)**

Albano, A. M., Miller, P. P., Zarate, R., P. P. Côté, G., & Barlow, D. H. (1997). Behavioral assessment and treatment of PTSD in prepubertal children: Attention to development factors and innovative strategies in the case study of a family. *Cognitive and Behavioral Practice, 4,* 245–262. **(Chap 5)**

Alcoholics Anonymous. (1990). Comments on A.A.'s triennial surveys. New York: Alcoholics Anonymous World Services. **(Chap 11)**

Alden, L. (1989). Short-term structured treatment for avoidant personality disorder. *Journal of Consulting and Clinical Psychology, 57,* 756–764. **(Chap 12)**

Alden, L. E., & Capreol, M. J. (1993). Avoidant personality disorder: Interpersonal problems as predictors of treatment response. *Behavior Therapy, 24,* 357–376. **(Chap 12)**

Alexander, F. (1950). *Psychosomatic medicine.* New York: Norton. **(Chap 9)**

Alexander, F. G. (1939). Emotional factors in essential hypertension: Presentation of a tentative hypothesis. *Psychosomatic Medicine, 1,* 175–179. **(Chap 9)**

Alexander F. G., & Selesnick, S. T. (1966). *The history of psychiatry: An evaluation of psychiatric thought and practice from prehistoric times to the present.* New York: Harper & Row, Publishers. **(Chap 1)**

Alfrey, A. C. (1986). Systemic toxicity of aluminum in man. *Neurobiology of Aging, 7,* 543–545. **(Chap 15)**

Allen, J., DeMyer, M., Norton, J., Pontius, W., & Yang, G. (1971). Intellectuality in parents of psychotic, subnormal, and normal children. *Journal of Autism and Childhood Schizophrenia, 1,* 311–326. **(Chap 14)**

Allen, J. M., Lam, R. W., Remick, R. A., & Sadovnick, A. D. (1993). Depressive symptoms and family history in seasonal and nonseasonal mood disorders. *American Journal of Psychiatry, 150*(3), 443–448. **(Chap 7)**

Allen, L. S., & Gorski, R. A. (1992). Sexual orientation and the size of the anterior commissure in the human brain. *Proceedings of the National Academy of Science, 89,* 7199–7202. **(Chap 10)**

Alloy, L. B., Kelly, K. A., Mineka, S., & Clements, C. M. (1990). Comorbidity of anxiety and depressive disorders: A helplessness-hopelessness perspective. In J. D. Maser & C. R. Cloninger (Eds.), *Comorbidity of mood and anxiety disorders* (pp. 499–543). Washington, DC: American Psychiatric Press. **(Chap 7)**

Alpert, M., Clark, A., & Pouget, E. R. (1994). The syntactic role of pauses in the speech of schizophrenic patients with alogia. *Journal of Abnormal Psychology, 103,* 750–757. **(Chap 13)**

American Bar Association, Standing Committee on Association Standards for Criminal Justice. (1984). *Criminal justice and mental health standards.* Chicago: Author. **(Chap 16)**

American Law Institute. (1962). *Model penal code: Proposed official draft.* Philadelphia: Author. **(Chap 16)**

American Psychiatric Association. (1980). *Diagnostic and statistical manual of mental disorders* (3rd ed.). Washington, DC: Author. **(Chaps 3, 5, 6, 7)**

American Psychiatric Association. (1982). *American Psychiatric Association statement on the insanity defense.* Washington, DC: Author. **(Chap 16)**

American Psychiatric Association. (1983). American Psychiatric Association statement on the insanity defense. *American Journal of Psychiatry, 140,* 681–688. **(Chap 16)**

American Psychiatric Association. (1987). *Diagnostic and statistical manual of mental disorders* (3rd ed. rev.). Washington, DC: Author. **(Chap 3)**

American Psychiatric Association. (1990). *Benzodiazepine dependence, toxicity, and abuse: A task force report of the American Psychiatric Association.* Washington, DC: Author. **(Chap 10)**

American Psychiatric Association. (1993). Practice guidelines for eating disorders. *American Journal of Psychiatry, 150*(2), 212–228. **(Chap 8)**

American Psychiatric Association. (1994). *Diagnostic and statistical manual of mental disorders* (4th ed.). Washington, DC: Author. **(Chaps 1, 3, 5, 6, 7, 8, 9, 11, 13, 14)**

American Psychiatric Association. (1997). Practice guidelines for the treatment of patients with schizophrenia. *The American Journal of Psychiatry, 154*(4) Supplement, 1–63. **(Chap 13)**

American Psychological Association. (1990). Ethical principles of psychologists. *American Psychologist, 45,* 390–395. (Chap 7)

American Psychological Association. (1992). Ethical principles of psychologists and code of conduct. *American Psychologist, 47,* 1597–1611. **(Chaps 4, 16)**

American Sleep Disorders Association. (1990). *The international classification of sleep disorders: Diagnostic and coding manual.* Rochester, MN: Author. **(Chap 18)**

Amir, N., Cashman, L., & Foa, E. B. (1997). Strategies of thought control and obsessive-compulsive disorder. *BRAT, 35,* 775–777. **(Chap 5)**

Anastasi, A. (1988). *Psychological testing* (6th ed.). New York: Oxford University Press. **(Chap 3)**

Anch, A. M., Browman, C. P., Mitler, M. M., & Walsh, J. K. (1988). *Sleep: A scientific perspective.* Englewood Cliffs, NJ: Prentice-Hall. **(Chap 18)**

Andersen, B. L. (1992). Psychological interventions for cancer patients to enhance the quality of life. Special issue: Behavioral medicine: An update for the 1990s. *Journal of Consulting and Clinical Psychology, 60*(4), 552–568. **(Chap 9)**

Andersen, B. L., Kiecolt-Glaser, J. K., & Glaser, R. (1994). A biobehavioral model of cancer stress and disease course. *American Psychologist, 49,* 389–404. **(Chap 9)**

Anderson, A. E. (1983). Anorexia nervosa and bulimia: A spectrum of eating disorders. *Journal of Adolescent Health Care, 4,* 15–21. **(Chap 8)**

Anderson, A. E., & Hay, A. (1985). Racial and socioeconomic influences in anorexia nervosa and bulimia. *International Journal of Eating Disorders, 4*(4), 479–487. **(Chap 8)**

Anderson, D. J., Noyes, R., & Crowe, R. R. (1984). A comparison of panic disorder and generalized anxiety disorder. *American Journal of Psychiatry, 141,* 572–575. **(Chap 5)**

Anderson, N. B., & Jackson, J. S. (1987). Race, ethnicity and health psychology: The example of essential hypertension. In C. M. Stone, S. M. Weiss, J. D. Matarazzo, N. E. Miller, J. Rodin, C. D. Belar, M. J. Follick, & J. E. Singer (Eds.), *Health psychology: A discipline and a profession.* Chicago: University of Chicago Press. **(Chap 9)**

Anderson, S. R., Avery, D. L., DiPietro, E. K., Edwards, G. L., & Christian, W. P. (1987). Intensive home-based early intervention with autistic children. *Education and Treatment of Children, 10,* 352–366. **(Chap 14)**

Andreasen, N. C. (1979). Thought, language, and communication disorders: I. Clinical assessment, definition of terms, and evaluation of their reliability. *Archives of General Psychiatry, 36,* 1315–1321. **(Chap 13)**

Andreasen, N. C. (1987). Creativity and mental illness: Prevalence rates in writers and their first-degree relatives. *American Journal of Psychiatry, 144*(10), 1288–1292. **(Chap 7)**

Andreasen, N. C. (1997). Linking mind and brain in the study of mental illnesses: A project for a scientific psychopathology. *Science, 275,* 1586–1593. **(Chap 13)**

Andreasen, N. C., & Bardach, J. (1977). Dysmorphophobia: Symptom or disease? *American Journal of Psychiatry, 134,* 673–676. **(Chap 6)**

Andreasen, N. C., & Flaum, M. A. (1990). Schizophrenia and related psychotic disorders. *Hospital and Community Psychiatry, 41,* 954–956. **(Chap 13)**

Andreasen, N. C., & Swayze, V. W. (1993). Neuroimaging. In J. A. Costa e Silva & C. C. Nadelson (Eds.), *International review of psychiatry* (Vol. 1). Washington, DC: American Psychiatric Press. **(Chap 3)**

Andreasen, N. C., Arndt, S., Alliger, R., Miller, D., & Flaum, M. (1995). Symptoms of schizophrenia: Methods, meanings, and mechanisms. *Archives of General Psychiatry, 52,* 341–351. **(Chap 13)**

Andreasen, N. C., Rezai, K., Alliger, R., Swayze, V. W., Flaum, M., Kirchner, P., Cohen, G., & O'Leary, D. S. (1992). Hypofrontality in neuroleptic-naive patients and in patients with chronic schizophrenia: Assessment with xenon 133 single-photon emission computed tomography with the Tower of London. *Archives of General Psychiatry, 49,* 943–958. **(Chap 13)**

Andreasen, N. C., Swayze, V. W., II, Flaum, M., Yates, W. R., Arndt, S., & McChesney, C. (1990). Ventricular enlargement in schizophrenia evaluated with computed tomographic scanning: Effects of gender, age, and stage of illness. *Archives of General Psychiatry, 47,* 1008–1015. **(Chap 13)**

Andrews, G., Morris-Yates, A., Howie, P., & Martin, N. G. (1991). Genetic factors in stuttering confirmed. *Archives of General Psychiatry, 48,* 1034–1035. **(Chap 14)**

Andrews, M. W., & Rosenblum, L. A. (1991). Attachment in monkey infants raised in variable- and low-demand environments. *Child Development, 62,* 686–693. **(Chap 2)**

Aneshensel, C. S., Pearlin, L. I., Mullan, J. T., Zarit, S. H., & Whitlatch, C. J. (1995). *Profiles in caregiving: The unexpected career.* San Diego, CA: Academic Press. **(Chap 15)**

Angst, J. (1988). Clinical course of affective disorders. In T. Helgason & R. J. Daly (Eds.), *Depressive illness: Prediction of course and outcome* (pp. 1–44). Berlin: Springer-Verlag. **(Chap 7)**

Angst, J., & Preizig, M. (1995). Course of a clinical cohort of unipolar, bipolar and schizoaffective patients: Results of a prospective study from 1959 to 1985. *Schweiz Archiv. Neurol. Psychiatr, 146,* 1–16. **(Chap 7)**

Anisman, H. (1984). Vulnerability to depression: Contribution of stress. In R. Post & J. Ballenger (Eds.), *Neurobiology of mood disorders.* Baltimore: Williams & Wilkins. **(Chap 2)**

Anthenelli, R. M., & Schuckit, M. A. (1997). Genetics. In J. H. Lowinson, P. Ruiz, R. B. Millman, & J. G. Langrod (Eds.), *Substance abuse: A comprehensive textbook* (pp. 41–51). Baltimore: Williams & Wilkins. **(Chap 11)**

Antoni, M. H., & Goodkin, K. (1991). The interaction of viral and psychological factors in the promotion of cervical neoplasia. In H. Balner & J. Have (Eds.), *Coping with cancer and beyond: Cancer treatment and mental health.* Amsterdam: Swets and Zeitlinger. **(Chaps 2, 9)**

Antoni, M. H., Baggett, L., Ironson, G., LaPerriere, A., August, S., Klimas, N., Schneiderman, N., & Fletcher, M. A. (1991). Cognitive-behavioral stress management intervention buffers distress responses and immunologic changes following notification of HIV-1 seropositivity. *Journal of Consulting and Clinical Psychology, 59*(6), 906–915. **(Chaps 2, 9)**

Antony, M. M., Brown, T. A., & Barlow, D. H. (1997a). Heterogeneity among specific phobia types in DSM-IV. *Behavior Research and Therapy, 35,* 1089–1100. **(Chap 5)**

Antony, M. M., Brown, T. A., & Barlow, D. H. (1997b). Response to hyperventilation and 5.5% CO_2 inhalation of subjects with types of specific phobia, panic disorder, or no mental disorder. *The American Journal of Psychiatry, 154,* 1089–1095. **(Chap 5)**

Antony, M. M., Brown, T. A., Craske, M. G., Barlow, D. H., Mitchell, W. B., & Meadows, E. A. (1993). *Accuracy of heart beat estimation in panic disorder, social phobic and non-anxious controls.* Manuscript submitted for publication. **(Chap 5)**

Antony, M. M., Craske, M. G., & Barlow, D. H. (1995). *Mastery of your specific phobia, client workbook.* San Antonio, TX: Graywind Publications Incorporated/The Psychological Corporation. **(Chap 5)**

Archer, R. P., & Krishnamurthy, R. (1996). The Minnesota Multiphasic Personality Inventory-Adolescent (MMPI-A). In C. S. Newmark (Ed.), *Major psychological assessment instruments* (pp. 59–107). Boston: Allyn & Bacon. **(Chap 3)**

Arens, R. (1974). *Insanity defense.* New York: Philosophical Library. **(Chap 16)**

Armstrong, H. E. (1993). Review of psychosocial treatments for schizophrenia. In D. L. Dunner (Ed.), *Current psychiatric therapy* (pp. 183–188). Philadelphia: W. B. Saunders. **(Chaps 8, 14)**

Arndt, S., Andreasen, N. C., Flaum, M., Miller, D., & Nopoulos, P. (1995). A longitudinal study of symptom dimensions in schizophrenia. *Archives of General Psychiatry, 52,* 352–350. **(Chap 13)**

Arnow, B., Kenardy, J., & Agras, W. S. (1992). Binge eating among the obese: A descriptive study. *Journal of Behavioral Medicine, 15*(2), 155–170. **(Chap 8)**

Asarnow, J. R. (1994). Annotation: Childhood-onset schizophrenia. *Journal of Child Psychology and Psychiatry, 35,* 1345–1371. **(Chap 13)**

Asberg, M., Nordstrom, P., & Traskman-Bendz, L. (1986). Cerebrospinal fluid studies in suicide: An overview. *Annals of the American Academy of Science, 487,* 243–255. **(Chap 7)**

Aschoff, J., & Wever, R. (1962). Spontanperiodik des Menschen die Ausschulus aller Zeitgeber. *Die Naturwissenschaften, 49,* 337–342. **(Chap 9)**

Asherson, P., Parfitt, E., Sargeant, M., Tidmarsh, S., Buckland, P., Taylor, C., Clements, A., Gill, M., McGuffin, P., & Owen, M. (1992). No evidence for a pseudoautosomal locus for schizophrenia linkage analysis of multiply affected families. *British Journal of Psychiatry, 161,* 63–68. **(Chap 13)**

Aspinwall, L. G., Kemeny, M. E., Taylor, S. E., Schneider, S. G., & Dudley, J. P. (1991). Psychosocial predictors of gay men's AIDS risk-reduction behavior. *Health Psychology, 10*(6), 432–444. **(Chap 9)**

Attie, I., & Brooks-Gunn, J. (1995). The development of eating regulation across the life span. In D. Cicchetti & D. J. Cohen (Eds.), *Developmental psychopathology,* (vol. 2). New York: Wiley. **(Chap 8)**

Attwood, A., Frith, U., & Hermelin, B. (1988). The understanding and use of interpersonal gesture by autistic and Down's syndrome children. *Journal of Autism and Developmental Disorders, 18,* 241–258. **(Chap 14)**

Ayllon, T., & Azrin, N. H. (1968). *The token economy: A motivational system for therapy and rehabilitation.* New York: Appleton-Century-Crofts. **(Chap 13)**

Azmitia, E. C. (1978). The serotonin-producing neurons of the midbrain median and dorsal raphe nuclei. In L. Iverson, S. Iverson, & S. Snyder (Eds.), *Handbook of psychopharmacology: Vol. 9. Chemical pathways in the brain* (pp. 233–314). New York: Plenum Press. **(Chap 2)**

Bach, A. K., Brown, T. A., & Barlow, D. H. (in press). The effects of false negative feedback on efficacy expectancies and sexual arousal in sexually functional males. *Behavior Therapy.* **(Chap 10)**

Bachrach, L. L. (1987). Deinstitutionalization in the United States: Promises and prospects. *New Directions for Mental Health Services, 35,* 75–90. **(Chap 16)**

Baer, D. M., Wolf, M. M., & Risley, T. R. (1968). Some current dimensions of applied behavior analysis. *Journal of Applied Behavior Analysis, 1,* 91–97. **(Chaps 3, 4)**

Baer, J. S., Marlatt, G. A., Kivlahan, D. R., Fromme, K., Larimer, M. E., & Williams, E. (1992). An experimental test of three methods of alcohol risk reduction with young adults. *Journal of Consulting and Clinical Psychology, 60,* 974–979. **(Chap 11)**

Bailey, J. M., & Benishay, D. S. (1993). Familial aggregation of female sexual orientation. *American Journal of Psychiatry, 150*(2), 272–277. **(Chap 10)**

Bailey, J. M., & Pillard, R. C. (1991). A genetic study of male sexual orientation. *Archives of General Psychiatry, 48,* 1089–1096. **(Chap 10)**

Bailey, J. M., Pillard, R. C., Neale, M. C., & Agyei, Y. (1993). Heritable factors influence sexual orientation in women. *Archives of General Psychiatry, 50,* 217–223. **(Chap 10)**

Baker, C. D., & DeSilva, P. (1988). The relationship between male sexual dysfunction and belief in Zilbergeld's myths: An empirical investigation. *Sexual and Marital Therapy, 3*(2), 229–238. **(Chap 10)**

Baker, T. B., Morse, E., & Sherman, J. E. (1987). The motivation to use drugs: A psychobiological analysis of urges. In P. Clayton Rivers (Ed.), *Alcohol and addictive behavior: Nebraska symposium on motivation 1986* (pp. 257–323). Lincoln: University of Nebraska Press. **(Chap 11)**

Baldessarini, R. J. (1989). Current status of antidepressants: Clinical pharmacology and therapy. *Journal of Clinical Psychiatry, 50*(4), 117–126. **(Chap 7)**

Baldwin, J. D., & Baldwin, J. I. (1989). The socialization of homosexuality and heterosexuality in a non-western society. *Archives of Sexual Behavior, 18,* 13–29. **(Chap 10)**

Ball, J. C., & Ross, A. (1991). *The effectiveness of methadone maintenance treatment.* New York: Springer-Verlag. **(Chap 11)**

Ball, S. G., & Otto, M. W. (1994). Cognitive behavioral treatment of choking phobia: Three case studies. *Psychotherapy and Psychosomatics, 62,* 207–211. **(Chap 5)**

Ballenger, J. C., Burrows, G. D., DuPont, R. L., Lesser, I. M., Noyes, R., Pecknold, J. C., Riskin, A., & Swinson, R. P. (1988). Alprazolam in panic disorder and agoraphobia: Results from a multi center trial: I. Efficacy in short-term treatment. *Archives of General Psychiatry, 45,* 413–422. **(Chap 5)**

Balter, M. B., & Bauer, M. L. (1975). Patterns of prescribing and use of hypnotic drugs in the United States. In A. D. Clift (Ed.), *Sleep disturbance and hypnotic drug dependence.* Amsterdam: Excerpta Medica. **(Chap 8)**

Bancroft, J. (1989). *Human sexuality and its problems* (2nd ed.). Edinburgh: Churchill Livingstone. **(Chap 10)**

Bancroft, J. (1994). Homosexual orientation: The search for a biological basis. *British Journal of Psychiatry, 164,* 437–440. **(Chap 10)**

Bancroft, J. (1997). Sexual problems. In D. M. Clark & C. G. Fairburn (Eds.), *Science and practice of cognitive behavior therapy* (pp. 243–257). New York: Oxford University Press. **(Chap 10)**

Bandura, A. (1973). *Aggression: A social learning analysis.* Englewood Cliffs, NJ: Prentice-Hall. **(Chap 2)**

Bandura, A. (1986). *Social foundations of thought and action: A social cognitive theory.* Englewood Cliffs, NJ: Prentice-Hall. **(Chaps 2, 5, 9)**

Bandura, A., O'Leary, A., Taylor, C. B., Gauthier, J., & Gossard, D. (1987). Perceived self-efficacy and pain control: Opioid and nonopioid mechanisms. *Journal of Personality and Social Psychology, 53,* 563–571. **(Chap 9)**

Bansal, S., Wincze, J. P., Nirenberg, T., Liepman, M. J., & Engle-Friedman, M. (1990). *Sex-steroid levels in chronic alcoholic males: Relationship to age and liver functions.* Unpublished manuscript, Brown University. **(Chap 10)**

Barinaga, M. (1995). New Alzheimer's gene found. *Science, 268,* 1845–1846. **(Chap 15)**

Barinaga, M. (1996). Finding new drugs to treat stroke. *Science, 272,* 664–666. **(Chap 15)**

Barinaga, M. (1996, January 19). Social status sculpts activity of crayfish neurons. *Science, 271,* 290–291. **(Chap 3)**

Barinaga, M. (1997, June 27). New imaging methods provide a better view into the brain. *Science, 276,* 1974–1976. **(Chap 3)**

Barkley, R. A. (1989). Attention deficit-hyperactivity disorder. In E. J. Mash & R. A. Barkley (Eds.), *Treatment of childhood disorders* (pp. 39–72). New York: Guilford Press. **(Chap 14)**

Barkley, R. A. (1990). *Attention deficit hyperactivity disorder: A handbook for diagnosis and treatment.* New York: Guilford Press. **(Chap 14)**

Barkley, R. A. (1997). Behavioral inhibition, sustained attention, and executive functions: Constructing a unifying theory of ADHD. *Psychological Bulletin, 121,* 65–94. **(Chap 14)**

Barkley, R. A., Murphy, K. R., & Kwasnik, D. (1996). Motor vehicle driving competencies and risks in teens and young adults with attention deficit hyperactivity disorder. *Pediatrics, 98,* 1089–1095. **(Chap 14)**

Barlow, D. H. (1986). Causes of sexual dysfunction: The role of anxiety and cognitive interference. *Journal of Consulting and Clinical Psychology, 54,* 140–148. **(Chap 10)**

Barlow, D. H. (1988). *Anxiety and its disorders: The nature and treatment of anxiety and panic.* New York: Guilford Press. **(Chap 5)**

Barlow, D. H. (1991). Disorders of emotion. *Psychological Inquiry, 2*(1), 58–71. **(Chaps 5, 7)**

Barlow, D. H. (1993). Covert sensitization for paraphilia. In J. R. Cautela & A. J. Kearney (Eds.), *Covert Conditioning Casebook* (pp. 187–198). Pacific Grove, CA: Brooks/Cole Publishing Company. **(Chap 10)**

Barlow, D. H. (in press). *Anxiety and its disorders: The nature and treatment of anxiety and panic* (2nd ed.). New York: Guilford Press. **(Chap 5)**

Barlow, D. H., & Craske, M. G. (1989). *Mastery of your anxiety and panic.* Albany, NY: Graywind Publications. **(Chap 5)**

Barlow, D. H., & Craske, M. G. (1994). *Mastery of your anxiety and panic* (MAP II). Albany, NY: Graywind Publications. **(Chap 5)**

Barlow, D. H., & Hersen, M. (1984). *Single case experimental design: Strategies for studying behavior change.* Elmsford, NY: Pergamon Press. **(Chap 4)**

Barlow, D. H., & Lehman, C. L. (1996). Advances in the psychosocial treatment of anxiety disorders: Implications for national health care. *Archives of General Psychiatry, 53,* 727–735. **(Chap 5)**

Barlow, D. H., & Liebowitz, M. R. (1995). Specific and social phobias. In H. I. Kaplan & B. J. Sadock (Eds.), *Comprehensive textbook of psychiatry: VI* (pp. 1204–1217). Baltimore: Williams & Wilkins. **(Chap 5)**

Barlow, D. H., & Rapee, R. M. (1991). *Mastering stress: A lifestyle approach.* Dallas, TX: American Health Publishing. **(Chap 9)**

Barlow, D. H., & Rapee, R. M., &. (1997). *Mastering stress: A lifestyle approach* (2nd ed.). Australia: Lifestyle Press. **(Chap 9)**

Barlow, D. H., & Wincze, J. P. (1980). Treatment of sexual deviations. In S. R. Leiblum & L. A. Pervin (Eds.), *Principles and practice of sex therapy* (pp. 347–375). New York: Guilford Press. **(Chap 10)**

Barlow, D. H., Abel, G. G., & Blanchard, E. B. (1979). Gender identity change in transsexuals: Follow-up and replications. *Archives of General Psychiatry, 36,* 1001–1007. **(Chap 10)**

Barlow, D. H., Becker, R., Leitenberg, H., & Agras, W. S. (1970). A mechanical strain gauge for recording penile circumference change. *Journal of Applied Behavior Analysis, 3,* 73–76. **(Chap 10)**

Barlow, D. H., Brown, T. A., & Craske, M. G. (1994). Definitions of panic attacks and panic disorder in DSM-IV: Implications for research. *Journal of Abnormal Psychology, 103,* 553–554. **(Chap 5)**

Barlow, D. H., Chorpita, B. F., & Turosvky, J. (1996). Fear, panic, anxiety, and disorders of emotion. In D. A. Hope (Ed.), *Perspectives on anxiety, panic and fear* (The 43rd Annual Nebraska Symposium on Motivation) (pp. 251–328). Lincoln: Nebraska University Press. **(Chap 5, 7)**

Barlow, D. H., Gorman, J. M., Shear, M. K. & Woods, S. W. (in press) Cognitive-behavioral treatment vs. imipramine and their combination for panic disorder: Primary outcome results. **(Chap 5)**

Barlow, D. H., Hayes, S. C., & Nelson, R. O. (1984). *The scientist practitioner: Research and accountability in clinical and educational settings.* Boston: Allyn & Bacon. **(Chap 1)**

Barlow, D. H., Hayes, S. C., Nelson, R. O., Steele, D. L., Meeler, M. E., & Mills, J. R. (1979). Sex role motor behavior: A behavioral checklist. *Behavioral Assessment, 1,* 119–138. **(Chap 10)**

Barlow, D. H., Reynolds, E. J., & Agras, W. S. (1973). Gender identity change in a transsexual. *Archives of General Psychiatry, 28,* 569–576. **(Chap 10)**

Barlow, D. H., Sakheim, D. K., & Beck, J. G. (1983). Anxiety increases sexual arousal. *Journal of Abnormal Psychology, 92,* 49–54. **(Chap 10)**

Barnes, J. (1981). Non-consummation of marriage. *Irish Medical Journal, 74,* 19–21. **(Chap 10)**

Barnes, J., Bowman, E. P., & Cullen, J. (1984). Biofeedback as an adjunct to psychotherapy in the treatment of vaginismus. *Biofeedback and Self-Regulation, 9,* 281–289. **(Chap 10)**

Barnett, P. A., & Gotlib, I. H. (1988). Psychosocial functioning and depression: Distinguishing among antecedents, concomitants and consequences. *Psychological Bulletin, 104*(1), 97–126. **(Chap 7)**

Baron, M., Gruen, R., Asnis, L., & Lord, S. (1985). Familial transmission of schizotypal and borderline personality disorders. *American Journal of Psychiatry, 142,* 927–934. **(Chap 12)**

Barrett, D. H., Resnick, H. S., Foy, D. W., Dansky, B. S., Flanders, W. D., & Stroup, N. E. (1996). Combat exposure and adult psychosocial adjustment among U. S. Army veterans serving in Vietnam, 1965-1971. *Journal of Abnormal Psychology, 105,* 575–581. **(Chap 12)**

Barrett, J. (1984). Naturalistic change over two years in neurotic depressive disorders (RDC categories). *Comprehensive Psychiatry, 25*(4), 404–418. **(Chap 7)**

Barrett, J. E., Barrett, J. A., Oxman, T. E., & Gerber, P. D. (1988). The prevalence of psychiatric disorders in a primary care practice. *Archives of General Psychiatry, 45,* 1100–1106. **(Chap 3)**

Barsky, A. J., & Wyshak, G. (1990). Hypochondriasis and somatosensory amplification. *British Journal of Psychiatry, 157,* 404–409. **(Chap 6)**

Barsky, A. J., Frank, C. B., Cleary, P. D., Wyshak, G., & Klerman, G. L. (1991). The relation between hypochondriasis and age. *American Journal of Psychiatry, 148,* 923–928. **(Chap 6)**

Barsky, A. J., Wyshak, G., & Klerman, G. L. (1986). Hypochondriasis: An evaluation of the DSM-III criteria in medical outpatients. *Archives of General Psychiatry, 43,* 493–500. **(Chap 6)**

Barsky, A. J., Wyshak, G., Klerman G. L., & Latham, K. S. (1990). The prevalence of hypochondriasis in medical outpatients. *Social Psychiatry & Psychiatric Epidemiology, 25,* 89–94. **(Chap 6)**

Bassett, A. S. (1989). Chromosome 5 and schizophrenia: Implications for genetic linkage studies, current and future. *Schizophrenia Bulletin, 15,* 393–402. **(Chap 13)**

Bassetti, C., & Aldrich, M. (1996). Narcolepsy. *Neurology Clinics, 14,* 545–571. **(Chap 8)**

Bates, M. D., Gingrich, J. A., Senogles, S. E., Falardeau, P., & Caron, M. G. (1991). Biochemical characterization of D1 and D2 dopamine receptors. In C. A. Tamminga & S. C. Schulz (Eds.), *Advances in neuropsychiatry and psychopharmacology, Volume1: Schizophrenia research* (pp. 3–11). New York: Raven Press. **(Chap 13)**

Bateson, G. (1959). Cultural problems posed by a study of schizophrenic process. In A. Auerback (Ed.), *Schizophrenia: An integrated approach.* New York: Ronald Press. **(Chap 13)**

Bauer, M. S., Calabrese, J., Dunner, D. L., Post, R., Whybrow, P. C., Gyulai, L., Tay, L. K., Younkin, S. R., Bynum, D., Lavori, P., & Price, R. A. (1994). Multisite data reanalysis of the validity of rapid cycling as a course modifier for bipolar disorder in DSM-IV. *American Journal of Psychiatry, 151,* 506–515. **(Chap 7)**

Baumgaertel, A., Wolraich, M. L., & Dietrich, M. (1995). Comparison of diagnostic criteria for attention deficit disorders in a German elementary school sample. *Journal of the American Academy of Child and Adolescent Psychiatry, 34,* 629–638. **(Chap 14)**

Baxter, L. R., Guze, B. H., & Reynolds, C. A. (1993). Neuroimaging: Uses in psychiatry. In D. L. Dunner (Ed.), *Current psychiatric therapy.* Philadelphia: W. B. Saunders. **(Chap 3)**

Baxter, L. R., Jr., Schwartz, J. M., Bergman, K. S., Szuba, M. P., Guze, B. H., Mazziotta, J. C., Alazraki, A., Selin, C. E., Ferng, H. K., Munford, P., & Phelps, M. E. (1992). Caudate glucose metabolic rate changes with both drug and behavior therapy for obsessive-compulsive disorder. *Archives of General Psychiatry, 49,* 681–689. **(Chap 2)**

Beach, S. R. H., Sandeen, E. E., & O'Leary, K. D. (1990). Depression in marriage: A model for etiology and treatment. In D. H. Barlow (Ed.), *Treatment manuals for practitioners.* New York: Guilford Press. **(Chap 7)**

Beard, G. M. (1869). Neurasthenia or nervous exhaustion. *Boston Medical Surgical Journal, 3,* 217–221. **(Chap 9)**

Beard, J. H., Malamud, T. J., & Rossman, E. (1978). Psychiatric rehabilitation and long-term rehospitalization rates: The findings of two research studies. *Schizophrenia Bulletin, 4,* 622–635. **(Chap 13)**

Beard, J. H., Propst, R. N., & Malamud, T. J. (1982). The Fountain House model of psychiatric rehabilitation. *Psychosocial Rehabilitation Journal, 5,* 47–53. **(Chap 13)**

Beardslee, W. R., Salt, P., Versage, E. M., Gladstone, T. R. G., Wright, E. J., & Rothberg, P. C. (1997). Sustained change in parents receiving preventive interventions for families with depression. *American Journal of Psychiatry, 154*(4), 510–515. **(Chap 7)**

Bebbington, P. E., Bowen, J., Hirsch, S. R., & Kuipers, E. A. (1995). Schizophrenia and psychosocial stresses. In S. R. Hirsch and D. R. Weinberger (Eds.), *Schizophrenia* (pp. 587–604). Oxford, England: Blackwell Science Ltd. **(Chap 13)**

Bebbington, P. E., Brugha, T., MacCarthy, B., Potter, J., Sturt, E., Wykes, T., Katz, R., & McGuffin, P. (1988). The Camberwell Collaborative Depression Study. I. Depressed probands: Adversity and the form of depression. *British Journal of Psychiatry, 152,* 754–765. **(Chap 2)**

Bebbington, P., Wilkins, S., Jones, P., Foerster, A., Murray, R., Toone, B., & Lewis, S. (1993). Life events and psychosis: Initial results from the Camberwell Collaborative Psychosis Study. *British Journal of Psychiatry, 162,* 72–79. **(Chap 13)**

Beck, A. T. (1967). *Depression: Clinical, experimental and theoretical aspects.* New York: Harper & Row. **(Chap 7)**

Beck, A. T. (1976). *Cognitive therapy and the emotional disorders.* New York: International Universities Press. **(Chaps 2, 7, 9)**

Beck, A. T. (1986). Hopelessness as a predictor of eventual suicide. *Annals of the New York Academy of Science, 487,* 90–96. **(Chap 7)**

Beck, A. T., & Emery, G. (1985). *Anxiety disorders and phobias.* New York: Basic Books. **(Chaps 1, 2, 5)**

Beck, A. T., & Freeman, A. (1990). *Cognitive therapy of personality disorders.* New York: Guilford Press. **(Chap 12)**

Beck, A. T., & Young, J. E. (1985). Depression. In D. H. Barlow (Ed.), *Clinical handbook of psychological disorders.* New York: Guilford Press. **(Chap 7, 9)**

Beck, A. T., Epstein, N., & Harrison, R. (1983). Cognitions, attitudes and personality dimensions in depression. *British Journal of Cognitive Psychotherapy, 1*(1), 1–16. **(Chap 7)**

Beck, A. T., Hollon, S. D., Young, J. E., Bedrosian, R. C., & Budenz, D. (1985). Treatment of depression with cognitive therapy and amitriptyline. *Archives of General Psychiatry, 42,* 142–148. **(Chap 7)**

Beck, A. T., Steer, R. A., Sanderson, W. C., & Skeie, T. M. (1991). Panic disorder and suicidal ideation and behavior: Discrepant findings in psychiatric outpatients. *American Journal of Psychiatry, 148*(9), 1195–1199. **(Chap 5)**

Beck, A. T., Steer, R., Kovacs, M., & Garrison, B. (1985). Hopelessness and eventual suicide: A 10-year prospective study of patients hospitalized with suicidal ideation. *American Journal of Psychiatry, 142,* 559–563. **(Chap 7)**

Beck, J. G. (1993). Vaginismus. In W. O'Donohue & J. H. Geer (Eds.), *Handbook of sexual dysfunctions: Assessment and treatment* (pp. 381–397). Boston, MA: Allyn and Bacon. **(Chap 10)**

Beck, J. G., & Barlow, D. H. (1984). Unraveling the nature of sex roles. In E. A. Blechman (Ed.), *Behavior modification with women* (pp. 34–59). New York: Guilford Press. **(Chap 10)**

Beck, J. G., & Stanley, M. A. (1997). Anxiety disorders in the elderly: The emerging role of behavior therapy. *Behavior Therapy, 28,* 83–100. **(Chap 5)**

Becker, J. V. (1990). Treating adolescent sexual offenders. *Professional Psychology: Research and Practice, 21,* 362–365. **(Chap 10)**

Belitsky, R., & McGlashan, T. H. (1993). The manifestations of schizophrenia in late life: A dearth of data. *Schizophrenia Bulletin, 19,* 683–685. **(Chap 13)**

Bell, C. C., Dixie-Bell, D. D., & Thompson, B. (1986). Further studies on the prevalence of isolated sleep paralysis in Black subjects. *Journal of the National Medical Association, 75,* 649–659. **(Chap 5)**

Bell, I. R. (1994). Somatization disorder: Health care costs in the decade of the brain. *Biological Psychiatry, 35,* 81–83. **(Chap 6)**

Bell, I. R., Jasnoski, M. L., Kagan, J., & King, D. S. (1991). Depression and allergies: Survey of a nonclinical population. *Psychotherapy and Psychosomatics, 55,* 24–31. **(Chap 4)**

Bell, K. E., & Stein, D. M. (1992). Behavioral treatments for pica: A review of empirical studies. *International Journal of Eating Disorders, 11,* 377–389. **(Chap 8)**

Bellack, A. S., & Mueser, K. T. (1992). Social skills training for schizophrenia? *Archives of General Psychiatry, 49,* 76. **(Chap 13)**

Bellack, A. S., & Mueser, K. T. (1993). Psychosocial treatment for schizophrenia. *Schizophrenia Bulletin, 19,* 317–336. **(Chap 13)**

Bellack, A., & Hersen, M. (1985). *Dictionary of behavior therapy techniques.* Elmsford, NY: Pergamon Press. **(Chap 12)**

Bellak, L. (1975). *The thematic apperception test, the children's apperception test, and the senior apperception technique in clinical use* (3rd ed.). New York: Grune & Stratton. **(Chap 3)**

Bellamy, G. T., Rhodes, L. E., Mank, D. M., & Albin, J. M. (1988). *Supported employment: A community implementation guide.* Baltimore: Paul H. Brookes. **(Chap 14)**

Bellis, D. J. (1981). *Heroin and politicians: The failure of public policy to control addiction in America.* Westport, CT: Greenwood Press. **(Chap 11)**

Bellivier, F., Leboyer, M. Courtet, P., Buresi, C., Beaufil, B., Samolyk, D., Allilaire, J-F., Feingold, J., Mallet, J., & Malafosse, A. (1998). Association between the tryptophan hydroxylase gene and manic-depressive illness. *Archives of General Psychiatry, 55,* 33–37. **(Chap 7)**

Bem, D. J. (1996). Exotic becomes erotic: A developmental theory of sexual orientation. *Psychological Review, 103,* 320–335. **(Chap 10)**

Benca, R. M., Obermeyer, W. H., Thisted, R. A., & Gillin, J. C. (1992). Sleep and psychiatric disorders: A meta-analysis. *Archives of General Psychiatry, 49,* 651–668. **(Chap 8)**

Benedetti, A, Perugi, G., Toni, C., Simonetti, B., Mata, B., & Cassano, G. B. (1997). Hypochondriasis and illness phobia in panic-agoraphobic patients. *Comprehensive Psychiatry, 38*(2), 124–131. **(Chap 6)**

Bennett, A. H. (1988). Venous arterialization for erectile impotence. *Urologic Clinics of North America, 15,* 111–113. **(Chap 10)**

Benowitz, N. L. (1992). Cigarette smoking and nicotine addiction. Medical Clinics of North America, 76, 415–437. **(Chap 11)**

Benson, H. (1975). *The relaxation response.* New York: William Morrow. **(Chap 9)**

Benson, H. (1984). *Beyond the relaxation response.* New York: Times Books. **(Chap 9)**

Berenbaum, H., & Oltmanns, T. F. (1992). Emotional experience and expression in schizophrenia and depression. *Journal of Abnormal Psychology, 101,* 37–44. **(Chap 13)**

Berkman, L. F., & Syme, S. L. (1979). Social networks, host resistance, and mortality: A nine-year follow-up study of Alameda county residents. *American Journal of Epidemiology, 109,* 186. **(Chap 2)**

Berlin, I. N. (1987). Suicide among American Indian adolescents: An overview. *Suicide and Life Threatening Behavior, 17*(3), 218–232. **(Chap 7)**

Berman, A. L., & Jobes, D. A. (1991). *Adolescent suicide: Assessment and intervention.* Washington, DC: American Psychological Association. **(Chap 7)**

Berman, K. F., & Weinberger, D. R. (1990). Lateralization of cortical function during cognitive tasks: Regional cerebral blood flow studies of normal individuals and patients with schizophrenia. *Journal of Neurology, Neurosurgery and Psychiatry, 53,* 150–160. **(Chap 13)**

Bernstein, D. A., & Borkovec, T. D. (1973). *Progressive relaxation training: A manual for the helping professions.* Champaign, IL: Research Press. **(Chap 9)**

Bernstein, D. P., Useda, D., & Siever, L. J. (1993). Paranoid personality disorder: Review of the literature and recommen-

dations for DSM-IV. *Journal of Personality Disorders, 7,* 53–62. **(Chap 12)**

Berstein, D. P., Useda, D., & Siever, L. J. (1995). Paranoid personality disorder. In W. J. Livesley (Ed.), *The DSM-IV personality disorders* (pp. 45–57). New York: Guilford Press. **(Chap 12)**

Bertelsen, B., Harvald, B., & Hauge, M. (1977). A Danish twin study of manic-depressive disorders. *British Journal of Psychiatry, 130,* 330–351. **(Chap 7)**

Bettelheim, B. (1967). *The empty fortress.* New York: Free Press. **(Chap 14)**

Biederman, J., Faraone, S. V., Keenan, K., Benjamin, J., Krifcher, B., Moore, C., Sprich-Buckminster, S., Ugaglia, K., Jellinek, M. S., Steingard, R., Spencer, T., Norman, D., Kolodny, R., Kraus, I., Perrin, J., Keller, M., & Tsuang, M. T. (1992). Further evidence for family-genetic risk factors in attention deficit hyperactivity disorder: Patterns of co-morbidity in probands and relatives in psychiatrically and pediatrically referred samples. *Archives of General Psychiatry, 49,* 728–738. **(Chap 14)**

Biederman, J., Rosenbaum, J. F., Hirshfeld, D. R., Farone, S. V., Bolduc, E. A., Gersten, M., Meminger, S. R., Kagan, J., Snidman, N. & Reznick, J. S. (1990). Psychiatric correlates of behavioral inhibition in young children of parents with and without psychiatric disorders. *Archives of General Psychiatry, 47,* 21–26. **(Chap 5)**

Biglan, A., Hops, H., Sherman, L., Friedman, L. S., Arthur, J., & Osteen, V. (1985). Problem solving interactions of depressed women and their husbands. *Behavior Therapy, 16,* 431–451. **(Chap 7)**

Billy, J. O. G., Tanfer, K., Grady, W. R., & Klepinger, D. H. (1993). The sexual behavior of men in the United States. *Family Planning Perspectives, 25,* 52–60. **(Chap 10)**

Birley, J., & Brown, G. W. (1970). Crisis andlife changes preceding the onset or relapse of acute schizophrenia: Clinical aspects. *British Journal of Psychiatry, 16,* 327–333. **(Chap 13)**

Biron, M., Risch, N., Hamburger, R., Mandel, B., Kushner, S., Newman, M., Drumer, D., & Belmaker, R. H. (1987). Genetic linkage between X-chromosome markers and bipolar affective illness. *Nature, 326,* 289–292. **(Chap 4)**

Bjorklund, D. F. (1989). *Children's thinking: Developmental function and individual differences.* Pacific Grove, CA: Brooks/Cole. **(Chap 3)**

Black, D. W., & Winokur, G. (1990). Suicide and psychiatric diagnosis. In S. J. Blumenthal & D. J. Kupfer (Eds.), *Suicide over the life cycle: Risk factors, assessment and treatment of suicidal patients.* Washington, DC: American Psychiatric Press. **(Chap 7)**

Black, D. W., Winokur, G., & Nasrallah, A. (1987). The treatment of depression: Electroconvulsive therapy vs. antidepressants: A naturalistic evaluation of 1,495 patients. *Comprehensive Psychiatry, 28*(2), 169–182. **(Chap 7)**

Blackburn, I.-M., & Moore, R. G. (1997). Controlled acute and follow-up trial of cognitive therapy and pharmacotherapy in out-patients with recurrent depression. *British Journal of Psychiatry, 171,* 328–334. **(Chap 7)**

Blanchard, C. G., Blanchard, E. B., & Becker, J. V. (1976). The young widow: Depressive symptomatology throughout the grief process. *Psychiatry, 39,* 394–399. **(Chap 7)**

Blanchard, E. B. (1987). Long-term effects of behavioral treatment of chronic headache. *Behavior Therapy, 18,* 375–385. **(Chap 9)**

Blanchard, E. B. (1992). Psychological treatment of benign headache disorders. Special issue: Behavioral medicine: An update for the 1990s. *Journal of Consulting and Clinical Psychology, 60*(4), 537–551. **(Chaps 3, 9)**

Blanchard, E. B., & Andrasik, F. (1982). Psychological assessment and treatment of headache: Recent developments and emerging issues. *Journal of Consulting and Clinical Psychology, 50*(6), 859–879. **(Chap 9)**

Blanchard, E. B., & Epstein, L. H. (1977). *A biofeedback primer.* Reading, MA: Addison-Wesley. **(Chap 9)**

Blanchard, E. B., Andrasik, F., Ahles, T. A., Teders, S. J., & O'Keefe, D. (1980). Migraine and tension headache: A meta-analytic review. *Behavior Therapy, 11,* 613–631. **(Chap 9)**

Blanchard, E. B., Appelbaum, K. A., Radnitz, C. L., Michultka, D., Morrill, B., Kirsh, C., Hillhouse, J., Evans, D. D., Guarnieri, P., Attanasio, V., Andrasik, F., Jaccard, J., & Dentinger, M. P. (1990). Placebo-controlled evaluation of abbreviated progressive muscle relaxation combined with cognitive therapy in the treatment of tension headache. *Journal of Consulting and Clinical Psychology, 58*(2), 210–215. **(Chap 9)**

Blanchard, E. B., Martin, J. E., & Dubbert, P. M. (1988). *Non-drug treatments for essential hypertension.* Elmsford, NY: Pergamon Press. **(Chap 3)**

Blanchard, J. J., & Neale, J. M. (1992). Medication effects: Conceptual and methodological issues in schizophrenia research. *Clinical Psychology Review, 12,* 345–361. **(Chap 13)**

Blanchard, R., & Bogaert, A. F. (1996). Homosexuality in men and number of older brothers. *American Journal of Psychiatry, 153,* 27–31. **(Chap 10)**

Blanchard, R., & Steiner, B. W. (1992). *Clinical management of gender identity disorders in children and adults.* Wash-ington, DC: American Psychiatric Press. **(Chap 10)**

Bland, R. C. (1997). Epidemiology of affective disorders: A review. *Canadian Journal of Psychiatry, 42,* 367–377. **(Chap 7)**

Blashfield, R. K., & Livesley, W. J. (1991). Metaphorical analysis of psychiatric classification as a psychological test. *Journal of Abnormal Psychology, 100*(3), 262–270. **(Chap 3)**

Blazer, D. G. (1989). Current concepts: Depression in the elderly. *New England Journal of Medicine, 320,* 164–166. **(Chap 7)**

Blazer, D. G., George, L., & Hughes, D. (1991). The epidemiology of anxiety disorders: An age comparison. In C. Salzman & B. Liebowitz (Eds.), *Anxiety disorders in the elderly* (pp. 17–30). New York: Springer. **(Chap 5)**

Blazer, D. G., Hughes, D., George, L. K., Swartz, M., & Boyer, R. (1991). Generalized anxiety disorder. In L. N. Robins & D. A. Regier (Eds.), *Psychiatric disorders in America* (pp. 180–203). New York: Free Press. **(Chap 5)**

Blehar, M. C., & Rosenthal, N. E. (1989). Seasonal affective disorder and phototherapy. *Archives of General Psychiatry, 46,* 469–474. **(Chap 7)**

Blehar, M. C., Weissman, M. M., Gershon, E. S., & Hirschfeld, R. M. A. (1988). Family and genetic studies of affective disorders. *Archives of General Psychiatry, 45,* 289–292. **(Chap 7)**

Bleuler, E. (1908). Die Prognose der Dementia praecox (Schizophreniegruppe). *Allgemeine Zeitschrift für Psychiatrie, 65,* 436–464. **(Chap 13)**

Bleuler, E. (1924). *Textbook of psychiatry.* A. A. Brill, Trans. New York: Macmillan. **(Chap 13)**

Blinder, B. J., Goodman, S. L., & Goldstein, R. (1988). Rumination: A critical review of diagnosis and treatment. In B. J. Blinder, B. F. Chaitin, & R. S. Goldstein (Eds.), *The eating disorders: Medical and psychological bases of diagnosis and treatment* (pp. 315–329). New York: PMA Publishing Corp. **(Chap 8)**

Bliss, E. L. (1984). A symptom profile of patients with multiple personalities including MMPI results. *Journal of Nervous and Mental Diseases, 172,* 197–211. **(Chap 6)**

Bliss, E. L. (1986). *Multiple personality allied disorders and hypnosis.* New York: Oxford University Press. **(Chap 6)**

Bloom, F. E., & Kupfer, D. J. (1995). *Psychopharmacology: The fourth generation of progress.* New York: Raven Press. **(Chap 2)**

Blue, A. V., & Gaines, A. D. (1992). The ethnopsychiatric répertoire: A review and overview of ethnopsychiatric studies. In A. D. Gaines (Ed.), *Ethnopsychiatry: The cultural construction of professional and folk psychiatries* (pp. 397–484). Albany: State University of New York Press. **(Chap 4)**

Blum, K., Noble, E. P., Sheridan, P. J., Montgomery, A., Ritchie, T., Jagadeeswaran, P., Nogami, H., Briggs, A. H., & Cohn, J. B. (1990). Allelic association of human dopamine D2 receptor gene in alcoholism. *Journal of the American Medical Association, 263,* 2055–2060. **(Chap 11)**

Blumenthal, S. J. (1990). An overview and synopsis of risk factors, assessment, and treatment of suicidal patients over the life cycle. In S. J. Blumenthal & D. J. Kupfer (Eds.), *Suicide over the life cycle: Risk factors, assessment and treatment of suicidal patients.* Washington, DC: American Psychiatric Press. **(Chap 7)**

Bock, G. R., & Goode, J. A. (Eds.). (1996). *Genetics of criminal and antisocial behaviour* (Ciba Foundation, Vol. 194). Chichester, England: Wiley. **(Chap 12)**

Bockoven, J. S. (1963). *Moral treatment in American psychiatry.* New York: Springer Publishing Company. **(Chap 1)**

Bodlund, O., & Kullgren, G. (1996). Transsexualism-general outcome and prognostic factors: A five-year follow-up study of nineteen transsexuals in the process of changing sex. *Archives of Sexual Behavior, 25,* 303–316. **(Chap 10)**

Bogerts, B. (1993). Images in psychiatry: Alois Alzheimer. *American Journal of Psychiatry, 150,* 1868. **(Chap 15)**

Bohman, M., Cloninger, C. R., von Knorring, A. L., & Sigvardsson, S. (1984). An adoption study of somatoform disorders: III. Cross-fostering analysis and genetic relationship to alcoholism and criminality. *Archives of General Psychiatry, 41,* 872–878. **(Chap 6)**

Bohman, M., Sigvardsson, S., & Cloninger, C. R. (1981). Maternal inheritance of alcohol abuse. *Archives of General Psychiatry, 38,* 965–969. **(Chap 11)**

Boivin, D. B., Czeisler, D. A., Dijk, D-J., Duffy, J. E., Folkard, S., Minors, D. S., Totterdell, P., & Waterhouse, J. M. (1997). Complex interaction of the sleep-wake cycle and circadian phase modulates mood in healthy subjects. *Archives of General Psychiatry, 54,* 145–152. **(Chap 8)**

Boll, T. J. (1985). Developing issues in clinical neuropsychology. *Journal of Clinical and Experimental Neuropsychology, 7*(5), 473–485. **(Chap 3)**

Bond, A., & Lader, M. L. (1979). Benzodiazepines and aggression. In M. Sandler (Ed.), *Psychopharmacology of aggression.* New York: Raven Press. **(Chap 2)**

Bond, C. F., DeCandia, C. G., & MacKinnon, J. (1988). Responses to race in a psychiatric setting: The role of patient's race. *Personality and Social Psychology Bulletin, 14,* 448–458. **(Chap 16)**

Bond, G. R., Drake, R. E., Mueser, K. T., & Becker, D. R. (1997). An update on supported employment for people with severe mental illness. *Psychiatric Services, 48,* 335–346. **(Chap 13)**

Boon, S., & Draijer, N. (1991). Diagnosing dissociative disorders in the Netherlands: A pilot study with the Structured Clinical Interview for DSM-III-R dissociative disorders. *American Journal of Psychiatry, 148,* 458–462. **(Chap 6)**

Boon, S., & Draijer, N. (1993). Multiple personality disorder in the Netherlands: A clinical investigation of 71 cases. *American Journal of Psychiatry, 150,* 489–494. **(Chap 6)**

Booth-Kewley, S., & Friedman, H. S. (1987). Psychological predictors of heart disease: A quantitative review. *Psychological Bulletin, 101*(3), 343–362. **(Chap 9)**

Bootzin, R. R., & Nicassio, P. M. (1978). Behavioral treatments of insomnia. In M. Hersen, R. Eisler, & P. M. Miller (Eds.), *Progress in behavior modification* (Vol. 6, pp. 1–45). New York: Academic Press. **(Chap 8)**

Bootzin, R. R., Engle-Friedman, M., & Hazelwood, L. (1983). Sleep disorders and the elderly. In P. M. Lewinson & L. Teri (Eds.), *Clinical geropsychology: New directions in assessment and treatment.* Elmsford, NY: Pergamon. **(Chap 4)**

Bootzin, R. R., Manber, R., Perlis, M. L., Salvio, M., & Wyatt, J. K. (1993). Sleep disorders. In P. B. Sutker & H. E. Adams (Eds.), *Comprehensive handbook of psychopathology* (2nd ed., pp. 531–561). New York: Plenum Press. **(Chaps 8, 11)**

Borkovec, T. D., & Costello, E. (1993). Efficacy of applied relaxation and cognitive-behavioral therapy in the treatment of generalized anxiety disorder. *Journal of Consulting and Clinical Psychology, 61*(4), 611–619. **(Chap 5)**

Borkovec, T. D., & Inz, J. (1990). The nature of worry in generalized anxiety disorder: A predominance of thought activity. *Behaviour Research and Therapy, 28,* 153–158. **(Chap 5)**

Borkovec, T. D., & Mathews, A. M. (1988). Treatment of nonphobic anxiety disorders: A comparison of nondirective, cognitive, and coping desensitization therapy. *Journal of Consulting and Clinical Psychology, 56,* 877–884. **(Chap 5)**

Borkovec, T. D., & Whisman, M. A. (1996). Psychososcial treatment for generalized anxiety disorder. In M. R. Mavissakalian & R. F. Prien (Eds.), *Long-term treatments of anxiety disorders.* Washington, DC: American Psychiatric Press. **(Chap 5)**

Borkovec, T. D., Shadick, R., & Hopkins, M. (1991). The nature of normal and pathological worry. In R. M. Rapee & D. H. Barlow (Eds.), *Chronic anxiety, generalized anxiety disorder, and mixed anxiety depression.* New York: Guilford Press. **(Chap 5)**

Bornstein, R. F. (1992). The dependent personality: Developmental, social, and clinical perspectives. *Psychological Bulletin, 112,* 3–23. **(Chap 12)**

Bornstein, R. F. (1997). Dependent personality disorder in the DSM-IV and beyond. *Clinical Psychology: Science and Practice, 4,* 175–187. **(Chap 12)**

Borysenko, M. (1987). Area review: Psychoneuroimmunology. *Annals of Behavioral Medicine, 9,* 3–10. **(Chap 9)**

Boskind-Lodahl, M. (1976). Cinderella's stepsisters: A feminist perspective on anorexia nervosa and bulimia. *Signs, 2,* 342–356. **(Chap 8)**

Bouchard, T. J., Jr., Lykken, D. T., McGue, M., Segal, N. L., & Tellegen, A. (1990). Sources of human psychological differences: The Minnesota study of twins reared apart. *Science, 250,* 223–228. **(Chap 2)**

Boulos, C., Kutcher, S., Marton, P., Simeon, J., Ferguson, B., & Roberts, N. (1991). Response to desipramine treatment in adolescent major depression. *Psychopharmacology Bulletin, 27*(1), 59–65. **(Chap 7)**

Bourgeois, M. S. (1992). Evaluating memory wallets in conversations with persons with dementia. *Journal of Speech and Hearing Research, 35,* 1344–1357. **(Chap 15)**

Bourgeois, M. S. (1993). Effects of memory aids on the dyadic conversations of individuals with dementia. *Journal of Applied Behavior Analysis, 26,* 77–87. **(Chap 14)**

Bowden, S., Bardenhagen, F., Ambrose, M., & Whelan, G. (1994). Alcohol, thiamin deficiency, and neuropsychological disorders. *Alcohol and Alcoholism Supplement, 2,* 267–272. **(Chap 15)**

Bower, G. H. (1981). Mood and memory. *American Psychologist, 36,* 129–148. **(Chap 2)**

Bowlby, J. (1977). The making and breaking of affectionate bonds. *British Journal of Psychiatry, 130,* 201–210. **(Chap 12)**

Bowman, E. S., & Nurnberger, J. I. (1993). Genetics of psychiatric diagnosis and treatment. In D. L. Dunner (Ed.), *Current psychiatric therapy* (pp. 46–53). Philadelphia: W. B. Saunders. **(Chap 14)**

Bracha, H. S., Torrey, E. F., Gottesman, I. I., Bigelow, L. B., & Cunniff, C. (1992). Second-trimester markers of fetal size in schizophrenia: A study of monozygotic twins. *American Journal of Psychiatry, 149,* 1355–1361. **(Chap 13)**

Bradford, J. (1997). Medical interventions in sexual deviance. In D. R. Laws & W. O'Donohue (Eds.), *Sexual deviance: Theory, assessment and treatment* (pp. 449–464). New York: Guilford Press. **(Chap 10)**

Bradley, B. P., & Mathews, A. (1988). Memory bias in recovered clinical depressives. Special issue: Information processing and the emotional disorders. *Cognition and Emotion, 2*(3), 235–245. **(Chap 7)**

Bradley, W. (1937). The behavior of children receiving Benzedrine. *American Journal of Psychiatry, 94,* 577–585. **(Chap 14)**

Brady, J. P. (1991). The pharmacology of stuttering: A critical review. *American Journal of Psychiatry, 148,* 1309–1316. **(Chap 14)**

Brady, J. P., & Lind, D. L. (1961). Experimental analysis of hysterical blindness. *Archives of General Psychiatry, 4,* 331–339. **(Chap 6)**

Brakel, S. J., Parry, J., & Weiner, B. A. (1985). *The mentally disabled and the law* (3rd ed.). Chicago: American Bar Association. (Chap **16**)

Brandon, S., Cowley, P., McDonald, C., Neville, P., Palmer, R., & Wellstood-Eason, S. (1984). Electroconvulsive therapy: Results in depressive illness from the Leicestershire trial. *British Medical Journal, 288*(6410), 22–25. **(Chap 7)**

Brandon, T. H., & Baker, T. B. (1992). The smoking consequences questionnaire: The subjective utility of smoking in college students. *Psychological Assessment: A Journal of Consulting and Clinical Psychology, 3,* 484–491. **(Chap 11)**

Brannon, L., & Feist, J. (1997). *Health psychology: An Introduction to behavior and health.* Pacific Grove, Brooks/Cole. **(Chap 9)**

Braswell, L., & Bloomquist, M. (1994). *Cognitive behavior therapy of ADHD.* New York: Guilford Press. **(Chap 14)**

Brauchi, J. T., & West, L. J. (1959). Sleep deprivation. *Journal of the American Medical Association, 171,* 11–14. **(Chap 8)**

Brazeau, R., & Burr, N. (1992). *International survey: Alcoholic beverage taxation and control policies.* Ottawa, Canada; Brewers Association of Canada. **(Chap 11)**

Breier, A. (1993). Paranoid disorder: Clinical features and treatment. In D. L. Dunner (Ed.), *Current psychiatric therapy* (pp. 154–159). Philadelphia: W. B. Saunders. **(Chap 14)**

Breier, A., Buchanan, R. W., Kirkpatrick, B., Davis, O. R., Irish, D., Summerfelt, A., & Carpenter, W. Y. (1994). Effects of clozapine on positive and negative symptoms in outpatients with schizophrenia. *American Journal of Psychiatry, 151,* 20–26. **(Chap 13)**

Brekke, J. S., Long, J. D., Nesbitt, N., Sobel, E. (1997). The impact of service characteristics on functional outcomes from community support programs for persons with schizophrenia: A growth curve analysis. *Journal of Consulting and Clinical Psychology, 65,* 464–475. **(Chap 13)**

Bremner, J. D., Licinio, J., Darnell, A., Krystal, A. H., Owens, M. J., Southwick, S. M., Nemeroff, C. B., & Charney, D. S. (1997). Elevated CSF corticotropin-releasing factor concentrations in posttraumatic stress disorder. *American Journal of Psychiatry, 154,* 624–629. **(Chap 5)**

Bremner, J. D., Randall, P. R., Scott, T. M., Bronen, R. A., Seibyl, J. P., Southwick, S. M., Delaney, R. C., McCarthy, G., Charney, D. S., & Innis R. B. (1995). MRI-based measurement of hippocampal volume in patients with combat-related posttraumatic stress disorder. *American Journal of Psychiatry, 152,* 973–981. **(Chap 5)**

Brenner, D. E., Kukull, W. A., van Belle, G. Bowen, J. D., McCormick, W. C., Teri, L., & Larson, E. B. (1993). Relationship between cigarette smoking and Alzheimer's disease in a population-based case-control study. *Neurology, 43,* 293–300. **(Chap 15)**

Brent, D. A., & Kolko, D. J. (1990). The assessment and treatment of children and adolescents at risk for suicide. In S. J. Blumenthal & D. J. Kupfer (Eds.), *Suicide over the life cycle: Risk factors, assessment and treatment of suicidal patients.* Washington, DC: American Psychiatric Press. **(Chap 7)**

Brent, D. A., Kerr, M. M., Goldstein, C., Bozigar, J., Wartella, M., & Allan, M. J. (1989). An outbreak of suicide and suicidal behavior in a high school. *Journal of the American Academy of Child and Adolescent Psychiatry, 28*(6), 918–924. **(Chap 7)**

Brent, D. A., Perper, J. A., Goldstein, C. E., Kolko, D. J., Allan, M. J., Allman, C. J., & Zellenak, J. P. (1988). Risk factors for adolescent suicide: A comparison of adolescent suicide victims with suicidal inpatients. *Archives of General Psychiatry, 45,* 581–588. **(Chap 7)**

Breslau, N., Davis, G. C., Andreski, M. A. (1995). Risk factors for PTSD-related traumatic events: A prospective analysis. *American Journal of Psychiatry, 152,* 529–535. **(Chap 5)**

Breslau, N., Kilbey, M. M., & Andreski, P. (1993). Nicotine dependence and ma-jor depression: New evidence from a prospective investigation. *Archives of General Psychiatry, 50,* 31–35. **(Chap 11)**

Breslau, N., Schultz, L., & Peterson, E. (1995). Sex differences in depression: A role for preexisting anxiety. *Psychiatry Research, 58,* 112. **(Chap 7)**

Breuer, J., & Freud, S. (1957). *Studies on hysteria.* New York: Basic Books. (Original work published 1895) **(Chaps 1, 2)**

Brewin, C. R., Andrews, B., & Gotlib, I. H. (1993). Psychopathology in early experience: A reappraisal of retrospective reports. *Psychological Bulletin, 113,* 82–98. **(Chap 6)**

Broadhead, W. E., Kaplan, B. H., & James, S. A. (1983). The epidemiologic evidence for a relationship between social support and health. *American Journal of Epidemiology, 117,* 521–537. **(Chaps 1, 9)**

Brody, M. J., Walsh, B. T., & Devlin, M. J. (1994). Binge eating disorder: Reliability and validity of a new diagnostic category. *Journal of Consulting and Clinical Psychology, 62,* 381–386. **(Chap 8)**

Broude, G. J., & Greene, S. J. (1980). Cross-cultural codes on 20 sexual attitudes and practices. In H. Barry, III, & A. Schlegel (Eds.), *Cross-cultural samples and codes* (pp. 313–333). Pittsburgh: University of Pittsburgh Press. **(Chap 10)**

Brown, D. R., Ahmed, F., Gary, L. E., & Milburn, N. G. (1995). Major depression in a community sample of African Americans. *American Journal of Psychiatry, 152,* 373–378. **(Chap 7)**

Brown, G. K., & Nicassio, P. M. (1987). The development of a questionnaire for the assessment of active and passive coping strategies in chronic pain patients. *Pain, 31,* 53–65. **(Chap 9)**

Brown, G. W. (1959). Experiences of discharged chronic schizophrenic mental hospital patients in various types of living group. *Millbank Memorial Fund Quarterly, 37,* 105–131. **(Chap 13)**

Brown, G. W. (1989). Depression. In G. W. Brown & T. O. Harris (Eds.), *Life events and illness* (pp. 49–93). New York: Guilford Press. **(Chap 7)**

Brown, G. W., & Birley, J. L. T. (1968). Crisis and life change and the onset of schizophrenia. *Journal of Health and Social Behavior, 9,* 203–214. **(Chap 13)**

Brown, G. W., & Harris, T. O. (1978). *Social origins of depression: A study of psychiatric disorder in women.* London: Tavistock. **(Chap 7)**

Brown, G. W., Harris, T. O., & Hepworth, C. (1994). Life events and endogenous depression. *Archives of General Psychiatry, 51,* 525–534. **(Chap 7)**

Brown, G. W., Monck, E. M., Carstairs, G. M., & Wing, J. K. (1962). Influence of family life on the course of schizophrenic illness. *British Journal of Preventive and Social Medicine, 16,* 55–68. **(Chap 14)**

Brown, J., & Finn, P. (1982). Drinking to get drunk: Findings of a survey of junior and senior high school students. *Journal of Alcohol and Drug Education, 27,* 13–25. **(Chap 4)**

Brown, J. H., D'Emidio-Caston, M., & Pollard, J. A. (1997). Students and substances: Social power in drug education. *Education Evaluation and Policy Analysis, 19,* 65–82. **(Chap 11)**

Brown, T. A., Barlow, D. H., & Liebowitz, M. R. (1994). The empirical basis of generalized anxiety disorder. *American Journal of Psychiatry, 15*(9), 1272–1280. **(Chap 5)**

Brown, T. A., Chorpita, B. F., & Barlow, D. H. (1998). Structural relationships among dimensions of the DSM-IV anxiety and mood disorders and dimensions of negative affect, positive affect, and autonomic arousal. *Journal of Abnormal Psychology.* **(Chap 7)**

Brown, T. A., Marten, P. A., & Barlow, D. H. (1995). Discriminant validity of the symptoms comprising the DSM-III-R and DSM-IV associated symptom criterion of generalized anxiety disorder. *Journal of Anxiety Disorders, 9,* 317–328. **(Chap 5)**

Brownell, K. D. (1991). Dieting and the search for the perfect body: Where physiology and culture collide. *Behavior Therapy, 22,* 1–12. **(Chap 8)**

Brownell, K. D., & Fairburn, C. G. (Eds.). (1995). *Eating disorders and obesity: A comprehensive handbook.* New York: Guilford Press. **(Chap 8)**

Brownell, K. D., & Rodin, J. (in press). The dieting maelstrom: Is it possible and advisable to lose weight? *American Psychologist.* **(Chap 8)**

Brownell, K. D., Hayes, S. C., & Barlow, D. H. (1977). Patterns of appropriate and deviant sexual arousal: The behavioral treatment of multiple sexual deviations. *Journal of Consulting and Clinical Psychology, 45*(6), 1144–1155. **(Chap 10)**

Brownmiller, S. (1984). *Femininity.* New York: Ballantine Books. **(Chap 6)**

Bruce, B., & Agras, W. S. (1992). Binge eating in females: A population based investigation. *International Journal of Eating Disorders, 12*(4), 365–373. **(Chap 8)**

Bruce, M. L., & Kim, K. M. (1992). Differences in the effects of divorce on major depression in men and women. *American Journal of Psychiatry, 149*(7), 914–917. **(Chap 7)**

Bruch, H. (1973). *Eating disorders: Obesity, anorexia nervosa, and the person within.* New York: Basic Books. **(Chap 8)**

Bruch, H. (1985). Four decades of eating disorders. In D. M. Garner & P. E. Garfinkel (Eds.), *Handbook of psychotherapy for anorexia nervosa and bulimia* (pp. 7–18). New York: Guilford Press. **(Chap 8)**

Bruch, H. (1986). Anorexia nervosa: The therapeutic task. In K. D. Brownell & J. P. Foreyt (Eds.), *Handbook of eating disorders: Physiology, psychology, and treatment of obesity, anorexia, and bulimia* (pp. 328–332). New York: Basic Books. **(Chap 8)**

Bruch, M. A., & Heimberg, R. G. (1994). Differences in perceptions of parental and personal characteristics between generalized and non-generalized social phobics. *Journal of Anxiety Disorders, 8,* 155–168. **(Chap 5)**

Bruck, M., Ceci, S., Francouer, E. & Renick, A. (1995). Anatomically detailed dolls do not facilitate preschoolers reports of a pediatric examination involving genital touching. *Journal of Experimental Psychology: Applied, 1,* 95–109. **(Chap 6)**

Bruininks, R. H., Woodcock, R. W., Weatherman, R. F., & Hill, B. K. (1984). *Scales of independent behavior.* Allen, TX: DLM/Teaching Resources. **(Chap 14)**

Brunner, H. G., Nelen, M. R., Van Zandvoort, P., Abeling, N. G. G. M., van Gennip, A. H., Wolters, E. C., Kuiper, M. A., Ropers, H. H., & Van Oost,

B. A. (1993). X-linked borderline mental retardation with prominent behavioral disturbance: Phenotype, genetic localization, and evidence for disturbed monoamine metabolism. *American Journal of Human Genetics, 52,* 1032–1039. **(Chap 12)**

Brunner, H. G., Nelen, M., Breakefield, X. O., Ropers, H. H., & van Oost, B. A. (1993). Abnormal behavior associated with a point mutation in the structural gene for monoamine oxidase A. *Science, 262,* 578–580. **(Chap 12)**

Buchwald, A. M., & Rudick-Davis, D. (1993). The symptoms of major depression. *Journal of Abnormal Psychology, 102*(2), 197–205. **(Chap 7)**

Buda, M., & Tsuang, M. T. (1990). The epidemiology of suicide: Implications for clinical practice. In S. J. Blumenthal & D. J. Kupfer (Eds.), *Suicide over the life cycle: Risk factors, assessment and treatment of suicidal patients.* Washington, DC: American Psychiatric Press. **(Chap 7)**

Budd, K. S., McGraw, T. E. Farbisz., R., Murphy, T. M., Hawkins, D., Heilman, N. Werle, M., Hochstadt, N. J. (1992). Psychosocial concomitants of children's feeding disorders. *Journal of Pediatric Psychology, 17,* 81–94. **(Chap 8)**

Buehler, R. E., Patterson, G. R., & Furniss, J. M. (1966). The reinforcement of behavior in institutional settings. *Behavior, Research, and Therapy, 4,* 157–167. **(Chap 4)**

Buffum, J. (1982). Pharmacosexology: The effects of drugs on sexual function—A review. *Journal of Psychoactive Drugs, 14,* 5–44. **(Chap 10)**

Bureau of the Census. (1983). *Statistical Abstract of the United States.* Washington, DC: U.S. Government Printing Office. **(Chap 8)**

Burish, T. G., Carey, M. P., Krozely, M. G., & Greco, F. A. (1987). Conditioned side effects induced by cancer chemotherapy: Prevention through behavioral treatment. *Journal of Consulting and Clinical Psychology, 55,* 42–48. **(Chap 9)**

Burke, K. C., Burke, J. D., Jr., Regier, D. A., & Rae, D. S. (1990). Age at onset of selected mental disorders in five community populations. *Archives of General Psychiatry, 47,* 511–518. **(Chap 7)**

Burnette, M. M., Koehn, K. A., Kenyon-Jump, R., Hutton, K., & Stark, C. (1991). Control of genital herpes recurrences using progressive muscle relaxation. *Behavior Therapy, 22,* 237–247. **(Chap 9)**

Burton, R. (1977). *Anatomy of melancholy.* (Reprint edition). New York: Random House. **(Chap 1)**

Bushman, B. J. (1993). Human aggression while under the influence of alcohol and other drugs: An integrative research review. *Psychological Science, 2,* 148–152. **(Chap 11)**

Bushnell, J. A., Wells, J. E., Hornblow, A. R., Oakley-Browne, M. A., & Joyce, P.

(1990). Prevalence of three bulimia syndromes in the general population. *Psychological Medicine, 20,* 671–680. **(Chap 8)**

Butcher, J. N., Graham, J. R., Williams, C. L., & Ben-Porath, Y. S. (1990). *Development and use of the MMPI-2 content scales.* Minneapolis: University of Minnesota Press. **(Chap 3)**

Butler, G., & Mathews, A. (1983). Cognitive processes in anxiety. *Advances in Behaviour Research and Therapy, 5,* 51–62. **(Chap 5)**

Butler, L. D., Duran, R. E. F., Jasiukaitis, P., Koopman, C., & Spiegel, D. (1996). Hypnotizability and traumatic experience: A diathesis stress model of dissociative symptomatology. *American Journal of Psychiatry, 153,* 42–63. **(Chap 6)**

Butters, N., & Cermak, L. S. (1980). *Alcoholic Korsakoff's syndrome: An information-processing approach to amnesia.* New York: Academic Press. **(Chap 15)**

Buysse, D. J., Reynolds, C. F., & Kupfer, D. J. (1993). Classification of sleep disorders: A preview of the DSM-IV. In D. L. Dunner (Ed.), *Current psychiatric therapy* (pp. 360–361). Philadelphia: W. B. Saunders. **(Chap 8)**

Byerly, W., Plaetke, R., Jensen, S., Holik, J., Hoff, M., Myles-Worsley, M., Wender, P., Reimherr, F., Leppert, M., O'Connell, P., Lalouel, J., & White, R. (1991). Linkage analysis of six schizophrenia pedigrees with 150 DNA markers. *Schizophrenia Research, 4* (Special Issue), 274–275. **(Chap 13)**

Byne, W., & Parsons, B. (1993). Human sexual orientation: The biologic theories reappraised. *Archives of General Psychiatry, 50,* 228–239. **(Chap 10)**

Byrne, D., & Schulte, L. (1990). Personality dispositions as mediators of sexual responses. *Annual Review of Sex Research, 1,* 93–117. **(Chap 10)**

Cadoret, R. J. (1978). Psychopathology in the adopted-away offspring of biologic parents with antisocial behavior. *Archives of General Psychiatry, 35,* 176–184. **(Chap 6)**

Cadoret, R. J., Yates, W. R., Troughton, E., Woodworth, G., & Stewart, M. A. (1995). Genetic-environment interaction in the genesis of aggressivity and conduct disorders. *Archives of General Psychiatry, 52,* 916–924. **(Chap 12)**

Callahan, L. A., McGreevy, M. A., Cirincione, C., & Steadman, H. J. (1992). Measuring the effects of the guilty but mentally ill (GBMI) verdict: Georgia's 1982 GBMI reform. *Law and Human Behavior, 16,* 447–462. **(Chap 16)**

Campbell, S. S., & Murphy, P. J. (1998). Extraocular circadian phototransduction in humans. *Science, 279,* 396–399. **(Chap 8)**

Candy, J. M., Klinowsky, J., Perry, R. H., Perry, E. K., Fairbairn, A., Oakley, A. E., Carpenter, T. A., Atack, J. R., Blessed, G., & Edwardson, J. A. (1986). Aluminosilicates and senile

plaque formation in Alzheimer's disease. *Lancet, 335,* 354–357. **(Chap 15)**

Cannon, T. D., Barr, C. E., & Mednick, S. A. (1991). Genetic and perinatal factors in the etiology of schizophrenia. In E. F. Walker (Ed.), *Schizophrenia: A life-course developmental perspective* (pp. 9–31). New York: Academic Press. **(Chap 13)**

Cannon, W. B. (1929). *Bodily changes in pain, hunger, fear and rage* (2nd ed.). New York: Appleton-Century-Crofts. **(Chap 2)**

Cannon, W. B. (1942). Voodoo death. *American Anthropologist, 44,* 169–181. **(Chap 2)**

Canter, A. (1996). The Bender-Gesalt Test (BGT). In C. S. Newmark (Ed.), *Major psychological assessment instruments* (pp. 400–430). Boston: Allyn & Bacon. **(Chap 3)**

Cantwell, D. P. (1996). Attention deficit disorder: A review of the past 10 years. *Journal of the American Academy of Child and Adolescent Psychiatry, 35,* 978–987. **(Chap 14)**

Cappell, H., & Greeley, J. (1987). Alcohol and tension reduction: An update on research and theory. In H. T. Blane & K. E. Leonard (Eds.), *Psychological theories of drinking and alcoholism* (pp. 15–54). New York: Guilford Press. **(Chap 11)**

Capruso, D. X., & Levin, H. S. (1992). Cognitive impairment following closed head injury. *Neurologic Clinics, 10,* 879–893. **(Chap 14)**

Cardeña, E., Lewis-Fernandez, R., Bear, D., Pakianathan, I., & Spiegel, D. (1996). Dissociative disorders. In T. A. Widiger, A. J. Frances, H. A. Pincus, R. Ross, M. B. First, & W. W. Davis (Eds.), *DSM-IV sourcebook* (Vol. 2, pp. 973–1005). Washington, DC: American Psychiatric Press. **(Chap 6)**

Cardon, L. R., Smith, S. D., Fulker, D. W., Kimberling, W. J., Pennington, B. F., & Defries, J. C. (1994). Quantitative trait locus for reading disability on chromosome 6. *Science, 266,* 276–279. **(Chap 14)**

Carey, G. (1992). Twin imitation for antisocial behavior: Implications for genetic and family environment research. *Journal of Abnormal Psychology, 101,* 18–25. **(Chap 4)**

Carey, M. P., & Burish, T. G. (1988). Etiology and treatment of the psychological side effects associated with cancer chemotherapy: A critical review and discussion. *Psychological Bulletin, 104*(3), 307–325. **(Chap 9)**

Carey, M. P., & Johnson, B. T. (1996). Effectiveness of yohimbine in the treatment of erectile disorder: Four meta-analytic integrations. *Archives of Sexual Behavior, 25,* 341–360. **(Chap 10)**

Carey, M. P., Wincze, J. P., & Meisler, A. W. (1993). Sexual dysfunction: Male erectile disorder. In D. H. Barlow (Ed.), *Clinical handbook of psychological disorders* (2nd ed., pp. 442–480). New York Guilford Press. **(Chap 10)**

Carlat, D. J., Camargo, C. A. (1991). Review of bulimia nervosa in males. *American Journal of Psychiatry, 148,* 831–843. **(Chap 8)**

Carlat, D. J., Camargo, C. A., Jr., & Herzog, D. B. (1997). Eating disorders in males: A report on 135 patients. *American Journal of Psychiatry, 154,* 1127–1132. **(Chap 8)**

Carlson, C. L., Lahey, B. B., & Neeper, R. (1984). Peer assessment of the social behavior of accepted, rejected, and neglected children. *Journal of Abnormal Child Psychology, 12,* 189–198. **(Chap 14)**

Carlson, E. B., & Putnam, F. W. (1989). Integrating research on dissociation and hypnotizability: Are there two pathways to hypnotizability? *Dissociation, 2,* 32–38. **(Chap 6)**

Carlson, G. A. (1990). Annotation: Child and adolescent mania-diagnostic considerations. *Journal of Child Psychology and Psychiatry, 31*(3), 331–341. **(Chap 7)**

Carlson, G. A., & Kashani, J. H. (1988). Phenomenology of major depression from childhood through adulthood: Analysis of three studies. *American Journal of Psychiatry, 145*(10), 1222–1225. **(Chap 7)**

Carlsson, A. (1978). Antipsychotic drugs, neurotransmitters and schizophrenia. *American Journal of Psychiatry, 135,* 164–173. **(Chap 13)**

Carlsson, A. (1995). The dopamine theory revisited. In S. R. Hirsch and D. R. Weinberger (Eds.), *Schizophrenia* (pp. 379–400). Oxford, England: Blackwell Science Ltd. **(Chap 13)**

Carmelli, D., Swan, G. E., Robinette, D., & Fabsitz, R. (1992). Genetic influences on smoking—A study of male twins. *New England Journal of Medicine, 327,* 829–833. **(Chap 11)**

Caron, C., & Rutter, M. (1991). Comorbidity in childhood psychopathology: Concepts, issues, and research strategies. *Journal of Child Psychology and Psychiatry, 32,* 1063–1080. **(Chap 12)**

Carpenter, W. T. (1992). The negative symptom challenge. *Archives of General Psychiatry, 49,* 236–237. **(Chap 13)**

Carpenter, W. T. (1994). The deficit syndrome. *American Journal of Psychiatry, 151,* 327–329. **(Chap 13)**

Carroll, B. J., Feinberg, M., Greden, J. F., Haskett, R. F., James, N. M., Steiner, M., & Tarika, J. (1980). Diagnosis of endogenous depression: Comparison of clinical, research, and neuroendocrine criteria. *Journal of Affective Disorders, 2,* 177–194. **(Chap 7)**

Carroll, B. J., Martin, F. I., & Davies, B. (1968). Resistance to suppression by dexamethasome of plasma 11-O.H.C.S. levels in severe depressive illness. *British Medical Journal, 3,* 285–287. **(Chap 7)**

Carroll, E. M., Rueger, D. B., Foy, D. W., & Donahoe, C. P. (1985). Vietnam combat veterans with posttraumatic stress disorder: Analysis of marital and cohabiting adjustment. *Journal of Abnormal Psychology, 94,* 329–337. **(Chap 5)**

Carson, R. C. (1991). Discussion: Dilemmas in the pathway of DSM-IV. *Journal of Abnormal Psychology, 100,* 302–307. **(Chap 3)**

Carson, R. C., & Sanislow, C. A. (1993). The schizophrenias. In P. B. Sutker & H. E. Adams (Eds.), *Comprehensive handbook of psychopathology* (pp. 295–333). New York: Plenum Press. **(Chap 13)**

Carson, Robert C. (1996). Aristotle, Galileo, and the *DSM* Taxonomy: The case of Schizophrenia. *Journal of Consulting and Clinical Psychology, 64*(6), 1133–1139. **(Chap 3)**

Casper, R. C. (1982). Treatment principles in anorexia nervosa. *Adolescent Psychiatry, 10,* 431–454. **(Chap 8)**

Casper, R. C., Redmond, D. E., Katz, M. M., Schaffer, C. B., Davis, J. M., & Koslow, S. H. (1985). Somatic symptoms in primary affective disorder: Presence and relationship to the classification of depression. *Archives of General Psychiatry, 42,* 1098–1104. **(Chap 7)**

Caspi, A., Elder, G. H., Jr., & Bem, D. L. (1987). Moving against the world: Life-course patterns of explosive children. *Developmental Psychology, 23,* 308–313. **(Chap 12)**

Cassidy, F., Forest, K., Murry, E., & Carroll, B. J. (1998). A factor analysis of the signs and symptoms of mania. *Archives of General Psychiatry, 55,* 27–32. **(Chap 7)**

Castonguay, L. G., Eldredge, K. L., & Agras, W. S. (1995). Binge eating disorder: Current state and directions. *Clinical Psychology Review, 15,* 815–890. **(Chap 8)**

Cautela, J. R. (1966). Treatment of compulsive behavior by covert sensitization. *Psychological Record, 16,* 33–41. **(Chap 11)**

Cautela, J. R. (1967). Covert sensitization. *Psychological Reports, 20,* 459–468. **(Chap 10)**

Cavior, N., & Marabotto, C. M. (1976). Monitoring verbal behaviors in a dyadic interaction: Valence of target behaviors, type, timing, and reactivity of monitoring. *Journal of Consulting and Clinical Psychology, 44,* 68–76. **(Chap 3)**

Ceci, S. (1995). False beliefs: Some developmental and clinical considerations. In D. L. Schacter (Ed.), *Memory distortion: How minds, brains, and societies reconstruct the past.* (pp. 91–125). Cambridge, MA: Harvard University Press. **(Chap 6)**

Ceci, S. J., Peters, D., & Plotkin, J. (1985). Human subjects review, personal values, and the regulation of social science research. *American Psychologist, 40,* 994–1002. **(Chap 4)**

Centers for Disease Control. (1988). CDC recommendations for a community plan for the prevention and containment of suicide clusters. *Morbidity and Mortality Weekly Report* (Supplement No. 5–6), *37,* 1–12. **(Chap 7)**

Centers for Disease Control. (1994, September). *HIV/AIDS surveillance.* Atlanta: U. S. Department of Health and Human Services, Public Health Services. **(Chaps 7, 9)**

Cepeda-Benito, A. (1993). Meta-analytical review of the efficacy of nicotine chewing gum in smoking treatment programs. *Journal of Consulting and Clinical Psychology, 61,* 822–830. **(Chap 11)**

Cesaroni, L., & Garber, M. (1991). Exploring the experience of autism through firsthand accounts. *Journal of Autism and Developmental Disorders, 21,* 303–313. **(Chap 14)**

Chambless, D. L., Cherney, J., Caputo, G. C., & Rheinstein, B. J. G. (1987). Anxiety disorders and alcoholism: A study with inpatient alcoholics. *Journal of Anxiety Disorders, 1,* 29–40. **(Chap 5)**

Chan, C. H., Janicak, P. G., Davis, J. M., & Altman, E. (1987). Response of psychotic and nonpsychotic depressed patients to tricyclic antidepressants. *Journal of Clinical Psychiatry, 48,* 197–200. **(Chap 7)**

Charlebois, P., LeBlanc, M., Gagnon, C., Larivée, S., & Tremblay, R. (1993). Age trends in early behavioral predictors of serious antisocial behaviors. *Journal of Psychopathology and Behavioral Assessment, 15,* 23–41. **(Chap 12)**

Charney, D. S., Deutch, A. Y., Krystal, J. H., Southwick, S. M., & Davis, M. (1993). Psychobiological mechanisms of posttraumatic stress disorder. *Archives of General Psychiatry, 50,* 294–305. **(Chap 5)**

Charney, D. S., Woods, S. W., Price, L. H., Goodman, W. K., Glazer, W. M., & Heninger, G. R. (1997). Noradrenergic dysregulation in panic disorder. In I. Boris-Wollner & R. D. Zimmerman (Eds.), *Neurobiology of panic disorder, frontiers of clinical neuroscience series.* New York: Alan R. Liss. **(Chap 2)**

Chassin, L., Pillow, D. R., Curran, P. J., Molina, B. S. G., & Barrera, M. (1993). Relation of parental alcoholism to early adolescent substance use: A test of three mediating mechanisms. *Journal of Abnormal Psychology, 102,* 3–19. **(Chap 11)**

Chesney, M. A. (1986, November). *Type A behavior: The biobehavioral interface.* Keynote address presented at the annual meeting of the Association for Advancement of Behavior Therapy, Chicago. **(Chap 2)**

Chesney, M. A. (1993). Health psychology in the 21st century: Acquired immunodeficiency syndrome as a harbinger of things to come. *Health Psychology, 12*(4), 259–268. **(Chap 9)**

Chilcott, L. A., & Shapiro, C. M. (1996). The socioeconomic impact of insomnia: An overview. *Pharmacoeconomics, 10,* 1–14. **(Chap 8)**

Chodoff, P. (1974). The diagnosis of hysteria: An overview. *American Journal of Psychiatry, 131,* 1073–1078. **(Chap 6)**

Chodoff, P. (1982). Hysteria in women. *American Journal of Psychiatry, 139,* 545–551. **(Chap 12)**

Chorpita, B. F., & Barlow, D. H. (in press). The development of anxiety: The role of control in the early environment. *Psychological Bulletin.* **(Chaps 5, 7)**

Chorpita, B. F., Vitali, A. E., & Barlow, D. H. (1997). Behavioral treatment of choking phobia in an adolescent: An experimental analysis. *Journal of Behavior Therapy & Experimental Psychiatry, 28*(4), 307–315. **(Chap 5)**

Christenson, R., & Blazer, D. (1984). Epidemiology of persecutory ideation in an elderly population in the community. *American Journal of Psychiatry, 141,* 1088–1091. **(Chap 12)**

Christiansen, B. A., Smith, G. T., Roehling, P. V., & Goldman, M. S. (1989). Using alcohol expectancies to predict adolescent drinking behavior after one year. *Journal of Consulting and Clinical Psychology, 57,* 93–99. **(Chap 12)**

Chung, S. Y., Luk, S. L., & Lee, P. W. H. (1990). A follow-up study of infantile autism in Hong Kong. *Journal of Autism and Developmental Disorders, 20,* 221–232. **(Chap 14)**

Cicchetti, D. (1991). A historical perspective on the discipline of developmental psychopathology. In J. Rolf, A. S. Masten, D. Cicchetti, K. H. Nuechterlein, & S. Weintraub (Eds.), *Risk and protective factors in the development of psychopathology* (pp. 2–28). New York: Cambridge University Press. **(Chap 2)**

Cipani, E. (1991). Educational classification and placement. In J. L. Matson & J. A. Mulick (Eds.), *Handbook of mental retardation* (2nd ed., pp. 181–191). Elmsford, NY: Pergamon Press. **(Chap 14)**

Clark, D. M. (1986). A cognitive approach to panic. *Behaviour Research and Therapy, 24,* 461–470. **(Chap 5)**

Clark, D. M. (1996). Panic disorder: From theory to therapy. In P. Salkovskis (Ed.), *Frontiers of cognitive therapy* (pp. 318–344). New York: Guilford Press. **(Chap 5)**

Clark, D. M., Salkovskis, P. M., Hackmann, A., Middleton, H., Anastasiades, P., & Gelder, M. (1994). A comparison of cognitive therapy, applied relaxation and imipramine in the treatment of panic disorder. *British Journal of Psychiatry.* **(Chap 5)**

Clark, L. A. (1993). *Manual for the Schedule of Nonadaptive and Adaptive Personality.* Minneapolis: University of Minnesota Press. **(Chap 12)**

Clark, L. A., & Watson, D. (1991). Tripartite model of anxiety and depression: Psychometric evidence and taxonomic implications. Special issue: Diagnoses, dimensions, and DSM-IV: The science of classification. *Journal of Abnormal Psychology, 100*(3), 316–336. **(Chap 7)**

Clarkin, J. F., Carpenter, D., Hull, J., Wilner, P., & Glick, I. (in press). The effect of psychoeducational marital intervention for bipolar patients and spouses. *Psychiatric Services.* **(Chap 7)**

Clarkin, J. F., Haas, G. L., & Glick, I. D. (1988). *Affective disorders in the family.* New York: Guilford Press. **(Chap 13)**

Classen, C., Diamond, S., Spiegel, D. (in press). Studies of life-extending psychosocial interventions. In J. Holland (Ed.), *Textbook of psycho-oncology.* Oxford Press. **(Chap 9)**

Clayton, P. J., & Darvish, H. S. (1979). Course of depressive symptoms following the stress of bereavement. In J. E. Barrett (Ed.), *Stress and mental disorder.* New York: Raven. **(Chap 7)**

Cleckley, H. M. (1982). *The mask of sanity* (6th ed.). St. Louis: Mosby. **(Chap 12)**

Cleghorn, J. M., & Albert, M. L. (1990). Modular disjunction in schizophrenia: A framework for a pathological psychophysiology. In A. Kales, C. N. Stefanis, & J. A. Talbot (Eds.), *Recent advances in schizophrenia* (pp. 59–80). New York: Springer-Verlag. **(Chap 13)**

Cleghorn, J. M., Franco, S., Szechtman, B., Kaplan, R. D., Szechtman, H., Brown, G. M., Nahmias, C., & Garnett, E. S. (1992). Toward a brain map of auditory hallucinations. *American Journal of Psychiatry, 149,* 1062–1069. **(Chap 13)**

Clement, U. (1990). Surveys of heterosexual behavior. *Annual Review of Sex Research, 1,* 45–74. **(Chap 10)**

Clementz, B. A., & Sweeney, J. A. (1990). Is eye movement dysfunction a biological marker for schizophrenia? A methodological review. *Psychological Bulletin, 108,* 77–92. **(Chap 13)**

Cloninger, C. R. (1978). The link between hysteria and sociopathy: An integrative model of pathogenesis based on clinical, genetic, and neurophysiological observations. In H. S. Akiskal & W. L. Webb (Eds.), *Psychiatric diagnosis: Exploration of biological predictors* (pp. 189–218). New York: Spectrum. **(Chaps 6, 12)**

Cloninger, C. R. (1987). A systematic method for clinical description and classification of personality variants: A proposal. *Archives of General Psychiatry, 44,* 573–588. **(Chaps 6, 12)**

Cloninger, C. R. (1989). Establishment of diagnostic validity in psychiatric illness: Robins and Guze's method revisited. In L. N. Robins & J. E. Barrett (Eds.), *The validity of psychiatric diagnosis* (pp. 9–16). New York: Raven Press. **(Chap 3)**

Cloninger, C. R. (1991). D2 dopamine receptor gene is associated but not linked with alcoholism. *Journal of the American Medical Association, 266,* 1833–1834. **(Chap 11)**

Cloninger, C. R. (1996). Somatization disorder. Literature review for DSM-IV sourcebook. Washington, DC: American Psychiatric Press. **(Chap 6)**

Cloninger, C. R., Bohman, M., & Sigvardsson, S. (1981). Inheritance of alcohol abuse. *Archives of General Psychiatry, 38,* 861–868. **(Chap 11)**

Closser, M. H. (1992). Cocaine epidemiology. In T. R. Kosten & H. D. Kleber (Eds.), *Clinician's guide to cocaine addiction: Theory, research, and treatment* (pp. 225–240). New York: Guilford Press. **(Chap 11)**

Coates, T. J. (1990). Strategies for modifying sexual behavior for primary and secondary prevention of HIV disease. *Journal of Consulting and Clinical Psychology, 58*(1), 57–69. **(Chap 9)**

Coates, T. J., McKusick, L., Kuno, R., & Stites, D. P. (1989). Stress management training reduced number of sexual partners but did not improve immune function in men infected with HIV. *American Journal of Public Health, 79,* 885–887. **(Chap 9)**

Cobb, S. (1976). Social support as a moderator of life stress. *Psychosomatic Medicine, 38,* 300. **(Chap 2)**

Cochran, S. D. (1984). Preventing medical noncompliance in the outpatient treatment of bipolar affective disorders. *Journal of Consulting and Clinical Psychology, 52*(5), 873–878. **(Chap 7)**

Cocores, J. A., Miller, N. S., Pottash, A. C., & Gold, M. S. (1988). Sexual dysfunction in abusers of cocaine and alcohol. *American Journal of Drug and Alcohol Abuse, 14,* 169–173. **(Chap 10)**

Cohen, D., & Eisdorfer, C. (1988). Depression in family members caring for a relative with Alzheimer's disease. *Journal of the American Geriatrics Society, 36,* 885–889. **(Chap 15)**

Cohen, F. (1996). Offenders with mental disorders in the criminal justice-correctional process. In B. D. Sales and D. W. Shuman (Eds.), *Law, mental health, and mental disorder* (pp. 397–413). Pacific Grove, CA: Brooks/Cole. **(Chap 16)**

Cohen, J. (1997, July 4). The daunting challenge of keeping HIV suppressed. *Science, 277,* 32–33. **(Chap 9)**

Cohen, J. B., & Reed, D. (1985). Type A behavior and coronary heart disease among Japanese men in Hawaii. *Journal of Behavioral Medicine, 8,* 343–352. **(Chap 9)**

Cohen, M. S., Rosen, B. R., & Brady, T. J. (1992). Ultrafast MRI permits expanded clinical role. *Magnetic Resonance, 2,* 26–37. **(Chap 3)**

Cohen, S. (1996). Psychological stress, immunity, and upper respiratory infections. *Current Directions in Psychological Science, 5,* 86–90. **(Chap 9)**

Cohen, S., & Herbert, T. B. (1996). Health Psychology: Psychological factors and physical disease from the perspective of human psychoneuroimmunology. *Annual Review of Psychology, 47,* 113–142. **(Chap 9)**

Cohen, S., Doyle, W. J., Skoner, D. P., Fireman, P., Gwaltney, J. M., Jr., Newsome, J. T. (1995). State and trait negative affect as predictors of objective and subjective symptoms of respiratory viral infections. *Journal of Personality and Social Psychology, 68,* 159–169. **(Chap 9)**

Cohen, S., Doyle, W., Skoner, D. P., Rabin, B. S., & Gwaltney, J. M. (1997). Social ties and susceptibility to the common cold. *Journal of the American Medical Association, 277,* 1940–1944. **(Chap 2)**

Cohen, S., Tyrrell, D. A., & Smith, A. P. (1993). Negative life events, perceived stress, negative affect, and susceptibility to the common cold. *Journal of Personality and Social Psychology, 64*(1), 131–140. **(Chap 9)**

Cohen, S., Tyrrell, D. A. J., & Smith, A. P. (1991). Psychological stress and susceptibility to the common cold. *New England Journal of Medicine, 325,* 606–612. **(Chap 9)**

Col, N., Fanale, J. E., & Kronholm, P. (1990). The role of medical noncompliance and adverse drug reactions in hospitalizations of the elderly. *Archives of Internal Medicine, 150,* 841–845. **(Chap 15)**

Cole, M., Winkelman, M. D., Morris, J. C., Simon, J. E., & Boyd, T. A. (1992). Thalamic amnesia: Korsakoff syndrome due to left thalamic infarction. *Journal of the Neurological Sciences, 110,* 62–67. **(Chap 15)**

Coleman, E., Bockting, W. O., & Gooren, L. (1993). Homosexual and bisexual identity in sex-reassigned female-to-male transsexuals. *Archives of Sexual Behavior, 22,* 37–50. **(Chap 10)**

Coleman, E., Colgan, P., & Gooren, L. (1992). Male cross-gender behavior in Myanmar (Burma): A description of the acault. *Archives of Sexual Behavior, 21*(3), 313–321. **(Chap 10)**

Comas-Diaz, L. (1981). Puerto Rican espiritismo and psychotherapy. *American Journal of Orthopsychiatry, 51*(4), 636–645. **(Chap 6)**

Compas, B. E., Oppedisano, G., Connor, J. K., Gerhardt, C. A., Hinden, B. R., Achenbach, T. M., & Hammen, C. (1997). Gender differences in depressive symptoms in adolescence: Comparison of national samples of clinically referred and nonreferred youths. *Journal of Consulting and Clinical Psychology, 65,* 617–626. **(Chap 7)**

Condelli, W. S., Fairbank, J. A., Dennis, M. L., & Rachal, J. V. (1991). Cocaine use by clients in methadone programs: Significance, scope, and behavioral interventions. *Journal of Substance Abuse Treatment, 8,* 203–212. **(Chap 11)**

Condon, W., Ogston, W., & Pacoe, L. (1969). Three faces of Eve revisited: A study of transient microstrabismus. *Journal of Abnormal Psychology, 74,* 618–620. **(Chap 6)**

Conn. Gen. Stat. Ann. (1992). 319:Part II 17a-495. **(Chap 16)**

Conwell, Y., Duberstein, P. R., Cox, C., Hermmann, J. H., Forbes, N. T., &

Caine, E. D. (1996). Relationships of age and axis I diagnoses in victims of completed suicide: A psychological autopsy study. *American Journal of Psychiatry, 153,* 1001–1008. **(Chap 7)**

Cook, C. C. H., & Gurling, H. M. D. (1991). Genetic factors in alcoholism. In T. N. Palmer (Ed.), *The molecular pathology of alcoholism* (pp. 182–210). New York: Oxford University Press. **(Chap 11)**

Cook, E. W., III, Hodes, R. L., & Lang, P. J. (1986). Preparedness and phobia: Effects of stimulus content on human visceral conditioning. *Journal of Abnormal Psychology, 95,* 195–207. **(Chap 2)**

Cook, P. J. (1993). The matter of tobacco use. *Science, 262,* 1750–1751. **(Chap 11)**

Coon, P. M. (1986). Treatment progress in 20 patients with multiple personality disorder. *Journal of Nervous and Mental Disease, 174,* 715–721. **(Chap 6)**

Cooney, N. L., Litt, M. D., Morse, P. A., Bauer, L. O., & Gaupp, L. (1997). Alcohol cue reactivity, negative-mood reactivity, and relapse in treated alcoholic men. *Journal of Abnormal Psychology, 106,* 243–250. **(Chap 11)**

Coons, P. M. (1994). Confirmation of childhood abuse in child and adolescent cases of multiple personality disorder not otherwise specified. *Journal of Nervous & Mental Disease, 182,* 461–464. **(Chap 6)**

Coons, P. M., Bowman, E. S., Kluft, R. P., & Milstein, V. (1991). The cross cultural occurrence of NPD: Additional cases from a recent survey. *Dissociation, 4,* 124–128. **(Chap 6)**

Cooper, A. J. (1988). Sexual dysfunction and cardiovascular disease. *Stress Medicine, 4,* 273–281. **(Chap 10)**

Cooper, A. M., & Ronningstam, E. (1992). Narcissistic personality disorder. In A. Tasman & M. B. Riba (Eds.), *Review of psychiatry* (Vol. 11, pp. 80–97). Washington, DC: Psychiatric Press. **(Chap 12)**

Cooper, M. (1957). *Pica.* Springfield, IL: Charles Thomas. **(Chap 8)**

Cooper, M. L., Russell, M., & George, W. H. (1988). Coping, expectancies, and alcohol abuse: A test of social learning formulations. *Journal of Abnormal Psychology, 97,* 218–230. **(Chap 11)**

Cooper, M. L., Russell, M., Skinner, J. B., Frone, M. R., & Mudar, P. (1992). Stress and alcohol use: Moderating effects of gender, coping, and alcohol expectancies. *Journal of Abnormal Psychology, 101,* 139–152. **(Chap 11)**

Copolov, D. L., Rubin, R. T., Mander, A. J., Sashidharan, S. P., Whitehouse, A. M., Blackburn, I. M., Freeman, C. P., & Blackwood, D. H. R. (1986). DSM-III melancholia: Do the criteria accurately and reliably distinguish endogenous pattern depression? *Journal of Affective Disorders, 10,* 191–202. **(Chap 7)**

Corder, E. H., Saunders, A. M., Strittmatter, W. J., Schmechel, D. E., Gaskell,

P. C., Small, G. W., Roses, A. D., Haines, J. L., & Pericak-Vance, M. A. (1993). Gene dose of apolipoprotein E type 4 allele and the risk of Alzheimer's disease in late onset families. *Science, 261,* 921–923. **(Chap 15)**

Corrigan, P. W., Wallace, C. J., Schade, M. L., & Green, M. F. (1994). Learning medication self-management skills in schizophrenia: Relationships with cognitive deficits and psychiatric symptoms. *Behavior Therapy, 25,* 5–15. **(Chap 13)**

Coryell, W., & Turner, R. (1985). Outcome with desipramine therapy in subtypes of nonpsychotic major depression. *Journal of Affective Disorders, 9,* 149–154. **(Chap 7)**

Coryell, W. H., & Zimmerman, M. (1989). Personality disorder in the families of depressed, schizophrenic, and never-ill probands. *American Journal of Psychiatry, 146,* 496–502. **(Chap 12)**

Coryell, W., Endicott, J., & Keller, M. (1992). Rapid cycling affective disorder: Demographics, diagnosis, family history, and course. *Archives of General Psychiatry, 49,* 126–131. **(Chap 7)**

Coryell, W., Endicott, J., Maser, J. D., Keller, M. B., Leon, A. C., & Akiskal, H. S. (1995). Long-term stability of polarity distinctions in the affective disorders. *American Journal of Psychiatry, 152,* 385–390. **(Chap 7)**

Coryell, W., Leon, A., Winokur, G., Endicott, J., Keller, M., Akiskal, H., & Solomon, D. (1996). Importance of psychotic features to long-term course in major depressive disorder. *American Journal of Psychiatry, 153,* 483–489. **(Chap 7)**

Costa e Silva, J. A., & DeGirolamo, G. (1990). Neurasthenia: History of a concept. In N. Sartorius, D. Goldberg, G. DeGirolamo, J. A. Costa e Silva, Y. Lecrubier, & U. Witttchen (Eds.), *Psychological disorders in general medical settings* (pp. 699–81). Toronto: Hogrefe and Huber. **(Chap 9)**

Costa, E. (1985). Benzodiazepine-GABA interactions: A model to investigate the neurobiology of anxiety. In A. H. Tuma & J. D. Maser (Eds.), *Anxiety and the anxiety disorders.* Hillsdale, NJ: Lawrence Erlbaum. **(Chap 2)**

Costa, P. T., & Widiger, T. A. (Eds.). (1994). *Personality disorders and the five-factor model of personality.* Washington, DC: American Psychological Association. **(Chap 12)**

Costa, P. T., Jr., & McCrae, R. R. (1990). Personality disorders and the five-factor model of personality. *Journal of Personality Disorders, 4,* 362–371. **(Chap 12)**

Côté, G., O'Leary, T., Barlow, D. H., Strain, J. J., Salkovskis, P. M., Warwick, H. M. C., Clark, D. M., Rapee, R., & Rasmussen, S. A. (1996). Hypochondriasis. In T. A. Widiger, A. J. Frances, H. A. Pincus, R. Ross, M. B. First, W. W. Davis (Eds.),

DSM-IV sourcebook. (Vol. 2, pp. 933–947). Washington, DC: American Psychiatric Association. **(Chap 6)**

Coughlin, A. M. (1994). Excusing women. *California Law Review, 82,* 1–93. **(Chap 16)**

Courchesne, E. (1991). Neuroanatomic imaging in autism. *Pediatrics, 87,* 781–790. **(Chaps 2, 14)**

Courchesne, E. (1997). Brainstem, cerebellar and limbic neuroanatomical abnormalities in autism. *Current Opinion in Neurobiology, 7,* 269–278. **(Chap 2)**

Courchesne, E., Hesselink, J. R., Jernigan, T. L., & Yeung-Courchesne, R. (1987). Abnormal neuroanatomy in a nonretarded person with autism: Unusual findings with magnetic resonance imaging. *Archives of Neurology, 44,* 335–341. **(Chap 14)**

Cox, A., Rutter, M., Newman, S., & Bartak, L. (1975). A comparative study of infantile autism and specific developmental receptive language disorder: II. Parental characteristics. *British Journal of Psychiatry, 126,* 146–159. **(Chap 14)**

Cox, B. C., Swinson, R. P., Schulman, I. D., Kuch, K, & Reikman, J. T. (1993). Gender effects in alcohol use in panic disorder with agoraphobia. *BRAT, 31*(4), 413–416. **(Chap 5)**

Coyne, J. C. (1976). Toward an interactional description of depression. *Psychiatry, 39*(1), 28–40. **(Chap 7)**

Crabbe, J. C., Belknap, J. K., & Buck, K. J. (1994). Genetic animal models of alcohol and drug abuse. *Science, 264,* 1715–1723. **(Chap 11)**

Crago, M. Shisslak, C. M., & Estes, L. S., (1997). Eating disturbances among American minority groups: A review. *The International Journal of Eating Disorders, 19,* 239–248. **(Chap 8)**

Craighead, L. W., & Agras, W. S. (1991). Mechanisms of action in cognitive-behavioral and pharmacological interventions for obesity and bulimia nervosa. *Journal of Consulting and Clinical Psychology, 59,* 115–125. **(Chap 8)**

Craighead, W. E., Ilardi, S. S., Greenberg, M. P., & Craighead, L. W. (1997). Cognitive psychology: Basic theory and clinical implications. In A. Tasman, J. Key, & J. A. Lieberman (Eds.), *Psychiatry* (Vol. 1, pp. 350–368). Philadelphia: W. B. Saunders. **(Chap 2)**

Craighead, W. E., Miklowitz, D. J., Vajk, F. C., & Frank, E. (1998). In P. E. Nathan & J. M. Gorman (Eds.), *A guide to treatments that work* (pp. 240–248). New York: Oxford University Press. **(Chap 7)**

Craske, M. G., & Barlow, D. H. (1988). A review of the relationship between panic and avoidance. *Clinical Psychology Review, 8,* 667–685. **(Chap 5)**

Craske, M. G., & Barlow, D. H. (1993). Panic disorder and agoraphobia. In D. H. Barlow (Ed.), *Clinical handbook of psychological disorders* (2nd ed.). New York: Guilford Press. **(Chap 5)**

Craske, M. G., & Rowe, M. K. (1997). Nocturnal panic. *Clinical Psychology: Science & Practice, 4,* 153–174. **(Chap 5)**

Craske, M. G., Antony, M. M., & Barlow, D. H. (1997). *Mastery of your specific phobia, therapist guide.* San Antonio, TX: Graywind Publications Incorporated/The Psychological Corporation. **(Chap 5)**

Craske, M. G., Barlow, D. H., & O'Leary, T. A. (1992). *Mastery of your anxiety and worry.* Albany, NY: Graywind Publications. **(Chap 5)**

Craske, M. G., Barlow, D. H., Clark, D. M., Curtis, G. C., Hill, E. M., Himle, J. A., Lee, Y.-J., Lewis, J. A., McNally, R. J., Ost, L.-G., Salkovskis, P. M., & Warwick, H. M. C. (1996). Specific (simple) phobia. In T. A. Widiger, A. J. Frances, H. A. Pincus, R. Ross, M. B. First, & W. W. Davis (Eds.), *DSM-IV sourcebook* (Vol. 2, pp. 473–506). Washington, DC: American Psychiatric Association. **(Chap 5)**

Craske, M. G., Brown, T. A., & Barlow, D. H. (1991). Behavioral treatment of panic disorder: A two year follow-up. *Behavior Therapy, 22,* 289–304. **(Chap 5)**

Craske, M. G., Rapee, R. M., & Barlow, D. H. (1988). The significance of panic expectancy for individual patterns of avoidance. *Behavior Therapy, 19,* 577–592. **(Chap 5)**

Creese, I., Burt, D. R., & Snyder, S. H. (1976). Dopamine receptor binding predicts clinical and pharmacological potencies of antischizophrenic drugs. *Science, 192,* 481–483. **(Chap 13)**

Crisp, A. H., Callender, J. S., Halek, C., & Hsu, L. K. G. (1992). Long-term mortality in anorexia nervosa: A 20-year follow-up of the St. George's and Aberdeen cohorts. *British Journal of Psychiatry, 161,* 104–107. **(Chap 8)**

Crocker, A. C. (1992). Data collection for the evaluation of mental retardation prevention activities: The fateful forty-three. *Mental Retardation, 30,* 303–317. **(Chap 14)**

Cross-National Collaborative Group. (1992). The changing rate of major depression: Cross-national comparisons. *Journal of the American Medical Association, 268,* 3098–3105. **(Chap 7)**

Crow, T. J. (1980). Molecular pathology of schizophrenia: More than one dimension of pathology? *British Medical Journal, 280,* 66–68. **(Chap 13)**

Crow, T. J. (1985). The two-syndrome concept: Origins and current status. *Schizophrenia Bulletin, 11,* 471–486. **(Chap 13)**

Crow, T. J. (1988). Sex chromosomes and psychosis: The case for pseudoautosomal locus. *British Journal of Psychiatry, 153,* 675–683. **(Chap 13)**

Crow, T. J., Cross, A. J., Owen, D., Ferrier, N., Johnstone, E. C., MacReadie, R. M., & Ownes, D. G. C. (1981). *Neurochemical studies on post mortem brains in schizophrenia: Changes in the dopamine receptor in relation to psychiatric and neurological symptoms.* Proceedings of the 134th Meeting of the American Psychiatric Association, p. 39. **(Chap 13)**

Crow, T. J., Deakin, J. F. W., Johnstone, E. C., et al. (1984). The Northwich Park ECT trial. Predictors of response to real and simulated ECT. *British Journal of Psychiatry, 144,* 227–237. **(Chap 7)**

Crowe, L. C., & George, W. H. (1989). Alcohol and human sexuality: Review and integration. *Psychological Bulletin, 105*(3), 374–386. **(Chap 10)**

Crowe, R. R. (1974). An adoption study of antisocial personality. *Archives of General Psychiatry, 31,* 785–791. **(Chap 12)**

Crowe, R. R. (1984). Electroconvulsive therapy: A current perspective. *New England Journal of Medicine, 311,* 163–167. **(Chap 7)**

Crowley, P. H., Hayden, T. L., & Gulati, D. K. (1982). Etiology of Down syndrome. In S. M. Pueschel & J. E. Rynders, (Eds.), *Down syndrome: Advances in biomedicine and behavioral sciences* (pp. 89–131). Cambridge, MA: Ware Press. **(Chap 14)**

Cruickshank, J. K., & Beevers, D. G. (1989). *Ethnic factors in health and disease.* London: Wright. **(Chap 15)**

Cummings, J. L. (1990). *Subcortical dementia.* New York: Oxford University Press. **(Chap 15)**

Curtis, G. C., Hill, E. M., & Lewis, J. A. (1990). *Heterogeneity of DSM-III-R simple phobia and the simple phobia/agoraphobia boundary: Evidence from the ECA study.* Preliminary report to the Simple Phobia subcommittee of the DSM-IV Anxiety Disorders Work Group. **(Chap 5)**

Curtis, G. C., Himle, J. A., Lewis, J. A., & Lee, Y-J. (1989). *Specific situational phobias: Variant of agoraphobia?* Paper requested by the Simple Phobia subcommittee of the DSM-IV Anxiety Disorders Work Group. **(Chap 5)**

Cutrona, C. E. (1984). Social support and stress in the transition to parenthood. *Journal of Abnormal Psychology, 93*(4), 378–390. **(Chap 7)**

Cutting, J. (1985). *The psychology of schizophrenia.* New York: Churchill Livingstone. **(Chap 13)**

Czeisler, C. A., & Allan, J. S. (1989). Pathologies of the sleep-wake schedule. In R. L. Williams, I. Karacan, & C. A. Morre (Eds.), *Sleep disorders: Diagnosis and treatment* (pp. 109–129). New York: John Wiley. **(Chap 8)**

Czeisler, C. A., Allan, J. S., Strogatz, S. H., Ronda, J. M., Sanchez, R., Rios, C. D., Frietag, W. O., Richardson, G. S., &

Kronauer, R. E. (1986). Bright light resets the human circadian pacemaker independent of the timing of the sleep-wake cycle. *Science, 233,* 667–671. **(Chap 8)**

Czeisler, C. A., Richardson, G. S., Coleman, R. M., Zimmerman, J. C., Moore-Ede, M. C., Dement, W. C., & Weitzman, E. D. (1981). Chronotherapy: Resetting the circadian clocks of patients with delayed sleep phase insomnia. *Sleep, 4,* 1–21. **(Chap 8)**

Dagan, Y., Dela, H., Omer, H., Hallis, D., & Dar, R. (1996). High prevalence of personality disorders among circadian rhythm sleep disorders (CRSD) patients. *Journal of Psychosomatic Research, 41,* 357–363. **(Chap 8)**

Dahl, A. A. (1993, Spring). The personality disorders: A critical review of family, twin, and adoption studies. *Journal of Personality Disorders,* Supplement, 86–99. **(Chap 12)**

Dalack, G. W., Glassman, A. H., & Covey, L. S. (1993). Nicotine use. In D. L. Dunner (Ed.), *Current psychiatric therapy* (pp. 114–118). Philadelphia: W. B. Saunders. **(Chap 11)**

Daly, R. J. (1983). Samuel Pepys and post traumatic stress disorder. *British Journal of Psychiatry, 143,* 64–68. **(Chap 5)**

d'Amato, T., Campion, D., Gorwood, P., Jay, M., Sabate, O., Petit, C., Abbar, M., Malafosse, A., Leboyer, M., Hillaire, D., Clerget-Darpoux, F., Feingold, J., Waksman, G., & Mallet, J. (1992). Evidence for a pseudoautosomal locus for schizophrenia. II: Replication of a nonrandom segregation of alleles at the DXYS14 locus. *British Journal of Psychiatry, 161,* 59–62. **(Chap 13)**

Dana, R. H. (1996). The Thematic Apperception Test (TAT). In C. S. Newmark (Ed.), *Major psychological assessment instruments* (pp. 166–205). Boston: Allyn & Bacon. **(Chap 3)**

Darwin, C. R. (1872). *The expression of emotions in man and animals.* London: John Murray. **(Chaps 1, 2, 5)**

Dassori, A. M., Miller, A. L., & Saldana, D. (1995). Schizophrenia among Hispanics: Epidemiology, phenomenology, course, and outcome. *Schizophrenia Bulletin, 21,* 303–312. **(Chap 13)**

Davidson, J., & Robertson, E. (1985). A follow-up study of postpartum illness, 1946–1978. *Acta Psychiatrica Scandinavica, 71*(15), 451–457. **(Chap 7)**

Davidson, J., Swartz, M., Storck, M., Krishnan, R. R., & Hammett, E. (1985). A diagnostic and family study of posttraumatic stress disorder. *American Journal of Psychiatry, 142,* 90–93. **(Chap 5)**

Davidson, J., Miller, R. D., Turnbull, C. D., & Sullivan, J. L. (1982). Atypical depression. *Archives of General Psychiatry, 39,* 527–534. **(Chap 7)**

Davidson, J. R. T., Hughes, D. L., Blazer, D. G., & George, L. K. (1991). Posttrau-matic stress in the community: An epidemiological study. *Journal of Psychological Medicine, 21,* 713–721. **(Chap 5)**

Davidson, M., Keefe, R. S. E., Mohs, R. C., Siever, L. J., Losonczy, M. F., Horvath, T. B., & Davis, K. L. (1987). L-Dopa challenge and relapse in schizophrenia. *American Journal of Psychiatry, 144,* 934–938. **(Chap 13)**

Davidson, R. J. (1993). Cerebral asymmetry and emotion: Methodological conundrums. *Cognition and Emotion, 7,* 115–138. **(Chap 7)**

Davis, C., Katzman, D. K., Kaptein, S., Kirsh, C., Brewer, H., Kalmbach, K., Olmsted, M. P., Woodside, D. B., & Kaplan, A. S. (1997). The prevalence of high-level exercise in the eating disorders: Etiological implications. *Comprehensive Psychiatry, 38,* 321–326. **(Chap 8)**

Davis, K. L., Kahn, R. S., Ko, G., & Davidson, M. (1991). Dopamine in schizophrenia: A review and reconceptualization. *American Journal of Psychiatry, 148,* 1474–1486. **(Chap 13)**

Davis, M. (1992). The role of the amygdala in fear and anxiety. *Annual Review of Neuroscience, 15,* 353–375. **(Chap 5)**

Davison, G. C. (1968). Elimination of a sadistic fantasy by a client-controlled counter-conditioning technique: A case study. *Journal of Abnormal Psychology, 73,* 91–99. **(Chap 10)**

Dawson, G., & McKissick, F. C. (1984). Self-recognition in autistic children. *Journal of Autism and Developmental Disorders, 14,* 383–394. **(Chap 14)**

Day, J., Grant, I., Atkinson, J. H., Brysk, L. T., McCutchan, J. A., Hesselink, J. R., Keaton, R. K., Weinrich, J. D., Spector, S. A., & Richman, D. D. (1992). Incidence of AIDS dementia in a 2-year follow-up of AIDS and ARC patients on an initial phase II AZT placebo-controlled study: San Diego cohort. *Journal of Neuropsychiatry and Clinical Neuroscience, 4,* 15–20. **(Chap 14)**

Day, R., Nielsen, J. A., Korten, A., Ernberg, G., Dube, K. C., Gebhart, J., Jablensky, A., Leon, C., Marsella, A., Olatawura, M., Sartorius, N., Stromgren, E., Takahashi, R., Wig, N., & Wynne, L. C. (1987). Stressful life events preceding the acute onset of schizophrenia: A cross-national study from the World Health Organization. *Cultural Medicine and Psychiatry, 11,* 123–205. **(Chap 15)**

Deakin, J. F. W., & Graeff, F. G. (1991). Critique: 5-HT and mechanisms of defence. *Journal of Psychopharmacology, 5*(4), 305–315. **(Chap 5)**

Deale, A., Chalder, T., Marks, I., & Wessely, S. (1997). Cognitive behavior therapy for chronic fatigue syndrome: A randomized controlled trial. *American Journal of Psychiatry, 154,* 408–414. **(Chap 9)**

de Almeidia-Filho, N., Santana, V. S., Pinto, I. M., & de Carvalho-Neto, J. A. (1991). Is there an epidemic of drug misuse in Brazil? A review of the epidemiological evidence (1977–1988). *International Journal of the Addictions, 26,* 355–369. **(Chap 11)**

Dean, C., & Kendell, R. E. (1981). The symptomatology of postpartum illness. *British Journal of Psychiatry, 139,* 128–133. **(Chap 7)**

Dean, R. R., Kelsey, J. E., Heller, M. R., & Ciaranello, R. D. (1993). Structural foundations of illness and treatment: Receptors. In D. L. Dunner (Ed.), *Current psychiatric therapy.* Philadelphia: W. B. Saunders. **(Chap 2)**

De Angelis, T. (1994). Experts see little impact from insanity plea ruling. *APA Monitor, 25,* 28. **(Chap 16)**

Debacker, G., Kittel, F., Kornitzer, M., & Dramaix, M. (1983). Behavior, stress, and psychosocial traits as risk factors. *Preventative Medicine, 12,* 32–36. **(Chap 9)**

DeBuono, B. A., Zinner, S. H., Daamen, M., & McCormack, W. M. (1990). Sexual behavior of college women in 1975, 1986 and 1989. *New England Journal of Medicine, 322*(12), 821–825. **(Chap 10)**

de la Monte, S. M., Hutchins, G. M., & Moore, G. W. (1989). Racial differences in the etiology of dementia and frequency of Alzheimer lesions in the brain. *Journal of the National Medical Association, 81,* 644–652. **(Chap 15)**

de Lissovoy, V. (1961). Head banging in early childhood. *Child Development, 33,* 43–56. **(Chap 14)**

Dembroski, T. M., & Costa, P. T., Jr. (1987). Coronary prone behavior: Components of the Type A pattern and hostility. *Journal of Personality, 55*(2), 211–235. **(Chap 9)**

Dembroski, T. M., MacDougall, J. M., Costa, P. T., & Grandits, G. A. (1989). Components of hostility as predictors of sudden death and myocardial infarction in the multiple risk factor intervention trial. *Psychosomatic Medicine, 51*(5), 514–522. **(Chap 9)**

Denzin, N. K. (1987). *The recovering alcoholic.* Newbury Park, CA: Sage Publications. **(Chap 11)**

Depression Guideline Panel. (1993, April). *Depression in primary care: Vol. 1. Detection and diagnosis* (AHCPR Publication No. 93–0550). Clinical practice guideline, No. 5. Rockville, MD: U.S. Department of Health and Human Services, Public Health Service, Agency for Health Care Policy and Research. **(Chap 7)**

Deptula, D., & Pomara, N. (1990). Effects of antidepressants on human performance: A review. *Journal of Clinical Psychopharmacology, 10,* 105–111. **(Chap 7)**

Depue, R. A. (in press). *Neurobehavioral systems, personality, and psychopathology.* New York: Springer-Verlag. **(Chap 2)**

Depue, R. A., & Iacono, W. G. (1989). Neurobehavioral aspects of affective disorders. *Annual Review of Psychology, 40,* 457–492. **(Chap 7)**

Depue, R. A., & Spoont, M. R. (1986). Conceptualizing a serotonin trait: A behavioral dimension of constraint. *Annals of the New York Academy of Sciences, 487,* 47–62. **(Chap 2)**

Depue, R. A., & Zald, D. (1993). Biological and environmental processes in nonpsychotic psychopathology: A neurobehavioral system perspective. In C. Costello (Ed.), *Basic issues in psychopathology.* New York: Guilford Press. **(Chap 2)**

Depue, R. A., Luciana, M., Arbisi, P., Collins, P., & Leon, A. (1994). Dopamine and the structure of personality: Relation of agonist-induced dopamine activity to positive emotionality. *Journal of Personality and Social Psychology.* **(Chap 2)**

Depue, R. A., Slater, J. F., Wolfstetter-Kausch, H., Klein, D., Goplerud, E., & Farr, D. (1981). A behavioral paradigm for identifying persons at risk for bipolar depressive disorder: A conceptual framework and five validation studies. *Journal of Abnormal Psychological Monographs, 90,* 381–437. **(Chap 7)**

Dershewitz, R. A., & Williamson, J. W. (1977). Prevention of childhood household injuries: A controlled clinical trial. *American Journal of Public Health, 67,* 1148–1153. **(Chap 9)**

Devinsky, O., Feldman, E., Burrowes, K., & Bromfield, E. (1989). Autoscopic phenomena with seizures. *Archives of Neurology, 46*(10), 1080–1088. **(Chap 6)**

Dewji, N. N., & Singer, S. J. (1996). Genetic clues to Alzheimer's disease. *Science, 271,* 159–160. **(Chap 15)**

Diamond, M. (1995). Biological aspects of sexual orientation and identity. In L. Diamant & R. D. McAnulty (Eds.), *The psychology of sexual orientation, behavior, and identity.* Westport, CT: Greenwood Press. **(Chap 10)**

Diamond, M., & Sigmundson, K. (1997). Sex reassignment at birth: Long-term review and clinical implications. *Archives of Pediatric and Adolescent Medicine, 151,* 298–304. **(Chap 10)**

DiBartolo, P. M., Brown, T. A., & Barlow, D. H. (1997). Effects of Anxiety on attentional allocation and task performance: An information processing analysis. *BRAT, 35,* 1101–1111. **(Chap 5)**

DiLalla, L. F., & Gottesman, I. I. (1991). Biological and genetic contributors to violence—Widom's untold tale. *Psychological Bulletin, 109,* 125–129. **(Chap 12)**

Dimberg, U., & Öhman, A. (1983). The effects of directional facial cues on electrodermal conditioning to facial stimuli. *Psychophysiology, 20,* 160–167. **(Chap 5)**

DiNardo, P. A. (1991). *MacArthur reanalysis of generalized anxiety disorder.* Unpublished manuscript. **(Chap 5)**

DiNardo, P. A., & Barlow, D. H. (1990). Syndrome and symptom comorbidity in the anxiety disorders. In J. D. Maser & C. R. Cloninger (Eds.), *Comorbidity of mood and anxiety disorders* (pp. 205–230). Washington, DC: American Psychiatric Press. **(Chap 7)**

DiNardo, P. A., Brown, T. A., & Barlow. D. H. (1994). *Anxiety disorders interview schedule for DSM-IV (ADIS-IV).* Albany, NY: Graywind Publications. **(Chap 3)**

DiNardo, P. A., Moras, K., Barlow, D. H., Rapee, R. M., & Brown, T. A. (1993). Reliability of DSM-III-R anxiety disorder categories: Using the Anxiety Disorders Interview Schedule-Revised (ADIS-R). *Archives of General Psychiatry, 50,* 251–256. **(Chap 3)**

DiNardo, P. A., O'Brien, G. T., Barlow, D. H., Waddell, M. T., & Blanchard, E. B. (1983). Reliability of DSM-III anxiety disorder categories using a new structured interview. *Archives of General Psychiatry, 40,* 1070–1074. **(Chap 3)**

Diokno, A. C., Brown, M. B., & Herzog, A. R. (1990). Sexual function in the elderly. *Archives of Internal Medicine, 150,* 197–200. **(Chap 10)**

Dishion, T. J., Patterson, G. R., & Reid, J. R. (1988). Parent and peer factors associated with drug sampling in early adolescence: Implications for treatment. In E. R. Rahdert & J. Gabowski (Eds.), *Adolescent drug abuse: Analyses of treatment research* (NIDA Research Monograph No. 77, DHHS Publication No. ADM88–1523, pp. 69–93). Rockville, MD: National Institute on Drug Abuse. **(Chap 11)**

Dissanayake, C., & Crossley, S. A. (1996). Proximity and sociable behaviours in autism: Evidence for attachment. *Journal of Child Psychology and Psychiatry, 37,* 149–156. **(Chap 14)**

Dixon, J. C. (1963). Depersonalization phenomena in a sample population of college students. *British Journal of Psychiatry, 109,* 371–375. **(Chap 6)**

Dixon, L. B., & Lehman, A. F. (1995). Family interventions for schizophrenia. *Schizophrenia Bulletin, 21,* 631–643. **(Chap 13)**

Docherty, N. M., DeRosa, M., & Andreasen, N. V. (1996). Communication disturbances in schizophrenia and mania. *Archives of General Psychiatry, 53,* 358–364. **(Chap 13)**

Docter, R. F., & Prince, V. (1997). Transvestism: A survey of 1032 cross-dressers. *Archives of Sexual Behavior, 26,* 589–605. **(Chap 10)**

Dohrenwend, B. P., & Dohrenwend, B. S. (1981). Socioenvironmental factors, stress and psychopathology. *American Journal of Community Psychology, 9*(2), 128–164. **(Chap 7)**

Dohrenwend, B. P., & Egri, G. (1981). Recent stressful life events and episodes of schizophrenia. *Schizophrenia Bulletin, 7,* 12–23. **(Chap 13)**

Donaldson, K. (1976). *Insanity inside out.* New York: Crown. **(Chap 16)**

Doyne, E. J., Ossip-Klein, D. J., Bowman, E. D., Osborn, K. M., McDougall-Wilson, I. B., & Neimeyer, R. A. (1987). Running versus weight lifting in the treatment of depression. Special issue: Eating disorders. *Journal of Consulting and Clinical Psychology, 55*(5), 748–754. **(Chap 7)**

Draguns, J. G. (1990). Normal and abnormal behavior in cross-cultural perspective: Specifying the nature of their relationship. In J. Berman (Ed.), *Cross-Cultural Perspectives: Nebraska Symposium on Motivation 1989* (pp. 235–277). Lincoln: University of Nebraska Press. **(Chap 2)**

Draguns, J. G. (1995). Cultural influences upon psychopathology: Clinical and practical implications. *Journal of Social Distress and the Homeless, 4,* 79–103. **(Chap 2)**

Drake, R. E., McHugo, G. J., Becker, D. R., Anthony, W. A., & Clark, R. E. (1996). The New Hampshire study of supported employment for people with severe mental illness. *Journal of Consulting and Clinical Psychology, 64,* 391–399. **(Chap 13)**

Drotar, D., & Sturm, L. (1991). Psychosocial influences in the etiology, diagnosis, and prognosis of nonorganic failure to thrive. In H. E. Fitzgerald, B. M. Lester, & M. W. Yogman, *Theory and research in behavioral pediatrics.* New York: Plenum Press. **(Chap 2)**

Dubovsky, S. L. (1983). Psychiatry in Saudi Arabia. *American Journal of Psychiatry, 140,* 1455–1459. **(Chap 4)**

Dulit, R. A., Marin, D. B., & Frances, A. J. (1993). Cluster B personality disorders. In D. L. Dunner (Ed.), *Current psychiatric therapy* (pp. 405–411). Philadelphia: W. B. Saunders. **(Chap 12)**

Dumas, J., & Wahler, R. G. (1983). Predictors of treatment outcome in parent training: Mother insularity and socioeconomic disadvantage. *Behavioral Assessment, 5,* 301–313. **(Chap 12)**

Dunner, D. D., & Fieve, R. (1974). Clinical factors in lithium carbonate prophylaxis failure. *Archives of General Psychiatry, 30,* 229–233. **(Chap 7)**

DuPaul, G. J., Anastopoulos, A. D., Kwasnik, D., Barkley, R. A., & McMurray, M. B. (1996). Methylphenidate effects on children with attention deficit hyperactivity disorder: Self-report of symptoms, side-effects, and self-esteem. *Journal of Attention Disorders, 1,* 3–15. **(Chap 14)**

Durand, V. M. (1990). *Severe behavior problems: A functional communication training approach.* New York: Guilford Press. **(Chap 14)**

Durand, V. M. (1993). Functional communication training using assistive devices: Effects on challenging behavior and affect. *Augmentative and Alternative Communication, 9,* 168–176. **(Chap 14)**

Durand, V. M. (1998). *Sleep better: A guide to improving the sleep of children with special needs.* Baltimore: Paul H. Brookes. **(Chap 8)**

Durand, V. M. (in press). New directions in educational programming for students with autism. To appear in D. Berkell-Zager (Ed.), *Autism: Identification, education, and treatment* (2nd ed.). Hillsdale, NJ: Erlbaum. **(Chap 14)**

Durand, V. M., & Carr, E. G. (1992). An analysis of maintenance following functional communication training. *Journal of Applied Behavior Analysis, 25,* 777–794. **(Chap 4)**

Durand, V. M., & Crimmins, D. B. (1988). Identifying the variables maintaining self-injurious behavior. *Journal of Autism and Developmental Disorders, 18,* 99–117. **(Chap 3)**

Durand, V. M., & Mindell, J. A. (1990). Behavioral treatment of multiple childhood sleep disorders. *Behavior Modification, 14,* 37–49. **(Chap 8)**

Durand, V. M., Blanchard, E. B., & Mindell, J. A. (1988). Training in projective testing: A survey of clinical training directors and internship directors. *Professional Psychology: Research and Practice, 19,* 236–238. **(Chap 3)**

Durham v. United States. (1954). 214 F.2d, 862, 874–875 (D.C. Cir.). **(Chap 16)**

Durham, M. L., & La Fond, J. Q. (1985). The empirical consequences and policy implications of broadening the statutory criteria for civil commitment. *Yale Law and Policy Review, 3,* 395–446. **(Chap 16)**

Durkheim, E. (1951). *Suicide: A study in sociology.* (J. A. Spaulding & G. Simpson, Trans.). New York: Free Press. **(Chap 7)**

Dwyer, E. (1992). Attendants and their world of work. In A. D. Gaines (Ed.), *Ethnopsychiatry: The cultural construction of professional and folk psychiatries* (pp. 291–305). Albany: State University of New York Press. **(Chap 4)**

Dwyer, J. T., Feldman, J. J., Seltzer, C. C., & Mayer, J. (1969). Body image in adolescents: Attitudes toward weight and perception of appearance. *American Journal of Clinical Nutrition, 20,* 1045–1056. **(Chap 8)**

Dykens, E., Leckman, J., Paul, R., & Watson, M. (1988). Cognitive, behavioral, and adaptive functioning in fragile X and non-fragile X retarded men. *Journal of Autism and Developmental Disorders, 18,* 41–52. **(Chap 14)**

Eagles, J. M., Johnston, M. I. Hunter, D., Lobban, M., & Millar, H. R. (1995). Increasing incidence of anorexia nervosa in the female population of northeast Scotland. *American Journal of Psychiatry, 152,* 1266–1271. **(Chap 8)**

Eaker, E. D., Pinsky, J., & Castelli, W. P. (1992). Myocardial infarction and coronary death among women: Psychosocial predictors from a 20-year follow-up of women in the Framingham study. *American Journal of Epidemiology, 135,* 854–864. **(Chap 9)**

Earnst, K. S., & Kring, A. M. (1997). Construct validity of negative symptoms. *Clinical Psychology Review, 17,* 167–189. **(Chap 13)**

Eaton, W. W., Anthony, J. C., Gallo, J., Cai, G., Tien, A., Romanoski, A., Lyketsos, C., & Chen, L.-S. (1997). Natural history of diagnostic interview schedule/DSM-IV major depression: The Baltimore Epidemiologic Catchment Area follow-up. *Archives of General Psychiatry, 54,* 993–999. **(Chap 7)**

Eaton, W. W., Kessler, R. C., Wittchen, H. U., & McGee, W. J. (1994). Panic and panic disorder in the United States. *American Journal of Psychiatry, 151,* 413–420. **(Chap 5)**

Ebigno, P. (1982). Development of a culture-specific screening scale of somatic complaints indicating psychiatric disturbance. *Culture, Medicine, and Psychiatry, 6,* 29–43. **(Chap 4)**

Ebigno, P. O. (1986). A cross sectional study of somatic complaints of Nigerian females using the Enugu Somatization Scale. *Culture, Medicine, and Psychiatry, 10,* 167–186. **(Chap 6)**

Eckman, T. A., Wirshing, W. C., Marder, S. R., Liberman, R. P., Johnston-Cronk, K., Zimmermann, K., & Mintz, J. (1992). Techniques for training schizophrenic patients in illness self-management: A controlled trial. *American Journal of Psychiatry, 149,* 1549–1555. **(Chap 13)**

Edwards, A. J. (1994). *When memory fails: Helping the Alzheimer's and dementia patient.* New York: Plenum Press. **(Chap 15)**

Efon, S. (1997, October 19). Tsunami of eating disorders sweeps across Asia. *San Francisco Examiner,* p. A27. **(Chap 8)**

Egeland, J. A., Gerhard, D. S., Pauls, D. L., Sussex, J. N., Kidd, K. K., Allen, C. R., Hosteller, A. M., & Housman, D. E. (1987). Bipolar affective disorders linked to DNA markers on chromosome 11. *Nature, 325*(6107), 783–787. **(Chaps 4, 7)**

Ehlers, A., & Breuer, P. (1992). Increased cardiac awareness in panic disorder. *Journal of Abnormal Psychology, 101*(3), 371–382. **(Chap 5)**

Ehrhardt, A. A., & Meyer-Bahlburg, H. F. L. (1981). Effects of prenatal sex hormones on gender-related behavior. *Science, 211,* 1312–1318. **(Chap 10)**

Ehrhardt, A. A., Meyer-Bahlburg, H. F. L., Rosen, L. R., Feldman, J. F., Veridiano, N. P., Zimmerman, I., & McEwen, B. (1985). Sexual orientation after prenatal exposure to exogenous estrogen. *Archives of Sexual Behavior, 14*(1), 57–77. **(Chap 10)**

Eisler, I., Dare, C., Russell, G. F. M., Szmukler, G., le Grange, D., & Dodge, E. (1997). Family and individual therapy in anorexia nervosa: A five year follow-up. *Archives of General Psychiatry, 54,* 1025–1030. **(Chap 8)**

Ekstrand, M. L., & Coates, T. J. (1990). Maintenance of safer sexual behaviors and predictors of risky sex: The San Francisco men's health study. *American Journal of Public Health, 80,* 973–977. **(Chap 9)**

Elbedour, S., Shulman, S., & Kedem, P. (1997). Children's fears: Cultural and developmental perspectives. *Behavior Research and Therapy, 35,* 491–496. **(Chap 2)**

Eldredge, K. L., & Agras, W. S. (1996). Weight and shape overconcern and emotional eating in binge eating disorder. *International Journal of Eating Disorders, 19,* 73–82. **(Chap 8)**

Elkin, I., Gibbons, R. D., Shea, M. T., Sotsky, S. M., Watkins, J. T., Pilkonis, P. A., & Hedeker, D. (1995). Initial severity and differential treatment outcome in the National Institute of Mental Health Treatment of Depression Collaborative Research Program. *Journal of Consulting and Clinical Psychology, 63,* 841–847. **(Chap 7)**

Elkin, I., Shea, M. T., Watkins, J. T., Imber, S. D., Sotsky, S. M., Collins, J. F., Glass, D. R., Pilkonis, P. A., Leber, W. R., Docherty, J. P., Fiester, S. J., & Parloff, M. B. (1989). National Institute of Mental Health Treatment of Depression Collaborative Research Program: General effectiveness of treatments. *Archives of General Psychiatry, 46*(11), 971–982. **(Chap 7)**

Ellason, J. W., & Ross, C. A. (1997). Two-year follow up of inpatients with dissociative identity disorder. *American Journal of Psychiatry., 154,* 832–839. **(Chap 6)**

Ellicott, A. G. (1988). *A prospective study of stressful life events and bipolar illness.* Unpublished doctoral dissertation, University of California, Los Angeles. **(Chap 7)**

Elliot, D. M. (1997). Traumatic events: Prevalence and delayed recall in the general population. *Journal of Consulting and Clinical Psychology, 65,* 811–820. **(Chap 6)**

Ellis, A. (1962). *Reason and emotion in psychotherapy.* Secaucus, NJ: Prentice-Hall. **(Chap 2)**

Ellis, N. R. (1970). Memory processes in retardates and normals. In N. R. Ellis (Ed.), *International review of research in mental retardation* (Vol. 4, pp. 1–32). New York: Academic Press. **(Chap 14)**

Emery, R. E. (1982). Interparental conflict and the children of discord and divorce. *Psychological Bulletin, 92,* 310–330. **(Chap 4)**

Emrick, C. D., Tonigan, J. S., Montgomery, H., & Little, L. (1993). Alcoholics

Anonymous: What is currently known? In B. S. McCrady & W. R. Miler (Eds.), *Research on Alcoholics Anonymous: Opportunities and alternatives* (pp. 41–76). New Brunswick, NJ: Rutgers Center of Alcohol Studies. **(Chap 11)**

Emslie, G. J., Rush, A. J., Weinberg, W. A., Rintelmann, J. W., & Roffwarg, H. P. (1994). Sleep EEG features of adolescents with major depression. *Biological Psychiatry, 36,* 573–581. **(Chap 8)**

Eppright, T. D., Kashani, J. H., Robison, B. D., & Reid, J. C. (1993). Comorbidity of conduct disorder and personality disorders in an incarcerated juvenile population. *American Journal of Psychiatry, 150,* 1233–1236. **(Chap 12)**

Erdberg, P. (1996). The Rorschach. In C. S. Newmark (Ed.), *Major psychological assessment instruments* (pp. 148–165). Boston: Allyn & Bacon. **(Chap 3)**

Erhardt, D., & Hinshaw, S. P. (1994). Initial sociometric impressions of attention-deficit hyperactivity disorder and comparison boys: Predictions from social behaviors and from nonbehavioral variables. *Journal of Consulting and Clinical Psychology, 62,* 833–842. **(Chap 14)**

Erikson, E. (1982). *The life cycle completed.* New York: Norton. **(Chap 2)**

Ernst, C., & Angst, J. (1995). Depression in old age: Is there a real decrease in prevalence? A review. *European Archives of Psychiatry and Clinical Neuroscience, 245*(6), 272–287. **(Chap 7)**

Ernst, R. L., & Hay, J. W. (1994). The US economic and social costs of Alzheimer's disease revisited. *American Journal of Public Health, 84,* 1261–1264. **(Chap 15)**

Ertekin, C., Colakoglu, Z., & Altay, B. (1995). Hand and genital sympathetic skin potentials in flaccid and erectile penile states in normal potent men and patients with premature ejaculation. *The Journal of Urology, 153,* 76–79. **(Chap 10)**

Escobar, J. I., & Canino, G. (1989). Unexplained physical complaints: Psychopathology and epidemiological correlates. *British Journal of Psychiatry, 154,* 24–27. **(Chap 6)**

Escobar, J. I., Burnam, A., Karno, M., Forsythe, A., & Golding, J. M. (1987). Somatization in the community. *Archives of General Psychiatry, 44,* 713–718. **(Chap 6)**

Eslinger, P. J., & Damasio, A. R. (1985). Severe disturbance of higher cognition after bilateral frontal lobe ablation: Patient EVR. *Neurology, 35,* 1731–1741. **(Chap 2)**

Esterling, B., Antoni, M., Schneiderman, N., LaPerriere, A., Ironson., G., Klimas, N., & Fletcher, M. A. (1992). Psychosocial modulation of antibody to Epstein-Barr viral capsid antigen and human herpes virus-Type 6 in HIV-1 infected and at-risk gay men.

Psychosomatic Medicine, 54, 354–371. **(Chap 9)**

Eth, S. (1990). Posttraumatic stress disorder in childhood. In M. Hersen & C. G. Last (Ed.), *Handbook of child and adult psychopathology: A longitudinal perspective.* Elmsford, NY: Pergamon Press. **(Chap 5)**

Evans, D. A., Funkenstein, H. H., Albert, M. S., Scherr, P. A., Cook, N. R., Chonn, M. J., Hebert, L. E., Hennekens, C. H., & Taylor, J. O. (1989). Prevalence of Alzheimer's disease in a community population of older persons. *Journal of the American Medical Association, 262,* 2551–2556. **(Chap 15)**

Evans, J. A., & Hammerton, J. L. (1985). Chromosomal anomalies. In A. M. Clarke, A. D. B. Clarke, & J. M. Berg (Eds.), *Mental deficiency: The changing outlook* (4th ed., pp. 213–266). New York: Free Press. **(Chap 14)**

Evans, M. D., Hollon, S. D., DeRubeis, R. J., Pinsecki, J. M., Grove, W. M., Garvey, J. J., & Tuason, V. B. (1992). Differential relapse following cognitive therapy and pharmacotherapy for depression. *Archives of General Psychiatry, 49*(10), 802–808. **(Chap 7)**

Exner, J. E. (1974). *The Rorschach: A comprehensive system* (Vol. 1). New York: John Wiley. **(Chap 3)**

Exner, J. E. (1978). *The Rorschach: A comprehensive system* (Vol. 2). *Current research and advanced interpretation.* New York: John Wiley. **(Chap 3)**

Exner, J. E. (1986). *The Rorschach: A comprehensive system* (Vol. 1, 2nd ed.). New York: John Wiley. **(Chap 3)**

Exner, J. E., & Weiner, I. B. (1982). *The Rorschach: A comprehensive system* (Vol 3). *Assessment of children and adolescents.* New York: John Wiley. **(Chap 3)**

Eysenck, H. J. (Ed.). (1967). *The biological basis of personality.* Springfield, IL: Charles C. Thomas. **(Chap 5)**

Eysenck, H. J., & Eysenck, S. B. G. (1975). *Manual for the Eysenck Personality Questionnaire.* London: Hodder & Stoughton. **(Chap 12)**

Eysenck, H. J., & Eysenck, S. B. G. (1978). Psychopathy, personality, and genetics. In R. D. Hare & D. Schalling (Eds.), *Psychopathic behaviour: Approaches to research* (pp. 197–223). Chichester, England: John Wiley. **(Chap 12)**

Eysenck, M. W. (1992). *Anxiety: The cognitive perspective.* Hove, United Kingdom: Lawrence Erlbaum. **(Chaps 2, 5)**

Ezzel, C. (1993). On borrowed time: Long-term survivors of HIV-1 infection. *The Journal of NIH Research, 5,* 77–82. **(Chap 9)**

Fackelmann, K. A. (1993). Marijuana and the brain: Scientists discover the brain's own THC. *Science, 143,* 88–94. **(Chap 10)**

Faden, R. R. (1987). Health psychology and public health. In G. L. Stone, S. M. Weiss, J. D. Matarazzo, N. E. Miller, J.

Rodin, C. D. Belar, M. J. Follick, & J. E. Singer (Eds.), *Health psychology: A discipline and a profession.* Chicago, IL: University of Chicago Press. **(Chap 9)**

Fahrner, E. M. (1987). Sexual dysfunction in male alcohol addicts: Prevalence and treatment. *Archives of Sexual Behavior, 16*(3), 247–257. **(Chap 10)**

Fairburn, C. G. (1985). Cognitive-behavioral treatment for bulimia. In D. M. Garner & P. E. Garfinkel (Eds.), *Handbook of psychotherapy for anorexia nervosa and bulimia* (pp. 160–192). New York: Guilford Press. **(Chap 8)**

Fairburn, C. G., & Beglin, S. J. (1990). Studies of the epidemiology of bulimia nervosa. *American Journal of Psychiatry, 147*(4), 401–409. **(Chap 8)**

Fairburn, C. G., & Cooper, P. J. (1984). Rumination in bulimia nervosa. *British Medical Journal, 288,* 826–827. **(Chap 8)**

Fairburn, C. G., & Cooper, Z. (in press). The schedule of the eating disorder examination. In C. G. Fairburn & G. T. Wilson (Eds.), *Binge eating: Nature, assessment, and treatment.* New York: Guilford Press. **(Chap 8)**

Fairburn, C. G., & Wilson, G. T. (in press). Binge eating: Definition and classification. In C. G. Fairburn & G. T. Wilson (Eds.), *Binge eating: Nature, assessment, and treatment.* New York: Guilford Press. **(Chap 8)**

Fairburn, C. G., Agras, W. S., & Wilson, G. T. (1992). The research on the treatment of bulimia nervosa: Practical and theoretical implications. In G. H. Anderson & S. H. Kennedy (Eds.), *The biology of feast and famine: Relevance to eating disorders* (pp. 317–340). New York: Academic Press. **(Chap 8)**

Fairburn, C. G., Cooper, Z., & Cooper, P. J. (1986). The clinical features and maintenance of bulimia nervosa. In K. D. Brownell & J. P. Foreyt (Eds.), *Handbook of eating disorders: Physiology, psychology, and treatment of obesity, anorexia, and bulimia* (pp. 389–404). New York: Basic Books. **(Chap 8)**

Fairburn, C. G., Hay, P. J., & Welch, S. L. (in press). Binge eating and bulimia nervosa: Distribution and determinants. In C. G. Fairburn & G. T. Wilson (Eds.), *Binge eating: Nature, assessment, and treatment.* New York: Guilford Press. **(Chap 8)**

Fairburn, C. G., Jones, R., Peveler, R. C., Hope, R. A., & O'Connor, M. (1993). Psychotherapy and bulimia nervosa: The longer-term effects of interpersonal psychotherapy, behaviour therapy and cognitive behaviour therapy. *Archives of General Psychiatry, 50,* 419–428. **(Chap 8)**

Fairburn, C. G., Marcus, M. D., & Wilson, G. T. (in press). Cognitive behaviour therapy for binge eating and bulimia nervosa: A comprehensive treatment manual. In C. G. Fairburn & G. T. Wilson (Eds.), *Binge eating: Nature, assessment, and treatment.* New York: Guilford Press. **(Chap 8)**

Fairburn, C. G., Norman, P. A., Welch, S. L., O'Connor, M. E., Doll, H., Peveler, R. C. (1995). A prospective study of outcome in bulimia nervosa and the long term effects of three psychological treatments. *Archives of General Psychiatry, 52,* 304–312. **(Chap 8)**

Falconer, D. S. (1965). The inheritance of liability to certain diseases, estimated from the incidence among relatives. *Annals of Human Genetics, 29,* 51–76. **(Chap 14)**

Fallon, A. (1990). Culture in the mirror: Sociocultural determinants of body image. In T. F. Cash & T. Pruzinsky (Eds.), *Body images: Development, deviance, and change* (pp. 80–109). New York: Guilford Press. **(Chap 6)**

Fallon, A. E., & Rozin, P. (1985). Sex differences in perceptions of desirable body shape. *Journal of Abnormal Psychology, 94,* 102–105. **(Chap 8)**

Falloon, I. R. H., Boyd, J. L., McGill, C. W., Williamson, M., Razani, J., Moss, H. B., Gilderman, A. M., & Simpson, G. M. (1985). Family management in the prevention of morbidity of schizophrenia. *Archives of General Psychiatry, 42,* 887–896. **(Chap 13)**

Falloon, I. R. H., Brooker, C., & Graham-Hole, V. (1992). Psychosocial interventions for schizophrenia. *Behaviour Change, 9,* 238–245. **(Chap 13)**

Farde, L., Gustavsson, J. P., & Jonsson, E. (1997). D2 dopamine receptors and personality traits. *Nature, 385,* 590. **(Chap 12)**

Farde, L., Wiesel, F. A., Stone-Elander, S., Halldin, C., Nordstrom, A. L., Hall, H., & Sedvall, G. (1990). D2 dopamine receptors in neuroleptic-naive patients: A positron emission tomography study with [11C] raclopride. *Archives of General Psychiatry, 47,* 213–219. **(Chap 13)**

Fava, G. A., Grandi, S., Zielezny, M., Rafanelli, C., & Canestrari, R. (1996). Four-year outcome for cognitive behavioral treatment of residual symptoms in major depression. *American Journal of Psychiatry, 153,* 945–947. **(Chap 7)**

Fava, M., & Rosenbaum, J. F. (1991). Suicidality and fluoxetine: Is there a relationship? *Journal of Clinical Psychiatry, 52*(3), 108–111. **(Chap 7)**

Fawzy, F. I., Cousins, N., Fawzy, N. W., Kemeny, M. E., Elashoff, R., & Morton, D. (1990). A structured psychiatric intervention for cancer patients: I.: Changes over time in methods of coping and affective disturbance. *Archives of General Psychiatry, 47,* 720–728. **(Chaps 2, 9)**

Fawzy, F. I., Fawzy, N. W., Arndt, L. A. & Pasnau, R. O. (1995). Critical review of psychosocial interventions in cancer care. *Archives of General Psychiatry, 52,* 100–113. **(Chap 2)**

Fawzy, F. I., Fawzy, N. W., Hyun, C. S., Elashoff, R., Guthrie, D., Fahey, J. L., & Morton, D. L. (1993). Malignant melanoma: Effects of an early structured psychiatric intervention, coping, and affective state on recurrence and survival 6 years later. *Archives of General Psychiatry, 50,* 681–689. **(Chaps 2, 9)**

Fawzy, F. I., Kemeny, M. E., Fawzy, N. W., Elashoff, R., Morton, D., Cousins, N., & Fahey, J. L. (1990). A structured psychiatric intervention for cancer patients: II. Changes over time in immunological measures. *Archives of General Psychiatry, 47,* 729–735. **(Chaps 2, 9)**

Fein, G., & Callaway, E. (1993). Electroencephalograms and event-related potentials in clinical psychiatry. In D. L. Dunner (Ed.), *Current psychiatric therapy* (pp. 18–26). Philadelphia: W. B. Saunders. **(Chap 3)**

Feinberg, M., & Carroll, B. J. (1984). Biological "markers" for endogenous depression: Effect of age, severity of illness, weight loss and polarity. *Archives of General Psychiatry, 41,* 1080–1085. **(Chap 7)**

Feingold, B. F. (1975). *Why your child is hyperactive.* New York: Random House. **(Chap 14)**

Feldman, H. A., Goldstein, I., Hatzichristou, D. G, Krane, R. J., & McKunlay, J. B. (1994). Impotence and its medical and psychosocial correlates: Results of the Massachusetts Male Aging Study. *Journal of Urology, 151,* 54–61. **(Chap 10)**

Fenske, E. C., Zalenski, S., Krantz, P. J., & McClannahan, L. E. (1985). Age at intervention and treatment outcome for autistic children in a comprehensive intervention program. *Analysis and Intervention in Developmental Disabilities, 5,* 7–31. **(Chap 14)**

Ferber, R. (1985). *Solve your child's sleep problems.* New York: Simon & Schuster. **(Chap 8)**

Fernandez, F., Levy, J. K., & Mansell, P. W. A. (1989). Management of delirium in terminally ill AIDS patients. *International Journal of Psychiatry Medicine, 19,* 165–172. **(Chap 15)**

Fernandez, F., Levy J. K., Lachar, B. L., & Small, G. W. (1995). The management of depression and anxiety in the elderly. *Journal of Clinical Psychiatry, 56*(Suppl. 2), 20–29. **(Chap 7)**

Ferster, C. B. (1961). Positive reinforcement and behavioral deficits of autistic children. *Child Development, 32,* 437–456. **(Chap 14)**

Ferster, C. B., & DeMyer, M. K. (1961). The development of performances in autistic children in an automatically controlled environment. *Journal of Chronic Diseases, 13,* 312–345. **(Chap 14)**

Ferster, C. B., & Skinner, B. F. (1957). *Schedules of reinforcement.* New York: Appleton-Century-Crofts. **(Chap 1)**

Feske, U., & Chambless, D. L. (1995). Cognitive behavioral versus exposure only treatment for social phobia: A meta-analysis. *Behavior Therapy, 26,* 695–720. **(Chap 5)**

Feuerstein, M., Labbe, E. E., & Kuczmierczyk, A. R. (1986). *Health psychology: A psychobiological perspective.* New York: Plenum Press. **(Chap 9)**

Fewell, R. R., & Glick, M. P. (1996). Program evaluation findings of an intensive early intervention program. *American Journal on Mental Retardation, 101,* 233–243. **(Chap 14)**

Field, T., Healy, B., Goldstein, S., Perry, S., Bendell, D., Schanberg, S., Zimmerman, E. A., & Kuhn, C. (1988). Infants of depressed mothers show "depressed" behavior even with nondepressed adults. *Child Development, 59*(6), 1569–1579. **(Chap 7)**

Fiester, S. J. (1995). Self-defeating personality disorder. In W. J. Livesley (Ed.), *The DSM-IV personality disorders* (pp. 341–358). New York: Guilford Press. **(Chap 12)**

Fiester, S. J., & Gay, M. (1995). Sadistic personality disorder. In W. J. Livesley (Ed.), *The DSM-IV personality disorders* (pp. 329–340). New York: Guilford Press. **(Chap 12)**

Figueira, I. V., & Versiani, M. (1996). Social phobia. In T. A. Widiger, A. J. Frances, H. A. Pincus, R. Ross, M .B. First, & W. W. Davis (Eds.), *DSM-IV sourcebook.* (Vol. 2, pp. 507–548). Washington, DC: American Psychiatric Association. **(Chap 5)**

Figueroa, E., & Silk, K. R. (1997). Biological implications of childhood sexual abuse in borderline personality disorder. *Journal of Personality Disorders, 11,* 71–92. **(Chap 12)**

Fils-Aime, M. L. (1993). Sedative-hypnotic abuse. In D. L. Dunner (Ed.), *Current psychiatric therapy* (pp. 124–131). Philadelphia: W. B. Saunders. **(Chap 11)**

Fincham, F. D., Beach, S. R. H., Harold, G. T., & Osborne, L. N. (1997). Marital satisfaction and depression: Different causal relationships for men and women? *Psychological Science, 8*(5), 351–357. **(Chap 7)**

Fink, M., & Sackeim, H. A. (1996). Convulsive therapy in schizophrenia? *Schizophrenia Bulletin, 22,* 27–39. **(Chap 13)**

Finnegan, L. P., & Kandall, S. R. (1997). Maternal and neonatal effects of alcohol and drugs. In J. H. Lowinson, P. Ruiz, R. B. Millman, & J. G. Langrod (Eds.), *Substance abuse: A comprehensive textbook* (pp. 513–534). Baltimore: Williams & Wilkins. **(Chap 11)**

Fiore, T. A., Becker, E. A., & Nero, R. C. (1993). Educational interventions for students with attention deficit disorder.

Exceptional Children, 60, 163-173. **(Chap 14)**

Fiorino, A. S. (1996). Sleep, genes and death: Fatal familial insomnia. *Brain Research Reviews, 22,* 258–264. **(Chap 8)**

Fischer, M. (1971). Psychoses in the offspring of schizophrenic monozygotic twins and their normal co-twins. *British Journal of Psychiatry, 118,* 43–52. **(Chap 13)**

Fish, B. (1977). Neurobiological antecedents of schizophrenia in children: Evidence for an inherited, congenital, neurointegrative defect. *Archives of General Psychiatry, 34,* 1297–1313. **(Chap 13)**

Fish, B. (1987). Infant predictors of the longitudinal course of schizophrenic development. *Schizophrenia Bulletin, 13,* 395–410. **(Chap 13)**

Fishbain, D. A., & Goldberg, M. (1991). The misdiagnosis of conversion disorder in a psychiatric emergency service. *General Hospital Psychiatry, 13*(3), 177–181. **(Chap 6)**

Fisher, J. E., & Carstensen, L. L. (1990). Behavior management of the dementias. *Clinical Psychology Review, 10,* 611–629. **(Chap 15)**

Fisher, M., & Zeaman, D. (1973). An attention-retention theory of retardate discrimination learning. In N. R. Ellis (Ed.), *International review of research in mental retardation* (Vol. 6, pp. 169–256). New York: Academic Press. **(Chap 14)**

Fisher, W. W. Piazza, C. C., Bowman, L. G., Kurtz, P. F., & Lachman, S. R. (1994). A preliminary evaluation of empirically derived consequences for the treatment of pica. *Journal of Applied Behavior Analysis, 27,* 447–457. **(Chap 8)**

Fitts, S. N., Gibson, P., Redding, C. A., & Deiter, P. J. (1989). Body dysmorphic disorder: Implications for its validity as a DSM-III-R clinical syndrome. *Psychological Reports, 64,* 655–658. **(Chap 6)**

Fleischman, M. J. (1981). A replication of Patterson's \"Intervention for boys with conduct problems." *Journal of Consulting and Clinical Psychology, 49,* 342–351. **(Chap 12)**

Fleming, J. E., Boyle, M. H., & Offord, D. R. (1993). The outcome of adolescent depression in the Ontario child health study follow-up. *Journal of the American Academy of Child and Adolescent Psychiatry, 32*(1), 28–33. **(Chap 7)**

Fleshner, C. L. (1995). First person account: Insight from a schizophrenia patient with depression. *Schizophrenia Bulletin, 21,* 703–707. **(Chap 13)**

Flint, J., Corley, R., DeFries, J. C., Fulker, D. W., Gray, J. A., Miller, S., & Collins, A. C. (1995). Chromosomal mapping of three loci determining quantitative variation of susceptibility to anxiety in the mouse. *Science, 268,* 1432–1435. **(Chap 5)**

Flor, H., & Turk, D. C. (1988). Chronic back pain and rheumatoid arthritis: Predicting pain and disability from cognitive variables. *Journal of Behavioral Medicine, 11,* 251–265. **(Chap 9)**

Flor, H. Elbert, T., Kenecht, S., Weinbruch, C., Pantev, C., Birbaumer, N., Larbig, W., & Taub, E. (1995). Phantom limb pain as a perceptual correlate of corticol reorganization following arm amputation. *Nature, 375,* 482–484. **(Chap 9)**

Foa, E. B., & Meadows, E. A. (1997). Psychosocial treatments for posttraumatic stress disorder: A critical review. *Annual Review of Psychology, 48,* 449–480. **(Chap 5)**

Foa, E. B., Jenike, M., Kozak, M. J., Joffe, R., Baer, L., Pauls, D., Beidel, D. C., Rasmussen, S. A., Goodman, W., Swinson, R. P., Hollander, E., & Turner, S. M. (1996). Obsessive-compulsive disorder. In T. A. Widiger, A. J. Frances, H. A. Pincus, M. R. Ross, M. B. First, & W. W. Davis (Eds.), *DSM-IV sourcebook* (Vol. 2, pp. 549–576). Washington, DC: American Psychiatric Association. **(Chap 5)**

Folks, D. G., Ford, C. U., & Regan, W. M. (1984). Conversion symptoms in a general hospital. *Psychosomatics, 25*(4), 285–295. **(Chap 6)**

Follete, W. C., & Houts, A. C. (1996). Models of scientific progress and the role of theory in taxonomy development: A case study of the *DSM. Journal of Consulting and Clinical Psychology, 64*(6), 1120–1132. **(Chaps 1, 3)**

Folstein, S., & Rutter, M. (1977). Genetic influences and infantile autism. *Nature, 265,* 726–728. **(Chap 14)**

Folstein, S. E., Brandt, J., & Folstein, M. F. (1990). Huntington's disease. In J. L. Cummings (Ed.), *Subcortical dementia* (pp. 87–107). New York: Oxford University Press. **(Chap 15)**

Ford, C., & Beach, F. (1951). *Patterns of sexual behavior.* New York: Harper & Row. **(Chap 10)**

Ford, C. V. (1985). Conversion disorders: An overview. *Psychosomatics, 26,* 371–383. **(Chap 6)**

Ford, D. E., & Kamerow, D. B. (1989). Epidemiologic study of sleep disturbances and psychiatric disorder: An opportunity for prevention? *Journal of the American Medical Association, 262,* 1479–1484. **(Chap 8)**

Ford, M. R., & Widiger, T. A. (1989). Sex bias in the diagnosis of histrionic and antisocial personality disorders. *Journal of Consulting and Clinical Psychology, 57,* 301–305. **(Chap 12)**

Fordyce, W. E. (1976). *Behavioral methods in chronic pain and illness.* St. Louis, MO: Mosby. **(Chap 9)**

Fordyce, W. E. (1988). Pain and suffering: A reappraisal. *American Psychologist, 43*(4), 276–283. **(Chap 9)**

Fowles, D. C. (1988). Psychophysiology and psychopathy: A motivational approach. *Psychophysiology, 25,* 373–391. **(Chap 12)**

Fowles, D. C. (1992a). Motivational approach to anxiety disorders. In D. G. Forgays, T. Sosnowski, & K. Wrzesniewski (Eds.), *Anxiety: Recent developments in cognitive, psychophysiological, and health research* (pp. 181–192). Washington: Hemisphere Publishing Corporation. **(Chap 5)**

Fowles, D. C. (1992b). Schizophrenia: Diathesis-stress revisited. *Annual Review of Psychology, 43,* 303–336. **(Chap 14)**

Fowles, D. C. (1993). A motivational theory of psychopathology. In W. Spaulding (Ed.), *Nebraska symposium on motivation: Integrated views of motivation, cognition, and emotion* (Vol. 41, pp. 181–238). Lincoln: University of Nebraska Press. **(Chap 5)**

Fox, P. T., Ingham, R. J., Ingham, J. C., Hirsch, T. B., Downs, J. H., Martin, C., Jerabek, P., Glass, T., & Lancaster, J. L., (1996). A PET study of the neural systems of stuttering. *Nature, 382,* 158–161. **(Chap 14)**

Foxx, R. M., & Martin, E. D. (1975). Treatment of scavenging behavior (coprophagy and pica) by overcorrection. *Behavior Research and Therapy, 13,* 153–162. **(Chap 8)**

Foy, D. W., Resnick, H. S., Sipprelle, R. C., & Carroll, E. M. (1987). Premilitary, military and postmilitary factors in the development of combat related posttraumatic stress disorder. *The Behavior Therapist, 10,* 3–9. **(Chap 5)**

Foy, D. W., Sipprelle, R. C., Rueger, D. B., & Carroll, E. M. (1984). Etiology of posttraumatic stress disorder in Vietnam veterans: Analysis of premilitary, military, and combat exposure influences. *Journal of Consulting and Clinical Psychology, 52,* 79–87. **(Chap 5)**

Frances, A., & Widiger, T. (1987). A critical review of four DSM-III personality disorders: Borderline, avoidant, dependent, and passive aggressive. In G. Tischler (Ed.), *Diagnosis and classification in psychiatry* (pp. 269–289). New York: Cambridge University Press. **(Chap 13)**

Frances, A., & Widiger, T. A. (1986). Methodological issues in personality disorder diagnosis. In T. Millon & G. Klerman (Ed.), *Contemporary directions in psychopathology.* New York: Guilford Press. **(Chap 3)**

Frances, R., Franklin, J., & Flavin, D. (1986). Suicide and alcoholism. *Annals of the New York Academy of Science, 287,* 316–326. **(Chap 7)**

Francis, G., & Hart, K. J. (1992). Depression and suicide. In V. B. Van Hasselt & D. J. Kolko (Eds.), *Inpatient behavior therapy for children and adolescents* (pp. 93–111). New York: Plenum Press. **(Chap 4)**

Francis, G., Last, C. G., & Strauss, C. C. (1987). Expression of separation anxiety disorder: The roles of age and gender. *Child Psychiatry and Human Development, 18,* 82–89. **(Chap 5)**

Francis, J., Martin, D., & Kapoor, W. N. (1990). A prospective study of delirium in hospitalized elderly. *Journal of the American Medical Association, 263,* 1097–1101. **(Chap 15)**

Frank, E., Anderson, B., Reynolds, C. F., Ritenour, A., & Kupfer, D. J. (1994). Life events and the research diagnostic criteria endogenous subtype. *Archives of General Psychiatry, 51,* 519–524. **(Chap 7)**

Frank, E., Anderson, C., & Rubinstein, D. (1978). Frequency of sexual dysfunction in "normal" couples. *New England Journal of Medicine, 299,* 111–115. **(Chap 10)**

Frank, E., Hlastala, S., Ritenour, A., Houck, P., Tu, X. M., Monk, T. H., Mallinger, A. G., & Kupfer, D. J. (1997). Inducing lifestyle regularity in recovering bipolar disorder patients: Results from the Maintenance Therapies in Bipolar Disorder Protocol. *Biological Psychiatry, 41,* 1165–1173. **(Chap 7)**

Frank, E., Kupfer, D. J., Perel, J. M., Cornes, C., Jarrett, D. B., Mallinger, A. G., Thase, M. E., McEachran, A. B., & Grochocinski, V. J. (1990). Three year outcomes for maintenance therapies in recurrent depression. *Archives of General Psychiatry, 47*(12), 1093–1099. **(Chap 7)**

Frank, E., Kupfer, D. J., Wagner, E. F., McEachran, A. B., & Cornes, C. (1991). Efficacy of interpersonal psychotherapy as a maintenance treatment for recurrent depression: Contributing factors. *Archives of General Psychiatry, 48,* 1053–1059. **(Chap 7)**

Franklin, D. (1990, November/December). Hooked-Not hooked: Why isn't everyone an addict? *Health,* pp. 39–52. **(Chap 11)**

Frasure-Smith, N. (1991). In-hospital symptoms of psychological stress as predictors of long-term outcome after acute myocardial infarction in men. *American Journal of Cardiology, 67,* 121–127. **(Chap 9)**

Frasure-Smith, N., Lesperance, F. & Talajic, M. (1993). Depression following myocardial infarction: Impact on six month's survival. *Journal of the American Medical Association, 270,* 1819–1825. **(Chap 9)**

Fratiglioni, L., Grut, M., Forsell, Y., Viitanen, M., Grafstrom, M., Holmen, K., Ericsson, K., Backman, L., Ahlbom, A., & Winblad, B. (1991). Prevalence of Alzheimer's disease and other dementias in an elderly urban population: Relationship with age, sex and education. *Neurology, 41,* 1886–1892. **(Chap 15)**

Fredrikson, M., & Matthews, K. A. (1990). Cardiovascular responses to behavioral stress and hypertension: A meta-analytic review. *Annals of Behavioral Medicine, 12*(1), 30–39. **(Chap 9)**

Fredrikson, M., Annas, P., Wik, G. (1997). Parental history, aversive exposure and the development of snake and spider phobia in women. *Behavior Research and Therapy, 35,* 23–28. **(Chap 2)**

Freedman, M. (1990). Parkinson's disease. In J. L. Cummings (Ed.), *Subcortical dementia* (pp. 108–122). New York: Oxford University Press. **(Chap 15)**

Freeman, A., Pretzer, J., Fleming, B., & Simon, K. M. (1990). *Clinical applications of cognitive therapy.* New York: Plenum Press. **(Chap 13)**

Freeman, L., Nixon, P. G. F., Sallabank, P., & Reaveley, D. (1987). Psychological stress and silent myocardial ischemia. *American Heart Journal, 114,* 477–482. **(Chap 9)**

Freinkel, A., Koopman, C., Spiegel, D. (1994). Dissociative symptoms in media eye witnesses of an execution. *American Journal of Psychiatry, 151,* 1335–1339. **(Chap 6)**

French-Belgian Collaborative Group. (1982). Ischemic heart disease and psychological patterns: Prevalence and incidence studies in Belgium and France. *Advances in Cardiology, 29,* 25–31. **(Chap 9)**

Freud, A. (1946). *Ego and the mechanisms of defense.* New York: International Universities Press. **(Chap 1)**

Freud, S. (1894). The neuro-psychoses of defence. In J. Strachey (Ed.), *The complete psychological works* (Vol. 3, pp. 45–62). London: Hogarth Press (1962). **(Chap 6)**

Freud, S. (1957). Mourning and melancholia. In J. Strachey (Ed. and Trans.), *The standard edition of the complete psychological works of Sigmund Freud* (Vol. 14). London: Hogarth Press. (Original work published 1917) **(Chap 7)**

Freud, S. (1974). On coca. In R. Byck (Ed.), *Cocaine papers by Sigmund Freud* (pp. 49–73). New York: Stonehill. (Original work published 1885) **(Chap 11)**

Freund, K., Seto, M. C., & Kuban, M. (1996). Two types of fetishism. *Behaviour Research and Therapy, 34,* 687–694. **(Chap 10)**

Frick, P. J., Strauss, C. C., Lahey, B. B., & Christ, M. A. G. (1993). Behavior disorders of children. In P. B. Sutker & H. E. Adams (Eds.), *Comprehensive handbook of psychopathology* (pp. 765–789). New York: Plenum. **(Chap 14)**

Friedman, M., & Rosenman, R. H. (1959). Association of specific overt behavior pattern with blood and cardiovascular findings. *Journal of the American Medical Association, 169,* 1286. **(Chap 9)**

Friedman, M., & Rosenman, R. H. (1974). *Type A behavior and your heart.* New York: Knopf. **(Chap 9)**

Friedman, M., Thoresen, C. E., Gill, J., Powell, L. H., Ulmer, D., Thompson, L., Price, V. A., Rabin, D. D., Breall, W. S., Dixon, T., Levy, R., & Bourg, E. (1984). Alteration of type A behavior and reduction in cardiac recurrences in post-myocardial infarction patients. *American Heart Journal, 108,* 237–248. **(Chap 9)**

Friedman, S., Jones, J. C., Chernen, L., & Barlow, D. H. (1992). Suicidal ideation and suicide attempts among patients with panic disorder: A survey of two outpatient clinics. *American Journal of Psychiatry, 149*(5), 680–685. **(Chap 5)**

Friedman, S., Paradis, C. M., & Hatch, M. (1994). Characteristics of African-American and white patients with panic disorder and agoraphobia. *Hospital & Community Psychiatry, 45,* 798–803. **(Chap 5)**

Fristad, M. A., Weller, E. B., & Weller, R. A. (1992). Bipolar disorder in children and adolescents. *Child and Adolescent Psychiatric Clinics of North America, 1*(1), 13–39. **(Chap 7)**

Fromm-Reichmann, F. (1948). Notes on the development of treatment of schizophrenics by psychoanalytic psychotherapy. *Psychiatry, 11,* 263–273. **(Chap 13)**

Frost, R. O., Sher, K. J., & Geen, T. (1986). Psychotherapy and personality characteristics of non-clinical compulsive checkers. *Behaviour Research and Therapy, 24,* 133–143. **(Chap 5)**

Fukuda, K., Straus, S. E., Hickie, I., Sharpe, M. B., Dobbins, J. G., & Komaroff, A. L. (1994). Chronic fatigue syndrome: A comprehensive approach to its diagnosis and management. *Annals of Internal Medicine, 121,* 953–959. **(Chap 9)**

Fyer, A., Liebowitz, M., Gorman, J., Compeas, R., Levin, A., Davies, S., Goetz, D., & Klein, D. (1987). Discontinuation of alprazolam treatment in panic patients. *American Journal of Psychiatry, 144,* 303–308. **(Chap 5)**

Fyer, A. J., Mannuzza, S., Chapman, T. F., Liebowitz, M. R., & Klein, D. F. (1993). A direct interview family study of social phobia. *Archives of General Psychiatry, 50,* 286–293. **(Chap 5)**

Fyer, A. J., Mannuzza, S., Gallops, M. S., Martin, L. Y., Aaronson, C., Gorman, J. M., Liebowitz, M. R., & Klein, D. F. (1990). Familial transmission of simple phobias and fears: A preliminary report. *Archives of General Psychiatry, 47,* 252–256. **(Chap 5)**

Gagnon, J. H. (1990). The explicit and implicit use of the scripting perspective in sex research. *Annual Review of Sex Research, 1,* 1–43. **(Chap 10)**

Gagnon, M., & Ladouceur, R. (1992). Behavioral treatment of child stutterers: Replication and extension. *Behavior Therapy, 23,* 113–129. **(Chap 14)**

Gajdusek, D. C. (1977). Unconventional viruses and the origin and disappearance of Kuru. *Science, 197,* 943. **(Chap 15)**

Gallagher-Thompson, D., & Osgood, N. J. (1997). Suicide later in life. *Behavior Therapy, 28,* 23–41. **(Chap 7)**

Garb, H. N. (1992). The *trained* psychologist as expert witness. *Clinical Psychology Review, 12,* 451–467. **(Chap 16)**

Garber, J., Weiss, B., & Shanley, N. (1993). Cognitions, depressive symptoms and development in adolescents. *Journal of Abnormal Psychology, 102*(1), 47–57. **(Chap 7)**

Garber, S. W., Garber, M. D., & Spizman, R. F. (1996). *Beyond Ritalin: Facts about medication and other strategies for helping children, adolescents, and adults with attention deficit disorders.* New York: Villard. **(Chap 14)**

Garcia, J., McGowan, B. K., & Green, K. F. (1972). Biological constraints on conditioning. In A. H. Black & W. F. Prokasy (Eds.), *Classical conditioning II: Current research and theory.* New York: Appleton-Century-Crofts. **(Chap 2)**

Gardner, D. L., & Cowdry, R. W. (1986). Alprazolam-induced dyscontrol in borderline personality disorder. *American Journal of Psychiatry, 143,* 519–522. **(Chap 12)**

Gardner, E. L. (1997). Brain reward mechanisms. In J. H. Lowinson, P. Ruiz, R. B. Millman, & J. G. Langrod (Eds.), *Substance abuse: A comprehensive textbook* (pp. 51–85). Baltimore: Williams & Wilkins. **(Chap 11)**

Garfinkel, P. E. (in press). Evidence in support of attitudes to shape and weight as a diagnostic criterion of bulimia nervosa. *International Journal of Eating Disorders.* **(Chap 8)**

Garfinkel, P. E., & Garner, D. M. (1982). *Anorexia nervosa: A multidimensional perspective.* New York: Brunner/Mazel. **(Chap 8)**

Garfinkel, P. E., Lin, E. Goering P., Spegg, C., Goldbloom, D. S., Kennedy, S. Caplan, A. S., & Woodside, D. B. (1995). Bulimia nervosa in a Canadian community sample: Prevalence in comparison of subgroups. *American Journal of Psychiatry, 152,* 1052–1058. **(Chap 8)**

Garfinkel, P. E., Moldofsky, H., & Garner, D. M. (1979). The heterogeneity of anorexia nervosa: Bulimia as a distinct subgroup. *Archives of General Psychiatry, 37,* 1036–1040. **(Chap 8)**

Garland, A. F., & Zigler, E. (1993). Adolescent suicide prevention: Current research and social policy implications. *American Psychologist, 48*(2), 169–182. **(Chap 7)**

Garmezy, N., & Rutter, M. (Eds.). (1983). *Stress, coping and development in children.* New York: McGraw-Hill. **(Chap 2)**

Garner, D. M., & Fairburn, C. G. (1988). Relationship between anorexia nervosa and bulimia nervosa: Diagnostic implications. In D. M. Garner & P. E. Garfinkel (Eds.), *Diagnostic issues in anorexia nervosa and bulimia nervosa.* New York: Brunner/Mazel. **(Chap 8)**

Garner, D. M., & Garfinkel, P. E. (Eds.) (1985). *Handbook of psychotherapy for anorexia nervosa and bulimia.* New York: Guilford Press. **(Chap 8)**

Garner, D. M., & Needleman, L. D. (1996). Step care and the decision-tree models for treating eating disorders. In J. K. Thompson (Ed.), *Body image, eating disorders and obesity* (pp. 225–252). Washington, DC: American Psychological Association. **(Chap 8)**

Garner, D. M., Garfinkel, P. E., & O'Shaughnessy, M. (1985). The validity of the distinction between bulimics with and without anorexia nervosa. *American Journal of Psychiatry, 142,* 581–587. **(Chap 8)**

Garner, D. M., Garfinkel, P. E., Rockert, W., & Olmsted, M. P. (1987). A prospective study of eating disturbances in the ballet. Ninth World Congress of the International College of Psychosomatic Medicine, Sydney, Australia. *Psychotherapy and Psychosomatics, 48,* 170–175. **(Chap 8)**

Garner, D. M., Garfinkel, P. E., Schwartz, D., & Thompson, M. (1980). Cultural expectation of thinness in women. *Psychological Reports, 47,* 483–491. **(Chap 8)**

Garvey, M., Hollon, S. D., DeRubeis, R. J., & Evans, M. D. (1990a). Does 24-h urinary MHPG predict treatment response to antidepressants? I. A review. *Journal of Affective Disorders, 20*(3), 173–179. **(Chap 7)**

Garvey, M., Hollon, S. D., DeRubeis, R. J., & Evans, M. D. (1990b). Does 24-h MHPG predict treatment response to antidepressants? II. Association between imipramine response and low MHPG. *Journal of Affective Disorders, 20*(3), 181–184. **(Chap 7)**

Gatchel, R. J. (1996). Psychological disorders and chronic pain: Cause-and-effect relationships. In R. J. Gatchel & D. C. Turk (Eds.), *Psychological approaches to pain management: A practitioner's handbook* (pp. 33–52). New York: Guilford Press. **(Chap 9)**

Gatchel, R. J., Polatin, P. B., & Kinney, R. K. (1995). Predicting outcome of chronic back pain using clinical predictors of psychopathology: A prospective analysis. *Health Psychology, 14,* 415–420. **(Chap 9)**

Gatz, M., & Smyer, M. A. (1992). The mental health system and older adults in the 1990s. *American Psychologist, 47*(6), 741–751. **(Chap 2)**

Gawin, F. H., Kleber, H. D., Byck, R., Rounsaville, B. J., Kosten, T. R., Jatlow, P. I., & Morgan, C. (1989). Desipramine facilitation of initial cocaine abstinence. *Archives of General Psychiatry, 46,* 117–121. **(Chap 11)**

Gearhart, J. P. (1989). Total ablation of the penis after circumcision electrocautery: A method of management and long term follow-up. *The Journal of Urology, 42,* 789–801. **(Chap 10)**

Geer, J. H., Morokoff, P., & Greenwood, P. (1974). Sexual arousal in women: The development of a measurement device for vaginal blood volume. *Archives of Sexual Behavior, 3,* 559–564. **(Chap 10)**

Geller, B., Cooper, T. B., Graham, D. L., Fetaer, H. M., Marsteller, F. A., & Wells, J. M. (1992). Pharmacokinetically designed double blind placebo controlled study of nortriptyline in 6–12 year olds with major depressive disorder: Outcome: Nortriptyline and hydroxy-nortriptyline plasma levels; EKG, BP and side effect measurements. *Journal of the American Academy of Child and Adolescent Psychiatry, 31,* 33–44. **(Chap 7)**

George, L. K. (1984). *The burden of caregiving: Center reports of advances in research* (Vol. 8). Durham, NC: Duke University Center for the Study of Aging and Human Development. **(Chap 15)**

George, L. K., Landoman, R., Blazer, D. G., & Anthony, J. C. (1991). Cognitive impairment. In L. N. Robins & D. A. Regier (Eds.), *Psychiatric disorders in America* (pp. 291–327). New York: Free Press. **(Chap 15)**

Gershon, E. S. (1990). Genetics. In F. K. Goodwin & K. R. Jamison (Eds.), *Manic-depressive illness* (pp. 373–401). New York: Oxford University Press. **(Chap 7)**

Gibb, W. R. G. (1989). Dementia and Parkinson's disease. *British Journal of Psychiatry, 154,* 596–614. **(Chap 15)**

Gibbons, J. L. (1964). Cortisol secretion rates in depressive illness. *Archives of General Psychiatry, 10,* 572–575. **(Chap 7)**

Giedd, J. N., Castellanos, F. X., Casey, B. J., Kozuch, P., King, A. C., Hamburger, S. D., & Rapport, J. L. (1994). Quantitative morphology of the corpus callosum in attention deficit hyperactivity disorder. *American Journal of Psychiatry, 151,* 665–669. **(Chap 14)**

Gil, K., Williams, D., Keefe, F., & Beckham, J. (1990). The relationship of negative thoughts to pain and psychological distress. *Behavior Therapy, 21,* 349–362. **(Chap 9)**

Giles, D. E., Kupfer, D. J., Rush, J., & Roffwarg, H. P. (1998). Controlled comparison of electrophysiological sleep in families of probands with unipolar depression. *American Journal of Psychiatry, 155,* 192–199. **(Chap 8)**

Gilham, J. E., Reivich, K. J., Jaycox, L. H., & Seligman, M. E. P. (1995). Prevention of depressive symptoms in schoolchildren: Two-year follow-up. *Psychological Science, 6*(6), 343–351. **(Chap 7)**

Gillberg, C. (1984). Infantile autism and other childhood psychoses in a Swedish urban region: Epidemiological aspects. *Journal of Child Psychology and Psychiatry, 25,* 35–43. **(Chap 14)**

Gillin, J. C. (1993). Clinical sleep-wake disorders in psychiatric practice: Dyssomnias. In D. L. Dunner (Ed.), *Current psychiatric therapy* (pp. 373–380). Philadelphia: W. B. Saunders. **(Chap 8)**

Gislason, I. L. (1988). Eating disorders in childhood (ages 4 through 11 years). In B. J. Blinder, B. F. Chaitin, & R. S. Goldstein (Eds.), *The eating disorders: Medical and psychological bases of diagnosis and treatment* (pp. 285–293). New York: PMA. **(Chap 8)**

Gitlin, M. J., Swendsen, J., Heller, T. L., & Hammen, C. (1995). Relapse and impairment in bipolar disorder. *American Journal of Psychiatry, 152,* 1635–1640. **(Chap 7)**

Gladstone, M., Best, C. T., & Davidson, R. J. (1989). Anomalous bimanual coordination among dyslexic boys. *Developmental Psychology, 25,* 236–246. **(Chap 2)**

Gladue, B. A., Green, R., & Hellman, R. E. (1984). Neuroendocrine response to estrogen and sexual orientation. *Science, 225,* 1496–1499. **(Chap 10)**

Glaser, R., Kennedy, S., Lafuse, W. P., Bonneau, R. H., Speicher, C. E., Hillhouse, J., & Kiecolt-Glaser, J. K. (1990). Psychological stress-induced modulation of 1L-2 receptor gene expression and 1L-2 production in peripheral blood leukocytes. *Archives of General Psychiatry, 47,* 707–712. **(Chap 9)**

Glaser, R., Kiecolt-Glaser, J. K., Speicher, C. E., & Holliday, J. E. (1985). Stress, loneliness, and changes in herpes virus latency. *Journal of Behavioral Medicine, 8,* 249–260. **(Chap 9)**

Glaser, R., Rice, J., Sheridan, J., Fertel, R., Stout, J., Speicher, C., Pinsky, D., Kotar, M., Post, A., Beck, M., & Kiecolt-Glaser, J. K. (1987). Stress-related immune suppression: Health implications. *Brain, Behavior, and Immunity, 1,* 7–20. **(Chap 9)**

Glassman, A. H., & Roose, S. P. (1981). Delusional depression: A distinct clinical entity? *Archives of General Psychiatry, 138,* 424–427. **(Chap 7)**

Glatt, A. E., Zinner, S. H., & McCormack, W. M. (1990). The prevalence of dyspareunia. *Obstetrics and Gynecology, 75,* 433–436. **(Chap 10)**

Gleaves, D. H. (1996). The sociognitive model of dissociative identity disorder: A reexamination of the evidence. *Psychological Bulletin, 120,* 42–59. **(Chap 6)**

Goedde, H. W., & Agarwal, D. P. (1987). Polymorphism of aldehyde dehydrogenase and alcohol sensitivity. *Enzyme, 37,* 29–44. **(Chap 11)**

Gold, J. H., Endicott, J., Parry, B. L., Severino, S. K., Stotland, N., & Frank, E. (1996). Late luteal phase dysphoric disorder. In T. A. Widiger, A. J. Frances, H. A. Pincus, Ross, R., First, M. B. & Davis, W. W. (Eds.), *DSM-IV sourcebook* (Vol. 2, pp. 317–394). Washington, DC: American Psychiatric Association. **(Chap 7)**

Gold, M. S. (1997). Cocaine (and crack): Clinical aspects. In J. H. Lowinson, P.

Ruiz, R. B. Millman, & J. G. Langrod (Eds.), *Substance abuse: A comprehensive textbook* (pp. 181–199). Baltimore: Williams & Wilkins. **(Chap 11)**

Gold, M. S., & Miller, N. S. (1997). Cocaine (and crack): Neurobiology. In J. H. Lowinson, P. Ruiz, R. B. Millman, & J. G. Langrod (Eds.), *Substance abuse: A comprehensive textbook* (pp. 166–181). Baltimore: Williams & Wilkins. **(Chap 11)**

Gold, P. W., Goodwin, F. K., & Chrousos, G. P. (1988). Clinical and biochemical manifestations of depression: Relation to the neurobiology of stress. *New England Journal of Medicine, 319,* 348–353. **(Chap 7)**

Goldberg, J. F., Harrow, M., & Grossman, L. S. (1995). Course and outcome in bipolar affective disorder: A longitudinal follow-up study. *American Journal of Psychiatry, 152,* 379–384. **(Chap 7)**

Goldberg, L. (1993). The structure of phenotypic personality traits. *American Psychologist, 48,* 26–34. **(Chap 12)**

Goldberg, S. C., Schultz, C., Resnick, R. J., Hamer, R. M., & Schultz, P. M. (1987). Differential prediction of response to thiothixene and placebo in borderline and schizotypal personality disorders. *Psychopharmacology Bulletin, 23,* 342–346. **(Chap 12)**

Golden, C. J., Hammeke, T. A., & Purisch, A. D. (1980). *The Luria-Nebraska Battery manual.* Palo Alto, CA: Western Psychological Services. **(Chap 3)**

Goldfarb, W. (1963). Self-awareness in schizophrenic children. *Archives of General Psychiatry, 8,* 63–76. **(Chap 14)**

Goldman, M. S., & Rather, B. C. (1993). Substance use disorders: Cognitive models and architecture. In K. S. Dobson & P. C. Kendall (Eds.), *Psychopathology and cognition* (pp. 245–292). New York: Academic Press. **(Chap 11)**

Goldman, S. J., D'Angelo, E. J., DeMaso, D. R., & Mezzacappa, E. (1992). Physical and sexual abuse histories among children with borderline personality disorder. *American Journal of Psychiatry, 149,* 1723–1726. **(Chap 12)**

Goldstein, A. (1994). *Addiction: From biology to drug policy.* New York: W. H. Freeman. **(Chap 11)**

Goldstein, G., & Shelly, C. (1984). Discriminative validity of various intelligence and neuropsychological tests. *Journal of Consulting and Clinical Psychology, 52,* 383–389. **(Chap 3)**

Goldstein, I., Lue, T. F., Padma-Nathan, H., Rosen, R. C., Steers, W. D., & Wicker, P. A., for the Sildenafil Study Group. (1998). Oral sildenafil in the treatment of erectile dysfunction. *The New England Journal of Medicine, 338,* 1397–1404. **(Chap 10)**

Gonzalez-Lavin, A., & Smolak, L. (1995, March). *Relationships between television and eating problems in middle school girls.* Paper presented at the meeting of the Society for Research in

Child Development, Indianapolis, IN. **(Chap 8)**

Good, B. J., & Kleinman, A. M. (1985). Culture and anxiety: Cross-cultural evidence for the patterning of anxiety disorders. In A. H. Tuma & J. D. Maser (Eds.), *Anxiety and the anxiety disorders.* Hillsdale, NJ: Lawrence Erlbaum. **(Chaps 2, 9)**

Goode, E. (1993). *Drugs in American society* (4th ed.). New York: McGraw-Hill. **(Chap 11)**

Goodwin, D. S. (1979). Alcoholism and heredity. *Archives of General Psychiatry, 36,* 57–61. **(Chap 11)**

Goodwin, D. W., & Gabrielli, W. F. (1997). Alcohol: Clinical aspects. In J. H. Lowinson, P. Ruiz, R. B. Millman, & J. G. Langrod (Eds.), *Substance abuse: A comprehensive textbook* (pp. 142–148). Baltimore: Williams & Wilkins. **(Chap 11)**

Goodwin, D. W., & Guze, S. B. (1984). *Psychiatric diagnosis* (3rd ed). New York: Oxford University Press. **(Chap 6)**

Goodwin, F. K., & Ghaemi, S. N. (1998). Understanding manic-depressive illness. *Archives of General Psychiatry, 55,* 23–25. **(Chap 7)**

Goodwin, F. K., & Jamison, K. R. (1990). *Manic depressive illness.* New York: Oxford University Press. **(Chap 7)**

Gordis, E. (1991). *Alcohol research: Promise for the decade.* Rockville, MD: National Institute of Alcohol Abuse and Alcoholism. **(Chap 11)**

Gorenstein, E. E., & Newman, J. P. (1980). Disinhibitory psychopathology: A new perspective and a model for research. *Psychological Review, 87,* 301–315. **(Chap 6)**

Gorman, J. M., Liebowitz, M. R., Fyer, A. J., & Stein, J. A. (1989, February). Neuroanatomical hypothesis for panic disorder. *American Journal of Psychiatry, 146,* 148–161. **(Chap 5)**

Gotlib, I. H., & Abramson, L. Y. (in press). Attributional theories of emotion. In T. Dalgleish & M. Power (Eds.), *Handbook of cognition and emotion.* **(Chap 7)**

Gotlib, I. H., & Beach, S. R. H. (1995). A marital/family discord model of depression: Implications for therapeutic intervention. In N. S. Jacobson & A. S. Gurman (Eds.), *Clinical handbook of couple therapy* (pp. 411–436). New York: Guilford Press. **(Chap 7)**

Gotlib, I. H., & Krasnoperova, E. (in press). Biased information processing as a vulnerability factor for depression. *Behavior Therapy.* **(Chap 7)**

Gotlib, I. H., & MacLeod, C. (1997). Information processing in anxiety and depression: A cognitive-developmental perspective. In J. Burack & J. Enns (Eds.), *Attention, development, and psychopathology* (pp. 350–378). New York: Guilford Press. **(Chap 7)**

Gotlib, I. H., & Nolan, S. A. (in press). Depression. In A. S. Bellack & M. Hersen

(Eds.), *Psychopathology in adulthood* (2nd ed.). Boston: Allyn and Bacon. **(Chap 6)**

Gotlib, I. H., Kurtzman, H. S. & Blehar, M. C. (1997). Cognition and depression: Issues and future directions. *Cognition and Emotion, 11(5/6),* 663–673. **(Chap 7)**

Gotlib, I. H., Ranganath, C., & Rosenfeld, J. P. (in press). Frontal EEG alpha assymmetry, depression, and cognitive functioning. *Cognition and Emotion.* **(Chap 7)**

Gotlib, I. H., Roberts, J. E., & Gilboa, E. (1996). Cognitive interference in depression. In I. G. Sarason, G. R. Pierce, & B. R. Sarason (Eds.), *Cognitive interference: Theories, methods, and findings* (pp. 347–377). Mawah, NJ: Erlbaum. **(Chap 7)**

Gotlib, I. H., Whiffen, V. E., Wallace, P. M., & Mount, J. H. (1991). Prospective investigation of postpartum depression: Factors involved in onset and recovery. *Journal of Abnormal Psychology, 100(2),* 122–132. **(Chap 7)**

Gottesman, I. I. (1991). *Schizophrenia genesis: The origins of madness.* New York: W. H. Freeman. **(Chaps 2, 4, 13)**

Gottesman, I. I. (1997, June 6). Twins: En route to QTLs for cognition. *Science, 276,* 1522–1523. **(Chap 2)**

Gottesman, I. I., & Bertelsen, A. (1989). Dual mating studies in psychiatry—Offspring of inpatients with examples from reactive (psychogenic) psychoses. *International Review of Psychiatry, 1,* 287–296. **(Chap 13)**

Gottesman, I. I., McGuffin, P., & Farmer, A. E. (1987). Clinical genetics as clues to the "real" genetics of schizophrenia: A decade of modest gains while playing for time. *Schizophrenia Bulletin, 13,* 23–47. **(Chap 13)**

Gould, M. S. (1990). Suicide clusters and media exposure. In S. J. Blumenthal & D. J. Kupfer (Eds.), *Suicide over the life cycle: Risk factors, assessment and treatment of suicidal patients.* Washington, DC: American Psychiatric Press. **(Chap 7)**

Gould, R. A., Otto, M. W., Pollack, M. H., & Yap, L. (1997). Cognitive behavioral and pharmacological treatment of generalized anxiety disorder: A preliminary meta-analysis. *Behavior Therapy, 28,* 285–305. **(Chap 5)**

Graeff, F. G. (1987). The anti-aversive action of drugs. In T. Thompson, P. B. Dews, & J. Barrett (Eds.), *Advances in behavioral pharmacology* (Vol. 6). Hillside, NJ: Erlbaum. **(Chap 5)**

Graeff, F. G., (1993). Role of 5-ht in defensive behavior and anxiety. *Review in the Neurosciences, 4,* 181–211. **(Chap 5)**

Graf, P., Squire, L. R., & Mandler, G. (1984). The information that amnesic patients do not forget. *Journal of Experimental Psychology: Learning, Memory, and Cognition, 10,* 164–178. **(Chap 2)**

Graham, J. R. (1990). *MMPI-2: Assessing personality and psychopathology.* New York: Oxford University Press. **(Chap 3)**

Grant, I., Patterson, T. L., & Yager, J. (1988). Social supports in relation to physical health and symptoms of depression in the elderly. *American Journal of Psychiatry, 145(10),* 1254–1258. **(Chaps 2, 7, 9)**

Gray, J. A. (1982). *The neuropsychology of anxiety.* New York: Oxford University Press. **(Chaps 2, 5, 6)**

Gray, J. A. (1985). Issues in the neuropsychology of anxiety. In A. H. Tuma & J. D. Maser (Eds.), *Anxiety and the anxiety disorders* (pp. 5–25). Hillside, NJ: Lawrence Erlbaum. **(Chaps 2, 5, 6, 7)**

Gray, J. A. (1987). *The psychology of fear and stress* (2nd ed.). New York: Cambridge University Press. **(Chap 2)**

Gray, J. A., & Buffery, A. W. H. (1971). Sex differences in emotional and cognitive behavior in mammals including man: Adaptive and neural bases. *Acta Psychologica, 35,* 89–111. **(Chap 6)**

Gray, J. A. & McNaughton, N. (1996). The neuropsychology of anxiety: Reprise. In DA. Hope (Ed.), *Perspectives on anxiety, panic and fear* (The 43rd Annual Nebraska Symposium on Motivation) (pp. 61–134). Lincoln, NE: Nebraska University Press. **(Chaps 2, 5)**

Greden, J. F., & Walters, A. (1997). Caffeine. In J. H. Lowinson, P. Ruiz, R. B. Millman, & J. G. Langrod (Eds.), *Substance abuse: A comprehensive textbook* (pp. 294–307). Baltimore: Williams & Wilkins. **(Chap 11)**

Green, A. I., Mooney, J. J., Posener, J. A., & Schildkraut, J. J. (1995). Mood disorders: Biochemical aspects. In H. I. Kaplan & B. J. Sadock (Eds.), *Comprehensive textbook of psychiatry* (6th ed., pp. 1089–1101). Baltimore: Williams & Wilkins. **(Chap 7)**

Green, B. L., Grace, M. C., Lindy, J. D., Titchener, J. L., & Lindy, J. G. (1983). Levels of functional impairment following a civilian disaster: The Beverly Hills Supper Club fire. *Journal of Consulting and Clinical Psychology, 51,* 573–580. **(Chap 5)**

Green, R. (1987). *The "sissy boy syndrome" and the development of homosexuality.* New Haven: Yale University Press. **(Chap 10)**

Green, R., & Fleming, D. T. (1990). Transsexual surgery follow-up: Status in the 1990s. *Annual Review of Sex Research, 1,* 163–174. **(Chap 10)**

Green, R., & Money, J. (1969). *Transsexualism and sex reassignment.* Baltimore: Johns Hopkins Press. **(Chap 10)**

Greenberg, D. R. & LaPorte, D. L. (1996). Racial differences in body type preferences of men for women. *International Journal of Eating Disorders, 19,* 275–278. **(Chap 8)**

Greenberg, M. S., & Beck, A. T. (1989). Depression versus anxiety: A test of the content specificity. *Journal of Abnormal Psychology, 98(1),* 9–13. **(Chap 7)**

Greenough, W. T., Withers, G. S., & Wallace, C. S. (1990). Morphological changes in the nervous system arising from behavioral experience: What is the evidence that they are involved in learning and memory? In L. R. Squire & E. Lindenlaub (Eds.), *The biology of memory, Symposia Medica Hoescht 23* (pp. 159–183). Stuttgart/New York: Schattauer Verlag. **(Chap 2)**

Gregoire, A. (1992). New treatments for erectile impotence. *British Journal of Psychiatry, 160,* 315–326. **(Chap 10)**

Greist, J. H. (1990). Treatment of obsessive compulsive disorder: Psychotherapies, drugs, and other somatic treatments. *Journal of Clinical Psychiatry, 51,* 44–50. **(Chap 5)**

Griffith, E. E. H., English, T., & Mayfield, U. (1980). Possession, prayer and testimony: Therapeutic aspects of the Wednesday night meeting in a black church. *Psychiatry, 43(5),* 120–128. **(Chap 6)**

Grinspoon, L., & Bakalar, J. B. (1980). Drug dependence: Non-narcotic agents. In H. I. Kaplan, A. M. Freedman, & B. J. Sadock (Eds.), *Comprehensive textbook of psychiatry* (3rd ed., pp. 1614–1629). Baltimore: Williams and Wilkins. **(Chap 11)**

Grinspoon, L., & Bakalar, J. B. (1997). Marihuana. In J. H. Lowinson, P. Ruiz, R. B. Millman, & J. G. Langrod (Eds.), *Substance abuse: A comprehensive textbook* (pp. 199–206). Baltimore: Williams & Wilkins. **(Chap 11)**

Grisso, T., & Appelbaum, P. S. (1992). Is it unethical to offer predictions of future violence? *Law and Human Behavior, 16,* 621–633. **(Chap 16)**

Grob, C. S. & Poland, R. E. (1997). In J. H. Lowinson, P. Ruiz, R. B. Millman, & J. G. Langrod (Eds.), *Substance abuse: A comprehensive textbook* (pp. 269–275). Baltimore: Williams & Wilkins. **(Chap 11)**

Gross, J., & Rosen, J. C. (1988). Bulimia in adolescents: Prevalence and psychosocial correlates. *International Journal of Eating Disorders, 7,* 51–61. **(Chap 8)**

Gross, J. J., & Levenson, R. W. (1997). Hiding feelings: The acute effects of inhibiting negative and positive emotion. *Journal of Abnormal Psychology, 108,* 95–103. **(Chap 2)**

Gross, J. J., & Munoz, R. F. (1995). Emotion regulation and mental health. *Clinical Psychology: Science and Practice, 2,* 151–164. **(Chap 2)**

Gross, R. T., & Borkovec, T. D. (1982). Effects of cognitive intrusion manipulation on sleep-onset latency of good sleepers. *Behavior Therapy, 13,* 112–116. **(Chap 8)**

Grosz, H. J., & Zimmerman, J. (1965). Experimental analysis of hysterical blindness: A follow-up report and new experimental data. *Archives of General Psychiatry, 13,* 255–260. **(Chap 6)**

Grosz, H. J., & Zimmerman, J. (1970). A second detailed case study of functional blindness: Further demonstration of the contribution of objective psychological laboratory data. *Behavior Therapy, 1,* 115–123. **(Chap 6)**

Grove, W. M., & Tellegen, A. (1991). Problems in the classification of personality disorders. *Journal of Personality Disorders, 5,* 31–42. **(Chap 12)**

Grove, W. M., Clementz, B. A., Iacono, W. G., & Katsanis, J. (1992). Smooth pursuit ocular motor dysfunction in schizophrenia: Evidence for a major gene. *American Journal of Psychiatry, 149,* 1362–1368. **(Chap 13)**

Gruder, C. L., Mermelstein, R. J., Kirkendol, S., Hedeker, D., Wong, S. C., Schreckengost, J., Warnecke, R. B., Burzette, R., & Miller, T. Q. (1993). Effects of social support and relapse prevention training as adjuncts to a televised smoking-cessation intervention. *Journal of Consulting and Clinical Psychology, 61,* 113–120. **(Chap 11)**

Guilleminault, C. (1989). Clinical features and evaluation of obstructive sleep apnea. In M. H. Kryger, T. Roth, & W. C. Dement (Eds.), *Principles and practice of sleep medicine* (pp. 552–558). Philadelphia: W. B. Saunders. **(Chap 8)**

Guilleminault, C., & Dement, W. C. (1988). Sleep apnea syndromes and related sleep disorders. In R. L. Williams, I. Karacan, & C. A. Moore (Eds.), *Sleep disorders: Diagnosis and treatment* (pp. 47–71). New York: John Wiley. **(Chap 8)**

Guilleminault, C., & Mondini, S. (1986). Mononucleosis and chronic daytime sleepiness. *Archives of Internal Medicine, 146,* 1333–1335. **(Chap 8)**

Gunderson, J. G. (1992). Diagnostic controversies. In A. Tasman & M. B. Riba (Eds.), *Review of psychiatry* (Vol. 11, pp. 9–24). Washington, DC: American Psychiatric Press. **(Chap 13)**

Gunderson, J. G., & Sabo, A. N. (1993). The phenomenological and conceptual interface between borderline personality disorder and PTSD. *American Journal of Psychiatry, 150,* 19–27. **(Chap 12)**

Gunderson, J. G., Ronningstam, E., & Smith, L. E. (1991). Narcissistic personality disorder: A review of data on DSM-III-R descriptions. *Journal of Personality Disorders, 5,* 167–177. **(Chap 12)**

Gunderson, J. G., Ronningstam, E., & Smith, L. E. (1995). Narcissistic personality disorder. In W. J. Livesley (Ed.), *The DSM-IV personality disorders* (pp. 201–212). New York: Guilford Press. **(Chap 12)**

Gunderson, J. G., Zanarini, M. C., & Kisiel, C. L. (1995). Borderline personality disorder. In W. J. Livesley (Ed.), *The DSM-IV personality disorders* (pp. 141–157). New York: Guilford Press. **(Chap 12)**

Gur, R. E., & Pearlson, G. D. (1993). Neuroimaging in schizophrenia research. *Schizophrenia Bulletin, 19,* 337–353. **(Chap 13)**

Gureje, O., Simon, G. E., Ustun, T. B., & Goldberg, D. P. (1997). Somatization in cross-cultural perspective: A World Health Organization study in primary care. *American Journal of Psychiatry, 154,* 989–995. **(Chap 6)**

Gurvits, T. V., Shenton, M. E., Hokama, H. Ohta, H., Lasko, N. B., Gilbertson, M. W., Orr, S. P., Kikinis, R., Jolesz, F. A., McCarley, R. W., & Pitman, R. K. (1996). Magnetic resonance imaging study of hippocampal volume in chronic, combat-related posttraumatic stress disorder. *Biological Psychiatry, 40,* 1091–1099. **(Chap 5)**

Gusella, J. F., Wexler, N. S., Conneally, P. M., Naylor, S. L., Anderson, M. A., Tanzi, R. E., Watkins, P. C., Ottina, K., Wallace, M. R., Sakaguchi, A. Y., Young, A. B., Shoulson, I., Bonilla, E., & Martin, J. B. (1983). A polymorphic DNA marker genetically linked to Huntington's disease. *Nature, 306,* 234–239. **(Chap 15)**

Guttmacher, M. S., & Weihofen, H. (1952). *Psychiatry and the law.* New York: Norton. **(Chap 16)**

Guze, S. B. (1976). *Criminality and psychiatric disorders.* New York: Oxford University Press. **(Chap 12)**

Guze, S. B., Cloninger, C. R., Martin, R. L., & Clayton, P. J. (1986). A follow-up and family study of Briquet's syndrome. *British Journal of Psychiatry, 149,* 17–23. **(Chap 6)**

Haas, A. P., & Hendin, H. (1987). The meaning of chronic marijuana use among adults: A psychosocial perspective. *Journal of Drug Issues, 17,* 333–348. **(Chap 11)**

Haber, S. N., & Barchas, P. R. (1983). The regulatory effect of social rank on behavior after amphetamine administration. In P. R. Barchas (Ed.), *Social hierarchies: Essays toward a sociophysiological perspective* (pp. 119–132). Westport, CT: Greenwood Press. **(Chap 2)**

Hackett, T. P., & Cassem, N. H. (1973). Psychological adaptation to convalescence in myocardial infarction patients. In J. P. Naughton, H. K. Hellerstein, & I. C. Mohler (Eds.), *Exercise testing and exercise training in coronary heart disease.* New York: Academic Press. **(Chap 9)**

Hademenos, G. J. (1997). The biophysics of stroke. *American Scientist, 85,* 226–235. **(Chap 15)**

Hagnell, O., Franck, A., Grasbeck, A., Ohman, R., Ojesjo, L., Otterbeck, L., & Rorsman, B. (1992). Vascular dementia in the Lundby study: I. A prospective, epidemiological study of incidence and risk from 1957 to 1972. *Neuropsychobiology, 26,* 43–49. **(Chap 15)**

Haley, W. E., Roth, D. L., Coleton, M. I., Ford, G. R., West, C. A., Collins, R. P., & Isobe, T. L. (1996). Appraisal, coping and social support as mediators of well-being in black and white family caregivers of patients with Alzheimer's disease. *Journal of Consulting and Clinical Psychology, 64,* 121–129. **(Chap 15)**

Hall, G. C. N. (1995). Sexual offender recidivism revisited: A meta-analysis of recent treatment studies. *Journal of Consulting and Clinical Psychology, 63,* 802–809. **(Chap 10)**

Hall, S. M., Muñoz, R. F., & Reus, V. I. (1994). Cognitive-behavioral intervention increases abstinence rates for depressive-history smokers. *Journal of Consulting and Clinical Psychology, 62,* 141–146. **(Chap 11)**

Hall, S. M., Muñoz, R. F., Reus, V. I., & Sees, K. L. (1993). Nicotine, negative affect, and depression. *Journal of Consulting and Clinical Psychology, 61,* 761–767. **(Chap 11)**

Hall, S. M., Muñoz, R. F., Reus, V. I., Sees, K. L., Duncan, C., Humfleet, G. L., & Hartz, D. T. (1996). Mood management and nicotine gum in smoking treatment: A therapeutic contact and placebo-controlled study. *Journal of Consulting and Clinical Psychology, 64,* 1003–1009. **(Chap 11)**

Halmi, K. A., Eckert, E., LaDu, T. J., & Cohen, J. (1986). Anorexia nervosa: Treatment efficacy of cyproheptadine and anitriptyline. *Archives of General Psychiatry, 43,* 177–181. **(Chap 8)**

Hamer, D. H., Hu, S., Magnuson, V. L., Hu, N., & Pattatucci, A. M. (1993). A linkage between DNA markers on the X chromosome and male sexual orientation. *Science, 261,* 321–327. **(Chap 10)**

Hammen, C., Burge, D., Burney, E., & Adrian, C. (1990). Longitudinal study of diagnoses in children of women with unipolar and bipolar affective disorder. *Archives of General Psychiatry, 47*(12), 1112–1117. **(Chap 7)**

Hammen, C., Marks, T., Mayol, A., & de Mayo, R. (1985). Depressive self-schemas, life stress, and vulnerability to depression. *Journal of Abnormal Psychology, 94,* 308–319. **(Chap 7)**

Hammill, D. D. (1993). A brief look at the learning disability movement in the United States. *Journal of Learning Disabilities, 26,* 295–310. **(Chap 14)**

Hanley, I. (1986). Reality orientation in the care of the elderly patient with dementia—three case studies. In I. Hanley & M. Gilhooly (Eds.), *Psychological therapies for the elderly* (pp. 65–79). New York: New York University Press. **(Chap 15)**

Hanley, I. G., & Lusty, K. (1984). Memory aids in reality orientation: A single-case study. *Behavior Research and Therapy, 22,* 709–712. **(Chap 15)**

Hanna, G. L. (1995). Demographic and clinical features of obsessive-compulsive disorder in children and adolescents. *Journal of the American Academy of Child and Adolescent Psychiatry, 34,* 19–27. **(Chap 5)**

Hans, S. L., & Marcus, J. (1991). Neurobehavioral development of infants at risk for schizophrenia: A review. In E. F. Walker (Ed.), *Schizophrenia: A lifecourse developmental perspective* (pp. 33–57). New York: Academic Press. **(Chap 13)**

Hans, V. P. (1986). An analysis of public attitudes toward the insanity defense. *Criminology, 4,* 393–415. **(Chap 16)**

Hanson, R. K., Steffy, R. A., and Gauthier, R. (1993). Long-term recidivism of child molesters. *Journal of Consulting and Clinical Psychology, 61,* 646–652. **(Chap 10)**

Harbert, T. L., Barlow, D. H., Hersen, M., & Austin, J. B. (1974). Measurement and modification of incestuous behavior: A case study. *Psychological Reports, 34,* 79–86. **(Chap 10)**

Hardy, J. A., Mann, D. M., Wester, P., & Winblad, B. (1986). An integrative hypothesis concerning the pathogenesis and progression of Alzheimer's disease. *Neurobiology of Aging, 7,* 489–502. **(Chap 15)**

Hare, R. D. (1970). *Psychopathy: Theory and research.* New York: John Wiley. **(Chap 12)**

Hare, R. D. (1983). Diagnosis of antisocial personality disorder in two prison populations. *American Journal of Psychiatry, 140,* 887–890. **(Chap 12)**

Hare, R. D. (1991). *Manual for the Revised Psychopathy Checklist.* Toronto: Multi-Health Systems. **(Chap 12)**

Hare, R. D. (1993). *Without conscience: The disturbing world of the psychopaths among us.* New York: Pocket Books. **(Chap 12)**

Hare, R. D., McPherson, L. M., & Forth, A. E. (1988). Male psychopaths and their criminal careers. *Journal of Consulting and Clinical Psychology, 56,* 710–714. **(Chap 12)**

Harpur, T. J., Hare, R. D., & Hakstian, A. R. (1989). Two-factor conceptualization of psychopathy: Construct validity and assessment implications. *Psychological Assessment: A Journal of Consulting and Clinical Psychology, 1,* 6–17. **(Chap 12)**

Harris, G. T., Rice, M. E., Quinsey, V. L., Chapling, T. C. & Earls, C. (1992). Maximizing the discriminant validity of phallometric assessment data. *Psychological Assessment, 4,* 502–511. **(Chap 11)**

Harris, S., Handleman, J. S., Kristoff, B., Bass, L., & Gordon, R. (1990). Changes in language development among autistic and peer children in segregated and integrated preschool settings. *Journal of Autism and Developmental Disorders, 20,* 23–32. **(Chap 14)**

Harrow, M., Sands, J. R., Silverstein, M. L., & Goldberg, J. F. (1997). Course and outcome for schizophrenia versus other psychotic patients: A longitudinal study. *Schizophrenia Bulletin, 23,* 287–303. **(Chap 13)**

Hart, E. L., Lahey, B. B., Loeber, R., Applegate, B., & Frick, P. J. (1995). Developmental change in attention-deficit hyperactivity disorder in boys: A four-year longitudinal study. *Journal of Abnormal Child Psychology, 23,* 729–749. **(Chap 14)**

Hart, S. D., Forth, A. E., & Hare, R. D. (1990). Performance of criminal psychopaths on selected neuropsychological tests. *Journal of Abnormal Psychology, 99,* 374–379. **(Chap 12)**

Haslam, J. (1809/1976). *Observations on madness and melancholy.* New York: Arno Press. **(Chap 13)**

Hatfield, E., Cacioppo, J. T., & Rapson, R. L. (1994). *Emotional contagion.* Cambridge: Cambridge University Press. **(Chap 1)**

Hatfield, E., Sprecher, S., Pillemer, J. T., Greenberger, D, et al. (1988). Gender differences in what is desired in the sexual relationship. *Journal of Psychology and Human Sexuality, 1*(2), 39–52. **(Chap 10)**

Hathaway, S. R., & McKinley, J. C. (1943). *Manual for the Minnesota Multiphasic Personality Inventory.* New York: Psychological Corporation. **(Chap 3)**

Hauri, P. (1982). *The sleep disorders* (2nd ed.). Kalamazoo, MI: Upjohn Company. **(Chap 8)**

Hauri, P. J. (1991). Sleep hygiene, relaxation therapy, and cognitive interventions. In P. J. Hauri (Ed.), *Case studies in insomnia* (pp. 65–84). New York: Plenum Medical Books Company. **(Chap 8)**

Hawkins, R. P. (1979). The functions of assessment: Implications for selection and development of devices for assessing repertoires in clinical, educational, and other settings. *Journal of Applied Behavior Analysis, 12,* 501–516. **(Chap 3)**

Hawton, K. (1995). Treatment of sexual dysfunctions of sex therapy and other approaches. *British Journal of Psychiatry, 167,* 307–314. **(Chap 10)**

Hay, P. J., & Hall, A. (1991). The prevalence of eating disorders in recently admitted psychiatric in-patients. *British Journal of Psychiatry, 159,* 562–565. **(Chap 8)**

Hayes, S. C., Wilson, K. G., Gifford, E. V., Follette, V. M., & Strosahl, K. (1996). Experiential avoidance and behavior disorders: A functional dimensional approach. *Journal of Consulting and Clinical Psychology, 64* (6), 1152–1168. **(Chap 3)**

Haynes, S. G., & Matthews, K. A. (1988). Area review: Coronary-prone behavior: Continuing evolution of the concept: Review and methodologic critique of recent studies on type A behavior and cardiovascular disease. *Annals of Behavioral Medicine, 10*(2), 47–59. **(Chap 9)**

Haynes, S. G., Feinleib, M., & Kannel, W. B. (1980). The relationship of psychosocial factors to coronary heart disease in the Framingham study: III. Eight-year incidence of coronary heart disease. *American Journal of Epidemiology, 111,* 37–58. **(Chap 9)**

Hayward, G., Killen, J. D., Hammer, L. D., Litt, I. F., Wilson, D. M., Simmonds, B., & Taylor, C. B. (1992). Pubertal stage and panic attack history in sixth- and seventh-grade girls. *American Journal of Psychiatry, 149,* 1239–1243. **(Chap 5)**

Heaton, R. K. (1988). Introduction to special series. *Journal of Consulting and Clinical Psychology, 56,* 787–788. **(Chap 14)**

Heaton, R. K., Velin, R. A., McCutchan, A., Gulevich, S. J., Atkinson, J. H., Waalace, M. R., Godfrey, H. P. D., Kirson, D. A., & Grant, I. (1994). Neuropsychological impairment in human immunodeficiency virus-infection: Implications for employment. *Psychosomatic Medicine, 56,* 8–17. **(Chap 15)**

Heiman, J. R., & LoPiccolo, J. (1983). *Effectiveness of daily versus weekly therapy in the treatment of sexual dysfunction.* Unpublished manuscript, State University of New York at Stony Brook. **(Chap 10)**

Heiman, J. R., & LoPiccolo, J. (1988). *Becoming orgasmic: A sexual and personal growth program for women* (rev. ed.). New York: Prentice-Hall. **(Chap 10)**

Heimberg, R. G., Dodge, C. S., Hope, D. A., Kennedy, C. R., Zollo, L., & Becker, R. E. (1990). Cognitive behavioral group treatment for social phobia: Comparison to a credible placebo control. *Cognitive Therapy and Research, 14,* 1–23. **(Chap 5)**

Heimberg, R. G., Klosko, J. S., Dodge, C. S., & Shadick, R. (1989). Anxiety disorders, depression and attributional style: A further test of the specificity of depressive attributions. *Cognitive Therapy and Research, 13*(1), 21–36. **(Chap 7)**

Heimberg, R. G., Liebowitz, M. R., Hope, D. A., Schneier, F. R., Holt, C. S., Welkowitz, L., Juster, H. R., Campeas, R., Bruch, M. A., Cloitre, M. Fallon, B., & Klein, D. F. (1997). *Cognitive-behavioral group therapy versus phenelzine in social phobia: 12-week outcome.* Manuscript submitted for publication. **(Chap 5)**

Heimberg, R. G., Salzman, D. G., Holt, C. S., & Blendell, K. A. (1993). Cognitive-behavioral group treatment for social phobia: Effectiveness at five-year follow up. *Cognitive Therapy and Research, 17,* 325–339. **(Chap 5)**

Helmes, E., & Reddon, J. R. (1993). A perspective on developments in assessing psychopathology: A critical review of the MMPI and MMPI-2. *Psychological Bulletin, 113,* 453–471. **(Chap 3)**

Helweg-Larsen, M., & Collins, B. E. (1997). A social psychological perspective on the role of knowledge about AIDS in AIDS prevention. *Current*

Directions in Psychological Science, 6, 23–26. **(Chap 9)**

Helzer, J. E., & Canino, G. (1992). Comparative analyses of alcoholism in 10 cultural regions. In J. Helzer & G. Canino (Eds.), *Alcoholism—North America, Europe and Asia: A coordinated analysis of population data from ten regions* (pp. 131–155). London: Oxford University Press. **(Chap 11)**

Herault, J., Petit, E., Buchler, M., Martineau, J., Cherpi, C., Perrot, A., Sauvage, D., Barthelemy, C., Muh, J. P., & Lelord, G. (1994). Lack of association between three genetic markers of brain growth factors and infantile autism. *Biological Psychiatry, 35,* 281–283. **(Chap 14)**

Herbert, T. B., & Cohen, S. (1993). Depression and immunity: A meta-analytic review. *Psychological Bulletin, 113*(3), 472–486. **(Chap 9)**

Herdt, G. H. (1987). *The Sambia: Ritual and gender in New Guinea.* New York: Holt, Rinehart and Winston. **(Chap 10)**

Herdt, G. H., & Stoller, R. J. (1989). Commentary to "The socialization of homosexuality and heterosexuality in a non-western society." *Archives of Sexual Behavior, 18,* 31–34. **(Chap 10)**

Herman, D. B., Susser, E. S., Jandorf, L., Lavelle, J., & Bromet, E. J. (1998). Homelessness among individuals with psychotic disorders hospitalized for the first time: Findings from the Suffolk County Mental Health Project. *American Journal of Psychiatry, 155,* 109–113. **(Chap 16)**

Herman, J. L., Perry, C., & van der Kolk, B. A. (1989). Childhood trauma in borderline personality disorder. *American Journal of Psychiatry, 146,* 490–495. **(Chap 12)**

Hersen, M., Van Hasselt, V. B., & Goreczny, A. J. (1993). Behavioral assessment of anxiety in older adults. *Behavior Modification, 17*(2), 99–112. **(Chap 5)**

Herzog, D. B. (1988). Eating disorders. In A. M. Nicoli, Jr. (Ed.), *The new Harvard guide to psychiatry* (pp. 434–445). Boston: Harvard University Press. **(Chap 8)**

Hetherington, E. M., & Blechman, E. A. (Eds.). (1996). *Stress, coping and resiliency in children and families.* Mahwah, NJ: Erlbaum. **(Chap 2)**

Hetherington, E. M., Stanley-Hagan, M., & Anderson, E. R. (1989). Marital transitions: A child's perspective. *American Psychologist, 44,* 303–312. **(Chap 12)**

Higgins, S. T., Budney, A. J., Bickel, W. K., Hughes, J. R., Foerg, F., & Badger, G. (1993). Achieving cocaine abstinence with a behavioral approach. *American Journal of Psychiatry, 150,* 763–769. **(Chap 11)**

Hilgard, E. R. (1992). Divided consciousness and dissociation. *Consciousness & Cognition, 1,* 16–31. **(Chap 2)**

Hill, A. E., & Rosenbloom, L. (1986). Disintegrative psychosis of childhood: Teenage follow-up. *Developmental Medicine and Child Neurology, 28,* 34–40. **(Chap 14)**

Hillman, E., Kripke, D. F., & Gillin, J. C. (1990). Sleep restriction, exercise, and bright lights: Alternate therapies for depression. In A. Tasman, C. Kaufman, & S. Goldfinger (Eds.), *American Psychiatric Press review of psychiatry: Section I: Treatment of refractory affective disorder.* (R. Post, section ed.) (Vol. 9, pp. 132–144). Washington, DC: American Psychiatric Press. **(Chap 8)**

Hilts, P. J. (1994, March 10). Agency faults a U.C.L.A. study for suffering of mental patients. *New York Times,* A1. **(Chap 16)**

Himle, J. A., & Hill, E. M. (1991). Alcohol abuse & the anxiety disorders: Evidence from the Epidemiological Catchment Survey. *Journal of Anxiety Disorders, 5,* 237–245. **(Chap 5)**

Himmelfarb, S., & Murrell, S. A. (1984). The prevalence and correlation of anxiety symptoms in older adults. *Journal of Psychiatry, 116,* 159–167. **(Chap 5)**

Himmelhoch, J. M., & Thase, M. E. (1989). The vagaries of atypical depression. In J. E. Havells (Ed.), *Modern perspectives in the psychiatry of depression* (pp. 223–242). New York: Brunner/Mazel. **(Chap 7)**

Hindley, J. A. & Hill, E. M. (1991). Alcohol abuse and the anxiety disorders: Evidence from the Epidemiological Catchment Area Survey. *Journal of Anxiety Disorders, 5,* 237–245. **(Chap 5)**

Hindmarch, I. (1986). The effects of psychoactive drugs on car handling and related psychomotor ability: A review. In J. F. O'Hanlon & J. J. Gier (Eds.), *Drugs and driving* (pp. 71–79). London: Taylor and Francis. **(Chap 5)**

Hindmarch, I. (1990). Cognitive impairment with anti-anxiety agents: A solvable problem? In D. Wheatley (Ed.), *The anxiolytic jungle: Where, next?* (pp. 49–61). Chichester, England: John Wiley. **(Chap 5)**

Hinshelwood, J. A. (1896). A case of dyslexia: A peculiar form of word-blindness. *Lancet, 2,* 1451–1454. **(Chap 14)**

Hirsch, S., Cramer, P., & Bowen, J. (1992). The triggering hypothesis of the role of life events in schizophrenia. *British Journal of Psychiatry, 161,* 84–87. **(Chap 13)**

Hirschfeld, D. R., Rosenbaum, J. F., Biederman, J., Bolduc, E. A., Farone, S. V., Snidman, N., Reznick, J. S., & Kagan, J. (1992). Stable behavioral inhibition and its association with anxiety disorder. *Journal of the American Academy of Child and Adolescent Psychiatry, 31,* 103–111. **(Chap 5)**

Hirschfeld, R. M., Shea, M. T., & Weise, R. E. (1991). Dependent personality disorder: Perspectives for DSM-IV. *Journal of Personality Disorders, 5,* 135–149. **(Chap 12)**

Hirschfeld, R. M. A., Keller, M. M., Panico, S., Arons, B. S., Barlow, D., Davidoff, F., Endicott, J., Froom, J., Goldstein, M., Gorman, J. M., Guthrie, D., Marek R. G., Maurer, T. A., Meyer, R., Phillips, K., Ross, J., Schwenk, T. L., Sharfstein, S. S., Thase, M. E., & Wyatt, R. J. (1997). The National Depressive and Manic-Depressive Association consensus statement on the undertreatment of depression. *Journal of the American Medical Association, 277*(4), 333–340. **(Chap 7)**

Hirschfeld, R. M. A., Shea, M. T., & Weise, R. (1995). Dependent personality disorder. In W. J. Livesley (Ed.), *The DSM-IV personality disorders* (pp. 239–256). New York: Guilford Press. **(Chap 12)**

Hitchcock, P. B., & Mathews, A. (1992). Interpretation of bodily symptoms in hypochondriasis. *Behaviour Research and Therapy, 30*(3), 223–234. **(Chap 6)**

Hodapp, R. M., & Dykens, E. M. (1994). Mental retardation's two cultures of behavioral research. *American Journal of Mental Retardation, 98,* 675–687. **(Chap 14)**

Hoehn-Saric, R., McLeod, D. R., & Zimmerli, W. D. (1989). Somatic manifestations in women with generalized anxiety disorder: Psychophysiological responses to psychological stress. *Archives of General Psychiatry, 46,* 1113–1119. **(Chap 5)**

Hoek, H. W., Bartelds, A. I. M., Bosveld, J. J. F., van der Graaf, Y., Limpens, V. E. L., Maiwald, M., & Spaaij, C. J. K. (1995). Impact of urbanization on detection rates of eating disorders. *American Journal of Psychiatry, 152,* 1272–1278. **(Chap 8)**

Hofmann, S. G., & Barlow, D. H. (1996). Ambulatory psychophysiological monitoring: A potentially useful tool when treating panic relapse. *Cognitive and Behavioral Practice, 3,* 53–61. **(Chap 5)**

Hofmann, S. G., Lehman, C. L., & Barlow, D. H. (1997). How specific are specific phobias? *Journal of Behavior Therapy and Experimental Psychiatry, 28,* 233–240. **(Chap 5)**

Hogarty, G. E., Anderson, C. M., Reiss, D. J., Kornblith, S. J., Greenwald, D. P., Javna, C. D., & Madonia, M. J. (1986). Family psychoeducation, social skills training, and maintenance chemotherapy in the aftercare treatment of schizophrenia: I. One year effects of a controlled study on relapse and expressed emotion. *Archives of General Psychiatry, 43,* 633–642. **(Chap 13)**

Hogarty, G. E., Anderson, C. M., Reiss, D. J., Kornblith, S. J., Greenwald, D. P., Ulrich, R. F., Carter, M., & The Environmental-Personal Indicators in the Course of Schizophrenia (EPICS) Research Group. (1991). Family psychoeducation, social skills training, and maintenance chemotherapy in the aftercare treatment of schizophrenia.

Archives of General Psychiatry, 48, 340–347. **(Chap 13)**

Hogarty, G. E., Reis, D., Kornblith, S. J., Greenwald, D., Ulrich, R., & Carter, M. (1992). In reply. *Archives of General Psychiatry, 49,* 76–77. **(Chap 13)**

Hoge, S. K., Appelbaum, P. S., Lawler, T., Beck, J. C., Litman, R., Greer, A., Gutheil, T. G., & Kaplan, E. (1990). A prospective, multicenter study of patients' refusal of antipsychotic medication. *Archives of General Psychiatry, 47,* 949–956. **(Chap 13)**

Hokanson, J. E., Rubert, M. P., Welker, R. A., Hollander, G. R., & Hedeen, C. (1989). Interpersonal concomitants and antecedents of depression among college students. *Journal of Abnormal Psychology, 98*(3), 209–217. **(Chap 7)**

Holden, C. (1997). NIH to explore St. John's Wort. *Science, 278,* 391. **(Chap 7)**

Holden, C. (1997, December 5). World AIDS-the worst is still to come. *Science, 278,* 1715. **(Chap 9)**

Hollander, E., Liebowitz, M. R., Winchel, R., Klumker, A., & Klein, D. F. (1989). Treatment of body-dysmorphic disorder with serotonin reuptake blockers. *American Journal of Psychiatry, 1989,* 146, 768–770. **(Chap 6)**

Hollender, E., Cohen, L. J., Simeon, D., & Rosen, J. (1994). Fluvoxamine treatment of body dysmorphic disorder. *Journal of Clinical Psychopharmacology, 14,* 75–77. **(Chap 6)**

Hollien, H. (1990). The expert witness: Ethics and responsibilities. *Journal of Forensic Sciences, 35,* 1414–1423. **(Chap 16)**

Hollifield, M., Katon, W., Spain, D., & Pule, L. (1990). Anxiety and depression in a village in Lesotho, Africa: A comparison with the United States. *British Journal of Psychiatry, 156,* 343–350. **(Chap 5)**

Hollis, J. F., Connett, J. E., Stevens, V. J., & Greenlick, M. R. (1990). Stressful life events, Type A behavior, and the prediction of cardiovascular and total mortality over six years. *Journal of Behavioral Medicine, 13*(3), 263–280. **(Chap 9)**

Hollon, S. D. (1993). Review of psychosocial treatments for mood disorders. In D. L. Dunner (Ed.), *Current psychiatric therapy.* Philadelphia: W. B. Saunders. **(Chap 7)**

Hollon, S. D., & Beck, A. T. (1994). Cognitive and cognitive behavioral therapies. In A. E. Bergin & S. L. Garfield (Eds.), *Handbook of psychotherapy and behavior change: An empirical analysis* (4th ed., pp. 428–466). **(Chap 7)**

Hollon, S. D., DeRubeis, R. J., Evans, M. D., Wiener, M. J., Garvey, M. J., Grose, W. M., & Tuason, V. B. (1992). Cognitive therapy and pharmacotherapy for depression: Singly and in combination. *Archives of General Psychiatry, 49*(10), 772–781. **(Chap 7)**

Hollon, S. D., Kendall, P. C., & Lumry, A. (1986). Specificity of depressotypic cognitions in clinical depression. *Journal of Abnormal Psychology, 95,* 52–59. **(Chap 7)**

Hollon, S. D., Shelton, R. C., & Loosen, P. T. (1991). Cognitive therapy and pharmacotherapy for depression. *Journal of Consulting and Clinical Psychology, 59*(1), 88–99. **(Chap 7)**

Holm, V. A., & Varley, C. K. (1989). Pharmacological treatment of autistic children. In G. Dawson (Ed.), *Autism: Nature, diagnosis, and treatment* (pp. 386–404). New York: Guilford Press. **(Chap 14)**

Holroyd, K. A., & Penzien, D. B. (1986). Client variables in the behavioral treatment of current tension headache: A meta-analytic review. *Journal of Behavioral Medicine, 9,* 515–536. **(Chap 9)**

Holroyd, K. A., Andrasik, F., & Noble, J. (1980). A comparison of EMG biofeedback and a credible pseudotherapy in treating tension headache. *Journal of Behavioral Medicine, 3,* 29–39. **(Chap 9)**

Holroyd, K. A., Nash, J. M., Pingel, J. D., Cordingley, G. E., & Jerome, A. (1991). A comparison of pharmacological (amitriptyline HCL) and nonpharmacological (cognitive-behavioral) therapies for chronic tension headaches. *Journal of Consulting and Clinical Psychology, 59*(3), 387–393. **(Chap 9)**

Holzman, P. S., & Levy, D. L. (1977). Smooth pursuit eye movements and functional psychoses: A review. *Schizophrenia Bulletin, 3,* 15–27. **(Chap 13)**

Hook, E. B. (1982). Epidemiology of Down syndrome. In S. M. Pueschel & J. E. Rynders (Eds.), *Down syndrome: Advances in biomedicine and the behavioral sciences* (pp. 11–88). Cambridge, MA: Ware Press. **(Chap 14)**

Hooley, J. M. (1985). Expressed emotion: A review of the critical literature. *Clinical Psychology Review, 5,* 119–139. **(Chap 13)**

Hoon, E. F., Hoon, P. W., Rand, K. H., Johnson, J., Hall, N. R., Edwards, N. B. (1991). A psycho-behavioral model of genital herpes recurrence. *Journal of Psychosomatic Research, 35,* 25–36. **(Chap 9)**

Hoon, P. W., Wincze, J. P., & Hoon, E. F. (1977). A test of reciprocal inhibition: Are anxiety and sexual arousal in women mutually inhibitory? *Journal of Abnormal Psychology, 86,* 65–74. **(Chap 10)**

Hope, D. A., & Heimberg, R. G. (1993). Social phobia and social anxiety. In D. H. Barlow (Ed.), *Clinical handbook of psychological disorders: A step-by-step treatment manual* (2nd ed., pp. 99–136). New York: Guilford Press. **(Chap 5)**

Hope, D. A., & Heimberg, R. G. (1993). Social phobia. In C. Last & M. Hersen

(Eds.), *Adult behavior therapy casebook.* New York: Plenum Press. **(Chap 5)**

Horgan, M. M., Sparrow, M. D., & Brazeau, R. (1986). *Alcoholic beverage taxation and control policies* (6th ed.). Ottawa: Brewers Association of Canada. **(Chap 11)**

Horikoshi, H. (1980). Asrama: An Islamic psychiatric institution in West Java. *Social Science and Medicine, 14,* 157–165. **(Chap 4)**

Hornig, C. D., & McNally, R. J. (1995). Panic disorder and suicide attempt: A reanalysis of data from the Epidemiologic Catchment Area Study. *British Journal of Psychiatry, 167,* 76–79. **(Chap 5)**

Horowitz, M. (1986). *Stress response syndromes.* London: Jason Aronson. **(Chap 5)**

Horowitz, M. J., Siegel, B., Holen, A., Bonanno, G. A., Milbrath, C., & Stinson, C. H. (1997). Diagnostic criteria for complicated grief disorder. *American Journal of Psychiatry, 154,* 904–910. **(Chap 7)**

Horvath, T. B. (1975). Clinical spectrum and epidemiological features of alcohol dementia. In J. G. Rankin (Ed.), *Alcohol, drugs and brain damage* (pp. 1–16). Toronto: Toronto Addiction Center. **(Chap 15)**

Horwath, E., & Weissman, M. (1997). Epidemiology of anxiety disorders across cultural groups. In S. Friedman (Ed.), *Cultural issues in the treatment of anxiety* (pp. 21–39.) New York: Guilford Press. **(Chap 5)**

House, J. S., Landis, K. R., & Umberson, D. (1988). Social relationships and health. *Science, 241,* 540–545. **(Chaps 1, 2, 7)**

House, J. S., Robbins, C., & Metzner, H. M. (1982). The association of social relationships and activities with mortality: Prospective evidence from the Tecumseh community health study. *American Journal of Epidemiology, 116,* 123. **(Chap 2)**

Houston, B. K., Chesney, M. A., Black, G. W., Cates, D. S., & Hecker, M. H. L. (1992). Behavioral clusters and coronary heart disease risk. *Psychosomatic Medicine, 54*(4), 447–461. **(Chap 9)**

Howard, R., Castle, D., Wessely, S., & Murray, R. (1993). A comparative study of 470 cases of early-onset and late-onset schizophrenia. *British Journal of Psychiatry, 163,* 352–357. **(Chap 13)**

Hoyson, M., Jamieson, B., & Strain, P. S. (1984). Individualized group instruction of normally developing and autistic-like children: A description and evaluation of the LEAP curriculum model. *Journal of the Division of Early Childhood, 8,* 157–171. **(Chap 14)**

Hser, Y., Anglin, M. D., & Powers, K. (1993). A 24-year follow-up of California narcotics addicts. *Archives of General Psychiatry, 50,* 577–584. **(Chap 11)**

Hsiao, J. K., Colison, J., Bartko, J. J., Doran, A. R., Konicki, P. E., Potter, W. Z., & Pickar, D. (1993). Monoamine neurotransmitter interactions in drug-free and neuroleptic-treated schizophrenics. *Archives of General Psychiatry, 50,* 606–614. **(Chap 13)**

Hsu, L. K. G. (1988). The outcome of anorexia nervosa: A reappraisal. *Psychological Medicine, 18,* 807–812. **(Chap 8)**

Hsu, L. K. G. (1990). *Eating disorders.* New York: Guilford Press. **(Chap 8)**

Hsu, L. K. G., & Zimmer, B. (1988). Eating disorders in old age. *International Journal of Eating Disorders, 7,* 133–138. **(Chap 8)**

Hsu, L. M. (1989). Random sampling, randomization, and equivalence of contrasted groups in psychotherapy outcome research. *Journal of Consulting and Clinical Psychology, 57,* 131–137. **(Chap 4)**

Hubert, N. C., Jay, S. M., Saltoun, M., & Hayes, M. (1988). Approach-avoidance and distress in children undergoing preparation for painful medical procedures. *Journal of Clinical Child Psychology, 17,* 194–202. **(Chap 9)**

Hucker, S. J. (1997). Sexual sadism: Psychopathology and theory. In D. R. Laws & W. T. O'Donohue (Eds.), *Sexual deviance: Theory, assessment, and treatment* (pp. 194–209). New York: The Guilford Press. **(Chap 10)**

Hudson, J., Pope, H., Jonas, J. M., & Yurgelun-Todd, D. (1983). Family history study of anorexia nervosa and bulimia. *British Journal of Psychiatry, 142,* 133–138. **(Chap 8)**

Hughes, J. R. (1993). Pharmacotherapy for smoking cessation: Unvalidated assumptions, anomalies, and suggestions for future research. *Journal of Consulting and Clinical Psychology, 61,* 751–760. **(Chap 11)**

Hughes, J. R., Gust, S. W., Skoog, K., Keenan, R. M., & Fenwick, J. W. (1991). Symptoms of tobacco withdrawal: A replication and extension. *Archives of General Psychiatry, 48,* 52–61. **(Chap 11)**

Humphrey, L. L. (1986). Structural analysis of parent-child relationships in eating disorders. *Journal of Abnormal Psychology, 95,* 395–402. **(Chap 8)**

Humphrey, L. L. (1988). Relationships within subtypes of anorexic, bulimic, and normal families. *Journal of the American Academy of Child and Adolescent Psychiatry, 27,* 544–551. **(Chap 8)**

Humphrey, L. L. (1989). Observed family interactions among subtypes of eating disorders using structural analysis of social behavior. *Journal of Consulting and Clinical Psychology, 57,* 206–214. **(Chap 8)**

Hunicutt, C. P., & Newman, I. A. (1993). Adolescent dieting practices and nutrition knowledge. Health Values: *The Journal of Health Behavior, Education and Promotion, 17*(4), 35–40. **(Chap 8)**

Hunt, W. A. (1980). History and classification. In A. E. Kazdin, A. S. Bellack, &

M. Hersen (Eds.), *New perspectives in abnormal psychology.* New York: Oxford University Press. **(Chap 1)**

Huntington's Disease Collaborative Research Group. (1993). A novel gene containing a trinucleotide repeat that is expanded and unstable on Huntington's disease chromosomes. *Cell, 72,* 971–983. **(Chap 15)**

Hurt, S. W., Schnurr, P. P., Severino, S. K., Freeman, E. W., Gise, L. H., Rivera-Tovar, A., & Steege, J. F. (1992). Late luteal phase dysphoric disorder in 670 women evaluated for premenstrual complaints. *American Journal of Psychiatry, 149,* 525–530. **(Chap 3)**

Hussian, R. A., & Brown, D. C. (1987). Use of two dimensional grid patterns to limit hazardous ambulation in demented patients. *Journal of Gerontology, 42,* 558–560. **(Chap 14)**

Hyler, S. E., Williams, J. B. W., & Spitzer, R. L. (1982). Reliability in the DSM-III field trials: Interview v. case summary. *Archives of General Psychiatry, 39,* 1275–1278. **(Chap 3)**

Hymowitz, P., Frances, A., Jacobsberg, L., Sickles, M., & Hoyt, R. (1986). Neuroleptic treatment of schizotypal personality disorder. *Comprehensive Psychiatry, 27,* 267–271. **(Chap 12)**

Hynd, G. W., & Semrud-Clikeman, M. (1989). Dyslexia and brain morphology. *Psychological Bulletin, 106,* 447–482. **(Chap 14)**

Ickovics, J. R., & Rodin, J. (1992). Women and AIDS in the United States: Epidemiology, natural history, and mediating mechanisms. *Health Psychology, 11*(1), 1–16. **(Chap 9)**

Iguchi, M. Y., Griffiths, R. R., Bickel, W. K., Handelsman, L., Childress, A. R., & McLellan, A. T. (1990). Relative abuse liability of benzodiazepines in methadone maintenance populations in three cities. *Problems of drug dependence* (pp. 364–365). (NIDA Publication Number ADM90–1663). Washington, DC: U.S. Government Printing Office. **(Chap 11)**

Ikels, C. (1991). Aging and disability in China: Cultural issues in measurement and interpretation. *Social Science Medicine, 32,* 649–665. **(Chap 15)**

Imber, S. D., Glanz, L. M., Elkin, I., Sotsky, S. M., Boyer, J. L., & Leber, W. R. (1986). Ethical issues in psychotherapy research: Problems in a collaborative clinical trials study. *American Psychologist, 41,* 137–146. **(Chap 4)**

Imperato-McGinley, J., Peterson, R. E., Gautier, T., & Sturla, E. (1979). Androgens and the evolution of male-gender identity among male pseudohermaphrodites with 5-alpha-reductase deficiency. *The New England Journal of Medicine, 300,* 1233–1237. **(Chap 10)**

Insel, T. R. (1992). Toward a neuroanatomy of obsessive-compulsive disorder. *Archives*

of General Psychiatry, 49, 739–744. **(Chap 2)**

Insel, T. R. (Ed.). (1984). *New findings in obsessive-compulsive disorder.* Washington, DC: American Psychiatric Press. **(Chap 5)**

Insel, T. R., Champoux, M., Scanlan, J. M., & Suomi, S. J. (1986, May). *Rearing condition and response to anxiogenic drug.* Paper presented at the annual meeting of the American Psychiatric Association, Washington, DC. **(Chap 2)**

Ironson, G., Friedman, A., Klimas, N., Antoni, M., Fletcher, M. A., LaPerriere, A., Simoneau, J., & Schneiderman, N. (1994). Distress, denial, and low adherence to behavioral interventions predict faster disease progression in gay men infected with human immunodeficiency virus. *International Journal of Behavioral Medicine, 1,* 90–105. **(Chap 9)**

Ironson, G., Taylor, C. B., Boltwood, M., Bartzokis, T., Dennis, C., Chesney, M., Spitzer, S., & Segall, G. M. (1992). Effects of anger on left ventricular ejection fraction in coronary artery disease. *American Journal of Cardiology, 70,* 281–285. **(Chaps 2, 9)**

Irwin, M., Daniels, M., Smith, T. L., Bloom, E., & Weiner, H. (1987). Impaired natural killer cell activity during bereavement. *Brain, Behavior, and Immunity, 1,* 98–104. **(Chap 9)**

Irwin, M., Mascovich, A., Gillin, J. C., Willoughby, R., Pike, J., & Smith, T. L. (1994). Partial sleep deprivation reduces natural killer cell activity in humans. *Psychosomatic Medicine, 56,* 493–498. **(Chap 8)**

Ito, T. A., Miller, N., & Pollock, V. E. (1996). Alcohol and aggression: A meta-analysis on the moderating effects of inhibitory cues, triggering events, and self-focused attention. *Psychological Bulletin, 120,* 60–82. **(Chap 11)**

Izard, C. E. (1992). Basic emotions, relations among emotions, and emotion-cognition relations. *Psychological Review, 99*(3), 561–565. **(Chap 2)**

Jablensky, A. (1995). Schizophrenia: The epidemiological horizon. In S. R. Hirsch and D. R. Weinberger (Eds.), *Schizophrenia* (pp. 206–252). Oxford, England: Blackwell Science, Ltd. **(Chap 13)**

Jackson v. Indiana, 406 U.S. 715 (1972). **(Chap 16)**

Jacobi, W., & Winkler, H. (1927). Encephalographische Studien an chronischen Schizophrenen. *Arch. Psychiatr. Nervenk.r, 81,* 299–332. **(Chap 13)**

Jacobs, S. (1993). *Pathologic grief: Maladaptation to loss.* Washington, DC: American Psychiatric Press. **(Chap 7)**

Jacobs, S., Hansen, F., Berkman, L., Kasl, S., & Ostfeld, A. (1989). Depressions of bereavement. *Comprehensive Psychiatry, 30*(3), 218–224. **(Chap 7)**

Jacobsen, P. B., Bovbjerg, D. H., Schwartz, M. D., Andrykowski, M. A., Futterman, A. D., Gilewski, T., Norton, L., & Redd, W. H. (1993). Formation of food aversions in cancer patients receiving repeated infusions of chemotherapy. *Behaviour Research and Therapy, 31,* 739–748. **(Chap 9)**

Jacobsen, P. B., Bovbjerg, D. H., Schwartz, M. D., Hudis, C. A., Gilewski, T. A., & Norton, L. (1995). Conditioned emotional distress in women receiving chemotherapy for breast cancer. *Journal of Consulting and Clinical Psychology, 63,* 108–114. **(Chap 9)**

Jacobson, E. (1938). *Progressive relaxation.* Chicago: University of Chicago Press. **(Chap 9)**

Jacobson, N. S., & Hollon, S. D. (1996). Cognitive behavior therapy vs. pharmacotherapy: Now that the jury's returned its verdict, it's time to present the rest of the evidence. *Journal of Consulting and Clinical Psychology, 64,* 74–80. **(Chap 7)**

Jacobson, N. S., & Hollon, S. D. (1996). Prospects for future comparisons between drugs and psychotherapy: Lessons from the CBT vs. pharmacotherapy exchange. *Journal of Consulting and Clinical Psychology, 64,* 104–108. **(Chap 7)**

Jacobson, N. S., & Truax, P. (1991). Clinical significance: A statistical approach to defining meaningful change in psychotherapy research. *Journal of Consulting and Clinical Psychology, 59,* 12–19. **(Chap 4)**

Jacobson, N. S., Dobson, K., Fruzzetti, A. E., Schmaling, K. B., & Salusky, S. (1991). Marital therapy as a treatment for depression. *Journal of Consulting and Clinical Psychology, 59*(4), 547–557. **(Chap 7)**

Jacobson, N. S., Dobson, K. S., Truax, P. A., Addis, M. E., Koerner, K., Gollan, J. K., Gortner, E., & Prince, S. E. (1996). A component analysis of cognitive-behavioral treatment for depression. *Journal of Consulting and Clinical Psychology, 64,* 295–304. **(Chap 7)**

Jacobson, N. S., Fruzzetti, A. E., Dobson, K., Whisman, M., & Hops, H. (1993). Couple therapy as a treatment for depression: II. The effects of relationship quality and therapy on depressive relapse. *Journal of Consulting and Clinical Psychology, 61*(3), 516–519. **(Chap 7)**

Jaffe, A. J., Rounsaville, B., Chang, G., Schottenfeld, R. S., Meyer, R. E., & O'Malley, S. O. (1996). Naltrexone, relapse prevention, and supportive therapy with alcoholics: An analysis of patient treatment matching. *Journal of Consulting and Clinical Psychology, 64,* 1044–1053. **(Chap 11)**

Jaffe, J. H., Knapp, C. M., & Ciraulo, D. A. (1997). Opiates: Clinical aspects. In J. H. Lowinson, P. Ruiz, R. B. Millman, & J. G. Langrod (Eds.), *Substance abuse: A comprehensive textbook* (pp. 158–166). Baltimore: Williams & Wilkins. **(Chap 11)**

Jamison, K. R. (1986). Suicide and bipolar disorders. *Annual New York Academy of Science, 487,* 301–315. **(Chap 7)**

Jamison, K. R. (1989). Mood disorders and patterns of creativity in British writers and artists. *Psychiatry, 52,* 125–134. **(Chap 7)**

Jamison, R. N., & Virts, K. L. (1990). The influence of family support on chronic pain. *Behaviour Research and Therapy, 28*(4), 283–287. **(Chap 9)**

Jamner, L. D., Shapiro, D., Goldstein, I. B., & Hug, R. (1991). Ambulatory blood pressure and heart rate in paramedics: Effects of cynical hostility and defensiveness. *Psychosomatic Medicine, 53,* 393–406. **(Chap 9)**

Jaspers, K. (1963). *General psychopathology* (J. Hoenig & M. W. Hamilton, Trans.). Manchester, England: Manchester University Press. **(Chap 13)**

Jay, S. M., Elliott, C. H., Ozolins, M., Olson, R. A., & Pruitt, S. D. (1985). Behavioral management of children's distress during painful medical procedures. *Behaviour Research and Therapy, 23*(5), 513–520. **(Chap 9)**

Jellinek, E. M. (1946). Phases in the drinking histories of alcoholics. *Quarterly Journal of Studies on Alcohol, 7,* 1–88. **(Chap 11)**

Jellinek, E. M. (1952). Phases of alcohol addiction. *Quarterly Journal of Studies on Alcohol, 13,* 673–684. **(Chap 11)**

Jellinek, E. M. (1960). *The disease concept of alcohol.* New Brunswick, NJ: Hillhouse Press. **(Chap 11)**

Jenike, M. A., Baer, L., & Minichiello, W. E. (Eds.). (1986). *Obsessive-compulsive disorders: Theory and management.* Littleton, MA: PSG Publishing. **(Chap 5)**

Jenike, M. A., Baer, L., Ballantine, H. T., Martuza, R. L., Tynes, S., Giriunas, I., Buttolph, M. L., & Cassem, N. H. (1991). Cingulotomy for refractory obsessive-compulsive disorder: A long-term follow-up of 33 patients. *Archives of General Psychiatry, 48,* 548–555. **(Chaps 2, 5)**

Jenkins, J. H., & Karno, M. (1992). The meaning of expressed emotion: Theoretical issues raised by cross-cultural research. *American Journal of Psychiatry, 149,* 9–21. **(Chap 13)**

Jenkins, J. H., Kleinman, A., & Good, B. J. (1990). Cross-cultural studies of depression. In J. Becker & A. Kleinman (Eds.), *Psychosocial aspects of depression.* Hillsdale, NJ: Lawrence Erlbaum. **(Chap 7)**

Jensen, E. J., Schmidt, E., Pedersen, B., & Dahl, R. (1991). Effect on smoking cessation of silver acetate, nicotine and ordinary chewing gum. *Psychopharmacology, 104,* 470–474. **(Chap 11)**

Jensen, G. B., & Pakkenberg, B. (1993). Do alcoholics drink their neurons away? *Lancet, 342,* 1201–1204. **(Chap 11)**

Jensen, M. P., Turner, J. A., Romano, J. M., & Karoly, P. (1991). Coping with chronic pain: A critical review of the literature. *Pain, 47,* 249–283. **(Chap 9)**

Jilek, W. G. (1982). Altered states of consciousness in North American Indian ceremonials. *Ethos, 10*(4), 326–343. **(Chap 6)**

Jobst, K. A., Hindley, N. J., King, E., & Smith, A. D. (1994). The diagnosis of Alzheimer's disease: A question of image? *Journal of Clinical Psychiatry, 55,* 22–31. **(Chap 15)**

Jockin, V., McGue, M., & Lykken, D. T. (1996). Personality and divorce: A genetic analysis. *Journal of Personality and Social Psychology, 71,* 288–299. **(Chap 2)**

Joffe, R., Segal, Z., & Singer, W. (1996). Change in thyroid hormone levels following response to cognitive therapy for major depression. *American Journal of Psychiatry, 153,* 411–413. **(Chap 7)**

Johns, M. B. et al. (1987). Primary care and health promotion: A model for preventive medicine. *American Journal of Preventive Medicine, 3*(6), 351. **(Chap 9)**

Johnson, A. M., Wadsworth, J., Wellings, K., Bradshaw, S., & Field, J. (1992). Sexual lifestyles and HIV risk. *Nature, 360,* 410–412. **(Chap 10)**

Johnson, B. A. (1991). Cannabis. In I. B. Glass (Ed.), *International handbook of addiction behaviour* (pp. 69–76). London: Tavistock/Routledge. **(Chap 10)**

Johnson, D. L. (1989). Schizophrenia as a brain disease: Implications for psychologists and families. *American Psychologist, 44,* 553–555. **(Chap 13)**

Johnson, J., Weissman, M. M., & Klerman, G. L. (1990). Panic disorder, comorbidity and suicide attempts. *Archives of General Psychiatry, 47,* 805–808. **(Chap 5)**

Johnson, J. M., Baumgart, D., Helmstetter, E., & Curry, C. (1996). *Augmenting basic communication in natural contexts.* Baltimore, MD: Paul H. Brookes. **(Chap 14)**

Johnson, R. E., Nahmias, A. J., Magder, L. S., Lee, F. K., Brooks, C. A., & Snowden, C. B. (1989). A seroepidemiologic survey of the prevalence of herpes simplex virus type 2 infection in the United States. *New England Journal of Medicine, 321,* 7–12. **(Chap 9)**

Johnson, S. L., & Miller, I. (1997). Negative life events and time to recovery from episodes of bipolar disorder. *Journal of Abnormal Psychology, 106*(3), 449–457. **(Chap 7)**

Johnson, S. L., & Roberts, J. E. (1995). Life events and bipolar disorder: Implications from biological theories. *Psychological Bulletin, 117*(3), 434–449. **(Chap 7)**

Johnston, C., Pelham, W. E., & Murphy, H. A. (1985). Peer relationships in ADHD and normal children: A developmental analysis of peer and teacher ratings. *Journal of Abnormal Child Psychology, 13,* 89–100. **(Chap 14)**

Johnston, D. W. (1997). Cardiovascular disease. In D. M. Clark & C. G. Fairburn (Eds.), *Science and practice of cognitive behaviour therapy* (pp. 341–358). Oxford, U. K.: Oxford University Press. **(Chap 9)**

Joiner, T. E. (1997). Shyness and low social support as interactive diatheses, with loneliness as mediator: Testing an interpersonal-personality view of vulnerability to depressive symptoms. *Journal of Abnormal Psychology, 106*(3), 386–394. **(Chap 7)**

Joiner, T. E., & Rudd, D. M. (1996). Toward a categorization of depression-related psychological constructs. *Cognitive Therapy and Research, 20,* 51–68. **(Chap 7)**

Joiner, T. F., Jr., Heatherton, T. F., & Keel, P. K. (1997). Ten year stability and predictive validity of five bulimia-related indicators. *American Journal of Psychiatry, 154,* 1133–1138. **(Chap 8)**

Jones, B. E., & Gray, B. A. (1986). Problems in diagnosing schizophrenia and affective disorders in Blacks. *Hospital and Community Psychiatry, 37,* 61–65. **(Chap 13)**

Jones, D. J., Fox, M. M., Babigan, H. M., & Hutton, H. E. (1980). Epidemiology of anorexia nervosa in Monroe County, New York: 1960–1976. *Psychosomatic Medicine, 42,* 551–558. **(Chap 8)**

Jones, J. C., & Barlow, D. H. (1990). The etiology of posttraumatic stress disorder. *Clinical Psychology Review, 10,* 299–328. **(Chap 5)**

Jones, K. L., & Smith, D. W. (1973). Recognition of the Fetal Alcohol Syndrome in early infancy. *Lancet, 2,* 999–1001. **(Chap 11)**

Jones, M. C. (1924a). The elimination of children's fears. *Journal of Experimental Psychology, 7,* 383–390. **(Chap 1)**

Jones, M. C. (1924b). A laboratory study of fear. The case of Peter. *Pedagogical Seminary, 31,* 308–315. **(Chap 1)**

Jones, R. T., & Haney, J. I. (1984). A primary preventive approach to the acquisition and maintenance of fire emergency responding: Comparison of external and self-instruction strategies. *Journal of Community Psychology, 12*(2), 180–191. **(Chap 9)**

Jones, R. T., & Kazdin, A. E. (1980). Teaching children how and when to make emergency telephone calls. *Behavior Therapy, 11*(4), 509–521. **(Chap 9)**

Judd, L. L., Akiskal, H. S., Maser, J. D., Zeller, P. J., Endicott, J., Coryell, W., Paulus, M. P., Kunovac, J. L., Leon, A. C., Mueller, T., Rie, J. A., & Keller, M. B. (in press). A prospective 12-year study of subsyndromal and syndromal depressive symptomatology in 431 patients with unipolar major depressive disorder. *Archives of General Psychiatry.* **(Chap 7)**

Junginger, J. (1997). Fetishism: Assessment and treatment. In D. R. Laws & W. O'Donohue (Eds.), *Sexual deviance: Theory, assessment and treatment* (pp.92–110). New York: Guilford Press. **(Chap 10)**

Kafka, M. P. (1997). A monoamine hypothesis for the pathophysiology of paraphilic disorders. *Archives of Sexual Behavior, 26,* 343–358. **(Chap 10)**

Kagan, J., & Snidman, N. (1991). Infant predictors of inhibited and uninhibited profiles. *Psychological Science, 2,* 40–44. **(Chap 5)**

Kagan, J., Reznick, J. S., & Snidman, N. (1988). Biological bases of childhood shyness. *Science, 240,* 167–171. **(Chaps 5, 13)**

Kahn, R. S., Davidson, M., Knott, P., Stern, R. G., Apter, S., & Davis, K. L. (1993). Effect of neuroleptic medication on cerebrospinal fluid monoamine metabolite concentrations in schizophrenia: Serotonin-dopamine interactions as a target for treatment. *Archives of General Psychiatry, 50,* 599–605. **(Chap 13)**

Kalant, H. (1989). The nature of addiction: An analysis of the problem. In A. Goldstein (Ed.), *Molecular and cellular aspects of the drug addictions* (pp. 1–28). New York: Springer-Verlag. **(Chap 11)**

Kales, A., Soldatos, C. R., Bixler, E. O., Ladda, R. L., Charney, D. S., Weber, G., & Schweitzer, P. K. (1980). Hereditary factors in sleepwalking and night terrors. *British Journal of Psychiatry, 137,* 111–118. **(Chap 8)**

Kales, A., Soldatos, C. R., Caldwell, A., Kales, J., Humphrey, F., Charney, D., & Schweitzer, P. (1980). Somnabulism: Clinical characteristics and personality patterns. *Archives of General Psychiatry, 37,* 1406–1410. **(Chap 8)**

Kallmann, F. J. (1938). *The genetics of schizophrenia.* New York: Augustin. **(Chap 13)**

Kalus, O., Bernstein, D. P., & Siever, L. J. (1993). Schizoid personality disorder: A review of current status and implications for DSM-IV. *Journal of Personality Disorders, 7,* 43–52. **(Chap 12)**

Kalus, O., Berstein, D. P., & Siever, L. J. (1995). Paranoid personality disorder. In W. J. Livesley (Ed.), *The DSM-IV personality disorders* (pp. 58–70). New York: Guilford Press. **(Chap 12)**

Kandel, D. B., Wu, P., & Davies, M. (1994). Maternal smoking during pregnancy and smoking by adolescent daughters. *American Journal of Public Health, 84,* 1407–1413. **(Chap 11)**

Kandel, E. R. (1983). From metapsychology to molecular biology: Explorations into the nature of anxiety. *American Journal of Psychiatry, 140,* 1277–1293. **(Chap 2)**

Kandel, E. R., Jessell, T. M., & Schacter, S. (1991). Early experience and the fine tuning of synaptic connections. In E. R. Kandel, J. H. Schwartz, T. M. Jessell, (Eds.), *Principles of neural science* (3rd ed., pp. 945–958). New York: Elsevier. **(Chap 2)**

Kane, J., Honigfeld, G., Singer, J., & Meltzer, H. Y. (1988). Clozapine for the treatment resistant schizophrenic. *Archives of General Psychiatry, 45,* 789–796. **(Chap 13)**

Kanigel, R. (1988, October/November). Nicotine becomes addictive. *Science Illustrated,* pp. 12–14, 19–21. **(Chap 11)**

Kanner, L. (1943). Autistic disturbances of affective contact. *Nervous Child, 2,* 217–250. **(Chap 14)**

Kanner, L. (1949). Problems of nosology and psychodynamics of early infantile autism. *American Journal of Orthopsychiatry, 19,* 416–426. **(Chap 14)**

Kansas v. Hendricks, 117 S. Ct. 2072 (1997). **(Chap 16)**

Kaplan, H. S. (1979). *Disorders of sexual desire.* New York: Brunner/Mazel. **(Chap 10)**

Kaplan, H. S. (1987). *Sexual aversion, sexual phobias, and panic disorder.* New York: Brunner/Mazel. **(Chap 10)**

Kaplan, M. (1983). A woman's view of DSM-III. *American Psychologist, 38,* 786–792. **(Chap 12)**

Kaplan, N. M. (1980). The control of hypertension: A therapeutic breakthrough. *American Scientist, 68,* 537–545. **(Chap 9)**

Karno, M., & Golding, J. M. (1991). Obsessive-compulsive disorder. In L. N. Robins & D. A. Regier (Eds.), *Psychiatric disorders in America: The epidemiologic catchment area study* (pp. 204–219). New York: Free Press. **(Chap 5)**

Kashani, J. H., Hoeper, E. W., Beck, N. C., & Corcoran, C. M. (1987). Personality, psychiatric disorders, and parental attitude among a community sample of adolescents. *Journal of the American Academy of Child and Adolescent Psychiatry, 26*(6), 879–885. **(Chap 7)**

Kasindorf, J. (1988, May 2). The real story of Billie Boggs: Was Koch right—Or the civil libertarians? *New York,* 36–44. **(Chap 17)**

Kass, D. J., Silvers, F. M., & Abrams, G. M. (1972). Behavioral group treatment of hysteria. *Archives of General Psychiatry, 26,* 42–50. **(Chap 12)**

Katon, W. (1993). Somatization disorder, hypochondriasis, and conversion disorder. In D. L. Dunner (Ed.), *Current psychiatric therapy* (pp. 314–320). Philadelphia: W. B. Saunders. **(Chap 6)**

Katon, W., & Roy-Byrne, P. P. (1991). Mixed anxiety and depression. *Journal of Abnormal Psychology, 100*(3), 337–345. **(Chap 3)**

Katon, W., Lin, E., Von Korff, M., Russo, J., Lipscomb, P., & Bush, T. (1991). Somatization: A spectrum of severity. *American Journal of Psychiatry, 148,* 34–40. **(Chap 6)**

Katz, I. R. (1993). Delirium. In D. L. Dunner (Ed.), *Current psychiatric therapy* (pp. 65–73). Philadelphia: W. B Saunders. **(Chap 14)**

Katz, I. R., Leshen, E., Kleban, M., & Jethanandani, V. (1989). Clinical features of depression in the nursing home. *International Psychogeriatrics, 1,* 5–15. **(Chap 7)**

Katz, J. L., Weiner, H., Gallagher, T. F., & Hellman, I. (1970). Stress, distress, and ego defenses: Psychoendocrine response to impending breast tumor biopsy. *Archives of General Psychiatry, 23,* 131–142. **(Chap 9)**

Kavale, K. A., & Forness, S. R. (1983). Hyperactivity and diet treatment: A meta-analysis of the Feingold Hypothesis. *Journal of Learning Disabilities, 16,* 324–330. **(Chap 14)**

Kawabata, S., Higgins, G. A., & Gordon, J. W. (1991). Amyloid plaques, neurofibrillary tangles and neuronal loss in brains of transgenic mice overexpressing a C-terminal fragment of human amyloid precursor protein. *Nature, 354,* 476–478. **(Chap 15)**

Kay, D. W. K. (1991). The epidemiology of dementia: A review of recent work. *Review of Clinical Gerontology, 1,* 55–66. **(Chap 15)**

Kaye, W. H., Weltzin, T. E., Hsu, L. K. G., McConaha, C. W., & Bolton, B. (1993). Amount of calories retained after binge eating and vomiting. *American Journal of Psychiatry, 150*(6), 969–971. **(Chap 8)**

Kaysen, S. (1993). *Girl, interrupted.* New York: Turtle Bay Books. **(Chap 12)**

Kazdin, A. E. (1979). Unobtrusive measures in behavioral assessment. *Journal of Applied Behavior Analysis, 12,* 713–724. **(Chap 3)**

Kazdin, A. E. (1981). Drawing valid inferences from case studies. *Journal of Consulting and Clinical Psychology, 49,* 183–192. **(Chap 4)**

Kazdin, A. E. (1983). Hopelessness, depression, and suicidal intent among psychiatrically disturbed inpatient children. *Journal of Consulting and Clinical Psychology, 51*(4), 504–510. **(Chap 7)**

Kazdin, A. E., & Mazurick, J. L. (1994). Dropping out of child psychotherapy: Distinguishing early and late dropouts over the course of treatment. *Journal of Consulting and Clinical Psychology, 62,* 1069–1074. **(Chap 12)**

Kazdin, A. E., Mazurick, J. L., & Bass, D. (1993). Risk for attrition in treatment of antisocial children and families. *Journal of Child Clinical Psychology, 22,* 2–16. **(Chap 12)**

Kearney, C. A., Albano, A. M., Eisen, A. R., Allan, W. D., & Barlow, D. H. (1997). The phenomenologoy of panic disorder in youngsters: An empirical study of a clinical sample. *Journal of Anxiety Disorders, 11*(10), 49–62. **(Chap 5)**

Keefe, F. J., Crisson, J., Urban, B. J., & Williams, D. A. (1990). Analyzing chronic low back pain: The relative contribution of pain coping strategies. *Pain, 40,* 293–301. **(Chap 9)**

Keefe, F. J., Dunsmore, J., & Burnett, R. (1992). Behavioral and cognitive-behavioral approaches to chronic pain: Recent advances and future directions. Special issue: Behavioral medicine: An update for the 1990s. *Journal of Consulting and Clinical Psychology, 60*(4), 528–536. **(Chap 9)**

Keel, P. K., & Mitchell, J. E. (1997) Outcome in bulimia nervosa. *American Journal of Psychiatry, 154,* 313–321. **(Chap 8)**

Keilitz, I. (1987). Researching and reforming the insanity defense. *Rutgers Law Review, 39,* 289–322. **(Chap 16)**

Keilitz, I., & Fulton, J. P. (1984). *The insanity defense and its alternatives: A guide for policymakers.* Williamsburg, VA: National Center for State Courts. **(Chap 16)**

Keitner, G. I., Ryan, C. E., Miller, I. W., Kohn, R., Bishop, D. S., & Epstein, N. B. (1995). Role of the family in recovery and major depression. *American Journal of Psychiatry, 152,* 1002–1008. **(Chap 7)**

Keller, M. B., & Wunder, J. (1990). Bipolar disorder in childhood. In M. Hersen & C. G. Last (Eds.), *Handbook of child and adult psychopathology: A longitudinal perspective.* Elmsford, NY: Pergamon Press. **(Chap 7)**

Keller, M. B., Baker, L. A., & Russell, C. W. (1993). Classification and treatment of dysthymia. In D. L. Dunner (Ed.), *Current psychiatric therapy.* Philadelphia: W. B. Saunders. **(Chap 7)**

Keller, M. B., Hirschfeld, R. M. A., & Hanks, D. L. (1997). Double depression: A distinctive subtype of unipolar depression. *Journal of Affective Disorders, 45,* 65–73. **(Chap 7)**

Keller, M. B., Klein, D. N., Hirschfeld, R. M. A., Kocsis, J. H., McCullough, J. P., Miller, I., First, M. B., Holzer, C. P., III, Keitner, G. I., Marin, D. B., and Shea, T. (1995). Results of the DSM-IV mood disorders field trial. *American Journal of Psychiatry, 152,* 843–849. **(Chap 7)**

Keller, M. B., Lavori, P. W., Endicott, J., Coryell, W., & Klerman, G. L. (1983). "Double depression": Two year follow-up. *American Journal of Psychiatry, 140*(6), 689–694. **(Chap 7)**

Keller, M. B., Lavori, P. W., Mueller, T. I., Endicott, J., Coryell, W., Hirschfeld, R. M. A., & Shea, T. (1992). Time to recovery, chronicity, and levels of psychopathology in major depression. *Archives of General Psychiatry, 49,* 809–816. **(Chap 7)**

Kellner, R. (1985). Functional somatic symptoms and hypochondriasis: A survey of empirical studies. *Archives of General Psychiatry, 42,* 821–833. **(Chap 6)**

Kellner, R. (1986). *Somatization and hypochondriasis.* New York: Praeger-Greenwood. **(Chap 6)**

Kellner, R. (1992). Diagnosis and treatments of hypochondriacal syndromes. *Psychosomatics, 33*(3), 278–279. **(Chap 6)**

Kellner, R., Hernandez, J., & Pathak, D. (1992). Hypochondriacal fears and beliefs, anxiety, and somatization. *British Journal of Psychiatry, 160,* 525–532. **(Chap 6)**

Kelly, J. A. (1995). *Changing HIV risk behavior: Practical strategies.* New York: Guilford Press. **(Chaps 7, 9)**

Kelly, J. A., Murphy, D. A., Sikkema, K. J., McAuliffe, T. L., Roffman, R. A., Solomon, L. J., Winett, R. A., Kalichman, S. C., & the Community HIV Prevention Research Collaborative (1997). Randomised, controlled community-level HIV-prevention intervention for sexual-risk behaviour among homosexual men in U.S. cities. *The Lancet, 350,* 1500–1505. **(Chap 10)**

Kelly, M. P., Strassberg, D. S., & Kircher, J. R. (1990). Attitudinal and experiential correlates of anorgasmia. *Archives of Sexual Behavior, 19*(2), 165–177. **(Chap 10)**

Kelsoe, J. R. (1997). The genetics of bipolar disorder. *Psychiatry Annual, 27,* 285–292. **(Chap 7)**

Kelsoe, J. R., Ginns, E. I., Egeland, J. A., Gerhard, D. S., Goldstein, A. M., Bale, S. J., Pauls, D. J., Long, R. T., Kidd, K. K., Conte, G., Housman, D. E., & Paul, S. M. (1989). Reevaluation of the linkage relationship between chromosome 11p loci and the gene for bipolar affective disorder in the Old Order Amish. *Nature, 342,* 238–243. **(Chap 7)**

Kemeny, M. E., Cohen, F., Zegans, L. S., & Conant, M. A. (1989). Psychological and immunological predictors of genital herpes recurrence. *Psychosomatic Medicine, 51,* 195–208. **(Chap 9)**

Kemp, S. (1990). *Medieval psychology.* New York: Greenwood Press. **(Chap 1)**

Kendall, P. C., Flannery-Schroeder, E., Panichelli-Mindell, M., Southam-Gerow, M., Henin, A., & Warman, M. (1997). Therapy for youths with anxiety disorder: A second randomized clinical trial. *Journal of Consulting and Clinical Psychology, 65,* 366–380. **(Chap 5)**

Kendell, R. (1985). Emotional and physical factors in the genesis of puerperal mental disorders. *Journal of Psychosomatic Research, 29,* 3–11. **(Chap 7)**

Kendler, K. S. (1982). Demography of paranoid psychosis (delusional disorder): A review and comparison with schizophrenia and affective illness. *Archives of General Psychiatry, 39,* 890–902. **(Chap 13)**

Kendler, K. S. (1995). Genetic epidemiology in psychiatry. *Archives of General Psychiatry, 52,* 895–899. **(Chap 2)**

Kendler, K. S., & Diehl, S. R. (1993). The genetics of schizophrenia: A current, genetic-epidemiologic perspective. *Schizophrenia Bulletin, 19,* 261–285. **(Chap 13)**

Kendler, K. S., & Gruenberg, A. M. (1982). Genetic relationship between paranoid personality disorder and the "schizophrenic spectrum" disorders. *American*

Journal of Psychiatry, 139, 1185–1186. **(Chap 12)**

Kendler, K. S., Heath, A. C., Neale, M. C., Kessler, R. C., & Eaves, L. J. (1992). A population-based twin study of alcoholism in women. *Journal of the American Medical Association, 268,* 1877–1882. **(Chap 11)**

Kendler, K. S., Kessler, R. C., Neale, M. C., Heath, A. C., & Eaves, L. J. (1993). The prediction of major depression in women: Toward an integrated etiologic model. *American Journal of Psychiatry, 150,* 1139–1148. **(Chap 4)**

Kendler, K. S., Kessler, R. C., Walters, E. E., MacLean, C., Neale, M. C., Heath, A. C., & Eaves, L. J. (1995). Stressful life events, genetic liability, and onset of an episode of major depression in women. *American Journal of Psychiatry, 152,* 833–842. **(Chap 2)**

Kendler, K. S., MacLean, C., Neale, M., Kessler, R., Heath, A., & Eaves, L. (1991). The genetic epidemiology of bulimia nervosa. *American Journal of Psychiatry, 148*(12), 1627–1637. **(Chap 8)**

Kendler, K. S., McGuire, M., Gruenberg, A. M., O'Hare, A., Spellman, M., & Walsh, D. (1993). The Roscommon Family Study: I. Methods, diagnosis of probands, and risk of schizophrenia in relatives. *Archives of General Psychiatry, 50,* 527–540. **(Chap 13)**

Kendler, K. S., Neale, M. C., Heath, A. C., Kessler, R. C., & Eaves, L. J. (1994). A twin-family study of alcoholism in women. *American Journal of Psychiatry, 151,* 707–715. **(Chap 11)**

Kendler, K. S., Neale, M. C., Kessler, R. C., Heath, A. C., & Eaves, L. J. (1992a). Generalized anxiety disorder in women: A population-based twin study. *Archives of General Psychiatry, 49,* 267–272. **(Chap 5)**

Kendler, K. S., Neale, M. C., Kessler, R. C., Heath, A. C., & Eaves, L. J. (1992b). Major depression and generalized anxiety disorder: Same genes, (partly) different environments? *Archives of General Psychiatry, 49,* 716–722. **(Chap 7)**

Kendler, K. S., Neale, M. C., MacLean, C. J., Heath, A. C., Eaves, L. J., & Kessler, R. C. (1993). Smoking and major depression: A causal analysis. *Archives of General Psychiatry, 50,* 36–43. **(Chap 11)**

Kendler, K. S., Neale, M. C., Kessler, R. C., Heath, A. C., & Eaves, L. J. (1993). A longitudinal twin study of 1-year prevalence of major depression in women. *Archives of General Psychiatry, 50,* 843–852. **(Chap 7)**

Kermani, E. J., & Drob, S. L. (1987). *Tarasoff* decision: A decade later dilemma still faces psychotherapists. *American Journal of Psychotherapy, 41,* 271–285. **(Chap 16)**

Kerns, R., Southwick, S., Giller, E., Haythornwaite, J., Jacob, M., & Rosenberg, R. (1991). The relationship between reports of pain-related social interactions and expressions of pain and affective distress. *Behavior Therapy, 22,* 101–111. **(Chap 9)**

Kertzner, R. M., & Gorman, J. M. (1992). Psychoneuroimmunology and HIV infection. In A. Tashan & M. B. Riba (Eds.), *Review of psychiatry* (Vol. 11). Washington, DC: American Psychiatric Press. **(Chap 9)**

Kessler, R. C. (1997). The effects of stressful life events on depression. *Annual Review of Psychology, 48,* 191–214. **(Chap 7)**

Kessler, R. C., McGonagle, K. A., Zhao, S., Nelson, C. B., Hughes, M., Eshleman, S., Wittchen, H. U., & Kendler, K. S. (1994). Lifetime and 12-month prevalence of DSM-III-R psychiatric disorders among persons aged 15–54 in the United States: Results from the national comorbidity survey. *Archives of General Psychiatry.* **(Chap 7)**

Kessler, R. C., Sonnega, A., Bromet, E., Hughes, M., & Nelson, C. B. (1995). Posttraumatic stress disorder in the national comorbidity survey. *Archives of General Psychiatry, 52,* 1048–1060. **(Chap 5)**

Kety, S. S. (1990). Genetic factors in suicide: Family, twin, and adoption studies. In S. J. Blumenthal & D. J. Kupfer (Eds.), *Suicide over the life cycle: Risk factors, assessment and treatment of suicidal patients* (pp. 127–133). Washington, DC: American Psychiatric Press. **(Chap 7)**

Kety, S. S., Rosenthal, D., Wender, P. H., Schulsinger, F., & Jacobsen, B. (1978). The biological and adoptive families of adoptive individuals who become schizophrenic. In L. C. Wynne, R. L. Cromwell, & S. Matthysse (Eds.), *The nature of schizophrenia* (pp. 25–37). New York: John Wiley. **(Chap 13)**

Keys, A., Brozek, J., Henschel, A., Michelson, O., & Taylor, H. L. (1950). *The biology of human starvation* (Vol. 1). Minneapolis: University of Minnesota Press. **(Chap 8)**

Khantzian, E. J., Gawin, F., Kleber, H. D., & Riordan, C. E. (1984). Methylphenidate (Ritalin) treatment of cocaine dependence: A preliminary report. *Journal of Substance Abuse Treatment, 1,* 107–112. **(Chap 11)**

Kiecolt-Glaser, J. K., & Glaser, R. (1987). Chronic stress and immunity in family caregivers of Alzheimer's disease victims. *Psychosomatic Medicine, 49*(5), 523–535. **(Chap 9)**

Kiecolt-Glaser, J. K., & Glaser, R. (1992). Psychoneuroimmunology: Can psychological interventions modulate immunity? Special issue: Behavioral medicine: An update for the 1990s. *Journal of Consulting and Clinical Psychology, 60*(4), 569–575. **(Chap 9)**

Kiecolt-Glaser, J. K., Malarkey, W. B., Cacioppo, J. T., Glaser, R. (1994). Stressful personal relationships: Immune and endocrine function. In R. Glaser & J. Kiecolt-Glaser (Eds.), *Handbook of human stress and immunity* (pp. 321–329). San Diego: Academic. **(Chap 9)**

Kiesler, C. A., & Sibulkin, A. E. (1987). *Mental hospitalization: Myths and facts about a national crisis.* Beverly Hills, CA: Sage. **(Chap 16)**

Kiesler, D. J. (1966). Some myths of psychotherapy research and the search for a paradigm. *Psychological Bulletin, 65,* 110–136. **(Chap 4)**

Kihlstrom, J. F. (1992). Dissociation and dissociations: A commentary on consciousness and cognition. *Consciousness & Cognition, 1,* 47–53. **(Chap 2)**

Kihlstrom, J. F. (1994). One hundred years of hysteria. In S. J. Lynn & J. W. Rhue (Eds.), *Dissociation: Clinical and theoretical perspectives.* New York: Guilford Press. **(Chap 6)**

Kihlstrom, J. F. (1997). Memory, abuse, and science. *American Psychologist, 52,* 994–995. **(Chap 6)**

Kihlstrom, J. F., Barnhardt, T. M., & Tataryn, D. J. (1992). The psychological unconscious: Found, lost, and regained. *American Psychologist, 47*(6), 788–791. **(Chap 2)**

Kihlstrom, J. F., Glisky, M. L., Anguilo, M. J. (1994). Dissociative tendencies and dissociative disorders. *Journal of Abnormal Psychology, 103,* 117–124. **(Chap 6)**

Killen, J. D. (1996). Development and evaluation of a school-based eating disorder symptoms prevention program. In L. Smolak, M. P. Levine & R. Striegel-Moore (Eds.), *The developmental psychopathology of eating disorders: Implications for research, prevention, and treatment* (pp. 313–339). Mahwah, NJ: Erlbaum. **(Chap 8)**

Killen, J. D., Taylor, C. B., Hayward, C., Wilson, D. M., Hammer, L. D., Robinson, T. N., Litt, I., Simmonds, B. A., Varady, A., & Kraemer, H. (1994). The pursuit of thinness and onset of eating disorder symptoms in a community sample of adolescent girls: A three-year prospective analysis. *International Journal of Eating Disorders, 16,* 227–238. **(Chap 8)**

Kilpatrick, D. G., Best, C. L., Veronen, L. J., Amick, A. E., Villeponteaux, L. A., & Ruff, G. A. (1985). Mental health correlates of criminal victimization: A random community survey. *Journal of Consulting and Clinical Psychology, 53,* 866–873. **(Chap 5)**

Kim, E. D., & Lipshultz, L. I. (1997, April 15). Advances in the treatment of organic erectile dysfunction. *Hospital Practice,* 101–120. **(Chap 10)**

King, A. C., Taylor, C. B., Albright, C. A., & Haskell, W. L. (1990). The relationship between repressive and defensive coping styles and blood pressure responses in healthy, middle-aged men and women. *Journal of Psychosomatic Research, 34,* 461–471. **(Chap 9)**

King, D. W., King, L. A., Foy, D. W., & Gudanowski, D. M. (1996). Prewar factors in combat related posttraumatic stress disorder: Structural equation modeling with a national sample of female and male Vietnam veterans. *Journal of Consulting and Clinical Psychology, 64,* 520–531. **(Chap 5)**

King, G. R., & Ellinwood, E. H. (1997). Amphetamines and other stimulants. In J. H. Lowinson, P. Ruiz, R. B. Millman, & J. G. Langrod (Eds.), *Substance abuse: A comprehensive textbook* (pp. 207–223). Baltimore: Williams & Wilkins. **(Chap 11)**

King, N. J. (1993). Simple and social phobias. In T. H. Ollendick & R. J. Prinz (Eds.), *Advances in clinical child psychology,* (Vol. 15, pp. 305–341). New York: Plenum Press. **(Chap 5)**

King, S. A., & Strain, J. J. (1991). *Pain disorders: A proposed classification for DSM-IV.* Paper presented at the 144th annual meeting of the American Psychiatric Association, New Orleans. **(Chap 6)**

Kinsey, A. C., Pomeroy, W. B., & Martin, C. E. (1948). *Sexual behavior in the human male.* Philadelphia: W. B. Saunders. **(Chap 10)**

Kinsey, A. C., Pomeroy, W. B., Martin, C. E., & Gebhard, P. H. (1953). *Sexual behavior in the human female.* Philadelphia: W. B. Saunders. **(Chap 10)**

Kinzie, J. D., Leung, P. K., Boehnlein, J., & Matsunaga, D. (1992). Psychiatric epidemiology of an Indian village: A 19-year replication study. *Journal of Nervous and Mental Disease, 180*(1), 33–39. **(Chap 7)**

Kirch, D. G. (1993). Infection and autoimmunity as etiologic factors in schizophrenia: A review and reappraisal. *Schizophrenia Bulletin, 19,* 355–370. **(Chap 13)**

Kirkley, B. A., Kolotkin, R. L., Hernandez, J. T., & Gallagher, P. N. (1992). A comparison of binge-purgers, obese binge eaters and obese nonbinge eaters on the MMPI. *International Journal of Eating Disorders, 12*(2), 221–228. **(Chap 8)**

Kirmayer, L. J. (1991). The place of culture in psychiatric nosology: Taijin kyofusho and DSM-III-R. *Journal of Nervous and Mental Disease, 179,* 19–28. **(Chap 5)**

Kirmayer, L. J., & Robbins, J. M. (1991). Three forms of somatization in primary care: Prevalence, co-occurrence, and sociodemographic characteristics. *Journal of Nervous and Mental Disease, 179,* 647–655. **(Chap 6)**

Kirmayer, L. J., & Weiss, M. (1993). *On cultural considerations for somatoform disorders in the DSM-IV.* In cultural proposals and supporting papers for DSM-IV. Submitted to the DSM-IV Task Force by the Steering Committee, NIMH-Sponsored Group on Culture and Diagnosis. **(Chap 6)**

Kirschenbaum, B., Nedergaard, M., Preuss, A., Barami, K., Fraser, R. A. & Goldman, S. A. (1994). In vitro neuronal production and differentiation by precursor cells derived from the adult human forebrain. *Cerebral Cortex, 4,* 576–589. **(Chap 15)**

Klein, D. F. (1964). Delineation of two drug responsive anxiety syndromes. *Psychopharmacologia, 5,* 397–408. **(Chap 5)**

Klein, D. F. (1989). The pharmacological validation of psychiatric diagnosis. In L. Robins & J. Barrett (Eds.), *Validity of psychiatric diagnosis.* New York: Raven Press. **(Chap 7)**

Klein, D. N., Lewinsohn, P. M., & Seeley, J. R. (1997). Psychosocial characteristics of adolescents with a past history of dysthymic disorder: Comparison with adolescents with past histories of major depressive and non-affective disorders, and never mentally ill controls. *Journal of Affective Disorders, 42,* 127–135. **(Chap 7)**

Klein, D. N., Taylor, E. B., Dickstein, S., & Harding, K. (1988). The early-late onset distinction in DSM-III-R dysthymia. *Journal of Affective Disorders, 14*(1), 25–33. **(Chap 7)**

Kleinknecht, R. A., Dinnel, D. L., Kleinknecht, E. E., Hiruma, N., & Harada, N. (1997). Cultural factors in social anxiety: A comparison of social phobia symptoms and *taijin kyofusho.* *Journal of Anxiety Disorders, 11,* 157–177. **(Chap 5)**

Kleinman, A. (1986). *Social origins of distress and disease: Depression neurasthenia, and pain in modern China.* New Haven, CT: Yale University Press. **(Chap 9)**

Klerman, G. L. (1988). Depression and related disorders of mood (affective disorders). In A. M. Nicholi, Jr. (Ed.), *The new Harvard guide to psychiatry.* Cambridge, MA: Harvard University Press. **(Chap 7)**

Klerman, G. L., & Weissman, M. M. (1989). Increasing rates of depression. *Journal of the American Medical Association, 261,* 2229–2235. **(Chap 7)**

Klerman, G. L., & Weissman, M. M. (1992). The course, morbidity, and costs of depression. *Archives of General Psychiatry, 49*(10), 831–834. **(Chap 7)**

Klerman, G. L., Weissman, M. M., Rounsaville, B. J., & Chevron, E. S. (1984). *Interpersonal psychotherapy of depression.* New York: Basic Books. **(Chaps 2, 7, 8)**

Klosko, J. S., Barlow, D. H., Tassinari, R., & Cerny, J. A. (1990). A comparison of alprazolam and behavior therapy in treatment of panic disorder. *Journal of Consulting and Clinical Psychology, 58,* 77–84. **(Chap 5)**

Kluft, R. P. (1984). Treatment of multiple personality disorder. *Psychiatric Clinics of North America, 7,* 9–29. **(Chap 6)**

Kluft, R. P. (1991). Multiple personality disorder. In A. Tasman, & S. W. Goldinger (Eds.), *Review of psychiatry* (Vol. 10). Washington, DC: American Psychiatric Press. **(Chap 6)**

Kluft, R. P. (1996). Treating the traumatic memories of patients with dissociative identity disorder. *American Journal of Psychiatry, 153,* 103–110. **(Chap 6)**

Knapp, C. (1997). *Drinking: A love story.* New York: Delta. **(Chap 11)**

Knight, R. A., & Prentky, R. A. (1990). Classifying sexual offenders: The development and corroboration of taxonomic models. In W. L. Marshall, D. R. Laws, & H. E. Barbaree (Eds.), *Handbook of sexual assault: Issues, theories and treatment of the offender* (pp. 23–52). New York: Plenum Press. **(Chap 10)**

Kocsis, O. H., Croughan, J. L., Katz, M. M., Butler, T. P., Secunda, S., Bowden, C. L., & Davis, J. M. (1990). Response to treatment with antidepressants of patients with severe or moderate nonpsychotic depression and of patients with psychotic depression. *American Journal of Psychiatry, 147,* 621–624. **(Chap 7)**

Koegel, L. K. (1995). Communication and language intervention. In R. L. Koegel and L. K. Koegel (Eds.), *Teaching children with autism: Strategies for initiating positive interactions and improving learning opportunities* (pp. 17–32). Baltimore, MD: Paul H. Brookes. **(Chap 14)**

Koegel, P., Burnam, M. A., & Farr, R. K. (1988). The prevalence of specific psychiatric disorders among homeless individuals in the inner city of Los Angeles. *Archives of General Psychiatry, 45,* 1085–1092. **(Chap 16)**

Koegel, R. L., Schreibman, L., O'Neill, R. E., & Burke, J. C. (1983). The personality and family interaction characteristics of parents of autistic children. *Journal of Consulting and Clinical Psychology, 51,* 683–692. **(Chap 14)**

Kogon, M. M., Biswas, A., Peral, D., Carlson, R. W. L., & Spiegel, D. (1997). Effects of medical and psychotherapeutic treatment on the survival of women with metastatic breast carcinoma. *Cancer, 80,* 225–230. **(Chap 2)**

Kohut, H. (1971). *The analysis of self.* New York: International Universities Press. **(Chap 12)**

Kohut, H. (1977). *The restoration of the self.* New York: International Universities Press. **(Chap 12)**

Kolata, G. (1992, November 10). New Alzheimer's study questions link to metal. *New York Times,* C2. **(Chap 15)**

Koob, G. F. (1992). Drugs of abuse: Anatomy, pharmacology and function of reward pathways. *Trends in Pharmacological Sciences, 13,* 177–184. **(Chap 11)**

Koocher, G. P. (1996). Pediatric oncology: Medical crisis intervention. In R. J. Resnick & R. H. Rozensky (Eds.), *Health psychology through the life span: Practice and research opportunities* (pp.

213–225). Washington, DC: American Psychological Association. **(Chap 9)**

Kopyov, O. V., Jacques, D., Lieberman, A., Duma, C. M., & Rogers, R. L. (1996). Clinical study of fetal mesencephalic intracerebral transplants for the treatment of Parkinson's disease. *Cell Transplantation, 5,* 327–337. **(Chap 15)**

Korczyn, A. D., Kahana, E., & Galper, Y. (1991). Epidemiology of dementia in Ashkelon, Israel. *Neuroepidemiology, 10,* 100. **(Chap 15)**

Korenman, S. G., & Barchas, J. D. (1993). *Biological basis of substance abuse.* New York: Oxford University Press. **(Chap 10)**

Kotsaftis, A., & Neale, J. M. (1993). Schizotypal personality disorder I: The clinical syndrome. *Clinical Psychology Review, 13,* 451–472. **(Chap 12)**

Kovacs, M., Akiskal, H. S., Gatsonis, C., & Parrone, P. L. (1994). Childhood-onset dysthymic disorder. *Archives of General Psychiatry, 51,* 365–374. **(Chap 7)**

Kovacs, M., Gatsonis, C., Paulauskas, S. L., & Richards, C. (1989). Depressive disorders in childhood: IV. A longitudinal study of comorbidity with and risk for anxiety disorders, 46(9), 776–782. **(Chap 7)**

Kovacs, M., Goldston, D., & Gatsonis, C. (1993). Suicidal behaviors and childhood-onset depressive disorders: A longitudinal investigation. *Journal of the American Academy of Child and Adolescent Psychiatry, 32,* 8–20. **(Chap 7)**

Kovacs, M., Rush, A. J., Beck, A. T., & Hollon, S. D. (1981). Depressed outpatients treated with cognitive therapy or pharmacotherapy: A one-year follow-up. *Archives of General Psychiatry, 38(1),* 33–39. **(Chap 7)**

Kraepelin, E. (1898). *The diagnosis and prognosis of dementia praecox.* Paper presented at the 29th Congress of Southwestern German Psychiatry, Heidelberg. **(Chap 13)**

Kraepelin, E. (1899). *Kompendium der Psychiatrie* (6th ed.). Leipzig: Abel. **(Chap 13)**

Kraepelin, E. (1913). *Psychiatry: A textbook.* Leipzig: Barth. **(Chaps 1, 3)**

Kraepelin, E. (1919). *Dementia praecox and paraphrenia.* (R. M. Barclay & G. M. Robertson, Trans.). New York: R. E. Krieger. **(Chap 13)**

Krantz, D. S., & Deckel, A. W. (1983). Coping with coronary heart disease and stroke. In T. G. Burish, & L. A. Bradley (Eds.), *Coping with chronic disease: Research and applications.* New York: Academic Press. **(Chap 9)**

Kraus, N., McGee, T. J., Carrell, T. D., Zecker, S. G., Nicol, T. G., & Koch, D. B. (1996). Auditory neurophysiologic responses and discrimination deficits in children with learning problems. *Science, 273,* 971–973. **(Chap 14)**

Kring, A. M., & Bachorowski, J. (in press). *Emotions and psychopathology.* **(Chap 2)**

Kring, A. M., & Neale, J. M. (1996). Do schizophrenic patients show a disjunctive relationship among expressive, experiential, and psychophysiological components of emotion? *Journal of Abnormal Psychology, 105,* 249–257. **(Chap 13)**

Krishnan, K. R., Doraiswamy, P. M., Venkataraman, S., Reed, D., & Richie, J. C. (1991). Current concepts in hypothalamo-pituitary-adrenal axis regulation. In J. A. McCubbin, P. G. Kaufmann, & C. B. Nemeroff (Eds.), *Stress, neuropeptides, and systemic disease* (pp. 19–35). San Diego: Academic Press. **(Chap 9)**

Krueger, R. F., Caspi, A., Moffitt, T. E., Silva, P. A., & McGee, R. (1996). Personality traits are differentially linked to mental disorders: A multitrait-multidiagnosis study of an adolescent birth cohort. *Journal of Abnormal Psychology, 105,* 299–312. **(Chap 12)**

Krug, E. G., Kresnow, M.-J., Peddicord, J. P., Dahlberg, L. L., Powell, K. E., Crosby, A. E., & Annest, J. L. (1998). Suicide after natural disasters. *New England Journal of Medicine, 338,* 373–378. **(Chap 7)**

Kuechenmeister, C. A., Linton, P. H., Mueller, T. V., & White, H. B. (1977). Eye tracking in relation to age, sex, and illness. *Archives of General Psychiatry, 34,* 578–579. **(Chap 13)**

Kuiper, B., & Cohen-Kettenis, P. (1988). Sex reassignment surgery: A study of 141 Dutch transsexuals. *Archives of Sexual Behaviour, 17,* 439–457. **(Chap 10)**

Kupfer, D. J. (1995). Sleep research in depressive illness: Clinical implications-A tasting menu. *Biological Psychiatry, 38,* 391–403. **(Chap 7)**

Kupfer, D. J., Frank, E., Perel, J. M., Cornes, C., Mallinger, A. G., Thase, M. E., McEachran, A. B., Gronchocinski, V. J. (1992). Five-year outcome for maintenance therapies in recurrent depression. *Archives of General Psychiatry, 49,* 769–773. **(Chap 7)**

Kurita, H., Kita, M., & Miyake, Y. (1992). A comparative study of development and symptoms among disintegrative psychosis and infantile autism with and without speech loss. *Journal of Autism and Developmental Disorders, 22,* 175–188. **(Chap 14)**

Kushner, M. G., Shear, K. J. & Beitman, B. D. (1990). The relation between alcohol problems and the anxiety disorders. *American Journal of Psychiatry, 147,* 685–695. **(Chap 5)**

Lacey, J. H. (1992). The treatment demand for bulimia: A catchment area report of referral rates and demography. *Psychiatric Bulletin, 16,* 203–205. **(Chap 8)**

Lacks, P., & Morin, C. M. (1992). Recent advances in the assessment and treatment of insomnia. *Journal of Consulting and Clinical Psychology, 60,* 586–594. **(Chap 8)**

Ladd, C. O., Owens, M. J., & Nemeroff, C. B. (1996). Persistent changes in corticotropin-releasing factor neuronal systems induced by maternal deprivation. *Endocrinology, 137(4),* 1212–1218. **(Chap 7)**

Ladee, G. A. (1966). *Hypochondriacal syndromes.* New York: Elsevier. **(Chap 6)**

Lader, M., & Sartorius, N. (1968). Anxiety in patients with hysterical conversion symptoms. *Journal of Neurology, Neurosurgery, and Psychiatry, 31,* 490–495. **(Chap 6)**

Lader, M. H. (1975). *The psychophysiology of mental illness.* London: Routledge & Kegan Paul. **(Chap 2)**

Lader, M. H., & Wing, L. (1964). Habituation of the psycho-galvanic reflex in patients with anxiety states and in normal subjects. *Journal of Neurology, Neurosurgery, and Psychiatry, 27,* 210–218. **(Chap 5)**

La Fond, J. Q. (1996). The impact of law on the delivery of involuntary mental health services. In B. D. Sales and D. W. Shuman (Eds.), *Law, mental health, and mental disorder* (pp. 219–239). Pacific Grove, CA: Brooks/Cole. **(Chap 16)**

La Fond, J. Q., & Durham, M. L. (1992). *Back to the asylum: The future of mental health law and policy in the United States.* New York: Oxford University Press. **(Chap 16)**

Laing, R. D. (1967). *The politics of experience.* New York: Pantheon. **(Chap 13)**

Lakin, M. M., Montague, D. K., Vanderbrug Medendorp, S., Tesar, L., & Schover, L. R. (1990). Intracavernous injection therapy: Analysis of results and complications. *Journal of Urology, 143,* 1138–1141. **(Chap 10)**

Lam, R. W., & Stewart, J. N. (1996). The validity of atypical depression in DSM-IV. *Comprehensive Psychiatry, 37(6),* 375–383. **(Chap 7)**

Lambert, M. C., Weisz, J. R., Knight, F., Desrosiers, M., Overly, K., & Thesiger, C. (1992). Jamaican and American adult perspectives on child psychopathology: Further explorations of the threshold model. *Journal of Consulting and Clinical Psychology, 60,* 146–149. **(Chap 4)**

Lambert, M. J., Shapiro, D. A., & Bergin, A. E. (1986). The effectiveness of psychotherapy. In S. L. Garfield & A. E. Bergin (Eds.), *Handbook of psychotherapy and behavior change* (3rd ed.). New York: John Wiley. **(Chap 4)**

Landis, S. E., Earp, J. L., & Koch, G. G. (1992). Impact of HIV testing and counseling on subsequent sexual behavior. *AIDS Education and Prevention, 4(1),* 61–70. **(Chap 9)**

Landry, D. W., Zhao, K., Yang, G. X. Q., Glickman, M., & Georgiadis, T. M. (1993). Antibody-catalyzed degradation of cocaine. *Science, 259,* 1899–1901. **(Chap 11)**

Landsberg, J. P., McDonald, B., & Watt, F. (1992). Absence of aluminum in neuritic plaque cores in Alzheimer's disease. *Nature, 360,* 65–68. **(Chap 15)**

Lang, P. J. (1979). A bio-informational theory of emotional imagery. *Psychophysiology, 16,* 495–512. **(Chap 2)**

Lang, P. J. (1985). The cognitive psychophysiology of emotion: Fear and anxiety. In A. H. Tuma & J. D. Maser (Eds.), *Anxiety and the anxiety disorders.* Hillsdale, NJ: Lawrence Erlbaum. **(Chap 2)**

Lapierre, Y. D. (1994). Pharmacological therapy of dysthymia. *Acta Psychiatrica Scandinavica Supplemental, 89*(383), 42–48. **(Chap 7)**

Larson, E. B. (1993). Illnesses causing dementia in the very elderly. *New England Journal of Medicine, 328,* 203–205. **(Chap 15)**

La Rue, A. (1992). *Aging and neuropsychological assessment.* New York: Plenum Press. **(Chap 15)**

Lasch, C. (1978). *The culture of narcissism: American life in an age of diminishing expectations.* New York: W. W. Norton. **(Chap 12)**

Last, C. G., Hersen, M., Kazdin, A. E., Finkelstein, R., & Strauss, C. C. (1987). Comparison of DSM-III separation anxiety and overanxious disorders: Demographic characteristics and patterns of comorbidity. *Journal of the American Academy of Child and Adolescent Psychiatry, 26,* 527–531. **(Chap 5)**

Laumann, E., Gagnon, J., Michael, R., Michaels, S. (1994). *The social organization of sexuality: Sexual practices in the United States.* Chicago: University of Chicago Press. **(Chap 10)**

Laws, D. R. (Ed.). (1989). *Relapse prevention with sex offenders.* New York: Guilford Press. **(Chap 10)**

Laws, D. R., & O'Donohue, W. (Eds.). (1997). *Sexual deviance: Theory, assessment and treatment.* New York: Guilford Press. **(Chap 10)**

Lawson, W. B., Hepler, N., Holladay, J., & Cuffel, B. (1994). Race as a factor in inpatient and outpatient admissions and diagnosis. *Hospital and Community Psychiatry, 45,* 72–74. **(Chap 16)**

Laxenaire, M., Ganne-Vevonec, M. O., & Streiff, O. (1982). Les problemes d'idendité chez les enfants des migrants. *Annales Medico-Psychologiques, 140,* 602–605. **(Chap 12)**

Laxova, R., Ridler, M. A. C., & Bowen-Bravery, M. (1977). An etiological survey of the severely retarded Hertfordshire children who were born between January 1, 1965 and December 31, 1967. *American Journal of Medical Genetics, 1,* 75–86. **(Chap 14)**

Lazare, D. (1989, October 18–24). Drugs 'R' Us. *In These Times,* pp. 12–13. **(Chap 11)**

Lazarus, R. A., & Folkman, S. (1984). *Stress, appraisal, and coping.* New York: Springer. **(Chap 9)**

Lazarus, R. S. (1968). Emotions and adaptation: Conceptual and empirical relations. In W. J. Arnold (Ed.), *Nebraska Symposium on Motivation* (Vol. 16). Lincoln: University of Nebraska Press. **(Chap 2)**

Lazarus, R. S. (1991). Progress on a cognitive-motivational relational theory of emotion. *American Psychologist, 46*(8), 819–834. **(Chap 2)**

Lebedinskaya, K. S., & Nikolskaya, O. S. (1993). Brief report: Analysis of autism and its treatment in modern Russian defectology. *Journal of Autism and Developmental Disorders, 23,* 675–697. **(Chap 14)**

Leccese, A. P. (1991). *Drugs and society: Behavioral medicines and abusable drugs.* Englewood Cliffs, NJ: Prentice-Hall. **(Chap 11)**

Leckman, J. F., Grice, D. E., Boardman, J., Zhang, H., Vitali, A., Bondi, C., Alsobrook, J., Peterson, B. S., Cohen, D. J., Rasmussen, S. A., Goodman, W. K., McDougle, C. J., & Pauls, D. L. (1997). Symptoms of obsessive-compulsive disorder. *American Journal of Psychiatry, 154,* 911–917. **(Chap 5)**

Leckman, J. F., Peterson, B. S., Anderson, G. M., Arnstein, A. F. T., Pauls, D. L., & Cohen, D. J. (1997). Pathogenesis of Tourette's syndrome. *Journal of Child Psychology and Psychiatry, 38,* 119–142. **(Chap 14)**

Leckman, J. F., Weissman, M. M., Merikangas, K. R., Pauls, D. L., & Prusoff, B. A. (1983). Panic disorder and major depression. *Archives of General Psychiatry, 40,* 1055–1060. **(Chap 7)**

Lecrubier, Y., Bakker, A., Dunbar, G. and the collaborative paroxetine panic study investigators. (1997). A comparison of paroxetine, clomipramine and placebo in the treatment of panic disorder. *Acta Psychiatrica Scandinavica, 95,* 145–152. **(Chap 5)**

Lecrubier, Y., Judge, R., & and the collaborative paroxetine panic study investigators. (1997). Long term evaluation of paroxetine, clomipramine and placebo in panic disorder. *Acta Psychiatrica Scandinavica, 95,* 153–160. **(Chap 5)**

LeDoux, J. E. *The emotional brain.* (1996). New York: Simon & Schuster. **(Chap 5)**

LeDoux, J. E. (1993). Emotional networks in the brain. In M. Lewis & J. M. Haviland (Eds.), *Handbook of Emotions* (pp. 109–118). New York: Guilford Press. **(Chap 2)**

LeDoux, J. E. (1995). In search of an emotional system in the brain: Leaping from fear to emotion to consciousness. In M. S. Gazzaniga (Ed.), *The cognitive neurosciences* (pp. 1049–1062). Cambridge, MA: MIT Press. **(Chap 2)**

Lee, C. K. (1992). Alcoholism in Korea. In J. Helzer & G. Canino (Eds.), *Alcoholism—North America, Europe and Asia: A coordinated analysis of population data from ten regions* (pp. 247–262). London: Oxford University Press. **(Chap 11)**

Lee, K. (1992). Pattern of night waking and crying of Korean infants from 3 months to 2 years old and its relation with various factors. *Journal of Developmental & Behavioral Pediatrics, 13,* 326–330. **(Chap 8)**

Lee, S., Hsu, L. K. G., & Wing, Y. K. (1992). Bulimia nervosa in Hong Kong Chinese patients. *British Journal of Psychiatry, 161,* 545–551. **(Chap 8)**

Lee, S., Leung, C. M., Wing, Y. K., Chiu, H. F. et al. (1991). Acne as a risk factor for anorexia nervosa in Chinese. *Australian and New Zealand Journal of Psychiatry, 25*(1), 134–137. **(Chap 8)**

Lee, T., & Tang, S. W. (1984). Lozapine and clozapine decrease serotonin (S2) but do not elevate dopamine (D2) receptor numbers in the rat brain. *Psychiatry Research, 12,* 277–285. **(Chap 13)**

Leff, J., Satorius, N., Jablensky, A., Korten, A., & Ernberg, G. (1992). The International Pilot Study of Schizophrenia: Five-year follow-up findings. *Psychological Medicine, 22,* 131–145. **(Chap 13)**

Lefrancois, G. R. (1990). *The lifespan* (3rd ed.). Belmont, CA: Wadsworth Publishing. **(Chap 4)**

le Grange, D., Telch, C. F., & Agras, W. S. (1997). Eating and general psychopathology in a sample of Caucasian and ethnic minority subjects. *International Journal of Eating Disorders, 21,* 285–293. **(Chap 8)**

Lehman, A. F. (1995). Vocational rehabilitation in schizophrenia. *Schizophrenia Bulletin, 21,* 645–656. **(Chap 13)**

Leiblum, S. R., & Rosen, R. C. (Eds.). (1988). *Sexual desire disorders.* New York: Guilford Press. **(Chap 10)**

Leitenberg, H., Detzer, M. J., & Srebnik, D. (1993). Gender differences in masturbation and the relation of masturbation experience in preadolescence and/or early adolescence to sexual behavior and sexual adjustment in young adulthood. *Archives of Sexual Behavior, 22*(2), 87–98. **(Chap 10)**

Lejeune, J., Gauthier, M., & Turpin, R. (1959). Étude des chromosomes somatiques de neuf enfants mongoliens. *Comptes Rendus Hebdomadaires des Seances de l'Academie des Sciences. D: Sciences Naturelles (Paris), 248,* 1721–1722. **(Chap 14)**

Lemoine, P., Harousseau, H., Borteyru, J. P., & Menuet, J. C. (1968). Les enfants de parents alcooliques: Anomalies observées. Á propos de 127 cas [Children of alcoholic parents: Anomalies observed in 127 cases]. *Quest Medicine, 21,* 476–482. **(Chap 11)**

Lenke, R. R., & Levy, H. (1980). Maternal phenylketonuria and hyperphenylalanemia: An international survey of the outcome of untreated and treated pregnancies. *New England Journal of Medicine, 303,* 1202–1208. **(Chap 14)**

Leo, J. (1983, August 15). Take me out to the ballgame. *Time,* p. 72. **(Chap 5)**

Lesch, K.-P., Bengel, D., Heils, A., Sabol, S. Z., Greenberg, B. D., Petri, S., Benjamin, J., Müller, C. R., Hamer, D. H., & Murphy, D. L. (1996, November 29). Association of anxiety-related traits with a polymorphism in the serotonin transporter gene regulatory region. *Science, 274,* 1527–1531. **(Chap 5)**

LeVay, S. (1991). A difference in hypothalamic structure between heterosexual and homosexual men. *Science, 253,* 1034–1037. **(Chap 10)**

Levin, A., & Hyler, S. (1986). DSM-III personality diagnosis in bulimia. *Comprehensive Psychiatry, 27,* 47. **(Chap 12)**

Levine, M. N., Guyatt, G. H., Gent, M., DePauw, S., Goodyear, M. D., Hryniuk, W. M., Arnold, A., Findlay, B., Skillings, J. R., Bramwell, V. H., Levin, L., Bush, H., Abu-Zahra, H., & Kotalik, J. (1988). Quality of life in stage II breast cancer: An instrument for clinical trials. *Journal of Clinical Oncology, 6,* 1798–1810. **(Chap 9)**

Levine, M. P., & Smolak, L. (1996). Media as a context for the development of disordered eating. In L. Smolak, M. P. Levine, & R. Striegel-Moore (Eds.), *The developmental psychopathology of eating disorders: Implications for research, prevention, and treatment* (pp. 235–257). Mahwah, NJ: Erlbaum. **(Chap 8)**

Levine, S. B., & Yost, M. A. (1976). Frequency of sexual dysfunction in a general gynecological clinic: An epidemiological approach. *Archives of Sexual Behavior, 5,* 229–238. **(Chap 10)**

Levitt, A. J., Joffe, R. T., Moul, D. F., Lam, R. W., Teicher, M. H., Lebegue, B., Murray, M. G., Oren, D. A., Schwartz, P., Buchanan, A., Glod, C. A., & Brown, J. (1993). Side effects of light therapy in seasonal affective disorder. *American Journal of Psychiatry, 150,* 650–652. **(Chap 7)**

Lewin, T. H. D. (1975). Psychiatric evidence in criminal cases for purposes other than the defense of insanity. *Syracuse Law Review, 26,* 1051–1115. **(Chap 16)**

Lewinsohn, P. M., & Clarke, G. N. (1984). Group treatment of depressed individuals: The "coping with depression" course. *Advances in Behaviour Research and Therapy, 6*(2), 99–114. **(Chap 7)**

Lewinsohn, P. M., & Gotlib, I. H. (1995). Behavioral therapy and treatment of depression. In E. E. Beckham & W. R. Leber (Eds.), *Handbook of depression.* (pp. 352–375). New York: Guilford Press. **(Chap 7)**

Lewinsohn, P. M., & Rosenbaum, M. (1987). Recall of parental behavior by acute depressives, remitted depressives and nondepressives. *Journal of Personality and Social Psychology, 52*(3), 611–619. **(Chap 7)**

Lewinsohn, P. M., Gotlib, I. H., & Seeley, J. R. (1997). Depression-related psychosocial variables: Are they specific to depression in adolescents? *Journal of Abnormal Psychology, 106*(3), 365–375. **(Chap 7)**

Lewinsohn, P. M., Hops, H., Roberts, R. E., Seeley, J. R., & Andrews, J. A. (1993). Adolescent psychopathology: I. Prevalence and incidence of depression and other DSM-III-R disorders in high school students. *Journal of Abnormal Psychology, 102*(1), 133–144. **(Chap 7)**

Lewinsohn, P. M., Rohde, P., & Seeley, J. R. (1993). Psychosocial characteristics of adolescents with a history of suicide attempt. *Journal of the American Academy of Child and Adolescent Psychiatry, 32*(1), 60–68. **(Chap 7)**

Lewinsohn, P. M., Rohde, P., Seeley, J. R., & Fischer, S. A. (1993). Age-cohort changes in the lifetime occurrence of depression and other mental disorders. *Journal of Abnormal Psychology, 102*(1), 110–120. **(Chap 7)**

Lewis, D. O., Yeager, C. A., Swica, Y., Pincus, J. H., & Lewis, M. (1997). Objective documentation of child abuse and dissociation in 12 murderers with dissociative identity disorder. *American Journal of Psychiatry, 154,* 1703–1710. **(Chap 6)**

Lewis, G., Croft-Jeffreys, C., & Anthony, D. (1990). Are British psychiatrists racist? *British Journal of Psychiatry, 157,* 410–415. **(Chap 13)**

Lewis, G., David, A., Andreasson, S., & Allsbeck, P. (1992). Schizophrenia and city life. *Lancet, 340,* 137–140. **(Chaps 2, 13)**

Lewis, G., Hawton, K., & Jones, P. (1997). Strategies for preventing suicide. *British Journal of Psychiatry, 171,* 351–354. **(Chap 7)**

Lewy, A. J. (1993). Seasonal mood disorders. In D. L. Dunner (Ed.), *Current psychiatric therapy* (pp. 220–225). Philadelphia: W. B. Saunders. **(Chap 7)**

Lewy, A. J., Kern, H. E., Rosenthal, N. E., & Wehr, T. A. (1982). Bright artificial light treatment of a manic-depressive patient with a seasonal mood cycle. *American Journal of Psychiatry, 139,* 1496–1498. **(Chap 7)**

Liberman, R. P., DeRisi, W. D., & Mueser, K. T. (1989). *Social skills training for psychiatric patients.* Boston, MA: Allyn & Bacon. **(Chap 13)**

Liberman, R. P., Kopelowicz, A., & Young, A. S. (1994). Biobehavioral treatment and rehabilitation of schizophrenia. *Behavior Therapy, 25,* 89–107. **(Chap 13)**

Liberman, R. P., Spaulding, W. D., & Corrigan, P. W. (1995). Cognitive-behavioural therapies in psychiatric rehabilitation. In S. R. Hirsch and D. R. Weinberger (Eds.), *Schizophrenia* (pp. 605–625). Oxford, England: Blackwell Science Ltd. **(Chap 13)**

Liddell, H. S. (1949). The role of vigilance in the development of animal neurosis. In P. Hoch & J. Zubin (Eds.), *Anxiety.* New York: Grune & Stratton. **(Chap 5)**

Lidz, C. W., Mulvey, E. P., Appelbaum, P. S., & Cleveland, S. (1989). Commitment: The consistency of clinicians and the use of legal standards. *American Journal of Psychiatry, 146,* 176–186. **(Chap 16)**

Lieberman, J. A., Jody, D., Alvir, J. M. J., Ashtari, M., Levy, D. L., Bogerts, B., Degreef, G., Mayeroff, D. I., & Cooper, T. (1993). Brain morphology, dopamine, and eye-tracking abnormalities in first-episode schizophrenia. *Archives of General Psychiatry, 50,* 357–368. **(Chap 13)**

Liebeskind, J. (1991). Pain can kill. *Pain, 44,* 3–4. **(Chap 9)**

Liebowitz, M. R., Heimberg, R. G., Schneier, F. R., Hope, D. A., Davies, S., Holt, C. S., Goetz, D., Juster, H. R., Lin, S.-H., Bruch, M. A., & Klein, D. F. (1997). *Cognitive-behavioral group therapy versus phenelzine in social phobia: Long term outcome.* Manuscript submitted for publication. **(Chap 5)**

Liebowitz, M. R., Salman, E., Jusino, C. M., Garfinkel, R., Street, L., Cardenas, D. L., Silvestre, J., Fyer, A. J., Carrasco, J. L., Davies, S. Guarnaccia, P, & Klein, D. F. (1994). Ataque de nervios and panic disorder. *American Journal of Psychiatry, 151,* 871–875. **(Chap 5)**

Liebowitz, M. R., Schneier, F., Campeas, R., Hollander, E., Hatterer, J., Fyer, A., Gorman, J., Papp, L., Davies, S., Gully, R., & Klein, D. F. (1992). Phenelzine vs. atenolol in social phobia: A placebo controlled comparison. *Archives of General Psychiatry, 49,* 290–300. **(Chap 5)**

Liggett, J. (1974). *The human face.* New York: Stein and Day. **(Chap 6)**

Lilienfeld, S. O. (1992). The association between antisocial personality and somatization disorders: A review and integration of theoretical models. *Clinical Psychology Review, 12,* 641–662. **(Chaps 6, 13)**

Lilienfeld, S. O., & Marino, L. (in press). Essentialism Revisited: Evolutionary Theory and the concept of mental disorder. *Journal of Abnormal Psychology.* **(Chap 1)**

Lilienfeld, S. O., VanValkenburg, C., Larntz, K., & Akiskal, H. S. (1986). The relationship of histrionic personality to antisocial personality and somatization disorders. *American Journal of Psychiatry, 143,* 718–722. **(Chap 12)**

Lin, K. M. (1986). Psychopathology and social disruption in refugees. In C. L. Williams & J. Westermeyer (Eds.), *Refugee mental health in resettlement countries* (pp.

61–73). Washington, DC: Hemisphere Publishing Corp. **(Chap 15)**

Lin, N., & Ensel, W. M. (1984). Depression-mobility and its social etiology: The role of life events and social support. *Journal of Health and Social Behavior, 25*(2), 176–188. **(Chap 7)**

Lindesay, J. (1991). Phobic disorders in the elderly. *British Journal of Psychiatry, 159,* 531–541. **(Chap 5)**

Lindquist, P., & Allebeck, P. (1990). Schizophrenia and crime: A longitudinal followup of 644 schizophrenics in Stockholm. *British Journal of Psychiatry, 157,* 345–350. **(Chap 16)**

Lindsey, K. P., & Paul, G. L. (1989). Involuntary commitments to public mental institutions: Issues involving the overrepresentation of blacks and assessment of relevant functioning. *Psychological Bulletin, 106,* 171–183. **(Chap 13)**

Linehan, M. M. (1987). Dialectical behavior therapy for borderline personality disorder: Theory and method. *Bulletin of the Menninger Clinic, 51,* 261–276. **(Chap 12)**

Linehan, M. M., & Kehrer, C. A. (1993). Borderline personality disorder. In D. H. Barlow (Ed.), *Clinical handbook of psychological disorders: A step by step treatment manual.* New York: Guilford Press. **(Chaps 7, 12)**

Linehan, M. M., Armstrong,, H. E., Suarez, A., Allmon, D., & Heard, H. L. (1991). Cognitive-behavioral treatment of chronically parasuicidal borderline patients. *Archives of General Psychiatry, 48,* 1060–1064. **(Chap 12)**

Linehan, M. M., Heard, H. L., & Armstrong, H. E. (1992). *Naturalistic follow-up of a behavioral treatment for chronically parasuicidal borderline patients.* Unpublished manuscript, University of Washington, Seattle. **(Chap 12)**

Links, P., Steiner, M., & Huxley, G. (1988). The occurrence of borderline personality disorder in families of borderline patients. *Journal of Personality Disorders, 2,* 14–20. **(Chap 12)**

Links, P. S., Steiner, M., Boiago, I., & Irwin, D. (1990). Lithium therapy for borderline patients: Preliminary findings. *Journal of Personality Disorders, 4,* 173–181. **(Chap 12)**

Lipowski, Z. J. (1983). Transient cognitive disorders (delirium, acute confusional states) in the elderly. *American Journal of Psychiatry, 140,* 1426–1436. **(Chap 15)**

Lipowski, Z. J. (1990). *Delirium: Acute confusional states.* New York: Oxford University Press. **(Chap 15)**

Lipska, B. K., Jaskiw, G. E., & Weinberger, D. R. (1993). Postpubertal emergence of hyperresponsiveness to stress and to amphetamine after neonatal excitotoxic hippocampal damage: A potential animal model of schizopherenia. *Neuropsychopharmacology, 9,* 67–75. **(Chap 13)**

Lisspers, J., & Öst, L. (1990). Long-term followup of migraine treatment: Do the effects remain up to six years? *Behaviour Research and Therapy, 28,* 313–322. **(Chap 9)**

Loebel, J. P., Dager, S. R., & Kitchell, M. A. (1993). Alzheimer's disease. In D. L. Dunner (Ed.), *Current psychiatric therapy* (pp. 59–65). Philadelphia: W. B. Saunders. **(Chap 15)**

Loeber, R. (1982). The stability of antisocial and delinquent child behavior: A review. *Child Development, 53,* 1431–1446. **(Chap 12)**

Loehlin, J. C. (1992). *Genes and environment in personality development.* Newbury Park, CA: Sage. **(Chap 2)**

Loftus, E. F., Coan, J. A., & Pickrell, J. E. (1996). Manufacturing false memories using bits of reality. In L. Reder (Ed.), *Implicit memory and metacognition* (pp. 195–220). Mahwah, NJ: Erlbaum. **(Chap 6)**

Loo, D. T., Copani, A., Pike, C. J., Whittemore, E. R., Walencewicz, A. J., & Cotman, C. W. (1993). Apoptosis is induced by B-amyloid in cultured central nervous system neurons. *Proceedings of the National Academy of Sciences, 90,* 7951–7955. **(Chap 15)**

LoPiccolo, J., & Friedman, J. M. (1988). Broad spectrum treatment of low sexual desire: Integration of cognitive, behavioral, and systemic therapy. In S. R. Leiblum & R. C. Rosen (Eds.), *Sexual desire disorders* (pp. 107–144). New York: Guilford Press. **(Chap 11)**

LoPiccolo, J., & Stock, W. E. (1987). Sexual function, dysfunction and counseling in gynecological practice. In Z. Rosenwaks, F. Benjamin, & M. L. Stone (Eds.), *Gynecology.* New York: Macmillan. **(Chap 10)**

LoPiccolo, J., Heiman, J. R., Hogan, D. R., & Roberts, C. W. (1985). Effectiveness of single therapists versus cotherapy teams in sex therapy. *Journal of Consulting and Clinical Psychology, 53*(3), 287–294. **(Chap 10)**

Lotter, V. (1966). Epidemiology of autistic conditions in young children: I. Prevalence. *Social Psychiatry, 1,* 124–137. **(Chap 14)**

Lovaas, O. I. (1977). *The autistic child: Language development through behavior modification.* New York: Irvington. **(Chap 14)**

Lovaas, O. I. (1987). Behavioral treatment and normal educational and intellectual functioning in young autistic children. *Journal of Consulting and Clinical Psychology, 55,* 3–9. **(Chap 14)**

Lovaas, O. I., Berberich, J. P., Perloff, B. F., & Schaeffer, B. (1966). Acquisition of imitative speech by schizophrenic children. *Science, 151,* 705–707. **(Chap 14)**

Lowing, P. A., Mirsky, A. F., & Pereira, R. (1983). The inheritance of schizophrenic spectrum disorders: A reanalysis of the Danish adoptee study data.

American Journal of Psychiatry, 140, 1167–1171. **(Chap 13)**

Lucas, A. R., Beard, C. M., O'Fallon, W. M., & Kurlan, L. T. (1991). 50-year trends in the incidence of anorexia nervosa in Rochester, Minn.: A population-based study. *American Journal of Psychiatry, 148,* 917–922. **(Chap 8)**

Luckasson, R., Coulter, D. L., Polloway, E. A., Reiss, S., Schalock, R. L., Snell, M. E., Spitalnik, D. M., & Stark, J. A. (1992). *Mental retardation: Definition, classification, and systems of supports* (9th ed.). Washington, DC: American Association on Mental Retardation. **(Chaps 3, 14)**

Ludwig, A., Brandsma, J., Wilbur, C., Bendfeldt, F., & Jameson, D. (1972). The objective study of a multiple personality. *Archives of General Psychiatry, 26,* 298–310. **(Chap 6)**

Ludwig, A. M. (1985). Cognitive processes associated with \"spontaneous" recovery from alcoholism. *Journal of Studies on Alcohol, 46,* 53–58. **(Chap 11)**

Lundh, L.-G., & Öst, L.-G. (1996). Recognition bias for critical faces in social phobics. *BRAT, 34,* 787–794. **(Chap 5)**

Lundstrom, B., Pauly, I., & Walinder, J. (1984). Outcome of sex reassignment surgery. *Acta Psychiatrica Scandinavica, 70,* 289–294. **(Chap 10)**

Lundy, A. (1985). The reliability of the thematic apperception test. *Journal of Personality Assessment, 49,* 141–145. **(Chap 3)**

Lutgendorf, S. K., Antoni, M. H., Ironson, G., Klimas, N., Kumar, M., Starr, K., & McCabe, P., Cleven, K., Fletcher, M. A., & Schneiderman, N. (1997). Cognitive-behavioral stress management decreases dysphoric mood and herpes simplex virus-type 2 antibody titers in symptomatic HIV-seropositive gay men. *Journal of Consulting and Clinical Psychology, 65,* 31–43. **(Chap 9)**

Lydiard, R. B., Brawman-Mintzer, O., & Ballenger, J. C. (1996). Recent developments in the psychopharmacology of anxiety disorders. *Journal of Consulting & Clinical Psychology, 64,* 660–668. **(Chap 5)**

Lykken, D. T. (1957). A study of anxiety in the sociopathic personality. *Journal of Abnormal and Social Psychology, 55,* 6–10. **(Chap 12)**

Lykken, D. T. (1982). Fearfulness: Its carefree charms and deadly risks. *Psychology Today, 16,* 20–28. **(Chap 12)**

Lynam, D. R. (1996). Early identification of chronic offenders: Who is a fledgling psychopath? *Psychological Bulletin, 120,* 209–234. **(Chap 12)**

Lyons, M. J., True, W. R., Eisen, S. A., Goldberg, J., Meyer, J. M., Faraone, S. V., Eaves, L. J., & Tsuang, M. T. (1995). Differential heritability of adult and juvenile antisocial traits. *Archives of General Psychiatry, 52,* 906–915. **(Chap 4)**

Maas, J. W., Bowden, C. L., Miller, A. L., Javors, M. A., Funderburg, L. G.,

Berman, N., & Weintraub, S. T. (1997). Schizophrenia, psychosis, and cerebral spinal fluid homovanillic acid concentrations. *Schizophrenia Bulletin, 23*, 147–154. **(Chap 13)**

Macciocchi, S. N., & Barth, J. T. (1996). The Halstead-Reitan Neuropsychological Test Battery (HRNTB). In C. S. Newmark (Ed.), *Major psychological assessment instruments* (pp. 431–459). Boston: Allyn & Bacon. **(Chap 3)**

Macdonald, P. T., Waldorf, D., Reinarman, C., & Murphy, S. (1988). Heavy cocaine use and sexual behavior. *Journal of Drug Issues, 18*, 437–455. **(Chap 10)**

MacDougall, J. M., Dembroski, T. M., Dimsdale, J. E., & Hackett, T. P. (1985). Components of Type A, hostility, and anger-in: Further relationships to angiographic findings. *Health Psychology, 4*(2), 137–152. **(Chap 2)**

Mace, C. J. (1992). Hysterical conversion II: A critique. *British Journal of Psychiatry, 161*, 378–389. **(Chap 6)**

MacLeod, C., & Mathews, A. M. (1991). Cognitive-experimental approaches to the emotional disorders. In P. R. Martin (Ed.), *Handbook of behavior therapy and psychological science: An integrative approach* (pp. 116–150). Elmsford, NY: Pergamon Press. **(Chap 5)**

MacLeod, C., Mathews, A., & Tata, P. (1986). Attentional bias in emotional disorders. *Journal of Abnormal Psychology, 95*, 15–20. **(Chap 5)**

Magee, W. J., Eaton, W. W., Wittchen, H.-U., McGonagle, K. A., & Kessler, R. C. (1996). Agoraphobia, simple phobia, and social phobia in the National Comorbidity Survey. *Archives of General Psychiatry, 53*, 159–168. **(Chap 5)**

Magne-Ingvar, U., Ojehagen, A., & Traskman-Bendz, L. (1992). The social network of people who attempt suicide. *Acta Psychiatrica Scandinavica, 86*, 153–158. **(Chap 7)**

Maher, B. A., & Maher, W. B. (1985a). Psychopathology: I. From ancient times to the eighteenth century. In G. A. Kimble & K. Schlesinger (Eds.), *Topics in the history of psychology* (pp. 251–294). Hillsdale, NJ: Lawrence Erlbaum. **(Chap 1)**

Maher, B. A., & Maher, W. B. (1985b). Psychopathology: II. From the eighteenth century to modern times. In G. A. Kimble & K. Schlesinger (Eds.), *Topics in the history of psychology* (pp. 295–329). Hillsdale, NJ: Lawrence Erlbaum. **(Chap 1)**

Maher, J. J. (1997). Exploring alcohol's effects on liver function. *Alcohol Health & Research World, 21*, 5–12. **(Chap 11)**

Maher, M. (1952). On childhood psychosis and schizophrenia: Autistic and symbiotic infantile psychosis. *Psychoanalytic Study of the Child, 7*, 286–305. **(Chap 14)**

Mahr, G., & Leith, W. (1992). Psychogenic stuttering of adult onset. *Journal of Speech and Hearing Research, 35*, 283–286. **(Chap 14)**

Maier, S. F. (1997, September). *Stressor controllability, anxiety, and serotonin*. Paper presented at the National Institute of Mental Health Workshop on Cognition and Anxiety, Rockville, MD. **(Chap 5)**

Malatesta, V. J., & Adams, H. E. (1984). The sexual dysfunctions. In H. E. Adams & P. B. Sutker (Eds.), *Comprehensive handbook of psychopathology* (pp. 725–775). New York: Plenum Press. **(Chap 10)**

Maletzky, B. M. (1991). *Treating the sexual offender*. Newbury Park, CA: Sage. **(Chap 10)**

Maletzky, B. M. (1998). The paraphilias: Research and treatment. In P. E. Nathan & J. M. Gorman (Eds.), *A guide to treatments that work* (pp. 472–500). New York: Oxford University Press. **(Chap 10)**

Malpass, R. S., & Poortinga, Y. H. (1986). Strategies for design and analysis. In W. J. Lonner & J. W. Berry (Eds.), *Field methods in cross-cultural research* (pp. 47–83). Beverly Hills, CA: Sage. **(Chap 4)**

Mandalos, G. E., & Szarek, B. L. (1990). Dose-related paranoid reaction associated with fluoxetine. *Journal of Nervous and Mental Disease, 178*(1), 57–58. **(Chap 7)**

Mandel, J. L., Monaco, A. P., Nelson, D. L., Schlessinger, D., & Willard, H. (1992). Genome analysis and the human X chromosome. *Science, 258*, 103–109. **(Chap 4)**

Mandell, A. J., & Knapp, S. (1979). Asymmetry and mood, emergent properties of seratonin regulation: A proposed mechanism of action of lithium. *Archives of General Psychiatry, 36*(8), 909–916. **(Chap 7)**

Mann, J. J., Malone, K. M., Diehl, D. J., Perel, J., Cooper, T. B., & Mintun, M. A. (1996). Demonstration in vivo of reduced serotonin responsivity in the brain of untreated depressed patients. *American Journal of Psychiatry, 153*, 174–182. **(Chap 7)**

Mann, J. M. (1991). Global AIDS: Critical issues for prevention in the 1990's. *International Journal of Health Sciences, 21*(3), 553–559. **(Chap 9)**

Mann, K., Klingler, T., Noe, S., Röschke, J., Müller, S., & Benkert, O. (1996). Effects of yohimbine on sexual experiences and nocturnal penile tumescence and rigidity in erectile dysfunction. *Archives of Sexual Behavior, 25*, 1–16. **(Chap 10)**

Manni, R., Ratti, M. T., & Tartara, A. (1997). Nocturnal eating: Prevalence and features in 120 insomniac referrals. *Sleep, 20*, 734–738. **(Chap 8)**

Mannuzza, S., Klein, R. G., Bessler, A., Malloy, P., & LaPadula, M. (1993). Adult outcome of hyperactive boys: Educational achievement, occupational rank, and psychiatric status. *Archives of General Psychiatry, 50*, 565–576. **(Chap 14)**

Manson, S. M., & Good, B. J. (1993, January). *Cultural considerations in the diagnosis of DSM-IV mood disorders*. Cultural proposals and supporting papers for DSM-IV. Submitted to the DSM-IV Task Force by the Steering Committee, NIMH-Sponsored Group on Culture and Diagnosis. **(Chap 7)**

Mar, J. (1993). New lead to an Alzheimer's mouse? *Science, 261*, 1520. **(Chap 14)**

Marcopulos, B. A., & Graves, R. E. (1990). Antidepressant effect on memory in depressed older persons. *Journal of Clinical and Experimental Neuropsychology, 12*(5), 655–663. **(Chap 7)**

Marcus, M. D., Smith, D., Santelli, R., & Kaye, W. (1992). Characterization of eating disordered behavior in obese binge eaters. *International Journal of Eating Disorders, 12*, 249–255. **(Chap 8)**

Marcus, M. D., Wing, R. R., & Hopkins, J. (1988). Obese binge eaters: Affect, cognitions, and response to behavioral weight control. *Journal of Consulting and Clinical Psychology, 3*, 433–439. **(Chap 8)**

Marcus, M. D., Wing, R. R., Ewing, L., Keern, E., Gooding, W., & McDermott, M. (1990). Psychiatric disorders among obese binge eaters. *International Journal of Eating Disorders, 9*, 69–77. **(Chap 8)**

Margo, A., Hemsley, D. R., & Slade, P. D. (1981). The effects of varying auditory input on schizophrenic hallucinations. *British Journal of Psychiatry, 139*, 122–127. **(Chap 13)**

Mariani, M. A., & Barkley, R. A. (1997). Neuropsychological and academic functioning in preschool boys with attention deficit hyperactivity disorder. *Developmental Neuropsychology, 13*, 111–129. **(Chap 14)**

Marks, I. M. (1985). Behavioural treatment of social phobia. *Psychopharmacology Bulletin, 21*, 615–618. **(Chap 5)**

Marks, I. M. (1988). Blood-injury phobia: A review. *American Journal of Psychiatry, 145*, 1207–1213. **(Chap 2)**

Marlatt, G. A. (1985). Relapse prevention: Theoretical rationale and overview of the model. In G. A. Marlatt & J. R. Gordon (Eds.), *Relapse prevention: Maintenance strategies in the treatment of addictive behaviors* (pp. 3–70). New York: Guilford Press. **(Chap 11)**

Marlatt, G. A., & Gordon, J. R. (1980). Determinants of relapse: Implications for the maintenance of behavior change. In P. O. Davidsen & S. M. Davidsen (Eds.), *Behavioral medicine: Changing health life-styles* (pp. 474–482). New York: Brunner/Mazel. **(Chap 11)**

Marlatt, G. A., Larimer, M. E., Baer, J. S., & Quigley, L. A. (1993). Harm reduction for alcohol problems: Moving beyond the controlled drinking controversy. *Behavior Therapy, 24,* 461–504. **(Chap 11)**

Marmot, M. G., & Syme, S. L. (1976). Acculturation and coronary heart disease in Japanese Americans. *American Journal of Epidemiology, 104,* 225–247. **(Chap 9)**

Marsden, C. D. (1986). Hysteria—a neurologist's view. *Psychological Medicine, 16,* 277–288. **(Chap 6)**

Marshall, P. S. (1993). Allergy and depression: A neurochemical threshold model of the relation between the illnesses. *Psychological Bulletin, 113,* 23–43. **(Chap 4)**

Marshall, W. L. (1997). Pedophilia: Psychopathology and theory. In D. R. Laws & W. O'Donohue (Eds.), *Sexual deviance: Theory, assessment and treatment* (pp.152–174). New York: Guilford Press. **(Chap 10)**

Marshall, W. L., Barbaree, H. E., & Christophe, D. (1986). Sexual offenders against female children: Sexual preferences for age of victims and type of behavior. *Canadian Journal of Behavioral Science, 18,* 424–439. **(Chap 10)**

Marten, P. A., Brown, T. A., Barlow, D. H., Borkovec, T. D., Shear, M. K., & Lydiard, M. B. (in press). Evaluation of the ratings comprising the associated symptom criterion of DSM-III-R generalized anxiety disorder. *Journal of Nervous and Mental Disease.* **(Chap 5)**

Martin, I. (1983). Human classical conditioning. In A. Gale & J. A. Edward (Eds.), *Physiological correlates of human behavior: Vol. 2. Attention and performance.* London: Academic Press. **(Chaps 2, 5)**

Martin, P. R., Pekovich, S. R., McCool, B. A., Whetsell, W. O., & Singleton, C. K. (1994). Thiamine utilization in the pathogenesis of alcohol-induced brain damage. *Alcohol and Alcoholism Supplement, 2,* 273–279. **(Chap 15)**

Martin, S. L., Ramey, C. T., & Ramey, S. L. (1990). The prevention of intellectual impairment in children of impoverished families: Findings of a randomized trial of educational daycare. *American Journal of Public Health, 80,* 844–847. **(Chap 14)**

Maser, J. D. (1985). List of phobias. In A. H. Tuma & J. D. Maser (Eds.), *Anxiety and the anxiety disorders.* Hillsdale, NJ: Lawrence Erlbaum. **(Chap 5)**

Maser, J. D., & Gallup, G. G. (1974). Tonic immobility in the chicken: Catalepsy potentiation by uncontrollable shock and alleviation by imipramine. *Psychosomatic Medicine, 36,* 199–205. **(Chap 2)**

Maser, J. D., Kaelber, C., & Weise, R. E. (1991). International use and attitudes toward DSM-III and DSM-III-R: Growing consensus in psychiatric classification. *Journal of Abnormal Psychology, 100*(3), 271–279. **(Chap 3)**

Mason, F. L. (1997). Fetishism: Psychopathology and theory. In D. R. Laws & W. O'Donohue (Eds.), *Sexual deviance: Theory, assessment and treatment* (pp. 75–91). New York: Guilford Press. **(Chap 10)**

Massie, H. N., Miranda, G., Snowdon, D. A., Greiner, L. H., Wekstein, D. R., Danner, D., Markesbery, W. R., Kemper, S. J., & Mortimer, J. A. (1996). Linguistic ability in early life and Alzheimer disease in late life. *The Journal of the American Medical Association, 275,* 1879. **(Chap 15)**

Masters, W. H., & Johnson, V. E. (1966). *Human sexual response.* Boston: Little, Brown. **(Chaps 4, 10)**

Masters, W. H., & Johnson, V. E. (1970). *Human sexual inadequacy.* Boston: Little, Brown. **(Chap 10)**

Mathews, A. (1997). Information processing biases in emotional disorders. In D. M. Clark & C. G. Fairburn (Eds.), *Science and practice of cognitive-behavior therapy* (pp. 47–66). Oxford: Oxford University Press. **(Chap 5)**

Mathews, A., & MacLeod, C. (1994). Cognitive approaches to emotion and emotional disorders. *Annual Review of Psychology, 45,* 25–50. **(Chap 2)**

Mathews, A., Mogg, K., Kentish, J., & Eysenck, M. (1995). Effective psychological treatment on cognitive bias and generalized anxiety disorder. *Behavior Research and Therapy, 33,* 293–303. **(Chap 5)**

Matsumoto, D. (1994). *People: Psychology from a cultural perspective.* Pacific Grove, CA: Brooks/Cole. **(Chap 11)**

Matsumoto, D. (1996). *Culture and psychology.* Pacific Grove, CA: Brooks/Cole. **(Chap 9)**

Mattay, V. S., Berman, K. F., Ostrem, J. L., Esposito, G., Van-Horn, J. D., Bigelow, L. B., & Weinberger, D. R. (1996). Dextroamphetamine enhances "neural network-specific" physiological signals: A positron-emission tomography rCBF study. *Journal of Neuroscience, 16,* 4816–4822. **(Chap 14)**

Matthews, K. A. (1988). Coronary heart disease and Type A behaviors: Update on and alternative to the Booth-Kewley and Friedman (1987) quantitative review. *Psychological Bulletin, 104*(3), 373–380. **(Chap 9)**

May, P. A., & Hymbaugh, K. J. (1983). A pilot project of fetal alcohol syndrome among American Indians. *Alcohol Health and Research World, 7,* 3–9. **(Chap 11)**

Mays, V. M., & Cochran, S. D. (1988). Issues in the perception of AIDS risk and risk reduction activities by black and Hispanic/Latino women. *American Psychologist, 43*(11), 949–957. **(Chap 9)**

McAdoo, W. G., & DeMyer, M. K. (1978). Research related to family factors in autism. *Journal of Pediatric Psychology, 2,* 162–166. **(Chap 14)**

McCaffrey, R. J., & Bellamy-Campbell, R. (1989). Psychometric detection of fabricated symptoms of combat-related posttraumatic stress disorder: A systematic replication. *Journal of Clinical Psychology, 45,* 76–79. **(Chap 16)**

McCann, U. D., Rossiter, E. M., King, R. J., & Agras, W. S. (1991). Nonpurging bulimia: A distinct subtype of bulimia nervosa. *International Journal of Eating Disorders, 10,* 679–687. **(Chap 8)**

McCaughrin, W. B. (1988). *Longitudinal trends of competitive employment for developmentally disabled adults: A benefit-cost analysis.* Unpublished doctoral dissertation, University of Illinois at Urbana-Champaign. **(Chap 14)**

McClearn, G. E., Johansson, B., Berg, S., Pedersen, N. L., Ahern, F., Petrill, S. A., & Plomin, R. (1997, June 6). Substantial genetic influence on cognitive abilities in twins 80 or more years old. *Science, 276,* 1560–1563. **(Chap 2)**

McCrae, R. R., & Costa, P. T. (1997). Personality trait structure as a human universal. *American Psychologist, 52,* 509–516. **(Chap 12)**

McCreery, J. M., & Walker, R. D. (1993). Alcohol problems. In D. L. Dunner (Ed.), *Current psychiatric therapy* (pp. 92–98). Philadelphia: W. B. Saunders. **(Chaps 4, 11)**

McDaniel, K. (1990). Thalmic degeneration. In J. L. Cummings (Ed.), *Subcortical dementia* (pp. 132–144). New York: Oxford University Press. **(Chap 14)**

McEachin, J. J., Smith, T., & Lovaas, O. I. (1993). Long-term outcome for children with autism who received early intensive behavioral treatment. *American Journal on Mental Retardation, 97,* 359–372. **(Chap 14)**

McElroy, S. L., & Keck, P. E. (1993). Rapid cycling. In D. L. Dunner (Ed.), *Current psychiatric therapy* (pp. 226–231). Philadelphia: W. B. Saunders. **(Chap 7)**

McElroy, S. L., Keck, P. E., Pope, H. G., Hudson, J. I., Faedda, G. L., & Swann, A. C. (1992). Clinical and research implications of the diagnosis of dysphoric or mixed mania or hypomania. *American Journal of Psychiatry, 149*(12), 1633–1644. **(Chap 7)**

McEwen, B. S., & Stellar, E. (1993). Stress and the individual: Mechanisms leading to disease. *Archives of Internal Medicine, 153,* 2093–2101. **(Chaps 2, 9)**

McGehee, D. S., Heath, M. J. S., Gelber, S., Devay, P., & Role, L. W. (1995). Nicotine enhancement of fast excitatory synaptic transmission in CNS by presynaptic receptors. *Science, 269,* 1692–1696. **(Chap 11)**

McGillivray, B. C., Bassett, A. S., Langlois, S., Pantzar, T., & Wood, S. (1990). Familial 5q11.2-q13.3 segmental duplication cosegregating with multiple anomalies, including schizophrenia. *American Journal of Medical Genetics, 35,* 10–13. **(Chap 13)**

McGinnis, J. M., & Foege, W. H. (1993, November 10). Actual causes of death in the United States. *JAMA, 270*(18), 2207–2212. **(Chap 9)**

McGlashan, T. H., & Fenton, W. S. (1991). Classical subtypes for schizophrenia: Literature review for DSM-IV. *Schizophrenia Bulletin, 17,* 609–623. **(Chap 13)**

McGowin, D. F. (1993). *Living in the labyrinth: A personal journey through the maze of Alzheimer's.* New York: Delacorte Press. **(Chap 15)**

McGrath, P. A., & DeVeber, L. L. (1986). The management of acute pain evoked by medical procedures in children with cancer. *Journal of Pain and Symptom Management, 1,* 145–150. **(Chap 9)**

McGue, M., & Christensen, K. (1997). Genetic and environmental contributions to depression symptomatology: Evidence from Danish twins 75 years of age and older. *Journal of Abnormal Psychology, 106*(3), 439–448. **(Chap 7)**

McGue, M., & Lykken, D. T. (1992). Genetic influence on risk of divorce. *Psychological Science, 3*(6), 368–373. **(Chaps 2, 4)**

McGue, M., Pickens, R. W., & Svikis, D. S. (1992). Sex and age effects on the inheritance of alcohol problems: A twin study. *Journal of Abnormal Psychology, 101,* 3–17. **(Chaps 4, 11)**

McGuffin, P., & Katz, R. (1989). The genetics of depression and manic-depressive disorder. *British Journal of Psychiatry, 155,* 294–304. **(Chap 7)**

McGuffin, P., & Reich, T. (1984). Psychopathology and genetics. In H. E. Adams & P. B. Sutker (Eds.), *Comprehensive handbook of psychopathology.* New York: Plenum Press. **(Chap 5)**

McGuffin, P., Katz, R., & Bebbington, P. (1988). The Camberwell Collaborative Depression Study. III. Depression and adversity in the relatives of depressed probands. *British Journal of Psychiatry, 152,* 775–782. **(Chap 2)**

McGuire, P. K., Shah, G. M. S., & Murray, R. M. (1993). Increased blood flow in Broca's area during auditory hallucinations in schizophrenia. *Lancet, 342,* 703–706. **(Chap 13)**

McIntosh, J. L., Santos, J. F., Hubbard, R. W., & Overholser, J. C. (1994). *Elder suicide: Research, theory and treatment.* Washington, DC: American Psychological Association. **(Chap 7)**

McKay, D., Todaro, J., Neziroglu, F., Campisi, T., Moritz, E. K., & Yaryura-Tobias, J. A. (1997). Body dysmorphic disorder: A preliminary evaluation of treatment and maintenance using exposure with response prevention. *Behaviour Research and Therapy, 35,* 67–70. **(Chap 6)**

McKenzie, S. J., Williamson, D. A., & Cubic, B. A. (1993). Stable and reactive body image disturbances in bulimia nervosa. *Behavior Therapy, 24,* 195–207. **(Chap 8)**

McKeon, P., & Murray, R. (1987). Familial aspects of obsessive-compulsive neuroses. *British Journal of Psychiatry, 151,* 528–534. **(Chap 12)**

McKim, W. A. (1991). *Drugs and behavior: An introduction to behavioral pharmacology* (2nd ed.). Englewood Cliffs, NJ: Prentice-Hall. **(Chap 11)**

McKinnon, W., Weisse, C. S., Reynolds, C. P., Bowles, C. A., & Baum, A. (1989). Chronic stress, leukocyte subpopulations, and hormonal response to latent viruses. *Health Psychology, 8,* 399–402. **(Chap 9)**

McKnight, D. L., Nelson-Gray, R. O., & Barnhill, J. (1992). Dexamethasone suppression test and response to cognitive therapy and antidepressant medication. *Behavior Therapy, 23*(1), 99–111. **(Chap 7)**

McLaren, J., & Bryson, S. E. (1987). Review of recent epidemiological studies of mental retardation: Prevalence, associated disorders, and etiology. *American Journal of Mental Retardation, 92,* 243–254. **(Chap 14)**

McLean, P., & Taylor, S. (1992). Severity of unipolar depression and choice of treatment. *Behaviour Research and Therapy, 30*(5), 443–451. **(Chap 7)**

McLeod, J. D., Kessler, R. C., & Landis, K. R. (1992). Speed of recovery from major depressive episodes in a community sample of married men and women. *Journal of Abnormal Psychology, 101*(2), 277–286. **(Chap 7)**

McNally, R. J. (1994a). Choking phobia: A review of the literature. *Comprehensive Psychiatry, 35,* 83–89. **(Chap 5)**

McNally, R. J. (1994b). *Panic disorder: A critical analysis.* New York: Guilford Press. **(Chap 5)**

McNally, R. J. (1996) Cognitive bias in the anxiety disorders. In D. A. Hope (Ed.), *Perspectives on anxiety, panic and fear* (The 43rd Annual Nebraska Symposium on Motivation) (pp. 211–250). Lincoln: Nebraska University Press. **(Chap 5)**

McNeil, E. B. (1970). *Neuroses and personality disorders.* Englewood Cliffs, NJ: Prentice-Hall. **(Chap 12)**

McNeil, T. F. (1987). Perinatal influences in the development of schizophrenia. In H. Helmchen & F. A. Henn (Eds.), *Biological perspectives of schizophrenia* (pp. 125–138). New York: John Wiley. **(Chap 13)**

McNiel, D. E., & Binder, R. L. (1987). Clinical assessment of the risk of violence among psychiatric inpatients. *American Journal of Psychiatry, 148,* 1317–1321. **(Chap 16)**

Medina vs. California. (1992). 112 S. Ct. 2575. **(Chap 16)**

Mednick, S. A., & Schulsinger, F. (1965). A longitudinal study of children with a high risk for schizophrenia: A preliminary report. In S. Vandenberg (Ed.), *Methods and goals in human behavior genetics* (pp. 255–296). New York: Academic Press. **(Chap 13)**

Mednick, S. A., & Schulsinger, F. (1968). Some premorbid characteristics related to breakdown in children with schizophrenic mothers. *Journal of Psychiatric Research, 6,* 267–291. **(Chap 13)**

Meehan, P. J., Lamb, J. A., Saltzman, L. E., & O'Carroll, P. W. (1992). Attempted suicide among young adults: Progress toward a meaningful estimate of prevalence. *American Journal of Psychiatry, 149*(1), 41–44. **(Chap 7)**

Meehl, P. E. (1945). The dynamics of "structured" personality tests. *Journal of Clinical Psychology, 1,* 296–303. **(Chap 3)**

Meehl, P. E. (1962). Schizotaxia, schizotypy, schizophrenia. *American Psychologist, 17,* 827–838. **(Chaps 12, 13)**

Meehl, P. E. (1989). Schizotaxia revisited. *Archives of General Psychiatry, 46,* 935–944. **(Chap 3)**

Melamed, B. G., & Siegel, L. J. (1975). Reduction of anxiety in children facing hospitalization and surgery by use of filmed modeling. *Journal of Consulting and Clinical Psychology, 43*(4), 511–521. **(Chap 9)**

Mellinger, G. D., Balter, M. B., & Uhlenhuth, E. H. (1985). Insomnia and its treatment: Prevalence and correlates. *Archives of General Psychiatry, 42,* 225–232. **(Chaps 4, 8)**

Melton, G. B., Petrila, J., Poythress, N. G., & Slobogin, C. (1987). *Psychological evaluations for the courts.* New York: Guilford. **(Chap 16)**

Meltzer, E. S., & Kumar, R. (1985). Puerperal mental illness, clinical features and classification: A study of 142 mother-and-baby admissions. *British Journal of Psychiatry, 147,* 647–654. **(Chap 7)**

Meltzer, H. Y. (1995). Atypical antipsychotic drug therapy for treatment-resistant schizophrenia. In S. R. Hirsch and D. R. Weinberger (Eds.), *Schizophrenia* (pp. 485–502). Oxford, England: Blackwell Science Ltd. **(Chap 13)**

Melzack, R., & Wall, P. D. (1965). Pain mechanisms: A new theory. *Science, 150,* 971–979. **(Chap 9)**

Melzack, R., & Wall, P. D. (1982). *The challenge of pain.* New York: Basic Books. **(Chap 9)**

Mendlewicz, J., & Rainer, J. D. (1977). Adoption study supporting genetic transmission in manic-depressive illness. *Nature, 268*(5618), 327–329. **(Chap 7)**

Merzenich, M. M., Jenkins, W. M., Johnston, P., Schreiner, C., Miller, S. L., & Tallal, P. (1996). Temporal processing deficits of language-learning impaired children ameliorated by training. *Science, 271,* 77–81. **(Chap 14)**

Meston, C. M., & Gorzalka, B. B. (1995). The effects of sympathetic activation on physiological and subjective sexual arousal in women. *Behaviour Research and Therapy, 33*, 651–664. **(Chap 10)**

Meyer, A. J., Nash, J. D., McAlister, A. L., Maccoby, M., & Farquhar, J. W. (1980). Skills training in a cardiovascular health education campaign. *Journal of Consulting and Clinical Psychology, 2*, 129–142. **(Chap 9)**

Meyer, L. H., Peck, C. A., & Brown, L. (1991). *Critical issues in the lives of people with severe disabilities.* Baltimore: Paul H. Brookes. **(Chap 14)**

Meyerowitz, B. E. (1983). Postmastectomy coping strategies and quality of life. *Health Psychology, 2*, 117–132. **(Chap 9)**

Meyers, A. (1991). Biobehavioral interactions in behavioral medicine. *Behavior Therapy, 22*, 129–131. **(Chap 9)**

Mezzich, J. E., Good, B. J., Lewis-Fernandez, R., Guarnaccia, P., Lin, K. M., Parron, D., O'Nell, T., Manson, S., Fleming, C., Weiss, M., & Hughes, C. (1993, September). *Cultural formulation guidelines.* Revised cultural proposals for DSM-IV. Submitted to the DSM-IV Task Force by the Steering Committee, NIMH-Sponsored Group on Culture and Diagnosis. **(Chap 3)**

Mezzich, J. E., Kleinman, A., Fabrega, H., Jr., Good, B., Johnson-Powell, G., Lin, K. M., Manson, S., & Parron, D. (1992). *Cultural proposals for DSM-IV.* Submitted to the DSM-IV Task Force by the Steering Committee, NIMH-Sponsored Group on Culture and Diagnosis. **(Chap 6)**

Michultka, D. M., Blanchard, E. B., Appelbaum, K. A., Jaccard, J., & Dentinger, M. P. (1989). The refractory headache patient. II. High medication consumption (analgesic rebound) headache. *Behaviour Research and Therapy, 27*, 411–420. **(Chap 9)**

Middleton, W., Burnett, P., Raphael, B., & Martinek, N. (1996). The bereavement response: A cluster analysis. *British Journal of Psychiatry, 169*, 167–171. **(Chap 7)**

Miklowitz, D. J., & Goldstein, M. J. (1990). Behavioral family treatment for patients with bipolar affective disorder. *Behavior Modification, 14*, 457–489. **(Chap 7)**

Miklowitz, D. J., Simoneau, T. L., Sachs-Ericsson, N., Warner, R., & Suddath, R. (1996). Family risk indicators in the course of bipolar affective disorder. In E. Mundt et al., *Interpersonal factors in the origin and course of affective disorders* (pp. 204–217). London: Gaskell Press. **(Chap 7)**

Milby, J. B., Williams, V., Hall, J. N., Khuder, S., McGill, T., & Wooten, V. (1993). Effectiveness of combined triazolam-behavior therapy for primary insomnia. *American Journal of Psychiatry, 150*, 1259–1260. **(Chap 8)**

Miller, I. W., & Norman, W. H. (1979). Learned helplessness in humans: A review and attribution-theory model. *Psychological Bulletin, 86*(1), 93–118. **(Chaps 2, 7)**

Miller, I. W., Keitner, G. I., Epstein, N. B., Bishop, D. S., & Ryan, C. E. (1991). *Families of bipolar patients: Dysfunction, course of illness, and pilot treatment study.* Paper presented at the annual meeting of the Association for the Advancement of Behavior Therapy, New York. **(Chap 7)**

Miller, I. W., Norman, W. H., Keitner, G. I. (1989). Cognitive-behavioral treatment of depressed inpatients: Six- and twelve-month follow-up. *American Journal of Psychiatry, 146*, 1274–1279. **(Chap 7)**

Miller, I. W., Norman, W. H., Keitner, G. I., Bishop, S. B., & Down, M. G. (1989). Cognitive-behavioral treatment of depressed inpatients. *Behavior Therapy, 20*(1), 25–47. **(Chap 7)**

Miller, N. E. (1969). Learning of visceral and glandular responses. *Science, 163*, 434–445. **(Chap 9)**

Miller, N. E. (1987). Education for a lifetime of learning. In G. C. Stone, S. M. Weiss, J. D. Matarazzo, N. E. Miller, J. Rodin, C. D. Belar, M. J. Follick, & J. E. Singer (Eds.), *Health psychology: A discipline and a profession.* Chicago: IL: University of Chicago Press. **(Chap 9)**

Miller, N. S., Gold, M. S., & Pottash, A. C. (1989). A 12-step treatment approach for marijuana (cannabis) dependence. *Journal of Substance Abuse Treatment, 6*, 241–250. **(Chap 11)**

Miller, P. M., Smith, G. T., & Goldman, M. S. (1990). Emergence of alcohol expectancies in childhood: A possible critical period. *Journal of Studies on Alcohol, 51*, 343–349. **(Chap 11)**

Miller, P. P., Albano, A. M., & Barlow, D. H. (1992). *Sibling modeling in the treatment of PTSD.* Paper presented at the annual meeting of the Association for the Advancement of Behavior Therapy, Boston, MA. **(Chap 5)**

Miller, S., & Watson, B. C. (1992). The relationship between communication attitude, anxiety, and depression in stutterers and nonstutterers. *Journal of Speech and Hearing Research, 35*, 789–798. **(Chap 14)**

Miller, S. D. (1989). Optical differences in cases of multiple personality disorder. *Journal of Nervous and Mental Disease, 177*(8), 480–486. **(Chap 6)**

Miller, T. Q., Smith, T. W., Turner, C. W., Guijarro, M. L., & Hallet, A. J. (1996). A meta-analytic review of research on hostility and physical health. *Psychological Bulletin, 119*(2), 322–348. **(Chap 9)**

Miller, W. R. (1985). Motivation for treatment: A review with special emphasis on alcoholism. Psychological Bulletin, *98*, 84–107. **(Chap 11)**

Miller, W. R., & Hester, R. K. (1986). Inpatient alcoholism treatment: Who benefits? *American Psychologist, 41*, 794–805. **(Chap 11)**

Miller, W. R., & McCrady, B. S. (1993). The importance of research on Alcoholics Anonymous. In B. S. McCrady & W. R. Miller (Eds.), *Research on Alcoholics Anonymous: Opportunities and alternatives* (pp. 3–11). New Brunswick, NJ: Rutgers Center of Alcohol Studies. **(Chap 11)**

Millon, T. (1981). *Disorders of personality: DSM-III, Axis II.* New York: John Wiley. **(Chap 12)**

Millon, T. (1986). Schizoid and avoidant personality disorders in DSM-III. *American Journal of Psychiatry, 143*, 1321–1322. **(Chap 12)**

Millon, T., & Martinez, A. (1995). Avoidant personality disorder. In W. J. Livesley (Ed.), *The DSM-IV personality disorders* (pp. 218–233). New York: Guilford Press. **(Chap 12)**

Mills, J. L., Holmes, L. B., Aarons, J. H., Simpson, J. L., Brown, Z. A., Jovanovic-Peterson, L. G., Conley, M. R., Graubard, B. I., Knopp, R. H., & Metzger, B. E. (1993). Moderate caffeine use and the risk of spontaneous abortion and intrauterine growth retardation. *Journal of the American Medical Association, 269*, 593–597. **(Chap 11)**

Mindell, J. A. (1993). Sleep disorders in children. *Health Psychology, 12*, 152–163. **(Chap 8)**

Mineka, S. (1985a). Animal models of anxiety based disorders: Their usefulness and limitations. In A. H. Tuma & J. D. Maser (Eds.), *Anxiety and the anxiety disorders.* Hillsdale, NJ: Lawrence Erlbaum. **(Chap 5)**

Mineka, S. (1985b). The frightful complexity of the origins of fears. In F. R. Bruch & J. B. Overmier (Eds.), *Affect, conditioning, and cognition: Essays on the determinants of behavior.* Hillsdale, NJ: Lawrence Erlbaum. **(Chaps 2, 5)**

Mineka, S., & Kelly, K. A. (1989). The relationship between anxiety, lack of control and loss of control. In A. Steptoe & A. Appels (Eds.), *Stress, personal control and worker health.* New York: John Wiley. **(Chap 7)**

Mineka, S., & Watson, D., & Clark, L. A. (1998). Comorbidity of anxiety and unipolar mood disorders. *Annual Review of Psychology, 49*, 377–412. **(Chap 5)**

Mineka, S., & Zinbarg, R. E. (1995) Animal-ethological models of social phobia. In R. Heimberg, M. Leibowitz, D. Hope, & F. Schneier (Eds.), *Social phobia: Diagnosis, assessment and treatment* (pp.134–162). New York: Guilford Press. **(Chap 5)**

Mineka, S., & Zinbarg, R. E. (1996). Conditioning and ethological models of anxiety disorders: Stress-in-dynamic-context anxiety models. In D. A. Hope (Ed.), *Perspectives on anxiety, panic and fear* (The 43rd Annual Nebraska Symposium on Motivation) (pp. 135–210). Lincoln: Nebraska University Press. **(Chap 5)**

Mineka, S., Davidson, M., Cook, M., & Keir, R. (1984). Observational conditioning of snake fear in rhesus monkeys. *Journal of Abnormal Psychology, 93,* 355–372. **(Chap 5)**

Mingdao, Z., & Zhenyi, X. (1990). Delivery systems and research for schizophrenia in China. In A. Kales, C. N. Stefanis, & J. A. Talbott (Eds.), *Recent advances in schizophrenia* (pp. 373–395). New York: Springer-Verlag. **(Chap 13)**

Minuchin, S., Rosman, B. L., & Baker, L. (1978). *Psychosomatic families.* Cambridge, MA: Harvard University Press. **(Chap 8)**

Mirsky, A. F. (1995). Israeli High-Risk Study: Editor's introduction. *Schizophrenia Bulletin, 21,* 179–182. **(Chap 13)**

Mitchell, J. E., & Pyle, R. L. (1988). The diagnosis and clinical characteristics of bulimia. In B. J. Blinder, B. F. Chaitin, & R. S. Goldstein (Eds.), *The eating disorders: Medical and psychological bases of diagnosis and treatment* (pp. 267–273). New York: PMA. **(Chap 8)**

Mitchell, W. B., DiBartolo, P. M., Brown, T. A., & Barlow, D. H. (in press). The effects of positive and negative affect on sexual arousal in sexually functional males. *Archives of Sexual Behavior.* **(Chap 10)**

Mogg, K., Bradley, B. P., Millar, N., & White, J. (1995). A follow-up study of cognitive bias in generalized anxiety disorder. *BRAT, 33,* 927–935. **(Chap 5)**

Mogg, K., Mathews, A., & Weinman, J. (1989). Selective processing of threat cues in anxiety states: A replication. *Behaviour Research and Therapy, 27,* 317–323. **(Chap 5)**

Mogil, J. S., Sternberg, W. F., Kest, B., Marek, P., & Liebeskind, J. C. (1993). Sex differences in the antagonism of swim stress-induced analgesia: Effects of gonadectomy and estrogen replacement. *Pain, 53,* 17–25. **(Chap 9)**

Mohr, D. C., & Beutler, L. E. (1990). Erectile dysfunction: A review of diagnostic and treatment procedures. *Clinical Psychology Review, 10*(1), 123–150. **(Chap 10)**

Moller-Madsen, S. & Nystrup, J. (1992). Incidence of anorexia nervosa in Denmark. *Acta Psychiatrica Scandinavica, 86,* 197–200. **(Chap 8)**

Monahan, J. (1984). The prediction of violent behavior: Toward a second generation of theory and policy. *American Journal of Psychiatry, 141,* 10–15. **(Chap 16)**

Money, J. (1992). *The Kaspar Hauser syndrome of \"psychosocial dwarfism": Deficient statural, intellectual, and social growth induced by child abuse.* Buffalo: Prometheus Books. **(Chap 2)**

Money, J., & Ehrhardt, A. (1972). *Man and woman, boy and girl.* Baltimore: Johns Hopkins University Press. **(Chap 10)**

Money, J., Annecillo, C., & Hutchison, J. W. (1985). Forensic and family psychiatry in abuse dwarfism: Munchausen's Syndrome by proxy, atonement, and addiction to abuse. *Journal of Sex and Marital Therapy, 11*(1), 30–40. **(Chap 2)**

Monk, T. H., & Moline, M. L. (1989). The timing of bedtime and waketime decisions in free-running subjects. *Psychophysiology, 26,* 304–310. **(Chap 8)**

Monroe, S. M., & Roberts, J. E. (1990). Conceptualizing and measuring life stress: Problems, principles, procedures, progress. Special issue: II-IV. Advances in measuring life stress. *Stress Medicine, 6*(3), 209–216. **(Chap 7)**

Monroe, S. M., Bromet, E. J., Connell, M. M., & Steiner, S. C. (1986). Social support, life events, and depressive symptoms: A 1 year prospective study. *Journal of Consulting and Clinical Psychology, 54*(4), 424–431. **(Chap 7)**

Monroe, S. M., Imhoff, D. F., Wise, B. D., & Harris, J. E. (1983). Prediction of psychological symptoms under high-risk psychosocial circumstances: Life events, social support, and symptom specificity. *Journal of Abnormal Psychology, 92*(2), 338–350. **(Chap 7)**

Monroe, S. M., Kupfer, D. J., & Frank, E. (1992). Life stress and treatment course of recurrent depression: I. Response during index episode. *Journal of Consulting and Clinical Psychology, 60*(5), 718–724. **(Chap 7)**

Monroe, S. M., Roberts, J. E., Kupfer, D. J., & Frank, E. (1996). Life stress and treatment course of recurrent depression: II. Postrecovery associations with attrition, symptom course, and recurrence over 3 years. *Journal of Abnormal Psychology, 105*(3), 313–328. **(Chap 7)**

Monroe, S. M., Thase, M. E., & Simons, A. D. (1992). Social factors and the psychobiology of depression: Relations between life stress and rapid eye movement sleep latency. *Journal of Abnormal Psychology, 101*(3), 528–537. **(Chap 7)**

Mooney, J. J., Schatzberg, A. F., Cole, J. O., & Samson, J. A. (1991). Urinary 3-methoxy-4-hydroxyphenylglycol and the depression-type score as predictors of differential responses to antidepressants. *Journal of Clinical Psychopharmacology, 11*(6), 339–343. **(Chap 7)**

Moore, R. Y. (1973). Retinohypothalamic projection in mammals: A comparative study. *Brain Research, 49,* 403–409. **(Chap 2)**

Moras, K., Clark, L. A., Katon, W., Roy-Byrne, P., Watson, D, & Barlow, D. H. (1996). Mixed anxiety-depression. In T. A. Widiger, A. J. Frances, H. A. Pincus, R. Ross, M. B. First, & W. W. Davis (Eds.), *DSM-IV sourcebook* (Vol. 2, pp. 623–643). Washington, DC: American Psychiatric Association. **(Chap 3)**

Moreau, D., & Weissman, M. M. (1992). Panic disorder in children and adolescents: A review. *American Journal of Psychiatry, 149,* 1306–1314. **(Chap 5)**

Morelli, G. A., Rogoff, B., Oppenheim, D., & Goldsmith, D. (1992). Cultural variation in infants' sleeping arrangements: Questions of independence. *Developmental Psychology, 28,* 604–613. **(Chap 8)**

Morenz, B., & Becker, J. (1995). The treatment of youthful sexual offenders. *Applied & Preventive Psychology, 4,* 247–256. **(Chap 10)**

Morey, L. C. (1988). Personality disorders in DSM-III and DSM-III-R: Convergence, coverage, and internal consistency. *American Journal of Psychiatry, 145,* 573–577. **(Chap 12)**

Morey, L. C., & Kurtz, J. E. (1989). *The place of neurasthenia in the DSM-IV.* Unpublished report to the DSM-IV subgroup on generalized anxiety disorder and mixed anxiety depression. **(Chap 9)**

Morey, L. C., & Ochoa, E. S. (1989). An investigation of adherence to diagnostic criteria: Clinical diagnosis of the DSM-III personality disorders. *Journal of Personality Disorders, 3*(3), 180–192. **(Chap 3)**

Morgan, H. W. (1981). *Drugs in America: A social history, 1800–1980.* Syracuse, NY: Syracuse University Press. **(Chap 11)**

Morgan, J. P. (1997). Designer drugs. In J. H. Lowinson, P. Ruiz, R. B. Millman, & J. G. Langrod (Eds.), *Substance abuse: A comprehensive textbook* (pp. 264–269). Baltimore: Williams & Wilkins. **(Chap 11)**

Morgenstern, H., & Glazer, W. M. (1993). Identifying risk factors for tardive dyskinesia among long-term outpatients maintained with neuroleptic medications: Results of the Yale tardive dyskinesia study. *Archives of General Psychiatry, 50,* 723–733. **(Chap 13)**

Morin, C. M. (1993a). *Insomnia: Psychological assessment and management.* New York: Guilford Press. **(Chap 8)**

Morin, C. M. (1993b). *Psychological management of insomnia.* New York: Guilford Press. **(Chap 8)**

Morin, C. M., & Azrin, N. H. (1988). Behavioral and cognitive treatments of geriatric insomnia. *Journal of Consulting and Clinical Psychology, 56,* 748–753. **(Chap 8)**

Morin, C. M., Kowatch, R. A., Barry, T., & Walton, E. (1993). Cognitive-behavior therapy for late-life insomnia. *Journal of Consulting and Clinical Psychology, 61,* 137–146. **(Chap 8)**

Morin, C. M., Stone, J., Trinkle, D., Mercer, J., & Remsberg, S. (in press). Dysfunctional beliefs and attitudes about sleep among older adults with and without insomnia complaints. *Psychology and Aging.* **(Chap 8)**

Morokoff, P. J. (1993). Female sexual arousal disorder. In W. O'Donohue & J. H. Geer (Eds.), *Handbook of sexual dysfunctions: Assessment and treatment* (pp.

157–199). Boston: Allyn & Bacon. **(Chap 10)**

Morokoff, P. J., & Heiman, J. R. (1980). Effects of erotic stimuli on sexually functional and dysfunctional women: Multiple measures before and after sex therapy. *Behaviour Research and Therapy, 18,* 127–137. **(Chap 10)**

Morris, D. (1985). *Body watching: A field guide to the human species.* New York: Crown. **(Chap 6)**

Morris, J. K., Cook, D. G., & Shaper, A. G. (1994). Loss of employment and mortality. *British Medical Journal, 308,* 1135–1139. **(Chap 9)**

Morris, M., Lack, L., & Dawson, D. (1990). Sleep-onset insomniacs have delayed temperature rhythms. *Sleep, 13,* 1–14. **(Chap 8)**

Morrow, G. R. (1986). Behavioral management of chemotherapy-induced nausea and vomiting in the cancer patient. *The Clinical Oncologist, 113,* 11–14. **(Chap 9)**

Morrow, G. R., & Dobkin, P. L. (1988). Anticipatory nausea and vomiting in cancer patients undergoing chemotherapy treatment: Prevalence, etiology, and behavioral interventions. *Clinical Psychology Review, 8,* 517–556. **(Chaps 1, 9)**

Morse, G. A. (1992). Causes of homelessness. In M. J. Robertson & M. Greenblatt (Eds.), *Homelessness: A national perspective* (pp. 3–17). New York: Plenum Press. **(Chap 16)**

Morton, A. (1992). *Diana: Her true story.* New York: Pocket Books. **(Chap 8)**

Mosher, D. L., & Sirkin, M. (1984). Measuring a macho personality constellation. *Journal of Research in Personality, 18,* 150–163. **(Chap 12)**

Mosko, S., Richard, C., & McKenna, J. C. (1997). Maternal sleep and arousals during bedsharing with infants. *Sleep, 20,* 142–150. **(Chap 8)**

Moss, A. R., & Bacchetti, P. (1989). Natural history of HIV infection. *AIDS, 3,* 55–61. **(Chap 9)**

Mucha, T. F., & Reinhardt, R. F. (1970). Conversion reactions in student aviators. *American Journal of Psychiatry, 127,* 493–497. **(Chap 6)**

Mueller, T., Keller, M. B., Leon, A. C., Solomon, D. A., Shea, M. T., Coryell, W., & Endicott, J. (1996). Recovery after 5 years of unremitting major depressive disorder. *Archives of General Psychiatry, 53,* 794–799. **(Chap 7)**

Mueser, K. T., & Glynn, S. M. (in press). Family interventions for schizophrenia. In K. S. Dobson & K. D. Craig (Eds.), *Best practices: Developing and promoting empirically supported interventions.* Newbury Park, CA: Sage Publications. **(Chap 13)**

Mueser, K. T., Bellack, A. S., Wade, J. H., Sayers, S. L., Tierney, A., & Haas, G. (1993). Expressed emotion, social skill, and response to negative affect in schiz-

ophrenia. *Journal of Abnormal Psychology, 102,* 339–351. **(Chap 13)**

Mueser, K. T., Liberman, R. P., & Glynn, S. M. (1990). Psychosocial interventions in schizophrenia. In A. Kales, C. N. Stefanis, & J. A. Talbott (Eds.), *Recent advances in schizophrenia* (pp. 213–235). New York: Springer-Verlag. **(Chap 13)**

Mumford, D. B., Whitehouse, A. M., & Platts, M. (1991). Sociocultural correlates of eating disorders among Asian schoolgirls in Bradford. *British Journal of Psychiatry, 158,* 222–228. **(Chap 8)**

Mundy, P., Sigman, M., & Kasari, C. (1990). A longitudinal study of joint attention and language development in autistic children. *Journal of Autism and Developmental Disorders, 20,* 115–128. **(Chap 14)**

Munjack, D. J. (1984). The onset of driving phobias. *Journal of Behavior Therapy and Experimental Psychiatry, 15,* 305–308. **(Chap 5)**

Muñoz, R. F. (1993). The prevention of depression: Current research and practice. *Applied and Preventative Psychology, 2,* 21–33. **(Chap 7)**

Murdoch, D., Pihl, R. O., & Ross, D. (1990). Alcohol and crimes of violence: Present issues. *International Journal of the Addictions, 25,* 1065–1081. **(Chap 11)**

Murphy, A., Lehrer, P., & Jurish, S. (1990). Cognitive coping skills training and relaxation training as treatments for tension headaches. *Behavior Therapy, 21,* 89–98. **(Chap 9)**

Murray, C. J. L. (1996). *Global health statistics.* Cambridge, MA: Harvard University Press. **(Chap 7)**

Murray, C. J. L., & Lopez, A. (Eds.) (1996). *The global burden of disease.* Cambridge, MA: Harvard University Press. **(Chap 7)**

Murray, M. E., Keele, D. K., & McCarver, J. W. (1976). Behavioral treatment of rumination. *Clinical Pediatrics, 15,* 591–596. **(Chap 8)**

Mustafa, G. (1990). Delivery systems for the care of schizophrenic patients in Africa—Sub-Sahara. In A. Kales, C. N. Stefanis, & J. A. Talbot (Eds.), *Recent advances in schizophrenia* (pp. 353–371). New York: Springer-Verlag. **(Chap 13)**

Musto, D. F. (1992). America's first cocaine epidemic: What did we learn? In T. R. Kosten & H. D. Kleber (Eds.), *Clinician's guide to cocaine addiction: Theory, research, and treatment* (pp. 3–15). New York: Guilford Press. **(Chap 11)**

Myers, J. K., Weissman, M. M., Tischler, C. E., Holzer, C. E., III, Orvaschel, H., Anthony, J. C., Boyd, J. H., Burke, J. D., Jr., Kramer, M., & Stoltzman, R. (1984). Six-month prevalence of psychiatric disorders in three communities. *Archives of General Psychiatry, 41,* 959–967. **(Chap 5)**

Nadig, P. W., Ware, J. C., & Blumoff, R. (1986). Noninvasive device to produce

and maintain an erection-like state. *Urology, 27,* 126–131. **(Chap 11)**

Nagel, D. B. (1991). Psychotherapy of schizophrenia: 1900–1920. In J. G. Howells (Ed.), *The concept of schizophrenia: Historical perspectives* (pp. 191–201). Washington, DC: American Psychiatric Press. **(Chap 13)**

Nasser, M. (1986). Comparative study of the prevalence of abnormal eating attitudes among Arab female students of both London and Cairo universities. *Psychological Medicine, 16,* 621–625. **(Chap 8)**

Nasser, M. (1988). Eating disorders: The cultural dimension. *Social Psychiatry and Psychiatric Epidemiology, 23,* 184–187. **(Chap 8)**

Nathan, P. E. (1993). Alcoholism: Psychopathology, etiology, and treatment. In P. B. Sutker & H. E. Adams (Eds.), *Comprehensive handbook of psychopathology* (pp. 451–476). New York: Plenum Press. **(Chap 11)**

Nathan, P. E., & Gorman, J. M., (1998). *A guide to treatments that work.* New York: Oxford University Press. **(Chap 10)**

National Center for Health Statistics. (1993). Advance report of final mortality statistics, 1990 (Monthly Vital Statistics Report, Vol, 41, No. 7, Suppl.). Hyattsville, MD: Public Health Service. **(Chap 7)**

National Institute on Drug Abuse. (1991). *National household survey on drug abuse, population estimates, 1991* (DHHS Publication No. ADM 91–1732). Washington, DC: U.S. Government Printing Office. **(Chap 11)**

National Institutes of Health (1993). *Learning disabilities* (NIH Publication No. 93–3611). Washington, DC: U. S. Government Printing Office. **(Chap 14)**

Navia, B. A. (1990). The AIDS dementia complex. In J. L. Cummings (Ed.), *Subcortical dementia* (pp. 181–198). New York: Oxford University Press. **(Chap 14)**

Neal, A. M., Nagle-Rich, L., & Smucker, W. D. (1994). The presence of panic disorder among African American hypertensives: A pilot study. *Journal of Black Psychology, 20,* 29–35. **(Chap 5)**

Neal-Barnett, A. M., & Smith, J., Sr. (1997). African Americans. In S. Friedman (Ed.), *Cultural issues in the treatment of anxiety* (pp. 154–174). New York: Guilford Press. **(Chap 5)**

Neighbors, H. W., Jackson, J. S., Campbell, L., & Williams, D. (1989). The influence of racial factors on psychiatric diagnosis: A review and suggestions for research. *Community Mental Health Journal, 25*(4), 301–311. **(Chap 7)**

Nelles, W. B. N., & Barlow, D. H. (1988). Do children panic? *Clinical Psychology Review, 8*(4), 359–372. **(Chap 5)**

Nelson, R. O., & Barlow, D. H. (1981). Behavioral assessment: Basic strategies and initial procedures. In D. H. Barlow (Ed.), *Behavioral assessment of adult disorders.* New York: Guilford Press. **(Chap 3)**

Nestadt, G., Romanoski, A. J., Chahal, R., Merchant, A., Folstein, M. F., Gruenberg, E. M., & McHugh, P. R. (1990). An epidemiological study of histrionic personality disorder. *Psychological Medicine, 20,* 413–422. **(Chap 12)**

New York Mental Hygiene Law. (1992). 1.03 (20). **(Chap 16)**

New York Times. (1994, February 2). **(Chap 16)**

Newlin, D. B. (1989). The skin-flushing response: Autonomic, self-report, and conditioned responses to repeated administrations of alcohol in Asian men. *Journal of Abnormal Psychology, 98,* 421–425. **(Chap 11)**

Newlin, D. B., & Thomson, J. B. (1990). Alcohol challenge with sons of alcoholics: A critical review and analysis. *Psychological Bulletin, 108,* 383–402. **(Chap 11)**

Newman, J. P., & Wallace, J. F. (1993). Psychopathy and cognition. In K. S. Dobson & P. C. Kendall (Eds.), *Psychopathology and cognition* (pp. 293–349). New York: Academic Press. **(Chap 12)**

Newman, J. P., Patterson, C. M., & Kosson, D. S. (1987). Response perseveration in psychopaths. *Journal of Abnormal Psychology, 96,* 145–148. **(Chap 12)**

Newman, J. P., Widom, C. S., & Nathan, S. (1985). Passive-avoidance in syndromes of disinhibition: Psychopathy and extraversion. *Journal of Personality and Social Psychology, 50,* 624–630. **(Chap 6)**

Newmark, C. S., & McCord, D. M. (1996). The Minnesota Multiphasic Personality Inventory-2 (MMPI-2). In C. S. Newmark (Ed.), *Major psychological assessment instruments* (pp. 1–58). Boston: Allyn & Bacon. **(Chap 3)**

NIDA Capsules, CAP 16 (1993). U. S. Department of Health and Human Services, National Institute on Drug Abuse. **(Chap 11)**

Nisbett, R. E., & Ross, L. (1980). *Human inference: Strategies and shortcomings in social judgement.* New York: Century. **(Chap 4)**

Nofzinger, E. A., Schwartz, C. F., Reynolds, C. F., Thase, M. E., Jennings, J. R., Frank, E., Fasiczka, A. L., Garamoni, G. L., & Kupfer, D. J. (1994). Affect intensity and phasic REM sleep in depressed men before and after treatment with cognitive-behavior therapy. *Journal of Consulting and Clinical Psychology, 62,* 83–91. **(Chap 8)**

Nolen-Hoeksema, S. (1987). Sex differences in unipolar depression: Evidence and theory. *Psychological Bulletin, 101*(2), 259–282. **(Chap 7)**

Nolen-Hoeksema, S. (1990). *Sex differences in depression.* Stanford, CA: Stanford University Press. **(Chap 7)**

Nolen-Hoeksema, S., Girgus, J. S., & Seligman, M. E. P. (1992). Predictors and consequences of childhood depressive symptoms: A 5-year longitudinal study. *Journal of Abnormal Psychology, 101*(3), 405–422. **(Chaps 4, 7)**

Noll, R. B., Zucker, R. A., & Greenberg, G. S. (1990). Identification of alcohol by smell among preschoolers: Evidence for early socialization about drugs occurring in the home. *Child Development, 61,* 1520–1527. **(Chap 11)**

Norman, W. H., Miller, I. W., & Dow, M. G. (1988). Characteristics of depressed patients with elevated levels of dysfunctional cognitions. *Cognitive Therapy and Research, 12,* 39–51. **(Chap 7)**

Norton, G. R., Harrison, B., Hauch, J., & Rhodes, L. (1985). Characteristics of people with infrequent panic attacks. *Journal of Abnormal Psychology, 94,* 216–221. **(Chap 5)**

Noyes, R., & Kletti, R. (1977). Depersonalization in response to life-threatening danger. *Comprehensive Psychiatry, 18,* 375–384. **(Chap 6)**

Noyes, R., Clarkson, C., Crowe, R. R., Yates, W. R., & McChesney, C. M. (1987). A family study of generalized anxiety disorder. *American Journal of Psychiatry, 144,* 1019–1024. **(Chap 5)**

Noyes, R., Garvey, M. J., Cook, B., & Suelzer, M. (1991). Controlled discontinuation of benzodiazepine treatment for patients with panic disorder. *American Journal of Psychiatry, 148,* 517–523. **(Chap 5)**

Noyes, R., Hoenk, P., Kuperman, S., & Slymen, D. (1977). Depersonalization in accident victims and psychiatric patients. *Journal of Nervous and Mental Disease, 164,* 401–407. **(Chap 6)**

Noyes, R., Woodman, C., Garvey, M. J., Cook, B. L., Suelzer, M., Clancy, J., & Anderson, D. J. (1992). Generalized anxiety disorder vs. panic disorder: Distinguishing characteristics and patterns of comorbidity. *Journal of Nervous and Mental Disease, 180,* 369–379. **(Chap 5)**

Nurnberg, H. G., Raskin, M., Levine, P. E., Pollack, S., Siegel, O., & Prince, R. (1991). The comorbidity of borderline personality and other DSM-III-R Axis II personality disorders. *American Journal of Psychiatry, 148,* 1371–1377. **(Chap 12)**

Nurnberger, J. I., & Gershon, E. S. (1992). Genetics. In E. S. Paykel (Ed.), *Handbook of affective disorders* (pp. 126–145). New York: Guilford Press. **(Chap 7)**

Nurnberger, J. I., Jr., Berrettini, W., Tamarkin, L., Hamovit, J., Norton, J., & Gershon, E. S. (1988). Supersensitivity to melatonin suppression by light in young people at high risk for affective disorder: A preliminary report. *Neuropsychopharmacology, 1,* 217–223. **(Chap 7)**

Nyhan, W. L. (1978). The Lesch-Nyhan syndrome. *Developmental Medicine and Child Neurology, 20,* 376–387. **(Chap 14)**

Oades, R. D. (1985). The role of noradrenaline in tuning and dopamine in switching between signals in the CNS. *Neuroscienceand Biobehavioral Reviews, 9,* 261–282. **(Chap 2)**

Oatley, K., & Jenkins, J. M. (1992). Human emotions: Function and dysfunction. *Annual Review of Psychology, 43,* 55–85. **(Chap 2)**

O'Brien, C. P. (1996). Recent developments in the pharmacotherapy of substance abuse. *Journal of Consulting and Clinical Psychology, 64,* 677–686. **(Chap 11)**

O'Brien, M. M., Trestman, R. L., & Siever, L. J. (1993). Cluster A personality disorders. In D. L. Dunner (Ed.), *Current psychiatric therapy* (pp. 399–404). Philadelphia: W. B. Saunders. **(Chap 12)**

O'Callaghan, E., Sham, P., Takei, N., Glover, G., & Murray, R. M. (1991). Schizophrenia after prenatal exposure to 1957 A2 influenza epidemic. *Lancet, 337,* 1248–1250. **(Chap 13)**

O'Carroll, P. W. (1990). Community strategies for suicide prevention and intervention. In S. J. Blumenthal & D. J. Kupfer (Eds.), *Suicide over the life cycle: Risk factors, assessment and treatment of suicidal patients.* Washington, DC: American Psychiatric Press. **(Chap 7)**

O'Connor v. Donaldson. (1975). 95 S. Ct. 2486. **(Chap 16)**

O'Connor, M., Sales, B. D., & Shuman, D. W. (1996). Mental health professional expertise in the courtroom. In B. D. Sales & D. W. Shuman (Eds.), *Law, mental health, and mental disorder* (pp. 40–59). Pacific Grove, CA: Brooks/ Cole. **(Chap 16)**

Office of Applied Studies (1997). *The 1996 National Household Survey on Drug Abuse.* Rockville, MD: Substance Abuse and Mental Health Services Administration. **(Chap 11)**

Ogata, S. N., Silk, K. R., Goodrich, S., Lohr, N. E., Westen, D., & Hill, E. M. (1990). Childhood sexual and physical abuse in adult patients with borderline personality disorder. *American Journal of Psychiatry, 147,* 1008–1013. **(Chap 12)**

Ogloff, J. P. R., Wong, S., & Greenwod, A. (1990). Treating criminal psychopaths in a therapeutic community program. *Sciences and the Law, 8,* 81–90. **(Chap 12)**

O'Hagan, S. (1992, February 22). Raving madness. *The Times Saturday Review,* pp. 10–12. **(Chap 11)**

O'Hanlon, J. F., Haak, J. W., Blaauw, G. J., & Riemersma, J. B. J. (1982). Diazepam impairs lateral position control in highway driving. *Science, 27,* 79–81. **(Chap 5)**

O'Hara, M. W. (1986). Social support, life events and depression during pregnancy and the puerperium. *Archives of*

General Psychiatry, 43(6), 569–575. **(Chap 7)**

O'Hara, M. W., Zekoski, E. M., Philipps, L. H., & Wright, E. J. (1990). Controlled prospective study of postpartum mood disorders: Comparison of child bearing and nonbearing women. *Journal of Abnormal Psychology, 99*(1), 3–15. **(Chap 7)**

Öhman, A. (1986). Face the beast and fear the face: Animal and social fears as prototypes for evolutionary analyses of emotion. *Psychophysiology, 23,* 123–145. **(Chap 5)**

Öhman, A., & Dimberg, U. (1978). Facial expressions as conditioned stimuli for electrodermal responses: A case of preparedness? *Journal of Personality and Social Psychology, 36*(11), 1251–1258. **(Chap 5)**

Olds, J. (1956). Pleasure centers in the brain. *Scientific American, 195,* 105–116. **(Chap 11)**

Olds, J., & Milner, P. M. (1954). Positive reinforcement produced by electrical stimulation of septal area and other regions of rat brain. *Journal of Comparative and Physiological Psychology, 47,* 419–427. **(Chap 11)**

O'Leary, A. (1990). Stress, emotion, and human immune function. *Psychological Bulletin, 108*(3), 363–382. **(Chap 9)**

O'Leary, A. (1992). Self-efficacy and health: Behavioral and stress-physiological mediation. *Cognitive Therapy and Research, 16*(2), 229–245. **(Chap 9)**

O'Leary, K. D., & Beach, S. R. (1990). Marital therapy: A viable treatment for depression and marital discord. *American Journal of Psychiatry, 147*(2), 183–186. **(Chap 7)**

Olin, S. S., Raine, A., Cannon, T. D., Parnas, J., Schulsinger, F., & Mednick, S. A. (1997). Childhood behavior precursors of schizotypal personality disorder. *Schizophrenia Bulletin, 23,* 93–103. **(Chap 12)**

Oliver, M. B., & Hyde, J. S. (1993). Gender differences in sexuality: A meta-analysis. *Psychological Bulletin, 114*(1), 29–51. **(Chap 10)**

Ollendick, T. H., & Huntzinger, R. M. (1990). Separation anxiety disorder in childhood. In M. Hersen & C. G. Last (Eds.), *Handbook of child and adult psychopathology: A longitudinal perspective.* Elmsford, NY: Pergamon Press. **(Chap 5)**

Ollendick, T. H., & Ollendick, D. G. (1990). Tics and Tourette syndrome. In A. M. Gross & R. S. Drabman (Eds.), *Handbook of clinical behavioral pediatrics* (pp. 243–252). New York: Plenum Press. **(Chap 14)**

O'Malley, S. S., Jaffe, A. J., Chang, G., Schottenfeld, R. S., Meyer, R. E., & Rounsaville, B. (1992). Naltrexone and coping skills therapy for alcohol dependence: A controlled study. *Archives of General Psychiatry, 49,* 881–887. **(Chap 11)**

Onstad, S., Skre, I., Torgersen, S., & Kringlen, E. (1991). Twin concordance for DSM-III-R schizophrenia. *Acta Psychiatrica Scandinavica, 83,* 395–401. **(Chap 13)**

Opjordsmoen, S. (1989). Delusional disorders. I. Comparative long-term outcome. *Acta Psychiatrica Scandia, 80,* 603–612. **(Chap 13)**

Orne, M. T., Dinges, D. F., & Orne, E. C. (1984). On the differential diagnosis of multiple personality in the forensic context. International *Journal of Clinical and Experimental Hypnosis, 32,* 118–169. **(Chap 6)**

Ortiz, A., & Medicna-Mora, M. E. (1988). Research on drugs in Mexico: Epidemiology of drug abuse and issues among Native American populations. In Community Epidemiology Work Group Proceedings, December, 1987. Contract No. 271-87-8321. Washington, DC: U.S. Government Printing Office. **(Chap 11)**

Ortony, A., & Turner, T. J. (1990). What's basic about basic emotions? *Psychological Review, 97,* 315–331. **(Chap 2)**

Oscar-Berman, M., Shagrin, B., Evert, D. L., & Epstein, C. (1997). Impairments of brain and behavior: The neurological effects of alcohol. *Alcohol Health & Research World, 21,* 65–75. **(Chap 11)**

Ossip-Klein, D. J., Doyne, E. J., Bowman, E. D., Osborn, K. M., McDougall-Wilson, I. B., & Neimeyer, R. A. (1989). Effects of running or weight lifting on self-concept in clinically depressed women. *Journal of Consulting and Clinical Psychology, 57*(1), 158–161. **(Chap 7)**

Öst, L. G. (1985). Mode of acquisition of phobias. *Acta Universitatis Uppsaliensis* (Abstracts of Uppsala Dissertations from the Faculty of Medicine), 529, 1–45. **(Chap 5)**

Öst, L. G. (1987). Age at onset in different phobias. *Journal of Abnormal Psychology, 96,* 223–229. **(Chap 5)**

Öst, L. G. (1989). *Blood phobia: A specific phobia subtype in DSM-IV.* Paper requested by the Simple Phobia subcommittee of the DSM-IV Anxiety Disorders Work Group. **(Chap 5)**

Öst, L. G. (1992). Blood and injection phobia: Background and cognitive, physiological, and behavioral variables. *Journal of Abnormal Psychology, 101*(1), 68–74. **(Chaps 2, 5)**

Öst, L. G., & Sterner, U. (1987). Applied tension: A specific behavioural method for treatment of blood phobia. *Behaviour Research and Therapy, 25,* 25–30. **(Chap 5)**

Öst, L. G., Ferebee, I., & Furmark, T. (1997). One session group therapy of spiderphobia: Direct vs. indirect treatments. *BRAT, 35,* 721–732. **(Chap 5)**

Osterberg, E. (1986). Alcohol-related problems in cross-national perspectives: Results of the ISACE study. Special issue: Alcohol and culture: Comparative perspectives from Europe and America (T. Babot, Ed.). *Annals of the New York Academy of Sciences, 472,* 10–20. **(Chap 11)**

O'Sullivan, K. (1979). Observations on vaginismus in Irish women. *Archives of General Psychiatry, 36,* 824–826. **(Chap 10)**

Ouimette, P. C., Finney, J. W., & Moos, R. H. (1997). Twelve-step and cognitive-behavioral treatment for substance abuse: A comparison of treatment effectiveness. *Journal of Consulting and Clinical Psychology, 65,* 230–240. **(Chap 11)**

Overall, J. E., & Hollister, L. E. (1982). Decision rules for phenomenological classification of psychiatric patients. *Journal of Consulting and Clinical Psychology, 50,* 535–545. **(Chap 3)**

Owens, M. J., Mulchahey, J. J., Stout, S. C., & Plotsky, P. M. (1997). Molecular and neurobiological mechanisms in the treatment of psychiatric disorders. In A. Tasman, J. Kay, & J. A. Lieberman (Eds.), *Psychiatry* (Vol. 1) (pp. 210–257). Philadelphia: W. B. Saunders. **(Chaps 2, 9)**

Oyama, O., & Andrasik, F. (1992). Behavioral strategies in the prevention of disease. In S. M. Turner, K. S. Calhoun & H. E. Adams (Eds.), *Handbook of clinical behavior therapy* (2nd ed., pp. 397–413). New York: John Wiley. **(Chap 9)**

Page, A. C. (1994). Blood-injury phobia. *Clinical Psychology Review, 14,* 443–461. **(Chap 2)**

Page, A. C. (1996). Blood-injury-injection fears in medical practice. *Medical Journal of Australia, 164,* 189. **(Chap 2)**

Page, G. G., Ben-Eliyahu, S., Yirmiya, R., & Liebeskind, J. C. (1993). Morphine attenuates surgery-induced enhancement of metastatic colonization in rats. *Pain, 54*(1), 21–28. **(Chap 9)**

Pahl, J. J., Swayze, V. W., & Andreasen, N. C. (1990). Diagnostic advances in anatomical and functional brain imaging in schizophrenia. In A. Kales, C. N. Stefanis, & J. A. Talbott (Eds.), *Recent advances in schizophrenia* (pp. 163–189). New York: Springer-Verlag. **(Chap 14)**

Palace, E. M. (1995). Modification of dysfunctional patterns of sexual response through autonomic arousal and false physiological feedback. *Journal of Consulting and Clinical Psychology, 63,* 604–615. **(Chap 10)**

Palace, E. M., & Gorzalka, B. B. (1990). The enhancing effects of anxiety on arousal in sexually dysfunctional and functional women. *Journal of Abnormal Psychology, 99*(4), 403–411. **(Chap 10)**

Pantaleo, G., Graziosi, C., & Fauci, A. S. (1993). The immunopathogenesis of human immunodeficiency virus infection. *New England Journal of Medicine, 328,* 327–335. **(Chap 9)**

Papillo, J. F., & Shapiro, D. (1990). The cardiovascular system. In J. T. Cacioppo &

L. G. Tassinaryo (Eds.), *Principles of psychophysiology: Physical, social, and inferential elements.* New York: Cambridge University Press. **(Chap 9)**

Paradis, C. M., Friedman, S., & Hatch, M. (1997). Isolated sleep paralysis in African-Americans with panic disorder. *Cultural Diversity & Mental Health, 3,* 69–76. **(Chap 5)**

Parker, G., & Hadzi-Pavlovic, D. (1990). Expressed emotion as a predictor of schizophrenic relapse: An analysis of aggregated data. *Psychological Medicine, 20,* 961–965. **(Chap 13)**

Parkes, J. D., & Block, C. (1989). Genetic factors in sleep disorders. *Journal of Neurology, Neurosurgery, and Psychiatry, 52,* 101–108. **(Chap 8)**

Parkinson, L., & Rachman, S. (1981a). Intrusive thoughts: The effects of an uncontrived stress. *Advances in Behaviour Research and Therapy, 3,* 111–118. **(Chap 5)**

Parkinson, L., & Rachman, S. (1981b). Speed of recovery from an uncontrived stress. *Advances in Behaviour Research and Therapy, 3,* 119–123. **(Chap 5)**

Parloff, M. B. (1986). Placebo controls in psychotherapy research: A sine qua non or a placebo for research problems? *Journal of Consulting and Clinical Psychology, 54,* 79–87. **(Chap 4)**

Parry-Jones, B. (1994). Mercycism or rumination disorder: A historical investigation and current assessment. *British Journal of Psychiatry, 165,* 303–314. **(Chap 8)**

Parry-Jones, W. Li., & Parry-Jones, B. (1994). Implications of historical evidence for the classification of eating disorders. *British Journal of Psychiatry, 165,* 287–292. **(Chap 8)**

Parsons, O. A., & Nixon, S. J. (1993). Behavioral disorders associated with central nervous system dysfunction. In P. B. Sutker & H. E. Adams (Eds.), *Comprehensive handbook of psychopathology* (pp. 689–733). New York: Plenum Press. **(Chap 14)**

Pasewark, R. A., & Seidenzahl, D. (1979). Opinions concerning the insanity plea and criminality among mental patients. *Bulletin of the American Academy of Psychiatry and Law, 7,* 199–202. **(Chap 16)**

Pataki, C. S., & Carlson, G. A. (1990). Major depression in childhood. In M. Hersen & C. Last (Eds.), *Handbook of child and adult psychopathology: A longitudinal perspective.* Elmsford, NY: Pergamon Press. **(Chap 7)**

Patterson, G. R. (1982). *Coercive family process.* Eugene, OR: Castalia Publishing Company. **(Chaps 4, 12)**

Patterson, G. R. (1986). Performance models for antisocial boys. *American Psychologist, 41,* 432–444. **(Chap 12)**

Patterson, G. R., Chamberlain, P., & Reid, J. B. (1982). A comparative evaluation of a parent-training program. *Behavior Therapy, 13,* 638–650. **(Chap 12)**

Patterson, G. R., Cobb, J. A., & Ray, R. S. (1972). Direct intervention in the classroom: A set of procedures for the aggressive child. In F. Clark, D. Evans, & L. Hamerlynck (Eds.), *Implementing behavioral programs for schools and clinics.* Champaign, IL: Research Press. **(Chap 4)**

Patterson, G. R., DeBaryshe, B. D., & Ramsey, E. (1989). A developmental perspective on antisocial behavior. *American Psychologist, 44,* 329–335. **(Chap 12)**

Patton, G. C. (1988). Mortality in eating disorders. *Psychological Medicine, 18*(4), 947–951. **(Chap 8)**

Patton, G. C., Johnson-Sabine, E., Wood, K., Mann, A. H., & Wakeling, A. (1990). Abnormal eating attitudes in London school girls—a prospective epidemiological study: Outcome at twelve month followup. *Psychological Medicine, 20,* 383–394. **(Chap 8)**

Paul, G. L., & Lentz, R. J. (1977). *Psychosocial treatment of chronic mental patients: Milieu versus social learning programs.* Cambridge, MA: Harvard University Press. **(Chap 13)**

Pavalko, E. K., Elder, G. H., Jr., & Clipp E. C. (1993). Worklives and longevity: Insights from a life course perspective. *Journal of Health and Social Behavior, 34,* 363–380. **(Chap 9)**

Paykel, E. S., & Weissman, M. M. (1973). Social adjustment and depression: A longitudinal study. *Archives of General Psychiatry, 28,* 659–663. **(Chap 7)**

Paykel, E. S., Brayne, C., Huppert, F. A., Gill, C., Barkley, C., Gehlhaar, E., Beardsall, L., Girling, D. M., Pollitt, P., & O'Connor, D. (1994). Incidence of dementia in a population older than 75 years in the United Kingdom. *Archives of General Psychiatry, 51,* 325–332. **(Chap 15)**

Paykel, E. S., Hollyman, J. A., Freeling, P., & Sedgwich, P. (1988). Predictor of therapeutic benefit from amitriptyline in mild depression: A general practice placebo-controlled trial. *Journal of Affective Disorders, 14,* 83–95. **(Chap 7)**

Pechnick, R. N., & Ungerleider, J. T. (1997). Hallucinogens. In J. H. Lowinson, P. Ruiz, R. B. Millman, & J. G. Langrod (Eds.), *Substance abuse: A comprehensive textbook* (pp. 230–238). Baltimore, MD: Williams & Wilkins. **(Chap 11)**

Pelham, W. E., & Milich, R. (1991). Individual differences in response to Ritalin in classwork and social behavior. In L. L. Greenhill & B. B. Osman (Eds.), *Ritalin: Theory and patient management* (pp. 203–221). New York: Liebert. **(Chap 14)**

Peltonen, L. (1995). All out for chromosome six. *Nature, 378,* 665–666. **(Chap 2)**

Pendery, M. L., Maltzman, I. M., & West, L. J. (1982). Controlled drinking by alcoholics? New findings and a reevaluation of a major affirmative study. *Science, 217,* 169–175. **(Chap 11)**

Pennington, B. F., & Smith, S. D. (1988). Genetic influences on learning disabilities: An update. *Journal of Consulting and Clinical Psychology, 56,* 817–823. **(Chap 14)**

Pepper, C. M., Klein, D. N., Anderson, R. L., Riso, L. P., Ouimette, P. C., & Lizardi, H. (1995). DSM-III-R Axis II comorbidity in dysthymia and major depression. *American Journal of Psychiatry, 152,* 239–247. **(Chap 7)**

Pericak-Vance, M. A., Johnson, C. C., Rimmler, J. B., Saunders, A. M., Robinson, L. C., D'Hondt, E. G., Jackson, C. E., & Haines, J. L. (1996). Alzheimer's disease and apolipoprotein E-4 allele in an Amish population. *Annals of Neurology, 39,* 700–704. **(Chap 15)**

Perlin, M. L. (1996). The voluntary delivery of mental health services in the community. In B. D. Sales and D. W. Shuman (Eds.), *Law, mental health, and mental disorder* (pp. 150–177). Pacific Grove, CA: Brooks/Cole. **(Chap 16)**

Perlin, M. L., & Dorfman, D. A. (1993). Sanism, social science, and the development of mental disability law jurisprudence. *Behavioral Sciences and the Law, 11,* 47–66. **(Chap 16)**

Peroutka, S. J., & Snyder, S. H. (1980). Relationship of neuroleptic drug effects at brain dopamine, serotonin, alpha-adrenergic, and histamine receptors to clinical potence. *American Journal of Psychiatry, 137,* 1518–1522. **(Chap 13)**

Perry, J. C. (1993). Longitudinal studies of personality disorders. *Journal of Personality Disorders, 7,* 63–85. **(Chap 12)**

Perry, S. (1993). Psychiatric treatment of adults with human immunodeficiency virus infection. In D. L. Dunner (Ed.), *Current psychiatric therapy* (pp. 475–482). Philadelphia: W. B. Saunders. **(Chap 14)**

Person, D. C., & Borkevec, T. D. (1995, August). *Anxiety disorders among the elderly: Patterns and issues.* Paper presented at the 103rd annual meeting of the American Psychological Association. New York, NY. **(Chap 5)**

Peselow, E. D., Fieve, R. R., Difiglia, C., & Sanfilipo, M. P. (1994). Lithium prophylaxis of bipolar illness: The value of combination treatment. *British Journal of Psychiatry, 164,* 208–214. **(Chap 7)**

Peters, C. P. (1991). Concepts of schizophrenia after Kraepelin and Bleuler. In J. G. Howells (Ed.), *The concept of schizophrenia: Historical perspectives* (pp. 93–107). Washington, DC: American Psychiatric Press. **(Chap 13)**

Petersen, A. C., Compas, B. E., Brooks-Gunn, J., Stemmler, M., Ey, S., & Grant, K. E. (1993). Depression in adolescence. *American Psychologist, 48*(2), 155–168. **(Chap 7)**

Peterson, B. S. (1995). Neuroimaging in child and adolescent neuropsychiatric disorders. *Journal of the American Academy of Child and Adolescent Psychiatry, 34,* 1560–1576. **(Chap 14)**

Peterson, D. R. (1968). *The clinical study of social behavior.* New York: Appleton-Century-Crofts. **(Chap 3)**

Peterson, L., & Roberts, M. C. (1992). Complacency, misdirection, and effective prevention of children's injuries. *American Psychologist, 47*(8), 1040–1044. **(Chap 9)**

Peterson, L., & Thiele, C. (1988). Home safety at school. *Child and Family Behavior Therapy, 10*(1), 1–8. **(Chap 9)**

Peterson, L., Farmer, J., & Kashani, J. H. (1990). Parental injury prevention endeavors: A function of health beliefs? *Health Psychology, 9*(2), 177–191. **(Chap 9)**

Pfohl, B. (1991). Histrionic personality disorder: A review of available data and recommendations for DSM-IV. *Journal of Personality Disorders, 5,* 150–166. **(Chap 12)**

Pfohl, B. (1993). Proposed DSM-IV criteria for personality disorders. In D. L. Dunner (Ed.), *Current psychiatric therapy* (pp. 397–399). Philadelphia: W. B. Saunders. **(Chap 12)**

Pfohl, B. (1995). Histrionic personality disorder. In W. J. Livesley (Ed.), *The DSM-IV personality disorders* (pp. 173–192). New York: Guilford Press. **(Chap 12)**

Pfohl, B., & Blum, N. (1995). Obsessive-compulsive personality disorder. In W. J. Livesley (Ed.), *The DSM-IV personality disorders* (pp. 261–276). New York: Guilford Press. **(Chap 12)**

Phibbs, C. S., Bateman, D. A., & Schwartz, R. M. (1991). The neonatal costs of maternal cocaine use. *Journal of the American Medical Association, 266,* 1521–1526. **(Chap 11)**

Phifer, J. F., & Murrell, S. A. (1986). Etiologic factors in the onset of depressive symptoms in older adults. *Journal of Abnormal Psychology, 95,* 282–291. **(Chap 7)**

Philips, H. C., & Grant, L. (1991). Acute back pain: A psychological analysis. *Behaviour Research and Therapy, 29,* 429–434. **(Chap 9)**

Phillips, K. A. (1991). Body dysmorphic disorder: The distress of imagined ugliness. *American Journal of Psychiatry, 148,* 1138–1149. **(Chap 6)**

Phillips, K. A., McElroy, S. L., Keck, P. E., Jr., Pope, H. G., Jr., & Hudson, J. I. (1993). Body dysmorphic disorder: 30 cases of imagined ugliness. *American Journal of Psychiatry, 150,* 302–308. **(Chap 6)**

Pickens, R. W., Svikis, D. S., McGue, M., Lykken, D. T., Heston, L. L., & Clay-ton, P. J. (1991). Heterogeneity in the inheritence of alcoholism. *Archives of General Psychiatry, 48,* 19–28. **(Chap 11)**

Pierce, J. P., & Gilpin, E. A. (1995). A historical analysis of tobacco marketing and the uptake of smoking by youth in the United States: 1890–1977. *Health Psychology, 14,* 500–508. **(Chap 11)**

Pihl, R. O., Peterson, J. B., & Lau, M. A. (1993). A biosocial model of the alcohol-aggression relationship. *Journal of Studies on Alcohol,* Supplement No. 11, 128–139. **(Chap 11)**

Pike, K. M., & Rodin, J. (1991). Mothers, daughters, and disordered eating. *Journal of Abnormal Psychology, 100*(2), 198–204. **(Chap 8)**

Pike, K. M., Loeb., K., & Vitousek, K. (1996). Cognitive-behavioral therapy for anorexia nervosa and bulimia nervosa. In J. K. Thompson (Ed.), *Body image, eating disorders and obesity* (pp. 253–302). Washington, DC: American Psychological Association. **(Chap 8)**

Pilowsky, I. (1970). Primary and secondary hypochondriasis. *Acta Psychiatrica Scandinavica, 46,* 273–285. **(Chap 6)**

Pinel, P. (1801/1962). *A treatise on insanity.* New York: Hafner. **(Chaps 12, 13)**

Pinel, P. H. (1809). *Traite medico-philosophique sur l'alienation mentale.* Paris: Chez J. Ant Brosson. **(Chap 13)**

Pirke, K. M., Schweiger, U., & Fichter, M. M. (1987). Hypothalamic-pituitary-ovarian axis in bulimia. In J. I. Hudson & H. G. Pope (Eds.), *The psychobiology of bulimia* (pp. 15–28). Washington, DC: American Psychiatric Press. **(Chap 8)**

Pithers, W. D., Martin, G. R., & Cumming, G. F. (1989). Vermont treatment program for sexual aggressors. In D. R. Laws (Ed.), *Relapse prevention with sex offenders* (pp. 292–310). New York: Guilford Press. **(Chap 10)**

Plomin, R. (1990). The role of inheritance in behavior. *Science, 248,* 183–188. **(Chaps 2, 4, 13)**

Plomin, R., DeFries, J. C., McClearn, G. E., & Rutter, M. (1997). *Behavioral Genetics: A Primer.* (3rd ed.) New York: Freeman. **(Chap 2)**

Plomin, R., McClearn, G. E., Smith, D. L., Skuder, P., Vignetti, S., Chorney, M. J., Charney, K., Kasarda, S., Thompson, L. A., Determan, D. K., Petrill, S. A., Dfaziels, J., Owen, M. J., & McGuffin, P. (1995). Allelic association between 100 DNA markers and high versus low IQ. *Intelligence, 21,* 31–48. **(Chap 2)**

Plomin, R., Owen, M. J., & McGuffin, P. (1994). The genetic basis of complex human behaviors. *Science, 264,* 1733–1739. **(Chaps 4, 13)**

Polich, J., Pollock, V. E., & Bloom, F. E. (1994). Meta-analysis of P300 amplitude from males at risk for alcoholism. *Psychological Bulletin, 115,* 55–73. **(Chap 11)**

Polivy, J. M., & Herman, C. P. (1993). Etiology of binge eating: Psychological mechanisms. In C. G. Fairburn & G. T. Wilson (Eds.), *Binge eating: Nature, assessment, and treatment.* New York: Guilford Press. **(Chap 8)**

Pollack, C., & Andrews, G. (1989). Defense styles associated with specific anxiety disorders. *American Journal of Psychiatry, 146,* 1500–1502. **(Chap 1)**

Pollack, M. H., Brotman, A. W., & Rosenbaum, J. F. (1989). Cocaine abuse and treatment. *Comprehensive Psychiatry, 30,* 31–44. **(Chap 11)**

Polloway, E. A., Schewel, R., & Patton, J. R. (1992). Learning disabilities in adulthood: Personal perspectives. *Journal of Learning Disabilities, 25,* 520–522. **(Chap 14)**

Pope, H. G., Ionescu-Pioggia, M., Aizley, H. G., & Varma, D. K. (1990). Drug use and life style among college undergraduates in 1989: A comparison with 1969 and 1978. *American Journal of Psychiatry, 147,* 998–1001. **(Chap 11)**

Pope, K. S. (1996). Memory, abuse and science: Questioning claims about the false memory syndrome epidemic. *American Psychologist, 51,* 957–974. **(Chap 6)**

Pope, K. S. (1997). Science as careful questioning: Are claims of a false memory syndrome epidemic based on empirical evidence? *American Psychologist, 52,* 997–1006. **(Chap 6)**

Portenoy, R. K., & Payne, R. (1997). Acute and chronic pain. In J. H. Lowinson, P. Ruiz, R. B. Millman, & J. G. Langrod (Eds.), *Substance abuse: A comprehensive textbook* (pp. 563–589). Baltimore, MD: Williams & Wilkins. **(Chap 11)**

Post, R. M. (1992). Transduction of psychosocial stress into the neurobiology of recurrent affective disorder. *American Journal of Psychiatry, 149*(8), 999–1010. **(Chap 7)**

Post, R. M., Rubinow, D. R., Uhde, T. W., Roy-Byrne, P. P., Linnoila, M., Rosoff, A., & Cowdry, R. (1989). Dysphoric mania: Clinical and biological correlates. *Archives of General Psychiatry, 46,* 353–358. **(Chap 7)**

Potkin, S. G., Albers, L. J., & Richmond, G. (1993). Schizophrenia: An overview of pharmacological treatment. In D. L. Dunner (Ed.), *Current psychiatric therapy* (pp. 142–154). Philadelphia: W. B. Saunders. **(Chap 13)**

Potter, W. Z., & Manji, H. K. (1993). Are monoamine metabolites in cerebral spinal fluid worth measuring? *Archives of General Psychiatry, 50,* 653–656. **(Chap 13)**

Poznanski, E. O., Israel, M. C., & Grossman, J. A. (1984). Hypomania in a four year old. *Journal of the American Academy of Child Psychiatry, 23*(1), 105–110. **(Chap 7)**

Prelior, E. F., Yutzy, S. H., Dean, J. T., & Wetzel, R. D. (1993). Briquet's syndrome, dissociation and abuse. *American*

Journal of Psychiatry, 150, 1507–1511. **(Chap 6)**

Preskorn, S. H. (1995). Comparison of the tolerability of bupropion, fluoxetine, imipramine, nefazodone, paroxetine, sertraline, and venlafaxine. *Journal of Clinical Psychiatry, 56*(Suppl. 6), 12–21. **(Chap 7)**

Presley, C. A., & Meilman, P. W. (1992). *Alcohol and drugs on American college campuses: A report to college presidents.* Carbondale: Southern Illinois University Press. **(Chap 11)**

Price, R., & Brew, B. (1988). The AIDS dementia complex. *Journal of Infectious Diseases, 158,* 1079–1083. **(Chap 15)**

Prien, R. F., & Kupfer, D. J. (1986). Continuation drug therapy for major depressive episodes: How long should it be maintained? *American Journal of Psychiatry, 143*(1), 18–23. **(Chap 7)**

Prien, R. F., & Potter, W. Z. (1993). Maintenance treatment for mood disorders. In D. L. Dunner (Ed.), *Current psychiatric therapy* (pp. 255–260). Philadelphia: W. B. Saunders. **(Chap 7)**

Prien, R. F., Kupfer, D. J., Mansky, P. A., Small, J. G., Tuason, V. B., Voss, C. B., & Johnson, W. E. (1984). Drug therapy in the prevention of recurrences in unipolar and bipolar affective disorders: Report of the NIMH collaborative study group comparing lithium carbonate, imipramine and a lithium carbonate-imipramine combination. *Archives of General Psychiatry, 41,* 1096–1104. **(Chap 7)**

Prince, M. (1906–1907). Hysteria from the point of view of dissociated personality. *Journal of Abnormal Psychology, 1,* 170–187. **(Chap 6)**

Pritchett, D. B., Lüddens, H., & Seeburg, P. H. (1989). Importance of a novel GABAA Receptor subunit for benzodiazepine pharmacology. *Nature, 338,* 582–585. **(Chap 2)**

Prizant, B. M., & Wetherby, A. M. (1989). Enhancing language and communication in autism: From theory to practice. In G. Dawson (Ed.), *Autism: Nature, diagnosis, and treatment* (pp. 282–309). New York: Guilford Press. **(Chap 14)**

Project MATCH Research Group (1993). Project MATCH: Rationale and methods for a multisite clinical trial matching patients to alcoholism treatment. *Alcoholism: Clinical and Experimental Research, 17,* 1130–1145. **(Chap 11)**

Project MATCH Research Group (1997). Matching alcoholism treatments to client heterogeneity: Project MATCH: Posttreatment drinking outcomes. *Journal of Studies on Alcohol, 58,* 7–29. **(Chap 11)**

Prudic, J., Sackeim, H. A., & Devanand, D. P. (1990). Medication resistance and clinical response to electroconvulsive therapy. *Psychiatry Research, 31,* 287–296. **(Chap 7)**

Pruzinsky, T. (1988). Collaboration of plastic surgeon and medical psychotherapist: Elective cosmetic surgery. *Medical Psychotherapy, 1,* 1–13. **(Chap 6)**

Pueschel, S. M., & Goldstein, A. (1991). Genetic counseling. In J. L. Matson & J. A. Mulick (Eds.), *Handbook of mental retardation* (2nd ed., pp. 279–291). Elmsford, NY: Pergamon Press. **(Chap 14)**

Pugliese, M. T., Weyman-Daun, M., Moses, N., & Lifshitz, F. (1987). Parental health beliefs as a cause of nonorganic failure to thrive. *Pediatrics, 80,* 175–182. **(Chap 8)**

Puig-Antich, J. (1982). Major depression and conduct disorder in prepuberty. *Journal of the American Academy of Child Psychiatry, 21,* 118–128. **(Chap 7)**

Puig-Antich, J., & Rabinovich, H. (1986). Relationship between affective and anxiety disorders in childhood. In R. G. Helman (Ed.), *Anxiety disorders of childhood* (pp. 136–156). New York: John Wiley. **(Chap 7)**

Purdie, F. R., Hareginan, B., & Rosen, P. (1981). Acute organic brain syndrome: A review of 100 cases. *Annual of Emergency Medicine, 10,* 455–461. **(Chap 15)**

Purdy, D., & Frank, E. (1993). Should postpartum mood disorders be given a more prominent or distinct place in DSM-IV? *Depression, 1,* 59–70. **(Chap 7)**

Pury, C. L. S., & Mineka, S. (1997). Covariation bias for blood-injury stimuli and aversion outcomes. *Behavior Research and Therapy, 35,* 35–47. **(Chaps 2, 5)**

Putnam, F. W. (1989). *Diagnosis and treatment of multiple personality disorder.* New York: Guilford Press. **(Chap 6)**

Putnam, F. W. (1991). Dissociative phenomena. In A. Tasman & S. M. Goldinger (Eds.), *American Psychiatric Press Review of Psychiatry* (Vol. 10). Washington, DC: American Psychiatric Press. **(Chap 6)**

Putnam, F. W. (1992). Altered states: Peeling away the layers of a multiple personality. *Sciences, 32*(6), 30–36. **(Chap 6)**

Putnam, F. W., & Loewenstein, R. J., (1993). Treatment of multiple personality disorder: A survey of current practices. *American Journal of Psychiatry, 150,* 1048–1052. **(Chap 6)**

Putnam, F. W., Guroff, J. J., Silberman, E. K., Barban, L., & Post, R. M. (1986). The clinical phenomenology of multiple personality disorder: Review of 100 recent cases. *Journal of Clinical Psychiatry, 47,* 285–293. **(Chap 6)**

Quality Assurance Project (1990). Treatment outlines for paranoid, schizotypal and schizoid personality disorders. *Australian and New Zealand Journal of Psychiatry, 24,* 339–350. **(Chap 12)**

Quay, H. C. (1965). Psychopathic personality as pathological stimulation seeking. *American Journal of Psychiatry, 122,* 180–183. **(Chap 12)**

Quay, H. C. (1993). The psychobiology of undersocialized aggressive conduct disorder: A theoretical perspective. *Development and Psychopathology, 5,* 165–180. **(Chap 12)**

Quitkin, F. M., Harrison, W., Stewart, J. W., McGrath, P., Tricamo, E., Ocepek-Welikson, K., Rabkin, J. G., Wager, S. G., Nunes, E., & Klein, D. F. (1991). Response to pheneizine and imipramine in placebo nonresponders with atypical depression: A new application of the crossover design. *Archives of General Psychiatry, 48,* 319–323. **(Chap 7)**

Quon, D., Wang, Y., Catalano, R., Scardina, J. M., Murakami, K., & Cordell, B. (1991). Formation of B-amyloid protein deposits in brains of transgenic mice. *Nature, 352,* 239–241. **(Chap 14)**

Rachman, S. (1978). *Fear and courage.* San Francisco: W. H. Freeman. **(Chap 5)**

Rachman, S. (1991). Neo-conditioning and the classical theory of fear acquisition. *Clinical Psychology Review, 11,* 155–173. **(Chap 5)**

Rachman, S., & Hodgson, R. (1968). Experimentally induced \"sexual fetishism": Replication and development. *Psychological Record, 18*(1), 25–27. **(Chap 10)**

Radnitz, C. L., Appelbaum, K. A., Blanchard, E. B., Elliott, L., & Andrasik, F. (1988). The effect of self-regulatory treatment on pain behavior in chronic headache. *Behaviour Research and Therapy, 26,* 253–260. **(Chap 9)**

Rado, S. (1962). Theory and therapy: The theory of schizotypal organization and its application to the treatment of decompensated schizotypal behavior. In S. Rado (Ed.), *Psychoanalysis of behavior* (Vol. 2, pp. 127–140). New York: Grune & Stratton. **(Chap 12)**

Raich, R. M., Rosen, J. C., Deus, J., Perez, O., Requiena, A., & Gross, J. (1992). Eating disorder symptoms among adolescents in the United States and Spain: A comparative study. *International Journal of Eating Disorders, 11,* 63–72. **(Chap 8)**

Raine, A., Venables, P. H., & Williams, M. (1990). Relationships between central and autonomic measures of arousal at age 15 years and criminality at age 24 years. *Archives of General Psychiatry, 47,* 1003–1007. **(Chap 12)**

Ramachandran, V. S. (1993). Filling in the gaps in perception II: Scotomas and phantom limbs. *Current Directions in Psychological Science, 2,* 56–65. **(Chap 9)**

Ramey, C. T., & Ramey, S. L. (1992). Effective early intervention. *Mental Retardation, 30,* 337–345. **(Chap 14)**

Rapee, R. M. (1991). The conceptual overlap between cognition and conditioning in clinical psychology. *Clinical Psychology Review, 11,* 193–203. **(Chap 2)**

Rapee, R. M. & Melville, L. F. (1997). Recall of family factors in social phobia and panic disorder: Comparison of mother and offspring reports. *Depression and Anxiety, 5,* 7–11. **(Chap 5)**

Rapkin, A. J., Chang, L. C., & Reading, A. E. (1989). Mood and cognitive style in premenstrual syndrome. *Obstetrics and Gynecology, 74,* 644–649. **(Chap 3)**

Rapp, S. R., Parisi, S. A., & Wallace, C. E. (1991). Comorbid psychiatric disorders in elderly medical patients: A 1-year prospective study. *Journal of the American Geriatrics Society, 39*(2), 124–131. **(Chap 7)**

Rasmussen, S. A., & Eisen, J. L. (1990). Epidemiology of obsessive-compulsive disorder. *Journal of Clinical Psychiatry, 51,* 10–14. **(Chap 5)**

Rasmussen, S. A., & Tsuang, M. T. (1984). The epidemiology of obsessive-compulsive disorder. *Journal of Clinical Psychiatry, 45,* 450–457. **(Chap 5)**

Rasmussen, S. A., & Tsuang, M. T. (1986). Clinical characteristics and family history in DSM-III obsessive-compulsive disorder. *American Journal of Psychiatry, 143,* 317–322. **(Chap 5)**

Ratnasuriya, R. H., Eisler, I., Szmuhter, G. I., & Russell, G. F. (1991). Anorexia nervosa: Outcome and prognostic factors after 20 years. *British Journal of Psychiatry, 158,* 495–502. **(Chap 8)**

Ray, W. A., Fought, R. L., & Decker, M. D. (1992). Psychoactive drugs and the risk of injurious motor vehicle crashes in elderly drivers. *American Journal of Epidemiology, 136,* 873–883. **(Chap 15)**

Ray, W. A., Griffin, M. R., Schaffner, W., Baugh, D. K., & Melton, L. J. (1987). Psychotropic drug use and the risk of hip fracture. *New England Journal of Medicine, 316,* 363–369. **(Chap 15)**

Ray, W. A., Gurwitz, J., Decker, M. D., & Kennedy, D. L. (1992). Medications and the safety of the older driver: Is there a basis for concern? Special issue: Safety and mobility of elderly drivers: II. *Human Factors, 34*(1), 33–47. **(Chap 5)**

Razran, G. (1961). The observable unconscious and the inferable conscious in current Soviet psychophysiology: Interoceptive conditioning, semantic conditioning, and the orienting reflex. *Psychological Review, 68,* 81–150. **(Chap 5)**

Redd, W. H., & Andrykowski, M. A. (1982). Behavioral intervention in cancer treatment: Controlling aversion reactions to chemotherapy. *Journal of Consulting and Clinical Psychology, 50,* 1018–1029. **(Chap 1)**

Redd, W. H., Andreason, G. V., & Minagawa, R. Y. (1982). Hypnotic control of anticipatory emesis in patients receiving cancer chemotherapy. *Journal of Consulting and Clinical Psychology, 50,* 14–19. **(Chap 9)**

Reeve, R. E., & Kauffman, J. M. (1988). Learning disabilities. In V. B. Van Hasselt, P. S. Strain, & M. Hersen (Eds.), *Handbook of developmental and physical disabilities* (pp. 316–335). Elmsford, NY: Pergamon Press. **(Chap 14)**

Rehm, L. P., Kaslow, N. J., & Rabin, A. S. (1987). Cognitive and behavioral targets in a self-control therapy program for depression. *Journal of Consulting and Clinical Psychology, 55*(1), 60–67. **(Chap 7)**

Reich, J. (1987). Sex distribution of DSM-III personality disorders in psychiatric outpatients. *American Journal of Psychiatry, 144,* 485–488. **(Chap 12)**

Reich, J., Yates, W., & Nduaguba, M. (1989). Prevalence of DSM-III personality disorders in the community. *Social Psychiatry and Psychiatric Epidemiology, 24,* 12–16. **(Chap 12)**

Reichle, J., Mirenda, P., Locke, P., Piche, L., & Johnston, S. (1992). Beginning augmentative communication systems. In S. F. Warren & J. Reichle (Eds.), *Causes and effects in communication and language intervention* (pp. 131–156). Baltimore: Paul H. Brookes. **(Chap 14)**

Reid, D. H., Wilson, P. G., & Faw, G. D. (1991). Teaching self-help skills. In J. L. Matson & J. A. Mulick (Eds.), *Handbook of mental retardation* (2nd ed., pp. 436–450). Elmsford, NY: Pergamon Press. **(Chap 14)**

Reid, W. J., & Crisafulli, A. (1990). Marital discord and child behavior problems: A meta-analysis. *Journal of Abnormal Child Psychology, 18,* 105–117. **(Chap 4)**

Reik, T. (1964). *Pagan rites in Judaism.* New York: Farrar, Strauss. **(Chap 3)**

Reiss, A. L. (1985). Developmental manifestations in a boy with prepubertal bipolar disorder. *Journal of Clinical Psychiatry, 46*(10), 441–443. **(Chap 7)**

Reitan, R. M., & Davison, I. A. (1974). *Clinical neuropsychology: Current status and applications.* Washington, DC: V. H. Winston. **(Chap 3)**

Rekers, G. A., Kilgus, M., & Rosen, A. C. (1990). Long-term effects of treatment for gender identity disorder of childhood. *Journal of Psychology & Human Sexuality, 3*(2), 121–153. **(Chap 10)**

Rende, R., & Plomin, R. (1992). Diathesis-stress models of psychopathology: A quantitative genetic perspective. *Applied & Preventive Psychology, 1,* 177–182. **(Chap 2)**

Renneberg, B., Goldstein, A. J., Phillips, D., & Chambless, D. L. (1990). Intensive behavioral group treatment of avoidant personality disorder. *Behavior Therapy, 21,* 363–377. **(Chap 12)**

Rennie, J. (1992). The mice that missed: Two models for Alzheimer's disease are retracted. *Scientific American, 267,* 20–26. **(Chap 15)**

Report of the Advisory Panel on Alzheimer's Disease (1995). *Alzheimer's disease and related dementias: Biomedical update.* Department of Health and Human Services. **(Chap 15)**

Repp, A. C., & Singh, N. N. (1990). *Perspectives on the use of nonaversive and aversive interventions for persons with developmental disabilities.* Sycamore, IL: Sycamore Publishing. **(Chap 14)**

Rescorla, R. A. (1988). Pavlovian conditioning: It's not what you think it is. *American Psychologist, 43*(3), 151–160. **(Chaps 1, 2)**

Resner, J., & Hartog, J. (1970). Concepts and terminology of mental disorders among Malays. *Journal of Cross-Cultural Psychology, 1,* 369–381. **(Chap 4)**

Resnick, H. S., Kilpatrick, D. G., Dansky, B. S., Saunders, B. E., & Best, C. L. (1993). Prevalence of civilian trauma in posttraumatic stress disorder in a representative national sample of women. *Journal of Consulting and Clinical Psychology, 61,* 984–991. **(Chap 5)**

Riccio, C. A., Hynd, G. W., Cohen, M. J., & Gonzalez, J. J. (1993). Neurological basis of attention deficit hyperactivity disorder. *Exceptional Children, 60,* 118–124. **(Chap 14)**

Rice, D. P., & MacKenzie, E. J. (1989). *Cost of injury in the United States: A report to Congress.* San Francisco: University of California and Injury Prevention Center, Institute for Health and Aging, and the Johns Hopkins University. **(Chap 9)**

Rice, J., Reich, T., Andreasen, N. C., Endicott, J., Van Eerdewegh, M., Fishman, R., Hirschfeld, R. M. A., & Klerman, G. L. (1987). The familiar transmission of bipolar illness. *Archives of General Psychiatry, 44,* 441–447. **(Chap 7)**

Rice, M. E., Harris, G. T., & Quinsey, V. L. (1990). A follow-up of rapists assessed in a maximum security psychiatric facility. *Journal of Interpersonal Violence, 4,* 435–448. **(Chap 12)**

Richardson, S. A., Katz, M., & Koller, H. (1986). Sex differences in number of children administratively classified as mildly mentally retarded: An epidemiological review. *American Journal of Mental Deficiency, 91,* 250–256. **(Chap 14)**

Richeimer, S. H. (1987). Psychological intervention in delirium: An important component of management. *Postgraduate Medicine, 81,* 173–180. **(Chap 14)**

Rickels, K., Downing, R., Schweizer, E., & Hassman, H. (1993). Antidepressants for the treatment of generalized anxiety disorder. *Archives of General Psychiatry, 50,* 884–895. **(Chap 5)**

Rickels, K., Schweizer, E., Case, W. G., & Greenblatt, D. J. (1990). Long-term therapeutic use of benzodiazepines. I. Effects of abrupt discontinuation. *Archives of General Psychiatry, 47,* 899–907. **(Chap 5)**

Riding, A. (1992, November 17). New catechism for Catholics defines sins of modern world. *New York Times,* A14. **(Chap 11)**

Riggins v. Nevada. (1992). 112 S. Ct. 1810. **(Chap 16)**

Riggs, D. S., & Foa, E. B. (1993). Obsessive compulsive disorder. In D. H. Barlow

(Ed.), *Clinical handbook of psychological disorders* (2nd ed.). New York: Guilford Press. **(Chap 5)**

Riggs, J. E. (1993). Smoking and Alzheimer's disease: Protective effect or differential survival bias? *Lancet, 342,* 793–794. **(Chap 15)**

Ritenbaugh, C., Shisstak, C., Teufel, N., Leonard-Green, T. K., & Prince, R. (1993). Eating disorders: A cross-cultural review in regard to DSM-IV. In J. E. Mezzich, A. Kleinman, H. Fabrega, B. Good, G. Johnson-Powell, K. M. Lin, S. Manson, & D. Parron (Eds.), *Cultural proposals and supporting papers for DSM-IV.* **(Chap 8)**

Ritvo, E. R., Freeman, B. J., Mason-Brothers, A., Mo, A., & Ritvo, A. M. (1985). Concordance for the syndrome of autism in 40 pairs of afflicted twins. *American Journal of Psychiatry, 142,* 74–77. **(Chap 14)**

Rivera-Tovar, A. D., & Frank, E. (1990). Late luteal phase dysphoric disorder in young women. *American Journal of Psychiatry, 147,* 1634–1636. **(Chap 3)**

Rivera-Tovar, A. D., Pilkonis, P., & Frank, E. (1992). Symptom patterns in late luteal-phase dysphoric disorder. *Journal of Psychopathology and Behavioral Assessment, 14,* 189–199. **(Chap 3)**

Roberts, G. A. (1991). Delusional belief and meaning in life: A preferred reality? *British Journal of Psychiatry, 159,* 20–29. **(Chap 13)**

Roberts, J., & Rowland, M. (1981). *Hypertension in adults 25–74 years of age.* United States, 1971–1975 (Series II No. 221). Washington, DC: U.S. Department of Health, Education, and Welfare, National Center for Health Statistics. **(Chap 9)**

Roberts, R. E., Kaplan, G. A., Shema, S. J., & Strawbridge, W. J. (1997). Does growing old increase the risk for depression? *American Journal of Psychiatry, 154,* 1384–1390. **(Chap 7)**

Robertson, M. J. (1986). Mental disorder among homeless people in the United States: An overview of recent empirical literature. *Administration in Mental Health, 4,* 14–27. **(Chap 16)**

Robertson, N. (1988). *Getting better: Inside Alcoholics Anonymous.* New York: William Morrow. **(Chap 11)**

Robins, C. J., Block, P., & Peselow, E. D. (1990). Endogenous and non-endogenous depressions: Relations to life events, dysfunctional attitudes and event perceptions. *British Journal of Clinical Psychology, 29,* 201–207. **(Chap 7)**

Robins, L. N. (1966). *Deviant children grown up: A sociological and psychiatric study of sociopathic personality.* Baltimore: Williams & Wilkins. **(Chap 12)**

Robins, L. N. (1978). Sturdy childhood predictors of adult antisocial behavior: Replications from longitudinal studies. *Psychological Medicine, 8,* 611–622. **(Chap 12)**

Robins, L. N., Helzer, J. E., & Davis, D. H. (1975). Narcotic use in Southeast Asia and afterwards. *Archives of General Psychiatry, 32,* 955–961. **(Chap 11)**

Rockney, R. M., & Lemke, T. (1992). Casualties from a junior-senior high school during the Persian Gulf war: Toxic poisoning or mass hysteria? *Developmental and Behavioral Pediatrics, 13*(5), 339–342. **(Chap 1)**

Rockwood, K., Stolee, P., & Brahim, A. (1991). Outcomes of admission to a psychogeriatric service. *Canadian Journal of Psychiatry, 36*(4), 275–279. **(Chap 7)**

Rodin, J., & Salovey, P. (1989). Health psychology. *Annual Review of Psychology, 40,* 533–579. **(Chap 9)**

Roehrich, L., & Kinder, B. N. (1991). Alcohol expectancies and male sexuality: Review and implications for sex therapy. *Journal of Sex and Marital Therapy, 17*(1), 45–54. **(Chap 10)**

Roemer, L., & Borkovec, T. D. (1993). Worry: Unwanted cognitive activity that controls unwanted somatic experience. In D. M. Wegner & J. W. Pennebaker (Eds.), *Handbook of mental control.* Englewood Cliffs, NJ: Prentice Hall. **(Chap 5)**

Roffman, R. A., & Barnhart, R. (1987). Assessing need for marijuana dependence treatment through an anonymous telephone interview. *International Journal of the Addictions, 22,* 639–651. **(Chap 11)**

Roffman, R. A., & Stephens, R. S. (1993). Cannabis dependence. In D. L. Dunner (Ed.), *Current psychiatric therapy* (pp. 105–109). Philadelphia: W. B. Saunders. **(Chap 11)**

Rogers, C. R. (1961). *On becoming a person.* Boston: Houghton Mifflin. **(Chap 1)**

Rogers, R. (1987). APA's position on the insanity defense: Empiricism versus emotionalism. *American Psychologist, 42,* 840–848. **(Chap 16)**

Rogers, S. J., & DiLalla, D. L. (1991). A comparative study of the effects of a developmentally based preschool curriculum on young children with autism and young children with other disorders of behavior and development. *Topics in Early Childhood Special Education, 11,* 29–47. **(Chap 14)**

Rogers, S. J., & Lewis, H. C. (1989). An effective day treatment model for young children with pervasive developmental disorders. *Journal of the American Academy of Child and Adolescent Psychiatry, 28,* 207–214. **(Chap 14)**

Rogers, S. J., Lewis, H. C., & Reis, K. (1987). An effective procedure for training early special education teams to implement a model program. *Journal of the Division of Early Childhood, 11,* 180–188. **(Chap 14)**

Rogers, S. L., & Friedhoff, L. T. (1996). The efficacy and safety of donepezil in patients with Alzheimer's disease: Results of a US multicentre, randomized, double-blind, placebo-controlled trial. The Donepezil Study Group. *Dementia, 7,* 293–303. **(Chap 15)**

Roitt, I. (1988). *Essential immunology* (6th ed.). Oxford, England: Blackwell. **(Chap 9)**

Room, R. (1993). Alcoholics Anonymous as a social movement. In B. S. McCrady & W. R. Miller (Eds.), *Research on Alcoholics Anonymous: Opportunities and alternatives* (pp. 167–187). New Brunswick, NJ: Rutgers Center of Alcohol Studies. **(Chap 11)**

Rorabaugh, W. J. (1991, Fall). Alcohol in America. *OAH Magazine of History,* pp. 17–19. **(Chap 11)**

Rorschach, H. (1951). *Psychodiagnostics.* New York: Grune & Stratton. (Original work published 1921) **(Chap 3)**

Rorsman, B., Hagnell, O., & Lanke, J. (1986). Prevalence and incidence of senile and multi-infarct dementia in the Lundby Study: A comparison between the time periods 1947–1957 and 1957–1974. *Neuropsychobiology, 15,* 122–129. **(Chap 15)**

Rosen, J. C., & Leitenberg, H. (1985). Exposure plus response prevention treatment of bulimia. In D. M. Garner & P. E. Garfinkel (Eds.), *Handbook of psychotherapy for anorexia nervosa and bulimia* (pp. 193–209). New York: Guilford Press. **(Chap 8)**

Rosen, L. W., Shafer, C. L., Dummer, G. M., Cross, L. K., Deuman, G. W., & Malmberg, S. R. (1988). Prevalence of pathogenic weight-control behaviors among Native American women and girls. *International Journal of Eating Disorders, 7*(6), 807–811. **(Chap 8)**

Rosen, R. C., & Beck, J. G. (1988). *Patterns of sexual arousal: Psychophysiological processes and clinical applications.* New York: Guilford Press. **(Chap 10)**

Rosen, R. C., Leiblum, S. R. (1995). Treatment of sexual disorders in the 1990's: An integrated approach. *Journal of Consulting and Clinical Psychology, 63,* 877–890. **(Chap 10)**

Rosenberg, H. (1993). Prediction of controlled drinking by alcoholics and problem drinkers. *Psychological Bulletin, 113,* 129–139. **(Chap 11)**

Rosenberg, R. N., Richter, R. W., Risser, R. C., Taubman, K., Prado-Farmer, I., Ebalo, E., Posey, J., Kingfisher, D., Dean, D., Weiner, M. F., Svetlik, D., Adams, P., Honig, L. S., Cullum, C. M. Schaefer, F. V., & Schellenberg, G. D. (1996). Genetic factors for the development of Alzheimer's disease in the Cherokee Indian. *Archives of Neurology, 53,* 997–1000. **(Chap 15)**

Rosenblatt, J., Bloom, P., & Koegel, R. L. (1995). Overselective responding: Description, implications, and intervention. In R. L. Koegel and L. K. Koegel (Eds.), *Teaching children with autism: Strategies for initiating positive interactions and improving learning opportunities* (pp. 33–42). Baltimore: Paul H. Brookes. **(Chap 14)**

Rosengren, A., Tibblin, G., & Wilhelmsen, L. (1991). Self-perceived psychological stress and incidence of coronary artery disease in middle-aged men. *American Journal of Cardiology, 68,* 1171–1175. **(Chap 9)**

Rosenman, R. H., Brand, R. J., Jenkins, C. D., Friedman, M., Straus, R., & Wurm, M. (1975). Coronary heart disease in the Western Collaborative Group Study: Final follow-up experience of 8 years. *Journal of the American Medical Association, 233,* 872–877. **(Chap 9)**

Rosenthal, D. (Ed.). (1963). *The Genain quadruplets: A case study and theoretical analysis of heredity and environment in schizophrenia.* New York: Basic Books. **(Chap 13)**

Rosenthal, D., Wender, P. H., Kety, S. S., Schulsinger, F., Welner, J., & Ostergaard, L. (1968). Schizophrenics' offspring reared in adoptive homes. In D. Rosenthal & S. S. Kety (Eds.), *The transmission of schizophrenia* (pp. 377–391). Oxford: Pergamon Press. **(Chap 13)**

Rosenthal, P. A., & Rosenthal, S. (1984). Suicidal behavior by preschool children. *American Journal of Psychiatry, 141,* 520–525. **(Chap 7)**

Rosowsky, E., & Gurian, B. (1992). Impact of borderline personality disorder in late life on systems of care. *Hospital and Community Psychiatry, 43,* 386–389. **(Chap 12)**

Ross, A. O., & Pelham, W. E. (1981). Child psychopathology. *Annual Review of Psychology, 32,* 243–278. **(Chap 14)**

Ross, C. A. (1991). Epidemiology of multiple personality disorder and dissociation. *Psychiatric Clinics of North America, 14,* 503–517. **(Chap 6)**

Ross, C. A. (1997). *Dissociative identity disorder.* New York: Wiley. **(Chap 6)**

Ross, C. A., Anderson, G., Fleisher, W. P., Norton, G. R. (1991). The frequency of multiple personality disorder among psychiatric inpatients. *American Journal of Psychiatry, 148,* 1717–1720. **(Chap 6)**

Ross, C. A., Miller, S. D., Reagor, P., Bjornson, L., Fraser, G. A., & Anderson, G. (1990). Structured interview data on 102 cases of multiple personality disorder from four centers. *American Journal of Psychiatry, 147,* 596–601. **(Chap 6)**

Ross, M. W., Walinder, J., Lundstrom, B., & Thuwe, I. (1981). Cross-cultural approaches to transsexualism: A comparison between Sweden and Australia. *Acta Psychiatrica Scandinavica, 63,* 75–82. **(Chap 10)**

Rounsaville, B. J., Sholomskas, D., & Prusoff, B. A. (1988). Chronic mood disorders in depressed outpatients: Diagnosis and response to pharmacotherapy. *Journal of Affective Disorders, 2,* 72–88. **(Chap 7)**

Roush, W. (1997, April 18). Herbert Benson: Mind-body maverick pushes the envelope. *Science, 276,* 357–359. **(Chap 9)**

Rowell, E. A., & Rowell, R. (1939). *On the trail of marihuana: The weed of madness.* Mountain View, CA: Pacific Press Publishing Association. **(Chap 11)**

Roy, A., Segal, N. L., & Sarchiapone, M. (1995). Attempted suicide among living co-twins of twin suicide victims. *American Journal of Psychiatry, 152,* 1075–1076. **(Chap 7)**

Rubin, R., & Balow, B. (1971). Learning and behavior disorders: A longitudinal study. *Exceptional Children, 38,* 293–299. **(Chap 14)**

Rubin, R. T. (1982). Koro (Shook Yang): A culture-bound psychogenic syndrome. In C. T. H. Friedmann & R. A. Fauger (Eds.), *Extraordinary disorders of human behavior* (pp. 155–172). New York: Plenum Press. **(Chap 6)**

Rubonis, A. V., Colby, S. M., Monti, P. M., Rohsenow, D. J., Gulliver, S. B., & Sirota, A. D. (1994). Alcohol cue reactivity and mood induction in male and female alcoholics. *Journal of Studies on Alcohol, 55,* 487–494. **(Chap 11)**

Rudd, M. D., Rajab, M. H., Orman, D. T., Stulman, D. A., Joiner, T., & Dixon, W. (1996). Effectiveness of an outpatient intervention targeting suicidal young adults: Preliminary results. *Journal of Consulting and Clinical Psychology, 64,* 179–190. **(Chap 7)**

Rupp, A., & Keith, S. J. (1993). The costs of schizophrenia: Assessing the burden. *Psychiatric Clinics of North America, 16,* 413–423. **(Chap 13)**

Rush, A. J., & Weissenburger, J. E. (1994). Melancholic symptom features and DSM-IV. *American Journal of Psychiatry, 151,* 489–498. **(Chap 7)**

Rush, A. J., Erman, M. K., Giles, D. E., Schlesser, M. A., Carpenter, G., Vasavada, N., & Roffwarg, H. P. (1986). Polysomnographic findings in recently drug-free and clinically remitted depressed patients. *Archives of General Psychiatry, 43,* 878–884. **(Chap 7)**

Rush, A. J., Giles, D. E., Schlesser, M. A., Orsulak, P. J., Weissenburger, J. E., Fulton, C. L., Fairchild, C. J., & Roffwarg, H. P. (1997). Dexamethasone response, thyrotropin-releasing hormone stimulation, rapid eye movement latency, and subtypes of Depression. *Biological Psychiatry, 41,* 915–928. **(Chap 7)**

Rush, B. (1812). *Medical inquiries and observations upon the diseases of the mind.* Philadelphia: Kimber and Richardson. **(Chap 7)**

Rush, J. A. (1993). Mood disorders in DSM-IV. In D. L. Dunner (Ed.), *Current psychiatric therapy* (pp. 189–195). Philadelphia: W. B. Saunders. **(Chap 7)**

Russell, G. F. M. (1979). Bulimia nervosa: An ominous variant of anorexia nervosa. *Psychological Medicine, 9,* 429–448. **(Chap 8)**

Russell, G. F. M., Szmukler, G. I., Dare, C., & Eisler, I. (1987). An evaluation of family therapy in anorexia nervosa and bulimia nervosa. *Archives of General Psychiatry, 44,* 1047–1056. **(Chap 8)**

Rutter, M., & Giller, H. (1984). *Juvenile delinquency: Trends and perspectives.* New York: Guilford Press. **(Chap 4)**

Rutter, M., & Schopler, E. (1992). Classification of pervasive developmental disorders: Some concepts and practical considerations. *Journal of Autism and Developmental Disorders, 22,* 459–482. **(Chap 14)**

Rutter, M., Macdonald, H., Le Couteur, A., Harrington, R., Bolton, P., & Baily, A. (1990). Genetic factors in child psychiatric disorders—II. Empirical findings. *Journal of Child Psychology and Psychiatry, 31,* 39–83. **(Chap 4)**

Rutter, M. L. (1997). Nature-nurture integration: The example of antisocial behavior. *American Psychologist, 52,* 390–398. **(Chap 12)**

Ryan, W. D. (1992). The pharmacologic treatment of child and adolescent depression. *Psychiatric Clinics of North America, 15,* 29–40. **(Chap 7)**

Saab, P. G., Llabre, M. M., Hurwitz, B. E., Frame, C. A., Reineke, I., Fins, A. I., McCalla, J., Cieply, L. K., & Schneiderman, N. (1992). Myocardial and peripheral vascular responses to behavioral challenges and their stability in Black and White Americans. *Psychophysiology, 29*(4), 384–397. **(Chap 9)**

Sachs, G. A., & Cassel, C. K. (1989). Ethical aspects of dementia. *Neurologic Clinics, 7,* 845–858. **(Chap 15)**

Sack, R. L., & Lewy, A. J. (1993). Human circadian rhythms: Lessons from the blind. *Annals of Medicine, 25,* 303–305. **(Chap 8)**

Sackeim, H. A., & Devanand, D. P. (1991). Dissociative disorders. In M. Hersen & S. M. Turner (Eds.), *Adult psychopathology & diagnosis* (2nd ed., pp. 279–322). New York: John Wiley. **(Chap 6)**

Sackeim, H. A., Nordlie, J. W., & Gur, R. C. (1979). A model of hysterical and hypnotic blindness: Cognition, motivation and awareness. *Journal of Abnormal Psychology, 88,* 474–489. **(Chap 6)**

Saigh, P. A. (1984). Pre- and postinvasion anxiety in Lebanon. *Behavior Therapy, 15,* 185–190. **(Chap 5)**

Sajwaj, T., Libet, J., & Agras, S. (1974). Lemon-juice therapy: The control of life threatening rumination in a six-month old infant. *Journal of Applied Behavior Analysis, 7*(4), 557–563. **(Chap 8)**

Sakel, M. (1958). *Schizophrenia.* New York: Philosophical Library Inc. **(Chap 1)**

Sakheim, D. K., Barlow, D. H., Abrahamson, D. J., & Beck, J. G. (1987). Distinguishing between organogenic and psychogenic erectile dysfunction. *Behaviour Research and Therapy, 25,* 379–390. **(Chap 10)**

Salge, R. A., Beck, J. G., & Logan, A. (1988). A community survey of panic.

Journal of Anxiety Disorder, 2, 157–167. **(Chap 5)**

Salkovskis, P. M., & Campbell, P. (1994). Thought suppression induces intrusion in naturally occurring negative intrusive thoughts. *Behaviour Research and Therapy, 32*(1), 1–8. **(Chap 5)**

Salkovskis, P. M., Atha, C., & Storer, D. (1990). Cognitive-behavioural problem solving in the treatment of patients who repeatedly attempt suicide: A controlled trial. *British Journal of Psychiatry, 157,* 871–876. **(Chap 7)**

Salzman, C. (1991). Pharmacologic treatment of the anxious elderly patient. In C. Salzman & B. D. Lebowitz (Eds.), *Anxiety in the elderly: Treatment and research* (pp. 149–173). New York: Springer. **(Chap 5)**

Sameroff, A. J., & Seifer, R. (1990). Early contributors to developmental risk. In J. Rolf, A. S. Masten, D. Cicchetti, K. H. Nuechterlein, & S. Weintrab (Eds.), *Risk and protective factors in the development of psychopathology* (pp. 52–66). Cambridge: Cambridge University Press. **(Chap 4)**

Sampson, R. J., Raudenbush, S. W., & Earls, F. (1997). Neighborhoods and violent crime: A multilevel study of collective efficacy. *Science, 277,* 918–924. **(Chap 12)**

Samson, J. A., Mirin, S. M., Hauser, S. T., Fenton, B. T., & Schildkraut, J. J. (1992). Learned helplessness and urinary MHPG levels in unipolar depression. *American Journal of Psychiatry, 149*(6), 806–809. **(Chap 7)**

Samuels, S. C., & Davis, K. L. (1997). A risk-benefit assessment of tacrine in the treatment of Alzheimer's disease. *Drug Safety, 16,* 66–77. **(Chap 15)**

Sanders, M. R. (1992). Enhancing the impact of behavioural family intervention with children: Emerging perspectives. *Behaviour Change, 9,* 115–119. **(Chap 12)**

Sanders, M. R., Dadds, M. R., Johnston, B. M., & Cash, R. (1992). Childhood depression and conduct disorder: I. Behavioral, affective and cognitive aspects of family problem solving interactions. *Journal of Abnormal Psychology, 101*(3), 495–504. **(Chap 7)**

Sanderson, C., & Clarkin, J. F. (1994). Use of the NEO-PI personality dimensions in differential treatment planning. In P. T. Costa & T. A. Widiger (Eds.), *Personality disorders and the five-factor model of personality* (pp. 219–235). Washington, D. C.: American Psychological Association. **(Chaps 3, 12)**

Sanderson, W. C., DiNardo, P. A., Rapee, R. M., & Barlow, D. H. (1990). Syndrome comorbidity in patients diagnosed with a DSM-III-R anxiety disorder. *Journal of Abnormal Psychology, 99,* 308–312. **(Chaps 5, 7)**

Sands, J. R., & Harrow, M. (1995). Vulnerability to psychosis in unipolar major depression: Is premorbid functioning involved? *American Journal of Psychiatry, 152,* 1009–1015. **(Chap 7)**

Sano, M., Ernesto, C., Thomas, R. G. Klauber, M. R., Schafer, K., Grundman, M., Woodbury, P., Growdon, J., Cotman, C. W., Pfeiffer, E., Schneider, L. S., & Thal, L. J. (1997). A controlled trial of selegiline, alphatocopherol, or both as treatment for Alzheimer's disease. *The New England Journal of Medicine, 336,* 1216–1222. **(Chap 15)**

Sansbury, L. L., & Wahler, R. G. (1992). Pathways to maladaptive parenting with mothers and their conduct disordered children. *Behavior Modification, 16,* 574–592. **(Chap 12)**

Saper, J. R. (1989). Chronic headache syndromes. *Neurologic Clinics, 7,* 387–411. **(Chap 9)**

Sapolsky, R. M. (1990, January). Stress in the wild. *Scientific American,* 116–123. **(Chap 9)**

Sapolsky, R., & Ray, J. C. (1989). Styles of dominance and their endocrine correlates among wild, live baboons. *American Journal of Primatology, 18*(1), 1–13. **(Chap 9)**

Sapolsky, R. M., & Meaney, M. J. (1986). Maturation of the adrenal stress response: Neuroendocrine control mechanisms and the stress hyporesponsive period. *Brain Research Review, 11,* 65–76. **(Chap 9)**

Sarbin, T., & Mancuso, J. (1980). *Schizophrenia: Medical diagnosis or moral verdict?* Elmsford, NY: Pergamon Press. **(Chap 13)**

Sarrel, P. M., & Masters, W. H. (1982). Sexual molestation of men by women. *Archives of Sexual Behavior, 11,* 117–131. **(Chap 10)**

Satel, S. (1992). Craving for and fear of cocaine: A phenomenologic update on cocaine craving and paranoia. In T. R. Kosten & H. D. Kleber (Eds.), *Clinician's guide to cocaine addiction: Theory, research, and treatment* (pp. 172–192). New York: Guilford Press. **(Chap 11)**

Saudino, J. J., Pedersen, N. L., Lichenstein, P. McClearn, G. E., & Plomin, R. (Jan. 1997). Can personality explain genetic influence on life events? *Journal of Personality & Social Psychology, 72* (1), 196–206. **(Chap 2)**

Saudino, K. J., & Plomin, R. (1996). Personality and behavioral genetics: Where have we been and where are we going? *Journal of Research in Personality, 30,* 335–347. **(Chap 2)**

Saudino, K. J., Plomin, R., & DeFries, J. C. (1996). Tester-rated temperament at 14, 20, and 24 months: Environmental change and genetic continuity. *British Journal of Developmental Psychology, 14,* 129–144. **(Chap 2)**

Saunders, A. M., Strittmatter, W. J., Schmechel, D., St. George-Hyslop, P. H., Pericak-Vance, M. A., Joo, S. H., Rosi, B. L., Gusella, J. F., Crapper-Maclachlan, D. R., Alberts, M. J., Hulette, C., Crain, B., Goldgaber, D., & Roses, A. D. (1993). Association of apolipoprotein E allele e4 with late-onset familial and sporadic Alzheimer's disease. *Neurology, 43,* 1467–1472. **(Chap 15)**

Saxe, G. N., van der Kolk, B. A., Berkowitz, R., Chinman, G., Hall, K., Leiberg, G., & Schwartz, J. (1993). Dissociative disorders in psychiatric inpatients. *American Journal of Psychiatry, 150,* 1037–1042. **(Chap 6)**

Saxena, S., & Prasad, K. (1989). DSM-III subclassifications of dissociative disorders applied to psychiatric outpatients in India. *American Journal of Psychiatry, 146,* 261–262. **(Chap 6)**

Sbrocco, T. & Barlow, D. H. (1997). Conceptualizing the cognitive component of sexual arousal: Implications for sexuality research and treatment. In P. M. Salkovskis (Ed.), *Frontiers of cognitive therapy* (pp. 419–449). New York: Guilford Press. **(Chap 10)**

Schacter, D. L. (Ed.). (1995). *Memory distortion: How minds, brains, and societies reconstruct the past.* Cambridge, MA: Harvard University Press. **(Chap 6)**

Schacter, D. L., Chiu, P., & Ochsner, K. N. (1993). Implicit memory: A selective review. *Annual Review of Neuroscience, 16,* 159–182. **(Chap 2)**

Schafer, J., & Brown, S. A. (1991). Marijuana and cocaine effect expectancies and drug use patterns. *Journal of Consulting and Clinical Psychology, 59,* 558–565. **(Chap 11)**

Scheerenberger, R. C. (1983). *A history of mental retardation.* Baltimore: Paul H. Brookes. **(Chap 14)**

Scheibel, A. B., & Conrad, A. S. (1993). Hippocampal dysgenesis in mutant mouse and schizophrenic man: Is there a relationship? *Schizophrenia Bulletin, 19,* 21–33. **(Chap 13)**

Scheier, M. F., Matthews, K. A., Owens, J. F., Magovern, G. J., Sr., Lefebvre, R. C., Abbott, R. A., & Carver, C. S. (1989). Dispositional optimism and recovery from coronary artery bypass surgery: The beneficial effects on physical and psychological well-being. *Journal of Personality and Social Psychology, 57*(6), 1024–1040. **(Chap 9)**

Schenk, L., & Bear, D. (1981). Multiple personality and related dissociative phenomena in patients with temporal lobe epilepsy. *American Journal of Psychiatry, 138,* 1311–1316. **(Chap 6)**

Schiavi, R. C. (1990). Chronic alcoholism and male sexual dysfunction. *Journal of Sex and Marital Therapy, 16,* 23–33. **(Chap 10)**

Schiavi, R. C., White, D, Mandeli, J., & Levine, A. C. (1997). Effect of testosterone administration on sexual behavior and mood in men with erectile dysfunction. *Archives of Sexual Behavior, 26,* 231–241. **(Chap 10)**

Schildkraut, J. J. (1965). The catecholamine hypothesis of affective disorders: A review of supporting evidence. *American Journal of Psychiatry, 122,* 509–522. **(Chaps 2, 7)**

Schizophrenia Collaborative Linkage Group (Chromosome 22). (1996). A combined analysis of D22S278 marlcer alleles in affected sib-pairs: Support for a susceptibility locus at chromosomen 22q12. *American Journal of Medical Genetics, Neuropsychiatric Genetics, 67,* 40–45. **(Chap 4)**

Schleifer, S. J., Keller, S. E., Bond, R. N., Cohen, J., & Stein, M. (1989). Major depressive disorder and immunity: Role of age, sex, severity, and hospitalization. *Archives of General Psychiatry, 46,* 81–87. **(Chap 9)**

Schlundt, O. G., & Johnson, W. G. (1990). *Eating disorders: Assessment and treatment.* Boston: Allyn & Bacon. **(Chap 8)**

Schmitz, J. M., Schneider, N. G., & Jarvik, M. E. (1997). Nicotine. In J. H. Lowinson, P. Ruiz, R. B. Millman, & J. G. Langrod (Eds.), *Substance abuse: A comprehensive textbook* (pp. 276–294). Baltimore: Williams & Wilkins. **(Chap 11)**

Schneiderman, J., Antoni., M., Ironson, G., Klimas, N. LaPerriere, A., et al. (1994) HIV-1, immunity, and behavior. In R. Glaser & J. Kiecolt-Glaser (Eds.), *Handbook of human stress and immunity* (pp. 267–300). New York: Academic. **(Chap 9)**

Schneiderman, N., Antoni, M. H., Ironson, G., LaPerriere, A., & Fletcher, M. A. (1992). Applied psychological science and HIV-1 spectrum disease. *Applied and Preventive Psychology, 1,* 67–82. **(Chaps 2, 9)**

Schneier, F. R., Liebowitz, M. R., Beidel, D. C., Fyer, A. J., George, M. S., Heimberg, R. G., Holt, C. S., Klein, D. G., Levin, A. P., Lydiard, R. B., Mannuzza, S., Martin, L. Y., Nardi, A. E., Terrill, D. R., Spitzer, R. L., Turner, S. M., Uhde, T. W., Figueira, I. V., & Versiani, M. (1996). Social phobia. In T. A. Widiger, A. J. Frances, H. A. Pincus, R. Ross, M. B. First, & W. W. Davis (Eds.), *DSM-IV sourcebook* (Vol. 2, pp. 507–548). Washington, DC: American Psychiatric Association. **(Chap 5)**

Schoenbach, V. J., Kaplan, B. H., Fredman, L., & Kleinbaum, D. G. (1986). Social ties and mortality in Evans County, Georgia. *American Journal of Epidemiology, 123,* 577. **(Chap 2)**

Schoeneman, T. J. (1977). The role of mental illness in the European witchhunts of the sixteenth and seventeenth centuries: An assessment. *Journal of the History of the Behavioral Sciences, 13,* 337–351. **(Chap 1)**

Schover, L. R. (1981). Unpublished data. Cited by Schover, L. R. & Jensen, S. B. (1988). *Sexuality and chronic illness: A comprehensive approach* (pp. 59–60, 126, 130–135). New York: Guilford Press. **(Chap 10)**

Schover, L. R., & Jensen, S. B. (1988). *Sexuality and chronic illness: A comprehensive approach.* New York: Guilford Press. **(Chap 10)**

Schover, L. R., & Newsom, C. D. (1976). Overselectivity, developmental level, and overtraining in autistic and normal children. *Journal of Abnormal Child Psychology, 4,* 289–298. **(Chap 14)**

Schreiber, F. R. (1973). *Sybil.* Chicago: Regnery. **(Chap 6)**

Schreiner-Engel, P., & Schiavi, R. C. (1986). Lifetime psychopathology in individuals with low sexual desire. *Journal of Nervous and Mental Disease, 174,* 646–651. **(Chap 10)**

Schroeder, M. L., Wormworth, J. A., & Livesley, W. J. (1993). Dimensions of personality disorder and the five-factor model of personality. In P. T. Costa, Jr., & T. A. Widiger (Eds.), *Personality disorders and the five-factor model of personality* (pp. 117–127). Washington, DC: American Psychological Association. **(Chap 12)**

Schubert, D. S., Burns, R., Paras, W., & Sioson, E. (1992). Increase of medical hospital length of stay by depression in stroke and amputation patients: A pilot study. *Psychotherapy and Psychosomatics, 57*(1–2), 61–66. **(Chap 2)**

Schuckit, M. A. (1993). Keeping current with the DSMs and substance use disorder. In D. L. Dunner (Ed.), *Current psychiatric therapy* (pp. 89–91). Philadelphia: W. B. Saunders. **(Chap 11)**

Schuckit, M. A. (1994). Low level of response to alcohol as a predictor of future alcoholism. *American Journal of Psychiatry, 151,* 184–189. **(Chap 11)**

Schuckit, M. A., Smith, T. L., Anthenelli, R., & Irwin, M. (1993). Clinical course of alcoholism in 636 male inpatients. *American Journal of Psychiatry, 150,* 786–792. **(Chap 11)**

Schulberg, H. C., Block, M. R., Madonia, M. J., Scott, C. P., Rodriguez, E., Imber, S. D., Perel, J., Lave, J., Houck, P. R., & Coulehan, J. L. (1996). Treating major depression in primary care practice: Eight-month clinical outcomes. *Archives of General Psychiatry, 53,* 913–919. **(Chap 7)**

Schulsinger, F., Kety, S. S., & Rosenthal, D. (1979). A family study of suicide. In M. Schou & E. Stromgren (Eds.), *Origin, prevention, and treatment of affective disorders.* New York: Academic Press. **(Chap 7)**

Schwalberg, M. D., Barlow, D. H., Alger, S. A., & Howard, L. J. (1992). Comparison of bulimics, obese binge eaters, social phobics, and individuals with panic disorder or comorbidity across DSM-III-R anxiety. *Journal of Abnormal Psychology, 101,* 675–681. **(Chap 8)**

Schwartz, A. J., & Whitaker, L. C. (1990). Suicide among college students: Assessment, treatment, and intervention. In S. J. Blumenthal & D. J. Kupfer (Eds.), *Suicide over the life cycle: Risk factors, assessment and treatment of suicidal patients.* Washington, DC: American Psychiatric Press. **(Chap 7)**

Schwartz, G. E., & Weiss, S. M. (1978). Behavioral medicine revisited: An amended definition. *Journal of Behavioral Medicine, 1,* 249–252. **(Chap 9)**

Schwartz, I. M. (1993). Affective reactions of American and Swedish women to the first premarital coitus: A cross-cultural comparison. *Journal of Sex Research, 30*(1), 18–26. **(Chap 10)**

Schwartz, J. M., Stoessel, P. W., Baxter, L. R., Martin, K. M., & Phelps, M. E. (1996). Systematic changes in cerebral glucose metabolic rate after successful behavior modification treatment of obsessive compulsive disorder. *Archives of General Psychiatry, 53,* 109–113. **(Chap 2)**

Schwartz, P. J., Brown, C., Wehr, T. A., & Rosenthal, N. E. (1996). Winter seasonal affective disorder: A follow-up study of the first 59 patients of the National Institute of Mental Health seasonal studies program. *American Journal of Psychiatry, 153,* 1028–1036. **(Chap 7)**

Schweizer, E. & Rickels, K. (1996). Pharmacological treatment for generalized anxiety disorder. In M. R. Mavissakalian & R. F. Prien (Eds.), *Long-term treatments of anxiety disorders.* Washington, DC: American Psychiatric Press, Inc. **(Chap 5)**

Schweizer, E., Rickels, K., Case, W. G., & Greenblatt, D. J. (1990). Long-term use of benzodiazepines. II. Effects of gradual taper. *Archives of General Psychiatry, 47,* 908–915. **(Chap 5)**

Scott, J. E., & Dixon, L. B. (1995). Assertive community treatment and case management for schizophrenia. *Schizophrenia Bulletin, 21,* 657–668. **(Chap 13)**

Scott, J. E., & Dixon, L. B. (1995). Psychological interventions for schizophrenia. *Schizophrenia Bulletin, 21,* 621–630. **(Chap 13)**

Scott, J. (1995). Psychotherapy for bipolar disorder. *British Journal of Psychiatry, 167,* 581–588. **(Chap 7)**

Scott, K. G., & Carran, D. T. (1987). The epidemiology and prevention of mental retardation. *American Psychologist, 42,* 801–804. **(Chap 14)**

Sedlmeier, P., & Gigerenzer, G. (1989). Do studies of statistical power have an effect on the power of studies? *Psychological Bulletin, 105,* 309–316. **(Chap 4)**

Seeman, P., Lee, T., Chau Wong, M. & Wong, K. (1976). Antipsychotic drug doses and neuroleptic/dopamine receptors. *Nature, 261,* 717–719. **(Chap 13)**

Segal, S. (1978). Attitudes toward the mentally ill: A review. *Social Work, 23,* 211–217. **(Chap 3)**

Segal, Z. V., Hood, J. E., Shaw, B. F., & Higgins, E. (1988). A structural analysis of the self-schema construct in major depression. *Cognitive Therapy and Research, 12*(5), 471–485. **(Chap 7)**

Segraves, R. T., & Althof, S. (1998). Psychotherapy and pharmacotherapy of sexual dysfunctions. In P. E. Nathan & J. M. Gorman (Eds.), *A guide to treatments that work* (pp. 447–471). New York: Oxford University Press. **(Chap 10)**

Seidman, S. N., & Rieder, R. O. (1994). A review of sexual behavior in the United States. *The American Journal of Psychiatry, 151,* 330–341. **(Chap 10)**

Seligman, M. E. P. (1971). Phobias and preparedness. *Behavior Therapy, 2,* 307–320. **(Chap 2)**

Seligman, M. E. P. (1975). *Helplessness: On depression, development and death.* San Francisco: W. H. Freeman. **(Chaps 7, 9)**

Selkoe, D. J. (1997). Alzheimer's disease: Genotypes, phenotype, and treatments. *Science, 275,* 630–631. **(Chap 15)**

Selye, H. (1936). A syndrome produced by diverse noxious agents. *Nature, 138,* 32. **(Chap 9)**

Selye, H. (1950). *The physiology and pathology of exposure to stress.* Montreal: Acta. **(Chap 9)**

Semans, J. H. (1956). Premature ejaculation: A new approach. *Southern Medical Journal, 49,* 353–358. **(Chap 10)**

Severino, S. K., & Moline, M. L. (1989). *Premenstrual syndrome: A clinician's guide.* New York: Guilford Press. **(Chap 3)**

Sexton, M. M. (1979). Behavioral epidemiology. In O. F. Pomerleau & J. P. Brady (Eds.), *Behavioral medicine: Theory and practice* (pp. 3–21). Baltimore: Williams & Wilkins. **(Chap 9)**

Shabecoff, P. (1987, October 14). Stress and the lure of harmless remedies. *New York Times,* p. 12. **(Chap 11)**

Shaffer, D. R. (1993). *Developmental psychology: Childhood and adolescence* (3rd ed.). Pacific Grove, CA: Brooks/Cole. **(Chap 2)**

Shaffer, D., Garland, A., Gould, M., Fisher, P., & Trautmen, P. (1988). Preventing teenage suicide: A critical review. *Journal of the American Academy of Child and Adolescent Psychiatry, 27,* 675–687. **(Chap 7)**

Shaffer, D., Garland, A., Vieland, V., Underwood, M., & Busner, C. (1991). The impact of curriculum based suicide prevention programs for teenagers. *Journal of the American Academy of Child and Adolescent Psychiatry, 30*(4), 588–596. **(Chap 7)**

Shapiro, D. (1965). *Neurotic styles.* New York: Basic Books. **(Chap 12)**

Shapiro, D. (1974). Operant-feedback control of human blood pressure: Some clinical issues. In P. A. Obrist, A. H. Black, J. Brener, & L. V. DiCara (Eds.), *Cardiovascular psychophysiology: Current issues in response mechanisms, biofeedback, and methodology.* Chicago: Aldine. **(Chap 9)**

Shapiro, D. A., Rees, A., Barkham, M., Hardy, G., Reynolds, S., & Startup, M. (1995). Effects of treatment duration and severity of depression on the maintenance of gains after cognitive-behavioral and psychodynamic-interpersonal psychotherapy. *Journal of Consulting and Clinical Psychology, 63,* 378–387. **(Chap 7)**

Shapiro, E. S., & Lentz, F. E. (1991). Vocational-technical programs: Follow-up of students with learning disabilities. *Exceptional Children, 58,* 47–59. **(Chap 14)**

Sharfstein, S. S. (1987). Reimbursement resistance to treatment and support for the long-term mental patient. *New Directions for Mental Health Services, 33,* 75–85. **(Chap 16)**

Sharpe, M. (1992). Fatigue and chronic fatigue syndrome. *Current Opinion in Psychiatry, 5,* 207–212. **(Chap 9)**

Sharpe, M. (1993). *Chronic fatigue syndrome* (pp. 298–317). Chichester, England: John Wiley. **(Chap 9)**

Sharpe, M. (1997). Chronic fatigue. In D. M. Clark & C. G. Fairburn (Eds.), *Science and practice of cognitive behavior therapy* (pp. 381–414). Oxford, U. K.: Oxford University Press. **(Chap 9)**

Shea, M. T., Elkin, I., Imber, S. D., Sotsky, S. M., Watkins, J. T., Collins, J. F., Pilkonis, P. A., Beckham, E., Glass, D. R., Dolan, R. T., & Parloff, M. B. (1992). Course of depressive symptoms over follow-up: Findings from the National Institute of Mental Health Treatment of Depression Collaborative Research Program. *Archives of General Psychiatry, 49* (10), 782–787. **(Chap 7)**

Shea, M. T., Pilkonis, P. A., Beckham, E., Collins, J. F., Elkin, I. Sotsky, S. M., & Docherty, J. P. (1990). Personality disorders and treatment outcome in the NIMH treatment of depression collaborative research program. *American Journal of Psychiatry, 147,* 711–718. **(Chap 12)**

Shear, M. K., Brown, T. A., Barlow, D. H., Money, R., Sholomskas, D. E., Woods, S. W., Gorman, J. M., & Papp, L. A. (1997). Multicenter collaborative panic disorder severity scale. *American Journal of Psychiatry, 154,* 1571–1575. **(Chap 5)**

Sheikh, J. I. (1992). Anxiety and its disorders in old age. In J. E. Birren, K. Sloan, & G. D. Cohen (Eds.), *Handbook of mental health and aging* (pp. 410–432). New York: Academic Press. **(Chap 5)**

Sherbourne, C. D., Hays, R. D., & Wells, K. B. (1995). Personal and psychosocial risk factors for physical and mental health outcomes and course of depression among depressed patients. *Journal of Consulting and Clinical Psychology, 63,* 345–355. **(Chap 7)**

Sherman, S. L., DeFries, J. C., Gottesman, I. I., Loehlin, J. C., Meyer, J. M., Pelias, M. Z., Rice, J., & Waldman, I. (1997). Recent developments in human behavioral genetics: Past accomplishments and future directions. *American Journal of Human Genetics, 60,* 1265–1275. **(Chaps 4, 13)**

Shiffman, S., Hickcox, M., Paty, J. A., Gnys, M., Kassel, J. D., & Richards, T. J. (1996). Progression from a smoking lapse to relapse: Prediction from abstinence violation effects, nicotine dependence, and lapse characteristics. *Journal of Consulting and Clinical Psychology, 64,* 993–1002. **(Chap 11)**

Shneidman, E. S. (1989). Approaches and commonalities of suicide. In R. F. W. Diekstra, R. Mariss, S. Platt, A. Schmidtke, & G. Sonneck (Eds.), *Suicide and its prevention: The role of attitude and imitation. Advances in Suicidology* (Vol. 1). Leiden, Netherlands: E. J. Brill. **(Chap 7)**

Shneidman, E. S., Farberow, N. L., & Litman, R. E. (Eds.) (1970). *The psychology of suicide.* New York: Science House. **(Chap 7)**

Shore, J. H., Tatum, E. L., & Vollmer, W. M. (1986). Evaluation of mental health effects of disaster. *American Journal of Public Health, 76,* 76–83. **(Chap 4)**

Show, M. (1985). Practical problems of lithium maintenance treatment. *Advances in Biochemical Psychopharmacology, 40,* 131–138. **(Chap 7)**

Shrout, P. E., Link, B. G., Dohrenwend, B. P., Skodol, A. E., Stueve, A., & Mirotznik, J. (1989). Characterizing life events as risk factors for depression: The role of fateful loss events. *Journal of Abnormal Psychology, 98,* 460–467. **(Chap 7)**

Sibley, D. C., & Blinder, B. J. (1988). Anorexia nervosa. In B. J. Blinder, B. F. Chaitin, & R. S. Goldstein (Eds.), *The eating disorders: Medical and psychological bases of diagnosis and treatment* (pp. 247–258). New York: PMA Publishing Corp. **(Chap 8)**

Sieck, W. A., & McFall, R. M. (1976). Some determinants of self-monitoring effects. *Journal of Consulting and Clinical Psychology, 44,* 958–965. **(Chap 3)**

Siever, L. J. (1992). Schizophrenia spectrum personality disorders. In A. Tasman & M. B. Riba (Eds.), *Review of psychiatry* (Vol. 11, pp. 25–42). Washington, DC: American Psychiatric Press. **(Chap 12)**

Siever, L. J., Bernstein, D. P., & Silverman, J. M. (1991). Schizotypal personality disorder: A review of its current status. *Journal of Personality Disorders, 5,* 178–193. **(Chap 12)**

Siever, L. J., Bernstein, D. P., & Silverman, J. M. (1995). Schizotypal personality disorder. In W. J. Livesley (Ed.), *The DSM-IV personality disorders* (pp. 71–90). New York: Guilford Press. **(Chap 12)**

Siever, L. J., Davis, K. L., & Gorman, L. K. (1991). Pathogenesis of mood disorders. In K. Davis, H. Klar, & J. T. Coyle, *Foundations of psychiatry.* Philadelphia: W. B. Saunders. **(Chap 2)**

Siffre, M. (1964). *Beyond time.* (H. Briffault, Ed. and Trans.) New York: McGraw-Hill. **(Chap 8)**

Sigman, M., & Ungerer, J. A. (1984). Attachment behaviors in autistic children. *Journal of Autism and Developmental Disorders, 14,* 231–244. **(Chap 14)**

Sigvardsson, S., Cloninger, C. R., Bohman, M., & von-Knorring, A. L. (1982). Predisposition to petty criminality in Swedish adoptees. *Archives of General Psychiatry, 39,* 1248–1253. **(Chap 12)**

Silbersweig, D. A., Stern, E., Frith, C., Cahill, C., Holmes, A., Grootoonk, S., Seaward, J., McKenna, P., Chua, S. E., Schnorr, L., Jones, T., & Frackowiak, R. S. J. (1995). A functional neuroanatomy of hallucinations in schizophrenia. *Nature, 378,* 176–179. **(Chap 13)**

Silva, P. A. (1980). The prevalence, stability and significance of developmental language delay in preschool children. *Developmental Medicine and Child Neurology, 22,* 768–777. **(Chap 14)**

Silver, E., Cirincione, C., & Steadman, H. J. (1994). Demythologizing inaccurate perceptions of the insanity defense. *Law and Human Behavior, 18,* 63–70. **(Chap 16)**

Silverman, K., Evans, S. M., Strain, E. C., & Griffiths, R. R. (1992). Withdrawal syndrome after the double-blind cessation of caffeine consumption. *New England Journal of Medicine, 327,* 1109–1114. **(Chap 11)**

Silverman, W. K., & Rabian, B. (1993). Simple phobias. *Child and Adolescent Psychiatric Clinics of North America, 2,* 603–622. **(Chap 5)**

Silverman, W. K., La Greca, A. M., & Wasserstein, S. (1995). What do children worry about? Worries & their relation to anxiety. *Child Development, 66,* 671–686. **(Chap 5)**

Silverstone, T. (1985). Dopamine in manic depressive illness: A pharmacological synthesis. *Journal of Affective Disorders, 8*(3), 225–231. **(Chap 7)**

Simeon, D., Gross, S., Guralnik, O., Stein, M. B., Schmeidler, J. & Hollander E. (1997). Thirty cases of DSM III-R depersonalization disorder. *American Journal of Psychiatry, 154,* 1107–1113. **(Chap 6)**

Simon, E. J. (1997). Opiates: Neurobiology. In J. H. Lowinson, P. Ruiz, R. B. Millman, & J. G. Langrod (Eds.), *Substance abuse: A comprehensive textbook* (pp. 148–158). Baltimore: Williams & Wilkins. **(Chap 11)**

Simon, R. J., & Aaronson, D. E. (1988). *The insanity defense: A critical assessment of law and policy in the post-Hinckley era.* New York: Praeger Press. **(Chap 16)**

Simonoff, E., Bolton, P., & Rutter, M. (1996). Mental retardation: Genetic findings, clinical implications and research agenda. *Journal of Child Psychology and Psychiatry, 37,* 259–280. **(Chap 14)**

Simons, A. D., Murphy, G. E., Levine, J. L., & Wetzel, R. D. (1986). Cognitive therapy and pharmacotherapy for depression: Sustained improvement over one year. *Archives of General Psychiatry, 43*(1), 43–48. **(Chap 7)**

Simpson, G. M., Pi, E. H., Gross, L., Baron, D., & November, M. (1988). Plasma levels and therapeutic response with trimipramine treatment of endogenous depression. *Journal of Clinical Psychiatry, 49,* 113–116. **(Chap 7)**

Singh, N. N., & Winton, A. S. W. (1984). Effects of a screening procedure on pica and collateral behaviors. *Journal of Behavior Therapy and Experimental Psychiatry, 15,* 59–65. **(Chap 8)**

Singh, N. N., Manning, P. J., & Angell, M. J. (1982). Effects of an oral hygiene punishment on chronic rumination and collateral behaviors in monozygotic twins. *Journal of Applied Behavioral Analysis, 15,* 309–314. **(Chap 8)**

Singhi, S., Singhi, P., & Adwani, G. B. (1981). Role of psychosocial stress in the cause of pica. *Clinical Pediatrics, 20,* 783–785. **(Chap 8)**

Siris, S. G. (1993). The treatment of schizoaffective disorder. In D. L. Dunner (Ed.), *Current psychiatric therapy* (pp. 160–165). Philadelphia: W. B. Saunders. **(Chap 13)**

Sisson, R. W., & Azrin, N. H. (1989). The community reinforcement approach. In R. K. Hester & W. R. Miller (Eds.), *Handbook of alcohol treatment approaches: Effective alternatives.* Elmsford: NY: Pergamon Press. **(Chap 11)**

Skhiri, D., Annabi, S., Bi, S., & Allani, D. (1982). Enfants d'immigrés: Facteurs de liens ou de rupture? *Annales Medico-Psychologiques, 140,* 597–602. **(Chap 12)**

Skinner, B. F. (1938). *The behavior of organisms.* New York: Appleton-Century-Crofts. **(Chap 1)**

Skinner, B. F. (1948). *Walden two.* New York: Macmillan. **(Chap 1)**

Skinner, B. F. (1971). *Beyond freedom and dignity.* New York: Knopf. **(Chap 1)**

Slutske, W. S., Heath, A. C., Dinwiddie, S. H., Madden, P. A. F., Bucholz, K. K., Dunne, M. P., Statham, D. J., & Martin, N. G. (1997). Modeling genetic and environmental influences in the etiology of conduct disorder: A study of 2,682 adult twin pairs. *Journal of Abnormal Psychology, 106,* 266–279. **(Chap 12)**

Small, G. W. (1991). Recognition and treatment of depression in the elderly. The clinician's challenge: Strategies for treatment of depression in the 1990's. *Journal of Clinical Psychiatry, 52,* 11–22. **(Chap 7)**

Smalley, S. L. (1991). Genetic influences in autism. *Psychiatric Clinics of North America, 14,* 125–139. **(Chap 14)**

Smith, D. E., Marcus, M. D., & Kaye, W. (1992). Cognitive-behavioral treatment of obese binge eaters. *International Journal of Eating Disorders, 12,* 257–262. **(Chap 8)**

Smith, G. A., & Hall, J. A. (1982). Evaluating Michigan's guilty but mentally ill verdict: An empirical study. *Journal of Law Reform, 16,* 75–112. **(Chap 16)**

Smith, G. R., Monson, R. A., & Ray, D. B. (1986). Psychiatric consultation in somatization disorder. *New England Journal of Medicine, 314,* 1407–1413. **(Chap 6)**

Smith, J. E., & Krejci, J. (1991). Minorities join the majority: Eating disturbances among Hispanic and Native American youth. *International Journal of Eating Disorders, 10,* 179–186. **(Chap 8)**

Smith, M. D. (1992). Community integration and supported employment. In D. E. Berkell (Ed.), *Autism: Identification, education, and treatment* (pp. 253–271). Hillsdale, NJ: Lawrence Erlbaum. **(Chap 14)**

Smith, P. G., & Cousens, S. N. (1996). Is the new variant of Creutzfeldt-Jakob disease from mad cows? *Science, 273,* 748. **(Chap 15)**

Smith, R. J. (1991). Somatization disorder: Defining its role in clinical medicine. *Journal of General Internal Medicine, 6,* 168–175. **(Chap 6)**

Smith, S. E. (1993). Cognitive deficits associated with fragile X syndrome. *Mental Retardation, 31,* 279–283. **(Chap 14)**

Smith, S. S., & Newman, J. P. (1990). Alcohol and drug abuse-dependence disorders in psychopathic and nonpsychopathic criminal offenders. *Journal of Abnormal Psychology, 99,* 430–439. **(Chap 12)**

Smith, S. S., O'Hara, B. F., Persico, A. M., Gorelick, D. A., Newlin, D. B., Vlahov, D., Solomon, L., Pickens, R., & Uhl, G. R. (1992). Genetic vulnerability to drug abuse: The D2 dopamine receptor Taq B1 restriction fragment length polymorphism appears more frequently in polysubstance abusers. *Archives of General Psychiatry, 49,* 723–727. **(Chap 11)**

Smith, T. E., Bellack, A. S., & Liberman, R. P. (1996). Social skills training for schizophrenia: Review and future directions. *Clinical Psychology Review, 16,* 599–617. **(Chap 13)**

Smith, T. W. (1992). Hostility and health: Current status of a psychosomatic hypothesis. *Health Psychology, 11*(3), 139–150. **(Chap 9)**

Smolak, L., & Levine, M. P. (1996). Adolescent transitions and the development of eating problems. In L. Smolak, M. P.

Levine, & R. Striegel-Moore (Eds.), *The developmental psychopathology of eating disorders: Implications for research, prevention, and treatment* (pp. 207–233). Mahwah, NJ: Erlbaum. **(Chap 8)**

Snyder, E. Y., Taylor, R. M., & Wolfe, J. H. (1995). Neural progenitor cell engraftment corrects lysosomal storage throughout the MPS VII mouse brain. *Nature, 374,* 367–370. **(Chap 14)**

Snyder, S. H. (1976). The dopamine hypothesis of schizophrenia: Focus on the dopamine receptor. *American Journal of Psychiatry, 133,* 197–202. **(Chap 2)**

Snyder, S. H. (1981). Opiate and benzodiazepine receptors. *Psychosomatics, 22*(11), 986–989. **(Chap 2)**

Snyder, S. H., Burt, D. R., & Creese, I. (1976). Dopamine receptor of mammalian brain: Direct demonstration of binding to agonist and antagonist states. *Neuroscience Symposia, 1,* 28–49. **(Chap 2)**

Sobell, M. B., & Sobell, L. C. (1978). *Behavioral treatment of alcohol problems.* New York: Plenum Press. **(Chap 11)**

Sobell, M. B., & Sobell, L. C. (1993). *Problem drinkers: Guided self-change treatment.* New York: Guilford Press. **(Chap 11)**

Society for Research in Child Development, Committee for Ethical Conduct in Child Development Research. (1990, Winter). SRCD ethical standards for research with children. *SRCD Newsletter,* Chicago. **(Chap 4)**

Soloff, P. H., George, A., Nathan, R. S., Schulz, P. M., Cornelius, J. R., Herring, J., & Perel, J. M. (1989). Amitriptyline versus haloperidol in borderlines: Final outcomes and predictors of response. *Journal of Clinical Psychopharmacology, 9,* 238–246. **(Chap 12)**

Solomon, D. A., Keller, M. B., Leon, A. C., Mueller, T. I., Shea, M. T., Warshaw, M., Maser, J. D., Coryell, W., & Endicott, J. (1997). Recovery from major depression: A 10-year prospective follow-up across multiple episodes. *Archives of General Psychiatry, 54,* 1001–1006. **(Chap 7)**

Somber news from the AIDS front. (1993). *Science, 260,* 1712–1713. **(Chap 2)**

Southwick, S. M., Krystal, J. H., & Charney, D. S. (1991). *Yohimbine in PTSD* (Abstract No. NR478). New research abstracts of the American Psychiatric Association 143rd annual meeting. **(Chap 5)**

Southwick, S. M., Krystal, J. H., Johnson, D. R., & Charney, D. S. (1992). Neurobiology of posttraumatic stress disorder. In A. Tasman & M. B. Riba (Eds.), *Review of psychiatry* (Vol. 11, pp. 347–367). Washington, DC: American Psychiatric Press. **(Chap 5)**

Spangler, D. L., Simons, A. D., Monroe, S. M., & Thase, M. E. (1996). Gender differences in cognitive diathesis-stress domain match: Implications for differential pathways to depression. *Journal of Abnormal Psychology, 105,* 653–657. **(Chap 7)**

Spangler, D. L., Simons, A. D., Monroe, S. M., & Thase, M. E. (1997). Comparison of cognitive models of depression: Relationships between cognitive constructs and cognitive diathesis-stress match. *Journal of Abnormal Psychology, 106,* 395–403. **(Chap 7)**

Spanos, N. P. (1996). *Multiple identities and false memories: A sociocognitive prospective.* Washington, DC: American Psychological Association. **(Chap 6)**

Spanos, N. P., James, B., & de Groot, H. P. (1990). Detection of simulated hypnotic amnesia. *Journal of Abnormal Psychology, 99*(2), 179–182. **(Chap 6)**

Spanos, N. P., Weeks, J. R., & Bertrand, L. D. (1985). Multiple personality: A social psychological perspective. *Journal of Abnormal Psychology, 92,* 362–376. **(Chap 6)**

Spector, I. P., & Carey, M. P. (1990). Incidence and prevalence of the sexual dysfunctions: A critical review of the empirical literature. *Archives of Sexual Behavior, 19*(4), 389–408. **(Chap 10)**

Speer, D. C. (1992). Clinically significant change: Jacobson and Truax (1991) revisited. *Journal of Consulting and Clinical Psychology, 60,* 402–408. **(Chap 4)**

Spiegel, D. (1995). Hypnosis and suggestion. In D. L. Schacter (Ed.), *Memory distortion: How minds, brains, and societies reconstruct the past.* Cambridge, MA: Harvard University Press. **(Chap 6)**

Spiegel, D. (1996). Cancer and depression. *British Journal of Psychiatry, 168*(suppl. 30), 109–116. **(Chap 2)**

Spiegel, D., & Cardena, E. (1991). Disintegrated experience: The dissociative disorders revisited. *Journal of Abnormal Psychology, 100*(3), 366–378. **(Chap 6)**

Spiegel, D., Bloom, J. R., Kramer, H. C., & Gotheil, E. (1989). Effect of psychosocial treatment on survival of patients with metastatic breast cancer. *Lancet, 14,* 880–1891. **(Chap 2)**

Spiegel, D., Bloom, J. R., Kramer, H. C., & Gotheil, E. (1989). Effect of psychosocial treatment on survival of patients with metastatic breast cancer. *Lancet, 14,* 888–891. **(Chaps 2, 9)**

Spiegel, D., Morrow, G. R., Classen, C., Riggs, G., Stott, P. B., Mudaliar, N., Pierce, H. I., Flynn, P. J., & Heard, L. (1996). Effects of group therapy on women with primary breast cancer. *The Breast Journal, 2*(1), 104–106. **(Chap 9)**

Spielberger, C. D., & Frank, R. G. (1992). Injury control: A promising field for psychologists. *American Psychologist, 47*(8), 1029–1030. **(Chap 9)**

Spielman, A. J., & Glovinsky, P. (1991). The varied nature of insomnia. In P. J. Hauri (Ed.), *Case studies in insomnia* (pp. 1–15). New York: Plenum Press. **(Chap 8)**

Spiker, D., & Ricks, M. (1984). Visual self-recognition in autistic children: Develop-

mental relationships. *Child Development, 55,* 214–225. **(Chap 14)**

Spiker, D. G., Weiss, J. C., Dealy, R. S., Griffin, S. J., Hanin, I., Neil, J. F., Perel, J. M., Rossi, A. J., & Soloff, P. H. (1985). The pharmacological treatment of delusional depression. *American Journal of Psychiatry, 142,* 430–436. **(Chap 7)**

Spira, A., Bajos, N., Bejin, A., Beltzer, N., Bozon, M., Ducot, M., Durandeau, A., Ferrand, A., Giami, A., Gilloire, A., Giraud, M., Leridon, H., Messiah, A., Ludwig, D., Moatti, J., Mounnier, L., Olomucki, H., Poplavsky, J., Riadney, B., Spencer, B., Sztalryd, J., & Touzard, H. (1992). AIDS and sexual behavior in France. *Nature, 360,* 407–409. **(Chap 10)**

Spitzer, R. L. (1991). An outsider-insider's views about revising the DSMs. *Journal of Abnormal Psychology, 100*(3), 294–296. **(Chap 3)**

Spitzer, R. L., Devlin, M. J., Walsh, B. T., Hasin, D., Wing, R., Marcus, M. D., Mitchell, J., & Nonas, C. (1991). Binge eating disorder: To be or not to be in DSM-IV. *International Journal of Eating Disorders, 10,* 627–629. **(Chap 8)**

Spitzer, R. L., Devlin, M. J., Walsh, B. T., Hasin, D., Wing, R., Marcus, M., Stunkard, A., Wadden, T., Yanovski, S., Agras, S., Mitchell, J., & Nonas, C. (1992). Binge eating disorder: A multisite field trial of the diagnostic criteria. *International Journal of Eating Disorders, 11,* 191–203. **(Chap 8)**

Spitzer, R. L., Forman, J. B. W., & Nee, J. (1979). DSM-III field trials: I. Initial interrater diagnostic reliability. *American Journal of Psychiatry, 136,* 815–817. **(Chap 3)**

Spitzer, R. L., Yanovski, Wadden, T., Wing, R., Marcus, M., Stunkard, A., Devlin, M., Mitchell, J., Hasin, D., & Horne, R. L. (1993). Binge eating disorder: Its further validation in a multi-site study. *International Journal of Eating Disorders, 13,* 137–153. **(Chap 8)**

Spoont, M. R. (1992). Modulatory role of serotonin in neural information processing: Implications for human psychopathology. *Psychological Bulletin, 112*(2), 330–350. **(Chaps 2, 7, 11)**

Spreen, O. (1988). Prognosis of learning disability. *Journal of Consulting and Clinical Psychology, 56,* 836–842. **(Chap 14)**

Spurrell, E. B., Wilfley, D. E., Tanofsky, M. B., Brownell, K. D. (1997). Age of onset for binge eating: Are there different pathways to binge eating? *International Journal of Eating Disorders, 21,* 55–65. **(Chap 8)**

Stacy, A. W. (1995). Memory association and ambiguous cues in models of alcohol and marijuana use. *Experimental and Clinical Psychopharmacology, 3,* 183–194. **(Chap 11)**

Stall, R., McKusick, L., Wiley, J., Coates, T. J., & Ostrow, D. G. (1986). Alcohol and drug use during sexual activity and compliance with safe sex guidelines for AIDS. *Health Education Quarterly, 13,* 359–371. **(Chap 9)**

Stam, H., & Steggles, S. (1987). Predicting the onset or progression of cancer from psychological characteristics: Psychometric and theoretical issues. *Journal of Psychosocial Oncology, 5*(2), 35–46. **(Chap 9)**

Stanley, M. A., Beck, J. G., & Glassco, J. D. (1997). Generalized anxiety in older adults: Treatment with cognitive-behavioral and supportive approaches. *Behavior Therapy, 27,* 565–581. **(Chap 5)**

State v. Campanaro. (1980). Nos. 632–79, 1309–79, 1317–79, 514–80, & 707–80 (Supreme Court of New Jersey Criminal Division, Union County). **(Chap 16)**

Steadman, H. J. (1979). *Beating a rap: Defendents found incompetent to stand trial.* Chicago: University of Chicago Press. **(Chap 16)**

Steadman, H. J. (1985). Empirical research on the insanity defense. *Annals of the American Academy of Political and Social Sciences, 477,* 58–71. **(Chap 16)**

Steadman, H. J., & Ribner, S. A. (1980). Changing perceptions of the mental health needs of inmates in local jails. *American Journal of Psychiatry, 137,* 1115–1116. **(Chap 16)**

Steele, C. M., & Josephs, R. A. (1990). Alcohol myopia: Its prized and dangerous effects. *American Psychologist, 45*(8), 921–933. **(Chap 11)**

Stefan, S. (1996). Issues relating to women and ethnic minorities in mental health treatment and law. In B. D. Sales and D. W. Shuman (Eds.), *Law, mental health, and mental disorder* (pp. 240–278). Pacific Grove, CA: Brooks/Cole. **(Chap 16)**

Steffenburg, S., Gillberg, C., Hellgren, L., Andersson, L., Gillberg, I. C., Jakobsson, G., & Bohman, M. (1989). A twin study of autism in Denmark, Finland, Iceland, Norway, and Sweden. *Journal of Child Psychology and Psychiatry, 30,* 405–416. **(Chap 14)**

Stein, M. B., Forde, D. R., Anderson, G., & Walker, J. R. (1997). Obsessive-compulsive disorder in the community: An epidemiologic survey with clinical reappraisal. *American Journal of Psychiatry, 154,* 1120–1126. **(Chap 5)**

Stein, M. I. (1978). Thematic apperception test and related methods. In B. B. Wolman (Ed.), *Clinical diagnosis of mental disorders: A handbook* (pp. 179–235). New York: Plenum Press. **(Chap 3)**

Stein, R. M., & Ellinwood, E. H. (1993). Stimulant use: Cocaine and amphetamine. In D. L. Dunner (Ed.), *Current psychiatric therapy* (pp. 98–105). Philadelphia: W. B. Saunders. **(Chap 11)**

Steinberg, M. (1991). The spectrum of depersonalization: Assessment and treat-

ment. *Annual Review of Psychiatry, 10,* 223–247. **(Chap 6)**

Steinglass, P., Weisstub, E., & Kaplan De-Nour, A. K. (1988). Perceived personal networks as mediators of stress reactions. *American Journal of Psychiatry, 145,* 1259–1264. **(Chap 2)**

Stephens, R. S., Roffman, R. A., & Simpson, E. E. (1994). Treating adult marijuana dependence: A test of the relapse prevention model. *Journal of Consulting and Clinical Psychology, 62,* 92–99. **(Chap 11)**

Stern, Y., Gurland, B., Tatemichi, T. K., Tang, M. X., Wilder, D., & Mayeux, R. (1994). Influence of education and occupation on the incidence of Alzheimer's disease. *Journal of the American Medical Association, 271,* 1004–1010. **(Chap 15)**

Sternberg, R. J. (1988). Intellectual development: Psychometric and information-processing approaches. In M. H. Bornstein & M. E. Lamb (Eds.), *Developmental psychology: An advanced textbook* (2nd ed.). Hillsdale, NJ: Lawrence Erlbaum. **(Chap 3)**

Stevens, J. (1987). *Storming heaven: LSD and the American dream.* New York: Atlantic Monthly Press. **(Chap 11)**

Stewart, J. W., Rabkin, J. G., Quitkin, F. M., McGrath, P. J., & Klein, D. F. (1993). Atypical depression. In D. L. Dunner (Ed.), *Current psychiatric therapy.* Philadelphia: W. B. Saunders. **(Chap 7)**

Stewart, S. H. (1996). Alcohol abuse in individuals exposed to trauma: A critical review. *Psychological Bulletin, 120,* 85–112. **(Chap 11)**

Stewart, W. F., Kawas, C., Corrada, M., Metter, E. J. (1997). Risk of Alzheimer's disease and duration of NSAID use. *Neurology, 48,* 626–632. **(Chap 15)**

Stice, E., Schupak-Neuberg, E., Shaw, H. E., & Stein, R. I. (1994). Relation of media exposure to eating disorder symptomatology: An examination of mediating mechanisms. *Journal of Abnormal Psychology, 103,* 836–840. **(Chap 8)**

Stock, W. (1993). Inhibited female orgasm. In W. O'Donohue & J. H. Geer (Eds.), *Handbook of Sexual Dysfunctions: Assessment and Treatment* (pp. 253–277). Boston, MA: Allyn and Bacon. **(Chap 10)**

Stoller, R. J. (1976). Two feminized male American Indians. *Archives of Sexual Behavior, 5,* 529–538. **(Chap 10)**

Stoller, R. J. (1982). Transvestism in women. *Archives of Sexual Behavior, 11,* 99–115. **(Chap 10)**

Stone, A. B., Pearlstein, T. B., & Brown, W. A. (1991). Fluoxetine in the treatment of late luteal phase dysphoric disorder. *Journal of Clinical Psychiatry, 52*(7), 290–293 **(Chap 3)**

Stone, M. (1983). Psychotherapy with schizotypal borderline patients. *Journal*

of the American Academy of Psychoanalysis, 11, 87–111. **(Chap 12)**

Stone, M. H. (1986). Borderline personality disorder. In A. M. Cooper, A. J. Frances, & M. H. Sacks (Eds.), *The personality disorders and neuroses* (pp. 203–217). New York: Basic Books. **(Chap 12)**

Stone, M. H. (1989). The course of borderline personality disorder. In A. Tasman, R. E. Hales, & A. J. Frances (Eds.), *Annual Review of Psychiatry* (Vol. 8, pp. 103–122). Washington, DC: American Psychiatric Press. **(Chap 12)**

Stone, M. H. (1993). Cluster C personality disorders. In D. L. Dunner (Ed.), *Current psychiatric therapy* (pp. 411–417). Philadelphia: W. B. Saunders. **(Chap 12)**

Stout, C. W., & Bloom, L. J. (1986). Genital herpes and personality. *Journal of Human Stress, 12,* 119–124. **(Chap 9)**

Strain, E. C., Mumford, G. K., Silverman, K., & Griffiths, R. R. (1994). Caffeine dependence syndrome: Evidence from case histories and experimental evaluations. *Journal of the American Medical Association, 272,* 1043–1048. **(Chap 11)**

Strassberg, D. S., Kelly, M. P., Carroll, C., & Kircher, J. C. (1987). The psychophysiological nature of premature ejaculation. *Archives of Sexual Behavior, 16,* 327–336. **(Chap 10)**

Straus, S. E., Tosato, G., Armstrong, G., Lawley, T., Preble, O. T., Henle, W., Davey, R., Pearson, G., Epstein, J., Brus, I., & Blaese, R. M. (1985). Persisting illness and fatigue in adults with evidence of Epstein Barr virus infection. *Annals of Internal Medicine, 102,* 7–16. **(Chap 9)**

Strauss, J., Carpenter, W. T., Jr., & Bartko, J. (1974). The diagnosis and understanding of schizophrenia: Part III. Speculations on the processes that underlie schizophrenic symptoms and signs. *Schizophrenia Bulletin, 1,* 61–69. **(Chap 13)**

Stravynski, A., Elie, R., & Franche, R. L. (1989). Perception of early parenting by patients diagnosed avoidant personality disorder: A test of the overprotection hypothesis. *Acta Psychiatrica Scandinavica, 80,* 415–420. **(Chap 12)**

Stravynski, A., Lesage, A., Marcouiller, M., & Elie, R. (1989). A test of the therapeutic mechanism in social skills training with avoidant personality disorder. *Journal of Nervous and Mental Disease, 177,* 739–744. **(Chap 12)**

Strickland, B. R. (1992). Women and depression. *Current Directions in Psychological Science, 1*(4), 132–135. **(Chap 7)**

Striegal-Moore, R. H., Silberstein, L. R., & Rodin, J. (1986). Toward an understanding of risk factors for bulimia. *American Psychologist, 3,* 246–263. **(Chap 8)**

Striegal-Moore, R. H., Silberstein, L. R., & Rodin, J. (1993). The social self in bulimia nervosa: Public self-consciousness, social anxiety, and perceived fraudulence. *Journal of Abnormal Psychology, 102*(2), 297–303. **(Chap 8)**

Strittmatter, A. M. Saunders, A. M., Schmechel, D., Pericak-Vance, M., Enghild, J., Salvesen, G. S., & Roses, A. D. (1993). Apolipoprotein E: High-avidity binding to B-amyloid and increased frequency of type 4 allele in late-onset familial Alzheimer disease. *Proceedings of the National Academy of Sciences, 90,* 1977–1981. **(Chap 15)**

Strober, M., & Humphrey, L. L. (1987). Familial contributions to the etiology and course of anorexia nervosa and bulimia. Special Issue: Eating disorders. *Journal of Consulting and Clinical Psychology, 55*(5), 654–659. **(Chap 8)**

Stuss, D. T., & Cummings, J. L. (1990). Subcortical vascular dementias. In J. L. Cummings (Ed.), *Subcortical dementia* (pp. 145–163). New York: Oxford University Press. **(Chap 15)**

Su, Y., Burke, J., O'Neill, F. A., Murphy, B., Nie, L., Kipps, B., Bray, J., Shinkwin, R., Ni Nuallain, M., MacLean, C. J., Walsh, D., Diehl, S. R., & Kendler, K. S. (1993). Exclusion of linkage between schizophrenia and D2 dopamine receptor gene region of chromosome 11q in 112 Irish multiplex familes. *Archives of General Psychiatry, 50,* 205–211. **(Chap 13)**

Suddath, R. L., Christison, G. W., Torrey, E. F., Casanova, M. F., & Weinberger, D. R. (1990). Anatomical abnormalities in the brains of monozygotic twins discordant for schizophrenia. *New England Journal of Medicine, 322,* 789–794. **(Chap 13)**

Sugiyama, T., & Abe, T. (1989). The prevalence of autism in Nagoya, Japan: A total population study. *Journal of Autism and Developmental Disorders, 19,* 87–96. **(Chap 14)**

Sullivan, P. F. (1995). Mortality in anorexia nervosa. *American Journal of Psychiatry, 152,* 1073–1074. **(Chap 8)**

Sulloway, F. (1979). *Freud, biologist of the mind.* London: Burnett. **(Chap 6)**

Sultzer, D. L., Levin, H. S., Mahler, M. E., High, W. M., & Cummings, J. L. (1993). A comparison of psychiatric symptoms in vascular dementia and Alzheimer's disease. *American Journal of Psychiatry, 150,* 1806–1812. **(Chap 15)**

Suppes, T., Baldessarini, R. J., Faedda, G. L., & Tohen, M. (1991). Risk of recurrence following discontinuation of lithium treatment in bipolar disorder. *Archives of General Psychiatry, 48*(12), 1082–1088. **(Chap 7)**

Sutherland, G. R., & Richards, R. I. (1994). Dynamic mutations. *American Scientist, 82,* 157–163. **(Chap 14)**

Sutker, P. B., Bugg, F., & West, J. A. (1993). Antisocial personality disorder. In P. B. Sutker & H. E. Adams (Eds.), *Comprehensive handbook of psychopathology* (2nd. ed., pp. 337–369). New York: Plenum Press. **(Chap 12)**

Swanson, J. M., McBurnett, K., Wigal, T., Pfiffner, L. J., Lerner, M. A., Williams, L., Christian, D. L., Tamm, L., Willcut, E., Crowley, K., Clevenger, W., Khouzam, N., Woo, C., Crinella, F. M., & Fisher, T. D. (1993). Effect of stimulant medication on children with attention deficit disorder: A "review of reviews." *Exceptional Children, 60,* 154–162. **(Chap 14)**

Swartz, M., Blazer, D., George, L., & Landerman, R. (1986). Somatization disorder in a community population. *American Journal of Psychiatry, 143,* 1403–1408. **(Chap 6)**

Swartz, M., Blazer, D., George, L., & Landerman, R. (1988). Somatization disorder in a southern community. *Psychiatric Annals, 18,* 335–339. **(Chap 6)**

Swartz, M., Blazer, D., Woodbury, M., George, L., & Landerman, R. (1986). Somatization disorder in a U.S. southern community: Use of a new procedure for analysis of medical classification. *Psychological Medicine, 16,* 595–609. **(Chap 6)**

Swartz, M., Landerman, R., George, L. K., Blazer, D. G., & Escobar, J. (1991). Somatization disorder. In L. N. Robins & D. A. Regier (Eds.), *Psychiatric disorders in America: The epidemiologic catchment area study* (pp. 220–257). New York: Free Press. **(Chap 6)**

Swedo, S. E., Pleeter, J. D., Richter, D. M., Hoffman, C. L., Allen, A. J., Hamburger, S. D., Turner, E. H., Yamada, E. M., & Rosenthal, N. F. (1995). Rates of seasonal affective disorder n children and adolescents. *American Journal of Psychiatry, 152,* 1016–1019. **(Chap 7)**

Szasz, T. (1961). *The myth of mental illness: Foundations of a theory of personal conduct.* New York: Hoeber-Harper. **(Chap 13)**

Szmukler, G. I., Eisler, I., Gillis, C., & Haywood, M. E. (1985). The implications of anorexia nervosa in a ballet school. *Journal of Psychiatric Research, 19,* 177–181. **(Chap 8)**

Takei, N., Lewis, S., Jones, P., Harvey, I., & Murray, R. M. (1996). Prenatal exposure to influenza and increased cerebrospinal fluid spaces in schizophrenia. *Schizophrenia Bulletin, 22,* 521–534. **(Chap 13)**

Talbott, J. A. (1990). Current perspectives in the United States on the chronically mentally ill. In A. Kales, C. N. Stefanis, & J. A. Talbott (Eds.), *Recent advances in schizophrenia* (pp. 279–295). New York: Springer-Verlag. **(Chap 13)**

Tan, E. S. (1980). Transcultural aspects of anxiety. In G. D. Burrows & B. Davies (Eds.), *Handbook of studies on anxiety.* Amsterdam: Elsevier/North-Holland. **(Chaps 2, 5)**

Tang, M. X., Jacobs, D., Stern, Y., Marder, K., Schofield, P., Gurland, B., Andrews, H., & Mayeux, R. (1996). Effects of estrogen during menopause on risk and age at onset of Alzheimer's disease. *Lancet, 348,* 429–432. **(Chap 15)**

Tanofsky, M. B., Wilfley, D. E., Spurrel, E. B., Welch, R., & Brownell, K. D. (1997). Comparison of Men and women with Binge Eating Disorder. *International Journal of Eating Disorders, 21,* 49–54. **(Chap 8)**

Tanzi, R. E., Gusella, F., Watkins, P. C., Bruns, G. A. P., St. George-Hyslop, P., Van Keunen, M. L., Patterson, D., Pagan, S., Kurnit, D. M., & Neve, R. L. (1987). Amyloid B protein gene: cDNA, mRNA distribution, and genetic linkage near the Alzheimer locus. *Science, 235,* 880–884. **(Chap 15)**

Tarasoff v. Regents of University of California ("Tarasoff I"), 529 P.2d 553 (Cal. Sup. Ct. 1974); ("Tarasoff II"), 551 P.2d 334 (Cal. Sup. Ct. 1976). **(Chap 16)**

Taylor, C. B., Sheikh, J., Agras, W. S., Roth, W. T., Margraf, J., Ehlers, A., Maddock, R. J., & Gossard, D. (1986). Self-report of panic attacks: Agreement with heart rate changes. *American Journal of Psychiatry, 143,* 478–482. **(Chap 5)**

Taylor, H. G. (1988). Learning disabilities. In E. J. Mash & L. G. Terdal (Eds.), *Behavioral assessment of childhood disorders* (2nd ed.). New York: Guilford Press. **(Chap 14)**

Taylor, M. A., & Abrams, R. (1981). Early and late-onset bipolar illness. *Archives of General Psychiatry, 38*(1), 58–61. **(Chap 7)**

Taylor, S. (1991). *Health psychology* (2nd ed.). New York: McGraw-Hill. **(Chap 9)**

Taylor, S. (1996). Meta-analysis of cognitive behavioral treatment for social phobia. *Journal of Behavior Therapy and Experimental Psychiatry, 27,* 1–9. **(Chap 5)**

Taylor, S., & Koch, W. J. (1995). Anxiety disorders due to motor vehicle accidents: Nature and treatment. *Clinical Psychology Review, 15,* 721–738. **(Chap 5)**

Taylor, S. E., Repetti, R. L., & Seeman, T. (1997). Health psychology: What is an unhealthy environment and how does it get under the skin? *Annual Review of Psychology, 48,* 411–447. **(Chap 9)**

Teasdale, J. D. (1993). Emotion and two kinds of meaning: Cognitive therapy and applied cognitive science. *Behaviour Research and Therapy, 31*(4), 339–354. **(Chap 2)**

Teicher, M. H., Glod, C., & Cole, J. O. (1990). Emergence of intense suicidal preoccupation during fluoxetine treatment. *American Journal of Psychiatry, 147*(1), 207–210. **(Chap 7)**

Telch, C. F., & Agras, W. S. (1993). The effects of a very low calorie diet on binge eating. *Behavior Therapy, 24,* 177–193. **(Chap 8)**

Telch, C. F., & Agras, W. S., (1994). Obesity binge eating and psychopathology: Are they related? *International Journal of Eating Disorders, 15,* 53–61. **(Chap 8)**

Telch, C. F., Agras, W. S., & Rossiter, E. M. (1988). Binge eating increases with increasing adiposity. *International Journal of Eating Disorders, 7,* 115–119. **(Chap 8)**

Telch, M. J. (1988). Combined pharmacologic and psychological treatments for panic sufferers. In S. Rachman & J. D. Maser (Eds.), *Panic: Psychological perspectives.* Hillsdale, NJ: Lawrence Erlbaum. **(Chap 5)**

Telch, M. J., Lucas, J. A., & Nelson, P. (1989). Nonclinical panic in college students: An investigation of prevalence and symptomatology. *Journal of Abnormal Psychology, 98,* 300–306. **(Chap 5)**

Telch, M. J., Tearnan, B. H., & Taylor, C. B. (1983). Antidepressant medication in the treatment of agoraphobia. A critical review. *Behaviour Research and Therapy, 21,* 505–527. **(Chap 5)**

Tellegen, A. (1978). *Manual for the Multidimensional Personality Questionnaire.* Unpublished manuscript, University of Minnesota, Minneapolis. **(Chap 12)**

Tellegen, A. (1985). Structures of mood and personality and their relevance to assessing anxiety, with an emphasis on self-report. In A. H. Tuma & J. D. Maser (Eds.), *Anxiety and the anxiety disorders* (pp. 681–706). Hillsdale, NJ: Lawrence Erlbaum. **(Chaps 5, 7)**

Teplin, L. A. (1984). Criminalizing mental disorder: The comparative arrest rate of the mentally ill. *American Psychologist, 39,* 794–803. **(Chap 16)**

Teplin, L. A. (1985). The criminality of the mentally ill: A dangerous misconception. *American Journal of Psychiatry, 142,* 593–599. **(Chap 16)**

Teplin, L. A., Abram, K. M., & McClelland, G. M. (1994). Does psychiatric disorder predict violent crime among released jail detainees? A six-year longitudinal study. *American Psychologist, 49,* 335–342. **(Chap 16)**

Terman, M. (1988). On the question of mechanism in phototherapy for seasonal affective disorder: Considerations of clinical efficacy and epidemiology. *Journal of Biological Rhythms, 3*(2), 155–172. **(Chap 7)**

Thase, M. E. (1990). Relapse and recurrence in unipolar major depression: Short-term and long-term approaches. *Journal of Clinical Psychiatry, 51*(6, Suppl.), 51–57. **(Chap 7)**

Thase, M. E., & Kupfer, D. J. (1996). Recent developments in the pharmacotherapy of mood disorders. *Journal of Consulting and Clinical Psychology, 64,* 646–659. **(Chap 7)**

Thase, M. E., Reynolds, C. F., III, Frank, E., Simons, A. D., McGeary, J., Fasiczka, A. L., Garamoni, G. G., Jennings, J. R., & Kupfer, D. J. (1994). Do depressed men and women respond similarly to cognitive behavior therapy? *American Journal of Psychiatry, 151,* 500–505. **(Chap 7)**

Thase, M. E., Simons, A. D., & Reynolds, C. F., III (1996). Abnormal electroencephalographic sleep profiles in major depression. *Archives of General Psychiatry, 53,* 99–108. **(Chap 7)**

Thayer, J. F., Friedman, B. H., & Borkovec, T. D. (1996). Autonomic characteristics of generalized anxiety disorder and worry. *Biological Psychiatry, 39,* 255–266. **(Chap 5)**

Theander, S. (1985). Outcome and prognosis in anorexia nervosa and bulimia: Some results of previous investigations, compared with those of the Swedish long-term study. *Journal of Psychiatric Research, 19,* 493–508. **(Chap 8)**

Thies-Flechtner, K., Muller-Oerlinghausen, B. Seibert, W., Walther, A., Greil, W. Effect of prophylactic treatment on suicide risk in patients with major affective disorders: Data from a randomized prospective trial. *Pharmacopsychiatry, 29,* 103–107. **(Chap 7)**

Thompson v. County of Alameda, 614 P.2d 728 (Cal. Sup. Ct. 1980). **(Chap 16)**

Thoresen, C. E., & Powell, L. H. (1992). Type A behavior pattern: New perspectives on theory, assessment and intervention. Special issue: Behavioral medicine: An update for the 1990s. *Journal of Consulting and Clinical Psychology, 60*(4), 595–604. **(Chap 9)**

Thorndike, R. L., Hagen, E. P., & Sattler, J. M. (1986). *The Stanford-Binet Intelligence Scale: Fourth edition. Guide for administering and scoring.* Chicago: Riverside Publishing Co. **(Chap 3)**

Thorpe, G. L., & Burns, L. E. (1983). *The agoraphobic syndrome.* New York: John Wiley. **(Chap 5)**

Thorpy, M., & Glovinsky, P. (1987). Parasomnias. *Psychiatric Clinics of North America, 10,* 623–639. **(Chap 8)**

Thyer, B. A. (1993). Childhood separation anxiety disorder and adult-onset agoraphobia: Review of evidence. In C. Last (Ed.), *Anxiety across the lifespan: A developmental perspective* (pp. 128–145). New York: Springer. **(Chap 5)**

Tienari, P. (1991). Interaction between genetic vulnerability and family environment: The Finnish adoptive family study of schizophrenia. *Acta Psychiatrica Scandinavica, 84,* 460–465. **(Chap 14)**

Tienari, P. (1992). Implications of adoption studies on schizophrenia. *British Journal of Psychiatry, 161,* 52–58. **(Chap 13)**

Tiffany, S. T. (1990). A cognitive model of drug urges and drug-use behavior: Role of automatic and nonautomatic processes. *Psychological Review, 97,* 147–168. **(Chap 11)**

Tinbergen, E. A., & Tinbergen, N. (1972). *Early childhood autism: An ethological approach.* Berlin: Paul Parey. **(Chap 14)**

Tingelstad, J. B. (1991). The cardiotoxicity of the tricyclics. *Journal of the American Academy of Child and Adolescent Psychiatry, 30,* 845–846. **(Chap 7)**

Tjio, J. H., & Levan, A. (1956). The chromosome number of man. *Hereditas, 42,* 1–6. **(Chap 14)**

Tollefson, G. D. (1993). Major depression. In D. L. Dunner (Ed.), *Current psychiatric therapy.* Philadelphia: W. B. Saunders. **(Chap 7)**

Tomac, A., Lindqvist, E., Lin, L. F. H., Ögren, S. O., Young, D., Hoffer, B. J., & L. Olson (1995). Protection and repair of the nigrostriatal dopaminergic system by GDNF in vivo. *Nature, 373,* 335–339. **(Chap 15)**

Tomarken, A. J., Sutton, S. K. & Mineka, S. (1995). Fear relevant illusory correlations: What types of associations promote judgmental bias? *Journal of Abnormal Psychology, 104,* 312–326. **(Chap 5)**

Tondo, L., Jamison, K. R., & Baldessarini, R. J. (in press). Effect of lithium maintenance on suicidal behavior in major mood disorders. *Annual of New York Academy of Sciences.* **(Chap 7)**

Torgersen, S. (1983). Genetic factors in anxiety disorders. *Archives of General Psychiatry, 40,* 1085–1089. **(Chap 5)**

Torgersen, S. (1986). Genetics of somatoform disorder. *Archives of General Psychiatry, 43,* 502–505. **(Chap 6)**

Torgersen, S., Onstad, S., Skre, I., Edvardsen, J., & Kringlen, E. (1993). "True" schizotypal personality disorder: A study of co-twins and relatives of schizophrenic probands. *American Journal of Psychiatry, 150,* 1661–1667. **(Chap 12)**

Torrey, E. F. (1988a). *Nowhere to go: The tragic odyssey of the homeless mentally ill.* New York: Harper & Row. **(Chap 16)**

Torrey, E. F. (1988b). Stalking the schizovirus. *Schizophrenia Bulletin, 14,* 223–229. **(Chap 13)**

Torrey, E. F., Bowler, A. E., Taylor, E. H., & Gottesman, I. I. (1994). *Schizophrenia and manic-depressive disorder: The biological roots of mental illness as revealed by the landmark study of identical twins.* New York: Basic Books. **(Chap 13)**

Torrey, E. F., Rawlings, R., & Waldman, I. (1988). Schizophrenic births and viral diseases in two states. *Schizophrenia Research, 1,* 73–77. **(Chap 13)**

Tracey, S. A., Chorpita, B. F., Douban, J., & Barlow, D. H. (1997). Empirical evaluation of DSM-IV generalized anxiety disorder criteria in children and adolescents. *Journal of Clinical Child Psychology, 26,* 404–414. **(Chap 5)**

Trebbe, A. (1979, September 15). Ideal is body beautiful and clean cut. *USA Today,* pp. 1–2. **(Chap 8)**

Trèves, T. A. (1991). Epidemiology of Alzheimer's disease. *The Psychiatric Clinics of North America, 14,* 251–265. **(Chap 15)**

Trimbell, M. R. (1981). *Neuropsychiatry.* Chichester, England: John Wiley. **(Chap 6)**

True, W. R., Rice, J., Eisen, S. A., Heath, A. C., Goldberg, J., Lyons, M. J., & Nowak, J. (1993). A twin study of genetic and environmental contributions to liability for posttraumatic stress symptoms. *Archives of General Psychiatry, 50,* 257–264. **(Chap 5)**

Trzepacz, P. T. (1996). Delirium: Advances in diagnosis, pathophysiology, and treatment. *The Psychiatric Clinics of North America, 19,* 429–448. **(Chap 15)**

Tsai, L. Y., & Ghaziuddin, M. (1992). Biomedical research in autism. In D. E. Berkell (Ed.), *Autism: Identification, education, and treatment* (pp. 53–74). Hillsdale, NJ: Lawrence Erlbaum. **(Chap 14)**

Tsuang, D., & Coryell, W. (1993). An 8-year follow-up of patients with DSM-III-R psychotic depression, schizoaffective disorder, and schizophrenia. *American Journal of Psychiatry, 150,* 1182–1188. **(Chap 13)**

Tuchman, B. (1978). *A distant mirror.* New York: Ballantine Books. **(Chap 1)**

Tucker, G. J. (1993). DSM-IV: Organic disorders. In D. L. Dunner (Ed.), *Current psychiatric therapy* (pp. 57–59). Philadelphia: W. B. Saunders. **(Chap 14)**

Tucker, G., Popkin, M., Caine, E., Folstein, M., & Grant, I. (1990). Reorganizing the "organic" disorders. *Hospital and Community Psychiatry, 41,* 722–724. **(Chap 15)**

Tucker, G. J., Ferrell, R. B., & Price, T. R. P. (1984). The hospital treatment of schizophrenia. In A. S. Bellack (Ed.), *Schizophrenia: Treatment, management, and rehabilitation* (pp. 175–191). New York: Grune & Stratton. **(Chap 13)**

Tukat, I. D., & Maisto, S. A. (1985). Personality disorders: Applications of the experimental method to the formulation and modification of personality disorders. In D. H. Barlow (Ed.), *Clinical handbook of psychological disorders.* New York: Guilford Press. **(Chap 12)**

Tupes, E. C., & Christal, R. E. (1992). Recurrent personality factors based on trait ratings. *Journal of Personality, 60,* 225–251. **(Chap 12)**

Turk, D. C. (1996). Biopsychosocial perspective on chronic pain. In R. J. Gatchel & D. C. Turk (Eds.), *Psychological approaches to pain management: A practitioner's handbook* (pp. 3–32). New York: Guilford Press. **(Chap 9)**

Turk, D. C., Meichenbaum, D., & Genest, M. (1983). *Pain and behavioral medicine: A cognitive-behavioral perspective.* New York: Guilford Press. **(Chap 9)**

Turkheimer, E., & Parry, C. D. H. (1992). Why the gap? Practice and policy in civil commitment hearings. *American Psychologist, 47,* 646–655. **(Chap 16)**

Turkington, C. (1994, January). Wexler wins Lasker award for her work on Huntington's. *APA Monitor,* pp. 20–21. **(Chap 15)**

Turovsky, J., & Barlow, D. H. (1996). Generalized anxiety disorder. In J. Margraf (Ed.), *Textbook of behavior therapy* (pp. 87–106). Berlin: Springer-Verlag. **(Chap 5)**

Tyler, D. B. (1955). Psychological changes during experimental sleep deprivation. *Diseases of the Nervous System, 16,* 293–299. **(Chap 8)**

Tynes, L. L., White, K., & Steketee, G. S. (1990). Toward a new nosology of obsessive-compulsive disorder. *Comprehensive Psychiatry, 31,* 465–480. **(Chap 6)**

Uchino, B. N., Cacioppo, J. T., & Kiecolt-Glaser, J. K. (1996). The relationship between social support and physiological processes: A review with emphasis on underlying mechanisms and implications for health. *Psychological Bulletin, 119*(3), 488–531. **(Chap 9)**

Uddo, M., Malow, R., & Sutker, P. B. (1993). Opioid and cocaine abuse and dependence disorders. In P. B. Sutker & H. E. Adams (Eds.), *Comprehensive handbook of psychopathology* (pp. 477–503). New York: Plenum Press. **(Chap 11)**

Uhde, T. (1994). The anxiety disorder: Phenomenology and treatment of core symptoms and associated sleep disturbance. In M. Kryger, T. Roth, & W. Dement (Eds.), *Principles and practice of sleep medicine* (pp. 871–898). Philadelphia: Saunders. **(Chap 5)**

Umbricht, D., & Kane, J. M. (1996). Medical complications of new antipsychotic drugs. *Schizophrenia Bulletin, 22,* 475–483. **(Chap 13)**

U.S. Congress, Office of Technology Assessment. (1992, September). *The biology of mental disorders,* OTA-BA-538. Washington, DC: U.S. Government Printing Office. **(Chap 7)**

U.S. Department of Health and Human Services. (1982). *The health consequences of smoking. Cancer: A report of the Surgeon General.* Washington, DC: U.S. Government Printing Office. **(Chap 9)**

U.S. Department of Health and Human Services. (1988). *The health consequences of smoking—nicotine addiction: A report of the surgeon general* (DHHS Publication No. CDC 88-8406). Washington, DC: U.S. Government Printing Office. **(Chap 11)**

U.S. Department of Health and Human Services. (1989). *Reducing the health consequences of smoking: 25 years of progress. A report of the Surgeon General, Executive summary* (DHHS Publication No. CDC 89-8411). Washington, DC: U.S. Goverment Printing Office. **(Chap 11)**

U.S. Department of Health and Human Services. (1990). *Seventh annual report to the U.S. Congress on alcohol and health from the Secretary of Health and Human Services.* Rockville, MD: National Institute on Alcohol Abuse and Alcoholism. **(Chaps 4, 11)**

U.S. Department of Health and Human Services. (1991). *Health and behavior research.* National Institutes of Health: Report to Congress. **(Chap 9)**

U.S. General Accounting Office (1995). *Prescription drugs and the elderly: Many still receive potentially harmful drugs despite recent improvements.* (GOA/HEHS-95-152). United States General Accounting Office: Report to Congress. **(Chap 15)**

U.S. Surgeon General. (1979). *Healthy people.* Washington, DC: Government Printing Office. **(Chap 9)**

Vaillant, G. (1983). *The natural history of alcoholism.* Cambridge, MA: Harvard University Press. **(Chap 11)**

Vaillant, G. E. (1976). Natural history of male psychological health V: The relation of choice of ego mechanisms of defense to adult adjustment. *Archives of General Psychiatry, 33,* 535–545. **(Chap 1)**

Vaillant, G. E. (1979). Natural history of male psychological health. *New England Journal of Medicine, 301,* 1249–1254. **(Chap 9)**

Vaillant, G. E. & Hiller-Sturmhöfel, S. (1997). The natural history of alcoholism. *Alcohol Health & Research, 20,* 152–161. **(Chap 11)**

Vaillant, G. E., Bond, M., & Vaillant, C. D. (1986). An empirically validated hierarchy of defense mechanisms. *Archives of General Psychiatry, 43,* 786–794. **(Chap 1)**

Van Acker, R. (1991). Rett syndrome: A review of current knowledge. *Journal of Autism and Developmental Disorders, 21,* 381–406. **(Chap 14)**

van der Molen, G. M., van den Hout, M. A., van Dieren, A. C., & Griez, E. (1989). Childhood separation anxiety and adult-onset panic disorders. *Journal of Anxiety Disorders, 3,* 97–106. **(Chap 5)**

Vander Plate, C., Aral, S. O., & Magder, L. (1988). The relationship among genital herpes simplex virus, stress, and social support. *Health Psychology, 7,* 159–168. **(Chap 9)**

van Kammen, D. P., Docherty, J. P., & Bunney, W. E. (1982). Prediction of early relapse after pimozide discontinuation by response to d-amphetamine during pimozide treatment. *Biological Psychiatry, 17,* 223–242. **(Chap 13)**

VanKammen, W. B., Loeber, R., & Stouthamer-Loeber, M. (1991). Substance use and its relationship to conduct problems and delinquency in young boys. *Journal of Youth and Adolescence, 20*, 399–413. **(Chap 12)**

Van Praag, H. M., & Korf, J. (1975). Central monamine deficiency in depressions: Causative of secondary phenomenon? *Pharmakopsychiatr Neuropsychopharmakol, 8*, 322–326. **(Chap 7)**

Veale, D., Boocock, A., Gournay, K., Dryden, W., Shah, F., Willson, R., & Walburn, J. (1996). Body dysmorphic disorder: A survey of 50 cases. *British Journal of Psychiatry, 169*, 196–201. **(Chap 6)**

Veale, D., Gournay, K., Dryden, W., Boocock, A., Shah, F., Willson, R., & Walburn, J. (1996). Body dysmorphic disorder: A cognitive behavioral model and pilot randomized control trial. *Behaviour Research and Therapy, 34*, 717–729. **(Chap 6)**

Venables, P. H. (1996). Schizotypy and maternal exposure to influenza and to cold temperature: The Mauritius Study. *Journal of Abnormal Psychology, 105*, 53–60. **(Chaps 12, 13)**

Ventura, J., Nuechterlein, K. H., Hardisty, J. P., & Gitlin, M. (1992). Life events and schizophrenic relapse after withdrawal of medication: A prospective study. *British Journal of Psychiatry, 161*, 615–620. **(Chap 13)**

Ventura, J., Nuechterlein, K. H., Lukoff, D., & Hardesty, J. P. (1989). A prospective study of stressful life events and schizophrenia relapse. *Journal of Abnormal Psychology, 98*, 407–411. **(Chap 13)**

Vernberg, E. M., LaGreca, A. M., Silverman, W. K., & Prinstein, M. J. (1996). Prediction of posttraumatic stress symptoms in children after Hurricane Andrew. *Journal of Abnormal Psychology, 105*, 237–248. **(Chap 5)**

Vinken, P. J., & Bruyn, G. W. (1972). The phakomatoses. In P. J. Vinken & G. W. Bruyn (Eds.), *Handbook of clinical neurology* (Vol. 14). New York: Elsevier. **(Chap 14)**

Visser, F. E., Aldenkamp, A. P., van Huffelen, A. C., Kuilman, M., Overweg, J., & van Wijk, J. (1997). Prospective study of the prevalence of Alzheimer-type dementia in institutionalized individuals with Down syndrome. *American Journal on Mental Retardation, 101*, 400–412. **(Chap 14)**

Volkmar, F. R., & Cohen, D. J. (1991). Nonautistic pervasive developmental disorders. In R. Michels (Ed.), *Psychiatry* (pp. 201–210). Philadelphia: J. B. Lippincott. **(Chap 14)**

Volkmar, F. R., Klin, A., Siegel, B., Szatmari, P., Lord, C., Campbell, M., Freeman, B. J., Cicchetti, D. V., Rutter, M., Kline, W., Buitelaar, J., Hattab, Y., Fombonne, E., Fuentes, J., Werry, J., Stone, W., Kerbeshian, J., Hoshino, Y., Bregman, J., Loveland, K., Szymanski, L., & Towbin, K. (1994). Field trial for autistic disorder in DSM-IV. *American Journal of Psychiatry, 151*, 1361–1367. **(Chap 14)**

Volkmar, F. R., Szatmari, P., & Sparrow, S. S. (1993). Sex differences in pervasive developmental disorders. *Journal of Autism and Developmental Disorders, 23*, 579–591. **(Chap 14)**

Volpicelli, J. R., Alterman, A. I., Hayashida, M., & O'Brien, C. P. (1992). Naltrexone in the treatment of alcohol dependence. *Archives of General Psychiatry, 49*, 876–880. **(Chap 11)**

von Braunsberg, M. J. (1994). Multiple personality disorder: An investigation of prevalence in three populations. *Dissertation Abstracts International*, University Microfilms, No. ADG94-08430. **(Chap 6)**

Von Knorring, A. L., Cloninger, C. R., Bohman, M., & Sigvardsson, S. (1983). An adoption study of depressive disorders and substance abuse. *Archives of General Psychiatry, 40*, 943–950. **(Chap 7)**

Vuchinich, S., Bank, L., & Patterson, G. R. (1992). Parenting, peers, and the stability of antisocial behavior in preadolescent boys. *Developmental Psychology, 28*, 510–521. **(Chap 12)**

Wagner, A. W., & Linehan, M. M. (1994). Relationship between childhood sexual abuse and topography of parasuicide among women with borderline personality disorder. *Journal of Personality Disorders, 8*, 1–9. **(Chap 12)**

Wagner, B. M. (1997). Family risk factors for child and adolescent suicidal behavior. *Psychological Bulletin, 121*, 246–298. **(Chap 7)**

Wagner, M. (1990, April). *The school programs and school performance of secondary students classified as learning disabled: Findings from the National Longitudinal Transition Study of special education students.* Paper presented at Division G, American Educational Research Association Annual Meeting, Boston. **(Chap 14)**

Wakefield, J. (1997). Diagnosing DSM-IV – Part 1: DSM-IV and the concept of disorder. *Behaviour Research and Therapy, 35*, 633–649. **(Chap 1)**

Wakefield, J. C. (1992). The concept of mental disorder: On the boundary between biological facts and social values. *American Psychologist, 47*, 373–388. **(Chap 1)**

Walker, E. (1991). Research on life-span development in schizophrenia. In E. F. Walker (Ed.), *Schizophrenia: A life-course developmental perspective* (pp. 1–6). New York: Academic Press. **(Chap 13)**

Walker, E. F., Grimes, K. E., Davis, D. M., & Smith, A. J. (1983). Childhood precursors of schizophrenia: Facial expressions of emotion. *American Journal of Psychiatry, 150*, 1654–1660. **(Chap 13)**

Wallace, C. S., Kilman, V. L., Withers, G. S., & Greenough, W. T. (1992). Increases in dendritic length in occipital cortex after 4 days of differential housing in weanling rats. *Behavioral and Neural Biology, 58*, 64–68. **(Chap 2)**

Wallace, J., & O'Hara, M. W. (1992). Increases in depressive symptomatology in the rural elderly: Results from a cross-sectional and longitudinal study. *Journal of Abnormal Psychology, 101*(3), 398–404. **(Chaps 4, 7)**

Waller, N. G., Putnam, F. W., Carlson, E. B. (1996). Types of dissociation and dissociative types: A taxometric analysis of dissociative experiences. *Psychological Methods, 1*, 300–321. **(Chap 6)**

Waller, N. G., Ross, C. A. (1997). The prevalence and biometric structure of pathological dissociation in the general population: Taxometric and behavior genetic findings. *Journal of Abnormal Psychology, 106*, 499–510. **(Chap 6)**

Walsh, B. T. (1991). Fluoxetine treatment of bulimia nervosa. *Journal of Psychosomatic Research, 35*, 471–475. **(Chap 8)**

Walsh, B. T. (1995). Pharmacotherapy of eating disorders. In K. D. Brownell & C. G. Fairburn (Eds.), *Eating disorders and obesity: A comprehensive handbook* (pp. 313–317). New York: Guilford Press. **(Chap 8)**

Walsh, B. T., Hadigan, C. M., Devlin, M. J., Gladis, M., & Roose, S. P. (1991). Long-term outcome of antidepressant treatment of bulimia nervosa. *Archives of General Psychiatry, 148*, 1206–1212. **(Chap 8)**

Walsh, B. T., Wilson G. T., Loeb, K. L., Devlin, M. J., Pike, K. M., Roose, S. P., Fleiss, J., & Waternaux, C. (1997). Medication and psychotherapy in the treatment of bulimia nervosa. *American Journal of Psychiatry, 154*, 523–531. **(Chap 8)**

Walters, E. E., & Kendler, K. S. (1995). Anorexia nervosa and anorexia-like syndromes in a population based female twin sample. *American Journal of Psychiatry, 152*, 64–71. **(Chap 8)**

Ward, M. M., Swan, G. E., & Chesney, M. A. (1987). Arousal-reduction treatments for mild hypertension: A meta-analysis of recent studies. *Handbook of hypertension, 9*, 285–302. **(Chap 9)**

Ware, J. C. (1988). Sleep and anxiety. In R. L. Williams, I. Karacan, & C. A. Moore (Eds.), *Sleep disorders: Diagnosis and treatment* (pp. 189–214). New York: John Wiley. **(Chap 8)**

Warneke, L. B. (1991). Benzodiazepines: Abuse and new use. *Canadian Journal of Psychiatry, 36*, 194–205. **(Chap 11)**

Warren, S. F., & Reichle, J. (1992). *Causes and effects in communication and language intervention.* Baltimore: Paul H. Brookes. **(Chap 14)**

Warwick, H. M. C., Clark, D. M., Cobb, A. M., & Salkovskis, P. M. (1996). A controlled trail of cognitive-behavioural treatment of hypochondriasis. *British Journal of Psychiatry, 169*, 189–195. **(Chap 6)**

Waterhouse, L., Morris, R., Allen, D., Dunn, M., Fein, D., Feinstein, C., Rapin, I., & Wing, L. (1996). Diagnosis and classification in autism. *Journal of Autism and Developmental Disorders, 26*, 59–86. **(Chap 14)**

Waterhouse, L., Wing, L., & Fein, D. (1989). Re-evaluating the syndrome of autism in light of empirical research. In G. Dawson (Ed.), *Autism: Nature, diagnosis and treatment* (pp. 263–281). New York: Guilford Press. **(Chap 14)**

Waterhouse, L., Wing, L., Spitzer, R., & Siegel, B. (1992). Pervasive developmental disorders: From DSM-III to DSM-III-R. *Journal of Autism and Developmental Disorders, 22*, 525–549. **(Chap 14)**

Waters, B. G. H. (1979). Early symptoms of bipolar affective psychosis: Research and clinical implications. *Canadian Psychiatric Association Journal, 2*, 55–60. **(Chap 7)**

Watson, D., & Kendall, P. C. (1989). Common and differentiating features of anxiety and depression: Current findings and future directions. In P. C. Kendall & D. Watson (Eds.), *Anxiety and depression: Distinctive and overlapping features* (pp. 493–508). San Diego, CA: Academic Press. **(Chap 7)**

Watson, D., Clark, L. A., & Harkness, A. R. (1994). Structures of personality and their relevance to psychopathology. *Journal of Abnormal Psychology, 103*, 18–31. **(Chap 12)**

Watson, G. C., & Buranen, C. (1979). The frequency and identification of false positive conversion reactions. *Journal of Nervous and Mental Disease, 167*, 243–247. **(Chap 6)**

Watson, J. B. (1913). Psychology as a behaviorist views it. *Psychology Review, 20*, 158–177. **(Chap 1)**

Weaver, D. R., Rivkees, S. A., & Reppert, S. M. (1992). D1-dopamine receptors activate c-fos expression in the fetal suprachiasmatic nuclei. *Proceedings of the National Academy of Science, 89*, 9201–9204. **(Chap 11)**

Webster-Stratton, C., & Hammond, M. (1997). Treating children with early-onset conduct problems: A comparison of child and parent training interventions. *Journal of Consulting and Clinical Psychology, 65*, 93–109. **(Chap 12)**

Wehr, T., Sack, D., Rosenthal, N. E., & Cowdry, R. W. (1988). Rapid cycling affective disorder: Contributing factors and treatment response on 51 patients. *American Journal of Psychiatry, 145*, 179–184. **(Chap 7)**

Wehr, T. A., & Sack, D. A. (1988). The relevance of sleep research to affective illness. In W. P. Koella, F. Obal, H. Schulz, & P. Visser, *Sleep '86* (pp. 207–211). New York: Gustav Fischer Verlag. **(Chap 7)**

Wehr, T. A., Goodwin, F. K., Wirz-Justice, A., Breitmeier, J., & Craig, C. (1982). Forty-eight-hour sleep-wake cycles in manic-depressive illness: Naturalistic observations and sleep-deprivation experiments. *Archives of General Psychiatry, 39*, 559–565. **(Chap 7)**

Weiden, P. J., Dixon, L., Frances, A., Appelbaum, P., Haas, G., & Rapkin, B. (1991). In C. A. Tamminga & S. C. Schulz (Eds.), *Advances in neuropsychiatry and psychopharmacology, Volume 1: Schizophrenia research* (pp. 285–296). New York: Raven Press. **(Chap 13)**

Weinberg, R. A. (1989). Intelligence and IQ: Landmark issues and great debates. *American Psychologist, 44*, 98–104. **(Chap 3)**

Weinberger, D. R. (1987). Implications of normal brain development for the pathogenesis of schizophrenia. *Archives of General Psychiatry, 44*, 660–669. **(Chap 13)**

Weinberger, D. R. (1995). Schizophrenia as a neurodevelopmental disorder. In S. R. Hirsch and D. R. Weinberger (Eds.), *Schizophrenia* (pp. 293–323). Oxford, England: Blackwell. **(Chap 13)**

Weinberger, D. R., Berman, K. F., & Chase, T. N. (1988). Mesocortical dopaminergic function and human cognition. *Annals of the New York Academy of Sciences, 537*, 330–338. **(Chap 13)**

Weinberger, D. R., Berman, K. F., Suddath, R., & Torrey, E. F. (1992). Evidence of dysfunction of a prefrontal-limbic network in schizophrenia: A magnetic resonance imaging and regional cerebral blood flow study of discordant monozygotic twins. *American Journal of Psychiatry, 149*, 890–897. **(Chap 13)**

Weiner, B. A., & Wettstein, R. M. (1993). *Legal issues in mental health care.* New York: Plenum Press. **(Chap 16)**

Weiner, D. N. (1996). *Premature ejaculation: An evaluation of sensitivity to erotica.* Unpublished doctoral dissertation, State University of New York, Albany. **(Chap 10)**

Weiskrantz, L. (1980). Varieties of residual experience. *Quarterly Journal of Experimental Psychology, 32*, 365–386. **(Chap 6)**

Weiskrantz, L. (1992, September/October). Unconscious vision: The strange phenomenon of blindsight. *The Sciences*, 23–28. **(Chap 2)**

Weiss, G., & Hechtman, L. (1986). *Hyperactive children grown up.* New York: Guilford Press. **(Chap 14)**

Weisse, C. S. (1992). Depression and immunocompetence: A review of the literature. *Psychological Bulletin, 111*(3), 475–489. **(Chap 9)**

Weisse, C. S., Pato, C. W., McAllister, C. G., Littman, R., & Breier, A. (1990). Differential effects of controllable and uncontrollable acute stress on lymphocyte proliferation and leukocyte percentages in humans. *Brain, Behavior, and Immunity, 4*, 339–351. **(Chap 9)**

Weissman, M. (1985). The epidemiology of anxiety disorders: Rates, risks, and familial patterns. In A. H. Tuma & J. D. Maser (Eds.), *Anxiety and the anxiety disorders.* Hillsdale, NJ: Lawrence Erlbaum. **(Chap 7)**

Weissman, M. (1995). *Mastering depression: A patient's guide to interpersonal psychotherapy.* Albany, NY: Graywind. **(Chaps 2, 7)**

Weissman, M. M. (1993). The epidemiology of personality disorders: A 1990 update. *Journal of Personality Disorders, Supplement, Spring*, 44–62. **(Chap 12)**

Weissman, M. M., & Klerman, G. L. (1977). Sex differences and the epidemiology of depression. *Archives of General Psychiatry, 34*, 98–111. **(Chap 7)**

Weissman, M. M., & Markowitz, J. C. (1994). Interpersonal psychotherapy: Current status. *Archives of General Psychiatry, 51*, 599–606. **(Chap 7)**

Weissman, M. M., & Olfson, M. (1995, August 11). Depression in women: Implications for health care research. *Science, 269*, 799–801. **(Chap 7)**

Weissman, M. M., Bruce, M. L., Leaf, P. J., Florio, L. P., & Holzer, C. (1991). Affective disorders. In L. N. Robins & D. A. Regier (Eds.), *Psychiatric disorders of America: The epidemiologic catchment area study* (pp. 53–80). New York: Free Press. **(Chap 7)**

Weissman, M. M., Klerman, G. L., Markowitz, J. S., & Ouellette, R. (1989). Suicidal ideation and suicide attempts in panic disorder and attacks. *New England Journal of Medicine, 321*, 1209–1214. **(Chap 5)**

Weitze, C., & Osburg, S. (1996). Transsexualism in Germany: Empirical data on epidemiology and application of the German transsexuals' act during its first ten years. *Archives of Sexual Behavior, 25*, 409–465. **(Chap 10)**

Weller, E. B., & Weller, R. A. (1988). Neuroendocrine changes in affectively ill children and adolescents. *Endocrinology and Metabolism Clinics of North America, 17*, 41–53. **(Chap 7)**

Wells, K. B., Stewart, A., Hays, R. D., Burnam, M. A., Rogers, W., Daniels, M., Berry, S., Greenfield, S., & Ware, J. (1989). The functioning and well-being of depressed patients: Results from the medical outcomes study. *Journal of the American Medical Association, 262*(7), 914–919. **(Chap 3)**

Wender, P. H., Kety, S. S., Rosenthal, D., Schlusinger, F., Ortmann, J., & Lunde, I. (1986). Psychiatric disorders in the biological and adoptive families of adopted individuals with affective disorders. *Archives of General Psychiatry, 43*, 923–929. **(Chap 7)**

Wesson, D. R., Smith, D. E., Ling, W. & Seymour, R. B. (1997). Sedative-hypnotics and tricyclics. In J. H. Lowinson, P. Ruiz, R. B. Millman, &

J. G. Langrod (Eds.), *Substance abuse: A comprehensive textbook* (pp. 223–230). Baltimore: Williams & Wilkins. **(Chap 11)**

Westen, D. (1997). Divergence between clinical and research methods for assessing personality disorders: Implications for research and the evolution of Axis II. *American Journal of Psychiatry, 154*, 895–903. **(Chap 12)**

Westermeyer, J. (1989). *Mental health for refugees and other migrants: Social and preventive approach.* Illinois: C. C. Thomas. **(Chap 15)**

Westphal, C. (1871). Die Agoraphobia: Eine neuropathische Eischeinung. *Archives für Psychiatrie und Nervenkrankheiten, 3*, 384–412. **(Chap 5)**

Wetter, D. W., Smith, S. S., Kenford, S. L., Jorenby, D. E., Fiore, M. C., Hurt, R. D., Offord, K. P., & Baker, T. B. (1994). Smoking outcome expectancies: Factor structure, predictive validity, and discriminant validity. *Journal of Abnormal Psychology, 103*, 801–811. **(Chap 11)**

Wheeler, R. E., Davidson, R. J., & Tomarken, A. J. (1993). Frontal brain asymmetry and emotional reactivity: A biological substrate of affective style. *Psychophysiology, 30*, 82–89. **(Chap 7)**

Whiffen, V. E. (1992). Is postpartum depression a distinct diagnosis? *Clinical Psychology Review, 12*(5), 485–508. **(Chap 7)**

Whiffen, V. E., & Gotlib, I. H. (1989). Stress and coping in maritally distressed and nondistressed couples. *Journal of Social and Personal Relationships, 6*(3), 327–344. **(Chap 7)**

Whiffen, V. E., & Gotlib, I. H. (1993). Comparison of postpartum and nonpostpartum depression: Clinical presentation, psychiatric history, and psychosocial functioning. *Journal of Consulting and Clinical Psychology, 61*(3), 485–494. **(Chap 7)**

White, J. L., Moffitt, T. E., & Silva, P. A. (1989). A prospective replication of the protective effects of IQ in subjects at high risk for juvenile delinquency. *Journal of Consulting and Clinical Psychology, 57*, 719–724. **(Chap 12)**

Whitehurst, G. J., Fischel, J. E., Lonigan, C. J., Valdez-Menchaca, M. C., DeBaryshe, B. D., & Caulfield, M. B. (1988). Verbal interaction in families of normal and expressive-language-delayed children. *Developmental Psychology, 24*, 690–699. **(Chap 14)**

Whitnam, F. L., Diamond, M., & Martin, J. (1993). Homosexual orientation in twins: A report on 61 pairs and three triplet sets. *Archives of Sexual Behavior, 22*(3), 187–206. **(Chap 10)**

Whitney, C. W., Enright, P. L., Newman, A. B., Bonekat, W., Foley, D., & Quan, S. F. (1998). Correlates of daytime sleepiness in 4578 elderly persons: The cardiovascular health study. *Sleep, 21*, 27–36. **(Chap 8)**

Wickramaratne, P. J., Weissman, M. M., Leaf, D. J., & Holford, T. R. (1989). Age, period and cohort effects on the risk of major depression: Results from five United States communities. *Journal of Clinical Epidemiology, 42*, 333–343. **(Chap 7)**

Widiger, T. A. (1991). Personality disorder dimensional models proposed for the DSM-IV. *Journal of Personality Disorders, 5*, 386–398. **(Chap 12)**

Widiger, T. A., & Corbitt, E. M. (1995). Antisocial personality disorder. In W. J. Livesley (Ed.), *The DSM-IV personality disorders* (pp. 103–126). New York: Guilford Press. **(Chap 12)**

Widiger, T. A., & Frances, A. (1985). The DSM-III personality disorders: Perspectives from psychology. *Archives of General Psychiatry, 42*, 615–623. **(Chap 12)**

Widiger, T. A., & Rogers, J. H. (1989). Prevalence and comorbidity of personality disorders. *Psychiatry Annual, 19*, 132. **(Chap 12)**

Widiger, T. A., & Spitzer, R. L. (1991). Sex bias in the diagnosis of personality disorders: Conceptual and methodological issues. *Clinical Psychology Review, 11*, 1–22. **(Chap 12)**

Widiger, T. A., & Trull, T. J. (1993). Borderline and narcissistic personality disorders. In P. B. Sutker & H. E. Adams (Eds.), *Comprehensive handbook of psychopathology* (2nd ed., pp. 371–394). New York: Plenum Press. **(Chap 12)**

Widiger, T. A., & Weissman, M. M. (1991). Epidemiology of borderline personality disorder. *Hospital and Community Psychiatry, 42*, 1015–1021. **(Chap 12)**

Widiger, T. A., Frances, A. J., Pincus, H. A., Ross, R., First, M. B., & Davis, W. W. (Eds.). (1996). *DSM-IV sourcebook* (Vol. 2). Washington, DC: American Psychiatric Association. **(Chap 3)**

Widom, C. S. (1977). A methodology for studying noninstitutionalized psychopaths. *Journal of Consulting and Clinical Psychology, 45*, 674–683. **(Chap 12)**

Widom, C. S. (1984). Sex roles, criminality, and psychopathology. In C. S. Widom (Ed.), *Sex roles and psychopathology* (pp. 183–217). New York: Plenum Press. **(Chap 6)**

Wilkins, R. (1985). A comparison of elective mutism and emotional disorders in children. *British Journal of Psychiatry, 146*, 198–203. **(Chap 14)**

Willi, J., & Grossman, S. (1983). Epidemiology of anorexia nervosa in a defined region of Switzerland. *American Journal of Psychiatry, 140*, 564–567. **(Chap 8)**

Williams, D. (1992). *Nobody nowhere: The extraordinary autobiography of an autistic.* New York: Times Books. **(Chap 14)**

Williams, L. (1994). Recall of childhood trauma: A prospective study of women's memories of child sexual abuse. *Journal of Consulting and Clinical Psychology, 62*, 1167–1176. **(Chap 6)**

Williams, R. B., Jr., Haney, T. L., Lee, K. L., Kong, V., & Blumenthal, J. A. (1980). Type A behavior, hostility, and coronary atherosclerosis. *Psychosomatic Medicine, 42*, 529–538. **(Chap 2)**

Willmuth, M. E., Leitenberg, H., Rosen, J. C., & Cado, S. (1988). A comparison of purging and nonpurging normal weight bulimics. *International Journal of Eating Disorders, 7*, 825–835. **(Chap 8)**

Wills, T. A., Vaccaro, D., McNamara, G., & Hirky, A. E. (1996). Escalated substance use: A longitudinal grouping analysis from early to middle adolescence. *Journal of Abnormal Psychology, 105*, 166–180. **(Chap 11)**

Willwerth, J. (1993, August 30). *Tinkering with madness. Time*, pp. 40–42 **(Chap 16)**

Wilson, G. T. (1977). Alcohol and human sexual behavior. *Behaviour Research and Therapy, 15*, 239–252. **(Chap 10)**

Wilson, G. T. (1987). Cognitive studies in alcoholism. *Journal of Consulting and Clinical Psychology, 55*, 325–331. **(Chap 11)**

Wilson, G. T. (1993). Psychological and pharmacological treatments of bulimia nervosa: A research update. *Applied and Preventive Psychology, 2*, 35–42. **(Chap 8)**

Wilson, G. T., & Pike, K. M. (1993). *Eating disorders.* **(Chap 8)**

Winchel, R. M., Stanley, B., & Stanley, M. (1990). Biochemical aspects of suicide. In S. J. Blumenthal & D. J. Kupfer (Eds.), *Suicide over the life cycle: Risk factors, assessment and treatment of suicidal patterns* (pp. 97–126). Washington, DC: American Psychiatric Press. **(Chap 7)**

Wincze, J. P., & Carey, M. P. (1991). *Sexual dysfunction: A guide for assessment and treatment.* New York: Guilford Press. **(Chap 10)**

Windgassen, K. (1992). Treatment with neuroleptics: The patient's perspective. *Acta Psychiatrica Scandinavica, 86*, 405–410. **(Chap 13)**

Wing, J. K., Cooper, J. E., & Sartorius, N. (1974). *The measurement and classification of psychiatric symptoms.* Cambridge, England: Cambridge University Press. **(Chap 3)**

Winick, B. J. (1997). *The right to refuse mental health treatment.* Washington, DC: American Psychological Association. **(Chap 16)**

Winker, M. A. (1994). Tacrine for Alzheimer's disease: Which patient, what dose? *Journal of the American Medical Association, 271*, 1023–1024. **(Chap 15)**

Winokur, G. (1985). Familial psychopathology in delusional disorder. *Comprehensive Psychiatry, 26*, 241–248. **(Chap 13)**

Winokur, G., Coryell, W., Endicott, J., & Akiskal, H. (1993). Further distinctions between manic-depressive illness (bipolar disorder) and primary depressive disorder (unipolar depression). *American Journal of Psychiatry, 150,* 1176–1181. **(Chap 7)**

Winokur, G., Pfohl, B., & Tsuang, M. (1987). A 40-year follow-up of hebephrenic-catatonic schizophrenia. In N. Miller & G. Cohen (Eds), *Schizophrenia and aging* (pp. 52–60). New York: Guilford Press. **(Chap 13)**

Wirak, D. O., Bayney, R., Ramabhadran, T. V., Fracasso, R. P., Hart, J. T., Hauer, P. E., Hsiau, P., Pekar, S. K., Scangos, G. A., Trapp, B. D., & Unterbeck, A. J. (1991). Deposits of amyloid B protein in the central nervous system of transgenic mice. *Science, 253,* 323–325. **(Chap 15)**

Wise, R. A. (1988). The neurobiology of craving: Implications for the understanding and treatment of addiction. *Journal of Abnormal Psychology, 97,* 118–132. **(Chap 11)**

Wiseman, C. V., Gray, J. J., Mosimann, J. E., & Ahrens, A. H. (1992). Cultural expectations of thinness in women: An update. *International Journal of Eating Disorders, 11,* 85–89. **(Chap 8)**

Wisocki, P. A. (1988). Worry as a phenomenon relevant to the elderly. *Behavior Therapy, 19,* 369–379. **(Chap 5)**

Wisocki, P. A., Handen, B., & Morse, C. K. (1986). The Worry Scale as a measure of anxiety among homebound and community active elderly. *The Behavior Therapist, 5,* 91–95. **(Chap 5)**

Witherington, R. (1988). Suction device therapy in the management of erectile impotence. *Urologic Clinics of North America, 15,* 123–128. **(Chap 10)**

Wittchen, H.-U., Knäuper, B., & Kessler, R. C. (1994). Lifetime risk of depression. *British Journal of Psychiatry, 165*(Suppl.26), 116–22. **(Chap 7)**

Wittchen, H. U., Zhao, S., Kessler, R. C. & Eaton, W. W. (1994). DSM-III-R generalized anxiety disorder in the national comorbidity survey. *Archives of General Psychiatry, 51,* 355–364. **(Chap 5)**

Wolanin, M. O., & Phillips, L. R. F. (1981). *Confusion.* St. Louis: C. V. Mosby. **(Chap 15)**

Wolf, M. M. (1978). Social validity: The case for subjective measurement or how applied behavior analysis is finding its heart. *Journal of Applied Behavior Analysis, 11,* 203–214. **(Chap 4)**

Wolf, S. S., Jones, D. W., Knable, M. B., Gorey, J. G., Lee, K. S., Hyde, T. M., Coppola, R., & Weinberger, D. R. (1996). Tourette syndrome: Prediction of phenotypic variation in monozygotic twins by caudate nucleus D2 receptor binding. *Science, 273,* 1225–1227. **(Chap 14)**

Wolfe, D. A. (1991). *Preventing physical and emotional abuse of children.* New York: Guilford Press. **(Chap 3)**

Wolff, S., Townshed, R., McGuire, R. J., & Weeks, D. J. (1991). "Schizoid" personality in childhood and adult life II: Adult adjustment and continuity with schizotypal personality disorder. *British Journal of Psychiatry, 159,* 615–620. **(Chap 12)**

Wolkin, A., Sanfilipo, M., Wolf, A. P., Angrist, B., Brodie, J. D., & Rotrosen, J. (1992). Negative symptoms and hypofrontality in chronic schizophrenia. *Archives of General Psychiatry, 49,* 959–965. **(Chap 13)**

Wolpe, J. (1958). *Psychotherapy by reciprocal inhibition.* Stanford, CA: Stanford University Press. **(Chaps 1, 4)**

Woods, E. R., Lin, Y. G., Middleman, A., Beckford, P., Chase, L., & DuRant, R. H. (1997). The associations of suicide attempts in adolescents. *Pediatrics, 99,* 791–796. **(Chap 7)**

Woods, N. S., Eyler, F. D., Behnke, M., & Conlon, M. (1992). Cocaine use during pregnancy: Maternal depressive symptoms and infant neurobehavior over first month. *Infant Behavior and Development, 16,* 83–98. **(Chap 11)**

Woodside, M. R., & Legg, B. H. (1990). Patient advocacy: A mental health perspective. *Journal of Mental Health Counseling, 12,* 38–50. **(Chap 16)**

Woody, G. E., & Cacciola, J. (1997). Diagnosis and classification: DSM-IV and ICD-10. In J. H. Lowinson, P. Ruiz, R. B. Millman, & J. G. Langrod (Eds.), *Substance abuse: A comprehensive textbook* (pp. 361–363). Baltimore: Williams & Wilkins. **(Chap 11)**

Wooten, V. (1990). Evaluation and management of sleep disorders in the elderly. *Psychiatric Annals, 20,* 466–473. **(Chap 8)**

Wootton, J. M., Frick, P. J., Shelton, K. K., & Silverthorn, P. (1997). Ineffective parenting and childhood conduct problems: The moderating role of callous-unemotional traits. *Journal of Consulting and Clinical Psychology, 65,* 301–308. **(Chap 12)**

Worell, J., & Remer, P. (1992). *Feminist perspectives in therapy: An empowerment model for women.* New York: John Wiley. **(Chap 3)**

World Health Organization. (1973). *The international pilot study of schizophrenia.* Geneva. **(Chap 13)**

Wulfert, E., Greenway, D. E., & Dougher, M. J. (1996). A logical functional analysis of reinforcement-based disorders: Alcoholism and pedophilia. *Journal of Consulting and Clinical Psychology, 64*(6), 1140–1151. **(Chap 3)**

Wyatt, R. J., Alexander, R. C., Egan, M. F., & Kirch, D. G. (1988). Schizophrenia: Just the facts. *Schizophrenia Research, 1,* 3–18. **(Chap 13)**

Wyatt v. Stickney, 344 F. Supp. 373 (Ala. 1972). **(Chap 16)**

Yairi, E., & Ambrose, N. (1992). Onset of stuttering in preschool children: Selected factors. *Journal of Speech and Hearing Research, 35,* 782–788. **(Chap 14)**

Yamamoto, J., Silva, A., Sasao, T., Wang, C., & Nguyen, L. (1993). Alcoholism in Peru. *American Journal of Psychiatry, 150,* 1059–1062. **(Chap 11)**

Yanovski, S. Z., Nelson, J. E., Duppert, B. K., & Spitzer, R. L. (1993). Association of binge eating disorder and psychiatric comorbidity in the obese. *American Journal of Psychiatry, 150,* 1472–1479. **(Chap 8)**

Yeaton, W. H., & Bailey, J. S. (1978). Teaching pedestrian safety skills to young children: An analysis and one-year follow-up. *Journal of Applied Behavior Analysis, 11,* 315–329. **(Chap 9)**

Yeh, S.-R., Fricke, R. A. & Edwards, D. H. (1996, January 19). The effect of social experience on serotonergic modulation of escape circuit of crayfish. *Science, 271,* 355–369. **(Chap 2)**

Yonkers, K. A., Warshaw, M. G., Massion, A. O., & Keller, M. B. (1996). Phenomenology and course of generalized anxiety disorder. *British Journal of Psychiatry, 168,* 308–313. **(Chap 5)**

Yoon, C. K. (1996). New light on seasonal disorder (SAD) therapy. *The Journal of NIH Research, 8,* 29–31. **(Chap 7)**

Yoshida, A., Huang, I-Y., & Ikawa, M. (1984). Molecular abnormality of an inactive aldehyde dehydrogenase variant commonly found in Orientals. *Proceedings of the National Academy of Sciences, 81,* 258–261. **(Chap 11)**

Young, A. M., & Herling, S. (1986). Drugs as reinforcers: Studies in laboratory animals. In S. R. Goldberg & I. P. Stolerman (Eds.), *Behavioral analysis of drug dependence* (pp. 9–67). Orlando, FL: Academic Press. **(Chap 11)**

Young, J. E., Beck, A. T., & Weinberger, A. (1993). Depression. In D. H. Barlow (Ed.), *Clinical handbook of psychological disorders* (2nd ed., pp. 240–277). New York: Guilford Press. **(Chap 7)**

Youngberg v. Romeo, 457 U.S. 307 (1982). **(Chap 16)**

Yutzy, S. H., Cloninger, C. R., Guze, S. B., Pribor, E. F., Martin, R. L., Kathol, R. G., Smith, G. R., & Strain, J. J. (1995). DSM-IV field trial: Testing a new proposal for somatization disorder. *American Journal of Psychiatry, 152,* 97–101. **(Chap 6)**

Zajonc, R. B. (1984). On the primacy of affect. *American Psychologist, 117–123.* **(Chap 2)**

Zakowski, S. G., McAllister, C. G., Deal, M., & Baum A. (1992). Stress, reactivity, and immune function in healthy men. *Health Psychology, 11,* 223–32. **(Chap 9)**

Zametkin, A. J., Nordahl, T., Gross, M., King, A. C., Semple, W. E., Rumsey, J., Hamburger, S., & Cohen, R. M. (1990). Cerebral glucose metabolism in adults with hyperactivity of childhood onset. *New England Journal of Medicine, 323,* 1361–1366. **(Chap 14)**

Zanarini, M., Gunderson, J., Marino, M., Schwartz, E., & Frankenburg, F. (1988). DSM-III disorders in the families of borderline outpatients. *Journal of Personality Disorders, 2,* 292–302. **(Chap 12)**

Zanarini, M. C., & Frankenberg, F. R. (1997). Pathways to the development of borderline personality disorder. *Journal of Personality Disorders, 11,* 93–104. **(Chap 12)**

Zanarini, M. C., Williams, A. A., Lewis, R. E., Reich, R. B., Vera, S. C., Marino, M. F., Levin, A., Yong, L., & Frankenberg, F. R. (1997). Reported pathological childhood experiences associated with the development of borderline personality disorder. *American Journal of Psychiatry, 154,* 1101–1106. **(Chap 12)**

Zhou, J. N., Hofman, M. A., Gooren, L. J., & Swaab, D. F. (1995, November 2). A sex difference in the human brain and its relation to transsexuality. *Nature, 378,* 68–70. **(Chap 10)**

Zigler, E., & Balla, D. (1982). *Mental retardation: The developmental-difference controversy.* Hillsdale, NJ: Lawrence Erlbaum. **(Chap 14)**

Zigler, E., & Cascione, R. (1984). Mental retardation: An overview. In E. S. Gollin (Ed.), *Malformations of develop-ment: Biological and psychological sources and consequences* (pp. 69–90). New York: Academic Press. **(Chap 14)**

Zigler, E., & Hodapp, R. M. (1986). *Understanding mental retardation.* Cambridge: Cambridge University Press. **(Chap 14)**

Zigler, E., Taussig, C., & Black, K. (1992). Early childhood intervention: A promising preventative for juvenile delinquency. *American Psychologist, 47,* 997–1006. **(Chap 12)**

Zigler, E. F., & Stevenson, M. F. (1993). *Children in a changing world: Development and social issues* (2nd ed.). Pacific Grove, CA: Brooks/Cole Publishing. **(Chap 14)**

Zilbergeld, B. (1992). *The new male sexuality.* New York: Bantam Books. **(Chap 10)**

Zilboorg, G., & Henry, G. (1941). *A history of medical psychology.* New York: W. W. Norton. **(Chap 1)**

Zillmann, D. (1983). Arousal and aggression. In R. G. Geen & E. Donnerstein (Eds.), *Aggression: Theoretical and empirical reviews* (Vol. 1). New York: Academic Press. **(Chap 9)**

Zimmerman, M., & Coryell, W. (1989). DSM-III personality disorder diagnoses in a nonpatient sample. *Archives of General Psychiatry, 46,* 682–689. **(Chap 12)**

Zimmerman, M., & Coryell, W. (1990). Diagnosing personality disorders in the community: A comparison of self-report and interview measures. *Archives of General Psychiatry, 47,* 527–531. **(Chap 12)**

Zinbarg, R. E., & Barlow, D. H. (1996). Structure of anxiety and the anxiety disorders: A hierarchical model. *Journal of Abnormal Psychology, 105,* 181–193. **(Chap 7)**

Zinbarg, R. E., Barlow, D. H., Liebowitz, M., Street, L., Broadhead, E., Katon, W., Roy-Byrne, P., Lepine, J. P., Teherani, M., Richards, J., Brantley, P. J., & Kraemer, H. (1994). The DSM-IV field trial for mixed anxiety depression. *American Journal of Psychiatry, 151,* 1153–1162. **(Chaps 3, 7)**

Zohar, J., Judge, R., & the OCD paroxetine study investigators. (1996). Paroxetine vs. clomipremine in the treatment of obsessive-compulsive disorder. *British Journal of Psychiatry, 169,* 468–474. **(Chap 5)**

Zonana, H. (1997). The civil commitment of sex offenders. *Science, 278,* 1248–1249. **(Chap 16)**

Zubin, J., Steinhauer, S. R., & Condray, R. (1992). Vulnerability to relapse in schizophrenia. *British Journal of Psychiatry, 161,* 13–18 **(Chap 13)**

subject index

name index

credits

This page constitutes an extension of the copyright page. We have made every effort to trace the ownership of all copyrighted material and to secure permission from copyright holders. In the event of any question arising as to the use of any material, we will be pleased to make the necessary corrections in future printings. Thanks are due to the following authors, publishers, and agents for permission to use the material indicated.

Three Studies," by G. A. Carlson, and J. H. Kashani, 1988, *American Journal of Psychiatry, 145*(10), 1222–1225. Copyright 1988 by the American Psychiatry Association. Reprinted by permission. **197:** Table 7.4 adapted and reprinted with the permission of The Free Press, a Division of Simon & Schuster from "Affective Disorders," by M. M. Weissman, M. L. Bruce, P. J. Leaf, L. P. Fiorio, and C. Holzer, in *Psychiatric Disorders in America: The Epidemiologic Catchment Area Study*, by Lee N. Robins, Ph.D. and Darrel A. Regier, M.D. Copyright © 1991 by Lee N. Robins and Darrel A. Regier. **198:** Table 7.5 from *Manic-Depressive Illness* by Frederick K. Goodwin and Kay Redfield Jamison, p. 347. Copyright © 1990 by Oxford University Press, Inc. Used by permission of Oxford University Press, Inc. **199:** Table 7.6 adapted from "The DSM-IV Field Trial for Mixed Anxiety Depression," by R. E. Zinbarg, D. H. Barlow, M. Liebowitz, L. Street, E. Broadhead, W. Katon, P. Roy-Byrne, J. P. Lepine, M. Teherani, J. Richards, P. J. Brantley, and H. Kraemer, (in press), *The American Journal of Psychiatry*. **201:** Figure 7.3 adapted from "A Danish Twin Study of Manic-Depressive Disorders," by A. Bertelsen, B. Harvald, and M. Hauge, 1977, *British Journal of Psychiatry, 130,* 330–351. Reprinted by permission. **204:** Figure 7.4 from "Life Events and Measurement," by G. W. Brown, 1989. In G. W. Brown and T. O. Harris (Eds.), *Life Events and Illness.* Copyright © 1989 by The Guilford Press. Reprinted by permission. **208:** Figure 7.6 from "Depression in Women: Implications for Health Care Research," by M. M. Weissman and M. Olfson, 1995, *Science, 269.* Copyright © 1995 American Association for the Advancement of Science. **217:** Figure 7.8 from "Differential Relapse Following Cognitive Therapy and Pharmacotherapy for Depression," by M. D. Evans, S. D. Hollon, R. J. DeRubeis, J. M. Piasecki, W. M. Grove, M. J. Garvey, and V. B. Tuason, 1992, *Archives of General Psychiatry, 49,* 802–808. Copyright 1992 by the American Medical Association. Reprinted by permission. **217:** Figure 7.9 adapted from "Families of Bipolar Patients: Dysfunction, Course of Illness, and Pilot Treatment Study," by I. W. Miller, G. I. Keitner, N. B. Epstein, D. S. Bishop, and C. E. Ryan, 1991. Paper presented at the annual meeting of the Association for the Advancement of Behavior Therapy, New York. Adapted by permission. **219:** Figure 7.10 from "The Epidemiology of Suicide: Implications for Clinical Practice," by M. Buda, and M. T. Tsuang, 1990. In S. J. Blumenthal and D. J. Kupfer (Eds.), *Suicide Over the Life Cycle: Risk Factors, Assessment, and Treatment of Suicidal Patients,* pp. 17–37. Copyright 1990 by the American Psychiatric Press, Inc. Reprinted by permission. **219:** Figure 7.11 from "The Epidemiology of Suicide: Implications for Clinical Practice," by M. Buda, and M. T. Tsuang, 1990. In S. J. Blumenthal and D. J. Kupfer

(Eds.), *Suicide Over the Life Cycle: Risk Factors, Assessment, and Treatment of Suicidal Patients,* pp. 17–37. Copyright 1990 by the American Psychiatric Press, Inc. **222:** Figure 7.12 from "Clinical Assessment and Treatment of Youth Suicide," by S. J. Blumenthal, and D. J. Kupfer, 1988, *Journal of Youth and Adolescence, 17,* 1–24. Copyright 1988 by Plenum Publishing Corporation. Reprinted by permission. **223:** Excerpts from *An Unquiet Mind,* by Kay Redfield Jamison. Copyright © 1995 Alfred A. Knopf, Inc. Reprinted by permission.

Chapter 8: 230: Figure 8.1 from "Relationship Between Anorexia Nervosa and Bulimia Nervosa: Diagnostic Implications," by D. M. Garner and C. G. Fairburn, 1988, p. 60. In D. M. Garner and P. E. Garfinkel (Eds.), *Diagnostic Issues in Anorexia Nervosa and Bulimia Nervosa.* Copyright 1988 by Brunner/Mazel, Inc. Reprinted with permission from Brunner/Mazel, Inc. **236:** Figure 8.2 from "The Genetic Epidemiology of Bulimia Nervosa," by K. S. Kendler, C. Maclean, M. Neale, R. Kessler, A. Heath, and L. Evans, 1991, *American Journal of Psychiatry, 148*(12), 1627–1637. Copyright © 1991 by the American Psychiatric Association. Reprinted by permission. **238:** Figure 8.3 from "Cultural Expectations of Thinness in Women: An Update," by C. V. Wiseman, J. J. Gray, J. E. Mosimann, and A. H. Ahrens, 1992, *International Journal of Eating Disorders, 11*(1), 85–89. Copyright © 1992 by John Wiley & Sons. Reprinted by permission of John Wiley & Sons, Inc. **244:** Figure 8.6 from "Psychotherapy and Bulimia Nervosa: The Longer-Term Effects of Interpersonal Psychotherapy, Behaviour Therapy and Cognitive Behaviour Therapy," by C. G. Fairburn, R. Jones, R. C. Peveler, R. A. Hope, and M. O'Connor, 1993, *Archives of General Psychiatry, 50,* 419–428. Copyright 1993 by the American Medical Association. Reprinted by permission. **245:** Table 8.1 from L. K. G. Hsu, *Eating Disorders,* p. 136, 1990. Copyright 1990 by Guilford Press. Reprinted by permission. **246:** Figure 8.7 from "Behavior Modification of Anorexia Nervosa," by W. S. Agras, D. H. Barlow, H. N. Chapin, G. G. Abel, H. Leitenberg, 1974, *Archives of General Psychiatry, 30,* 279–286. Copyright 1974 by the American Medical Association. Reprinted by permission. **246:** Table 8.2 from "Development and Evaluation of a School-Based Eating Disorder Symptoms Prevention Program," by J. D. Killen in *The Developmental Psychopathology of Eating Disorders: Implications for Research, Prevention, and Treatment,* pp. 313–339. Copyright © 1996 by Lawrence Erlbaum Associates. Reprinted by permission. **260:** Excerpts from *Feeding the Hungry Heart: The Experience of Compulsive Eating,* by Geneen Roth. Copyright © 1993 Penguin Books.

Chapter 9: 266: Figure 9.1 from "Control of Genital Herpes Recurrences Using Pro-

gressive Muscle Relaxation," by M. M. Burnette, K. A. Koehn, R. Kenyon-Jump, and C. Stark, 1991, *Behavior Therapy, 22,* 237–247. Copyright 1991 by the Association for Advancement of Behavior Therapy. Reprinted by permission of the publisher and author. **270:** Figure 9.3 from "Styles of Dominance and Their Endocrine Correlates Among Wild, Live Baboons," by R. Sapolsky, and J. C. Ray, 1989, *American Journal of Primatology, 18*(1), 1–13. Copyright 1989 by Wiley-Liss, Inc. Reprinted by permission of Wiley-Liss, Inc. a subsidiary of John Wiley & Sons. **271:** Figure 9.4 from *Mastering Stress: A Lifestyle Approach* by D. H. Barlow and R. M. Rapee, 1991. Copyright 1991 by American Health Publishing Co. Reprinted by permission. **275:** Figure 9.7 from "Cognitive-Behavioral Stress Management Decreases Dysphoric Mood and Herpes Simplex Virus-Type 2 Antibody Titers in Symptomatic HIV-Seropositive Gay Men," by S. K. Lutgendorf, N. H. Antoni, G. Ironson, N. Klinas, M. Kunar, K. Starr, P. McCabe, K. Cleven, M. A. Fletcher, and N. Schneiderman, 1997, *Journal of Consulting and Clinical Psychology, 65,* 31–43. Copyright 1997 by the American Psychological Association. Reprinted by permission. **276:** Figure 9.8 adapted from "Effect of Psychosocial Treatment on Survival of Patients with Metastatic Breast Cancer," by D. Spiegel, J. R. Bloom, H. C. Kramer, and E. Gotheil, 1989, *Lancet, 14,* 888–891. © by The Lancet Ltd. 1989. Reprinted by permission. **280:** Figure 9.9 from "In-Hospital Symptoms of Psychological Stress as Predictors of Long-Term Outcome After Acute Myocardial Infarction in Men," by N. Frasure-Smith, 1991, *The American Journal of Cardiology, 67,* 121–127. Copyright 1991 by Cahners Publishing Company. Reprinted by permission. **285:** Figure 9.10 from "Chronic Fatigue," by M. Sharpe in Science and Practice of Cognitive Behavior, edited by D. M. Clark and C. G. Fairburn, pp. 381–414. Copyright © 1997 by Oxford University Press, Inc. **286:** Table 9.3 from "Cognitive Behavior Therapy for Chronic Fatigue Syndrome: A Randomized Controlled Trial," by A. Deale, T. Chalder, I. Marks, and S. Wessely, 1997, *American Journal of Psychiatry, 154,* 408–414. Copyright 1997 by the American Psychiatric Association. Reprinted by permission. **288:** Figure 9.11 from *Mastering Stress: A Lifestyle Approach* by D. H. Barlow, and R. M. Rapee, 1991. Copyright 1991 by the American Health Publishing. Reprinted by permission. **288:** Table 9.4 from *Mastering Stress: A Lifestyle Approach* by D. H. Barlow, and R. M. Rapee, 1991. Copyright 1991 by the American Health Publishing. Reprinted by permission. **290:** Table 9.5 from "Primary Care and Health Promotion: A Model for Preventive Medicine," by M. B. Johns et al, 1987, *American Journal of Preventive Medicine, 3*(6), 351. Copyright 1987 American Journal of Preventive Medicine. Reprinted by permission. **292:** Table 9.7 from "Strate-

Psychiatry, 161, 52–58. Reprinted by permission of the Royal College of Psychiatrists. **429:** Table 13.2 adapted from a table in American Psychiatric Association Practice Guidelines for the Treatment of Patients with Schizophrenia (1997). *The American Journal of Psychiatry, 154*(4) Supplement, 1-63 (p. 10) **432:** Table 13.3 from "Techniques for Training Schizophrenic Patients in Illness Self-Management: A Controlled Trial," by T. A. Eckman, W. C. Wirshing, S. R. Marder, R. P. Liberman, K. Johnston-Cronk, K. Zimmermann, and J. Mintz, 1992, *American Journal of Psychiatry, 149,* 1549–1555. Copyright 1992 by the American Psychiatric Association. Reprinted by permission. **433:** Figure 13.10 from "Psychosocial Interventions for Schizophrenia," by I. R. H. Falloon, C. Brooker, and V. Graham-Hole, 1992, *Behaviour Change, 9,* 238–245. Copyright 1992 by Australian Behaviour Modification Association. Reprinted by permission. **434:** Excerpts from *When the Music's Over: My Journey into Schizophrenia,* by R. D. Burke. Copyright © 1995 Basic Books.

Chapter 14: 462: Figure 14.4 adapted from *Understanding Mental Retardation,* by E. Zigler and R. M. Hodapp. Copyright 1986 by Cambridge University Press. **464:** Excerpts from *Nobody Nowhere: The Extraordinary Autobiography of an Autistic,* by Donna Williams. Copyright © 1992 by Donna Williams. Reprinted by permission of Times Books, a division of Random House, Inc.

Chapter 15: 474: Figure 15.2 adapted and reprinted with the permission of The Free Press, an imprint of Simon & Schuster, from *Psychiatric Disorders in America: The Epidemiologic Catchment Area Study* by Lee N. Robins, Ph.D. and Darrel A. Regier, M.D., p. 327. Copyright © 1991 by Lee N. Robins and Darrel A. Regier. **475:** Table 15.1 adapted from the Mini Mental State Examination Form, Folstein, Folstein, and McHugh, reprinted in *The Merck Manual of Geriatrics.* **478:** Table 15.2 adapted from *Subcortical Dementia,* edited by Jeffrey L. Cummings. Copyright © 1990 Oxford University Press, Inc. Reprinted by permission. **484:** Table 15.4 adapted from *When Memory Fails: Helping the Alzheimer's and Dementia Patient,* by A. J. Edwards, page 174. Copyright © 1994 by Plenum Press. Adapted by permission. **486:** Excerpts from *Living in the Labyrinth: A Personal Journey Through the Maze of Alzheimer's,* by Diana Friel McGowin. Copyright © 1993 by Elder Books. Used by permission of Del Books, a division of Bantam Doubleday Dell Publishing Group, Inc.

Chapter 16: 499: Table 16.2 from "Demythologizing Inaccurate Perceptions of the Insanity Defense," by E. Silver, C. Cirincione, and H. J. Steadman, 1994, *Law and Human Behavior, 18,* 63–70. Copyright 1994 by Plenum Press. Reprinted by permission.

506: Table 16.3 from *Template for Developing Guidelines: Interventions for Mental Disorders and Psychosocial Aspects of Physical Disorders,* by American Psychological Association Board of Professional Affairs Task Force on Psychological Intervention Guidelines, 1995. Approved by APA Council of Representatives, February, 1995, Washington D.C. Copyright © 1995 by the American Psychological Association. Reprinted with permission.

Photo Credits

Chapter 1: 1 Giraudon/Art Resource NY/ Rene Magritte 1898–1967: *Person meditating upon madness.* Private collection © 1998 C. Herscovici, Brussels/ARS (ARS), NY; **3 (top)** © Jim Sugar Photography/Corbis; **(bottom)** © Adam Woolfit/Corbis; **4** AP/ Wide World; **6** © Pablo Corral V/Corbis; **8** Mary Evans Picture Library; **9 (top)** Mary Evans Picture Library, **(bottom)** Culver Pictures, Inc.; **10** © Henry Dilitz/Corbis; **11** Scala/Art Resource/*Removal of the Stone of Folly* by Hieronymus Bosch, Prado, Madrid; **12** Frank K.Vizetelly/Illustrated London News/Mary Evans Picture Library; **14** Stock Montage; **15** Stock Montage; **16 (top left)** Scala/Art Resource/*Hypnotic Session* by Sven Richard Berg, 1887, National Museum, Stockholm, **(top right)** Mary Evans Picture Library, **(bottom)** Corbis–Bettmann; **17 (top)** Mary Evans Picture Library, **(bottom)** Scala/Art Resource ©VAGA, New York; **19** Stock Montage; **22** CHARMET/Science Photo Library/Photo Researchers; **23** Archives of the History of American Psychology; **24** Corbis–Bettmann/UPI.

Chapter 2: 27 Robert J. Western; **29** © Natsuko Utsumi/Gamma Liaison; **31** © Bio-Photo Associates/Science Source/ Photo Researchers; **32 (left)** © Dan McCoy/Rainbow, **(right)** © Will & Demi McIntyre/Photo Researchers; **33 (top)** © Peter Byron, **(bottom)** © T. K. Wanstall/The Image Works; **37 (both)** © David Young-Wolff/Photo Edit; **41** courtesy J. James Frost, MD, PhD/Johns Hopkins University School of Medicine; **42** University of California @ San Francisco/photo created with Midas-Software; **43** University of California @ San Francisco/photo created with MidasSoftware; **44 (both)** University of California @ San Francisco/photo created with Midas-Software; **45** Lewis Baxter Jr. M.D.; **47** Johns Hopkins University School of Medicine; **48 (left)** Thomas Insel/1986 Study/National Institute of Mental Health, **(right)** courtesy of Thomas Insel; **49** William Greenough/ University of Illinois; **51** courtesy of Martin Seligman; **53** Charles Darwin; Evolution of The Species 1896; **55 (left)** © John T. Barr/Gamma-Liaison, **(right)** © Phil Schermeister/Corbis; **56** © K. McGlynn/The Image Works; **57 (left)** © David H. Wells/Corbis, **(right)** © A. Ramey/Woodfin Camp; **59** © Bill Luster/Corbis; **60** © Louise Gubb/The Image Works.

Chapter 3: 63 © Blair Seltz/Photo Researchers, Inc.; **65** Richard Heinzen/Super-Stock; **74** © Bob Daemmrich/Stock Boston; **76 (top)** PhotoDisc, Inc., **(bottom)** Dr. Monty Buchsbaum/Peter Arnold; **77 (all)** Carl Fristom of Stichman Medical Equipment, Medford, Mass.; **79** Mary Evans Picture Library; **80** Stock Montage; **82** courtesy of Dr. Allen Francis; **83** © Bonnie Kamin/ PhotoEdit; **84** Rob Rowan/© Corbis–Bettmann; **85** © Jim Sugar/Corbis.

Chapter 4: 89 PhotoDisc, Inc.; **93** © Sue Klemens/Stock Boston; **96** © Stephanie Maze/Corbis–Bettmann; **98 (left)** © Robert Brenner/PhotoEdit, **(right)** © Michael Schwarz/The Image Works; **102** © Jim Sugar/Corbis–Bettmann; **106 (left)** © Henry Diltz/Corbis–Bettmann, **(right)** © 1994 Jack Kurtz/Impact Visuals; **107 (left)** © B. Daemmrich/The Image Works, **(right)** © 1997 Michele Burgess/Stock Boston.

Chapter 5: 111 Bill Luster/© Corbis–Bettmann; **113** Abnormal Psychology Inside Out, produced by Ira Wohl, Only Child Motion Pictures; **119** courtesy of Dr. Tom Borkovec; **122 (left)** © NBC News Photo, **(right)** courtesy of Dr. M. Craske; **131 (top)** © Tim Thompson/Corbis, **(bottom)** courtesy of Dr. Tom Ollendick; **132** © Paul A.Souders/Corbis; **134 (top)** © Joel Gordon 1993, **(bottom)** courtesy of Dr. Peter DiNardo; **137** courtesy of Dr. Jerome Kagan; **139** © David Turnley/Corbis; **145** Abnormal Psychology Inside Out, produced by Ira Wohl, Only Child Motion Pictures.

Chapter 6: 152 © Rousseau/The Image Works; **155** Michael Newman/PhotoEdit; **158** Corbis–Bettmann; **163** © 1995 Donna Binder/Impact Visuals; **166** © Kevin Morris/Corbis–Bettmann; **167 (left)** Archive Photos/Fotos International, **(right)** Corbis–Bettmann/Reuters; **168** AP/Wide World; **172 (top)** Corbis–Bettmann/UPI, **(bottom)** AP/Wide World; **175** Francoise Sauze/Science Photo Library/Photo Researchers.

Chapter 7: 182 © 1991 Paul Figura/ Liaison International; **185** Corbis–Bettmann/ UPI; **188** Corbis–Bettmann; **190** Abnormal Psychology Inside Out, produced by Ira Wohl, Only Child Motion Pictures; **191** Abnormal Psychology Inside Out, produced by Ira Wohl, Only Child Motion Pictures; **193** © photograph Erich Lessing/Art Resource/Abram Jefimovich Arkhipov (1862–1930), *Sunset in a winter landscape,* 1902/Musee d'Orsay, Paris, France; **197 (top)** © Robert Ginn/PhotoEdit, **(bottom)** © Robert Maass/Corbis; **198** Corbis–Bettmann; **204** courtesy of Dr. David Kupfer; **205** Christopher Morris/Black Star; **209** © J.Y. Rabeuf/The Image Works; **212 (top left)** © Scott Camazine/Photo Researchers, **(top right)** © Patrick Johns/ Corbis–Bettmann, **(bottom)** © Tom Wolff/ Knopf; **215 (both)** courtesy of Dr. Myrna

Weisman; **216** courtesy of Dr. Ellen Frank; **220** AP/Wide World.

Chapter 8: 228 © James Amos/Corbis–Bettmann; **230** © Topham/PA/John Stilwell/The Image Works; **232** courtesy of Dr. Harold Lietenberg; **233** Mary Ann Smith/The Image Bank; **234 (both)** B. Bodine/Custom Medical Stock; **236** © Kelly-Mooney Photography/Corbis–Bettmann; **239 (top left)** © Erich Lessing/Art Resource/Pierre-Auguste Renoir (1841–1919), *The lady with blond hair*, 1904–1906/Neue Galerie, Vienna, Austria, **(top right)** © Rose Hartman/Corbis–Bettmann, **(bottom)** Abnormal Psychology Inside Out, produced by Ira Wohl, Only Child Motion Pictures; **241** courtesy of Dr. Judith Rodin; **243 (left)** courtesy of Dr. Tim Walsh, **(right)** courtesy of Dr. Christopher Fairburn; **245** courtesy of Dr. Stewart Agras; **249** © Will and Demi McIntyre/Photo Researchers, Inc.; **252 (left)** © Annie Griffiths/Corbis-Bettmann, **(right)** © Michelle Bridwell/PhotoEdit; **253** Spencer Grant/Monkmeyer; **257** courtesy of Dr. William C. Dement; **259** Erika Stone/Photo Researchers, Inc.

Chapter 9: 264 © B. Daemmrich/The Image Works; **269 (top)** © W. McIntyre/Photo Researchers, Inc., **(bottom)** © Peter Johnson/Corbis–Bettmann; **273 (left)** Dr. Andrejs Liepins/Science Photo Library/Photo Researchers, **(right)** courtesy of Dr. Robert Ader; **276** Custom Medical Stock Photo; **277 (top)** courtesy of Dr. David Spiegel, **(bottom)** Bob Daemmrich/The Image Works; **279** Bob Daemmrich/The Image Works; **281** Dave Bartruff/Stock Boston; **282** Myrleen Ferguson/PhotoEdit; **283** Richards-Liaison/Gamma Liaison; **286** © Tony Freeman/PhotoEdit; **287** courtesy of Dr. Edward Blanchard; **291 (left)** courtesy of Dr. Lizette Peterson, **(right)** Corbis–Bettmann/UPI; **292** © Meryl Levin/Impact Visuals.

Chapter 10: 298 © Eastcott/M/The Image Works; **300** © Esbin-Anderson/The Image Works; **302** courtesy of Dr. John Bancroft; **304** courtesy of Dr. J. Michael Bailey; **305 (left)** © Mitchell Gerber/Corbis–Bettmann, **(right)** © Mitchell Gerber/Corbis–Bettmann; **306** Corbis–Bettmann/UPI; **314 (top left)** courtesy of Dr. John Wincze, **(top right)** courtesy of Michael

Carey, Ph.D., **(bottom left)** courtesy of Dr. Ray Rosen, **(bottom right)** courtesy of Dr. J. Gayle Beck; **315** Abnormal Psychology Inside Out, produced by Ira Wohl, Only Child Motion Pictures; **321** Martin/Custom Medical Stock; **322** Larry Mulvehill/The Image Works; **323** © Doug Vargas/The Image Works; **325** Corbis–Bettmann/UPI; **327** © Crosby/Liaison/Gamma Liaison.

Chapter 11: 336 © Blair Seltz/Photo Researchers, Inc.; **338** © Steve Azzara/Gamma Liaison; **339 (top left)** © Owen Franken/Corbis, **(top right)** © Philip Gould/Corbis, **(bottom left)** © Kelly-Mooney Photography/Corbis, **(bottom right)** © B. Daemmrich/The Image Works; **343** Abnormal Psychology Inside Out, produced by Ira Wohl, Only Child Motion Pictures; **344 (bottom left)** Science Source/Photo Researchers, Inc., **(bottom right)** Martin Rotker/Science Source/Photo Researchers, Inc.; **345 (top)** Dr. Adolf Pfefferbaum, Stanford University, with the support from the National Institute on Alcohol Abuse and Alcoholism and the Department of Veteran Affairs, **(bottom)** © David H. Wells/Corbis; **346** Michael Yamashita/Corbis-Bettmann; **347** © Monika Anderson/Stock Boston; **349** © David Hartung/Gamma Liaison; **350 (top)** Nancy Seisel/NYT Pictures, **(bottom)** Savariau/Gamma Liaison; **354** courtesy of the DEA; **356** courtesy of the DEA; **357** Ted Streshinsky/Corbis–Bettmann; **362** © Kevin Fleming/Corbis; **363** © Dean Conger/Corbis.

Chapter 12: 374 © Stephanie Maze/Corbis–Bettmann; **378** © Paula Lerner/Woodfin Camp; **379** © Bob Daemmrich/Stock Boston; **381** © Paul Souders/Corbis-Bettmann; **385** courtesy of Dr. Robert Hare; **387** Abnormal Psychology Inside Out, produced by Ira Wohl, Only Child Motion Pictures; **388** © James Wilson/Woodfin Camp; **389** courtesy of Dr. D.T. Lykken; **391** © Joe Sohm/The Image Works; **393** Dr. P. Marazzi/Science Photo Library/Photo Researchers; **395** © Vic Bider/PhotoEdit; **397** Christie's, London/SuperStock.

Chapter 13: 404 © Nik Kleinberg/Stock Boston; **406** Corbis–Bettmann/UPI; **409** Abnormal Psychology Inside Out, produced by Ira Wohl, Only Child Motion Pictures; **411** Robert Gauthier; **412** N.R. Rowan/

Stock Boston; **417** © Robbie Jack/Corbis–Bettmann; **418 (top)** Dr. Allan F. Mirsky/National Institute of Mental Health, **(bottom)** courtesy of Dr. Irving Gottesman; **421** Dr. Dean F. Wong, Division of Nuclear Medicine and Radiation Health Sciences, Department of Radiology, The Johns Hopkins University School of Medicine; **425** Dr. E. Fuller Torrey and Dr. Manuel Casanova/National Institute for Mental Health; **427** courtesy of Jill Hooley; **428** The Surgeon by Jan Sanders van Hemessen/SuperStock; **430** Robert Gauthier; **431** Robert Gauthier; **433** © Kevin R. Morris/Corbis.

Chapter 14: 438 © Myrleen Ferguson/Photo Edit; **441** © Dan McCoy/Rainbow; **442** Dr. F. Xavier Castellanos/NIMH; **445** Courtesy National Institute of Mental Health; **447** Scientific Learning; **448 (left)** Robert Fish//Monterey County Herald, **(right)** © D. Kahn Kalas/Stock Boston; **449 (left)** © David Grossman/Photo Researchers, **(right)** © Michael Schwarz; **450** Courtesy Lee-Yun Chu; **453** Eric Courchesne, PhD, Autism and Brain Development Research Laboratory, LaJolla, CA; **455** Robert Fish/Monterey County Herald; **456** © Bonnie Schiffman/Onyx; **457** © Bob Daemmrich/Stock Boston; **459** © Stephanie Maze/Corbis; **460** © Lawrence Migdale/Stock Boston; **461** © Saturn Stills/Science Photo Library; **463** Research Collections/University Archive/Lovejoy Library.

Chapter 15: 468 © R. Llewellyn/SuperStock; **471** © Ed Lallo 1993/Liaison International; **475 (both)** Tim Beddow/Science Source/Photo Researchers, Inc.; **476** © Jeff Greenberg/Photo Researchers, Inc.; **478** © J. Griffin/The Image Works; **479** © Peter Ginter; **484** © John Livzey; **485** Abnormal Psychology Inside Out, produced by Ira Wohl, Only Child Motion Pictures.

Chapter 16: 490 © Kevin Fleming/Corbis–Bettmann; **491 (left)** © Earl Kowall/Corbis–Bettmann, **(right)** Peter Menzel/Stock Boston; **493** Corbis–Bettmann/UPI; **494 (both)** AP/Wide World; **495** AP/Wide World; **496** © Jerry Berndt/Stock Boston; **499** AP/Wide World Photos; **500 (both)** AP/Wide World Photos; **502** AP/Wide World; **505** © Mojgan B. Azimi/Onyx.